This Chart Supplement is a Civil Fli[g...]   [tran]sportation,
Federal Aviation Administration, Ae[ronautical...]
It is designed for use with Aeronauti[cal...]   [standar]ds.

The Airport/Facility Directory section [...] [an]d selected
private use facilities specifically requ[ested... Department of Defense] (DoD) for which a DoD Instrument Approach Procedure has
been published in the U.S. Terminal Procedures Publication. Additionally, this publication contains communications data,
navigational facilities and certain special notices and procedures.

Military data contained within this publication is provided by the National Geospatial-Intelligence Agency and is intended to provide
reference data for military and/or joint use airports. Not all military data contained in this publication is applicable to civil users.

CORRECTIONS, COMMENTS, AND/OR PROCUREMENT

CRITICAL information such as equipment malfunction, abnormal field conditions, hazards to flight, etc., should be reported as
soon as possible.

FOR COMMENTS OR CORRECTIONS: https://www.faa.gov/air_traffic/flight_info/aeronav/aero_data/
  FAA, Aeronautical Information Services
  1305 East West Highway
  SSMC-4 Suite 4400
  Silver Spring, MD 20910-3281
  Telephone 1-800-638-8972

  NOTICE: Changes must be received by Aeronautical Information Services as soon as possible but not later than the "cut-off"
  dates listed below to assure publication on the desired effective date. Information cut-off dates that fall on a federal
  holiday must be received the previous work day.

Effective Date	Airport Information Cut-off date	Airspace Information* Cut-off date
25 Jan 24	13 Dec 23	28 Nov 23
21 Mar 24	7 Feb 24	23 Jan 24
16 May 24	3 Apr 24	19 Mar 24
11 Jul 24	29 May 24	14 May 24
5 Sep 24	24 Jul 24	9 Jul 24
31 Oct 24	18 Sep 24	3 Sep 24

*Airspace Information includes changes to preferred routes and graphic depictions on charts.

FOR PROCUREMENT:
  For digital products, visit our website at:
  http://www.faa.gov/air_traffic/flight_info/aeronav/digital_products/

  For a list of approved FAA Print Providers, visit our website at:
  http://www.faa.gov/air_traffic/flight_info/aeronav/print_providers/

THIS PUBLICATION COMPRISES PART OF THE FOLLOWING SECTIONS OF THE UNITED STATES AERONAUTICAL INFORMATION
PUBLICATION (AIP): GEN, ENR AND AD.

GENERAL INFORMATION
TABLE OF CONTENTS

1

GENERAL INFORMATION .... Inside Front Cover
   City/Military Airport Cross Reference 2
   Seaplane Landing Areas 3
   Abbreviations 4
SECTION 1: AIRPORT/FACILITY DIRECTORY LEGEND 12
SECTION 2: AIRPORT/FACILITY DIRECTORY
   Arkansas 32
   Louisiana 86
   Mississippi 130
   Oklahoma 175
   Texas 238
SECTION 3: NOTICES
   Special Notices 452
   Regulatory Notices 466
SECTION 4: ASSOCIATED DATA
   FAA Telephone Numbers and National Weather Service 467
   NWS Upper Air Observing Stations 470
   Air Route Traffic Control Centers 471
   Flight Service Station Communication Frequencies 476
   VOR Receiver Checkpoints and VOR Test Facilities 479
   Parachute Jumping Areas 482
   Supplemental Communication Reference 486
   Preferred IFR Routes 492
   Tower Enroute Control 510
   Minimum Operational Network (MON) Airport Listing 513
SECTION 5: AIRPORT DIAGRAMS
   Airport Diagrams Legend 514
   Airport Hot Spots 516
   Airport Diagrams 520
PIREP Form 636

GENERAL INFORMATION

CITY/MILITARY AIRPORT CROSS REFERENCE

Military airports are listed alphabetically by state and official airport name. The following city/military airport cross-reference listing provides alphabetical listing by state and city name for all military airport published in this directory.

STATE	CITY NAME	AIRPORT NAME
AR	JACKSONVILLE	LITTLE ROCK AFB
LA	BOSSIER CITY	BARKSDALE AFB
LA	FORT POLK	MAKS AAF
LA	NEW ORLEANS	NEW ORLEANS NAS JRB (ALVIN CALLENDER FLD)
MS	BILOXI	KEESLER AFB
MS	COLUMBUS	COLUMBUS AFB
MS	MERIDIAN	JOE WILLIAMS NOLF
MS	MERIDIAN	MERIDIAN NAS (MC CAIN FLD)
OK	ALTUS	ALTUS AFB
OK	ENID	VANCE AFB
OK	FORT SILL	HENRY POST AAF (FORT SILL)
OK	LEXINGTON	MULDROW AHP
OK	OKLAHOMA CITY	TINKER AFB
TX	ABILENE	DYESS AFB
TX	BERCLAIR	GOLIAD NOLF
TX	CORPUS CHRISTI	CABANISS FLD NOLF
TX	CORPUS CHRISTI	CORPUS CHRISTI NAS (TRUAX FLD)
TX	CORPUS CHRISTI	WALDRON FLD NOLF
TX	DEL RIO	LAUGHLIN AFB
TX	FORT BLISS (EL PASO)	BIGGS AAF (FORT BLISS)
TX	FORT CAVAZOS (KILLEEN)	ROBERT GRAY AAF
TX	FORT CAVAZOS (KILLEEN)	YOAKUM-DEFRENN AHP
TX	FORT WORTH	FORT WORTH NAS JRB (CARSWELL FLD)
TX	KINGSVILLE	KINGSVILLE NAS
TX	ORANGE GROVE	ORANGE GROVE NALF
TX	SAN ANTONIO	KELLY FLD
TX	UNIVERSAL CITY	RANDOLPH AFB
TX	WICHITA FALLS	SHEPPARD AFB/WICHITA FALLS MUNI

GENERAL INFORMATION

SEAPLANE LANDING AREAS

The following locations have Seaplane Landing Areas (Waterways). See alphabetical listing for complete data on these facilities.

STATE	CITY NAME	FACILITY NAME
LA	NEW IBERIA	ACADIANA RGNL
LA	PATTERSON	HARRY P. WILLIAMS MEM
LA	PINEVILLE	PINEVILLE MUNI
TX	FRANKSTON	AERO ESTATES
TX	HOUSTON	DAVID WAYNE HOOKS MEM

GENERAL INFORMATION
ABBREVIATIONS

The following abbreviations/acronyms are those commonly used within this Directory. Other abbreviations/acronyms may be found in the Legend and are not duplicated below. The abbreviations presented are intended to represent grammatical variations of the basic form. (Example—"req" may mean "request", "requesting", "requested", or "requests").

For additional FAA approved abbreviations/acronyms please see FAA Order JO 7340.2 —Contractions

Abbreviation	Description
A/G	air/ground
AAF	Army Air Field
AAS	Airport Advisory Service
AB	Airbase
abm	abeam
ABn	Aerodrome Beacon
abv	above
ACC	Air Combat Command Area Control Center
acft	aircraft
ACLS	Automatic Carrier Landing System
ACN	Aircraft Classification Number
ACR	Aircraft Classification Rating
act	activity
ACWS	Aircraft Control and Warning Squadron
ADA	Advisory Area
ADCC	Air Defense Control Center
ADCUS	Advise Customs
addn	addition
ADF	Automatic Direction Finder
adj	adjacent
admin	administration
ADR	Advisory Route
advs	advise
advsy	advisory
AEIS	Aeronautical Enroute Information Service
AER	approach end rwy
AFA	Army Flight Activity
AFB	Air Force Base
afct	affect
AFFF	Aqueous Film Forming Foam
AFHP	Air Force Heliport
AFIS	Automatic Flight Information Service
afld	airfield
AFOD	Army Flight Operations Detachment
AFR	Air Force Regulation
AFRC	Armed Forces Reserve Center/Air Force Reserve Command
AFRS	American Forces Radio Stations
AFS	Air Force Station
AFTN	Aeronautical Fixed Telecommunication Network
AG	Agriculture
A-G, A-GEAR	Arresting Gear
agcy	Agency
AGL	above ground level
AHP	Army heliport
AID	Airport Information Desk
AIS	Aeronautical Information Services
AL	Approach and Landing Chart
ALF	Auxiliary Landing Field
ALS	Approach Light System
ALSF-1	High Intensity ALS Category I configuration with sequenced Flashers (code)
ALSF-2	High Intensity ALS Category II configuration with sequenced Flashers (code)

Abbreviation	Description
alt	altitude
altn	alternate
AM	Amplitude Modulation, midnight til noon
AMC	Air Mobility Command
amdt	amendment
AMSL	Above Mean Sea Level
ANGS	Air National Guard Station
ant	antenna
AOE	Airport/Aerodrome of Entry
AP	Area Planning
APAPI	Abbreviated Precision Approach Path Indicator
apch	approach
apn	apron
APP	Approach Control
Apr	April
aprx	approximate
APU	Auxiliary Power Unit
apv, apvl	approve, approval
ARB	Air Reserve Base
ARCAL (CANADA)	Aircraft Radio Control of Aerodrome Lighting
ARFF	Aircraft Rescue and Fire Fighting
ARINC	Aeronautical Radio Inc
arng	arrange
arpt	airport
arr	arrive
ARS	Air Reserve Station
ARSA	Airport Radar Service Area
ARSR	Air Route Surveillance Radar
ARTCC	Air Route Traffic Control Center
AS	Air Station
ASAP	as soon as possible
ASDA	Accelerate-Stop Distance Available
ASDE	Airport Surface Detection
ASDE-X	Airport Surface Detection Equipment-Model X
asgn	assign
ASL	Above Sea Level
ASOS	Automated Surface Observing System
ASR	Airport Surveillance Radar
ASSC	Airport Surface Surveillance Capability
ASU	Aircraft Starting Unit
ATA	Actual Time of Arrival
ATC	Air Traffic Control
ATCC	Air Traffic Control Center
ATCT	Airport Traffic Control Tower
ATD	Actual Time of Departure Along Track Distance
ATIS	Automatic Terminal Information Service
ATS	Air Traffic Service
attn	attention
Aug	August
auth	authority
auto	automatic
AUW	All Up Weight (gross weight)
aux	auxiliary
AVASI	abbreviated VASI
avbl	available

GENERAL INFORMATION

Abbreviation	Description
AvGas	Aviation gasoline
avn	aviation
AvOil	aviation oil
AWOS	Automatic Weather Observing System
AWSS	Automated Weather Sensor System
awt	await
awy	airway
az	azimuth
BA	braking action
BASH	Bird Aircraft Strike Hazard
BC	back course
bcn	beacon
bcst	broadcast
bdry	boundary
bldg	building
blkd	blocked
blo, blw	below
BOQ	Bachelor Officers Quarters
brg	bearing
btn	between
bus	business
byd	beyond
C	Commercial Circuit (Telephone)
CAC	Centralized Approach Control
cap	capacity
cat	category
CAT	Clear Air Turbulence
CCW or cntclkws	counterclockwise
ceil	ceiling
CERAP	Center Radar Approach Control
CG	Coast Guard
CGAF	Coast Guard Air Facility
CGAS	Coast Guard Air Station
CH, chan	channel
CHAPI	Chase Helicopter Approach Path Indicator
chg	change
cht	chart
cir	circle, circling
CIV, civ	Civil, civil, civilian
ck	check
CL	Centerline Lighting System
cl	class
clnc	clearance
clsd	closed
CNATRA	Chief of Naval Air Training
cnl	cancel
cntr	center
cntrln	centerline
Co	Company, County
CO	Commanding Officer
com	communication
comd	command
Comdr	Commander
coml	commercial
compul	compulsory
comsn	commission
conc	concrete
cond	condition
const	construction
cont	continue
CONUS	Continental United States
convl	conventional
coord	coordinate

Abbreviation	Description
copter	helicopter
corr	correct
CPDLC	Controller Pilot Data Link Communication
crdr	corridor
cros	cross
CRP	Compulsory Reporting Point
crs	course
CS	call sign
CSTMS	Customs
CTA	Control Area
CTAF	Common Traffic Advisory Frequency
ctc	contact
ctl	control
ctn	caution
CTLZ	Control Zone
CVFR	Controlled Visual Flight Rules Areas
CW	Clockwise, Continuous Wave, Carrier Wave
dalgt	daylight
D-ATIS	Digital Automatic Terminal Information Service
daylt	daylight
db	decibel
DCL	Departure Clearance
Dec	December
decom	decommission
deg	degree
del	delivery
dep	depart
DEP	Departure Control
destn	destination
det	detachment
DF	Direction Finder
DH	Decision Height
DIAP	DoD Instrument Approach Procedure
direc	directional
disem	disseminate
displ	displace
dist	district, distance
div	division
DL	Direct Line to FSS
dlt	delete
dly	daily
DME	Distance Measuring Equipment (UHF standard, TACAN compatible)
DNVT	Digital Non-Secure Voice Telephone
DoD	Department of Defense
drct	direct
DSN	Defense Switching Network (Telephone)
DSN	Defense Switching Network
dsplcd	displaced
DT	Daylight Savings Time
dur	during
durn	duration
DV	Distinguished Visitor
E	East
ea	each
EAT	Expected Approach Time
ECN	Enroute Change Notice
eff	effective, effect
E-HA	Enroute High Altitude
E-LA	Enroute Low Altitude

GENERAL INFORMATION

Abbreviation	Description
elev	elevation
ELT	Emergency Locator Transmitter
EMAS	Engineered Material Arresting System
emerg	emergency
eng	engine
EOR	End of Runway
eqpt	equipment
ERDA	Energy Research and Development Administration
E-S	Enroute Supplement
est	estimate
estab	establish
ETA	Estimated Time of Arrival
ETD	Estimated Time of Departure
ETE	Estimated Time Enroute
ETS	European Telephone System
EUR	European (ICAO Region)
ev	every
evac	evacuate
exc	except
excld	exclude
exer	exercise
exm	exempt
exp	expect
extd	extend
extn	extension
extv	extensive
F/W	Fixed Wing
FAA	Federal Aviation Administration
fac	facility
FAWS	Flight Advisory Weather Service
fax	facsimile
FBO	Fixed Base Operator
FCC	Flight Control Center
FCG	Foreign Clearance Guide
FCLP	field carrier landing practice
fcst	forecast
Feb	February
FIC	Flight Information Center
FIH	Flight Information Handbook
FIR	Flight Information Region
FIS	Flight Information Service
FL	flight level
fld	field
flg	flashing
FLIP	Flight Information Publication
flt	flight
flw	follow
FM	Fan Marker, Frequency Modulation
FOC	Flight Operations Center
FOD	Foreign Object Damage
fone	telephone
FPL	Flight Plan
fpm	feet per minute
fr	from
freq	frequency, frequent
Fri	Friday
frng	firing
FSS	Flight Service Station
ft	foot
ftr	fighter

Abbreviation	Description
GA	Glide Angle
gal	gallon
GAT	General Air Traffic (Europe-Asia)
GCA	Ground Control Approach
GCO	Ground Communication Outlet
gldr	glider
GND	Ground Control
gnd	ground
govt	government
GP	Glide Path
Gp	Group
GPI	Ground Point of Intercept
grad	gradient
grd	guard
GS	glide slope
GWT	gross weight
H	Enroute High Altitude Chart (followed by identification)
H+	Hours or hours plus...minutes past the hour
H24	continuous operation
HAA	Height Above Airport/Aerodrome
HAL	Height Above Landing Area
HAR	Height Above Runway
HAT	Height Above Touchdown
haz	hazard
hdg	heading
HDTA	High Density Traffic Airport/Aerodrome
HF	High Frequency (3000 to 30,000 KHz)
hgr	hangar
hgt	height
hi	high
HIRL	High Intensity Runway Lights
HO	Service available to meet operational requirements
hol	holiday
HOLF	Helicopter Outlying Field
hosp	hospital
HQ	Headquarters
hr	hour
HS	Service available during hours of scheduled operations
hsg	housing
hvy	heavy
HW	Heavy Weight
hwy	highway
HX	station having no specific working hours
Hz	Hertz (cycles per second)
I	Island
IAP	Instrument Approach Procedure
IAS	Indicated Air Speed
IAW	in accordance with
ICAO	International Civil Aviation Organization
ident	identification
IFF	Identification, Friend or Foe
IFR	Instrument Flight Rules
IFR-S	FLIP IFR Supplement
ILS	Instrument Landing System
IM	Inner Marker
IMC	Instrument Meteorological Conditions
IMG	Immigration

GENERAL INFORMATION

Abbreviation	Description
immed	immediate
inbd	inbound
Inc	Incorporated
incl	include
incr	increase
indef	indefinite
info	information
inop	inoperative
inst	instrument
instl	install
instr	instruction
int	intersection
intcntl	intercontinental
intcp	intercept
intl	international
intmt	intermittent
ints	intense, intensity
invof	in the vicinity of
irreg	Irregularly
Jan	January
JASU	Jet Aircraft Starting Unit
JATO	Jet Assisted Take-Off
JOAP	Joint Oil Analysis Program
JOSAC	Joint Operational Support Airlift Center
JRB	Joint Reserve Base
Jul	July
Jun	June
K or Kt	Knots
kHz	kilohertz
KIAS	Knots Indicated Airspeed
KLIZ	Korea Limited Identification Zone
km	Kilometer
kw	kilowatt
L	Compass locator (Component of ILS system) under 25 Watts, 15 NM, Enroute Low Altitude Chart (followed by identification)
L	Local Time
LAHSO	Land and Hold-Short Operations
L-AOE	Limited Airport of Entry
LAWRS	Limited Aviation Weather Reporting Station
lb, lbs	pound (weight)
LC	local call
lcl	local
LCP	French Peripheral Classification Line
lctd	located
lctn	location
lctr	locator
LCVASI	Low Cost Visual Approach Slope Indicator
lczr	localizer
LD	long distance
LDA	Landing Distance Available
ldg	landing
LDIN	Lead-in Lights
LDOCF	Long Distance Operations Control Facility
len	length
lgt, lgtd, lgts	light, lighted, lights
LIRL	Low Intensity Runway Lights
LLWAS	Low-Level Wind Shear Alert System

Abbreviation	Description
LLZ	Localizer (Instrument Approach Procedures Identification only)
LMM	Compass locator at Middle Marker ILS
lo	low
LoALT or LA	Low Altitude
LOC	Localizer
LOM	Compass locator at Outer Marker ILS
LR	Long Range, Lead Radial
LRA	Landing Rights Airport
LRRS	Long Range RADAR Station
LSB	lower side band
ltd	limited
M	meters, magnetic (after a bearing), Military Circuit (Telephone)
MACC	Military Area Control Center
mag	magnetic
maint	maintain, maintenance
maj	major
MALS	Medium Intensity Approach Lighting System
MALSF	MALS with Sequenced Flashers
MALSR	MALS with Runway Alignment Indicator Lights
Mar	March
MARA	Military Activity Restricted Area
MATO	Military Air Traffic Operations
MATZ	Military Aerodrome Traffic Zone
max	maximum
mb	millibars
MCAC	Military Common Area Control
MCAF	Marine Corps Air Facility
MCALF	Marine Corps Auxiliary Landing Field
MCAS	Marine Corps Air Station
MCB	Marine Corps Base
MCC	Military Climb Corridor
MCOLF	Marine Corps Outlying Field
MDA	Minimum Descent Altitude
MEA	Minimum Enroute Altitude
med	medium
MEHT	Minimum Eye Height over Threshold
mem	memorial
MET	Meteorological, Meteorology
METAR	Aviation Routine Weather Report (in international MET figure code)
METRO	Pilot-to-Metro voice cell
MF	Medium Frequency (300 to 3000 KHz), Mandatory Frequency (Canada)
MFA	Minimum Flight Altitude
mgmt	Management
mgr	manager
MHz	Megahertz
mi	mile
MID/ASIA	Middle East/Asia (ICAO Region)
MIJI	Meaconing, Intrusion, Jamming, and Interference
Mil, mil	military
min	minimum, minute
MIRL	Medium Intensity Runway Lights
misl	missile
mkr	marker (beacon)
MM	Middle Marker of ILS
mnt	monitor
MOA	Military Operations Area

GENERAL INFORMATION

Abbreviation	Description
MOCA	Minimum Obstruction Clearance Altitude
mod	modify
MOG	Maximum (aircraft) on the Ground
MON	Minimum Operational Network
Mon	Monday
MP	Maintenance Period
MR	Medium Range
MRA	Minimum Reception Altitude
mrk	mark, marker
MSAW	minimum safe altitude warning
msg	message
MSL	Mean Sea Level
msn	Mission
mt	mount, mountain
MTAF	Mandatory Traffic Advisory Frequency
MTCA	Military Terminal Control Area
mthly	monthly
MUAC	Military Upper Area Control
muni	municipal
MWARA	Major World Air Route Area
N	North
N/A	not applicable
NA	not authorized (For Instrument Approach Procedure take–off and alternate MINIMA only)
NAAS	Naval Auxiliary Air Station
NADC	Naval Air Development Center
NADEP	Naval Air Depot
NAEC	Naval Air Engineering Center
NAES	Naval Air Engineering Station
NAF	Naval Air Facility
NALCO	Naval Air Logistics Control Office
NALF	Naval Auxiliary Landing Field
NALO	Navy Air Logistics Office
NAS	Naval Air Station
NAT	North Atlantic (ICAO Region)
natl	national
nav	navigation
navaid	navigation aid
NAVMTO	Navy Material Transportation Office
NAWC	Naval Air Warfare Center
NAWS	Naval Air Weapons Station
NCRP	Non–Compulsory Reporting Point
NDB	Non–Directional Radio Beacon
NE	Northeast
nec	necessary
NEW	Net Explosives Weight
ngt	night
NM	nautical miles
nml	normal
NMR	nautical mile radius
No or Nr	number
NOLF	Naval Outlying Field
NORDO	Lost communications or no radio installed/available in aircraft
NOTAM	Notice to Air Missions
Nov	November
npi	non precision instrument
Nr or No	number
NS	Naval Station
NS ABTMT	Noise Abatement
NSA	Naval Support Activity
NSF	Naval Support Facility

Abbreviation	Description
NSTD, nstd	nonstandard
ntc	notice
NVD	Night Vision Devices
NVG	Night Vision Goggles
NW	Northwest
NWC	Naval Weapons Center
O/A	On or about
O/S	out of service
O/R	On Request
OAT	Operational Air Traffic
obsn	observation
obst	obstruction
OCA	Oceanic Control Area
ocnl	occasional
Oct	October
ODALS	Omnidirectional Approach Lighting System
ODO	Operations Duty Officer
offl	official
OIC	Officer In Charge
OLF	Outlying Field
OLS	Optical Landing System
OM	Outer Marker, ILS
opr	operate, operator, operational
OPS, ops	operations
orig	original
OROCA	Off Route Obstruction Clearance Altitude
ORTCA	Off Route Terrain Clearance Altitude
OT	other times
OTS	out of service
outbd	outbound
ovft	overflight
ovrn	overrun
OX	oxygen
P/L	plain language
PAC	Pacific (ICAO Region)
PAEW	personnel and equipment working
PALS	Precision Approach and Landing System (NAVY)
PAPI	Precision Approach Path Indicator
PAR	Precision Approach Radar
para	paragraph
parl	parallel
pat	pattern
PAX	Passenger
PCL	pilot controlled lighting
PCN	Pavement Classification Number
PCR	Pavement Classification Rating
PDC	Pre–Departure Clearance
pent	penetrate
perm	permanent
perms	permission
pers	personnel
PFC	Porous Friction Courses
PJE	Parachuting Activities/Exercises
p–line	power line
PM	Post meridian, noon til midnight
PMRF	Pacific Missile Range Facility
PMSV	Pilot–to–Metro Service
PN	prior notice
POB	persons on board
POL	Petrol, Oils and Lubricants
posn	position

SC, 25 JAN 2024 to 21 MAR 2024

GENERAL INFORMATION

Abbreviation	Description
PPR	prior permission required
prcht	parachute
pref	prefer
prev	previous
prim	primary
prk	park
PRM	Precision Runway Monitor
pro	procedure
proh	prohibited
pt	point
PTD	Pilot to Dispatcher
pub	publication
publ	publish
PVASI	Pulsating Visual Approach Slope Indicator
pvt	private
pwr	power
QFE	Altimeter Setting above station
QNE	Altimeter Setting of 29.92 inches which provides height above standard datum plane
QNH	Altimeter Setting which provides height above mean sea level
qtrs	quarters
quad	quadrant
R/T	Radiotelephony
R/W	Rotary/Wing
RACON	Radar Beacon
rad	radius, radial
RAIL	Runway Alignment Indicator Lights
RAMCC	Regional Air Movement Control Center
R–AOE	Regular Airport of Entry
RAPCON	Radar Approach Control (USAF)
RATCF	Radar Air Traffic Control Facility (Navy)
RCAG	Remote Center Air to Ground Facility
RCAGL	Remote Center Air to Ground Facility Long Range
RCL	runway centerline
RCLS	Runway Centerline Light System
RCO	Remote Communications Outlet
rcpt	reception
RCR	Runway Condition Reading
rcv	receive
rcvr	receiver
rdo	radio
reconst	reconstruct
reful	refueling
reg	regulation, regular
REIL	Runway End Identifier Lights
rel	reliable
relctd	relocated
REP	Reporting Point
req	request
RETIL	Rapid Exit Taxiway Indicator Light
Rgn	Region
Rgnl	Regional
rgt	right
rgt tfc	right traffic
rlgd	realigned
RLLS	Runway Lead-in Light System
rmk	remark
rng	range, radio range
RNP	Required Navigation Performance

Abbreviation	Description
RON	Remain Overnight
Rot Lt or Bcn	Rotating Light or Beacon
RPI	Runway Point of Intercept
rpt	report
rqr	require
RR	Railroad
RRP	Runway Reference Point
RSC	Runway Surface Condition
RSDU	Radar Storm Detection Unit
RSE	Runway Starter Extension/Starter Strip
RSRS	Reduced Same Runway Separation
rstd	restricted
rte	route
ruf	rough
RVR	Runway Visual Range
RVSM	Reduced Vertical Separation Minima
rwy	runway
S	South
S/D	Seadrome
SALS	Short Approach Lighting System
SAR	Search and Rescue
Sat	Saturday
SAVASI	Simplified Abbreviated Visual Approach Slope Indicator
SAWRS	Supplement Aviation Weather Reporting Station
sby	standby
Sched	scheduled services
sctr	sector
SDF	Simplified Directional Facility
SE	Southeast
sec	second, section
secd	secondary
SELCAL	Selective Calling System
SELF	Strategic Expeditionary Landing Field
SEng	Single Engine
Sep	September
SFA	Single Frequency Approach
SFB	Space Force Base
sfc	surface
SFL	Sequence Flashing Lights
SFRA	Special Flight Rules Area
SID	Standard Instrument Departure
SIDA	Secure Identification Display Area
SIF	Selective Identification Feature
sked	schedule
SM	statute miles
SOAP	Spectrometric Oil Analysis Program
SOF	Supervisor of Flying
SPB	Seaplane Base
SR	sunrise
SRE	Surveillance Radar Element of GCA (Instrument Approach Procedures Identification only)
SS	sunset
SSALS/R	Simplified Short Approach Lighting System/with RAIL
SSB	Single Sideband
SSR	Secondary Surveillance Radar
STA	Straight-in Approach
std	standard
stn	station
stor	storage
str–in	Straight–in

SC, 25 JAN 2024 to 21 MAR 2024

GENERAL INFORMATION

Abbreviation	Description
stu	student
subj	subject
survl	survival, surveillance
sum	summer
Sun	Sunday
sur	surround
suspd	suspended
sUAS	small Unmanned Aerial Systems
svc	service
svcg	servicing
SW	Southwest
sys	system
TA	Transition Altitude
TAC	Tactical Air Command
TAF	Aerodrome (terminal or alternate) forecast in abbreviated form
TALCE	Tanker Aircraft Control Element
TCA	Terminal Control Area
TCH	Threshold Crossing Height
TCTA	Transcontinental Control Area
TD	Touchdown
TDWR	Terminal Doppler Weather Radar
TDZ	Touchdown Zone
TDZL	Touchdown Zone Lights
tfc	traffic
thld	threshold
thou	thousand
thru	through
Thu	Thursday
til	until
tkf, tkof	take-off
TLv	Transition Level
tmpry	temporary
TODA	Take-Off Distance Available
TORA	Take-Off Run Available
TP	Tire Pressure
TPA	Traffic Pattern Altitude
TRACON	Terminal Radar Approach Control (FAA)
tran	transient
trans	transmit
trml	terminal
trng	training
trns	transition
TRSA	Terminal Radar Service Area
Tue	Tuesday
TV	Television
twr	tower
twy	taxiway
UACC	Upper Area Control Center (used outside US)
UAS	Unmanned Aerial Systems
UC	Under Construction
UCN	Urgent Change Notice
UDA	Upper Advisory Area
UDF	Ultra High Frequency Direction Finder
UFN	until further notice
UHF	Ultra High Frequency (300 to 3000 MHz)
UIR	Upper Flight Information Region
una	unable
unauthd	unauthorized
unavbl	unavailable
unctl	uncontrolled
unk	unknown
unlgtd	unlighted

Abbreviation	Description
unltd	unlimited
unmrk	unmarked
unmto	unmonitored
unrel	unreliable
unrstd	unrestricted
unsatfy	unsatisfactory
unsked	unscheduled
unsvc	unserviceable
unuse, unusbl	unusable
USA	United States Army
USAF	United States Air Force
USB	Upper Side Band
USCG	United States Coast Guard
USMC	United States Marine Corps
USSF	United States Space Force
USN	United States Navy
UTA	Upper Control Area
UTC	Coordinated Universal Time
V	Defense Switching Network (telephone, formerly AUTOVON)
V/STOL	Vertical and Short Take-off and Landing aircraft
VAL	Visiting Aircraft Line
var	variation (magnetic variation)
VASI	Visual Approach Slope Indicator
vcnty	vicinity
VDF	Very High Frequency Direction Finder
veh	vehicle
vert	vertical
VFR	Visual Flight Rules
VFR-S	FLIP VFR Supplement
VHF	Very High Frequency (30 to 300 MHz)
VIP	Very Important Person
vis	visibility
VMC	Visual Meteorological Conditions
VOIP	Voice Over Internet Protocol
VOT	VOR Receiver Testing Facility
W	Warning Area (followed by identification), Watts, West, White
WCH	Wheel Crossing Height
Wed	Wednesday
Wg	Wing
WIE	with immediate effect
win	winter
WIP	work in progress
WSO	Weather Service Office
WSFO	Weather Service Forecast Office
wk	week
wkd	weekday
wkly	weekly
wng	warning
wo	without
WSP	Weather System Processor
wt	weight
wx	weather
yd	yard
yr	year
Z	Greenwich Mean Time (time groups only)

SC, 25 JAN 2024 to 21 MAR 2024

INTENTIONALLY
LEFT
BLANK

AIRPORT/FACILITY DIRECTORY LEGEND

SAMPLE

① **CITY NAME**
② **AIRPORT NAME** ③ (ALTERNATE NAME) ④ (LTS)(KLTS) ⑤ CIV/MIL ⑥ 3 N ⑦ UTC–6(–5DT) N34°41.93´ W99°20.20´ ⑧ JACKSONVILLE COPTER
⑪ 200 ⑫ B ⑬ TPA—1000(800) ⑭ AOE ⑮ LRA Class IV, ARFF Index A ⑯ NOTAM FILE ORL ⑰ Not insp. ⑱ MON Airport H–4G, L–19C
IAP, DIAP, AD

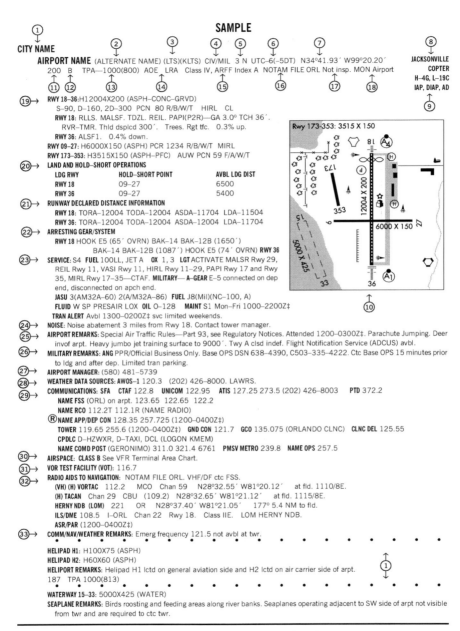

⑲ **RWY 18–36:** H12004X200 (ASPH–CONC–GRVD)
  S–90, D–160, 2D–300 PCN 80 R/B/W/T HIRL CL
  RWY 18: RLLS. MALSF. TDZL. REIL. PAPI(P2R)—GA 3.0° TCH 36´.
    RVR–TMR. Thld dsplcd 300´. Trees. Rgt tfc. 0.3% up.
  RWY 36: ALSF1. 0.4% down.
  RWY 09–27: H6000X150 (ASPH) PCR 1234 R/B/W/T MIRL
  RWY 173–353: H3515X150 (ASPH–PFC) AUW PCN 59 F/A/W/T

⑳ **LAND AND HOLD–SHORT OPERATIONS**
LDG RWY	HOLD–SHORT POINT	AVBL LDG DIST
RWY 18	09–27	6500
RWY 36	09–27	5400

㉑ **RUNWAY DECLARED DISTANCE INFORMATION**
  RWY 18: TORA–12004 TODA–12004 ASDA–11704 LDA–11504
  RWY 36: TORA–12004 TODA–12004 ASDA–12004 LDA–11704

㉒ **ARRESTING GEAR/SYSTEM**
  RWY 18 HOOK E5 (65´ OVRN) BAK–14 BAK–12B (1650´)
           BAK–14 BAK–12B (1087´) HOOK E5 (74´ OVRN) **RWY 36**

㉓ **SERVICE:** S4 **FUEL** 100LL, JET A **OX** 1, 3 **LGT** ACTIVATE MALSR Rwy 29,
  REIL Rwy 11, VASI Rwy 11, HIRL Rwy 11–29, PAPI Rwy 17 and Rwy
  35, MIRL Rwy 17–35–CTAF. **MILITARY**— **A–GEAR** E–5 connected on dep
  end, disconnected on apch end.
  JASU 3(AM32A–60) 2(A/M32A–86) **FUEL** J8(Mil)(NC–100, A)
  FLUID W SP PRESAIR LOX **OIL** O–128 **MAINT** S1 Mon–Fri 1000–2200Z‡
  TRAN ALERT Avbl 1300–0200Z‡ svc limited weekends.

㉔ **NOISE:** Noise abatement 3 miles from Rwy 18. Contact tower manager.
㉕ **AIRPORT REMARKS:** Special Air Traffic Rules—Part 93, see Regulatory Notices. Attended 1200–0300Z‡. Parachute Jumping. Deer invof arpt. Heavy jumbo jet training surface to 9000´. Twy A clsd indef. Flight Notification Service (ADCUS) avbl.
㉖ **MILITARY REMARKS:** ANG PPR/Official Business Only. Base OPS DSN 638–4390, C503–335–4222. Ctc Base OPS 15 minutes prior to ldg and after dep. Limited tran parking.
㉗ **AIRPORT MANAGER:** (580) 481–5739
㉘ **WEATHER DATA SOURCES:** AWOS–1 120.3   (202) 426–8000. LAWRS.
㉙ **COMMUNICATIONS:** SFA **CTAF** 122.8 **UNICOM** 122.95 **ATIS** 127.25 273.5 (202) 426–8003   **PTD** 372.2
  NAME FSS (ORL) on arpt. 123.65 122.65 122.2
  NAME RCO 112.2T 112.1R (NAME RADIO)
  Ⓡ **NAME APP/DEP CON** 128.35 257.725 (1200–0400Z‡)
  TOWER 119.65 255.6 (1200–0400Z‡) **GND CON** 121.7 **GCO** 135.075 (ORLANDO CLNC) **CLNC DEL** 125.55
  CPDLC D–HZWXR, D–TAXI, DCL (LOGON KMEM)
  NAME COMD POST (GERONIMO) 311.0 321.4 6761 **PMSV METRO** 239.8 **NAME OPS** 257.5
㉚ **AIRSPACE: CLASS B** See VFR Terminal Area Chart.
㉛ **VOR TEST FACILITY (VOT):** 116.7
㉜ **RADIO AIDS TO NAVIGATION:** NOTAM FILE ORL. VHF/DF ctc FSS.
  (VH) (H) VORTAC 112.2   MCO   Chan 59   N28°32.55´ W81°20.12´   at fld. 1110/8E.
  (H) TACAN Chan 29 CBU (109.2) N28°32.65´ W81°21.12´   at fld. 1115/8E.
  HERNY NDB (LOM) 221   OR   N28°37.40´ W81°21.05´   177° 5.4 NM to fld.
  ILS/DME 108.5 I–ORL Chan 22 Rwy 18.   Class IIE. LOM HERNY NDB.
  ASR/PAR (1200–0400Z‡)
㉝ **COMM/NAV/WEATHER REMARKS:** Emerg frequency 121.5 not avbl at twr.

HELIPAD H1: H100X75 (ASPH)
HELIPAD H2: H60X60 (ASPH)
HELIPORT REMARKS: Helipad H1 lctd on general aviation side and H2 lctd on air carrier side of arpt.
187 TPA 1000(813)

• • • • • • • • • • • • •

WATERWAY 15–33: 5000X425 (WATER)
SEAPLANE REMARKS: Birds roosting and feeding areas along river banks. Seaplanes operating adjacent to SW side of arpt not visible from twr and are required to ctc twr.

All bearings and radials are magnetic unless otherwise specified. All mileages are nautical unless otherwise noted.
All times are Coordinated Universal Time (UTC) except as noted. All elevations are in feet above/below Mean Sea Level (MSL) unless otherwise noted.
The horizontal reference datum of this publication is North American Datum of 1983 (NAD83), which for charting purposes is considered equivalent to World Geodetic System 1984 (WGS 84).

AIRPORT/FACILITY DIRECTORY LEGEND

⑩ SKETCH LEGEND

RUNWAYS/LANDING AREAS

- Hard Surface
- Metal Surface
- Other than Hard Surface Runways
- Water Runway
- Under Construction
- Closed Rwy
- Closed Pavement
- Helicopter Landings Area
- Displaced Threshold
- Taxiway, Apron and Stopways

RADIO AIDS TO NAVIGATION

- VORTAC
- VOR
- VOR/DME
- NDB
- TACAN
- NDB/DME
- DME

MISCELLANEOUS AERONAUTICAL FEATURES

- Airport Beacon
- Wind Cone
- Landing Tee
- Tetrahedron
- Control Tower ... TWR

When control tower and rotating beacon are co-located beacon symbol will be used and further identified as TWR.

MISCELLANEOUS BASE AND CULTURAL FEATURES

- Buildings
- Power Lines
- Towers
- Wind Turbine
- Tanks
- Oil Well
- Smoke Stack
- Obstruction ... 5812
- Controlling Obstruction ... +5812
- Trees
- Populated Places
- Cuts and Fills ... Cut / Fill
- Cliffs and Depressions
- Ditch
- Hill

APPROACH LIGHTING SYSTEMS

A dot "●" portrayed with approach lighting letter identifier indicates sequenced flashing lights (F) installed with the approach lighting system e.g. (A) Negative symbology, e.g., (A1) ⓥ indicates Pilot Controlled Lighting (PCL).

- Runway Centerline Lighting
- Ⓐ Approach Lighting System ALSF-2
- Ⓐ1 Approach Lighting System ALSF-1
- Ⓐ2 Short Approach Lighting System SALS/SALSF
- Ⓐ3 Simplified Short Approach Lighting System (SSALR) with RAIL
- Ⓐ4 Medium Intensity Approach Lighting System (MALS and MALSF)/(SSALS and SSALF)
- Ⓐ5 Medium Intensity Approach Lighting System (MALSR) and RAIL
- Ⓞ Omnidirectional Approach Lighting System (ODALS)
- Ⓓ Navy Parallel Row and Cross Bar
- Ⓕ Air Force Overrun
- Ⓥ Visual Approach Slope Indicator with Standard Threshold Clearance provided
- Ⓥ2 Pulsating Visual Approach Slope Indicator (PVASI)
- Ⓥ3 Visual Approach Slope Indicator with a threshold crossing height to accomodate long bodied or jumbo aircraft
- Ⓥ4 Tri-color Visual Approach Slope Indicator (TRCV)
- Ⓥ5 Approach Path Alignment Panel (APAP)
- Ⓟ Precision Approach Path Indicator (PAPI)

SC, 25 JAN 2024 to 21 MAR 2024

AIRPORT/FACILITY DIRECTORY LEGEND

LEGEND

This directory is a listing of data on record with the FAA on public–use airports, military airports and selected private–use airports specifically requested by the Department of Defense (DoD) for which a DoD Instrument Approach Procedure has been published in the U.S. Terminal Procedures Publication. Additionally this listing contains data for associated terminal control facilities, air route traffic control centers, and radio aids to navigation within the conterminous United States, Puerto Rico and the Virgin Islands. Civil airports and joint Civil/Military airports which are open to the public are listed alphabetically by state, associated city and airport name and cross–referenced by airport name. Military airports and private–use (limited civil access) joint Military/Civil airports are listed alphabetically by state and official airport name and cross–referenced by associated city name. Navaids, flight service stations and remote communication outlets that are associated with an airport, but with a different name, are listed alphabetically under their own name, as well as under the airport with which they are associated.

The listing of an airport as open to the public in this directory merely indicates the airport operator's willingness to accommodate transient aircraft, and does not represent that the airport conforms with any Federal or local standards, or that it has been approved for use on the part of the general public. Military airports, private–use airports, and private–use (limited civil access) joint Military/Civil airports are open to civil pilots only in an emergency or with prior permission. See Special Notice Section, Civil Use of Military Fields.

The information on obstructions is taken from reports submitted to the FAA. Obstruction data has not been verified in all cases. Pilots are cautioned that objects not indicated in this tabulation (or on the airports sketches and/or charts) may exist which can create a hazard to flight operation. Detailed specifics concerning services and facilities tabulated within this directory are contained in the Aeronautical Information Manual, Basic Flight Information and ATC Procedures.

The legend items that follow explain in detail the contents of this Directory and are keyed to the circled numbers on the sample on the preceding pages.

① CITY/AIRPORT NAME
Civil and joint Civil/Military airports which are open to the public are listed alphabetically by state and associated city. Where the city name is different from the airport name the city name will appear on the line above the airport name. Airports with the same associated city name will be listed alphabetically by airport name and will be separated by a dashed rule line. A solid rule line will separate all others. FAA approved helipads and seaplane landing areas associated with a land airport will be separated by a dotted line. Military airports and private–use (limited civil access) joint Military/Civil airports are listed alphabetically by state and official airport name.

② ALTERNATE NAME
Alternate names, if any, will be shown in parentheses.

③ LOCATION IDENTIFIER
The location identifier is a three or four character FAA code followed by a four–character ICAO code, when assigned, to airports. If two different military codes are assigned, both codes will be shown with the primary operating agency's code listed first. These identifiers are used by ATC in lieu of the airport name in flight plans, flight strips and other written records and computer operations. Zeros will appear with a slash to differentiate them from the letter "O".

④ OPERATING AGENCY
Airports within this directory are classified into two categories, Military/Federal Government and Civil airports open to the general public, plus selected private–use airports. The operating agency is shown for military, private–use and joint use airports. The operating agency is shown by an abbreviation as listed below. When an organization is a tenant, the abbreviation is enclosed in parentheses. No classification indicates the airport is open to the general public with no military tenant.

A	US Army	MC	Marine Corps
AFRC	Air Force Reserve Command	MIL/CIV	Joint Use Military/Civil Limited Civil Access
AF	US Air Force	N	Navy
ANG	Air National Guard	NAF	Naval Air Facility
AR	US Army Reserve	NAS	Naval Air Station
ARNG	US Army National Guard	NASA	National Air and Space Administration
CG	US Coast Guard	P	US Civil Airport Wherein Permit Covers Use by Transient Military Aircraft
CIV/MIL	Joint Use Civil/Military Open to the Public		
DND	Department of National Defense Canada	PVT	Private Use Only (Closed to the Public)
DOE	Department of Energy		

⑤ AIRPORT LOCATION
Airport location is expressed as distance and direction from the center of the associated city in nautical miles and cardinal points, e.g., 3 N.

⑥ TIME CONVERSION
Hours of operation of all facilities are expressed in Coordinated Universal Time (UTC) and shown as "Z" time. The directory indicates the number of hours to be subtracted from UTC to obtain local standard time and local daylight saving time UTC–5(–4DT). The symbol ‡ indicates that during periods of Daylight Saving Time (DST) effective hours will be one hour earlier than shown. In those areas where daylight saving time is not observed the (–4DT) and ‡ will not be shown. Daylight saving time is in effect from 0200 local time the second Sunday in March to 0200 local time the first Sunday in November. Canada and all U.S. Conterminous States observe daylight saving time except Arizona and Puerto Rico, and the Virgin Islands. If the state observes daylight saving time and the operating times are other than daylight saving times, the operating hours will include the dates, times and no ‡ symbol will be shown, i.e., April 15–Aug 31 0630–1700Z, Sep 1–Apr 14 0600–1700Z.

AIRPORT/FACILITY DIRECTORY LEGEND

⑦ GEOGRAPHIC POSITION OF AIRPORT—AIRPORT REFERENCE POINT (ARP)
Positions are shown as hemisphere, degrees, minutes and hundredths of a minute and represent the approximate geometric center of all usable runway surfaces.

⑧ CHARTS
Charts refer to the Sectional Chart and Low and High Altitude Enroute Chart and panel on which the airport or facility is depicted. Pacific Enroute Chart will be indicated by P. Area Enroute Charts will be indicated by A. Helicopter Chart depictions will be indicated as COPTER. IFR Gulf of Mexico West and IFR Gulf of Mexico Central will be referenced as GOMW and GOMC.

⑨ INSTRUMENT APPROACH PROCEDURES, AIRPORT DIAGRAMS
IAP indicates an airport for which a prescribed (Public Use) FAA Instrument Approach Procedure has been published. DIAP indicates an airport for which a prescribed DoD Instrument Approach Procedure has been published in the U.S. Terminal Procedures. See the Special Notice Section of this directory, Civil Use of Military Fields and the Aeronautical Information Manual 5-4-5 Instrument Approach Procedure Charts for additional information. AD indicates an airport for which an airport diagram has been published. Airport diagrams are located in the back of each Chart Supplement volume alphabetically by associated city and airport name.

⑩ AIRPORT SKETCH
The airport sketch, when provided, depicts the airport and related topographical information as seen from the air and should be used in conjunction with the text. It is intended as a guide for pilots in VFR conditions. Symbology that is not self-explanatory will be reflected in the sketch legend. The airport sketch will be oriented with True North at the top.

⑪ ELEVATION
The highest point of an airport's usable runways measured in feet from mean sea level. When elevation is sea level it will be indicated as "00". When elevation is below sea level a minus "−" sign will precede the figure.

⑫ ROTATING LIGHT BEACON
B indicates rotating beacon is available. Rotating beacons operate sunset to sunrise unless otherwise indicated in the AIRPORT REMARKS or MILITARY REMARKS segment of the airport entry.

⑬ TRAFFIC PATTERN ALTITUDE
Traffic Pattern Altitude (TPA)—The first figure shown is TPA above mean sea level. The second figure in parentheses is TPA above airport elevation. TPA will only be published if they differ from the recommended altitudes as described in the AIM, Traffic Patterns. Multiple TPA shall be shown as "TPA—See Remarks" and detailed information shall be shown in the Airport or Military Remarks Section. Traffic pattern data for USAF bases, USN facilities, and U.S. Army airports (including those on which ACC or U.S. Army is a tenant) that deviate from standard pattern altitudes shall be shown in Military Remarks.

⑭ AIRPORT OF ENTRY, LANDING RIGHTS, AND CUSTOMS USER FEE AIRPORTS
U.S. CUSTOMS USER FEE AIRPORT—Private Aircraft operators are frequently required to pay the costs associated with customs processing.

AOE—Airport of Entry. A customs Airport of Entry where permission from U.S. Customs is not required to land. However, at least one hour advance notice of arrival is required.

LRA—Landing Rights Airport. Application for permission to land must be submitted in advance to U.S. Customs. At least one hour advance notice of arrival is required.

NOTE: Advance notice of arrival at both an AOE and LRA airport may be included in the flight plan when filed in Canada or Mexico. Where Flight Notification Service (ADCUS) is available the airport remark will indicate this service. This notice will also be treated as an application for permission to land in the case of an LRA. Although advance notice of arrival may be relayed to Customs through Mexico, Canada, and U.S. Communications facilities by flight plan, the aircraft operator is solely responsible for ensuring that Customs receives the notification. (See Customs, Immigration and Naturalization, Public Health and Agriculture Department requirements in the International Flight Information Manual for further details.)

U.S. CUSTOMS AIR AND SEA PORTS, INSPECTORS AND AGENTS

Northeast Sector (New England and Atlantic States—ME to MD)	407-975-1740
Southeast Sector (Atlantic States—DC, WV, VA to FL)	407-975-1780
Central Sector (Interior of the US, including Gulf states—MS, AL, LA)	407-975-1760
Southwest East Sector (OK and eastern TX)	407-975-1840
Southwest West Sector (Western TX, NM and AZ)	407-975-1820
Southwest West Sector (Western TX, NM and AZ)	407-975-1820
Pacific Sector (WA, OR, CA, HI and AK)	407-975-1800

AIRPORT/FACILITY DIRECTORY LEGEND

⑮ CERTIFICATED AIRPORT (14 CFR PART 139)

Airports serving Department of Transportation certified carriers and certified under 14 CFR part 139 are indicated by the Class and the ARFF Index; e.g. Class I, ARFF Index A, which relates to the availability of crash, fire, rescue equipment. Class I airports can have an ARFF Index A through E, depending on the aircraft length and scheduled departures. Class II, III, and IV will always carry an Index A.

AIRPORT CLASSIFICATIONS

Type of Air Carrier Operation	Class I	Class II	Class III	Class IV
Scheduled Air Carrier Aircraft with 31 or more passenger seats	X			
Unscheduled Air Carrier Aircraft with 31 or more passengers seats	X	X		X
Scheduled Air Carrier Aircraft with 10 to 30 passenger seats	X	X	X	

INDICES AND AIRCRAFT RESCUE AND FIRE FIGHTING EQUIPMENT REQUIREMENTS

Airport Index	Required No. Vehicles	Aircraft Length	Scheduled Departures	Agent + Water for Foam
A	1	<90'	≥1	500#DC or HALON 1211 or 450#DC + 100 gal H_2O
B	1 or 2	≥90', <126'	≥5	Index A + 1500 gal H_2O
		≥126', <159'	<5	
C	2 or 3	≥126', <159'	≥5	Index A + 3000 gal H_2O
		≥159', <200'	<5	
D	3	≥159', <200'		Index A + 4000 gal H_2O
		>200'	<5	
E	3	≥200'	≥5	Index A + 6000 gal H_2O

> Greater Than; < Less Than; ≥ Equal or Greater Than; ≤ Equal or Less Than; H_2O–Water; DC–Dry Chemical.

NOTE: The listing of ARFF index does not necessarily assure coverage for non–air carrier operations or at other than prescribed times for air carrier. ARFF Index Ltd.—indicates ARFF coverage may or may not be available, for information contact airport manager prior to flight.

⑯ NOTAM SERVICE

All public use landing areas are provided NOTAM service. A NOTAM FILE identifier is shown for individual landing areas, e.g., "NOTAM FILE BNA". See the AIM, Basic Flight Information and ATC Procedures for a detailed description of NOTAMs. Current NOTAMs are available from flight service stations at 1–800–WX–BRIEF (992–7433) or online through the FAA PilotWeb at https://pilotweb.nas.faa.gov. Military NOTAMs are available using the Defense Internet NOTAM Service (DINS) at https://www.notams.faa.gov. Pilots flying to or from airports not available through the FAA PilotWeb or DINS can obtain assistance from Flight Service.

⑰ FAA INSPECTION

All airports not inspected by FAA will be identified by the note: Not insp. This indicates that the airport information has been provided by the owner or operator of the field.

⑱ MINIMUM OPERATIONAL NETWORK (MON) AIRPORT DESIGNATION

MON Airports have at least one VOR or ILS instrument approach procedure that can be flown without the need for GPS, WAAS, DME, NDB or RADAR. The primary purpose of the MON designation is for recovery in case of GPS outage.

⑲ RUNWAY DATA

Runway information is shown on two lines. That information common to the entire runway is shown on the first line while information concerning the runway ends is shown on the second or following line. Runway direction, surface, length, width, weight bearing capacity, lighting, and slope, when available are shown for each runway. Multiple runways are shown with the longest runway first. Direction, length, width, and lighting are shown for sea–lanes. The full dimensions of helipads are shown, e.g., 50X150. Runway data that requires clarification will be placed in the remarks section.

RUNWAY DESIGNATION

Runways are normally numbered in relation to their magnetic orientation rounded off to the nearest 10 degrees. Parallel runways can be designated L (left)/R (right)/C (center). Runways may be designated as Ultralight or assault strips. Assault strips are shown by magnetic bearing.

RUNWAY DIMENSIONS

Runway length and width are shown in feet. Length shown is runway end to end including displaced thresholds, but excluding those areas designed as overruns.

AIRPORT/FACILITY DIRECTORY LEGEND

RUNWAY SURFACE AND SURFACE TREATMENT

Runway lengths prefixed by the letter "H" indicate that the runways are hard surfaced (concrete, asphalt, or part asphalt–concrete). If the runway length is not prefixed, the surface is sod, clay, etc. The runway surface composition is indicated in parentheses after runway length as follows:

- (AFSC)—Aggregate friction seal coat
- (AM2)—Temporary metal planks coated with nonskid material
- (ASPH)—Asphalt
- (CONC)—Concrete
- (DIRT)—Dirt
- (GRVD)—Grooved
- (GRVL)—Gravel, or cinders
- (MATS)—Pierced steel planking, landing mats, membranes
- (PEM)—Part concrete, part asphalt
- (PFC)—Porous friction courses
- (PSP)—Pierced steel plank
- (RFSC)—Rubberized friction seal coat
- (SAND)—Sand
- (TURF)—Turf
- (TRTD)—Treated
- (WC)—Wire combed

RUNWAY WEIGHT BEARING CAPACITY

Runway strength data shown in this publication is derived from available information and is a realistic estimate of capability at an average level of activity. It is not intended as a maximum allowable weight or as an operating limitation. Many airport pavements are capable of supporting limited operations with gross weights in excess of the published figures. Permissible operating weights, insofar as runway strengths are concerned, are a matter of agreement between the owner and user. When desiring to operate into any airport at weights in excess of those published in the publication, users should contact the airport management for permission. Runway strength figures are shown in thousand of pounds, with the last three figures being omitted. Add 000 to figure following S, D, 2S, 2T, AUW, SWL, etc., for gross weight capacity. A blank space following the letter designator is used to indicate the runway can sustain aircraft with this type landing gear, although definite runway weight bearing capacity figures are not available, e.g., S, D. Applicable codes for typical gear configurations with S=Single, D=Dual, T=Triple and Q=Quadruple:

CURRENT	NEW	NEW DESCRIPTION
S	S	Single wheel type landing gear (DC3), (C47), (F15), etc.
D	D	Dual wheel type landing gear (BE1900), (B737), (A319), etc.
T	D	Dual wheel type landing gear (P3, C9).
ST	2S	Two single wheels in tandem type landing gear (C130).
TRT	2T	Two triple wheels in tandem type landing gear (C17), etc.
DT	2D	Two dual wheels in tandem type landing gear (B707), etc.
TT	2D	Two dual wheels in tandem type landing gear (B757, KC135).
SBTT	2D/D1	Two dual wheels in tandem/dual wheel body gear type landing gear (KC10).
None	2D/2D1	Two dual wheels in tandem/two dual wheels in tandem body gear type landing gear (A340–600).
DDT	2D/2D2	Two dual wheels in tandem/two dual wheels in double tandem body gear type landing gear (B747, E4).
TTT	3D	Three dual wheels in tandem type landing gear (B777), etc.
TT	D2	Dual wheel gear two struts per side main gear type landing gear (B52).
TDT	C5	Complex dual wheel and quadruple wheel combination landing gear (C5).

AUW—All up weight. Maximum weight bearing capacity for any aircraft irrespective of landing gear configuration.

SWL—Single Wheel Loading. (This includes information submitted in terms of Equivalent Single Wheel Loading (ESWL) and Single Isolated Wheel Loading).

PSI—Pounds per square inch. PSI is the actual figure expressing maximum pounds per square inch runway will support, e.g., (SWL 000/PSI 535).

Omission of weight bearing capacity indicates information unknown.

The ACN/PCN System is the ICAO standard method of reporting pavement strength for pavements with bearing strengths greater than 12,500 pounds. The Pavement Classification Number (PCN) is established by an engineering assessment of the runway. The PCN is for use in conjunction with an Aircraft Classification Number (ACN). Consult the Aircraft Flight Manual, Flight Information Handbook, or other appropriate source for ACN tables or charts. Currently, ACN data may not be available for all aircraft. If an ACN table or chart is available, the ACN can be calculated by taking into account the aircraft weight, the pavement type, and the subgrade category. For runways that have been evaluated under the ACN/PCN system, the PCN will be shown as a five-part code (e.g. PCN 80 R/B/W/T). Details of the coded format are as follows:

NOTE: ICAO adopted the ACR/PCR System as the new standard method for reporting pavement strength in July 2020. The ACR/PCR System methodology remains unchanged from the ACN/PCN system described above. The Pavement Classification Rating (PCR) remains a five-part code (e.g. PCR 460 R/B/W/T) with the number being one order of magnitude higher than PCNs. The details of the code below are not changed with PCR. ICAO has established a four year transition period during which time a PCN or a PCR may be reported. Currently Aircraft Classification Rating (ACR) data may not be available for all aircraft.

AIRPORT/FACILITY DIRECTORY LEGEND

NOTE: Prior permission from the airport controlling authority is required when the ACN/ACR of the aircraft exceeds the published PCN/PCR or aircraft tire pressure exceeds the published limits.

(1) The PCN/PCR NUMBER—The reported PCN/PCR indicates that an aircraft with an ACN/ACR equal or less than the reported PCN/PCR can operate on the pavement subject to any limitation on the tire pressure.

(2) The type of pavement:
  R — Rigid
  F — Flexible

(3) The pavement subgrade category:
  A — High
  B — Medium
  C — Low
  D — Ultra-low

(4) The maximum tire pressure authorized for the pavement:
  W — Unlimited, no pressure limit
  X — High, limited to 254 psi (1.75 MPa)
  Y — Medium, limited to 181 psi (1.25MPa)
  Z — Low, limited to 73 psi (0.50 MPa)

(5) Pavement evaluation method:
  T — Technical evaluation
  U — By experience of aircraft using the pavement

RUNWAY LIGHTING

Lights are in operation sunset to sunrise. Lighting available by prior arrangement only or operating part of the night and/or pilot controlled lighting with specific operating hours are indicated under airport or military remarks. At USN/USMC facilities lights are available only during airport hours of operation. Since obstructions are usually lighted, obstruction lighting is not included in this code. Unlighted obstructions on or surrounding an airport will be noted in airport or military remarks. Runway lights nonstandard (NSTD) are systems for which the light fixtures are not FAA approved L–800 series: color, intensity, or spacing does not meet FAA standards. Nonstandard runway lights, VASI, or any other system not listed below will be shown in airport remarks or military service. Temporary, emergency or limited runway edge lighting such as flares, smudge pots, lanterns or portable runway lights will also be shown in airport remarks or military service. Types of lighting are shown with the runway or runway end they serve.

NSTD—Light system fails to meet FAA standards.
LIRL—Low Intensity Runway Lights.
MIRL—Medium Intensity Runway Lights.
HIRL—High Intensity Runway Lights.
RAIL—Runway Alignment Indicator Lights.
REIL—Runway End Identifier Lights.
CL—Centerline Lights.
TDZL—Touchdown Zone Lights.
ODALS—Omni Directional Approach Lighting System.
AF OVRN—Air Force Overrun 1000´ Standard Approach Lighting System.
MALS—Medium Intensity Approach Lighting System.
MALSF—Medium Intensity Approach Lighting System with Sequenced Flashing Lights.
MALSR—Medium Intensity Approach Lighting System with Runway Alignment Indicator Lights.
RLLS—Runway Lead-in Light System

SALS—Short Approach Lighting System.
SALSF—Short Approach Lighting System with Sequenced Flashing Lights.
SSALS—Simplified Short Approach Lighting System.
SSALF—Simplified Short Approach Lighting System with Sequenced Flashing Lights.
SSALR—Simplified Short Approach Lighting System with Runway Alignment Indicator Lights.
ALSAF—High Intensity Approach Lighting System with Sequenced Flashing Lights.
ALSF1—High Intensity Approach Lighting System with Sequenced Flashing Lights, Category I, Configuration.
ALSF2—High Intensity Approach Lighting System with Sequenced Flashing Lights, Category II, Configuration.
SF—Sequenced Flashing Lights.
OLS—Optical Landing System.
WAVE-OFF.

NOTE: Civil ALSF2 may be operated as SSALR during favorable weather conditions. When runway edge lights are positioned more than 10 feet from the edge of the usable runway surface a remark will be added in the "Remarks" portion of the airport entry. This is applicable to Air Force, Air National Guard and Air Force Reserve Bases, and those joint use airfields on which they are tenants.

VISUAL GLIDESLOPE INDICATORS

APAP—A system of panels, which may or may not be lighted, used for alignment of approach path.
  PNIL   APAP on left side of runway
  PNIR   APAP on right side of runway

PAPI—Precision Approach Path Indicator
  P2L   2-identical light units placed on left side of runway
  P2R   2-identical light units placed on right side of runway
  P4L   4-identical light units placed on left side of runway
  P4R   4-identical light units placed on right side of runway

PVASI—Pulsating/steady burning visual approach slope indicator, normally a single light unit projecting two colors.
  PSIL   PVASI on left side of runway
  PSIR   PVASI on right side of runway

SAVASI—Simplified Abbreviated Visual Approach Slope Indicator
  S2L   2-box SAVASI on left side of runway
  S2R   2-box SAVASI on right side of runway

AIRPORT/FACILITY DIRECTORY LEGEND

SAVASI—Simplified Abbreviated Visual Approach Slope Indicator
    S2L   2–box SAVASI on left side of runway   S2R   2–box SAVASI on right side of runway

TRCV—Tri-color visual approach slope indicator, normally a single light unit projecting three colors.
    TRIL   TRCV on left side of runway   TRIR   TRCV on right side of runway

VASI—Visual Approach Slope Indicator
V2L	2–box VASI on left side of runway	V6L	6–box VASI on left side of runway
V2R	2–box VASI on right side of runway	V6R	6–box VASI on right side of runway
V4L	4–box VASI on left side of runway	V12	12–box VASI on both sides of runway
V4R	4–box VASI on right side of runway	V16	16–box VASI on both sides of runway

NOTE: Approach slope angle and threshold crossing height will be shown when available; i.e., –GA 3.5° TCH 37′.

PILOT CONTROL OF AIRPORT LIGHTING

Key Mike	Function
7 times within 5 seconds	Highest intensity available
5 times within 5 seconds	Medium or lower intensity (Lower REIL or REIL–Off)
3 times within 5 seconds	Lowest intensity available (Lower REIL or REIL–Off)

Available systems will be indicated in the Service section, e.g., **LGT** ACTIVATE HIRL Rwy 07–25, MALSR Rwy 07, and VASI Rwy 07—122.8.

Where the airport is not served by an instrument approach procedure and/or has an independent type system of different specification installed by the airport sponsor, descriptions of the type lights, method of control, and operating frequency will be explained in clear text. See AIM, "Aeronautical Lighting and Other Airport Visual Aids," for a detailed description of pilot control of airport lighting.

RUNWAY SLOPE
When available, runway slope data will be provided. Runway slope will be shown only when it is 0.3 percent or greater. On runways less than 8000 feet, the direction of the slope up will be indicated, e.g., 0.3% up NW. On runways 8000 feet or greater, the slope will be shown (up or down) on the runway end line, e.g., RWY 13: 0.3% up., RWY 31: Pole. Rgt tfc. 0.4% down.

RUNWAY END DATA
Information pertaining to the runway approach end such as approach lights, touchdown zone lights, runway end identification lights, visual glideslope indicators, displaced thresholds, controlling obstruction, and right hand traffic pattern, will be shown on the specific runway end. "Rgt tfc"—Right traffic indicates right turns should be made on landing and takeoff for specified runway end. Runway Visual Range shall be shown as "RVR" appended with "T" for touchdown, "M" for midpoint, and "R" for rollout; e.g., RVR-TMR.

⑳ LAND AND HOLD–SHORT OPERATIONS (LAHSO)
LAHSO is an acronym for "Land and Hold-Short Operations" These operations include landing and holding short of an intersection runway, an intersecting taxiway, or other predetermined points on the runway other than a runway or taxiway. Measured distance represents the available landing distance on the landing runway, in feet.
Specific questions regarding these distances should be referred to the air traffic manager of the facility concerned. The Aeronautical Information Manual contains specific details on hold-short operations and markings.

㉑ RUNWAY DECLARED DISTANCE INFORMATION
TORA—Take-off Run Available. The length of runway declared available and suitable for the ground run of an aeroplane take-off.
TODA—Take-off Distance Available. The length of the take-off run available plus the length of the clearway, if provided.
ASDA—Accelerate-Stop Distance Available. The length of the take-off run available plus the length of the stopway, if provided.
LDA—Landing Distance Available. The length of runway which is declared available and suitable for the ground run of an aeroplane landing.

㉒ ARRESTING GEAR/SYSTEMS
Arresting gear is shown as it is located on the runway. The a-gear distance from the end of the appropriate runway (or into the overrun) is indicated in parentheses. A-Gear which has a bi-direction capability and can be utilized for emergency approach end engagement is indicated by a (B). Up to 15 minutes advance notice may be required for rigging A-Gear for approach and engagement. Airport listing may show availability of other than US Systems. This information is provided for emergency requirements only. Refer to current aircraft operating manuals for specific engagement weight and speed criteria based on aircraft structural restrictions and arresting system limitations.

Following is a list of current systems referenced in this publication identified by both Air Force and Navy terminology:
BI-DIRECTIONAL CABLE (B)

TYPE	DESCRIPTION
BAK–9	Rotary friction brake.
BAK–12A	Standard BAK–12 with 950 foot run out, 1–inch cable and 40,000 pound weight setting. Rotary friction brake.
BAK–12B	Extended BAK–12 with 1200 foot run, 1¼ inch Cable and 50,000 pounds weight setting. Rotary friction brake.
E28	Rotary Hydraulic (Water Brake).
M21	Rotary Hydraulic (Water Brake) Mobile.

AIRPORT/FACILITY DIRECTORY LEGEND

The following device is used in conjunction with some aircraft arresting systems:

BAK–14	A device that raises a hook cable out of a slot in the runway surface and is remotely positioned for engagement by the tower on request. (In addition to personnel reaction time, the system requires up to five seconds to fully raise the cable.)
H	A device that raises a hook cable out of a slot in the runway surface and is remotely positioned for engagement by the tower on request. (In addition to personnel reaction time, the system requires up to one and one–half seconds to fully raise the cable.)

UNI–DIRECTIONAL CABLE

TYPE	DESCRIPTION
MB60	Textile brake—an emergency one–time use, modular braking system employing the tearing of specially woven textile straps to absorb the kinetic energy.
E5/E5–1/E5–3	Chain Type. At USN/USMC stations E–5 A–GEAR systems are rated, e.g., E–5 RATING–13R–1100 HW (DRY), 31L/R–1200 STD (WET). This rating is a function of the A–GEAR chain weight and length and is used to determine the maximum aircraft engaging speed. A dry rating applies to a stabilized surface (dry or wet) while a wet rating takes into account the amount (if any) of wet overrun that is not capable of withstanding the aircraft weight. These ratings are published under Service/Military/A-Gear in the entry.

FOREIGN CABLE

TYPE	DESCRIPTION	US EQUIVALENT
44B–3H	Rotary Hydraulic (Water Brake)	
CHAG	Chain	E–5

UNI–DIRECTIONAL BARRIER

TYPE	DESCRIPTION
MA–1A	Web barrier between stanchions attached to a chain energy absorber.
BAK–15	Web barrier between stanchions attached to an energy absorber (water squeezer, rotary friction, chain). Designed for wing engagement.

NOTE: Landing short of the runway threshold on a runway with a BAK–15 in the underrun is a significant hazard. The barrier in the down position still protrudes several inches above the underrun. Aircraft contact with the barrier short of the runway threshold can cause damage to the barrier and substantial damage to the aircraft.

OTHER

TYPE	DESCRIPTION
EMAS	Engineered Material Arresting System, located beyond the departure end of the runway, consisting of high energy absorbing materials which will crush under the weight of an aircraft.

㉓ SERVICE

SERVICING—CIVIL

S1:	Minor airframe repairs.	S5:	Major airframe repairs.
S2:	Minor airframe and minor powerplant repairs.	S6:	Minor airframe and major powerplant repairs.
S3:	Major airframe and minor powerplant repairs.	S7:	Major powerplant repairs.
S4:	Major airframe and major powerplant repairs.	S8:	Minor powerplant repairs.

FUEL

CODE	FUEL	CODE	FUEL
100	Grade 100 gasoline (Green)	J5 (JP5)	(JP–5 military specification) Kerosene with FS–II, FP** minus 46°C.
100LL	100LL gasoline (low lead) (Blue)		
A	Jet A, Kerosene, without FS–II*, FP** minus 40° C.	J8 (JP8)	(JP–8 military specification) Jet A–1, Kerosene with FS–II*, CI/LI#, SDA##, FP** minus 47°C.
A+	Jet A, Kerosene, with FS–II*, FP** minus 40°C.		
A++	Jet A, Kerosene, with FS–II*, CI/LI#, SDA##, FP** minus 40°C.	J8+100	(JP–8 military specification) Jet A–1, Kerosene with FS–II*, CI/LI#, SDA##, FP** minus 47°C, with +100 fuel additive that improves thermal stability characteristics of kerosene jet fuels.
A++100	Jet A, Kerosene, with FS–II*, CI/LI#, SDA##, FP** minus 40°C, with +100 fuel additive that improves thermal stability characteristics of kerosene jet fuels.	J	(Jet Fuel Type Unknown)
		MOGAS	Automobile gasoline which is to be used as aircraft fuel.
A1	Jet A–1, Kerosene, without FS–II*, FP** minus 47°C.	UL91	Unleaded Grade 91 gasoline
		UL94	Unleaded Grade 94 gasoline
A1+	Jet A–1, Kerosene with FS–II*, FP** minus 47° C.	UL100	Unleaded Grade 100 gasoline

*(Fuel System Icing Inhibitor)   **(Freeze Point)   # (Corrosion Inhibitors/Lubricity Improvers)   ## (Static Dissipator Additive)

AIRPORT/FACILITY DIRECTORY LEGEND

NOTE: Certain automobile gasoline may be used in specific aircraft engines if a FAA supplemental type certificate has been obtained. Automobile gasoline, which is to be used in aircraft engines, will be identified as "MOGAS", however, the grade/type and other octane rating will not be published.

Data shown on fuel availability represents the most recent information the publisher has been able to acquire. Because of a variety of factors, the fuel listed may not always be obtainable by transient civil pilots. Confirmation of availability of fuel should be made directly with fuel suppliers at locations where refueling is planned.

OXYGEN—CIVIL

OX 1	High Pressure	OX 3	High Pressure—Replacement Bottles
OX 2	Low Pressure	OX 4	Low Pressure—Replacement Bottles

SERVICE—MILITARY

Specific military services available at the airport are listed under this general heading. Remarks applicable to any military service are shown in the individual service listing.

JET AIRCRAFT STARTING UNITS (JASU)—MILITARY

The numeral preceding the type of unit indicates the number of units available. The absence of the numeral indicates ten or more units available. If the number of units is unknown, the number one will be shown. Absence of JASU designation indicates non–availability. The following is a list of current JASU systems referenced in this publication:

USAF JASU (For variations in technical data, refer to T.O. 35–1–7.)

ELECTRICAL STARTING UNITS:
- A/M32A–86   AC: 115/200v, 3 phase, 90 kva, 0.8 pf, 4 wire
                   DC: 28v, 1500 amp, 72 kw (with TR pack)
- MC–1A   AC: 115/208v, 400 cycle, 3 phase, 37.5 kva, 0.8 pf, 108 amp, 4 wire
                   DC: 28v, 500 amp, 14 kw
- MD–3   AC: 115/208v, 400 cycle, 3 phase, 60 kva, 0.75 pf, 4 wire
                   DC: 28v, 1500 amp, 45 kw, split bus
- MD–3A   AC: 115/208v, 400 cycle, 3 phase, 60 kva, 0.75 pf, 4 wire
                   DC: 28v, 1500 amp, 45 kw, split bus
- MD–3M   AC: 115/208v, 400 cycle, 3 phase, 60 kva, 0.75 pf, 4 wire
                   DC: 28v, 500 amp, 15 kw
- MD–4   AC: 120/208v, 400 cycle, 3 phase, 62.5 kva, 0.8 pf, 175 amp, "WYE" neutral ground, 4 wire, 120v, 400 cycle, 3 phase, 62.5 kva, 0.8 pf, 303 amp, "DELTA" 3 wire, 120v, 400 cycle, 1 phase, 62.5 kva, 0.8 pf, 520 amp, 2 wire

AIR STARTING UNITS
- AM32–95   150 +/– 5 lb/min (2055 +/– 68 cfm) at 51 +/– 2 psia
- AM32A–95   150 +/– 5 lb/min @ 49 +/– 2 psia (35 +/– 2 psig)
- LASS   150 +/– 5 lb/min @ 49 +/– 2 psia
- MA–1A   82 lb/min (1123 cfm) at 130° air inlet temp, 45 psia (min) air outlet press
- MC–1   15 cfm, 3500 psia
- MC–1A   15 cfm, 3500 psia
- MC–2A   15 cfm, 200 psia
- MC–11   8,000 cu in cap, 4000 psig, 15 cfm

COMBINED AIR AND ELECTRICAL STARTING UNITS:
- AGPU   AC: 115/200v, 400 cycle, 3 phase, 30 kw gen
                   DC: 28v, 700 amp
                   AIR: 60 lb/min @ 40 psig @ sea level
- AM32A–60*   AIR: 120 +/– 4 lb/min (1644 +/– 55 cfm) at 49 +/– 2 psia
                   AC: 120/208v, 400 cycle, 3 phase, 75 kva, 0.75 pf, 4 wire, 120v, 1 phase, 25 kva
                   DC: 28v, 500 amp, 15 kw
- AM32A–60A   AIR: 150 +/– 5 lb/min (2055 +/– 68 cfm at 51 +/– psia
                   AC: 120/208v, 400 cycle, 3 phase, 75 kva, 0.75 pf, 4 wire
                   DC: 28v, 200 amp, 5.6 kw
- AM32A–60B*   AIR: 130 lb/min, 50 psia
                   AC: 120/208v, 400 cycle, 3 phase, 75 kva, 0.75 pf, 4 wire
                   DC: 28v, 200 amp, 5.6 kw

*NOTE: During combined air and electrical loads, the pneumatic circuitry takes preference and will limit the amount of electrical power available.

AIRPORT/FACILITY DIRECTORY LEGEND

USN JASU
ELECTRICAL STARTING UNITS:
- NC-8A/A1 — DC: 500 amp constant, 750 amp intermittent, 28v; AC: 60 kva @ .8 pf, 115/200v, 3 phase, 400 Hz.
- NC-10A/A1/B/C — DC: 750 amp constant, 1000 amp intermittent, 28v; AC: 90 kva, 115/200v, 3 phase, 400 Hz.

AIR STARTING UNITS:
- GTC-85/GTE-85 — 120 lbs/min @ 45 psi.
- MSU-200NAV/A/U47A-5 — 204 lbs/min @ 56 psia.
- WELLS AIR START SYSTEM — 180 lbs/min @ 75 psi or 120 lbs/min @ 45 psi. Simultaneous multiple start capability.

COMBINED AIR AND ELECTRICAL STARTING UNITS:
- NCPP-105/RCPT — 180 lbs/min @ 75 psi or 120 lbs/min @ 45 psi. 700 amp, 28v DC. 120/208v, 400 Hz AC, 30 kva.

ARMY JASU
- 59B2-1B — 28v, 7.5 kw, 280 amp.

OTHER JASU
ELECTRICAL STARTING UNITS (DND):
- CE12 — AC 115/200v, 140 kva, 400 Hz, 3 phase
- CE13 — AC 115/200v, 60 kva, 400 Hz, 3 phase
- CE14 — AC/DC 115/200v, 140 kva, 400 Hz, 3 phase, 28vDC, 1500 amp
- CE15 — DC 22-35v, 500 amp continuous 1100 amp intermittent
- CE16 — DC 22-35v, 500 amp continuous 1100 amp intermittent soft start

AIR STARTING UNITS (DND):
- CA2 — ASA 45.5 psig, 116.4 lb/min

COMBINED AIR AND ELECTRICAL STARTING UNITS (DND)
- CEA1 — AC 120/208v, 60 kva, 400 Hz, 3 phase DC 28v, 75 amp AIR 112.5 lb/min, 47 psig

ELECTRICAL STARTING UNITS (OTHER):
- C-26 — 28v 45kw 115-200v 15kw 380-800 Hz 1 phase 2 wire
- C-26-B, C-26-C — 28v 45kw: Split Bus: 115-200v 15kw 380-800 Hz 1 phase 2 wire
- E3 — DC 28v/10kw

AIR STARTING UNITS (OTHER):
- A4 — 40 psi/2 lb/sec (LPAS Mk12, Mk12L, Mk12A, Mk1, Mk2B)
- MA-1 — 150 Air HP, 115 lb/min 50 psia
- MA-2 — 250 Air HP, 150 lb/min 75 psia

CARTRIDGE:
- MXU-4A — USAF

FUEL—MILITARY

Fuel available through US Military Base supply, DESC Into-Plane Contracts and/or reciprocal agreement is listed first and is followed by (Mil). At commercial airports where Into-Plane contracts are in place, the name of the refueling agent is shown. Military fuel should be used first if it is available. When military fuel cannot be obtained but Into-Plane contract fuel is available, Government aircraft must refuel with the contract fuel and applicable refueling agent to avoid any breach in contract terms and conditions. Fuel not available through the above is shown preceded by NC (no contract). When fuel is obtained from NC sources, local purchase procedures must be followed. The US Military Aircraft Identaplates DD Form 1896 (Jet Fuel), DD Form 1897 (Avgas) and AF Form 1245 (Avgas) are used at military installations only. The US Government Aviation Into-Plane Reimbursement (AIR) Card (currently issued by AVCARD) is the instrument to be used to obtain fuel under a DESC Into-Plane Contract and for NC purchases if the refueling agent at the commercial airport accepts the AVCARD. A current list of contract fuel locations is available online at https://cis.energy.dla.mil/ip_cis/. See legend item 14 for fuel code and description.

SUPPORTING FLUIDS AND SYSTEMS—MILITARY

CODE	
ADI	Anti-Detonation Injection Fluid—Reciprocating Engine Aircraft.
W	Water Thrust Augmentation—Jet Aircraft.
WAI	Water-Alcohol Injection Type, Thrust Augmentation—Jet Aircraft.
SP	Single Point Refueling.
PRESAIR	Air Compressors rated 3,000 PSI or more.
De-Ice	Anti-icing/De-icing/Defrosting Fluid (MIL-A-8243).

AIRPORT/FACILITY DIRECTORY LEGEND

OXYGEN:

LPOX	Low pressure oxygen servicing.
HPOX	High pressure oxygen servicing.
LHOX	Low and high pressure oxygen servicing.
LOX	Liquid oxygen servicing.
OXRB	Oxygen replacement bottles. (Maintained primarily at Naval stations for use in acft where oxygen can be replenished only by replacement of cylinders.)
OX	Indicates oxygen servicing when type of servicing is unknown.

NOTE: Combinations of above items is used to indicate complete oxygen servicing available;

LHOXRB	Low and high pressure oxygen servicing and replacement bottles;
LPOXRB	Low pressure oxygen replacement bottles only, etc.

NOTE: Aircraft will be serviced with oxygen procured under military specifications only. Aircraft will not be serviced with medical oxygen.

NITROGEN:

LPNIT — Low pressure nitrogen servicing.
HPNIT — High pressure nitrogen servicing.
LHNIT — Low and high pressure nitrogen servicing.

OIL—MILITARY

US AVIATION OILS (MIL SPECS):

CODE	GRADE, TYPE
O-113	1065, Reciprocating Engine Oil (MIL-L-6082)
O-117	1100, Reciprocating Engine Oil (MIL-L-6082)
O-117+	1100, O-117 plus cyclohexanone (MIL-L-6082)
O-123	1065, (Dispersant), Reciprocating Engine Oil (MIL-L-22851 Type III)
O-128	1100, (Dispersant), Reciprocating Engine Oil (MIL-L-22851 Type II)
O-132	1005, Jet Engine Oil (MIL-L-6081)
O-133	1010, Jet Engine Oil (MIL-L-6081)
O-147	None, MIL-L-6085A Lubricating Oil, Instrument, Synthetic
O-148	None, MIL-L-7808 (Synthetic Base) Turbine Engine Oil
O-149	None, Aircraft Turbine Engine Synthetic, 7.5c St
O-155	None, MIL-L-6086C, Aircraft, Medium Grade
O-156	None, MIL-L-23699 (Synthetic Base), Turboprop and Turboshaft Engines
JOAP/SOAP	Joint Oil Analysis Program. JOAP support is furnished during normal duty hours, other times on request. (JOAP and SOAP programs provide essentially the same service, JOAP is now the standard joint service supported program.)

TRANSIENT ALERT (TRAN ALERT)—MILITARY

Tran Alert service is considered to include all services required for normal aircraft turn–around, e.g., servicing (fuel, oil, oxygen, etc.), debriefing to determine requirements for maintenance, minor maintenance, inspection and parking assistance of transient aircraft. Drag chute repack, specialized maintenance, or extensive repairs will be provided within the capabilities and priorities of the base. Delays can be anticipated after normal duty hours/holidays/weekends regardless of the hours of transient maintenance operation. Pilots should not expect aircraft to be serviced for TURN–AROUNDS during time periods when servicing or maintenance manpower is not available. In the case of airports not operated exclusively by US military, the servicing indicated by the remarks will not always be available for US military aircraft. When transient alert services are not shown, facilities are unknown. NO PRIORITY BASIS—means that transient alert services will be provided only after all the requirements for mission/tactical assigned aircraft have been accomplished.

(24) NOISE

Remarks that indicate noise information and/or abatement measures that exist in the vicinity of the airport.

(25) AIRPORT REMARKS

The Attendance Schedule is the months, days and hours the airport is actually attended. Airport attendance does not mean watchman duties or telephone accessibility, but rather an attendant or operator on duty to provide at least minimum services (e.g., repairs, fuel, transportation).

Airport Remarks have been grouped in order of applicability. Airport remarks are limited to those items of information that are determined essential for operational use, i.e., conditions of a permanent or indefinite nature and conditions that will remain in effect for more than 30 days concerning aeronautical facilities, services, maintenance available, procedures or hazards, knowledge of which is essential for safe and efficient operation of aircraft. Information concerning permanent closing of a runway or taxiway will not be shown. A note "See Special Notices" shall be applied within this remarks section when a special notice applicable to the entry is contained in the Special Notices section of this publication.

Parachute Jumping indicates parachute jumping areas associated with the airport. See Parachute Jumping Area section of this publication for additional information.

Landing Fee indicates landing charges for private or non–revenue producing aircraft. In addition, fees may be charged for planes that remain over a couple of hours and buy no services, or at major airline terminals for all aircraft.

Note: Unless otherwise stated, remarks including runway ends refer to the runway's approach end.

AIRPORT/FACILITY DIRECTORY LEGEND

㉖ MILITARY REMARKS

Joint Civil/Military airports contain both Airport Remarks and Military Remarks. Military Remarks published for these airports are applicable only to the military. Military and joint Military/Civil airports contain only Military Remarks. Remarks contained in this section may not be applicable to civil users. When both sets of remarks exist, the first set is applicable to the primary operator of the airport. Remarks applicable to a tenant on the airport are shown preceded by the tenant organization, i.e., (A) (AF) (N) (ANG), etc. Military airports operate 24 hours unless otherwise specified. Airport operating hours are listed first (airport operating hours will only be listed if they are different than the airport attended hours or if the attended hours are unavailable) followed by pertinent remarks in order of applicability. Remarks will include information on restrictions, hazards, traffic pattern, noise abatement, customs/agriculture/immigration, and miscellaneous information applicable to the Military.

Type of restrictions:

CLOSED: When designated closed, the airport is restricted from use by all aircraft unless stated otherwise. Any closure applying to specific type of aircraft or operation will be so stated. USN/USMC/USAF airports are considered closed during non-operating hours. Closed airports may be utilized during an emergency provided there is a safe landing area.

OFFICIAL BUSINESS ONLY: The airfield is closed to all transient military aircraft for obtaining routine services such as fueling, passenger drop off or pickup, practice approaches, parking, etc. The airfield may be used by aircrews and aircraft if official government business (including civilian) must be conducted on or near the airfield and prior permission is received from the airfield manager.

AF OFFICIAL BUSINESS ONLY OR NAVY OFFICIAL BUSINESS ONLY: Indicates that the restriction applies only to service indicated.

PRIOR PERMISSION REQUIRED (PPR): Airport is closed to transient aircraft unless approval for operation is obtained from the appropriate commander through Chief, Airfield Management or Airfield Operations Officer. Official Business or PPR does not preclude the use of US Military airports as an alternate for IFR flights. If a non-US military airport is used as a weather alternate and requires a PPR, the PPR must be requested and confirmed before the flight departs. The purpose of PPR is to control volume and flow of traffic rather than to prohibit it. Prior permission is required for all aircraft requiring transient alert service outside the published transient alert duty hours. All aircraft carrying hazardous materials must obtain prior permission as outlined in AFJI 11-204, AR 95-27, OPNAVINST 3710.7.

Note: OFFICIAL BUSINESS ONLY AND PPR restrictions are not applicable to Special Air Mission (SAM) or Special Air Resource (SPAR) aircraft providing person or persons on aboard are designated Code 6 or higher as explained in AFJMAN 11-213, AR 95-11, OPNAVINST 3722-8J. Official Business Only or PPR do not preclude the use of the airport as an alternate for IFR flights.

㉗ AIRPORT MANAGER

The phone number of the airport manager.

㉘ WEATHER DATA SOURCES

Weather data sources will be listed alphabetically followed by their assigned frequencies and/or telephone number and hours of operation.

ASOS—Automated Surface Observing System. Reports the same as an AWOS-3 plus precipitation identification and intensity, and freezing rain occurrence;

AWOS—Automated Weather Observing System

AWOS-A—reports altimeter setting (all other information is advisory only).

AWOS-AV—reports altimeter and visibility.

AWOS-1—reports altimeter setting, wind data and usually temperature, dew point and density altitude.

AWOS-2—reports the same as AWOS-1 plus visibility.

AWOS-3—reports the same as AWOS-1 plus visibility and cloud/ceiling data.

AWOS-3P reports the same as the AWOS-3 system, plus a precipitation identification sensor.

AWOS-3PT reports the same as the AWOS-3 system, plus precipitation identification sensor and a thunderstorm/lightning reporting capability.

AWOS-3T reports the same as AWOS-3 system and includes a thunderstorm/lightning reporting capability.

See AIM, Basic Flight Information and ATC Procedures for detailed description of Weather Data Sources.

AWOS-4—reports same as AWOS-3 system, plus precipitation occurrence, type and accumulation, freezing rain, thunderstorm and runway surface sensors.

LAWRS—Limited Aviation Weather Reporting Station where observers report cloud height, weather, obstructions to vision, temperature and dewpoint (in most cases), surface wind, altimeter and pertinent remarks.

LLWAS—indicates a Low Level Wind Shear Alert System consisting of a center field and several field perimeter anemometers.

SAWRS—identifies airports that have a Supplemental Aviation Weather Reporting Station available to pilots for current weather information.

SWSL—Supplemental Weather Service Location providing current local weather information via radio and telephone.

TDWR—indicates airports that have Terminal Doppler Weather Radar.

WSP—indicates airports that have Weather System Processor.

When the automated weather source is broadcast over an associated airport NAVAID frequency (see NAVAID line), it shall be indicated by a bold ASOS or AWOS followed by the frequency, identifier and phone number, if available.

AIRPORT/FACILITY DIRECTORY LEGEND

㉙ COMMUNICATIONS

Airport terminal control facilities and radio communications associated with the airport shall be shown. When the call sign is not the same as the airport name the call sign will be shown. Frequencies shall normally be shown in ascending order with the primary frequency listed first. Frequencies will be listed, together with sectorization indicated by outbound radials, and hours of operation. Communications will be listed in sequence as follows:

Single Frequency Approach (SFA), Common Traffic Advisory Frequency (CTAF), Aeronautical Advisory Stations (UNICOM) or (AUNICOM), and Automatic Terminal Information Service (AT S) along with their frequency is shown, where available, on the line following the heading "COMMUNICATIONS." When the CTAF and UNICOM frequencies are the same, the frequency will be shown as CTAF/UNICOM 122.8.

The FSS telephone nationwide is toll free 1–800–WX–BRIEF (1–800–992–7433). When the FSS is located on the field it will be indicated as "on arpt". Frequencies available at the FSS will fo low in descending order. Remote Communications Outlet (RCO) providing service to the airport followed by the frequency and FSS RADIO name will be shown when available. FSS's provide information on airport conditions, radio aids and other facilities, and process flight plans. Airport Advisory Service (AAS) is provided on the CTAF by FSS's for select non–tower airports or airports where the tower is not in operation.

(See AIM, Para 4–1–9 Traffic Advisory Practices at Airports Without Operating Control Towers or AC 90–42C.)

Aviation weather briefing service is provided by FSS specialists. Flight and weather briefing services are also available by calling the telephone numbers listed.

Remote Communications Outlet (RCO)—An unmanned air/ground communications facility that is remotely controlled and provides UHF or VHF communications capability to extend the service range of an FSS.

Civil Communications Frequencies–Civil communications frequencies used in the FSS air/ground system are operated on 122.0, 122.2, 123.6; emergency 121.5; plus receive–only on 122.1.

   a. 122.2 is assigned as a common enroute frequency.
   b. 123.6 is assigned as the airport advisory frequency at select non–tower locations. At airports with a tower, FSS may provide airport advisories on the tower frequency when tower is closed.
   c. 122.1 is the primary receive–only frequency at VOR's.
   d. Some FSS's are assigned 50 kHz frequencies in the 122–126 MHz band (eg. 122.45). Pilots using the FSS A/G system should refer to this directory or appropriate charts to determine frequencies available at the FSS or remoted facility through which they wish to communicate.

Emergency frequency 121.5 and 243.0 are available at all Flight Service Stations, most Towers, Approach Control and RADAR facilities.

Frequencies published followed by the letter "T" or "R", indicate that the facility will only transmit or receive respectively on that frequency. All radio aids to navigation (NAVAID) frequencies are transmit only. In cases where communications frequencies are annotated with (R) or (E), (R) indicates Radar Capability and (E) indicates Emergency Frequency.

TERMINAL SERVICES

SFA—Single Frequency Approach.

CTAF—A program designed to get all vehicles and aircraft at airports without an operating control tower on a common frequency.

ATIS—A continuous broadcast of recorded non–control information in selected terminal areas.

D–ATIS—Digital ATIS provides ATIS information in text form outside the standard reception range of conventional ATIS via landline & data link communications and voice message within range of existing transmitters.

AUNICOM—Automated UNICOM is a computerized, command response system that provides automated weather, radio check capability and airport advisory information selected from an automated menu by microphone clicks.

UNICOM—A non–government air/ground radio communications facility which may provide airport information.

PTD—Pilot to Dispatcher.

APP CON—Approach Control. The symbol ® indicates radar approach control.

TOWER—Control tower.

GCA—Ground Control Approach System.

GND CON—Ground Control.

GCO—Ground Communication Outlet—An unstaffed, remotely controlled, ground/ground communications facility. Pilots at uncontrolled airports may contact ATC and FSS via VHF to a telephone connection to obtain an instrument clearance or close a VFR or IFR flight plan. They may also get an updated weather briefing prior to takeoff. Pilots will use four "key clicks" on the VHF radio to contact the appropriate ATC facility or six "key clicks" to contact the FSS. The GCO system is intended to be used only on the ground.

DEP CON—Departure Control. The symbol ® indicates radar departure control.

CLNC DEL—Clearance Delivery.

CPDLC—Controller Pilot Data Link Communication. FANS ATC data communication capability from the aircraft to the ATC Data Link system.

PDC—Pre-Departure Clearance. ACARS-based clearance delivery capability from tower to gate printer or aircraft.

PRE TAXI CLNC—Pre taxi clearance.

VFR ADVSY SVC—VFR Advisory Service. Service provided by Non–Radar Approach Control.
   Advisory Service for VFR aircraft (upon a workload basis) ctc APP CON.

COMD POST—Command Post followed by the operator call sign in parenthesis.

PMSV—Pilot-to-Metro Service call sign, frequency and hours of operation, when full service is other than continuous. PMSV installations at which weather observation service is available shall be indicated, following the frequency and/or hours of operation as "Wx obsn svc 1900–0000Z‡" or "other times" may be used when no specific time is given. PMSV facilities manned by forecasters are considered "Full Service". PMSV facilities manned by weather observers are listed as "Limited Service".

OPS—Operations followed by the operator call sign in parenthesis.

CON

RANGE

FLT FLW—Flight Following

MEDIVAC

NOTE: Communication frequencies followed by the letter "X" indicate frequency available on request.

㉚ AIRSPACE

Information concerning Class B, C, and part-time D and E surface area airspace shall be published with effective times, if available.

CLASS B—Radar Sequencing and Separation Service for all aircraft in CLASS B airspace.

CLASS C—Separation between IFR and VFR aircraft and sequencing of VFR arrivals to the primary airport.

TRSA—Radar Sequencing and Separation Service for participating VFR Aircraft within a Terminal Radar Service Area.

Class C, D, and E airspace described in this publication is that airspace usually consisting of a 5 NM radius core surface area that begins at the surface and extends upward to an altitude above the airport elevation (charted in MSL for Class C and Class D).
Class E surface airspace normally extends from the surface up to but not including the overlying controlled airspace.

When part-time Class C or Class D airspace defaults to Class E, the core surface area becomes Class E. This will be formatted as:
AIRSPACE: CLASS C svc "times" ctc **APP CON** other times CLASS E:
or
AIRSPACE: CLASS D svc "times" other times CLASS E.

When a part-time Class C, Class D or Class E surface area defaults to Class G, the core surface area becomes Class G up to, but not including, the overlying controlled airspace. Normally, the overlying controlled airspace is Class E airspace beginning at either 700′ or 1200′ AGL and may be determined by consulting the relevant VFR Sectional or Terminal Area Charts. This will be formatted as:
AIRSPACE: CLASS C svc "times" ctc **APP CON** other times CLASS G
or
AIRSPACE: CLASS D svc "times" other times CLASS G
or
AIRSPACE: CLASS E svc "times" other times CLASS G

NOTE: AIRSPACE SVC "TIMES" INCLUDE ALL ASSOCIATED ARRIVAL EXTENSIONS. Surface area arrival extensions for instrument approach procedures become part of the primary core surface area. These extensions may be either Class D or Class E airspace and are effective concurrent with the times of the primary core surface area. For example, when a part-time Class C, Class D or Class E surface area defaults to Class G, the associated arrival extensions will default to Class G at the same time. When a part-time Class C or Class D surface area defaults to Class E, the arrival extensions will remain in effect as Class E airspace.

NOTE: CLASS E AIRSPACE EXTENDING UPWARD FROM 700 FEET OR MORE ABOVE THE SURFACE, DESIGNATED IN CONJUNCTION WITH AN AIRPORT WITH AN APPROVED INSTRUMENT PROCEDURE.

Class E 700′ AGL (shown as magenta vignette on sectional charts) and 1200′ AGL (blue vignette) areas are designated when necessary to provide controlled airspace for transitioning to/from the terminal and enroute environments. Unless otherwise specified, these 700′/1200′ AGL Class E airspace areas remain in effect continuously, regardless of airport operating hours or surface area status. These transition areas should not be confused with surface areas or arrival extensions.

(See Chapter 3, AIRSPACE, in the Aeronautical Information Manual for further details)

㉛ VOR TEST FACILITY (VOT)

The VOT transmits a signal which provided users a convenient means to determine the operational status and accuracy of an aircraft VOR receiver while on the ground. Ground based VOTs and the associated frequency shall be shown when available. VOTs are also shown with identifier, frequency and referenced remarks in the VOR Receiver Check section in the back of this publication.

AIRPORT/FACILITY DIRECTORY LEGEND

㉜ RADIO AIDS TO NAVIGATION

The Airport/Facility Directory section of the Chart Supplement lists, by facility name, all Radio Aids to Navigation that appear on FAA, Aeronautical Information Services Visual or IFR Aeronautical Charts and those upon which the FAA has approved an Instrument Approach Procedure, with exception of selected TACANs. All VOR, VORTAC, TACAN and ILS equipment in the National Airspace System has an automatic monitoring and shutdown feature in the event of malfunction. Unmonitored, as used in this publication, for any navigational aid, means that monitoring personnel cannot observe the malfunction or shutdown signal. The NAVAID NOTAM file identifier will be shown as "NOTAM FILE IAD" and will be listed on the Radio Aids to Navigation line. When two or more NAVAIDS are listed and the NOTAM file identifier is different from that shown on the Radio Aids to Navigation line, it will be shown with the NAVAID listing. NOTAM file identifiers for ILSs and its components (e.g., NDB (LOM) are the same as the associated airports and are not repeated. Automated Surface Observing System (ASOS) and Automated Weather Observing System (AWOS) will be shown when this service is broadcast over selected NAVAIDs.

NAVAID information is tabulated as indicated in the following sample:

ASR/PAR—Indicates that Surveillance (ASR) or Precision (PAR) radar instrument approach minimums are published in the U.S. Terminal Procedures. Only part-time hours of operation will be shown.

RADIO CLASS DESIGNATIONS
VOR/DME/TACAN Standard Service Volume (SSV) Classifications

SSV Class	Altitudes	Distance (NM)
(T) Terminal	1000′ to 12,000′	25
(L) Low Altitude	1000′ to 18,000′	40
(H) High Altitude	1000′ to 14,500′	40
	14,500′ to 18,000′	100
	18,000′ to 45,000′	130
	45,000′ to 60,000′	100
(VL) VOR Low	1000′ to 5,000′	40
	5,000′ to 18,000′	70
(VH) VOR High	1000′ to 5,000′	40
	5,000′ to 14,500′	70
	14,500′ to 18,000′	100
	18,000′ to 45,000′	130
	45,000′ to 60,000′	100
(DL) DME Low & (DH) DME High*	1000′ to 12,900′	40 increasing to 130
(DL) DME Low	12,900′ to 18,000′	130
(DH) DME High	12,900′ to 45,000′	130
	45,000′ to 60,000′	100

*Between 1000′ to 12,900′, DME service volume follows a parabolic curve used by flight management computers.

NOTES: Additionally, High Altitude facilities provide Low Altitude and Terminal service volume and Low Altitude facilities provide Terminal service volume. Altitudes are with respect to the station's site elevation. Coverage is not available in a cone of airspace directly above the facility. In some cases local conditions (terrain, buildings, trees, etc.) may require that the service volume be restricted. The public shall be informed of any such restriction by a remark in the NAVAID entry in this publication or by a Notice to Airmen (NOTAM).

AIRPORT/FACILITY DIRECTORY LEGEND

The term VOR is, operationally, a general term covering the VHF omnidirectional bearing type of facility without regard to the fact that the power, the frequency protected service volume, the equipment configuration, and operational requirements may vary between facilities at different locations.

AB	Automatic Weather Broadcast.
DF	Direction Finding Service.
DME	UHF standard (TACAN compatible) distance measuring equipment.
DME(Y)	UHF standard (TACAN compatible) distance measuring equipment that require TACAN to be placed in the "Y" mode to receive DME.
GS	Glide slope.
H	Non–directional radio beacon (homing), power 50 watts to less than 2,000 watts (50 NM at all altitudes).
HH	Non–directional radio beacon (homing), power 2,000 watts or more (75 NM at all altitudes).
H–SAB	Non–directional radio beacons providing automatic transcribed weather service.
ILS	Instrument Landing System (voice, where available, on localizer channel).
IM	Inner marker.
LDA	Localizer Directional Aid.
LMM	Compass locator station when installed at middle marker site (15 NM at all altitudes).
LOM	Compass locator station when installed at outer marker site (15 NM at all altitudes).
MH	Non–directional radio beacon (homing) power less than 50 watts (25 NM at all altitudes).
MM	Middle marker.
OM	Outer marker.
S	Simultaneous range homing signal and/or voice.
SABH	Non–directional radio beacon not authorized for IFR or ATC. Provides automatic weather broadcasts.
SDF	Simplified Direction Facility.
TACAN	UHF navigational facility–omnidirectional course and distance information.
VOR	VHF navigational facility–omnidirectional course only.
VOR/DME	Collocated VOR navigational facility and UHF standard distance measuring equipment.
VORTAC	Collocated VOR and TACAN navigational facilities.
W	Without voice on radio facility frequency.
Z	VHF station location marker at a LF radio facility.

AIRPORT/FACILITY DIRECTORY LEGEND

ILS FACILITY PERFORMANCE CLASSIFICATION CODES

Codes define the ability of an ILS to support autoland operations. The two portions of the code represent Official Category and farthest point along a Category I, II, or III approach that the Localizer meets Category III structure tolerances.

Official Category: I, II, or III; the lowest minima on published or unpublished procedures supported by the ILS.

Farthest point of satisfactory Category III Localizer performance for Category I, II, or III approaches: A – 4 NM prior to runway threshold, B – 3500 ft prior to runway threshold, C – glide angle dependent but generally 750–1000 ft prior to threshold, T – runway threshold, D – 3000 ft after runway threshold, and E – 2000 ft prior to stop end of runway.

ILS information is tabulated as indicated in the following sample:

ILS/DME 108.5 I-ORL Chan 22 Rwy 18. Class IIE. LOM HERNY NDB.

ILS Facility Performance Classification Code

FREQUENCY PAIRING TABLE

VHF FREQUENCY	TACAN CHANNEL	VHF FREQUENCY	TACAN CHANNEL	VHF FREQUENCY	TACAN CHANNEL	VHF FREQUENCY	TACAN CHANNEL
108.10	18X	108.55	22Y	111.05	47Y	114.85	95Y
108.30	20X	108.65	23Y	111.15	48Y	114.95	96Y
108.50	22X	108.75	24Y	111.25	49Y	115.05	97Y
108.70	24X	108.85	25Y	111.35	50Y	115.15	98Y
108.90	26X	108.95	26Y	111.45	51Y	115.25	99Y
109.10	28X	109.05	27Y	111.55	52Y	115.35	100Y
109.30	30X	109.15	28Y	111.65	53Y	115.45	101Y
109.50	32X	109.25	29Y	111.75	54Y	115.55	102Y
109.70	34X	109.35	30Y	111.85	55Y	115.65	103Y
109.90	36X	109.45	31Y	111.95	56Y	115.75	104Y
110.10	38X	109.55	32Y	113.35	80Y	115.85	105Y
110.30	40X	109.65	33Y	113.45	81Y	115.95	106Y
110.50	42X	109.75	34Y	113.55	82Y	116.05	107Y
110.70	44X	109.85	35Y	113.65	83Y	116.15	108Y
110.90	46X	109.95	36Y	113.75	84Y	116.25	109Y
111.10	48X	110.05	37Y	113.85	85Y	116.35	110Y
111.30	50X	110.15	38Y	113.95	86Y	116.45	111Y
111.50	52X	110.25	39Y	114.05	87Y	116.55	112Y
111.70	54X	110.35	40Y	114.15	88Y	116.65	113Y
111.90	56X	110.45	41Y	114.25	89Y	116.75	114Y
108.05	17Y	110.55	42Y	114.35	90Y	116.85	115Y
108.15	18Y	110.65	43Y	114.45	91Y	116.95	116Y
108.25	19Y	110.75	44Y	114.55	92Y	117.05	117Y
108.35	20Y	110.85	45Y	114.65	93Y	117.15	118Y
108.45	21Y	110.95	46Y	114.75	94Y	117.25	119Y

AIRPORT/FACILITY DIRECTORY LEGEND

FREQUENCY PAIRING TABLE
The following is a list of paired VOR/ILS VHF frequencies with TACAN channels.

TACAN CHANNEL	VHF FREQUENCY	TACAN CHANNEL	VHF FREQUENCY	TACAN CHANNEL	VHF FREQUENCY	TACAN CHANNEL	VHF FREQUENCY
2X	134.50	43X	110.60	72X	112.50	101X	115.40
2Y	134.55	43Y	110.65	72Y	112.55	101Y	115.45
11X	135.40	44X	110.70	73X	112.60	102X	115.50
11Y	135.45	44Y	110.75	73Y	112.65	102Y	115.55
12X	135.50	45X	110.80	74X	112.70	103X	115.60
12Y	135.55	45Y	110.85	74Y	112.75	103Y	115.65
17X	108.00	46X	110.90	75X	112.80	104X	115.70
17Y	108.05	46Y	110.95	75Y	112.85	104Y	115.75
18X	108.10	47X	111.00	76X	112.90	105X	115.80
18Y	108.15	47Y	111.05	76Y	112.95	105Y	115.85
19X	108.20	48X	111.10	77X	113.00	106X	115.90
19Y	108.25	48Y	111.15	77Y	113.05	106Y	115.95
20X	108.30	49X	111.20	78X	113.10	107X	116.00
20Y	108.35	49Y	111.25	78Y	113.15	107Y	116.05
21X	108.40	50X	111.30	79X	113.20	108X	116.10
21Y	108.45	50Y	111.35	79Y	113.25	108Y	116.15
22X	108.50	51X	111.40	80X	113.30	109X	116.20
22Y	108.55	51Y	111.45	80Y	113.35	109Y	116.25
23X	108.60	52X	111.50	81X	133.40	110X	116.30
23Y	108.65	52Y	111.55	81Y	113.45	110Y	116.35
24X	108.70	53X	111.60	82X	113.50	111X	116.40
24Y	108.75	53Y	111.65	82Y	113.55	111Y	116.45
25X	108.80	54X	111.70	83X	113.60	112X	116.50
25Y	108.85	54Y	111.75	83Y	113.65	112Y	116.55
26X	108.90	55X	111.80	84X	113.70	113X	116.60
26Y	108.95	55Y	111.85	84Y	113.75	113Y	116.65
27X	109.00	56X	111.90	85X	113.80	114X	116.70
27Y	109.05	56Y	111.95	85Y	113.85	114Y	116.75
28X	109.10	57X	112.00	86X	113.90	115X	116.80
28Y	109.15	57Y	112.05	86Y	113.95	115Y	116.85
29X	109.20	58X	112.10	87X	114.00	116X	116.90
29Y	109.25	58Y	112.15	87Y	114.05	116Y	116.95
30X	109.30	59X	112.20	88X	114.10	117X	117.00
30Y	109.35	59Y	112.25	88Y	114.15	117Y	117.05
31X	109.40	60X	133.30	89X	114.20	118X	117.10
31Y	109.45	60Y	133.35	89Y	114.25	118Y	117.15
32X	109.50	61X	133.40	90X	114.30	119X	117.20
32Y	109.55	61Y	133.45	90Y	114.35	119Y	117.25
33X	109.60	62X	133.50	91X	114.40	120X	117.30
33Y	109.65	62Y	133.55	91Y	114.45	120Y	117.35
34X	109.70	63X	133.60	92X	114.50	121X	117.40
34Y	109.75	63Y	133.65	92Y	114.55	121Y	117.45
35X	109.80	64X	133.70	93X	114.60	122X	117.50
35Y	109.85	64Y	133.75	93Y	114.65	122Y	117.55
36X	109.90	65X	133.80	94X	114.70	123X	117.60
36Y	109.95	65Y	133.85	94Y	114.75	123Y	117.65
37X	110.00	66X	133.90	95X	114.80	124X	117.70
37Y	110.05	66Y	133.95	95Y	114.85	124Y	117.75
38X	110.10	67X	134.00	96X	114.90	125X	117.80
38Y	110.15	67Y	134.05	96Y	114.95	125Y	117.85
39X	110.20	68X	134.10	97X	115.00	126X	117.90
39Y	110.25	68Y	134.15	97Y	115.05	126Y	117.95
40X	110.30	69X	134.20	98X	115.10		
40Y	110.35	69Y	134.25	98Y	115.15		
41X	110.40	70X	112.30	99X	115.20		
41Y	110.45	70Y	112.35	99Y	115.25		
42X	110.50	71X	112.40	100X	115.30		
42Y	110.55	71Y	112.45	100Y	115.35		

(33) **COMM/NAV/WEATHER REMARKS:** These remarks consist of pertinent information affecting the current status of communications, NAVAIDs, weather, and in the absence of air-ground radio outlets identified in the Communications section some approach control facilities will have a clearance delivery phone number listed here.

SC, 25 JAN 2024 to 21 MAR 2024

INTENTIONALLY LEFT BLANK

ARKANSAS

ALMND N35°42.19´ W91°47.86´ NOTAM FILE BVX. MEMPHIS
    NDB (LOMW) 335 BV 078° 7.5 NM to Batesville Rgnl. 1193/1E. L–16G

ALMYRA MUNI (M73) 3 W UTC–6(–5DT) N34°24.75´ W91°27.92´ MEMPHIS
  210 B NOTAM FILE JBR L–18F
  RWY 18–36: H3494X60 (ASPH) S–4 MIRL IAP
    RWY 18: PAPI(P2R)—GA 3.0° TCH 39´. Thld dsplcd 38´. Road.
    RWY 36: PAPI(P2L)—GA 3.0° TCH 37´.
  RWY 10–28: H3000X50 (ASPH) S–4
    RWY 28: Trees.
  SERVICE: S2 **FUEL** 100LL **LGT** ACTIVATE MIRL Rwy 18–36, PAPI Rwy 18 and Rwy 36—CTAF.
  AIRPORT REMARKS: Attended Mon–Fri 1400–2300Z‡. For svc aft hrs call 870–830–1231. Migratory birds on and invof arpt Nov–Feb. Numerous agricultural acft opns. 100LL self serve avbl with credit card. Rwy 18 markings faded.
  AIRPORT MANAGER: (870) 830-1231
  COMMUNICATIONS: CTAF/UNICOM 123.0
    LITTLE ROCK APP/DEP CON 119.85
    CLNC DEL 119.85
  CLEARANCE DELIVERY PHONE: For CD when una via freq ctc Little Rock Apch 501-379-2908 or Little Rock ATCT 501-379-2911
  RADIO AIDS TO NAVIGATION: NOTAM FILE PBF.
    PINE BLUFF (L)(L) VORW/DME 116.0 PBF Chan 107 N34°14.81´ W91°55.57´ 062° 25.0 NM to fld. 212/4E.
    VOR unusable:
      140°–145° byd 35 NM blo 4,900´
      260°–275° byd 25 NM

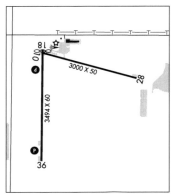

ARKADELPHIA
DEXTER B FLORENCE MEML FLD (ADF)(KADF) 1 S UTC–6(–5DT) N34°05.99´ W93°03.97´ MEMPHIS
  182 B NOTAM FILE ADF H–6I, L–17E
  RWY 04–22: H5002X75 (ASPH) S–50, D–60, 2D–100 MIRL IAP
    RWY 04: REIL. PAPI(P2L)—GA 3.0° TCH 23´. Rgt tfc.
    RWY 22: REIL. PAPI(P2L)—GA 3.0° TCH 32´. Trees.
  SERVICE: S4 **FUEL** 100LL, JET A **LGT** Actvt REIL Rwys 04 and 22; MIRL Rwy 04–22—CTAF. PAPI Rwy 04 and 22 oper consly. Rwy 22 PAPI unusbl byd 8 degs right of cntrln.
  AIRPORT REMARKS: Attended Mon–Fri 1300–2330Z‡. For arpt attendant after hours call 870–246–8945—fee charged. Self-serve fuel avbl 24 hrs with credit card (100LL & Jet A, full service avbl upon request). Significant student pilot activity.
  AIRPORT MANAGER: (870) 246-8945
  WEATHER DATA SOURCES: AWOS–3PT 118.175 (870) 403–0945.
  COMMUNICATIONS: CTAF/UNICOM 122.7
  Ⓡ **MEMPHIS CENTER APP/DEP CON** 128.475
  CLEARANCE DELIVERY PHONE: For CD ctc Memphis ARTCC at 901-368-8453/8449.
  RADIO AIDS TO NAVIGATION: NOTAM FILE ELD.
    EL DORADO (VH)(DH) VORW/DME 115.5 ELD Chan 102 N33°15.37´ W92°44.64´ 335° 53.0 NM to fld. 230/7E.
    DME unusable:
      020°–035° blo 2,000´
      036°–019° byd 30 NM blo 3,200´
    VOR unusable:
      110°–120° byd 40 NM

ARKANSAS INTL (See BLYTHEVILLE on page 37)

ARKAVALLEY (See GREENBRIER on page 52)

ARKANSAS 33

ASH FLAT
SHARP CO RGNL (CVK)(KCVK)   3 NE   UTC–6(–5DT)   N36°15.89′ W91°33.76′   **KANSAS CITY**
717   B   NOTAM FILE JBR   **H–6J, L–16G**
RWY 04–22: H5158X75 (ASPH)   S–12.5   MIRL   0.9% up NE   **IAP**
  RWY 04: PAPI(P2L)—GA 3.0° TCH 40′. Trees.
  RWY 22: PAPI(P2L)—GA 3.0° TCH 40′. Thld dsplcd 154′. Tree.
SERVICE: S4   **FUEL** 100LL, JET A   **LGT** ACTIVATE MIRL Rwy
  04–22—CTAF.
AIRPORT REMARKS: Attended Mon–Fri 1400–2200Z‡. Self service fuel avbl
  24 hrs with credit card (100LL & Jet A). Rwy 22 has 15′ + drop off
  150′ from end of pavement (304′ from dsplcd thld).
AIRPORT MANAGER: 360-620-6121
COMMUNICATIONS: CTAF/UNICOM 122.7
®**MEMPHIS CENTER APP/DEP CON** 120.075
CLEARANCE DELIVERY PHONE: For CD ctc Memphis ARTCC at
  901-368-8453/8449.
RADIO AIDS TO NAVIGATION: NOTAM FILE ARG.
  WALNUT RIDGE (VH) (H) VORTAC 114.5   ARG   Chan 92   N36°06.00′
  W90°57.22′   284° 31.0 NM to fld. 265/4E.
  TACAN AZIMUTH unusable:
   011°–021° byd 15 NM blo 5,000′
  VOR unusable:
   010°–021° byd 40 NM blo 3,000′
   010°–021° byd 55 NM
   011°–021° byd 8 NM blo 4,000′
   022°–052° byd 40 NM
   053°–078° byd 40 NM blo 2,300′
   053°–078° byd 64 NM
   079°–175° byd 40 NM blo 18,000′
   195°–216° byd 40 NM blo 18,000′
   217°–278° byd 40 NM blo 3,000′
   217°–278° byd 61 NM blo 18,000′
   279°–350° byd 40 NM blo 3,400′
   279°–350° byd 59 NM

AUGUSTA
WOODRUFF CO (M60)   4 E   UTC–6(–5DT)   N35°16.31′ W91°16.22′   **MEMPHIS**
200   B   NOTAM FILE JBR   **L–16G**
RWY 09–27: H3797X75 (ASPH)   MIRL   **IAP**
  RWY 09: PAPI(P2L)—GA 3.0° TCH 44′. Road.
  RWY 27: PAPI(P2L)—GA 3.04° TCH 45′. Trees.
SERVICE: **LGT** ACTIVATE MIRL Rwy 09–27—CTAF.
AIRPORT REMARKS: Unattended. Deer on and invof arpt.
AIRPORT MANAGER: 870-731-5516
COMMUNICATIONS: CTAF 122.9
®**MEMPHIS CENTER APP/DEP CON** 135.3
CLEARANCE DELIVERY PHONE: For CD ctc Memphis ARTCC at
  901-368-8453/8449.
RADIO AIDS TO NAVIGATION: NOTAM FILE ARG.
  WALNUT RIDGE (VH) (H) VORTAC 114.5   ARG   Chan 92   N36°06.60′
  W90°57.22′   193° 52.5 NM to fld. 265/4E.
  TACAN AZIMUTH unusable:
   011°–021° byd 15 NM blo 5,000′
  VOR unusable:
   010°–021° byd 40 NM blo 3,000′
   010°–021° byd 55 NM
   011°–021° byd 8 NM blo 4,000′
   022°–052° byd 40 NM
   053°–078° byd 40 NM blo 2,300′
   053°–078° byd 64 NM
   079°–175° byd 40 NM blo 18,000′
   195°–216° byd 40 NM blo 18,000′
   217°–278° byd 40 NM blo 3,000′
   217°–278° byd 61 NM blo 18,000′
   279°–350° byd 40 NM blo 3,400′
   279°–350° byd 59 NM

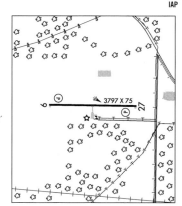

SC, 25 JAN 2024 to 21 MAR 2024

ARKANSAS

BALD KNOB MUNI (M74) 0 SE UTC–6(–5DT) N35°17.97′ W91°33.46′ MEMPHIS
212 B NOTAM FILE JBR
RWY 09–27: H2228X50 (ASPH) MIRL
  RWY 09: Thld dsplcd 246′. Tree.
  RWY 27: Thld dsplcd 146′. Tree.
RWY 04–22: 1850X100 (TURF)
  RWY 04: Road.
  RWY 22: Road.
SERVICE: S2 **LGT** ACTIVATE MIRL Rwy 09–27—CTAF.
AIRPORT REMARKS: Unattended.
AIRPORT MANAGER: 501-281-1218
COMMUNICATIONS: CTAF 122.9
CLEARANCE DELIVERY PHONE: For CD ctc Little Rock Apch 501-379-2908 or Little Rock ATCT 501-379-2911.

BATESVILLE RGNL (BVX)(KBVX) 3 S UTC–6(–5DT) N35°43.57′ W91°38.85′ MEMPHIS
465 B TPA—1250(785) NOTAM FILE BVX H–6J, L–16G
RWY 08–26: H6002X150 (ASPH) S–35, D–50, 2D–80 MIRL IAP
  RWY 08: REIL. PAPI(P2L)—GA 3.0° TCH 44′.
  RWY 26: REIL. PAPI(P2L)—GA 3.0° TCH 45′. Tree.
RWY 18–36: H2804X60 (ASPH) S–8 0.9% up S
  RWY 18: Tree.
  RWY 36: Road.
SERVICE: S4 **FUEL** 100LL, JET A+ **LGT** ACTVT REIL Rwy 08 and 26
  and MIRL Rwy 08–26—CTAF.
AIRPORT REMARKS: Attended 1330–2330Z‡, 2330–1330Z‡ on call.
  100LL fuel self serve avbl with credit card, for service other hours, call
  870-251-1244, fee charged.
AIRPORT MANAGER: 870-251-1244
WEATHER DATA SOURCES: AWOS–3PT 126.375 (870) 251-1369. AWOS–3
  ceiling unreliable.
COMMUNICATIONS: CTAF/UNICOM 122.8
  RCO 122.3 (JONESBORO RADIO)
®**MEMPHIS CENTER APP/DEP CON** 126.85
CLEARANCE DELIVERY PHONE: For CD ctc Memphis ARTCC at
  901-368-8453/8449.
RADIO AIDS TO NAVIGATION: NOTAM FILE ARG.
  WALNUT RIDGE (VH) (H) VORTAC 114.5 ARG Chan 92 N36°06.60′ W90°57.22′ 232° 40.9 NM to fld. 265/4E.
  TACAN AZIMUTH unusable:
    011°–021° byd 15 NM blo 5,000′
  VOR unusable:
    010°–021° byd 40 NM blo 3,000′
    010°–021° byd 55 NM
    011°–021° byd 8 NM blo 4,000′
    022°–052° byd 40 NM
    053°–078° byd 40 NM blo 2,300′
    053°–078° byd 64 NM
    079°–175° byd 40 NM blo 18,000′
    195°–216° byd 40 NM blo 18,000′
    217°–278° byd 40 NM blo 3,000′
    217°–278° byd 61 NM blo 18,000′
    279°–350° byd 40 NM blo 3,400′
    279°–350° byd 59 NM
  ALMND NDB (LOMW) 335 BV N35°42.19′ W91°47.86′ 078° 7.5 NM to fld. 1193/1E. NOTAM FILE BVX.
  LOC/DME 109.7 I–BVX Chan 34 Rwy 08. LOM ALMND NDB. LOC/DME unmonitored indef. DME unusable byd 25°
    right of course.

RWY 18-36 : 2804 X 60

BAXTER CO (See MOUNTAIN HOME on page 69)

BEARCE (See MOUNT IDA on page 68)

ARKANSAS

BENTON

SALINE CO RGNL (SUZ)(KSUZ)　5 E　UTC–6(–5DT)　N34°35.42′ W92°28.77′　　**MEMPHIS**
389　B　NOTAM FILE JBR　MON Airport　　**H–6I, L–14E**
RWY 02–20: H5002X100 (ASPH)　S–54, D–65, 2D–111　MIRL　　**IAP**
　RWY 02: REIL. PAPI(P4L)—GA 3.0° TCH 56′. Trees. Rgt tfc.
　RWY 20: REIL. PAPI(P4L)—GA 3.0° TCH 63′. Tree.
SERVICE: S6　**FUEL** 100LL, JET A+　**LGT** ACTVT REIL Rwys 02 and 20; MIRL Rwy 02–20—CTAF.
AIRPORT REMARKS: Attended Mon–Fri 1400–2230Z‡. Self svc 100LL and Jet A avbl 24/7, for svc after hours call 501–672–9809 call out fee. 100LL: Self svc fuel avbl 24 hrs with credit card. Courtesy car avbl. Aft hrs, ctc AMGR for trml bldg entry code.
AIRPORT MANAGER: (501) 672-9809
WEATHER DATA SOURCES: AWOS–3 132.125 (501) 847–3883.
COMMUNICATIONS: CTAF/UNICOM 122.8
Ⓡ **LITTLE ROCK APP/DEP CON** 119.5
CLEARANCE DELIVERY PHONE: For CD ctc Little Rock Apch 501-379-2908 or Little Rock ATCT 501-379-2911.
RADIO AIDS TO NAVIGATION: NOTAM FILE LIT.
　LITTLE ROCK (H) (H) VORTACW 113.9　LIT　Chan 86　N34°40.66′ W92°10.83′　246° 15.7 NM to fld. 240/5E.
　TACAN AZIMUTH & DME unusable:
　　221°–228° byd 20 NM blo 2,800′
　　229°–239° byd 20 NM blo 2,500′
　　260°–280° byd 35 NM blo 5,000′
　TACAN AZIMUTH unusable:
　　320°–335° byd 5 NM
　ILS/DME 111.95　I–SUZ　Chan 56(Y)　Rwy 02.　Class IT.　Glideslope unusable byd 5° right of course. Unmonitored.

BENTONVILLE MUNI/LOUISE M THADEN FLD (VBT)(KVBT)　2 S　UTC–6(–5DT)　N36°20.72′　　**KANSAS CITY**
W94°13.17′　　**L–16F**
1298　B　NOTAM FILE VBT　　**IAP**
RWY 18–36: H4426X75 (ASPH)　S–12.5, D–21.5　MIRL
　RWY 18: REIL. PAPI(P2L)—GA 3.0° TCH 45′. Thld dspldc 230′. Brush.
　RWY 36: REIL. PAPI(P2R)—GA 3.0° TCH 45′. Pole.
RWY 17–35: 2448X75 (TURF)
RUNWAY DECLARED DISTANCE INFORMATION
　RWY 17: TORA–2448　TODA–2448
　RWY 18:　　　　　　　　　　LDA–4196
　RWY 35: TORA–2448　TODA–2448
　RWY 36:　　　　　　　　ASDA–4196　LDA–4196
SERVICE: S4　**FUEL** 100LL, JET A　**OX** 3　**LGT** ACTIVATE MIRL Rwy 18–36, PAPI Rwy 18–36—CTAF.
AIRPORT REMARKS: Attended Oct–Mar 1400–2300Z‡, Apr–Sep 1300–0100Z‡. For svc after hours call 479–367–9800. Migratory birds on and invof arpt. Beginning 60′ byd north end of Rwy 18 pavement, ground has approximately 12′ drop over 60′ length to pond. Rwy 18 and Rwy 36 marking faded. Rwy 17–35 VFR dalgt opns only. Simul use of rwys 17/35 and 18/36 NA.
AIRPORT MANAGER: 479-254-2028
WEATHER DATA SOURCES: AWOS–3PT 134.975 (479) 273–9198.
COMMUNICATIONS: CTAF/UNICOM 122.975
Ⓡ **RAZORBACK APP/DEP CON** 121.0 (1130–0500Z‡)
　MEMPHIS CENTER APP/DEP CON 126.1 (0500–1130Z‡)
　CLNC DEL 121.05
CLEARANCE DELIVERY PHONE: For CD ctc Razorback Apch 479-649-2416, when Apch clsd ctc Memphis ARTCC at 901-368-8453/8449.

CONTINUED ON NEXT PAGE

ARKANSAS

CONTINUED FROM PRECEDING PAGE

AIRSPACE: CLASS E svc 1130–0500Z‡; other times CLASS G.
RADIO AIDS TO NAVIGATION: NOTAM FILE JBR.
  RAZORBACK (VH) (H) VORTACW 116.4   RZC   Chan 111   N36°14.79´ W94°07.28´   317° 7.6 NM to fld. 1332/4E.
  VOR unusable:
    025°–035° byd 40 NM
    025°–150° byd 22 NM blo 4,000´
    070°–080° byd 40 NM
    093°–103° byd 124 NM
    093°–103° byd 40 NM blo 17,000´
    104°–144° byd 40 NM
    145°–155° byd 40 NM blo 6,500´
    145°–155° byd 67 NM blo 9,500´
    145°–155° byd 80 NM
    150°–210° byd 22 NM blo 3,500´
    156°–170° byd 40 NM
    195°–215° byd 40 NM
    210°–220° byd 22 NM blo 3,000´
    234°–245° byd 40 NM
    310°–025° byd 22 NM blo 3,000´
  TACAN AZIMUTH unusable:
    148°–160°
    225°–240°

BERRYVILLE

CARROLL CO (4M1)   3 W   UTC–6(–5DT)   N36°22.88´ W93°37.47´   KANSAS CITY
  1206   B   NOTAM FILE JBR   L-16F
  RWY 07–25: H3555X75 (ASPH)   S-12   MIRL   1.1% up E   IAP
    RWY 07: REIL. PAPI(P2L)—GA 3.0° TCH 33´. Trees.
    RWY 25: REIL. PAPI(P2L)—GA 3.0° TCH 22´. Trees.
  SERVICE: S4   FUEL 100LL   LGT ACTVT REIL Rwy 07 and Rwy 25; PAPI
    Rwys 07 and Rwy 25, MIRL Rwy 07–25; twy lgts—CTAF.
  AIRPORT REMARKS: Attended Tue–Sat 1400–2300Z‡. Deer, turkey on &
    invof arpt. Ultralight activity on and invof arpt. Fuel avbl 24 hrs self
    service with credit card. No line of sight btn rwy ends.
  AIRPORT MANAGER: 870-423-8393
  COMMUNICATIONS: CTAF 122.9
  Ⓡ RAZORBACK APP/DEP CON 126.6 (1130–0500Z‡)
  Ⓡ MEMPHIS CENTER APP/DEP CON 126.1 (0500–1130Z‡)
  CLEARANCE DELIVERY PHONE: For CD ctc Razorback Apch 479-649-2416,
    when Apch clsd ctc Memphis ARTCC at 901-368-8453/8449.
  RADIO AIDS TO NAVIGATION: NOTAM FILE JBR.
    RAZORBACK (VH) (H) VORTACW 116.4   RZC   Chan 111   N36°14.79´
      W94°07.28´   067° 25.4 NM to fld. 1332/4E.
    VOR unusable:
      025°–035° byd 40 NM
      025°–150° byd 22 NM blo 4,000´
      070°–080° byd 40 NM
      093°–103° byd 124 NM
      093°–103° byd 40 NM blo 17,000´
      104°–144° byd 40 NM
      145°–155° byd 40 NM blo 6,500´
      145°–155° byd 67 NM blo 9,500´
      145°–155° byd 80 NM
      150°–210° byd 22 NM blo 3,500´
      156°–170° byd 40 NM
      195°–215° byd 40 NM
      210°–220° byd 22 NM blo 3,000´
      234°–245° byd 40 NM
      310°–025° byd 22 NM blo 3,000´
    TACAN AZIMUTH unusable:
      148°–160°
      225°–240°

ARKANSAS 37

TRIGGER GAP (17A) 5 SW   UTC−6(−5DT)   N36°19.70′ W93°37.33′   KANSAS CITY
  1650   NOTAM FILE JBR
  RWY 10−28: 3000X75 (TURF)   1.4% up E
    RWY 10: Tree. Rgt tfc.
    RWY 28: Trees.
  AIRPORT REMARKS: Unattended. Deer on and invof arpt.
  AIRPORT MANAGER: 817-938-3334
  COMMUNICATIONS: CTAF 122.9
  CLEARANCE DELIVERY PHONE: For CD ctc Razorback Apch 479-649-2416, when Apch clsd ctc Memphis ARTCC at
    901-368-8453/8449.

BILL AND HILLARY CLINTON NTL/ADAMS FLD (See LITTLE ROCK on page 61)

BILLY FREE MUNI (See DUMAS on page 46)

BLYTHEVILLE

ARKANSAS INTL (BYH)(KBYH)   3 NW   UTC−6(−5DT)   N35°57.86′ W89°56.64′   MEMPHIS
  254   B   NOTAM FILE BYH   H−6J, L−16H
  RWY 18−36: H11602X150 (CONC)   S−155, D−235, 2D−455   IAP
    HIRL(NSTD)
  RWY 36: VASI(V4L)—GA 3.0° TCH 51′.
  SERVICE: S5 **FUEL** 100LL, JET A **LGT** Dusk−Dawn. Actvt HIRL Rwy
    18−36—CTAF. Rwy 18−36 Nstd HIRL; lctd 77′ fm rwy edge and nstd
    dstc fm cntrln. Dpt perception problems may exist durg pds of
    darkness. Rwy 36 VASI OTS indefly.
  AIRPORT REMARKS: Attended Mon−Fri 1400−2300Z‡. Arpt unattended
    holidays. Fuel avbl 24 hrs self serve with credit card (100 LL). No fee
    charged for svc after hrs ctc/leave msg 870−532−5628. Twy A btn
    Twy B and Twy D tkof and ldg avbl to mil acft.
  AIRPORT MANAGER: 870-532-5628
  COMMUNICATIONS: CTAF/UNICOM 122.7
  ®**MEMPHIS CENTER APP/DEP CON** 134.65
  CLEARANCE DELIVERY PHONE: For CD ctc Memphis ARTCC at
    901-368-8453/8449.
  RADIO AIDS TO NAVIGATION: NOTAM FILE DYR.
    DYERSBURG (L) TACAN   Chan 115   DYR (116.8)   N36°01.11′
      W89°19.06′   261° 30.7 NM to fld. 389/3E.
    ILS/DME 110.3 I−BYH Chan 40   Rwy 18. Class
      IT. Unmonitored.

BLYTHEVILLE MUNI (HKA)(KHKA)   3 E   UTC−6(−5DT)   N35°56.43′ W89°49.85′   MEMPHIS
  256   B   TPA—See Remarks   NOTAM FILE HKA   L−16H
  RWY 18−36: H4999X75 (ASPH)   S−15   MIRL   IAP
    RWY 18: PAPI(P4L)—GA 3.0° TCH 48′.
    RWY 36: PAPI(P4L)—GA 3.0° TCH 48′.
  SERVICE: S2 **FUEL** 100LL, JET A **LGT** ACTIVATE MIRL Rwy
    18−36—CTAF. PAPI Rwy 18 and Rwy 36 opr continuously. Wind
    indicator lgt temporarily OTS.
  AIRPORT REMARKS: Attended 1330−2330Z‡. For arpt attendant after hours
    call 870−740−0798/0660. Numerous agricultural acft ops from
    Feb−Nov 250′ AGL and below, right and left TPA.
  AIRPORT MANAGER: 870-763-0200
  WEATHER DATA SOURCES: ASOS 135.025 (870) 763−82C6.
  COMMUNICATIONS: CTAF/UNICOM 123.05
  ®**MEMPHIS CENTER APP/DEP CON** 134.65
  CLEARANCE DELIVERY PHONE: For CD ctc Memphis ARTCC at
    901-368-8453/8449.
  RADIO AIDS TO NAVIGATION: NOTAM FILE DYR.
    DYERSBURG (L) TACAN   Chan 115   DYR (116.8)   N36°01.11′
      W89°19.06′   257° 25.4 NM to fld. 389/3E.

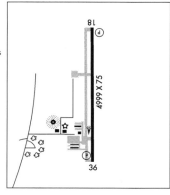

BOONE CO (See HARRISON on page 53)

SC, 25 JAN 2024 to 21 MAR 2024

ARKANSAS

BOONEVILLE MUNI (4M2) 3 E   UTC–6(–5DT)   N35°08.97´ W93°51.80´ MEMPHIS
468 B   NOTAM FILE JBR   L–17E
RWY 09–27: H3254X50 (ASPH)   MIRL   0.6% up W
 RWY 09: Trees.
 RWY 27: Trees.
SERVICE: S4 FUEL 100LL LGT ACTIVATE MIRL Rwy 09–27—CTAF.
AIRPORT REMARKS: Attended Mon–Fri 1400–2300Z‡. Self–serve fuel avbl 24 hrs with credit card.
AIRPORT MANAGER: 479-518-5890
COMMUNICATIONS: CTAF/UNICOM 122.8
CLEARANCE DELIVERY PHONE: For CD ctc Razorback Apch at 479-649-2416, when Apch clsd ctc Memphis ARTCC at 901-368-8453/8449.
RADIO AIDS TO NAVIGATION: NOTAM FILE FSM.
 FORT SMITH (L) (L) VORTACW 110.4   FSM   Chan 41   N35°23.30´ W94°16.29´   118° 24.6 NM to fld. 432/7E.

BRINKLEY

FRANK FEDERER MEML (M36) 0 SE   UTC–6(–5DT)   N34°52.82´ W91°10.59´ MEMPHIS
195 B   NOTAM FILE JBR   L–18F
RWY 02–20: H4002X75 (ASPH) S–12 MIRL   IAP
 RWY 02: PAPI(P2L)—GA 3.0° TCH 45´. Thld dsplcd 248´. Pole. Rgt tfc.
 RWY 20: PAPI(P2L)—GA 3.0° TCH 48´. Thld dsplcd 150´. Tree.
SERVICE: S4 FUEL 100LL LGT ACTIVATE MIRL Rwy 02–20—CTAF.
 Rwy 02 PAPI unusbl byd 5 degs left of cntrln. Rwy 20 PAPI unusbl byd
 4 degs left of cntrln and byd 7 degs right of cntrln.
AIRPORT REMARKS: Attended Mar–Sep Mon–Sat 1400–2300Z‡, Oct–Feb
 Mon–Fri 1400–2300Z‡. Migratory birds on and invof arpt. Numerous
 agricultural acft ops from Feb–Nov 500´ AGL and below. Fuel avbl 24
 hrs self svc with credit card. Water tank NW.
AIRPORT MANAGER: 870-734-5059
COMMUNICATIONS: CTAF/UNICOM 122.8
®MEMPHIS CENTER APP/DEP CON 135.3
CLEARANCE DELIVERY PHONE: For CD ctc Memphis ARTCC at
 901-368-8453/8449.
RADIO AIDS TO NAVIGATION: NOTAM FILE JBR.
 GILMORE (L) (L) VORW/DME 113.0   GQE   Chan 77   N35°20.82´
 W90°28.69´   227° 44.3 NM to fld. 211/4E.

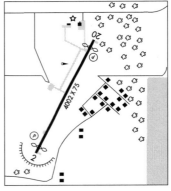

CALICO ROCK–IZARD CO (37T) 3 NW   UTC–6(–5DT)   N36°09.87´ W92°08.67´ KANSAS CITY
733   NOTAM FILE JBR   L–16G
RWY 15–33: H3000X60 (ASPH)   S–12.5   MIRL   1.2% up NW
 RWY 15: REIL. PAPI(P2L)—GA 4.0° TCH 29´.
 RWY 33: REIL. PAPI(P2L)—GA 4.0° TCH 29´. Trees.
SERVICE: LGT Actvt REIL, PAPI and MIRL 15–33—CTAF. Rwy 33 visual
 glide slope indicator OTS indef.
AIRPORT REMARKS: Unattended. Rwy 15 mkgs in poor cond.
AIRPORT MANAGER: (870) 291-1200
COMMUNICATIONS: CTAF 122.9
CLEARANCE DELIVERY PHONE: For CD ctc Memphis ARTCC at
 901-368-8453/8449.
RADIO AIDS TO NAVIGATION: NOTAM FILE FLP.
 FLIPPIN (DH) DME 116.05   FLP   Chan 107(Y)   N36°17.98´
 W92°27.50´   118° 17.3 NM to fld. 782.
 DME unusable:
  020°–050° byd 26 NM blo 3,500´
  020°–050° byd 32 NM blo 4,500´
  075°–105° byd 39 NM blo 4,500´
  105°–135° byd 35 NM blo 4,500´

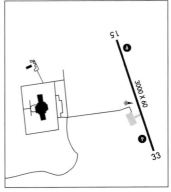

ARKANSAS

CAMDEN

HARRELL FLD (CDH)(KCDH)   5 NE   UTC−6(−5DT)   N33°37.37′ W92°45.80′   **MEMPHIS**
130   B   NOTAM FILE JBR   **H−6I, L−17E**
  RWY 01−19: H6502X100 (ASPH−GRVD)   S−86, D−112, 2S−142,   **IAP**
    2D−180   MIRL
    RWY 01: REIL. PAPI(P2L)—GA 3.0° TCH 45′. Trees.
    RWY 19: REIL. PAPI(P2L)—GA 3.0° TCH 43′. Trees.
  SERVICE: FUEL 100LL, JET A   LGT Actvt MIRL Rwy 18−36, PAPI Rwys
    18 and 36 and REIL Rwys 18 and 36—CTAF.
  AIRPORT REMARKS: Attended Mon−Fri 1400−2230Z‡. For svc aft hrs call
    870−818−3408. Fuel avbl self serve 24 hrs with credit card (100LL
    & JET A). Ultralight activity on and invof arpt. Deer on and in vicinity
    of arpt. NOTE: See Special Notice−Controlled Firing.
  AIRPORT MANAGER: 870−818−3408
  WEATHER DATA SOURCES: AWOS−3 125.2 (870) 574−1011.
  COMMUNICATIONS: CTAF/UNICOM 122.7
  ® FORT WORTH CENTER APP/DEP CON 128.2
  CLEARANCE DELIVERY PHONE: For CD ctc Fort Worth ARTCC at
    817−858−7584.
  RADIO AIDS TO NAVIGATION: NOTAM FILE ELD.
    EL DORADO (VH) (DH) VORW/DME 115.5   ELD   Chan 102
      N33°15.37′ W92°44.64′   350° 22.0 NM to fld. 230/7E.
      DME unusable:
        020°−035° blo 2,000′
        036°−019° byd 30 NM blo 3,200′
      VOR unusable:
        110°−120° byd 40 NM

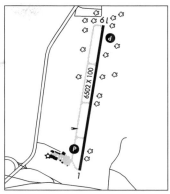

CARLISLE MUNI   (4M3)   2 NE   UTC−6(−5DT)   N34°48.49′ W91°42.73′   **MEMPHIS**
241   B   NOTAM FILE JBR   **L−18F**
  RWY 09−27: H4501X75 (ASPH)   S−17   MIRL   **IAP**
    RWY 09: PAPI(P2L)—GA 3.0° TCH 48′.
    RWY 27: PAPI(P2L)—GA 3.0° TCH 47′. Berm.
  RWY 18−36: H4494X75 (ASPH)   S−17   MIRL
    RWY 18: PAPI(P2L)—GA 3.25° TCH 40′.
    RWY 36: PAPI(P2L)—GA 3.25° TCH 40′. Brush.
  SERVICE: S4   FUEL 100LL   LGT ACTVT PAPI Rwys 09 and 27 and Rwys
    18 and 36; MIRL Rwy 09−27 and Rwy 18−36—CTAF.
  AIRPORT REMARKS: Unattended. Migratory birds invof arpt Nov to Mar.
    Numerous agriculture operations year round. Self serve fuel avbl 24 hrs
    with credit card. Rwy 18 Markings Faded.
  AIRPORT MANAGER: 870−552−5225
  WEATHER DATA SOURCES: AWOS−2 119.275 (870) 552−1445.
  COMMUNICATIONS: CTAF/UNICOM 122.8
  ® LITTLE ROCK APP/DEP CON 135.4
    CLNC DEL 135.4
  CLEARANCE DELIVERY PHONE: For CD when una via freq ctc Little Rock Apch
    501−379−2908 or Little Rock ATCT 501−379−2911
  RADIO AIDS TO NAVIGATION: NOTAM FILE LIT.
    LITTLE ROCK (H) (H) VORTACW 113.9   LIT   Chan 8E   N34°40.66′
      W92°10.83′   066° 24.4 NM to fld. 240/5E.
      TACAN AZIMUTH & DME unusable:
        221°−228° byd 20 NM blo 2,800′
        229°−239° byd 20 NM blo 2,500′
        260°−280° byd 35 NM blo 5,000′
      TACAN AZIMUTH unusable:
        320°−335° byd 5 NM

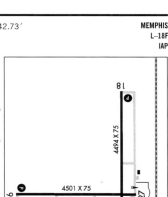

CARROLL CO   (See BERRYVILLE on page 36)

CERCY   N35°07.35′ W91°45.70′   NOTAM FILE SRC.   **MEMPHIS**
  NDB (LOMW) 375   DS   011° 5.4 NM to Searcy Muni   223/2E.

ARKANSAS

CLARENDON MUNI (4M8) 5 SW UTC–6(–5DT) N34°38.80´ W91°23.68´   MEMPHIS
213 B NOTAM FILE JBR   L–18F
RWY 18–36: H3256X60 (ASPH) S–4 MIRL 0.3% up NORTH
　RWY 18: Thld dsplcd 55´. Road.
SERVICE: S2 **FUEL** 100LL **LGT** Actvt MIRL Rwy 18–36—122.7.
AIRPORT REMARKS: Attended Mon–Fri 1400–2300Z‡. Fuel avbl 24 hrs self serve. Migratory birds invof arpt. Rwy 18–36 agriculture acft use turf 2400´ by 100´ area east side of paved rwy, soft when wet. Rwy 18 and 36 markings faded.
AIRPORT MANAGER: 870-241-3781
COMMUNICATIONS: CTAF/UNICOM 122.8
CLEARANCE DELIVERY PHONE: For CD ctc Memphis ARTCC at 901-368-8453/8449.
RADIO AIDS TO NAVIGATION: NOTAM FILE PBF.
　PINE BLUFF (L) (L) VORW/DME 116.0   PBF   Chan 107   N34°14.81´ W91°55.57´   044° 35.6 NM to fld. 212/4E.
　VOR unusable:
　　140°–145° byd 35 NM blo 4,900´
　　260°–275° byd 25 NM

CLARKSVILLE MUNI (H35) 3 E UTC–6(–5DT) N35°28.24´ W93°25.63´   MEMPHIS
481 B TPA—1448(967) NOTAM FILE JBR   L–16F
RWY 09–27: H4504X75 (ASPH) S–19 MIRL 0.7% up E   IAP
　RWY 09: PAPI(P2L)—GA 4.0° TCH 86´. Trees.
　RWY 27: PAPI(P2L)—GA 4.0° TCH 37´. Tree.
SERVICE: S4 **FUEL** 100LL, JET A **LGT** PAPI Rwy 09 & 27 opr consly; MIRL Rwy 09–27 on SS–SR. PAPI unusbl byd 8 degs right of cntrln.
AIRPORT REMARKS: Attended daylight hours. Wildlife on and invof arpt. Self svc fuel avbl 24 hrs with credit card (100LL and Jet A).
AIRPORT MANAGER: 479-264-8408
COMMUNICATIONS: CTAF/UNICOM 122.8
®**MEMPHIS CENTER APP/DEP CON** 128.475
CLEARANCE DELIVERY PHONE: For CD ctc Memphis ARTCC at 901-368-8453/8449.
RADIO AIDS TO NAVIGATION: NOTAM FILE FSM.
　FORT SMITH (L) (L) VORTACW 110.4   FSM   Chan 41   N35°23.30´ W94°16.29´   076° 41.7 NM to fld. 432/7E.

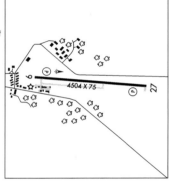

ARKANSAS 41

CLINTON

CLINTON MUNI (CCA)(KCCA)   1 NE   UTC–6(–5DT)   N35°35.87´ W92°27.10´   MEMPHIS
514   B   NOTAM FILE CCA   L–16G
RWY 13–31: H4007X60 (ASPH)   MIRL   0.3% up NW   IAP
  RWY 13: REIL. Trees.
  RWY 31: REIL. PAPI(P2L)—GA 4.0° TCH 69´. Trees.
SERVICE: S4   **FUEL** 100LL   **LGT** Dusk–dawn. Actvt REIL Rwy 13–31; PAPI Rwy 31; MIRL Rwy 13–31—CTAF.
AIRPORT REMARKS: Attended Mon–Fri 1400–2300Z‡. Deer on and invof arpt. 24 hr self svc fuel avbl with credit card. Use extreme care rapidly rising terrain 3 miles southwest thru northeast. Use extreme care rapidly rising terrain 3 miles northwest of arpt.
AIRPORT MANAGER: 501-745-6550
WEATHER DATA SOURCES: AWOS–3 118.725 (501) 745–5000.
COMMUNICATIONS: CTAF/UNICOM 122.7
®**MEMPHIS CENTER APP/DEP CON** 126.850
CLEARANCE DELIVERY PHONE: For CD ctc Memphis ARTCC at 901-368-8453/8449.
AIRSPACE: CLASS E.
RADIO AIDS TO NAVIGATION: NOTAM FILE LIT.
  LITTLE ROCK (H) (H) VORTACW 113.9   LIT   Chan 86   N34°40.66´ W92°10.83´   341° 56.7 NM to fld. 240/5E.
  TACAN AZIMUTH & DME unusable:
    221°–228° byd 20 NM blo 2,800´
    229°–239° byd 20 NM blo 2,500´
    260°–280° byd 35 NM blo 5,000´
  TACAN AZIMUTH unusable:
    320°–335° byd 5 NM

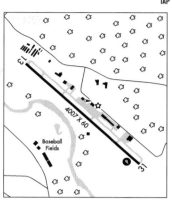

HOLLEY MOUNTAIN AIRPARK (2A2)   5 NE   UTC–6(–5DT)   N35°39.04´ W92°24.23´   MEMPHIS
1270   B   NOTAM FILE JBR   L–16G
RWY 05–23: H4795X50 (ASPH)   MIRL   IAP
  RWY 05: REIL. VASI(V2L)—GA 3.5° TCH 31´. Thld dsplcd 398´. Trees.
  RWY 23: REIL. PAPI(P2L)—GA 3.0° TCH 47´. Trees. Rgt tfc.
SERVICE: **LGT** ACTIVATE REIL Rwy 05 and Rwy 23, VASI Rwy 05; MIRL Rwy 05–23—CTAF. Rwy 05 VASI unusable byd 2° left and 7° right of centerline.
AIRPORT REMARKS: Unattended. Deer on and invof rwy. Rwy 05–23 CLOSED to acft gross weight greater than 12,500 lbs. Beginning 10 ft byd east end of Rwy 23 pavement, gnd has aprx 10 ft drop over 40 ft len. Beginning 50 ft byd west end of Rwy 05 pavement, gnd has aprx 25 ft drop over 125 ft len.
AIRPORT MANAGER: 501-253-4590
COMMUNICATIONS: CTAF/UNICOM 122.7
®**MEMPHIS CENTER APP/DEP CON** 126.85
CLEARANCE DELIVERY PHONE: For CD ctc Memphis ARTCC at 901-368-8453/8449.
RADIO AIDS TO NAVIGATION: NOTAM FILE LIT.
  LITTLE ROCK (H) (H) VORTACW 113.9   LIT   Chan 86   N34°40.66´ W92°10.83´   344° 59.3 NM to fld. 240/5E.
  TACAN AZIMUTH & DME unusable:
    221°–228° byd 20 NM blo 2,800´
    229°–239° byd 20 NM blo 2,500´
    260°–280° byd 35 NM blo 5,000´
  TACAN AZIMUTH unusable:
    320°–335° byd 5 NM
COMM/NAV/WEATHER REMARKS: Wx Info–CTAF (6 clicks).

ARKANSAS

COLT

DELTA RGNL (DRP)(KDRP)   1 SW   UTC−6(−5DT)   N35°07.20′ W90°49.59′   **MEMPHIS**
239   B   NOTAM FILE JBR   H−6J, L−16F
RWY 18−36: H5003X75 (ASPH) S−30 HIRL   IAP
  RWY 18: REIL. PAPI(P2L)—GA 3.0° TCH 44′.
  RWY 36: REIL. PAPI(P2L)—GA 3.0° TCH 44′.
SERVICE: **FUEL** 100LL, JET A   **LGT** Actvt REIL Rwys 18 and 36; HIRL
  Rwy 18−36—CTAF. PAPI Rwys 18 and 36 opers continuously.
AIRPORT REMARKS: Attended Mon−Fri 1300−2230Z‡ For svc aft hrs call
  901−490−5165. Fuel avbl self serve after hrs with credit card.
AIRPORT MANAGER: 870−633−6083
WEATHER DATA SOURCES: AWOS−3 120.0 (870) 630−8144.
COMMUNICATIONS: CTAF/UNICOM 123.0
®MEMPHIS CENTER APP/DEP CON 135.3
CLEARANCE DELIVERY PHONE: For CD ctc Memphis ARTCC at
  901−368−8453/8449.
RADIO AIDS TO NAVIGATION: NOTAM FILE JBR.
  GILMORE (L) (L) VORW/DME 113.0   GQE   Chan 77   N35°20.82′
  W90°28.69′   228° 21.9 NM to fld. 211/4E.

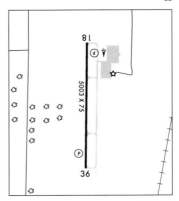

CONWAY RGNL (CXW)(KCXW)   7 SW   UTC−6(−5DT)   N35°01.19′ W92°33.31′   **MEMPHIS**
276   B   NOTAM FILE JBR   H−6I, L−17E
RWY 04−22: H5500X100 (CONC−GRVD) S−30, D−60, 2D−120   MIRL   IAP
  RWY 04: REIL. PAPI(P2L)—GA 3.0° TCH 40′.
  RWY 22: REIL. PAPI(P2L)—GA 3.0° TCH 40′.
SERVICE: S4 **FUEL** 100LL, JET A   **LGT** ACTIVATE REIL, PAPI and MIRL
  Rwy 04 and Rwy 22—CTAF.
AIRPORT REMARKS: Attended 1400−0000Z‡. For svc aft hrs call
  501−697−6476. 100LL avbl 24 hrs self service with credit card. Ldg
  fee, fee waived if fuel is purchased.
AIRPORT MANAGER: 501−358−6200
WEATHER DATA SOURCES: AWOS−2 118.775 (501) 358−6209.
COMMUNICATIONS: CTAF/UNICOM 123.05
® LITTLE ROCK APP CON 119.5 (240°−039°)   135.4 (040°−239°)
® LITTLE ROCK DEP CON 119.5
CLNC DEL 121.2
CLEARANCE DELIVERY PHONE: For CD when una via freq ctc Little Rock Apch
  501−379−2908 or Little Rock ATCT 501−379−2911
RADIO AIDS TO NAVIGATION: NOTAM FILE LIT.
  LITTLE ROCK (H) (H) VORTACW 113.9   LIT   Chan 86   N34°40.66′
  W92°10.83′   313° 27.6 NM to fld. 240/5E.
  TACAN AZIMUTH & DME unusable:
    221°−228° byd 20 NM blo 2,800′
    229°−239° byd 20 NM blo 2,500′
    260°−280° byd 35 NM blo 5,000′
  TACAN AZIMUTH unusable:
    320°−335° byd 5 NM

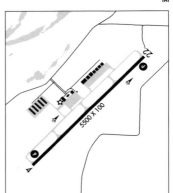

SC, 25 JAN 2024 to 21 MAR 2024

ARKANSAS 43

CORNING MUNI (4M9)   3 W   UTC−6(−5DT)   N36°24.25′ W90°38.88′   ST LOUIS
293   B   NOTAM FILE JBR   L−16H
RWY 18−36: H4299X60 (ASPH)   S−12.5   MIRL   IAP
  RWY 18: REIL. PAPI(P2L)—GA 3.0° TCH 40′. Pole.
  RWY 36: REIL. PAPI(P2L)—GA 3.0° TCH 40′. Road.
SERVICE: S4   FUEL 100LL, JET A   LGT ACTIVATE REIL Rwy 18 and Rwy 36, PAPI Rwy 18 and Rwy 36, MIRL Rwy 18−36 and twy lgts—CTAF.
AIRPORT REMARKS: Attended Mon−Fri 1300−0100Z‡, Sat 1400−1800Z‡ and Sun unattended. Self svc fuel avbl 24 hrs with credit card.
AIRPORT MANAGER: 870-323-0304
WEATHER DATA SOURCES: AWOS−3 118.325 (870) 857−9702.
COMMUNICATIONS: CTAF/UNICOM 123.0
®MEMPHIS CENTER APP/DEP CON 120.075
CLEARANCE DELIVERY PHONE: For CD ctc Memphis ARTCC at 901-368-8453/8449.
RADIO AIDS TO NAVIGATION: NOTAM FILE ARG.
  WALNUT RIDGE (VH) (H) VORTAC 114.5   ARG   Chan 92   N36°06.60′ W90°57.22′   036° 23.0 NM to fld. 265/4E
  TACAN AZIMUTH unusable:
    011°−021° byd 15 NM blo 5,000′
  VOR unusable:
    010°−021° byd 40 NM blo 3,000′
    010°−021° byd 55 NM
    011°−021° byd 8 NM blo 4,000′
    022°−052° byd 40 NM
    053°−078° byd 40 NM blo 2,300′
    053°−078° byd 64 NM
    079°−175° byd 40 NM blo 18,000′
    195°−216° byd 40 NM blo 18,000′
    217°−278° byd 40 NM blo 3,000′
    217°−278° byd 61 NM blo 18,000′
    279°−350° byd 40 NM blo 3,400′
    279°−350° byd 59 NM

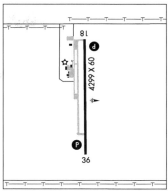

CROSSETT

Z M JACK STELL FLD (CRT)(KCRT)   5 NE   UTC−6(−5DT)   N33°10.70′ W91°52.81′   MEMPHIS
184   B   NOTAM FILE JBR   H−6J, L−18F
RWY 05−23: H5010X75 (ASPH)   S−19   MIRL   IAP
  RWY 05: PAPI(P2L)—GA 3.25° TCH 42′. Trees.
  RWY 23: PAPI(P2L)—GA 3.25° TCH 42′.
SERVICE: FUEL 100LL, JET A   LGT Rwy 05 and Rwy 23 PAPI nightime only.
AIRPORT REMARKS: Attended Mon−Fri irregularly. Self serve 100LL avbl 24 hrs with credit card. Assitance avbl if needed. Midfield twy clsd to acft over 6000 lbs. Lndg fee chrgd acft gtr than 8645 lbs unless fuel purchased.
AIRPORT MANAGER: 870-304-6361
COMMUNICATIONS: CTAF/UNICOM 122.8
®MEMPHIS CENTER APP/DEP CON 135.875
CLEARANCE DELIVERY PHONE: For CD ctc Memphis ARTCC at 901-368-8453/8449.
RADIO AIDS TO NAVIGATION: NOTAM FILE JBR.
  MONTICELLO (L) DME 111.6   MON   Chan 53   N33°33.72′ W91°42.93′   200° 24.4 NM to fld. 208.

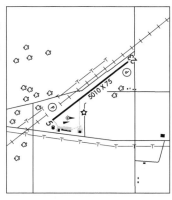

CRYSTAL LAKE (See DECATUR on page 45)

SC, 25 JAN 2024 to 21 MAR 2024

ARKANSAS

DANVILLE MUNI (32A) 3 NW UTC–6(–5DT) N35°05.24´ W93°25.74´ MEMPHIS
393 B NOTAM FILE JBR H–6I, L–17E
RWY 11–29: H4466X75 (ASPH) S–12.5 MIRL 0.4% up E IAP
SERVICE: FUEL 100LL LGT ACTVT MIRL Rwy 11–29 —CTAF.
AIRPORT REMARKS: Unattended. For svc call Yell County sheriff
 501–495–4881. Self-serve fuel avbl 24 hrs with credit card OTS
 indef.
AIRPORT MANAGER: 479–495–0722
COMMUNICATIONS: CTAF 122.9
®**MEMPHIS CENTER APP/DEP CON** 128.475
CLEARANCE DELIVERY PHONE: For CD ctc Memphis ARTCC at
 901–368–8453/8449.
AIRSPACE: CLASS E.
RADIO AIDS TO NAVIGATION: NOTAM FILE HOT.
 HOT SPRINGS (L) (L) VOR/DME 110.0 HOT Chan 37 N34°28.72´
  W93°05.44´ 331° 40.1 NM to fld. 529/4E.
 VOR unusable:
  030°–045° byd 25 NM
  056°–074° byd 20 NM blo 6,500´
  075°–095° byd 15 NM blo 6,500´
  096°–140° byd 11 NM blo 3,000´
  141°–187° byd 14 NM blo 5,000´
  141°–227° byd 20 NM blo 3,500´
  141°–227° byd 26 NM blo 5,500´
  228°–311° byd 20 NM blo 3,500´
  312°–345° byd 6 NM blo 4,500´
  312°–345° byd 15 NM blo 5,500´
  312°–345° byd 32 NM blo 9,500´
  346°–055° byd 20 NM blo 3,500´
  349°–359° byd 20 NM blo 4,500´
 DME unusable:
  025°–055° byd 32 NM blo 4,500´
  056°–070° byd 35 NM blo 6,000´
  071°–095° byd 35 NM blo 4,000´
  096°–140° byd 13 NM blo 4,000´
  096°–140° byd 8 NM blo 3,000´
  184°–215° byd 15 NM blo 7,500´
  184°–215° byd 35 NM blo 3,000´
  316°–055° byd 15 NM blo 7,500´
  316°–055° byd 18 NM blo 4,500´
  316°–055° byd 20 NM blo 9,500´
  316°–055° byd 28 NM blo 11,500´
  316°–055° byd 35 NM blo 17,500´
  316°–055° byd 5 NM blo 5,500´
  345°–360° byd 35 NM

DE QUEEN
 J LYNN HELMS SEVIER CO (DEQ)(KDEQ) 3 W UTC–6(–5DT) N34°02.82´ W94°23.96´ MEMPHIS
 355 B NOTAM FILE DEQ H–6I, L–17D
 RWY 08–26: H5001X75 (ASPH) S–27 MIRL IAP
  RWY 08: REIL. PAPI(P2L)—GA 3.0° TCH 44´. Tree.
  RWY 26: REIL. PAPI(P2L)—GA 3.0° TCH 49´. Trees.
 SERVICE: FUEL 100LL, JET A LGT Dusk–Dawn. Actvt REIL Rwy 08 and
  26; PAPI Rwy 08 and 26; MIRL Rwy 08–26—CTAF.
 AIRPORT REMARKS: Unattended. Fuel avbl 24 hr self serve with major credit
  card (100LL & Jet A).
 AIRPORT MANAGER: 870–582–2492
 WEATHER DATA SOURCES: ASOS 134.075 (870) 642–7829.
 COMMUNICATIONS: CTAF/UNICOM 122.8
 ®**FORT WORTH CENTER APP/DEP CON** 123.925
 CLEARANCE DELIVERY PHONE: For CD ctc Fort Worth ARTCC at
  817–858–7584.
 RADIO AIDS TO NAVIGATION: NOTAM FILE TXK.
  TEXARKANA (VH) (H) VORTACW 116.3 TXK Chan 110 N33°30.83´
   W94°04.39´ 326° 35.9 NM to fld. 273/7E.

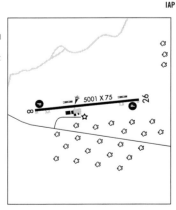

SC, 25 JAN 2024 to 21 MAR 2024

ARKANSAS   45

DE WITT

DEWITT MUNI/WHITCOMB FLD (5M1)   3 SE   LTC–6(–5DT)   N34°15.74′ W91°18.45′   **MEMPHIS**
189   B   NOTAM FILE JBR   L–18F
RWY 18–36: H3205X60 (ASPH)   S–12   MIRL   IAP
  RWY 18: REIL. PAPI(P2L)—GA 3.0° TCH 40′. Road.
  RWY 36: REIL. PAPI(P2L)—GA 3.0° TCH 40′.
SERVICE: S4   **FUEL** 100LL   **LGT** ACTVT REIL Rwy 18 and Rwy 36; PAPI
  Rwy 18 and Rwy 36; MIRL Rwy 18–36—CTAF.
AIRPORT REMARKS: Attended Mon–Fri 1400–2300Z‡, Mar–Aug Sat
  1300–1800Z‡. For svc aft hrs call 870–830–3091 or
  870–946–1745. Fuel avbl 24 hr self serve with credit card.
AIRPORT MANAGER: 870–830–3091
COMMUNICATIONS: CTAF 122.9
®**MEMPHIS CENTER APP/DEP CON** 135.3
CLEARANCE DELIVERY PHONE: For CD ctc Memphis ARTCC at
  901–368–8453/8449.
RADIO AIDS TO NAVIGATION: NOTAM FILE PBF.
  PINE BLUFF (L) (L) VORW/DME 116.0   PBF   Chan 107   N34°14.81′
    W91°55.57′   084° 30.8 NM to fld. 212/4E
    VOR unusable:
      140°–145° byd 35 NM blo 4,900′
      260°–275° byd 25 NM

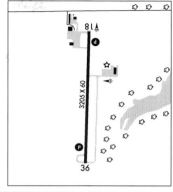

DECATUR

CRYSTAL LAKE (5M5)   2 NE   UTC–6(–5DT)   N36°20.62′ W94°26.69′   **KANSAS CITY**
1178   NOTAM FILE JBR   L–16F
RWY 13–31: H3863X75 (ASPH)   S–10   LIRL   0.6% up SE   IAP
  RWY 13: VASI(V2L)—GA 3.5° TCH 53′. Trees.
  RWY 31: VASI(V2L)—GA 3.5° TCH 37′. Trees.
SERVICE: S4   **LGT** Rwy 13 VASI OTS indef. Rwy 31 VASI OTS indef.
AIRPORT REMARKS: Unattended. Deer and geese on and invof arpt. Rwy
  13–31 NSTD thld markings due to size. Be alert for +176′ tower
  approximately 1300′ north of Rwy 13. Rwy 13–31 unmarked.
AIRPORT MANAGER: 479–220–5047
COMMUNICATIONS: CTAF/UNICOM 122.8
®**RAZORBACK APP/DEP CON** 121.0 (1130–0500Z‡)
®**MEMPHIS CENTER APP/DEP CON** 126.1 (0500–1130Z‡)
  CLNC DEL 126.6
CLEARANCE DELIVERY PHONE: For CD ctc Razorback Apch 479–649–2416,
  when Apch clsd ctc Memphis ARTCC at 901–368–8453/8449.
RADIO AIDS TO NAVIGATION: NOTAM FILE JBR.
  RAZORBACK (VH) (H) VORTACW 116.4   RZC   Chan 111   N36°14.79′
    W94°07.28′   286° 16.7 NM to fld. 1332/4E.
    VOR unusable:
      025°–035° byd 40 NM
      025°–150° byd 22 NM blo 4,000′
      070°–080° byd 40 NM
      093°–103° byd 124 NM
      093°–103° byd 40 NM blo 17,000′
      104°–144° byd 40 NM
      145°–155° byd 40 NM blo 6,500′
      145°–155° byd 67 NM blo 9,500′
      145°–155° byd 80 NM
      150°–210° byd 22 NM blo 3,500′
      156°–170° byd 40 NM
      195°–215° byd 40 NM
      210°–220° byd 22 NM blo 3,000′
      234°–245° byd 40 NM
      310°–025° byd 22 NM blo 3,000′
    TACAN AZIMUTH unusable:
      148°–160°
      225°–240°

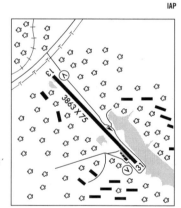

DELTA RGNL (See COLT on page 42)

SC, 25 JAN 2024 to 21 MAR 2024

ARKANSAS

DERMOTT MUNI (4M5) 3 SW UTC–6(–5DT) N33°29.28′ W91°26.56′ MEMPHIS
135 B NOTAM FILE JBR
RWY 01–19: H2980X50 (ASPH)
  RWY 01: Tree.
SERVICE: LGT Rotating bcn OTS indef.
AIRPORT REMARKS: Unattended. Nmrs agricultural acft ops Feb–Nov 500′ AGL and below. Rwy 01–19 nmrs cracks, and crumbling thrut rwy. Rwy 01 and Rwy 19 markings faded.
AIRPORT MANAGER: 870-866-5203
COMMUNICATIONS: CTAF 122.9
CLEARANCE DELIVERY PHONE: For CD ctc Memphis ARTCC at 901-368-8453/8449.

DEWITT MUNI/WHITCOMB FLD (See DE WITT on page 45)

DEXTER B FLORENCE MEML FLD (See ARKADELPHIA on page 32)

DRAKE FLD (See FAYETTEVILLE on page 48)

DUMAS

BILLY FREE MUNI (ØMØ) 2 W UTC–6(–5DT) N33°53.07′ W91°32.06′ MEMPHIS
164 B NOTAM FILE JBR H–6J, L–18F
RWY 18–36: H5003X75 (ASPH) S–15 MIRL IAP
  RWY 36: PAPI(P2L)—GA 3.0° TCH 40′.
SERVICE: S4 **FUEL** 100LL, JET A **LGT** ACTVT PAPI Rwy 36; MIRL Rwy 18–36—CTAF. Bcn temp OTS.
AIRPORT REMARKS: Attended Mon–Fri 1400–2300Z‡. Migratory birds on and invof arpt Nov–Feb. For arpt attendant after hrs call 870-299-3861. Self service fuel avbl 24 hrs with credit card (100LL & Jet A).
AIRPORT MANAGER: 870-382-2216
COMMUNICATIONS: CTAF/UNICOM 122.8
®**MEMPHIS CENTER APP/DEP CON** 135.875
CLEARANCE DELIVERY PHONE: For CD ctc Memphis ARTCC at 901-368-8453/8449.
RADIO AIDS TO NAVIGATION: NOTAM FILE JBR.
  MONTICELLO (L) DME 111.6 MON Chan 53 N33°33.72′ W91°42.93′ 025° 21.3 NM to fld. 208.

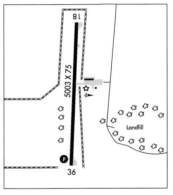

EL DORADO

EL DORADO DOWNTOWN–STEVENS FLD (F43) 0 S UTC–6(–5DT) N33°11.48′ W92°39.79′ MEMPHIS
256 B NOTAM FILE JBR L–17E
RWY 18–36: H3000X60 (ASPH) S–7 LIRL
  RWY 18: Trees.
  RWY 36: PAPI(P2L)—GA 3.5° TCH 32′. Trees.
SERVICE: S4 **FUEL** 100LL
AIRPORT REMARKS: Attended Mon–Fri 1400–2300Z‡. For svc after hrs call 870-310-0310; 24 hr self svc fuel with credit card avbl. Ultralight activity on and invof arpt. Rwy 18 ground drops off 10′ + approx 40′ from rwy end. Rwy 36 ground drops off 10′ + approx 30′ from rwy end.
AIRPORT MANAGER: 870-863-5068
COMMUNICATIONS: CTAF/UNICOM 122.8
CLEARANCE DELIVERY PHONE: For CD ctc Fort Worth ARTCC at 817-858-7584.
RADIO AIDS TO NAVIGATION: NOTAM FILE ELD.
  (VH) (DH) VORW/DME 115.5 ELD Chan 102 N33°15.37′ W92°44.64′ 127° 5.6 NM to fld. 230/7E.
  DME unusable:
    020°–035° blo 2,000′
    036°–019° byd 30 NM blo 3,200′
  VOR unusable:
    110°–120° byd 40 NM

ARKANSAS

SOUTH ARKANSAS RGNL AT GOODWIN FLD (ELD)(KELD) 8 W   UTC–6(–5DT)   N33°13.27′   **MEMPHIS**
W92°48.70′   **H–6I, L–17E**
277   B   NOTAM FILE ELD   **IAP**
RWY 04–22: H6601X150 (ASPH–AFSC)   S–75, D–200, 2S–175   HIRL
  RWY 04: PAPI(P4L)—GA 3.0° TCH 50′. Trees.
  RWY 22: MALSR. PAPI(P4L)—GA 3.0° TCH 53′.
RWY 13–31: H5100X100 (ASPH)   S–25   MIRL   0.7% up NW
  RWY 13: PAPI(P2L)—GA 4.0° TCH 43′.
  RWY 31: PAPI(P2R)—GA 4.0° TCH 43′.
SERVICE: S4   **FUEL** 100LL, JET A+   **LGT** HIRL Rwy 04–22 preset low intst; to incr intst and actvt MIRL Rwy 13–31; MALSR Rwy 22 and twy lgts—CTAF. Rwy 13 PAPI unusbl byd 9 degs left and 6 degs right of cntrln. Rwy 31 PAPI unusbl byd 7 degs left and right of cntrln.
AIRPORT REMARKS: Attended Mon–Fri 1200–2330Z‡, Sat 1630–2330Z‡, Sun 1630–2330Z‡. For svc aft hrs call 870–312–6255; fee chrgd.
NOTE: See Special Notices—Controlled Firing.
AIRPORT MANAGER: 870–881–4192
WEATHER DATA SOURCES: ASOS 118.325 (870) 862–3090.
COMMUNICATIONS: CTAF/UNICOM 123.0
  EL DORADO RCO 122.2 (JONESBORO RADIO)
Ⓡ **FORT WORTH CENTER APP/DEP CON** 128.2
CLEARANCE DELIVERY PHONE: For CD if una to ctc on FSS freq, ctc Fort Worth ARTCC at 817-858-7584.
AIRSPACE: CLASS E.
RADIO AIDS TO NAVIGATION: NOTAM FILE ELD.
EL DORADO (VH) (DH) VORW/DME 115.5   ELD   Char 102   N33°15.37′ W92°44.64′   232° 4.0 NM to fld. 230/7E.
  DME unusable:
    020°–035° blo 2,000′
    036°–019° byd 30 NM blo 3,200′
  VOR unusable:
    110°–120° byd 40 NM
LADOS NDB (LOMW) 418   EL   N33°17.16′ W92°43.69′   224° 5.7 NM to fld. 140/3E.
ILS/DME 111.1   I–ELD   Chan 48   Rwy 22.   Class IA.   LOM LADOS NDB. ILS/DME unmonitored when ATCT closed..
  LOM unmonitored. DME unusable byd 021° right of course.

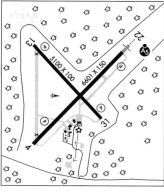

ARKANSAS

FAYETTEVILLE

DRAKE FLD (FYV)(KFYV) 3 S UTC−6(−5DT) N36°00.31′ W94°10.20′
1252 B TPA—2101(849) Class IV, ARFF Index A NOTAM FILE FYV

KANSAS CITY
H−6I, L−16F
IAP, AD

RWY 16−34: H6005X100 (ASPH−GRVD) S−90, D−150, 2S−175, 2D−175 MIRL
  RWY 16: ODALS. PAPI(P4L)—GA 3.0° TCH 50′.
  RWY 34: ODALS. PAPI(P4L)—GA 3.5° TCH 58′. Tree.
RUNWAY DECLARED DISTANCE INFORMATION
  RWY 16: TORA−6005 TODA−6005 ASDA−6005 LDA−6005
  RWY 34: TORA−6005 TODA−6005 ASDA−6005 LDA−6005
SERVICE: S2 **FUEL** 100LL, JET A **LGT** When ATCT clsd MIRL Rwy 16−34 preset med intst. Actvt ODALS Rwy 16 and 34; PAPI Rwy 34—CTAF.
AIRPORT REMARKS: Attended Mon−Fri 1200−0400Z‡, Sat−Sun 1400−0200Z‡. Deer on and invof arpt. For fuel after hrs call 479−443−4343, fee charged. Self service avbl 24hrs. 24 hr PPR for air carrier ops with more than 30 passenger seats call arpt manager 479−718−7642 and fax FBO 479−718−7646.
AIRPORT MANAGER: (479) 718−7644
WEATHER DATA SOURCES: ASOS 119.575 (479) 442−5237.
COMMUNICATIONS: CTAF 128.0 ATIS 119.575 UNICOM 122.95
  FAYETTEVILLE RCO 122.3 (JONESBORO RADIO)
  Ⓡ **RAZORBACK APP/DEP CON** 121.0 (1130−0500Z‡)
  Ⓡ **MEMPHIS CENTER APP/DEP CON** 126.1 (0500−1130Z‡)
  TOWER 128.0 (1200−0400Z‡) **GND CON** 121.8
CLEARANCE DELIVERY PHONE: For CD ctc Memphis ARTCC at 901−368−8453/8449.
AIRSPACE: CLASS D svc 1200−0400Z‡; other times CLASS E.
RADIO AIDS TO NAVIGATION: NOTAM FILE JBR.
  RAZORBACK (VH) (H) VORTACW 116.4 RZC Chan 111 N36°14.79′ W94°07.28′ 185° 14.7 NM to fld. 1332/4E.
  VOR unusable:
    025°−035° byd 40 NM
    025°−150° byd 22 NM blo 4,000′
    070°−080° byd 40 NM
    093°−103° byd 124 NM
    093°−103° byd 40 NM blo 17,000′
    104°−144° byd 40 NM
    145°−155° byd 40 NM blo 6,500′
    145°−155° byd 67 NM blo 9,500′
    145°−155° byd 80 NM
    150°−210° byd 22 NM blo 3,500′
    156°−170° byd 40 NM
    195°−215° byd 40 NM
    210°−220° byd 22 NM blo 3,000′
    234°−245° byd 40 NM
    310°−025° byd 22 NM blo 3,000′
  TACAN AZIMUTH unusable:
    148°−160°
    225°−240°
  LOC/DME 111.9 I−FYV Chan 56 Rwy 16. LOC/DME unmonitored when ATCT clsd. LOC unusable wi 0.0 NM abv 2,500′ 1.2 DME; unusable wi 2.5 NM abv 3,200′ 3.7 DME.
  LDA/DME 111.9 I−LFH Chan 56 Rwy 34. LOC unusable byd 10 NM blw 3,500′; byd 10° right of course. DME unusable byd 10° right of course; byd 8 NM byd 3,000′; byd 10 NM blo 3,500′ byd 15 NM.
  ASR (1200−0400Z‡)

FAYETTEVILLE N36°00.50′ W94°10.83′
RCO 122.3 (JONESBORO RADIO)

KANSAS CITY
L−16F

ARKANSAS

FAYETTEVILLE/SPRINGDALE/ROGERS

NORTHWEST ARKANSAS NTL (XNA)(KXNA) 15 NW UTC–6(–5DT) N36°16.89´ W94°18.47´   KANSAS CITY
1288 B Class I, ARFF Index B NOTAM FILE XNA   H–6I, L–16F
RWY 16L–34R: H8801X150 (CONC–GRVD) S–120, D–223, 2D–404   IAP, AD
  PCN 68 R/B/W/T HIRL
  RWY 16L: MALSR. PAPI(P4L)—GA 3.0° TCH 52´. RVR–TR
  RWY 34R: MALSR. PAPI(P4L)—GA 3.0° TCH 51´. RVR–TR
RWY 16R–34L: H8800X150 (CONC–GRVD) S–75, D–150, 2D–350
  MIRL
RUNWAY DECLARED DISTANCE INFORMATION
  RWY 16L: TORA–8800 TODA–8800 ASDA–8800 LDA–8800
  RWY 16R: TORA–8800 TODA–8800 ASDA–8800 LDA–8800
  RWY 34L: TORA–8800 TODA–8800 ASDA–8800 LDA–8800
  RWY 34R: TORA–8800 TODA–8800 ASDA–8800 LDA–8800
SERVICE: **FUEL** 100LL, JET A **OX** 2 **LGT** When ATCT clsd actvt
  MALSR Rwy 16L & 34R; HIRL Rwy 16L–34R—CTAF. PAPI Rwy 16L
  & 34R oper consly. Caution: elevated rwy thld lgts AER Rwys 16L &
  34R.
AIRPORT REMARKS: Attended continuously. Bird activity on and invof arpt.
  For fuel svcs use freq 130.05. Distance and direction to arpt from
  Springdale is 10 NM northwest and from Rogers MSA is 9 NM
  southwest.
AIRPORT MANAGER: 479–205–1000
WEATHER DATA SOURCES: ASOS 119.425 (479) 203–0109.
COMMUNICATIONS: CTAF 127.1 **ATIS** 119.425
  FAYETTEVILLE/SPRINGDALE/ROGERS RCO 122.55 (JONESBORO RADIO)
Ⓡ **RAZORBACK APP/DEP CON** 121.0 (West) 126.6 (East) (1130–0500Z‡)
Ⓡ **MEMPHIS CENTER APP/DEP CON** 126.1 (0500–1130Z‡)
  TOWER 127.1 (1130–0500Z‡) **GND CON** 121.9
CLEARANCE DELIVERY PHONE: For CD ctc Memphis ARTCC at 901–368–8453/8449.
AIRSPACE: CLASS C svc ctc **APP CON** svc 1130–0500Z‡ other times CLASS G.
RADIO AIDS TO NAVIGATION: NOTAM FILE JBR.
  RAZORBACK (VH) (H) VORTACW 116.4   RZC   Chan 111   N36°14.79´ W94°07.28´   279° 9.3 NM to fld. 1332/4E.
  VOR unusable:
    025°–035° byd 40 NM
    025°–150° byd 22 NM blo 4,000´
    070°–080° byd 40 NM
    093°–103° byd 124 NM
    093°–103° byd 40 NM blo 17,000´
    104°–144° byd 40 NM
    145°–155° byd 40 NM blo 6,500´
    145°–155° byd 67 NM blo 9,500´
    145°–155° byd 80 NM
    150°–210° byd 22 NM blo 3,500´
    156°–170° byd 40 NM
    195°–215° byd 40 NM
    210°–220° byd 22 NM blo 3,000´
    234°–245° byd 40 NM
    310°–025° byd 22 NM blo 3,000´
  TACAN AZIMUTH unusable:
    148°–160°
    225°–240°
  ILS/DME 111.55 I–XNA Chan 52(Y) Rwy 16L. Class IE.
  ILS/DME 111.55 I–FBS Chan 52(Y) Rwy 34R. Class IE.

ARKANSAS

FLIPPIN

MARION CO RGNL (FLP)(KFLP) 1 N UTC–6(–5DT) N36°17.45′ W92°35.42′ KANSAS CITY
720 B NOTAM FILE FLP H–6I, L–16G
  IAP
RWY 04–22: H5001X75 (ASPH) S–30 MIRL 1.3% up NE
  RWY 04: REIL. PAPI(P2L)—GA 3.5° TCH 71′. Tree.
  RWY 22: REIL. PAPI(P2L)—GA 3.5° TCH 52′. Trees.
SERVICE: S2 **FUEL** 100LL, JET A **LGT** Actvt MIRL Rwy 04–22; PAPI and
  REIL Rwy 04 and 22—CTAF.
AIRPORT REMARKS: Attended Mon–Sat 1500–2100Z‡. For srvc aft hrs call
  918–760–4438. Wildlife on and invof arpt. Ultralight activity on and
  invof arpt. Fuel avbl 24 hrs self svc (100LL and Jet A). No line of sight
  between rwy ends.
AIRPORT MANAGER: 870-453-2241
WEATHER DATA SOURCES: AWOS–3PT 132.075 (870) 453–2380.
COMMUNICATIONS: CTAF/UNICOM 123.0
  FLIPPIN RCO 122.35 (JONESBORO RADIO)
  ®**MEMPHIS CENTER APP/DEP CON** 126.85
CLEARANCE DELIVERY PHONE: For CD ctc Memphis ARTCC at
  901-368-8453/8449.
RADIO AIDS TO NAVIGATION: NOTAM FILE FLP.
  FLIPPIN (DH) DME 116.05 FLP Chan 107(Y) N36°17.98′
  W92°27.50′ 265° 6.4 NM to fld. 782.
  DME unusable:
    020°–050° byd 26 NM blo 3,500′
    020°–050° byd 32 NM blo 4,500′
    075°–105° byd 39 NM blo 4,500′
    105°–135° byd 35 NM blo 4,500′

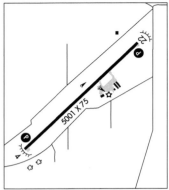

FORDYCE MUNI (5M4) 3 NE UTC–6(–5DT) N33°50.75′ W92°21.93′ MEMPHIS
193 B NOTAM FILE JBR L–18F
RWY 05–23: H3183X60 (ASPH) S–4 MIRL
  RWY 05: Trees.
  RWY 23: Trees.
SERVICE: **FUEL** 100LL **LGT** Rwy 05–23 MIRL oprs Dusk–0700Z‡. Bcn
  oprs dusk–0700Z+.
AIRPORT REMARKS: Unattended. Deer & migratory birds on & invof airport.
  Fuel avbl 24 hr self service with credit card.
AIRPORT MANAGER: 870-313-2870
COMMUNICATIONS: CTAF 122.9
CLEARANCE DELIVERY PHONE: For CD ctc Memphis ARTCC at
  901-368-8453/8449.
RADIO AIDS TO NAVIGATION: NOTAM FILE PBF.
  PINE BLUFF (L) (L) VORW/DME 116.0 PBF Chan 107 N34°14.81′
  W91°55.57′ 218° 32.5 NM to fld. 212/4E.
  VOR unusable:
    140°–145° byd 35 NM blo 4,900′
    260°–275° byd 25 NM

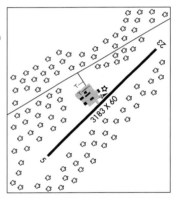

SC, 25 JAN 2024 to 21 MAR 2024

ARKANSAS 51

FORREST CITY

HUTFLY (FCY)(KFCY) 4 S UTC–6(–5DT) N34°56.52´ W90°46.50´ **MEMPHIS**
249 B NOTAM FILE JBR L–18F
RWY 18–36: H3014X50 (ASPH) S–20 MIRL
 RWY 18: REIL. PAPI(P2L)—GA 4.0° TCH 36´.
 RWY 36: REIL. PAPI(P2R)—GA 4.0° TCH 36´. Trees.
SERVICE: S4 **FUEL** JET A **LGT** Dusk–Dawn. Actvt PAPI Rwy 18 and 36; MIRL Rwy 18–36—CTAF. Rotg bcn OTS indefly. Rwy 18–36 REIL OTS indefly. Rwy 18–36 PAPI OTS indefly.
AIRPORT REMARKS: Attended Mon–Fri 1400–2300Z‡. Rwy 36 ditch 201´ from south end of rwy. 494´ lgtd twr 3 miles north on centerline.
AIRPORT MANAGER: 870-633-4511
COMMUNICATIONS: CTAF/UNICOM 122.8
®**MEMPHIS CENTER APP/DEP CON** 135.3
CLEARANCE DELIVERY PHONE: For CD ctc Memphis Apch at 901-842-8457.

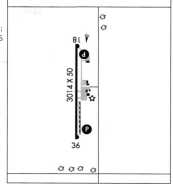

FORT SMITH RGNL (FSM)(KFSM) P (ANG) 3 SE UTC–6(–5DT) N35°20.20´ W94°21.97´ **MEMPHIS**
469 B Class I, ARFF Index B NOTAM FILE FSM H–6I, L–16F
RWY 08–26: H9318X150 (ASPH–GRVD) S–75, D–175, 2D–295 IAP, AD
 HIRL
 RWY 08: MALSR. PAPI(P4R)—GA 3.0° TCH 51´. RVR–R Tree.
 RWY 26: MALSR. PAPI(P4L)—GA 3.0° TCH 50´. RVR–T Tree.
RWY 02–20: H5001X150 (ASPH–GRVD) S–55, D–70, 2D–120 MIRL
 RWY 02: PAPI(P4R)—GA 3.0° TCH 50´. Railroad.
 RWY 20: PAPI(P4L)—GA 3.0° TCH 40´. Tree.
RUNWAY DECLARED DISTANCE INFORMATION
 RWY 02: TORA–5001 TODA–5001 ASDA–5001 LDA–5001
 RWY 20: TORA–5001 TODA–5001 ASDA–5001 LDA–5001
SERVICE: S4 **FUEL** 100LL, JET A **LGT** When ATCT clsd actvt MALSR Rwy 08 and 26; MIRL Rwy 02–20; HIRL Rwy 08–26—CTAF. Rwy 02 PAPI unusbl 8 degs left of cntrln. Rwy 20 PAPI unusbl 5 deg right of cntrln. **MILITARY— FUEL** A+ (C479–646–1611.) (NC–100LL – avbl H24 self svc; A – not avbl 0400Z‡ Sat – 1200Z‡ Sun and 0400Z‡ Sun – 1200Z‡ Mon.) **FLUID** PRESAIR LOX **OIL** O–128–(133–148 Mil) SOAP
AIRPORT REMARKS: Attended continuously. Flock of migratory birds on and in vicinity of arpt. Fuel 100LL avbl 24 hrs self serve. For Jet A Sat and Sun 0400–1200Z‡ call 479–646–1611. Rwy 02 aiming points 1390´ fm thld. Landing fee for all FAR 121 and FAR 135 opns above 12,500 lbs. PPR for all acft (including U.S. government) above 100,000 lbs contact arpt manager Mon–Fri 1400–2300Z‡ 479–452–7000 minimum 24 hrs in advance. 24 hrs PPR for unscheduled air carrier ops with more than 30 passenger seats call arpt manager 479–452–7000.
AIRPORT MANAGER: 479-452-7000
WEATHER DATA SOURCES: ASOS (479) 649–2425 LLWAS.
COMMUNICATIONS: CTAF 118.3 **ATIS** 124.775 **UNICOM** 122.95
 RCO 122.2 (JONESBORO RADIO)
®**RAZORBACK APP/DEP CON** 120.9 (1130–0500Z‡)
®**MEMPHIS CENTER APP/DEP CON** 126.1 (0500–1130Z‡)
 TOWER 118.3 (1130–0500Z‡) **GND CON** 121.9 **CLNC DEL** 133.85
CLEARANCE DELIVERY PHONE: For CD ctc Memphis ARTCC at 901-368-8453/8449.
AIRSPACE: CLASS D svc 1130–0500Z‡; other times CLASS E.
 TRSA svc ctc **APP CON** within 25 NM. **TRSA** service not provided within R2401 and R2402 when activated.
RADIO AIDS TO NAVIGATION: NOTAM FILE FSM.
 (L) (L) VORTACW 110.4 FSM Chan 41 N35°23.30´ W94°16.29´ 229° 5.4 NM to fld. 432/7E.
 ILS 111.3 I–GKV Rwy 08. Class IE. Unmonitored when ATCT clsd.
 ILS 111.3 I–FSM Rwy 26. Class IT. Unmonitored when ATCT clsd. LOC unusable byd 20° right of course.
 ASR

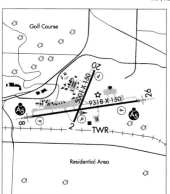

ARKANSAS

FRANK FEDERER MEML (See BRINKLEY on page 38)

GASTONS (See LAKEVIEW on page 60)

GILMORE N35°20.82′ W90°28.69′ NOTAM FILE JBR. MEMPHIS
(L) (L) **VORW/DME** 113.0   GQE   Chan 77   015° 11.8 NM to Marked Tree Muni. 211/4E. H–6J, L–16H

GREENBRIER

ARKAVALLEY (12A)   5 SE   UTC–6(–5DT)   N35°10.65′ W92°20.10′ MEMPHIS
329   NOTAM FILE JBR L–16G
RWY 18–36: H3133X40 (ASPH)   MIRL
  RWY 18: Tree.
SERVICE: **LGT** ACTIVATE MIRL Rwy 18–36—CTAF.
AIRPORT REMARKS: Unattended. Rising terrain north end.
AIRPORT MANAGER: 501-514-0204
COMMUNICATIONS: CTAF/UNICOM 122.8
CLEARANCE DELIVERY PHONE: For CD ctc Little Rock Apch 501-379-2908 or Little Rock ATCT 501-379-2911.
RADIO AIDS TO NAVIGATION: NOTAM FILE LIT.
  LITTLE ROCK (H) (H) **VORTACW** 113.9   LIT   Chan 86   N34°40.66′ W92°10.83′   341° 30.9 NM to fld. 240/5E.
  TACAN AZIMUTH & DME unusable:
    221°–228° byd 20 NM blo 2,800′
    229°–239° byd 20 NM blo 2,500′
    260°–280° byd 35 NM blo 5,000′
  TACAN AZIMUTH unusable:
    320°–335° byd 5 NM

GURDON LOWE FLD (5M8)   1 NW   UTC–6(–5DT)   N33°55.43′ W93°10.09′ MEMPHIS
229   B   NOTAM FILE JBR L–17E
RWY 08–26: H4403X60 (ASPH)   S–12.5   MIRL
  RWY 08: Trees.
  RWY 26: Thld dsplcd 114′. Road. Rgt tfc.
SERVICE: **FUEL** 100LL   **LGT** ACTIVATE MIRL Rwy 08–26—122.9. Rwy 26 NSTD dsplcd thld lights, thld lights at rwy end.
AIRPORT REMARKS: Unattended. For fuel call 870-353-7119 or after hrs call 870-353-7119. Deer on and invof arpt. Ultralight activity on and invof arpt.
AIRPORT MANAGER: (870) 353-7119
COMMUNICATIONS: CTAF 122.9
CLEARANCE DELIVERY PHONE: For CD ctc Fort Worth ARTCC at 817-858-7584.
RADIO AIDS TO NAVIGATION: NOTAM FILE ELD.
  EL DORADO (VH) (DH) **VORW/DME** 115.5   ELD   Chan 102   N33°15.37′ W92°44.64′   325° 45.3 NM to fld. 230/7E.
  DME unusable:
    020°–035° blo 2,000′
    036°–019° byd 30 NM blo 3,200′
  VOR unusable:
    110°–120° byd 40 NM

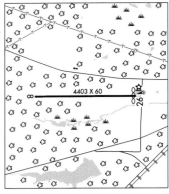

SC, 25 JAN 2024 to 21 MAR 2024

ARKANSAS   53

HAMPTON MUNI (ØR6)   2 SE   UTC–6(–5DT)   N33°31.36´ W92°27.62´   **MEMPHIS**
178   NOTAM FILE JBR   **L–18F**
RWY 02–20: H4326X50 (ASPH)
  RWY 02: Trees.
  RWY 20: Trees.
AIRPORT REMARKS: Unattended. Deer on and invof arpt. Rwy 02–20
  potholes northern third of rwy. Rwy 02 and 20 markings faded.
AIRPORT MANAGER: 870–798–4818
COMMUNICATIONS: CTAF 122.9
CLEARANCE DELIVERY PHONE: For CD ctc Memphis ARTCC at
  901–368–8453/8449.
RADIO AIDS TO NAVIGATION: NOTAM FILE ELD.
  EL DORADO (VH) (DH) VORW/DME 115.5   ELD   Chan 102
    N33°15.37´ W92°44.64´   035° 21.4 NM to fld. 230/7E.
  DME unusable:
    020°–035° blo 2,000´
    036°–019° byd 30 NM blo 3,200´
  VOR unusable:
    110°–120° byd 40 NM

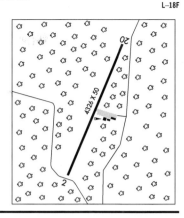

HARRELL FLD (See CAMDEN on page 39)

HARRISON
BOONE CO   (HRO)(KHRO)   3 NW   UTC–6(–5DT)   N36°15.69´ W93°09.28´   **KANSAS CITY**
1365   B   TPA—2201(836)   NOTAM FILE HRC   **H–6I, L–16F**
RWY 18–36: H6161X150 (ASPH–GRVD)   S–38, D–53, 2D–84   HIRL   **IAP**
  RWY 18: REIL. VASI(V4L)—GA 3.0° TCH 50´.
  RWY 36: MALSR. VASI(V4L)—GA 3.0° TCH 50´.
SERVICE: S2   **FUEL** 100LL, JET A   **LGT** ACTIVATE MALSR Rwy 36, REIL
  Rwy 18 and HIRL Rwy 18–36—CTAF.
AIRPORT REMARKS: Attended 1300–0100Z‡. 100LL avbl 24 hrs self serve.
  For service after hrs call 870–741–4510; fee charged; call ahead if
  possible. Deer and birds on and invof arpt.
AIRPORT MANAGER: 870–741–6954
WEATHER DATA SOURCES: ASOS 121.125 (870) 365–8550.
COMMUNICATIONS: CTAF/UNICOM 123.0
  HARRISON RCO 122.45 (JONESBORO RADIO)
®**MEMPHIS CENTER APP/DEP CON** 126.85
CLEARANCE DELIVERY PHONE: For CD ctc Memphis ARTCC at
  901–368–8453/8449.
AIRSPACE: CLASS E svc 1200–0400Z‡; other times CLASS G.
RADIO AIDS TO NAVIGATION: NOTAM FILE HRO.
  HARRISON (VL) (L) VORW/DME 112.5   HRO   Chan 72   N36°19.10´
    W93°12.80´   136° 4.4 NM to fld. 1400/4E.
  DME unusable:
    245°–260° byd 30 NM blo 4,500´
  VOR unusable:
    000°–086° byd 40 NM
    087°–097° byd 40 NM blo 3,000´
    087°–097° byd 55 NM
    098°–166° byd 40 NM
    165°–215° byd 20 NM blo 5,000´
    165°–215° byd 30 NM blo 6,500´
    167°–177° byd 40 NM blo 10,000´
    167°–177° byd 69 NM
    178°–250° byd 40 NM
    300°–359° byd 40 NM
  ILS/DME 111.7   I–HRO   Chan 54   Rwy 36.

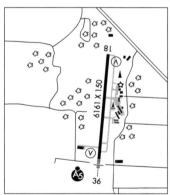

SC, 25 JAN 2024 to 21 MAR 2024

ARKANSAS

HAZEN MUNI DAVID DUCH FLD (6MØ)   3 SW   UTC–6(–5DT)   N34°45.55′ W91°38.28′   MEMPHIS
230   B   NOTAM FILE JBR   L–18F
RWY 18–36: H4048X150 (ASPH)   S–12   MIRL
  RWY 18: PAPI(P2L)—GA 3.0° TCH 52′.
  RWY 36: PAPI(P2L)—GA 3.0° TCH 52′.
SERVICE: S4   **FUEL** 100LL   **LGT** Actvt MIRL Rwy 18–36—CTAF.
AIRPORT REMARKS: Attended dalgt hrs. For svc after hrs call 501–554–6590.
  Migratory birds invof arpt Oct–Mar. Extensive agriculture operations
  Jan–Sep. 100LL avbl 24 hrs self serve with credit card.
AIRPORT MANAGER: 501-554-6590
COMMUNICATIONS: CTAF/UNICOM 122.8
CLEARANCE DELIVERY PHONE: For CD ctc Little Rock Apch 501-379-2908 or
  Little Rock ATCT 501-379-2911.
RADIO AIDS TO NAVIGATION: NOTAM FILE LIT.
  LITTLE ROCK (H) (H) VORTACW 113.9   LIT   Chan 86   N34°40.66′
    W92°10.83′   075° 27.3 NM to fld. 240/5E.
  TACAN AZIMUTH & DME unusable:
    221°–228° byd 20 NM blo 2,800′
    229°–239° byd 20 NM blo 2,500′
    260°–280° byd 35 NM blo 5,000′
  TACAN AZIMUTH unusable:
    320°–335° byd 5 NM

HEBER SPRINGS MUNI (HBZ)(KHBZ)   2 NE   UTC–6(–5DT)   N35°30.70′ W92°00.78′   MEMPHIS
632   B   TPA—1430(798)   NOTAM FILE JBR   L–16G
RWY 06–24: H4002X75 (ASPH)   S–12.5   MIRL   IAP
  RWY 06: REIL. PAPI(P2L)—GA 3.0° TCH 36′. Trees.
  RWY 24: REIL. PAPI(P2L)—GA 3.0° TCH 39′.
SERVICE: S4   **FUEL** 100LL, JET A   **OX** 4   **LGT** ACTIVATE REIL Rwy 06–24 and MIRL Rwy 06–24—CTAF.
AIRPORT REMARKS: Attended 1400–2300Z‡. Deer on and invof arpt. Self svc fuel avbl 24 hrs with credit card (100LL and Jet
  A). Rwy 06–24 no line of sight btn rwy ends.
AIRPORT MANAGER: 501-362-3294
COMMUNICATIONS: CTAF/UNICOM 122.7
Ⓡ**MEMPHIS CENTER APP/DEP CON** 126.85
CLEARANCE DELIVERY PHONE: For CD ctc Memphis ARTCC at 901-368-8453/8449.
RADIO AIDS TO NAVIGATION: NOTAM FILE LIT.
  LITTLE ROCK (H) (H) VORTACW 113.9   LIT   Chan 86   N34°40.66′ W92°10.83′   004° 50.6 NM to fld. 240/5E.
  TACAN AZIMUTH & DME unusable:
    221°–228° byd 20 NM blo 2,800′
    229°–239° byd 20 NM blo 2,500′
    260°–280° byd 35 NM blo 5,000′
  TACAN AZIMUTH unusable:
    320°–335° byd 5 NM

ARKANSAS 55

HELENA/WEST HELENA

THOMPSON–ROBBINS (HEE)(KHEE) 5 NW UTC–6(–5DT) N34°34.59′ W90°40.55′   **MEMPHIS**
  242   B   TPA—1202(960)   NOTAM FILE JBR   H–6J, L–18F
  RWY 18–36: H5001X100 (ASPH–GRVD)   S–15   MIRL   IAP
    RWY 18: REIL. PAPI(P4L)—GA 3.0° TCH 48′.
    RWY 36: REIL. PAPI(P4L)—GA 3.0° TCH 48′.
  RWY 09–27: H3011X60 (ASPH)   S–16   MIRL
    RWY 09: Tree.
  SERVICE: S4   **FUEL** 100LL, JET A   **LGT** ACTVT MIRL Rwy 09–27 and
    Rwy 18–36—CTAF. PAPI Rwy 18 and 36 on consly.
  AIRPORT REMARKS: Attended Mon–Fri daylight hours, Sat 1400–1800Z‡.
    Numerous agriculture ops Feb thru Oct.
  AIRPORT MANAGER: 870-714-1844
  COMMUNICATIONS: CTAF/UNICOM 122.8
  ®**MEMPHIS CENTER APP/DEP CON** 135.3
  CLEARANCE DELIVERY PHONE: For CD ctc Memphis ARTCC at
    901-368-8453/8449.
  RADIO AIDS TO NAVIGATION: NOTAM FILE JBR.
    MARVELL (VL) (L) VORW/DME 113.65   UJM   Chan 83(Y)
      N34°34.50′ W90°40.46′   at fld. 243/1E.
    DME unusable:
      030°–064°
      065°–094° byd 27 NM blo 3,500′
      095°–114° byd 29 NM blo 4,000′
      115°–129° byd 29 NM blo 3,500′
      130°–190° byd 34 NM blo 2,800′

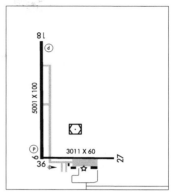

HOLLEY MOUNTAIN AIRPARK (See CLINTON on page 41)

HOLLY GROVE MUNI (2A6) 1 SE UTC–6(–5DT) N34°34.95′ W91°09.91′   MEMPHIS
  176   B   NOTAM FILE JBR   L–18F
  RWY 15–33: H4469X50 (ASPH)   S–12.5   MIRL
    RWY 15: TRCV(TRIL)—GA 3.0° TCH 10′. Tree.
    RWY 33: TRCV(TRIL)—GA 3.0° TCH 10′. Fence.
  SERVICE: **LGT** Bcn OTS indef. Rwy 15 TRIL OTS indef. ACTIVATE MIRL
    Rwy 15–33, VASI Rwy 15 and Rwy 33—CTAF.
  AIRPORT REMARKS: Attended Mon–Sat 1400–2300Z‡. For attendant aft hrs
    call 870–672–1807. Deer on and invof arpt.
  AIRPORT MANAGER: 870-462-3675
  COMMUNICATIONS: CTAF 122.9
  CLEARANCE DELIVERY PHONE: For CD ctc Memphis ARTCC at
    901-368-8453/8449.
  RADIO AIDS TO NAVIGATION: NOTAM FILE PBF.
    PINE BLUFF (L) (L) VORW/DME 116.0   PBF   Chan 107   N34°14.81′
      W91°55.57′   058° 42.8 NM to fld. 212/4E.
    VOR unusable:
      140°–145° byd 35 NM blo 4,900′
      260°–275° byd 25 NM

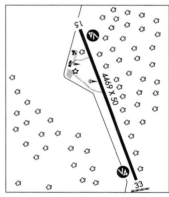

SC, 25 JAN 2024 to 21 MAR 2024

ARKANSAS

HOPE MUNI (M18) 4 NW UTC−6(−5DT) N33°43.20´ W93°39.53´ MEMPHIS
359 B NOTAM FILE JBR H−6I, L−17E
RWY 16−34: H5501X100 (CONC) S−40, D−55, 2S−70, 2D−105 IAP
  MIRL(NSTD) 0.3% up NW
  RWY 16: REIL. PAPI(P2L)—GA 3.0° TCH 43´. Tree.
  RWY 34: REIL. PAPI(P2L)—GA 3.0° TCH 44´. Trees.
RWY 04−22: H5301X100 (CONC) S−40, D−55, 2S−70, 2D−105
  0.4% up NE
  RWY 04: Thld dsplcd 1190´. Trees.
  RWY 22: Thld dsplcd 344´.
SERVICE: S2 **FUEL** 100LL, JET A **LGT** PAPI Rwy 16 and 34—CTAF.
  MIRL Rwy 16−34 oper dusk−0400Z‡; aft 0400Z‡ ACTVT—CTAF.
AIRPORT REMARKS: Attended Mon–Fri 1400−2300Z‡. Deer on and invof
  arpt. For svc aft hrs call 870−777−3434 (Hope P.D.). Self−serve fuel
  avbl 24 hrs (100LL & Jet A). Rwy 16−34 nstd MIRL lgts lctd
  approximately 35´ from marked rwy edge. Rwy 04−22 and Rwy
  16−34 cntrln and thr mkgs faded.
AIRPORT MANAGER: 870−777−3444
COMMUNICATIONS: CTAF/UNICOM 122.8
Ⓡ**FORT WORTH CENTER APP/DEP CON** 123.925
CLEARANCE DELIVERY PHONE: For CD ctc Fort Worth ARTCC at
  817−858−7584.
RADIO AIDS TO NAVIGATION: NOTAM FILE TXK.
  TEXARKANA (VH) (H) VORTACW 116.3 TXK Chan 110 N33°30.83´ W94°04.39´ 052° 24.2 NM to fld. 273/7E.

HORSESHOE BEND (6M2) 1 NE UTC−6(−5DT) N36°13.28´ W91°45.33´ KANSAS CITY
782 B NOTAM FILE JBR L−16G
RWY 13−31: H4502X60 (ASPH) S−4 MIRL IAP
  RWY 13: Thld dsplcd 994´. Trees.
  RWY 31: PAPI(P2L)—GA 3.0° TCH 40´. Tree.
SERVICE: S4 **FUEL** 100LL **LGT** Dusk−dawn ACTVT MIRL Rwy
  13−31—CTAF. PAPI Rwy 31 opr consly.
AIRPORT REMARKS: Unattended. Deer on and invof arpt. 100LL self serve
  fuel. Rwy 13 tkof recommended due to rapidly rising trrn NW of arpt.
AIRPORT MANAGER: 304−268−3666
COMMUNICATIONS: CTAF/UNICOM 122.8
Ⓡ**MEMPHIS CENTER APP/DEP CON** 120.075
CLEARANCE DELIVERY PHONE: For CD ctc Memphis ARTCC at
  901−368−8453/8449.
RADIO AIDS TO NAVIGATION: NOTAM FILE ARG.
  WALNUT RIDGE (VH) (H) VORTAC 114.5 ARG Chan 92 N36°06.60´
  W90°57.22´ 276° 39.5 NM to fld. 265/4E.
  TACAN AZIMUTH unusable:
    011°−021° byd 15 NM blo 5,000´
  VOR unusable:
    010°−021° byd 40 NM blo 3,000´
    010°−021° byd 55 NM
    011°−021° byd 8 NM blo 4,000´
    022°−052° byd 40 NM
    053°−078° byd 40 NM blo 2,300´
    053°−078° byd 64 NM
    079°−175° byd 40 NM blo 18,000´
    195°−216° byd 40 NM blo 18,000´
    217°−278° byd 40 NM blo 3,000´
    217°−278° byd 61 NM blo 18,000´
    279°−350° byd 40 NM blo 3,400´
    279°−350° byd 59 NM

HOSSY N34°25.35´ W93°11.38´ NOTAM FILE HOT. MEMPHIS
  NDB (LOMW) 385 HO 053° 5.7 NM to Meml Fld. 471/1E. L−17E
    mntrd by HOT & LIT ATCT

ARKANSAS

HOT SPRINGS

MEML FLD (HOT)(KHOT)   3 SW   UTC–6(–5DT)   N34°28.68´ W93°05.77´   **MEMPHIS**
540   B   Class II, ARFF Index A   NOTAM FILE HOT   H–6I, L–17E
RWY 05–23: H6595X150 (ASPH–GRVD)   S–75, D–125, 2S–158,   IAP
2D–210, 2D/2D2–400 PCN 54 F/D/X/U HIRL 0.6% up NE
  RWY 05: MALSR. Rgt tfc.
  RWY 23: PAPI(P4L)—GA 3.0° TCH 40´. Pole.
RWY 13–31: H4098X100 (ASPH)   S–28, D–36, 2D–63
PCN 25 F/D/Y/T MIRL 0.4% up NW
  RWY 13: REIL. Trees. Rgt tfc.
  RWY 31: Pole.
RUNWAY DECLARED DISTANCE INFORMATION
  RWY 05: TORA–6595 TODA–6595 ASDA–6595 LDA–6595
  RWY 13: TORA–3210 TODA–4098 ASDA–4098 LDA–4098
  RWY 23: TORA–6595 TODA–6595 ASDA–6235 LDA–6235
  RWY 31: TORA–4098 TODA–4098 ASDA–4098 LDA–3210
SERVICE: S4 **FUEL** 100LL, JET A   **LGT** ACTIVATE HIRL Rwy 05–23,
MIRL Rwy 13–31, MALSR Rwy 05, PAPI Rwy 23, REIL Rwy
13—CTAF. Rwy 23 PAPI unusbl byd 6° right of cntrln.
AIRPORT REMARKS: Attended 1100–0400Z‡. For fuel after hrs call
501–617–0324 or 501–609–6523.
AIRPORT MANAGER: 501-321-6750
WEATHER DATA SOURCES: ASOS 119.925 (501) 624–7633.
COMMUNICATIONS: CTAF/UNICOM 123.0
  RCO 122.1R 110.0T (JONESBORO RADIO)
®**MEMPHIS CENTER APP/DEP CON** 128.475
CLEARANCE DELIVERY PHONE: For CD ctc Memphis ARTCC at 901-368-8453.
AIRSPACE: **CLASS E** svc 1200–0400Z‡; other times CLASS G.
RADIO AIDS TO NAVIGATION: NOTAM FILE HOT.
  HOT SPRINGS (L) (L) VOR/DME 110.0 HOT   Chan 37   N34°28.72´ W93°05.44´   at fld. 529/4E.
  VOR unusable:
    030°–045° byd 25 NM
    056°–074° byd 20 NM blo 6,500´
    075°–095° byd 15 NM blo 6,500´
    096°–140° byd 11 NM blo 3,000´
    141°–187° byd 14 NM blo 5,000´
    141°–227° byd 20 NM blo 3,500´
    141°–227° byd 26 NM blo 5,500´
    228°–311° byd 20 NM blo 3,500´
    312°–345° byd 6 NM blo 4,500´
    312°–345° byd 15 NM blo 5,500´
    312°–345° byd 32 NM blo 9,500´
    346°–055° byd 20 NM blo 3,500´
    349°–359° byd 20 NM blo 4,500´
  DME unusable:
    025°–055° byd 32 NM blo 4,500´
    056°–070° byd 35 NM blo 6,000´
    071°–095° byd 35 NM blo 4,000´
    096°–140° byd 13 NM blo 4,000´
    096°–140° byd 8 NM blo 3,000´
    184°–215° byd 15 NM blo 7,500´
    184°–215° byd 35 NM blo 3,000´
    316°–055° byd 15 NM blo 7,500´
    316°–055° byd 18 NM blo 4,500´
    316°–055° byd 20 NM blo 9,500´
    316°–055° byd 28 NM blo 11,500´
    316°–055° byd 35 NM blo 17,500´
    316°–055° byd 5 NM blo 5,500´
    345°–360° byd 35 NM
  HOSSY NDB (LOMW) 385   HO   N34°25.35´ W93°11.38´   053° 5.7 NM to fld. 471/1E.
    mntrd by HOT & LIT ATCT
  ILS/DME 111.5 I–HOT Chan 52 Rwy 05. Class IA. LOM HOSSY NDB. ILS and LOM unmonitored.

HOWARD CO (See NASHVILLE on page 70)

ARKANSAS

HUNTSVILLE MUNI (H34)   2 SW   UTC−6(−5DT)   N36°04.69′ W93°45.29′   KANSAS CITY
1748   B   NOTAM FILE JBR   L−16F
RWY 12−30: H3601X60 (ASPH)   S−12.5   MIRL   IAP
RWY 03−21: 1250X60 (TURF)
  RWY 03: Trees.
SERVICE: **FUEL** 100LL   **LGT** ACTIVATE MIRL Rwy 12−30—CTAF.
AIRPORT REMARKS: Unattended. Self service fuel avbl 24 hrs with credit card. Rwy 03 and Rwy 21 steep dropoffs at Rwy ends. Ultralight activity on and invof arpt.
AIRPORT MANAGER: 479-738-7287
COMMUNICATIONS: CTAF/UNICOM 122.8
® **RAZORBACK APP/DEP CON** 126.6 (1130−0500Z‡)
  MEMPHIS CENTER APP/DEP CON 126.1 (0500−1130Z‡)
CLEARANCE DELIVERY PHONE: For CD ctc Razorback Apch 479-649-2416, when Apch clsd ctc Memphis ARTCC at 901-368-8453/8449.
RADIO AIDS TO NAVIGATION: NOTAM FILE JBR.
  RAZORBACK (VH) (H) VORTACW 116.4   RZC   Chan 111   N36°14.79′ W94°07.28′   115° 20.5 NM to fld. 1332/4E.
  VOR unusable:
   025°−035° byd 40 NM
   025°−150° byd 22 NM blo 4,000′
   070°−080° byd 40 NM
   093°−103° byd 124 NM
   093°−103° byd 40 NM blo 17,000′
   104°−144° byd 40 NM
   145°−155° byd 40 NM blo 6,500′
   145°−155° byd 67 NM blo 9,500′
   145°−155° byd 80 NM
   150°−210° byd 22 NM blo 3,500′
   156°−170° byd 40 NM
   195°−215° byd 40 NM
   210°−220° byd 22 NM blo 3,000′
   234°−245° byd 40 NM
   310°−025° byd 22 NM blo 3,000′
  TACAN AZIMUTH unusable:
   148°−160°
   225°−240°

HUTFLY (See FORREST CITY on page 51)

J LYNN HELMS SEVIER CO (See DE QUEEN on page 44)

JACKSONVILLE   N34°55.08′ W92°09.46′   NOTAM FILE JBR.   MEMPHIS
(T) **TACAN** 109.2   LRF   Chan 29   at Little Rock AFB. 359/1W.   L−18F
  No NOTAM MP: 1000−1430Z‡ Tue
  DME unusable:
   300°−315° byd 35 NM blo 3,000′
   355°−056° byd 38 NM blo 3,000′

ARKANSAS

JONESBORO MUNI (JBR)(KJBR)   3 E   UTC–6(–5DT)   N35°49.90′ W90°38.79′   MEMPHIS
262   B   NOTAM FILE JBR   MON Airport   H–6J, L–16H
RWY 05–23: H6200X150 (ASPH–GRVD)   S–40, D–48, 2D–76   MIRL   IAP
   RWY 23: ODALS. VASI(V4L)—GA 3.0° TCH 54′.
RWY 13–31: H4099X150 (ASPH–GRVD)   S–50, D–60, 2D–95   MIRL
   0.3% up NW
   RWY 13: Road.
   RWY 31: Tree.
SERVICE: S4   FUEL 100LL, JET A   LGT ACTVT ODA_S Rwy 23; VASI Rwy
   23; MIRL Rwy 05–23 and Rwy 13–31; twy lgts—CTAF.
AIRPORT REMARKS: Attended 1200–0300Z‡. For svc after hrs, call
   870–935–1770.
AIRPORT MANAGER: 870-761-4149
WEATHER DATA SOURCES: ASOS 118.525 (870) 932–4C10.
COMMUNICATIONS: CTAF/UNICOM 123.0
   RCO 122.2 (JONESBORO RADIO)
®MEMPHIS CENTER APP/DEP CON 120.075
CLEARANCE DELIVERY PHONE: For CD ctc Memphis ARTCC at
   901-368-8453/8449.
AIRSPACE: CLASS E svc continuous.
RADIO AIDS TO NAVIGATION: NOTAM FILE JBR.
   (VL) (L) VORW/DME 115.85   JBR   Chan 105(Y)   N35°52.49′
   W90°35.31′   228° 3.8 NM to fld. 247/0W.
   DME unusable:
      235°–270° byd 37 NM blo 3,000′
      310°–010° byd 33 NM blo 4,000′
   VOR unusable:
      015°–025° byd 14 NM blo 5,000′
      015°–025° byd 27 NM blo 8,000′
      035°–155° byd 40 NM
      040°–069° byd 10 NM blo 5,000′
      040°–069° byd 25 NM blo 7,000′
      070°–090° byd 10 NM blo 7,000′
      100°–114° byd 18 NM blo 7,000′
      115°–150° byd 15 NM blo 7,000′
      175°–200° byd 40 NM
      182°–192° byd 22 NM blo 5,000′
      238°–250° byd 40 NM
      253°–027° byd 40 NM
      310°–345° byd 14 NM blo 4,000′
      310°–345° byd 25 NM blo 7,000′
   ILS 110.15   I–JBR   Rwy 23.   Class IT.

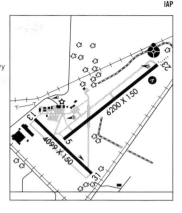

KIRK FLD (See PARAGOULD on page 72)

KIZER FLD (See PRESCOTT on page 75)

LADOS   N33°17.16′ W92°43.69′   NOTAM FILE ELD.   MEMPHIS
   NDB (LOMW) 418   EL   224° 5.7 NM to South Arkansas Rgnl at Goodwin Fld. 140/3E.

ARKANSAS

LAKE VILLAGE MUNI (M32) 2 W UTC–6(–5DT) N33°20.79´ W91°18.93´   MEMPHIS
126 B NOTAM FILE JBR   L–18F
RWY 01–19: H4400X75 (ASPH) S–18 MIRL   IAP
  RWY 01: PAPI(P2L)—GA 3.0° TCH 24´. Trees.
  RWY 19: PAPI(P2L)—GA 3.0° TCH 33´. Trees.
SERVICE: FUEL 100LL, JET A   **LGT** Actvt MIRL Rwy 01–19, PAPI Rwy 01 and 19—CTAF.
AIRPORT REMARKS: Attended Mon–Fri 1300–2300Z‡, Sat 1300–1800Z‡. Numerous agriculture ops Feb–Oct below 500´.
AIRPORT MANAGER: 870-265-2723
COMMUNICATIONS: CTAF 122.9
Ⓡ **MEMPHIS CENTER APP/DEP CON** 135.875
CLEARANCE DELIVERY PHONE: For CD ctc Memphis ARTCC at 901-368-8453/8449.
RADIO AIDS TO NAVIGATION: NOTAM FILE GLH.
  GREENVILLE (VL) (DH) VOR/DME 114.25   GLH   Chan 89(Y)
    N33°31.41´ W90°58.98´   234° 19.8 NM to fld. 130/4E.
  VOR unusable:
    144°–157° byd 40 NM

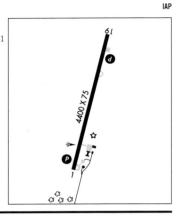

LAKEVIEW

GASTONS (3M0) 1 S UTC–6(–5DT) N36°20.94´ W92°33.35´   KANSAS CITY
479 TPA—1300(821) NOTAM FILE JBR
RWY 06–24: 3200X55 (TURF)
  RWY 06: Road.
  RWY 24: Tree.
SERVICE: FUEL 100LL
AIRPORT REMARKS: Attended 1230–0300Z‡. Fuel avbl dalgt only. Rwy 24 has 20´ drop 50´ from end of rwy. All acft land Rwy 24, takeoff Rwy 06.
AIRPORT MANAGER: 870-431-5202
COMMUNICATIONS: CTAF/UNICOM 122.8
CLEARANCE DELIVERY PHONE: For CD ctc Memphis ARTCC at 901-368-8453/8449.

LASKY N34°40.14´ W92°18.32´ NOTAM FILE LIT.   MEMPHIS
  NDB (LOMW) 353   LI   048° 5.4 NM to Bill And Hillary Clinton Ntl/Adams Fld. 248/0E.   L–18F

LAWRENCE CO N36°12.42´ W90°55.39´ NOTAM FILE ARG.   ST LOUIS
  NDB (MHW) 227   TNZ   180° 4.9 NM to Walnut Ridge Rgnl. 262/1E. NDB unmonitored 2300–1300Z‡.   L–16G

ARKANSAS

LITTLE ROCK
BILL AND HILLARY CLINTON NTL/ADAMS FLD (LIT)(KLIT) 2 E UTC−6(−5DT) N34°43.77′
W92°13.49′
266 B LRA Class I, ARFF Index C NOTAM FILE LIT
MEMPHIS
H−6I, L−18F
IAP, AD

RWY 04L−22R: H8273X150 (CONC−GRVD) S−75, D−200, 2S−175, 2D−350 HIRL CL
  RWY 04L: MALSR. TDZL. PAPI(P4L)—GA 3.0° TCH 50′. RVR−TMR Thld dsplcd 297′. Railroad.
  RWY 22R: ALSF2. TDZL. PAPI(P4R)—GA 3.0° TCH 58′. RVR−TMR Rgt tfc.
RWY 04R−22L: H8251X150 (CONC−GRVD) S−75, D−200, 2S−175, 2D−350 HIRL CL
  RWY 04R: MALSR. TDZL. PAPI(P4R)—GA 3.0° TCH 50′. RVR−TR Thld dsplcd 1050′. Pole. Rgt tfc.
  RWY 22L: MALSF. TDZL. PAPI(P4L)—GA 3.0° TCH 50′. RVR−TR Trees.
RWY 18−36: H6224X150 (CONC−GRVD) S−75, D−100, 2S−127, 2D−135 MIRL
  RWY 18: PAPI(P4L)—GA 3.0° TCH 50′. Tree.
  RWY 36: PAPI(P4R)—GA 3.75° TCH 63′. Thld dsplcd 164′. Trees.
RUNWAY DECLARED DISTANCE INFORMATION
  RWY 04L: TORA−8273 TODA−8273 ASDA−8250 LDA−7976
  RWY 04R: TORA−8250 TODA−8250 ASDA−8250 LDA−7200
  RWY 18: TORA−6060 TODA−6060 ASDA−6060 LDA−6060
  RWY 22L: TORA−7200 TODA−7200 ASDA−7200 LDA−7200
  RWY 22R: TORA−8273 TODA−8273 ASDA−8273 LDA−8273
  RWY 36: TORA−6224 TODA−6224 ASDA−6224 LDA−6060
ARRESTING GEAR/SYSTEM
  RWY 22R: EMAS
SERVICE: S4 **FUEL** 100LL, JET A **OX** 1, 3
AIRPORT REMARKS: Attended continuously. Large concentrations of birds invof arpt most activity between SR−SS up to 1500′ MSL. Be alert North Little Rock Muni arpt is lctd 6 miles north−northwest with similar rwy configurations. Twy A 315′ south of Twy L intersection to Rwy 36 clsd except acft with wingspan less than 79′. No general aviation parking on terminal or cargo ramp. Cargo and terminal ramps are non−movement areas. Landing fee.
AIRPORT MANAGER: 501−372−3439
WEATHER DATA SOURCES: ASOS (501) 376−0247 LLWAS.
COMMUNICATIONS: D−ATIS 125.65 (501) 379−2915 **UNICOM** 122.95
  LITTLE ROCK RCO 122.4 (JONESBORO RADIO)
  ® **LITTLE ROCK APP/DEP CON** 135.4 (040°−239°) 119.5 (240°−039°)
  TOWER 118.7 **GND CON** 121.9 **CLNC DEL** 118.95 **PRE TAXI CLNC** 118.95
  PDC
CLEARANCE DELIVERY PHONE: For CD when una via freq ctc Little Rock Apch 501−379−2908 or Little Rock ATCT 501−379−2911.
AIRSPACE: CLASS C svc ctc **APP CON.**
RADIO AIDS TO NAVIGATION: NOTAM FILE LIT.
  LITTLE ROCK (H) (H) VORTACW 113.9 LIT Chan 86 N34°40.66′ W92°10.83′ 320° 3.8 NM to fld. 240/5E.
  TACAN AZIMUTH & DME unusable:
    221°−228° byd 20 NM blo 2,800′
    229°−239° byd 20 NM blo 2,500′
    260°−280° byd 35 NM blo 5,000′
  TACAN AZIMUTH unusable:
    320°−335° byd 5 NM
  LASKY NDB (LOMW) 353 LI N34°40.14′ W92°18.32′ 048° 5.4 NM to fld. 248/0E.
  ILS/DME 110.3 I−LIT Chan 40 Rwy 04L. Class IA. LOM LASKY NDB. DME also serves Rwy 22R. DME unusable byd 30° left and byd 15° right of course.
  ILS/DME 111.3 I−CNL Chan 50 Rwy 04R. Class IA.
  ILS/DME 110.7 I−BWY Chan 44 Rwy 22L. Class IB. LOC offset 1.87 degs.
  ILS/DME 110.3 I−AAY Chan 40 Rwy 22R. Class IIIE. DME also serves Rwy 04L.

ARKANSAS

LITTLE ROCK AFB (LRF)(KLRF) AF (ANG)   1 SE   UTC−6(−5DT)   N34°55.05′ W92°08.70′   **MEMPHIS**
312   B   TPA—See Remarks   NOTAM FILE LRF   Not insp.   H−6I, L−18F
RWY 07−25: H12007X150 (CONC)   PCN 38 R/D/W/T   HIRL   CL   DIAP, AD
  RWY 07: ALSF (NSTD) PAPI(P4L)—GA 2.83° TCH 50′. RVR−TMR
  RWY 25: ALSF2. TDZL. PAPI(P4L)—GA 3.0° TCH 56′. RVR−TMR Rgt tfc.
RWY 07L−25L: H3499X60 (CONC)
SERVICE: LGT SFL ints unctl may be turned off O/R. NSTD infra−red lgt co−lctd with Rwy 07, 25 and 250° edge lgt and one NSTD infra−red strobe lctd end of Rwy 07 and 250° ovrn. Infra−red strobe lctd end of Rwy 25 co—ctd with rwy end lgt. These lgt are vis only thru NVD. Rwy 07 NSTD ALSF−1 (missing last centerline barrette prior to thld). Rwy 25 ILS and PAPI GS not coincidental. **MILITARY—JASU** 5(A/M 32A−86) **FUEL** A−Min POL capability 2200−0600Z‡ Mon−Fri, exp 2−4 hr delay dur lcl flying. **FLUID** SP PRESAIR LHOX LOX **OIL** O−133−148−156 **TRAN ALERT** Svc avbl 1300−0100Z‡ Mon thru Fri, no weekend support. After hr support for Higher HQ msn only.
NOISE: Noise abatement: Departing heavy acft climb rwy heading to 1500′ AGL prior to turning on course.
MILITARY REMARKS: Opr continuously. Arpt normally clsd fed hol from 0300Z‡ thru 1300Z‡ succeeding day. **RSTD** Degraded firefighting capability for B−2, C−5, VC−25, E−4, KC−10, MD−11, 747 and 777 acft−coordinate 48 hours prior to arrival for PPR and SVC. Confirm rescue and firefighting capability prior ldg or tkf. PPR except AIREVAC and Armed Forces Courier. Official Business Only weekdays 1700−2100Z‡, except AIREVAC and Armed Forces Courier obtain PPR 72 hrs prior to arrival, call DSN 731−6123, PPR is valid +/− 30 minutes of proposed ETA. No practice apch or landing during local flying. Dep acft remain at or blo 1400′ until dep end of rwy. Fighter acft unable to ctc dep until airborne. B52 acft prohibited. Use of alert apron (x−mas tree) stub 1 rqr prior coordination with airfield management. NSTD rwy markings−assault strip marked (3500′X60′) painted on Rwy 25. Rwy 25 centerline markings obscured by rubber deposits. **CAUTION** Extensive turbo prop training Mon−Fri 1300−0600Z‡. Tran ramp marking may not be appropriate for large acft follow marshallers instructions. Significant increase in bird activity Apr−May, Sep−Nov. Deer hazard. Phase II in effect Apr−May and Sep−Nov. High potential for hydroplaning on Rwy 07−25 during periods of wet wx. Numerous unlighted obstructions located in primary surface. Afld lgt intermittent between SS/SR due to local ngt vision training, non participating acft ctc twr prior to entering Class D airspace and to incr ints. **TFC PAT** TPA—Rectangular 1400 (1090), overhead 1900 (1590).
MISC AN/FMQ−19 automated obsn system in use, augmented by human obsn when necessary during afld hrs. No COMSEC avbl for tran issue. No classified material stor at AM OPS, stor avbl at comd post. Backup wx obsn view ltd, rstd from 060°−280° by flightline facilities and trees. ATC Personnel in accordance with cooperative wx watch will alert wx personnel on any unreported wx condition that could affect flt safety. All tran acft ctc Comd Post 20 minutes prior to arrival. Ltd aircrew transportation on weekends. Aerodrome for NVG ops tran acft should receive briefing from 19 OSS Tactics at DNS 731−7013 or 19OSS.OSKTACTICS@US.AF.MIL. To ensure aircrew transportation avbl upon arrival, ctc afld management at least 20 min prior to ldg. NOTE: See Special Notices—CAUTION—High density student flying. ARFF−CAT 3, with 14 performance, 4880−5000 gallon of capability, ctc AMOP 731−6123 for updated ARFF status.
AIRPORT MANAGER: 501-987-3103
COMMUNICATIONS: SFA (Tfc permitting.) **ATIS** 119.175 251.1 (Mon−Fri 1200−0500Z‡, Sat−Sun 1500−2300Z‡ except holidays.) **PTD** 372.2
®**APP/DEP CON** 119.5 306.2
  TOWER 120.6 269.075 Opr continuously. (Hol, arpt CLOSED from 0300Z‡ preceding day thru 1300Z‡ succeeding day. Holiday on Mon, CLOSED 0500Z‡ preceding Sat thru 1300Z‡ succeeding Tue. CLOSED Dec 24, 0300Z‡ thru Dec 26, 1300Z‡ and CLOSED Dec 31, 0300Z‡ thru Jan 2 1300Z‡)
  GND CON 132.8 275.8 **CLNC DEL** 253.5 (weekdays 1300−0500Z‡, other times or VHF only acft ctc Gnd Con. Ctc Clnc Del for engine start and req prior to taxi.)
  COMD POST (ROCK OPS) 349.4
  ANG COMD POST 138.6 225.45 **PMSV METRO** 239.8 WX svc avbl 24 hr unless aerodrome CLOSED at DSN 731−6152/6444, C501−987−6152/6444. AN/FMQ automated sys in use, augmented by human observation when necessary. Vis of afld rstd for base WX ops southeast−south during manual augmentation by WX forecaster. Contact 26 OPR WX squadron DSN 731−2651/2652, C318−529−2651/2652 dur wx flt closure or evac.
CLEARANCE DELIVERY PHONE: For CD when una via freq ctc Little Rock Apch 501-379-2908 or Little Rock ATCT 501-379-2911.
AIRSPACE: CLASS D svc continuous.
RADIO AIDS TO NAVIGATION: NOTAM FILE JBR.
  JACKSONVILLE (T) TACAN   Chan 29   LRF (109.2)   N34°55.08′ W92°09.46′   at fld. 359/1W.
    No NOTAM MP: 1000−1430Z‡ Tue
  DME unusable:
    300°−315° byd 35 NM blo 3,000′
    355°−056° byd 38 NM blo 3,000′
  ILS 109.9   I-TYV   Rwy 25.   Class IIE.   No NOTAM MP: ILS 1000−1430Z‡ Wed/Thu.
COMM/NAV/WEATHER REMARKS: Radar see Terminal FLIP for Radar Minima.

ARKANSAS 63

MAGNOLIA

RALPH C WEISER FLD (AGO)(KAGO) 3 SE UTC−6(−5DT) N33°13.65′ W93°13.02′ MEMPHIS
319 B NOTAM FILE JBR H−61, L−17E
RWY 18−36: H5007X100 (ASPH) S−50, D−75, 2D−130 MIRL IAP
 0.4% up S
 RWY 18: REIL. PAPI(P2L)—GA 3.0° TCH 34′. Trees.
 RWY 36: REIL. PAPI(P2L)—GA 4.0° TCH 40′.
SERVICE: **FUEL** 100LL, JET A **LGT** PAPI Rwys 18 and 36 on 24/7. Actvt REIL and MIRL Rwy 18−36—CTAF.
AIRPORT REMARKS: Attended Mon−Fri 1400−2300Z‡. Self serve fuel avbl 24 hrs with credit card. For svc after hrs call 870−904−6731.
AIRPORT MANAGER: (870) 904−6731
WEATHER DATA SOURCES: AWOS−3 118.05 (870) 901−3532.
COMMUNICATIONS: CTAF/UNICOM 122.8
Ⓡ **FORT WORTH CENTER APP/DEP CON** 128.2
CLEARANCE DELIVERY PHONE: For CD ctc Fort Worth ARTCC at 817-858-7584.
RADIO AIDS TO NAVIGATION: NOTAM FILE ELD.
 EL DORADO (VH) (DH) VORW/DME 115.3 ELD Chan 102
  N33°15.37′ W92°44.64′ 259° 23.9 NM to fld. 230/7E.
 DME unusable:
  020°−035° blo 2,000′
  036°−019° byd 30 NM blo 3,200′
 VOR unusable:
  110°−120° byd 40 NM

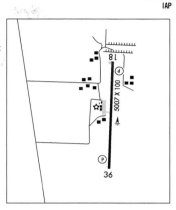

MALVERN MUNI (M78) 3 SE UTC−6(−5DT) N34°20.00′ W92°45.69′ MEMPHIS
538 B NOTAM FILE JBR L−17E
RWY 04−22: H3188X60 (ASPH) S−10 MIRL IAP
 RWY 22: Thld dsplcd 376′. Trees.
SERVICE: S4 **FUEL** 100LL **LGT** Actvt MIRL Rwy 04−22—CTAF.
AIRPORT REMARKS: Attended Mon−Fri 1330−2230Z‡. For svc aft hrs call 501−315−9004.
AIRPORT MANAGER: 501−337−9939
COMMUNICATIONS: CTAF/UNICOM 122.8
Ⓡ **MEMPHIS CENTER APP/DEP CON** 128.475
CLEARANCE DELIVERY PHONE: For CD ctc Little Rock Apch 501−379−2908 or Little Rock ATCT 501−379−2911.
RADIO AIDS TO NAVIGATION: NOTAM FILE LIT.
 LITTLE ROCK (H) (H) VORTACW 113.9 LIT Chan 86 N34°40.66′
  W92°10.83′ 230° 35.4 NM to fld. 240/5E.
 TACAN AZIMUTH & DME unusable:
  221°−228° byd 20 NM blo 2,800′
  229°−239° byd 20 NM blo 2,500′
  260°−280° byd 35 NM blo 5,000′
 TACAN AZIMUTH unusable:
  320°−335° byd 5 NM

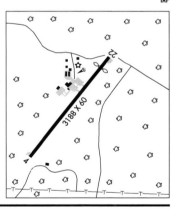

ARKANSAS

MANILA MUNI (MXA)(KMXA) 2 NE UTC−6(−5DT) N35°53.67´ W90°09.27´ MEMPHIS
243 B NOTAM FILE JBR L−16H
RWY 18−36: H4201X75 (ASPH) S−15 MIRL IAP
  RWY 18: REIL. PAPI(P2R)—GA 4.0° TCH 48´. Tree.
  RWY 36: REIL. PAPI(P2L)—GA 4.0° TCH 28´. Thld dsplcd 60´. Road.
    Rgt tfc.
SERVICE: S4 **FUEL** 100LL **LGT** Actvt REIL Rwy 18 and 36; MIRL Rwy
  18−36; and PAPI Rwy 18 and—CTAF. Local arpt WX 4 clicks.
AIRPORT REMARKS: Attended dalgt hours. For svc aft hrs call
  901−605−1094 our 479−757−0722 no fee. No fee 100LL avbl with
  credit card 1400Z.to 2300Z‡. Numerous agricultural acft ops from
  Feb−Nov 500´ AGL and below.
AIRPORT MANAGER: 479−757−0722
COMMUNICATIONS: CTAF/UNICOM 122.8
®**MEMPHIS CENTER APP/DEP CON** 120.075
CLEARANCE DELIVERY PHONE: For CD ctc Memphis ARTCC at
  901−368−8453/8449.
RADIO AIDS TO NAVIGATION: NOTAM FILE JBR.
  GILMORE (L) (L) VORW/DME 113.0 GQE Chan 77 N35°20.82´
    W90°28.69´ 022° 36.4 NM to fld. 211/4E.
COMM/NAV/WEATHER REMARKS: UNICOM freq: 4 clicks for temp, wind, and
  density alt.

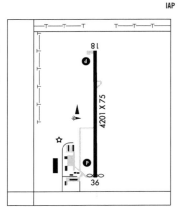

MARIANNA/LEE CO−STEVE EDWARDS FLD (6M7) 3 W UTC−6(−5DT) N34°46.97´ W90°48.60´ MEMPHIS
219 B NOTAM FILE JBR L−18F
RWY 18−36: H4021X75 (ASPH) MIRL IAP
  RWY 18: REIL. PAPI(P2L)—GA 3.0° TCH 52´. Tree.
  RWY 36: REIL. PAPI(P2L)—GA 3.0° TCH 53´. Tree.
SERVICE: **FUEL** 100LL **LGT** Actvt REIL Rwy 18 & 36; PAPI Rwy 18 &
  36; MIRL Rwy 18−36—CTAF.
AIRPORT REMARKS: Attended Mon−Fri dalgt hours, Sat sunrise−1800Z‡. For
  fuel other hours call 870−295−3485. Numerous agriculture ops
  Feb−Oct. Rwy 36 75´ unlgtd p−line 2300´ S of thld.
AIRPORT MANAGER: 870−295−3485
COMMUNICATIONS: CTAF/UNICOM 122.8
®**MEMPHIS CENTER APP/DEP CON** 135.3
CLEARANCE DELIVERY PHONE: For CD ctc Memphis ARTCC at
  901−368−8453/8449.
RADIO AIDS TO NAVIGATION: NOTAM FILE JBR.
  GILMORE (L) (L) VORW/DME 113.0 GQE Chan 77 N35°20.82´
    W90°28.69´ 202° 37.5 NM to fld. 211/4E.

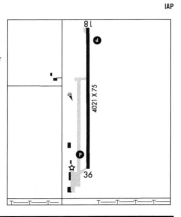

MARION CO RGNL (See FLIPPIN on page 50)

MARKED TREE MUNI (6M8) 1 E UTC−6(−5DT) N35°31.99´ W90°24.01´ MEMPHIS
219 B NOTAM FILE JBR L−16H
RWY 18−36: H3200X60 (ASPH) S−8 MIRL
  RWY 18: PAPI(P2L)—GA 3.0° TCH 40´.
  RWY 36: PAPI(P2L)—GA 3.0° TCH 40´. Road.
SERVICE: **LGT** ACTIVATE MIRL Rwy 18−36—CTAF.
AIRPORT REMARKS: Attended irregularly. For svc aft hrs call 870−358−2024. Numerous agricultural acft ops from Feb−Nov
  500´ AGL and below.
AIRPORT MANAGER: (870) 375−3025
COMMUNICATIONS: CTAF/UNICOM 122.8
CLEARANCE DELIVERY PHONE: For CD ctc Memphis Apch at 901−842−8457.
RADIO AIDS TO NAVIGATION: NOTAM FILE JBR.
  GILMORE (L) (L) VORW/DME 113.0 GQE Chan 77 N35°20.82´ W90°28.69´ 015° 11.8 NM to fld. 211/4E.

ARKANSAS

MARSHALL

SEARCY CO (4A5) 1 SW UTC–6(–5DT) N35°53.92′ W92°39.38′ MEMPHIS
964 B NOTAM FILE JBR L–16G
IAP
RWY 05–23: H4003X75 (ASPH) S–12.5 MIRL 1.0% up NE
  RWY 05: REIL. PAPI(P2L)—GA 3.25° TCH 43′.
  RWY 23: REIL. PAPI(P2L)—GA 3.25° TCH 44′. Rgt tfc.
SERVICE: FUEL 100LL LGT Actvt REIL Rwy 05 and 23; MIRL Rwy 05–23—CTAF. Rwy 05 PAPI unusbl 9° each side of cntrln. Rwy 23 PAPI unusbl byd 7° right of cntrln. Rwy 05 REIL OTS indefly. Rwy 23 REIL OTS indefly.
AIRPORT REMARKS: Unattended. Fuel 100LL: self svc avbl H24 with credit card. Deer on and invof arpt. Lgtd twr 2059′ MSL/299′ AGL on mt top 1 mile E of arpt.
AIRPORT MANAGER: 512-618-5331
COMMUNICATIONS: CTAF 122.9
® MEMPHIS CENTER APP/DEP CON 126.850
CLEARANCE DELIVERY PHONE: For CD ctc Memphis ARTCC at 901-368-8453/8449.
AIRSPACE: CLASS E.
RADIO AIDS TO NAVIGATION: NOTAM FILE FLP.
  FLIPPIN (DH) DME 116.05 FLP Chan 107(Y) N36°17.98′ W92°27.50′ 202° 25.9 NM to fld. 782.
  DME unusable:
    020°–050° byd 26 NM blo 3,500′
    020°–050° byd 32 NM blo 4,500′
    075°–105° byd 39 NM blo 4,500′
    105°–135° byd 35 NM blo 4,500′

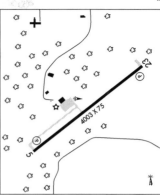

MARVELL N34°34.50′ W90°40.46′ NOTAM FILE JBR.   MEMPHIS
H–6J, L–18F
(VL) (L) VORW/DME 113.65 UJM Chan 83(Y) at Thompson–Robbins. 243/1E.
DME unusable:
  030°–064°
  065°–094° byd 27 NM blo 3,500′
  095°–114° byd 29 NM blo 4,000′
  115°–129° byd 29 NM blo 3,500′
  130°–190° byd 34 NM blo 2,800′

MC GEHEE MUNI (7M1) 2 E UTC–6(–5DT) N33°37.21′ W91°21.89′ MEMPHIS
141 B NOTAM FILE JBR L–18F
IAP
RWY 18–36: H4007X75 (ASPH) S–12.5 MIRL
  RWY 18: Trees.
SERVICE: FUEL 100LL, JET A
AIRPORT REMARKS: Attended Feb–Oct Mon–Fri 1400–2300Z‡. For srvc aft hrs call 870–644–0069 or 870–222–8830. 24 hr self svc fuel avbl with credit card. Numerous agriculture acft ops frcm Feb–Nov 500′ AGL and blo. Rwy 36 turnaround has 3–4′ drop-off on east and north side.
AIRPORT MANAGER: 870-919-5172
COMMUNICATIONS: CTAF 122.9
  MEMPHIS CENTER APP/DEP CON 135.875
CLEARANCE DELIVERY PHONE: For CD ctc Memphis ARTCC at 901-368-8453/8449.
RADIO AIDS TO NAVIGATION: NOTAM FILE JBR.
  MONTICELLO (L) DME 111.6 MON Chan 53 N33°33.72′ W91°42.93′ 079° 17.9 NM to fld. 208.

ARKANSAS

MELBOURNE MUNI – JOHN E MILLER FLD (42A)　3 E　UTC−6(−5DT)　N36°04.26′ W91°49.81′　KANSAS CITY
735　B　NOTAM FILE JBR　L−16G
RWY 03−21: H4003X75 (ASPH)　MIRL　0.6% up SW　IAP
　RWY 03: REIL. PAPI(P2L)—GA 3.0° TCH 45′. Tree.
　RWY 21: REIL. PAPI(P2L)—GA 3.0° TCH 43′. Tree.
SERVICE: S4　**FUEL** 100LL, JET A　**LGT** Actvt MIRL Rwy 03−21 and REIL 03−21—CTAF.
AIRPORT REMARKS: Attended Mon–Sat dalgt. Self serve fuel H24 with credit card. 150 ft paved stopway each end–full strength.
AIRPORT MANAGER: (870) 291-1227
WEATHER DATA SOURCES: AWOS−3PT 121.575 (870) 916−2768.
COMMUNICATIONS: CTAF 122.9
®**MEMPHIS CENTER APP/DEP CON** 126.85
CLEARANCE DELIVERY PHONE: For CD ctc Memphis ARTCC at 901-368-8453/8449.
RADIO AIDS TO NAVIGATION: NOTAM FILE FLP.
　FLIPPIN (DH) DME 116.05　FLP　Chan 107(Y)　N36°17.98′
　　W92°27.50′　114° 33.4 NM to fld. 782.
　DME unusable:
　　020°−050° byd 26 NM blo 3,500′
　　020°−050° byd 32 NM blo 4,500′
　　075°−105° byd 39 NM blo 4,500′
　　105°−135° byd 35 NM blo 4,500′

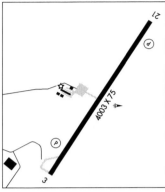

MEML FLD (See HOT SPRINGS on page 57)

MENA INTERMOUNTAIN MUNI (MEZ)(KMEZ)　2 SE　UTC−6(−5DT)　N34°32.73′ W94°12.14′　MEMPHIS
1080　B　NOTAM FILE MEZ　H−6I, L−17E
RWY 09−27: H5485X100 (ASPH)　S−75, D−200, 2S−175, 2D−300　IAP, AD
　MIRL　0.5% up W
　RWY 09: REIL. PAPI(P4L)—GA 3.5° TCH 44′.
　RWY 27: REIL. PAPI(P4L)—GA 3.0° TCH 49′.
RWY 17−35: H5001X75 (ASPH)　S−75, D−100, 2S−127, 2D−160
　MIRL　0.8% up S
　RWY 17: PAPI(P4R)—GA 3.0° TCH 50′. Tree.
　RWY 35: REIL. Tree.
SERVICE: S4　**FUEL** 100LL, JET A　**OX** 4　**LGT** MIRL Rwys 09−27 and 17−35 opr SS−SR; ACTVT PAPI Rwys 09, 17 and 27—CTAF. PAPI Rwy 09 unusbl byd 7 deg right of cntrln.
AIRPORT REMARKS: Attended dawn–dusk. Migratory birds and deer on and invof arpt. Mountains north and south southwest of arpt.
AIRPORT MANAGER: 479-394-4077
WEATHER DATA SOURCES: AWOS−3 118.025 (479) 394−5149.
COMMUNICATIONS: CTAF/UNICOM 122.8
®**MEMPHIS CENTER APP/DEP CON** 126.1
CLEARANCE DELIVERY PHONE: For CD ctc Memphis ARTCC at 901-368-8453/8449.
RADIO AIDS TO NAVIGATION: NOTAM FILE MLC.
　RICH MOUNTAIN (VL) (L) VORTACW 113.5　PGO　Chan 82　N34°40.83′ W94°36.54′　108° 21.7 NM to fld. 2700/4E.
　VOR unusable:
　　016°−021° byd 40 NM
　　028°−029° byd 40 NM
　　030°−040°
　　050°−075° blo 4,000′
　　090°−145°
　　167°−169° byd 40 NM
　　170°−200°
　　235°−245° byd 30 NM blo 5,000′
　　260°−280° byd 35 NM blo 5,000′
　　329°−335° byd 40 NM
　　340°−345° blo 5,000′
　　358°−002° byd 40 NM
　ILS/DME 108.7　I-VMU　Chan 24　Rwy 27.　Unmonitored.

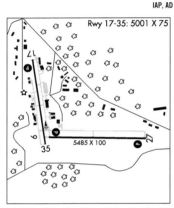

SC, 25 JAN 2024 to 21 MAR 2024

ARKANSAS

MONTICELLO MUNI/ELLIS FLD (LLQ)(KLLQ) 2 E UTC–6(–5DT) N33°38.31´ W91°45.06´ **MEMPHIS**
268 B NOTAM FILE LLQ H–6J, L–18F
RWY 03–21: H5020X75 (ASPH) S–17 MIRL 0.7% up SW IAP
  RWY 03: REIL. PAPI(P2L)—GA 3.0° TCH 52´. P–line.
  RWY 21: REIL. PAPI(P2L)—GA 3.0° TCH 52´. Road.
SERVICE: S2 FUEL 100LL, JET A LGT Actvt MIRL Rwy 03–21, PAPI Rwy 03 and 21 and REIL Rwy 03 and 21—CTAF.
AIRPORT REMARKS: Attended Mon–Fri 1400–2300Z‡. Self service fuel avbl 24 hrs with credit card (100LL and Jet A).
AIRPORT MANAGER: 870-367-4450
WEATHER DATA SOURCES: ASOS 133.325 (870) 367-1019.
COMMUNICATIONS: CTAF/UNICOM 122.8
  MEMPHIS CENTER APP/DEP CON 135.875
  CLEARANCE DELIVERY PHONE: For CD ctc Memphis ARTCC at 901-368-8453/8449.
RADIO AIDS TO NAVIGATION: NOTAM FILE JBR.
  (L) DME 111.6 MON Chan 53 N33°33.72´ W91°42.93´ 339° 4.9 NM to fld. 208.

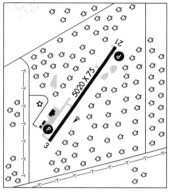

MONTICELLO N33°33.72´ W91°42.93´ NOTAM FILE JBR. **MEMPHIS**
  (L) DME 111.6 MON Chan 53 339° 4.9 NM to Monticello Muni/Ellis Fld. 208. L–18F

MORRILTON

MORRILTON MUNI (BDQ)(KBDQ) 2 SE UTC–6(–5DT) N35°08.17´ W92°42.82´ **MEMPHIS**
321 B NOTAM FILE JBR L–17E
RWY 09–27: H3998X75 (ASPH) S–4 MIRL 0.3% up W IAP
  RWY 09: Tree.
  RWY 27: Trees.
SERVICE: S4 FUEL 100LL, JET A+ LGT ACTVT MIRL Rwy 09–27—122.9.
AIRPORT REMARKS: Attended 1400–0000Z‡. For after hrs svc please call 501-306-5656. Jet A and 100LL fuel self service with credit card. Ultralight activity on and invof arpt. Deer on and invof arpt. Rwy 09 and Rwy 27 markings faded.
AIRPORT MANAGER: (501) 306-5656
COMMUNICATIONS: CTAF/UNICOM 122.8
  ®MEMPHIS CENTER APP/DEP CON 128.475
  CLEARANCE DELIVERY PHONE: For CD ctc Memphis ARTCC at 901-368-8453/8449.
RADIO AIDS TO NAVIGATION: NOTAM FILE LIT.
  LITTLE ROCK (H) (H) VORTACW 113.9 LIT Chan 86 N34°40.66´ W92°10.83´ 311° 38.0 NM to fld. 240/5E.
  TACAN AZIMUTH & DME unusable:
    221°–228° byd 20 NM blo 2,800´
    229°–239° byd 20 NM blo 2,500´
    260°–280° byd 35 NM blo 5,000´
  TACAN AZIMUTH unusable:
    320°–335° byd 5 NM

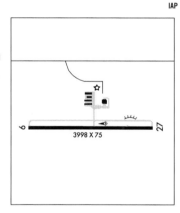

ARKANSAS

PETIT JEAN PARK (MPJ)(KMPJ) 8 W UTC–6(–5DT) N35°08.33′ W92°54.55′ MEMPHIS
923 B NOTAM FILE JBR H–6I, L–17E
RWY 03–21: H5852X75 (ASPH) S–17 MIRL 0.6% up NE IAP
  RWY 03: PAPI(P2R)—GA 4.0° TCH 50′. Thld dsplcd 438′. Trees.
  RWY 21: PAPI(P2L)—GA 4.0° TCH 44′. Thld dsplcd 190′. Trees.
SERVICE: FUEL 100LL, JET A **LGT** Actvt PAPI Rwy 03 and 21; MIRL Rwy 03–21—CTAF. PAPI Rwy 03 and 21 unavbl 0400–1000Z‡. Actvt rotg bcn—CTAF. Bcn unavbl 0400–1000Z‡. Rwy 03–21 MIRL OTS indefly.
AIRPORT REMARKS: Unattended. Deer and migratory birds on and invof arpt. Ultralight activity on and invof arpt. For service call 501–727–5441. Self serve fuel avbl 24 hr with credit card (100LL and Jet A).
AIRPORT MANAGER: 501-727-5441
COMMUNICATIONS: CTAF 122.9
®**MEMPHIS CENTER APP/DEP CON** 128.475
CLEARANCE DELIVERY PHONE: For CD ctc Memphis ARTCC at 901-368-8453/8449.
RADIO AIDS TO NAVIGATION: NOTAM FILE LIT.
  LITTLE ROCK (H) (H) VORTACW 113.9 LIT Chan 86 N34°40.66′ W92°10.83′ 303° 45.3 NM to fld. 240/5E.
  TACAN AZIMUTH & DME unusable:
    221°–228° byd 20 NM blo 2,800′
    229°–239° byd 20 NM blo 2,500′
    260°–280° byd 35 NM blo 5,000′
  TACAN AZIMUTH unusable:
    320°–335° byd 5 NM

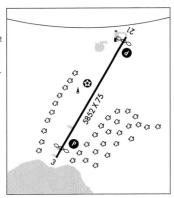

MOUNT IDA

BEARCE (7M3) 5 E UTC–6(–5DT) N34°31.74′ W93°31.77′ MEMPHIS
644 B NOTAM FILE JBR L–17E
RWY 08–26: H4000X75 (ASPH) S–6.5, D–12.5 MIRL
  RWY 08: PAPI(P2R)—GA 4.0° TCH 70′. Tree.
  RWY 26: PAPI(P2R)—GA 4.0° TCH 72′. Thld dsplcd 180′. Trees. Rgt tfc.
SERVICE: FUEL 100LL, JET A **LGT** ACTVT PAPI Rwy 08 and Rwy 26; MIRL Rwy 08–26—CTAF. Rwy 08 PAPI unusbl byd 8 degs left and byd 5 degs right of cntrln. Rwy 26 PAPI unusbl byd 8 degs right of cntrln.
AIRPORT REMARKS: Unatndd. Deer and coyotes on and invof arpt. Self service fuel avbl 24 hrs with credit card (Jet A and 100LL). Rwy 08 and 26 mkgs faded.
AIRPORT MANAGER: 817-999-3310
COMMUNICATIONS: CTAF 122.9
CLEARANCE DELIVERY PHONE: For CD ctc Memphis ARTCC at 901-368-8453/8449.
RADIO AIDS TO NAVIGATION: NOTAM FILE LIT.
  LITTLE ROCK (H) (H) VORTACW 113.9 LIT Chan 86 N34°40.66′ W92°10.83′ 258° 67.4 NM to fld. 240/5E.
  TACAN AZIMUTH & DME unusable:
    221°–228° byd 20 NM blo 2,800′
    229°–239° byd 20 NM blo 2,500′
    260°–280° byd 35 NM blo 5,000′
  TACAN AZIMUTH unusable:
    320°–335° byd 5 NM

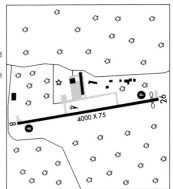

ARKANSAS

MOUNTAIN HOME
BAXTER CO (BPK)(KBPK) 4 NW UTC–6(–5DT) N36°22.14´ W92°28.23´　　　　**KANSAS CITY**
928 B NOTAM FILE BPK　　　　　　　　　　　　　　　　　　　　　　　　　　　　　H–6I, L–16G
　RWY 05–23: H5000X75 (ASPH) S–17 MIRL 0.3% up SW　　　　　　　　　　　　　**IAP**
　　RWY 05: REIL. PAPI(P4R)—GA 3.0° TCH 38´. Road.
　　RWY 23: REIL. PAPI(P2L)—GA 4.0° TCH 46´. P–line.
　SERVICE: S4 **FUEL** 100LL, JET A **OX** 3 **LGT** Actvt REIL Rwy 05 and
　　23; PAPI Rwy 05 and 23; MIRL 05–23—CTAF.
　AIRPORT REMARKS: Attended Mon–Fri 1300–2230Z‡. For svc aft hrs call
　　870–402–9000. No ARFF svcs avbl until further notice. FBO on
　　870–402–9000.
　AIRPORT MANAGER: 870–481–5418
　WEATHER DATA SOURCES: ASOS 133.975 (870) 481–5946.
　COMMUNICATIONS: CTAF/UNICOM 123.0
　®**MEMPHIS CENTER APP/DEP CON** 126.85
　CLEARANCE DELIVERY PHONE: For CD ctc Memphis ARTCC flight data on
　　901–368–8453/8449.
　RADIO AIDS TO NAVIGATION: NOTAM FILE FLP.
　　FLIPPIN (DH) DME 116.05　FLP　Chan 107(Y)　N36°17.98´
　　　W92°27.50´　352° 4.2 NM to fld. 782.
　　DME unusable:
　　　020°–050° byd 26 NM blo 3,500´
　　　020°–050° byd 32 NM blo 4,500´
　　　075°–105° byd 39 NM blo 4,500´
　　　105°–135° byd 35 NM blo 4,500´
　　ILS/DME 111.95 I–BPK　Chan 56(Y)　Rwy 05.　Class IT.　Unmonitored. Glideslope unusable blw 1,200´; byd 3° left
　　　of course; byd 5° r of course.

MOUNTAIN VIEW WILCOX MEML FLD (7M2)　2 E　UTC–6(–5DT)　N35°51.87´ W92°05.42´　　　**MEMPHIS**
805 B NOTAM FILE JBR　　　　　　　　　　　　　　　　　　　　　　　　　　　　　L–16G
　RWY 09–27: H4502X70 (ASPH)　　MIRL　0.5% up W　　　　　　　　　　　　　　　**IAP**
　　RWY 09: Bldg.
　　RWY 27: Tower.
　SERVICE: **FUEL** 100LL
　AIRPORT REMARKS: Unatndd. Self-service fuel avbl 24 hrs with credit card.
　　For svc after hrs call 501–203–8644. Deer & coyotes on & invof arpt.
　　Rwy 27 has a 15 ft dropoff 400 ft from thld.
　AIRPORT MANAGER: 501–203–8644
　COMMUNICATIONS: CTAF/UNICOM 122.7
　®**MEMPHIS CENTER APP/DEP CON** 126.85
　CLEARANCE DELIVERY PHONE: For CD ctc Memphis ARTCC at
　　901–368–8453/8449.
　RADIO AIDS TO NAVIGATION: NOTAM FILE ARG.
　　WALNUT RIDGE (VH) (H) VORTAC 114.5　ARG　Chan 92　N36°06.60´
　　　W90°57.22´　251° 57.3 NM to fld. 265/4E.
　　TACAN AZIMUTH unusable:
　　　011°–021° byd 15 NM blo 5,000´
　　VOR unusable:
　　　010°–021° byd 40 NM blo 3,000´
　　　010°–021° byd 55 NM
　　　011°–021° byd 8 NM blo 4,000´
　　　022°–052° byd 40 NM
　　　053°–078° byd 40 NM blo 2,300´
　　　053°–078° byd 64 NM
　　　079°–175° byd 40 NM blo 18,000´
　　　195°–216° byd 40 NM blo 18,000´
　　　217°–278° byd 40 NM blo 3,000´
　　　217°–278° byd 61 NM blo 18,000´
　　　279°–350° byd 40 NM blo 3,400´
　　　279°–350° byd 59 NM

NASHVILLE

HOWARD CO (M77)   3 N   UTC–6(–5DT)   N33°59.83´ W93°50.29´   MEMPHIS
553   B   NOTAM FILE JBR   L–17E
RWY 01–19: H3994X75 (ASPH)   S–8   MIRL   0.5% up N   IAP
  RWY 01: PAPI(P2L)—GA 3.0° TCH 40´. Thld dsplcd 115´. Trees.
  RWY 19: PAPI(P2L)—GA 3.0° TCH 40´. Trees.
SERVICE: FUEL 100LL   LGT ACTIVATE MIRL Rwy 01–19; PAPI Rwy 01 and Rwy 19 —CTAF.
AIRPORT REMARKS: Unattended. 100LL self serve fuel avbl 24 hrs. Rwy 19 turnaround has a 10´ drop off. Rwy 01 fence 3´ and road 7´ below thld 200´ from rwy end.
AIRPORT MANAGER: 870-845-7501
COMMUNICATIONS: CTAF 122.9
®FORT WORTH CENTER APP/DEP CON 123.925
CLEARANCE DELIVERY PHONE: For CD ctc Fort Worth ARTCC at 817-858-7584.
RADIO AIDS TO NAVIGATION: NOTAM FILE TXK.
  TEXARKANA (VH) (H) VORTACW 116.3   TXK   Chan 110   N33°30.83´ W94°04.39´   015° 31.2 NM to fld. 273/7E.

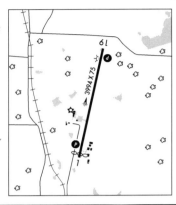

NEWPORT RGNL (M19)   5 NE   UTC–6(–5DT)   N35°38.26´ W91°10.58´   MEMPHIS
239   B   NOTAM FILE M19   H–6J, L–16G
RWY 04–22: H5002X150 (CONC)   S–30   IAP
  RWY 04: Rgt tfc.
RWY 18–36: H5002X150 (CONC)   S–30   MIRL
  RWY 18: REIL. PAPI(P4L)—GA 3.0° TCH 44´. P-line.
  RWY 36: REIL. PAPI(P4R)—GA 3.0° TCH 44´. Rgt tfc.
SERVICE: FUEL 100LL, JET A   LGT Dusk–Dawn.Actvt MIRL Rwy 18–36—CTAF.
AIRPORT REMARKS: Attended Mon–Fri 1400–2300Z‡, Sat 1400–1800Z‡. For svc aft hrs call 870-217-1400. Self svc fuel avbl after hrs with credit card Jet A and 100LL. Numerous agricultural opns March thru August.
AIRPORT MANAGER: 870-523-3613
WEATHER DATA SOURCES: AWOS–3PT 118.15 (870) 523–2189.
COMMUNICATIONS: CTAF/UNICOM 122.8
®MEMPHIS CENTER APP/DEP CON 120.075
CLEARANCE DELIVERY PHONE: For CD ctc Memphis ARTCC at 901-368-8453/8449.
RADIO AIDS TO NAVIGATION: NOTAM FILE ARG.
  WALNUT RIDGE (VH) (H) VORTAC 114.5   ARG   Chan 92   N36°06.60´ W90°57.22´   197° 30.3 NM to fld. 265/4E.
  TACAN AZIMUTH unusable:
    011°–021° byd 15 NM blo 5,000´
  VOR unusable:
    010°–021° byd 40 NM blo 3,000´
    010°–021° byd 55 NM
    011°–021° byd 8 NM blo 4,000´
    022°–052° byd 40 NM
    053°–078° byd 40 NM blo 2,300´
    053°–078° byd 64 NM
    079°–175° byd 40 NM blo 18,000´
    195°–216° byd 40 NM blo 18,000´
    217°–278° byd 40 NM blo 3,000´
    217°–278° byd 61 NM blo 18,000´
    279°–350° byd 40 NM blo 3,400´
    279°–350° byd 59 NM

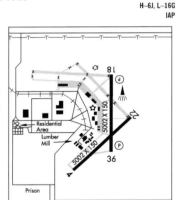

ARKANSAS

NORTH LITTLE ROCK MUNI (ORK)(KORK) 4 N UTC−6(−5DT) N34°49.99′ W92°15.25′ **MEMPHIS**
545 B TPA—See Remarks NOTAM FILE JBR **H−6I, L−18F**
RWY 05−23: H5002X75 (CONC) S−30, D−60 MIRL 0.5% up SW **IAP**
 RWY 05: REIL. PAPI(P2R)—GA 3.0° TCH 49′. Trees.
 RWY 23: REIL. PAPI(P2L)—GA 3.0° TCH 43′. Rgt tfc.
RWY 17−35: H3019X75 (ASPH) S−17 MIRL
 RWY 17: REIL. PAPI(P2L)—GA 3.0° TCH 44′. Ground. Rgt tfc.
 RWY 35: PAPI(P2L)—GA 3.0° TCH 44′. Trees.
SERVICE: S4 FUEL 100LL, JET A LGT Actvt REIL Rwys 05, 23, 17;
 MIRL Rwys 05−23 and 17−35—CTAF. PAPI Rwys 05, 23, 17 and 35
 opr consly.
AIRPORT REMARKS: Attended 1200−0200Z‡. For arpt access call
 501−835−5654, 501−529−1051. Deer on and invof arpt. Ultralight
 activity on and invof arpt. 100LL avbl 24 hr self service with credit
 card. Rwy 35 calm wind preferred tkf/ldg to the north when possible.
 Rwy 23 thld not visible from Rwy 17 thld. Rwy 17−35 500′ blast pad
 north end. TPA—helicopters 1045 (500), prop acft 1545 (1000),
 turboprop 2045 (1500).
AIRPORT MANAGER: 501-835-5654
WEATHER DATA SOURCES: AWOS−3PT 123.775 (501) 906−6529.
COMMUNICATIONS: CTAF/UNICOM 123.075
®LITTLE ROCK APP/DEP CON 119.5
CLNC DEL 121.6
CLEARANCE DELIVERY PHONE: For CD when una via freq ctc Little Rock Apch 501−379−2908 or Little Rock ATCT 501−379−2911
RADIO AIDS TO NAVIGATION: NOTAM FILE LIT.
 LITTLE ROCK (H) (H) VORTACW 113.9 LIT Chan 86 N34°40.66′ W92°10.83′ 334° 10.0 NM to fld. 240/5E.
 TACAN AZIMUTH & DME unusable:
  221°−228° byd 20 NM blo 2,800′
  229°−239° byd 20 NM blo 2,500′
  260°−280° byd 35 NM blo 5,000′
 TACAN AZIMUTH unusable:
  320°−335° byd 5 NM
 LOC/DME 111.9 I−ORK Chan 56 Rwy 05. DME unusable byd 20° right of course.

NORTHWEST ARKANSAS NTL (See FAYETTEVILLE/SPRINGDALE/ROGERS on page 49)

OSCEOLA MUNI (7M4) 2 SW UTC−6(−5DT) N35°41.47′ W90°00.61′ **MEMPHIS**
235 B NOTAM FILE JBR **L−16H**
RWY 01−19: H3799X75 (ASPH) S−8.5 MIRL **IAP**
 RWY 01: REIL. Tree.
 RWY 19: REIL. Pole.
SERVICE: FUEL 100LL LGT ACTVT REIL Rwy 19; MIRL Rwy 01−19—CTAF.
AIRPORT REMARKS: Unattended. For arpt attendant call 479−522−1150. Fuel avbl 24 hrs with credit card.
AIRPORT MANAGER: 479-522-1150
COMMUNICATIONS: CTAF/UNICOM 122.8
®MEMPHIS APP/DEP CON 119.1
CLEARANCE DELIVERY PHONE: For CD ctc Memphis Apch at 901−842−8457.
RADIO AIDS TO NAVIGATION: NOTAM FILE JBR.
 GILMORE (L) (L) VORW/DME 113.0 GQE Chan 77 N35°20.82′ W90°28.69′ 044° 30.8 NM to fld. 211/4E.

SC, 25 JAN 2024 to 21 MAR 2024

ARKANSAS

OZARK/FRANKLIN CO (7M5)   2 NW   UTC−6(−5DT)   N35°30.64′ W93°50.36′
648 B   NOTAM FILE JBR
RWY 04−22: H3302X75 (ASPH)   S−12   MIRL   1.3% up NE
  RWY 04: PAPI(P2L)—GA 3.0° TCH 17′. Bldg.
  RWY 22: PAPI(P2L)—GA 4.0° TCH 22′. Tree.
SERVICE: FUEL 100LL   LGT Lgts dusk−dawn. Actvt MIRL Rwy 04−22, PAPI Rwy 04 and 22—CTAF. Rwy 22 PAPI unusable byd 2° right of cntrln. Rwy 22 PAPI does not prvd obstn clnc byd 4 NM from thld, unusable byd 4 NM. Bcn OTS.
AIRPORT REMARKS: Unattended. Use extreme caution, wildlife may be on field. Self svc fuel avbl 24 hrs with credit card.
AIRPORT MANAGER: 479-667-7618
COMMUNICATIONS: CTAF/UNICOM 122.8
®**RAZORBACK APP/DEP CON** 120.9 (1130−0500Z‡)
  MEMPHIS CENTER APP/DEP CON 128.475 (0500−1130Z‡)
CLEARANCE DELIVERY PHONE: For CD ctc Razorback Apch at 479-649-2416, when Apch clsd ctc Memphis ARTCC at 901-368-8453/8449.
RADIO AIDS TO NAVIGATION: NOTAM FILE FSM.
  FORT SMITH (L) (L) VORTACW 110.4   FSM   Chan 41   N35°23.30′ W94°16.29′   064° 22.4 NM to fld. 432/7E.

MEMPHIS
L−16F
IAP

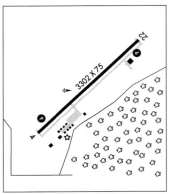

PARAGOULD
KIRK FLD (PGR)(KPGR)   1 NW   UTC−6(−5DT)   N36°03.83′ W90°30.55′
290 B TPA—1099(809)   NOTAM FILE JBR
RWY 04−22: H4500X75 (ASPH)   S−12.5   MIRL
  RWY 04: REIL. PAPI(P2L)—GA 3.0° TCH 18′. Thld dsplcd 489′. Road.
  RWY 22: REIL. PAPI(P2L)—GA 4.0° TCH 59′. Thld dsplcd 148′. Road.
RWY 08−26: 2792X100 (TURF)
  RWY 08: P−line.
  RWY 26: Trees.
SERVICE: FUEL 100LL, JET A   LGT Actvt MIRL Rwy 04−22, REIL and PAPI Rwys 04 and 22—CTAF.
AIRPORT REMARKS: Attended Mon−Fri 1300−2200Z‡. Wildlife on and invof rwy and twy. For svc after hrs call 870−450−7599 fee charged. 24 hr self svc fuel avbl with credit card (100LL & Jet A). Unlgtd twr 250′ AGL 0.17 miles east southeast AER 04. Rwy 08−26 soft when wet.
AIRPORT MANAGER: 870-239-7505
COMMUNICATIONS: CTAF/UNICOM 122.8
®**MEMPHIS CENTER APP/DEP CON** 120.075
CLEARANCE DELIVERY PHONE: For CD ctc Memphis ARTCC at 901-368-8453/8449.

ST LOUIS
L−16H
IAP

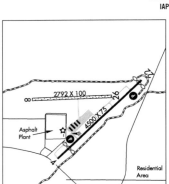

CONTINUED ON NEXT PAGE

ARKANSAS

CONTINUED FROM PRECEDING PAGE

RADIO AIDS TO NAVIGATION: NOTAM FILE ARG.
WALNUT RIDGE (VH) (H) VORTAC 114.5   ARG   Chan 92   N36°06.60′ W90°57.22′   093° 21.8 NM to fld. 265/4E.
  TACAN AZIMUTH unusable:
    011°–021° byd 15 NM blo 5,000′
  VOR unusable:
    010°–021° byd 40 NM blo 3,000′
    010°–021° byd 55 NM
    011°–021° byd 8 NM blo 4,000′
    022°–052° byd 40 NM
    053°–078° byd 40 NM blo 2,300′
    053°–078° byd 64 NM
    079°–175° byd 40 NM blo 18,000′
    195°–216° byd 40 NM blo 18,000′
    217°–278° byd 40 NM blo 3,000′
    217°–278° byd 61 NM blo 18,000′
    279°–350° byd 40 NM blo 3,400′
    279°–350° byd 59 NM
JONESBORO (VL) (L) VORW/DME 115.85   JBR   Chan 105(Y)   N35°52.49′ W90°35.31′   019° 12.0 NM to fld.
  247/0W. NOTAM FILE JBR.
  DME unusable:
    235°–270° byd 37 NM blo 3,000′
    310°–010° byd 33 NM blo 4,000′
  VOR unusable:
    015°–025° byd 14 NM blo 5,000′
    015°–025° byd 27 NM blo 8,000′
    035°–155° byd 40 NM
    040°–069° byd 10 NM blo 5,000′
    040°–069° byd 25 NM blo 7,000′
    070°–090° byd 10 NM blo 7,000′
    100°–114° byd 18 NM blo 7,000′
    115°–150° byd 15 NM blo 7,000′
    175°–200° byd 40 NM
    182°–192° byd 22 NM blo 5,000′
    238°–250° byd 40 NM
    253°–027° byd 40 NM
    310°–345° byd 14 NM blo 4,000′
    310°–345° byd 25 NM blo 7,000′

PARIS (SUBIACO)
PARIS MUNI (7M6)   2 E   UTC–6(–5DT)   N35°17.95′ W93°40.90′   MEMPHIS
  430   B   NOTAM FILE JBR
  RWY 03–21: H2710X60 (ASPH)   S–10   MIRL   0.7% up SW
    RWY 03: Road.
    RWY 21: PAPI(P2L)—GA 3.0° TCH 43′. Tree.
  SERVICE: LGT Actvt MIRL Rwy 03–21—CTAF.
  AIRPORT REMARKS: Unattended. Agriculture ops Feb–Oct blo 500′ AGL.
  AIRPORT MANAGER: 479-963-2450
  COMMUNICATIONS: CTAF 122.9
  CLEARANCE DELIVERY PHONE: For CD ctc Memphis ARTCC at 901-368-8453/8449.

PETIT JEAN PARK (See MORRILTON on page 68)

PIGGOTT MUNI   (7M7)   2 E   UTC–6(–5DT)   N36°22.69′ W90°09.97′   ST LOUIS
  275   B   NOTAM FILE JBR
  RWY 18–36: H2550X50 (ASPH)   S–10   MIRL
    RWY 18: Thld dsplcd 550′.
    RWY 36: Thld dsplcd 230′. Trees.
  SERVICE: LGT ACTVT MIRL Rwy 18–36—CTAF.
  AIRPORT REMARKS: Unattended. South end of Rwy 18–36 flooded after heavy rain.
  AIRPORT MANAGER: 870-324-2358
  COMMUNICATIONS: CTAF 122.9
  CLEARANCE DELIVERY PHONE: For CD ctc Memphis ARTCC at 901-368-8453/8449.

ARKANSAS

PINE BLUFF

PINEBLUFF RGNL/GRIDER FLD (PBF)(KPBF) P (NG) 4 SE UTC−6(−5DT) N34°10.47′ W91°56.14′ **MEMPHIS**
206 B TPA—1200(994) NOTAM FILE PBF
H−6J, L−18F
IAP
RWY 18−36: H5998X150 (ASPH) S−40, D−56, 2D−90 MIRL
  RWY 18: MALSR. VASI(V4L)—GA 3.0° TCH 52′.
  RWY 36: VASI(V4L)—GA 3.0° TCH 52′.
SERVICE: S4 **FUEL** 100LL, JET A **LGT** ACTIVATE MIRL Rwy 18−36 and MALSR Rwy 18—CTAF.
  MILITARY—FUEL (NC−100LL, A − Self svc avbl H24 with credit card)
AIRPORT REMARKS: Attended 1400−0000Z‡. For arpt attendant after hours call 870−540−9439. Self svc fuel avbl 24 hrs with credit card (100LL and JET A). Arpt CLOSED to acft with 30 or more passengers. Migratory birds invof arpt. Numerous AG ops on and invof arpt year round.
AIRPORT MANAGER: 870-534-4131
WEATHER DATA SOURCES: ASOS 120.775 (870) 536-0228.
COMMUNICATIONS: CTAF/UNICOM 123.0
  PINE BLUFF RCO 122.6 (JONESBORO RADIO)
 Ⓡ **LITTLE ROCK APP/DEP CON** 119.85
  CLNC DEL 119.85 (501) 379-2908
CLEARANCE DELIVERY PHONE: For CD ctc Memphis ARTCC at 901-368-8453/8449.
AIRSPACE: CLASS E.
RADIO AIDS TO NAVIGATION: NOTAM FILE PBF.
  PINE BLUFF (L) (L) VORW/DME 116.0 PBF Chan 107 N34°14.81′ W91°55.57′ 182° 4.4 NM to fld. 212/4E.
  VOR unusable:
    140°−145° byd 35 NM blo 4,900′
    260°−275° byd 25 NM
  ILS 111.7 I−PBF Rwy 18. Class IT. Unmonitored indef. Autopilot cpd apch NA blw 900 MSL.

PINEBLUFF RGNL/GRIDER FLD (See PINE BLUFF on page 74)

ARKANSAS 75

POCAHONTAS MUNI (M70) 1 SE UTC−6(−5DT) N36°14.73′ W90°57.31′   ST LOUIS
273   B   NOTAM FILE JBR   L−16G
  RWY 18−36: H4000X75 (ASPH) S−19 MIRL   IAP
    RWY 18: REIL. PAPI(P2L)—GA 3.0° TCH 43′. Tree.
    RWY 36: REIL. PAPI(P2L)—GA 3.0° TCH 40′. Road.
  SERVICE: S4   **FUEL** 100LL, JET A   **LGT** Actvt REIL Rwy 18 and 36;
    MIRL Rwy 18−36—CTAF. PAPI Rwy 18 and 36 oper cons.
  AIRPORT REMARKS: Attended 1400−2300Z‡. For srvc aftr hrs call
    870−260−8283. 24 hr self serve fuel avbl with credit card (100LL,
    Jet A). Full svc avbl (Jet A).
  AIRPORT MANAGER: 870-248-1141
  COMMUNICATIONS: CTAF/UNICOM 122.8
  ®**MEMPHIS CENTER APP/DEP CON** 120.075
  CLEARANCE DELIVERY PHONE: For CD ctc Memphis ARTCC at
    901-368-8453/8449.
  RADIO AIDS TO NAVIGATION: NOTAM FILE ARG.
    WALNUT RIDGE (VH) (H) VORTAC 114.5   ARG   Chan 92   N36°06.60′
      W90°57.22′   355° 8.1 NM to fld. 265/4E.
    TACAN AZIMUTH unusable:
      011°−021° byd 15 NM blo 5,000′
    VOR unusable:
      010°−021° byd 40 NM blo 3,000′
      010°−021° byd 55 NM
      011°−021° byd 8 NM blo 4,000′
      022°−052° byd 40 NM
      053°−078° byd 40 NM blo 2,300′
      053°−078° byd 64 NM
      079°−175° byd 40 NM blo 18,000′
      195°−216° byd 40 NM blo 18,000′
      217°−278° byd 40 NM blo 3,000′
      217°−278° byd 61 NM blo 18,000′
      279°−350° byd 40 NM blo 3,400′
      279°−350° byd 59 NM

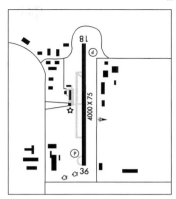

PRESCOTT

KIZER FLD (4F7) 1 E UTC−6(−5DT) N33°48.23′ W93°21.73′   MEMPHIS
319   B   NOTAM FILE JBR   L−17E
  RWY 18−36: H3464X50 (ASPH) S−12 MIRL
    RWY 18: Road.
    RWY 36: Trees.
  AIRPORT REMARKS: Unattended. Arpt gate locked from 0300−1100Z‡, call
    police for access 870−887−2676. Rwy 36 apch ground slope
    downward 6′ in 100′; 100′ from rwy end.
  AIRPORT MANAGER: 870-887-2210
  COMMUNICATIONS: CTAF 122.9
  CLEARANCE DELIVERY PHONE: For CD ctc Fort Worth ARTCC at
    817-858-7584.
  RADIO AIDS TO NAVIGATION: NOTAM FILE TXK.
    TEXARKANA (VH) (H) VORTACW 116.3   TXK   Chan 110   N33°30.83′
      W94°04.39′   057° 39.6 NM to fld. 273/7E.

RALPH C WEISER FLD (See MAGNOLIA on page 63)

SC, 25 JAN 2024 to 21 MAR 2024

ARKANSAS

RAZORBACK N36°14.79´ W94°07.28´ NOTAM FILE JBR.
  (VH) (H) VORTACW 116.4 RZC Chan 111 175° 4.2 NM to Springdale Muni. 1332/4E.

KANSAS CITY
H–6I, L–16F

  VOR unusable:
    025°–035° byd 40 NM
    025°–150° byd 22 NM blo 4,000´
    070°–080° byd 40 NM
    093°–103° byd 124 NM
    093°–103° byd 40 NM blo 17,000´
    104°–144° byd 40 NM
    145°–155° byd 40 NM blo 6,500´
    145°–155° byd 67 NM blo 9,500´
    145°–155° byd 80 NM
    150°–210° byd 22 NM blo 3,500´
    156°–170° byd 40 NM
    195°–215° byd 40 NM
    210°–220° byd 22 NM blo 3,000´
    234°–245° byd 40 NM
    310°–025° byd 22 NM blo 3,000´
  TACAN AZIMUTH unusable:
    148°–160°
    225°–240°

RECTOR (7M8) 2 SW UTC–6(–5DT) N36°15.00´ W90°19.17´
  281 B NOTAM FILE JBR

ST LOUIS
L–16H

  RWY 18–36: H3405X60 (ASPH) S–5 MIRL
    RWY 18: Tree.
    RWY 36: Thld dsplcd 266´. Tree.
  SERVICE: **LGT** ACTIVATE MIRL Rwy 18–36—CTAF.
  AIRPORT REMARKS: Unattended.
  AIRPORT MANAGER: 870-243-8421
  COMMUNICATIONS: CTAF 122.9
  CLEARANCE DELIVERY PHONE: For CD ctc Memphis ARTCC at
    901-368-8453/8449.

ARKANSAS

ROGERS EXEC – CARTER FLD (ROG)(KROG)   2 N   UTC–6(–5DT)   N36°22.35´ W94°06.42´   KANSAS CITY
1359   B   TPA—2358(999)   NOTAM FILE ROG   H–6I, L–16F
RWY 02–20: H6011X100 (ASPH–GRVD)   S–45, D–100, 2S–92   IAP, AD
    PCN 42 F/B/X/T   HIRL   0.3% up S
RWY 02: REIL. PAPI(P4L)—GA 3.0° TCH 55´.
RWY 20: MALSR. PAPI(P4L)—GA 3.0° TCH 55´.
SERVICE: S4   **FUEL** 100LL, JET A   **OX** 3   **LGT** When twr clsd ACTIVATE
    HIRL Rwy 02–20, REIL Rwy 02, twy lgts, MALSR Rwy 20, PAPI Rwy
    02 and Rwy 20—CTAF.
AIRPORT REMARKS: Attended Mon–Fri 1000–0300Z‡, Sat–Sun
    1300–0100Z‡. For fuel after hrs call 479–636–9400, fee charged.
    Bird activity on and invof arpt. Deer and coyote on and invof arpt. Rwy
    20 designated calm wind rwy. ARFF available upon request.
AIRPORT MANAGER: 479-631-1400
WEATHER DATA SOURCES: AWOS–3PT 134.375 (479) 631–9196. LAWRS.
COMMUNICATIONS: CTAF 119.375
® **RAZORBACK APP/DEP CON** 126.3 (1130–0500Z‡)
    MEMPHIS CENTER APP/DEP CON 126.1 (0500–1130Z‡)
    TOWER 119.375 (Mon–Fri 1130–0130Z‡, Sat–Sun 1400–0100Z‡)
    GND CON 118.0   **CLNC DEL** 121.75
CLEARANCE DELIVERY PHONE: For CD when una via freq ctc Razorback Apch
    479-649-2416, when Apch clsd ctc Memphis ARTCC at
    901-368-8453/8449.
AIRSPACE: CLASS D svc 1130–0130Z‡ Mon–Fri, 1400–0100Z‡ Sat–Sun; other times CLASS E.
RADIO AIDS TO NAVIGATION: NOTAM FILE JBR.
    RAZORBACK (VH) (H) VORTACW 116.4   RZC   Chan 111   N36°14.79´ W94°07.28´   001° 7.6 NM to fld. 1332/4E.
    VOR unusable:
       025°–035° byd 40 NM
       025°–150° byd 22 NM blo 4,000´
       070°–080° byd 40 NM
       093°–103° byd 124 NM
       093°–103° byd 40 NM blo 17,000´
       104°–144° byd 40 NM
       145°–155° byd 40 NM blo 6,500´
       145°–155° byd 67 NM blo 9,500´
       145°–155° byd 80 NM
       150°–210° byd 22 NM blo 3,500´
       156°–170° byd 40 NM
       195°–215° byd 40 NM
       210°–220° byd 22 NM blo 3,000´
       234°–245° byd 40 NM
       310°–025° byd 22 NM blo 3,000´
    TACAN AZIMUTH unusable:
       148°–160°
       225°–240°
ILS/DME 111.5   I–ROG   Chan 52   Rwy 20.   Class IB.   Glideslope unusable byd 5° right of course. Glideslope unusable
    for auto coupled apchs blo 1,632´. Unmonitored.

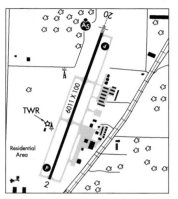

ARKANSAS

RUSSELLVILLE RGNL (RUE)(KRUE) 2 SE UTC−6(−5DT) N35°15.56′ W93°05.56′   **MEMPHIS**
409 B TPA—1414(1005) NOTAM FILE RUE   H−6I, L−16F
RWY 07−25: H5505X75 (ASPH) S−32, D−46 MIRL 0.7% up NE   IAP
  RWY 07: REIL. PAPI(P4L)—GA 3.0° TCH 60′. Tree.
  RWY 25: REIL. PAPI(P4L)—GA 4.0° TCH 83′. Thld dsplcd 706′. Tree.
SERVICE: FUEL 100LL, JET A **LGT** Dusk−dawn.Actvt REIL Rwys 07 and 25; PAPI Rwys 07 and 25; MIRL Rwy 07−25—CTAF.
AIRPORT REMARKS: Attended Mar–Nov Mon–Fri 1330–0030Z‡; Nov–Mar Mon–Fri 1330–2330Z‡; Sat–Sun 1400–0000Z‡. For svc aft hrs call 479–857–0362 or 479–857–4076. Deer on & invof rwy. Flocks of migratory birds invof arpt. Self svc fuel avbl 24 hrs with credit card (100LL). Heli service center on fld.
AIRPORT MANAGER: 479-967-1227
WEATHER DATA SOURCES: ASOS 132.475 (479) 968–2267.
COMMUNICATIONS: CTAF/UNICOM 122.7
®**MEMPHIS CENTER APP/DEP CON** 128.475
CLEARANCE DELIVERY PHONE: For CD ctc Memphis ARTCC at 901-368-8453/8449.
RADIO AIDS TO NAVIGATION: NOTAM FILE LIT.
  LITTLE ROCK (H) (H) VORTACW 113.9 LIT Chan 86 N34°40.66′ W92°10.83′ 303° 56.9 NM to fld. 240/5E.
  TACAN AZIMUTH & DME unusable:
    221°–228° byd 20 NM blo 2,800′
    229°–239° byd 20 NM blo 2,500′
    260°–280° byd 35 NM blo 5,000′
  TACAN AZIMUTH unusable:
    320°–335° byd 5 NM
  NDB (MHW) 379 RUE N35°15.42′ W93°05.68′ at fld. 379/3E. NOTAM FILE RUE. NDB unmonitored.

SALEM (7M9) 1 S UTC−6(−5DT) N36°21.35′ W91°49.86′   **KANSAS CITY**
787 B NOTAM FILE JBR   L−16G
RWY 02−20: H3489X50 (ASPH) MIRL
  RWY 02: Thld dsplcd 1233′. Hill.
  RWY 20: Thld dsplcd 248′. Tree.
SERVICE: FUEL 100LL **LGT** ACTIVATE MIRL Rwy 02−20—CTAF. Obstruction lgts OTS indef.
AIRPORT REMARKS: Unattended. Fuel: For svc call 870–371–0756 or 870–371–1025 (no fee). Deer on and invof rwy. All acft land Rwy 20, tkf Rwy 02. Rwy 02 has 3′ ditch at end of rwy extending 700′ along east side of rwy.
AIRPORT MANAGER: (870) 371-0756
COMMUNICATIONS: CTAF 122.9
CLEARANCE DELIVERY PHONE: For CD ctc Memphis ARTCC at 901-368-8453/8449.
RADIO AIDS TO NAVIGATION: NOTAM FILE ARG.
  WALNUT RIDGE (VH) (H) VORTAC 114.5 ARG Chan 92 N36°06.60′ W90°57.22′ 285° 45.1 NM to fld. 265/4E.
  TACAN AZIMUTH unusable:
    011°–021° byd 15 NM blo 5,000′
  VOR unusable:
    010°–021° byd 40 NM blo 3,000′
    010°–021° byd 55 NM
    011°–021° byd 8 NM blo 4,000′
    022°–052° byd 40 NM
    053°–078° byd 40 NM blo 2,300′
    053°–078° byd 64 NM
    079°–175° byd 40 NM blo 18,000′
    195°–216° byd 40 NM blo 18,000′
    217°–278° byd 40 NM blo 3,000′
    217°–278° byd 61 NM blo 18,000′
    279°–350° byd 40 NM blo 3,400′
    279°–350° byd 59 NM

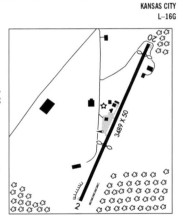

SALINE CO RGNL (See BENTON on page 35)

SALLY WOFFORD (See WEINER on page 85)

SEARCY CO (See MARSHALL on page 65)

ARKANSAS 79

SEARCY MUNI (SRC)(KSRC) 3 S UTC−6(−5DT) N35°12.64′ W91°44.25′ **MEMPHIS**
265 B TPA—1065(800) NOTAM FILE SRC H−6J, L−16G
RWY 01−19: H6008X100 (ASPH) S−24 MIRL 0.5% up N IAP
  RWY 01: MALSR. PAPI(P4L)—GA 3.0° TCH 57′.
  RWY 19: REIL. PAPI(P4L)—GA 3.0° TCH 40′. Tree.
SERVICE: S4 **FUEL** 100LL, JET A **OX** 1, 3 **LGT** Dusk−Dawn. MIRL Rwy
  01−19 preset low ints, to increase ints ACTIVATE—CTAF.
AIRPORT REMARKS: Attended 1300−0000Z‡. 100LL avbl self serve with
  credit card. For JET A fuel or svc after hours call 501−279−1080.
  Numerous gyrocopter ops dalgt hours. Numerous student pilot ops. No
  line of sight between rwy ends—small acft. Numerous agricultural acft
  opns from Feb−Nov 500 ft AGL and below.
AIRPORT MANAGER: 501−279−1080
WEATHER DATA SOURCES: AWOS−3PT 128.325 (501) 263−4280.
COMMUNICATIONS: CTAF/UNICOM 122.7
  LITTLE ROCK APP/DEP CON 119.75
  CLNC DEL 119.75
CLEARANCE DELIVERY PHONE: For CD when una via freq ctc Little Rock Apch
  501-379-2908 or Little Rock ATCT 501-379-2911.
RADIO AIDS TO NAVIGATION: NOTAM FILE LIT.
  LITTLE ROCK (H) (H) VORTACW 113.9 LIT Chan 86 N34°40.66′
    W92°10.83′ 029° 38.7 NM to fld. 240/5E.
  TACAN AZIMUTH & DME unusable:
    221°−228° byd 20 NM blo 2,800′
    229°−239° byd 20 NM blo 2,500′
    260°−280° byd 35 NM blo 5,000′
  TACAN AZIMUTH unusable:
    320°−335° byd 5 NM
  CERCY NDB (LOMW) 375 DS N35°07.35′ W91°45.70′ 011° 5.4 NM to fld. 223/2E. NOTAM FILE SRC.
  ILS/DME 110.1 I−DSY Chan 38 Rwy 01. Class IE. LOM CERCY NDB. Unmonitored indef.

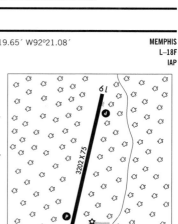

SHARP CO RGNL (See ASH FLAT on page 33)

SHERIDAN−GRANT CO RGNL (9M8) 3 E UTC−6(−5DT) N34°19.65′ W92°21.08′ **MEMPHIS**
236 B NOTAM FILE JBR L−18F
RWY 01−19: H3202X75 (ASPH) S−12.5 MIRL IAP
  RWY 01: PAPI(P2L)—GA 3.75° TCH 38′. Trees.
  RWY 19: PAPI(P2L)—GA 3.25° TCH 43′. Trees.
SERVICE: **FUEL** 100LL **LGT** Actvt PAPI Rwys 01 and 19; MIRL Rwy
  01−19—CTAF. Rwy 01 PAPI unusable byd 6° left of centerline.
AIRPORT REMARKS: Unattended. Self svc fuel avbl 24 hrs with credit card.
AIRPORT MANAGER: 870-941-9595
COMMUNICATIONS: CTAF/UNICOM 122.8
Ⓡ **LITTLE ROCK APP/DEP CON** 135.4 353.6
CLEARANCE DELIVERY PHONE: For CD ctc Little Rock Apch 501-379-2908 or
  Little Rock ATCT 501-379-2911.
AIRSPACE: CLASS E.
RADIO AIDS TO NAVIGATION: NOTAM FILE LIT.
  LITTLE ROCK (H) (H) VORTACW 113.9 LIT Chan 86 N34°40.66′
    W92°10.83′ 197° 22.6 NM to fld. 240/5E.
  TACAN AZIMUTH & DME unusable:
    221°−228° byd 20 NM blo 2,800′
    229°−239° byd 20 NM blo 2,500′
    260°−280° byd 35 NM blo 5,000′
  TACAN AZIMUTH unusable:
    320°−335° byd 5 NM

ARKANSAS

SHERRILL

SMITH'S INTL (99A) 1 NW UTC−6(−5DT) N34°24.37´ W91°57.53´ **MEMPHIS**
218 NOTAM FILE JBR
RWY 17−35: 3800X75 (TURF)
 RWY 17: Road.
 RWY 35: Trees. Rgt tfc.
AIRPORT REMARKS: Unattended.
AIRPORT MANAGER: (870) 766-4619
COMMUNICATIONS: CTAF 122.9
CLEARANCE DELIVERY PHONE: For CD ctc Little Rock Apch 501-379-2908 or Little Rock ATCT 501-379-2911.

SILOAM SPRINGS

SMITH FLD (SLG)(KSLG) 3 NE UTC−6(−5DT) N36°11.51´ W94°29.40´ **KANSAS CITY**
1191 B NOTAM FILE SLG **L−16F**
  IAP
RWY 18−36: H4997X75 (ASPH) S−24 MIRL 0.3% up N
 RWY 18: REIL. PAPI(P2L)—GA 3.0° TCH 44´.
 RWY 36: REIL. PAPI(P2L)—GA 3.0° TCH 43´.
SERVICE: S4 **FUEL** 100LL, JET A **LGT** Actvt REIL Rwy 18 and 36; PAPI
 Rwy 18 and 36 MIRL Rwy 18−36—CTAF. Rwy 36 VGSI unusbl byd 7°
 right of cntrln.
AIRPORT REMARKS: Attended Mon−Fri 1400−2300Z‡. For svc aft hrs call
 479-524-4103. Self-serve 100LL available 24 hrs with credit card.
AIRPORT MANAGER: 479-524-4103
WEATHER DATA SOURCES: AWOS−3PT 118.375 (479) 524-9893.
COMMUNICATIONS: CTAF/UNICOM 122.8
®**RAZORBACK APP/DEP CON** 121.0 (1130−0500Z‡)
®**MEMPHIS CENTER APP/DEP CON** 126.1 (0500−1130Z‡)
CLEARANCE DELIVERY PHONE: For CD ctc Razorback Apch 479-649-2416,
 when Apch clsd ctc Memphis ARTCC at 901-368-8453/8449.
RADIO AIDS TO NAVIGATION: NOTAM FILE JBR.
 RAZORBACK (VH) (H) VORTACW 116.4 RZC Chan 111 N36°14.79´
 W94°07.28´ 256° 18.2 NM to fld. 1332/4E.

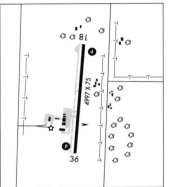

 VOR unusable:
  025°−035° byd 40 NM
  025°−150° byd 22 NM blo 4,000´
  070°−080° byd 40 NM
  093°−103° byd 124 NM
  093°−103° byd 40 NM blo 17,000´
  104°−144° byd 40 NM
  145°−155° byd 40 NM blo 6,500´
  145°−155° byd 67 NM blo 9,500´
  145°−155° byd 80 NM
  150°−210° byd 22 NM blo 3,500´
  156°−170° byd 40 NM
  195°−215° byd 40 NM
  210°−220° byd 22 NM blo 3,000´
  234°−245° byd 40 NM
  310°−025° byd 22 NM blo 3,000´
 TACAN AZIMUTH unusable:
  148°−160°
  225°−240°
 SILOAM SPRINGS NDB (MHW) 284 SLG N36°11.35´ W94°29.31´ at fld. 1625/4E. NOTAM FILE SLG. VFR only.

SILOAM SPRINGS   N36°11.35´ W94°29.31´   NOTAM FILE SLG. **KANSAS CITY**
NDB (MHW) 284   SLG   at Smith Fld. 1625/4E. (VFR only).

SMITH FLD (See SILOAM SPRINGS on page 80)

SMITH'S INTL (See SHERRILL on page 80)

SOCIAL HILL   N34°17.75´ W92°57.98´ **MEMPHIS**
RCO 122.2 (JONESBORO RADIO) **L−17E**

SOUTH ARKANSAS RGNL AT GOODWIN FLD (See EL DORADO on page 47)

ARKANSAS

SPRINGDALE MUNI (ASG)(KASG)   1 SE   UTC−6(−5DT)   N36°10.58′ W94°07.16′   KANSAS CITY
1353   B   NOTAM FILE ASG   MON Airport   H−6I, L−16F
RWY 18−36: H5302X76 (ASPH)   S−35, D−50, 2D−90   HIRL   IAP, AD
  RWY 18: MALSF. REIL. PAPI(P4L)—GA 3.0° TCH 43′. Thld dsplcd
    363′.
  RWY 36: REIL. PAPI(P4R)—GA 3.0° TCH 40′. Trees.
  SERVICE: S4 **FUEL** 100LL, JET A **OX** 4 **LGT** ACTIVATE HIRL Rwy
    18−36—CTAF. When twr clsd ACTIVATE MALSF Rwy 18—CTAF.
    ACTIVATE REIL Rwy 18 and Rwy 36—122.8.
  AIRPORT REMARKS: Attended 1200−0300Z‡. For svc after hours call
    479−751−4462. 100LL avbl 24 hrs self serve with credit card. All acft
    left overnight will be charged a ramp fee unless fuel has been
    purchased.
  AIRPORT MANAGER: 479-750-8135
  WEATHER DATA SOURCES: AWOS−3 124.675 (479) 750−2967. LAWRS
    (1200−0300Z‡).
  COMMUNICATIONS: CTAF 118.2 **UNICOM** 122.95
  ®**RAZORBACK APP/DEP CON** 126.6 (1130−0500Z‡)
    MEMPHIS CENTER APP/DEP CON 126.1 (0500−1130Z‡)
    TOWER 118.2 (1200−0300Z‡) **GND CON** 121.6
  CLEARANCE DELIVERY PHONE: For CD when una via freq ctc Razorback Apch
    479−649−2416, when Apch clsd ctc Memphis ARTCC at
    901−368−8453/8449.
  AIRSPACE: CLASS D svc 1200−0300Z‡; other times CLASS E.
  RADIO AIDS TO NAVIGATION: NOTAM FILE JBR.
    RAZORBACK (VH) (H) VORTACW 116.4   RZC   Chan 111   N36°14.79′ W94°07.28′   175° 4.2 NM to fld. 1332/4E.
    VOR unusable:
      025°−035° byd 40 NM
      025°−150° byd 22 NM blo 4,000′
      070°−080° byd 40 NM
      093°−103° byd 124 NM
      093°−103° byd 40 NM blo 17,000′
      104°−144° byd 40 NM
      145°−155° byd 40 NM blo 6,500′
      145°−155° byd 67 NM blo 9,500′
      145°−155° byd 80 NM
      150°−210° byd 22 NM blo 3,500′
      156°−170° byd 40 NM
      195°−215° byd 40 NM
      210°−220° byd 22 NM blo 3,000′
      234°−245° byd 40 NM
      310°−025° byd 22 NM blo 3,000′
    TACAN AZIMUTH unusable:
      148°−160°
      225°−240°
    ILS 110.9   I−ASG   Rwy 18.   Autopilot cpld apch NA blo 1,900′. Rate of change/reversal at 1.4NM fm thr.

STAR CITY MUNI (55M)   2 SW   UTC−6(−5DT)   N33°55.59′ W91°51.67′   MEMPHIS
398   NOTAM FILE JBR   L−18F
  RWY 18−36: H3000X60 (ASPH)   S−4
    RWY 18: Tree.
    RWY 36: Tree.
  SERVICE: **FUEL** 100LL
  AIRPORT REMARKS: Unattended. Self serve fuel avbl 24 hrs with credit card.
    Rwy 18 markings faded. Rwy 36 markings faded.
  AIRPORT MANAGER: 870−329−0484
  COMMUNICATIONS: CTAF 122.9
  CLEARANCE DELIVERY PHONE: For CD ctc Memphis ARTCC at
    901−368−8453/8449.
  RADIO AIDS TO NAVIGATION: NOTAM FILE PBF.
    PINE BLUFF (L) (L) VORW/DME 116.0   PBF   Chan 107   N34°14.81′
      W91°55.57′   166° 19.5 NM to fld. 212/4E.
    VOR unusable:
      140°−145° byd 35 NM blo 4,900′
      260°−275° byd 25 NM

82   ARKANSAS

STEPHENS

WILSON (4F8)   2 NE   UTC−6(−5DT)   N33°26.59′ W93°03.26′   MEMPHIS
230   B   NOTAM FILE JBR   L−17E
     RWY 02−20: H3000X50 (ASPH)   S−4   MIRL
        RWY 02: Trees.
        RWY 20: Trees.
        SERVICE: LGT Beacon OTS indef. Rwy lights OTS indef.
     AIRPORT REMARKS: Unattended. Deer on and invof arpt. Rwy 02−20 many
        longitudinal cracks with vegetation. Rwy 02−20 markings faded.
     AIRPORT MANAGER: 870-510-5874
     COMMUNICATIONS: CTAF 122.9
     CLEARANCE DELIVERY PHONE: For CD ctc Fort Worth ARTCC at
        817-858-7584.
     RADIO AIDS TO NAVIGATION: NOTAM FILE ELD.
        EL DORADO (VH) (DH) VORW/DME 115.5   ELD   Chan 102   N33°15.37′
        W92°44.64′   299° 19.2 NM to fld. 230/7E.
        DME unusable:
          020°−035° blo 2,000′
          036°−019° byd 30 NM blo 3,200′
        VOR unusable:
          110°−120° byd 40 NM

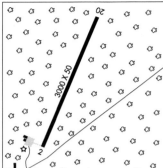

STUTTGART MUNI CARL HUMPHREY FLD   (SGT)(KSGT)   7 N   UTC−6(−5DT)   N34°35.97′ W91°34.50′   MEMPHIS
224   B   NOTAM FILE SGT   H−6J, L−18F
     RWY 18−36: H6015X100 (ASPH−GRVD)   S−75, D−150, 2S−82,   IAP
        2D−200, 2D/2D2−300   MIRL
        RWY 18: REIL.
        RWY 36: MALSF.
     RWY 09−27: H5002X150 (CONC)   S−25, D−65, 2S−82, 2D−120   MIRL
        RWY 27: REIL.
     SERVICE: FUEL 100LL, JET A   LGT Actvt MALSF Rwy 36; REIL Rwy 18
        and 27; MIRL Rwy 09−27 and 18−36—CTAF.
     AIRPORT REMARKS: Attended Nov-Jan 1400−0200Z‡, Feb-Oct Mon-Fri
        1400−2200Z‡. Numerous agricultural acft ops from Feb-Sep 500′
        AGL and below. For svc aft hrs call 870−672−2005. 100LL fuel avbl
        24 hrs self−serve with credit card. For fuel nights call
        870−672−2005. Migratory birds on and invof arpt Nov-Feb.
     AIRPORT MANAGER: 870-673-2960
     WEATHER DATA SOURCES: AWOS−3PT 119.025 (870) 673−1884.
     COMMUNICATIONS: CTAF/UNICOM 122.8
     ® LITTLE ROCK APP/DEP CON 135.4
     CLNC DEL 123.7
     CLEARANCE DELIVERY PHONE: For CD when una via freq ctc Little Rock Apch
        501−379−2908 or Little Rock ATCT 501−379−2911
     RADIO AIDS TO NAVIGATION: NOTAM FILE PBF.
        PINE BLUFF (L) (L) VORW/DME 116.0   PBF   Chan 107   N34°14.81′ W91°55.57′   035° 27.4 NM to fld. 212/4E.
        VOR unusable:
          140°−145° byd 35 NM blo 4,900′
          260°−275° byd 25 NM
        NDB (LOMW) 338   TT   N34°30.35′ W91°34.91′   001° 5.6 NM to fld. 196/2E.   NOTAM FILE SGT.
        ILS/DME 110.55   I−TTL   Chan 42(Y)   Rwy 36.   Class IE.   LOM STUTT NDB. Unmonitored.

STUTT   N34°30.35′ W91°34.91′   NOTAM FILE SGT.   MEMPHIS
     NDB (LOMW) 338   TT   001° 5.6 NM to Stuttgart Muni Carl Humphrey Fld. 196/2E.   L−18F

TECCO   N33°31.44′ W93°54.36′   NOTAM FILE TXK.   MEMPHIS
     NDB (LOMW) 234   TX   220° 6.0 NM to Texarkana Rgnl−Webb Fld. 260/5E.   L−17E

ARKANSAS

TEXARKANA RGNL–WEBB FLD (TXK)(KTXK) 3 NE UTC–6(–5DT) N33°27.22´ W93°59.46´   MEMPHIS
390 B TPA—1590(1200) Class I, ARFF Index A NOTAM FILE TXK MON Airport   H–6I, L–17E
RWY 04–22: H6602X150 (ASPH–GRVD) S–50, D–86, 2S–109,   IAP, AD
  2D–120 HIRL 0.7% up NE
  RWY 04: VASI(V4L)—GA 3.0° TCH 52´. Trees.
  RWY 22: MALSR. Trees.
RWY 13–31: H5200X100 (ASPH–GRVD) S–25 MIRL 0.5% up SE
  RWY 13: PAPI(P4L)—GA 3.0° TCH 48´. Thld dsplcd 641´. Railroad.
  RWY 31: PAPI(P4L)—GA 3.0° TCH 39´. Tree.
RUNWAY DECLARED DISTANCE INFORMATION
  RWY 04: TORA–6602 TODA–6602 ASDA–6602 LDA–6602
  RWY 13: TORA–5200 TODA–5200 ASDA–5200 LDA–4559
  RWY 22: TORA–6602 TODA–6602 ASDA–6602 LDA–6602
  RWY 31: TORA–5200 TODA–5200 ASDA–4559 LDA–4559
SERVICE: S4 FUEL 100LL, JET A OX 3 LGT When ATCT clsd actvt
  MALSR rwy 22; HIRL rwy 04/22; MIRL rwy 13/31—CTAF.
AIRPORT REMARKS: Attended 1200–0400Z‡. Deer on and invof arpt. Birds
  on and invof arpt. Ldg Fee. NOTE: See SPECIAL NOTICE—Controlled
  Firing.
AIRPORT MANAGER: 870-774-2171
WEATHER DATA SOURCES: ASOS 120.2 (870) 774–0404.
COMMUNICATIONS: CTAF 123.875 ATIS 120.2
  RCO 122.2 (JONESBORO RADIO)
®FORT WORTH CENTER APP/DEP CON 123.925
  TOWER 123.875 (1200–0400Z‡) GND CON 119.225
CLEARANCE DELIVERY PHONE: For CD if una to ctc on FSS freq, ctc Fort Worth ARTCC at 817-858-7584.
AIRSPACE: CLASS D svc 1200–0400Z‡; other times CLASS E.
RADIO AIDS TO NAVIGATION: NOTAM FILE TXK.
  (VH) (H) VORTACW 116.3 TXK Chan 110 N33°30.83´ W94°04.39´ 124° 5.5 NM to fld. 273/7E.
  TECCO NDB (LOMW) 234 TX N33°31.44´ W93°54.36´ 220° 6.0 NM to fld. 260/5E.
  ILS/DME 111.9 I–TXK Chan 56 Rwy 22. Class IA. LOM TECCO NDB. Unmonitored when ATCT clsd. DME unusable byd 32° right of course.

THOMPSON–ROBBINS (See HELENA/WEST HELENA on page 55)

TRIGGER GAP (See BERRYVILLE on page 37)

WALDRON MUNI (M27) 2 SW UTC–6(–5DT) N34°52.56´ W94°06.53´   MEMPHIS
705 B NOTAM FILE JBR   L–17E
RWY 09–27: H3650X60 (ASPH) S–4 MIRL 0.5% up E
  RWY 09: Trees.
  RWY 27: Tree.
SERVICE: LGT Actvt MIRL Rwy 09–27—CTAF.
AIRPORT REMARKS: Unattended. Deer on and invof arpt.
AIRPORT MANAGER: 479-637-3181
COMMUNICATIONS: CTAF 122.9
CLEARANCE DELIVERY PHONE: For CD ctc Razorback Apch at 479-649-2416, when Apch clsd ctc Memphis ARTCC at
  901-368-8453/8449.
RADIO AIDS TO NAVIGATION: NOTAM FILE MLC.
  RICH MOUNTAIN (VL) (L) VORTACW 113.5 PGO Chan 82 N34°40.83´ W94°36.54´ 061° 27.4 NM to fld. 2700/4E.
  VOR unusable:
    016°–021° byd 40 NM
    028°–029° byd 40 NM
    030°–040°
    050°–075° blo 4,000´
    090°–145°
    167°–169° byd 40 NM
    170°–200°
    235°–245° byd 30 NM blo 5,000´
    260°–280° byd 35 NM blo 5,000´
    329°–335° byd 40 NM
    340°–345° blo 5,000´
    358°–002° byd 40 NM

ARKANSAS

WALNUT RIDGE RGNL (ARG)(KARG) 4 NE UTC–6(–5DT) N36°07.48′ W90°55.51′ **MEMPHIS**
279 B NOTAM FILE ARG H–6J, L–16G
RWY 04–22: H6001X150 (ASPH) S–40, D–60, 2D–110 MIRL IAP
  RWY 04: MALSF.
  RWY 22: PAPI(P4L)—GA 3.0° TCH 47′.
RWY 13–31: H5003X150 (CONC) S–40, D–60, 2D–110
  RWY 13: Road.
  RWY 31: Berm.
RWY 18–36: H5001X150 (CONC) S–40, D–60, 2D–110 MIRL
  RWY 18: ODALS. REIL. Road.
SERVICE: S4 **FUEL** 100LL, JET A **LGT** ACTVT MALSF Rwy 04; ODALS Rwy 18; REIL Rwy 18; MIRL Rwy 04–22, Rwy 18–36—CTAF.
AIRPORT REMARKS: Attended 1400–2300Z‡. If arpt attendant not avbl, call 870–886–5432. Fee chrg unless prior arrangements made. Self svc fuel avbl 24 hrs with credit card. Government contract fuel avbl. Agricultural ops on and invof arpt Apr—Sep. Migratory birds invof arpt Oct—Jan.
AIRPORT MANAGER: 870–886–5432
WEATHER DATA SOURCES: AWOS–3PT 126.525 (870) 886–2537.
COMMUNICATIONS: CTAF/UNICOM 122.8
  RCO 122.1R 114.5T (JONESBORO RADIO)
  RCO 122.5 (JONESBORO RADIO)
®**MEMPHIS CENTER APP/DEP CON** 120.075
CLEARANCE DELIVERY PHONE: For CD ctc Memphis ARTCC at 901-368-8453/8449.
RADIO AIDS TO NAVIGATION: NOTAM FILE ARG.
  (VH) (H) VORTAC 114.5 ARG Chan 92 N36°06.60′ W90°57.22′ 054° 1.6 NM to fld. 265/4E.
  TACAN AZIMUTH unusable:
    011°–021° byd 15 NM blo 5,000′
  VOR unusable:
    010°–021° byd 40 NM blo 3,000′
    010°–021° byd 55 NM
    011°–021° byd 8 NM blo 4,000′
    022°–052° byd 40 NM
    053°–078° byd 40 NM blo 2,300′
    053°–078° byd 64 NM
    079°–175° byd 40 NM blo 18,000′
    195°–216° byd 40 NM blo 18,000′
    217°–278° byd 40 NM blo 3,000′
    217°–278° byd 61 NM blo 18,000′
    279°–350° byd 40 NM blo 3,400′
    279°–350° byd 59 NM
  LAWRENCE COUNTY NDB (MHW) 227 TNZ N36°12.42′ W90°55.39′ 180° 4.9 NM to fld. 262/1E. NDB unmonitored 2300–1300Z‡.
  LOC 111.1 I–ARG Rwy 18. LOC unmonitored 2300–1300Z‡.

WARREN MUNI (3M9) 3 S UTC–6(–5DT) N33°33.63′ W92°05.12′ **MEMPHIS**
235 B NOTAM FILE JBR L–18F
RWY 03–21: H3829X75 (ASPH) S–4 LIRL 1.0% up NE IAP
  RWY 03: PAPI(P2L)—GA 3.0° TCH 40′. Trees.
  RWY 21: PAPI(P2L)—GA 3.5° TCH 40′. Road.
SERVICE: **FUEL** 100LL **LGT** ACTVT LIRL and PAPI Rwy 03–21—CTAF. Rwy 03 PAPI unusbl byd 2 degs left of cntrln. Rwy 21 PAPI unusbl byd 3 degs right and left of cntrln.
AIRPORT REMARKS: Unattended. Self svc fuel avbl 24 hrs with credit card. For services call 870–226–6743 or after hrs 870–226–3703. Deer on and invof arpt. Ctc police 870–226–3703 to clear rwy.
AIRPORT MANAGER: 870–820–9119
COMMUNICATIONS: CTAF 122.9
®**MEMPHIS CENTER APP/DEP CON** 135.875
RADIO AIDS TO NAVIGATION: NOTAM FILE JBR.
  MONTICELLO (L) DME 111.6 MON Chan 53 N33°33.72′ W91°42.93′ 270° 18.5 NM to fld. 208.

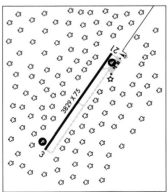

ARKANSAS

WEINER

SALLY WOFFORD (8M2) 3 S UTC–6(–5DT) N35°35.42′ W90°54.82′ MEMPHIS
245 NOTAM FILE JBR
RWY 01–19: H2330X160 (ASPH–TURF)
AIRPORT REMARKS: Unattended. Numerous agricultural acft ops. Rwy 01–19 2000 ft X 28 ft asph superimposed on Rwy 19 end, remainder turf.
AIRPORT MANAGER: (870) 930-4555
COMMUNICATIONS: CTAF 122.9
CLEARANCE DELIVERY PHONE: For CD ctc Memphis ARTCC at 901-368-8453/8449.

WEST MEMPHIS MUNI (AWM)(KAWM) 3 W UTC–6(–5DT) N35°08.10′ W90°14.07′ MEMPHIS
213 B NOTAM FILE AWM H–6J, L–16H
RWY 17–35: H6003X100 (CONC) S–85, D–104, 2D–167 IAP
PCN 33 R/D/W/T MIRL
RWY 17: MALSR.
RWY 35: REIL. PAPI(P4L)—GA 3.0° TCH 40′.
SERVICE: S4 FUEL 100LL, JET A **LGT** MIRL Rwy 17–35 preset low ints, to increase ints and ACTIVATE MALSR Rwy 17; PAPI Rwy 35; REIL Rwy 35—CTAF.
AIRPORT REMARKS: Attended Mon–Fri 1300–0100Z‡, Sat–Sun 1400–2300Z‡. For svc after hrs call 870–735–4656, fee charged. 100LL avbl 24 hr self service with credit card.
AIRPORT MANAGER: 870-735-4656
WEATHER DATA SOURCES: ASOS 118.175 (870) 733–9987.
COMMUNICATIONS: CTAF/UNICOM 123.05
Ⓡ **MEMPHIS APP CON** 119.1
Ⓡ **MEMPHIS DEP CON** 124.65
CLNC DEL 121.7
CLEARANCE DELIVERY PHONE: For CD ctc Memphis Apch at 901-842-8457.
RADIO AIDS TO NAVIGATION: NOTAM FILE JBR.
GILMORE (L) (L) VORW/DME 113.0 GQE Chan 77 N35°20.82′ W90°28.69′ 133° 17.5 NM to fld. 211/4E.
ILS/DME 110.7 I-LWR Chan 44 Rwy 17. Class IE. Unmonitored indef. Autopilot cpd apch NA blw 620′.

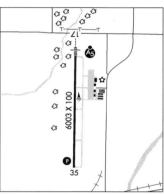

WILSON (See STEPHENS on page 82)

WOODRUFF CO (See AUGUSTA on page 33)

Z M JACK STELL FLD (See CROSSETT on page 43)

ABBEVILLE CHRIS CRUSTA MEML (IYA)(KIYA)   3 E   UTC–6(–5DT)   N29°58.55´   HOUSTON
W92°05.05´   H–7D, L–21B, 22E, GOMC
16   B   TPA—See Remarks   NOTAM FILE DRI   IAP
RWY 16–34: H5000X75 (ASPH)   S–17   MIRL
 RWY 16: REIL. PAPI(P2L)—GA 3.0° TCH 50´. Fence.
 RWY 34: REIL. PAPI(P2L)—GA 3.0° TCH 50´. Trees.
SERVICE: S4   **FUEL** 100LL, JET A   **LGT** MIRL Rwy 16–34; REIL Rwy 16
 and 34 preset on low intst dusk to dawn; to incr intst actvt—CTAF.
AIRPORT REMARKS: Attended daylight hours. TPA—352 (336) ultralight
 within 3 miles of arpt.
AIRPORT MANAGER: (337) 898-4206
WEATHER DATA SOURCES: AWOS–3 118.875 (337) 892–0526.
COMMUNICATIONS: CTAF/UNICOM 122.8
®**LAFAYETTE APP/DEP CON** 121.1 (1130–0430Z‡)
 HOUSTON CENTER APP/DEP CON 126.35 (0430–1130Z‡)
 GCO 135.075 (LAFAYETTE APCH and DE RIDDER FSS)
CLEARANCE DELIVERY PHONE: For CD ctc Lafayette Apch at 337-262-2729,
 when Apch clsd ctc Houston ARTCC at 281-230-5622.
RADIO AIDS TO NAVIGATION: NOTAM FILE LFT.
 LAFAYETTE (L) (L) VORTACW 109.8   LFT   Chan 35   N30°11.63´
  W91°59.55´   197° 13.9 NM to fld. 36/3E.
  TACAN AZIMUTH unusable:
  295°–320° blo 4,000´
 NDB (MHW) 230   BNZ   N30°03.67´ W92°07.40´   156° 5.5 NM to fld. 13/2E.   NOTAM FILE DRI.
 LOC 110.95   I–IYA   Rwy 16.

ACADIANA RGNL (See NEW IBERIA on page 113)

ALEXANDRIA
ALEXANDRIA INTL (AEX)(KAEX) P (ANG)   4 W   UTC–6(–5DT)   N31°19.64´ W92°32.91´   HOUSTON
88   B   TPA—See Remarks   Class I, ARFF Index D   NOTAM FILE AEX   H–6I, L–21B, 22E
                                                                                                                                                  IAP, AD
RWY 14–32: H9352X150 (CONC–GRVD)   S–81, D–180, 2S–175,
 2D–330, 2D/2D2–850   HIRL
 RWY 14: MALSR. TDZL. PAPI(P4L)—GA 3.0° TCH 71´. RVR–TR
 RWY 32: REIL. PAPI(P4L)—GA 3.0° TCH 80´. RVR–TR
RWY 18–36: H7001X150 (ASPH–CONC–GRVD)   S–75, D–130,
 2S–165, 2D–191, 2D/2D2–502   HIRL
 RWY 18: REIL. PAPI(P4L)—GA 3.0° TCH 79´.
 RWY 36: REIL. PAPI(P4L)—GA 3.0° TCH 77´. Trees.
RUNWAY DECLARED DISTANCE INFORMATION
 RWY 14: TORA–9352   TODA–9352   ASDA–9352   LDA–9352
 RWY 18: TORA–7001   TODA–7001   ASDA–7001   LDA–7001
 RWY 32: TORA–9352   TODA–9352   ASDA–9352   LDA–9352
 RWY 36: TORA–7001   TODA–7001   ASDA–7001   LDA–7001
SERVICE: S4   **FUEL** 100, JET A, MOGAS   **OX** 2, 4   **MILITARY— FUEL** A+
 (C318–443–5566.) (NC–100LL, A)
AIRPORT REMARKS: Attended continuously. Extensive helicopter tfc during
 military exercises. Center 75´ of first 3000´ of Rwy 18 is concrete,
 remainder is asphalt. Light acft frequently cross apch zones to Rwy
 14–32 blo 2000´ MSL. Extensive lgt acft tfc (cropdusters) below
 900´ to civ arpt 3.5 NM west southwest of field. TPA—right
 rectangular 1289 (1200), left overhead 1789 (1700). Commercial and lifeguard acft only on Commercial Terminal Ramp,
 all other acft utilize Twy A to FBO.
AIRPORT MANAGER: 318-427-6419
WEATHER DATA SOURCES: ASOS 123.975 (318) 442–6583.
COMMUNICATIONS: CTAF 127.35
 RCO 122.2 (DE RIDDER RADIO)
®**POLK APP/DEP CON** 125.4
 TOWER 127.35   **GND CON** 121.9   **CLNC DEL** 121.9

CONTINUED ON NEXT PAGE

LOUISIANA

CONTINUED FROM PRECEDING PAGE

AIRSPACE: CLASS D.
RADIO AIDS TO NAVIGATION: NOTAM FILE AEX.
  (H) (H) VORTACW 116.1   AEX   Chan 108   N31°15.40´ W92°30.06´   327° 4.9 NM to fld. 76/3E.
  VOR unusable:
    035°–065° blo 2,000´
    066°–094° byd 35 NM blo 3,000´
    185°–200° byd 35 NM blo 3,000´
    201°–214° byd 35 NM blo 2,000´
    215°–260° blo 2,000´
    261°–285° byd 35 NM blo 2,000´
    357°–034° byd 35 NM blo 3,000´
  ILS 110.1 I–ERJ Rwy 14. Class IT.
  ASR/PAR
COMM/NAV/WEATHER REMARKS: Multicom frequency 130.0 avbl.

ESLER RGNL (ESF)(KESF) P (ARNG) 10 NE UTC–6(–5DT) N31°23.69´ W92°17.75´   **HOUSTON**
  112 B   NOTAM FILE ESF   H–6I, L–21B, 22E
  RWY 09–27: H5998X150 (ASPH–GRVD) S–75, D–150, 2S–175,   IAP
    2D–220 HIRL
  RWY 09: REIL. PAPI(P4L)—GA 3.0° TCH 51´. Trees.
  RWY 27: MALSR.
  RWY 14–32: H5600X150 (ASPH–GRVD) S–75, D–150, 2S–175,
    2D–220 MIRL 0.4% up NW
  RWY 14: REIL. PAPI(P4L)—GA 3.0° TCH 36´. Trees.
  RWY 32: REIL. VASI(V4L)—GA 3.0° TCH 56´. Fence.
  SERVICE: **FUEL** 100LL, JET A   **LGT** ACTVT MALSR Rwy 27; REIL Rwy
    09, 14–32; MIRL Rwy 14–32; HIRL Rwy 09–27; twy lgts Twys A,
    B, C, D and E—CTAF. **MILITARY**— **FUEL** A+ (avbl 1300–2300Z‡
    Tue–Fri; OT, C318–443–5566.) (NC–100LL)
  AIRPORT REMARKS: Attended Tue–Fri 1300–2330Z‡. Fuel avbl Tue–Fri
    1300–2300Z‡ Sat–Mon on call in advance 318–443–5566. Birds
    on and invof arpt seasonally. PAEW adjacent rwys and twys. Rwy 14
    and Rwy 32 rwy markings severely faded.
  AIRPORT MANAGER: 985-750-0485
  WEATHER DATA SOURCES: ASOS 119.425 (318) 484–9031.
  COMMUNICATIONS: CTAF/UNICOM 122.8
  ® **POLK APP/DEP CON** 125.4
  CLEARANCE DELIVERY PHONE: For CD ctc Polk Apch at 337-531-2352.
  RADIO AIDS TO NAVIGATION: NOTAM FILE AEX.
    ALEXANDRIA (H) (H) VORTACW 116.1   AEX   Chan 108   N31°15.40´ W92°30.06´   049° 13.4 NM to fld. 76/3E.
    VOR unusable:
      035°–065° blo 2,000´
      066°–094° byd 35 NM blo 3,000´
      185°–200° byd 35 NM blo 3,000´
      201°–214° byd 35 NM blo 2,000´
      215°–260° blo 2,000´
      261°–285° byd 35 NM blo 2,000´
      357°–034° byd 35 NM blo 3,000´
    ILS/DME 111.5 I–ESF   Chan 52   Rwy 27. Class IA. ILS/DME unmonitored. DME unusable byd 25° right of course.

ALLEN PARISH (See OAKDALE on page 118)

ALVIN CALLENDER FLD (See NEW ORLEANS NAS JRB (ALVIN CALLENDER FLD) on page 116)

ANGER   N30°36.38´ W90°25.27´   NOTAM FILE DRI.   **NEW ORLEANS**
  NDB (LOMW) 212 HP 178° 5.1 NM to Hammond Northshore Rgnl. 94/0E.

LOUISIANA

ARCADIA–BIENVILLE PARISH (5F0)   2 SW   UTC–6(–5DT)   N32°31.93′ W92°57.17′   MEMPHIS
440   B   NOTAM FILE DRI   L–17E
RWY 14–32: H3000X75 (ASPH)   S–16   MIRL
 RWY 14: Trees.
 RWY 32: Trees.
SERVICE: LGT ACTVT MIRL Rwy 14–32—CTAF. MIRL Rwy 14–32 OTS indefly. Rotating bcn 0.5 mile southeast of arpt OTS.
AIRPORT REMARKS: Unattended. For arpt attendant call 318–263–2013. Golf crs adj to arpt. Hold shrt line nstd dist fm rwy.
AIRPORT MANAGER: 318-263-8456
COMMUNICATIONS: CTAF 122.9
CLEARANCE DELIVERY PHONE: For CD ctc Fort Worth ARTCC at 817-858-7584.
RADIO AIDS TO NAVIGATION: NOTAM FILE DRI.
 ELM GROVE (L) (L) VORTACW 111.2   EMG   Chan 49   N32°24.02′ W93°35.71′   069° 33.5 NM to fld. 160/7E.
  controlled by SHV RAPCON
  TACAN unusable:
   Byd 30 NM blo 2,000′
  VOR unusable:
   Byd 30.0NM blo 2,000′

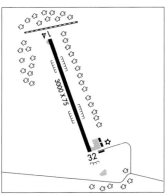

BARKSDALE AFB (BAD)(KBAD) AF   3 E   UTC–6(–5DT)   N32°30.12′ W93°39.76′   MEMPHIS
165   B   NOTAM FILE DRI   Not insp.   H–6I, L–17E
RWY 15–33: H11758X299 (PEM)   PCN 83 R/C/W/T   HIRL   DIAP, AD
 RWY 15: ALSF1. REIL. PAPI(P4L)—GA 2.5° TCH 53′. RVR–T.
 RWY 33: ALSF1. REIL. PAPI(P4L)—GA 2.5° TCH 50′. RVR–T.
ARRESTING GEAR/SYSTEM
                                                                                   BAK–12(B) (1102′). **RWY 33**
SERVICE: S4   **FUEL** JET A++   OX 2   **LGT** Rwy 15 ALSF–1 NSTD confign–dist fm thr lgt to pre–thr lgt is 128 ft; pre–thr lgt to term bar is 128 ft. **MILITARY— A–GEAR** BAK–12B avbl upon req 1 hr prior. W side A-Gear mrk perm removed.MP every third Fri fr 1200–1400Z‡. **JASU** 1(MA–1A) 7(A/M32A–86) 1(AM32A–95) 1(AM32A–60) **FLUID** W SP PRESAIR LHOX LOX OIL O–132–133–148–156 JOAP **TRAN ALERT** Tran maint svc hr 1400–0100Z‡ Mon–Fri; 1400–2400Z‡ Sat–Sun; clsd hol. No priority basis. Exp svc delays of 2 hr or more. Ltd fleet svc avbl. Potable water unavbl.
MILITARY REMARKS: Opr 1200Z–0630Z‡ Mon–Fri, 1400Z–2200Z‡ wkends; clsd AFGSC family days and fed hol. **RSTD** PPR, call Afld OPS DSN 781–3226/4978 or C318–456–3226. All tran aircrews must rpt to Afld OPS. Practice apch may be restricted by twr, depending on tfc and time of day. PPR issued up to 7 days prior to arr. PPR good for +/– 15 minute PPR time. Coordination of PPR outside of block time by telephone is rqr or PPR Number will be considered cancelled. 180° deg turns for C135 and hvy acft are auth in the first 750 ft Rwy 15 and the first 1000 ft Rwy 33. Tran acft with ordnance not authorized. Twy C unlgtd, open to all acft for daytime ops only exc for B–52. Twy E and Twy E1 unlighted and usable for daylgt VFR only. Training for tran acft will not be permitted to interfere with local acft opr. Non-AFGSC acft may be subjected to less than rqr Quantity–Distance separation due munitions opr. Aircrews should exercise appropriate risk management in determining afld suitability. **CAUTION** Lgt acft and prcht opr invof Shreveport Downtown 3.3 NM NW dur final apch Rwy 15 and dep Rwy 33. **TFC PAT** Rectangular 1200 ft, Overhead 1700 ft. VFR copter enter tfc pat at 700 ft fm E and 1000 ft fm W. Ovft of munitions stor area E–NE of fld not auth. **MISC** Wx svc avbl 1300–0400Z‡Mon–Fri 1400–2200Z‡wkends; Clsd AFGSC Family Day and Federal hol. DSN 781–3136, C318–456–3136. AN/FMQ–19 ASOS in use; augmented by human obsn when nec. Dur evac of wx flt ctc 26 OWS at nr abv. Observed surface visibility restricted from 150° to 330° by obstructions and lack of visibility markers byd 2 NM. Acft with distinguished visitor ctc PTD or Comd Post at least 20 minutes prior to ETA. Afld ops unable to issue COMSEC and has no storage capability. USAF Afld Mgmt pers do not determine/rpt a Rwy Cond Code (RwyCC) nor issue FAA formatted fld cond NOTAM (FICON). **RWY** First 1184 ft Rwy 15 and first 1600 ft Rwy 33 is concrete. Middle 8972 ft is asphalt with first 3000 ft at each end having a 75 ft wide concrete keel sfc in cntr and the mid 2972 ft having a 50 ft conc keel sfc. NSTD spacing of 150 ft btn Rwy 15 and Rwy 33 overrun mrks.
AIRPORT MANAGER: 318-456-3226
COMMUNICATIONS: ATIS 307.025   **PTD** 254.425
®**SHREVEPORT APP/DEP CON** 123.75 360.725 (320°–152°) 119.9 335.55 (153°–319°)
 TOWER 128.25 278.3   (Opr 1300–0400Z‡Mon–Fri 1400–2200Z‡ Wkends: clsd AFGSC family days, federal hol.)
 GND CON 121.8 253.5
 COMD POST (Call RAYMOND 06) 311.0 321.0 **PMSV METRO** 227.4

CONTINUED ON NEXT PAGE

SC, 25 JAN 2024 to 21 MAR 2024

LOUISIANA

CONTINUED FROM PRECEDING PAGE

AIRSPACE: CLASS C svc ctc APP CON.
RADIO AIDS TO NAVIGATION: NOTAM FILE DRI.
   (L) TACAN Chan 105   BAD (115.8)   N32°30.20´ W93°40.07´   at fld. 162/2E.
     No NOTAM MP: 1600–1800Z‡ Wed. mnt dur publ opr hr only
    TACAN AZIMUTH unusable:
      010°–053° byd 30 NM blo 5,000´
      054°–064° byd 20 NM blo 5,000´
      065°–104° byd 30 blo 5,000´
      105°–115° byd 18 NM blo 5,000´
      116°–277° byd 30 NM blo 3,000´
      278°–288° byd 30 NM
      289°–330° byd 30 NM blo 5,000´
    TACAN DME unusable:
      010°–053° byd 30 NM blo 5,000´
      054°–064° byd 20 NM blo 5,000´
      065°–104° byd 30 blo 5,000´
      105°–115° byd 18 NM blo 5,000´
      116°–277° byd 30 NM blo 3,000´
      278°–288° byd 30 NM
      289°–330° byd 30 NM blo 5,000´
   BELCHER (H) (H) VORTACW 117.4   EIC   Chan 121   N32°46.28´ W93°48.60´   148° 17.8 NM to fld.
     190/7E.   NOTAM FILE SHV.
   ELM GROVE (L) (L) VORTACW 111.2   EMG   Chan 49   N32°24.02´ W93°35.71´   324° 7.0 NM to fld. 160/7E.
     controlled by SHV RAPCON
    TACAN unusable:
     Byd 30 NM blo 2,000´
    VOR unusable:
     Byd 30.0NM blo 2,000´
   ILS 108.9   I–JKC   Rwy 15.
   ILS 109.9   I–BAD   Rwy 33.   Unmonitored when ATCT clsd.. No NOTAM MP: 1100–1400Z‡ Tue, Thu. Mnt dur publ
     opr hr only. Glide SLOPE unusable for cpd apchs blw 425´ MSL.
   ASR/PAR
   COMM/NAV/WEATHER REMARKS: Radar see Terminal FLIF for Radar Minima.

BASTROP

MOREHOUSE MEML (BQP)(KBQP)   2 SE   UTC–6(–5DT)   N32°45.37´ W91°52.84´   **MEMPHIS**
  168   B   TPA—1201(1033)   NOTAM FILE DRI   **L–18F**
  RWY 16–34: H4002X100 (ASPH)   S–15.5   MIRL   **IAP**
    RWY 16: REIL. PAPI(P2L)—GA 3.0° TCH 50´.
    RWY 34: REIL. PAPI(P2L)—GA 3.0° TCH 50´.
  SERVICE: S2   **FUEL** 100LL   **LGT** Dusk–Dawn. REIL Rwys 16 and 34;
    MIRL Rwy 16–34 preset low intst dusk–dawn, to incr intst
    ACTVT—CTAF. PAPI Rwy 16 OTS indef. Rwy 34 REIL OTS indefly.
  AIRPORT REMARKS: Attended Mon–Fri 1315–2100Z‡. Deer on and invof
    rwy. Self serve fuel avbl 24 hrs with credit card. Rwy 16 mkgs in poor
    cond due to fading and mold growth. Rwy 34 cracking, fading, and
    mold growth on rwy mkgs.
  AIRPORT MANAGER: 318-281-2018
  WEATHER DATA SOURCES: AWOS–3PT 118.375 (318) 281–1443. Wind unrel.
  COMMUNICATIONS: CTAF/UNICOM 122.8
  ® **MONROE APP/DEP CON** 126.9 (1200–0400Z‡)
  ® **FORT WORTH CENTER APP/DEP CON** 126.325 (0400–1200Z‡)

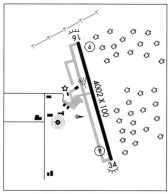

CONTINUED ON NEXT PAGE

LOUISIANA

CONTINUED FROM PRECEDING PAGE

CLEARANCE DELIVERY PHONE: For CD ctc Monroe Apch at 318-327-5641, if unavbl, ctc Fort Worth ARTCC at 817-858-7584.
RADIO AIDS TO NAVIGATION: NOTAM FILE MLU.
  MONROE (VL) (L) VORTACW 117.2   MLU   Chan 119   N32°31.01´ W92°02.16´   026° 16.3 NM to fld. 77/3E.
  VOR unusable:
    010°–040° byd 40 NM
    125°–135° byd 40 NM
    215°–231° byd 40 NM
    232°–242° byd 40 NM blo 8,000´
    232°–242° byd 83 NM
    243°–255° byd 40 NM blo 7,000´
    243°–255° byd 56 NM
    256°–267° byd 40 NM blo 18,000´
    256°–267° byd 45 NM
    268°–271° byd 40 NM
    272°–282° byd 40 NM blo 2,000´
    272°–282° byd 51 NM
    283°–315° byd 40 NM
  BASTROP NDB (MHW) 329   BQP   N32°45.28´ W91°53.01´   at fld. 159/3E.   NOTAM FILE DRI.
    AWOS broadcasted on NDB

BATON ROUGE METRO, RYAN FLD (BTR)(KBTR)   4 N   UTC–6(–5DT)   N30°31.98´ W91°08.99´   **HOUSTON**
70   B   LRA   ARFF Index—See Remarks   NOTAM FILE BTR   MON Airport   **H–7D, L–21B, 22F**
RWY 04L–22R: H7500X150 (CONC–GRVD)   S–120, D–170, 2S–175,   **IAP, AD**
  2D–300 PCN 70 R/A/W/T   HIRL   CL
  RWY 04L: RVR–TR Pole.
  RWY 22R: MALSR. TDZL. PAPI(P4L)—GA 3.0° TCH 56´. RVR–TR Rgt
    tfc.
RWY 13–31: H7005X150 (ASPH–GRVD)   S–120, D–170, 2S–175,
  2D–300 PCN 95 F/C/X/T   HIRL
  RWY 13: MALSR. RVR–T Thld dsplcd 597´. Pole.
  RWY 31: MALS. VASI(V4L)—GA 3.0° TCH 64´. RVR–R Thld dsplcd
    314´. Road.
RWY 04R–22L: H3799X75 (ASPH)   S–30, D–45 PCN 26 F/C/X/T   MIRL
  RWY 04R: PAPI(P2L)—GA 3.0°. Rgt tfc.
  RWY 22L: PAPI(P2L)—GA 3.0°.

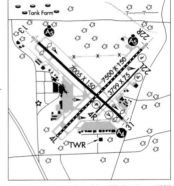

RUNWAY DECLARED DISTANCE INFORMATION
  RWY 04L: TORA–7500 TODA–7500 ASDA–7500 LDA–7500
  RWY 04R: TORA–3799 TODA–3799 ASDA–3799 LDA–3799
  RWY 13: TORA–7004 TODA–7004 ASDA–6317 LDA–5720
  RWY 22L: TORA–3799 TODA–3799 ASDA–3799 LDA–3799
  RWY 22R: TORA–7500 TODA–7500 ASDA–7500 LDA–7500
  RWY 31: TORA–7004 TODA–7004 ASDA–6407 LDA–6094
SERVICE: S4   **FUEL** 100LL, JET A   **OX** 1, 3   **LGT** ACTVT MALSR Rwy 22R & 13 and MALS Rwy 31—CTAF. When ATCT
  clsd HIRL Rwys 13–31 & 04L–22R preset low intst; to incr intst ACTVT—CTAF. MIRL Rwy 04R–22L not avbl.
AIRPORT REMARKS: Attended 1100–0600Z‡. Migratory birds on and in vicinity of arpt during months of Mar, Apr, Sep and Oct.
  Class I ARFF Index C, 24 hrs PPR for unscheduled air carrier ops with more than 30 passenger seats 0600–1100Z‡, call
  arpt manager 225–355–2068/0333. When twr clsd use 121.9 to ctc ARFF for emergency request. Rwy 04R–22L not
  avbl for air carrier ops with more than 30 passenger seats. Rwy 04R–22L and Twy E are similar in appearance. Use
  caution when exiting Rwy 13–31. Ramp and twy lane adjacent to the commercial air carrier terminal building is limited
  to commercial air carrier and passenger airtaxi acft only. Twy E weight restrictions: single 44,000 lbs, dual 55,000 lbs,
  dual tandem 93,000 lbs. Twy E, Twy F btn Rwy 04R–22L and AER 31 not avbl for skedd acr ops. Twy F btn Rwy 04–22L
  and 31 RDCS to 40 ft wid.
AIRPORT MANAGER: 225-355-0333
WEATHER DATA SOURCES: ASOS (225) 354–2138 LLWAS.
COMMUNICATIONS: CTAF 118.45   ATIS 125.2 225–354–2170   UNICOM 122.95
  RCO 122.2 (DE RIDDER RADIO)
® APP/DEP CON 120.3 WEST 133.225 EAST (1100–0600Z‡)
® HOUSTON CENTER APP/DEP CON 126.35 (0600–1100Z‡)
  TOWER 118.45 (1100–0600Z‡)   GND CON 121.9   CLNC DEL 119.4
CLEARANCE DELIVERY PHONE: For CD if una to ctc on FSS freq, ctc Houston ARTCC at 281-230-5622.
AIRSPACE: CLASS C svc ctc APP CON svc (per TWR/NOTAM 1100–0600Z‡); other times CLASS E.
RADIO AIDS TO NAVIGATION: NOTAM FILE BTR.
  FIGHTING TIGER (VL) (L) VORTACW 116.5   LSU   Chan 112   N30°29.11´ W91°17.64´   063° 8.0 NM to fld. 20/6E.
  RUNDI NDB (LOMW) 284   BT   N30°34.98´ W91°12.66´   133° 4.4 NM to fld. 69/0E.
  ILS/DME 110.3 I–BTR   Chan 40   Rwy 13.   Class ID.   LOM RUNDI NDB. Unmonitored when ATCT closed.
  ILS/DME 108.7 I–CLZ   Chan 24   Rwy 22R.   Class IIE.   Unmonitored when ATCT closed.
  ASR (1100–0600Z‡)

LOUISIANA 91

BEAUREGARD RGNL (See DE RIDDER on page 94)

BELCHER N32°46.28′ W93°48.60′ NOTAM FILE SHV.   **MEMPHIS**
  (H) (H) VORTACW 117.4   EIC   Chan 121   159° 14.2 NM to Shreveport Downtown. 190/7E.   **H–6I, L–17E**

BLOCK WR29   WBF   N26°55.83′ W90°30.42′/130
  AWOS–3 118.525 (985) 773–5497 Winds unrel.   **L–21B, GOMC**

BLUEBIRD HILL (See KEITHVILLE on page 103)

BOGALUSA

GEORGE R CARR MEML AIR FLD (BXA)(KBXA)   2 N   UTC–6(–5DT)   N30°48.82′ W89°51.90′   **NEW ORLEANS**
  119   B   NOTAM FILE DRI   **H–6J, 8F, L–21B, 22F**
  RWY 18–36: H5002X100 (ASPH)   S–22   MIRL   **IAP**
    RWY 18: REIL. PAPI(P2L)—GA 3.0° TCH 50′. Trees.
    RWY 36: REIL. PAPI(P2L)—GA 3.0° TCH 52′. Trees.
    SERVICE: S4   FUEL 100LL, JET A   LGT Dusk–Dawn. REIL Rwys 18 and
      36; MIRL Rwy 18–36 preset low intst dusk–dawn; to incr intst—CTAF.
    AIRPORT REMARKS: Attended 1400–2300Z‡. Fuel avbl 24 hrs self svc with
      credit card. Single point and overwing fueling avbl.
    AIRPORT MANAGER: 985-732-6200
    WEATHER DATA SOURCES: AWOS–3PT 118.025 (985) 732–6224.
    COMMUNICATIONS: CTAF/UNICOM 122.8
    ® HOUSTON CENTER APP/DEP CON 126.8
    CLEARANCE DELIVERY PHONE: For CD ctc Houston ARTCC at 281-230-5622.
    RADIO AIDS TO NAVIGATION: NOTAM FILE GWO.
      PICAYUNE (L) (L) VORW/DME 113.95   PCU   Chan 86(Y)   N30°33.67′
        W89°43.83′   330° 16.6 NM to fld. 70/5E.
      VOR unusable:
        285°–305° byd 6 NM blo 4,000′
        325°–076° byd 26 NM blo 2,500′
      DME unusable:
        078°–180° byd 32 NM blo 3,000′
        331°–064° byd 27 NM blo 4,000′
      BOGALUSA NDB (MHW) 353   GVB   N30°52.90′ W89°51.73′   182° 4.1 NM to fld. 148/0W.   NOTAM FILE DRI.
        NDB unmonitored indef.
      LOC 111.1   I–BXA   Rwy 18.

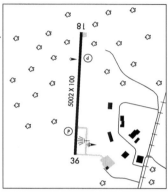

BUNKIE MUNI (2R6)   2 S   UTC–6(–5DT)   N30°57.40′ W92°14.05′   **HOUSTON**
  62   B   NOTAM FILE DRI   **L–21B, 22E**
  RWY 18–36: H3005X75 (ASPH)   S–8   MIRL   **IAP**
    RWY 18: REIL. PAPI(P2L)—GA 3.0° TCH 25′.
    RWY 36: REIL. PAPI(P2L)—GA 3.25° TCH 26′. Trees.
    SERVICE: FUEL 100LL   LGT ActvtREIL rwy 18 and rwy 36; MIRL rwy
      18–36—CTAF. MIRL rwy 18–36 preset low intst dusk–dawn; incr
      intst—CTAF.
    AIRPORT REMARKS: Unattended. 100LL fuel avbl by appt call
      318–346–2371.
    AIRPORT MANAGER: (318) 264-2922
    COMMUNICATIONS: CTAF 122.9
    ® POLK APP/DEP CON 125.3
    CLEARANCE DELIVERY PHONE: For CD ctc Polk Apch at 337-531-2352.
    RADIO AIDS TO NAVIGATION: NOTAM FILE AEX.
      ALEXANDRIA (H) (H) VORTACW 116.1   AEX   Chan 108   N31°15.40′
        W92°30.06′   139° 22.6 NM to fld. 76/3E.
      VOR unusable:
        035°–065° blo 2,000′
        066°–094° byd 35 NM blo 3,000′
        185°–200° byd 35 NM blo 3,000′
        201°–214° byd 35 NM blo 2,000′
        215°–260° blo 2,000′
        261°–285° byd 35 NM blo 2,000′
        357°–034° byd 35 NM blo 3,000′

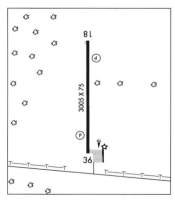

BYERLEY (See LAKE PROVIDENCE on page 106)

SC, 25 JAN 2024 to 21 MAR 2024

LOUISIANA

C E 'RUSTY' WILLIAMS (See MANSFIELD on page 108)

CALDWELL PARISH (See COLUMBIA on page 92)

CHENNAULT INTL (See LAKE CHARLES on page 105)

COLUMBIA
CALDWELL PARISH (F86) 2 NE UTC–6(–5DT) N32°07.33′ W92°03.27′ MEMPHIS
67 B NOTAM FILE DRI L–18F
RWY 01–19: H3501X75 (ASPH) S–6 MIRL
  RWY 01: REIL. PAPI(P2L)—GA 3.5° TCH 63′. Trees.
  RWY 19: REIL. PAPI(P2L)—GA 3.0° TCH 53′.
SERVICE: LGT ACTIVATE MIRL Rwy 01–19—CTAF. REIL Rwy 01–19 opr continuously. Rwy 01 REIL OTS approach end Rwy 01. Rwy 19 REIL OTS approach end Rwy 19.
AIRPORT REMARKS: Unattended. Birds invof arpt. Foreign objects and debris present on apron. Grass growing through cracks. Windsock OTS temp.
AIRPORT MANAGER: (318) 331-3888
COMMUNICATIONS: CTAF 122.9
CLEARANCE DELIVERY PHONE: For CD ctc Monroe Apch at 318-327-5641, if unavbl, ctc Fort Worth ARTCC at 817-858-7584.
RADIO AIDS TO NAVIGATION: NOTAM FILE MLU.
  MONROE (VL) (L) VORTACW 117.2 MLU Chan 119 N32°31.01′
  W92°02.16′ 179° 23.7 NM to fld. 77/3E.
  VOR unusable:
  010°–040° byd 40 NM
  125°–135° byd 40 NM
  215°–231° byd 40 NM
  232°–242° byd 40 NM blo 8,000′
  232°–242° byd 83 NM
  243°–255° byd 40 NM blo 7,000′
  243°–255° byd 56 NM
  256°–267° byd 40 NM blo 18,000′
  256°–267° byd 45 NM
  268°–271° byd 40 NM
  272°–282° byd 40 NM blo 2,000′
  272°–282° byd 51 NM
  283°–315° byd 40 NM

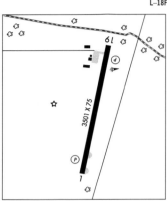

CONCORDIA PARISH (See VIDALIA on page 127)

COUSHATTA
THE RED RIVER (0R7) 2 SE UTC–6(–5DT) N31°59.42′ W93°18.46′ HOUSTON
177 B NOTAM FILE DRI H–6I, L–22E
  IAP
RWY 18–36: H5002X74 (ASPH) S–44 MIRL
  RWY 18: REIL. PAPI(P2L)—GA 3.0° TCH 50′. Trees.
  RWY 36: REIL. PAPI(P2L)—GA 3.0° TCH 50′. Trees.
SERVICE: LGT MIRL Rwy 18–36, REIL Rwy 18 and 36 preset low intst dusk-dawn, to incr intst actvt—CTAF. Rwy 18 and 36 REILS out of service. Rwy 18 and 36 PAPI out of service. Airport beacon out of service.
AIRPORT REMARKS: Unattended. 66′ trees 253′ east of rwy centerline full length. NOTE: See Special Notices—Aerobatic Practice Area.
AIRPORT MANAGER: 318-932-5710
COMMUNICATIONS: CTAF 122.9
®**POLK APP/DEP CON** 132.05
CLEARANCE DELIVERY PHONE: For CD ctc Fort Worth ARTCC at 817-858-7584.
RADIO AIDS TO NAVIGATION: NOTAM FILE SHV.
  BELCHER (H) (H) VORTACW 117.4 EIC Chan 121 N32°46.28′
  W93°48.60′ 144° 53.3 NM to fld. 190/7E.

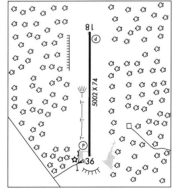

LOUISIANA 93

COVINGTON

ST TAMMANY RGNL (L31) 6 SE UTC−6(−5DT) N30°26.70′ W89°59.33′ **NEW ORLEANS**
39 B NOTAM FILE DRI L−21B, 22F
RWY 18−36: H2999X75 (ASPH) S−17.5 MIRL
  RWY 18: Trees.
  RWY 36: Trees.
SERVICE: S2 FUEL 100LL LGT MIRL Rwy 18−36 preset med int.
AIRPORT REMARKS: Attended Mon−Fri 1400−2100Z‡. Self service fuel avbl 24 hrs with credit card. Parachute jumping activities and skydiving act on weekends.
AIRPORT MANAGER: (985) 898−2792
COMMUNICATIONS: CTAF/UNICOM 122.8
®NEW ORLEANS APP/DEP CON 133.15
CLEARANCE DELIVERY PHONE: For CD ctc New Orleans Apch at 504−471−4350.
RADIO AIDS TO NAVIGATION: NOTAM FILE GWO.
  PICAYUNE (L) (L) VORW/DME 113.95 PCU Chan 86(Y) N30°33.67′
    W89°43.83′ 238° 15.1 NM to fld. 70/5E.
  VOR unusable:
    285°−305° byd 6 NM blo 4,000′
    325°−076° byd 26 NM blo 2,500′
  DME unusable:
    078°−180° byd 32 NM blo 3,000′
    331°−064° byd 27 NM blo 4,000′

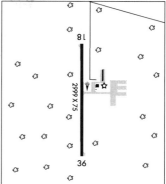

CROWLEY

LE GROS MEML (3R2) 7 SW UTC−6(−5DT) N30°09.71′ W92°29.04′ **HOUSTON**
14 B NOTAM FILE DRI L−21B, 22E
RWY 04−22: H4304X150 (CONC) S−30, D−47, 2D−87 MIRL
  RWY 04: REIL. PAPI(P2L)—GA 3.0° TCH 50′.
  RWY 22: REIL. PAPI(P2L)—GA 3.0° TCH 50′.
RWY 13−31: H4003X150 (CONC) S−30, D−47, 2D−87
  RWY 13: Thld dsplcd 240′. Tree.
SERVICE: LGT MIRL Rwy 04−22, REIL Rwy 04 and Rwy 22 preset low ints, to increase ints ACTIVATE—CTAF.
AIRPORT REMARKS: Attended Mon−Fri 1400−2300Z‡. NOTE: See Special Notices—Aerobatic Practice Area.
AIRPORT MANAGER: 318−788−8800
COMMUNICATIONS: CTAF 122.9
CLEARANCE DELIVERY PHONE: For CD ctc Lafayette Apch at 337−262−2729, when Apch clsd ctc Houston ARTCC at 281−230−5622.
RADIO AIDS TO NAVIGATION: NOTAM FILE LFT.
  LAFAYETTE (L) (L) VORTACW 109.8 LFT Chan 35 N30°11.63′
    W91°59.55′ 263° 25.6 NM to fld. 36/3E.
  TACAN AZIMUTH unusable:
    295°−320° blo 4,000′

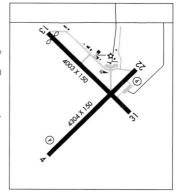

DAVID G JOYCE (See WINNFIELD on page 128)

SC, 25 JAN 2024 to 21 MAR 2024

LOUISIANA

DE QUINCY INDUSTRIAL AIRPARK (5R8) 2 SW UTC–6(–5DT) N30°26.47´ W93°28.42´ HOUSTON
83 B NOTAM FILE 5R8   L–21B, 22E
                                                                                          IAP
RWY 16–34: H4997X75 (ASPH) S–18 MIRL
  RWY 16: REIL. PAPI(P2L)—GA 3.0° TCH 50´. Tree.
  RWY 34: REIL. PAPI(P2L)—GA 3.0° TCH 50´. Trees.
SERVICE: S2 FUEL 100LL LGT MIRL Rwy 16–34, REIL Rwy 16 and
  Rwy 34 preset low ints dusk–dawn, to increase ints ACTIVATE—CTAF.
AIRPORT REMARKS: Attended Mon–Thurs 1300–2200Z‡, Fri
  1300–1700Z‡. Self svc fuel with credit card. Emerg airframe rpr avbl
  call arpt mgr for details. Emerg pwr plant rpr avbl call arpt mgr for
  details. Courtesy car and pilots lounge avbl.
AIRPORT MANAGER: 337-660-3488
WEATHER DATA SOURCES: AWOS–3PT 121.2 (337) 786–1518.
COMMUNICATIONS: CTAF/UNICOM 122.8
®LAKE CHARLES APP/DEP CON 119.35 (1200–0400Z‡)
®HOUSTON CENTER APP/DEP CON 124.7 (0400–1200Z‡)
CLEARANCE DELIVERY PHONE: For CD ctc Lake Charles Apch at
  337-480-3103, when Apch clsd ctc Houston ARTCC at
  281-230-5622.
RADIO AIDS TO NAVIGATION: NOTAM FILE LCH.
  LAKE CHARLES (H) (H) VORTACW 113.4   LCH Chan 81 N30°08.49´
    W93°06.33´   306° 26.2 NM to fld. 20/7E.
  VOR unusable:
    181°–359° byd 30 NM blo 1,500´

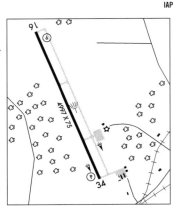

DE RIDDER

BEAUREGARD RGNL (DRI)(KDRI) 3 SW UTC–6(–5DT) N30°49.90´ W93°20.39´ HOUSTON
202 B TPA—1202(1000) NOTAM FILE DRI   H–6I, L–21B, 22E
                                                                                          IAP
RWY 18–36: H5494X100 (ASPH–CONC–AFSC) S–60 MIRL
  RWY 18: REIL. PAPI(P4R)—GA 3.0° TCH 50´. Trees.
  RWY 36: ODALS. PAPI(P4L)—GA 3.0° TCH 50´. Trees.
RWY 14–32: H4218X60 (ASPH)
  RWY 14: Thld dsplcd 454´. Trees.
  RWY 32: Trees.
SERVICE: S2 FUEL 100LL, JET A LGT REIL Rwy 18 andMIRL Rwy
  18–36 preset low intst dusk–dawn; to incr intst ACTVT—CTAF.
AIRPORT REMARKS: Attended Mon–Fri 1400–2300Z‡. For attendant other
  times call 337-401-2967. 100LL avbl 24 hrs self svc with credit
  card. For Jet A aft hrs and hols call 337-401-2967. Rwy 18 and Rwy
  36 markings faded.
AIRPORT MANAGER: 337-463-8250
WEATHER DATA SOURCES: AWOS–3PT 118.225 (337) 463–8278.
COMMUNICATIONS: CTAF/UNICOM 122.8
®POLK APP/DEP CON 123.7
CLEARANCE DELIVERY PHONE: For CD if una to ctc on FSS freq, ctc Polk Apch
  at 337-531-2352.
RADIO AIDS TO NAVIGATION: NOTAM FILE LCH.
  LAKE CHARLES (H) (H) VORTACW 113.4   LCH Chan 81 N30°08.49´
    W93°06.33´   337° 43.1 NM to fld. 20/7E.
  VOR unusable:
    181°–359° byd 30 NM blo 1,500´
  DE RIDDER NDB (MHW) 385   DXB   N30°45.13´ W93°20.08´   353° 4.8 NM to fld. 164/4E.   NOTAM FILE DRI. NDB
    unmonitored 0100–1300Z‡.
  LOC 111.1 I–DRI Rwy 36. LOC unmonitored 0100–1300Z‡.

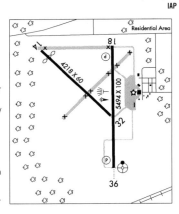

SC, 25 JAN 2024 to 21 MAR 2024

LOUISIANA

DELHI MUNI (0M9) 3 S UTC−6(−5DT) N32°24.64′ W91°29.91′   MEMPHIS
91 B NOTAM FILE DRI   L−18F
RWY 18−36: H3000X75 (ASPH) S−5 MIRL
  RWY 18: REIL. Trees.
  RWY 36: REIL. Road.
SERVICE: **LGT** MIRL Rwy 18−36, REIL Rwy 18 and Rwy 36 preset low
  ints dusk−dawn, to incr ints ACTIVATE—CTAF.
AIRPORT REMARKS: Unattended. Rwy 18−36 4′ fence 123′ from centerline
  on both sides of rwy.
AIRPORT MANAGER: (318) 614-9210
COMMUNICATIONS: CTAF 122.9
CLEARANCE DELIVERY PHONE: For CD ctc Monroe Apch at 318-327-5641, if
  unavbl, ctc Fort Worth ARTCC at 817-858-7584.
RADIO AIDS TO NAVIGATION: NOTAM FILE MLU.
  MONROE (VL) (L) VORTACW 117.2   MLU   Chan 119   N32°31.01′
    W92°02.16′   100° 28.0 NM to fld. 77/3E.
  VOR unusable:
    010°−040° byd 40 NM
    125°−135° byd 40 NM
    215°−231° byd 40 NM
    232°−242° byd 40 NM blo 8,000′
    232°−242° byd 83 NM
    243°−255° byd 40 NM blo 7,000′
    243°−255° byd 56 NM
    256°−267° byd 40 NM blo 18,000′
    256°−267° byd 45 NM
    268°−271° byd 40 NM
    272°−282° byd 40 NM blo 2,000′
    272°−282° byd 51 NM
    283°−315° byd 40 NM

DURALDE   N30°33.59′ W92°26.88′   NOTAM FILE DRI.   HOUSTON
NDB (MHW) 263   ECY   165° 5.7 NM to Eunice. 2E.   H−7D, L−21B, 22E

EAST CAMERON 321A   EZP   N28°13.19′ W92°47.66′/100   HOUSTON
AWOS−3 119.050 (504) 323−0220   L−21B, GOMC

ELM GROVE   N32°24.02′ W93°35.71′   NOTAM FILE DRI.   MEMPHIS
(L) (L) VORTACW 111.2   EMG   Chan 49   324° 7.0 NM to Barksdale AFB. 160/7E.   H−6I, L−17E
  controlled by SHV RAPCON
  TACAN unusable:
    Byd 30 NM blo 2,000′
  VOR unusable:
    Byd 30.0NM blo 2,000′

ESLER RGNL (See ALEXANDRIA on page 87)

EUGENE ISLAND 251A   EKE   N28°29.83′ W91°34.21′/104   HOUSTON
AWOS−3P 119.925 (985) 510−2076   L−21B, GOMC

LOUISIANA

EUNICE (4R7) 2 S UTC–6(–5DT) N30°27.98´ W92°25.43´ HOUSTON
42 B NOTAM FILE DRI H–7D, L–21B, 22E, GOMC
RWY 16–34: H5001X75 (ASPH) S–21 MIRL IAP
  RWY 16: REIL. PAPI(P2L)—GA 3.0° TCH 50´. Trees.
  RWY 34: REIL. PAPI(P2L)—GA 3.0° TCH 50´. Trees.
SERVICE: S2 **FUEL** 100LL, JET A, MOGAS **LGT** REIL Rwy 16–34, MIRL
  Rwy 16–34 preset low ints dusk to dawn; to incr ints ACTIVATE—CTAF.
  Rwy 16 PAPI unusbl byd 6° left of cntrln.
AIRPORT REMARKS: Attended Mon–Fri 1400–2300Z‡, Sat and Sun on call.
  For fuel after hours call 337–457–6585. Rwy 16 and 34 runway
  markings severely faded.
AIRPORT MANAGER: 337–457–6585
COMMUNICATIONS: CTAF/UNICOM 122.8
®**LAFAYETTE APP/DEP CON** 128.7 (1030–0530Z‡)
  HOUSTON CENTER APP/DEP CON 126.35 (0530–1030Z‡)
  GCO 135.075 (LAFAYETTE APCH and DE RIDDER FSS)
CLEARANCE DELIVERY PHONE: For CD ctc Lafayette Apch at 337–262–2729,
  when Apch clsd ctc Houston ARTCC at 281–230–5622.
RADIO AIDS TO NAVIGATION: NOTAM FILE LFT.
  LAFAYETTE (L) (L) VORTACW 109.8 LFT Chan 35 N30°11.63´
  W91°59.55´ 303° 27.7 NM to fld. 36/3E.
  TACAN AZIMUTH unusable:
  295°–320° blo 4,000´.
DURALDE NDB (MHW) 263 ECY N30°33.59´ W92°26.88´ 165° 5.7 NM to fld. 2E. NOTAM FILE DRI.

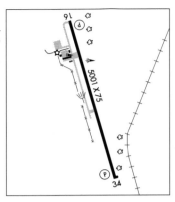

FALSE RIVER RGNL (See NEW ROADS on page 117)

FARMERVILLE

UNION PARISH (F87) 4 SE UTC–6(–5DT) N32°43.50´ W92°20.23´ MEMPHIS
121 B NOTAM FILE DRI L–22E
RWY 16–34: H3003X75 (ASPH) S–8 MIRL
  RWY 16: REIL. PAPI(P2L)—GA 3.83° TCH 63´. Trees.
  RWY 34: REIL. PAPI(P2L)—GA 3.0° TCH 50´. Trees.
SERVICE: **FUEL** 100LL **LGT** MIRL Rwy 16–34, REIL Rwy 16 and Rwy 34
  preset low ints dusk–dawn, to incr intst ACTIVATE—CTAF.
AIRPORT REMARKS: Unattended. Rwy 16–34 CLOSED to acft over 12,500
  lbs. Oxidation pond with 6´ fence 150´ west of centerline on the north
  end of Rwy 16. NOTE: See Special Notices—Aerobatic Practice Area.
AIRPORT MANAGER: 318–243–4155
COMMUNICATIONS: CTAF 122.9
CLEARANCE DELIVERY PHONE: For CD ctc Monroe Apch at 318–327–5641, if
  unavbl, ctc Fort Worth ARTCC at 817–858–7584.

FELICIANA AIRPARK (See JACKSON on page 101)

FIGHTING TIGER N30°29.11´ W91°17.64´ NOTAM FILE BTR. HOUSTON
(VL) (L) VORTACW 116.5 LSU Chan 112 063° 8.0 NM to Baton Rouge Metro, Ryan Fld. 20/6E. H–7D, L–21B, 22F
RCO 122.2 (DE RIDDER RADIO)

LOUISIANA 97

FRANKLINTON (2R7) 3 SE UTC–6(–5DT) N30°49.17´ W90°06.75´   NEW ORLEANS
175   B   NOTAM FILE DRI   L–21B, 22F
RWY 13–31: H3000X75 (ASPH)   S–20   MIRL
  RWY 13: REIL. PAPI(P2L)—GA 3.0° TCH 50´. Trees.
  RWY 31: REIL. PAPI(P2L)—GA 3.0° TCH 50´. Trees.
SERVICE: LGT MIRL Rwy 13–31 preset low intst; to incr intst
  ACTVT—CTAF. Rwy 13 and Rwy 31 REILs OTS. Rwy 13 and Rwy 31
  PAPI OTS indefly. Arpt lgtg OTS. VFR only.
AIRPORT REMARKS: Unattended. Golf course .25 miles north of arpt. Rwy 13
  and Rwy 31 runway markings chipped and faded.
AIRPORT MANAGER: (225) 333-1579
COMMUNICATIONS: CTAF 122.9
CLEARANCE DELIVERY PHONE: For CD ctc Houston ARTCC at 281-230-5622.
RADIO AIDS TO NAVIGATION: NOTAM FILE GWO.
  PICAYUNE (L) (L) VORW/DME 113.95   PCU   Chan 86(Y)   N30°33.67´
    W89°43.83´   303° 25.1 NM to fld. 70/5E.
  VOR unusable:
    285°–305° byd 6 NM blo 4,000´
    325°–076° byd 26 NM blo 2,500´
  DME unusable:
    078°–180° byd 32 NM blo 3,000´
    331°–064° byd 27 NM blo 4,000´

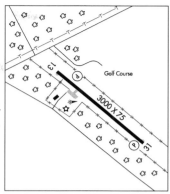

GALLIANO
SOUTH LAFOURCHE LEONARD MILLER JR (GAO)(KGAO)   1 E   UTC–6(–5DT)   N29°26.47´   NEW ORLEANS
W90°15.67´   H–7E, L–21B, 22F, GOMC
00   B   LRA   NOTAM FILE DRI   IAP
RWY 18–36: H6500X100 (ASPH)   S–60, D–75   MIRL
  RWY 18: REIL. PAPI(P4L)—GA 3.0° TCH 38´. Trees.
  RWY 36: SSALR. PAPI(P4L)—GA 3.0° TCH 50´.
SERVICE: FUEL 100LL, JET A1+   LGT SSALR Rwy 36; REIL Rwy 18;
  MIRL Rwy 18–36 preset low intensity dusk to dawn; to increase
  intensity ACTIVATE—CTAF.
AIRPORT REMARKS: Attended continuously. Fuel avbl 24/7 with credit card.
  All sfcs work in progress mowing. Bird activity invof Rwy 18–36.
AIRPORT MANAGER: 985-291-0818
WEATHER DATA SOURCES: AWOS–3PT 118.175 (985) 475–5178.
COMMUNICATIONS: CTAF/UNICOM 123.0
®NEW ORLEANS APP/DEP CON 120.85
  CLNC DEL 120.85
CLEARANCE DELIVERY PHONE: For CD ctc New Orleans Apch at
  504-471-4350 or 120.85.
RADIO AIDS TO NAVIGATION: NOTAM FILE DRI.
  LEEVILLE (VH) (H) VORTAC 113.5   LEV   Chan 82   N29°10.51´
    W90°06.24´   331° 17.9 NM to fld. 2/2E.
  ILS/DME 109.1   I-GAO   Chan 28   Rwy 36.   Class 1B.   Glideslope
    unusable byd 005 degrees right of course.

• • • • • • • • • • • •

HELIPAD H1: H60X60 (CONC)
HELIPORT REMARKS: H1 CLOSED indef.

GALLIANO   2LS   N29°24.82´ W90°17.73´/–2   NEW ORLEANS
AWOS–3PT 118.175 (985) 475–5178 AWOS is assocd with heli 2LSO.   L–22F

GARDEN BANKS 172   GHB   N27°50.42´ W91°59.27´
AWOS–3 118.025 Winds unreliable.   L–21B, GOMC

GARDEN BANKS 426   AGI   N27°32.77´ W92°26.61´/134
AWOS–3PT 118.375 (504) 425–5011   L21–B, GOMC

GARDEN BANKS 783   GBK   N27°12.23´ W92°12.15´
AWOS–3 118.825 Winds unreliable.   L–21B, GOMC

GEORGE R CARR MEML AIR FLD (See BOGALUSA on page 91)

LOUISIANA

GONZALES

LOUISIANA RGNL (REG)(KREG) 2 S UTC−6(−5DT) N30°10.28′ W90°56.42′ NEW ORLEANS
14 B LRA NOTAM FILE DRI L−21B, 22F, GOMC
RWY 17−35: H5003X100 (ASPH) S−30, D−60 MIRL IAP
  RWY 17: REIL. PAPI(P2L)—GA 3.0° TCH 50′. Trees.
  RWY 35: REIL. PAPI(P2L)—GA 3.0° TCH 50′. Trees.
SERVICE: S2 **FUEL** 100LL, JET A+ **LGT** Dusk−dawn. MIRL Rwy 17−35 and REIL Rwy 17 and 35 preset low intst dusk to dawn; to incr intst actvt—CTAF.
AIRPORT REMARKS: Attended 1400−2300Z‡. Deer on and invof arpt. 100LL avbl self service with credit card, Jet A avbl after hours call 225−644−1959.
AIRPORT MANAGER: 225−644−1959
WEATHER DATA SOURCES: AWOS−3PT 121.175 (225) 644−4014.
COMMUNICATIONS: CTAF/UNICOM 123.0
Ⓡ **BATON ROUGE APP/DEP CON** 133.225 (1100−0600Z‡)
  HOUSTON CENTER APP/DEP CON 126.35 (0600−1100Z‡)
  GCO 135.075 (BATON ROUGE APCH and DE RIDDER FSS)
  CLEARANCE DELIVERY PHONE: For CD if una via GCO ctc Baton Rouge Apch at 225−354−2142 or Houston ARTCC at 281−230−5622.
RADIO AIDS TO NAVIGATION: NOTAM FILE BTR.
  FIGHTING TIGER (VL) (L) VORTACW 116.5 LSU Chan 112
    N30°29.11′ W91°17.64′   130° 26.3 NM to fld. 20/6E.

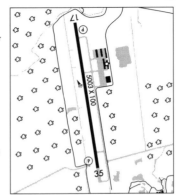

GREEN CANYON 19 XER N27°56.76′ W90°59.82′/130
  AWOS−3 118.55 L−21B, GOMC

GREEN CANYON 338 GRY N27°37.48′ W90°26.47′
  AWOS−3 118.875 Winds unreliable. L−21B, GOMC

GREEN CANYON 787 ATP N27°11.73′ W90°01.62′
  AWOS−3 119.525 (979) 235−2225 L−21B, GOMC

GREEN CANYON BLK 433 MKQ N27°31.18′ W90°05.88′/133
  AWOS−3 118.150 L−21B, GOMC

GREEN CANYON BLK 763 ANR N27°13.58′ W91°11.40′/302
  AWOS−3P 118.975 L−21B, GOMC

GULF OF MEXICO JSL N26°14.20′ W91°15.40′/146
  AWOS−3 119.575 (985) 773−5178 NADIN/METAR wx disem for this Gulf of Mexico (GOMEX) AWOS on the oil rig. L−21B, GOMC

LOUISIANA

HAMMOND NORTHSHORE RGNL (HDC)(KHDC)   3 NE   UTC–6(–5DT)   N30°31.30′
W90°25.10′

NEW ORLEANS
H–7D, L–21B, 22F, GOMC
IAP, AD

46   B   TPA—1002(956)   NOTAM FILE DRI
RWY 13–31: H6502X100 (ASPH–CONC)   S–22, D–33   MIRL
  RWY 13: REIL. PAPI(P4L)—GA 3.3° TCH 50′.
  RWY 31: REIL. PAPI(P4L)—GA 3.3° TCH 56′. Thld dsplcd 690′. Trees.
RWY 18–36: H5001X150 (CONC)   S–27, D–41   MIRL
  RWY 18: MALSR. PAPI(P4L)—GA 3.0° TCH 52′.
  RWY 36: REIL. PAPI(P4L)—GA 3.0° TCH 52′.
SERVICE: S4   **FUEL** 100LL, JET A   **LGT** Actvt MALSR Rwy 18; REIL Rwy 13, 31, and 36; MIRL Rwy 13–31 and 18–36; preset low intst dusk–dawn; to incr intst—CTAF. Rwy 31 right side REIL OTS.
AIRPORT REMARKS: Attended Mon–Fri 1200–0200Z‡, Sat–Sun 1400–0000Z‡. Birds, deer and coyotes on and invof arpt. Mil and govt acft serviced at NW apron at FBO. Rwy 18–36 all safety areas NSTD. Twy D unmrk and unlgtd.
AIRPORT MANAGER: 985-277-5667
WEATHER DATA SOURCES: AWOS–3PT (985) 277–5670
COMMUNICATIONS: CTAF 120.575 ATIS 118.325
Ⓡ **NEW ORLEANS APP/DEP CON** 119.3
  TOWER 120.575 (1400–0000Z‡)   **GND CON** 119.85
  CLNC DEL 119.3 (when twr closed)
CLEARANCE DELIVERY PHONE: For CD when ATCT is clsd ctc MSY Apch at 504-471-4350 or 119.3.
AIRSPACE: CLASS D svc 1400–0000Z‡; other times CLASS G.
RADIO AIDS TO NAVIGATION: NOTAM FILE MSY.
  RESERVE (L) (L) VORW/DME 110.8   RQR   Chan 45   N30°05.25′ W90°35.32′   017° 27.5 NM to fld. 5/2E.
  ANGER NDB (LOMW) 212   HP   N30°36.38′ W90°25.27′   178° 5.1 NM to fld. 94/0E.   NOTAM FILE DRI.
  ILS 111.5   I–HPF   Rwy 18.   Class ID.   LOM ANGER NDB. ILS and LOM unmonitored.

HARRY P WILLIAMS MEML (See PATTERSON on page 119)

HART (See MANY on page 109)

HARVEY   N29°51.01′ W90°00.18′   NOTAM FILE NEW.
(VH) (H) VORTACW 114.1   HRV   Chan 88   351° 11.6 NM to Lakefront. 2/2E.

NEW ORLEANS
H–7E, 8F, L–21B, 22F, GOMC

  VOR unusable:
    000°–014° byd 40 NM
    015°–025° byd 40 NM blo 18,000′
    026°–050° byd 40 NM
    040°–060° byd 34 NM blo 2,500′
    051°–068° byd 40 NM blo 3,500′
    051°–068° byd 66 NM
    069°–252° byd 40 NM
    253°–263° byd 40 NM blo 17,000′
    264°–296° byd 40 NM
    270°–280° byd 28 NM blo 4,000′
    270°–280° byd 35 NM blo 5,000′
    297°–307° byd 40 NM blo 18,000′
    308°–359° byd 40 NM
    325°–330° byd 28 NM blo 3,000′
  TACAN AZIMUTH unusable:
    040°–060° byd 24 NM blo 2,500′
  DME unusable:
    040°–060° byd 34 NM blo 2,500′
    070°–090° blo 2,400′
    070°–090° byd 26 NM blo 3,400′

LOUISIANA

HOMER MUNI (5F4)   3 E   UTC−6(−5DT)   N32°47.31′ W93°00.22′   MEMPHIS
244   B   NOTAM FILE DRI   L−17E
RWY 12−30: H3200X60 (ASPH)   S−12   MIRL   0.5% up NW
  RWY 12: REIL. Trees.
  RWY 30: REIL. Trees.
SERVICE: LGT REIL Rwy 12−30 MIRL Rwy 12−30 preset low ints
  dusk−dawn; to incr intst actvt—CTAF.
AIRPORT REMARKS: Unattended. Excessive rwy edge lips exist after overlay
  project, pilots are cautioned to stay in the center of the rwy and twy.
AIRPORT MANAGER: 318−225−0911
COMMUNICATIONS: CTAF 122.9
CLEARANCE DELIVERY PHONE: For CD ctc Fort Worth ARTCC at
  817−858−7584.
RADIO AIDS TO NAVIGATION: NOTAM FILE SHV.
  BELCHER (H) (H) VORTACW 117.4   EIC   Chan 121   N32°46.28′
  W93°48.60′   081° 40.8 NM to fld. 190/7E.

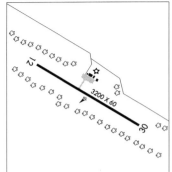

HOUMA−TERREBONNE (HUM)(KHUM)   3 SE   UTC−6(−5DT)   N29°33.99′ W90°39.63′   NEW ORLEANS
9   B   LRA   NOTAM FILE HUM   H−7D, L−21B, 22F
RWY 18−36: H6508X150 (CONC−GRVD)   S−116, D−224, 2S−89,   IAP, AD
  2D−406, 2D/2D2−907 PCN 63 R/B/W/T   MIRL
  RWY 18: MALSR. PAPI(P2L)—GA 3.0° TCH 50′. Trees.
  RWY 36: REIL. PAPI(P2L)—GA 3.0° TCH 50′. Trees.
RWY 12−30: H4999X185 (CONC)   S−50, D−70, 2S−89, 2D−137   MIRL
  RWY 12: REIL. PAPI(P2L)—GA 3.0° TCH 44′. Trees.
  RWY 30: REIL. PAPI(P2L)—GA 3.0° TCH 39′.
SERVICE: S4   FUEL 100LL, JET A   OX 1, 2, 3, 4   LGT ACTIVATE MIRL
  Rwy 12−30 and Rwy 18−36; MALSR Rwy 18 and REIL Rwy 12, Rwy
  30 and Rwy 36—CTAF.
AIRPORT REMARKS: Attended 1200−0100Z‡. Fuel avbl 24 hrs with credit
  card. Birds on and invof arpt, numerous birds 500′ AGL and blo 2.8
  NM south−southwest AER 36, avoidance advised. Extensive helicopter
  ops south thru west of arpt. Rwy 12−30 surface skid resistance fair
  when wet.
AIRPORT MANAGER: 985−872−4646
WEATHER DATA SOURCES: AWOS−3PT 120.25 (985) 876−4055. LAWRS.
COMMUNICATIONS: CTAF 125.3   ATIS 120.25   UNICOM 122.95
®NEW ORLEANS APP/DEP CON 118.9
  TOWER 125.3 (1200−0100Z‡)   GND CON 123.875
  CLNC DEL 118.9 (when twr closed)
CLEARANCE DELIVERY PHONE: For CD when ATCT is clsd ctc MSY Apch at 504−471−4350 or 118.9.
AIRSPACE: CLASS D svc 1200−0100Z‡; other times CLASS G.
RADIO AIDS TO NAVIGATION: NOTAM FILE DRI.
  TIBBY (L) (L) VOR/DME 112.0   TBD   Chan 57   N29°39.86′ W90°49.75′   122° 10.6 NM to fld. 10/2E.
  ILS 108.5   I−HUM   Rwy 18.   Class IE.   Unmonitored when ATCT clsd.

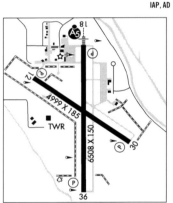

IDAS HELIPORT (L87)   0 N   UTC−6(−5DT)   N33°00.26′ W93°53.59′   MEMPHIS
286   NOTAM FILE DRI
HELIPAD H1: H40X40 (CONC)   PERIMETER LGTS
SERVICE: LGT For perimeter lgts call 318−284−3231.
HELIPORT REMARKS: Attended continuously. Helipad markings faded. Helipad H1 apch 200°−departure 020°.
AIRPORT MANAGER: (903) 826−8608
COMMUNICATIONS: CTAF 122.9
CLEARANCE DELIVERY PHONE: For CD ctc Fort Worth ARTCC at 817−858−7584.

INTRACOASTAL CITY LA9   N29°47.22′ W92°09.27′/2   HOUSTON
AWOS−3 123.875 (337) 500−1178 AWOS associated with airport LA09.   L−22E

LOUISIANA

JACKSON

FELICIANA AIRPARK (LA3) 2 S UTC–6(–5DT) N30°48.47′ W91°12.80′ **HOUSTON**
204 NOTAM FILE DRI **L–22F**
RWY 15–33: H3000X75 (ASPH) S–12
 RWY 15: Trees. Rgt tfc.
 RWY 33: Trees.
AIRPORT REMARKS: Unattended. Rwy 15–33 closed SS–SR. PAJA operations are prohibited on arpt. Rwy 15–33 has cracks with overgrown grass. 50′ downslopes begin 80′ outboard from both ends of the rwy.
AIRPORT MANAGER: (225) 405-8901
COMMUNICATIONS: CTAF 122.9
CLEARANCE DELIVERY PHONE: For CD ctc Baton Rouge Apch at 225-354-2142, when Apch clsd ctc Houston ARTCC at 281-230-5622.

JEANERETTE

LE MAIRE MEML (2R1) 1 S UTC–6(–5DT) N29°53.94′ W91°39.96′ **HOUSTON**
14 B NOTAM FILE DRI **L–21B, 22F**
RWY 04–22: H3000X75 (ASPH) S–6 MIRL
 RWY 04: REIL. PAPI(P2L)—GA 4.5° TCH 75′. Trees.
 RWY 22: REIL. PAPI(P2L)—GA 3.75° TCH 63′. Thld dsplcd 603′. Trees.
SERVICE: FUEL 100LL LGT MIRL Rwy 04–22 and REIL Rwys 04 and Rwy 22 preset low ints SS–SR, to incr ints ACTIVATE–122.9.
AIRPORT REMARKS: Unattended. For arpt attended call 337-365-7202. Fuel avbl 24 hrs self svc with credit card SS–SR. Rwy 22 pavement roughness, mdt to sev longitudinal cracking, raveling producing FOD approximately 1000 ft fm EOR 22.
AIRPORT MANAGER: 337-365-7202
COMMUNICATIONS: CTAF 122.9
CLEARANCE DELIVERY PHONE: For CD ctc Lafayette Apch at 337-262-2729, when Apch clsd ctc Houston ARTCC at 281-230-5622.
RADIO AIDS TO NAVIGATION: NOTAM FILE LFT.
 LAFAYETTE (L) (L) VORTACW 109.8 LFT Chan 35 N30°11.63′ W91°59.55′ 133° 24.5 NM to fld. 36/3E.
 TACAN AZIMUTH unusable:
  295°–320° blo 4,000′.

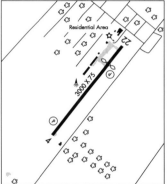

JENA

JENA (1R1) 2 SW UTC–6(–5DT) N31°40.13′ W92°09.46′ **HOUSTON**
216 B NOTAM FILE DRI **L–22E**
RWY 18–36: H4901X75 (ASPH) S–12 MIRL
 RWY 18: REIL. PAPI(P2L)—GA 3.0° TCH 50′. Thld dsplcd 1101′. Trees.
 RWY 36: REIL. PAPI(P2L)—GA 3.0° TCH 50′. Trees.
SERVICE: LGT Dusk–Dawn. MIRL Rwy 18–36 and REIL Rwy 18 and 36 preset low intst dusk–dawn, to incr intst ACTVT—CTAF. Rwy 36 REIL OTS. Rwy 36 PAPI OTS.
AIRPORT REMARKS: Unattended.
AIRPORT MANAGER: (318) 992-3004
COMMUNICATIONS: CTAF 122.9
CLEARANCE DELIVERY PHONE: For CD ctc Polk Apch at 337-531-2352.
RADIO AIDS TO NAVIGATION: NOTAM FILE AEX.
 ALEXANDRIA (H) (H) VORTACW 116.1 AEX Chan 108 N31°15.40′ W92°30.06′ 032° 30.3 NM to fld. 76/3E.
 VOR unusable:
  035°–065° blo 2,000′
  066°–094° byd 35 NM blo 3,000′
  185°–200° byd 35 NM blo 3,000′
  201°–214° byd 35 NM blo 2,000′
  215°–260° blo 2,000′
  261°–285° byd 35 NM blo 2,000′
  357°–034° byd 35 NM blo 3,000′

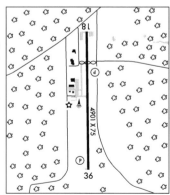

LOUISIANA

JENNINGS (3R7) 1 NW UTC−6(−5DT) N30°14.56´ W92°40.41´   HOUSTON
23   B   NOTAM FILE DRI   H−7D, L−21B, 22E, GOMW
RWY 08−26: H5002X75 (ASPH) S−12 MIRL   IAP
  RWY 08: REIL. PAPI(P2L)—GA 3.0° TCH 50´. Trees.
  RWY 26: REIL. PAPI(P2L)—GA 3.0° TCH 50´. Pole. Rgt tfc.
RWY 13−31: H3601X75 (ASPH) S−12 MIRL
  RWY 13: REIL. PAPI(P2L)—GA 3.0° TCH 50´. Sign. Rgt tfc.
  RWY 31: REIL. PAPI(P2L)—GA 3.0° TCH 50´. Thld dsplcd 588´. Bldg.
RWY 17−35: 1977X150 (TURF)
  RWY 17: Pole. Rgt tfc.
  RWY 35: P−line.
SERVICE: FUEL 100LL, JET A   **LGT** Actvt MIRL Rwy 08−26, Rwy 13−31—CTAF.
AIRPORT REMARKS: Attended Mon−Fri 1200−2200Z‡. Ultralight activity invof arpt. Numerous agricultural acft invof arpt. Self svc fuel avbl after hrs with credit card. Rwy 17−35 and thld outlined with orange cones. 20´ unlgtd tower 150´ from approach end Rwy 35. NOTE: See Special Notices—Aerobatic Practice Area.
AIRPORT MANAGER: 337−616−2370
WEATHER DATA SOURCES: AWOS−3PT 121.150 (337) 824−0517.
COMMUNICATIONS: CTAF/UNICOM 122.8
®**LAKE CHARLES APP/DEP CON** 119.8 (1200−0400Z‡)
®**HOUSTON CENTER APP/DEP CON** 124.7 (0400−1200Z‡)
CLEARANCE DELIVERY PHONE: For CD ctc Houston ARTCC at 281−230−5622.
RADIO AIDS TO NAVIGATION: NOTAM FILE LCH.
  LAKE CHARLES (H) (H) VORTACW 113.4 LCH Chan 81 N30°08.49´ W93°06.33´   068° 23.3 NM to fld. 20/7E.
  VOR unusable:
    181°−359° byd 30 NM blo 1,500´

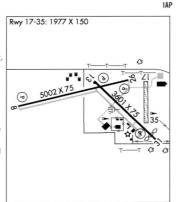

Rwy 17-35: 1977 X 150

JOHN H HOOKS JR MEML (See RAYVILLE on page 120)

JONESBORO (F88) 3 S UTC−6(−5DT) N32°12.12´ W92°43.98´   MEMPHIS
256   B   NOTAM FILE DRI   L−17E
RWY 18−36: H3204X75 (ASPH) S−28 MIRL   IAP
  RWY 18: REIL. PAPI(P2L)—GA 3.0° TCH 50´. Trees.
  RWY 36: REIL. PAPI(P2L)—GA 3.0° TCH 50´. Trees.
SERVICE: **LGT** REIL Rwy 18 and 36 and MIRL Rwy 18−36, preset low intst; to incr intst actvt—CTAF. PAPI Rwy 36 OTS indefinitely. Lgtd windsock OTS midfield.
AIRPORT REMARKS: Unattended. Deer and wildlife on and invof arpt. South hold line NSTD distance from rwy centerline.
AIRPORT MANAGER: 318−533−7811
COMMUNICATIONS: CTAF 122.9
®**MONROE APP/DEP CON** 126.9 (1200−0400Z‡)
®**FORT WORTH CENTER APP/DEP CON** 126.325 (0400−1200Z‡)
CLEARANCE DELIVERY PHONE: For CD ctc Monroe Apch at 318−327−5641, if unavbl, ctc Fort Worth ARTCC at 817−858−7584.
RADIO AIDS TO NAVIGATION: NOTAM FILE MLU.
  MONROE (VL) (L) VORTACW 117.2 MLU Chan 119 N32°31.01´ W92°02.16´   239° 40.1 NM to fld. 77/3E.
  VOR unusable:
    010°−040° byd 40 NM
    125°−135° byd 40 NM
    215°−231° byd 40 NM
    232°−242° byd 40 NM blo 8,000´
    232°−242° byd 83 NM
    243°−255° byd 40 NM blo 7,000´
    243°−255° byd 56 NM
    256°−267° byd 40 NM blo 18,000´
    256°−267° byd 45 NM
    268°−271° byd 40 NM
    272°−282° byd 40 NM blo 2,000´
    272°−282° byd 51 NM
    283°−315° byd 40 NM

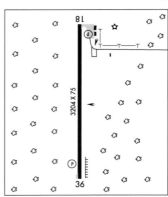

LOUISIANA

JONESVILLE (L32) 0 W UTC−6(−5DT) N31°37.22′ W91°50.06′ HOUSTON
56 B NOTAM FILE DRI L−22E
RWY 06−24: H3000X75 (ASPH) S−16 MIRL
  RWY 06: REIL. PAPI(P2L)—GA 4.0° TCH 66′. Trees.
  RWY 24: REIL. PAPI(P2L)—GA 4.0° TCH 68′. Trees.
SERVICE: S2 **FUEL** 100LL, JET A **LGT** Rwy 24 PAPI obstructed by trees
  OTS indef. Rwy 06 PAPI obstructed by trees OTS indef. MIRL Rwy
  06−24, REIL Rwy 06 and Rwy 24 preset low ints dusk to dawn, to incr
  ints ACTIVATE—CTAF.
AIRPORT REMARKS: Attended Mon−Fri 1400−2300Z‡. For fuel after hrs call
  318−339−4747.
AIRPORT MANAGER: 318−339−4747
COMMUNICATIONS: CTAF 122.9
CLEARANCE DELIVERY PHONE: For CD ctc Polk Apch at 337−531−2352.
RADIO AIDS TO NAVIGATION: NOTAM FILE AEX.
  ALEXANDRIA (H) (H) VORTACW 116.1 AEX Chan 108 N31°15.40′
  W92°30.06′ 054° 40.6 NM to fld. 76/3E.
  VOR unusable:
    035°−065° blo 2,000′
    066°−094° byd 35 NM blo 3,000′
    185°−200° byd 35 NM blo 3,000′
    201°−214° byd 35 NM blo 2,000′
    215°−260° blo 2,000′
    261°−285° byd 35 NM blo 2,000′
    357°−034° byd 35 NM blo 3,000′

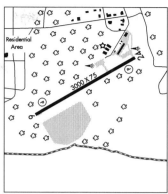

KEITHVILLE

BLUEBIRD HILL (5F5) 2 NE UTC−6(−5DT) N32°20.68′ W93°47.99′ MEMPHIS
180 B NOTAM FILE DRI
RWY 18−36: H3000X40 (ASPH−TURF) LIRL
  RWY 18: Thld dsplcd 430′. Trees.
  RWY 36: Thld dsplcd 850′. Trees.
SERVICE: S2 **LGT** Apt bcn OTS.
AIRPORT REMARKS: Attended continuously. Rwy 18−36 CLOSED SS−SR. Rwy 18−36 430 ft asph on Rwy 18 end, 2570 ft turf
  on Rwy 36 end. Rwy 18−36 dsplcd thrs mkd with one orange cone on each side. Rwy ends stop at 50 ft: trees.
AIRPORT MANAGER: 903−503−8505
COMMUNICATIONS: CTAF 122.9
CLEARANCE DELIVERY PHONE: For CD ctc Fort Worth ARTCC at 817−858−7584.

KELLY−DUMAS (See OAK GROVE on page 117)

LOUISIANA

LAFAYETTE RGNL/PAUL FOURNET FLD (LFT)(KLFT) P (AR) 2 SE UTC−6(−5DT) HOUSTON
N30°12.30′ W91°59.27′ H−7D, L−21B, 22E, GOMC
42 B LRA Class I, ARFF Index B NOTAM FILE LFT IAP, AD
RWY 04R−22L: H8000X150 (ASPH−GRVD) S−140, D−170, 2S−175,
2D−290 PCN 67 F/C/X/T HIRL
 RWY 04R: REIL. PAPI(P4L)—GA 3.0° TCH 50′. RVR−R Pole. Rgt tfc.
 RWY 22L: MALSR. PAPI(P4L)—GA 3.0° TCH 50′. RVR−T Thld dsplcd
  342′. Trees.
RWY 11−29: H5400X148 (ASPH−GRVD) S−85, D−110, 2S−140,
2D−175 PCN 5 F/D/X/T MIRL
 RWY 11: REIL. PAPI(P4L)—GA 3.0° TCH 36′. Trees. Rgt tfc.
 RWY 29: REIL. PAPI(P4L)—GA 3.0° TCH 51′. Tree.
RWY 04L−22R: H4099X75 (ASPH) S−25, D−32 PCN 11 F/D/X/T MIRL
 RWY 04L: REIL. PAPI(P2L)—GA 3.0° TCH 26′. Tree.
 RWY 22R: REIL. PAPI(P2L)—GA 3.0° TCH 26′. Tree. Rgt tfc.
RUNWAY DECLARED DISTANCE INFORMATION
 RWY 04L: TORA−4099 TODA−4099 ASDA−4099 LDA−4099
 RWY 04R: TORA−8000 TODA−8000 ASDA−8000 LDA−8000
 RWY 22L: TORA−8000 TODA−8000 ASDA−8000 LDA−7659
 RWY 22R: TORA−4099 TODA−4099 ASDA−4099 LDA−4099
ARRESTING GEAR/SYSTEM
 RWY 04R: EMAS
 RWY 11: EMAS
 RWY 22L: EMAS
 RWY 29: EMAS
SERVICE: S4 **FUEL** 100LL, JET A, A+ **OX** 1, 4 **LGT** Dusk−Dawn. When ATCT clsd actvt MALSR Rwy 22L —CTAF; MIRL
Rwy 04L−22R not avbl. Rwy 11−29; Rwy 04L/22R and Rwy 04R/22L lgtd distance remaining signs.
 MILITARY— A−GEAR Rwy 22L EMAS 380.67′ x 170′. Rwy 04R EMAS 223′ x 170′. Rwy 29 EMAS 170′ x 448′. **FUEL**
A+ (C337−288−3940). (NC−100LL, A)
AIRPORT REMARKS: Attended continuously. Migratory birds on and invof arpt. For A+ call 337−703−4800. PPR for
unscheduled acr opns with more than 30 psgr seats call amgr. 337−266−4400. Rwy 04L−22R not avbl for acr opns with
more than 30 psgr seats, rwy closed 0430−1130Z‡. Rwy 11−29 clsd UFN. Ctc ground control prior to push back from
terminal. 155′ oil rig 1 NM southeast of arpt. Use caution: twr blind spots on Twy M east and west of Twy E. Taxilane A
and all prkg ramps are non−movement areas. ATCT has ltd vis of north prkg ramp.
AIRPORT MANAGER: 337−703−4800
WEATHER DATA SOURCES: ASOS 134.05 (337) 262−2757.
COMMUNICATIONS: CTAF 118.5 **ATIS** 134.05 **UNICOM** 122.95
 RCO 122.35 (DE RIDDER RADIO)
®️ **APP/DEP CON** 121.1 (020°−210°) 128.7 (211°−019°) (1130−0430Z‡)
®️ **HOUSTON CENTER APP/DEP CON** 126.35 (0430−1130Z‡)
  TOWER 118.5 (1130−0430Z‡) **GND CON** 121.8 **CLNC DEL** 125.55
CLEARANCE DELIVERY PHONE: For CD if una to ctc on FSS freq, ctc Houston ARTCC at 281−230−5622.
AIRSPACE: CLASS C svc ctc APP CON svc 1130−0430Z‡; other times CLASS E.
RADIO AIDS TO NAVIGATION: NOTAM FILE LFT.
 (L) (L) VORTACW 109.8 LFT Chan 35 N30°11.63′ W91°59.55′ at fld. 36/3E.
  TACAN AZIMUTH unusable:
   295°−320° blo 4,000′
 LAFFS NDB (LOMW) 375 LF N30°17.36′ W91°54.47′ 216° 6.5 NM to fld. 21/3E.
 ILS/DME 110.9 I−TYN Chan 46 Rwy 04R. Class IE.
 ILS/DME 109.5 I−LFT Chan 32 Rwy 22L. Class IE. LOM LAFFS NDB. ILS and LOM unmonitored when ATCT clsd.
 ASR (1130−0430Z‡)

LAFFS N30°17.36′ W91°54.47′ NOTAM FILE LFT. HOUSTON
 NDB (LOMW) 375 LF 216° 6.5 NM to Lafayette Rgnl/Paul Fournet Fld. 21/3E. L−21B, 22E

LOUISIANA

LAKE CHARLES

CHENNAULT INTL (CWF)(KCWF) 4 E UTC−6(−5DT) N30°12.64′ W93°08.59′ **HOUSTON**
17 B TPA—1500(1483) LRA ARFF Index—See Remarks NOTAM FILE CWF H−7D, L−21B, 22E, GOMW
RWY 15−33: H10702X200 (CONC) S−120, D−250, 2S−175, 2D−542, IAP, AD
  2D/2D2−750 PCN 92 R/C/W/T HIRL
  RWY 15: MALSR. PAPI(P4L)—GA 3.0° TCH 53′.
  RWY 33: REIL. PAPI(P4L)—GA 3.0° TCH 53′. Rgt tfc.
RUNWAY DECLARED DISTANCE INFORMATION
  RWY 15: TORA−10702 TODA−10702 ASDA−10702 LDA−10702
  RWY 33: TORA−10702 TODA−10702 ASDA−10702 LDA−10702
SERVICE: **FUEL** 100LL, JET A1+ **OX** 4 **LGT** When ATCT clsd ACTVT
  MALSR Rwy 15; REIL Rwy 33; PAPI Rwy 15 and 33; HIRL Rwy
  15−33—CTAF.
AIRPORT REMARKS: Attended 1200−0400Z‡. After hrs call
  337−433−7766. Birds on and invof arpt. For fuel call
  337−436−4877. Self svc avbl 24 hrs with credit card. Class IV, ARFF
  Index A. 6 hrs PPR for ACR opns with more than 30 psgr seats AMGR
  337−491−9961. ARFF index E available 24/7. PFR reqd for/helo ops
  in the industrial area. For Port of Entry req, contact the Dir of Ops at
  least 3 bus days (M−F) prior to planned arr.
AIRPORT MANAGER: 337−491−9961
WEATHER DATA SOURCES: AWOS−3 120.0 (337) 436−3452. LAWRS.
COMMUNICATIONS: CTAF 124.2 **ATIS** 120.0 **UNICOM** 122.95
Ⓡ **LAKE CHARLES APP/DEP CON** 119.8 (1200−0400Z‡)
Ⓡ **HOUSTON CENTER APP/DEP CON** 124.7 (0400−1200Z≠)
  TOWER 124.2 (1200−0400Z‡) **GND CON** 121.65
  CLEARANCE DELIVERY PHONE: When ATCT clsd, for CD c⁻c Houston ARTCC at 281−230−5622.
AIRSPACE: CLASS D svc 1200−0400Z‡; other times CLASS G.
RADIO AIDS TO NAVIGATION: NOTAM FILE LCH.
  LAKE CHARLES (H) (H) VORTACW 113.4 LCH Chan 81 N30°08.49′ W93°06.33′ 328° 4.6 NM to fld. 20/7E.
  VOR unusable:
    181°−359° byd 30 NM blo 1,500′
  MOSSY NDB (LOMW) 418 CW N30°18.40′ W93°11.77′ 154° 6.4 NM to fld. 23/0E. NOTAM FILE CWF.
  ILS 110.7 I−CWF Rwy 15. Class IE. LOM MOSSY NDB. Unmonitored when ATCT clsd.
  ASR (1200−0400Z‡)

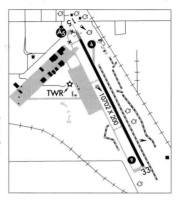

LOUISIANA

LAKE CHARLES RGNL (LCH)(KLCH)   5 S   UTC–6(–5DT)   N30°07.57´ W93°13.41´   **HOUSTON**
15   B   LRA   Class I, ARFF Index B   NOTAM FILE LCH   MON Airport   H–7D, L–21B, 22E, GOMW
RWY 15–33: H6500X150 (CONC–GRVD)   S–100, D–145, 2S–175,   IAP, AD
2D–260   HIRL
  RWY 15: MALSR. PAPI(P4L)—GA 3.0° TCH 70´. RVR–TM Pole. Rgt tfc.
  RWY 33: MALSF. PAPI(P4R)—GA 3.0° TCH 54´. RVR–M
RWY 05–23: H5200X100 (ASPH)   S–70, D–90, 2S–114, 2D–140
  MIRL
  RWY 05: REIL. PAPI(P4L)—GA 3.0° TCH 49´. Tree.
  RWY 23: REIL. VASI(V4L)—GA 3.0° TCH 47´. Rgt tfc.
RUNWAY DECLARED DISTANCE INFORMATION
  RWY 05: TORA–5200   TODA–5200   ASDA–5200   LDA–5200
  RWY 15: TORA–6500   TODA–6500   ASDA–6500   LDA–6500
  RWY 23: TORA–5200   TODA–5200   ASDA–5200   LDA–5200
  RWY 33: TORA–6500   TODA–6500   ASDA–6500   LDA–6500
SERVICE: S4   **FUEL** 100LL, JET A1+   **LGT** When twr clsd ACTIVATE
MALSR Rwy 15, MALSF Rwy 33, HIRL Rwy 15–33, MIRL Rwy
05–23—CTAF. PAPI Rwy 33 opr consly.
AIRPORT REMARKS: Attended 1100–0430Z‡. Birds on and in vicinity of arpt.
Svc available on request Mon–Fri 1400–2230Z‡ except holidays call
arpt manager 337–477–6051 ext 0. Control twr blind spot on Taxiway
J. Rwy 15–33 south 900´ grooved. Flight Notification Service
(ADCUS) available.
AIRPORT MANAGER: 337-477-6051
WEATHER DATA SOURCES: ASOS (337) 477–3371 LAWRS.
COMMUNICATIONS: CTAF 120.7 **ATIS** 118.75 **UNICOM** 122.95
  RCO 122.3 (DE RIDDER RADIO)
® **APP/DEP CON** 119.35 (West) 119.8 (East) 119.75 (Offshore helicopter opr) (1200–0400Z‡) 119.75 OTS indef.
® **HOUSTON CENTER APP/DEP CON** 124.7 (0400–1200Z‡)
  TOWER 120.7 (1200–0400Z‡)   **GND CON** 121.8   **CLNC DEL** 126.25
CLEARANCE DELIVERY PHONE: For CD if una to ctc on FSS freq, ctc Houston ARTCC at 281-230-5622.
AIRSPACE: CLASS D svc 1200–0400Z‡; other times CLASS E.
TRSA ctc **APP CON** within 30 NM
RADIO AIDS TO NAVIGATION: NOTAM FILE LCH.
  (H) (H) VORTACW 113.4   LCH   Chan 81   N30°08.49´ W93°06.33´   254° 6.2 NM to fld. 20/7E.
  VOR unusable:
    181°–359° byd 30 NM blo 1,500´
  ILS/DME 109.1   I–LCH   Chan 28   Rwy 15.   Class IB.   Unmonitored when ATCT clsd.
  ASR (1200–0400Z‡)

LAKE PROVIDENCE
BYERLEY (ØM8)   2 N   UTC–6(–5DT)   N32°49.55´ W91°11.26´   **MEMPHIS**
106   B   NOTAM FILE DRI   L–18F
RWY 17–35: H3196X75 (ASPH)   S–4
  RWY 17: Thld dsplcd 175´. Road.
  RWY 35: Thld dsplcd 530´. Trees.
SERVICE: **LGT** Dsplcd thld lgts OTS indef. Rotating bcn OTS indef.
AIRPORT REMARKS: Unattended. Day VFR only. Rwy 17 dsplcd thld
markings NSTD, no arrows or chevrons. Rwy 35 dsplcd thld markings
incomplete—no arrows/chevrons. No hold short line east side of Rwy
35. West apron gravel and potholes.
AIRPORT MANAGER: (318) 282-9263
COMMUNICATIONS: CTAF 122.9
CLEARANCE DELIVERY PHONE: For CD ctc Memphis ARTCC at
901-368-8453/8449.
RADIO AIDS TO NAVIGATION: NOTAM FILE GLH.
  GREENVILLE (VL) (DH) VOR/DME 114.25   GLH   Chan 89(Y)
    N33°31.41´ W90°58.98´   190° 43.0 NM to fld. 130/4E.
  VOR unusable:
    144°–157° byd 40 NM

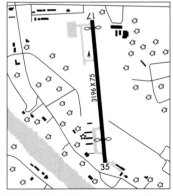

LAKEFRONT   (See NEW ORLEANS on page 114)

SC, 25 JAN 2024 to 21 MAR 2024

LOUISIANA 107

LE GROS MEML (See CROWLEY on page 93)

LE MAIRE MEML (See JEANERETTE on page 101)

LEESVILLE (L39)   4 W   UTC−6(−5DT)   N31°10.09′ W93°20.55′   **HOUSTON**
282   B   NOTAM FILE DRI   **L−21B, 22E**
RWY 18−36: H3807X75 (ASPH)   S−31, D−47 PCN 11 F/C/X/T   MIRL   **IAP**
  0.4% up N
  RWY 18: REIL. PAPI(P2L)—GA 3.0° TCH 48′. Trees.
  RWY 36: REIL. PAPI(P2L)—GA 3.0° TCH 54′. Trees.
SERVICE: **FUEL** 100LL, JET A   **LGT** Dusk−Dawn. MIRL Rwy 18−36, REIL
  Rwy 18 and 36 preset low intst dusk−dawn; to incr intst actvt—CTAF
  122.8. Rwy 36 REIL OTS.
AIRPORT REMARKS: Attended continuously. Wildlife on and invof arpt. Fuel,
  restroom, and terminal lobby avbl 24/7, manager hrs part−time on call.
  Fuel avbl 24 hrs with credit card. Use rwy end turnabouts to avoid
  locked wheel and sharp turns on rwy sfc. Rwy 18−36, 15 ft terrain drop
  east side of rwy.
AIRPORT MANAGER: 337-238-5968
COMMUNICATIONS: CTAF/UNICOM 122.8
® **POLK APP/DEP CON** 123.7
CLEARANCE DELIVERY PHONE: For CD ctc Polk Apch at 337-531-2352.
RADIO AIDS TO NAVIGATION: NOTAM FILE AEX.
  ALEXANDRIA (H) (H) VORTACW 116.1   AEX   Chan 108   N31°15.40′
  W92°30.06′   260° 43.6 NM to fld. 76/3E.
  VOR unusable:
    035°−065° blo 2,000′
    066°−094° byd 35 NM blo 3,000′
    185°−200° byd 35 NM blo 3,000′
    201°−214° byd 35 NM blo 2,000′
    215°−260° blo 2,000′
    261°−285° byd 35 NM blo 2,000′
    357°−034° byd 35 NM blo 3,000′

LEEVILLE   N29°10.51′ W90°06.24′   NOTAM FILE DRI.   **NEW ORLEANS**
  (VH) (H) VORTAC 113.5   LEV   Chan 82   331° 17.9 NM to South Lafourche Leonard Miller Jr. **H−7E, 8F, L−21B, 22E, GOMC**
  2/2E.
  RCO 122.1R 113.5T (DE RIDDER RADIO)

LITTLE PECAN   3L4   N29°47.71′ W92°48.01′/8   **HOUSTON**
  AWOS−3 118.825 (337) 538−2321 3l4 AWOS−3 is associated with Little Pecan Island airport 3LA4.   **L−22E**

LOUIS ARMSTRONG NEW ORLEANS INTL (See NEW ORLEANS on page 115)

LOUISIANA RGNL (See GONZALES on page 98)

LUCIUS   18H   N26°07.70′ W92°02.00′/190
  AWOS−3 118.075 (832) 636−9295   **L−21B, GOMC**

LOUISIANA

MAKS AAF (POE)(KPOE) A 7 SE UTC–6(–5DT) N31°02.69´ W93°11.50´ **HOUSTON**
330 B TPA—See Remarks NOTAM FILE POE L–21B, 22E
RWY 16–34: H4107X100 (ASPH) PCN 52 F/A/W/T HIRL DIAP, AD
  RWY 16: REIL. PAPI(P4R)—GA 3.0° TCH 44´. Thld dsplcd 194´. Trees.
  RWY 34: ALSF1. REIL. PAPI(P4L)—GA 3.0° TCH 45´. Trees.
SERVICE: **MILITARY**— **FUEL** A++. **OIL** O–156 **TRAN ALERT** Ltd svc.
MILITARY REMARKS: Attended 1400–0600Z‡ Mon–Fri, clsd hol. Afld mgmt opr 1400–0600Z‡ Mon–Fri, clsd hol. Airfield Operations contact number is DSN 863–4831, C337–531–4831. See flip AP/1 supplementary arpt info. C130 parking ltd to 2 acft. C130 may land only when parking is avbl. **RSTD** Prior Permission Required (PPR)–Fixed wing aircraft only must obtain a PPR number at DSN 863–4831, C337–531–4831. **TFC PAT** All patterns west of fld. TPA—Fixed Wing tfc 1800´, Rotary Wing tfc 1000´. **MISC** Special VFR dalgt 500–1, ngt unaided/Night Vision Devices 500–2. Surface visibility observation blocked NW–SE by hills, building and trees. Units utilizing range facility/restricted areas or staging operations at Polk AAF (KPOE) must contact AT&A officer at DSN 863–1151, C337–531–1151 for briefing. Wx svc avbl 1400–0600Z‡ dly and 24/7 dly during JRTC rotations when sptd by 1–5 avn, DSN 863–4100, C337–531–4100. Wx sensor automated 24/7. Hours will vary with lcl msn sked.
AIRPORT MANAGER: 337-531-6195
WEATHER DATA SOURCES: ASOS 134.85 (337) 531–4100. Wx opr full service 1400–0600Z‡; will vary with lcl msn sked. ASOS FMQ–23: Rwy 16
COMMUNICATIONS: CTAF 119.0 **ATIS** 134.85 282.2
®**APP/DEP CON** 123.7 261.3
  TOWER 119.0 257.75 41.5 (1300–0500Z‡ daily.) **GND CON** 121.8 239.25
  PMSV METRO 134.1 249.75 **POE OPS** 118.575 374.2 **RANGE CON** 143.2 373.3 40.95
  MEDEVAC OPS 42.50 **FLT FOLLOWING** 123.7 254.8 (All flights ctc Polk apch 30 NM out.)
CLEARANCE DELIVERY PHONE: When ATCT clsd, for CD ctc Polk app 123.7, 261.3.
AIRSPACE: CLASS D svc 1300–0500Z‡; other times CLASS E.
RADIO AIDS TO NAVIGATION: NOTAM FILE DRI.
  POLK (T) VORW 108.4 FXU N31°06.69´ W93°13.15´ 158° 4.2 NM to fld. 312/2E.
    VOR unusable:
    185°–205° byd 6 NM blo 7,000´
  ASR/PAR 1400–0600Z‡
COMM/NAV/WEATHER REMARKS: Radar see Terminal FLIP for Radar Minima. Wx svc avbl 1400–0600Z‡ dly and 24/7 dly during JRTC rotations when sptd by 1–5 AVN, DSN 863–4100, C337–531–4100. Wx sensor automated 24/7. Hours will vary with lcl msn sked.

MANSFIELD

C E 'RUSTY' WILLIAMS (3F3) 3 NW UTC–6(–5DT) N32°04.37´ W93°45.94´ **MEMPHIS**
324 B NOTAM FILE DRI H–6I, L–17E
RWY 18–36: H5005X100 (ASPH) S–12 MIRL IAP
  RWY 18: REIL. PAPI(P2L)—GA 3.0° TCH 50´. Trees.
  RWY 36: REIL. PAPI(P2L)—GA 3.5° TCH 58´. Trees.
SERVICE: **FUEL** 100LL, JET A **LGT** MIRL Rwy 18–36, preset low ints dusk to dawn, to incr ints ACTVT REIL Rwy 18 and Rwy 36—CTAF.
AIRPORT REMARKS: Attended Mon–Fri 1400–2300Z‡, Sat–Sun irregularly. Fuel avbl 24 hrs with credit card. Parachute Jumping.
AIRPORT MANAGER: (318) 871-7900
WEATHER DATA SOURCES: AWOS–3PT 119.125 (318) 872–3537.
COMMUNICATIONS: CTAF/UNICOM 122.8
®**SHREVEPORT APP/DEP CON** 119.9
CLEARANCE DELIVERY PHONE: For CD ctc Fort Worth ARTCC at 817-858-7584.
RADIO AIDS TO NAVIGATION: NOTAM FILE SHV.
  BELCHER (H) (H) VORTACW 117.4 EIC Chan 121 N32°46.28´ W93°48.60´ 170° 41.9 NM to fld. 190/7E.

LOUISIANA

MANY

HART (3R4) 2 SW UTC–6(–5DT) N31°32.65′ W93°29.03′
319 B NOTAM FILE DRI
RWY 12–30: H4402X75 (ASPH) S–6 MIRL 0.3% up NW
  RWY 12: REIL. PAPI(P2L)—GA 3.0° TCH 50′. Trees.
  RWY 30: REIL. PAPI(P2L)—GA 3.5° TCH 56′. Trees.
SERVICE: FUEL 100LL LGT MIRL Rwy 12–30, REIL Rwy 12 and Rwy 30 preset low ints dusk to dawn to incr ints ACTIVATE—CTAF.
AIRPORT REMARKS: Unattended. Self svc fuel avbl after hrs with credit card. Beacon lctd .44 mi from apch end Rwy 12.
AIRPORT MANAGER: 318-256-5857
COMMUNICATIONS: CTAF/UNICOM 122.8
  RCO 122.3 (DE RIDDER RADIO)
® POLK APP/DEP CON 123.7
  GCO 135.075 (POLK APCH and DE RIDDER FSS)
CLEARANCE DELIVERY PHONE: For CD ctc if una via GCO ctc Polk Apch at 337-531-2352.
RADIO AIDS TO NAVIGATION: NOTAM FILE AEX.
  ALEXANDRIA (H)(H) VORTACW 116.1 AEX Chan 108 N31°15.40′
    W92°30.06′ 286° 53.3 NM to fld. 76/3E.
  VOR unusable:
    035°–065° blo 2,000′
    066°–094° byd 35 NM blo 3,000′
    185°–200° byd 35 NM blo 3,000′
    201°–214° byd 35 NM blo 2,000′
    215°–260° blo 2,000′
    261°–285° byd 35 NM blo 2,000′
    357°–034° byd 35 NM blo 3,000′

HOUSTON
L–22E
IAP

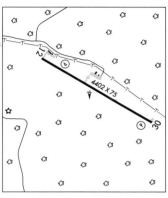

MARKSVILLE MUNI (MKV)(KMKV) 1 S UTC–6(–5DT) N31°05.68′ W92°04.14′
78 B NOTAM FILE DRI
RWY 04–22: H3799X75 (ASPH) S–19 MIRL
  RWY 04: REIL. PAPI(P2L)—GA 3.0° TCH 50′.
  RWY 22: REIL. PAPI(P2L)—GA 3.0° TCH 50′. Pole.
SERVICE: FUEL 100LL LGT ActvtREIL Rwy 04 and 22; MIRL Rwy 04–22 preset low intst; to incr intst—CTAF.
AIRPORT REMARKS: Attended Mon–Fri 1300–2000Z‡. Aerial spraying invof arpt. Fuel avbl 24/7 with credit card. Northeast apron pavement failed. Northeast apron holding position NSTD.
AIRPORT MANAGER: 225-266-4196
COMMUNICATIONS: CTAF 122.9
® POLK APP/DEP CON 125.4
CLEARANCE DELIVERY PHONE: For CD ctc Polk Apch at 337-531-2352.
RADIO AIDS TO NAVIGATION: NOTAM FILE AEX.
  ALEXANDRIA (H)(H) VORTACW 116.1 AEX Chan 108 N31°15.40′
    W92°30.06′ 110° 24.3 NM to fld. 76/3E.
  VOR unusable:
    035°–065° blo 2,000′
    066°–094° byd 35 NM blo 3,000′
    185°–200° byd 35 NM blo 3,000′
    201°–214° byd 35 NM blo 2,000′
    215°–260° blo 2,000′
    261°–285° byd 35 NM blo 2,000′
    357°–034° byd 35 NM blo 3,000′

HOUSTON
L–21B, 22E
IAP

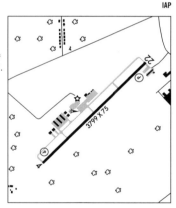

MELVILLE

PETE ANTIE MUNI HELIPORT (7L9) 0 N UTC–6(–5DT) N30°41.66′ W91°44.78′
30 B NOTAM FILE DRI
HELIPAD H1: H40X30 (CONC) PERIMETER LGTS
SERVICE: LGT Bcn OTS indefinitely.
AIRPORT REMARKS: Unattended.
HELIPORT REMARKS: Unattended. Oak trees 48 ft in height, 268 ft from the FATO penetrates the approach to H1. Current Slope 5:1. Windsock OTS.
AIRPORT MANAGER: 337-623-4226
COMMUNICATIONS: CTAF 122.9
CLEARANCE DELIVERY PHONE: For CD ctc Baton Rouge Apch at 225-354-2142, when Apch clsd ctc Houston ARTCC at 281-230-5622.

HOUSTON
COPTER

LOUISIANA

MINDEN (MNE)(KMNE) 2 NW UTC–6(–5DT) N32°38.76´ W93°17.89´
278 B TPA—1300(1022) NOTAM FILE FTW
RWY 01–19: H5004X75 (ASPH) S–30, D–45 MIRL 0.3% up S
  RWY 01: REIL. PAPI(P2L)—GA 3.15° TCH 53´. Trees.
  RWY 19: REIL. PAPI(P2L)—GA 3.75° TCH 64´. Trees.
SERVICE: **FUEL** 100LL, JET A+ **LGT** ACTIVATE MIRL Rwy 01–19—CTAF.
AIRPORT REMARKS: Attended 1400–0000Z‡. For arpt attendant after hrs call 318–377–2144. Birds on and invof arpt.
AIRPORT MANAGER: 318-371-7862
WEATHER DATA SOURCES: AWOS–3PT 119.325 (318) 371–7874.
COMMUNICATIONS: CTAF/UNICOM 122.8
Ⓡ **SHREVEPORT APP/DEP CON** 123.75
  GCO 135.075 (THRU BAD RAPON)
CLEARANCE DELIVERY PHONE: For CD if una via GCO ctc Fort Worth ARTCC at 817-858-7584.
RADIO AIDS TO NAVIGATION: NOTAM FILE SHV.
  BELCHER (H) (H) VORTACW 117.4 EIC Chan 121 N32°46.28´ W93°48.60´ 099° 27.0 NM to fld. 190/7E.

MEMPHIS
H–6I, L–17E
IAP

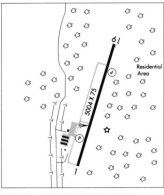

MISSISSIPPI CANYON 650 DSF N28°20.56´ W88°15.89´/130
AWOS–3 119.925 (985) 773–7295 Winds unrel.

NEW ORLEANS
L–21C, GOMC

MISSISSIPPI CANYON 724 GLX N28°14.08´ W88°59.06´/104
AWOS–3 118.225 (713) 357–3575

NEW ORLEANS
L–21C, GOMC

MISSISSIPPI CANYON BLK 807 CYD N28°10.17´ W89°13.37´/151
AWOS–3 119.025 (504) 425–1521

NEW ORLEANS
L–21C, GOMC

MISSISSIPPI CANYON BLK 941 ETO N28°02.02´ W89°06.05´/140
AWOS–3 118.65 (713) 405–7529

NEW ORLEANS
L–21C, GOMC

LOUISIANA

MONROE RGNL (MLU)(KMLU)   3 E   UTC−6(−5DT)   N32°30.63′ W92°02.17′   **MEMPHIS**
79   B   Class I, ARFF Index B   NOTAM FILE MLU   H−6J, L−18F
RWY 04−22: H7504X150 (ASPH−GRVD)   S−75, D−170, 2S−175,   IAP, AD
2D−290 PCN 111F/D/X/T   HIRL
RWY 04: MALSR. PAPI(P4L)—GA 3.0° TCH 50′. RVR−T
RWY 22: MALSR. PAPI(P4L)—GA 3.0° TCH 50′. RVR−R
RWY 14−32: H6301X150 (ASPH)   S−75, D−170, 2S−175, 2D−290
PCN 32 R/C/X/T   MIRL
RWY 14: REIL. PAPI(P4L)—GA 3.0° TCH 50′.
RWY 32: REIL. PAPI(P4L)—GA 3.0° TCH 53′.
RUNWAY DECLARED DISTANCE INFORMATION
RWY 04: TORA−7504   TODA−7504   ASDA−7504   LDA−7504
RWY 14: TORA−6301   TODA−6301   ASDA−6301   LDA−6301
RWY 22: TORA−7504   TODA−7504   ASDA−7504   LDA−7504
RWY 32: TORA−6301   TODA−6301   ASDA−6301   LDA−6301
SERVICE: S4   FUEL 100LL, JET A   OX 1   LGT When ATCT clsd actvt
MALSR Rwys 04 and 22; HIRL Rwy 04−22; MIRL Rwy 14−32; Twy
lgts—CTAF. PAPI Rwy 04, 22, 14 and 32 opr consly.
AIRPORT REMARKS: Attended continuously. Bird activity on and invof arpt.
Twys J and E east of Rwy 04−22 not avbl for air carrier ops with over
9 passenger seats. SW 6000′ grvd ASPH. Taxiway E east of Rwy
04−22 restricted to acft with wingspan under 90 ft. Twy C turnaround
btn apch end Rwy 22 and Twy C1 clsd to acft wingspan more than 49 ft. Twy C2 clsd.
AIRPORT MANAGER: 318-329-2460
WEATHER DATA SOURCES: ASOS (318) 327−5675 LLWAS.
COMMUNICATIONS: CTAF 118.9   ATIS 125.05   UNICOM 122.95
RCO 122.4 (DE RIDDER RADIO)
®APP/DEP CON 118.15 (Within 20 NM blw 4000′)   126.9 (1200−0400Z‡)
®FORT WORTH CENTER APP/DEP CON 126.325 (0400−1200Z‡)
TOWER 118.9 (1200−0400Z‡)   GND CON 121.9   CLNC DEL 121.65
CLEARANCE DELIVERY PHONE: For CD when ATCT is clsd ctc Fort Worth ARTCC at 817-858-7584
AIRSPACE: CLASS D svc 1200−0400Z‡; other times CLASS E.
TRSA svc ctc APP CON within 25 NM below 7000
RADIO AIDS TO NAVIGATION: NOTAM FILE MLU
(VL) (L) VORTACW 117.2   MLU   Chan 119   N32°31.01′ W92°02.16′   at fld. 77/3E.
VOR unusable:
010°−040° byd 40 NM
125°−135° byd 40 NM
215°−231° byd 40 NM
232°−242° byd 40 NM blo 8,000′
232°−242° byd 83 NM
243°−255° byd 40 NM blo 7,000′
243°−255° byd 56 NM
256°−267° byd 40 NM blo 18,000′
256°−267° byd 45 NM
268°−271° byd 40 NM
272°−282° byd 40 NM blo 2,000′
272°−282° byd 51 NM
283°−315° byd 40 NM
SABAR NDB (LOMW) 392   ML   N32°27.24′ W92°06.26′   043° 4.8 NM to fld. 75/3E.
ILS 109.5   I−MLU   Rwy 04.   Class IB.   LOM SABAR NDB. ILS and LOM unmonitored when ATCT clsd.
ILS 109.5   I−MZR   Rwy 22.   Class IT.   Unmonitored when ATCT clsd. LOC usable byd 20° right of course.
ASR (1200−0400Z‡)

MOREHOUSE MEML (See BASTROP on page 89)

MOSSY   N30°18.40′ W93°11.77′   NOTAM FILE CWF.   **HOUSTON**
NDB (LOMW) 418   CW   154° 6.4 NM to Chennault Intl. 23/0E.

NATCHITOCHES RGNL (IER)(KIER)   2 S   UTC–6(–5DT)   N31°44.14´ W93°05.95´   HOUSTON
121   B   NOTAM FILE IER   H–6I, L–22E
RWY 17–35: H5003X150 (ASPH)   S–30   MIRL   IAP
 RWY 17: REIL. PAPI(P4L)—GA 3.0° TCH 45´. Tree.
 RWY 35: ODALS. PAPI(P4L)—GA 3.0° TCH 43´. Trees.
RWY 07–25: H4000X100 (ASPH)   S–21   MIRL
 RWY 07: REIL. PAPI(P2L)—GA 3.0° TCH 50´. Trees.
 RWY 25: PAPI(P2L)—GA 3.0° TCH 50´. Tree.
SERVICE: S4   **FUEL** 100LL, JET A1+   **LGT** MIRL Rwy 17–35 and Rwy
 07–25 preset low ints dusk to dawn, to increase ints ACTIVATE
 —CTAF. ODALS Rwy 35, REIL Rwy 07 and Rwy 17 preset low ints
 continuously, to increase ints ACTIVATE—CTAF.
AIRPORT REMARKS: Attended dawn–dusk. For arpt attendant after hrs call
 318–471–2106. Fuel avbl 24/7 with credit card.
AIRPORT MANAGER: 318-352-0994
WEATHER DATA SOURCES: AWOS–3 119.025 (318) 352–1575.
COMMUNICATIONS: CTAF/UNICOM 122.8
®**POLK APP/DEP CON** 125.4
 GCO Avbl on freq 135.075 (Thru FORT POLK APCH–4 clicks; and
 FSS—6 clicks).
CLEARANCE DELIVERY PHONE: For CD if una via GCO ctc Polk Apch at
 337-531-2352.
RADIO AIDS TO NAVIGATION: NOTAM FILE AEX.
 ALEXANDRIA (H) (H) VORTACW 116.1   AEX   Chan 108   N31°15.40´ W92°30.06´   310° 42.0 NM to fld. 76/3E.
 VOR unusable:
  035°–065° blo 2,000´
  066°–094° byd 35 NM blo 3,000´
  185°–200° byd 35 NM blo 3,000´
  201°–214° byd 35 NM blo 2,000´
  215°–260° blo 2,000´
  261°–285° byd 35 NM blo 2,000´
  357°–034° byd 35 NM blo 3,000´
 NDB (MHW) 407   OOC   N31°39.45´ W93°04.66´   343° 4.8 NM to fld. 115/4E.   NOTAM FILE IER.
  LOC 110.5   I–IER   Rwy 35.   LOC unmonitored when FBO is clsd.

NEW IBERIA

ACADIANA RGNL (ARA)(KARA)   4 NW   UTC–6(–5DT)   N30°02.27´ W91°53.03´   **HOUSTON**
24   B   LRA   ARFF Index—See Remarks   NOTAM FILE ARA   H–7D, L–21B, 22E, GOMC
RWY 17–35: H8002X200 (CONC–GRVD)   D–105, 2S–133, 2D–163,   IAP, AD
2D/2D2–400 PCN 39 R/B/W/T   HIRL
  RWY 17: ODALS. PAPI(P4L)—GA 3.0° TCH 51´.
  RWY 35: MALSR. PAPI(P4L)—GA 3.0° TCH 52´. Rgt tfc.
RUNWAY DECLARED DISTANCE INFORMATION
  RWY 17: TORA–8002   TODA–8002   ASDA–8002   LDA–8002
  RWY 35: TORA–8002   TODA–8002   ASDA–8002   LDA–8002
SERVICE: S2   **FUEL** 100LL, JET A   **OX** 4   **LGT** When ATCT clsd HIRL
Rwy 17–35 preset low intst. To incr intst—CTAF. MALSR Rwy 35 on
consly. ACTVT seaway edge lgts Rwy 17W–35W–122.7 3 clicks on 7
clicks off.
AIRPORT REMARKS: Attended 1300–0300Z‡. For fuel after hrs call
337–367–1401, FAX 337–367–1404. Seaplane landing area (water
channel) W of and adjacent/parallel to runway. Bird activity on and
invof arpt. Class IV, ARFF Index A. ARFF Index B btn 0200Z‡ and
1030Z‡ Mon thru Fri. PPR for more than 30 psgr seats call AMGR
337–365–7202 (M–F 1430–2230Z‡). Rotor wing movement and
landing area between the rwy and seaway. Intensive helicopter
training. Compass rose not avbl.
AIRPORT MANAGER: (337) 365-7202
WEATHER DATA SOURCES: ASOS 133.325 (337) 365–0128.
COMMUNICATIONS: CTAF 125.0   **UNICOM** 122.95
®**LAFAYETTE APP/DEP CON** 121.1 (1130–0430Z‡)
  HOUSTON CENTER APP/DEP CON 126.35 (0430–1130Z‡)
  TOWER 125.0 (1200–0300Z‡)   **GND CON** 121.7 **CLNC DEL** 121.7
  LAFAYETTE CLNC DEL 118.05 (When twr clsd)
CLEARANCE DELIVERY PHONE: For CD when Apch clsd ctc Houston ARTCC at 281-230-5622.
AIRSPACE: CLASS D svc 1200–0300Z‡; other times CLASS G.
RADIO AIDS TO NAVIGATION: NOTAM FILE LFT.
  LAFAYETTE (L) (L) VORTACW 109.8   LFT   Chan 35   N30°11.63´ W91°59.55´   146° 10.9 NM to fld. 36/3E.
  TACAN AZIMUTH unusable:
    295°–320° blo 4,000´
  ILS/DME 108.9   I–ARA   Chan 26   Rwy 35. Class IE.

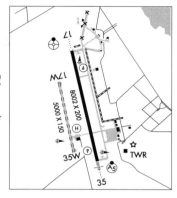

WATERWAY 17W–35W: 5000X150 (WATER)   MIRL
  WATERWAY 17W: Rgt tfc.
RUNWAY DECLARED DISTANCE INFORMATION
  RWY 17W: TORA–5000   TODA–5000   ASDA–5000   LDA–5000
  RWY 35W: TORA–5000   TODA–5000   ASDA–5000   LDA–5000
SEAPLANE REMARKS: Waterway 17–35 NSTD seaway edge lgts green, thld lgts amber. ACTIVATE seaway edge lgts Waterway
17–35—122.7. 3 clicks on 7 clicks off.

LOUISIANA

NEW ORLEANS

LAKEFRONT (NEW)(KNEW) P (ARNG)   4 NE   UTC−6(−5DT)   N30°02.55′ W90°01.70′   NEW ORLEANS
7   B   LRA   NOTAM FILE NEW   H−7E, 8F, L−21B, 22F, GOMC
IAP, AD
RWY 18R−36L: H6879X150 (ASPH−GRVD)   S−60, D−175, 2S−175,
  2D−200, 2D/2D2−350   MIRL
  RWY 18R: MALSR. PAPI(P4L)—GA 3.0° TCH 51′. Thld dsplcd 239′.
    Rgt tfc.
  RWY 36L: REIL. PAPI(P4L)—GA 3.0° TCH 50′. Thld dsplcd 820′.
    Berm.
RWY 18L−36R: H3697X75 (ASPH)   S−35, D−55, 2D−80   MIRL
  RWY 18L: REIL.
  RWY 36R: REIL. PAPI(P4L)—GA 3.0° TCH 45′. Bldg. Rgt tfc.
RWY 09−27: H3114X75 (ASPH)   S−50, D−80, 2S−102, 2D−100   MIRL
  RWY 09: REIL. PAPI(P4L)—GA 3.0° TCH 40′. Berm.
  RWY 27: PAPI(P4R)—GA 3.2° TCH 43′. Road. Rgt tfc.
RUNWAY DECLARED DISTANCE INFORMATION
  RWY 09: TORA−3113   TODA−3113   ASDA−3113   LDA−3113
  RWY 18L: TORA−3697   TODA−3697   ASDA−3697   LDA−3697
  RWY 18R: TORA−6880   TODA−6880   ASDA−6035   LDA−5510
  RWY 27: TORA−3113   TODA−3113   ASDA−3113   LDA−3113
  RWY 36L: TORA−6880   TODA−6880   ASDA−5955   LDA−5135
  RWY 36R: TORA−3697   TODA−3697   ASDA−3697   LDA−3697
SERVICE: S4   **FUEL** 100LL, JET A   **OX** 1, 3   **LGT** When twr clsd, actvt
  MALSR Rwy 18R; MIRL Rwy 18R−36L; Twy B, C, D, E, F, H, East Hngrln—preset low intst. Actvt 5 clicks for med and
  7 clicks for high—CTAF. Rwy 36R PAPI unusbl btn 0300−1300Z‡ (2100−0700 local). For arpt bcn ctc ATCT.
AIRPORT REMARKS: Attended continuously. Birds on and invof arpt. For assistance after 0300Z‡ contact arpt mgmt
  504−874−0459. For field conditions after hrs contact ARFF 504−606−9264. New AD fuel not avbl within 100′ of
  terminal bldg. Boats as high as 80′ pass within 400′ of Rwy 09 thld. Boat masts up to 80′ within 0.5 NM of AER Rwy
  27. Rwy 18R−36L few low spots near intersection of Rwy 09−27 holding water. Twy A uneven pavement. Caution Twy F
  btn terminal ramp and flight line, first ramp irregular surface. Arpt windcone on ball park ramp lgts OTS perm. ARFF
  capability equivalent to Index B. PPR required for acft trnspg any items listed in Part 175 Title 49, contact
  504−606−9264. Overnight parking on terminal ramp must be coordinated with FBO.
AIRPORT MANAGER: 504−243−4010
WEATHER DATA SOURCES: ASOS (504) 245−4366 LAWRS.
COMMUNICATIONS: CTAF 118.95 **ATIS** 124.9
  NEW ORLEANS RCO 122.6 (DE RIDDER RADIO)
® **NEW ORLEANS APP/DEP CON** 133.15 (North) 123.85 (South)
  TOWER 118.95 (1300−0300Z‡) **GND CON** 121.7 **CLNC DEL** 127.4
CLEARANCE DELIVERY PHONE: For CD when ATCT is clsd ctc MSY Apch at 504−471−4350 or 127.4
AIRSPACE: CLASS D svc 1300−0300Z‡; other times CLASS E.
RADIO AIDS TO NAVIGATION: NOTAM FILE NEW.
  HARVEY (VH) (H) VORTACW 114.1   HRV   Chan 88   N29°51.01′ W90°00.18′   351° 11.6 NM to fld. 2/2E.
  VOR unusable:
    000°−014° byd 40 NM
    015°−025° byd 40 NM blo 18,000′
    026°−050° byd 40 NM
    040°−060° byd 34 NM blo 2,500′
    051°−068° byd 40 NM blo 3,500′
    051°−068° byd 66 NM
    069°−252° byd 40 NM
    253°−263° byd 40 NM blo 17,000′
    264°−296° byd 40 NM
    270°−280° byd 28 NM blo 4,000′
    270°−280° byd 35 NM blo 5,000′
    297°−307° byd 40 NM blo 18,000′
    308°−359° byd 40 NM
    325°−330° byd 28 NM blo 3,000′
  TACAN AZIMUTH unusable:
    040°−060° byd 24 NM blo 2,500′
  DME unusable:
    040°−060° byd 34 NM blo 2,500′
    070°−090° blo 2,400′
    070°−090° byd 26 NM blo 3,400′
  ILS/DME 111.3   I−NEW   Chan 50   Rwy 18R.   Class IE.

LOUISIANA 115

LOUIS ARMSTRONG NEW ORLEANS INTL (MSY)(KMSY) 10 W UTC–6(–5DT) N29°59.60´ **NEW ORLEANS**
W90°15.54´ H–7E, L–21B, 22F, GOMC
  4   B   LRA   Class I, ARFF Index D   NOTAM FILE MSY   MON Airport IAP, AD
  RWY 11–29: H10104X150 (CONC–GRVD)   S–75, D–180, 2S–175,
    2D–380 PCN 123R/C/W/T   HIRL   CL
    RWY 11: ALSF2. TDZL. PAPI(P4R)—GA 2.8° TCH 55´. RVR–TMR
    RWY 29: MALSR. PAPI(P4R)—GA 3.0° TCH 68´. RVR–TMR Thld
      dsplcd 304´. Tree.
  RWY 02–20: H7001X150 (CONC–GRVD)   S–75, D–180, 2D–380
    PCN 64 R/C/W/T   HIRL   CL
    RWY 02: RLLS. PAPI(P4L)—GA 3.0° TCH 52´. RVR–TR Road.
    RWY 20: MALS. PAPI(P4L)—GA 3.0° TCH 52´. RVR–TR Road.
  RUNWAY DECLARED DISTANCE INFORMATION
    RWY 02: TORA–7001   TODA–7001   ASDA–7001   LDA–7001
    RWY 11: TORA–10104 TODA–10104 ASDA–9800   LDA–9800
    RWY 20: TORA–7001   TODA–7001   ASDA–7001   LDA–7001
    RWY 29: TORA–10104 TODA–10104 ASDA–10104 LDA–9800
  SERVICE: **FUEL** 100LL, JET A
  NOISE: Rwy 11 noise sensitive for dep; avbl for opr necessity. All rwys
    noise sensitive for arr. Arriving turbojets must make 5 mile final apch
    to minimize noise.
  AIRPORT REMARKS: Attended continuously. Flocks of birds on and invof
    arpt. ASSC in use. Operate transponders with altitude reporting mode and ADS–B (if equipped) enabled on all airport
    surfaces. 180° and locked wheel turns prohibited on asph sfc acft 12,500 lbs and over. Twy G btn Rwy 11–29 and Twy
    S sfc mov guidance and ctl system U/S perm. Ldg fee. Flight Notification Service (ADCUS) available.
  AIRPORT MANAGER: (504) 303-7652
  WEATHER DATA SOURCES: ASOS (504) 471–4486 TDWR.
  COMMUNICATIONS: D–ATIS 127.55 (504) 471–4417 **UNICOM** 122.95
  ® NEW ORLEANS APP/DEP CON 133.15 (East) 125.5 (West)
    TOWER 119.5   **GND CON** 121.9   **CLNC DEL** 120.925   **PRE TAXI CLNC** 120.925
    CPDLC (LOGON KUSA)
    PDC
  AIRSPACE: CLASS B See VFR Terminal Area Chart.
  RADIO AIDS TO NAVIGATION: NOTAM FILE MSY.
    RESERVE (L) (L) VORW/DME 110.8   RQR   Chan 45   N30°05.25´ W90°35.32´   106° 18.1 NM to fld. 5/2E.
    ILS/DME 111.7   I–JFI   Chan 54   Rwy 02.   Class IE.   DME also serves Rwy 20. Autopilot cpd approaches NA blw
      880´ MSL.
    ILS/DME 109.9   I–MSY   Chan 36   Rwy 11.   Class IIIE.   Lczr Rwy 11/29 interlocked. I–MSY front course, I–HOX back
      course. DME also serves Rwy 29.
    LOC/DME 111.7   I–ONW   Chan 54   Rwy 20.   DME also serves Rwy 02. DME unusable byd 25° right of course. LOC
      unusable byd 24° right of course.
    ILS/DME 109.9   I–HOX   Chan 36   Rwy 29.   Class IE.   DME also serves Rwy 11.

LOUISIANA

NEW ORLEANS NAS JRB (ALVIN CALLENDER FLD) (NBG)(KNBG) NAS (ANG CG) 3 S
NEW ORLEANS
H–7E, 8F, L–21B, 22F, GOMC
DIAP, AD

UTC–6(–5DT) N29°49.63´ W90°01.60´
2 B TPA—See Remarks AOE NOTAM FILE NBG Not insp.
RWY 04–22: H10000X200 (PEM) PCN 44 R/B/W/T HIRL(NSTD)
  RWY 04: ALSF1. OLS. WAVE–OFF. REIL. PAPI(P4L)—GA 3.0° TCH 49´.
  RWY 22: ALSF1. OLS. WAVE–OFF. REIL. PAPI(P4L)—GA 3.0° TCH 44´. Rgt tfc.
RWY 14–32: H6000X200 (PEM) PCN 60 R/B/W/T HIRL
  RWY 14: REIL. PAPI(P4L)—GA 3.0° TCH 54´.
  RWY 32: SALS. OLS. REIL. PAPI(P4L)—GA 3.0° TCH 50´.
ARRESTING GEAR/SYSTEM
  RWY 04 HOOK E28 (B) (1500')   HOOK E28(B) (1501') **RWY 22**
  RWY 14 HOOK E28(B) (1025')   HOOK E28(B) (1025') **RWY 32**
SERVICE: MILITARY— LGT Carrier deck lgt on Rwy 04 for FCLP´s avbl upon req one hr prior. Carrier deck Rwy 32 unlit VFR/Day use only. Double yellow twy end lgt at end of Twy K/O, L and P not instld. PCL are NSTD. 3 clicks Rwy 04 med ints. 5 clicks Rwy 22 med ints. 7 clicks Rwy 04 hi ints. Rwy 14–32 med ints all settings. Only PCL Rwy 04–22 HIRL and Rwy 32 SALS, response time for PCL is NSTD with approx 10 sec delay from pilot input to light intens change. PCL freq 123.8 or 340.2. **A–GEAR** Maint in raised posn and in battery at all times, do not land drct on A–GEAR cable. **JASU** 4(NC–10C) 4(A/M47A–4) Ltd DC pwr. **FUEL** J8. Opr 1330–0430Z‡. Fuel delays Fri–Sun. Tran acft exp some delay for svc outside nml working hr. **FLUID** PRESAIR LHOX LOX **OIL** O–128–156
MILITARY REMARKS: Attended 1300–0500Z‡ Mon–Fri, 1500–2300Z‡ Sat–Sun, clsd hol exc by NOTAM. Base OPS opr 1300–2100Z‡ Mon–Fri, clsd Sat–Sun. Wx svc avbl 1100–0500Z‡ Mon–Fri, 1400–2300Z‡ Sat–Sun. See FLIP AP/1 Supplementary Arpt info. Carrier deck lighting on Rwy 04 for field carrier landing practice is avbl upon req. Req a hr prior. For civ acft ldg pmt (CALP) info ctc afld mgr C504–678–4592. **RSTD** PPR all acft 48 hr prior notice DSN 678–3602/3 C504–678–3602/3. **CAUTION** Numerous civilian acft opr to/from canals vicinity afld. Bird hazard. 180° turns and pivots on asph unauthorized. **TFC PAT** TPA—Overhead break alt 1500´. Pat alt 1000´. Rwy–22 rgt tfc. Rwy–14 rgt tfc.
CSTMS/AG/IMG Avbl to mil acft/personnel only, coordinate with afld svcs DSN 678–3602, C504–678–3602. Other CSTMS requirements ctc C504–623–6600 for appointment. **MISC** Ctc Base Ops DSN 678–3101, C504–678–3101 or fax DSN 678–9575, C504–678–9575. OT civ acft trns Class D, ctc ATC on 123.8 for clnc. No lavatory svc avbl. Fire department status Cat II. **ANG** LA ANG AM OPS opr 1330–2130Z‡ Tues–Fri and unit trng act weekend. LA ANG AM OPS, DSN 457–8637, C504–391–8637, fax DSN 457–8671, C504–391–8671. **CG** Opr rstd 0500–1300Z‡ to CG. C504–393–6032.
COMMUNICATIONS: ATIS 279.55
Ⓡ **APP/DEP CON** 123.85 256.9
NAVY NEW ORLEANS TOWER 123.8 340.2 (1300–0500Z‡ Mon–Fri, 1500–2300Z‡ Sat–Sun, clsd hol exc by NOTAM).
NAVY NEW ORLEANS GND CON 121.6 270.35 **CLNC DEL** 128.35 263.0
PMSV METRO 265.8 (Opr 1100–0500Z‡ Mon–Sat, 1400–2300Z‡ Sat, Sun) **BASE OPS** 289.6 (Opr 1300–2100Z‡ Mon–Fri, clsd Sat–Sun) **CG** 345.0X 5696X 8984 (ctc New Orleans air)
AIRSPACE: CLASS D svc 1300–0500Z‡ Mon–Fri, 1500–2300Z‡ Sat–Sun, clsd hol exc by NOTAM; other times CLASS E.
RADIO AIDS TO NAVIGATION: NOTAM FILE NEW.
  HARVEY (VH) (H) VORTACW 114.1   HRV   Chan 88   N29°51.01´ W90°00.18´   220° 1.8 NM to fld. 2/2E.
  VOR unusable:
    000°–014° byd 40 NM
    015°–025° byd 40 NM blo 18,000´
    026°–050° byd 40 NM
    040°–060° byd 34 NM blo 2,500´
    051°–068° byd 40 NM blo 3,500´
    051°–068° byd 66 NM
    069°–252° byd 40 NM
    253°–263° byd 40 NM blo 17,000´
    264°–296° byd 40 NM
    270°–280° byd 28 NM blo 4,000´
    270°–280° byd 35 NM blo 5,000´
    297°–307° byd 40 NM blo 18,000´
    308°–359° byd 40 NM
    325°–330° byd 28 NM blo 3,000´
  TACAN AZIMUTH unusable:
    040°–060° byd 24 NM blo 2,500´
  DME unusable:
    040°–060° byd 34 NM blo 2,500´
    070°–090° blo 2,400´
    070°–090° byd 26 NM blo 3,400´
  ILS 109.5 I–NBG Rwy 04. Unmonitored during unmanned tower operations.
    ASR (Mon–Fri 1300–0500Z‡, Sat–Sun 1500–2300Z‡) / **PAR**
COMM/NAV/WEATHER REMARKS: Radar see Terminal FLIP for Radar Minima.

LOUISIANA 117

NEW ROADS

FALSE RIVER RGNL (HZR)(KHZR) 2 NW UTC−6(−5DT) N30°43.10′ W91°28.72′ **HOUSTON**
 39   B   TPA—See Remarks   NOTAM FILE DRI   **H−7D, L−21B, 22F**
 RWY 18−36: H5003X75 (ASPH) S−30 MIRL   **IAP**
 RWY 18: REIL. PAPI(P2L)—GA 3.0° TCH 50′.
 RWY 36: ODALS. PAPI(P2L)—GA 3.0° TCH 50′.
 SERVICE: **FUEL** 100LL **LGT** ACTIVATE REIL Rwy 18—122.8. MIRL
   Rwy 18−36; ODALS Rwy 36 preset low ints, to incr ints —122.8. Dual
   lighting system ops in effect due to testing of LED MIRL and twy lgts
   indef.
 AIRPORT REMARKS: Attended Mon−Fri 1400−2200Z‡. For attendant after
   hrs call 225−978−8367. Fuel avbl 24 hrs self svc with credit card.
   TPA—299 (260) ultralight, 499 (460) helicopter. 999 (960) fixed
   wing within 3 NM of arpt. Rwy 18−36 surface condition not reported
   0300−1900Z‡ Mon−Fri and 1100−1059Z‡ on weekends and
   holidays.
 AIRPORT MANAGER: 225−638−3192
 WEATHER DATA SOURCES: AWOS−3PT 121.250 (225) 638−3107.
 COMMUNICATIONS: CTAF/UNICOM 122.8
 ® **BATON ROUGE APP/DEP CON** 120.3 (1100−0600Z‡)
 ® **HOUSTON CENTER APP/DEP CON** 126.35 (0600−1100Z‡)
 CLEARANCE DELIVERY PHONE: For CD ctc Houston ARTCC at 281−230−5622.
 RADIO AIDS TO NAVIGATION: NOTAM FILE BTR.
   FIGHTING TIGER (VL) (L) VORTACW 116.5   LSU   Chan 112   N30°29.11′ W91°17.64′   320° 16.9 NM to fld. 20/6E.
   LOC/DME 111.9 I−HZR Chan 56 Rwy 36.

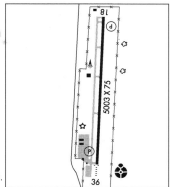

OAK GROVE

KELLY−DUMAS (9M6) 1 SW UTC−6(−5DT) N32°50.86′ W91°24.24′ **MEMPHIS**
 112 B NOTAM FILE DRI   **L−18F**
 RWY 18−36: H3799X60 (ASPH) S−10 MIRL
 RWY 18: REIL. PAPI(P2R)—GA 3.5° TCH 52′. Thld dsplcd 250′. Trees.
 RWY 36: REIL. PAPI(P2L)—GA 3.0° TCH 53′. Trees.
 SERVICE: S4 **FUEL** 100LL, JET A **LGT** MIRL Rwy 18−36, REIL Rwy 18
   and Rwy 36 preset low inst dusk−dawn; to incr intst ACTVT—CTAF.
   PAPI Rwy 18 and Rwy 36 dusk−dawn—CTAF.
 AIRPORT REMARKS: Attended Mon−Fri 1330−2300Z‡. Fuel avbl 24 hrs with
   credit card.
 AIRPORT MANAGER: 318−428−3129
 COMMUNICATIONS: CTAF 122.9
 CLEARANCE DELIVERY PHONE: For CD ctc Memphis ARTCC at
   901−368−8453/8449.
 RADIO AIDS TO NAVIGATION: NOTAM FILE MLU.
   MONROE (VL) (L) VORTACW 117.2   MLU   Chan 119   N32°31.01′
     W92°02.16′   055° 37.6 NM to fld. 77/3E.
   VOR unusable:
     010°−040° byd 40 NM
     125°−135° byd 40 NM
     215°−231° byd 40 NM
     232°−242° byd 40 NM blo 8,000′
     232°−242° byd 83 NM
     243°−255° byd 40 NM blo 7,000′
     243°−255° byd 56 NM
     256°−267° byd 40 NM blo 18,000′
     256°−267° byd 45 NM
     268°−271° byd 40 NM
     272°−282° byd 40 NM blo 2,000′
     272°−282° byd 51 NM
     283°−315° byd 40 NM

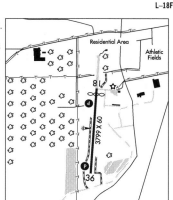

SC, 25 JAN 2024 to 21 MAR 2024

LOUISIANA

OAKDALE

ALLEN PARISH (ACP)(KACP) 4 S UTC–6(–5DT) N30°45.03´ W92°41.31´ HOUSTON
107 B NOTAM FILE DRI   H–7D, L–21B, 22E
RWY 18–36: H5000X75 (ASPH) S–11 MIRL   IAP
 RWY 18: REIL. PAPI(P2L)—GA 3.0° TCH 50´. Trees.
 RWY 36: REIL. PAPI(P2L)—GA 3.0° TCH 51´. Trees.
SERVICE: FUEL 100LL, JET A LGT MIRL Rwy 18–36; REIL Rwy 18 and
 Rwy 36 preset low ints dusk to dawn, to incr ints ACTIVATE—CTAF.
AIRPORT REMARKS: Attended continuously. Fuel avbl self service with credit
 card. Standing water on rwy at midfield after rain.
AIRPORT MANAGER: 318-215-0090
WEATHER DATA SOURCES: AWOS–3PT 118.275 (318) 215–9728.
COMMUNICATIONS: CTAF/UNICOM 122.8
Ⓡ POLK APP/DEP CON 123.7
 GCO 135.075 (POLK APCH CTL and Flight Services)
CLEARANCE DELIVERY PHONE: For CD if una via GCO, ctc Polk Apch at
 337-531-2352.
RADIO AIDS TO NAVIGATION: NOTAM FILE AEX.
 ALEXANDRIA (H) (H) VORTACW 116.1 AEX Chan 108 N31°15.40´
  W92°30.06´ 195° 31.8 NM to fld. 76/3E.
 VOR unusable:
  035°–065° blo 2,000´
  066°–094° byd 35 NM blo 3,000´
  185°–200° byd 35 NM blo 3,000´
  201°–214° byd 35 NM blo 2,000´
  215°–260° blo 2,000´
  261°–285° byd 35 NM blo 2,000´
  357°–034° byd 35 NM blo 3,000´

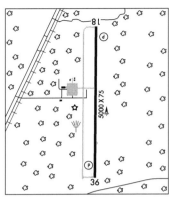

OPELOUSAS

ST LANDRY PARISH (OPL)(KOPL) 2 NW UTC–6(–5DT) N30°33.50´ W92°05.96´ HOUSTON
74 B NOTAM FILE OPL   H–7D, L–21B, 22E
RWY 18–36: H5999X100 (CONC) S–30 MIRL   IAP
 RWY 18: REIL. PAPI(P2L)—GA 3.5° TCH 58´. Thld dsplcd 150´. Tree.
  Rgt tfc.
 RWY 36: REIL. PAPI(P2L)—GA 3.5° TCH 59´. Thld dsplcd 789´. Road.
RWY 06–24: H4051X100 (CONC) S–30
 RWY 06: Thld dsplcd 165´. Trees.
 RWY 24: Thld dsplcd 169´. Trees. Rgt tfc.
SERVICE: S2 FUEL 100LL, JET A+ LGT REIL Rwy 18 & 36; MIRL Rwy
 18–36, preset low intst dusk–dawn; to incr intst ACTVT—CTAF.
AIRPORT REMARKS: Attended Mon–Fri 1400–2230Z‡, Sat 1400–1800Z‡.
 Parachute Jumping. Ctc aprt mgr for acceptable forms of payment for
 fuel. Rwy 06–24 markings are faded. Rwy 06–24 has some cracks
 with grass growing thru cracks. Rwy end 06: Rwy markings are faded.
 Rwy end 24: Rwy markings are faded.
AIRPORT MANAGER: 337-407-1551
WEATHER DATA SOURCES: AWOS–3PT 118.775 (337) 948–8560.
COMMUNICATIONS: CTAF/UNICOM 123.0
Ⓡ LAFAYETTE APP/DEP CON 128.7 (1130–0430Z‡)
 HOUSTON CENTER APP/DEP CON 126.35 (0430–1130Z‡)
CLEARANCE DELIVERY PHONE: For CD ctc Lafayette Apch at 337-262-2729,
 when Apch clsd ctc Houston ARTCC at 281-230-5622.
RADIO AIDS TO NAVIGATION: NOTAM FILE LFT.
 LAFAYETTE (L) (L) VORTACW 109.8 LFT Chan 35 N30°11.63´ W91°59.55´ 343° 22.5 NM to fld. 36/3E.
 TACAN AZIMUTH unusable:
  295°–320° blo 4,000´

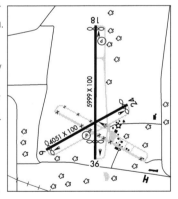

SC, 25 JAN 2024 to 21 MAR 2024

LOUISIANA 119

PATTERSON

HARRY P WILLIAMS MEML (PTN)(KPTN) 2 NW UTC−6(−5DT) N29°42.57′ W91°20.34′   **HOUSTON**
9   B LRA   NOTAM FILE PTN   **H−7D, L−21B, 22F, GOMC**
RWY 06−24: H5399X150 (ASPH) S−32 MIRL   **IAP**
  RWY 06: REIL. PAPI(P2L)—GA 3.0° TCH 50′. Thld dsplcd 394′. Trees.
  RWY 24: MALSR. PAPI(P2L)—GA 3.0° TCH 50′. Rgt tfc.
SERVICE: S4 **FUEL** 100LL, JET A **LGT** Actvt MALSR Rwy 24; MIRL
  Rwy 06−24 preset med intst, to incr intst—CTAF.
AIRPORT REMARKS: Attended continuously. 4500′ by 100′ waterwy hdg
  04−22 lctd 1100′ south of conc rwy. Dual land/sea operation.
AIRPORT MANAGER: 337-828-4100
WEATHER DATA SOURCES: AWOS−3PT 134.575 (985) 395−6735.
COMMUNICATIONS: CTAF/UNICOM 122.8
  PATTERSON RCO 122.5 (DE RIDDER RADIO)
®NEW ORLEANS APP/DEP CON 124.3
  CLNC DEL 124.3
CLEARANCE DELIVERY PHONE: For CD ctc New Orleans Apch at
  504-471-4350 or 124.3.
RADIO AIDS TO NAVIGATION: NOTAM FILE DRI.
  TIBBY (L) (L) VOR/DME 112.0   TBD   Chan 57   N29°39.86′
    W90°49.75′   274° 26.8 NM to fld. 10/2E.
  ILS/DME 108.3 I−PTN   Chan 20   Rwy 24.   Class IA.   ILS mnt by
    FBO durg NMI oprg hrs.

WATERWAY 04W−22W: 4500X100 (WATER)
  WATERWAY 04W: Road. Rgt tfc.

PETE ANTIE MUNI HELIPORT (See MELVILLE on page 109)

PINEVILLE MUNI (2L0) 2 N UTC−6(−5DT) N31°20.53′ W92°26.61′   **HOUSTON**
100 B TPA—See Remarks NOTAM FILE DRI   **L−21B, 22E**
RWY 18−36: H3000X75 (ASPH) S−15.5 MIRL 0.5% up N
  RWY 18: REIL. PAPI(P2L)—GA 4.0° TCH 68′. Trees.
  RWY 36: REIL. PAPI(P2R)—GA 3.0° TCH 49′. Trees.
SERVICE: S4 **FUEL** 100LL, MOGAS OX 1, 2 **LGT** MIRL Rwy 18−36,
  REIL Rwy 18 and Rwy 36 preset low ints dusk−dawn. To increase ints
  ACTIVATE—CTAF. REILS OTS approach end Rwy 18. REILS OTS
  approach end Rwy 36.
AIRPORT REMARKS: Attended Mon−Fri 1400−0000Z‡, Sat 1500−2000Z‡.
  Fuel avbl 24/7 with credit card. Rwy 18 drop off 95′ from end of rwy.
  Rwy 36 lake 96′ from end of rwy. TPA—780 (700) acft for water Rwy
  05W−23W, 1100 (1000) fixed wing for Rwy 18−36. All Rwy 18−36
  safety areas NSTD.
AIRPORT MANAGER: 318-449-5679
COMMUNICATIONS: CTAF/UNICOM 122.8
CLEARANCE DELIVERY PHONE: For CD ctc Polk Apch at 337-531-2352.
RADIO AIDS TO NAVIGATION: NOTAM FILE AEX.
  ALEXANDRIA (H) (H) VORTACW 116.1   AEX   Chan 108   N31°15.40′
    W92°30.06′   027° 5.9 NM to fld. 76/3E.
  VOR unusable:
    035°−065° blo 2,000′
    066°−094° byd 35 NM blo 3,000′
    185°−200° byd 35 NM blo 3,000′
    201°−214° byd 35 NM blo 2,000′
    215°−260° blo 2,000′
    261°−285° byd 35 NM blo 2,000′
    357°−034° byd 35 NM blo 3,000′

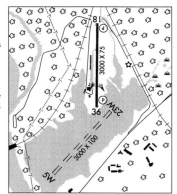

WATERWAY 05W−23W: 3000X100 (WATER)
  WATERWAY 23W: Rgt tfc.
SEAPLANE REMARKS: Waterway elevation 80′.

SC, 25 JAN 2024 to 21 MAR 2024

LOUISIANA

POLLOCK MUNI (L66) 4 SW UTC−6(−5DT) N31°28.65′ W92°27.67′   HOUSTON
203 B NOTAM FILE DRI   L−21B, 22E
RWY 18−36: H4499X75 (ASPH) S−49 MIRL
  RWY 18: Trees.
  RWY 36: Trees.
SERVICE: **LGT** Rotating bcn OTS indef. MIRL Rwy 18−36 preset low ints, to incr ints ACTIVATE−122.7.
AIRPORT REMARKS: Unattended. Rwy 18−36 north 1000′ of rwy CLOSED indef. Rwy 18−36 cracking and grass growing through cracks. Cracks in rwy > 1/4 inch. Surface rough. Ponding/standing water on Rwy near Rwys 18 and 36 apch end. Helicopter running landings not authorized on Rwy 18−36. Extensive military operations. Rotating bcn located 1/2 mile southeast of arpt.
AIRPORT MANAGER: 318-623-2436
COMMUNICATIONS: CTAF 122.9
CLEARANCE DELIVERY PHONE: For CD ctc Polk Apch at 337-531-2352.
RADIO AIDS TO NAVIGATION: NOTAM FILE AEX.
  ALEXANDRIA (H) (H) VORTACW 116.1   AEX   Chan 108   N31°15.40′ W92°30.06′   006° 13.4 NM to fld. 76/3E.
    VOR unusable:
      035°−065° blo 2,000′
      066°−094° byd 35 NM blo 3,000′
      185°−200° byd 35 NM blo 3,000′
      201°−214° byd 35 NM blo 2,000′
      215°−260° blo 2,000′
      261°−285° byd 35 NM blo 2,000′
      357°−034° byd 35 NM blo 3,000′

PORT OF SOUTH LOUISIANA EXEC RGNL (See RESERVE on page 121)

RAYVILLE

JOHN H HOOKS JR MEML (M79) 1 NW UTC−6(−5DT) N32°29.13′ W91°46.26′   MEMPHIS
83 B NOTAM FILE DRI   L−18F
RWY 18−36: H3998X75 (ASPH) S−12 MIRL   IAP
  RWY 18: REIL. PAPI(P2L)—GA 3.0° TCH 50′. Trees.
  RWY 36: REIL. PAPI(P2L)—GA 3.0° TCH 50′. Thld dsplcd 291′. Trees.
SERVICE: S4 **LGT** MIRL Rwy 18−36, REIL Rwy 18 and Rwy 36 preset low ints dusk to dawn, to increase ints ACTIVATE—CTAF.
AIRPORT REMARKS: Unattended. For svcs after hrs call 318−235−3177. Rwy 18-36 40−80′ trees west side of rwy penetrate transition slope.
AIRPORT MANAGER: 318-235-0187
COMMUNICATIONS: CTAF/UNICOM 122.8
®**MONROE APP/DEP CON** 126.9 (1200−0400Z‡)
®**FORT WORTH CENTER APP/DEP CON** 126.325 (0400−1200Z‡)
CLEARANCE DELIVERY PHONE: For CD ctc Monroe Apch at 318-327-5641, if unavbl, ctc Fort Worth ARTCC at 817-858-7584.
RADIO AIDS TO NAVIGATION: NOTAM FILE MLU.
  MONROE (VL) (L) VORTACW 117.2   MLU   Chan 119   N32°31.01′ W92°02.16′   095° 13.6 NM to fld. 77/3E.
    VOR unusable:
      010°−040° byd 40 NM
      125°−135° byd 40 NM
      215°−231° byd 40 NM
      232°−242° byd 40 NM blo 8,000′
      232°−242° byd 83 NM
      243°−255° byd 40 NM blo 7,000′
      243°−255° byd 56 NM
      256°−267° byd 40 NM blo 18,000′
      256°−267° byd 45 NM
      268°−271° byd 40 NM
      272°−282° byd 40 NM blo 2,000′
      272°−282° byd 51 NM
      283°−315° byd 40 NM

LOUISIANA 121

RESERVE

PORT OF SOUTH LOUISIANA EXEC RGNL (APS)(KAPS)   2 NW   UTC–6(–5DT)   N30°05.25′   **NEW ORLEANS**
W90°34.97′   L–21B, 22F, GOMC
7   B   NOTAM FILE APS   IAP
RWY 17–35: H5151X75 (ASPH)   MIRL
  RWY 17: REIL. PAPI(P2L)—GA 3.0° TCH 50′. Thld dsplcd 746′. Trees.
  RWY 35: REIL. PAPI(P2L)—GA 3.0° TCH 50′. Rgt tfc.
SERVICE: **FUEL** 100LL, JET A   **LGT** REIL Rwy 17 and 35; MIRL Rwy
  17–35 preset low intst; to incr intst actvt—CTAF.
AIRPORT REMARKS: Attended Mon–Fri 1300–2230Z‡. Self svc 24 hrs. Full
  svc weekend and after hrs by request. Birds on and invof arpt.
  Ultralight activity.
AIRPORT MANAGER: 985-212-1712
WEATHER DATA SOURCES: AWOS–3PT 125.45 (985) 536–1009.
COMMUNICATIONS: CTAF/UNICOM 122.7
®**NEW ORLEANS APP/DEP CON** 125.5
CLEARANCE DELIVERY PHONE: For CD ctc New Orleans Apch at
  504-471-4350.
RADIO AIDS TO NAVIGATION: NOTAM FILE MSY.
  RESERVE (L) (L) VORW/DME 110.8   RQR   Chan 45   N30°05.25′
  W90°35.32′   at fld. 5/2E.

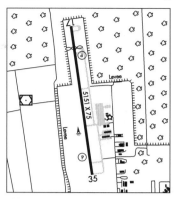

RUNDI   N30°34.98′ W91°12.66′   NOTAM FILE BTR.   **HOUSTON**
  NDB (LOMW) 284   BT   133° 4.4 NM to Baton Rouge Metro, Ryan Fld. 69/0E.   L–21B, 22F

RUSTON RGNL   (RSN)(KRSN)   3 E   UTC–6(–5DT)   N32°30.79′ W92°35.31′   **MEMPHIS**
317   B   TPA—1317(1000)   NOTAM FILE RSN   H–6I, L–17E
RWY 18–36: H6002X100 (ASPH)   S–78, D–119 PCN 30 F/B/X/T   IAP
  MIRL   0.7% up S
  RWY 18: REIL. PAPI(P4L)—GA 3.0° TCH 50′. Trees.
  RWY 36: REIL. PAPI(P4L)—GA 3.0° TCH 55′.
SERVICE: S2   **FUEL** 100LL, JET A   **LGT** REIL Rwy 18 and 36; MIRL Rwy
  18–36—preset low intst dusk–dawn; to incr intst ACTVT—CTAF. Rwy
  18 PAPI OTS.
AIRPORT REMARKS: Attended 1300–0100Z‡. Men and equipment operating
  near the rwy March–October. Numerous training acft in vicinity. For fuel
  after hrs call in advance during working hrs 318–251–9098.
AIRPORT MANAGER: 318-242-7703
WEATHER DATA SOURCES: AWOS–3PT 119.525 (318) 242–0062.
COMMUNICATIONS: CTAF/UNICOM 122.7
  RCO 122.3 (DE RIDDER RADIO)
®**MONROE APP/DEP CON** 126.9 (1200–0400Z‡)   **CLNC DEL** 118.8
®**FORT WORTH CENTER APP/DEP CON** 126.325 (0400–1200Z‡)
CLEARANCE DELIVERY PHONE: For CD ctc Monroe Apch at 318-327-5641 or
  118.8, if unavbl, ctc Fort Worth ARTCC at 817-858-7584
RADIO AIDS TO NAVIGATION: NOTAM FILE MLU.
  MONROE (VL) (L) VORTACW 117.2   MLU   Chan 119   N32°31.01′
  W92°02.16′   267° 28.0 NM to fld. 77/3E.
  VOR unusable:
    010°–040° byd 40 NM
    125°–135° byd 40 NM
    215°–231° byd 40 NM
    232°–242° byd 40 NM blo 8,000′
    232°–242° byd 83 NM
    243°–255° byd 40 NM blo 7,000′
    243°–255° byd 56 NM
    256°–267° byd 40 NM blo 18,000′
    256°–267° byd 45 NM
    268°–271° byd 40 NM
    272°–282° byd 40 NM blo 2,000′
    272°–282° byd 51 NM
    283°–315° byd 40 NM

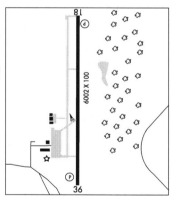

SABAR   N32°27.24′ W92°06.26′   NOTAM FILE MLU.   **MEMPHIS**
  NDB (LOMW) 392   ML   043° 4.8 NM to Monroe Rgnl. 75/3E.   L–18F

SC, 25 JAN 2024 to 21 MAR 2024

ST JOSEPH

TENSAS PARISH (L33) 4 NE UTC–6(–5DT) N31°58.39′ W91°14.32′ **HOUSTON**
74 B NOTAM FILE DRI L–18F
RWY 16–34: H3509X75 (ASPH) S–12 MIRL
  RWY 16: Road.
  RWY 34: Trees.
SERVICE: **FUEL** 100LL **LGT** MIRL Rwy 16–34 preset low ints, to increase ints ACTIVATE—CTAF. Windsock OTS tempoly.
AIRPORT REMARKS: Unattended. For arpt attendant call 318–282–0348 or 318–372–7277. Birds invof arpt.
AIRPORT MANAGER: (318) 537-1475
COMMUNICATIONS: CTAF 122.9
CLEARANCE DELIVERY PHONE: For CD ctc Memphis ARTCC at 901-368-8453/8449.
RADIO AIDS TO NAVIGATION: NOTAM FILE MLU.
  MONROE (VL) (L) VORTACW 117.2 MLU Chan 119 N32°31.01′ W92°02.16′ 126° 52.0 NM to fld. 77/3E.
  VOR unusable:
   010°–040° byd 40 NM
   125°–135° byd 40 NM
   215°–231° byd 40 NM
   232°–242° byd 40 NM blo 8,000′
   232°–242° byd 83 NM
   243°–255° byd 40 NM blo 7,000′
   243°–255° byd 56 NM
   256°–267° byd 40 NM blo 18,000′
   256°–267° byd 45 NM
   268°–271° byd 40 NM
   272°–282° byd 40 NM blo 2,000′
   272°–282° byd 51 NM
   283°–315° byd 40 NM

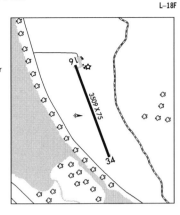

ST LANDRY PARISH (See OPELOUSAS on page 118)

ST TAMMANY RGNL (See COVINGTON on page 93)

SAWMILL N31°58.39′ W92°40.63′ NOTAM FILE DRI. **HOUSTON**
(H) (DH) VORW/DME 113.75 SWB Chan 84(Y) 122° 1.0 NM to David G Joyce. 164/2E. H–6I, L–22F
  VOR unusable:
   001°–240° byd 6 NM
   001°–360° blo 4,000′
   241°–360° byd 25 NM
  DME unusable:
   211°–229° blo 13,000′
   230°–239°
   240°–210° blo 2,500′

SCOTT (See TALLULAH on page 125)

SHIP SHOAL 241 PZZ N28°26.06′ W91°02.07′/130 **HOUSTON**
AWOS-3 121.125 (985) 288-6254 L–21B, GOMC

LOUISIANA

SHREVEPORT

SHREVEPORT DOWNTOWN (DTN)(KDTN) 3 N UTC–6(–5DT) N32°32.45´ W93°44.63´ MEMPHIS
179 B NOTAM FILE DTN H–6I, L–13D, 17E
RWY 14–32: H5016X150 (ASPH) S–35, D–55 HIRL IAP, AD
  RWY 14: REIL. PAPI(P4L)—GA 3.0° TCH 43´. Trees.
  RWY 32: REIL. PAPI(P4R)—GA 3.0° TCH 27´. Trees.
RWY 05–23: H4198X75 (ASPH) S–12.5 MIRL
  RWY 05: REIL. PAPI(P2L)—GA 3.0° TCH 42´. Fence.
  RWY 23: REIL. PAPI(P2L)—GA 3.0° TCH 39´. Trees.
SERVICE: S4 **FUEL** 100LL, JET A **OX** 2, 3 **LGT** Rwy 05 REIL OTS indef.
Rwy 23 REIL OTS indef. Rwy 14 PAPI unusable byd 8° right of centerline.
AIRPORT REMARKS: Attended 1300–0400Z‡. 100LL avbl 24 hrs self svc with credit card. For Jet A after hrs call 318–510–4330. Avbl 24 hrs self svc with credit card. All VFR tfc remain within 1 1/2 miles northeast thru southwest from the center of the arpt due to Shreveport/Barksdale AFB CLASS C airspace. Wildlife–deer & birds on & invof arpt. Rwy 14 designated calm wind rwy. Acft/vehicles not vsbl from ATCT on N 685 ft of Twy F.
AIRPORT MANAGER: 318-349-8330
WEATHER DATA SOURCES: ASOS 118.525 (318) 425–7967.
COMMUNICATIONS: CTAF 120.225 UNICOM 122.95
  SHREVEPORT RCO 122.6 (DE RIDDER RADIO)
(R) **SHREVEPORT APP/DEP CON** 119.9 (153°–319°) 123.75 (320°–152°)
  CLNC DEL 121.65 (When ATCT clsd CLNC DEL provided by SHV DEP CON on 119.9)
  TOWER 120.225 (1300–0400Z‡) **GND CON** 121.65
AIRSPACE: CLASS D svc 1300–0400Z‡; other times CLASS G.
RADIO AIDS TO NAVIGATION: NOTAM FILE SHV.
  BELCHER (H) (H) VORTACW 117.4 EIC Chan 121 N32°46.28´ W93°48.60´ 159° 14.2 NM to fld. 190/7E.
  LOC/DME 111.7 I–DTN Chan 54 Rwy 14.

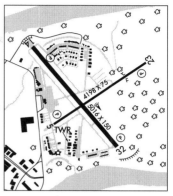

SHREVEPORT RGNL (SHV)(KSHV) 4 SW UTC–6(–5DT) N32°26.79´ W93°49.56´ MEMPHIS
258 B LRA Class I, ARFF Index B NOTAM FILE SHV MON Airport H–6I, L–17E
RWY 14–32: H8348X200 (ASPH–GRVD) S–75, D–190, 2S–175, IAP, AD
2D–400 PCN 46 F/A/Y/T HIRL CL
  RWY 14: ALSF2. TDZL. PAPI(P4R)—GA 3.0° TCH 50´. RVR–TMR 0.7% down.
  RWY 32: MALSR. RVR–TMR Thld dsplcd 373´. Railroad.
RWY 06–24: H7003X150 (ASPH–GRVD) S–75, D–158, 2D–280 PCN 49 F/C/Y/T MIRL
  RWY 06: REIL. PAPI(P4L)—GA 3.0° TCH 51´. Trees.
  RWY 24: REIL. Trees.
RUNWAY DECLARED DISTANCE INFORMATION
  RWY 06: TORA–7003 TODA–7003 ASDA–7003 LDA–7003
  RWY 14: TORA–8348 TODA–8348 ASDA–8118 LDA–8118
  RWY 24: TORA–7003 TODA–7003 ASDA–7003 LDA–7003
  RWY 32: TORA–8348 TODA–8348 ASDA–8348 LDA–7975
SERVICE: S4 **FUEL** 100LL, JET A **OX** 3
AIRPORT REMARKS: Attended continuously. Bird activity invof arpt. Landing fee for all commercial aircraft. Flight Notification Service (ADCUS) available Mon–Fri 1400–2300Z‡, other times by appointment call 318–635–7873 or 800–973–2867.
AIRPORT MANAGER: 318-673-5370
WEATHER DATA SOURCES: ASOS 128.45 (318) 636–5767. LLWAS.
COMMUNICATIONS: UNICOM 122.95 ATIS 128.45
(R) **APP/DEP CON** 119.9
  TOWER 121.4 **GND CON** 121.175 **CLNC DEL** 124.65
AIRSPACE: CLASS C svc ctc APP CON.
VOR TEST FACILITY (VOT) 108.2
RADIO AIDS TO NAVIGATION: NOTAM FILE SHV.
  BELCHER (H) (H) VORTACW 117.4 EIC Chan 121 N32°46.28´ W93°48.60´ 175° 19.5 NM to fld. 190/7E.
  LOC/DME 109.1 I–MWP Chan 28 Rwy 06.
  ILS/DME 110.7 I–SHV Chan 44 Rwy 14. Class IIE. LOM CRAKK NDB.
  ILS 110.3 I–FOG Rwy 32. Class IA.
  ASR

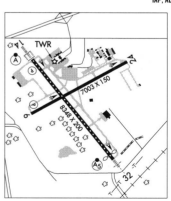

SLIDELL (ASD)(KASD) 4 NW UTC−6(−5DT) N30°20.78´ W89°49.25´ NEW ORLEANS
28 B NOTAM FILE ASD H−7E, 8F, L−21B, 22F, GOMC
RWY 18−36: H5002X100 (ASPH) S−48 MIRL IAP
  RWY 18: REIL. PAPI(P2L)—GA 3.0° TCH 50´. Thld dsplcd 944´. Trees.
  RWY 36: REIL. PAPI(P2L)—GA 3.0° TCH 50´. Trees.
RUNWAY DECLARED DISTANCE INFORMATION
  RWY 18: TORA−5001 TODA−5001 ASDA−5001 LDA−4057
  RWY 36: TORA−5001 TODA−5001 ASDA−5001 LDA−5001
SERVICE: S4 FUEL 100LL, JET A+ OX 3 LGT MIRL Rwy 18−36, REIL Rwy 18 and Rwy 36 preset low ints dusk−dawn, to increase ints ACTIVATE—CTAF.
AIRPORT REMARKS: Attended 1300−2200Z‡. Arpt unatndd Thanksgiving, Christmas, New Years Day. Parachute Jumping. Wildlife on and invof rwy. 100LL avbl 24 hrs with credit card. For JET fuel after hrs call 985−259−2460. Parachute jumping area on weekends.
AIRPORT MANAGER: 985−641−7590
WEATHER DATA SOURCES: ASOS 132.475 (985) 643−7263.
COMMUNICATIONS: CTAF/UNICOM 122.8
® NEW ORLEANS APP/DEP CON 133.15
  GCO 135.075 (NEW ORLEANS APCH and DE RIDDER FSS)
CLEARANCE DELIVERY PHONE: For CD ctc New Orleans Apch at 504−471−4350.
RADIO AIDS TO NAVIGATION: NOTAM FILE GWO.
  PICAYUNE (L) (L) VORW/DME 113.95 PCU Chan 86(Y) N30°33.67´ W89°43.83´ 195° 13.7 NM to fld. 70/5E.
  VOR unusable:
    285°−305° byd 6 NM blo 4,000´
    325°−076° byd 26 NM blo 2,500´
  DME unusable:
    078°−180° byd 32 NM blo 3,000´
    331°−064° byd 27 NM blo 4,000´

SOUTH LAFOURCHE LEONARD MILLER JR (See GALLIANO on page 97)

SOUTH PASS 89E−B MTK N28°41.80´ W89°23.75´/206 NEW ORLEANS
AWOS−3 124.175 (337) 761−8234 L−21C, GOMC

SOUTH TIMBALIER BLK 52 OYE N28°52.02´ W90°29.47´/98 NEW ORLEANS
AWOS−3 118.35 (281) 560−2390 L−21C, GOMC

SOUTHLAND FLD (See SULPHUR on page 125)

SPRINGHILL (SPH)(KSPH) 3 E UTC−6(−5DT) N32°59.02´ W93°24.55´ MEMPHIS
218 B NOTAM FILE DRI L−17E
RWY 18−36: H4202X75 (ASPH) MIRL 0.3% up S IAP
  RWY 18: PAPI(P2L)—GA 3.0° TCH 49´. Trees.
  RWY 36: PAPI(P2L)—GA 3.0° TCH 54´. Trees.
SERVICE: LGT MIRL Rwy 18−36 preset low intst dusk−dawn; to incr intst actvt—CTAF. Rwy 18 PAPI unusbl byd 9° right of cntrln.
AIRPORT REMARKS: Unattended. Airport beacon located .52 miles from the approach end of Rwy 18 right of centerline. Ultralight activity on and in vicinity of airport. NOTE: See Special Notices—Aerobatic Practice Area.
AIRPORT MANAGER: 318−453−7327
COMMUNICATIONS: CTAF/UNICOM 122.8
® SHREVEPORT APP/DEP CON 123.75
CLEARANCE DELIVERY PHONE: For CD ctc Fort Worth ARTCC at 817−858−7584.
RADIO AIDS TO NAVIGATION: NOTAM FILE SHV.
  BELCHER (H) (H) VORTACW 117.4 EIC Chan 121 N32°46.28´ W93°48.60´ 051° 23.9 NM to fld. 190/7E.

LOUISIANA

SULPHUR

SOUTHLAND FLD (UXL)(KUXL)   5 S   UTC−6(−5DT)   N30°07.89′ W93°22.57′   **HOUSTON**
10   B   NOTAM FILE UXL   H−7D, L−21B, 22E, GOMW
 RWY 15−33: H5001X75 (ASPH)   S−30, D−50   MIRL   IAP
  RWY 15: ODALS. PAPI(P4L)—GA 3.0° TCH 50′. Tree.
  RWY 33: REIL. PAPI(P4L)—GA 3.0° TCH 50′. Tree.
 SERVICE: S4   FUEL 100LL, JET A   LGT ODALS Rwy 15; REIL Rwy 33;
  MIRL Rwy 15−33 preset low intst dusk−dawn. To incr intst—CTAF.
  PAPI Rwy 15 and 33 opr consly.
 AIRPORT REMARKS: Attended 1200−0200Z‡. For fuel after hrs call
  337−302−4280, fee charged. NOTE: See Special Notices—Aerobatic
  Practice Area.
 AIRPORT MANAGER: 337−607−4550
 WEATHER DATA SOURCES: AWOS−3PT 118.175 (337) 558−5321.
 COMMUNICATIONS: CTAF/UNICOM 122.8
 ®LAKE CHARLES APP/DEP CON 119.35 (1200−0400Z‡)
 ®HOUSTON CENTER APP/DEP CON 124.7 (0400−1200Z‡)
 CLEARANCE DELIVERY PHONE: For CD ctc Lake Charles Apch at
  337−480−3103, when Apch clsd ctc Houston ARTCC at
  281−230−5622.
 RADIO AIDS TO NAVIGATION: NOTAM FILE LCH.
  LAKE CHARLES (H) (H) VORTACW 113.4   LCH   Chan 81   N30°08.49′
   W93°06.33′   261° 14.1 NM to fld. 20/7E.
  VOR unusable:
   181°−359° byd 30 NM blo 1,500′
  SULPHUR NDB (MHW) 278   AUR   N30°11.91′ W93°25.24′   146° 4.6 NM to fld. 10/4E.   NOTAM FILE DRI.
  LOC 109.3   I−UXL   Rwy 15.

SULPHUR
N30°11.91′ W93°25.24′   NOTAM FILE DRI.   **HOUSTON**
 NDB (MHW) 278   AUR   146° 4.6 NM to Southland Fld. 10/4E.   L−21B, 22E, GOMC

TALLULAH

SCOTT (M80)   2 E   UTC−6(−5DT)   N32°24.98′ W91°08.94′   **MEMPHIS**
86   B   NOTAM FILE DRI   L−18F
 RWY 18−36: H3003X75 (ASPH)   S−12   MIRL
  RWY 36: Thld dsplcd 250′.
 RWY 17−35: 2642X140 (TURF)
  RWY 35: Thld dsplcd 572′. Acft.
 SERVICE: LGT Wind indicator lgt OTS indef. Arpt bcn OTS. Actvt MIRL Rwy 18−36—CTAF.
 AIRPORT REMARKS: Attended on call. For attendant call 318−282−7462. Aerobatic box on fld check NOTAMS. Numerous
  agricultural and ultralight ops at arpt. Rwy 36 dsplcd thld daylight ops only. Acft parking apron 200′ south of Rwy 35 thld.
 AIRPORT MANAGER: 318−282−7462
 COMMUNICATIONS: CTAF/UNICOM 122.8
 CLEARANCE DELIVERY PHONE: For CD ctc Memphis ARTCC at 901−368−8453/8449.
 RADIO AIDS TO NAVIGATION: NOTAM FILE MLU.
  MONROE (VL) (L) VORTACW 117.2   MLU   Chan 119   N32°31.01′ W92°02.16′   094° 45.4 NM to fld. 77/3E.
  VOR unusable:
   010°−040° byd 40 NM
   125°−135° byd 40 NM
   215°−231° byd 40 NM
   232°−242° byd 40 NM blo 8,000′
   232°−242° byd 83 NM
   243°−255° byd 40 NM blo 7,000′
   243°−255° byd 56 NM
   256°−267° byd 40 NM blo 18,000′
   256°−267° byd 45 NM
   268°−271° byd 40 NM
   272°−282° byd 40 NM blo 2,000′
   272°−282° byd 51 NM
   283°−315° byd 40 NM

SC, 25 JAN 2024 to 21 MAR 2024

LOUISIANA

VICKSBURG TALLULAH RGNL (TVR)(KTVR) 9 E UTC–6(–5DT) N32°21.10′ W91°01.66′ MEMPHIS
86 B TPA—1086(1000) NOTAM FILE TVR H–6J, L–18F
RWY 18–36: H5002X100 (ASPH) S–60, D–75 MIRL IAP
 RWY 18: REIL. PAPI(P4L)—GA 3.0° TCH 50′. Trees.
 RWY 36: SSALR. PAPI(P4L)—GA 3.0° TCH 50′. Trees.
RUNWAY DECLARED DISTANCE INFORMATION
 RWY 18: TORA–5002 TODA–5002 ASDA–5002 LDA–5002
 RWY 36: TORA–5002 TODA–5002 ASDA–5002 LDA–5002
SERVICE: S4 FUEL 100LL, JET A LGT MIRL Rwy 18–36, REIL Rwy
 18, SSALR Rwy 36 preset low ints dusk–dawn, to increase ints
 ACTIVATE—CTAF.
AIRPORT REMARKS: Attended 1300–0100Z‡. For arpt mgr aft hrs call
 318–366–1615. PAEW on arpt. Migratory birds invof arpt. Crop
 dusting activity 2 NM radius of arpt. Pilots in tfc pattern are requested
 to avoid over flight of Mound, LA 1/2 mile south and east of Rwy 36.
AIRPORT MANAGER: 318-574-5841
WEATHER DATA SOURCES: ASOS 118.525 (318) 574–4866.
COMMUNICATIONS: CTAF/UNICOM 123.0
 MEMPHIS CENTER APP/DEP CON 132.5
CLEARANCE DELIVERY PHONE: For CD ctc Memphis ARTCC at
 901-368-8453/8449.
RADIO AIDS TO NAVIGATION: NOTAM FILE GWO.
 MAGNOLIA (VH) (H) VORTACW 113.2 MHZ Chan 79 N32°26.04′ W90°05.99′ 265° 47.4 NM to fld. 407/1W.
  TACAN AZIMUTH unusable:
  240°–275° byd 30 NM blo 2,000′
  DME unsbl 240–275 byd 30 NM blo 2000′
 TALLULAH NDB (MHW/LOM) 344 TKH N32°14.72′ W91°01.55′ 357° 6.4 NM to fld. 79/2E. NOTAM FILE DRI.
 ILS 109.7 I–TVR Rwy 36. Class ID.

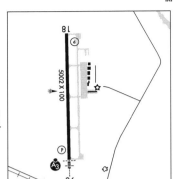

TENSAS PARISH (See ST JOSEPH on page 122)

THE RED RIVER (See COUSHATTA on page 92)

THIBODAUX MUNI (L83) 3 S UTC–6(–5DT) N29°44.87′ W90°49.97′ NEW ORLEANS
9 B NOTAM FILE DRI L–21B, 22F, GOMC
RWY 08–26: H2999X75 (ASPH) S–6 MIRL IAP
 RWY 08: REIL. Trees.
 RWY 26: REIL. Thld dsplcd 90′. Trees.
SERVICE: S2 FUEL 100LL LGT MIRL Rwy 08–26, REIL Rwy 08 and
 Rwy 26 preset low ints, to increase ints ACTVT—CTAF.
AIRPORT REMARKS: Attended 1400–2300Z‡. For arpt attendant after hrs call
 985–209–4697. Wildlife on or near the rwy safety area. 100LL fuel
 avbl by appt call 985–209–4697. Rwy 08–26 agriculture washdown
 pad 500′ north of rwy at midfield. Trees 60 ft tall; 160 ft north and
 south of cntrln pent the 7:1 trsnl slp Rwy 08.
AIRPORT MANAGER: 985-446-7208
COMMUNICATIONS: CTAF/UNICOM 122.8
®NEW ORLEANS APP/DEP CON 118.9
CLEARANCE DELIVERY PHONE: For CD ctc New Orleans Apch at
 504-471-4350.
RADIO AIDS TO NAVIGATION: NOTAM FILE DRI.
 TIBBY (L) (L) VOR/DME 112.0 TBD Chan 57 N29°39.86′
  W90°49.75′ 356° 5.0 NM to fld. 10/2E.

TIBBY N29°39.86′ W90°49.75′ NOTAM FILE DRI. NEW ORLEANS
 (L) (L) VOR/DME 112.0 TBD Chan 57 356° 5.0 NM to Thibodaux Muni. 10/2E. H–7D, L–21B, 22F, GOMC
 RCO 122.1R 112.0T (DE RIDDER RADIO)

UNION PARISH (See FARMERVILLE on page 96)

VICKSBURG TALLULAH RGNL (See TALLULAH on page 126)

LOUISIANA

VIDALIA

CONCORDIA PARISH (0R4)   4 W   UTC–6(–5DT)   N31°33.72′ W91°30.39′   HOUSTON
55   B   NOTAM FILE DRI   L–22F
RWY 14–32: H3701X75 (ASPH)   S–12   MIRL   IAP
  RWY 14: REIL. PAPI(P2L)—GA 3.0° TCH 50′. Trees.
  RWY 32: REIL. PAPI(P2L)—GA 3.0° TCH 50′.
SERVICE: FUEL 100LL   LGT REIL Rwys 14 and 32; MIRL Rwy 14–32
  preset low intst; to incr intst ACTVT—CTAF. PAPI Rwy 14 and Rwy 32
  opr consly. PAPI unusbl byd 8 deg right of cntrln.
AIRPORT REMARKS: Unattended. 100LL avbl 24 hrs self svc with credit
  card. 400′ twr 2 miles north of approach end Rwy 14. Rwy 32 75′
  trees east of rwy penetrate transition slope.
AIRPORT MANAGER: 318-336-8537
WEATHER DATA SOURCES: AWOS–3 118.2 (318) 336–8028.
COMMUNICATIONS: CTAF/UNICOM 122.8
® **HOUSTON CENTER APP/DEP CON** 120.975
CLEARANCE DELIVERY PHONE: For CD ctc Houston ARTCC at 281-230-5622.
RADIO AIDS TO NAVIGATION: NOTAM FILE AEX.
  ALEXANDRIA (H) (H) VORTACW 116.1   AEX   Chan 108   N31°15.40′
  W92°30.06′   067° 54.2 NM to fld. 76/3E.
  VOR unusable:
   035°–065° blo 2,000′
   066°–094° byd 35 NM blo 3,000′
   185°–200° byd 35 NM blo 3,000′
   201°–214° byd 35 NM blo 2,000′
   215°–260° blo 2,000′
   261°–285° byd 35 NM blo 2,000′
   357°–034° byd 35 NM blo 3,000′

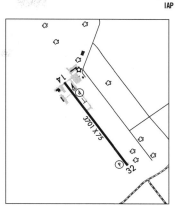

VIOSCAL KNOLL 786A   VOA   N29°13.73′ W87°46.85′   NEW ORLEANS
AWOS–3 118.925 (985) 773–7883 Winds unreliable 335°–005°.   L–21C, 22H, GOMC

VIVIAN (3F4)   2 SW   UTC–6(–5DT)   N32°51.68′ W94°00.61′   MEMPHIS
260   B   NOTAM FILE DRI   L–13D, 17E
RWY 09–27: H2998X75 (ASPH)   S–12   MIRL   0.4% up E   IAP
  RWY 09: REIL. PAPI(P2L)—GA 3.0° TCH 52′. Trees.
  RWY 27: REIL. Trees.
SERVICE: S4   FUEL 100LL   LGT MIRL Rwy 09–27 and REIL Rwy 09
  preset low intst dusk–dawn; to incr intst ACTVT—CTAF. Rwy 09 PAPI
  out of service. Rwy 27 REIL OTS.
AIRPORT REMARKS: Attended Mon–Sat dawn–dusk. Fuel avbl 24 hrs self svc
  with credit card.
AIRPORT MANAGER: (318) 455-5499
COMMUNICATIONS: CTAF/UNICOM 122.8
® **SHREVEPORT APP/DEP CON** 119.9
  GCO 135.075 (BARKSDALE APCH CTL and FLIGHT SERVICES)
CLEARANCE DELIVERY PHONE: For CD if una via GCO ctc Fort Worth ARTCC at
  817-858-7584.
RADIO AIDS TO NAVIGATION: NOTAM FILE SHV.
  BELCHER (H) (H) VORTACW 117.4   EIC   Chan 121   N32°46.28′
  W93°48.60′   291° 11.5 NM to fld. 190/7E.

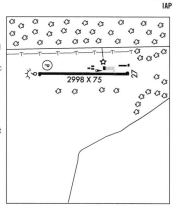

LOUISIANA

WELSH (6R1) 0 NW UTC−6(−5DT) N30°14.51′ W92°49.84′ HOUSTON
18 B NOTAM FILE DRI L−21B, 22E, GOMW
RWY 07−25: H2700X50 (ASPH) S−6 MIRL IAP
  RWY 07: Trees.
  RWY 25: Trees.
RWY 09−27: 2200X150 (TURF)
  RWY 09: Trees.
  RWY 27: Trees.
AIRPORT REMARKS: Attended irregularly. Rwy 07−25 has some small longitudinal cracks with grass growth. Block cracks with grass growth Rwy 07 turnaround. Gravel FOD present in places.
AIRPORT MANAGER: 337-570-4590
COMMUNICATIONS: CTAF/UNICOM 122.8
® LAKE CHARLES APP/DEP CON 119.8 (1200−0400Z‡)
® HOUSTON CENTER APP/DEP CON 124.7 (0400−1200Z‡)
CLEARANCE DELIVERY PHONE: For CD ctc Lake Charles Apch at 337-480-3103, when Apch clsd ctc Houston ARTCC at 281-230-5622.
RADIO AIDS TO NAVIGATION: NOTAM FILE LCH.
  LAKE CHARLES (H) (H) VORTACW 113.4 LCH Chan 81 N30°08.49′ W93°06.33′ 060° 15.5 NM to fld. 20/7E.
  VOR unusable:
    181°−359° byd 30 NM blo 1,500′

WHITE LAKE N29°39.79′ W92°22.42′ NOTAM FILE DRI. HOUSTON
(L) (L) VORW/DME 114.95 LLA Chan 96(Y) 5/4E. H−7D, L−21B, 22E, GOMC, GOMW

WINNFIELD

DAVID G JOYCE (0R5) 3 NW UTC−6(−5DT) N31°57.82′ W92°39.62′ HOUSTON
146 B NOTAM FILE DRI L−22E
RWY 09−27: H3002X100 (ASPH) S−4 MIRL 0.9% up W IAP
  RWY 09: REIL. PAPI(P2L)—GA 3.0° TCH 45′. Trees.
  RWY 27: REIL. PAPI(P2L)—GA 3.45° TCH 62′. Trees.
SERVICE: LGT MIRL 09−27 opr SS−SR and preset low intst; to incr intst and ACTVT REIL Rwy 09 and 27—CTAF.
AIRPORT REMARKS: Unattended. Rotating bcn obscured by trees south, west and east.
AIRPORT MANAGER: (318) 628-3939
COMMUNICATIONS: CTAF/UNICOM 122.7
® POLK APP/DEP CON 125.4
CLEARANCE DELIVERY PHONE: For CD ctc Polk Apch at 337-531-2352.
RADIO AIDS TO NAVIGATION: NOTAM FILE DRI.
  SAWMILL (H) (DH) VORW/DME 113.75 SWB Chan 84(Y)
    N31°58.39′ W92°40.63′ 122° 1.0 NM to fld. 164/2E.
  VOR unusable:
    001°−240° byd 6 NM
    001°−360° blo 4,000′
    241°−360° byd 25 NM
  DME unusable:
    211°−229° blo 13,000′
    230°−239°
    240°−210° blo 2,500′

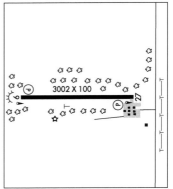

LOUISIANA 129

WINNSBORO MUNI (F89) 1 E UTC−6(−5DT) N32°09.18´ W91°41.92´ **MEMPHIS**
78 B NOTAM FILE DRI **L−18F**
RWY 18−36: H3001X75 (ASPH) S−11 MIRL
  RWY 18: PAPI(P2L)—GA 3.75° TCH 63´. Trees.
  RWY 36: REIL. PAPI(P2L)—GA 3.1° TCH 52´. Tree.
SERVICE: S2 **FUEL** 100LL **LGT** MIRL Rwy 18−36 preset on low ints dusk to dawn, to incr ints actvt—CTAF.
AIRPORT REMARKS: Attended continuously. Arpt attended on call 318−282−4524. 100LL avbl 24 hrs self serve with credit card. Heavy agricultural aircraft opr June−Oct. Rwy 18−36 trees west of rwy obstruct view of operating acft.
AIRPORT MANAGER: (318) 439-3676
COMMUNICATIONS: CTAF/UNICOM 122.8
CLEARANCE DELIVERY PHONE: For CD ctc Monroe Apch at 318-327-5641, if unavbl, ctc Fort Worth ARTCC at 817-858-7584.
RADIO AIDS TO NAVIGATION: NOTAM FILE MLU.
  MONROE (VL) (L) VORTACW 117.2   MLU Chan 119   N32°31.01´
  W92°02.16´   139° 27.7 NM to fld. 77/3E.
  VOR unusable:
    010°−040° byd 40 NM
    125°−135° byd 40 NM
    215°−231° byd 40 NM
    232°−242° byd 40 NM blo 8,000´
    232°−242° byd 83 NM
    243°−255° byd 40 NM blo 7,000´
    243°−255° byd 56 NM
    256°−267° byd 40 NM blo 18,000´
    256°−267° byd 45 NM
    268°−271° byd 40 NM
    272°−282° byd 40 NM blo 2,000´
    272°−282° byd 51 NM
    283°−315° byd 40 NM

WOODWORTH (1R4) 2 S UTC−6(−5DT) N31°07.58´ W92°30.08´ **HOUSTON**
140 B NOTAM FILE DRI **L−21B, 22E**
RWY 01−19: H3100X75 (ASPH) S−12 MIRL
  RWY 01: SAVASI(S2R)—GA 4.0° TCH 20´. Trees.
  RWY 19: SAVASI(S2R)—GA 4.0° TCH 20´. Trees.
SERVICE: **LGT** SAVASI Rwy 01 and Rwy 19 OTS indef. Windsock lghts OTS indef. ACTIVATE MIRL Rwy 01−19—122.8.
AIRPORT REMARKS: Unattended. Helicopter tfc on fld. Numerous 2 inch cracks on rwy.
AIRPORT MANAGER: 225-952-8074
COMMUNICATIONS: CTAF 122.9
CLEARANCE DELIVERY PHONE: For CD ctc Polk Apch at 337-531-2352.
RADIO AIDS TO NAVIGATION: NOTAM FILE AEX.
  ALEXANDRIA (H) (H) VORTACW 116.1   AEX Chan 108   N31°15.40´ W92°30.06´   177° 7.8 NM to fld. 76/3E.
  VOR unusable:
    035°−065° blo 2,000´
    066°−094° byd 35 NM blo 3,000´
    185°−200° byd 35 NM blo 3,000´
    201°−214° byd 35 NM blo 2,000´
    215°−260° blo 2,000´
    261°−285° byd 35 NM blo 2,000´
    357°−034° byd 35 NM blo 3,000´

SC, 25 JAN 2024 to 21 MAR 2024

MISSISSIPPI

ABERDEEN/AMORY
MONROE CO (M4Ø)   4 NE   UTC–6(–5DT)   N33°52.43´ W88°29.38´   MEMPHIS
226   B   NOTAM FILE GWO   L–18H
RWY 18–36: H4999X75 (ASPH)   S–21   MIRL   IAP
 RWY 18: REIL. PAPI(P4L)—GA 3.0° TCH 40´. Trees.
 RWY 36: REIL. PAPI(P4L)—GA 3.0° TCH 40´. Trees.
SERVICE: S4   FUEL 100LL, JET A   LGT ACTVT REIL Rwy 18 and 36;
 MIRL Rwy 18–36; twy lgts—CTAF. PAPI Rwy 18 and 36 opr consly.
 Rwy 36 unusbl byd 9° R of cntrln.
AIRPORT REMARKS: Attended 1400–2300Z‡. 110LL 24 hr with credit
 card. After hrs Jet A fuel call 662–436–6122. Pilots must provide
 their own tiedown ropes. Courtesy car avbl.
AIRPORT MANAGER: 662-369-4800
WEATHER DATA SOURCES: AWOS–3P 118.475 (662) 369–3498.
COMMUNICATIONS: CTAF/UNICOM 122.8
®COLUMBUS APP/DEP CON 126.075 (1300–0100Z‡ Mon–Fri,
 1800–2300Z‡ Sun, clsd Sat and hols.)
®MEMPHIS CENTER APP/DEP CON 127.1 (0100–1300Z‡ Mon–Fri,
 2300Z–1800Z‡ Sun, Sat and hols.)
CLEARANCE DELIVERY PHONE: For CD ctc Columbus Apch at 662-434-3044.
RADIO AIDS TO NAVIGATION: NOTAM FILE GWO.
 BIGBEE (L) (L) VORTACW 116.2   IGB   Chan 109   N33°29.13´
  W88°30.82´   359° 23.3 NM to fld. 245/4E.
  VOR portion unusable:
   010°–020°
   200°–260° blo 5,000´

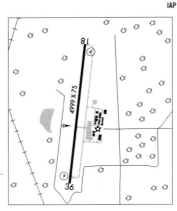

ACKERMAN CHOCTAW CO (9M4)   3 W   UTC–6(–5DT)   N33°18.21´ W89°13.70´   MEMPHIS
552   B   NOTAM FILE GWO   L–18G
RWY 01–19: H3000X75 (ASPH)   S–19.5   MIRL
 RWY 01: PAPI(P2L)—GA 3.0° TCH 42´.
 RWY 19: PAPI(P2L)—GA 3.0° TCH 34´. Tree.
AIRPORT REMARKS: Unattended. Wildlife on and invof arpt. Rwy 01 and 19
 markings faded.
AIRPORT MANAGER: 662-285-7633
COMMUNICATIONS: CTAF 122.9
CLEARANCE DELIVERY PHONE: For CD ctc Memphis ARTCC at
 901-368-8453/8449.
RADIO AIDS TO NAVIGATION: NOTAM FILE GWO.
 BIGBEE (L) (L) VORTACW 116.2   IGB   Chan 109   N33°29.13´
  W88°30.82´   249° 37.5 NM to fld. 245/4E.
  VOR portion unusable:
   010°–020°
   200°–260° blo 5,000´

ALLEN   N32°24.75´ W90°07.17´   NOTAM FILE JAN.   MEMPHIS
 NDB (LOMW) 365   JA   161° 6.5 NM to Jackson–Medgar Wiley Evers Intl. 330/1W.   L–18G

MISSISSIPPI 131

BATESVILLE

PANOLA CO (PMU)(KPMU) 4 NE UTC−6(−5DT) N34°21.81´ W89°53.57´ **MEMPHIS**
221 B NOTAM FILE GWO **H−6J, L−18G**
RWY 01−19: H5001X75 (ASPH) S−30 MIRL **IAP**
   RWY 01: PAPI(P2L)—GA 4.0° TCH 42´. Thld dsplcd 589´. Trees.
   RWY 19: PAPI(P2L)—GA 4.0° TCH 45´. Trees.
SERVICE: S4 **FUEL** 100LL, JET A **LGT** MIRL Rwy 01−19 opr dusk to 0400Z‡, aft 0400Z‡—CTAF. PAPI Rwy 01 and 19 opr consly.
AIRPORT REMARKS: Attended dalgt hrs. Ultralight act on and invof arpt. 100LL self svc with credit card 24 hrs; full svc avbl. Airframe and pwr plant repairs 662−501−5559. Pilots must provide their own tiedown ropes. Crew car avbl; coml car rental nearby.
AIRPORT MANAGER: 662-563-4100
WEATHER DATA SOURCES: AWOS−3PT 118.225 (662) 563−6267.
COMMUNICATIONS: CTAF/UNICOM 122.8
Ⓡ **MEMPHIS CENTER APP/DEP CON** 128.5
CLEARANCE DELIVERY PHONE: For CD ctc Memphis ARTCC at 901-368-8453/8449.
RADIO AIDS TO NAVIGATION: NOTAM FILE GWO.
   HOLLY SPRINGS (L) (L) **VORTACW** 112.4 HLI Chan 71 N34°46.21´ W89°29.79´ 216° 31.3 NM to fld. 624/3E.
   VOR UNUSABL:
     172°−192° byd 25 NM blo 2,400´

BAY SPRINGS

THIGPEN FLD (0ØM) 3 SE UTC−6(−5DT) N31°57.23´ W89°14.12´ **NEW ORLEANS**
351 B NOTAM FILE GWO **L−18G**
RWY 16−34: H3000X50 (ASPH) S−8 MIRL
   RWY 16: Tree.
   RWY 34: Trees.
AIRPORT REMARKS: Unattended.
AIRPORT MANAGER: (601) 580-0469
COMMUNICATIONS: CTAF 122.9
CLEARANCE DELIVERY PHONE: For CD ctc Memphis ARTCC at 901-368-8453/8449.
RADIO AIDS TO NAVIGATION: NOTAM FILE GWO.
   EATON (L) (L) **VORTACW** 110.6 LBY Chan 43 N31°25.12´ W89°20.26´ 004° 32.5 NM to fld. 290/5E.
   VORTAC unusable:
     300°−000° byd 30 NM
   VOR portion unusable:
     111°−164° byd 10 NM blo 2,000´
     241°−251°
   TACAN unusable:
     025°−035° byd 10 NM blo 3,000´
     268°−274° byd 30 NM blo 5,000´

BAY ST LOUIS

STENNIS INTL (HSA)(KHSA)   8 NW   UTC–6(–5DT)   N30°22.07´ W89°27.28´
23   B   LRA   ARFF Index—See Remarks   NOTAM FILE HSA
RWY 18–36: H8498X150 (ASPH–GRVD)   2S–175, 2D–472,
  2D/2D2–955 PCN 62 F/B/X/T   HIRL
  RWY 18: MALSR. PAPI(P4L)—GA 3.0° TCH 56´. Tree.
  RWY 36: REIL. PAPI(P4L)—GA 3.0° TCH 55´. Trees.
RUNWAY DECLARED DISTANCE INFORMATION
  RWY 18: TORA–8498   TODA–8498   ASDA–8498   LDA–8498
  RWY 36: TORA–8498   TODA–8498   ASDA–8498   LDA–8498
SERVICE: S4   **FUEL** 100LL, JET A+   **LGT** ACTVT MALSR Rwy 18; REIL
  Rwy 36; PAPI Rwy 18 and 36; HIRL Rwy 18–36—CTAF.
NOISE: Avoid overflying schools 0.4 NM E of Rwy 18–36 when poss.
AIRPORT REMARKS: Attended Mon–Fri 1300–0100Z‡, Sat–Sun
  1400–0200Z‡. Aft hrs callout—228–463–2389. Birds on and invof
  arpt. Nmrs low flying fish spotter acft ops near shoreline btn Gulfport
  and Bay St. Louis. FBO atndd Mon–Fri 1300–0200Z‡, Sat–Sun
  1400–0000Z‡. Class IV, ARFF Index A. ARFF Index: acr acft of at
  least 31 pax seats or more or cargo ops rqrg incrd ARFF Index, 48 hrs
  PPR 228–342–5415. CLOSED to acft ops with more than 09 psgr
  seat except 48 hr PPR call amgr.
AIRPORT MANAGER: 228-467-7070
WEATHER DATA SOURCES: AWOS–3PT 118.375 (228) 466–9320.
COMMUNICATIONS: CTAF 127.15   UNICOM 122.95
®**GULFPORT APP/DEP CON** 124.6 (130°–309°) 127.5 (310°–129°) (1200–0500Z‡)
®**HOUSTON CENTER APP/DEP CON** 132.6 (0500–1200Z‡)
  TOWER 127.15 (1300–0300Z‡)   **GND CON** 121.725 229.4
CLEARANCE DELIVERY PHONE: When ATCT clsd, for CD ctc Houston ARTCC at 281-230-5622.
AIRSPACE: CLASS D svc 1300–0300Z‡; other times CLASS G.
RADIO AIDS TO NAVIGATION: NOTAM FILE GPT.
  GULFPORT (L) (L) VORTAC 109.0   GPT   Chan 27   N30°24.41´ W89°04.61´   261° 19.7 NM to fld. 25/2E.
  TACAN AZIMUTH unusable:
    195°–217°
    266°–275° byd 12 NM
  VOR unusable:
    035°–086° blo 5,000´
    293°–303°
  HANCO NDB (MHW) 221   HS   N30°27.08´ W89°27.33´   181° 5.0 NM to fld. 94/2W.   NOTAM FILE HSA.
  ILS 110.35   I–HSA   Rwy 18.   Class IE.   LOM HANCO NDB.
COMM/NAV/WEATHER REMARKS: For fuel and FBO svcs aft hrs call 228–463–2389. For all airframe rprs call 228–463–2389.

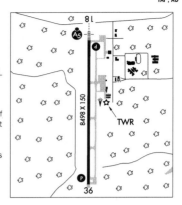

BAYOU   N30°29.14´ W89°09.74´   NOTAM FILE GPT.
  NDB (LOMW) 360   GP   136° 6.7 NM to Gulfport–Biloxi Intl. 83/2W.
  NDB unusable:
    085°–270° byd 10 NM

MISSISSIPPI

BELMONT

TISHOMINGO CO (Ø1M) 2 S UTC–6(–5DT) N34°29.51´ W88°12.07´   **MEMPHIS**
584 B NOTAM FILE GWO   L–18H
RWY 17–35: H4026X59 (ASPH) S–20 MIRL
  RWY 17: Thld dsplcd 512´. Trees.
  RWY 35: Tree.
SERVICE: **FUEL** 100LL **LGT** ACTVT MIRL Rwy 17–35—CTAF.
AIRPORT REMARKS: Unattended. 110LL fuel svc 24 hrs with credit card. For fuel and svc aft hrs call 662–279–0310.
AIRPORT MANAGER: 662–279–0310
COMMUNICATIONS: CTAF/UNICOM 122.8
CLEARANCE DELIVERY PHONE: For CD ctc Memphis ARTCC at 901–368–8453/8449.

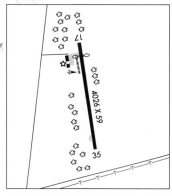

BELZONI MUNI (1M2) 3 SW UTC–6(–5DT) N33°08.71´ W90°30.92´   **MEMPHIS**
110 B NOTAM FILE GWO   L–18G
RWY 03–21: H3000X50 (ASPH) S–24 MIRL
  RWY 03: PAPI(P2L)—GA 3.0° TCH 40´. P–line.
  RWY 21: PAPI(P2L)—GA 3.0° TCH 40´.
SERVICE: **LGT** MIRL Rwy 03–21 preset low intst; higher intst actvt—CTAF. PAPI Rwy 21 OTS indefly. Rwy 21 VGSI OTS indef.
AIRPORT REMARKS: Unattended. Arpt CLOSED at ngt.
AIRPORT MANAGER: 662-962-4840
COMMUNICATIONS: CTAF 122.9
CLEARANCE DELIVERY PHONE: For CD ctc Memphis ARTCC at 901–368–8453/8449.
RADIO AIDS TO NAVIGATION: NOTAM FILE GWO.
  SIDON (VH) (H) VORTAC 114.7 SQS Chan 94 N33°27.83´ W90°16.64´ 209° 22.5 NM to fld. 127/3E.
  VOR unusable:
    059°–069° byd 40 NM

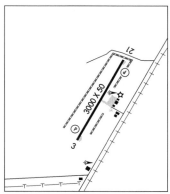

BIGBEE N33°29.13´ W88°30.82´ NOTAM FILE GWO.   **MEMPHIS**
(L) (L) **VORTACW** 116.2 IGB Chan 109 236° 4.5 NM to Golden Triangle Rgnl. 245/4E.   H–6J, L–18H
  VOR portion unusable:
    010°–020°
    200°–260° blo 5,000´
RCO 122.4 (GREENWOOD RADIO)

MISSISSIPPI

BOONEVILLE/BALDWYN (8M1) 6 SW UTC−6(−5DT) N34°35.51′ W88°38.91′
392 B NOTAM FILE GWO
RWY 15−33: H5003X75 (ASPH−GRVD) S−20 MIRL 0.3% up NW
 RWY 15: REIL. PAPI(P2L)—GA 3.0° TCH 40′. Trees.
 RWY 33: REIL. PAPI(P2L)—GA 3.0° TCH 40′. Trees.
SERVICE: **FUEL** 100LL, JET A **LGT** ACTIVATE MIRL Rwy 15−33—CTAF.
AIRPORT REMARKS: Attended 1400−2000Z‡. 100LL avbl 24 hrs with credit card.
AIRPORT MANAGER: 662-210-1773
COMMUNICATIONS: CTAF/UNICOM 122.8
®**MEMPHIS CENTER APP/DEP CON** 135.9
CLEARANCE DELIVERY PHONE: For CD ctc Memphis ARTCC at 901-368-8453/8449.
RADIO AIDS TO NAVIGATION: NOTAM FILE TUP.
 TUPELO (L) (L) VORW/DME 109.8 OTB Chan 35 N34°13.43′
 W88°47.84′ 014° 23.2 NM to fld. 364/4E.
 VOR portion unusable:
 190°−220°

MEMPHIS
H−6J, L−18G
IAP

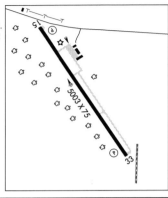

BRENZ N32°24.78′ W90°15.68′ NOTAM FILE HKS.
 NDB (MHW/LOM) 260 JH 157° 5.1 NM to Hawkins Fld. 314/0W. NDB unmonitored when ATCT clsd.

MEMPHIS
L−18G

BROOKHAVEN−LINCOLN CO (1R7) 3 NE UTC−6(−5DT) N31°36.35′ W90°24.56′
492 B NOTAM FILE GWO
RWY 05−23: H5000X75 (ASPH) S−27 MIRL
 RWY 05: PAPI(P2L)—GA 3.0° TCH 40′. Thld dsplcd 635′. Trees.
 RWY 23: PAPI(P2L)—GA 3.0° TCH 40′. Thld dsplcd 994′. Trees.
SERVICE: **FUEL** 100LL, JET A+ **LGT** Actvt MIRL Rwy 05−23—CTAF. PAPI Rwy 05 opr dusk−dawn. PAPI Rwy 23 opr consly. Wind indicator lgt opr dusk−dawn.
AIRPORT REMARKS: Attended Mon−Friday 1400−2300Z‡. Aft hrs 601−754−6588. PAEW at random times. 100LL svc avbl 24 hrs with credit card. Airframe rprs avbl−601−695−9874. Tall trees on AER 23.
AIRPORT MANAGER: 601-833-0999
WEATHER DATA SOURCES: AWOS−3P 118.125 (601) 833-3209.
COMMUNICATIONS: CTAF/UNICOM 122.8
®**HOUSTON CENTER APP/DEP CON** 126.8
CLEARANCE DELIVERY PHONE: For CD ctc Houston ARTCC at 281-230-5622.
RADIO AIDS TO NAVIGATION: NOTAM FILE MCB.
 MC COMB (H) (H) VORTAC 116.7 MCB Chan 114 N31°18.27′
 W90°15.49′ 334° 19.6 NM to fld. 440/3E.

NEW ORLEANS
H−6J, L−22F
IAP

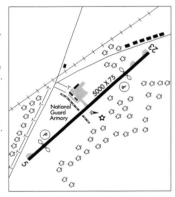

BRUCE CAMPBELL FLD (See MADISON on page 156)

C A MOORE (See LEXINGTON on page 154)

CALEDONIA N33°38.49′ W88°26.31′ NOTAM FILE CBM.
 (L) (L) VORTACW 115.2 CBM Chan 99 at Columbus AFB. 250/0E.
 military use: mnt 1300−0100Z‡ Mon−Fri; 1800−2300Z‡ Sun. No NOTAM MP: 0200−0400Z‡ Sun
 VOR unusable:
  317°−223°
 TACAN AZIMUTH unusable:
  015°−030° byd 20 NM blo 4,000′
 DME unusable:
  015°−030° byd 20 NM blo 4,000′
  080°−100° byd 35 NM blo 3,500′

MEMPHIS
L−18H

CALHOUN CO (See PITTSBORO on page 165)

MISSISSIPPI

CARTHAGE–LEAKE CO (Ø8M)   2 N   UTC–6(–5DT)   N32°45.70′ W89°31.82′   MEMPHIS
457   B   NOTAM FILE GWO   L–18G
RWY 17–35: H3000X75 (ASPH) S–20   MIRL
 RWY 17: Trees.
 RWY 35: Tree.
SERVICE: S2   **FUEL** 100LL   **LGT** Dusk–0400Z‡. Aft 0400Z‡ actvt MIRL Rwy 17–35—CTAF.
AIRPORT REMARKS: Unattended. 100LL fuel avbl 24 hrs with credit card. Pilots must prvd their own tiedown ropes.
AIRPORT MANAGER: 601-267-9327
COMMUNICATIONS: CTAF 122.9
CLEARANCE DELIVERY PHONE: For CD ctc Memphis ARTCC at 901-368-8453/8449.
RADIO AIDS TO NAVIGATION: NOTAM FILE GWO.
 MAGNOLIA (VH) (H) VORTACW 113.2   MHZ   Chan 79   N32°26.04′ W90°05.99′   057° 34.9 NM to fld. 407/1W.
 TACAN AZIMUTH unusable:
  240°–275° byd 30 NM blo 2,000′
  DME unsbl 240–275 byd 30 NM blo 2000′

CHARLESTON MUNI (Ø9M)   2 S   UTC–6(–5DT)   N33°59.48′ W90°04.71′   MEMPHIS
175   B   NOTAM FILE GWO   L–18G
RWY 18–36: H3000X50 (ASPH)   S–18   MIRL
 RWY 18: Tree.
 RWY 36: Pole.
AIRPORT REMARKS: Unattended. Public phone avbl 662-647-9484.
AIRPORT MANAGER: 662-515-8391
COMMUNICATIONS: CTAF 122.9
CLEARANCE DELIVERY PHONE: For CD ctc Memphis ARTCC at 901-368-8453/8449.
RADIO AIDS TO NAVIGATION: NOTAM FILE GWO.
 SIDON (VH) (H) VORTAC 114.7   SQS   Chan 94   N33°27.83′ W90°16.64′   014° 33.1 NM to fld. 127/3E.
 VOR unusable:
  059°–069° byd 40 NM

CLARKE CO (See QUITMAN on page 167)

CLARKSDALE

FLETCHER FLD (CKM)(KCKM)   7 NE   UTC–6(–5DT)   N34°17.98′ W90°30.74′   MEMPHIS
173   B   NOTAM FILE GWO   H–6J, L–18G
RWY 18–36: H5404X100 (ASPH–GRVD)   S–25, D–32 PCN 30 F/A/W/T   IAP
 MIRL
 RWY 18: REIL. PAPI(P2L)—GA 3.0° TCH 26′.
 RWY 36: REIL. PAPI(P2L)—GA 3.0° TCH 26′. Trees.
SERVICE: S7   **FUEL** 100LL, JET A   **LGT** Actvt REIL Rwy 18 and 36; PAPI Rwy 18 and 36; MIRL Rwy 18–36—CTAF.
AIRPORT REMARKS: Attended dalgt hrs. Nmrs agricultural acft ops W of N/S twy. Acft dep N and land S. 100LL avbl 24 hrs with credit card. Twy lgts on S stub twy to apn. Rwy 18–36, 1 hr PPR for acft over 30000 lbs, call 662-624-5554 or 662-902-1893. Pilots must provide their own tiedown ropes.
AIRPORT MANAGER: 662-627-4126
WEATHER DATA SOURCES: AWOS–3 120.675 (662) 624–9777.
COMMUNICATIONS: CTAF/UNICOM 122.8
Ⓡ**MEMPHIS CENTER APP/DEP CON** 135.2
CLEARANCE DELIVERY PHONE: For CD ctc Memphis ARTCC at 901-368-8453/8449.
RADIO AIDS TO NAVIGATION: NOTAM FILE JBR.
 MARVELL (VL) (L) VORW/DME 113.65   UJM   Chan 83(Y)   N34°34.50′ W90°40.46′   153° 18.3 NM to fld. 243/1E.
 DME unusable:
  030°–064°
  065°–094° byd 27 NM blo 3,500′
  095°–114° byd 29 NM blo 4,000′
  115°–129° byd 29 NM blo 3,500′
  130°–190° byd 34 NM blo 2,800′

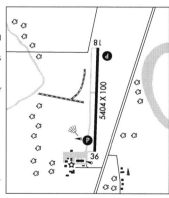

SC, 25 JAN 2024 to 21 MAR 2024

MISSISSIPPI

CLEVELAND MUNI (RNV)(KRNV) 2 NW UTC–6(–5DT) N33°45.75′ W90°45.48′ MEMPHIS
140 B NOTAM FILE GWO L–18F
RWY 18–36: H5005X75 (ASPH) S–26 MIRL IAP
  RWY 18: REIL. PAPI(P4L)—GA 3.0° TCH 42′.
  RWY 36: REIL. PAPI(P4R)—GA 3.25° TCH 46′. Trees.
SERVICE: S4 **FUEL** 100LL, JET A **LGT** ACTIVATE REIL Rwy 18–36; MIRL
  Rwy 18–36—CTAF. PAPI Rwy 18 and Rwy 36 opr continuously.
AIRPORT REMARKS: Attended Mon–Fri 1400–2300Z‡, Sat–Sun on call.
  100LL fuel avbl with credit card 24 hrs. Student act on and invof arpt.
AIRPORT MANAGER: 662-719-1189
WEATHER DATA SOURCES: AWOS–3PT 124.175 (662) 843–3021.
COMMUNICATIONS: CTAF/UNICOM 122.725
®**MEMPHIS CENTER APP/DEP CON** 135.875
CLEARANCE DELIVERY PHONE: For CD ctc Memphis ARTCC at
  901-368-8453/8449.
RADIO AIDS TO NAVIGATION: NOTAM FILE GLH.
  GREENVILLE (VL) (DH) VOR/DME 114.25 GLH Chan 89(Y)
    N33°31.41′ W90°58.98′ 034° 18.2 NM to fld. 130/4E.
  VOR unusable:
    144°–157° byd 40 NM

COLUMBIA/MARION CO (ØRØ) 3 N UTC–6(–5DT) N31°17.87′ W89°48.69′ NEW ORLEANS
270 B NOTAM FILE GWO L–21B, 22F
RWY 05–23: H5500X100 (ASPH) S–63, D–90, 2D–174 IAP
  PCN 23 F/B/X/T MIRL 0.5% up NE
  RWY 05: REIL. PAPI(P4L)—GA 3.0° TCH 42′. Trees.
  RWY 23: REIL. PAPI(P4L)—GA 3.0° TCH 43′. Tree.
SERVICE: **FUEL** 100LL, JET A **LGT** Actvt REIL Rwy 05 and 23; MIRL
  Rwy 05–23—CTAF. PAPI Rwy 05 and 23 opr consly.
AIRPORT REMARKS: Attended on call. For svc call 601–441–0299 or
  601–441–1867. Fuel svc avbl 24 hrs with credit card. Pub Fone avbl
  601–736–9295.
AIRPORT MANAGER: 601-736-9295
WEATHER DATA SOURCES: AWOS–3PT 120.675 (601) 736–4983.
COMMUNICATIONS: CTAF/UNICOM 122.8
®**HOUSTON CENTER APP/DEP CON** 126.8
CLEARANCE DELIVERY PHONE: For CD ctc Houston ARTCC at 281-230-5622.
RADIO AIDS TO NAVIGATION: NOTAM FILE GWO.
  EATON (L) (L) VORTACW 110.6 LBY Chan 43 N31°25.12′
    W89°20.26′ 249° 25.4 NM to fld. 290/5E.
  VORTAC unusable:
    300°–000° byd 30 NM
  VOR portion unusable:
    111°–164° byd 10 NM blo 2,000′
    241°–251°
  TACAN unusable:
    025°–035° byd 10 NM blo 3,000′
    268°–274° byd 30 NM blo 5,000′

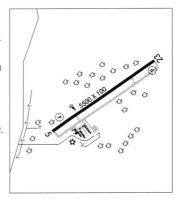

SC, 25 JAN 2024 to 21 MAR 2024

MISSISSIPPI

COLUMBUS AFB (CBM)(KCBM) AF   9 N   UTC–6(–5DT)   N33°38.71′ W88°26.76′   **MEMPHIS**
218   B   TPA—See Remarks   NOTAM FILE CBM   Not insp.   **H–6J, L–18H**
RWY 13C–31C: H12004X300 (ASPH–CONC)   PCN 55 R/B/W/T   HIRL   **DIAP, AD**
  RWY 13C: ALSF1. PAPI(P4L)—GA 3.0° TCH 47′.
  RWY 31C: ALSF1. PAPI(P4L)—GA 3.0° TCH 47′.
RWY 13L–31R: H8001X150 (ASPH–CONC)   PCN 28 R/B/W/T   HIRL
  RWY 13L: PAPI(P4L)—GA 3.0° TCH 40′.
  RWY 31R: PAPI(P4L)—GA 3.0° TCH 36′.
RWY 13R–31L: H6320X175 (CONC)   PCN 33 R/B/W/T   MIRL
  RWY 13R: PAPI(P4L)—GA 3.0° TCH 39′.
  RWY 31L: PAPI(P4L)—GA 3.0° TCH 37′.
ARRESTING GEAR/SYSTEM
  RWY 13C MA–1A CHAG (111 FT OVRN)   MA–1A CHAG (111 FT OVRN) **RWY 31C**
  RWY 13L BAK–15 CHAG (130 FT OVRN)   BAK–15 CHAG (130 FT OVRN) **RWY 31R**
SERVICE: S4   **FUEL** JET A++   **OX** 2, 4   **MILITARY**— **A–GEAR** MA–1A cont raised posn on dep end of cntr rwy, down and disconnected on apch end. BAK–15 Rwy 13L–31R uncertified/unsvc. Sun only. **JASU** 1(MD–3) 2(A/M32A–86) 3(AM32–95) **FUEL** A++. **FLUID** LPOX LOX **OIL** O–148–156; SOAP–results avbl Mon–Fri.
  TRAN ALERT Tran opr 1300–2300Z‡ wkd; no tran svc Sun wo prior cnd; clsd Sat and hol. OT by NOTAM.
NOISE: Noise abatement: Quiet hr daily 0400–1200Z‡.
MILITARY REMARKS: Opr 1300–0100Z‡ Mon–Fri, 1800–2300Z‡ Sun. Clsd Sat and hols; adnl dates/times intmt by NOTAM. **RSTD:** PPR; only 4 acft per hr dur stu trng. Overhead apch not auth dur stu trng opr. Rwy 13R–31L for lcl use only dur stu trng. All tsnt aircrews ck in with Base Ops. Exp radar vector for full stop ldg dur stu trng. Alt rstd for VMC dep acft. **CAUTION** Uncontrolled vehicle tfc on twy and ramps. Do not mistake parl twy to Rwy 13R–31L for rwy. Rwy 13R–31L addn mkgs for base asgn T–38 emerg lndg only. Rwy 13R overrun 1000 ft full strength pavement, Rwy 31C overrun 1635 ft full strength pavement. Exer caution when braking wet; ponding cond exists on asphalt portions of all rwys. Rwy 13R rwy hold sign at Twy A not collocated with pavement mrk. BA less than exp, reduced rwy skid resistance and hi potential for hydroplaning all rwy when wet. Rwy CC not rptd. Use caution at int Twy G and C, and J and C. Both apn edges inside require 25 ft from twy cntrln. T–1 ramp E of ctl twr is lctd in Rwy 31L clear zone. All 50 ft shoulders not marked with deceptive shoulder markings. Numerous signs on airfield are outside dist and sitting criteria. Acft within Rwy Supervisory Unit (RSU) practice area are not Class C participants. Potential transit/divert UAS ops within trml area. BASH–Phase II bird act for migratory season Sep–Apr. Peak act occurs within 1 hr of SR and SS, see AP/1 Chap 3 for more info. Obtain current bird watch conditions on ATIS. **TFC PAT** TPA—Overhead–1700 ft, Rectangular–1200 ft, Copter–700 ft. **MISC** Ltd hgr space avbl Apr–Dec. First 1000 ft Rwy 13L–31R is concrete, mid 6000 ft asphalt. Rwy 13R–31L is grooved concrete. Rwy 13C–31C cntr 200′ grooved concrete, 50′ outside portions asphalt. Rwy 13R–31L contr 75′ grooved conc outside portions asphalt. Augmented wx observation view limited, restricted from 140°–320° by flightline facilities and trees. Std USAF RSRS applied. ATC pers IAW the cooperative wx (CCW) watch will alert pers on any unreported wx cond that could afct flt safety. Auto AN/FMQ–19 ASOS in use H24 lctd near GS Rwy 13C–31C. Augmented/backed up AN/FMQ–19 ASOS in use when req dur opr hr and for resource protect on. Opr hr may vary with lcl flying sched. Winds are est due to FMQ–13 wind sensors being accurate to within only +/– 4 kt. ATC wx will not incl/relay wind corr into fcst/phraseology. Therefore, aircrews will incorporate a +/– 4 kt accuracy into their decision making process for flying ops. Afld ops does not have ability to store COMSEC. Ctc Comd Post, DSN 742–7020, C–662–434–7020 for COMSEC storage. ASR apch svc avbl for emergency and other time contingent upon manpower and equipment availability. Secondary ASR is MSSR.
AIRPORT MANAGER: 662-434-2993
WEATHER DATA SOURCES: ASOS 354.6.
COMMUNICATIONS: ATIS 115.2 273.5 (Mon–Fri 1300–0100Z‡, Sun 1800–2300Z‡, clsd Sat and hols.) **PTD** 376.0
®**COLUMBUS APP CON** 126.075 239.25 (310°–090°)   134.55 291.65 350.3 (090°–165°)   135.6 323.275 (165°–310°) 133.25 307.8(ARR)   121.075 134.55 263.15 317.15
  MEMPHIS CENTER APP/DEP CON 127.1 (0100–1300Z‡ Mon–Fri, 2300Z–1800Z‡ Sun, Sat and hols.)
  COLUMBUS TOWER 126.65 379.925 (1300–0100Z‡ Mon–Fri, 1800–2300Z‡ Sun, clsd Sat and hols.)
  GND CON 121.9 275.8 **CLNC DEL** 269.55
®**COLUMBUS DEP CON** 134.55 263.15 350.3 135.6 291.65 (090°–165°)   323.275   **COMD POST** 251.25 **PMSV METRO** 354.6 Wx opr H24 0600Z‡ Mon thru 0100Z‡ Sat, 1500–2300Z‡ Sun, clsd Sat and hols; opr hrs may vary by lcl flying sked. Ctc C662–434–2992/DSN 742–2992. Remote briefing svc avbl Barksdale AFB fr 26 OWS DSN 331–2651/2/3, C318–529–2651/2/3. **SOF** 252.1.
AIRSPACE: CLASS C svc ctc **APP CON** svc 1300–0100Z‡ Mon–Fri, 1800–2300Z‡ Sun, clsd Sat and hols, adnl dates/times intmt by NOTAM; other times CLASS G..

CONTINUED ON NEXT PAGE

MISSISSIPPI

CONTINUED FROM PRECEDING PAGE

RADIO AIDS TO NAVIGATION: NOTAM FILE CBM.
  CALEDONIA (L) (L) VORTACW 115.2   CBM   Chan 99   N33°38.49´ W88°26.31´   at fld. 250/0E.
    military use: mnt 1300–0100Z‡ Mon–Fri; 1800–2300Z‡ Sun. No NOTAM MP: 0200–0400Z‡ Sun
    VOR unusable:
      317°–223°
    TACAN AZIMUTH unusable:
      015°–030° byd 20 NM blo 4,000´
    DME unusable:
      015°–030° byd 20 NM blo 4,000´
      080°–100° byd 35 NM blo 3,500´
  BIGBEE (L) (L) VORTACW 116.2   IGB   Chan 109   N33°29.13´ W88°30.82´   016° 10.1 NM to fld.
    245/4E. NOTAM FILE GWO.
    VOR portion unusable:
      010°–020°
      200°–260° blo 5,000´
  ILS 109.3   I–CBM   Rwy 13C.   Class ID.   ILS mnt 1300–0100Z‡ Mon–Fri; 1800–2300Z‡ Sun, clsd Sat and hol. No
    NOTAM MP: 2400Z‡ Sun. Radar–See Terminal FLIP for Radar Minima.
  ILS 108.7   I–TBB   Rwy 31C.   Class IE.   ILS mnt 1300–0100Z‡ Mon–Fri; 1800–2300Z‡ Sun, clsd Sat and hol.

COLUMBUS–LOWNDES CO (UBS)(KUBS)   3 SE   UTC–6(–5DT)   N33°27.92´ W88°22.85´   **MEMPHIS**
188   B   NOTAM FILE GWO   **L–18H**
RWY 18–36: H4503X100 (ASPH)   S–40, D–70, 2S–89, 2D–120   MIRL   **IAP**
  RWY 18: PAPI(P2L)—GA 3.0° TCH 40´. Trees.
  RWY 36: PAPI(P2L)—GA 3.0° TCH 40´. Trees.
SERVICE: S4 **FUEL** 100LL, JET A+ **LGT** MIRL Rwy 18–36 opr
  dusk–0400Z‡, aft 0400Z‡ Actvt—CTAF. PAPI Rwy 18 and 36 opr
  consly. Rwy 36 VGSI OTS UFN.
AIRPORT REMARKS: Attended Mon–Fri 1500–0000Z‡, Sat–Sun on call. Fuel
  avbl 24 hrs with credit card. Call ahead for hangar space. Courtesy car
  avbl.
AIRPORT MANAGER: 662-251-4650
COMMUNICATIONS: CTAF/UNICOM 122.8
®**COLUMBUS APP/DEP CON** 135.6 (1300–0100Z‡) Mon–Fri, 1800–2300Z‡
  Sun, clsd Sat and hols.)
®**MEMPHIS CENTER APP/DEP CON** 127.1 (0100–1300Z‡ Mon–Fri,
  2300Z–1800Z‡ Sun, Sat and hols.)
CLEARANCE DELIVERY PHONE: For CD ctc Memphis ARTCC at
  901-368-8453/8449.
RADIO AIDS TO NAVIGATION: NOTAM FILE GWO.
  BIGBEE (L) (L) VORTACW 116.2   IGB   Chan 109   N33°29.13´
    W88°30.82´   096° 6.8 NM to fld. 245/4E.
  VOR portion unusable:
    010°–020°
    200°–260° blo 5,000´

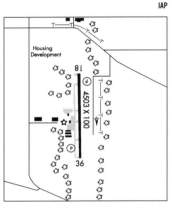

SC, 25 JAN 2024 to 21 MAR 2024

MISSISSIPPI

COLUMBUS/W POINT/STARKVILLE

GOLDEN TRIANGLE RGNL (GTR)(KGTR)   10 W   UTC−6(−5DT)   N33°26.90′ W88°35.48′   **MEMPHIS**
264 B ARFF Index—See Remarks NOTAM FILE GTR   H−6J, L−18H
RWY 18−36: H8003X150 (ASPH−GRVD) S−120, D−239, 2D−385,   IAP, AD
 2D/2D2−669 PCN 63 F/C/X/T HIRL
 RWY 18: MALSR. PAPI(P4R)—GA 3.0° TCH 56′.
 RWY 36: PAPI(P4L)—GA 3.0° TCH 55′.
SERVICE: S2 **FUEL** 100LL, JET A, A+ **LGT** Actvt MALSR rwy 18; PAPI
 rwy 18 and rwy 36; HIRL rwy 18−36; twy lgts—CTAF.
AIRPORT REMARKS: Attended continuously. Birds and wildlife invof arpt.
 Arpt and rwy conds not mnt 0400−1100Z‡. Class I, ARFF Index A.
 Index B ARFF eqpt avbl ctc arpt manager 662−327−4422.
AIRPORT MANAGER: 662-327-4422
WEATHER DATA SOURCES: AWOS−3PT 126.375 (662) 328−7798.
COMMUNICATIONS: CTAF 118.2 ATIS 126.375 UNICOM 122.95
®**COLUMBUS APP/DEP CON** 135.6 (1300−0100Z‡ Mon−Fri,
 1800−2300Z‡ Sun, clsd Sat and hols.)
®**MEMPHIS CENTER APP/DEP CON** 127.1 (0100−1300Z‡ Mon−Fri,
 2300Z−1800Z‡ Sun, Sat and hols.)
 COLUMBUS CLNC DEL 126.25
 TOWER 118.2 (1200−0200Z‡) **GND CON** 135.375 **CLNC DEL** 135.375
AIRSPACE: CLASS D svc 1200−0200Z‡; other times CLASS E.
RADIO AIDS TO NAVIGATION: NOTAM FILE GWO.
 BIGBEE (L) (L) VORTACW 116.2   IGB   Chan 109   N33°29.13′ W88°30.82′   236° 4.5 NM to fld. 245/4E.
 VOR portion unusable:
  010°−020°
  200°−260° blo 5,000′
 ILS 110.7 I−GTR Rwy 18.
 ILS/DME 111.15 I−RVT Chan 48(Y) Rwy 36. Class IA.

COPIAH CO (See CRYSTAL SPRINGS on page 140)

CORINTH

ROSCOE TURNER (CRX)(KCRX)   4 SW   UTC−6(−5DT)   N34°54.90′ W88°36.21′   **MEMPHIS**
425 B NOTAM FILE GWO   H−6J, L−18G
RWY 18−36: H6500X100 (ASPH−GRVD) S−30 MIRL 0.3% up S   IAP
 RWY 18: MALSR. PAPI(P2L)—GA 3.0° TCH 50′.
 RWY 36: PAPI(P2L)—GA 3.0° TCH 59′.
SERVICE: S4 **FUEL** 100LL, JET A **LGT** ACTVT MALSR Rwy 18; MIRL
 Rwy 18−36—CTAF.
AIRPORT REMARKS: Attended Mon−Sun 1300−2300Z‡. Clsd Christmas and
 Thanksgiving. Fuel avbl 24 hrs credit card svc.
AIRPORT MANAGER: 662-287-3223
WEATHER DATA SOURCES: AWOS−3PT 118.675 (662) 287−5103.
COMMUNICATIONS: CTAF/UNICOM 122.8
®**MEMPHIS CENTER APP/DEP CON** 135.9
CLEARANCE DELIVERY PHONE: For CD ctc Memphis ARTCC at
 901-368-8453/8449.
RADIO AIDS TO NAVIGATION: NOTAM FILE GWO.
 SEYER NDB (LOMW) 334 UU N35°00.94′
  W88°36.94′   176° 6.1 NM to fld. 510/2W.
 ILS 111.1 I−UUR Rwy 18. Class IA. LOM SEYER NDB. Autopilot
  coupled approaches NA blo 1,040′ MSL.

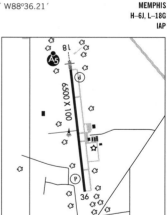

MISSISSIPPI

CROSBY MUNI (C71)   1 NE   UTC–6(–5DT)   N31°17.78´ W91°03.15´   HOUSTON
336   NOTAM FILE GWO   L–21B, 22F
RWY 17–35: H3127X60 (ASPH)   S–16
  RWY 17: Trees.
  RWY 35: Trees.
SERVICE: **LGT** Wind indicator lgts OTS.
AIRPORT REMARKS: Unattended. Deer on and invof arpt. Rwy markings are faded. Pilots must provide their own tiedown ropes.
AIRPORT MANAGER: 601-639-4516
COMMUNICATIONS: CTAF 122.9
CLEARANCE DELIVERY PHONE: For CD ctc Houston ARTCC at 281-230-5622.
RADIO AIDS TO NAVIGATION: NOTAM FILE HEZ.
  NATCHEZ (L) DME 110.0   HEZ   Chan 37   N31°37.09´ W91°17.98´   147° 23.1 NM to fld. 280.
  DME unusable:
    Byd 25 NM blo 4,000´

CRYSTAL SPRINGS

COPIAH CO (M11)   4 S   UTC–6(–5DT)   N31°54.15´ W90°22.01´   NEW ORLEANS
435   B   NOTAM FILE GWO   L–22F
    IAP
RWY 18–36: H4007X75 (ASPH)   S–10   MIRL
  RWY 18: REIL. PAPI(P2R)—GA 4.0° TCH 48´.
  RWY 36: REIL. PAPI(P2L)—GA 3.0° TCH 44´. Trees.
SERVICE: S4   **FUEL** 100LL, JET A1
AIRPORT REMARKS: Attended Mon–Sat 1400–2300Z‡. Aft hr ctc AMGR.
Fuel 24 hrs with credit card. Pilots must provide tiedown ropes.
Courtesy car avbl.
AIRPORT MANAGER: 601-594-2204
COMMUNICATIONS: CTAF 122.9
®**MEMPHIS CENTER APP/DEP CON** 132.5
CLEARANCE DELIVERY PHONE: For CD ctc Memphis ARTCC at
901-368-8453/8449.
RADIO AIDS TO NAVIGATION: NOTAM FILE MCB.
  MC COMB (H) (H) VORTAC 116.7   MCB   Chan 114   N31°18.27´
  W90°15.49´   348° 36.2 NM to fld. 440/3E.

MISSISSIPPI 141

DEAN GRIFFIN MEML (See WIGGINS on page 173)

DIAMONDHEAD (66Y)   0 SW   UTC–6(–5DT)   N30°21.78′ W89°23.26′   **NEW ORLEANS**
14   NOTAM FILE GWO   **L–21C, 22G**
RWY 18–36: H3800X75 (ASPH)   S–12   RWY LGTS(NSTD)
  RWY 18: Thld dsplcd 613′. Trees.
SERVICE: S4   **FUEL** 100LL   **LGT** Rwy 18 LIRL dthr bar and lgts lctd 423′ S of pavement end.
AIRPORT REMARKS: Attended Mon–Fri 1400–2300Z‡, Sat 1330–2230Z‡. Wildlife invof of rwy. Fuel avbl 24 hrs with credit card.
AIRPORT MANAGER: (228) 216-1935
COMMUNICATIONS: CTAF/UNICOM 123.0
CLEARANCE DELIVERY PHONE: For CD ctc Gulfport Apch at 228-265-6151, when Apch clsd ctc Houston ARTCC at 281-230-5622.
RADIO AIDS TO NAVIGATION: NOTAM FILE GPT.
  GULFPORT (L) (L) VORTAC 109.0   GPT   Chan 27   N30°24.41′ W89°04.61′   259° 16.3 NM to fld. 25/2E.
    TACAN AZIMUTH unusable:
      195°–217°
      266°–275° byd 12 NM
    VOR unusable:
      035°–086° blo 5,000′
      293°–303°

DREW

RULEVILLE–DREW (M37)   2 S   UTC–6(–5DT)   N33°46.58′ W90°31.50′   **MEMPHIS**
137   B   NOTAM FILE GWO   **L–18G**
RWY 18–36: H3000X60 (ASPH)   S–16   MIRL   **IAP**
  RWY 18: PAPI(P2L)—GA 3.0° TCH 40′.
  RWY 36: PAPI(P2L)—GA 3.0° TCH 40′.
SERVICE: **LGT** MIRL Rwy 18–36 ops dusk–0400Z‡; aft 0400Z‡
  ACTVT—CTAF. PAPI Rwy 18 and 36 opr consly. Bcn OTS indef.
AIRPORT REMARKS: Attended irregularly. Pilots must provide their own tiedown ropes.
AIRPORT MANAGER: 662-745-2733
COMMUNICATIONS: CTAF 122.9
Ⓡ**MEMPHIS CENTER APP/DEP CON** 135.875
CLEARANCE DELIVERY PHONE: For CD ctc Memphis ARTCC at 901-368-8453/8449.
RADIO AIDS TO NAVIGATION: NOTAM FILE GWO.
  SIDON (VH) (H) VORTAC 114.7   SQS   Chan 94   N33°27.83′ W90°16.64′   324° 22.5 NM to fld. 127/3E.
    VOR unusable:
      059°–069° byd 40 NM

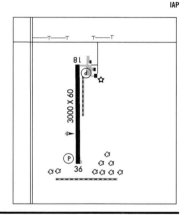

EAGLES RIDGE (See HERNANDO on page 147)

EATON   N31°25.12′ W89°20.26′   NOTAM FILE GWO.   **NEW ORLEANS**
(L) (L) **VORTACW** 110.6   LBY   Chan 43   356° 2.9 NM to Hattiesburg/Laurel Rgnl. 290/5E.   **H–6J, L–22G**
  VORTAC unusable:
    300°–000° byd 30 NM
  VOR portion unusable:
    111°–164° byd 10 NM blo 2,000′
    241°–251°
  TACAN unusable:
    025°–035° byd 10 NM blo 3,000′
    268°–274° byd 30 NM blo 5,000′

SC, 25 JAN 2024 to 21 MAR 2024

MISSISSIPPI

EUPORA (Ø6M) 2 W UTC−6(−5DT) N33°32.09′ W89°18.79′ MEMPHIS
450 B NOTAM FILE GWO L−18G
RWY 14−32: H3000X60 (ASPH) S−20 MIRL
  RWY 14: PAPI(P2L)—GA 3.0° TCH 35′. Tree.
  RWY 32: PAPI(P2L)—GA 3.0° TCH 42′.
SERVICE: **LGT** Actvt PAPI Rwy 14 and 32; MIRL Rwy 14−32—CTAF.
AIRPORT REMARKS: Unattended.
AIRPORT MANAGER: 662-258-2291
COMMUNICATIONS: CTAF 122.9
CLEARANCE DELIVERY PHONE: For CD ctc Memphis ARTCC at 901-368-8453/8449.
RADIO AIDS TO NAVIGATION: NOTAM FILE GWO.
  BIGBEE (L) (L) VORTACW 116.2 IGB Chan 109 N33°29.13′ W88°30.82′ 270° 40.2 NM to fld. 245/4E.
  VOR portion unusable:
    010°−020°
    200°−260° blo 5,000′

FERNI N31°15.27′ W90°30.62′ NOTAM FILE MCB. NEW ORLEANS
NDB (MHW/LOM) 413 MC 157° 5.0 NM to Mc Comb/Pike Co/John E Lewis Fld. 447/1W. L−21B, 22F

FLETCHER FLD (See CLARKSDALE on page 135)

FOREST

G V MONTGOMERY (2M4) 1 S UTC−6(−5DT) N32°21.30′ W89°29.29′ MEMPHIS
518 B NOTAM FILE GWO L−18G
RWY 17−35: H3602X75 (ASPH) S−25 MIRL
  RWY 17: Trees.
  RWY 35: Tree.
SERVICE: **LGT** MIRL Rwy 17−35 opr 2300−0400Z‡, after 0400Z‡ ACTIVATE—CTAF.
AIRPORT REMARKS: Unattended. Pilots must provide their own tiedown ropes.
AIRPORT MANAGER: 601-900-8255
COMMUNICATIONS: CTAF/UNICOM 122.8
CLEARANCE DELIVERY PHONE: For CD ctc Memphis ARTCC at 901-368-8453/8449.
RADIO AIDS TO NAVIGATION: NOTAM FILE MEI.
  MERIDIAN (VH) (H) VORTAC 117.0 MEI Chan 117 N32°22.71′ W88°48.26′ 263° 34.8 NM to fld. 578/5E.
  VOR unusable:
    000°−042° byd 40 NM
    054°−061° byd 40 NM blo 24,000′
    062°−082° byd 40 NM blo 16,000′
    083°−192° byd 40 NM
    193°−203° byd 40 NM blo 18,000′
    204°−209° byd 40 NM
    210°−230° byd 40 NM blo 3,000′
    210°−230° byd 49 NM blo 12,000′
    210°−230° byd 60 NM blo 18,000′
    231°−281° byd 40 NM
    282°−292° byd 40 NM blo 6,000′
    293°−359° byd 40 NM

G V MONTGOMERY (See FOREST on page 142)

GEORGE M BRYAN (See STARKVILLE on page 169)

GOLDEN TRIANGLE RGNL (See COLUMBUS/W POINT/STARKVILLE on page 139)

GREENE CO N31°05.88′ W88°29.17′ NOTAM FILE GWO. NEW ORLEANS
(H) TACAN 115.7 GCV Chan 104 030° 25.9 NM to Roy Wilcox. 300/5E. H−6J, L−21C, 22G

MISSISSIPPI 143

GREENVILLE MID–DELTA (GLH)(KGLH) 5 NE UTC–6(–5DT) N33°29.11′ W90°59.07′ **MEMPHIS**
131 B NOTAM FILE GLH H–6J, L–18F
RWY 18L–36R: H8001X150 (ASPH–GRVD) S–75, D–112, 2S–142, IAP, AD
2D–182, 2D/2D2–540 PCN 61 F/D/X/T HIRL
 RWY 18L: MALSR. RVR–T
 RWY 36R: REIL. PAPI(P4L)—GA 3.0° TCH 60′. Tree. Rgt tfc.
RWY 18R–36L: H7019X150 (ASPH–CONC–GRVD) S–29, D–47, 2D–78
PCN 11 R/C/X/T MIRL
 RWY 18R: PAPI(P4L)—GA 3.0° TCH 52′. Rgt tfc.
 RWY 36L: PAPI(P4L)—GA 3.0° TCH 52′. Trees.
RUNWAY DECLARED DISTANCE INFORMATION
 RWY 18L:TORA–8001 TODA–8001 ASDA–7981 LDA–7981
 RWY 36R:TORA–8001 TODA–8001 ASDA–8001 LDA–8001
SERVICE: S4 **FUEL** 100LL, JET A **LGT** When twr clsd ACTIVATE MALSR
Rwy 18L; HIRL Rwy 18L–36R preset med ints, to increase ints—CTAF.
PAPI Rwy 36R opr continuously.
AIRPORT REMARKS: Attended 1300–0100Z‡. Sgfnt bird act invof rwys. Fuel
avbl 1300–2300Z‡ dly, aft hrs call 662–822–5269. Rwy 18R–36L no
tkof or lndg auth for ACR acft. Twy C, D are clsd, and Twy F not avbl for
acr use. Rwy 18R–36L uneven pavement. Rwy 18R and Rwy 36L
markings faded. Index A ARFF equip avbl upon req only. Clsd to sked
acr ops with more than 9 pax seat and unsked acr ops with more than
30 pax seats.
AIRPORT MANAGER: 662-334-3121
WEATHER DATA SOURCES: ASOS 125.525 (662) 332–0853. LAWRS.
COMMUNICATIONS: CTAF 119.0 **UNICOM** 122.95
 RCO 122.1R 114.25T (GREENWOOD RADIO)
®**MEMPHIS CENTER APP/DEP CON** 135.875
 TOWER 119.0 (1300–0100Z‡) **GND CON** 121.5
CLEARANCE DELIVERY PHONE: For CD ctc Memphis ARTCC at 901-368-8453/8449.
AIRSPACE: CLASS D svc 1300–0100Z‡; other times CLASS G.
RADIO AIDS TO NAVIGATION: NOTAM FILE GLH.
 (VL) (DH) VOR/DME 114.25 GLH Chan 89(Y) N33°31.41′ W90°58.98′ 178° 2.3 NM to fld. 130/4E.
 VOR unusable:
  144°–157° byd 40 NM
 METCALF NDB (MHW) 359 MTQ N33°25.52′ W90°58.93′ 359° 3.6 NM to fld. 120/1W.
 ILS 109.1 I–GLH Rwy 18L. Class IE. Unmonitored when ATCT closed. LOC usable byd 25° left and right of
  course.

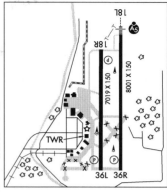

MISSISSIPPI

GREENWOOD–LEFLORE (GWO)(KGWO) 6 E UTC–6(–5DT) N33°29.60′ W90°05.20′
MEMPHIS
H–6J, L–18G
IAP, AD

162 B NOTAM FILE GWO MON Airport
RWY 18–36: H6501X150 (ASPH) S–100, D–176, 2S–175, 2D–300, 2D/2D2–560 HIRL
  RWY 18: MALSR.
  RWY 36: REIL. PAPI(P4L)—GA 3.0° TCH 50′.
RWY 05–23: H5011X150 (ASPH) S–30 MIRL 0.3% up NE
  RWY 05: VASI(V4L)—GA 3.0° TCH 33′. Trees.
  RWY 23: REIL. PVASI(PSIR). Trees.
SERVICE: S4 **FUEL** 100LL, JET A, A1+ **LGT** When twr clsd, actvt MALSR Rwy 18; PAPI Rwy 36; MIRL Rwy 05–23; HIRL Rwy 18–36—CTAF. VASI Rwy 05 opr consly. Rwy 05–23 lgts OTS indef.
AIRPORT REMARKS: Attended continuously. CLSD 2 days each at Thanksgiving and Christmas, 1 day for New Year′s. Fuel avbl Mon–Fri 1500–0000Z‡, Sat–Sun 1600–2200Z‡. Fee for fuel aft hrs call 662–392–3988, 662–392–8899 or 662–455–5530 for svc after hrs. Powerplant and airframe repairs in emerg or by appt. AMGR limits GWT Rwy 05–23 to S–42, D–60 in unusual situations. Pilots must provide their own tiedown ropes.
AIRPORT MANAGER: 662-453-1526
WEATHER DATA SOURCES: ASOS 119.975 (662) 453–3304.
COMMUNICATIONS: CTAF 118.35 **UNICOM** 122.95
  RCO 122.2 (GREENWOOD RADIO)
Ⓡ **MEMPHIS CENTER APP/DEP CON** 132.5
  TOWER 118.35 (1400–0000Z‡) **GND CON** 125.55 **CLNC DEL** 125.55
CLEARANCE DELIVERY PHONE: For CD ctc Memphis ARTCC at 901-368-8453/8449.
AIRSPACE: CLASS D svc 1400–0000Z‡; other times CLASS E.
RADIO AIDS TO NAVIGATION: NOTAM FILE GWO.
  SIDON (VH) (H) VORTAC 114.7 SQS Chan 94 N33°27.83′ W90°16.64′ 077° 9.7 NM to fld. 127/3E.
    VOR unusable:
      059°–069° byd 40 NM
  TEOCK NDB (LOMW) 349 GW N33°35.52′ W90°05.06′ 182° 5.9 NM to fld. 140/1W.
  ILS 111.3 I–GWO Rwy 18. Class IT. LOM TEOCK NDB.

GRENADA MUNI (GNF)(KGNF) 3 N UTC–6(–5DT) N33°49.95′ W89°47.89′
MEMPHIS
H–6J, L–18G
IAP

208 B NOTAM FILE GWO
RWY 13–31: H7000X150 (ASPH) S–60, D–200, 2S–175, 2D–300 MIRL
  RWY 13: MALSR. VASI(V4L)—GA 3.0° TCH 52′.
  RWY 31: VASI(V4L)—GA 3.0° TCH 56′. Trees.
RWY 04–22: H4998X99 (ASPH) S–60, D–200, 2S–175, 2D–300
  RWY 04: Trees.
  RWY 22: Thld dsplcd 272′. Road.
SERVICE: **FUEL** 100LL, JET A
AIRPORT REMARKS: Attended Mon–Sat on call 662–230–3646, Sun 1900–2300Z‡. Birds and deer invof arpt. Aerobatic acft dalgt hrs; 7000 ft and blw within 3 NM of arpt. Extsv agriculture ops invof arpt SR–SS Mar–Oct. For fuel call 662–230–3646; aft hrs call 662–417–7029 or 662–699–9460. Rwy 13 and 31 200 ft by 150 ft asph ovrn avbl. Rwy 04–22 asph cracked and has depressions. Rwy 04–22 markings faded. Pilots musts prvd their own tiedown ropes.
AIRPORT MANAGER: 662-227-8402
WEATHER DATA SOURCES: AWOS–3PT 118.025 (662) 227–3407.
COMMUNICATIONS: CTAF/UNICOM 122.8
Ⓡ **MEMPHIS CENTER APP/DEP CON** 128.5
CLEARANCE DELIVERY PHONE: For CD ctc Memphis ARTCC at 901-368-8453/8449.
RADIO AIDS TO NAVIGATION: NOTAM FILE GWO.
  SIDON (VH) (H) VORTAC 114.7 SQS Chan 94 N33°27.83′ W90°16.64′ 044° 32.6 NM to fld. 127/3E.
    VOR unusable:
      059°–069° byd 40 NM

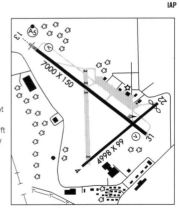

MISSISSIPPI 145

GULFPORT–BILOXI INTL (GPT)(KGPT) P (ANG ARNG)   3 NE   UTC–6(–5DT)   N30°24.44´   **NEW ORLEANS**
W89°04.21´   **H–7E, 8F, L–21C, 22G, GOMC**
28   B   TPA—See Remarks   LRA   Class I, ARFF Index B   NOTAM FILE GPT   **IAP, AD**
  RWY 14–32: H9002X150 (ASPH–CONC–GRVD)   S–81, D–300, 2S–175,
    2D–555, 2D/2D2–870 PCR 960 F/B/X/T   HIRL
    RWY 14: MALSR. PAPI(P4R)—GA 3.0° TCH 73´. RVR–T Trees.
    RWY 32: MALSR. PAPI(P4L)—GA 3.0° TCH 72´. RVR–T Tower.
  RWY 18–36: H4935X150 (ASPH–GRVD)   S–20, 2D–115
    PCN 147F/B/W/T   MIRL
    RWY 18: PAPI(P4R)—GA 3.0° TCH 50´. Tree.
    RWY 36: PAPI(P4L)—GA 3.0° TCH 50´. Trees.
  ARRESTING GEAR/SYSTEM
    RWY 14 BAK–14 BAK–12B(B) (1800 FT).
               BAK–14 BAK–12B(B) (1300 FT). **RWY 32**
  SERVICE: S4   **FUEL** 100LL, JET A   **LGT** When ATCT clsd actvt MALSR
    Rwy 14 and 32; HIRL Rwy 14–32; MIRL Rwy 18–36—CTAF. MIRL
    Rwy 18–36 not avbl when ATCT clsd and Rwy 14–32 actv.
    MILITARY— A–GEAR BAK–14 avbl dur ANG OPS with 30 min PN. **JASU**
    6(A/M32A–86) 3(AM32A–60A) **FUEL** A+ (MIL) A (C228–701–0400).
    OIL O–128–133–148(Mil)   **TRAN ALERT** Svc avbl pr or coord.
  AIRPORT REMARKS: Attended continuously. 150´ AGL crane 4600´ N of Rwy

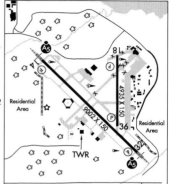

    18 thld. Numerous low flying fish spotter acft opr near shoreline
    between Pascagoula and Gulfport SR–SS. Maverick pad apron area on N end of Twy C restricted to military acft use only.
    TPA— 800 ft AGL lgt sngl–eng, 1200 ft AGL conventional, 1500 ft AGL jets. Acft over 115,000 lbs are restricted from
    180° turns on Rwy 18–36. Acft with wingspan greater than 223´ are restricted from opr on Twy C between Twy A and
    AER 32. Civil acft with wingspan of 132´ or greater and all air carrier acft must be escorted along Twy A north of Twy C
    by gnd handling agent. Acft opr as scheduled or charter passenger svc shall not taxi on Twy A north of Twy B intersection
    without escort from gnd handling agent or arpt authority. Acft over 155,000 lbs are restricted from using the N part of
    Twy A at Rwy 18–36. Acft over 316,000 lbs are restricted from using the S part of Twy A between Twy C and Rwy 14–32.
    Due to apron activity, acft with wingspan greater than 170´ should be alert on Twy A between Twy C and Twy B. Taxilane
    F20 between FBO and taxilane G clsd to acft with wingspan greater than 49´. Pole adj taxilane F20 not lgtd. Rwy 18–36
    not avbl for skedd acr ops with more than 9 pax seats or unsked acr ops at least 31 pax seats.
  MILITARY REMARKS: RSTD Military acft or acft supporting a mil mission with wingspan of 132´ or greater must have an escort
    or coordinate taxi procedures with gnd handling agent prior to taxiing on Twy A. Power check pad between Rwy 18–36
    and Twy A rstd to military acft only. C–5 acft parking rstd to 1 acft at a time due to twy width unless coordinated. Prk
    rstd wi 100 ft LOX fac lctd NE corner apron 1. **CAUTION** BASH Phase I bird act May–Sep. BASH Phase II in effect Apr–May
    and Aug–Oct. Ctc Afld Mgmt, for current Bird Watch Cond. **CSTMS/AG/IMG** Requestor of PPR responsible for notifying
    CSTMS 48 hr prior notice. **ANG** No COMSEC stor. CRTC Afld Mgmt Ops opr 1300–2130Z‡ Mon; 1300–2230Z‡ Tues–Fri
    and Unit Trng Assembly (UTA) wknds, normally first wknd of month; clsd hol. 48 hr pn PPR rqr ctc CRTC AM ops. Ctc
    guard ops 15 min prior to arr 377.800. DSN 363–6027; C228–214–6027; fax DSN 363–6031;
    C228–214–6031. **ARNG** MSAVCRAD ops opr 1300–2130Z‡ Mon; 1300–2230Z‡ Tue–Fri and unit trng assembly (UTA)
    wknd. PPR rqr ctc ARNG Ops, DSN 293–1378/1312, C228–214–1378/1312. Acft inbd to ARNG Ramp ctc Blackjack
    Ops (241.0/41.6) 10 min prior to ldg for prk instr.
  AIRPORT MANAGER: 228-863-5951
  WEATHER DATA SOURCES: ASOS 119.45 (228) 867–9937. LAWRS.
  COMMUNICATIONS: CTAF 123.7 **ATIS** 119.45 **UNICOM** 122.95
    RCO 122.1R 109.0T (GREENWOOD RADIO)
  ® **GULFPORT APP/DEP CON** 124.6 (130°–309°) 127.5 (310°–129°) (1200–0500Z‡)
  ® **HOUSTON CENTER APP/DEP CON** 127.65 (0500–1200Z‡)
    TOWER 123.7 (1200–0500Z‡) **GND CON** 120.4
  AIRSPACE: CLASS D svc 1200–0500Z‡; other times CLASS G.
    TRSA svc ctc **APP CON**
  RADIO AIDS TO NAVIGATION: NOTAM FILE GPT.
    (L) (L) **VORTAC** 109.0   GPT   Chan 27   N30°24.41´ W89°04.61´   at fld. 25/2E.
    TACAN AZIMUTH unusable:
      195°–217°
      266°–275° byd 12 NM
    VOR unusable:
      035°–086° blo 5,000´
      293°–303°
    BAYOU NDB (LOMW) 360   GP   N30°29.14´ W89°09.74´   136° 6.7 NM to fld. 83/2W.
    NDB unusable:
      085°–270° byd 10 NM
    ILS 110.9   I–GPT   Rwy 14.   Class IE.   LOM EAYOU NDB. Unmonitored when ATCT clsd. Glideslope unusable byd 7°
      right of course.
    ILS 108.3   I–UXI   Rwy 32.   Class IT.   Unmonitored when ATCT clsd.
    ASR (1200–0500Z‡)

MISSISSIPPI

HANCO N30°27.08′ W89°27.33′ NOTAM FILE HSA.
NDB (MHW) 221 HS 181° 5.0 NM to Stennis Intl. 94/2W.

NEW ORLEANS
L–21B, 22G, GOMC

HARDY–ANDERS FLD/NATCHEZ–ADAMS CO (See NATCHEZ on page 160)

HATTIESBURG BOBBY L CHAIN MUNI (HBG)(KHBG) 4 SE UTC–6(–5DT) N31°15.90′
W89°15.17′
151 B NOTAM FILE HBG
RWY 13–31: H6094X150 (ASPH–GRVD) S–48, D–68, 2S–114,
2D–145 MIRL
  RWY 13: REIL. PAPI(P4L)—GA 3.0° TCH 50′. Thld dsplcd 996′. Trees.
  RWY 31: PAPI(P4L)—GA 3.0° TCH 44′. Trees.
SERVICE: S4 **FUEL** 100LL, JET A **OX 3** **LGT** Actvt REIL Rwy 13; MIRL
  Rwy 13–31—CTAF. PAPI Rwy 13 and 31 opr consly.
AIRPORT REMARKS: Attended dalgt hours. 100L fuel svc avbl 24 hrs with
  credit card. Run–on landings by skid helicopters are not allowed.
AIRPORT MANAGER: (601) 544-8661
WEATHER DATA SOURCES: ASOS 135.425 (601) 544–2185.
COMMUNICATIONS: CTAF/UNICOM 122.8
®**HOUSTON CENTER APP/DEP CON** 126.8
CLEARANCE DELIVERY PHONE: For CD ctc Houston ARTCC at 281-230-5622.
RADIO AIDS TO NAVIGATION: NOTAM FILE GWO.
  EATON (L) (L) VORTACW 110.6 LBY Chan 43 N31°25.12′
    W89°20.26′ 150° 10.2 NM to fld. 290/5E.
  VORTAC unusable:
    300°–000° byd 30 NM
  VOR portion unusable:
    111°–164° byd 10 NM blo 2,000′
    241°–251°
  TACAN unusable:
    025°–035° byd 10 NM blo 3,000′
    268°–274° byd 30 NM blo 5,000′

NEW ORLEANS
H–6J, L–21C, 22G
IAP

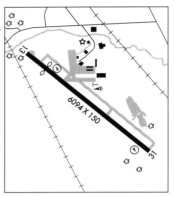

HATTIESBURG–LAUREL

HATTIESBURG/LAUREL RGNL (PIB)(KPIB) 9 N UTC–6(–5DT) N31°28.03′ W89°20.22′
298 B ARFF Index—See Remarks NOTAM FILE PIB
RWY 18–36: H6502X150 (ASPH–GRVD) S–125, D–225, 2S–175,
2D–275 PCN 72 F/B/X/T HIRL
  RWY 18: MALSR. REIL. PAPI(P4L)—GA 3.0° TCH 58′.
  RWY 36: REIL. PAPI(P4L)—GA 3.0° TCH 44′.
RUNWAY DECLARED DISTANCE INFORMATION
  RWY 18: TORA–6502 TODA–6502 ASDA–6502 LDA–6502
  RWY 36: TORA–6502 TODA–6502 ASDA–6502 LDA–6502
SERVICE: S2 **FUEL** 100, JET A **LGT** Actvt MALSR Rwy 18; REILS Rwys
  18 and 36; HIRL Rwy 18–36 preset to med intst, to incr intst—CTAF. PAPIs Rwys 18 and 36 opr consly.
AIRPORT REMARKS: Attended 1100–0500Z‡. ARFF Index clsd to acr ops
  with more than 30 pax seats excp 24 hr PPR, call arpt mgr
  601-545-3111.
AIRPORT MANAGER: 601-545-3111
WEATHER DATA SOURCES: AWOS–3PT 128.325 (601) 584–6701. LAWRS.
COMMUNICATIONS: CTAF/UNICOM 123.0
®**HOUSTON CENTER APP/DEP CON** 126.8
CLEARANCE DELIVERY PHONE: For CD ctc Houston ARTCC at 281-230-5622.
AIRSPACE: CLASS E svc 1200–0400Z‡; other times CLASS G.
RADIO AIDS TO NAVIGATION: NOTAM FILE GWO.
  EATON (L) (L) VORTACW 110.6 LBY Chan 43 N31°25.12′ W89°20.26′ 356° 2.9 NM to fld. 290/5E.
  VORTAC unusable:
    300°–000° byd 30 NM
  VOR portion unusable:
    111°–164° byd 10 NM blo 2,000′
    241°–251°
  TACAN unusable:
    025°–035° byd 10 NM blo 3,000′
    268°–274° byd 30 NM blo 5,000′
  ILS 109.5 I–PIB Rwy 18. Class IB.

NEW ORLEANS
H–6J, L–22G
IAP

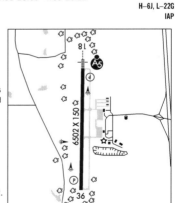

SC, 25 JAN 2024 to 21 MAR 2024

MISSISSIPPI 147

HATTIESBURG/LAUREL RGNL (See HATTIESBURG–LAUREL on page 146)

HAWKINS FLD (See JACKSON on page 150)

HERNANDO

EAGLES RIDGE (MS9)   5 SE   UTC–6(–5DT)   N34°47.79´ W89°54.79´   MEMPHIS
262   NOTAM FILE GWO   L–18G
RWY 10–28: H3300X40 (CONC)
 RWY 10: Thld dsplcd 922´. Trees. Rgt tfc.
 RWY 28: Trees.
SERVICE: FUEL 100
AIRPORT REMARKS: Unattended. Migratory waterfowl area 0.2 NM SE of arpt. Fuel avail 24 hrs with credit card, for svc call 901–387–9890. Rcmd all acft land Rwy 28 tkof Rwy 10. Rwy 10 and Rwy 28 markings badly faded.
AIRPORT MANAGER: 901-438-5127
COMMUNICATIONS: CTAF 122.9
CLEARANCE DELIVERY PHONE: For CD ctc Memphis ARTCC at 901-368-8453/8449.

HERNANDO VILLAGE AIRPARK   (H75)   2 SW   UTC–6(–5DT)   N34°47.89´ W90°02.22´   MEMPHIS
242   NOTAM FILE GWO
RWY 14–32: 3340X65 (TURF)   S–12
 RWY 14: Trees.
 RWY 32: Tower.
AIRPORT REMARKS: Attended dalgt hrs.
AIRPORT MANAGER: 901-359-6912
COMMUNICATIONS: CTAF/UNICOM 122.8
CLEARANCE DELIVERY PHONE: For CD ctc mem Apch at 901-842-8457.

HESLER–NOBLE FLD   (See LAUREL on page 154)

HOLLANDALE MUNI   (14M)   2 NE   UTC–6(–5DT)   N33°10.95´ W90°49.83´   MEMPHIS
114   B   NOTAM FILE GWO   L–18F
RWY 08–26: H3000X60 (ASPH)   S–21   MIRL
 RWY 08: PAPI(P2L)—GA 3.0° TCH 40´.
 RWY 26: PAPI(P2L)—GA 3.0° TCH 40´.
SERVICE: LGT Bcn OTS indefly. Ops 2300–0400Z‡; aft 0400Z‡ ACTVT MIRL Rwy 08–26—CTAF. Rwy 26 VGSI OTS indefly.
AIRPORT REMARKS: Unattended. Pilots must prvd their own tiedown ropes.
AIRPORT MANAGER: 662-827-2241
COMMUNICATIONS: CTAF 122.9
CLEARANCE DELIVERY PHONE: For CD ctc Memphis ARTCC at 901-368-8453/8449.
RADIO AIDS TO NAVIGATION: NOTAM FILE GLH.
 GREENVILLE **(VL) (DH)** VOR/DME 114.25   GLH   Chan 89(Y)   N33°31.41´ W90°58.98´   155° 21.8 NM to fld.
 130/4E.
 VOR unusable:
  144°–157° byd 40 NM

MISSISSIPPI

HOLLY SPRINGS–MARSHALL CO (M41)   4 W   UTC–6(–5DT)   N34°48.26′ W89°31.27′   MEMPHIS
551   B   NOTAM FILE GWO   L–18G
RWY 18–36: H3202X60 (ASPH)   S–15   MIRL   1.1% up S   IAP
 RWY 18: PAPI(P2L)—GA 2.75° TCH 86′.
 RWY 36: PAPI(P2L)—GA 3.25° TCH 65′.
SERVICE: S4   **FUEL** 100LL, JET A
AIRPORT REMARKS: Attended Mon–Fri 1400–2300Z‡. 100LL svc avbl 24 hrs with credit card. Pilots must supply their own tiedown ropes.
AIRPORT MANAGER: 901-230-3421
COMMUNICATIONS: CTAF/UNICOM 122.8
 RCO 122.3 (GREENWOOD RADIO)
Ⓡ **MEMPHIS APP CON** 125.8 120.075
Ⓡ **MEMPHIS DEP CON** 124.15
CLEARANCE DELIVERY PHONE: For CD ctc Memphis ARTCC at 901-368-8453/8449.
RADIO AIDS TO NAVIGATION: NOTAM FILE GWO.
 (L) (L) VORTACW 112.4   HLI   Chan 71   N34°46.21′
  W89°29.79′   326° 2.4 NM to fld. 624/3E.
 VOR UNUSABL:
  172°–192° byd 25 NM blo 2,400′

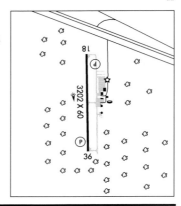

HOUSTON MUNI (M44)   2 SW   UTC–6(–5DT)   N33°53.19′ W89°01.38′   MEMPHIS
337   B   NOTAM FILE GWO   L–18G
RWY 03–21: H4400X75 (ASPH)   S–26   MIRL
 RWY 03: PAPI(P2L)—GA 3.0° TCH 40′. Trees.
 RWY 21: PAPI(P2L)—GA 3.0° TCH 40′. Trees.
SERVICE: S2   **FUEL** 100LL   **LGT** Actvt MIRL Rwy 03–21—CTAF. PAPI Rwy 03 and Rwy 21 opr consly.
AIRPORT REMARKS: Attended continuously. Fuel abvl 24 hrs with credit card. For arpt attendant Sat and Sun call 662-456-8484. Pilots must provide their own tiedown ropes.
AIRPORT MANAGER: (662) 456-8484
COMMUNICATIONS: CTAF 122.9
CLEARANCE DELIVERY PHONE: For CD ctc Memphis ARTCC at 901-368-8453/8449.
RADIO AIDS TO NAVIGATION: NOTAM FILE CBM.
 CALEDONIA (L) (L) VORTACW 115.2   CBM   Chan 99   N33°38.49′ W88°26.31′   297° 32.7 NM to fld. 250/0E.
  military use: mnt 1300–0100Z‡ Mon–Fri; 1800–2300Z‡ Sun. No NOTAM MP: 0200–0400Z‡ Sun
 VOR unusable:
  317°–223°
 TACAN AZIMUTH unusable:
  015°–030° byd 20 NM blo 4,000′
 DME unusable:
  015°–030° byd 20 NM blo 4,000′
  080°–100° byd 35 NM blo 3,500′

I H BASS JR MEML (See LUMBERTON on page 155)

MISSISSIPPI

149

INDIANOLA MUNI (IDL)(KIDL)   2 NW   UTC–6(–5DT)   N33°29.14′ W90°40.73′   **MEMPHIS**
126   B   NOTAM FILE GWO   H–6J, L–18F
RWY 18–36: H7004X150 (CONC)   S–20   MIRL   IAP
  RWY 18: Trees.
SERVICE: S4   **FUEL** 100LL   **LGT** Actvt MIRL Rwy 18–36—CTAF.
AIRPORT REMARKS: Attended Mon–Fri 1400–2300Z‡. Pilots must prvd their
  own tiedown ropes. Twy lgts on E–W Twy to apn only.
AIRPORT MANAGER: 662-588-0580
COMMUNICATIONS: CTAF/UNICOM 122.8
Ⓡ **MEMPHIS CENTER APP/DEP CON** 135.875
CLEARANCE DELIVERY PHONE: For CD ctc Memphis ARTCC at
  901-368-8453/8449.
RADIO AIDS TO NAVIGATION: NOTAM FILE GWO.
  SIDON (VH) (H) VORTAC 114.7   SQS   Chan 94   N33°27.83′
    W90°16.64′   271° 20.2 NM to fld. 127/3E.
  VOR unusable:
    059°–069° byd 40 NM

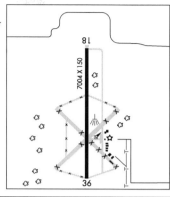

IUKA (15M)   3 SE   UTC–6(–5DT)   N34°46.40′ W88°09.97′   **MEMPHIS**
626   B   NOTAM FILE GWO   L–18H
RWY 01–19: H4001X75 (ASPH–GRVD)   S–30   MIRL   IAP
  RWY 01: PAPI(P4L)—GA 3.0° TCH 42′. Trees.
  RWY 19: PAPI(P4L)—GA 4.0° TCH 52′. Trees.
SERVICE: **FUEL** 100LL   **LGT** Actvt REIL Rwy 01 and 19; PAPI Rwy 01–19; MIRL Rwy 01–19—CTAF. Rwy lgt intst can be
  chgd M–H.
AIRPORT REMARKS: Attended dalgt hours. For aft hr svc ctc AMGR. 100LL avbl 24 hrs with credit card. Rwy 01 +8′ fence
  200′ fm thr 100′ L. Pilots must provide their own tiedown ropes.
AIRPORT MANAGER: 662-424-2356
COMMUNICATIONS: CTAF 122.9
Ⓡ **MEMPHIS CENTER APP/DEP CON** 124.35
CLEARANCE DELIVERY PHONE: For CD ctc Memphis ARTCC at 901-368-8453/8449.

MISSISSIPPI

JACKSON

HAWKINS FLD (HKS)(KHKS) P (ARNG)   3 NW   UTC–6(–5DT)   N32°20.09′ W90°13.35′   **MEMPHIS**
341   B   NOTAM FILE HKS   H–6J, L–18G
RWY 16–34: H5387X150 (ASPH–GRVD)   S–30, D–40, 2D–80   HIRL   IAP, AD
0.7% up NW
  RWY 16: MALSR. PAPI(P4L)—GA 3.0° TCH 57′.
  RWY 34: REIL. Trees.
RWY 11–29: H3431X150 (CONC)   S–30, D–40, 2D–80   MIRL
0.3% up SE
  RWY 11: P–line.
  RWY 29: Trees.
RUNWAY DECLARED DISTANCE INFORMATION
  RWY 11: TORA–4021   TODA–4400   ASDA–4250   LDA–3431
  RWY 29: TORA–3810   TODA–4400   ASDA–3810   LDA–3431
SERVICE: S4   **FUEL** 100LL, JET A+   **LGT** Actvt MALSR Rwy 16; REIL
Rwy 34; HIRL Rwy 16–34—CTAF. MIRL Rwy 11–29 ATCT–Ctl. When
ATCT clsd MIRL Rwy 11–29 unavbl. S Apn not lgtd.
  MILITARY— FUEL A+ (avbl 1200–0200Z‡, Mon–Fri, 1300–0100Z‡,
Sat–Sun, C800–521–4106, OT 30 min PN rqr, C601–948–8778.
$60 svc fee.) (NC–100LL)
AIRPORT REMARKS: Attended 1300–0300Z‡. Twys F and G clsd indef.
PAEW rwys nightly by NOTAM. Pilots must provide their own tiedown
ropes.
MILITARY REMARKS: ARNG OPS 1300–2230Z‡.   **ARNG** DSN 293–2117, C601–313–2117.
AIRPORT MANAGER: (601) 939–5631
WEATHER DATA SOURCES: ASOS 120.625 (601) 354–4037.
COMMUNICATIONS: CTAF 119.65 **UNICOM** 122.95
®**JACKSON APP/DEP CON** 123.9 (333°–152°) 125.25
(153°–332°)(1200–0500Z‡)
®**MEMPHIS CENTER APP/DEP CON** 132.5 (0500–1200Z‡)
  TOWER 119.65 (1300–0300Z‡) **GND CON** 121.9
  JACKSON CLNC DEL 121.9
CLEARANCE DELIVERY PHONE: When Apch clsd, for CD ctc Memphis ARTCC at 901–368–8453/8449.
AIRSPACE: CLASS D svc 1300–0300Z‡; other times CLASS G.
RADIO AIDS TO NAVIGATION: NOTAM FILE GWO.
  MAGNOLIA (VH) (H) VORTACW 113.2   MHZ   Chan 79   N32°26.04′ W90°05.99′   227° 8.6 NM to fld. 407/1W.
  TACAN AZIMUTH unusable:
    240°–275° byd 30 NM blo 2,000′
    DME unsbl 240–275 byd 30 NM blo 2000′
  BRENZ NDB (MHW/LOM) 260   JH   N32°24.78′ W90°15.68′   157° 5.1 NM to fld. 314/0W.   NOTAM FILE HKS.
  NDB unmonitored when ATCT clsd.
  ILS 111.7   I–JHF   Rwy 16.   Class IT.   LOM BRENZ NDB. Unmonitored when ATCT clsd. Marker/NDB jh unmonitored
when ATCT clsd.

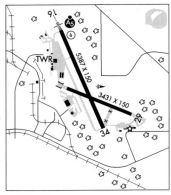

MISSISSIPPI 151

JACKSON–MEDGAR WILEY EVERS INTL (JAN)(KJAN) P (ANG)   5 E   UTC–6(–5DT)   N32°18.67′   **MEMPHIS**
W90°04.55′   H–6J, L–18G
346   B   LRA   Class I, ARFF Index C   NOTAM FILE JAN   MON Airport   IAP, DIAP, AD
  RWY 16L–34R: H8500X150 (ASPH–GRVD)   S–75, D–200, 2S–175,
    2T–585, 2D–390, 2D/2D2–850 PCN 88 F/C/W/T   HIRL   CL
    RWY 16L: ALSF2. TDZL. PAPI(P4L)—GA 3.0° TCH 71′. RVR–TMR
    Trees. 0.3% up.
    RWY 34R: REIL. PAPI(P4R)—GA 3.0° TCH 66′. RVR–TMR Trees.
    0.7% down.
  RWY 16R–34L: H8500X150 (ASPH–GRVD)   S–130, D–140, 2S–175,
    2T–585, 2D–250, 2D/2D2–720 PCN 59 F/B/X/U   HIRL   CL
    RWY 16R: REIL. PAPI(P4L)—GA 3.0° TCH 80′. RVR–R 0.4% up.
    RWY 34L: MALSR. TDZL. RVR–T Trees.
  SERVICE: S4   **FUEL** 100LL, JET A, A+   **OX** 1, 2, 3, 4   **LGT** When twr
    clsd actvt MALSR Rwy 34L; REIL Rwy 16R and 34R; HIRL Rwy
    16L–34R and 16R–34L—CTAF. Rwy 16L ALSF–2 preset on med intst
    exc SFL not avbl. **MILITARY**— JASU 8(A/M32A–86D) 3(MC–1A) **FUEL** A+,
    A (C601–939–9366) (NC–100LL)
  AIRPORT REMARKS: Attended continuously. Wt brg cpty for Rwys 16L–34R
    and Rwy 16R–34L are TRT–585 to accommodate C–17 acft. Be alert
    when xng AER 16R. Hold area 1 and 2 cmsnd on term apron btn Twy
    B3 and Twy B5. Ldg fee for non–coml acft over 25500 lbs; fee waived
    for lrgr non–sked acft with suf fuel purchase.

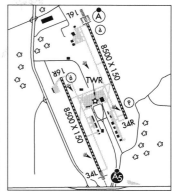

  MILITARY REMARKS: See FLIP AP/1 supplementary arpt remark. **CAUTION** Bash Phase II period July–October. Ctc afld mgmt or
    Comd Post for current bird watch cond. **ANG** Ofl bus. All tran acft 48 hr PPR. Ltd prk use. Ctc afld mgmt. Tran acft use
    FBO for svc. Afld mgmt opr 1300–0230Z‡ wkd, DSN 828–8372, C601–405–8372. Command Post opr 1200–0630Z‡
    wkd, DSN 828–8350. Mil acft use Twy C7 to aces the FBO apron unless otrw drctd by ATC.
  AIRPORT MANAGER: 601-939-5631
  WEATHER DATA SOURCES: ASOS 121.05 (601) 932–2822. LLWAS.
  COMMUNICATIONS: CTAF 120.9 ATIS 121.05 UNICOM 122.95
    RCO 122.2 (GREENWOOD RADIO)
  Ⓡ **APP/DEP CON** 123.9   317.7 (333°–152°)   125.25   319.2 (153°–332°)(1200–0500Z‡)
  Ⓡ **MEMPHIS CENTER APP/DEP CON** 132.5   259.1 (0500–1200Z‡)
    TOWER 120.9 352.0 (1200–0500Z‡)   **GND CON** 121.7 348.6
    ANG COMD POST 264.6 (172nd AW CP)
  CLEARANCE DELIVERY PHONE: For CD ctc Memphis ARTCC at 901-368-8453/8449.
  AIRSPACE: CLASS C svc ctc **APP CON** svc 1200–0500Z‡; other times CLASS E.
  VOR TEST FACILITY (VOT) 111.0
  RADIO AIDS TO NAVIGATION: NOTAM FILE GWO.
    MAGNOLIA (VH) (H) VORTACW 113.2   MHZ   Chan 79   N32°26.04′ W90°05.99′   172°   7.5 NM to fld. 407/1W.
    TACAN AZIMUTH unusable:
      240°–275° byd 30 NM blo 2,000′
      DME unsbl 240–275 byd 30 NM blo 2000′
    ALLEN NDB (LOMW) 365   JA   N32°24.75′ W90°07.17′   161°   6.5 NM to fld. 330/1W.   NOTAM FILE JAN.
    ILS 110.5   I–JAN   Rwy 16L.   Class IIIE.   LOM ALLEN NDB. Unmonitored 0500–1200Z‡ radar – see terminal flip for
      radar minima.
    ILS 109.3   I–FRL   Rwy 34L.   Class IB.   Unmonitored. Localizer restricted byd 25° left and right of course.
    ASR (1200–0500Z‡)

JAMES H EASOM FLD (See NEWTON on page 161)

JOE WILLIAMS NOLF   (NJW)(KNJW) N   UTC–6(–5DT)   N32°47.94′ W88°50.07′   **MEMPHIS**
  AIRSPACE: CLASS D svc 1400Z‡–2200Z‡ Mon–Fri; other times CLASS G..   H–6J, L–18G

JOHN BELL WILLIAMS (See RAYMOND on page 167)

SC, 25 JAN 2024 to 21 MAR 2024

MISSISSIPPI

KEESLER AFB (BIX)(KBIX) AF (AFRC) 0 W UTC–6(–5DT) N30°24.63´ W88°55.47´ NEW ORLEANS
33 B TPA—See Remarks NOTAM FILE BIX Not insp. H–7E, 8F, L–21C, 22G, GOMC
RWY 04–22: H7630X150 (PEM) PCN 32 F/B/W/T HIRL DIAP, AD
  RWY 04: REIL. PAPI(P4L)—GA 3.0° TCH 48´. Thld dsplcd 1600´. Trees–l.
  RWY 22: ALSF1. PAPI(P4L)—GA 3.0° TCH 55´. Thld dsplcd 1000´. Trees–l. Rgt tfc.
SERVICE: S4 **FUEL** JET A++ OX2 **LGT** NSTD rwy edge and twy lgts; svrl lgts gtr than 200 ft dist apart on rwy, svrl missing twy exit lgts. SFL OTS UFN. Rwy 22 lgts: ALSF–1 NSTD len 2000´. Rwy 04 REIL OTS. **MILITARY**— **JASU** 1(MA–1A) 3(A/M32A–86A) **FUEL** A++ **FLUID** Sp PRESAIR LPOX LOX **OIL** O–148–156 **TRAN ALERT** Tran maint opr 1400–2300Z‡ Mon–Fri, OT with prior coord; ctc AMOPS DSN 597–2120.
MILITARY REMARKS: Opr 1400–0500Z‡ Mon–Fri, clsd hol; weekend hrs: Unit Trng Assembly (UTA) weekends normally first weekend of month, Sat 1700–2300Z‡, Sun 1630–0500Z‡. All non–UTA weekends afld will be clsd but avbl to open with prior coord; ctc AMOPS DSN 597–2120. PPR All acft, PPR all acft after tran maint opr ctc Afld mgmt OPS at DSN 597–2120. See FLIP AP/1 Supplementary Arpt Remark. **RSTD** PPR all tran acft; ctc afld mgmt DSN 597–2120. Twy E 50 ft wide. Acft rinse fac (bird bath) Twy C avbl to C–130 and lrgr. No HOP on Ramp 3. Air crews ctc gnd prior to acft eng start. All C–130 or lrgr must face N on Twy B for maint runs or eng run–ups. Pilots will avoid flying ovr USAF Medical Cntr lctd on Back Bay 1 NM E of rwy & VA Hospital on Back Bay 1 NM W of rwy. Tran acft ron must arr by 2100Z‡ Mon–Fri by 2200Z‡ Sun. **CAUTION** GS ant 250´ W of cntrln and 1050´ from AER 22. BASH Phase II in eff 1 Jun–30 Sep; exp heavier bird act SR–SS. Marina trees hinder wind, low wind speed on Rwy 22 when wind dir from 280°–340°. Dur augmentation/backup; ltd wx obsn to E and vis mkr byd 1 sm avbl in the W to N sector, night flood lgt hinder cloud and vis obsn, and ceil fre 100´–200´ lower than obsn on Rwy 22 apch from Nov–Mar. Ctc twr with req to back taxi. Rwy edge lgts past thresholds greater than 10´ from full strength pavement. Spot 24/25 (Twy B and Twy F) light–alls used when C–17 park during hrs of darkness and inclement wx. First 100 ft conc spherical bollards lctd 440 ft sw of cntln. Rwy hazard men or equipment opr randomly to include within 100´ of rwy daily. Large frame and heavy acft will make 180° turns on concrete portion of rwy. Night vision devices training Tue and Thu 0200–0400Z‡. **TFC PAT** TPA—Overhead 1500(1467), Conventional 1000(967), Helicopter 500(467). Rwy 04–22 eff len 5030´ for tgl ops. **MISC** Rwy 04 displ thld dimensions and sfc—1st 200´ is concrete, next 800´ mid 75´ is concrete outer with 37.5´ non–wt brg asphalt edge ea side, and remaining 598´ X 150´ is concrete. Rwy 22 displ thld dimensions and sfc—1st 200 X 150 is concrete, next 800 X 75 is concrete with 37.5´ non–wt brg asphalt edge ea side. VIP acft ctc PTD 372.2 15 minutes prior to ldg with firm chock time. During opr hours, LIFEGUARD/MEDEVAC/SAR/MSN essential acft ctc Afld Management OPS DSN 597–2120, C228–377–2120 1 hour prior to arr for proper coordination, during non–opr hours, ctc Command Post DSN 597–4330, C228–377–4330 1 hour prior to req airfield be opened. Hangar space not avbl for severe weather. Rwy 04 avbl tkf 6632´ from key–hole. Rwy 22 avbl tkf 6034´ from key–hole. See US Terminal Low Arpt Sketch for NSTD Rwy 04–22 configuration. COMSEC materials are not avbl. Assault Zone marker on rwy. Rwy Surface Condition/Rwy Condition Reading not reported during published afld clsd times. **403 WG AFRC** C130/WC130 acft opr weekdays.
AIRPORT MANAGER: 228–377–2123
COMMUNICATIONS: ATIS 281.55 (Opr 1400–0500Z‡ Mon–Fri, 1700–2300Z‡ Sat and Sun, clsd hol, Unit Trng Assemblies 1700–2300Z‡ Sun) **PTD** 372.2
® **GULFPORT APP/DEP CON** 124.6 354.1 (130°–309°) 127.5 254.25 (310°–129°) (1200–0500Z‡)
® **HOUSTON CENTER APP/DEP CON** 132.6 316.075 (0500–1200Z‡)
  TOWER 120.75 269.075 (Opr 1400–0500Z‡ Mon–Fri, 1700–2300Z‡ Sat and Sun, clsd hol, Unit Trng Assemblies 1700–2300Z‡ Sun)
  GND CON 121.8 275.8 **CLNC DEL** 121.8 275.8
  403 WG AFRC COMD 252.8 (Call ACCOUNTANT) **PMSV METRO** 267.4 Full svc avbl 24 hrs from 0400Z‡ Mon thru 0500Z‡ Sat (2200 Local Sun thru 2300L Fri), clsd weekends and hol exc for unit trng assembly (UTA) weekends; UTA opr hrs 1600–2300Z‡ Sat and 1300Z‡ Sun–0400Z‡ Mon. Remote briefing svc avbl from 26 OWS Barksdale AFB, LA, DSN 331–2651, C318–529–2651. Automatic FMQ–19 in use 24/7. Augmented/backed up FMQ–19 in use when required during opr hrs and for resource protection. ASOS obsn avbl at DSN 597–0438 or C228–377–0438.
AIRSPACE: CLASS D svc 1400–0500Z‡ Mon–Fri, 1700–2300Z‡ Sat and Sun, clsd hol, uta 1900–0500Z‡ Sun; other times CLASS E.

CONTINUED ON NEXT PAGE

MISSISSIPPI
CONTINUED FROM PRECEDING PAGE

RADIO AIDS TO NAVIGATION: NOTAM FILE BIX.
 (T) TACAN Chan 55 BIX (111.8) N30°24.43′ W88°55.78′ at fld. 20/2W.
  mnt dur publ opr hr only
  No NOTAM MP: 1200–1400Z‡ Wed (1000/2+1)
  TACAN AZIMUTH unusable:
   110°–120° byd 15 NM
   148°–158° byd 15 NM
  DME unusable:
   110°–120° byd 15 NM
   148°–158° byd 15 NM
 GULFPORT (L)(L) VORTAC 109.0 GPT Chan 27 N30°24.41′ W89°04.61′ 086° 7.9 NM to fld. 25/2E. NOTAM FILE GPT.
  TACAN AZIMUTH unusable:
   195°–217°
   266°–275° byd 12 NM
  VOR unusable:
   035°–086° blo 5,000′
   293°–303°
 ILS 109.7 I–BIX Rwy 22. Class IB. Mnt 1400–0500Z‡. No NOTAM MP: 1200–1400Z‡ Tue and Thu (1,000/2+1). ILS critical area not protected. Radar: See Terminal FLIP for Radar Minima.

KEWANEE N32°22.06′ W88°27.43′ NOTAM FILE GWO.   MEMPHIS
 (L) DME 113.8 EWA Chan 85 131° 22.4 NM to Butler/Choctaw Co. 342.   L–18H
  DME unusable:
   Byd 30 NM blo 3,000′

KEY FLD (See MERIDIAN on page 158)

KOSCIUSKO–ATTALA CO (OSX)(KOSX) 3 NE UTC–6(–5DT) N33°05.42′ W89°32.52′   MEMPHIS
 494 B NOTAM FILE GWO   H–6J, L–18G
 RWY 14–32: H5009X75 (ASPH) S–18 MIRL 0.5% up NW   IAP
  RWY 14: PAPI(P2L)—GA 3.5° TCH 38′. Trees.
  RWY 32: PAPI(P2L)—GA 3.5° TCH 49′. Trees.
 SERVICE: FUEL 100LL, JET A **LGT** ACTVT MIRL Rwy 14–32—CTAF.
  PAPI Rwy 14 and Rwy 32 opr consly.
 AIRPORT REMARKS: Unattended. RC model airplane flying off rwy end.
  Courtesy car avbl. 100LL self svc avbl 24 hrs via credit card.
 AIRPORT MANAGER: 662-289-1226
 COMMUNICATIONS: CTAF 122.9
 ®**MEMPHIS CENTER APP/DEP CON** 132.75
 CLEARANCE DELIVERY PHONE: For CD ctc Memphis ARTCC at
  901-368-8453/8449.
 RADIO AIDS TO NAVIGATION: NOTAM FILE GWO.
  SIDON (VH)(H) VORTAC 114.7 SQS Chan 94 N33°27.83′
   W90°16.64′ 118° 43.2 NM to fld. 127/3E.
  VOR unusable:
   059°–069° byd 40 NM

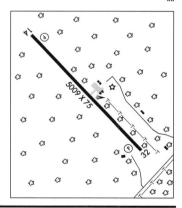

MISSISSIPPI

LAUREL

HESLER–NOBLE FLD (LUL)(KLUL) 3 SW UTC–6(–5DT) N31°40.38′ W89°10.37′ **NEW ORLEANS**
238 B NOTAM FILE GWO H–6J, L–22G
RWY 13–31: H5513X150 (ASPH) S–41, D–65, 2S–83, 2D–110 HIRL IAP
  RWY 13: REIL. PAPI(P4L)—GA 3.0° TCH 40′.
  RWY 31: PAPI(P4L)—GA 3.0° TCH 40′. Trees.
SERVICE: S2 FUEL 100LL, JET A1+ LGT Actvt REIL Rwy 13; HIRL Rwy
  13–31—CTAF. PAPI Rwy 13 and 31 opr consly.
AIRPORT REMARKS: Attended Mon–Fri 1330–0000Z‡, Sat 1500–0000Z‡,
  Sun 1900–0000Z‡. After hrs svc call 601–426–2626. Full svc fuel with
  credit card. Ultralight and crop dust activity invof arpt. Courtesy vehicle
  avbl.
AIRPORT MANAGER: 601-425-5121
WEATHER DATA SOURCES: AWOS–3PT 119.275 (601) 425–9792.
COMMUNICATIONS: CTAF/UNICOM 123.05
  LAUREL RCO 122.3 (GREENWOOD RADIO)
®HOUSTON CENTER APP/DEP CON 126.8
CLEARANCE DELIVERY PHONE: For CD if una to ctc on FSS freq, ctc Houston
  ARTCC at 281-230-5622.
RADIO AIDS TO NAVIGATION: NOTAM FILE GWO.
  EATON (L) (L) VORTACW 110.6 LBY Chan 43 N31°25.12′
    W89°20.26′ 024° 17.4 NM to fld. 290/5E.
  VORTAC unusable:
    300°–000° byd 30 NM
  VOR portion unusable:
    111°–164° byd 10 NM blo 2,000′
    241°–251°
  TACAN unusable:
    025°–035° byd 10 NM blo 3,000′
    268°–274° byd 30 NM blo 5,000′

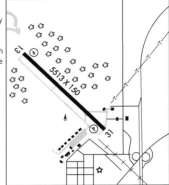

LEXINGTON

C A MOORE (19M) 2 NE UTC–6(–5DT) N33°07.53′ W90°01.53′ **MEMPHIS**
340 B NOTAM FILE GWO L–18G
RWY 01–19: H3199X60 (ASPH) S–20 MIRL 0.5% up N IAP
  RWY 01: PAPI(P2L)—GA 3.0° TCH 40′. Trees.
  RWY 19: PAPI(P2L)—GA 4.0° TCH 40′. Tree.
AIRPORT REMARKS: Unattended.
AIRPORT MANAGER: 662-834-1261
COMMUNICATIONS: CTAF 122.9
®MEMPHIS CENTER APP/DEP CON 132.5
CLEARANCE DELIVERY PHONE: For CD ctc Memphis ARTCC at 901-368-8453/8449.
RADIO AIDS TO NAVIGATION: NOTAM FILE GWO.
  SIDON (VH) (H) VORTAC 114.7 SQS Chan 94 N33°27.83′ W90°16.64′ 145° 23.9 NM to fld. 127/3E.
  VOR unusable:
    059°–069° byd 40 NM

SC, 25 JAN 2024 to 21 MAR 2024

MISSISSIPPI   155

LOUISVILLE/WINSTON CO (LMS)(KLMS) 1 N   UTC−6(−5DT)   N33°08.76′ W89°03.75′   **MEMPHIS**
575   B   NOTAM FILE GWO   L−18G
RWY 17−35: H4669X75 (ASPH−GRVD) S−50   MIRL   0.5% up S   IAP
  RWY 17: PAPI(P2L)—GA 3.25° TCH 48′. Trees.
  RWY 35: PAPI(P2L)—GA 3.0° TCH 40′. Trees.
SERVICE: **FUEL** 100LL, JET A   **LGT** Actvt MIRL Rwy 17−35—CTAF.
  PAPI Rwy 17 and 35 opr consly.
AIRPORT REMARKS: Unattended. For svc ctc AMGR. Fuel avbl 24 hrs with
  credit card. Assisted svc avbl. Pilots must provide their own tiedown
  ropes. Courtesy car avbl.
AIRPORT MANAGER: 662-705-4212
WEATHER DATA SOURCES: AWOS−3PT 118.325.
COMMUNICATIONS: CTAF/AUNICOM 122.7
®**MEMPHIS CENTER APP/DEP CON** 132.75
CLEARANCE DELIVERY PHONE: For CD ctc Memphis ARTCC at
  901-368-8453/8449.
RADIO AIDS TO NAVIGATION: NOTAM FILE GWO.
  BIGBEE (L) (L) VORTACW 116.3   IGB   Chan 109   N33°29.13′
    W88°30.82′   230° 34.3 NM to fld. 245/4E.
  VOR portion unusable:
    010°−020°
    200°−260° blo 5,000′
COMM/NAV/WEATHER REMARKS: Automated UNICOM; 4 clicks WX ADZY.

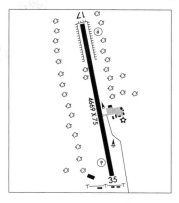

LUMBERTON

I H BASS JR MEML (4R1)   2 NW   UTC−6(−5DT)   N31°00.92′ W89°28.95′   **NEW ORLEANS**
310   B   NOTAM FILE GWO   L−21B, 22G
RWY 14−32: H3000X75 (ASPH)   S−22   MIRL
  RWY 14: PAPI(P2L). Trees.
  RWY 32: PAPI(P2L). Trees.
SERVICE: **LGT** ACTIVATE PAPI Rwy 14 and Rwy 32, MIRL Rwy 14−32—CTAF.
AIRPORT REMARKS: Unattended. Pilots must prvd their own tiedown ropes.
AIRPORT MANAGER: 601-325-4513
COMMUNICATIONS: CTAF/UNICOM 122.8
CLEARANCE DELIVERY PHONE: For CD ctc Houston ARTCC at 281-230-5622.
RADIO AIDS TO NAVIGATION: NOTAM FILE GWO.
  EATON (L) (L) VORTACW 110.3   LBY   Chan 43   N31°25.12′ W89°20.26′   192° 25.3 NM to fld. 290/5E.
  VORTAC unusable:
    300°−000° byd 30 NM
  VOR portion unusable:
    111°−164° byd 10 NM blo 2,000′
    241°−251°
  TACAN unusable:
    025°−035° byd 10 NM blo 3,000′
    268°−274° byd 30 NM blo 5,000′

MISSISSIPPI

MACON MUNI (2ØM) 2 E UTC–6(–5DT) N33°08.02´ W88°32.16´
MEMPHIS
L–18H
238 B NOTAM FILE GWO
RWY 18–36: H3000X50 (ASPH) S–28 MIRL
  RWY 18: PAPI(P2L)—GA 3.0° TCH 20´.
  RWY 36: PAPI(P2L)—GA 3.0° TCH 20´. Trees.
SERVICE: FUEL 100LL LGT Actvt MIRL Rwy 18–36—CTAF.
AIRPORT REMARKS: Unattended. 100LL avbl 24 hrs with credit card. Due to lmtd ln of sight all acft are rqrd to annc tkof and lndg on CTAF. Pilots must provide their own tiedown ropes.
AIRPORT MANAGER: 662-726-5847
COMMUNICATIONS: CTAF/UNICOM 122.7
CLEARANCE DELIVERY PHONE: For CD ctc Meridian Apch 601-679-3691, when Meridian Apch clsd ctc Memphis ARTCC at 901-368-8453/8449.
RADIO AIDS TO NAVIGATION: NOTAM FILE GWO.
  BIGBEE (L) (L) VORTACW 116.2 IGB Chan 109 N33°29.13´ W88°30.82´ 179° 21.1 NM to fld. 245/4E.
  VOR portion unusable:
    010°–020°
    200°–260° blo 5,000´

MADISON

BRUCE CAMPBELL FLD (MBO)(KMBO) 2 SE UTC–6(–5DT) N32°26.32´ W90°06.19´
MEMPHIS
L–18G
IAP
325 B NOTAM FILE GWO
RWY 17–35: H4444X75 (ASPH) S–25 MIRL
  RWY 17: PAPI(P2L)—GA 3.0° TCH 38´. Trees.
  RWY 35: PAPI(P2L)—GA 4.0° TCH 54´. Trees.
SERVICE: S2 FUEL 100LL, JET A1+ LGT Actvt PAPI Rwy 17 and 35; MIRL Rwy 17–35—CTAF. Rwy 35 PAPI OTS indef.
AIRPORT REMARKS: Attended Mon–Fri 1200–0200Z‡, Sat–Sun 1300–0100Z‡.
AIRPORT MANAGER: 601-853-1960
WEATHER DATA SOURCES: AWOS–3PT 119.125 (601) 605–8137.
COMMUNICATIONS: CTAF/UNICOM 122.8
®JACKSON APP/DEP CON 123.9 (333°–152°) 125.25 (153°–332°) (1200–0500Z‡)
®MEMPHIS CENTER APP/DEP CON 132.5 (0500–1200Z‡)
  CLNC DEL 125.9
CLEARANCE DELIVERY PHONE: When Apch clsd, for CD ctc Memphis ARTCC at 901-368-8453/8449.
RADIO AIDS TO NAVIGATION: NOTAM FILE GWO.
  MAGNOLIA (VH) (H) VORTACW 113.2 MHZ Chan 79 N32°26.04´ W90°05.99´ at fld. 407/1W.
  TACAN AZIMUTH unusable:
    240°–275° byd 30 NM blo 2,000´
    DME unsbl 240–275 byd 30 NM blo 2000¥

MAGEE MUNI (17M) 3 W UTC–6(–5DT) N31°51.77´ W89°48.04´
NEW ORLEANS
L–22F
IAP
556 B NOTAM FILE GWO
RWY 18–36: H3103X60 (ASPH) S–19 PCN 15 F/C/Y/T MIRL
  RWY 18: PAPI(P2L)—GA 3.0° TCH 43´. Trees.
  RWY 36: Trees.
SERVICE: FUEL 100LL LGT Actvt MIRL Rwy 18–36—CTAF.
AIRPORT REMARKS: Attended continuously. 100L fuel avbl 24 hrs with credit card. Rwy 36 4´ deep ditch 250´ fm thr.
AIRPORT MANAGER: 601-382-5752
COMMUNICATIONS: CTAF/UNICOM 122.8
®MEMPHIS CENTER APP/DEP CON 125.975
CLEARANCE DELIVERY PHONE: For CD ctc Memphis ARTCC at 901-368-8453/8449.
RADIO AIDS TO NAVIGATION: NOTAM FILE GWO.
  EATON (L) (L) VORTACW 110.6 LBY Chan 43 N31°25.12´ W89°20.26´ 313° 35.6 NM to fld. 290/5E.
  VORTAC unusable:
    300°–000° byd 30 NM
  VOR portion unusable:
    111°–164° byd 10 NM blo 2,000´
    241°–251°
  TACAN unusable:
    025°–035° byd 10 NM blo 3,000´
    268°–274° byd 30 NM blo 5,000´

MISSISSIPPI

MAGNOLIA N32°26.04′ W90°05.99′ NOTAM FILE GWO.   MEMPHIS
(VH) (H) VORTACW 113.2 MHZ Chan 79 at Bruce Campbell Fld. 407/1W.   L–18G
TACAN AZIMUTH unusable:
240°–275° byd 30 NM blo 2,000′
DME unsbl 240–275 byd 30 NM blo 2000′

MARKS

SELFS (MMS)(KMMS) 2 SW UTC–6(–5DT) N34°13.89′ W90°17.37′   MEMPHIS
162 NOTAM FILE GWO   L–18G
RWY 02–20: H3346X70 (ASPH) S–10 MIRL   IAP
 RWY 20: Trees.
SERVICE: S4
AIRPORT REMARKS: Attended Mon–Fri 1400–2300Z‡, Sat and Sun irregularly. For atndnc hrs Sat and Sun call 662–444–4736. Public phone avbl 662–326–9404. Rwy 02 markings badly faded.
AIRPORT MANAGER: 662-444-4736
COMMUNICATIONS: CTAF 122.9
 ®MEMPHIS CENTER APP/DEP CON 135.3
CLEARANCE DELIVERY PHONE: For CD ctc Memphis ARTCC at 901-368-8453/8449.
RADIO AIDS TO NAVIGATION: NOTAM FILE GWO.
 SIDON (VH) (H) VORTAC 114.7 SQS Chan 94 N33°27.83′ W90°16.64′ 356° 46.0 NM to fld. 127/3E.
 VOR unusable:
  059°–069° byd 40 NM

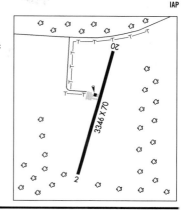

MC CAIN FLD (See MERIDIAN NAS (MC CAIN FLD) on page 159)

MC COMB/PIKE CO/JOHN E LEWIS FLD (MCB)(KMCB) 4 S UTC–6(–5DT) N31°10.71′   NEW ORLEANS
W90°28.31′   H–6J, L–21B, 22F
413 B NOTAM FILE MCB MON Airport   IAP
RWY 16–34: H5000X100 (ASPH–GRVD) S–25, D–172, 2D–308
 PCN 40 F/A/Y/T MIRL 0.5% up NW
 RWY 16: MALSF. PAPI(P4L)—GA 3.0° TCH 43′.
 RWY 34: PAPI(P2L)—GA 3.0° TCH 40′.
SERVICE: S2 **FUEL** 100LL, JET A1+ **LGT** Actvt MALSF Rwy 16—CTAF. MIRL Rwy 16–34 preset low intst dusk–0600Z‡, aft 0600Z‡ incr intst—CTAF.
AIRPORT REMARKS: Attended 1330–2330Z‡. For attendant and fuel after hrs call 601–684–8950. Courtesy car avbl. Pilots must provide their own tiedown ropes.
AIRPORT MANAGER: 601-684-8950
WEATHER DATA SOURCES: ASOS 119.025 (601) 249–3223.
COMMUNICATIONS: CTAF/UNICOM 123.05
 RCO 122.2 (GREENWOOD RADIO)
 RCO 122.1R 116.7T (GREENWOOD RADIO)
 ®HOUSTON CENTER APP/DEP CON 126.8
CLEARANCE DELIVERY PHONE: For CD if una to ctc on FSS freq, ctc Houston ARTCC at 281-230-5622.
AIRSPACE: CLASS E.
RADIO AIDS TO NAVIGATION: NOTAM FILE MCB.
 (H) (H) VORTAC 116.7 MCB Chan 114 N31°18.27′ W90°15.49′ 233° 13.3 NM to fld. 440/3E.
 FERNI NDB (MHW/LOM) 413 MC N31°15.27′ W90°30.62′ 157° 5.0 NM to fld. 447/1W.
 ILS 109.1 I–MCB Rwy 16. Class IA. LOM FERNI NDB. Glideslope unusable byd 5° left of course. LOC unusable 0.5 NM inbound.

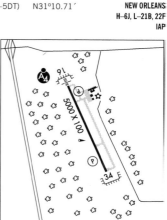

MCCHAREN FLD (See WEST POINT on page 173)

MERIDIAN

KEY FLD (MEI)(KMEI) P (ANG ARNG) 3 SW UTC–6(–5DT) N32°19.96´ W88°45.11´ **MEMPHIS**
298 B Class I, ARFF Index A NOTAM FILE MEI H–6J, L–18G
  IAP, AD

RWY 01–19: H10003X150 (ASPH–CONC) S–120, D–250, 2D–550
  PCN 104F/C/W/T HIRL
  RWY 01: MALSR. PAPI(P4L)—GA 3.0° TCH 54´. RVR–T Thld dsplcd 990´.
  RWY 19: MALSR. PAPI(P4L)—GA 3.0° TCH 69´. RVR–T Thld dsplcd 990´.
RWY 04–22: H4599X150 (ASPH) S–120, D–213, 2D–345
  PCN 61 F/C/W/U MIRL
  RWY 04: PAPI(P2L)—GA 3.13° TCH 19´. Trees.
  RWY 22: PAPI(P2L)—GA 3.59° TCH 20´. Pole.
RUNWAY DECLARED DISTANCE INFORMATION
  RWY 01: TORA–10003 TODA–10003 ASDA–10003 LDA–9013
  RWY 04: TORA–4599 TODA–4599 ASDA–4599 LDA–4599
  RWY 19: TORA–10003 TODA–10003 ASDA–10003 LDA–9013
  RWY 22: TORA–4599 TODA–4599 ASDA–4599 LDA–4599
SERVICE: S4 **FUEL** 100LL, JET A, A++ **OX** 1, 2 **LGT** ACTIVATE MALSR Rwy 01 and Rwy 19, MIRL Rwy 04–22, HIRL Rwy 01–19, twy lgts—CTAF. **MILITARY**— **JASU** 10(M32A–60) (MD–3A) (MA–1A) (MC–1) (MC–2A) **FUEL** A++(Mil) A+(avbl 1100–0400Z‡, C601–693–7282, OT 2 hr PN rqr.) (NC–100LL, A) **FLUID** SP PRESAIR **OIL** O–132–133–148(Mil)

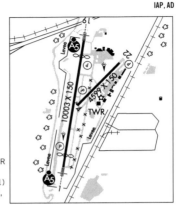

AIRPORT REMARKS: Attended 1200–0400Z‡. For attendant after hrs call 601–693–7282. ANG provides ATC services at KMEI. Rwy 01–19 dthr conc. ANG ltd prkg use; rsc info avbl for ANG Ops durg nml duty hrs. All tran acft 48 hr PPR. OBO. Rwy 01–19 non–std RESA due to sfc varns.
MILITARY REMARKS: Opr 1200–0400Z‡, OT fone C601–693–7282. **CAUTION** BASH Phase II period Mar–May, Sep–Nov. Ctc Afld Mgmt or Comd Post for current bird watch Cond. **ANG** Attended 1300–2230Z‡ Mon–Fri exc hol. ANG ramp clsd exc PPR, 601–484–9734/9714. ANG DSN 293–2829 C601–696–8829. RCR info avbl fr ANG OPS dur nml duty hr.
AIRPORT MANAGER: 601-482-0364
WEATHER DATA SOURCES: ASOS (601) 693–5650
COMMUNICATIONS: CTAF 133.975 **ATIS** 126.475 **UNICOM** 122.95
  MERIDIAN RCO 122.1R 117.0T (GREENWOOD RADIO)
Ⓡ **MERIDIAN APP/DEP CON** 120.5 Opr 1200–0400Z‡ other times by NOTAM. Other times ctc
Ⓡ **MEMPHIS CENTER APP/DEP CON** 125.975
  TOWER 133.975 (1200–0400Z‡), other times by NOTAM.
  GND CON 121.9 **CLNC DEL** 121.9
CLEARANCE DELIVERY PHONE: For CD ctc Memphis ARTCC at 901-368-8453/8449.
AIRSPACE: CLASS D svc 1200–0400Z‡; other times by NOTAM; other times CLASS G.
RADIO AIDS TO NAVIGATION: NOTAM FILE MEI.
  MERIDIAN (VH) (H) VORTAC 117.0 MEI Chan 117 N32°22.71´ W88°48.26´ 131° 3.8 NM to fld. 578/5E.
  VOR unusable:
   000°–042° byd 40 NM
   054°–061° byd 40 NM blo 24,000´
   062°–082° byd 40 NM blo 16,000´
   083°–192° byd 40 NM
   193°–203° byd 40 NM blo 18,000´
   204°–209° byd 40 NM
   210°–230° byd 40 NM blo 3,000´
   210°–230° byd 49 NM blo 12,000´
   210°–230° byd 60 NM blo 18,000´
   231°–281° byd 40 NM
   282°–292° byd 40 NM blo 6,000´
   293°–359° byd 40 NM
  ILS 110.1 I–MEI Rwy 01. Class IA. Unmonitored when ATCT closed.
  ILS/DME 111.35 I–IKQ Chan 50(Y) Rwy 19.
  ASR/PAR

MISSISSIPPI

MERIDIAN NAS (MC CAIN FLD) (NMM)(KNMM) N 11 NE UTC−6(−5DT) N32°53.21′ W88°33.32′   MEMPHIS
316 B TPA—1216(900) NOTAM FILE NMM Not insp.   H−6J, L−18H
    RWY 01L−19R: H8003X200 (CONC) PCN 65 R/C/W/T HIRL CL   DIAP, AD
        RWY 01L: ALSF1. OLS. WAVE-OFF. NSTD. 0.5% up.
        RWY 19R: PAPI(P4R)—GA 3.0° TCH 40′.
    RWY 01R−19L: H8000X200 (CONC) PCN 71 R/C/W/T HIRL CL
        RWY 01R: OLS. RVR-R
        RWY 19L: MALSR. OLS. WAVE-OFF. NSTD. RVR-T 0.6% down.
    RWY 10−28: H6402X200 (CONC) PCN 29 R/C/W/T HIRL
    ARRESTING GEAR/SYSTEM
      RWY 01L HOOK E28(B) (1750′)   HOOK E28(B) (1251′) **RWY 19R**
      RWY 01R HOOK E28(B) (1250′)   HOOK E28(B) (1748′) **RWY 19L**
      RWY 10 HOOK E28(B) (1250′)   HOOK E28(B) (1250′) **RWY 28**
    SERVICE: **FUEL** 100LL, JET A++, J8 **LGT** Portable OLS avbl Rwy 01L, 01R, 19L, 19R and 28. **MILITARY—A−GEAR** normally rigged on all rwys. **JASU** 2(NC−8A) (GTC−85) 1(NCPP−105) **FUEL** A++. Svc avbl during airfield hrs of ops. Expect 1 hr refuel delays. **TRAN ALERT** Svc avbl 1300−0500Z‡ Mon−Thu, 1300−2300Z‡ Fri. Drag chute repack unavbl. Ltd airstart capabilities for tran acft. CTC 601−679−2342 to verify status prior to req PPR.
    MILITARY REMARKS: Opr Mon−Thur 1300−0400Z‡, Fri 1200−2200Z‡, clsd Sat, Sun and hol exc by NOTAM; hr subject to chg in support CTW−1 flt OPS. Base OPS 1300−0500Z‡ Mon−Thur, 1300−2300Z‡ Fri, clsd Sat, Sun and hol exc by NOTAM. **RSTD** All acft rqr PPR, ctc Base OPS DSN 637−2470/2505, C601−679−2470/2505. PPR good for +/− 1 hr PPR time. For CALP processing ctc AFM via base ops. Arpt subj to short notice closure. Coord of PPR outside of block time by telephone is rqr or PPR Nr will be cancelled. Arpt subject to no notice closure. PPR civilian acft Official Business. **CAUTION** Rwy 19L and 19R have 1 percent down gradient first 6000′. Wildlife in vicinity all rwy. Mat and twy south of hangar not visible from twr. Ints student jet training during fld opr hr. **TFC PAT** Break 1400′, Tran acft expect visual apch. VFR acft ctc Meridian APP within 25 NM. **MISC** Ramp elev 283′. Expect arr/dep delay during extensive student training. No classified materials storage avbl. Scheduling point: 187 FW, AL ANG. Location: Montgomery, AL DSN: 358−9255 C334−394−7255.
    AIRPORT MANAGER: 601 6792470/2505
    COMMUNICATIONS: ATIS 290.525, (Mon−Thu 1300−0500Z‡, Fri 1300−2300Z‡, clsd Sat, Sun and holidays exc by NOTAM) ATIS hrs subject to change is support CTW−1 flt opr.
    Ⓡ **APP CON** 276.4 121.275 348.7(E) 120.5 269.325(S) 120.95 276.4(W) 379.275(N) (Mon−Thu 1300−0500Z‡, Fri 1300−2300Z‡, clsd Sat, Sun and holidays exc by NOTAM), other times ctc
    Ⓡ **MEMPHIS CENTER APP CON** 125.975 351.7
        MC CAIN TOWER 126.2 340.2 (Rwy 01L, Rwy 19L, Rwy 28) 126.2 360.2 (Rwy 01R, Rwy 19R, Rwy 10)
    MC CAIN GND CON 336.4 **CLNC DEL** 301.0
    Ⓡ **DEP CON** 276.4 124.8(S) 343.7(E) (Mon−Thu 1300−0500Z‡, Fri 1300−2300Z‡, clsd Sat, Sun and holidays exc by NOTAM), other times ctc
    Ⓡ **MEMPHIS CENTER DEP CON** 125.975 351.7
      PMSV METRO 282.525 (Avbl Mon−Thu 1100−0500Z‡, Fri 1100−2300Z‡.) **BASE OPS** 352.2
    CLEARANCE DELIVERY PHONE: For CD when una via freq ctc Meridian Apch 601−679−3691, when Meridian Apch clsd ctc Memphis ARTCC at 901−368−8453/8449.
    AIRSPACE: CLASS D svc 1300−0500Z‡ Mon−Thu, 1300−2300Z‡ Fri, clsd Sat−Sun, hol exc by NOTAM; other times CLASS G.
    RADIO AIDS TO NAVIGATION: NOTAM FILE GWO.
      (L) TACAN Chan 56 NMM (111.9) N32°34.70′ W88°32.71′ 201° 1.6 NM to fld. 309/2W.
      TACAN AZIMUTH unusable:
        013°−088° byd 21 NM blo 3,000′
        108°−113°
        opr dur flt opr hr only
      TACAN DME unusable:
        013°−088° byd 21 NM blo 3,000′
        108°−113°
      ILS/DME 109.7 I−NMM Chan 34 Rwy 19L. Class IE. Glideslope unusable byd 6° left of course.
      ASR/PAR 1300−0500Z‡
    COMM/NAV/WEATHER REMARKS: Radar see Terminal FLIP for Radar Minima.

METCALF N33°25.52′ W90°58.93′ NOTAM FILE GLH.   MEMPHIS
    NDB (MHW) 359 MTQ 359° 3.6 NM to Greenville Mid-Delta. 120/1W.   L−18F

MISSISSIPPI CANYON 474 IKT N28°31.25′ W88°17.33′   NEW ORLEANS
    AWOS−3 118.025 (979) 230−4223   L−21C, GOMC

MONROE CO (See ABERDEEN/AMORY on page 130)

MISSISSIPPI

NATCHEZ

HARDY–ANDERS FLD/NATCHEZ–ADAMS CO (HEZ)(KHEZ) 6 NE UTC–6(–5DT) N31°36.82′   HOUSTON
W91°17.84′   H–6J, L–22F
272 B Class IV, ARFF Index A NOTAM FILE HEZ   IAP
RWY 14–32: H6500X150 (ASPH–GRVD) S–50, D–78, 2D–172
  PCN 39 F/B/Y/T HIRL
  RWY 14: MALSR. PAPI(P4R)—GA 3.0° TCH 55′.
  RWY 32: PAPI(P4L)—GA 3.0° TCH 43′. Trees.
RWY 18–36: H5000X150 (ASPH) S–83, D–113, 2S–143, 2D–65
  PCN 35 F/B/Y/T MIRL
  RWY 18: VASI(V4L)—GA 3.0° TCH 30′.
  RWY 36: Trees.
SERVICE: S2 **FUEL** 100LL, JET A **LGT** ACTVT MALSR Rwy 14; PAPI Rwy 14 and Rwy 32; VASI Rwy 18; MIRL Rwy 18–36—CTAF.
AIRPORT REMARKS: Attended 1200–0200Z‡. Deer on and invof rwys. Twy A & C1 not avbl for acr use. Clsd for skedd acr ops with more than 30 pax seats excp 48 hrs PPR call AMGR. Gnd pwr unit avbl on field. Rwy 14–32 uneven pavement. Rwy 14 and Rwy 32 markings obscured. Rwy 18–36 widespread cracking and uneven pavement. Rwy 18–36 not avbl for skedd acr ops with more than 9 pax seats or unsked acr at least 31 pax seats. Rwy 18 and Rwy 36 markings faded.
AIRPORT MANAGER: 601-442-5171
WEATHER DATA SOURCES: AWOS–3PT 124.675 (601) 446–8022. LAWRS.
COMMUNICATIONS: CTAF/UNICOM 122.8
  NATCHEZ RCO 122.6 (GREENWOOD RADIO)
®**HOUSTON CENTER APP/DEP CON** 120.975
RADIO AIDS TO NAVIGATION: NOTAM FILE HEZ.
  NATCHEZ (L) DME 110.0 HEZ Chan 37 N31°37.09′ W91°17.98′ at fld. 280.
    DME unusable:
      Byd 25 NM blo 4,000′
  NATCHEZ–ADAMS COUNTY NDB (MHW) 388 HAH N31°41.42′ W91°17.59′ 183° 4.6 NM to fld. 114/0E.
  ILS 111.35 I–HEZ Rwy 14. Class IA. Glideslope unmonitored.

NATCHEZ N31°37.09′ W91°17.98′ NOTAM FILE HEZ.   HOUSTON
(L) DME 110.0 HEZ Chan 37 at Hardy–Anders Fld/Natchez–Adams Co. 280.   L–22F
  DME unusable:
    Byd 25 NM blo 4,000′
  RCO 122.6 (GREENWOOD RADIO)

NEW ALBANY/UNION CO (M72) 3 N UTC–6(–5DT) N34°32.94′ W89°01.47′   MEMPHIS
413 B NOTAM FILE GWO   L–18G
RWY 18–36: H3903X75 (ASPH) S–20 MIRL 0.4% up NW   IAP
  RWY 18: PAPI(P2L)—GA 3.0° TCH 40′. Trees.
  RWY 36: PAPI(P2L)—GA 3.0° TCH 40′. Trees.
SERVICE: FUEL 100LL **LGT** MIRL Rwy 18–36 opr dusk–0400Z‡.
AIRPORT REMARKS: Attended Mon–Fri dalgt hrs. 100LL fuel 24 hrs with credit card. Airframe and power plant rprs on req.
AIRPORT MANAGER: 662-534-1050
COMMUNICATIONS: CTAF/UNICOM 122.8
®**MEMPHIS CENTER APP/DEP CON** 135.9
CLEARANCE DELIVERY PHONE: For CD ctc Memphis ARTCC at 901–368–8453/8449.
RADIO AIDS TO NAVIGATION: NOTAM FILE GWO.
  HOLLY SPRINGS (L) (L) VORTACW 112.4 HLI Chan 71 N34°46.21′ W89°29.79′ 116° 26.9 NM to fld. 624/3E.
    VOR UNUSABL:
      172°–192° byd 25 NM blo 2,400′

MISSISSIPPI 161

NEWTON
JAMES H EASOM FLD (M23) 1 SE UTC−6(−5DT) N32°18.72′ W89°08.14′ **MEMPHIS**
370 B NOTAM FILE GWO **L−18G**
RWY 14−32: H3000X75 (ASPH) S−21 MIRL
   RWY 14: PVASI(PSIL). Trees.
   RWY 32: PVASI(PSIL)—GA 7.0° TCH 26′. Trees.
SERVICE: S4 **FUEL** 100LL **LGT** Actvt MIRL Rwy 14−32—CTAF. PAPI Rwy 32 opr consly.
AIRPORT REMARKS: Attended on call—601−357−0213. For attendant aft hrs and emerg only call 601−527−6249. 24 hr fuel avbl with credit card. Airframe repairs: to schedule, call 601−357−0115, also for power plant repairs. Pilots must provide their own tiedown ropes. Rwy 14−32 mkgs faded.
AIRPORT MANAGER: 601-357-0213
COMMUNICATIONS: CTAF/UNICOM 122.8
CLEARANCE DELIVERY PHONE: For CD ctc Meridian Apch 601-679-3691, when Meridian Apch clsd ctc Memphis ARTCC at 901-368-8453/8449.
RADIO AIDS TO NAVIGATION: NOTAM FILE MEI.
   MERIDIAN (VH) (H) VORTAC 117.0 MEI Chan 117 N32°22.71′ W88°48.26′ 252° 17.3 NM to fld. 578/5E.
     VOR unusable:
       000°–042° byd 40 NM
       054°–061° byd 40 NM blo 24,000′
       062°–082° byd 40 NM blo 16,000′
       083°–192° byd 40 NM
       193°–203° byd 40 NM blo 18,000′
       204°–209° byd 40 NM
       210°–230° byd 40 NM blo 3,000′
       210°–230° byd 49 NM blo 12,000′
       210°–230° byd 60 NM blo 18,000′
       231°–281° byd 40 NM
       282°–292° byd 40 NM blo 6,000′
       293°–359° byd 40 NM

OCEAN SPRINGS (5R2) 3 E UTC−6(−5DT) N30°23.37′ W88°45.21′ **NEW ORLEANS**
20 B NOTAM FILE GWO **L−21C, 22G**
RWY 18−36: H3500X50 (ASPH) S−10 MIRL
   RWY 18: REIL. Trees.
   RWY 36: REIL. Trees.
SERVICE: **FUEL** 100LL **LGT** Actvt non std REIL Rwy 18 and 36; MIRL Rwy 18−36—CTAF. Actvt lgtd windsock—CTAF. Bcn OTS.
AIRPORT REMARKS: Unattended.
AIRPORT MANAGER: 228-872-1962
COMMUNICATIONS: CTAF/UNICOM 122.7
   APP/DEP CON 124.6130−309
CLEARANCE DELIVERY PHONE: For CD ctc Gulfport Apch at 228-265-6151, when Apch clsd ctc Houston ARTCC at 281-230-5622.
RADIO AIDS TO NAVIGATION: NOTAM FILE ANB.
   SEMMES (VH) (H) VORTACW 115.3 SJI Chan 10C N30°43.56′ W88°21.56′ 220° 28.7 NM to fld. 190/5E.
     VOR unusable:
       010°–022° byd 40 NM
       023°–033°
       045°–075° byd 40 NM
       076°–088° byd 40 NM blo 3,100′
       076°–088° byd 49 NM
       097°–198° byd 40 NM
       199°–209°
       210°–228° byd 40 NM
       211°–221° byd 30 NM blo 6,000′
       229°–249° byd 40 NM blo 18,000′
       233°–243° byd 22 NM blo 5,000′
       250°–254° byd 40 NM
       255°–270° byd 40 NM blo 18,000′
       303°–329° byd 40 NM
       310°–320° byd 22 NM blo 8,000′
       330°–340°
       355°–015° byd 20 blo 4,000′
       358°–004° byd 40 NM
     TACAN AZIMUTH unusable:
       120°–130°
       268°–274° byd 30 NM blo 5,000′
     DME unusable:
       268°–274° byd 30 NM blo 5,000′

MISSISSIPPI

OKOLONA MUNI/RICHARD STOVALL FLD (5A4) 2 NE UTC–6(–5DT) N34°00.95´ W88°43.57´   MEMPHIS
337   B   NOTAM FILE GWO   L–18G
  RWY 18–36: H3197X60 (ASPH)   S–12.5   MIRL   IAP
    RWY 36: Trees.
  SERVICE: S4   **FUEL** 100LL   **LGT** Actvt MIRL Rwy 18–36—CTAF.
  AIRPORT REMARKS: Unattended. 100LL avbl 24 hr with credit card. Rwy
    18–36 terrain drops off abruptly 200´ fm both ends.
  AIRPORT MANAGER: 662-447-5461
  COMMUNICATIONS: CTAF 122.9
  Ⓡ **COLUMBUS APP/DEP CON** 126.075 (1300–0100Z‡ Mon–Fri,
    1800–2300Z‡ Sun, clsd Sat and hols.)
  Ⓡ **MEMPHIS CENTER APP/DEP CON** 128.5 (0100–1300Z‡ Mon–Fri,
    2300Z–1800Z‡ Sun, Sat and hols.)
  CLEARANCE DELIVERY PHONE: For CD ctc Memphis ARTCC at
    901-368-8453/8449.
  RADIO AIDS TO NAVIGATION: NOTAM FILE TUP.
    TUPELO (L) (L) VORW/DME 109.8   OTB   Chan 35   N34°13.43´
    W88°47.84´   160° 13.0 NM to fld. 364/4E.
    VOR portion unusable:
    190°–220°

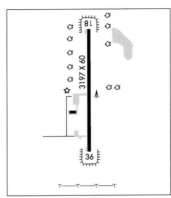

OKTIBBEHA (See STARKVILLE on page 169)

OLIVE BRANCH/TAYLOR FLD (OLV)(KOLV) 3 NE UTC–6(–5DT) N34°58.73´ W89°47.21´   MEMPHIS
402   B   TPA—1202(800)   NOTAM FILE OLV   H–6J, L–18G
  RWY 18–36: H6000X100 (ASPH–GRVD)   S–110, D–151, 2D–205,   IAP, AD
    2D/2D2–599 PCN 459F/D/X/T   HIRL
    RWY 18: MALSR. VASI(V4L)—GA 3.0° TCH 51´.
    RWY 36: VASI(V4L)—GA 3.0° TCH 31´. Trees.
  SERVICE: S4   **FUEL** 100LL, JET A   **OX** 3   **LGT** Actvt MALSR Rwy
    18—CTAF.
  AIRPORT REMARKS: Attended 1200–0300Z‡ Mon–Fri, 1400–2300Z‡
    Sat-Sun. Clsd Thanksgiving, Christmas and Easter. 100LL avbl 24 hrs
    with credit card. Bottle oxygen avbl on request call 662–895–2978.
    Read back rqrd of all hold back instructions. Twy H clsd exc to sngl and
    lgt twin acft only. Fixed dist mkrs.
  AIRPORT MANAGER: 662-895-2978
  WEATHER DATA SOURCES: AWOS–3 119.925 (662) 893–5906. LAWRS.
  COMMUNICATIONS: CTAF 125.275 **ATIS** 119.925 **UNICOM** 122.95
  Ⓡ **MEMPHIS APP CON** 125.8   120.075
  Ⓡ **MEMPHIS DEP CON** 124.15
    TOWER 125.275 (1300–0300Z‡)   **GND CON** 121.2   **CLNC DEL** 121.2
    CLNC DEL 121.3 (When twr clsd)
  AIRSPACE: CLASS D svc 1300–0300Z‡; other times CLASS G.
  RADIO AIDS TO NAVIGATION: NOTAM FILE MEM.
    MEMPHIS (H) (H) VORTACW 117.5   MEM   Chan 122   N35°00.91´   W89°58.99´   102° 9.9 NM to fld. 363/1E.
    ILS/DME 109.3   I–OLV   Chan 30   Rwy 18.   Class IA.   Unmonitored when ATCT is clsd.
    LOC/DME 111.55   I–EVO   Chan 52(Y)   Rwy 36.

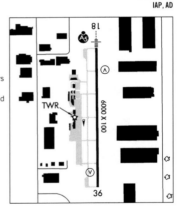

MISSISSIPPI

OXFORD

UNIVERSITY–OXFORD (UOX)(KUOX) 2 NW UTC–6(–5DT) N34°23.06′ W89°32.21′ MEMPHIS
452 B TPA—See Remarks ARFF Index—See Remarks NOTAM FILE GWO H–6J, L–18G
RWY 09–27: H5600X100 (ASPH) S–38, D–55, 2D–90 PCN 29 F/C/X/T IAP
  MIRL 0.7% up E
  RWY 09: REIL. PAPI(P4L)—GA 3.0° TCH 40′.
  RWY 27: REIL. PAPI(P4L)—GA 3.6° TCH 56′. Tree.
SERVICE: S1 **FUEL** 100LL, JET A, A+ **LGT** MIRL Rwy 09–27 oprs
  dusk–0400Z‡. Aft 0400Z‡, actvt REIL Rwy 09 & 27; PAPI Rwy 09;
  MIRL Rwy 09–27—CTAF. PAPI Rwy 27 opr consly. PAPI Rwy 27 unusbl
  byd 6 deg L of cntrln.
AIRPORT REMARKS: Attended 1300–0000Z‡. For arpt attendant ngts call
  662–234–2036. Class IV ARFF Index A. Clsd to acr ops with more than
  30 pax seats excp PPR call AMGR 662–234–2035. TPA—1252 (800)
  light acft, 1652 (1200) high speed acft.
AIRPORT MANAGER: 662–234–2036
WEATHER DATA SOURCES: AWOS–3PT 132.725 (662) 234–9751.
COMMUNICATIONS: CTAF/UNICOM 123.0
®**MEMPHIS CENTER APP/DEP CON** 128.5
  GCO 135.075 FOR MEMPHIS ARTCC (ZME))
CLEARANCE DELIVERY PHONE: For CD if una via GCO ctc Memphis ARTCC at
  901–368–8453/8449.
RADIO AIDS TO NAVIGATION: NOTAM FILE GWO.
HOLLY SPRINGS (L) (L) VORTACW 112.4 HLI Char 71 N34°46.21′ W89°29.79′ 182° 23.2 NM to fld. 624/3E.
  VOR UNUSABL:
    172°–192° byd 25 NM blo 2,400′
  TUNNG NDB (LOMW) 426 UV N34°23.11′ W89°37.56′ 092° 4.4 NM to fld. 410/1W. LOC & NDB unmonitored
    2300–1400Z‡.
  LOC 111.7 I–UVD Rwy 09. LOM TUNNG NDB. LOC and OM unmonitored 2300–1400Z‡.

PANOLA CO (See BATESVILLE on page 131)

PASCAGOULA

TRENT LOTT INTL (PQL)(KPQL) 6 N UTC–6(–5DT) N30°27.77′ W88°31.75′ NEW ORLEANS
17 B LRA NOTAM FILE PQL H–7E, 8F, L–21C, 22G, GOMC
RWY 17–35: H6501X150 (ASPH–GRVD) D–196, 2D–315, IAP, AD
  2D/2D2–753 PCN 57 F/C/X/T MIRL
  RWY 17: MALSR. PAPI(P4L)—GA 3.0° TCH 50′.
  RWY 35: PAPI(P4L)—GA 3.0° TCH 40′.
SERVICE: S4 **FUEL** 100LL, JET A **LGT** Actvt MALSR Rwy 17; PAPI Rwy
  35; MIRL Rwy 17–35—CTAF.
AIRPORT REMARKS: Attended continuously. Nmrs low flying fish spotter acft
  oprg near shoreline btn Bay St Louis and Pascagoula SR–SS. Mil contr
  100LL fuel avbl. ARFF 24hrs.
AIRPORT MANAGER: 228–475–1371
WEATHER DATA SOURCES: ASOS 135.175 (228) 474–2836.
COMMUNICATIONS: CTAF 118.575 **ATIS** 135.175 **UNICOM** 122.8
®**MOBILE APP/DEP CON** 121.0 (1200–0500Z‡)
®**HOUSTON CENTER APP/DEP CON** 127.65 (0500–1200Z‡)
  TOWER 118.575 (Mon–Fri 1200–0200Z‡; Sat–Sun
  1400–0000Z‡.) **GND CON** 121.725 **CLNC DEL** 121.725
CLEARANCE DELIVERY PHONE: For CD when ATCT clsd ctc Mobile Apch at
  251–662–6236, when Apch clsd ctc Houston ARTCC at
  281–230–5622.

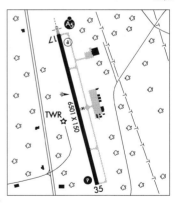

CONTINUED ON NEXT PAGE

MISSISSIPPI

CONTINUED FROM PRECEDING PAGE

AIRSPACE: CLASS D svc 1200–0200Z‡ Mon–Fri, 1400–0000Z‡ Sat–Sun; other times CLASS G.
RADIO AIDS TO NAVIGATION: NOTAM FILE ANB.
  SEMMES (VH) (H) VORTACW 115.3   SJI   Chan 100   N30°43.56´ W88°21.56´   204° 18.0 NM to fld. 190/5E.
    VOR unusable:
      010°–022° byd 40 NM
      023°–033°
      045°–075° byd 40 NM
      076°–088° byd 40 NM blo 3,100´
      076°–088° byd 49 NM
      097°–198° byd 40 NM
      199°–209°
      210°–228° byd 40 NM
      211°–221° byd 30 NM blo 6,000´
      229°–249° byd 40 NM blo 18,000´
      233°–243° byd 22 NM blo 5,000´
      250°–254° byd 40 NM
      255°–270° byd 40 NM blo 18,000´
      303°–329° byd 40 NM
      310°–320° byd 22 NM blo 8,000´
      330°–340°
      355°–015° byd 20 blo 4,000´
      358°–004° byd 40 NM
    TACAN AZIMUTH unusable:
      120°–130°
      268°–274° byd 30 NM blo 5,000´
    DME unusable:
      268°–274° byd 30 NM blo 5,000´
  ILS/DME 110.1   I-PQL   Chan 38   Rwy 17.   Class IA.

PAUL PITTMAN MEML (See TYLERTOWN on page 172)

PHILADELPHIA MUNI (MPE)(KMPE)   2 NW   UTC–6(–5DT)   N32°47.95´ W89°07.56´   **MEMPHIS**
458   B   NOTAM FILE GWO   H–6J, L–18G
  RWY 18–36: H5001X75 (ASPH) S–30 MIRL 0.4% up S   IAP
    RWY 18: REIL. PAPI(P2L)—GA 3.0° TCH 44´. Trees.
    RWY 36: REIL. PAPI(P2L)—GA 3.0° TCH 40´. Trees.
  SERVICE: **FUEL** 100LL, JET A   **LGT** ACTVT REIL Rwy 18 and 36; PAPI Rwy 18 and 36; MIRL Rwy 18–36—CTAF.
  AIRPORT REMARKS: Attended Mon–Sun 1300–2300Z‡. After hrs svc call 601–728–9682. Fuel: No self–serve; CC accepted. Rwy 18–36 markings faded.
  AIRPORT MANAGER: 601–656–0203
  WEATHER DATA SOURCES: AWOS–3P 118.725 (601) 663–0040.
  COMMUNICATIONS: CTAF/UNICOM 123.0
  Ⓡ **MEMPHIS CENTER APP/DEP CON** 132.75
  CLEARANCE DELIVERY PHONE: For CD ctc Memphis ARTCC at 901–368–8453/8449.
  RADIO AIDS TO NAVIGATION: NOTAM FILE MEI.
  MERIDIAN (VH) (H) VORTAC 117.0   MEI   Chan 117   N32°22.71´ W88°48.26´   322° 30.0 NM to fld. 578/5E.
    VOR unusable:
      000°–042° byd 40 NM
      054°–061° byd 40 NM blo 24,000´
      062°–082° byd 40 NM blo 16,000´
      083°–192° byd 40 NM
      193°–203° byd 40 NM blo 18,000´
      204°–209° byd 40 NM
      210°–230° byd 40 NM blo 3,000´
      210°–230° byd 49 NM blo 12,000´
      210°–230° byd 60 NM blo 18,000´
      231°–281° byd 40 NM
      282°–292° byd 40 NM blo 6,000´
      293°–359° byd 40 NM

MISSISSIPPI

PICAYUNE MUNI (MJD)(KMJD) 2 SE UTC−6(−5DT) N30°29.25´ W89°39.07´ NEW ORLEANS
55 B NOTAM FILE GWO H−7E, 8F, L−21B, 22G
RWY 18−36: H5000X75 (ASPH) S−30 MIRL IAP
  RWY 18: PAPI(P2L)—GA 3.0° TCH 36´. Trees.
  RWY 36: PAPI(P2L)—GA 3.0° TCH 43´. Tree.
SERVICE: S4 **FUEL** 100LL, JET A **LGT** ACTIVATE PAPI Rwy 18 and Rwy 36; MIRL Rwy 18−36—CTAF.
AIRPORT REMARKS: Attended 1400−2300Z‡. Birds and geese invof arpt. Fuel avbl 24 hrs with credit card. Closed circuit television at terminal and fuel pumps.
AIRPORT MANAGER: 601-590-0260
WEATHER DATA SOURCES: AWOS−3PT 119.075 (601) 798−4136.
COMMUNICATIONS: CTAF/UNICOM 122.8
® **GULFPORT APP/DEP CON** 124.6 (1200−0500Z‡)
® **HOUSTON CENTER APP/DEP CON** 127.65 (0500−1200Z‡)
CLEARANCE DELIVERY PHONE: For CD ctc Gulfport Apch at 228-265-6151, when Apch clsd ctc Houston ARTCC at 281-230-5622.
RADIO AIDS TO NAVIGATION: NOTAM FILE GWO.
  (L) (L) **VORW/DME** 113.95 PCU Chan 86(Y) N30°33.67´ W89°43.83´ 132° 6.0 NM to fld. 70/5E.
  VOR unusable:
    285°−305° byd 6 NM blo 4,000´
    325°−076° byd 26 NM blo 2,500´
  DME unusable:
    078°−180° byd 32 NM blo 3,000´
    331°−064° byd 27 NM blo 4,000´

PITTSBORO

CALHOUN CO (04M) 1 SW UTC−6(−5DT) N33°55.81´ W89°20.60´ MEMPHIS
387 B NOTAM FILE GWO L−18G
RWY 15−33: H3200X60 (ASPH) S−15 MIRL
  RWY 15: PAPI(P4L)—GA 3.0° TCH 40´. Trees.
  RWY 33: PAPI(P4L)—GA 3.0° TCH 40´. Trees.
SERVICE: **FUEL** 100LL **LGT** Actvt PAPI Rwy 15−33—CTAF; MIRL Rwy 15−33 on SS−SR.
AIRPORT REMARKS: Unattended. Fuel 24 hr credit card svc avbl. Courtesy car avbl.
AIRPORT MANAGER: 662-414-0975
COMMUNICATIONS: CTAF 122.9
CLEARANCE DELIVERY PHONE: For CD ctc Memphis ARTCC at 901-368-8453/8449.
RADIO AIDS TO NAVIGATION: NOTAM FILE CBM.
  CALEDONIA (L) (L) **VORTACW** 115.2 CBM Chan 99 N33°38.49´ W88°26.31´ 291° 48.4 NM to fld. 250/0E.
  military use: mnt 1300−0100Z‡ Mon−Fri; 1800−2300Z‡ Sun. No NOTAM MP: 0200−0400Z‡ Sun
  VOR unusable:
    317°−223°
  TACAN AZIMUTH unusable:
    015°−030° byd 20 NM blo 4,000´
  DME unusable:
    015°−030° byd 20 NM blo 4,000´
    080°−100° byd 35 NM blo 3,500´

PONTOTOC CO (22M) 2 NW UTC−6(−5DT) N34°16.53´ W89°02.28´ MEMPHIS
440 B NOTAM FILE GWO L−18G
RWY 11−29: H3000X50 (ASPH) S−16 MIRL 0.9% up SE
  RWY 11: Tree.
  RWY 29: Trees.
SERVICE: S4 **FUEL** 100LL
AIRPORT REMARKS: Unattended. For attendant and emerg svc call 662−489−3111. 110LL avbl 24 hrs with credit card. Pilots must provide their own tiedown ropes.
AIRPORT MANAGER: (662) 891-5593
COMMUNICATIONS: CTAF/UNICOM 122.8
CLEARANCE DELIVERY PHONE: For CD ctc Memphis ARTCC at 901-368-8453/8449.
RADIO AIDS TO NAVIGATION: NOTAM FILE GWO.
  HOLLY SPRINGS (L) (L) **VORTACW** 112.4 HLI Chan 71 N34°46.21´ W89°29.79´ 139° 37.3 NM to fld. 624/3E.
  VOR UNUSABL:
    172°−192° byd 25 NM blo 2,400´

MISSISSIPPI

POPLARVILLE/PEARL RIVER CO (M13)   3 SE   UTC–6(–5DT)   N30°47.19′ W89°30.27′   NEW ORLEANS
319   B   NOTAM FILE GWO   L–21B, 22G
RWY 16–34: H4000X100 (ASPH)   S–25.2   MIRL   0.4% up S   IAP
  RWY 16: PAPI(P2L)—GA 3.0° TCH 45′. Trees.
  RWY 34: PAPI(P2L)—GA 3.0° TCH 41′. Trees.
SERVICE: S4   **FUEL** 100LL   **LGT** PAPI Rwy 16 and 34; MIRL Rwy
  16–34 oper dusk–0300Z‡. Aft 0300Z‡ actvt—CTAF.
AIRPORT REMARKS: Unattended. Fuel 24 hr self svc with credit card.
  Ultralight act on and invof arpt. Rwy 34, terrn drops off abruptly 200′
  fm thr. Rwy 16, 335′ AGL ant twr on L downwind pat.
AIRPORT MANAGER: 601-550-3059
COMMUNICATIONS: CTAF 122.9
®**GULFPORT APP/DEP CON** 124.6   354.1 (1200–0500Z‡)
®**HOUSTON CENTER APP/DEP CON** 126.8   327.8 (0500–1200Z‡)
CLEARANCE DELIVERY PHONE: For CD ctc Gulfport Apch at 228-265-6151,
  when Apch clsd ctc Houston ARTCC at 281-230-5622.
RADIO AIDS TO NAVIGATION: NOTAM FILE GWO.
  PICAYUNE (L) (L) VORW/DME 113.95   PCU   Chan 86(Y)
    N30°33.67′ W89°43.83′   036° 17.9 NM to fld. 70/5E.
    VOR unusable:
      285°–305° byd 6 NM blo 4,000′
      325°–076° byd 26 NM blo 2,500′
    DME unusable:
      078°–180° byd 32 NM blo 3,000′
      331°–064° byd 27 NM blo 4,000′

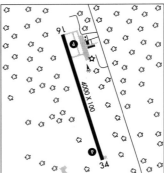

PRENTISS—JEFFERSON DAVIS CO (M43)   2 W   UTC–6(–5DT)   N31°35.72′ W89°54.39′   NEW ORLEANS
455   B   NOTAM FILE GWO   L–22F
RWY 12–30: H3197X60 (ASPH)   S–20   MIRL   IAP
  RWY 12: PAPI(P2L)—GA 2.75° TCH 45′.
  RWY 30: PAPI(P2L)—GA 2.75° TCH 45′. Trees.
SERVICE: **FUEL** 100LL   **LGT** ACTIVATE MIRL Rwy 12–30—CTAF.
AIRPORT REMARKS: Unattended. Fuel avbl 24 hrs with credit card. For
  emergency call police department 601–792–5198.
AIRPORT MANAGER: 601-466-4959
COMMUNICATIONS: CTAF/UNICOM 122.8
®**HOUSTON CENTER APP/DEP CON** 126.8
CLEARANCE DELIVERY PHONE: For CD ctc Houston ARTCC at 281-230-5622.
RADIO AIDS TO NAVIGATION: NOTAM FILE MCB.
  MC COMB (H) (H) VORTAC 116.7   MCB   Chan 114   N31°18.27′
    W90°15.49′   043° 25.1 NM to fld. 440/3E.

MISSISSIPPI

QUITMAN

CLARKE CO (23M) 3 N UTC−6(−5DT) N32°05.16′ W88°44.34′ MEMPHIS
321 B NOTAM FILE GWO L−17D, 18G
RWY 16−34: H3295X59 (ASPH) S−12.5 MIRL
 RWY 16: PAPI(P2L)—GA 4.0° TCH 56′. Trees.
 RWY 34: Trees.
SERVICE: **FUEL** 100LL **LGT** Lgts opr dusk−0400Z‡. Aft 0400Z‡ actvt MIRL Rwy 16−34—CTAF.
AIRPORT REMARKS: Attended Mon−Sat 1400−2300Z‡, Sun 1900−2300Z‡. Ultralight activity on and invof arpt. Credit card accepted in terminal. Gnd drops abruptly 250′ fm Rwy 16 thld. Gnd drops abruptly 240′ fm Rwy 34 thr. Pilots must provide their own tiedown ropes.
AIRPORT MANAGER: 601−776−6312
COMMUNICATIONS: CTAF/UNICOM 122.8
CLEARANCE DELIVERY PHONE: For CD ctc Meridian Apch 601−679−3691, when Meridian Apch clsd ctc Memphis ARTCC at 901−368−8453/8449.
RADIO AIDS TO NAVIGATION: NOTAM FILE MEI.
 MERIDIAN (VH) (H) VORTAC 117.0 MEI Chan 117 N32°22.71′ W88°48.26′ 164° 17.8 NM to fld. 578/5E.
  VOR unusable:
   000°−042° byd 40 NM
   054°−061° byd 40 NM blo 24,000′
   062°−082° byd 40 NM blo 16,000′
   083°−192° byd 40 NM
   193°−203° byd 40 NM blo 18,000′
   204°−209° byd 40 NM
   210°−230° byd 40 NM blo 3,000′
   210°−230° byd 49 NM blo 12,000′
   210°−230° byd 60 NM blo 18,000′
   231°−281° byd 40 NM
   282°−292° byd 40 NM blo 6,000′
   293°−359° byd 40 NM

RALPH M SHARPE (See TUNICA on page 170)

RAYMOND

JOHN BELL WILLIAMS (JVW)(KJVW) 3 NE UTC−6(−5DT) N32°18.27′ W90°24.63′ MEMPHIS
247 B NOTAM FILE GWO H−6J, L−18G
RWY 12−30: H5499X100 (ASPH−RFSC) S−60, D−75 MIRL IAP
 RWY 12: REIL. PAPI(P4L)—GA 3.0° TCH 38′.
 RWY 30: REIL. PAPI(P2L)—GA 4.0° TCH 50′. Trees.
SERVICE: S4 **FUEL** 100LL, JET A **LGT** Actvt REIL Rwy 12 and 30; MIRL Rwy 12−30—CTAF. PAPI Rwy 12 and 30 opr consly.
AIRPORT REMARKS: Attended Mon−Fri 1400−2300Z‡, Sat 1400−1800Z‡. Fuel avbl 24 hrs with card. Pilots must provide their own tiedown ropes. Paint fac.
AIRPORT MANAGER: 601−857−3884
WEATHER DATA SOURCES: AWOS−3PT 118.675 (601) 857−3887.
COMMUNICATIONS: CTAF/UNICOM 123.0
 JACKSON APP/DEP CON 125.25 (153°−332°) (1200−0500Z‡)
 ® MEMPHIS CENTER APP/DEP CON 132.5 (0500−1200Z‡)
CLEARANCE DELIVERY PHONE: When Apch clsd, for CD ctc Memphis ARTCC at 901−368−8453/8449.
RADIO AIDS TO NAVIGATION: NOTAM FILE GWO.
 MAGNOLIA (VH) (H) VORTACW 113.2 MHZ Chan 79 N32°26.04′ W90°05.99′ 245° 17.6 NM to fld. 407/1W.
  TACAN AZIMUTH unusable:
   240°−275° byd 30 NM blo 2,000′
   DME unsbl 240−275 byd 30 NM blo 2000′
 ILS/DME 108.55 I−JVW Chan 22(Y) Rwy 12.
COMM/NAV/WEATHER REMARKS: IFR clearances issued by Jackson App via recorded phone line call 601−965−4425.

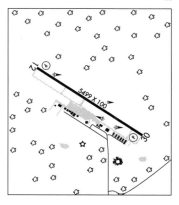

MISSISSIPPI

RICHTON–PERRY CO (M59) 2 S UTC–6(–5DT) N31°19.02′ W88°56.09′ NEW ORLEANS
167 B NOTAM FILE GWO L–21C, 22G
RWY 18–36: H3000X60 (ASPH) S–20 MIRL
  RWY 18: PAPI(P2L). Trees.
  RWY 36: PAPI(P2L). Trees.
SERVICE: **LGT** ACTIVATE PAPI Rwy 18 and Rwy 36; MIRL Rwy 18–36—CTAF.
AIRPORT REMARKS: Unattended.
AIRPORT MANAGER: 601-788-7770
COMMUNICATIONS: CTAF 122.9
CLEARANCE DELIVERY PHONE: For CD ctc Houston ARTCC at 281-230-5622.
RADIO AIDS TO NAVIGATION: NOTAM FILE GWO.
  EATON (L) (L) VORTACW 110.6 LBY Chan 43 N31°25.12′ W89°20.26′ 101° 21.6 NM to fld. 290/5E.
  VORTAC unusable:
    300°–000° byd 30 NM
  VOR portion unusable:
    111°–164° byd 10 NM blo 2,000′
    241°–251°
  TACAN unusable:
    025°–035° byd 10 NM blo 3,000′
    268°–274° byd 30 NM blo 5,000′

RIPLEY (25M) 3 W UTC–6(–5DT) N34°43.36′ W89°00.88′ MEMPHIS
467 B NOTAM FILE GWO L–18G
RWY 03–21: H4400X75 (ASPH) S–20 MIRL 0.8% up NE IAP
  RWY 03: PAPI(P2L)—GA 3.25° TCH 15′. Tree.
  RWY 21: PAPI(P2L)—GA 3.5° TCH 16′. Trees.
SERVICE: **FUEL** 100LL, JET A **LGT** Dusk–0400Z‡. After 0400Z‡ actvt PAPI Rwy 03 and 21; MIRL Rwy 03–21—CTAF.
AIRPORT REMARKS: Unattended. 100LL fuel avbl 24 hrs with credit card. Courtesy van avbl.
AIRPORT MANAGER: 662-587-9500
COMMUNICATIONS: CTAF/UNICOM 122.8
®**MEMPHIS CENTER APP/DEP CON** 135.9
CLEARANCE DELIVERY PHONE: For CD ctc Memphis ARTCC at 901-368-8453/8449.
RADIO AIDS TO NAVIGATION: NOTAM FILE GWO.
  HOLLY SPRINGS (L) (L) VORTACW 112.4 HLI Chan 71 N34°46.21′ W89°29.79′ 094° 24.0 NM to fld. 624/3E.
  VOR UNUSABL:
    172°–192° byd 25 NM blo 2,400′

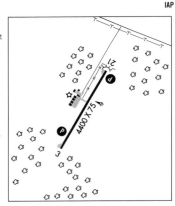

ROSCOE TURNER (See CORINTH on page 139)

RULEVILLE–DREW (See DREW on page 141)

SELFS (See MARKS on page 157)

SEYER N35°00.94′ W88°36.94′ NOTAM FILE GWO. MEMPHIS
  NDB (LOMW) 334 UU 176° 6.1 NM to Roscoe Turner. 510/2W.

SIDON N33°27.83′ W90°16.64′ NOTAM FILE GWO. MEMPHIS
(VH) (H) VORTAC 114.7 SQS Chan 94 077° 9.7 NM to Greenwood–Leflore. 127/3E. H–6J, 5C, L–18G
  VOR unusable:
    059°–069° byd 40 NM
  RCO 122.1R 114.7T (GREENWOOD RADIO)

MISSISSIPPI

STARKVILLE

GEORGE M BRYAN (STF)(KSTF) 3 SW   UTC–6(–5DT)   N33°25.99´ W88°50.92´
333   B   NOTAM FILE GWO
RWY 18–36: H5550X150 (ASPH–CONC) S–25, D–30 HIRL
  RWY 18: PAPI(P2L)—GA 3.0° TCH 36´. Thld dsplcd 1379´. Sign.
  RWY 36: REIL. PAPI(P2L)—GA 3.0° TCH 40´.
SERVICE: S4 FUEL 100LL, JET A LGT 1400–223CZ‡; aft hr ACTVT
  REIL Rwy 36; HIRL Rwy 18–36; CTAF. PAPI Rwy 18 and 36 opr
  consly.
AIRPORT REMARKS: Attended Mon–Sat 1400–2300Z‡, Sun
  1900–2300Z‡. Jet A full svc aft hrs–ctc AMGR. Fuel avbl 24 hrs with
  credit card. Experimental acft on and invof of arpt. Pilots must provide
  their own tiedown ropes.
AIRPORT MANAGER: 662-418-5900
WEATHER DATA SOURCES: AWOS–3PT 118.975 (662) 323–4966.
COMMUNICATIONS: CTAF/UNICOM 122.7
Ⓡ COLUMBUS APP/DEP CON 135.6 (1300–0100Z‡ Mon–Fri,
  1800–2300Z‡ Sun, clsd Sat and hols.)
Ⓡ MEMPHIS CENTER APP/DEP CON 127.1 (0100–1300Z⁼ Mon–Fri,
  2300Z–1800Z‡ Sun, Sat and hols.)
COLUMBUS CLNC DEL 126.25
CLEARANCE DELIVERY PHONE: For CD ctc Columbus Apch at 662-434-3044.
RADIO AIDS TO NAVIGATION: NOTAM FILE GWO.
  BIGBEE (L) (L) VORTACW 116.2   IGB Chan 109   N33°29.13´
  W88°30.82´   256° 17.1 NM to fld. 245/4E.
  VOR portion unusable:
    010°–020°
    200°–260° blo 5,000´.
  LOC/DME 109.9 I-STF   Chan 36   Rwy 36.

MEMPHIS
H–6J, L–18G
IAP

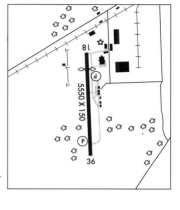

OKTIBBEHA (M51) 7 NE   UTC–6(–5DT)   N33°29.86´ W88°40.89´
250   NOTAM FILE GWO
RWY 14–32: 2600X150 (TURF)
  RWY 14: Trees.
  RWY 32: Trees.
RWY 01–19: 2237X150 (TURF)
  RWY 01: Trees.
  RWY 19: Trees.
AIRPORT REMARKS: Attended Sat–Sun. Rwy 14–32 marked by mowing and
  white jugs 75´ apart. Rwy 01–19 marked by mowing and white jugs
  75´ apart.
AIRPORT MANAGER: 662-341-2345
COMMUNICATIONS: CTAF/UNICOM 122.8
Ⓡ COLUMBUS APP/DEP CON 135.6 (1300–0100Z‡ Mon–Fri, 1800–2300Z‡
  Sun, clsd Sat and hols.)
Ⓡ MEMPHIS CENTER APP/DEP CON 127.1 (0100–1300Z⁼ Mon–Fri,
  2300Z–1800Z‡ Sun, Sat and hols.)
CLEARANCE DELIVERY PHONE: For CD ctc Memphis ARTCC at
  901-368-8453/8449.
RADIO AIDS TO NAVIGATION: NOTAM FILE GWO.
  BIGBEE (L) (L) VORTACW 116.2   IGB Chan 109   N33°29.13´
  W88°30.82´   271° 8.5 NM to fld. 245/4E.
  VOR portion unusable:
    010°–020°
    200°–260° blo 5,000´.
COMM/NAV/WEATHER REMARKS: UNICOM OTS indef.

MEMPHIS
L–18G
IAP

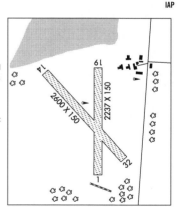

STENNIS INTL (See BAY ST LOUIS on page 132)

MISSISSIPPI

TALLULAH

VICKSBURG TALLULAH RGNL (TVR)(KTVR)   9 E   UTC–6(–5DT)   N32°21.10´ W91°01.66´   **MEMPHIS**
86   B   TPA—1086(1000)   NOTAM FILE TVR   H–6J, L–18F
RWY 18–36: H5002X100 (ASPH)   S–60, D–75   MIRL   IAP
  RWY 18: REIL. PAPI(P4L)—GA 3.0° TCH 50´. Trees.
  RWY 36: SSALR. PAPI(P4L)—GA 3.0° TCH 50´. Trees.
RUNWAY DECLARED DISTANCE INFORMATION
  RWY 18: TORA–5002   TODA–5002   ASDA–5002   LDA–5002
  RWY 36: TORA–5002   TODA–5002   ASDA–5002   LDA–5002
SERVICE: S4   **FUEL** 100LL, JET A   **LGT** MIRL Rwy 18–36, REIL Rwy 18, SSALR Rwy 36 preset low ints dusk–dawn, to increase ints ACTIVATE—CTAF.
AIRPORT REMARKS: Attended 1300–0100Z‡. For arpt mgr aft hrs call 318–366–1615. PAEW on arpt. Migratory birds invof arpt. Crop dusting activity 2 NM radius of arpt. Pilots in tfc pattern are requested to avoid over flight of Mound, LA 1/2 mile south and east of Rwy 36.
AIRPORT MANAGER: 318-574-5841
WEATHER DATA SOURCES: ASOS 118.525 (318) 574–4866.
COMMUNICATIONS: CTAF/UNICOM 123.0
  MEMPHIS CENTER APP/DEP CON 132.5
CLEARANCE DELIVERY PHONE: For CD ctc Memphis ARTCC at 901-368-8453/8449.
RADIO AIDS TO NAVIGATION: NOTAM FILE GWO.
  MAGNOLIA (VH) (H) VORTACW 113.2   MHZ   Chan 79   N32°26.04´ W90°05.99´   265° 47.4 NM to fld. 407/1W.
    TACAN AZIMUTH unusable:
      240°–275° byd 30 NM blo 2,000´
      DME unsbl 240–275 byd 30 NM blo 2000´
  TALLULAH NDB (MWH/LOM) 344   TKH   N32°14.72´ W91°01.55´   357° 6.4 NM to fld. 79/2E.   NOTAM FILE DRI.
  ILS 109.7   I–TVR   Rwy 36.   Class ID.

TEOCK   N33°35.52´ W90°05.06´   NOTAM FILE GWO.   **MEMPHIS**
NDB (LOMW) 349   GW   182° 5.9 NM to Greenwood–Leflore. 140/1W.   L–18G

THIGPEN FLD   (See BAY SPRINGS on page 131)

TISHOMINGO CO   (See BELMONT on page 133)

TRENT LOTT INTL   (See PASCAGOULA on page 163)

TUNICA

RALPH M SHARPE   (3ØM)   2 S   UTC–6(–5DT)   N34°39.55´ W90°22.57´   **MEMPHIS**
195   NOTAM FILE GWO
RWY 01–19: H2508X14 (ASPH)
  RWY 01: Thld dsplcd 108´.
AIRPORT REMARKS: Attended Mar–Oct dalgt hrs, Nov–Feb Mon–Fri irregularly, call manager. Rwy 01–19 80´ trees E side S of rwy violate 7:1 trsn slp. Call ahead to reserve hangar transient storage. Rwy 01 is 14 ft wid by 1800 ft long; Rwy 19 is 18 ft wid by 708 ft long.
AIRPORT MANAGER: 662-363-1461
COMMUNICATIONS: CTAF/UNICOM 122.8
CLEARANCE DELIVERY PHONE: For CD ctc Memphis Apch at 901-842-8457.

MISSISSIPPI

TUNICA MUNI (UTA)(KUTA) 1 E UTC−6(−5DT) N34°41.10′ W90°20.87′ **MEMPHIS**
194 B NOTAM FILE UTA MON Airport H−6J, L−18G
RWY 17−35: H8500X150 (ASPH−GRVD) S−94, D−215, 2T−510, IAP
  2D−460, 2D/2D2−720 PCN 45 F/B/X/U HIRL
  RWY 17: PAPI(P4L)—GA 3.0° TCH 50′.
  RWY 35: MALSR. PAPI(P4L)—GA 3.0° TCH 47′. Rgt tfc.
SERVICE: S4 **FUEL** 100LL, JET A **OX** 1, 3 **LGT** Actvt MALSR Rwy 35;
  HIRL Rwy 17−35—CTAF.
AIRPORT REMARKS: Attended 1200−0300Z‡. Large flocks of geese invof
  arpt Nov−Feb. Agricultural acft activity invof the arpt during daylight
  hours all days. Aft hrs fuel ctc AMGR 662−357−7330. 24 hr PPR
  coml flgts over 30 seats. Call AMGR 662−357−7320. Clsd to sked
  acr ops with more than 9 pax seats and unsked acr ops with more
  than 30 pax seats. Rwy 35 designated calm wind rwy.
AIRPORT MANAGER: 662-357-7320
WEATHER DATA SOURCES: AWOS−3 118.075 (662) 363−1652.
COMMUNICATIONS: CTAF/UNICOM 123.0
Ⓡ **MEMPHIS APP/DEP CON** 119.1
  CLNC DEL 118.9
CLEARANCE DELIVERY PHONE: For CD ctc Memphis Apch at 901-842-8457.
RADIO AIDS TO NAVIGATION: NOTAM FILE MEM.
  MEMPHIS (H) (H) VORTACW 117.5 MEM Chan 122 N35°00.91′
   W89°58.99′   221° 26.7 NM to fld. 363/1E.
  ILS/DME 110.95 I−UTA Chan 46(Y) Rwy 35. Class 1E.

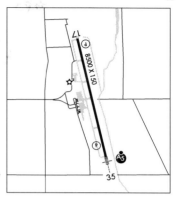

TUNNG N34°23.11′ W89°37.56′ NOTAM FILE GWO. **MEMPHIS**
  NDB (LOMW) 426 UV 092° 4.4 NM to University−Oxford. 410/1W. LOC & NDB unmonitored 2300−1400Z‡. L−18G

TUPELO RGNL (TUP)(KTUP) P (ARNG) 3 W UTC−6(−5D⁻) N34°16.14′ W88°46.19′ **MEMPHIS**
347 B Class I, ARFF Index A NOTAM FILE TUP H−6J, L−18G
RWY 18−36: H7150X150 (ASPH−GRVD) S−69, D−91, 2D−163 IAP, DIAP, AD
  PCN 72 F/C/W/T HIRL
  RWY 18: REIL. PAPI(P4R)—GA 3.0° TCH 45′.
  RWY 36: MALSR.
SERVICE: S4 **FUEL** 100LL, JET A, A+, A1+ **OX** 3, 4 **LGT** ACTIVATE
  MALSR Rwy 36; REIL Rwy 18; HIRL Rwy 18−36—CTAF. PAPI Rwy
  18 opr continuously.
  MILITARY—FUEL A+ (avbl 1200−0400Z‡, C931−492−2160. OT
  C931−492−2160, $50 fee, 30 min PN.) (NC-100LL, A1+)
AIRPORT REMARKS: Attended 1200−0400Z‡. A+ fuel svc avbl 24 hrs
  with credit card. Hel ops all hrs 700 ft AGL E of rwy 18/36−ctc CTAF
  for adzy. Acr ramp rstrd to acr ops excp with PPR Call amgr Mon−Fri
  1400−2300Z‡; 662-841-6570. PPR for unsked acr ops with more
  than 30 pax seats call amgr 662-841-6570. Index B ARFF eqpt
  avbl only during sked acr ops.
MILITARY REMARKS: CAUTION Hel ops all hrs 700 ft AGL E of Rwy
  18−36−ctc CTAF for adzy. **ARNG** Support fac opr Mon−Fri
  1300−2200Z‡ exc hol. Ltd prk avbl. No tsnt fuel avbl. DSN
  293-3438, C662-891-4438.
AIRPORT MANAGER: 662-841-6570
WEATHER DATA SOURCES: ASOS 133.525 (662) 840−8528.
COMMUNICATIONS: CTAF 118.775
  TUPELO RCO 122.5 (GREENWOOD RADIO)
Ⓡ **MEMPHIS CENTER APP/DEP CON** 128.5
  TOWER 118.775 (1200−0400Z‡) **GND CON** 121.825
AIRSPACE: CLASS D svc 1200−0400Z‡; other times CLASS E.
RADIO AIDS TO NAVIGATION: NOTAM FILE TUP.
  (L) (L) VORW/DME 109.8 OTB Chan 35 N34°13.43′ W88°47.84′ 023° 3.0 NM to fld. 364/4E.
   VOR portion unusable:
    190°−220°
  VERON NDB (LOMW) 420 TU N34°10.82′ W88°46.12′ 001° 5.3 NM to fld. 325/2W.
  ILS/DME 108.5 I−TUP Chan 22 Rwy 36. Class IA. LOM VERON NDB. Unmonitored 0500−1100Z‡. LOC front
   course unusable beyond 025° right of course

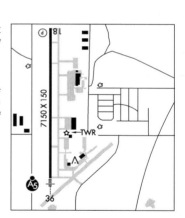

MISSISSIPPI

TYLERTOWN
PAUL PITTMAN MEML (T36)   3 NW   UTC–6(–5DT)   N31°08.76´ W90°10.09´   NEW ORLEANS
384   B   NOTAM FILE GWO   L–21B, 22F
RWY 18–36: H3000X60 (ASPH)   S–20   MIRL
  RWY 18: PAPI(P2L)—GA 3.0° TCH 40´. Trees.
  RWY 36: PAPI(P2L)—GA 3.0° TCH 41´.
SERVICE: FUEL 100LL   LGT PAPIs OTS indefly.
AIRPORT REMARKS: Unattended. 10LL avbl 24 hrs with credit card. Pilots must provide their own tiedown ropes. Pub fone 601–876–9327.
AIRPORT MANAGER: 601–814–9021
COMMUNICATIONS: CTAF/UNICOM 122.8
CLEARANCE DELIVERY PHONE: For CD ctc Houston ARTCC at 281–230–5622.
RADIO AIDS TO NAVIGATION: NOTAM FILE MCB.
  MC COMB (H) (H) VORTAC 116.7   MCB   Chan 114   N31°18.27´ W90°15.49´   151° 10.6 NM to fld. 440/3E.

UNIVERSITY–OXFORD (See OXFORD on page 163)

VERON   N34°10.82´ W88°46.12´   NOTAM FILE TUP.   MEMPHIS
NDB (LOMW) 420   TU   001° 5.3 NM to Tupelo Rgnl. 325/2W.   L–18G

VICKSBURG MUNI (VKS)(KVKS)   7 SW   UTC–6(–5DT)   N32°14.35´ W90°55.69´   MEMPHIS
107   B   NOTAM FILE GWO   H–6J, L–18F
   IAP
RWY 01–19: H5000X100 (ASPH)   S–30, D–50, 2D–90   MIRL
  RWY 01: PAPI(P2R)—GA 3.0° TCH 39´. Thld dsplcd 299´. Trees.
  RWY 19: PAPI(P2L)—GA 3.0° TCH 44´. Thld dsplcd 471´. Tree.
SERVICE: FUEL 100LL, JET A1+   LGT ACTVT PAPI Rwy 19; MIRL Rwy 01–19—CTAF. PAPI Rwy 01 opr consly.
AIRPORT REMARKS: Attended Mon–Fri 1200–2300Z‡. Aft hrs call 601–218–5428. Call out fee rqrd. 100LL 24 hrs with credit card. N parl twy clsd. Term stub twy only. Airframe rprs: avbl 601–529–2909. Pwr plant rprs: avbl 601–529–2909.
AIRPORT MANAGER: 601–218–5789
WEATHER DATA SOURCES: AWOS–3 118.85 (601) 801–5376.
COMMUNICATIONS: CTAF/UNICOM 122.8
®MEMPHIS CENTER APP/DEP CON 132.5
CLEARANCE DELIVERY PHONE: For CD ctc Memphis ARTCC at 901–368–8453/8449.
RADIO AIDS TO NAVIGATION: NOTAM FILE GWO.
  MAGNOLIA (VH) (H) VORTACW 113.2   MHZ   Chan 79   N32°26.04´ W90°05.99´   256° 43.7 NM to fld. 407/1W.
  TACAN AZIMUTH unusable:
    240°–275° byd 30 NM blo 2,000´
    DME unsbl 240–275 byd 30 NM blo 2000´

VICKSBURG TALLULAH RGNL (See TALLULAH on page 170)

WATER VALLEY MUNI (33M)   3 NW   UTC–6(–5DT)   N34°10.07´ W89°41.09´   MEMPHIS
270   B   NOTAM FILE GWO   L–18G
RWY 15–33: H3000X50 (ASPH)   S–20   LIRL
  RWY 15: PAPI(P2L)—GA 3.0° TCH 47´.
  RWY 33: PAPI(P2L)—GA 3.0° TCH 40´. Tree.
SERVICE: FUEL 100LL   LGT LIRL Rwy 15–33 preset low intst; to incr—CTAF. PAPIs oper continuously.
AIRPORT REMARKS: Attended on call. Lrg flocks of ducks ovr lake. For part–time attendant call 662–473–7676. 100LL avbl 24 hrs with credit card. Pilots must provide their own tie ropes.
AIRPORT MANAGER: 662–473–4229
COMMUNICATIONS: CTAF 122.9
CLEARANCE DELIVERY PHONE: For CD ctc Memphis ARTCC at 901–368–8453/8449.
RADIO AIDS TO NAVIGATION: NOTAM FILE GWO.
  HOLLY SPRINGS (L) (L) VORTACW 112.4   HLI   Chan 71   N34°46.21´ W89°29.79´   192° 37.3 NM to fld. 624/3E.
  VOR UNUSABL:
    172°–192° byd 25 NM blo 2,400´

MISSISSIPPI

WAYNESBORO MUNI (2R0) 2 S UTC–6(–5DT) N31°33.61′ W88°38.11′
169 B NOTAM FILE GWO
NEW ORLEANS
H–6J, L–22G

RWY 02–20: H5000X75 (ASPH) S–15 MIRL
  RWY 02: PAPI(P2L). Trees.
  RWY 20: PAPI(P2L). Thld dsplcd 665′. Railroad.
SERVICE: **FUEL** 100LL **LGT** ACTVT PAPI Rwy 02 and Rwy 20; MIRL Rwy 02–20—CTAF.
AIRPORT REMARKS: Attended Mon–Fri 1200–2000Z‡. Wildlife nr Rwy 20. Aft hrs svc ctc AMGR (401) 404–8959. 24 hr credit card svc avbl.
AIRPORT MANAGER: 601-735-9682
COMMUNICATIONS: CTAF/UNICOM 122.8
CLEARANCE DELIVERY PHONE: For CD ctc Memphis ARTCC at 901-368-8453/8449.
RADIO AIDS TO NAVIGATION: NOTAM FILE GWO.
  GREENE COUNTY (H) TACAN Chan 104 GCV (115 7) N31°05.88′ W88°29.17′ 342° 33.5 NM to fld. 300/5E.

WEST DELTA DLP N29°07.28′ W89°32.83′
AWOS–3 120.425
NEW ORLEANS
L–21B, 22G, GOMC

WEST POINT
MCCHAREN FLD (M83) 2 S UTC–6(–5DT) N33°35.04′ W88°40.00′
205 B NOTAM FILE GWO
MEMPHIS
L–18G
IAP

RWY 18–36: H3850X75 (ASPH) S–30, D–36 MIRL
  RWY 18: Thld dsplcd 390′. Tree.
  RWY 36: Road.
SERVICE: **FUEL** 100LL, JET A **LGT** Dusk–0400Z‡. Aft 0400Z‡, actvt MIRL Rwy 18–36—CTAF.
AIRPORT REMARKS: Unattended. 100LL svc avbl 24 hr with credit card. Public phone avbl 662–494–9854. Courtesy car avbl.
AIRPORT MANAGER: 662-524-0039
COMMUNICATIONS: CTAF 122.9
®**COLUMBUS APP/DEP CON** 135.6 (1300–0100Z‡ Mon–Fri, 1800–2300Z‡ Sun, clsd Sat and hols.)
®**MEMPHIS CENTER APP/DEP CON** 127.1 (0100–1300Z‡ Mon–Fri, 2300Z–1800Z‡ Sun, Sat and hols.)
CLEARANCE DELIVERY PHONE: For CD ctc Columbus Apch at 662-434-3044, when clsd ctc Memphis ARTCC at 901-368-8453/8449.
RADIO AIDS TO NAVIGATION: NOTAM FILE GWO.
  BIGBEE (L) (L) VORTACW 116.2 IGB Chan 109 N33°29.13′ W88°30.82′ 304° 9.7 NM to fld. 245/4E.
  VOR portion unusable:
    010°–020°
    200°–260° blo 5,000′

WIGGINS
DEAN GRIFFIN MEML (M24) 1 W UTC–6(–5D⁻) N30°50.58′ W89°09.69′
273 B NOTAM FILE GWO
NEW ORLEANS
L–21C, 22G
IAP

RWY 17–35: H3500X75 (ASPH) S–20 PCN 10 F/A/Y/T MIRL 0.8% up N
  RWY 17: PAPI(P2L)—GA 3.0° TCH 35′. Thld dsplcd 500′. Tree.
  RWY 35: PAPI(P2L)—GA 3.0° TCH 50′. Trees.
SERVICE: **FUEL** 100LL **LGT** ACTIVATE MIRL Rwy 17–35—CTAF. PAPI Rwy 17 and Rwy 35 opr continuously.
AIRPORT REMARKS: Attended 1400–2300Z‡. 100LL avbl 24 hrs with credit card. Pilots must provide their own tiedown ropes.
AIRPORT MANAGER: 601-928-7221
COMMUNICATIONS: CTAF/UNICOM 122.8
®**GULFPORT APP/DEP CON** 127.5 (1200–0500Z‡)
®**HOUSTON CENTER APP/DEP CON** 126.8 (0500–1200Z‡)
CLEARANCE DELIVERY PHONE: For CD ctc Gulfport Apch at 228-265-6151, when Apch clsd ctc Houston ARTCC at 281-230-5622.
RADIO AIDS TO NAVIGATION: NOTAM FILE GWO.
  PICAYUNE (L) (L) VORW/DME 113.95 PCU Chan 86(Y) N30°33.67′ W89°43.83′ 055° 33.9 NM to fld. 70/5E.
  VOR unusable:
    285°–305° byd 6 NM blo 4,000′
    325°–076° byd 26 NM blo 2,500′
  DME unusable:
    078°–180° byd 32 NM blo 3,000′
    331°–064° byd 27 NM blo 4,000′

MISSISSIPPI

WINONA–MONTGOMERY CO (5A6)   1 S   UTC–6(–5DT)   N33°27.90´ W89°43.81´   MEMPHIS
364   B   NOTAM FILE GWO   L–18G
RWY 03–21: H4000X60 (ASPH) S–18   MIRL   0.4% up NE   IAP
  RWY 03: PAPI(P2L)—GA 4.0° TCH 30´. Trees.
  RWY 21: PAPI(P2L)—GA 4.0° TCH 30´. Trees.
SERVICE: S2   **FUEL** 100LL   **LGT** Actvt PAPI Rwy 03 and 21; MIRL Rwy 03–21—CTAF. MIRL opr dusk–0400Z‡.
AIRPORT REMARKS: Attended continuously. Fuel 24 hr credit card svc avbl. Powerplant and airframe repairs avbl in emerg or with pn 662–283–9833. Pilots must provide their own tiedown ropes.
AIRPORT MANAGER: (662) 310-2001
WEATHER DATA SOURCES: AWOS–3PT 120.175 (662) 283–2172.
COMMUNICATIONS: CTAF 122.9
®**MEMPHIS CENTER APP/DEP CON** 128.5
CLEARANCE DELIVERY PHONE: For CD ctc Memphis ARTCC at 901-368-8453/8449.
RADIO AIDS TO NAVIGATION: NOTAM FILE GWO.
  SIDON (VH) (H) VORTAC 114.7   SQS   Chan 94   N33°27.83´ W90°16.64´   087° 27.5 NM to fld. 127/3E.
  VOR unusable:
    059°–069° byd 40 NM

YAZOO CITY

YAZOO CO (87I)   4 NW   UTC–6(–5DT)   N32°53.01´ W90°27.84´   MEMPHIS
105   B   NOTAM FILE GWO   H–6J, L–18G
RWY 17–35: H5000X100 (ASPH)   S–30, 2D–64   MIRL   IAP
  RWY 17: PAPI(P2L)—GA 3.0° TCH 40´.
  RWY 35: PAPI(P2L)—GA 3.0° TCH 40´. Trees.
SERVICE: **FUEL** 100LL, JET A1+   **LGT** MIRL Rwy 17–35 preset low intst dusk–0400Z‡, aft 0400Z‡ actvt or incr intst—CTAF.
AIRPORT REMARKS: Unattended. Parachute Jumping. Fuel avbl 24 hrs with credit card. Pilots must provide their own tiedown ropes.
AIRPORT MANAGER: 662-571-1392
COMMUNICATIONS: CTAF/UNICOM 122.8
®**MEMPHIS CENTER APP/DEP CON** 132.5
CLEARANCE DELIVERY PHONE: For CD ctc Memphis ARTCC at 901-368-8453/8449.
RADIO AIDS TO NAVIGATION: NOTAM FILE GWO.
  MAGNOLIA (VH) (H) VORTACW 113.2   MHZ   Chan 79   N32°26.04´ W90°05.99´   327° 32.6 NM to fld. 407/1W.
  TACAN AZIMUTH unusable:
    240°–275° byd 30 NM blo 2,000´
    DME unsbl 240–275 byd 30 NM blo 2000´

YAZOO CO (See YAZOO CITY on page 174)

OKLAHOMA

ADA RGNL (ADH)(KADH) 2 N UTC–6(–5DT) N34°48.26′ W96°40.27′ **DALLAS–FT WORTH**
1016 B NOTAM FILE ADH H–6H, L–17C
RWY 18–36: H6203X100 (ASPH) S–50, D–140, 2S–175, 2D–224 IAP
  MIRL 0.6% up N
  RWY 18: ODALS. PAPI(P4L)—GA 3.0° TCH 31′. Trees.
  RWY 36: REIL. PAPI(P4L)—GA 3.0° TCH 43′. Thld dsplcd 100′. Trees.
RWY 13–31: H2717X50 (ASPH–CONC) S–50, D–171, 2S–175,
  2D–280 0.9% up NW
SERVICE: S4 FUEL 100LL, JET A+ OX 1, 2 LGT ACTVT ODALS Rwy
  18; REILs Rwy 36; MIRL Rwy 18–36—CTAF. PAPI Rwy 18 and 36
  on consly. VGSI unusbl byd 7 degs right of cntrln
AIRPORT REMARKS: Attended Mon–Sat 1400–2300Z‡, Sun
  1800–2300Z‡. For 100LL fuel aft hr call 580–235–5279. Rwy
  13–31 svr cracking and raveling asph ptn. Rwy 13 and Rwy 31
  markings svrly faded. Lndg fee for acft weight 50,000 lbs or gtr.
AIRPORT MANAGER: 580-436-8190
WEATHER DATA SOURCES: AWOS–3 118.725 (580) 332–5222.
COMMUNICATIONS: CTAF/UNICOM 122.8
®FORT WORTH CENTER APP/DEP CON 132.2
CLEARANCE DELIVERY PHONE: For CD ctc Fort Worth ARTCC at
  817-858-7584.
RADIO AIDS TO NAVIGATION: NOTAM FILE ADM.
  ARDMORE (VH) (H) VORTACW 116.7 ADM Chan 114 N34°12.70′ W97°10.09′ 029° 43.2 NM to fld. 937/6E.
  VOR unusable:
   150°–160° byd 40 NM
   150°–160° byd 6 NM blo 14,000′
   297°–306° byd 40 NM blo 15,000′
   307°–314° blo 3,500′
   307°–314° byd 15 NM
   314°–333°
  TACAN AZIMUTH unusable:
   314°–333°
  DME unusable:
   314°–333°
   334°–011° byd 39 NM blo 3,100′

• • • • • • • • • • • • • • •
HELIPAD H1: H40X40 (CONC) PERIMETER LGTS

ADDMO N34°13.94′ W96°55.99′ NOTAM FILE ADM. **DALLAS–FT WORTH**
  NDB (LOMW) 400 AI 309° 6.1 NM to Ardmore Muni. 710/6E.

AFTON
GRAND LAKE RGNL (309) 10 SE UTC–6(–5DT) N36°34.65′ W94°51.71′ **KANSAS CITY**
792 NOTAM FILE MLC L–16F
RWY 17–35: H3925X60 (CONC) S–30, D–60, 2D–80 MIRL
  RWY 17: REIL. VASI(V2L)—GA 4.25° TCH 35′. Thld dsplcd 230′.
   Trees.
  RWY 35: VASI(V2L)—GA 3.75° TCH 29′. Thld dsplcd 230′.
SERVICE: LGT Actvt REIL Rwy 17; VASI Rwy 17 and 35; MIRL Rwy
  17–35—CTAF. VASI Rwy17 and 35 OTS indefly. REIL Rwy 17 OTS
  indefly.
AIRPORT REMARKS: Attended Apr–Oct 1200–0300Z‡; Nov–Mar
  1300–0100Z‡. Birds on and invof arpt. +130′ twr 1,200′ east of
  Rwy 17. Rwy 17 end is 30′ higher than Rwy 35 end. Rwy 17–35
  230′ safety zone on either end of rwy marked as dsplcd thld. Ldg fee.
AIRPORT MANAGER: 918-257-2011
COMMUNICATIONS: CTAF/UNICOM 122.8
CLEARANCE DELIVERY PHONE: For CD ctc Kansas City ARTCC at
  913-254-8508.

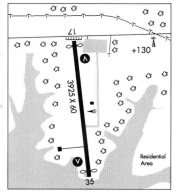

OKLAHOMA

ALTUS AFB (LTS)(KLTS) AF   3 E   UTC−6(−5DT)   N34°40.08´ W99°16.07´   DALLAS−FT WORTH
1382   B   TPA—See Remarks   NOTAM FILE LTS   Not insp.   H−6H, L−17B
RWY 18R−36L: H13440X150 (CONC)   PCN 61 R/B/W/T   HIRL   DIAP, AD
  RWY 18R: SALSF. PAPI(P4L)—GA 3.0° TCH 53´. RVR−T
  RWY 36L: ALSF1. PAPI(P4L)—GA 3.0° TCH 54´. RVR−T Rgt tfc.
RWY 18L−36R: H9001X150 (CONC−GRVD)   PCN 32 R/B/W/T   HIRL
  RWY 18L: SALSF. PAPI(P4L)—GA 3.0° TCH 46´. RVR−T
  RWY 36R: ALSF1. PAPI(P4L)—GA 3.0° TCH 52´. RVR−T
RWY 176−356: H3500X90 (CONC)   PCN 121R/B/W/T   HIRL
SERVICE: S4   **OX** 2, 4   **LGT** Reducd pri sfc obstn lgts for Rwy 18L−36R durg nvd ops. Rwy 18R, 18L, 36R and 36L sfl O/S
UFN. **MILITARY— JASU** (A/M32A−86) (AM32A−95) (MXU−4A−A) **FUEL** A++ **FLUID** W SP PRESAIR LHOX LOX **OIL**
O−133−148−156 SOAP (24 hr PN) **TRAN ALERT** Svc avbl 1500−0001Z‡ Mon−Fri; clsd Sat, Sun and hol. Tran maint and parts support extremely ltd. Transient maint unable to perform a magnetic chip indicator inspection on F16 acft with GE F110 engines.
MILITARY REMARKS: Opr 1500−0830Z‡ Mon−Fri, clsd weekends and holidays. Tran acft: 1530−0830Z‡, clsd weekends and holidays. See FLIP AP/1 Supplementary Arpt Info. **RSTD** PPR rqr 48 hr prior notice rqr. (training or operational) Ctc Afld Management Ops DSN 866−6200/6415, C580−481−6200/6415. PPR valid +/− 30 min prior/after ETA. Early/late arrival/ departure must re−coordinate with afld management ops. Transient aircrews must contact afld management ops for pattern work request. Limited to one apch Mon−Fri. Altus acft take priority over tran acft. Rwy 176−356 for assault strip trng only. Trans acft req assault strip use ctc Current Ops for sched/apvl DSN 866 6544. Due to unscheduled afld closings, aircrews utilizing Altus AFB as an alternate must advise their dep Afld Management Ops or local FSS to include KLTSYXYX as an addressee on the orig DD 175 Flight Plan and on any change, delay, dep and cancel message. All inbound passenger/cargo acft ctc command post (Geronimo 349.4) no later than 30 min prior to ldg. All acft with haz cargo (including MJU7 and MJU10 flares) notify Afld Management Ops (PTD 372.2) and Command Post no later than 30 min prior to ldg. Minimum Communications Security aids and overnight storage avbl for transient aircrews only. **CAUTION** Hvy/jumbo jet trng sfc to 9000´ within 25 NMR. Exer extreme caution for acft (1425´) taxiing 350´ east of dep end assault Rwy 176. Rwy 18R−36L marked with white non−reflective 90´ X 3500´ assault LZ mrk. Nstd Wing tip clnc trng line mrkgs lctd at Twy B & B2 intxn, Twy B & D intxn, and Twy A & C intxn. Ngt Vision Devices trng aprx 1 hr after SS til afld closure. IAW 97 OG NVD/white−light ops mou all tran acft req pattern trng between 1 hr after SS until afld closure must be opr under letter of agreement that includes NVD ops. To obtain Letter of Agreement, ctc current ops DSN 866−6544. All tran acft will ctc Afld Management Ops (327.2) or Comd Post (Geronimo 349.4) 30 min prior to arrival. No twy edge lgt Twy D south side to Twy B to Rwy 36L; retro reflective mkrs in place. Obst twr lgt OTS (3500´ west of Rwy 18R−36L thr) 1516 MSL (161 AGL). NSTD mark: C17 star turn markings lctd on the North Ramp, Twy J, and Twy L/M ground ops area. BASH phase II in eff 15 Nov thru 28−29 Feb for migratory birds. No tkof or ldg wi 1 hr of SR−SS, 97 OG/CC waiver auth. Ctc twr for current bird watch cond. **TFC PAT** TPA East, ovhd Rwy 18L−36R and 176−356 3400´ west, ovhd Rwy 18L−36R 3400´, east rectangular 2900´, West, (97 AMW acft only) retangular 2900´, copter 1900´.
MISC Twr vis obst of Rwy 36L apch end and Twy C, south of Twy E1 intxn. Rwy 18L−36R first 1000´ is conc. Middle 7001´ of Rwy 18L−36R is porous friction sfc.
AIRPORT MANAGER: 580−481−5739
COMMUNICATIONS: ATIS 109.8 273.5 PTD 372.2
Ⓡ **APP CON** 125.1 353.7 (1500−0830Z‡ Mon−Fri, clsd weekends and holidays.)
Ⓡ **FORT WORTH CENTER APP CON** 128.4 269.375 133.5 350.35 (0830−1500Z‡ Mon−Fri, 24 hrs weekends and holidays.)
TOWER 119.65 254.4 (1500−0830Z‡ Mon−Fri, clsd weekends and holidays.) **GND CON** 121.85 275.8 **CLNC DEL** 120.65 284.7
Ⓡ **DEP CON** 125.1 290.9, (1500−0830Z‡ Mon−Fri, clsd weekends and holidays.)
Ⓡ **FORT WORTH CENTER DEP CON** 128.4 269.375 133.5 350.35 (0830−1500Z‡ Mon−Fri, 24 hrs weekends and holidays.)
COMD POST (Call GERONIMO) 321.0 349.4 6761 **SOF** 349.4
PMSV METRO 239.8 (Opr H24 fm 0600Z‡ Mon thru 0800Z‡ Sat or end of flying Fri. Wx fcst svc avbl H24 fm 0600Z‡ Mon thru 0800Z‡ Sat or end of flying day Fri. Clsd wkend and hol. Remote briefing svc avbl 26 OWS, Barksdale AFB, DSN 331−2619, C318−529−2619. Afld WX is mnt by AN/FMQ−19, augmented as required dur afld opr hr. Auto obsn when afld clsd)

CONTINUED ON NEXT PAGE

OKLAHOMA

CONTINUED FROM PRECEDING PAGE

AIRSPACE: CLASS D svc 1500–0830Z‡ Mon–Fri, clsd Sat–Sun and hol; other times CLASS G.
   TRSA svc ctc **APP CON**
RADIO AIDS TO NAVIGATION: NOTAM FILE LTS.
   (L) (L) VORTACW 109.8   LTS   Chan 35   N34°39.78′   W99°16.27′   at fld. 1361/5E.
    No NOTAM MP: 1100–1400Z‡ Mon, Wed
    VOR unusable:
      033°–093° byd 35 NM blo 4,000′
      093°–118° byd 35 NM blo 5,000′
      149°–159° byd 10 NM
      213°–278° byd 35 NM blo 3,500′
      278°–303° byd 35 NM blo 4,000′
      303°–353° byd 30 NM blo 2,500′
      303°–353° byd 35 NM blo 4,000′
      353°–033° byd 30 NM blo 4,000′
      353°–033° byd 35 NM blo 5,000′
    TACAN AZIMUTH unusable:
      065°–080° byd 17 NM
      358°–008° byd 25 NM blo 6,000′
    DME unusable:
      065°–080° byd 17 NM
      358°–008° byd 25 NM blo 6,000′
   ILS 110.55 I–RUK Rwy 18L. No NOTAM MP: Rwy 18R–36L and 18L–3Rr 1100–1400Z‡ Tue, Thu.
   ILS 111.3 I–ALT Rwy 18R. No NOTAM MP: Rwy 18R–36L and 18L–36R 1100–1400Z‡ Tue, Thu. Ap coupled apch
    NA blw 1,740′ MSL.
   ILS 110.3 I–LTS Rwy 36L. No NOTAM MP: Rwy 18R–36L and 18L–36R 1100–1400Z‡ Tue, Thu.
   ILS 110.55 I–FNM Rwy 36R. Class IE. No NOTAM MP: Rwy 18R–36L and 18L–36R 1100–1400Z‡ Tue, Thu.
   ASR No–NOTAM MP 0800–1330Z‡ Mon–Fri.

ALTUS/QUARTZ MOUNTAIN RGNL (AXS)(KAXS) 3 N UTC–6(–5DT) N34°41.93′ W99°20.31′ **DALLAS–FT WORTH**
   1433 B NOTAM FILE AXS   **H–6H, L–17B**
   RWY 17–35: H5501X75 (CONC) S–30, D–48, 2D–90 MIRL   **IAP**
    0.3% up N
   RWY 17: ODALS. PAPI(P4L)—GA 3.0° TCH 40′. Rgt tfc.
   RWY 35: REIL. PAPI(P4L)—GA 3.0° TCH 40′.
   SERVICE: S4 **FUEL** 100LL, JET A+ **LGT** Actvt ODALS Rwy 17; REIL Rwy
    35; MIRL Rwy 17–35—CTAF. PAPI Rwy 17 and 35 on consly.
   AIRPORT REMARKS: Attended 1400–0000Z‡. Svc aft hr 580–471–0992.
    Do not mistake arpt for Altus AFB 4 miles SE. 320′ twr 2.6 mi S. Mil
    jet, agricultural and ultralight act and invof arpt.
   AIRPORT MANAGER: 580-482-8833
   WEATHER DATA SOURCES: AWOS–3PT 118.825 (580) 477–1745.
   COMMUNICATIONS: CTAF/UNICOM 122.8
   ® **APP/DEP CON** 125.1 (1500–0830Z‡, clsd weekends and holidays. Other
    times ctc)
   ® **FORT WORTH CENTER APP/DEP CON** 128.4 133.5
   CLEARANCE DELIVERY PHONE: For CD ctc Fort Worth ARTCC at
    817-858-7584.
   RADIO AIDS TO NAVIGATION: NOTAM FILE LTS.
    (L) (L) VORTACW 109.8 LTS Chan 35 N34°39.78′
    W99°16.27′ 298° 4.0 NM to fld. 1361/5E.
    No NOTAM MP: 1100–1400Z‡ Mon, Wed
    VOR unusable:
      033°–093° byd 35 NM blo 4,000′
      093°–118° byd 35 NM blo 5,000′
      149°–159° byd 10 NM
      213°–278° byd 35 NM blo 3,500′
      278°–303° byd 35 NM blo 4,000′
      303°–353° byd 30 NM blo 2,500′
      303°–353° byd 35 NM blo 4,000′
      353°–033° byd 30 NM blo 4,000′
      353°–033° byd 35 NM blo 5,000′
    TACAN AZIMUTH unusable:
      065°–080° byd 17 NM
      358°–008° byd 25 NM blo 6,000′
    DME unusable:
      065°–080° byd 17 NM
      358°–008° byd 25 NM blo 6,000′

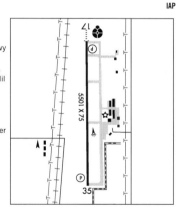

SC, 25 JAN 2024 to 21 MAR 2024

OKLAHOMA

ALVA RGNL (AVK)(KAVK)　2 S　UTC–6(–5DT)　N36°46.41′ W98°40.27′　　　WICHITA
1477　B　NOTAM FILE AVK　　　　　　　　　　　　　　　　　　　　　　　　H–6H, L–15D
RWY 18–36: H5001X75 (CONC)　MIRL　　　　　　　　　　　　　　　　　　　IAP
　RWY 18: ODALS. PAPI(P4L)—GA 3.0° TCH 47′.
　RWY 36: REIL. PAPI(P4L)—GA 3.0° TCH 40′.
RWY 09–27: 1390X170 (TURF)　　0.3% up W
SERVICE: S4　**FUEL** 100LL, JET A　**LGT** Actvt ODALS Rwy 18; REIL Rwy
　36; MIRL Rwy 18–36—CTAF. PAPI Rwy 18 and 36 on consly.
AIRPORT REMARKS: Attended 1400–2300Z‡. 100LL fuel avbl H24 with 24
　hr credit card.
AIRPORT MANAGER: 580-327-2898
WEATHER DATA SOURCES: AWOS–3PT 121.125 (580) 327-6778.
COMMUNICATIONS: CTAF/UNICOM 122.8
Ⓡ **VANCE APP/DEP CON** 126.75 (1300–0200Z‡ wkd, 1900–2300Z‡ Sun;
　clsd Sat & federal hol. Gnd ctl and clnc del svc avbl 15 min prior to
　afld opening. Other times by NOTAM)
Ⓡ **KANSAS CITY CENTER APP/DEP CON** 127.8 (0200–1300Z‡ wkd,
　2300–1900Z‡ Sun; 24 Sat & federal hol. Gnd ctl and clnc del svc avbl
　15 min prior to afld opening)
CLEARANCE DELIVERY PHONE: For CD ctc Vance Apch at 580-213-6765.
　When Vance Apch is clsd, ctc Kansas City ARTCC at 913-254-8508.
RADIO AIDS TO NAVIGATION: NOTAM FILE WDG.
　WOODRING (T) (T) VORW/DME 109.0　　ODG　Chan 27　N36°22.43′ W97°47.29′　　292° 48.9 NM to fld. 1151/8E.

ANADARKO MUNI (F68)　2 SW　UTC–6(–5DT)　N35°03.13′ W98°15.84′　　　DALLAS–FT WORTH
1291　B　NOTAM FILE MLC　　　　　　　　　　　　　　　　　　　　　　　　L–17C
RWY 17–35: H3100X50 (ASPH)　S–12.5　MIRL　1.1% up S
　RWY 17: Road.
　RWY 35: Trees.
SERVICE:　**LGT** MIRL Rwy 17–35 preset to low intensity; to
　increase—CTAF.
AIRPORT REMARKS: Unattended.
AIRPORT MANAGER: 405-247-2483
COMMUNICATIONS: CTAF 122.9
CLEARANCE DELIVERY PHONE: For CD ctc Fort Worth ARTCC at
　817-858-7584.
RADIO AIDS TO NAVIGATION: NOTAM FILE OKC.
　WILL ROGERS (H) (H) VORTACW 114.1　　IRW　Chan 88　N35°21.52′
　W97°36.55′　　234° 37.1 NM to fld. 1230/7E.

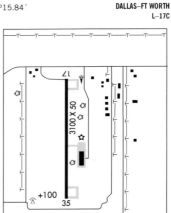

OKLAHOMA

ANTLERS MUNI (8Ø F)   3 SW   UTC–6(–5DT)   N34°11.61´ W95°38.99´
577   B   NOTAM FILE MLC
RWY 17–35: H4001X60 (ASPH)   S–12   MIRL
  RWY 17: PAPI(P2L)—GA 3.0° TCH 40´. Tree.
  RWY 35: PAPI(P2L)—GA 3.0° TCH 43´.
SERVICE: FUEL 100LL   LGT Actvt MIRL Rwy 17–35—CTAF. PAPI Rwy 17 and 35 on cnsly. Rwy 17 PAPI unusbl.
AIRPORT REMARKS: Unattended. 100LL avbl 24 hr with credit card.
AIRPORT MANAGER: 580-298-5635
COMMUNICATIONS: CTAF 122.9
®FORT WORTH CENTER APP/DEP CON 124.875
CLEARANCE DELIVERY PHONE: For CD ctc Fort Worth ARTCC at 817-858-7584.
RADIO AIDS TO NAVIGATION: NOTAM FILE MLC.
  MC ALESTER (L) TACAN   Chan 57   MLC (112.0)   N34°50.97´ W95°46.94´   162° 39.8 NM to fld. 782/8E.

DALLAS–FT WORTH
L–17D
IAP

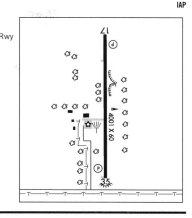

ARDMORE

ARDMORE DOWNTOWN EXEC (1F Ø)   1 SE   UTC–6(–5DT)   N34°08.82´ W97°07.36´
845   B   NOTAM FILE 1F0
RWY 17–35: H5014X75 (ASPH)   S–20   MIRL
  RWY 17: REIL. PAPI(P4L)—GA 4.0° TCH 41´. Trees.
  RWY 35: REIL. PAPI(P4L)—GA 3.0° TCH 40´. Road. Rgt tfc.
SERVICE: S2   FUEL 100LL, JET A   LGT ACTIVATE REIL Rwy 17 and Rwy 35, MIRL Rwy 17–35—CTAF.
AIRPORT REMARKS: Attended Mon–Fri 1400–2200Z‡, Sat 1400–1800Z‡, Sun on call (on call number: 580–223–5500). Fuel avbl 24 hrs with credit card.
AIRPORT MANAGER: (580) 389-5238
WEATHER DATA SOURCES: AWOS–3 118.15 (580) 226–1536.
COMMUNICATIONS: CTAF/UNICOM 122.7
®FORT WORTH CENTER APP/DEP CON 124.75
CLEARANCE DELIVERY PHONE: For CD ctc Fort Worth ARTCC at 817-858-7584.
RADIO AIDS TO NAVIGATION: NOTAM FILE ADM.
  (VH) (H) VORTACW 116.7   ADM   Chan 114   N34°12.70´ W97°10.09´   144° 4.5 NM to fld. 937/6E.
  VOR unusable:
    150°–160° byd 40 NM
    150°–160° byd 6 NM blo 14,000´
    297°–306° byd 40 NM blo 15,000´
    307°–314° blo 3,500´
    307°–314° byd 15 NM
    314°–333°
  TACAN AZIMUTH unusable:
    314°–333°
  DME unusable:
    314°–333°
    334°–011° byd 39 NM blo 3,100´

DALLAS–FT WORTH
H–6H, L–17C
IAP

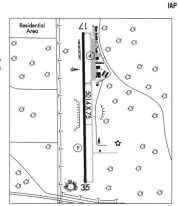

OKLAHOMA

ARDMORE MUNI (ADM)(KADM) 10 NE UTC−6(−5DT) N34°18.23´ W97°01.24´ DALLAS−FT WORTH
777 B NOTAM FILE ADM MON Airport H−6H, L−17C
RWY 13−31: H9002X150 (CONC) HIRL IAP, AD
  RWY 13: PAPI(P4L)—GA 3.0° TCH 57´. Trees. 0.7% down..
  RWY 31: MALS. VASI(V4L)—GA 3.0° TCH 49´. Trees. 0.3% up.
RWY 17−35: H5404X100 (ASPH) S−36 MIRL 0.5% up N
  RWY 35: Thld dsplcd 397´.
RUNWAY DECLARED DISTANCE INFORMATION
  RWY 17: TORA−5007 TODA−5007 ASDA−5007 LDA−5007
  RWY 35: TORA−5404 TODA−5404 ASDA−5404 LDA−5404
SERVICE: S4 **FUEL** 100LL, JET A OX 3 **LGT** When ATCT clsd ACTVT
  MALS Rwy 31—CTAF. HIRL Rwy 13−31; MIRL Rwy 17−35 on
  dusk−dawn. MALS Rwy 31 set to fixed intst; cannot incr or dcr.
AIRPORT REMARKS: Attended Mon−Fri 1300−0500Z‡, Sat−Sun
  1300−2300Z‡.
AIRPORT MANAGER: 580-389-5238
WEATHER DATA SOURCES: AWOS−3 125.6 (580) 389−5078. LAWRS.
COMMUNICATIONS: CTAF 118.5 **ATIS** 125.6 **UNICOM** 122.95
  RCO 122.6 (MC ALESTER RADIO)
®**FORT WORTH CENTER APP/DEP CON** 124.75
  TOWER 118.5 (1300−0500Z‡ Mon−Fri; 1300−2300Z‡ Sat−Sun)
  GND CON 121.8
CLEARANCE DELIVERY PHONE: For CD if una to ctc on FSS freq, ctc Fort Worth ARTCC at 817-858-7584.
AIRSPACE: CLASS D svc 1300−0500Z‡ Mon−Fri, 1300−2300Z‡ Sat−Sun; other times CLASS G.
RADIO AIDS TO NAVIGATION: NOTAM FILE ADM.
  (VH) (H) VORTACW 116.7 ADM Chan 114 N34°12.70´ W97°10.09´ 047° 9.2 NM to fld. 937/6E.
  VOR unusable:
    150°−160° byd 40 NM
    150°−160° byd 6 NM blo 14,000´
    297°−306° byd 40 NM blo 15,000´
    307°−314° blo 3,500´
    307°−314° byd 15 NM
    314°−333°
  TACAN AZIMUTH unusable:
    314°−333°
  DME unusable:
    314°−333°
    334°−011° byd 39 NM blo 3,100´
  ADDMO NDB (LOMW) 400 AI N34°13.94´ W96°55.99´ 309° 6.1 NM to fld. 710/6E.
  ILS 108.9 I−AIW Rwy 31. Class IT. LOM ADDMO NDB. Unmonitored when ATCT clsd.

ATOKA MUNI (AQR)(KAQR) 1 NW UTC−6(−5DT) N34°23.90´ W96°08.88´ DALLAS−FT WORTH
590 B NOTAM FILE AQR L−17D
RWY 18−36: H3015X60 (ASPH) S−4 MIRL 0.3% up N
  RWY 18: PAPI(P2L)—GA 3.0° TCH 44´. Thld dsplcd 197´. Trees.
  RWY 36: PAPI(P2L)—GA 3.0° TCH 43´. Thld dsplcd 233´. Trees.
SERVICE: FUEL 100LL **LGT** MIRL Rwy 18−36 ops SS−SR. Actvt PAPI Rwy 18—CTAF. Rwy 36 PAPI: unusbl byd 6 degs
  left and 9 degs right of cntrln.
AIRPORT REMARKS: Unattended. 100LL avbl H24 hr with credit card.
AIRPORT MANAGER: 580-889-3341
WEATHER DATA SOURCES: AWOS−3 121.125 (580) 889−6924.
COMMUNICATIONS: CTAF 122.9
CLEARANCE DELIVERY PHONE: For CD ctc Fort Worth ARTCC at 817-858-7584.
RADIO AIDS TO NAVIGATION: NOTAM FILE MLC.
  MC ALESTER (L) TACAN Chan 57 MLC (112.0) N34°50.97´ W95°46.94´ 206° 32.5 NM to fld. 782/8E.

OKLAHOMA

BARTLESVILLE MUNI (BVO)(KBVO) 2 NW UTC−6(−5DT) N36°45.80´ W96°00.67´   KANSAS CITY
717 B NOTAM FILE BVO H−6I, L−15E
RWY 17−35: H6850X100 (CONC−GRVD) S−50, D−100, 2S−127, IAP
  2D−170 MIRL 0.4% up S
  RWY 17: MALSR. PAPI(P4L)—GA 3.0° TCH 53´. Trees. Rgt tfc.
  RWY 35: REIL. PAPI(P4L)—GA 3.0° TCH 45´. Thld dsplcd 649´.
RUNWAY DECLARED DISTANCE INFORMATION
  RWY 17: TORA−6201 TODA−6201 ASDA−6201 LDA−6201
  RWY 35: TORA−6850 TODA−6850 ASDA−6850 LDA−6201
SERVICE: S4 FUEL 100LL, JET A+ OX 4 LGT ACTVT MALSR Rwy 17;
  REIL Rwy 35; PAPI Rwy 17 and Rwy 35—CTAF MIRL Rwy 17−35
  oper SS to SR and preset low intst, incr intst—CTAF.
AIRPORT REMARKS: Attended Mon−Thu 1300−0100Z‡, Fri−Sun
  1300−0000Z‡.
AIRPORT MANAGER: (918) 661-3500
WEATHER DATA SOURCES: ASOS 132.675 (918) 336−2070.
COMMUNICATIONS: CTAF 122.825
  RCO 122.4 (MC ALESTER RADIO)
® KANSAS CITY CENTER APP/DEP CON 128.6
  BARTLESVILLE ADVISORY 122.825 (Monitored Mon−Fri during business
  hrs)
CLEARANCE DELIVERY PHONE: For CD if una to ctc on FSS freq, ctc Kansas City
  ARTCC at 913-254-8508.
AIRSPACE: CLASS E svc Mon−Thu 1300−0100Z‡, Fri 1300−2300Z‡; other times CLASS G.
RADIO AIDS TO NAVIGATION: NOTAM FILE BVO.
  (L) (L) VORW/DME 117.9 BVO Chan 126 N36°50.06´ W96°01.11´ 167° 4.3 NM to fld. 930/8E.
  LOC 111.3 I−BVO Rwy 17. LOC unusable byd 20° right of course. LOC unmonitored.

BEAVER MUNI (K44) 1 SW UTC−6(−5DT) N36°47.88´ W100°31.61´   WICHITA
2491 B NOTAM FILE MLC L−15C
RWY 17−35: H4050X60 (ASPH) S−4 MIRL
  RWY 17: REIL. P−line.
  RWY 35: REIL. Trees.
RWY 04−22: 2000X130 (TURF) 1.5% up SW
  RWY 04: Road.
SERVICE: LGT ACTIVATE MIRL Rwy 17−35, REIL Rwy 17 and Rwy 35—CTAF.
AIRPORT REMARKS: Unattended.
AIRPORT MANAGER: 580-625-3331
COMMUNICATIONS: CTAF 122.9
CLEARANCE DELIVERY PHONE: For CD ctc Kansas City ARTCC at 913-254-8508.

BLACKWELL−TONKAWA MUNI (BKN)(KBKN) 5 SW UTC−6(−5DT) N36°44.71´ W97°20.98´   WICHITA
1030 B NOTAM FILE MLC L−15D
RWY 17−35: H3501X60 (ASPH) S−30, D−48, 2D−98 MIRL IAP
  0.6% up N
  RWY 17: PAPI(P2L)—GA 3.0° TCH 40´.
  RWY 35: PAPI(P2L)—GA 3.0° TCH 40´.
SERVICE: FUEL 100LL LGT Actvt and incr MIRL Rwy 17−35—CTAF.
  PAPI Rwy 17 and 35 opr consly.
AIRPORT REMARKS: Attended irregularly. Fuel avbl 24 hrs thru automated
  credit card system.
AIRPORT MANAGER: 580-363-4242
WEATHER DATA SOURCES: AWOS−3PT 120.575 (580) 363−0688.
COMMUNICATIONS: CTAF/UNICOM 122.8
® KANSAS CITY CENTER APP/DEP CON 127.8
CLEARANCE DELIVERY PHONE: For CD ctc Kansas City ARTCC at
  913-254-8508.
RADIO AIDS TO NAVIGATION: NOTAM FILE PNC.
  PIONEER (VH) (H) VORTACW 113.2 PER Chan 79 N36°44.79´
    W97°09.61´ 264° 9.1 NM to fld. 1054/6E.
  TACAN AZIMUTH unusable:
    184°−194° blo 3,000´

SC, 25 JAN 2024 to 21 MAR 2024

OKLAHOMA

BOISE CITY (17K)   3 N   UTC–6(–5DT)   N36°46.46´ W102°30.63´   WICHITA
4174   B   NOTAM FILE MLC   L–15B
RWY 04–22: H4211X60 (ASPH)   S–4   MIRL   IAP
  RWY 04: PAPI(P4L)—GA 3.0° TCH 42´. Trees.
  RWY 22: PAPI(P4L)—GA 3.0° TCH 42´. Road.
SERVICE: LGT ACTVT PAPI Rwy 04 and 22—CTAF. MIRL Rwy 04–22
  SS–SR; preset low intst; incr intst —CTAF. Rwy 04 PAPI unusbl byd 5
  degs left of cntrln.
AIRPORT REMARKS: Unattended.
AIRPORT MANAGER: 580-544-2271
COMMUNICATIONS: CTAF 122.9
®**ALBUQUERQUE CENTER APP/DEP CON** 127.85
CLEARANCE DELIVERY PHONE: For CD ctc Albuquerque ARTCC at
  505-856-4861.
RADIO AIDS TO NAVIGATION: NOTAM FILE DHT.
  DALHART (L) (L) VORTACW 112.0   DHT   Chan 57   N36°05.49´
  W102°32.68´   350° 40.9 NM to fld. 4020/12E.
  TAC AZM unusable:
    240°–255° byd 15 NM
    320°–350° byd 15 NM

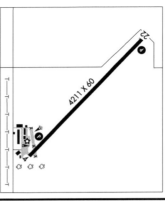

BRISTOW

JONES MEML   (3F7)   3 SW   UTC–6(–5DT)   N35°48.42´ W96°25.27´   DALLAS–FT WORTH
870   B   NOTAM FILE MLC   L–15E
RWY 18–36: H4001X75 (ASPH)   S–4   MIRL   1.4% up S   IAP
  RWY 36: Tree.
SERVICE: **FUEL** 100LL   **LGT** MIRL Rwy 18–36 on dusk–dawn. Incr
  intst—CTAF.
AIRPORT REMARKS: Unattended. 24 hr automated fuel service system.
  NOTE: See Special Notices— Aerobatic Practice Area.
AIRPORT MANAGER: 832-392-9040
COMMUNICATIONS: CTAF 122.9
®**KANSAS CITY CENTER APP/DEP CON** 127.8
CLEARANCE DELIVERY PHONE: For CD ctc Kansas City ARTCC at
  913-254-8508.
RADIO AIDS TO NAVIGATION: NOTAM FILE TUL.
  TULSA (H) (H) VORTACW 114.4   TUL   Chan 91   N36°11.78´
  W95°47.29´   225° 38.6 NM to fld. 788/8E.
  TACAN AZIMUTH unusable:
    248°–258° byd 23 NM blo 3,100´
  DME unusable:
    248°–258° byd 23 NM blo 3,100´

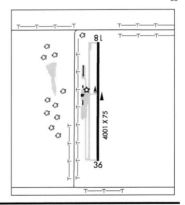

SC, 25 JAN 2024 to 21 MAR 2024

OKLAHOMA 183

BROKEN BOW (9ØF) 2 SW UTC–6(–5DT) N34°00.79′ W94°45.50′   **MEMPHIS**
404   B   NOTAM FILE MLC   **L–17D**
RWY 17–35: H3200X50 (ASPH)   S–17   MIRL
  RWY 17: PAPI(P2L)—GA 2.0° TCH 26′. Trees.
  RWY 35: PAPI(P2L)—GA 2.0° TCH 26′. Trees.
AIRPORT REMARKS: Unattended. High speed, low altitude military activity in vicinity of Broken Bow Lake.
AIRPORT MANAGER: 580-584-2885
COMMUNICATIONS: CTAF 122.9
CLEARANCE DELIVERY PHONE: For CD ctc Fort Worth ARTCC at 817-858-7584.
RADIO AIDS TO NAVIGATION: NOTAM FILE MLC.
  RICH MOUNTAIN (VL) (L) VORTACW 113.5   PGO   Chan 82
    N34°40.83′ W94°36.54′   187° 40.7 NM to fld. 2700/4E.
  VOR unusable:
    016°–021° byd 40 NM
    028°–029° byd 40 NM
    030°–040°
    050°–075° blo 4,000′
    090°–145°
    167°–169° byd 40 NM
    170°–200°
    235°–245° byd 30 NM blo 5,000′
    260°–280° byd 35 NM blo 5,000′
    329°–335° byd 40 NM
    340°–345° blo 5,000′
    358°–002° byd 40 NM

BUFFALO MUNI (BFK)(KBFK) 2 N UTC–6(–5DT) N36°51.80′ W99°37.12′   **WICHITA**
1822   B   NOTAM FILE MLC   **L–15C**
RWY 17–35: H4000X60 (ASPH)   S–4   MIRL   0.7% up N   **IAP**
  RWY 17: Pole.
  RWY 35: Tree.
SERVICE: **LGT** ACTIVATE MIRL Rwy 17–35—CTAF.
AIRPORT REMARKS: Unattended.
AIRPORT MANAGER: 580-735-2521
COMMUNICATIONS: CTAF 122.9
®**KANSAS CITY CENTER APP/DEP CON** 126.95
CLEARANCE DELIVERY PHONE: For CD ctc Kansas City ARTCC at 913-254-8508.
RADIO AIDS TO NAVIGATION: NOTAM FILE GAG.
  MITBEE (VH) (H) VORTACW 115.6   MMB   Chan 103   N36°20.62′ W99°52.81′   012° 33.6 NM to fld. 2426/10E.

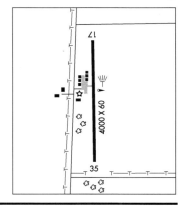

OKLAHOMA

BURNS FLAT

CLINTON/SHERMAN (CSM)(KCSM) 2 SW UTC−6(−5DT) N35°20.39′ W99°12.03′ DALLAS−FT WORTH
1922 B NOTAM FILE CSM H−6H, L−15C
  IAP, AD
RWY 17R−35L: H13503X200 (CONC) S−50, D−200, 2S−175, 2D−390
  HIRL(NSTD)
  RWY 17R: REIL. PAPI(P4L)—GA 3.0° TCH 54′. Rgt tfc.
  RWY 35L: REIL. PAPI(P4L)—GA 3.0° TCH 50′.
RWY 17L−35R: H5193X75 (CONC) S−50, D−200, 2S−175, 2D−390
  RWY 35R: Rgt tfc.
SERVICE: S4 FUEL JET A OX 3 LGT Actvt REIL 17R and 35L; HIRL
  Rwy 17R−35L; Twy lgt; wdi lgt—CTAF. PAPI Rwy 17R and 35L on
  consly. Rwy 17R−35L nstd; 75′ fm rwy edge.
AIRPORT REMARKS: Attended Mon−Fri 1500−0700Z‡. ATCT clsd fed hol. 24
  hr Jet−A fuel and otr svc avbl−ctc 405−267−4010. Rwy 17L−35R laid
  out and mrkd on Rwy 17L−35R parl twy. Rwy 17L−35R dalgt VFR
  only. Mil jet trng: hvy jets sfc to 5000′ wi 25 NMR. Extsv student pilot
  trng fm sfc to 5000′ wi 10 NMR btn 1500−1800Z‡. Mil jet ngt vision
  trng: ctc ATCT 10 mins prior to ldg aft SS to adjust arpt lgts. VFR acft
  adzd to ctc ATC 15 NM out for seqg. Ldg fee for acft gtr than 50,000
  lbs. See Special Notices—Space Launch Activity Area.
AIRPORT MANAGER: 580−309−3223
WEATHER DATA SOURCES: ASOS 118.450 (580) 562−4811. LAWRS.
COMMUNICATIONS: CTAF 119.6 UNICOM 122.95
  CLINTON−SHERMAN RCO 122.5 (MC ALESTER RADIO)
® FORT WORTH CENTER APP/DEP CON 128.4
  TOWER 119.6 (1500−0700Z‡ Mon−Fri; except federal holidays.) GND CON 121.7
AIRSPACE: CLASS D svc 1500−0700Z‡ Mon−Fri, exc fed hol; other times CLASS G.
RADIO AIDS TO NAVIGATION: NOTAM FILE CSM.
  BURNS FLAT (L) (L) VORTACW 110.0 BFV Chan 37 N35°14.22′ W99°12.37′ 358° 6.2 NM to fld. 1780/5E.
  FOSSI NDB (MHW/LOM) 393 BZ N35°27.04′ W99°12.09′ 175° 6.6 NM to fld. 5E. NDB unmonitored when
    Clinton−Sherman ATCT closed.
  ILS 109.5 I−BZF Rwy 17R. LOM FOSSI NDB. ILS and NDB/LOM unmonitored when ATCT closed.

BURNS FLAT N35°14.22′ W99°12.37′ NOTAM FILE CSM. DALLAS−FT. WORTH
  (L) (L) VORTACW 110.0 BFV Chan 37 358° 6.2 NM to Clinton/Sherman. 1780/5E. L−15C

BUZZARDS ROOST (See INOLA on page 205)

CANADIAN

CARLTON LANDING FLD (91F) 3 E UTC−6(−5DT) N35°09.38′ W95°37.29′ DALLAS−FT WORTH
851 B NOTAM FILE MLC L−17D
RWY 15−33: H3500X60 (ASPH) S−19 MIRL 0.6% up SE
  RWY 15: REIL. PAPI(P2L)—GA 3.0° TCH 43′.
  RWY 33: REIL. PAPI(P2L)—GA 3.0° TCH 43′.
SERVICE: FUEL 100LL LGT REIL Rwy 15 and 33; MIRL Rwy
  15−33—SS−SR. PAPI Rwy 15 and 33 on consly.
AIRPORT REMARKS: Unattended. Deer on and invof rwy. 24 hr self svc fuel
  avbl with credit card.
AIRPORT MANAGER: (405) 410−2050
COMMUNICATIONS: CTAF 122.9
CLEARANCE DELIVERY PHONE: For CD ctc Fort Worth ARTCC at
  817−858−7584.
RADIO AIDS TO NAVIGATION: NOTAM FILE MLC.
  MC ALESTER (L) TACAN Chan 57 MLC (112.0) N34°50.97′
    W95°46.94′ 015° 20.0 NM to fld. 782/8E.

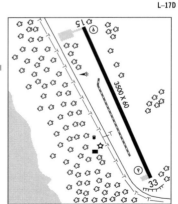

CARLTON LANDING FLD (See CANADIAN on page 184)

OKLAHOMA 185

CARNEGIE MUNI (86F) 2 NE UTC–6(–5DT) N35°07.42´ W98°34.51´ DALLAS–FT WORTH
1354 B NOTAM FILE MLC L–15D
RWY 17–35: H3000X60 (ASPH–CONC) S–11 MIRL 0.3% up S
  RWY 17: PAPI(P2L)—GA 3.0° TCH 40´.
  RWY 35: PAPI(P2R)—GA 3.0° TCH 40´.
SERVICE: LGT ACTVT MIRL Rwy 17–35—CTAF. PAPI Rwy 17 and 35 on consly.
AIRPORT REMARKS: Unattended.
AIRPORT MANAGER: (580) 574-3140
COMMUNICATIONS: CTAF 122.9
CLEARANCE DELIVERY PHONE: For CD ctc Fort Worth ARTCC at
  817-858-7584.
RADIO AIDS TO NAVIGATION: NOTAM FILE HBR.
  HOBART (L) (L) VORTACW 111.8 HBR Chan 55 N34°51.99´
    W99°03.80´ 047° 28.6 NM to fld. 1472/10E.
  VOR unusable:
    080°–120° byd 30 NM blo 4,000´
  TACAN AZIMUTH unusable:
    080°–090° byd 25 NM blo 4,500´
    100°–112° byd 25 NM blo 4,500´
    240°–270° byd 25 NM blo 4,500´
  DME unusable:
    080°–090° byd 25 NM blo 4,500´
    100°–112° byd 25 NM blo 4,500´
    240°–270° byd 25 NM blo 4,500´

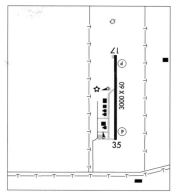

CATOOSA

PORT OF CATOOSA HELIPORT (O64) 3 N UTC–6(–5DT) N36°13.85´ W95°44.38´ KANSAS CITY
601 NOTAM FILE MLC
HELIPAD H1: H50X50 (CONC) PERIMETER LGTS
HELIPORT REMARKS: Attended irregularly. Helipad H1 perimeter lgts. Helipad H1 ingress/egress 030°–210°.
AIRPORT MANAGER: 918-266-2291
COMMUNICATIONS: CTAF 122.9
CLEARANCE DELIVERY PHONE: For CD ctc Tulsa Apch at 918-831-6714/6720.

CHANDLER RGNL (CQB)(KCQB) 3 NE UTC–6(–5DT) N35°43.45´ W96°49.22´ DALLAS–FT WORTH
985 B NOTAM FILE CQB L–15E
RWY 17–35: H4000X60 (ASPH) S–12.5 MIRL C.6% up S IAP
  RWY 17: PAPI(P4L)—GA 3.0° TCH 42´.
  RWY 35: PAPI(P4L)—GA 3.0° TCH 42´. Tree.
SERVICE: FUEL 100LL, JET A1+ LGT ACTVT PAPI Rwy 17 and Rwy
  35; MIRL Rwy 17–35——CTAF.
AIRPORT REMARKS: Unattended. Fuel avbl 24 hrs with credit card adps.
AIRPORT MANAGER: 405-258-3200
WEATHER DATA SOURCES: AWOS–3PT 119.275 (405) 253–6724.
COMMUNICATIONS: CTAF 122.9
®**KANSAS CITY CENTER APP/DEP CON** 127.8
CLEARANCE DELIVERY PHONE: For CD ctc Kansas City ARTCC at
  913-254-8508.
RADIO AIDS TO NAVIGATION: NOTAM FILE OKC.
  WILL ROGERS (H) (H) VORTACW 114.1 IRW Chan 88 N35°21.52´
    W97°36.55´ 053° 44.4 NM to fld. 1230/7E.

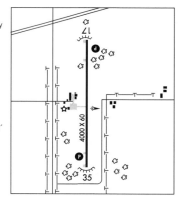

SC, 25 JAN 2024 to 21 MAR 2024

OKLAHOMA

CHATTANOOGA SKY HARBOR (92F)   3 SW   UTC−6(−5DT)   N34°22.13′ W98°40.93′   DALLAS–FT WORTH
1135   B   NOTAM FILE MLC   L−17B
RWY 17−35: H3400X60 (ASPH)   S−7   MIRL
AIRPORT REMARKS: Attended irregularly. Ultralights on and invof arpt.
AIRPORT MANAGER: 580-597-3390
COMMUNICATIONS: CTAF 122.9
CLEARANCE DELIVERY PHONE: For CD ctc Fort Worth ARTCC at 817-858-7584.
RADIO AIDS TO NAVIGATION: NOTAM FILE SPS.
   WICHITA FALLS (H) (H) VORTACW 112.7   SPS   Chan 74   N33°59.24′
      W98°35.61′   339° 23.3 NM to fld. 1133/10E.

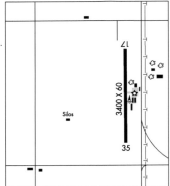

CHEROKEE MUNI (4O5)   2 N   UTC−6(−5DT)   N36°47.30′ W98°21.51′   WICHITA
1179   B   NOTAM FILE MLC   L−15D
RWY 17−35: H3770X60 (ASPH)   S−4   MIRL
   RWY 17: Thld dsplcd 200′.
   RWY 35: Thld dsplcd 200′.
SERVICE: **LGT** ACTIVATE MIRL Rwy 17−35—CTAF.
AIRPORT REMARKS: Unattended.
AIRPORT MANAGER: 580-596-3052
COMMUNICATIONS: CTAF 122.9
CLEARANCE DELIVERY PHONE: For CD ctc Vance Apch at 580-213-6765.
   when Vance Apch is clsd, ctc Kansas City ARTCC at 913-254-8508.

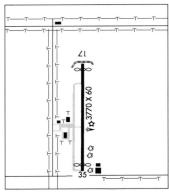

CHEYENNE

MIGNON LAIRD MUNI (93F) 2 W UTC–6(–5DT) N35°36.19´ W99°42.18´ DALLAS–FT WORTH
2093 B NOTAM FILE MLC L–15C
RWY 18–36: H4022X60 (ASPH) S–4 MIRL 1.2% up S
  RWY 18: PAPI(P2L)—GA 3.0° TCH 40´.
  RWY 36: PAPI(P2L)—GA 3.0° TCH 40´.
SERVICE: **FUEL** 100LL **LGT** MIRL Rwy 18–36 preset low intst SS–SR.
  ACTVT and incr intst—CTAF.
AIRPORT REMARKS: Unattended. Fuel avbl 24 hrs.
AIRPORT MANAGER: 580-878-1122
COMMUNICATIONS: CTAF 122.9
CLEARANCE DELIVERY PHONE: For CD ctc Fort Worth ARTCC at
  817-858-7584.

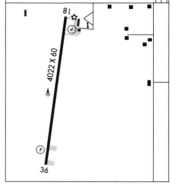

CHICKASHA MUNI (CHK)(KCHK) 3 NW UTC–6(–5DT) N35°05.83´ W97°58.06´ DALLAS–FT WORTH
1152 B NOTAM FILE CHK H–6H, L–17C
RWY 18–36: H5101X100 (CONC) S–40, D–52 MIRL 0.4% up N IAP
  RWY 18: PAPI(P4L)—GA 3.0° TCH 40´.
  RWY 36: PAPI(P4L)—GA 3.0° TCH 40´. Trees.
RWY 02–20: 2404X100 (TURF) 0.3% up N
  RWY 20: Tree.
RWY 01–19: 2232X100 (TURF) 0.3% up N
SERVICE: S2 **FUEL** 100LL, JET A+ **LGT** Actvt MIRL Rwy 18–36
  —CTAF. MIRL Rwy 18–36 preset low intst; to incr intst—CTAF.
AIRPORT REMARKS: Attended 1400–2300Z‡; excp hols. 110LL Fuel avbl
  H24 with credit card.
AIRPORT MANAGER: (405) 222-6045
WEATHER DATA SOURCES: AWOS–3 118.175 (405) 574–1016.
COMMUNICATIONS: CTAF/UNICOM 123.0
®**OKE CITY APP/DEP CON** 124.6
CLEARANCE DELIVERY PHONE: For CD ctc Oke City Apch at 405-681-5683.
RADIO AIDS TO NAVIGATION: NOTAM FILE OKC.
  WILL ROGERS (H) (H) VORTACW 114.1 IRW Chan 88 N35°21.52´
  W97°36.55´ 221° 23.6 NM to fld. 1230/7E.

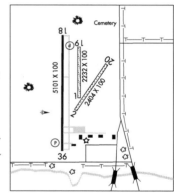

CHRISTMAN AIRFIELD (See OKEENE on page 212)

CITY OF COALGATE (See COALGATE on page 189)

OKLAHOMA

CLAREMORE

CLAREMORE RGNL (GCM)(KGCM) 7 E UTC–6(–5DT) N36°17.56´ W95°28.78´ KANSAS CITY
733 B NOTAM FILE GCM H–6I, L–15E
RWY 18–36: H5200X75 (ASPH) S–30, D–58.5, 2D–119.5 MIRL IAP
0.7% up S
  RWY 18: ODALS. PAPI(P4L)—GA 3.0° TCH 43´. Trees.
  RWY 36: REIL. PAPI(P4L)—GA 3.0° TCH 28´. Trees.
SERVICE: S4 FUEL 100LL, JET A LGT Actvt ODALS Rwy 18; REIL Rwy 36—CTAF. MIRL Rwy 18–36 SS–SR. PAPI Rwy 18 and 36 on consly.
AIRPORT REMARKS: Attended 1400–2300Z‡, unattended federal hols. 24 hr auto fuel svc sys for 100LL and Jet A.
AIRPORT MANAGER: 918-343-0931
WEATHER DATA SOURCES: AWOS–3PT 119.925 (918) 343–0184.
COMMUNICATIONS: CTAF/UNICOM 122.7
®TULSA APP/DEP CON 119.1
CLEARANCE DELIVERY PHONE: For CD ctc Tulsa Apch at 918-831-6714/6720.
RADIO AIDS TO NAVIGATION: NOTAM FILE TUL.
  TULSA (H) (H) VORTACW 114.4 TUL Chan 91 N36°11.78´ W95°47.29´ 061° 16.0 NM to fld. 788/8E.
  TACAN AZIMUTH unusable:
    248°–258° byd 23 NM blo 3,100´
  DME unusable:
    248°–258° byd 23 NM blo 3,100´

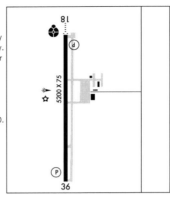

SAM RIGGS AIRPARK (K11) 7 S UTC–6(–5DT) N36°13.09´ W95°39.11´ KANSAS CITY
580 NOTAM FILE MLC
RWY 04–22: 2760X35 (TURF)
  RWY 04: Trees. Rgt tfc.
  RWY 22: Trees.
RWY 18–36: 1550X110 (TURF)
  RWY 18: Tree.
  RWY 36: Trees.
AIRPORT REMARKS: Unattended. Rwy 04–22 CLOSED indef. Rwy 04–22 ruf rwy sfc covd in tall grass & weeds. Trees & brush along edges. Rwy 18–36 covered in tall grass & weeds. Surface rough. Rwy unidentifiable. Rwy 18–36 ends unidentifiable.
AIRPORT MANAGER: 214-853-5751
COMMUNICATIONS: CTAF 122.9
CLEARANCE DELIVERY PHONE: For CD ctc Tulsa Apch at 918-831-6714/6720.

CLARENCE E PAGE MUNI (See OKLAHOMA CITY on page 213)

CLEVELAND MUNI (95F) 2 S UTC–6(–5DT) N36°17.05´ W96°27.80´ KANSAS CITY
976 B NOTAM FILE MLC L–15E
RWY 18–36: H4000X60 (ASPH) S–4 MIRL
  RWY 18: PAPI(P2L)—GA 2.75°. P–line.
  RWY 36: PAPI(P2L)—GA 2.75°. Tree.
SERVICE: LGT ACTIVATE MIRL Rwy 18–36—CTAF.
AIRPORT REMARKS: Unatndd. Golfers on and invof arpt.
AIRPORT MANAGER: 918-358-3506
COMMUNICATIONS: CTAF 122.9
CLEARANCE DELIVERY PHONE: For CD ctc Tulsa Apch at 918-831-6714/6720.
RADIO AIDS TO NAVIGATION: NOTAM FILE TUL.
  TULSA (H) (H) VORTACW 114.4 TUL Chan 91 N36°11.78´ W95°47.29´ 271° 33.2 NM to fld. 788/8E.
  TACAN AZIMUTH unusable:
    248°–258° byd 23 NM blo 3,100´
  DME unusable:
    248°–258° byd 23 NM blo 3,100´

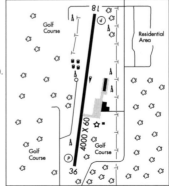

OKLAHOMA 189

CLINTON RGNL (CLK)(KCLK)   3 NE   UTC−6(−5DT)   N35°32.30′ W98°55.97′   DALLAS–FT WORTH
1616   B   NOTAM FILE CLK   L–15C
RWY 17–35: H4305X72 (ASPH)   S–7   MIRL   0.3% up N   IAP
  RWY 17: REIL. PAPI(P4L)—GA 3.0° TCH 40′.
  RWY 35: REIL. PAPI(P4R)—GA 3.0° TCH 40′.
RWY 13–31: 1348X245 (TURF)   1.0% up SE
SERVICE: S4   **FUEL** 100LL, JET A+   **LGT** ACTVT and incr intst REIL Rwy 17 and Rwy 35—CTAF. PAPI Rwy 17 and Rwy 35 on consly. MIRL Rwy 17–35; twy lgts on low intst dusk–dawn; incr intst—CTAF.
AIRPORT REMARKS: Attended 1400–2300Z‡. 100LL fuel avbl 24 hrs–self svc. Rwy 13–31 orange barrels mkd boundaries.
AIRPORT MANAGER: 580-323-5782
WEATHER DATA SOURCES: AWOS–3 119.225 (580) 323–3477.
COMMUNICATIONS: CTAF/UNICOM 122.8
Ⓡ **FORT WORTH CENTER APP/DEP CON** 128.4
CLEARANCE DELIVERY PHONE: For CD ctc Fort Worth ARTCC at 817-858-7584.
RADIO AIDS TO NAVIGATION: NOTAM FILE CSM.
  BURNS FLAT (L) (L) VORTACW 110.0   BFV   Chan 37   N35°14.22′ W99°12.37′   032° 22.5 NM to fld. 1780/5E.

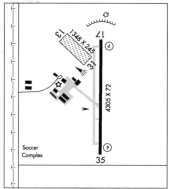

CLINTON/SHERMAN (See BURNS FLAT on page 184)

COALGATE

CITY OF COALGATE (08F)   1 W   UTC−6(−5DT)   N34°31.91′ W96°13.98′   DALLAS–FT WORTH
615   NOTAM FILE MLC
RWY 17–35: H2584X80 (CONC)
  RWY 17: Thld dsplcd 250′.
  RWY 35: Thld dsplcd 275′.
AIRPORT REMARKS: Unattended. Rwy 17 185′ water twrs 1320′ fm thr 350′ L. Rwy 17 and 35 marking nstd size.
AIRPORT MANAGER: 580-927-3914
COMMUNICATIONS: CTAF 122.9
CLEARANCE DELIVERY PHONE: For CD ctc Fort Worth ARTCC at 817-858-7584.

COOKSON

TENKILLER LAKE AIRPARK (44M)   1 SW   UTC−6(−5DT)   N35°42.30′ W94°56.17′   MEMPHIS
877   B   NOTAM FILE MLC
RWY 05–23: 2600X75 (TURF)   LIRL   1.3% up NE
  RWY 05: VASI(V2L)—GA 3.0° TCH 31′. Trees.
  RWY 23: VASI(V2L)—GA 3.5° TCH 33′. Trees.
SERVICE: **FUEL** 100LL   **LGT** ACTVT VASI Rwy 05 and Rwy 23—CTAF. LIRL Rwy 05–23 dusk–dawn. Rotating bcn OTS indef.
AIRPORT REMARKS: Attended irregularly. For fuel or after hrs assistance call 918–457–4095 or 918–931–0601. Ctn: Deer on and invof rwy. NOTE: See Special Notices—Aerobatic Practice Area.
AIRPORT MANAGER: 918-456-4121
COMMUNICATIONS: CTAF/UNICOM 122.8
CLEARANCE DELIVERY PHONE: For CD ctc Razorback Apch 479-649-2416, when Apch clsd ctc Memphis ARTCC at 901-368-8453/8449.

SC, 25 JAN 2024 to 21 MAR 2024

OKLAHOMA

CORDELL MUNI (F36)   1 E   UTC−6(−5DT)   N35°17.78′ W98°58.06′   DALLAS−FT WORTH
1589   B   NOTAM FILE MLC   L−15C
RWY 17−35: H3430X60 (ASPH)   S−12.6   MIRL
 RWY 17: PAPI(P2L)—GA 3.0° TCH 44′.
 RWY 35: PAPI(P2L)—GA 3.0° TCH 43′.
RWY 04−22: 1886X100 (TURF)
 RWY 04: Road.
SERVICE: **LGT** Actvt MIRL Rwy 17−35—CTAF. PAPI Rwy 17 and 35 on consly.
AIRPORT REMARKS: Attended Mon−Fri 1400−2300Z‡. Aft hr 580−660−0417 or Police Dept 580−832−3046.
AIRPORT MANAGER: 580-660-0417
COMMUNICATIONS: CTAF 122.9
CLEARANCE DELIVERY PHONE: For CD ctc Fort Worth ARTCC at 817-858-7584.
RADIO AIDS TO NAVIGATION: NOTAM FILE CSM.
 BURNS FLAT (L) (L) VORTACW 110.0   BFV   Chan 37   N35°14.22′ W99°12.37′   068° 12.2 NM to fld. 1780/5E.

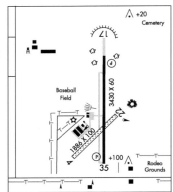

CUSHING MUNI (CUH)(KCUH)   2 S   UTC−6(−5DT)   N35°57.00′ W96°46.41′   DALLAS−FT WORTH
925   B   NOTAM FILE CUH   H−6H, L−15E
RWY 18−36: H5201X100 (CONC−TRTD−GRVD)   S−30 PCN 4 R/B/X/T   IAP
 MIRL   0.7% up N
 RWY 18: REIL. PAPI(P4L)—GA 3.0° TCH 26′.
 RWY 36: REIL. PAPI(P4L)—GA 3.0° TCH 33′. Trees.
RWY 08−26: 2700X40 (TURF)   0.9% up W
 RWY 08: Trees.
RWY 02−20: 2650X60 (TURF)   0.5% up N
 RWY 02: Trees.
RWY 11−29: 2500X50 (TURF)   1.4% up W
 RWY 11: Trees.
RUNWAY DECLARED DISTANCE INFORMATION
 RWY 18: TORA−5201   TODA−5201   ASDA−4986   LDA−4986
 RWY 36: TORA−5201   TODA−5201   ASDA−5201   LDA−5201
SERVICE: S4   **FUEL** 100LL, JET A   **OX** 2, 4   **LGT** Actvt REIL Rwy 18 and 36—CTAF. PAPI Rwy 18 and 36 on consly; MIRL Rwy 18−36 SS−SR preset med intst; incr intst—CTAF.
AIRPORT REMARKS: Attended Mon−Fri 1400−2300Z‡. Unatndd on fed hol. Parachute Jumping. Fuel avbl H24 with credit card. Rwy 08−26 and 11−29 soft when wet.
AIRPORT MANAGER: 918-225-0881
WEATHER DATA SOURCES: AWOS−3PT 118.25 (918) 225−6072.
COMMUNICATIONS: CTAF/UNICOM 122.8
Ⓡ **KANSAS CITY CENTER APP/DEP CON** 127.8
CLEARANCE DELIVERY PHONE: For CD ctc Kansas City ARTCC at 913-254-8508.
RADIO AIDS TO NAVIGATION: NOTAM FILE TUL.
 TULSA (H) (H) VORTACW 114.4   TUL   Chan 91   N36°11.78′ W95°47.29′   245° 50.1 NM to fld. 788/8E.
  TACAN AZIMUTH unusable:
   248°−258° byd 23 NM blo 3,100′
  DME unusable:
   248°−258° byd 23 NM blo 3,100′

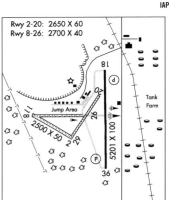

DAVID JAY PERRY (See GOLDSBY on page 197)

DECKER FLD (See MENO on page 209)

DOBIE'S (See INOLA on page 205)

OKLAHOMA 191

DUNCAN

HALLIBURTON FLD (DUC)(KDUC) 2 S UTC−6(−5DT) N34°28.25′ W97°57.59′ DALLAS−FT WORTH
1114 B NOTAM FILE DUC H−6H, L−17C
RWY 17−35: H6650X100 (CONC) S−44, D−56, 2D/2D2−101 MIRL IAP
  0.4% up N
RWY 17: ODALS. PAPI(P4R)—GA 3.0° TCH 53′.
RWY 35: REIL. VASI(V4L)—GA 3.0° TCH 42′. Thld dsplcd 325′.
RUNWAY DECLARED DISTANCE INFORMATION
  RWY 17: TORA−6325 TODA−6325 ASDA−6325 LDA−6325
  RWY 35: TORA−6650 TODA−6650 ASDA−6650 LDA−6325
SERVICE: S4 FUEL 100LL, JET A+ OX 1, 2 LGT ACTVT ODALS Rwy 17 med and high intst only; REIL Rwy 35; PAPI Rwy 17; VASI Rwy 35; MIRL Rwy 17−35—CTAF.
AIRPORT REMARKS: Attended 1400−2300Z‡. For fuel aft hrs call 580−656−2020 or 580−583−7196.
AIRPORT MANAGER: 580−470−2095
WEATHER DATA SOURCES: AWOS−3 119.075 (580) 252−4547.
COMMUNICATIONS: CTAF/UNICOM 122.8
®FORT SILL APP/DEP CON 118.6
  CLNC DEL 118.4
CLEARANCE DELIVERY PHONE: For CD ctc Fort Worth ARTCC at 817−858−7584.
RADIO AIDS TO NAVIGATION: NOTAM FILE LAW.
  LAWTON (L) (L) VORW/DME 116.85 LAW Chan 115(Y) N34°29.77′ W98°24.79′ 085° 22.5 NM to fld. 1105/9E.
  VOR unusable:
    270°−305° blo 3,900′
    270°−305° byd 10 NM

DURANT RGNL/EAKER FLD (DUA)(KDUA) 3 SW UTC−6(−5DT) N33°56.38′ W96°23.70′ DALLAS−FT WORTH
699 B NOTAM FILE DUA H−6H, L−17C
RWY 17−35: H6800X100 (ASPH) S−35, D−50 PCN 24 F/B/X/U MIRL IAP
RWY 17: ODALS. PAPI(P4L)—GA 3.0° TCH 43′. Trees.
RWY 35: PAPI(P4L)—GA 3.0° TCH 42′. Trees.
SERVICE: S4 FUEL 100LL, JET A LGT Actvt ODALS Rwy 17; MIRL Rwy 17−35; twy lgts—CTAF. PAPI Rwy 17 and 35 opr consly.
AIRPORT REMARKS: Attended Mon−Fri 1300−0100Z‡, Sat−Sun 1300−0100Z‡. Aft hr on req. Student trng invof arpt and over Lake Texoma. Aft hr 580−579−5024. For 100LL aft hrs call 580−579−5024. 372′ twr 2.5 mi N.
AIRPORT MANAGER: 580−579−5024
WEATHER DATA SOURCES: AWOS−3 124.175 (580) 931−3790.
COMMUNICATIONS: CTAF/UNICOM 123.05
®FORT WORTH CENTER APP/DEP CON 124.75
CLEARANCE DELIVERY PHONE: For CD ctc Fort Worth ARTCC at 817−858−7584.
RADIO AIDS TO NAVIGATION: NOTAM FILE DUA.
  TEXOMA (L) DME 114.3 URH Chan 90 N33°56.65′ W96°23.51′ at fld. 682.
  DME unusable:
    207°−240° byd 35 NM blo 2,500′
    335°−350° byd 35 NM blo 2,500′

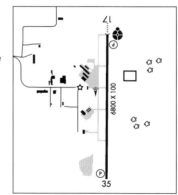

SC, 25 JAN 2024 to 21 MAR 2024

OKLAHOMA

EL RENO RGNL (RQO)(KRQO)   4 SW   UTC−6(−5DT)   N35°28.36´ W98°00.35´   DALLAS−FT WORTH
1420   B   NOTAM FILE RQO   H−6H, L−15D
  RWY 17−35: H5600X75 (CONC−TRTD)   S−30   MIRL   IAP
    RWY 17: REIL. PAPI(P4L)—GA 2.0° TCH 34´. P−line.
    RWY 35: REIL. PAPI(P4L)—GA 2.0° TCH 34´. Road. Rgt tfc.
  RWY 18−36: 4017X190 (TURF)
    RWY 18: Road. Rgt tfc.
    RWY 36: P−line.
  SERVICE: S4   FUEL 100LL, JET A   LGT Actvt REIL Rwy 17 and 35; MIRL Rwy 17−35—CTAF.
  AIRPORT REMARKS: Attended Mon−Fri 1400−2300Z‡, Sat−Sun 1500−2200Z‡. 100LL fuel avbl H24 with credit card. A fuel
    full svc avbl.
  AIRPORT MANAGER: 405-295-9343
  WEATHER DATA SOURCES: AWOS−3 118.475 (405) 262−0087.
  COMMUNICATIONS: CTAF/UNICOM 122.8
  ®OKE CITY APP/DEP CON 124.3
  CLEARANCE DELIVERY PHONE: For CD ctc Oke City Apch at 405-681-5683.
  RADIO AIDS TO NAVIGATION: NOTAM FILE OKC.
    WILL ROGERS (H) (H) VORTACW 114.1   IRW   Chan 88   N35°21.52´ W97°36.55´   282° 20.6 NM to fld. 1230/7E.
    KINGFISHER (H) TACAN   Chan 94   IFI (114.7)   N35°48.32´ W98°00.23´   171° 19.9 NM to fld. 1112/9E.   NOTAM
    FILE MLC.

ELK CITY RGNL BUSINESS (ELK)(KELK)   1 NE   UTC−6(−5DT)   N35°25.85´ W99°23.66´   DALLAS−FT WORTH
2013   B   NOTAM FILE MLC   H−6H, L−15C
  RWY 17−35: H5399X75 (CONC)   S−30   MIRL   0.5% up N   IAP
    RWY 17: ODALS. PAPI(P2L)—GA 3.0° TCH 42´.
    RWY 35: REIL. PAPI(P2L)—GA 3.5° TCH 39´. Pole.
  SERVICE: S4   FUEL 100LL, JET A+   LGT Actvt ODALS Rwy 17; REIL Rwy
    35, MIRL Rwy 17−35—CTAF. PAPI Rwys 17 and 35 opr consly.
  AIRPORT REMARKS: Attended Mon−Sat 1400−2300Z‡. Aft
    hr−580−225−7700. 100LL H24 with credit card. Ditch NW side of
    parl twy.
  AIRPORT MANAGER: 580-225-7700
  WEATHER DATA SOURCES: AWOS−3 118.225 (580) 303−9147.
  COMMUNICATIONS: CTAF/UNICOM 122.8
  ®FORT WORTH CENTER APP/DEP CON 128.4
  CLEARANCE DELIVERY PHONE: For CD ctc Fort Worth ARTCC at
    817-858-7584.
  RADIO AIDS TO NAVIGATION: NOTAM FILE CSM.
    BURNS FLAT (L) (L) VORTACW 110.0   BFV   Chan 37   N35°14.22´
    W99°12.37´   317° 14.8 NM to fld. 1780/5E.

SC, 25 JAN 2024 to 21 MAR 2024

OKLAHOMA

ENID WOODRING RGNL (WDG)(KWDG) 4 SE UTC–6(–5DT) N36°22.56′ W97°47.37′
1167 B NOTAM FILE WDG
WICHITA
H–6H, L–15D
IAP, AD
RWY 17–35: H8613X100 (CONC–GRVD) S–60, D–73, 2S–111, 2D–131 PCN 21 R/C/W/T MIRL
RWY 17: REIL. PAPI(P4L)—GA 3.0° TCH 52′. Thld dsplcd 611′. Road. 0.4% down.
RWY 35: MALSR. PAPI(P4L)—GA 3.0° TCH 49′. Rgt tfc. 0.3% up.
RWY 13–31: H3150X108 (ASPH) S–16 MIRL
RWY 13: Thld dsplcd 112′.
RWY 31: Rgt tfc.
SERVICE: S2 **FUEL** 100LL, JET A **LGT** When ATCT clsd actvt MALSR Rwy 35; REIL Rwy 17; MIRL Rwy 17–35 and 13–31—CTAF. PAPI Rwy 17 and 35 oper consly.
NOISE: Noise sensitive area 3/4 NM NW. All acft dep rwy 35 climb 500 ft AGL prior to turning crosswind to west.
AIRPORT REMARKS: Attended 1200–0330Z‡. Fuel avbl 24 hrs. Self svc AvGas avbl. For Jet A fuel aft hrs call 580–231–0189. Mil jet trng dalgt hrs invof arpt. Rwy 13–31 moderate to severe cracking, raveling, ponding and grass growing through cracks.
AIRPORT MANAGER: 580-616-7386
WEATHER DATA SOURCES: AWOS–3PT 123.725 (580) 237–1475. LAWRS.
COMMUNICATIONS: CTAF 118.9
WOODRING RCO 122.6 (MC ALESTER RADIO)
®**VANCE APP/DEP CON** 121.3 (1300–0200Z‡ wkd, 1900–2300Z‡ Sun; clsd Sat & federal hol. Gnd ctl and clnc del svc avbl 15 min prior to afld opening. Other times by NOTAM)
®**KANSAS CITY CENTER APP/DEP CON** 127.8 (0200–1300Z‡ wkd, 2300–1900Z‡ Sun; 24 Sat & federal hol. Gnd ctl and clnc del svc avbl 15 min prior to afld opening)
WOODRING TOWER 118.9 (1230–0300Z‡). **GND CON** 121.925
CLEARANCE DELIVERY PHONE: For CD ctc Vance Apch c580-213-6765. When Vance Apch clsd, ctc Kansas City ARTCC 913-254-8508.
AIRSPACE: CLASS D svc 1230–0300Z‡; other times CLASS E.
RADIO AIDS TO NAVIGATION: NOTAM FILE WDG.
WOODRING (T) (T) VORW/DME 109.0 ODG Chan 27 N36°22.43′ W97°47.29′ at fld. 1151/8E.
GARFY NDB (LOMW) 341 EI N36°16.50′ W97°47.45′ 356° 6.0 NM to fld. 1104/5E.
ILS 108.3 I–EIU Rwy 35. Class IE. LOM GARFY NDB. Unmonitored when ATCT clsd.

ERICK

HADDOCK FLD (O13) 1 SW UTC–6(–5DT) N35°12.05′ W99°52.86′
2097 NOTAM FILE MLC
DALLAS–FT WORTH
RWY 17–35: H2650X35 (ASPH) S–4
SERVICE: **LGT** Bcn OTS indefly.
AIRPORT REMARKS: Unattended. Military helicopter traffic on and invof arpt. Svr cracking and grass encroachment.
AIRPORT MANAGER: (580) 243-9190
COMMUNICATIONS: CTAF 122.9
CLEARANCE DELIVERY PHONE: For CD ctc Fort Worth ARTCC at 817-858-7584.

OKLAHOMA

EUFAULA

EUFAULA MUNI (F08) 2 W UTC–6(–5DT) N35°17.90´ W95°37.64´   DALLAS–FT WORTH
635   B   NOTAM FILE MLC   L–15E
RWY 17–35: H3000X60 (ASPH)   S–4   MIRL   0.4% up N
    RWY 17: PAPI(P2L)—GA 3.5° TCH 46´. Trees.
    RWY 35: PAPI(P2L)—GA 3.5° TCH 45´. Tree.
SERVICE: **FUEL** 100LL   **LGT** MIRL Rwy 17–35 preset low ints, to incr ints, ACTIVATE—CTAF.
AIRPORT REMARKS: Unattended. Ultralgts on and invof arpt. 100LL 24 hr self–service.
AIRPORT MANAGER: 918–689–2534
COMMUNICATIONS: CTAF 122.9
CLEARANCE DELIVERY PHONE: For CD ctc Fort Worth ARTCC at 817–858–7584.
RADIO AIDS TO NAVIGATION: NOTAM FILE MLC.
    MC ALESTER (L) TACAN   Chan 57   MLC (112.0)   N34°50.97´ W95°46.94´   008° 28.0 NM to fld. 782/8E.

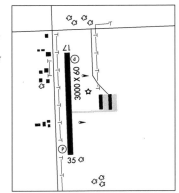

FOUNTAINHEAD LODGE AIRPARK (0F7)   6 N   UTC–6(–5DT)   N35°23.32´ W95°36.02´   DALLAS–FT WORTH
670   NOTAM FILE MLC   L–15E
RWY 18–36: H3000X50 (ASPH)   S–8
    RWY 36: Tree.
SERVICE: **LGT** MIRL OTS indef.
AIRPORT REMARKS: Unattended. Deer on and invof rwy.
AIRPORT MANAGER: 918–689–5311
COMMUNICATIONS: CTAF 122.9
CLEARANCE DELIVERY PHONE: For CD ctc Fort Worth ARTCC at 817–858–7584.

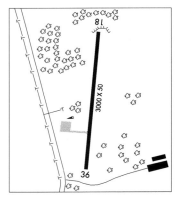

FAIRMONT FLD (1OK)   2 NE   UTC–6(–5DT)   N36°21.91´ W97°40.07´   WICHITA
1170   NOTAM FILE   Not insp.
RWY 17–35: 2540X65 (TURF)   0.3% up S
SERVICE: **FUEL** MOGAS
AIRPORT REMARKS: Unattended. Wildlife on and invof arpt. 4 ft seasonal crops at both apch ends Rwy 17–35. Ldg fee.
AIRPORT MANAGER: 580–242–6627
COMMUNICATIONS: CTAF 122.9
CLEARANCE DELIVERY PHONE: For CD ctc Vance Apch at580–213–6765. When Vance Apch is clsd, ctc Kansas City ARTCC at 913–254–8508.

OKLAHOMA

FAIRVIEW MUNI (6K4)   1 N   UTC−6(−5DT)   N36°17.47′ W98°28.55′   **WICHITA**
1274   B   NOTAM FILE MLC   L−15D
RWY 17−35: H4400X75 (ASPH−CONC)   S−30   MIRL   IAP
  RWY 35: Trees.
SERVICE: FUEL 100LL
AIRPORT REMARKS: Attended Mon−Sat dalgt hours. 1COLL avbl durg wint months.
AIRPORT MANAGER: 580-227-3788
COMMUNICATIONS: CTAF/UNICOM 122.8
®VANCE APP/DEP CON 126.75 (1300−0200Z‡ wkd, 1900−2300Z‡ Sun; clsd Sat & federal hol. Gnd ctl and clnc del svc avtl 15 min prior to afld opening. Other times by NOTAM.
®KANSAS CITY CENTER APP/DEP CON 127.8 (0200−1300Z‡ wkd, 2300−1900Z‡ Sun; 24 Sat & federal hol. Gnd ctl and clnc del svc avbl 15 min prior to afld opening)
CLEARANCE DELIVERY PHONE: For CD ctc Vance Apch at 580-213-6765.
When Vance Apch is clsd, ctc Kansas City ARTCC at 913-254-8508.
RADIO AIDS TO NAVIGATION: NOTAM FILE MLC.
  KINGFISHER (H) TACAN   Chan 94   IFI (114.7)   N35°48.32′ W98°00.23′   313° 37.1 NM to fld. 1112/9E.

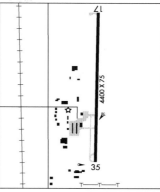

FORT SILL (See HENRY POST AAF (FORT SILL) on page 200)

FOSSI   N35°27.04′ W99°12.09′   NOTAM FILE CSM.   **DALLAS−FT. WORTH**
NDB (MHW/LOM) 393   BZ   175° 6.6 NM to Clinton/Sherman. 5E. NDB unmonitored when Clinton−Sherman ATCT closed.   L−15C

FOUNTAINHEAD LODGE AIRPARK (See EUFAULA on page 194)

FREDERICK RGNL (FDR)(KFDR)   3 SE   UTC−6(−5DT)   N34°21.13′ W98°59.03′   **DALLAS−FT WORTH**
1258   B   NOTAM FILE FDR   H−6H, L−17B
RWY 17−35: H6099X150 (ASPH)   S−35, D−50, 2D−100   MIRL   0.3% up N   IAP
  RWY 17: PAPI(P4L)—GA 3.09° TCH 50′.
  RWY 35: PAPI(P4R)—GA 3.09° TCH 46′.
RWY 03−21: H4812X60 (CONC)   S−30   0.4% up NE
  RWY 21: Road.
RWY 12−30: H4578X75 (CONC)   S−30
  RWY 30: Road.
SERVICE: FUEL 100LL   LGT ACTIVATE MIRL Rwy 17−35—CTAF.
AIRPORT REMARKS: Attended Mon−Sat 1400−2300Z‡, Sun 1900−2300Z‡. Self svc fuel avbl 24 hrs, for assistance call 580−335−1948. Rwy 12−30 marked to 75′ wide, pavement 150′ wide. Rwy 12−30 moderate cracking and deterioration. Rwy 03−21 marked to 60′ wide, pavement 150′ wide. Rwy 03−21 moderate cracking and deterioration. Arpt used as Sheppard AFB auxiliary: military tfc dalgt Mon−Fri. Ctc UNICOM for advisory. Military tfc will use rgt 360° overhead apchs to Rwy 17.
AIRPORT MANAGER: 580-335-2421
WEATHER DATA SOURCES: ASOS 132.675 (580) 335−7591.
COMMUNICATIONS: CTAF/UNICOM 123.05
®ALTUS APP/DEP CON 125.1 (1500−0830Z‡, clsd weekends and holidays. Other times ctc)
®FORT WORTH CENTER APP/DEP CON 128.4 133.5
CLEARANCE DELIVERY PHONE: For CD ctc Fort Worth ARTCC at 817-858-7584.
RADIO AIDS TO NAVIGATION: NOTAM FILE SPS.
  WICHITA FALLS (H) (H) VORTACW 112.7   SPS   Chan 74   N33°59.24′ W98°35.61′   308° 29.2 NM to fld. 1133/10E.

OKLAHOMA

FREEDOM MUNI (K77) 1 SE UTC–6(–5DT) N36°45.51´ W99°06.12´
1517 NOTAM FILE MLC
RWY 12–30: H3000X35 (ASPH)
 RWY 12: Trees.
AIRPORT REMARKS: Unattended. Rwy 12–30 edges & thlds unidbl. First 150 ft of Rwy 12 & first 400 ft of Rwy 30 cvrd in grass. Rwy sfc rough & uneven. Broken asph, rocks, & tall grass entr sfc. Ocnl equip on rwy sfc.
AIRPORT MANAGER: (580) 621-3302
COMMUNICATIONS: CTAF 122.9
CLEARANCE DELIVERY PHONE: For CD ctc Kansas City ARTCC at 913-254-8508.
RADIO AIDS TO NAVIGATION: NOTAM FILE GAG.
 MITBEE (VH) (H) VORTACW 115.6   MMB   Chan 103   N36°20.62´ W99°52.81´   046° 45.1 NM to fld. 2426/10E.

WICHITA
L–15C

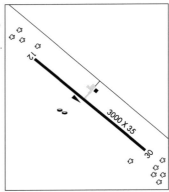

GAGE (GAG)(KGAG) 2 SW UTC–6(–5DT) N36°17.75´ W99°46.59´
2223 B NOTAM FILE GAG
RWY 17–35: H5033X75 (ASPH) S–4 LIRL(NSTD) 0.8% up S
SERVICE: **LGT** Actvt LIRL Rwy 17–35—123.0. Rwy 17–35 Intens rwy lgts nstd; Rwy 17 has no thr lgts; Rwy 35 has four thr lgts.
AIRPORT REMARKS: Unattended. Ultralight act on and invof arpt. Twys clsd; use midway stub and back taxi. Jet acft over 15,000 lbs NA.
AIRPORT MANAGER: (580) 923-7727
WEATHER DATA SOURCES: ASOS 128.625 (580) 923–7581.
COMMUNICATIONS: CTAF 122.9
 RCO 122.3 (MC ALESTER RADIO)
CLEARANCE DELIVERY PHONE: For CD if una to ctc on FSS freq, ctc Kansas City ARTCC at 913-254-8508.
RADIO AIDS TO NAVIGATION: NOTAM FILE GAG.
 MITBEE (VH) (H) VORTACW 115.6   MMB   Chan 103   N36°20.62´ W99°52.81´   110° 5.8 NM to fld. 2426/10E.

WICHITA
H–6H, L–15C

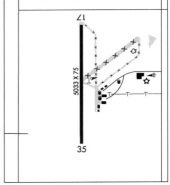

GARFY N36°16.50´ W97°47.45´ NOTAM FILE WDG.
 NDB (LOMW) 341 EI 356° 6.0 NM to Enid Woodring Rgnl. 1104/5E.

WICHITA

GLENPOOL N35°55.25´ W95°58.12´ NOTAM FILE MLC.
 (T) DME 110.6 GNP Chan 43 354° 7.2 NM to Tulsa Riverside. 810.

DALLAS–FT WORTH
L–15E

OKLAHOMA

GOLDSBY

DAVID JAY PERRY (1K4)   1 NE   UTC–6(–5DT)   N35°09.30′ W97°28.22′   DALLAS–FT WORTH
1169   B   NOTAM FILE MLC   L–15D
RWY 13–31: H3004X60 (CONC–GRVD)   S–30   MIRL   0.3% up NW   IAP
  RWY 13: Trees.
  RWY 31: Trees.
RWY 17–35: H1801X60 (ASPH)   S–4   0.4% up N
  RWY 17: Trees.
SERVICE: FUEL 100LL   LGT ACTVT MIRL Rwy 13–31 dusk–dawn—CTAF.
AIRPORT REMARKS: Attended Mon–Fri 1400–2300Z‡. 24 hr automated fuel servicing system. Coyotes on and invof rwy. Ultra ight act on and invof arpt. Intensive student training dalgt hrs.
AIRPORT MANAGER: 405-570-8399
COMMUNICATIONS: CTAF/UNICOM 122.7
®OKE CITY APP/DEP CON 120.45
CLEARANCE DELIVERY PHONE: For CD ctc Oke City Apch at 405-681-5683.
RADIO AIDS TO NAVIGATION: NOTAM FILE OKC.
  WILL ROGERS (H) (H) VORTACW 114.1   IRW   Chan 88   N35°21.52′
  W97°36.55′   144°   14.0 NM to fld. 1230/7E.

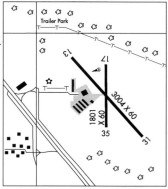

GRAND LAKE RGNL (See AFTON on page 175)

GRANDFIELD MUNI (101)   3 W   UTC–6(–5DT)   N34°14.26′ W98°44.52′   DALLAS–FT WORTH
1128   B   NOTAM FILE MLC   L–17B
RWY 17–35: H3100X75 (ASPH)   S–11   MIRL
RWY 08–26: H1540X75 (ASPH)
SERVICE: LGT ACTVT MIRL Rwy 17–35—CTAF.
AIRPORT REMARKS: Unattended. Parachute Jumping. Rwy 08–26 pavement exhibiting svr cracking, mod vegetation encroachment, and gen deterioration. Tower 1073 ft AGL 12,000 ft SSE of arpt. Tower 1059 ft AGL 8,500 ft SE of arpt. Rwy 08 and Rwy 26 markings unreadable.
AIRPORT MANAGER: 580-704-0016
COMMUNICATIONS: CTAF 122.9
CLEARANCE DELIVERY PHONE: For CD ctc Fort Worth ARTCC at 817-858-7584.
RADIO AIDS TO NAVIGATION: NOTAM FILE SPS.
  WICHITA FALLS (H) (H) VORTACW 112.7   SPS   Chan 74   N33°59.24′
  W98°35.61′   324°   16.7 NM to fld. 1133/10E.

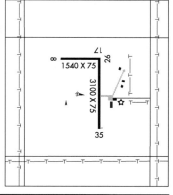

OKLAHOMA

GROVE RGNL (GMJ)(KGMJ) 2 NE UTC–6(–5DT) N36°36.41′ W94°44.31′ KANSAS CITY
831 B NOTAM FILE GMJ H–6I, L–16F
RWY 18–36: H5200X75 (ASPH) S–30 MIRL IAP
 RWY 18: PAPI(P4L)—GA 2.75° TCH 31′. Trees.
 RWY 36: PAPI(P4L)—GA 2.75° TCH 28′. Trees.
SERVICE: S4 **FUEL** 100LL, JET A+ **OX** 4 **LGT** MIRL Rwy 18–36
 preset medium ints dusk–dawn, to incr ints and ACTIVATE twy
 lgts—CTAF.
AIRPORT REMARKS: Attended 1400–2300Z‡. Arpt unattended
 Thanksgiving and Christmas. Terminal building/FBO lctd on west side
 of runway. Rwy 18 markings faded.
AIRPORT MANAGER: 918-786-6150
WEATHER DATA SOURCES: AWOS–3PT 119.025 (918) 786–8350. Dewpoint
 unreliable.
COMMUNICATIONS: CTAF/UNICOM 122.8
 ®**KANSAS CITY CENTER APP/DEP CON** 128.6
CLEARANCE DELIVERY PHONE: For CD ctc Kansas City ARTCC at
 913-254-8508.
RADIO AIDS TO NAVIGATION: NOTAM FILE JBR.
 RAZORBACK (VH) (H) VORTACW 116.4 RZC Chan 111 N36°14.79′
  W94°07.28′ 302° 36.9 NM to fld. 1332/4E.
 VOR unusable:
  025°–035° byd 40 NM
  025°–150° byd 22 NM blo 4,000′
  070°–080° byd 40 NM
  093°–103° byd 124 NM
  093°–103° byd 40 NM blo 17,000′
  104°–144° byd 40 NM
  145°–155° byd 40 NM blo 6,500′
  145°–155° byd 67 NM blo 9,500′
  145°–155° byd 80 NM
  150°–210° byd 22 NM blo 3,500′
  156°–170° byd 40 NM
  195°–215° byd 40 NM
  210°–220° byd 22 NM blo 3,000′
  234°–245° byd 40 NM
  310°–025° byd 22 NM blo 3,000′
 TACAN AZIMUTH unusable:
  148°–160°
  225°–240°

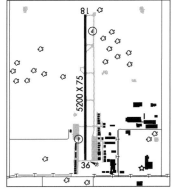

GUNDYS (See OWASSO on page 216)

GUTHRIE/EDMOND RGNL (GOK)(KGOK) 2 S UTC–6(–5DT) N35°51.09′ W97°24.97′ DALLAS–FT WORTH
1069 B NOTAM FILE GOK H–6H, L–15D
RWY 16–34: H5001X75 (CONC) S–30, D–48, 2D–78 MIRL IAP
 0.3% up S
 RWY 16: ODALS. REIL. PAPI(P4L)—GA 3.0° TCH 45′.
 RWY 34: REIL. PAPI(P4L)—GA 3.0° TCH 45′. Trees.
SERVICE: S4 **FUEL** 100LL, JET A **LGT** ACTVT ODALS Rwy 16; REIL
 Rwy 34—CTAF. MIRL Rwy 16–34 SS–SR preset med intst; incr
 intst—CTAF. PAPI Rwy 16 and 34 on consly.
AIRPORT REMARKS: Attended 1200–0000Z‡. Bird and otr wildlife act on
 and invof arpt. Rwy 16 calm wind rwy.
AIRPORT MANAGER: 405-282-2312
WEATHER DATA SOURCES: ASOS 133.975 (405) 282-0478.
COMMUNICATIONS: CTAF/UNICOM 122.8
 ®**OKE CITY APP/DEP CON** 124.2
CLEARANCE DELIVERY PHONE: For CD ctc Oke City Apch at 405-681-5683
RADIO AIDS TO NAVIGATION: NOTAM FILE MLC.
 KINGFISHER (H) TACAN Chan 94 IFI (114.7) N35°48.32′
  W98°00.23′ 075° 28.8 NM to fld. 1112/9E.

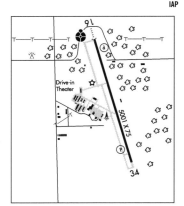

SC, 25 JAN 2024 to 21 MAR 2024

OKLAHOMA

GUYMON MUNI (GUY)(KGUY)   1 W   UTC–6(–5DT)   N36°41.05′ W101°30.42′   **WICHITA**
3125   B   NOTAM FILE GUY   **H–6G, L–15B**
RWY 18–36: H5904X100 (ASPH)   S–10   MIRL   **IAP**
   RWY 18: ODALS. VASI(V4L)—GA 3.0° TCH 25′. Rgt tfc.
   RWY 36: PAPI(P4L)—GA 3.0° TCH 35′. Road.
RWY 06–24: 1795X200 (TURF)   1.3% up SW
SERVICE: S4   **FUEL** 100LL, JET A   **OX** 1, 2   **LGT** ACTVT ODALS Rwy 18; VASI Rwy 18; PAPI Rwy 36; MIRL Rwy 18–36—CTAF. MIRL Rwy 18–36 preset low intst, incr intst—CTAF.
AIRPORT REMARKS: Attended Mon–Fri 1300–0030Z‡, Sat 1300–0000Z‡, Sun 1400–2300Z‡. For attendant after hours call 580–338–0481/7700. Numerous waterfowl invof arpt SR and SS. Rwy 06 dep NA. Rwy 06 edges marked with raised wooden mrkrs.
AIRPORT MANAGER: 580-338-7700
WEATHER DATA SOURCES: ASOS 119.925 (580) 468–1476.
COMMUNICATIONS: CTAF/UNICOM 122.7
Ⓡ **KANSAS CITY CENTER APP/DEP CON** 134.0
CLEARANCE DELIVERY PHONE: For CD ctc Kansas City ARTCC at 913-254-8508.
RADIO AIDS TO NAVIGATION: NOTAM FILE GUY.
   NDB (MHW) 275   GUY   N36°42.32′ W101°30.31′   175° 1.3 NM to fld. 3128/9E.

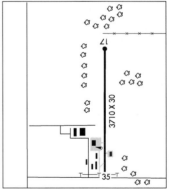

HADDOCK FLD (See ERICK on page 193)

HALLIBURTON FLD (See DUNCAN on page 191)

HARVEY YOUNG (See TULSA on page 230)

HASKELL   (2K9)   1 NE   UTC–6(–5DT)   N35°49.97′ W95°40.05′   **DALLAS–FT WORTH**
588   NOTAM FILE MLC   **L–15E**
RWY 17–35: H3710X30 (ASPH)
   RWY 17: Trees.
SERVICE: **FUEL** 100LL
AIRPORT REMARKS: Attended irregularly. Dalgt ops only. Ultralight act on and invof arpt. Rwy 17 ultralight use right tfc. Rwy 17 and 35 sml nrs and nstd cntrln. NOTE: See Special Notices—Model Aircraft Activity.
AIRPORT MANAGER: 918-231-3232
COMMUNICATIONS: CTAF 122.9
CLEARANCE DELIVERY PHONE: For CD ctc Tulsa approach at 918-831-6714.
RADIO AIDS TO NAVIGATION: NOTAM FILE TUL.
   TULSA (H) (H) VORTACW 114.4   TUL   Chan 91   N36°11.78′ W95°47.29′   157° 22.6 NM to fld. 788/8E.
   TACAN AZIMUTH unusable:
     248°–258° byd 23 NM blo 3,100′
   DME unusable:
     248°–258° byd 23 NM blo 3,100′

OKLAHOMA

HEALDTON MUNI (F32) 2 NE UTC−6(−5DT) N34°15.29′ W97°28.38′   DALLAS−FT WORTH
956   NOTAM FILE MLC   L−17C
RWY 17−35: H3020X60 (ASPH)   S−12.5
AIRPORT REMARKS: Unattended. Daylight ops only.
AIRPORT MANAGER: 580-229-1283
COMMUNICATIONS: CTAF 122.9
CLEARANCE DELIVERY PHONE: For CD ctc Fort Worth ARTCC at 817-858-7584.
RADIO AIDS TO NAVIGATION: NOTAM FILE ADM.
   ARDMORE (VH) (H) VORTACW 116.7   ADM   Chan 114   N34°12.70′
   W97°10.09′   274° 15.4 NM to fld. 937/6E.
   VOR unusable:
     150°−160° byd 40 NM
     150°−160° byd 6 NM blo 14,000′
     297°−306° byd 40 NM blo 15,000′
     307°−314° blo 3,500′
     307°−314° byd 15 NM
     314°−333°
   TACAN AZIMUTH unusable:
     314°−333°
   DME unusable:
     314°−333°
     334°−011° byd 39 NM blo 3,100′

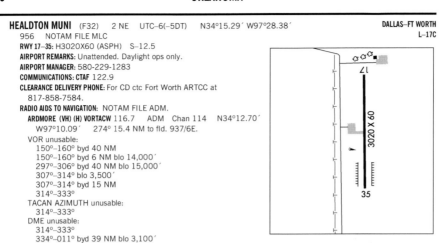

HEFNER−EASLEY (See WAGONER on page 234)

HENRY POST AAF (FORT SILL) (FSI)(KFSI) A   1 SE   UTC−6(−5DT)   N34°38.99′ W98°24.13′   DALLAS−FT WORTH
1188   B   TPA—See Remarks   NOTAM FILE FSI   Not insp.   H−6H, L−17C
RWY 18−36: H5002X150 (CONC)   PCN 61 R/B/W/T   HIRL   0.4% up N   DIAP
   RWY 18: REIL. PAPI(P4L)—GA 3.0° TCH 44′.
   RWY 36: SALS. PAPI(P4L)—GA 3.0° TCH 61′.
SERVICE: **LGT** Actvt PAPI Rwy 18 on 124.95. Apch, PAPI and Rwy 36 lgt opr O/R to twr or APP. **MILITARY**— **FUEL** A++. Avbl with 48 hr PN, ctc Afld Mgmt. **TRAN ALERT** No tran maintenance, limited svc. Tran aircrew must remain with acft to provide technical drct/assist in servicing.
MILITARY REMARKS: RSTD Afld cond unmto when Afld Mgmt Clsd. 24 hr PPR all trans acft. Rwy 18−36 nstd safety are byd each end due to terrain grade, no paved overruns. Twy A and Twy C PCN GWT rstd, C−130 and LRGR must use Twy B for rwy entry and exit. **TFC PAT** TPA—rotary wing 1900 (712) MSL, fixed wing 2700 (1512). **MISC** Afld Mgmt opr 1230−2100Z‡ Mon−Fri exc hol, other svcs avbl as published/NOTAM. DSN 639−4643/2023, C580−442−4643/2023, wx DSN 639−4000/4887, C580−442−4000/4887. Weather forecast avbl Mon−Fri 1200−0400Z‡ except holidays. Potential for bird activity near pond NW of AER Rwy 18. Remote briefing svc avbl 26 OWS Barksdale AFB DSN 331−2651, C318−529−2651, https://26ows.us.af.mil/. Wx obsn automated 24/7. Wx obsn augmented (as required) during hrs wx forecast avbl. wx obsn visibility ltd to 0.25 SM north and northeast when sfc wx obsn visibility sensor augmented. Wind cones located 353 feet from runway edge. Rwy edge lighting located 26 feet from runway edge line.
AIRPORT MANAGER: 580-442-4643
COMMUNICATIONS: CTAF 124.95   **ATIS** 135.425   354.025
Ⓡ **FORT SILL APP/DEP CON** 118.6 290.375 (VFR),   120.55 322.4 (IFR)
   POST TOWER 124.95   229.4 (Opr by NOTAM)
   POST GND CON/CLNC DEL 121.7   279.575
   PMSV METRO 306.5 (Svc avbl Mon−Fri 1200−0600Z‡, except holidays)
RADIO AIDS TO NAVIGATION: NOTAM FILE LAW.
   LAWTON (L) (L) VORW/DME 116.85   LAW   Chan 115(Y)   N34°29.77′ W98°24.79′   354° 9.2 NM to fld. 1105/9E.
   VOR unusable:
     270°−305° blo 3,900′
     270°−305° byd 10 NM
   ASR
COMM/NAV/WEATHER REMARKS: Radar see Terminal FLIP for Radar Minima.

SC, 25 JAN 2024 to 21 MAR 2024

OKLAHOMA

HENRYETTA MUNI (F10)   3 SW   UTC–6(–5DT)   N35°24.41´ W96°00.95´   DALLAS–FT WORTH
849   B   NOTAM FILE MLC   L–6H, 15E
RWY 18–36: H3501X50 (ASPH)   S–12   MIRL   0.5% up S   IAP
  RWY 18: PVASI(PSIL)—GA 3.5° TCH 45´. Trees.
  RWY 36: Trees.
SERVICE: LGT Dusk–Dawn. ACTIVATE MIRL Rwy 18–36—CTAF. Rwy
  18 PVASI OTS indefly.
AIRPORT REMARKS: Unatndd. Rwy 18–36 markings severely faded.
AIRPORT MANAGER: 918-652-3348
COMMUNICATIONS: CTAF/UNICOM 122.8
®FORT WORTH CENTER APP/DEP CON 132.2
CLEARANCE DELIVERY PHONE: For CD ctc Fort Worth ARTCC at
  817-858-7584.
RADIO AIDS TO NAVIGATION: NOTAM FILE MLC.
  MC ALESTER (L) TACAN   Chan 57   MLC (112.0)   N34°50.97´
    W95°46.94´   333° 35.3 NM to fld. 782/8E.
  NDB (MHW) 267   HET   N35°24.27´ W96°00.33´   at fld.
    849/4E. unmonitored.

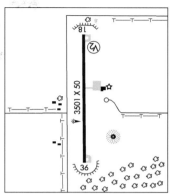

HINTON MUNI (2O8)   2 NE   UTC–6(–5DT)   N35°30.43´ W98°20.55´   DALLAS–FT WORTH
1587   B   NOTAM FILE MLC   L–15D
RWY 18–36: H4001X60 (ASPH)   MIRL   IAP
  RWY 18: PAPI(P2L)—GA 3.0° TCH 42´.
  RWY 36: PAPI(P2L)—GA 3.0° TCH 43´.
SERVICE: FUEL 100LL   LGT PAPI Rwy 18 and 36 on consly, preset low intst at ngt. Incr intst 5 or 7 mic clicks—CTAF;
  MIRL Rwy 18–36 SS–SR preset low intst, incr intst 5 or 7 mic clicks—CTAF.
AIRPORT REMARKS: Attended Mon–Sat 1500–2300Z‡, Sun 1900–2300Z‡. Glider act on and invof arpt. 100LL avbl 24 hr
  with adp sys.
AIRPORT MANAGER: 405-542-3993
COMMUNICATIONS: CTAF/UNICOM 123.05
®FORT WORTH CENTER APP/DEP CON 128.4
CLEARANCE DELIVERY PHONE: For CD ctc Fort Worth AR⁻CC at 817-858-7584.
RADIO AIDS TO NAVIGATION: NOTAM FILE OKC.
  WILL ROGERS (H) (H) VORTACW 114.1   IRW   Chan 88   N35°21.52´ W97°36.55´   277° 37.0 NM to fld. 1230/7E.

OKLAHOMA

HOBART RGNL (HBR)(KHBR)   3 SE   UTC–6(–5DT)   N34°59.40´ W99°03.18´   DALLAS–FT WORTH
1563   B   NOTAM FILE HBR   MON Airport   H–6H, L–17B
RWY 17–35: H5507X100 (ASPH)   S–20   MIRL   0.4% up S   IAP
 RWY 17: PAPI(P4L)—GA 3.0° TCH 35´.
 RWY 35: PAPI(P4L)—GA 3.0° TCH 42´.
RWY 03–21: H2975X60 (ASPH)   S–9.4   0.5% up SW
SERVICE: FUEL 100LL, JET A+
AIRPORT REMARKS: Attended Mon–Fri 1400–2200Z‡. Fuel avbl 24 hr self svc with major credit card. Rwy 03 markings svrly faded. Rwy 21 markings svrly faded.
AIRPORT MANAGER: 580-726-2719
WEATHER DATA SOURCES: ASOS 133.325 (580) 726–6651.
COMMUNICATIONS: CTAF/UNICOM 122.8
 RCO 122.2 (MC ALESTER RADIO)
Ⓡ **ALTUS APP/DEP CON** 125.1 (Mon–Fri 1500–0830Z‡, clsd weekends and holidays. Other times ctc)
Ⓡ **FORT WORTH CENTER APP/DEP CON** 128.4
CLEARANCE DELIVERY PHONE: For CD if una to ctc on FSS freq, ctc Fort Worth ARTCC at 817-858-7584.
AIRSPACE: CLASS E.
RADIO AIDS TO NAVIGATION: NOTAM FILE HBR.
 (L) (L) VORTACW 111.8   HBR   Chan 55   N34°51.99´ W99°03.80´   354° 7.4 NM to fld. 1472/10E.
 VOR unusable:
  080°–120° byd 30 NM blo 4,000´
 TACAN AZIMUTH unusable:
  080°–090° byd 25 NM blo 4,500´
  100°–112° byd 25 NM blo 4,500´
  240°–270° byd 25 NM blo 4,500´
 DME unusable:
  080°–090° byd 25 NM blo 4,500´
  100°–112° byd 25 NM blo 4,500´
  240°–270° byd 25 NM blo 4,500´

HOLDENVILLE MUNI (F99)   1 NW   UTC–6(–5DT)   N35°05.15´ W96°25.00´   DALLAS–FT WORTH
861   B   NOTAM FILE MLC   L–17D
RWY 17–35: H3251X100 (CONC)   S–30, D–42   MIRL(NSTD)   IAP
 RWY 35: Tree.
SERVICE: LGT Rwy 17–35 intens rwy lgts nstd dist fm rwy edge.
AIRPORT REMARKS: Unattended.   125´ AGL silo, .3 nm W Rwy 35 thld.
AIRPORT MANAGER: 254-368-4635
COMMUNICATIONS: CTAF 122.9
Ⓡ **FORT WORTH CENTER APP/DEP CON** 132.2
CLEARANCE DELIVERY PHONE: For CD ctc Fort Worth ARTCC at 817-858-7584.
RADIO AIDS TO NAVIGATION: NOTAM FILE OKM.
 OKMULGEE (VH) (DH) VORW/DME 114.9   OKM   Chan 96   N35°41.58´ W95°51.96´   209° 45.3 NM to fld. 774/8E.

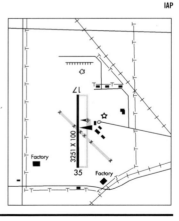

OKLAHOMA

HOLLIS MUNI (O35)   2 N   UTC−6(−5DT)   N34°42.32′ W99°54.51′   DALLAS–FT WORTH
1659   B   NOTAM FILE MLC   L–17B
RWY 18–36: H3000X60 (ASPH)   S–4   MIRL   IAP
  RWY 18: Road.
SERVICE: **FUEL** 100LL   **LGT** ACTIVATE MIRL Rwy 18–36—CTAF.
AIRPORT REMARKS: Attended irregularly. For fuel call Police 580-688-9216.
AIRPORT MANAGER: 580-688-9245
COMMUNICATIONS: CTAF 122.9
®**ALTUS APP/DEP CON** 125.1 (Mon–Fri 1500–0830Z‡, clsd weekends and holidays. Other times ctc)
®**FORT WORTH CENTER APP/DEP CON** 128.4   133.5
CLEARANCE DELIVERY PHONE: For CD ctc Fort Worth ARTCC at 817-858-7584.
RADIO AIDS TO NAVIGATION: NOTAM FILE CDS.
  CHILDRESS (VL) (H) VORTACW 117.0   CDS   Chan 117   N34°22.14′ W100°17.34′   033° 27.6 NM to fld. 1920/10E.

HOMINY MUNI (H92)   2 N   UTC−6(−5DT)   N36°26.57′ W96°23.23′   KANSAS CITY
825   B   NOTAM FILE MLC   L–15E
RWY 17–35: H3210X60 (ASPH)   S–8   MIRL
  RWY 17: PAPI(P4L). Thld dsplcd 180′. Trees.
  RWY 35: PAPI(P4L). Thld dsplcd 180′. Trees.
SERVICE: **FUEL** 100LL   **LGT** ACTIVATE MIRL Rwy 17–35—CTAF.
AIRPORT REMARKS: Unattended. Fuel avbl 24 hrs self svc with credit card. Ultralight activity on and invof arpt.
AIRPORT MANAGER: 918-885-2164
COMMUNICATIONS: CTAF 122.9
CLEARANCE DELIVERY PHONE: For CD ctc Kansas City ARTCC at 913-254-8508.
RADIO AIDS TO NAVIGATION: NOTAM FILE BVO.
  BARTLESVILLE (L) (L) VORW/DME 117.9   BVO   Chan 126   N36°50.06′ W96°01.11′   209° 29.5 NM to fld. 930/8E.

SC, 25 JAN 2024 to 21 MAR 2024

OKLAHOMA

HOOKER MUNI (O45) 1 W UTC–6(–5DT) N36°51.42´ W101°13.63´   WICHITA
3000 B NOTAM FILE MLC   L–15B
RWY 17–35: H3312X60 (ASPH)   MIRL
  RWY 17: PAPI(P2L)—GA 3.0° TCH 40´. Rgt tfc.
  RWY 35: PAPI(P2L)—GA 3.5° TCH 51´. P–line.
SERVICE: **FUEL** 100LL   **LGT** Actvt MIRL Rwy 17–35—CTAF.
AIRPORT REMARKS: Unattended. Self serve fuel avbl H24.
AIRPORT MANAGER: 580-652-2885
COMMUNICATIONS: CTAF 122.9
CLEARANCE DELIVERY PHONE: For CD ctc Kansas City ARTCC at 913-254-8508.

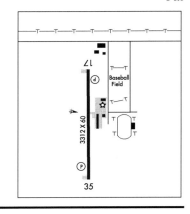

HUGO

STAN STAMPER MUNI (HHW)(KHHW) 2 NW UTC–6(–5DT) N34°02.02´ W95°32.52´   DALLAS–FT WORTH
572 B NOTAM FILE MLC   L–17D
RWY 17–35: H4007X75 (ASPH) S–12.5   MIRL   IAP
  RWY 17: REIL. PAPI(P2L)—GA 3.0° TCH 44´. Trees.
  RWY 35: REIL. PAPI(P2L)—GA 3.0° TCH 43´. Trees.
SERVICE: **FUEL** 100LL, JET A   **LGT** ACTIVATE MIRL Rwy 17–35, REIL Rwy 17–35—CTAF.
AIRPORT REMARKS: Attended Mon–Fri 1300–2200Z‡. For arpt attendant after hrs call 580–326–2302. Fuel avbl 24 hr self svc with major credit card.
AIRPORT MANAGER: 580-317-3513
WEATHER DATA SOURCES: AWOS–3 119.025 (580) 326–2134.
COMMUNICATIONS: CTAF/UNICOM 122.8
Ⓡ **FORT WORTH CENTER APP/DEP CON** 127.6
CLEARANCE DELIVERY PHONE: For CD ctc Fort Worth ARTCC at 817-858-7584.
RADIO AIDS TO NAVIGATION: NOTAM FILE MLC.
  MC ALESTER (L) TACAN Chan 57 MLC (112.0) N34°50.97´ W95°46.94´ 158° 50.3 NM to fld. 782/8E.

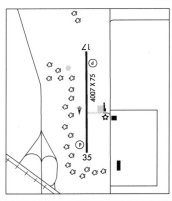

IDABEL

MC CURTAIN CO RGNL (4O4) 2 NW UTC–6(–5DT) N33°54.56´ W94°51.56´   MEMPHIS
472 B NOTAM FILE 4O4   H–6I, L–17D
RWY 02–20: H5002X75 (ASPH) S–30 MIRL   IAP
  RWY 02: REIL. PAPI(P4L)—GA 3.0° TCH 40´.
  RWY 20: ODALS. PAPI(P4L)—GA 3.0° TCH 41´. Trees. Rgt tfc.
SERVICE: S7 **FUEL** JET A+   **LGT** Actvt ODALS Rwy 20; REIL Rwy 02; PAPI Rwy 02 and 20; MIRL Rwy 02–20—CTAF.
AIRPORT REMARKS: Attended Mon–Fri 1300–2200Z‡.
AIRPORT MANAGER: 580-286-3558
WEATHER DATA SOURCES: AWOS–3 120.0 (580) 286–2217.
COMMUNICATIONS: CTAF/UNICOM 122.8
Ⓡ **FORT WORTH CENTER APP/DEP CON** 123.925
CLEARANCE DELIVERY PHONE: For CD ctc Fort Worth ARTCC at 817-858-7584.
RADIO AIDS TO NAVIGATION: NOTAM FILE TXK.
  TEXARKANA (VH) (H) VORTACW 116.3 TXK Chan 110 N33°30.83´ W94°04.39´ 294° 45.9 NM to fld. 273/7E.

OKLAHOMA 205

INOLA

BUZZARDS ROOST (O18)   4 E   UTC–6(–5DT)   N36°08.64′ W95°25.06′   KANSAS CITY
  661   NOTAM FILE MLC
  RWY 17–35: 2555X80 (TURF)
    RWY 17: Road. Rgt tfc.
    RWY 35: Fence. Rgt tfc.
  AIRPORT REMARKS: Unattended.
  AIRPORT MANAGER: 918-805-3284
  COMMUNICATIONS: CTAF 122.9
  CLEARANCE DELIVERY PHONE: For CD ctc Tulsa Apch at 918-831-6714/6720.

DOBIE'S (0K6)   4 NW   UTC–6(–5DT)   N36°10.76′ W95°34.82′   KANSAS CITY
  610   NOTAM FILE MLC
  RWY 17–35: 1575X150 (TURF)
    RWY 17: Trees.
    RWY 35: Fence. Rgt tfc.
  AIRPORT REMARKS: Attended irregularly.
  AIRPORT MANAGER: (918) 697-3263
  COMMUNICATIONS: CTAF 122.9
  CLEARANCE DELIVERY PHONE: For CD ctc Tulsa Apch at 918-831-6714/6720.

JONES MEML (See BRISTOW on page 182)

KETCHUM

SOUTH GRAND LAKE RGNL (1K8)   1 NE   UTC–5(–5DT)   N36°32.78′ W95°00.81′   KANSAS CITY
  783   NOTAM FILE MLC   L–15E
  RWY 18–36: H4730X75 (ASPH)   S–30, D–60   MIRL   IAP
    RWY 18: PAPI(P4L)—GA 4.0° TCH 42′. Thld dsplcd 442′. Road.
    RWY 36: PAPI(P4L)—GA 3.0° TCH 36′. Thld dsplcd 432′. Road.
  RUNWAY DECLARED DISTANCE INFORMATION
    RWY 18: TORA–4299   TODA–4299   ASDA–4670   LDA–4228
    RWY 36: TORA–4287   TODA–4287   ASDA–4670   LDA–4238
  SERVICE: S2   FUEL 100LL, JET A   LGT Actvt MIRL Rwy
    18–36—CTAF. PAPI Rwy 18 and 36 on consly.
  AIRPORT REMARKS: Attended Thu–Mon 1500–2300Z‡, Sun–Wed
    irregularly. Svc aft hr–918–629–3913.
  AIRPORT MANAGER: 937-623-0039
  WEATHER DATA SOURCES: AWOS–3PT 118.150 (918) 782–2047.
  COMMUNICATIONS: CTAF 122.9
  ®KANSAS CITY CENTER APP/DEP CON 128.6
  CLEARANCE DELIVERY PHONE: For CD ctc Kansas City ARTCC at
    913-254-8508.
  RADIO AIDS TO NAVIGATION: NOTAM FILE TUL.
    TULSA (H) (H) VORTACW 114.4   TUL   Chan 91   N36°11.78′
    W95°47.29′   053° 43.0 NM to fld. 788/8E.
    TACAN AZIMUTH unusable:
      248°–258° byd 23 NM blo 3,100′
    DME unusable:
      248°–258° byd 23 NM blo 3,100′

KINGFISHER (F92)   1 NW   UTC–6(–5DT)   N35°52.60′ W97°57.18′   DALLAS–FT WORTH
  1072   NOTAM FILE MLC
  RWY 18–36: H2800X60 (CONC)   PCN 4 R/D/Z/U   MIRL   0.7% up N
    RWY 18: Trees.
    RWY 36: Rgt tfc.
  SERVICE: FUEL 100LL   LGT Dusk–dawn; MIRL Rwy 18–36 preset low intst; to incr intst actvt—CTAF.
  AIRPORT REMARKS: Unattended. 100LL avbl with credit card. Heli auto rot practice on pavement NA.
  AIRPORT MANAGER: 405-375-4886
  COMMUNICATIONS: CTAF 122.9
  CLEARANCE DELIVERY PHONE: For CD ctc Oke City Apch at 405-681-5683.

KINGFISHER   N35°48.32′ W98°00.23′   NOTAM FILE MLC.
  (H) TACAN 114.7   IFI   Chan 94   271° 20.6 NM tc Watonga Rgnl. 1112/9E.   H–6H, L–15D

OKLAHOMA

KINGSTON

LAKE TEXOMA STATE PARK (F31) 4 E UTC–6(–5DT) N33°59.46′ W96°38.56′ **DALLAS–FT WORTH**
693 B NOTAM FILE MLC **L–17C**
RWY 18–36: H3000X50 (ASPH) S–4 MIRL
 RWY 18: Road.
 RWY 36: Trees.
SERVICE: **LGT** Actvt MIRL Rwy 18–36—CTAF. MIRL Rwy 18–36 preset low intst; incr intst—CTAF. Rotating bcn OTS indef.
AIRPORT REMARKS: Unattended. Deer and geese on and invof rwy. After hrs contact: 580–564–5515.
AIRPORT MANAGER: 580-564-2566
COMMUNICATIONS: CTAF/UNICOM 122.8
CLEARANCE DELIVERY PHONE: For CD ctc Fort Worth ARTCC at 817-858-7584.
RADIO AIDS TO NAVIGATION: NOTAM FILE ADM.
 ARDMORE (VH) (H) VORTACW 116.7 ADM Chan 114 N34°12.70′ W97°10.09′ 111° 29.3 NM to fld. 937/6E.
 VOR unusable:
  150°–160° byd 40 NM
  150°–160° byd 6 NM blo 14,000′
  297°–306° byd 40 NM blo 15,000′
  307°–314° blo 3,500′
  307°–314° byd 15 NM
  314°–333°
 TACAN AZIMUTH unusable:
  314°–333°
 DME unusable:
  314°–333°
  334°–011° byd 39 NM blo 3,100′

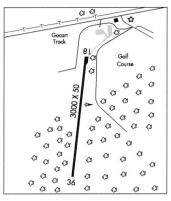

LAKE TEXOMA STATE PARK (See KINGSTON on page 206)

LAWTON–FORT SILL RGNL (LAW)(KLAW) 2 S UTC–6(–5DT) N34°34.06′ W98°25.00′ **DALLAS–FT WORTH**
1110 B ARFF Index—See Remarks NOTAM FILE LAW MON Airport **H–6H, L–17C**
RWY 17–35: H8599X150 (CONC–WC) S–45, D–179, 2S–175, 2D–344 HIRL **IAP, AD**
 RWY 17: REIL. PAPI(P4R)—GA 4.0° TCH 47′. Pole. 0.3% down.
 RWY 35: MALSR. 0.6% up.
RUNWAY DECLARED DISTANCE INFORMATION
 RWY 17: TORA–8599 TODA–8599 ASDA–8599 LDA–8599
 RWY 35: TORA–8599 TODA–8599 ASDA–8599 LDA–8599
SERVICE: S4 **FUEL** 100LL, JET A1+ **OX** 1, 2 **LGT** When ATCT clsd actvt MALSR Rwy 35—CTAF. HIRL Rwy 17–35 preset med intst; incr intst—CTAF.
AIRPORT REMARKS: Attended Mon–Fri 1130–0200Z‡ Sat–Sun 1130–0100Z‡. Birds on and invof arpt. When twr clsd ARFF avbl through Fort Sill apch control. ARFF Index PPR for unsked Part 121 acr ops with more than 30 pax seats—AMGR. Twy F clsd exc acft more than 110,000 lbs. 12 hr PPR 580–585–1321.
AIRPORT MANAGER: 580-353-4869
WEATHER DATA SOURCES: ASOS 120.75 (580) 581–1351.
COMMUNICATIONS: CTAF 119.9 **ATIS** 120.75 **UNICOM** 122.95
 ® **FORT SILL APP/DEP CON** 120.55
 TOWER 119.9 (1400–0100Z‡) **GND CON** 121.9
CLEARANCE DELIVERY PHONE: When ATCT clsd, for CD ctc Fort Worth ARTCC at 817-858-7584.
AIRSPACE: CLASS D svc 1400–0100Z‡; other times CLASS E.
RADIO AIDS TO NAVIGATION: NOTAM FILE LAW.
 (L) (L) VORW/DME 116.85 LAW Chan 115(Y) N34°29.77′ W98°24.79′ 349° 4.3 NM to fld. 1105/9E.
 VOR unusable:
  270°–305° blo 3,900′
  270°–305° byd 10 NM
 ILS 109.1 I–LAW Rwy 35. Class IB. Unmonitored when ATCT clsd. Glideslope unusable for coupled apchs blo 2,000′ MSL.
COMM/NAV/WEATHER REMARKS: When twr clsd weather avbl through Fort Sill apch control.

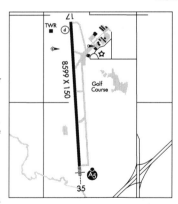

SC, 25 JAN 2024 to 21 MAR 2024

OKLAHOMA   207

LEXINGTON

MC CASLIN (O44)   4 N   UTC–6(–5DT)   N35°05.54′ W97°20.19′   DALLAS–FT WORTH
1135   NOTAM FILE MLC
RWY 17–35: 2135X80 (TURF)
  RWY 17: Fence.
  RWY 35: Bldg.
AIRPORT REMARKS: Unattended. +35′ powerline 145′ east of rwy, full length. 30 ft power line 478 ft fm Rwy 35 thr both sides.
AIRPORT MANAGER: (214) 642-6570
COMMUNICATIONS: CTAF 122.9
CLEARANCE DELIVERY PHONE: For CD ctc Oke City Apch at 405-681-5683.

LINDSAY MUNI (1K2)   2 NE   UTC–6(–5DT)   N34°50.97′ W97°35.12′   DALLAS–FT WORTH
968   B   NOTAM FILE MLC   L–17C
RWY 01–19: H3010X60 (ASPH)   S–4   MIRL
SERVICE: **LGT** ACTIVATE MIRL Rwy 01–19—CTAF.
AIRPORT REMARKS: Unattended. 660′ AGL antenna 3.2 miles north.
AIRPORT MANAGER: 405-756-2019
COMMUNICATIONS: CTAF 122.9
CLEARANCE DELIVERY PHONE: For CD ctc Fort Worth ARTCC at 817-858-7584.
RADIO AIDS TO NAVIGATION: NOTAM FILE OKC.
  WILL ROGERS (H) (H) VORTACW 114.1   IRW   Chan 88   N35°21.52′
  W97°36.55′   171° 30.5 NM to fld. 1230/7E.

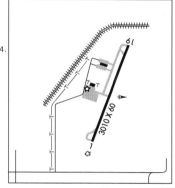

MADILL MUNI (1F4)   3 NW   UTC–6(–5DT)   N34°08.42′ W96°48.72′   DALLAS–FT WORTH
890   B   NOTAM FILE MLC   L–17C
                                                                                      IAP
RWY 18–36: H3005X60 (ASPH)   S–8   MIRL   0.6% up S
  RWY 18: REIL. Trees.
  RWY 36: REIL. Tree.
SERVICE: **LGT** MIRL Rwy 18–36 preset med ints dusk–0600Z‡, after 0600Z‡ ACTIVATE—CTAF. Rwy 18 left side REIL OTS indef.
AIRPORT REMARKS: Unattended. +1694′ twr 6.2 miles south of Rwy 36 end.
AIRPORT MANAGER: 580-795-4017
COMMUNICATIONS: CTAF 122.9
®**FORT WORTH CENTER APP/DEP CON** 124.75
CLEARANCE DELIVERY PHONE: For CD ctc Fort Worth ARTCC at 817-858-7584.
RADIO AIDS TO NAVIGATION: NOTAM FILE ADM.
  ARDMORE (VH) (H) VORTACW 116.7   ADM   Chan 114   N34°12.70′
  W97°10.09′   097° 18.2 NM to fld. 937/6E.
  VOR unusable:
    150°–160° byd 40 NM
    150°–160° byd 6 NM blo 14,000′
    297°–306° byd 40 NM blo 15,000′
    307°–314° blo 3,500′
    307°–314° byd 15 NM
    314°–333°
  TACAN AZIMUTH unusable:
    314°–333°
  DME unusable:
    314°–333°
    334°–011° byd 39 NM blo 3,100′

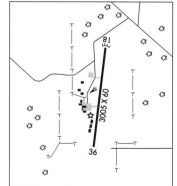

SC, 25 JAN 2024 to 21 MAR 2024

OKLAHOMA

MANGUM

SCOTT FLD (2K4) 2 NW UTC–6(–5DT) N34°53.56´ W99°31.69´ DALLAS–FT WORTH
1644 B NOTAM FILE MLC L–17B
RWY 17–35: H4199X75 (ASPH) S–12.5 MIRL 0.5% up S IAP
 RWY 35: Trees.
SERVICE: S4 FUEL 100LL
AIRPORT REMARKS: Unattended. Fuel 100LL: 24 hr automated credit card sys. Ultralights on and invof arpt. Drainage ditch adj Rwy 17 75 ft west. 30 ft pwr line 500 ft east end Rwy 35.
AIRPORT MANAGER: 580-782-2250
COMMUNICATIONS: CTAF 122.9
®ALTUS APP/DEP CON 125.1 (Mon–Fri 1500–0830Z‡, clsd weekends and holidays. Other times ctc)
®FORT WORTH CENTER APP/DEP CON 128.4
CLEARANCE DELIVERY PHONE: For CD ctc Fort Worth ARTCC at 817-858-7584.
RADIO AIDS TO NAVIGATION: NOTAM FILE HBR.
 HOBART (L) (L) VORTACW 111.8 HBR Chan 55 N34°51.99´
  W99°03.80´ 264° 23.0 NM to fld. 1472/10E.
 VOR unusable:
  080°–120° byd 30 NM blo 4,000´
 TACAN AZIMUTH unusable:
  080°–090° byd 25 NM blo 4,500´
  100°–112° byd 25 NM blo 4,500´
  240°–270° byd 25 NM blo 4,500´
 DME unusable:
  080°–090° byd 25 NM blo 4,500´
  100°–112° byd 25 NM blo 4,500´
  240°–270° byd 25 NM blo 4,500´

MC ALESTER RGNL (MLC)(KMLC) 3 SW UTC–6(–5DT) N34°52.94´ W95°47.01´ DALLAS–FT WORTH
771 B NOTAM FILE MLC H–6I, L–17D
RWY 02–20: H5602X100 (CONC) S–52, D–70, 2S–89, 2D–120 IAP
 MIRL 0.5% up NE
 RWY 02: MALS. PAPI(P4L)—GA 3.0° TCH 42´.
 RWY 20: REIL. PAPI(P4L)—GA 3.0° TCH 43´.
SERVICE: S4 FUEL 100LL, JET A LGT Actvt MALS Rwy 02; REIL Rwy 20; PAPI Rwy 02 and 20; MIRL Rwy 02–20—CTAF. MIRL Rwy 02–20 set low intst; incr intst—CTAF.
AIRPORT REMARKS: Attended 1130Z‡–dusk. Aft hr 918–329–8330. Wildlife on and invof arpt.
AIRPORT MANAGER: 918-470-4996
WEATHER DATA SOURCES: ASOS 120.425 (918) 426-7674.
COMMUNICATIONS: CTAF/UNICOM 122.95
 RCO 122.3 (MC ALESTER RADIO)
®FORT WORTH CENTER APP/DEP CON 132.2
CLEARANCE DELIVERY PHONE: For CD if una to ctc on FSS freq, ctc Fort Worth ARTCC at 817-858-7584.
AIRSPACE: CLASS E.
RADIO AIDS TO NAVIGATION: NOTAM FILE MLC.
 (L) TACAN Chan 57 MLC (112.0) N34°50.97´
  W95°46.94´ 350° 2.0 NM to fld. 782/8E.

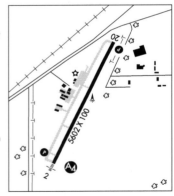

MC CASLIN (See LEXINGTON on page 207)

MC CURTAIN CO RGNL (See IDABEL on page 204)

OKLAHOMA

MEDFORD MUNI (O53) 1 SW UTC−6(−5DT) N36°47.44′ W97°44.94′ **WICHITA**
1092 B NOTAM FILE MLC L−15D
RWY 17−35: H3007X60 (ASPH) S−13 MIRL IAP
 RWY 17: PAPI(P2L)—GA 3.51° TCH 31′.
 RWY 35: PAPI(P2L)—GA 3.51° TCH 33′.
SERVICE: FUEL 100LL LGT Dusk−dawn ACTIVATE MIRL Rwy 17−35—CTAF.
AIRPORT REMARKS: Attended irregularly. For fuel call a-pt attendant 580−395−3176 or sheriff's office 580−395−2356. 100′ refinery 1 NM southwest of arpt.
AIRPORT MANAGER: 580-395-2875
COMMUNICATIONS: CTAF/UNICOM 122.8
®VANCE APP/DEP CON 118.075 (1300−0200Z‡ wkd, 1900−2300Z‡ Sun; clsd Sat & federal hol. Gnd ctl and clnc del svc avbl 15 min prior to afld opening. Other times by NOTAM.)
®KANSAS CITY CENTER APP/DEP CON 127.8 (0200−1300Z‡ wkd, 2300−1900Z‡ Sun; 24 Sat & federal hol. Gnd ctl and clnc del svc avbl 15 min prior to afld opening)
CLEARANCE DELIVERY PHONE: For CD ctc Vance Apch at 580-213-6765. When Vance Apch is clsd, ctc Kansas City ARTCC at 913-254-8508.
RADIO AIDS TO NAVIGATION: NOTAM FILE PNC.
 PIONEER (VH) (H) VORTACW 113.2 PER Chan 79 N36°44.79′ W97°09.61′ 269° 28.5 NM to fld. 1054/6E.
 TACAN AZIMUTH unusable:
  184°−194° blo 3,000′

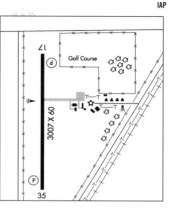

MENO

DECKER FLD (4O7) 1 S UTC−6(−5DT) N36°22.33′ W98°10.71′ **WICHITA**
1330 NOTAM FILE MLC
RWY 03−21: 2215X75 (TURF) 0.3% up NE
 RWY 21: Road.
SERVICE: S4
AIRPORT REMARKS: Attended 1300−0100Z‡. 35 rwy marked power line 480′ from Rwy 21 end.
AIRPORT MANAGER: 580-554-2814
COMMUNICATIONS: CTAF 122.9
CLEARANCE DELIVERY PHONE: For CD ctc Vance Apch at 580-213-6765. When Vance Apch is clsd, ctc Kansas City ARTCC at 913-254-8508.

MIAMI RGNL (MIO)(KMIO) 2 NW UTC−6(−5DT) N36°54.55′ W94°53.25′ **KANSAS CITY**
806 B NOTAM FILE MLC H−6I, L−16F
RWY 17−35: H5020X100 (ASPH) S−23 MIRL IAP
 RWY 17: ODALS. PAPI(P4L)—GA 3.0° TCH 42′. Trees. Rgt tfc.
 RWY 35: REIL. PAPI(P4L)—GA 3.0° TCH 42′.
SERVICE: S4 FUEL 100LL, JET A LGT ACTIVATE ODALS Rwy 17; REIL Rwy 35; MIRL Rwy 17−35—CTAF.
AIRPORT REMARKS: Attended Mon−Sat 1400−2300Z‡, Sun 1800−2300Z‡. Arpt unattended Thanksgiving and Christmas. Fuel avbl 24 hrs with credit card. Parachute Jumping.
AIRPORT MANAGER: (918) 541-2290
WEATHER DATA SOURCES: AWOS−3PT 119.675 (918) 544−6164.
COMMUNICATIONS: CTAF/UNICOM 122.8
®KANSAS CITY CENTER APP/DEP CON 128.6
CLEARANCE DELIVERY PHONE: For CD ctc Kansas City ARTCC at 913-254-8508.
RADIO AIDS TO NAVIGATION: NOTAM FILE ICT.
 OSWEGO (L) DME 117.6 OSW Chan 123 N37°09.45′ W95°12.22′ 134° 21.3 NM to fld. 928.

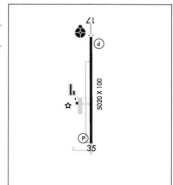

MID−AMERICA INDUSTRIAL (See PRYOR on page 220)

MIGNON LAIRD MUNI (See CHEYENNE on page 187)

OKLAHOMA

MITBEE N36°20.62′ W99°52.81′ NOTAM FILE GAG. — WICHITA
(VH) (H) VORTACW 115.6 MMB Chan 103 110° 5.8 NM to Gage. 2426/10E.

MOORELAND MUNI (MDF)(KMDF) 3 N UTC−6(−5DT) N36°29.09′ W99°11.65′ — WICHITA
1970 B NOTAM FILE MLC — L−15C
RWY 17−35: H3500X60 (ASPH) S−4 MIRL — IAP
  RWY 35: Trees.
SERVICE: **LGT** Dusk−dawn ACTIVATE MIRL Rwy 17−35—CTAF. Rotating bcn OTS indef.
AIRPORT REMARKS: Unattended. For arpt attendant call 580−334−5842. Twy A clsd indef, back taxi required for Rwy 17−35.
AIRPORT MANAGER: 580−994−5924
COMMUNICATIONS: CTAF/UNICOM 122.8
Ⓡ **KANSAS CITY CENTER APP/DEP CON** 126.95
CLEARANCE DELIVERY PHONE: For CD ctc Kansas City ARTCC at 913−254−8508.
RADIO AIDS TO NAVIGATION: NOTAM FILE GAG.
  MITBEE (VH) (H) VORTACW 115.6 MMB Chan 103 N36°20.62′ W99°52.81′ 066° 34.3 NM to fld. 2426/10E.

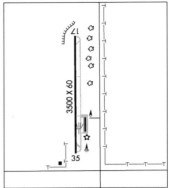

MULDROW AHP HELIPORT (HMY)(KHMY) A (ARNG) 4 E UTC−6(−5DT) N35°01.58′ — DALLAS−FT WORTH
W97°13.90′ — L−17C
1091 B NOTAM FILE MLC Not insp. — DIAP
HELIPAD H1: H75X75 (CONC) PERIMETER LGTS
HELIPAD H2: H75X75 (CONC) PERIMETER LGTS
HELIPAD 17−35: H2005X75 (CONC) LIRL
  HELIPAD 17: Road.
  HELIPAD 35: Road.
SERVICE: **FUEL** JET A++ **LGT** Actvt LIRL Rwy 17−35; perimeter lgts H1 and H2; twy lgts—C405−217−8100. Rotg bcn fone—C405−217−8100. **MILITARY— JASU** 1 AGPU F. **FUEL** J8 **FLUID** SP OIL.
MILITARY REMARKS: Opr Tue−Thurs 1130−0500Z‡; Mon and Fri. 1130−2230Z‡; slct wkends 1300−2200Z‡; Otr times—C405−595−8844. H1 dsgnd northpad. H2 dsgnd southpad. **RSTD** PPR for tsnt fuel, prk and night ops−D628−8101/C405−217−8101. **CAUTION** Hel prkg ramp has perimeter fence.
AIRPORT MANAGER: 405−217−8190
COMMUNICATIONS: OKLAHOMA CITY APP/DEP CON 124.2 336.4 **MULDROW OPS** (Advisory svc only)−139.425 227.2 46.9 (CTAF).
CLEARANCE DELIVERY PHONE: For CD ctc okc city Apch at 405−681−5683.

OKLAHOMA

MUSKOGEE–DAVIS RGNL (MKO)(KMKO) 6 S UTC−6(−5DT) N35°39.47′ W95°21.70′ DALLAS–FT WORTH
612 B NOTAM FILE MKO H−6I, L−15E
RWY 13–31: H7202X150 (ASPH) S−59, D−78, 2S−99, 2D−131 MIRL IAP
0.4% up NW
RWY 13: REIL. PAPI(P4L)—GA 3.0° TCH 50′.
RWY 31: MALS. PAPI(P4L)—GA 3.0° TCH 53′.
RWY 04–22: H4498X75 (ASPH) 0.3% up SW
RWY 18–36: H1904X60 (ASPH)
SERVICE: S2 **FUEL** 100LL, JET A **LGT** ACTVT MALS Rwy 31; REIL Rwy 13; MIRL Rwy 13–31—CTAF. PAPI Rwy 13 and 31 on consly.
AIRPORT REMARKS: Attended Mon–Sat 1400–2300Z‡. 100LL avbl 24 hrs self-svc. After hrs fuel call 918−869−8410. Arpt used for Oklahoma National Guard ATC training events− irregular schedule, contact twr on 118.95 when operational. Occasional coyotes on & invof rwy. Twy B clsd to acft over 25,000 lbs.
AIRPORT MANAGER: (918) 684-6343
WEATHER DATA SOURCES: ASOS 135.025 (918) 683−6987.
COMMUNICATIONS: CTAF/UNICOM 122.8
  RCO 122.5 (MC ALESTER RADIO)
® **FORT WORTH CENTER APP/DEP CON** 132.2
CLEARANCE DELIVERY PHONE: For CD if una to ctc on FSS freq, ctc Fort Worth ARTCC at 817-858-7584.
RADIO AIDS TO NAVIGATION: NOTAM FILE TUL.
  TULSA (H) (H) VORTACW 114.4 TUL Chan 91 N36°11.78′ W95°47.29′ 139° 38.4 NM to fld. 788/8E.
  TACAN AZIMUTH unusable:
    248°–258° byd 23 NM blo 3,100′
  DME unusable:
    248°–258° byd 23 NM blo 3,100′

Rwy 18-36: 1904 X 60

NINNEKAH
SKYROADS (O14) 9 SW UTC−6(−5DT) N34°53.42′ W97°59.89′ DALLAS–FT WORTH
1200 NOTAM FILE MLC
RWY 17–35: 2725X60 (TURF) 0.5% up S
RWY 17: Trees.
RWY 35: Tree.
AIRPORT REMARKS: Attended irregularly. 255′ twr 1.5 NM north–northwest and 350′ twr 2.4 NM east. Rwy 17–35 south 225′ clsd indef.
AIRPORT MANAGER: (910) 265-7596
COMMUNICATIONS: CTAF 122.9
CLEARANCE DELIVERY PHONE: For CD ctc Fort Worth ARTCC at 817-858-7584.

OKLAHOMA

NORMAN

UNIVERSITY OF OKLAHOMA WESTHEIMER (OUN)(KOUN) P (ARNG)   3 NW   UTC−6(−5DT)   DALLAS−FT WORTH
N35°14.73′ W97°28.33′   H−6H, L−15D
1182   B   TPA—See Remarks   NOTAM FILE OUN   IAP, AD
RWY 18−36: H5199X100 (ASPH−GRVD)   S−30, D−50, 2D−100   MIRL
 RWY 18: MALSR. PAPI(P4L)—GA 3.0° TCH 55′. Rgt tfc.
 RWY 36: REIL. PAPI(P4L)—GA 3.0° TCH 40′.
RWY 03−21: H4748X100 (ASPH)   S−30, D−50, 2D−100   MIRL
 RWY 03: MALS. PAPI(P4L)—GA 3.0° TCH 40′.
 RWY 21: PAPI(P4L)—GA 3.0° TCH 40′. Rgt tfc.
SERVICE: S4   FUEL 100LL, JET A   LGT When twr clsd, ACTIVATE MIRL
 Rwy 03−21 and Rwy 18−36; REIL Rwy 36; MALSR Rwy 18; MALS
 Rwy 03—CTAF. MILITARY— FUEL A+ (avbl 1300−0400Z‡,
 C405−329−8062, OT 2 hr PN C405−623−2099, $60 fee.)
 (NC−100LL, A)
AIRPORT REMARKS: Attended 1200−0400Z‡. Use extreme care coyotes on
 and invof rwys. High density student ops invof arpt and 5 miles south.
 180° turns prohibited on runways for all other than single engine light
 aircraft. TPA for hels 1682(500), Single engine 2182(1000);
 Multi−engine and jets 2682(1500). Lndg fee: Spl event fee for all acft
 the day before and day of a university home football game.
AIRPORT MANAGER: 405−325−7233
WEATHER DATA SOURCES: AWOS−3PT 119.55 (405) 325−7302.
COMMUNICATIONS: CTAF 118.0   UNICOM 122.95
 NORMAN RCO 122.4 (MC ALESTER RADIO)
®OKE CITY APP/DEP CON 120.45
 TOWER 118.0 (1400−0400Z‡)   GND CON 121.6
 CLEARANCE DELIVERY PHONE: For CD ifun to ctc twr, ctc Oke City Apch at 405−681−5683.
AIRSPACE: CLASS D svc 1400−0400Z‡; other times CLASS E.
RADIO AIDS TO NAVIGATION: NOTAM FILE OKC.
 WILL ROGERS (H) (H) VORTACW 114.1   IRW   Chan 88   N35°21.52′ W97°36.55′   128° 9.5 NM to fld. 1230/7E.
 LOC/DME 111.1   I−PHY   Chan 48   Rwy 03.   LOC/DME unmonitored when ATCT clsd.
 ILS/DME 111.95   I−BWM   Chan 56(Y)   Rwy 18.   Class IE.   DME unusable byd 30° left of course.

NOWATA MUNI (H66)   2 NE   UTC−6(−5DT)   N36°43.26′ W95°37.52′   KANSAS CITY
679   NOTAM FILE MLC
RWY 17−35: H2500X45 (ASPH)   S−4
 RWY 17: Trees.
 RWY 35: Trees.
RWY 05−23: 2440X45 (TURF)
 RWY 05: P−line.
 RWY 23: Trees.
AIRPORT REMARKS: Unattended. Rwy 05−23 clsd indefly, unusbl. Rwy unusbl. Rwy 05−23 unidentifiable; pline and road cross
 rwy. Rwy extremely rough & covered with tall grass & hay bales. Connector twy and apron pvmt failed. −2 ft ditch at Rwy
 23 thld; −12 ft ditch 220 ft fm Rwy 35 thld. NOTE: See Special Notices—Aerobatic Practice Area.
AIRPORT MANAGER: (918) 273−3538
COMMUNICATIONS: CTAF 122.9
CLEARANCE DELIVERY PHONE: For CD ctc Kansas City ARTCC at 913−254−8508.

OILLR   N36°05.85′ W95°53.33′   NOTAM FILE TUL.   KANSAS CITY
 NDB (LOMW) 338   TU   357° 6.0 NM to Tulsa Intl. 710/3E.

OKEENE

CHRISTMAN AIRFIELD (O65)   1 SE   UTC−6(−5DT)   N36°06.75′ W98°18.52′   WICHITA
1208   B   NOTAM FILE MLC   L−15D
RWY 17−35: H3000X60 (ASPH)   S−12   MIRL
 RWY 17: Tree.
SERVICE: LGT MIRL Rwy 17−35 preset low ints, to incr ints—CTAF.
AIRPORT REMARKS: Unattended.
AIRPORT MANAGER: 580−822−3035
COMMUNICATIONS: CTAF 122.9
CLEARANCE DELIVERY PHONE: For CD ctc Vance Apch at 580−213−6765. when Vance Apch is clsd, ctc Kansas City ARTCC at
 913−254−8508.
RADIO AIDS TO NAVIGATION: NOTAM FILE MLC.
 KINGFISHER (H) TACAN   Chan 94   IFI (114.7)   N35°48.32′ W98°00.23′   312° 23.6 NM to fld. 1112/9E.

SC, 25 JAN 2024 to 21 MAR 2024

OKLAHOMA 213

OKEMAH MUNI (F81)   2 S   UTC–6(–5DT)   N35°24.32′ W96°18.33′   DALLAS–FT WORTH
876   B   NOTAM FILE MLC   L–15E
RWY 18–36: H3400X60 (ASPH)   MIRL
 RWY 18: Trees.
SERVICE: **LGT** ACTIVATE MIRL Rwy 18–36—122.9.
AIRPORT REMARKS: Unattended.
AIRPORT MANAGER: 918-623-1050
COMMUNICATIONS: CTAF 122.9
CLEARANCE DELIVERY PHONE: For CD ctc Fort Worth ARTCC at 817-858-7584.

OKLAHOMA CITY

CLARENCE E PAGE MUNI (RCE)(KRCE)   15 W   UTC–6(–5DT)   N35°29.29′ W97°49.41′   DALLAS–FT WORTH
1354   B   NOTAM FILE MLC   H–6H, L–15D
RWY 17R–35L: H6014X100 (CONC)   S–40, D–60   HIRL   IAP, AD
 RWY 17R: PAPI(P4L)—GA 3.0° TCH 52′. Fence. Rgt tfc.
 RWY 35L: PAPI(P4L)—GA 3.0° TCH 41′. Trees.
RWY 17L–35R: H3502X75 (CONC)   S–17   MIRL
 RWY 35R: Rgt tfc.
SERVICE: S4   **FUEL** 100LL, JET A   **OX** 3   **LGT** Dusk–Dawn. ACTIVATE
  HIRL Rwy 17R–35L; MIRL Rwy 17L–35R—CTAF.
AIRPORT REMARKS: Attended Mon–Sat 1330–2330Z‡. Deer on and invof
  rwy. Aerobatic acft blo 6400′ 1NM radius of arpt. Surface conditions
  reported Mon–Fri 1400–2300Z‡.
AIRPORT MANAGER: 405-316-4061
WEATHER DATA SOURCES: AWOS–3 125.05 (405) 354–2517.
COMMUNICATIONS: CTAF/UNICOM 123.0
Ⓡ **OKE CITY APP/DEP CON** 124.6
CLEARANCE DELIVERY PHONE: For CD ctc Oke City Apch at 405-681-5683.
RADIO AIDS TO NAVIGATION: NOTAM FILE OKC.
 WILL ROGERS (H) (H) VORTACW 114.1   IRW   Chan 88   N35°21.52′
  W97°36.55′   299° 13.1 NM to fld. 1230/7E.

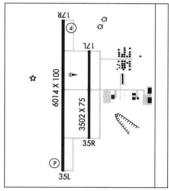
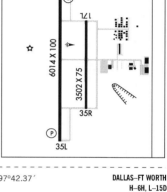

SUNDANCE (HSD)(KHSD)   12 NW   UTC–6(–5DT)   N35°36.11′ W97°42.37′   DALLAS–FT WORTH
1193   B   NOTAM FILE HSD   H–6H, L–15D
RWY 18–36: H5001X100 (CONC)   MIRL   0.8% up S   IAP
 RWY 18: VASI(V2L)—GA 3.0° TCH 30′. Rgt tfc.
 RWY 36: VASI(V2L)—GA 3.0° TCH 21′. Trees.
SERVICE: S4   **FUEL** 100LL, JET A   **OX** 1, 2, 3, 4   **LGT** Actvt VASI Rwy
  18 and 36; MIRL Rwy 18–36—CTAF. Rwy 18 VASI unusbl byd 7°
  right and left of cntrln. Rwy 36 VASI unusbl byd 7° left of cntrln.
AIRPORT REMARKS: Attended 1400–0000Z‡. 100LL se f svc avbl 24 hr with
  credit card. Bulk oxygen and bottle oxygen avbl durg ops hr Mon–Sat.
AIRPORT MANAGER: 405-568-1663
WEATHER DATA SOURCES: AWOS–3 120.975 (405) 283–9848.
COMMUNICATIONS: CTAF/UNICOM 122.7
Ⓡ **OKE CITY APP/DEP CON** 124.6
 CLNC DEL 123.7
CLEARANCE DELIVERY PHONE: For CD ctc Oke City Apch at 405-681-5683.
RADIO AIDS TO NAVIGATION: NOTAM FILE OKC.
 WILL ROGERS (H) (H) VORTACW 114.1   IRW   Chan 88   N35°21.52′
  W97°36.55′   335° 15.3 NM to fld. 1230/7E.

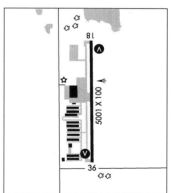

SC, 25 JAN 2024 to 21 MAR 2024

OKLAHOMA

WILEY POST (PWA)(KPWA) 7 NW UTC−6(−5DT) N35°32.05′ W97°38.82′   DALLAS–FT WORTH
1300 B TPA—See Remarks NOTAM FILE PWA   H−6H, L−15D
RWY 17L−35R: H7199X150 (CONC−GRVD) S−35, D−50, 2D−90 HIRL   IAP, AD
  RWY 17L: MALSR. PAPI(P4L)—GA 3.0° TCH 54′. Rgt tfc.
  RWY 35R: MALSR. PAPI(P4L)—GA 3.0° TCH 54′. Thld dsplcd 355′.
RWY 17R−35L: H5002X75 (ASPH−CONC) S−26, D−45 MIRL
  RWY 17R: REIL. PAPI(P4L)—GA 3.0° TCH 43′. Rgt tfc.
  RWY 35L: REIL. PAPI(P4L)—GA 3.0° TCH 42′.
RWY 13−31: H4214X100 (CONC) S−35, D−50, 2D−90 MIRL
  0.6% up SE
  RWY 13: Rgt tfc.
RUNWAY DECLARED DISTANCE INFORMATION
  RWY 13: TORA−4214   TODA−4214   ASDA−4214   LDA−4214
  RWY 17L: TORA−7199   TODA−7199   ASDA−6844   LDA−6844
  RWY 17R: TORA−5002   TODA−5002   ASDA−5002   LDA−5002
  RWY 31: TORA−4214   TODA−4214   ASDA−4214   LDA−4214
  RWY 35L: TORA−5001   TODA−5001   ASDA−5001   LDA−5001
  RWY 35R: TORA−7198   TODA−7198   ASDA−7198   LDA−6844
SERVICE: S4 **FUEL** 100LL, JET A+   **OX** 1, 2, 3, 4   **LGT** Dusk−Dawn.
  When ATCT clsd ACTVT MALSR Rwy 17L and 35R; HIRL Rwy
  17L−35R—CTAF. Rwy 13−31, 17R−35L unlgtd 0300−1200Z‡.
NOISE: Rwy 17L−35R noise abatement proc in efct: Dep acft 12,500 lbs
  or gtr climb at a max rate consistent with safety to 1500′ AGL then reduce pwr and climb rate to 3000′ AGL or 2 NM
  fm arpt depending on ATC and safety conds.
AIRPORT REMARKS: Attended continuously. Birds on and invof arpt. 100LL avbl H24 self svc with credit card. Sfc cond rprtd
  Mon−Fri 1300−2200Z‡. Rwy 13−31 CLOSED 0300−1200Z‡; acft over 12,500 lbs GWT NA. Exp ponding durg wet cond
  on Rwy 17L−35R at int of Rwy 13−31. TPA—Rwy 17R/35L 1900 (600), 2300 (1000) all other rwys.
AIRPORT MANAGER: 405-316-4061
WEATHER DATA SOURCES: ASOS (405) 798−2013
COMMUNICATIONS: CTAF 126.9 (0400−1300Z‡) **ATIS** 128.725 (405)−798−2059 **UNICOM** 122.95
  RCO 122.4 (MC ALESTER RADIO)
® **OKE CITY APP/DEP CON** 124.6 (171°−360°) 120.45 (081°−170°) 124.2 (001°−080°)
  TOWER 126.9 (1300−0400Z‡) **GND CON** 121.7
CLEARANCE DELIVERY PHONE: For CD ifun to ctc gnd con, ctc Oke City Apch at 405−681−5683.
AIRSPACE: CLASS D svc 1300−0400Z‡; other times CLASS E.
RADIO AIDS TO NAVIGATION: NOTAM FILE PWA.
  (T) (T) VORW/DME 113.4   PWA   Chan 81   N35°31.98′ W97°38.83′   at fld. 1271/8E.
  ILS 110.15   I−PWA   Rwy 17L.   Class I/B.   Unmonitored when ATCT clsd. DME also serves Rwy 35R.
  ILS/DME 110.15   I−TFM   Chan 38(Y)   Rwy 35R.   Class IT.   DME also serves Rwy 17L.

OKLAHOMA 215

WILL ROGERS WORLD (OKC)(KOKC) P (ANG)   6 SW   UTC−6(−5DT)   N35°23.58′ W97°36.05′   **DALLAS−FT WORTH**
1296   B   LRA   Class I, ARFF Index C   NOTAM FILE OKC   H−6H, L−15D
RWY 17L−35R: H9803X150 (CONC−GRVD)   S−120, D−250, 2S−175,   IAP, AD
  2D−550 PCN 98 R/B/W/T   HIRL   CL
  RWY 17L: MALSR. RVR−TMR
  RWY 35R: ALSF2. TDZL. RVR−TMR Rgt tfc.
RWY 17R−35L: H9801X150 (CONC−GRVD)   S−120, D−250, 2S−175,
  2D−550 PCN 98 R/B/W/T   HIRL   CL
  RWY 17R: MALSR. PAPI(P4L)—GA 3.0° TCH 60′. RVR−TR Rgt tfc.
  RWY 35L: MALSR. RVR−TR 0.3% up.
RWY 13−31: H7800X150 (ASPH−CONC−GRVD)   S−120, D−250,
  2S−175, 2D−489 PCN 91 F/C/W/T   MIRL
  RWY 13: REIL. PAPI(P4L)—GA 3.0° TCH 52′. Rgt tfc.
  RWY 31: REIL. PAPI(P4L)—GA 3.0° TCH 52′.
RWY 18−36: H3078X75 (ASPH)   S−116, D−164, 2S−175, 2D−269
  PCN 46 F/C/W/T
  RWY 18: Rgt tfc.
RUNWAY DECLARED DISTANCE INFORMATION
  RWY 13: TORA−7800   TODA−7800   ASDA−7800   LDA−7800
  RWY 17L: TORA−9802   TODA−9802   ASDA−9802   LDA−9802
  RWY 17R: TORA−9800   TODA−9800   ASDA−9800   LDA−9800
  RWY 18: TORA−3079   TODA−3079   ASDA−3079   LDA−3079
  RWY 31: TORA−7800   TODA−7800   ASDA−7800   LDA−7800
  RWY 35L: TORA−9800   TODA−9800   ASDA−9800   LDA−9800
  RWY 35R: TORA−9802   TODA−9802   ASDA−9802   LDA−9802
  RWY 36: TORA−3079   TODA−3079   ASDA−3079   LDA−3079
SERVICE: S4   **FUEL** 100LL, JET A   **OX** 1, 2, 3, 4   **LGT** Rwy 17R PAPI unusbl 4 degs right of rwy cntrln. **MILITARY**— **JASU**
  2(MA−1A) (CE12) (CE13) 4(CE16) **FUEL** A, A+ (405−218−3000 ext 1.) (NC−100LL) **FLUID** LPOX **OIL** O−128−156(Mil).
AIRPORT REMARKS: Attended continuously. Numerous birds on and invof arpt. PPR for parking on FAA Aeronautical Center ramp
  phone 405−954−9783 and email MXC@FAA.gov. Pilots of acft with wing spans greater than 118′ must use judgement
  over steering at all twy intersections. Rwy 18−36 600′ west of Rwy 17R−35L on existing twy. Rwy 18−36 VFR dalgt
  operations only except for Air National Guard. Rwy 18−36 used as taxiway when not used as rwy. Rwy 18−36, Twy G
  west of Rwy 17R−35L, Twy A2 east of Twy A, Twy D southwest of Rwy 13−31, Twy A1, Twy A3, Twy A4, Twy A6, Twy
  B, and C2, not avbl for air carrier ops with over 9 passenger seats. Twy G west of Twy B clsd to all except U.S. Marshals
  Service acft. Twy C2 clsd to all ops except Metro Tech tfc. Twys H2 and G east of Twy H clsd indef. Compass rose restricted
  to acft under 95,000 lbs except ANG C−130. Twy B north of compass rose restricted to acft under 120,000 lbs except
  ANG C−130. All ramps are uncontrolled. Flight Notification Service (ADCUS) available.
AIRPORT MANAGER: 405−316−3260
WEATHER DATA SOURCES: ASOS (405) 686−4711 TDWR.
COMMUNICATIONS: D−ATIS, ARR/DEP 125.85   (405) 686−4707
®**OKE CITY APP/DEP CON** 124.6 (171°−360°)   120.45 (081°−170°)   124.2 (001°−080°)
  ROGERS TOWER 119.35   120.25 **GND CON** 121.9 **CLNC DEL** 124.35 **PRE−TAXI CLNC** 124.35
  PDC
AIRSPACE: CLASS C svc ctc APP CON.
VOR TEST FACILITY (VOT) 112.15
RADIO AIDS TO NAVIGATION: NOTAM FILE OKC.
  (H) (H) VORTACW 114.1   IRW   Chan 88   N35°21.52′ W97°36.55′   004° 2.1 NM to fld. 1230/7E.
  ILS/DME 110.9   I−EXR   Chan 46   Rwy 17L.   Class IA.   Autopilot cpd apch na blw 1,480′ MSL.
  ILS/DME 110.7   I−OKC   Chan 44   Rwy 17R.   Class IE.   DME also SERVE Rwy 35L. LOC unusable 33° left and right
    of rcl.
  ILS/DME 110.7   I−LIK   Chan 44   Rwy 35L.   Class IE.   LOC unusable byd 30° right of course.
  ILS/DME 110.9   I−RGR   Chan 46   Rwy 35R.   Class IIE.
  ASR

OKLAHOMA

OKMULGEE RGNL/PAUL AND BETTY ABBOTT FLD (OKM)(KOKM)   3 N   UTC–6(–5DT)
DALLAS–FT WORTH
H–6I, L–15E
IAP

N35°40.09′ W95°56.91′
720   B   NOTAM FILE OKM
RWY 18–36: H5150X101 (CONC)   S–30, D–48, 2D–78   MIRL   0.7% up N
  RWY 18: MALSR. PAPI(P4L)—GA 3.0° TCH 51′.
  RWY 36: PAPI(P4L)—GA 3.0° TCH 40′.
SERVICE: S7   **FUEL** 100LL, JET A+   **LGT** ACTVT MALSR Rwy 18 and incr intst—CTAF; PAPI Rwy 18 and Rwy 36 on consly; MIRL Rwy 18–36 on low SS–SR, incr intst–CTAF.
AIRPORT REMARKS: Attended Mon–Fri 1400–2300Z‡. Parachute Jumping. Flocks of migratory birds and deer on and invof arpt. 24 hr fuel automated credit card system.
AIRPORT MANAGER: 918-756-0312
WEATHER DATA SOURCES: AWOS–3PT 118.225 (918) 756-9502.
COMMUNICATIONS: CTAF/UNICOM 123.0
®**TULSA APP/DEP CON** 119.85
CLEARANCE DELIVERY PHONE: For CD ctc Tulsa app/dep ctl at 918-831-6714.
RADIO AIDS TO NAVIGATION: NOTAM FILE OKM.
  (VH) (DH) VORW/DME 114.9   OKM   Chan 96   N35°41.58′
  W95°51.96′   242° 4.3 NM to fld. 774/8E.
  TULSA (H) (H) VORTACW 114.4   TUL   Chan 91   N36°11.78′
  W95°47.29′   186° 32.6 NM to fld. 788/8E. NOTAM FILE TUL.
  TACAN AZIMUTH unusable:
   248°–258° byd 23 NM blo 3,100′
  DME unusable:
   248°–258° byd 23 NM blo 3,100′
  ILS 109.1   I–OKM   Rwy 18.   Unmonitored.

OLUSTEE MUNI   (F09)   3 S   UTC–6(–5DT)   N34°30.75′ W99°25.77′
DALLAS–FT WORTH

1346   NOTAM FILE MLC
RWY 17–35: H2000X50 (ASPH)   S–12
AIRPORT REMARKS: Unattended. Rwy 17–35 has sev cracking and tall grass growing thru cracks.
AIRPORT MANAGER: 580-450-2288
COMMUNICATIONS: CTAF 122.9
CLEARANCE DELIVERY PHONE: For CD ctc Fort Worth ARTCC at 817-858-7584.

OWASSO

GUNDYS   (O38)   3 E   UTC–6(–5DT)   N36°16.01′ W95°47.02′
KANSAS CITY

720   B   NOTAM FILE MLC
RWY 17L–35R: H2600X40 (ASPH)   MIRL(NSTD)
  RWY 17L: Tree.
RWY 17R–35L: 1760X100 (TURF)
  RWY 17R: Bldg.
  RWY 35L: Trees.
SERVICE: **FUEL** 100LL   **LGT** Rwy 17L–35R NSTD MIRL, lgts located 35′ from rwy edge, thld lights missing.
AIRPORT REMARKS: Attended irregularly. Fuel: 24 hr automated system.
AIRPORT MANAGER: 918-272-1523
COMMUNICATIONS: CTAF 122.9
CLEARANCE DELIVERY PHONE: For CD ctc Tulsa Apch at 918-831-6714/6720.

OKLAHOMA

217

PAULS VALLEY MUNI (PVJ)(KPVJ) 2 S UTC–6(–5DT) N34°42.57´ W97°13.40´   DALLAS–FT WORTH
971 B NOTAM FILE PVJ   H–6H, L–17C
RWY 17–35: H5001X100 (CONC) S–42, D–55, 2D–110 MIRL   IAP
  0.4% up N
  RWY 17: REIL. PAPI(P4L)—GA 3.0° TCH 45´. Trees.
  RWY 35: REIL. PAPI(P4L)—GA 3.0° TCH 45´.
SERVICE: S4 **FUEL** 100LL, JET A **OX** 1 **LGT** ACTIVATE REIL Rwy 17
  and Rwy 35; PAPI Rwy 17 and Rwy 35; MIRL Rwy 17–35—CTAF.
AIRPORT REMARKS: Attended Mon–Fri 1400–2300Z‡. 100L avbl H24 hr
  with credit card. Fuel A on request. Ultralights on and invof arpt.
AIRPORT MANAGER: 405-238-7338
WEATHER DATA SOURCES: AWOS–3 118.675 (405) 238–4452.
COMMUNICATIONS: CTAF/UNICOM 122.8
®**FORT WORTH CENTER APP/DEP CON** 124.75
CLEARANCE DELIVERY PHONE: For CD ctc Fort Worth ARTCC at
  817-858-7584.
RADIO AIDS TO NAVIGATION: NOTAM FILE ADM.
  ARDMORE (VH) (H) VORTACW 116.7 ADM Chan 114 N34°12.70´
    W97°10.09´ 349° 30.0 NM to fld. 937/6E.
  VOR unusable:
    150°–160° byd 40 NM
    150°–160° byd 6 NM blo 14,000´
    297°–306° byd 40 NM blo 15,000´
    307°–314° blo 3,500´
    307°–314° byd 15 NM
    314°–333°
  TACAN AZIMUTH unusable:
    314°–333°
  DME unusable:
    314°–333°
    334°–011° byd 39 NM blo 3,100´

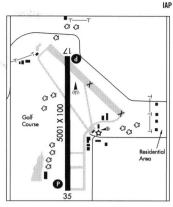

PAWHUSKA MUNI (H76) 4 W UTC–6(–5DT) N36°40.30´ W96°24.33´   KANSAS CITY
1000 B NOTAM FILE MLC   L–15E
RWY 17–35: H3200X60 (ASPH) S–12.5 MIRL
SERVICE: **LGT** MIRL Rwy 17–35 preset low ints SS–SR, to increase ints
  ACTIVATE—CTAF.
AIRPORT REMARKS: Unattended.
AIRPORT MANAGER: 918-287-3040
COMMUNICATIONS: CTAF 122.9
CLEARANCE DELIVERY PHONE: For CD ctc Kansas City ARTCC at
  913-254-8508.
RADIO AIDS TO NAVIGATION: NOTAM FILE BVO.
  BARTLESVILLE (L) (L) VORW/DME 117.9 BVO Chan 126 N36°50.06´
    W96°01.11´ 235° 21.1 NM to fld. 930/8E.

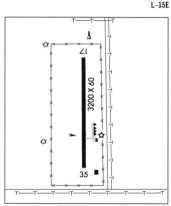

PAWNEE MUNI (H97) 2 N UTC–6(–5DT) N36°22.64´ W96°48.31´   KANSAS CITY
875 NOTAM FILE MLC
RWY 18–36: 2133X100 (TURF) 0.4% up N
  RWY 18: Trees.
  RWY 36: Trees.
AIRPORT REMARKS: Unattended. For arpt attendant call police dept 918–762–3166. Rwy 18–36 south 300´ muddy and soft
  when wet.
AIRPORT MANAGER: 918-762-2658
COMMUNICATIONS: CTAF 122.9
CLEARANCE DELIVERY PHONE: For CD ctc Kansas City ARTCC at 913-254-8508.

OKLAHOMA

PERRY MUNI (F22) 5 N UTC–6(–5DT) N36°23.14′ W97°16.63′   WICHITA
1003 B NOTAM FILE MLC   H–6H, L–15D
RWY 17–35: H5103X75 (ASPH) S–75, D–130 MIRL 0.5% up S   IAP
  RWY 17: REIL. PAPI(P2L)—GA 3.0° TCH 46′.
  RWY 35: REIL. PAPI(P2L)—GA 3.0° TCH 46′. Road.
SERVICE: S2 FUEL 100LL, JET A LGT ACTIVATE MIRL Rwy 17–35 and
  REIL Rwy 17 and Rwy 35—CTAF.
AIRPORT REMARKS: Attended 1400–2300Z‡. Unattended Christmas day.
  Heavy mil jet tfc dalgt. Ultralight activity on and invof arpt.
AIRPORT MANAGER: 580-336-4001
COMMUNICATIONS: CTAF/UNICOM 122.8
Ⓡ KANSAS CITY CENTER APP/DEP CON 127.8
CLEARANCE DELIVERY PHONE: For CD ctc Kansas City ARTCC at
  913-254-8508.
RADIO AIDS TO NAVIGATION: NOTAM FILE PNC.
  PIONEER (VH) (H) VORTACW 113.2   PER   Chan 79   N36°44.79′
    W97°09.61′   189° 22.4 NM to fld. 1054/6E.
  TACAN AZIMUTH unusable:
    184°–194° blo 3,000′

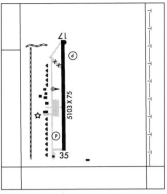

PIONEER N36°44.79′ W97°09.61′   NOTAM FILE PNC.   WICHITA
(VH) (H) VORTACW 113.2   PER   Chan 79   101° 3.0 NM to Ponca City Rgnl. 1054/6E.   H–6H, L–15D
  TACAN AZIMUTH unusable:
    184°–194° blo 3,000′

PONCA CITY RGNL (PNC)(KPNC) 2 NW UTC–6(–5DT) N36°43.92′ W97°05.99′   WICHITA
1009 B NOTAM FILE PNC MON Airport   H–6H, L–15D
RWY 17–35: H7201X100 (CONC-GRVD) S–51, D–65, 2S–83,   IAP
  2D–122 HIRL
  RWY 17: MALSR. PAPI(P4L)—GA 3.0° TCH 52′. Rgt tfc.
  RWY 35: ODALS. PAPI(P4L)—GA 3.0° TCH 46′. Bldg.
SERVICE: S4 FUEL 100LL, JET A OX 4 LGT Actvt MALSR Rwy 17;
  ODALS Rwy 35; HIRL Rwy 17–35—CTAF. PAPI Rwy 17 and 35 on
  consly. Rwy 35 PAPI unusbl byd 8 degs right of cntrln. FUEL 100LL
  avbl 24 hr.; Jet A and svc avbl 1300Z‡–dusk; otr times
  580–767–0429.
AIRPORT REMARKS: Attended 1300–0100Z‡. Ultralights on and invof arpt.
  Rwy 17–35 north 2400′ nstd plastic grooving entire width; 25′ each
  edge at remaining of 4801′.
AIRPORT MANAGER: 580-767-0470
WEATHER DATA SOURCES: ASOS 134.075 (580) 765-0049.
COMMUNICATIONS: CTAF/UNICOM 123.0
  RCO 122.2 (MC ALESTER RADIO)
Ⓡ KANSAS CITY CENTER APP/DEP CON 127.8
CLEARANCE DELIVERY PHONE: For CD if una to ctc on FSS freq, ctc Kansas City
  ARTCC at 913-254-8508.
AIRSPACE: CLASS E.
RADIO AIDS TO NAVIGATION: NOTAM FILE PNC.
  PIONEER (VH) (H) VORTACW 113.2   PER   Chan 79   N36°44.79′ W97°09.61′   101° 3.0 NM to fld. 1054/6E.
  TACAN AZIMUTH unusable:
    184°–194° blo 3,000′
  NDB (MHW/LOM) 515   PN   N36°49.50′ W97°06.03′   175° 5.6 NM to fld. 1038/5E.
  ILS/DME 111.9 I–PNC Chan 56 Rwy 17. LOM PONCA NDB. Unmonitored.

OKLAHOMA

POND CREEK MUNI (2K1)   0 SW   UTC−6(−5DT)   N36°39.75′ W97°48.52′   WICHITA
  1061   NOTAM FILE MLC
  RWY 17−35: 2320X430 (TURF)
    RWY 17: Pole.
  RWY 15−33: H1220X30 (ASPH)
    RWY 15: Trees.
  AIRPORT REMARKS: Unattended. Rwy 17−35 full width of rwy not maintained, use middle of rwy surface. Rwy 15−33 pvt maintained. Thld lgts NSTD all green lenses.
  AIRPORT MANAGER: 580-532-4915
  COMMUNICATIONS: CTAF 122.9
  CLEARANCE DELIVERY PHONE: For CD ctc Vance Apch at 580-213-6765. When Vance Apch is clsd, ctc Kansas City ARTCC at 913-254-8508.

PORT OF CATOOSA HELIPORT (See CATOOSA on page 185)

POTEAU

ROBERT S KERR   (RKR)(KRKR)   2 S   UTC−6(−5DT)   N35°01.30′ W94°37.28′   MEMPHIS
  451   B   NOTAM FILE RKR   L−17D
  RWY 18−36: H4007X75 (ASPH)   S−27   MIRL   IAP
    RWY 18: ODALS. PAPI(P4L)—GA 3.0° TCH 42′. Trees.
    RWY 36: REIL. PAPI(P4L)—GA 3.0° TCH 42′.
  SERVICE: S4   **FUEL** 100LL, JET A+   **LGT** Actvt ODALS Rwy 18; REIL Rwy 36—CTAF. MIRL Rwy 18−36−SS−SR, incr intst—CTAF.
  AIRPORT REMARKS: Attended 1400−2300Z‡. Ultralight activity on and invof arpt. 100LL avbl H24 with credit card. Rwy 18 and 36 markings faded.
  AIRPORT MANAGER: 918-647-4226
  WEATHER DATA SOURCES: AWOS−3 120.625 (918) 647−4063.
  COMMUNICATIONS: CTAF/UNICOM 122.8
  Ⓡ **RAZORBACK APP/DEP CON** 120.9 (1130−0500Z‡)
  Ⓡ **MEMPHIS CENTER APP/DEP CON** 126.1 (0500−1130Z‡)
  CLEARANCE DELIVERY PHONE: For CD ctc Razorback Apch 479-649-2416, when Apch clsd ctc Memphis ARTCC at 901-368-8453/8449.
  RADIO AIDS TO NAVIGATION: NOTAM FILE MLC.
    RICH MOUNTAIN (VL) (L) VORTACW 113.5   PGO   Chan 82
      N34°40.83′ W94°36.54′   354° 20.4 NM to fld. 2700/4E.
      VOR unusable:
        016°−021° byd 40 NM
        028°−029° byd 40 NM
        030°−040°
        050°−075° blo 4,000′
        090°−145°
        167°−169° byd 40 NM
        170°−200°
        235°−245° byd 30 NM blo 5,000′
        260°−280° byd 35 NM blo 5,000′
        329°−335° byd 40 NM
        340°−345° blo 5,000′
        358°−002° byd 40 NM

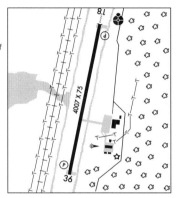

OKLAHOMA

PRAGUE MUNI (O47)   2 W   UTC−6(−5DT)   N35°28.85′ W96°43.13′   DALLAS−FT WORTH
1041   B   NOTAM FILE MLC   L−15E
RWY 17−35: H3600X60 (ASPH)   S−4   MIRL   0.9% up N   IAP
  RWY 17: PAPI(P2L)—GA 3.0° TCH 40′. Thld dsplcd 110′. Tree.
  RWY 35: PAPI(P2L)—GA 3.0° TCH 40′.
SERVICE: S4   **FUEL** 100LL   **LGT** MIRL Rwy 17−35 on SS−SR, preset low
  intst. Incr intst—CTAF.
AIRPORT REMARKS: Unatndd. Fuel avbl 24 hrs credit card adps.
AIRPORT MANAGER: 405-567-2270
COMMUNICATIONS: CTAF 122.9
®**FORT WORTH CENTER APP/DEP CON** 132.2
CLEARANCE DELIVERY PHONE: For CD ctc Fort Worth ARTCC at
  817-858-7584.
RADIO AIDS TO NAVIGATION: NOTAM FILE OKC.
  WILL ROGERS (H) (H) VORTACW 114.1   IRW   Chan 88   N35°21.52′
    W97°36.55′   073° 44.3 NM to fld. 1230/7E.
COMM/NAV/WEATHER REMARKS: CTAF OTS indefly.

PRYOR

MID−AMERICA INDUSTRIAL (H71)   6 S   UTC−6(−5DT)   N36°13.52′ W95°19.80′   KANSAS CITY
622   B   NOTAM FILE MLC   H−6I, L−15E
RWY 18−36: H5001X72 (ASPH)   S−30   MIRL   0.4% up N   IAP
  RWY 18: REIL. PAPI(P4L)—GA 3.0° TCH 40′. Rgt tfc.
  RWY 36: REIL. PAPI(P4L)—GA 3.0° TCH 40′.
SERVICE: **FUEL** 100LL, JET A   **LGT** ACTIVATE REIL Rwy 18 and Rwy
  36; MIRL Rwy 18−36—CTAF. Rwy 18 VGSI unusbl byd 9 deg right of
  cntrln.
AIRPORT REMARKS: Attended Mon−Fri 1400−2300Z‡. Wkend gldr ops on
  and invof arpt. 100LL avbl H24 hrs credit card. Aft hr svc call
  918−855−6464 or 918−636−0238.
AIRPORT MANAGER: 918-825-3500
WEATHER DATA SOURCES: AWOS−3PT 120.1 (918) 476−0517.
COMMUNICATIONS: CTAF/UNICOM 122.8
®**TULSA APP/DEP CON** 119.1
CLEARANCE DELIVERY PHONE: For CD ctc Tulsa Apch at 918-831-6714.
RADIO AIDS TO NAVIGATION: NOTAM FILE TUL.
  TULSA (H) (H) VORTACW 114.4   TUL   Chan 91   N36°11.78′
    W95°47.29′   077° 22.3 NM to fld. 788/8E.
  TACAN AZIMUTH unusable:
    248°−258° byd 23 NM blo 3,100′
  DME unusable:
    248°−258° byd 23 NM blo 3,100′

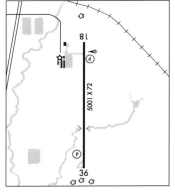

SC, 25 JAN 2024 to 21 MAR 2024

OKLAHOMA

PURCELL MUNI – STEVEN E SHEPHARD FLD (303)   2 SW   UTC–6(–5DT)   N34°59.00´   DALLAS–FT WORTH
W97°22.96´   L–17C
  1143   B   NOTAM FILE MLC
RWY 17–35: H3003X60 (ASPH)   S–9.5   MIRL
SERVICE: FUEL 100LL   **LGT** MIRL Rwy 17–35 preset low ints, to incr ints
    ACTIVATE—CTAF.
AIRPORT REMARKS: Attended 1600–2200Z‡ Mon–Fri. Fuel avbl 24 hrs with
    credit card.
AIRPORT MANAGER: 405-527-6563
COMMUNICATIONS: CTAF 122.9
CLEARANCE DELIVERY PHONE: For CD ctc Oke City Apch at 405-681-5683.
RADIO AIDS TO NAVIGATION: NOTAM FILE OKC.
  WILL ROGERS (H) (H) VORTACW 114.1   IRW   Chan 88   N35°21.52´
      W97°36.55´   147° 25.1 NM to fld. 1230/7E.

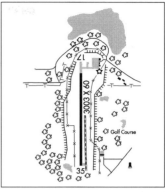

RICH MOUNTAIN   N34°40.83´ W94°36.54´   NOTAM FILE MLC.   MEMPHIS
  (VL) (L) VORTACW 113.5   PGO   Chan 82   354° 20.4 NM to Robert S Kerr. 2700/4E.   H–6I, L–17D
    VOR unusable:
      016°–021° byd 40 NM
      028°–029° byd 40 NM
      030°–040°
      050°–075° blo 4,000´
      090°–145°
      167°–169° byd 40 NM
      170°–200°
      235°–245° byd 30 NM blo 5,000´
      260°–280° byd 35 NM blo 5,000´
      329°–335° byd 40 NM
      340°–345° blo 5,000´
      358°–002° byd 40 NM
  RCO 122.6 (MC ALESTER RADIO)

ROBERT S KERR   (See POTEAU on page 219)

SALLISAW MUNI   (JSV)(KJSV)   1 SW   UTC–6(–5DT)   N35°26.30´ W94°48.18´   MEMPHIS
  527   B   NOTAM FILE JSV   L–16F
RWY 17–35: H4006X75 (ASPH)   MIRL   0.3% up N   IAP
  RWY 17: PAPI(P2R)—GA 3.0° TCH 40´.
  RWY 35: PAPI(P2L)—GA 3.0° TCH 40´.
SERVICE: S4   **FUEL** 100LL, JET A
AIRPORT REMARKS: Attended 1400–2300Z‡. Arpt unattended federal
    holidays. 100LL fuel avbl 24 hrs with a major credit card. For Jet A or
    addnl svcs call 918-773-2076. +200´ tower/antenna 2.2 miles north
    on extended centerline.
AIRPORT MANAGER: 918-775-6241
WEATHER DATA SOURCES: AWOS–3 118.475 (918) 775-4136.
COMMUNICATIONS: CTAF/UNICOM 122.7
  ®**RAZORBACK APP/DEP CON** 120.9 (1130–0500Z‡)
  ®**MEMPHIS CENTER APP/DEP CON** 126.1 (0500–1130Z‡)
CLEARANCE DELIVERY PHONE: For CD ctc Razorback Apch 479-649-2416,
    when Apch clsd ctc Memphis ARTCC at 901-368-8453/8449.
RADIO AIDS TO NAVIGATION: NOTAM FILE FSM.
  FORT SMITH (L) (L) VORTACW 110.4   FSM   Chan 41   N35°23.30´
      W94°16.29´   270° 26.2 NM to fld. 432/7E.

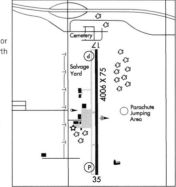

SAM RIGGS AIRPARK   (See CLAREMORE on page 188)

OKLAHOMA

SAND SPRINGS

WILLIAM R POGUE MUNI (OWP)(KOWP) 3 NW UTC–6(–5DT) N36°10.52´ W96°09.11´   KANSAS CITY
892 B NOTAM FILE MLC   H–6H, L–15E
RWY 17–35: H5799X100 (ASPH) S–30, D–58 MIRL   IAP
 RWY 17: PAPI(P4L)—GA 3.0° TCH 31´. Trees.
 RWY 35: ODALS. PAPI(P4L)—GA 3.0° TCH 33´.
SERVICE: FUEL 100LL LGT ODALS RWY 35; PAPI RWY 17 and RWY 35; MIRL RWY 17–35—OPR CONSLY. PAPI UNUSBL BYD 8 degs left, right of RCL.
AIRPORT REMARKS: Attended Mon–Sat 1400–2300Z‡, Sun 1600–2300Z‡. Arpt unattended Thanksgiving, Christmas and New Years Day. For assistance and for arpt attendant after hrs call 918–638–6895. Fuel avbl 24 hrs with major credit card. Deer invof arpt. Rwy 17 rgt tfc for helicopters. Helicopter training west twy and west ramp.
AIRPORT MANAGER: 918–246–2605
WEATHER DATA SOURCES: AWOS–3T 118.325 (918) 246–2635.
COMMUNICATIONS: CTAF/UNICOM 122.7
®TULSA APP/DEP CON 124.0
CLEARANCE DELIVERY PHONE: For CD ctc Tulsa Apch at 918-831-6714/6720.
RADIO AIDS TO NAVIGATION: NOTAM FILE MLC.
 GLENPOOL (T) DME 110.6 GNP Chan 43 N35°55.25´ W95°58.12´ 330° 17.7 NM to fld. 810.

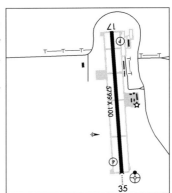

SAYRE MUNI (304) 7 S UTC–6(–5DT) N35°10.06´ W99°39.47´   DALLAS–FT WORTH
1937 B NOTAM FILE MLC   L–15C
RWY 17–35: H4276X130 (CONC) S–30 MIRL 0.5% up S
 RWY 17: PAPI(P2L)—GA 3.0° TCH 41´.
 RWY 35: PAPI(P2L)—GA 3.0° TCH 45´.
SERVICE: FUEL 100LL LGT ACTVT MIRL Rwy 17–35—CTAF.
AIRPORT REMARKS: Unattended. Self svc fuel avbl 24 hrs with credit card.
AIRPORT MANAGER: 580-928-8260
COMMUNICATIONS: CTAF 122.9
CLEARANCE DELIVERY PHONE: For CD ctc Fort Worth ARTCC at 817-858-7584.

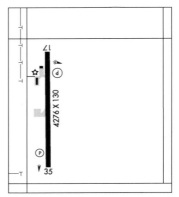

SCOTT FLD (See MANGUM on page 208)

SEILING (1S4) 0 NW UTC–6(–5DT) N36°09.32´ W98°56.02´   WICHITA
1746 NOTAM FILE MLC
RWY 17–35: H2435X38 (ASPH) LIRL(NSTD) 0.4% up N
 RWY 35: Tree.
SERVICE: LGT Rwy 17–35 nstd LIRL due to spacing and hgt.
AIRPORT REMARKS: Unattended. 496´ AGL unlgtd twr 18 NM S. S wgt thsd less than 4000 lbs. Rwy 17–35 edge mkd only.
AIRPORT MANAGER: 580-922-4460
COMMUNICATIONS: CTAF 122.9
CLEARANCE DELIVERY PHONE: For CD ctc Kansas City ARTCC at 913-254-8508.

OKLAHOMA

SEMINOLE MUNI (SRE)(KSRE) 3 N UTC–6(–5DT) N35°16.47´ W96°40.52´ DALLAS–FT WORTH
1023 B NOTAM FILE SRE   H–6H, L–15E
RWY 16–34: H5004X75 (ASPH) S–16 MIRL 0.5% up N   IAP
  RWY 16: REIL. PAPI(P4L)—GA 3.0° TCH 27´. Trees.
  RWY 34: REIL. PAPI(P4L)—GA 3.0° TCH 49´. Trees.
RWY 05–23: 2000X150 (TURF) 0.9% up NE
SERVICE: S4 FUEL 100LL, JET A LGT MIRL Rwy 16–34 preset low
  intst, incr intst—CTAF. FUEL 100LL self svc avbl H24. A svc and aft
  hrs—405–808–4045.
AIRPORT REMARKS: Attended Mon–Fri 1400–2300Z‡, Sat 1400–1800Z‡.
AIRPORT MANAGER: 405–382–2180
WEATHER DATA SOURCES: AWOS–3 118.625 (405) 382–0111.
COMMUNICATIONS: CTAF/UNICOM 122.8
®FORT WORTH CENTER APP/DEP CON 132.2
CLEARANCE DELIVERY PHONE: For CD ctc Fort Worth ARTCC at
  817-858-7584.
RADIO AIDS TO NAVIGATION: NOTAM FILE MLC.
  MC ALESTER (L) TACAN Chan 57 MLC (112.0) N34°50.97´
  W95°46.94´ 292° 50.8 NM to fld. 782/8E.

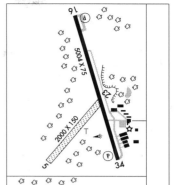

SHAWNEE RGNL (SNL)(KSNL) 2 NW UTC–6(–5DT) N35°21.44´ W96°56.57´ DALLAS–FT WORTH
1073 B NOTAM FILE SNL   H–6H, L–15D
RWY 17–35: H5997X100 (ASPH) S–30, D–40, 2D–60 MIRL   IAP
  RWY 17: MALSR. REIL. PAPI(P4L)—GA 3.0° TCH 52´. P–line. Rgt tfc.
  RWY 35: REIL. PAPI(P4L)—GA 3.0° TCH 42´. Thld dsplcd 404´. Trees.
SERVICE: S2 FUEL 100LL, JET A OX 3 LGT MIRL Rwy 17–35 preset
  low intst; to incr intst and ACTVT MALSR Rwy 17—CTAF.
AIRPORT REMARKS: Attended 1400–2300Z‡. Fuel avbl 24 hrs with credit
  card.
AIRPORT MANAGER: 405–878–1625
WEATHER DATA SOURCES: AWOS–3 118.275 (405) 878–1745.
COMMUNICATIONS: CTAF/UNICOM 122.7
®OKE CITY APP/DEP CON 120.45
CLEARANCE DELIVERY PHONE: For CD ctc oke Apch at 405–681–5683.
RADIO AIDS TO NAVIGATION: NOTAM FILE OKC.
  WILL ROGERS (H) (H) VORTACW 114.1 IRW Chan 88 N35°21.52´
  W97°36.55´ 083° 32.7 NM to fld. 1230/7E.
  ILS/DME 108.75 I–HNQ Chan 24(Y) Rwy 17. Class IE.

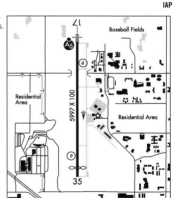

SKIATOOK MUNI (2F6) 1 SW UTC–6(–5DT) N36°21.31´ W96°00.64´ KANSAS CITY
671 B NOTAM FILE MLC   L–15E
RWY 18–36: H3002X60 (CONC) S–4 MIRL 0.4% up N
  RWY 18: PAPI(P2L)—GA 3.0° TCH 40´.
  RWY 36: Thld dsplcd 90´. Tree.
RWY N–S: 2600X40 (TURF)
  RWY N: Tree.
  RWY S: Tree.
SERVICE: FUEL 100LL LGT Actvt MIRL Rwy 18–36—CTAF. PAPI Rwy 18 on consly. PAPI unusbl.
AIRPORT REMARKS: Unattended. Parachute Jumping. Turf Rwy N–S CLOSED indef. 100LL avbl 24 hr with automated credit
  card adp sys.
AIRPORT MANAGER: 918–396–2797
COMMUNICATIONS: CTAF/UNICOM 122.8
CLEARANCE DELIVERY PHONE: For CD ctc Tulsa Apch at 918-831-6714/6720.

SKYROADS (See NINNEKAH on page 211)

OKLAHOMA

SNYDER (4O1) 4 SW UTC–6(–5DT) N34°37.66´ W99°00.84´ **DALLAS–FT WORTH**
1325 NOTAM FILE MLC
RWY 17–35: H2125X30 (ASPH)
  RWY 35: Trees.
SERVICE: FUEL 100LL, JET A
AIRPORT REMARKS: Attended irregularly. Fuel avbl on request call 580–569–2222.
AIRPORT MANAGER: 580-569-2222
COMMUNICATIONS: CTAF 122.9
CLEARANCE DELIVERY PHONE: For CD ctc Fort Worth ARTCC at 817-858-7584.

SOUTH GRAND LAKE RGNL (See KETCHUM on page 205)

STAN STAMPER MUNI (See HUGO on page 204)

STIGLER RGNL (GZL)(KGZL) 3 NE UTC–6(–5DT) N35°17.29´ W95°05.63´ **DALLAS–FT WORTH**
600 B NOTAM FILE MLC **L–15E**
RWY 17–35: H4296X60 (ASPH) S–12.5 LIRL **IAP**
  RWY 17: PAPI(P2L)—GA 2.75° TCH 40´. Thld dsplcd 95´. P–line.
  RWY 35: PAPI(P2L)—GA 3.0° TCH 40´.
RUNWAY DECLARED DISTANCE INFORMATION
  RWY 17: TORA–4296 TODA–4296 ASDA–4296 LDA–4200
  RWY 35: TORA–4296 TODA–4296 ASDA–4296 LDA–4296
SERVICE: FUEL 100LL **LGT** Actvt LIRL Rwy 17–35—CTAF. PAPI Rwy
  17 & 35 on consly.
AIRPORT REMARKS: Unattended. Self svc fuel is avbl 24 hrs.
AIRPORT MANAGER: 918-967-2164
WEATHER DATA SOURCES: AWOS–3PT 118.575 (918) 967–8982.
COMMUNICATIONS: CTAF 122.9
® **FORT WORTH CENTER APP/DEP CON** 132.2
CLEARANCE DELIVERY PHONE: For CD ctc Fort Worth ARTCC at
  817-858-7584.
RADIO AIDS TO NAVIGATION: NOTAM FILE FSM.
  FORT SMITH (L) (L) VORTACW 110.4 FSM Chan 41 N35°23.30´
  W94°16.29´ 255° 40.8 NM to fld. 432/7E.

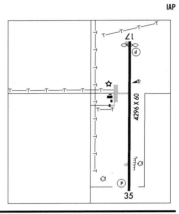

SC, 25 JAN 2024 to 21 MAR 2024

OKLAHOMA

STILLWATER RGNL (SWO)(KSWO) 3 NW UTC−6(−5DT) N36°09.68′ W97°05.15′ **WICHITA**
1000 B TPA—See Remarks ARFF Index—See Remarks NOTAM FILE SWO H−6H, L−15D
RWY 17−35: H7401X100 (CONC−GRVD) S−100, D−157, 2S−175, 2D−310 MIRL 0.5% up N IAP, AD
  RWY 17: MALSR. PAPI(P4L)—GA 3.0° TCH 50′.
  RWY 35: REIL. PAPI(P4L)—GA 3.0° TCH 38′.
RWY 04−22: H5002X75 (ASPH) S−34, D−60 MIRL 0.5% up NE
  RWY 04: PAPI(P4L)—GA 3.0° TCH 35′. Ground.
  RWY 22: PAPI(P4L)—GA 3.0° TCH 39′.
RUNWAY DECLARED DISTANCE INFORMATION
  RWY 04: TORA−5002 TODA−5002 ASDA−5002 LDA−5002
  RWY 17: TORA−7401 TODA−7401 ASDA−7401 LDA−7401
  RWY 22: TORA−5002 TODA−5002 ASDA−5002 LDA−5002
  RWY 35: TORA−7401 TODA−7401 ASDA−7401 LDA−7401
SERVICE: S4 FUEL 100LL, JET A LGT Actvt MALSR Rwy 17; REIL Rwy 35; PAPI Rwy 22; MIRL Rwy 04−22 and
  17−35—CTAF. MIRL Rwy 17−35 preset low intst; incr intst—CTAF. Rwy 04 unusbl byd 9 degs right of cntrln. Rwy 17 byd
  9 degs left and right of cntrln. Rwy 35 unusbl byd 9 degs left and 8 degs right of cntrln.
AIRPORT REMARKS: Attended 1100−0600Z‡. Student ops and birds on and invof arpt. All ramps are uncontrolled. Aft hr fuel
  405−377−5326. Aft hrs fuel avbl with PPR; ctc 405−624−5463. Class I, ARFF Index B. ARFF Index 24 hrs PPR for
  unsked acft ops with more than 9 pax call amgr 405−533−2222. ARFF index B maintained; ARFF index C PPR.
  TPA—light acft 1800 (800), turbo props/jets 2500 (1500). Ptn of Twy F north of T−hngr 2 not vsbl from ATCT. For GA
  tsnt prkg on Hangar 1 ramp ctc FBO on UNICOM or fone 405−624−5463.
AIRPORT MANAGER: 405-533-8425
WEATHER DATA SOURCES: ASOS 135.725 (405) 743−8150.
COMMUNICATIONS: CTAF 125.35 UNICOM 122.95
  RCO 122.3 (MC ALESTER RADIO)
®KANSAS CITY CENTER APP/DEP CON 127.8
  TOWER 125.35 (1400−0400Z‡) GND CON 121.6
CLEARANCE DELIVERY PHONE: For CD if una to ctc on FSS freq, ctc Kansas City ARTCC at 913−254−8508.
AIRSPACE: CLASS D svc 1400−0400Z‡ daily; other times CLASS G.
RADIO AIDS TO NAVIGATION: NOTAM FILE SWO.
  (T) (T) VORW/DME 108.4 SWO Chan 21 N36°13.45′ W97°04.88′ 176° 3.8 NM to fld. 1022/7E.
  GABEH NDB (LOMW) 255 SW N36°14.17′ W97°05.24′ 174° 4.5 NM to fld. 975/5E.
  ILS/DME 109.15 I−SWO Chan 28(Y) Rwy 17. Class IB. LOM GABEH NDB. Unmonitored when ATCT clsd.

STROUD MUNI (SUD)(KSUD) 3 N UTC−6(−5DT) N35°47.38′ W96°39.34′ **DALLAS−FT WORTH**
901 B NOTAM FILE MLC L−15E
RWY 18−36: H3000X60 (ASPH) S−12.5 MIRL
  RWY 18: PAPI(P2L). Trees.
  RWY 36: PAPI(P2L).
SERVICE: S4 FUEL 100LL, JET A LGT ACTIVATE PAPI Rwy 18 and Rwy 36; MIRL Rwy 18−36—CTAF.
AIRPORT REMARKS: Unattended. Fuel avbl 24 hr with credit card. 30′ unmrk powerline lctd approx 990′ from Rwy 18 end.
AIRPORT MANAGER: (918) 290−0787
COMMUNICATIONS: CTAF 122.9
CLEARANCE DELIVERY PHONE: For CD ctc Kansas City ARTCC at 913−254−8508.
RADIO AIDS TO NAVIGATION: NOTAM FILE OKM.
  OKMULGEE (VH) (DH) VORW/DME 114.9 OKM Chan 96 N35°41.58′ W95°51.96′ 271° 39.0 NM to fld. 774/8E.

OKLAHOMA

SULPHUR MUNI (F3Ø) 2 NW UTC–6(–5DT) N34°31.62′ W96°59.41′ DALLAS–FT WORTH
1071 B NOTAM FILE MLC L–17C
RWY 17–35: H3500X60 (ASPH) S–12.5 MIRL 1.1% up N
 RWY 17: Trees. Rgt tfc.
SERVICE: S4 **LGT** ACTIVATE MIRL Rwy 17–35—CTAF.
AIRPORT REMARKS: Unattended.
AIRPORT MANAGER: 580-622-5096
COMMUNICATIONS: CTAF 122.9
CLEARANCE DELIVERY PHONE: For CD ctc Fort Worth ARTCC at 817-858-7584.
RADIO AIDS TO NAVIGATION: NOTAM FILE ADM.
 ARDMORE (VH) (H) VORTACW 116.7 ADM Chan 114 N34°12.70′ W97°10.09′ 019° 20.9 NM to fld. 937/6E.
  VOR unusable:
   150°–160° byd 40 NM
   150°–160° byd 6 NM blo 14,000′
   297°–306° byd 40 NM blo 15,000′
   307°–314° blo 3,500′
   307°–314° byd 15 NM
   314°–333°
  TACAN AZIMUTH unusable:
   314°–333°
  DME unusable:
   314°–333°
   334°–011° byd 39 NM blo 3,100′

SUNDANCE (See OKLAHOMA CITY on page 213)

TAHLEQUAH MUNI (TQH)(KTQH) 2 NW UTC–6(–5DT) N35°55.82′ W95°00.27′ DALLAS–FT WORTH
874 B NOTAM FILE TQH H–6I, L–15E
RWY 17–35: H5001X75 (ASPH) S–26 MIRL 0.4% up N IAP
 RWY 17: REIL. PAPI(P4L)—GA 3.5° TCH 39′. Trees.
 RWY 35: REIL. PAPI(P4L)—GA 3.0° TCH 39′. Trees.
SERVICE: S2 **FUEL** 100LL, JET A **LGT** Actvt REIL Rwy 17 and 35; MIRL Rwy 17–35—CTAF. PAPI Rwy 17 and 35 on consly. Rwy 35 PAPI unusbl byd 8° right of cntrln.
AIRPORT REMARKS: Attended Mon–Fri 1400–2300Z‡. Parachute Jumping.
AIRPORT MANAGER: (918) 708-5600
WEATHER DATA SOURCES: AWOS–3P 118.425 (918) 453-2729.
 Thunderstorm sensor na – perm disabld.
COMMUNICATIONS: CTAF/UNICOM 122.8
® **MEMPHIS CENTER APP/DEP CON** 126.1
CLEARANCE DELIVERY PHONE: For CD ctc Memphis ARTCC at 901-368-8453/8449.
RADIO AIDS TO NAVIGATION: NOTAM FILE TUL.
 TULSA (H) (H) VORTACW 114.4 TUL Chan 91 N36°11.78′ W95°47.29′ 104° 41.3 NM to fld. 788/8E.
  TACAN AZIMUTH unusable:
   248°–258° byd 23 NM blo 3,100′
  DME unusable:
   248°–258° byd 23 NM blo 3,100′

OKLAHOMA

TALIHINA MUNI (6F1)   3 SW   UTC–6(–5DT)   N34°42.47′ W95°04.43′   DALLAS–FT WORTH
687   B   NOTAM FILE MLC   L–17D
RWY 01–19: H3300X60 (ASPH)   S–12   MIRL
  RWY 19: Trees.
SERVICE: LGT Actvt MIRL Rwy 01–19—CTAF. Actvt WDI lights–CTAF.
AIRPORT REMARKS: Unattended.
AIRPORT MANAGER: (918) 413-2088
COMMUNICATIONS: CTAF 122.9
CLEARANCE DELIVERY PHONE: For CD ctc Fort Worth ARTCC at
  817-858-7584.
RADIO AIDS TO NAVIGATION: NOTAM FILE MLC.
  RICH MOUNTAIN (VL) (L) VORTACW 113.5   PGO   Chan 82
    N34°40.83′ W94°36.54′   270° 23.1 NM to fld. 2700/4E.
  VOR unusable:
    016°–021° byd 40 NM
    028°–029° byd 40 NM
    030°–040°
    050°–075° blo 4,000′
    090°–145°
    167°–169° byd 40 NM
    170°–200°
    235°–245° byd 30 NM blo 5,000′
    260°–280° byd 35 NM blo 5,000′
    329°–335° byd 40 NM
    340°–345° blo 5,000′
    358°–002° byd 40 NM

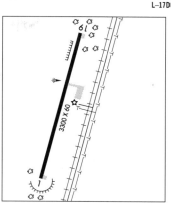

TENKILLER LAKE AIRPARK (See COOKSON on page 189)

TEXHOMA MUNI (K49)   1 W   UTC–6(–5DT)   N36°30.34′ W101°48.82′   WICHITA
3468   NOTAM FILE MLC   L–15B
RWY 03–21: H3564X48 (ASPH)   MIRL
  RWY 03: Thld dsplcd 590′. Road.
  RWY 21: Thld dsplcd 340′. Fence.
RWY 17–35: 2340X75 (TURF)
  RWY 17: Fence.
  RWY 35: Road.
SERVICE: FUEL 100LL   LGT ACTVT MIRL RWY 03–21—CTAF. RWY
  03-21 MIRL OTS INDEF.
AIRPORT REMARKS: Unattended. Ultralight activity on and invof arpt. For fuel
  call 580-522-2009. Rwy 03–21 not mkd. Wind turbines 350 ft AGL
  lctd 2 mi south of arpt.
AIRPORT MANAGER: 806-753-6567
COMMUNICATIONS: CTAF 122.9
CLEARANCE DELIVERY PHONE: For CD ctc Albuquerque ARTCC at
  505-856-4861.
RADIO AIDS TO NAVIGATION: NOTAM FILE DHT.
  DALHART (L) (L) VORTACW 112.0   DHT   Chan 57   N36°05.49′
    W102°32.68′   043° 43.3 NM to fld. 4020/12E.
  TAC AZM unusable:
    240°–255° byd 15 NM
    320°–350° byd 15 NM

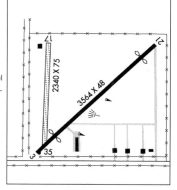

TEXOMA   N33°56.65′ W96°23.51′   NOTAM FILE DUA.   DALLAS–FT. WORTH
(L) DME 114.3   URH   Chan 90   at Durant Rgnl/Eaker Fld. 682.   H–6H, L–17D
  DME unusable:
    207°–240° byd 35 NM blo 2,500′
    335°–350° byd 35 NM blo 2,500′

OKLAHOMA

THOMAS MUNI (104) 1 SE UTC−6(−5DT) N35°44.02′ W98°43.83′   DALLAS–FT WORTH
1733   B   NOTAM FILE MLC   L−15D
RWY 17−35: H3771X60 (ASPH)   S−4   MIRL   IAP
  RWY 17: PAPI(P2L)—GA 3.0° TCH 40′. Thld dsplcd 212′. Road.
  RWY 35: PAPI(P2L)—GA 3.0° TCH 40′. Rgt tfc.
SERVICE: **FUEL** 100LL   **LGT** Rwy 17 PAPI unusable byd 8° right of centerline. MIRL Rwy 17−35 preset on low ints, to incr ints ACTIVATE—CTAF.
AIRPORT REMARKS: Attended Mon–Fri 1400–2300Z‡. Fuel ABVL 24 HRS self serve with credit card.
AIRPORT MANAGER: 580-603-2636
COMMUNICATIONS: CTAF 122.9
®**FORT WORTH CENTER APP/DEP CON** 128.4
CLEARANCE DELIVERY PHONE: For CD ctc Fort Worth ARTCC at 817-858-7584.
RADIO AIDS TO NAVIGATION: NOTAM FILE MLC.
  KINGFISHER (H) TACAN Chan 94   IFI (114.7)   N35°48.32′ W98°00.23′   254° 35.7 NM to fld. 1112/9E.

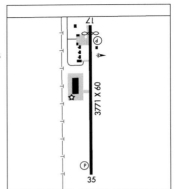

TINKER AFB (TIK)(KTIK) AF   8 SE   UTC−6(−5DT)   N35°24.89′ W97°23.20′   DALLAS–FT WORTH
1291   B   TPA—See Remarks   NOTAM FILE MLC   Not insp.   H−6H, L−15D
RWY 18−36: H11100X200 (PEM)   PCN 73 R/C/W/T   HIRL   DIAP, AD
  RWY 18: SALSF. PAPI(P4L)—GA 2.8° TCH 51′. RVR−T 0.3% up.
  RWY 36: ALSF1. PAPI(P4L)—GA 2.6° TCH 52′. RVR−T Rgt tfc.
RWY 13−31: H10000X200 (PEM)   PCN 59 R/C/W/T   HIRL
  RWY 13: SALS. PAPI(P4L)—GA 2.8° TCH 47′. Rgt tfc. 0.5% up.
  RWY 31: SALS. PAPI(P4L)—GA 3.0° TCH 71′.
SERVICE: S4   **OX** 1, 2, 4   **LGT** ALS Rwy 18 nstd for Cat I ILS. ALS Rwy 13−31 nstd. **MILITARY**— **JASU** 1(MC−1A) 1(MC−2A) (A/M32A−86) 8(AM32A−60) 6(AM32A−95) **FUEL** A++ (Mil) 115 B+ **FLUID** PRESAIR LHOX LOX LHNIT SP **OIL** O−148−156 SOAP-Results avbl 1345−1730Z‡, 1830−0600Z‡ wkd exc hol, results not avbl OT. **TRAN ALERT** Opr 1400−0530Z‡. Ltd Fleet Svc (lavatory and water only).
NOISE: Noise abatement: Practice circling apch to Rwy 18 prohibited. Night quiet hr in effect 0500−1200Z‡, practice apch are restricted.
MILITARY REMARKS: See FLIP AP/1 Supplementary Arpt Remark. **RSTD** PPR tran acft, ctc base ops DSN 884−2191, C405−734−2191. Notify Base OPS of 1 hr or more ETA chg and PPR CNL. No tran acft arr/dep 0530−1400Z‡. Tran acft may exp only one apch dur periods of ints lcl trng. **CAUTION** Exer ctn while tax; portions of ALC Ramp, KC−46 Ramp, and munitions fac not vis fm twr. Hold short of ramp for individual acft flw−me assistance. Use caution Rwy 13−31, N−S VFR corridor surface −3000′ 1 NM off dep end Rwy 31. Unlgtd fences around airfield. Unlighted bldgs NW, W, SW and E of Rwy 18−36. **TFC PAT** TPA Rectangular and clsd tfc pat 3000 (1709) (includes fighter/trainer acft), overhead tfc pat on req 3500 (2209). Use 124.45 while in tfc pat, monitor 251.05 to maximum extent possible. **CSTMS/AG/IMG:** See foreign clearance guide KTIK entry. **MISC** VIP acft ctc Base OPS 30 min prior to ETA with firm chock time. Rwy 13−31 apch end 1000′ conc, remaining rwy keel 75′ conc, non-keel asphalt. Rwy 18−36 apch ends 1000′ conc, remaining rwy keel 75′ conc, non-keel asphalt, mid 8100′ rwy grooved. Twy A clsd east side Rwy 18−36. Twy M NSTD due to 50′ wide. Rwy C NSTD shoulders btn trim pad and Rwy 13−31. Hgr space for tran acft dur inclement WX extremely ltd. Tran svc for B52, B1, C5, C17, C130, KC10 and C135 extremely ltd, acft should have crew chief on board. Anti-icing/De-icing capabilities for tran acft limited, tran aircrews must ctc Base OPS with deicing req prior to arrival. Rwy Cond Code (RwyCC) and Field Condition NOTAM (FICON) not determined/rprtd. Air terminal svc (ATOC) and contingency/deployment OPR avail 1300−0100Z‡ dly. Acft loading/offloading req outside publ times ctc DSN 339−5553, C405−734−2751. Std USAF RSRS applied. Veh transportation for tran aircews avbl Mon−Thur 1230−0430Z‡, Fri 1230−0200Z‡, exc hol. Air terminal svc (ATOC) and contingency/deployment opr avbl 1300−0100Z‡ dly. Acft loading/offloading req outside publ times ctc DSN 339−5553, C405−734−2751. Std USAF reduced same rwy separation applied.
AIRPORT MANAGER: 405-732-1110
COMMUNICATIONS: SFA 354.125 (Sooner Con/Okie Ops 228.45 311.0) **ATIS** 270.1 (1100−0400Z‡) DSN 884−5152, C405−734−5152. **PTD** 134.1 372.2
®**OKE CITY APP/DEP CON** 120.45 288.325 (081°−170°) 124.2 336.4 (001°−080°) 124.6 266.8 (261°−360°) 126.65 263.075 (171°−260°)
  TOWER 124.45 251.05 **GND CON** 121.8 275.8 **CLNC DEL** 119.7 335.8
TIK COMD POST (Arrow Ctl) 139.95 141.65 225.875 305.6
  PMSV METRO 261.025 (Forecast svc avbl during afld opr hr.) DSN 884−3196, C405−734−3196. Alternate wx location DSN 884−3529, C405−734−3529. **TINKER ATOC** 119.15
AFMC FLT TEST 382.6 (OC−ALC PDM input acft ctc Sabre Control 30 min prior arrival.)

CONTINUED ON NEXT PAGE
SC, 25 JAN 2024 to 21 MAR 2024

OKLAHOMA

CONTINUED FROM PRECEDING PAGE

AIRSPACE: CLASS C svc ctc **APP CON.**
RADIO AIDS TO NAVIGATION: NOTAM FILE PWA.
  WILEY POST (T) (T) VORW/DME 113.4   PWA   Chan 81   N35°31.98′ W97°38.83′   111° 14.6 NM to fld. 1271/8E.
  WILL ROGERS (H) (H) VORTACW 114.1   IRW   Chan 88   N35°21.52′ W97°36.55′   066° 11.4 NM to fld.
    1230/7E.   NOTAM FILE OKC.
  (T) TACAN   Chan 105   TIK (115.8)   N35°26.19′ W97°22.78′   192° 1.3 NM to fld. 1251/3E.   NOTAM FILE
    MLC.
  TACAN AZIMUTH unusable:
    051°–061° byd 20 NM blo 3,400′
    154°–174° byd 23 NM blo 3,400′
  DME unusable:
    051°–061° byd 20 NM blo 3,400′
    154°–174° byd 23 NM blo 3,400′
    No NOTAM MP: 1300–1500Z‡ 1st & 3rd Tue each Month
  LOC 111.7   I–EVG   Rwy 13.
  ILS 111.3   I–FRJ   Rwy 18.   Glideslope signal not protected fm psbl reflective interference caused by vehicle tfc. Acft
    with AN/ARN–58 localizer rcvr may experience course deviations due to interference. LOC unusable byd 15° right of
    course centerline; fm 0.1 NM to rwy thld. No NOTAM MP: 1300–1500Z‡ 1st and 3rd Tue each Month.
  LOC 111.7   I–PLH   Rwy 31.
  ILS 109.5   I–TIK   Rwy 36.   Acft with AN/ARN–58 localizer rcvr may experience course deviations due to interference.
    No NOTAM MP: 1300–1500Z‡ 1st and 3rd Tue each Month.
  PAR
COMM/NAV/WEATHER REMARKS: Radar see Terminal FLIP for Radar Minima. Acft with AN/ARN–58 localizer receiver may
  experience course deviations due to interference.

TIPTON MUNI (1O8)   3 SW   UTC–6(–5DT)   N34°27.52′ W99°10.28′   **DALLAS–FT WORTH**
1248   B   NOTAM FILE MLC   **L–17B**
RWY 17–35: H3062X50 (ASPH)   S–12   MIRL   **IAP**
  RWY 17: Pole.
  RWY 35: Pole.
AIRPORT REMARKS: Unattended. Rwy 17–35 moderate to severe cracking
  and grass growing through cracks.
AIRPORT MANAGER: 580-667-5211
COMMUNICATIONS: CTAF 122.9
® **ALTUS APP/DEP CON** 125.1 (1500–0830Z‡ Mon-Fri, clsd weekends and
  holidays, other times ctc)
® **FORT WORTH CENTER APP/DEP CON** 128.4 133.5
CLEARANCE DELIVERY PHONE: For CD ctc Fort Worth ARTCC at
  817-858-7584.
RADIO AIDS TO NAVIGATION: NOTAM FILE HBR.
  HOBART (L) (L) VORTACW 111.8   HBR   Chan 55   N34°51.99′
    W99°03.80′   182° 25.0 NM to fld. 1472/10E.
  VOR unusable:
    080°–120° byd 30 NM blo 4,000′
  TACAN AZIMUTH unusable:
    080°–090° byd 25 NM blo 4,500′
    100°–112° byd 25 NM blo 4,500′
    240°–270° byd 25 NM blo 4,500′
  DME unusable:
    080°–090° byd 25 NM blo 4,500′
    100°–112° byd 25 NM blo 4,500′
    240°–270° byd 25 NM blo 4,500′

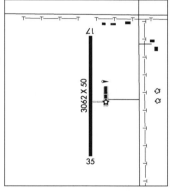

SC, 25 JAN 2024 to 21 MAR 2024

OKLAHOMA

TISHOMINGO AIRPARK (0F9) 2 S UTC−6(−5DT) N34°11.91′ W96°40.47′
DALLAS–FT WORTH
L−17C
647 B NOTAM FILE MLC
RWY 17−35: H3100X60 (ASPH) S−12 RWY LGTS(NSTD)
 RWY 17: Trees.
 RWY 35: Trees.
SERVICE: **LGT** Nstd solar LIRL Rwy 17−35 SS−SR. Rwy 17−35 nstd due to thld lgts all red and edge lgts all yellow. Rotating bcn OTS indef.
AIRPORT REMARKS: Unattended.
AIRPORT MANAGER: (580) 371-8605
COMMUNICATIONS: CTAF 122.9
CLEARANCE DELIVERY PHONE: For CD ctc Fort Worth ARTCC at 817-858-7584.
RADIO AIDS TO NAVIGATION: NOTAM FILE ADM.
 ARDMORE (VH) (H) VORTACW 116.7   ADM   Chan 114   N34°12.70′
 W97°10.09′   086° 24.6 NM to fld. 937/6E.
 VOR unusable:
  150°−160° byd 40 NM
  150°−160° byd 6 NM blo 14,000′
  297°−306° byd 40 NM blo 15,000′
  307°−314° blo 3,500′
  307°−314° byd 15 NM
  314°−333°
 TACAN AZIMUTH unusable:
  314°−333°
 DME unusable:
  314°−333°
  334°−011° byd 39 NM blo 3,100′

TULSA

HARVEY YOUNG (1H6) 8 E UTC−6(−5DT) N36°08.34′ W95°49.50′
KANSAS CITY
750 B NOTAM FILE MLC
RWY 17−35: H2580X40 (ASPH)
 RWY 17: Trees.
 RWY 35: Trees.
RWY N−S: 2580X80 (TURF)
 RWY N: Trees.
 RWY S: Trees.
SERVICE: S2 **FUEL** 100LL
AIRPORT REMARKS: Attended Mon−Fri 1400−2300Z‡. Arpt unattended federal holidays. Birds on and invof airport. Ultralights on and invof arpt. Rwy 17 rgt tfc for helicopters. Twys thin & soft in hot weather. Rwy 17−35 severe cracking and raveling. Rwy 17 markings severely faded. Rwy 35 markings svrly faded; nos unrdbl. Rwy N/S rough and uneven.
AIRPORT MANAGER: 918-298-4044
COMMUNICATIONS: CTAF/UNICOM 122.8
CLEARANCE DELIVERY PHONE: For CD ctc Tulsa Apch at 918-831-6714/6720.

OKLAHOMA

TULSA INTL (TUL)(KTUL) P (ANG ARNG)   5 NE   UTC−6(−5DT)   N36°11.90′ W95°53.29′   KANSAS CITY
678   B   LRA   Class I, ARFF Index C   NOTAM FILE TUL   H−6I, L−15E
RWY 18L−36R: H10000X150 (CONC−GRVD)   S−75, D−200, 2S−175,   IAP, AD
  2D−400 PCN 88 R/B/W/T   HIRL   CL
  RWY 18L: MALSR. PAPI(P4L)—GA 2.75° TCH 56′. RVR−TMR Tree.
    0.4% up.
  RWY 36R: ALSF2. TDZL. PAPI(P4L)—GA 3.0° TCH 52′. RVR−TMR
    Tree. Rgt tfc.
RWY 08−26: H7376X150 (CONC−GRVD)   S−75, D−200, 2S−175,
  2D−350 PCN 68 R/B/W/T   HIRL   0.5% up W
  RWY 08: REIL. PAPI(P4L)—GA 3.0° TCH 52′. Tree.
  RWY 26: MALSR. PAPI(P4L)—GA 3.0° TCH 57′.
RWY 18R−36L: H6101X100 (ASPH−GRVD)   S−100, D−140, 2S−127
  PCN 47 R/C/X/T   HIRL   0.7% up S
  RWY 18R: REIL. PAPI(P4L)—GA 2.75° TCH 42′. Thld dsplcd 600′.
    Tree. Rgt tfc.
  RWY 36L: REIL. PAPI(P4L)—GA 3.0° TCH 45′. Road.

RUNWAY DECLARED DISTANCE INFORMATION
RWY 08: TORA−7376   TODA−7376   ASDA−7375   LDA−7376
RWY 18L: TORA−10000 TODA−10000   ASDA−10000   LDA−10000
RWY 18R: TORA−6101   TODA−6101   ASDA−5701   LDA−5101
RWY 26: TORA−7376   TODA−7376   ASDA−7375   LDA−7375
RWY 36L: TORA−6101   TODA−6101   ASDA−5101   LDA−5101
RWY 36R: TORA−10000 TODA−10000   ASDA−10000   LDA−10000
ARRESTING GEAR/SYSTEM
RWY 18L BAK−14 BAK−12A(B) (1500 FT).   BAK−14 BAK−12A(B) (1500 FT). **RWY 36R**
RWY 08 BAK−14 BAK−12A(B) (1500 FT).   BAK−14 BAK−12A(B) (1500 FT). **RWY 26**
SERVICE: S4   **FUEL** 100LL, JET A   **OX** 1, 2, 3, 4   **LGT** Rwy 08 PAPI unusbl byd 8 deg left & right of rwy cntrln. Rwy 26
  PAPI unusbl byd 7 degs right & 9 degs left of cntrln.   **MILITARY—** **A−GEAR** BAK−12A(B) raised by BAK−14 device O/R to twr.
  JASU 2(A/M32A−86) 3(MD−3M) 3(MA−1A) 4(AM32A−60A) 6(AM32A−60B) **FUEL** A, A+ (C918−836−6592,
  1000−0600Z‡. OT 1 hr PN, $100 fee.) (NC−100LL, A1, B) **FLUID** SP PRESAIR LPOX LOX **OIL** O−128−148; SOAP−Avbl
  dur ANG opr hr.
NOISE: Noise abatement all rwys; climb to 3000′ asap aft tkof.
AIRPORT REMARKS: Attended continuously. Birds on and invof arpt.. Ctn: 4000 ft blacktop track 1.5 NM E Rwy 26; do not
  mistake for rwy. Rwy 18R ireg wind pat. Twy L3 not vsb from ATCT. Txl LA, NN, and QQ not vsb fm ATCT. Twy L north of
  Rwy 08−26 S−93/D−140/DT209. Twy M−2 S−81/D−140/DT186. Wt rstrd areas: Twy JJ S−35; Twy M2
  S−81/D−140/DT−186; Twy HH S−55/D−60; Twy L north of Rwy 08−26 S−93/D−140/DT209; Twy L btn Twy C & Twy L2
  S−120/D−250/DT−372; Twy L2 S−70/D−100/DT−166. Apvd acft run up area: 0500−1200Z‡ N end Twy J acft
  orientation N & S. 24 hr apch end Rwy 26 acft orientation E & W. 1200−0500Z‡ N end Twy L acft orientation N and S.
AIRPORT MANAGER: 918-838-5000
WEATHER DATA SOURCES: ASOS (918) 831−6772 LLWAS. TDWR.
COMMUNICATIONS: UNICOM 122.95 **D−ATIS** 124.9   377.2 (918−831−6718) **PTD** 260.4
  RCO 122.2 (MC ALESTER RADIO)
®**APP/DEP CON** 119.1 (355°−174°) (FINAL 119.85   355°−174°)   124.0 (175°−354°) (FINAL 132.1 175°−354°)
  TOWER 121.2   310.8 (Rwy 18L−36R and Rwy 08−26) 118.7   257.8 (Rwy 18R−36L) **GND CON** 121.9 348.6
  CLNC DEL PRE−TAXI CLNC 134.05   284.7 **ARNG OPS** 46.9 **ANG OPS** 335.47
  PDC
AIRSPACE: CLASS C svc ctc **APP CON.**
VOR TEST FACILITY (VOT) 109.0
RADIO AIDS TO NAVIGATION: NOTAM FILE TUL.
  (H) (H) VORTACW 114.4   TUL   Chan 91   N36°11.78′ W95°47.29′   264° 4.9 NM to fld. 788/8E.
    TACAN AZIMUTH unusable:
    248°−258° byd 23 NM blo 3,100′
    DME unusable:
    248°−258° byd 23 NM blo 3,100′
  OILLR NDB (LOMW) 338   TU   N36°05.85′ W95°53.33′   357° 6.0 NM to fld. 710/3E.
  ILS/DME 109.7   I−DWE   Chan 34   Rwy 18L.   Class IE.   Autopilot coupled apchs NA blw 813′ MSL. 813′ MSL is blw
    the Cat I DH.
  ILS 111.1   I−TJY   Rwy 18R.   Class IA.
  ILS/DME 110.3   I−TUL   Chan 40   Rwy 36R.   Class IIE.   LOM OILLR NDB.
  ASR

OKLAHOMA

TULSA RIVERSIDE (RVS)(KRVS)   5 S   UTC−6(−5DT)   N36°02.38′ W95°59.08′   KANSAS CITY
638   B   TPA—See Remarks   NOTAM FILE RVS   H−6I, L−15E
  RWY 01L−19R: H5102X100 (ASPH−GRVD)   S−61, D−87, 2D−168   IAP, AD
    PCN 27 F/B/X/T   HIRL   0.3% up N
    RWY 01L: REIL. PAPI(P4L)—GA 3.0° TCH 48′. Tree.
    RWY 19R: REIL. PAPI(P4L)—GA 3.2° TCH 43′. Trees. Rgt tfc.
  RWY 01R−19L: H4208X100 (ASPH)   S−30, D−60   MIRL   0.3% up N
    RWY 01R: PAPI(P4L)—GA 2.83° TCH 40′. Rgt tfc.
    RWY 19L: PAPI(P4L)—GA 2.83° TCH 40′. Thld dsplcd 142′. Road.
  RWY 13−31: H2641X50 (ASPH)   S−30   MIRL   0.3% up NW
    RWY 31: Rgt tfc.

  RUNWAY DECLARED DISTANCE INFORMATION
    RWY 01L: TORA−5102   TODA−5102   ASDA−5102   LDA−5102
    RWY 01R: TORA−4208   TODA−4208   ASDA−4208   LDA−4208
    RWY 13: TORA−2641   TODA−2641   ASDA−2641   LDA−2641
    RWY 19L: TORA−4208   TODA−4208   ASDA−4208   LDA−4066
    RWY 19R: TORA−5102   TODA−5102   ASDA−5102   LDA−5102
    RWY 31: TORA−2641   TODA−2641   ASDA−2641   LDA−2641
  SERVICE: S4   **FUEL** 100LL, JET A   **OX** 4   **LGT** When ATCT clsd actvt
    MIRL Rwy 01R−19L and 13−31; HIRL Rwy 01L−19R; Twys H, L, T
    and Z; Txl DD−CTAF. HIRL Rwy 01L−19R preset med intst incr
    intst−CTAF.
  NOISE: Noise Abatement: No turns on dep prior to 1500′ MSL NA.
  AIRPORT REMARKS: Attended 1200−0400Z‡. After hr PPR. Birds on and invof arpt. Rwy 13 L turn on dep bfr 1500′ MSL NA.
    Rwy 31 mntn TPA until abeam AER on downwind leg. NE, NW and SW ramps, ptns of Txl CC, DD and GG not vsb fm
    ATCT. Txl BB and NW pvt hngr area txl 20′ wide. NE and NW pvt hngr area wingspan gtr than 49 NA; wt lmt 12500 lb.
    Rwy 01L−19R only cntr 80′ grvd.
  AIRPORT MANAGER: 918−299−5886
  WEATHER DATA SOURCES: ASOS 126.5 (918) 299−0740. LAWRS.
  COMMUNICATIONS: CTAF 120.3 **ATIS** 126.5 **UNICOM** 122.95
® **TULSA APP/DEP CON** 134.7 (175°−355°) 119.85 (356°−174°)
    RIVERSIDE TOWER 120.3 119.2 (1300−0400Z‡) **GND CON** 121.7
    CLNC DEL PRE−TAXI CLNC 124.5
  AIRSPACE: CLASS D svc 1300−0400Z‡; other times CLASS G.
  RADIO AIDS TO NAVIGATION: NOTAM FILE TUL.
    (H) (H) VORTACW 114.4   TUL   Chan 91   N36°11.78′ W95°47.29′   218° 13.4 NM to fld. 788/8E.
      TACAN AZIMUTH unusable:
        248°−258° byd 23 NM blo 3,100′
      DME unusable:
        248°−258° byd 23 NM blo 3,100′
    GLENPOOL (T) DME 110.6   GNP   Chan 43   N35°55.25′ W95°58.12′   354° 7.2 NM to fld. 810. NOTAM FILE
      MLC.
    ILS 109.95   I−RVS   Rwy 01L.   Class IT.
  COMM/NAV/WEATHER REMARKS: Only use 119.2 lcl/twr frequency when advised to do so by RVS ATC or when broadcasted on
    RVS ATIS.

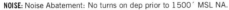

UNIVERSITY OF OKLAHOMA WESTHEIMER   (See NORMAN on page 212)

OKLAHOMA

VANCE AFB (END)(KEND) AF 3 S UTC–6(–5DT) N36°20.39´ W97°55.03´   **WICHITA**
1313 B NOTAM FILE MLC Not insp.   **H–6H, L–15D**
RWY 17C–35C: H9217X150 (PEM–GRVD) PCN 15 R/C/W/T HIRL   **DIAP, AD**
   RWY 17C: SALSF. PAPI(P4L)—GA 2.5° TCH 51´. RVR–T
   RWY 35C: SALSF. PAPI(P4L)—GA 2.5° TCH 41´. RVR–T
RWY 17R–35L: H9217X150 (PEM–GRVD) PCN 57 R/B/W/T HIRL
   RWY 17R: SALS. PAPI(P4L)—GA 2.5° TCH 48´.
   RWY 35L: SALS. PAPI(P4L)—GA 2.5° TCH 49´.
RWY 17L–35R: H5024X150 (CONC–GRVD) PCN 36 R/C/W/T MIRL
   RWY 17L: REIL. PAPI(P4L)—GA 3.0° TCH 54´.
   RWY 35R: REIL. PAPI(P4L)—GA 3.0° TCH 50´.
ARRESTING GEAR/SYSTEM
   RWY 17C BAK–15 CHAG (154 FT OVRN).   BAK–15 CHAG (154 FT OVRN). **RWY 35C**
   RWY 17R BAK–15 CHAG (152 FT OVRN).   BAK–15 CHAG (152 FT OVRN). **RWY 35L**
SERVICE: S4 **OX** 2, 4 **LGT** Rwy 17C–35C apch lgts nstd installed on precision rwy. Rwy 17C–35C and 17L–35R 4–lgt PAPI lctd both sides. Rwy 35R PAPI unubl byd 9 degs right and left of cntrln. **MILITARY**— **JASU** 8(A/M32A–86) 10(AM32–95) **FUEL** A++ (Mil) B+ **FLUID** SP PRESAIR LPOX LOX **OIL** O–148–156 SOAP **TRAN ALERT** Avbl durg publ/NOTAM ops hrs; no fleet svc avbl; tsnt deicing unavbl.
MILITARY REMARKS: Opr Mon–Fri, 1300–0200Z‡ Sun 1900–2300Z‡. Clsd Sat and Fed hol; ot by NOTAM. Apch lighting system Rwy 17C–35C NSTD (SALS) installed on precision runway). Rwy 17R–35L 4 lgt PAPI located both sides of rwy. First 3350 ft Rwy 17C and first 1000 ft Rwy 35C is grooved conc, mid 4950 ft is grooved asph. Rwy 17L–35R middle 2000´ is grooved. **RSTD** Rwy 17C–35C CLSD til aprx Apr 2025. PPR at least 24 hrs in adv ctc Vance afld mgt ops DSN 448–7426, C580–213–7426. Offl bus; submit req to afld mgmt at DSN 448–7426, C580–213–7426. Durg VMC, dep acft rmn blw 2300´ until DER to ensure sepn fm VFR ovhd pat unless otrw cleared by ATC. **CAUTION:** Barriers not connected to energy absorber at AER. Some obst lgts nstd; only vis to 3 mi. Led obst lgts may not be vis nvd or ngt vision goggles. Acft sunshades 735´ E of Rwy 17R–35R. **MISC** DV code 7 or hyr ctc Vance OPS 20 min prior to ETA. Wx obs lmtd all quad; all EOR not vis fm obs pt; when fog and/or lo clouds ovr AER 17–35 cond rpt fm obs pt may not be representative. Wind sock unlgtd when rwy unlgtd. Wx opr 0800–0500Z‡ Mon–Fri, 1400–2200Z‡ Sun; clsd Sat/federal hol; OT by NOTAM. Migratory bird act BASH (Phase II) 15 Apr–31 May and 1 Nov–28 Feb or active via NOTAM.
AIRPORT MANAGER: 580-213-7424
COMMUNICATIONS: SFA 392.1 **ATIS** 115.4 263.15 (1 May–31Oct) Mon–Fri 1300–0200Z‡ (1 Nov–30 Apr) Mon–Fri 1300–0100Z‡, Sun 2000–0000Z‡, clsd Sat and federal holidays. **PTD** 372.2
® **APP CON** 120.525 306.3 (169°–007° 10000´ to FL 240, 337°–169° FL 230 to FL 240) 118.075 273.475 (337°–037° to 19 DME at or blo FL 220) 121.3 291.1 (037°–169° at or blo 6500´) 125.45 388.2 (7000´ to FL 220) 126.75 346.325 (209°–337° to 18 DME at or blo FL 240) 119.775 244.875 (169°–007° within 18 DME at or blo 9500´) (1300–0200Z‡ wkd, 1900–2300Z‡ Sun; clsd Sat & federal hol. Gnd ctl and clnc del svc avbl 15 min prior to afld opening. Other times by NOTAM) Frequencies 126.75 and 346.325 unreliable byd 60 NM from rwy end.
® **KANSAS CITY CENTER APP CON** 127.8 319.1 (0200–1300Z‡ wkd, 2300–1900Z‡ Sun; 24 Sat & federal hol. Gnd ctl and clnc del svc avbl 15 min prior to afld opening.
   TOWER 124.05 259.1 (1300–0200Z‡ wkd, 1900–2300Z‡ Sun; clsd Sat and federal hol. Gnd ctl and clnc del svc avbl 15 min prior to afld opening. Other times by NOTAM)
   GND CON 121.675 289.4 **CLNC DEL** 225.4 **COMD POST** 237.15 (Call BOOMER OPS)
® **DEP CON** 120.525 306.3 1300–0200Z‡ Mon–Fri, 1900–2300Z‡, Sun, clsd Sat and federal holidays. Other times by NOTAM.)
® **KANSAS CITY CENTER DEP CON** 127.8 319.1 (0200–1300Z‡ wkd, 2300–1900Z‡ Sun, 24 hr Sat and Federal hol. Gnd ctl and clnc del svc avbl 15 min prior to afld opening)
   PMSV METRO 342.55
AIRSPACE: CLASS D svc 1300–0200Z‡ Mon–Fri, 1900–2300Z‡ Sun, clsd Sat and fed hol; other times by NOTAM; other times CLASS E.
RADIO AIDS TO NAVIGATION: NOTAM FILE MLC.
   (H) (H) VORTACW 115.4 END Chan 101 N36°20.70´ W97°55.10´ at fld. 1276/5E.
     mntnd drg ops hr
     MP 1000–1230Z‡ Mon–Fri, 1400–2200Z‡ Sat, 1400–1800Z‡ Sun
     VOR unusable:
      103°–117° byd 25 NM
   WOODRING (T) (T) VORW/DME 109.0 ODG Chan 27 N36°22.43´ W97°47.29´ 244° 6.6 NM to fld.
     1151/8E. NOTAM FILE WDG.
   ILS 108.9 I–LVC Rwy 17C. Class IE. Mnt dur publ opr hr only. Operates simultaneously with I–END. No NOTAM MP: 1100–1230Z‡ Tue and Wed. Autopilot cpd apch NA blw 1,500´ MSL
   ILS/DME 108.5 I–EZQ Chan 22 Rwy 17R.
   ILS 110.1 I–END Rwy 35C. Class IT. Mnt dur publ opr hr only. Operates simultaneously with I–LVC. No NOTAM MP: 1000–1230Z‡ Mon–Fri, 1400–2200Z‡ Sat, 1400–1800Z‡ Sun.
   ILS/DME 111.55 I–JUS Chan 52(Y) Rwy 35L.
COMM/NAV/WEATHER REMARKS: AWOS–Durg ops hr; obs augmented.

OKLAHOMA

VICI MUNI (5O1) 1 S UTC–6(–5DT) N36°08.46´ W99°18.20´ WICHITA
2268 NOTAM FILE MLC
RWY 16–34: H2565X50 (ASPH) S–8 RWY LGTS(NSTD) 1.0% up N
 RWY 16: Pole.
SERVICE: **LGT** SS–SR. Rwy 16–34 intens rwy lgts NSTD.
AIRPORT REMARKS: Unattended. Rwy 16 145´ Grain elevator 3200´ NE fm end of thr. Rwy 34 30´ drop off only 10´ from thr.
AIRPORT MANAGER: 580-995-4442
COMMUNICATIONS: CTAF 122.9
CLEARANCE DELIVERY PHONE: For CD ctc Kansas City ARTCC at 913-254-8508.

VINITA MUNI (H04) 2 SE UTC–6(–5DT) N36°36.88´ W95°09.10´ KANSAS CITY
695 B NOTAM FILE MLC L–15E
RWY 17–35: H4209X60 (ASPH–CONC) MIRL 0.4% up N IAP
 RWY 17: PAPI(P2L)—GA 3.0° TCH 45´. Thld dsplcd 210´. Fence.
 RWY 35: PAPI(P2L)—GA 3.0° TCH 43´. Trees.
SERVICE: **FUEL** 100LL **LGT** ACTIVATE MIRL Rwy 17–35—CTAF.
AIRPORT REMARKS: Unattended. Ultralight activity on and invof arpt. 24/7 self serve 100LL available w/ cc. Interstate highway 425 ft north of Rwy 17 end.
AIRPORT MANAGER: 918-244-2704
COMMUNICATIONS: CTAF 122.9
Ⓡ **KANSAS CITY CENTER APP/DEP CON** 128.6
CLEARANCE DELIVERY PHONE: For CD ctc Kansas City ARTCC at 913-254-8508.
RADIO AIDS TO NAVIGATION: NOTAM FILE TUL.
 TULSA (H) (H) VORTACW 114.4   TUL   Chan 91   N36°11.78´ W95°47.29´   043° 39.7 NM to fld. 788/8E.
  TACAN AZIMUTH unusable:
   248°–258° byd 23 NM blo 3,100´
  DME unusable:
   248°–258° byd 23 NM blo 3,100´

WAGONER

HEFNER–EASLEY (H68) 2 E UTC–6(–5DT) N35°57.94´ W95°20.51´ DALLAS–FT WORTH
599 B NOTAM FILE MLC L–15E
RWY 18–36: H3401X60 (ASPH) S–12.5 MIRL 0.4% up S IAP
 RWY 18: PAPI(P2L)—GA 3.0° TCH 40´. Trees.
 RWY 36: PAPI(P2R)—GA 3.0° TCH 35´. Tree.
SERVICE: S4 **LGT** PAPI Rwy 18 and Rwy 36 oper consly; MIRL Rwy 18–36 on dusk–dawn.
AIRPORT REMARKS: Unattended. N–S turf used for twy only. Ultralights on and invof arpt.
AIRPORT MANAGER: 918-485-2554
COMMUNICATIONS: CTAF 122.9
Ⓡ **TULSA APP/DEP CON** 119.1
CLEARANCE DELIVERY PHONE: For CD ctc Memphis ARTCC at 901-368-8453/8449.
RADIO AIDS TO NAVIGATION: NOTAM FILE TUL.
 TULSA (H) (H) VORTACW 114.4   TUL   Chan 91   N36°11.78´ W95°47.29´   114° 25.7 NM to fld. 788/8E.
  TACAN AZIMUTH unusable:
   248°–258° byd 23 NM blo 3,100´
  DME unusable:
   248°–258° byd 23 NM blo 3,100´

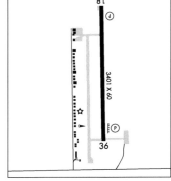

WALTERS MUNI (3O5) 5 W UTC–6(–5DT) N34°22.36´ W98°24.35´ DALLAS–FT WORTH
1058 B NOTAM FILE MLC
RWY 16–34: H2900X50 (ASPH) S–7 MIRL
AIRPORT REMARKS: Unattended. Rwy cntrln markings faded.
AIRPORT MANAGER: 580-875-3337
COMMUNICATIONS: CTAF 122.9
CLEARANCE DELIVERY PHONE: For CD ctc Fort Worth ARTCC at 817-858-7584.

OKLAHOMA 235

WATONGA RGNL (JWG)(KJWG) 1 NW UTC–6(–5DT) N35°51.87´ W98°25.25´   **DALLAS–FT WORTH**
1551   B   NOTAM FILE JWG   **L–15D**
RWY 17–35: H4001X60 (ASPH) S–12.5 MIRL 0.5% up N   **IAP**
  RWY 17: PAPI(P2L)—GA 3.0° TCH 40´. Rgt tfc.
  RWY 35: PAPI(P2L)—GA 3.5° TCH 46´. Tree.
SERVICE: **FUEL** 100LL, JET A   **LGT** MIRL Rwy 17–35 preset low intst;
  to incr intst actvt—CTAF.
AIRPORT REMARKS: Attended Mon–Fri 1400–2300Z‡. Aft hr—
  405–434–3122. Self svc fuel avbl.
AIRPORT MANAGER: 580–623–7350
WEATHER DATA SOURCES: AWOS–3 134.175 (580) 623–7388.
COMMUNICATIONS: CTAF/UNICOM 122.8
Ⓡ **VANCE APP/DEP CON** 126.75 (1300–0200Z‡ wkd, 1900–2300Z‡ Sun;
  clsd Sat & federal hol. Gnd ctl and clnc del svc avbl 15 min prior to
  afld opening. Other times by NOTAM)
Ⓡ **KANSAS CITY CENTER APP/DEP CON** 126.95 (0200–1300Z‡ wkd,
  2300–1900Z‡ Sun; 24 Sat & federal hol. Gnd ctl and clnc del svc
  avbl 15 min prior to afld opening)
CLEARANCE DELIVERY PHONE: For CD ctc Vance Apch at 580–213–6765.
  when Vance Apch is clsd, ctc Kansas City ARTCC at 913–254–8508.
RADIO AIDS TO NAVIGATION: NOTAM FILE MLC.
  KINGFISHER (H) TACAN Chan 94   IFI (114.7)   N35°48.32´
    W98°00.23´   271° 20.6 NM to fld. 1112/9E.

WAYNOKA MUNI (1K5) 1 SE UTC–6(–5DT) N36°34.28´ W98°51.28´   **WICHITA**
1544   B   NOTAM FILE MLC   **L–15D**
RWY 17–35: H3532X60 (ASPH) S–8 MIRL 0.3% up N
  RWY 35: Rgt tfc.
SERVICE: **LGT** ACTIVATE MIRL Rwy 17–35 dusk–dawn—CTAF.
AIRPORT REMARKS: Unattended. Parallel twy clsd indef.
AIRPORT MANAGER: (720) 256–3442
COMMUNICATIONS: CTAF 122.9
CLEARANCE DELIVERY PHONE: For CD ctc Kansas City ARTCC at
  913–254–8508.

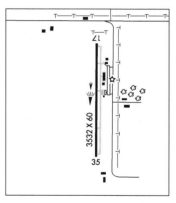

SC, 25 JAN 2024 to 21 MAR 2024

OKLAHOMA

WEATHERFORD STAFFORD (OJA)(KOJA) 2 NE UTC–6(–5DT) N35°32.75´ W98°40.11´   DALLAS–FT WORTH
1605 B NOTAM FILE MLC   H–6H, L–150
RWY 17–35: H5100X75 (CONC) S–30, D–48 MIRL   IAP
  RWY 17: REIL. PAPI(P2L)—GA 3.34° TCH 57´. Trees.
  RWY 35: REIL. PAPI(P2L)—GA 2.92° TCH 41´. P–line.
SERVICE: S4 **FUEL** 100LL, JET A+ **OX** 3, 4 **LGT** REIL Rwy 17 and 35;
  MIRL Rwy 17–35 on SS–SR; incr intst—CTAF. PAPI Rwy 17 and 35 on
  consly.
AIRPORT REMARKS: Attended Mon–Fri 1400–2330Z‡, Sat 1400–2300Z‡,
  Sun 1800–2300Z‡. FBO clsd some hols. Courtesy car avbl.
AIRPORT MANAGER: 580-774-1971
WEATHER DATA SOURCES: AWOS–3PT 118.575 (580) 772–7020.
COMMUNICATIONS: CTAF/UNICOM 122.8
®**FORT WORTH CENTER APP/DEP CON** 128.4
CLEARANCE DELIVERY PHONE: For CD ctc Fort Worth ARTCC at 817-858-7584.
RADIO AIDS TO NAVIGATION: NOTAM FILE MLC.
  KINGFISHER (H) TACAN Chan 94 IFI (114.7) N35°48.32´
  W98°00.23´ 236° 36.0 NM to fld. 1112/9E.

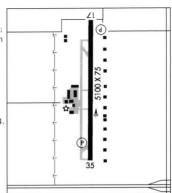

WEST WOODWARD (See WOODWARD on page 237)

WESTPORT (4F1) 2 E UTC–6(–5DT) N36°13.29´ W96°20.79´   KANSAS CITY
901 TPA—1501(600) NOTAM FILE MLC
RWY 03–21: H2900X42 (ASPH) S–10, D–12.5 MIRL 1.0% up NE
SERVICE: **LGT** ACTIVATE MIRL Rwy 03–21—CTAF. Activate Rwy lgts for all ops day & night. Use highest ints for daytime
  ops.
AIRPORT REMARKS: Attended irregularly. Rwy 21 steep uphill slope up to +60´ hill at rwy end and 50´ right of centerline. Gross
  weight limited by airport operator to 6000 lbs single wheel gear.
AIRPORT MANAGER: 918-358-6031
COMMUNICATIONS: CTAF 122.9
CLEARANCE DELIVERY PHONE: For CD ctc Tulsa Apch at 918-831-6714/6720.

WILBURTON MUNI (H05) 4 W UTC–6(–5DT) N34°55.21´ W95°23.63´   DALLAS–FT WORTH
670 B NOTAM FILE MLC   L–17D
RWY 17–35: H3000X60 (ASPH) S–2 MIRL
  RWY 17: PAPI(P2L)—GA 3.0° TCH 40´. Trees.
  RWY 35: PAPI(P2L)—GA 3.0° TCH 40´. Trees.
SERVICE: **LGT** ACTIVATE MIRL Rwy 17–35—CTAF.
AIRPORT REMARKS: Unattended. Deer on and invof rwy. Parl twy pavement
  failed; use south cnctr twy to apn.
AIRPORT MANAGER: 918-465-5361
COMMUNICATIONS: CTAF 122.9
CLEARANCE DELIVERY PHONE: For CD ctc Fort Worth ARTCC at
  817-858-7584.
RADIO AIDS TO NAVIGATION: NOTAM FILE MLC.
  MC ALESTER (L) TACAN Chan 57 MLC (112.0) N34°50.97´
  W95°46.94´ 069° 19.6 NM to fld. 782/8E.

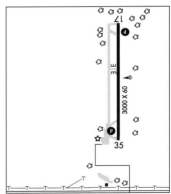

WILEY POST (See OKLAHOMA CITY on page 214)

WILL ROGERS WORLD (See OKLAHOMA CITY on page 215)

WILLIAM R POGUE MUNI (See SAND SPRINGS on page 222)

OKLAHOMA 237

WOODRING   N36°22.43′ W97°47.29′   NOTAM FILE WDG.   **WICHITA**
  (T) (T) **VORW/DME** 109.0   ODG   Chan 27   at Enid Woodring Rgnl. 1151/8E.   **L–15D**
  RCO 122.6 (MC ALESTER RADIO)

WOODWARD

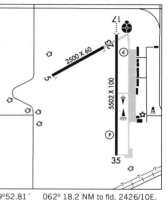

  WEST WOODWARD   (WWR)(KWWR)   6 W   UTC–6(–5DT)   N36°26.28′ W99°31.36′   **WICHITA**
  2189   B   NOTAM FILE WWR   **H–6H, L–15C**
  RWY 17–35: H5502X100 (CONC)   S–30, D–60   M RL   0.5% up S   **IAP**
    RWY 17: ODALS. PAPI(P4L)—GA 3.0° TCH 39′.
    RWY 35: REIL. PAPI(P4L)—GA 3.0° TCH 40′.
  RWY 05–23: H2500X60 (ASPH)   MIRL
    RWY 23: Rgt tfc.
  SERVICE: S2   **FUEL** 100LL, JET A+   **LGT** Actvt and incr intst ODALS Rwy
    17; REIL Rwy 35; MIRL Rwy 17/35, 05/23–CTAF. PAPI Rwy 17 & 35
    24–HR Photo Cell.
  AIRPORT REMARKS: Attended Mon–Fri 1400–0000Z‡; Sat 1400–2200Z‡.
    Unattend Sun and hol. Deer & coyotes on & invof arpt. Ultralight activity
    on and invof arpt. Self svc fuel avbl 24/7. Aft hrs ctc 580–216–8233;
    call out fee. Tetrahedron OTS. 24 hr lounge. Rwy 05 markings faded &
    obscd. Rwy 23 markings faded & obscd.
  AIRPORT MANAGER: 580-334-5786
  WEATHER DATA SOURCES: AWOS–3 118.425 (580) 254–5217.
  COMMUNICATIONS: CTAF/UNICOM 122.8
  ®**KANSAS CITY CENTER APP/DEP CON** 126.95
  CLEARANCE DELIVERY PHONE: For CD ctc Kansas City ARTCC at
    913-254-5289.
  RADIO AIDS TO NAVIGATION: NOTAM FILE GAG.
    MITBEE (VH) (H) VORTACW 115.6   MMB   Chan 103   N36°20.62′ W99°52.81′   062° 18.2 NM to fld. 2426/10E.

SC, 25 JAN 2024 to 21 MAR 2024

TEXAS

ABILENE RGNL (ABI)(KABI) 3 SE UTC−6(−5DT) N32°24.68′ W99°40.91′ DALLAS−FT WORTH
1791 B ARFF Index—See Remarks NOTAM FILE ABI H−6H, L−17B
RWY 17R−35L: H7208X150 (ASPH−GRVD) S−85, D−160, 2S−175, IAP, AD
  2D−160 PCN 61 F/D/X/T HIRL 0.4% up S
  RWY 17R: PAPI(P4L)—GA 3.0° TCH 63′. Rgt tfc.
  RWY 35L: REIL. PAPI(P4L)—GA 3.0° TCH 54′.
RWY 17L−35R: H7198X150 (ASPH−GRVD) S−85, D−160, 2S−165,
  2D−160 PCN 57 F/C/X/T HIRL
  RWY 17L: PAPI(P4L)—GA 3.0° TCH 54′. RVR−R Ground.
  RWY 35R: MALSR. RVR−T Rgt tfc.
RUNWAY DECLARED DISTANCE INFORMATION
  RWY 17L: TORA−7198 TODA−7198 ASDA−7198 LDA−7198
  RWY 17R: TORA−7202 TODA−7202 ASDA−7202 LDA−7202
  RWY 35L: TORA−7202 TODA−7202 ASDA−7202 LDA−7202
  RWY 35R: TORA−7198 TODA−7198 ASDA−7198 LDA−7198
SERVICE: S4 **FUEL** 100LL, JET A, A1+ **OX** 1, 2
AIRPORT REMARKS: Attended continuously. Uncontrolled arpt 2 NM NE of
  arpt pat alt 2300′. Class I, ARFF Index B; ARFF Index C avbl with
  PPR. Mil avn svcs avbl at arpt. Rwy 04−22 permly clsd, not avbl for
  acft opns.
AIRPORT MANAGER: 325-676-6367
WEATHER DATA SOURCES: ASOS (325) 201−9467
COMMUNICATIONS: ATIS 118.25 325−201−9495 **UNICOM** 122.95
  RCO 122.6 (FORT WORTH RADIO)
® **APP/DEP CON** 125.0 EAST 127.2 WEST
  TOWER 120.1 **GND CON** 121.7
AIRSPACE: CLASS C svc ctc APP CON.
RADIO AIDS TO NAVIGATION: NOTAM FILE ABI.
  (VH) (H) VORTACW 113.7 ABI Chan 84 N32°28.88′ W99°51.81′ 104° 10.1 NM to fld. 1809/10E.
  VOR unusable:
    163°−236° byd 40 NM blo 18,000′
    237°−247° byd 40 NM blo 7,000′
    248°−250° byd 40 NM blo 18,000′
    251°−255° byd 40 NM blo 4,500′
    251°−255° byd 46 NM blo 18,000′
  TUSCOLA (L) (L) VORW/DME 111.6 TQA Chan 53 N32°14.14′ W99°49.01′ 023° 12.6 NM to fld.
    2058/10E. NOTAM FILE FTW.
  TOMHI NDB (LOMW) 353 AB N32°17.93′ W99°40.45′ 352° 6.7 NM to fld. 1895/5E.
  LOC/DME 109.75 I−EMB Chan 34(Y) Rwy 17R.
  ILS/DME 110.3 I−ABI Chan 40 Rwy 35R. Class IE. LOM TOMHI NDB. DME unusable byd 17 DME (16 NM).
  ASR

ADDISON (See DALLAS on page 284)

AERO COUNTRY (See MC KINNEY on page 377)

AERO ESTATES (See FRANKSTON on page 313)

AERO ESTATES SPB (See FRANKSTON on page 313)

AERO VALLEY (See ROANOKE on page 409)

SC, 25 JAN 2024 to 21 MAR 2024

TEXAS

AGUA DULCE
OLD HOPPE PLACE (67T) 3 E UTC–6(–5DT) N27°47.98´ W97°51.05´ BROWNSVILLE
96 B NOTAM FILE SJT
RWY 16–34: H3164X30 (CONC) LIRL
  RWY 16: REIL. VASI(V2L)—GA 3.0°. Tn exceeds a 45 deg slope..
  RWY 34: REIL. VASI(V2L)—GA 3.75°. Pole.
SERVICE: LGT For REIL Rwy 16 and Rwy 34; VASI Rwy 16 and Rwy 34; LIRL Rwy 16–34 prior arngmts rqrd. Call 361–998–2516. Arpt bcn dusk–0700Z‡. Rwy lgts are srrndd by 18 in high stakes and razor wire. Rwy 16 and Rwy 34 VASI srndd by 2 ft high razor wire. Rwy 16 and Rwy 34 REIL are non–frangible and are srrndd with 18 inch razor wire.
AIRPORT REMARKS: Attended Mon–Fri 1400–2230Z‡. Wildlife on and invof arpt. Rwy 34, 99 ft AGL lgtd twr 0.35 mile SSE, 140 ft L of rwy cntrln. Rwys 16 and 34 have 40 ft blast pads 30 ft wide. Ldg fee.
AIRPORT MANAGER: 361-998-2516
COMMUNICATIONS: CTAF 122.9
CLEARANCE DELIVERY PHONE: For CD ctc Houston ARTCC at 281-230-5622.

AIR PARK–DALLAS (See DALLAS on page 285)

AIRPARK EAST (See DALLAS on page 285)

AKROVILLE (See SLIDELL on page 426)

ALAMINOS CANYON 25 HHV N26°56.35´ W94°41.32´
AWOS–3 119.075 (713) 431–9699
L–20J, 21A, GOMW

ALAMINOS CANYON BLK 857 GYF N26°07.75´ W94°53.88´/212
AWOS–3P 120.275
L–20J, 21A, GOMW

ALAMINOS CANYON BLOCK 773 AQA N26°13.73´ W94°40.41´/183
AWOS–3PT 119.275 (504) 425–5965
L–20J, 21A, GOMW

ALBANY MUNI (T23) 2 E UTC–6(–5DT) N32°43.28´ W99°16.06´ DALLAS–FT WORTH
1415 B NOTAM FILE FTW H–6H, L–17B
RWY 17–35: H5000X75 (ASPH) S–30 MIRL 0.5% up S IAP
  RWY 17: PAPI(P2L)—GA 3.0° TCH 40´. Road.
  RWY 35: PAPI(P2L)—GA 3.0° TCH 40´. Trees. Rgt tfc.
SERVICE: FUEL 100LL, JET A LGT MIRL Rwy 17–35 preset low intst; to incr intst and ACTVT PAPI Rwy 17 and Rwy 35—123.5.
AIRPORT REMARKS: Attended irregularly. 100LL and JET A avbl 24 hrs self serve.
AIRPORT MANAGER: 325-762-0383
COMMUNICATIONS: CTAF 122.9
®ABILENE APP/DEP CON 125.0
CLEARANCE DELIVERY PHONE: For CD ctc Fort Worth ARTCC at 817-858-7584.
RADIO AIDS TO NAVIGATION: NOTAM FILE ABI.
  ABILENE (VH) (H) VORTACW 113.7 ABI Chan 84 N32°28.88´ W99°51.81´ 054° 33.4 NM to fld. 1809/10E.
  VOR unusable:
    163°–236° byd 40 NM blo 18,000´
    237°–247° byd 40 NM blo 7,000´
    248°–250° byd 40 NM blo 18,000´
    251°–255° byd 40 NM blo 4,500´
    251°–255° byd 46 NM blo 18,000´

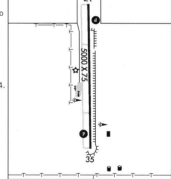

ALFRED C 'BUBBA' THOMAS (See SINTON on page 425)

ALIBI N30°25.92´ W95°28.58´ NOTAM FILE CXO. HOUSTON
NDB (LOMW) 281 CX 141° 5.7 NM to Conroe/North Houston Rgnl. 371/5E.

ALICE INTL (ALI)(KALI) 3 SE UTC−6(−5DT) N27°44.45′ W98°01.62′ BROWNSVILLE
178 B NOTAM FILE ALI H−7B, L−20H
RWY 13−31: H5997X100 (ASPH) S−30 MIRL IAP
  RWY 13: REIL. PAPI(P4L)—GA 3.0° TCH 50′. Road.
  RWY 31: MALS.
RWY 17−35: H4490X100 (ASPH) S−23 MIRL
  RWY 17: PAPI(P2L)—GA 3.0° TCH 44′. Trees.
  RWY 35: PAPI(P2L)—GA 3.0° TCH 44′. P−line.
SERVICE: FUEL 100LL, JET A OX 1, 2, 3, 4 LGT ACTVT MALS Rwy 31; REIL Rwy 13; PAPI Rwy 17 and Rwy 35—CTAF. MIRL Rwy 13−31 and Rwy 17−35 preset low intst dusk−0500Z‡; to incr intst ACTVT—CTAF aft 0500Z‡.
AIRPORT REMARKS: Attended 1400−2300Z‡. Aft hrs svc, call 361−664−2656. 100LL avbl 24 hrs at self−svc pump.
AIRPORT MANAGER: 361-460-0997
WEATHER DATA SOURCES: ASOS 119.225 (361) 668−0069.
COMMUNICATIONS: CTAF/UNICOM 123.0
  RCO 122.6 (SAN ANGELO RADIO)
Ⓡ **KINGSVILLE APP/DEP CON** 119.9 (1345−0600Z‡ Mon−Thu; 1345−2345Z‡ Fri; clsd Sat; Sun and hol exc by NOTAM, hrs subj to chg)
Ⓡ **HOUSTON CENTER APP/DEP CON** 128.15 (0500−1300Z‡ Mon−Thu; 2200−1300Z‡ Fri; 24 Sat, Sun and hol by NOTAM)
CLEARANCE DELIVERY PHONE: For CD if una to ctc on FSS freq, ctc Houston ARTCC at 281-230-5622.
RADIO AIDS TO NAVIGATION: NOTAM FILE CRP.
  CORPUS CHRISTI (VH) (H) VORTACW 115.5 CRP Chan 102 N27°54.23′ W97°26.69′ 244° 32.5 NM to fld. 60/9E.
  TACAN AZIMUTH & DME unusable:
    024°−036° byd 35 NM blo 1,700′
    037°−023° byd 35 NM blo 2,000′
    265°−275°
  VOR unusable:
    340°−005° byd 40 NM blo 7,000′
    340°−005° byd 84 NM
    Byd 30 NM blo 1,500′
  TACAN AZIMUTH unusable:
    080°−085° byd 30 NM
  (VL) VORW 114.5 ALI N27°44.39′ W98°01.28′ at fld. 170/6E. NOTAM FILE ALI.
  VOR unusable:
    352°−002° byd 40 NM
  LOC/DME 109.3 I−ALI Chan 30 Rwy 31. LOC/DME unmonitored.

TEXAS

ALPINE

ALPINE–CASPARIS MUNI (E38)   2 NW   UTC–6(–5DT)   N30°23.05´ W103°41.02´   EL PASO
4514   B   NOTAM FILE E38   H–7A, L–6J
RWY 01–19: H6002X75 (ASPH)   S–12.5   MIRL   1.1% up S   IAP
  RWY 01: PAPI(P2L)—GA 3.5° TCH 40´. P–line.
  RWY 19: PAPI(P2L)—GA 3.0° TCH 40´. Fence.
RWY 05–23: H5018X60 (ASPH)   S–12.5   MIRL   1.2% up SW
  RWY 05: Fence.
  RWY 23: Road.
SERVICE: S4   FUEL 100LL, JET A, A1+   LGT Dusk–dawn. MIRL Rwy 01–19 preset low intst; to incr intst and actvt MIRL Rwy 05–23—CTAF. PAPI Rwy 01 does not prvd obstn clnc byd 2 NM fm thr.
AIRPORT REMARKS: Attended Mon–Fri 1400–2300Z‡, Sat–Sun 1400–2200Z‡. Unatndd major hols. Aft hrs call–in fee.
AIRPORT MANAGER: 432-837-5929
WEATHER DATA SOURCES: AWOS–3 119.025 (432) 837-9613.
COMMUNICATIONS: CTAF/UNICOM 122.8
®ALBUQUERQUE CENTER APP/DEP CON 135.875
CLEARANCE DELIVERY PHONE: For CD ctc Albuquerque ARTCC at 505-856-4861.
RADIO AIDS TO NAVIGATION: NOTAM FILE FST.
  FORT STOCKTON (VH) (H) VORTACW 116.9   FST   Chan 116
  N30°57.13´ W102°58.54´   216° 50.0 NM to fld. 2893/11E.
  VOR unusable:
    020°–055° byd 20 NM blo 6,900´
    070°–086° byd 35 NM blo 6,400´
    106°–132° byd 30 NM blo 5,900´
    125°–202° byd 40 NM
    203°–213° byd 40 NM blo 18,000´
    214°–230° byd 40 NM
    245°–255° byd 40 NM
    315°–330° byd 30 NM blo 5,400´

TERLINGUA RANCH (1E2)   57 SE   UTC–6(–5DT)   N29°27.09´ W103°23.86´   EL PASO
3769   NOTAM FILE SJT
RWY 02–20: 4700X80 (GRVL–DIRT)   2.8% up SW
  RWY 02: Trees.
  RWY 20: Road.
AIRPORT REMARKS: Unattended. Wildlife on and invof arpt. Four–wheelers xng rwy. Arpt srndd by +500´–600´ mtns. 5–15´ brush/trees srnd rwy at edge, 80´ rwy wid may nct be avbl full len. Rwy 02–20 rwy rough and uneven gravel. Rwy slopes up fm NE to SW 128´ (2.7%).
AIRPORT MANAGER: 210-415-3040
COMMUNICATIONS: CTAF 122.9
CLEARANCE DELIVERY PHONE: For CD ctc Albuquerque ARTCC at 505-856-4861.

ALVIN AIRPARK (6R5)   3 W   UTC–6(–5DT)   N29°24.89´ W95°17.34´   HOUSTON
43   NOTAM FILE CXO   COPTER
RWY 06–24: 1500X80 (TURF)
  RWY 06: P–line.
  RWY 24: Trees.
RWY 03–21: 1420X75 (TURF)
  RWY 03: Trees.
  RWY 21: Trees.
RWY 12–30: 830X60 (TURF)
  RWY 12: P–line.
  RWY 30: Trees.
AIRPORT REMARKS: Unattended. Radio control model acft oprg area adj to arpt, NW. Rwy 03, 6 ft fence 40 ft SE of cntrln alg SE edge. +50 ft trees alg Rwy 03 right of cntrln. Rwy 21, 6 ft fence 20 ft fm thr 0B. 30 ft trees alg Rwy 21 left of cntrln. 6 ft arpt scty fence. All gates locked. For ingress or egress, ctc amgr. Rwy 03–21, Rwy 06–24, and Rwy 12–30 surfaces defined by mowing. Dfclt to dtrm rwy dimensions. Rwy sfc rough & uneven.
AIRPORT MANAGER: (713) 208-8707
COMMUNICATIONS: CTAF 122.9
CLEARANCE DELIVERY PHONE: For CD ctc Houston Apch at 281-443-5844 to cnl IFR call 281-443-5888.

AMARILLO

BUFFALO (1E7) 9 S UTC−6(−5DT) N35°03.83′ W101°52.66′   DALLAS–FT WORTH
3640 B NOTAM FILE FTW
RWY 02–20: 6200X150 (TURF)   LIRL(NSTD)
  RWY 02: Fence.
  RWY 20: Tree. Rgt tfc.
RWY 08–26: 1600X102 (TURF)
  RWY 08: P–line.
  RWY 26: Road.
SERVICE: LGT Dusk–0700Z‡. Rwy 02–20 Nonstd LIRL; first 3000′ north end of rwy lgtd. Thr lgts at north end only.
AIRPORT REMARKS: Attended irregularly. Radio controlled model acft act north end of arpt. Rwy 02–20 and Rwy 08–26 not mntnd, not mowed publd len and wid.
AIRPORT MANAGER: (806) 236-1109
COMMUNICATIONS: CTAF/UNICOM 122.8
CLEARANCE DELIVERY PHONE: For CD ctc Albuquerque ARTCC at 505-856-4861.

PALO DURO (1E4) 3 S UTC−6(−5DT) N35°08.62′ W101°50.35′   DALLAS–FT WORTH
3639 NOTAM FILE FTW
RWY 17–35: 3700X50 (TURF-GRVL)
  RWY 17: P–line.
  RWY 35: Fence.
AIRPORT REMARKS: Unattended. Arpt fenced, gates locked, no aces. Rwy not suitable for acft. Arpt hazus for tsnts; rwy not mkd or defined; 63′ transmission line acrs thr Rwy 17. Rwy 17–35 soft when wet on S end; loose grvl on rwy, vegetation on rwy.
AIRPORT MANAGER: 806-376-5853
COMMUNICATIONS: CTAF 122.9
CLEARANCE DELIVERY PHONE: For CD ctc Albuquerque ARTCC at 505-856-4861.

RICK HUSBAND AMARILLO INTL (AMA)(KAMA) 7 E UTC−6(−5DT) N35°13.16′ W101°42.36′   DALLAS–FT WORTH
3607 B TPA—See Remarks LRA ARFF Index—See Remarks NOTAM FILE AMA   H–6G, L–15B
RWY 04–22: H13502X200 (CONC–GRVD) S–100, D–200, 2S–175,   IAP, AD
  2D–400 PCN 176R/C/W/T HIRL(NSTD)
  RWY 04: MALSR. PAPI(P4L)—GA 3.0° TCH 61′. RVR–T
  RWY 22: MALSR. PAPI(P4L)—GA 3.0° TCH 77′. RVR–R
RWY 13–31: H7901X150 (CONC–GRVD) S–100, D–200, 2S–175,
  2D–400 PCN 89 R/B/W/T HIRL
  RWY 13: REIL. PAPI(P4L)—GA 3.0° TCH 52′.
  RWY 31: PAPI(P4L)—GA 3.0° TCH 52′.
RUNWAY DECLARED DISTANCE INFORMATION
  RWY 04: TORA–13502 TODA–13502 ASDA–13502 LDA–13502
  RWY 13: TORA–7901 TODA–7901 ASDA–7901 LDA–7901
  RWY 22: TORA–13502 TODA–13502 ASDA–13502 LDA–13502
  RWY 31: TORA–7901 TODA–7901 ASDA–7901 LDA–7901
SERVICE: S4 FUEL 100LL, JET A1+ OX 2, 4 LGT When ATCT clsd, to incr intst and ACTVT MALSR Rwys 04 and 22; REIL Rwy 13; HIRL Rwys 04–22, 13–31; all twys—CTAF.
AIRPORT REMARKS: Attended continuously. Tiltrotor acft activity invof arpt. Class I, ARFF Index B. Index C equip avbl upon req. TPA for propeller acft 4502 (895), turbojet acft 5002 (1395), overhead 5502 (1895). Rwy 04–22 center 130′ grvd full length. RWY 04 RVR AVBL 1200–0600Z‡ CTC TWR. Rwy 04–22 NSTD HIRL due to spacing. HIRL 50 ft from rwy edge, NSTD dstc fm cntrln–pavement outside rwy edge stripes may not be full strength and depth perception problems may exist during periods of darkness. Flight Notification Service (ADCUS) available. Lndg fee.
AIRPORT MANAGER: 806-354-7721
WEATHER DATA SOURCES: ASOS 118.85 (806) 335–1060.
COMMUNICATIONS: CTAF 118.3 ATIS 118.85 UNICOM 122.95
  AMARILLO RCO 122.3 (FORT WORTH RADIO) (0600–1200Z‡)
Ⓡ APP/DEP CON 119.5 (1200–0600Z‡)
Ⓡ ALBUQUERQUE CENTER APP/DEP CON 127.85 (0600–1200Z‡)
  TOWER 118.3 (1200–0600Z‡) GND CON 121.9 CLNC DEL 121.65
CLEARANCE DELIVERY PHONE: For CD if una to ctc on FSS freq, ctc Albuquerque ARTCC at 505-856-4561.
AIRSPACE: CLASS C svc ctc APP CON svc 1200–0600Z‡; other times CLASS E.

CONTINUED ON NEXT PAGE

TEXAS

CONTINUED FROM PRECEDING PAGE

    RADIO AIDS TO NAVIGATION: NOTAM FILE FTW.
      PANHANDLE (H) (H) VORTACW 116.6   PNH   Chan 113   N35°14.10´ W101°41.94´   at fld. 3595/8E.
      PANDE NDB (LOMW) 251   AM   N35°08.79´ W101°48.33´   040° 6.6 NM to fld. 3609/8E.   NOTAM FILE AMA.
         NDB unmonitored when ATCT clsd.
      ILS 110.3   I–AMA   Rwy 04.   Class IB.   LOM PANDE NDB. Unmonitored when ATCT clsd.
      LDA/DME 111.1   I–RIQ   Chan 48   Rwy 22.
      ASR (1200–0600Z‡)

RIVER FALLS (H81)   9 SE   UTC–6(–5DT)   N35°04.89´ W101°45.35´   **DALLAS–FT WORTH**
3585   B   NOTAM FILE H81   **H–6G, L–15B**
RWY 17–35: H6015X60 (ASPH)   MIRL
    RWY 17: Thld dsplcd 151´. Road.
    RWY 35: Rgt tfc.
RWY 04–22: 3200X70 (TURF)
    RWY 04: Rgt tfc.
    RWY 22: Bldg.
SERVICE: S2   **FUEL** 100LL, JET A1+   **LGT** ACTVT MIRL Rwy 17–35—CTAF. PCL click PTT slowly no more than once per second. Rwy 17 nonstd dsplcd thr lgts–incor colors.
AIRPORT REMARKS: Unattended. For fuel call 806–340–6790. Rwy 17 dsplcd thr not mkd. Dsplcd thr lgts 416 fm rwy end. 5599 ft avbl ngts. Rwy 35 markings faded.
AIRPORT MANAGER: (806) 670–5836
COMMUNICATIONS: CTAF/UNICOM 122.725
CLEARANCE DELIVERY PHONE: For CD ctc Albuquerque ARTCC at 505–856–4861.
RADIO AIDS TO NAVIGATION: NOTAM FILE FTW.
    PANHANDLE (H) (H) VORTACW 116.6   PNH   Chan 113   N35°14.10´ W101°41.94´   189° 9.6 NM to fld. 3595/8E.

TRADEWIND (TDW)(KTDW)   3 SE   UTC–6(–5DT)   N35°10.19´ W101°49.55´   **DALLAS–FT WORTH**
3649   B   NOTAM FILE FTW   **H–6G, L–15B**
RWY 17–35: H5098X60 (ASPH)   S–16   MIRL   **IAP**
    RWY 17: REIL. PVASI(PSIL)—GA 3.0° TCH 25´. Thld dsplcd 290´. Fence. Rgt tfc.
    RWY 35: REIL. Thld dsplcd 289´. Trees.
RWY 05–23: H3000X60 (ASPH)   S–20   MIRL   0.5% up SW
    RWY 05: Fence.
    RWY 23: Pole. Rgt tfc.
SERVICE: S4   **FUEL** 100LL, JET A1+   **OX** 3   **LGT** Actvt MIRL Rwys 05–23 and 17–35—CTAF.
AIRPORT REMARKS: Attended 1300–0400Z‡. Aft hrs svc 806–376–1008. Housing and school surrounds Rwy 23 end.
AIRPORT MANAGER: 806-376-1008
WEATHER DATA SOURCES: AWOS–AV 118.475 (806) 350–7407.
COMMUNICATIONS: CTAF/UNICOM 122.8
®**AMARILLO APP/DEP CON** 119.5 (1200–0600Z‡)
®**ALBUQUERQUE CENTER APP/DEP CON** 127.85 (0600–1200Z‡)
    CLNC DEL 125.4
CLEARANCE DELIVERY PHONE: For CD ctc Albuquerque ARTCC at 505–856–4861.
RADIO AIDS TO NAVIGATION: NOTAM FILE FTW.
    PANHANDLE (H) (H) VORTACW 116.6   PNH   Chan 113   N35°14.10´ W101°41.94´   230° 7.4 NM to fld. 3595/8E.
    PANDE NDB (LOMW) 251   AM   N35°08.79´ W101°48.33´   317° 1.7 NM to fld. 3609/8E.   NOTAM FILE AMA.
        NDB unmonitored when ATCT clsd.

• • • • • • • • • • • • • • •

HELIPAD H1: H50X50 (ASPH)

AMASON   N31°49.97´ W94°09.23´   NOTAM FILE CXO.   **HOUSTON**
    NDB (MHW) 341   CZJ   at Center Muni. 329/4E.   **L–19E**

AMBASSADOR   N32°35.13´ W95°06.79´   NOTAM FILE FTW.   **DALLAS–FT. WORTH**
    NDB (MHW) 404   ABG   424/7E. (VFR only).

ANAHUAC

CHAMBERS CO (T00) 1 E UTC−6(−5DT) N29°46.19′ W94°39.81′ HOUSTON
21 B NOTAM FILE CXO L−19E, 21A, GOMW
RWY 12−30: H3005X60 (ASPH) S−13 MIRL IAP
 RWY 12: PAPI(P2L)—GA 4.0° TCH 28′. Pole.
 RWY 30: Road. Rgt tfc.
RWY 17−35: 1900X300 (TURF)
 RWY 17: Trees.
 RWY 35: Road. Rgt tfc.
SERVICE: FUEL 100LL, JET A, A1+ **LGT** Dusk−dawn. MIRL Rwy 12−30 preset low intst; to incr intst actvt—CTAF.
AIRPORT REMARKS: Attended Mon−Fri 1400−2300Z‡. 100LL 24 hr self−serve. Rwy 17−35 soft when wet. Rwy 17, PAPI Rwy 12 in Rwy 17 apch, do not land bfr xng Rwy 12.
AIRPORT MANAGER: 409−267−2719
COMMUNICATIONS: CTAF 122.9
®**HOUSTON APP/DEP CON** 134.35
CLEARANCE DELIVERY PHONE: For CD ctc Houston Apch at 281−443−5844 to cnl IFR call 281−443−5888.
RADIO AIDS TO NAVIGATION: NOTAM FILE CXO.
 TRINITY (VL) (DL) VORW/DME 114.75 MHF Chan 94(Y) N29°32.78′ W94°44.85′ 011° 14.1 NM to fld. 38/7E.
 VOR unusable:
  060°−079° byd 40 NM
  080°−090° byd 40 NM blo 6,000′
  080°−090° byd 50 NM blo 8,000′
  091°−109° byd 40 NM
  110°−190° blo 2,000′

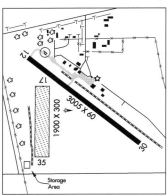

ANDREWS CO (E11) 1 NE UTC−6(−5DT) N32°19.85′ W102°31.78′ ALBUQUERQUE
3174 B NOTAM FILE SJT H−6G, L−6H
RWY 16−34: H5816X75 (ASPH) S−23, D−37 MIRL IAP
 RWY 16: REIL. PAPI(P4L)—GA 3.0° TCH 37′. Ground.
 RWY 34: REIL. PAPI(P4L)—GA 3.0° TCH 34′. Trees. Rgt tfc.
RWY 02−20: H3893X75 (ASPH) S−23 MIRL
 RWY 02: PAPI(P2L)—GA 3.0° TCH 26′. Thld dsplcd 954′. Trees. Rgt tfc.
 RWY 20: PAPI(P2L)—GA 3.0° TCH 42′. Trees.
RWY 11−29: H3048X75 (ASPH) S−17 0.3% up W
 RWY 11: Trees.
 RWY 29: Road. Rgt tfc.
SERVICE: S2 **FUEL** 100LL, JET A **LGT** Actvt REIL Rwy 16 and 34; PAPI Rwy 02−20; MIRL Rwy 02−20 and 16−34—CTAF. PAPI Rwy 16 and 34 opr consly.
AIRPORT REMARKS: Attended Mon−Fri 1400−2300Z‡. 5′−10′ dirt mounds 465′ fm Rwy 16 thr across extdd cntrln.
AIRPORT MANAGER: 432−524−1447
WEATHER DATA SOURCES: AWOS−3 118.2 (432) 524−2471.
COMMUNICATIONS: CTAF/UNICOM 122.8
®**MIDLAND APP/DEP CON** 124.6 (1200−0600Z‡)
®**FORT WORTH CENTER APP/DEP CON** 133.1 (0600−1200Z‡)
CLEARANCE DELIVERY PHONE: For CD ctc midland Apch at 432−563−2123. when Apch clsd ctc Fort Worth ARTCC at 817−858−7584.
RADIO AIDS TO NAVIGATION: NOTAM FILE MAF.
 MIDLAND (L) (L) VORTACW 114.8 MAF Chan 95 N32°00.56′ W102°11.42′ 307° 25.9 NM to fld. 2860/11E.
 VOR unusable:
  010°−020° byd 8 NM blo 8,000′

HELIPAD H1: H25X25 (ASPH)
HELIPORT REMARKS: Helipad H1 60′ pole 204′ east.

ANGELINA CO (See LUFKIN on page 370)

TEXAS

ANGLETON

BAILES (7R9) 2 E UTC–6(–5DT) N29°09.90′ W95°24.07′   HOUSTON
   21   NOTAM FILE CXO
  RWY 17–35: 2060X50 (TURF)
    RWY 17: Tree.
    RWY 35: Trees. Rgt tfc.
  AIRPORT REMARKS: Unattended. Rwy 17 end mkd w/conc. pad. Rwy 35 end mkd with white tires, 500 ft north of tree line at south bdry. Rwy mkgs obsc by vegetation.
  AIRPORT MANAGER: 979-549-6848
  COMMUNICATIONS: CTAF 122.9
  CLEARANCE DELIVERY PHONE: For CD ctc Houston Apch at 281-443-5844 to cnl IFR call 281-443-5888.

FLYIN TIGER (81D) 6 N UTC–6(–5DT) N29°15.90′ W95°24.75′   HOUSTON
   30   NOTAM FILE CXO   COPTER
  RWY 16–34: 2261X90 (TURF)
    RWY 16: Trees.
    RWY 34: Trees.
  RWY 17–35: 2200X80 (TURF)
    RWY 17: Tree.
    RWY 35: Trees.
  AIRPORT REMARKS: Unattended. Power lines buried in Rwy 16 and Rwy 17 apch. Rwy 16–34, 3 ft berm at south th. Rwy 16 and Rwy 17, 15 ft rd acrs rwy end.
  AIRPORT MANAGER: 281-889-8078
  COMMUNICATIONS: CTAF 122.9
  CLEARANCE DELIVERY PHONE: For CD ctc Houston Apch at 281-443-5844 to cnl IFR call 281-443-5888.

ANGLETON/LAKE JACKSON

TEXAS GULF COAST RGNL (LBX)(KLBX) 4 SW UTC–6(–5DT) N29°06.52′ W95°27.73′   HOUSTON
   25   B   Class IV, ARFF Index A   NOTAM FILE LBX   H–7C, L–19D, 21A, GOMW
  RWY 17–35: H7000X100 (CONC–GRVD) S–60, D–95, 2S–120, 2D–120 MIRL   IAP
    RWY 17: MALSR. PAPI(P4L)—GA 3.0° TCH 52′. Rgt tfc.
    RWY 35: PAPI(P4L)—GA 3.0° TCH 40′.
  RUNWAY DECLARED DISTANCE INFORMATION
    RWY 17: TORA–7000 TODA–7000 ASDA–7000 LDA–7000
    RWY 35: TORA–7000 TODA–7000 ASDA–7000 LDA–7000
  SERVICE: S6 **FUEL** 100LL, JET A **OX** 4 **LGT** MIRL Rwy 17–35 preset low intst; to incr intst and ACTVT MALSR Rwy 17—CTAF. PAPI Rwys 17 and 35 opr consly.
  AIRPORT REMARKS: Attended Mon–Fri 1230–0030Z‡, Sat–Sun 1400–0030Z‡. 100LL fuel avbl 24 hrs self service. For Jet A fuel after hrs call 979–319–2740. Arpt located 4.6 NM NW of Lake Jackson. Air carrier ops involving acft with more than 30 passengers are not authorized in excess of 15 min before or after scheduled arrival or departure times without prior coordination with arpt manager and confirmation that ARFF svcs are avbl prior to ldg or tkf.
  AIRPORT MANAGER: 979-849-5755
  WEATHER DATA SOURCES: ASOS 119.925 (979) 849–3319.
  COMMUNICATIONS: CTAF/UNICOM 123.0
  ®**HOUSTON APP/DEP CON** 134.35
    CLNC DEL 125.2
  CLEARANCE DELIVERY PHONE: For CD ctc Houston Apch at 281-443-5844. To cnl IFR ctc Houston Apch at 281-443-5888.
  RADIO AIDS TO NAVIGATION: NOTAM FILE GLS.
    SCHOLES (VH) (DH) VORW/DME 113.0 VUH Chan 77 N29°16.16′ W94°52.06′ 247° 32.7 NM to fld. 4/6E.
      VOR unusable:
        285°–295° byd 35 NM blo 2,500′
    ILS/DME 109.1 I–LBX Chan 28 Rwy 17. Class IE.

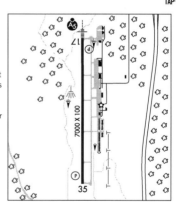

ARANSAS CO (See ROCKPORT on page 411)

ARCHER CITY MUNI (T39) 1 SE UTC–6(–5DT) N33°34.94´ W98°37.12´   DALLAS–FT WORTH
1065 NOTAM FILE FTW   L–17B
RWY 17–35: H3200X60 (ASPH–TURF) S–12.5
  RWY 17: Road.
SERVICE: S2
AIRPORT REMARKS: Unattended. Wildlife on and invof arpt. Rwy 17–35
  CLOSED indefly; under repair. Rwy 17–35 loose grvl, tall grass on rwy.
  Rwy mostly turf.
AIRPORT MANAGER: 940-631-4519
COMMUNICATIONS: CTAF 122.9
CLEARANCE DELIVERY PHONE: For CD ctc Fort Worth ARTCC at
  817-858-7584.
RADIO AIDS TO NAVIGATION: NOTAM FILE SPS.
  WICHITA FALLS (H) (H) VORTACW 112.7   SPS Chan 74   N33°59.24´
    W98°35.61´   173° 24.3 NM to fld. 1133/10E.

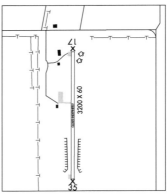

ARESTI AERODROME (See GODLEY on page 320)

ARLEDGE FLD (See STAMFORD on page 429)

ARLINGTON MUNI (GKY)(KGKY) 4 S   UTC–6(–5DT) N32°39.83´ W97°05.66´   DALLAS–FT WORTH
628 B NOTAM FILE GKY   COPTER
RWY 16–34: H6080X100 (CONC) S–60 MIRL 0.5% up NW   H–6H, L–17C, A
  RWY 16: REIL. PAPI(P4L)—GA 3.0° TCH 42´.   IAP, AD
  RWY 34: MALSR. PAPI(P4L)—GA 3.0° TCH 55´.
SERVICE: S4 **FUEL** 100LL, JET A OX 4 **LGT** MIRL Rwy 16–34 preset
  med intst; higher intst by ATCT req. When ATCT clsd ACTVT MALSR
  Rwy 34—CTAF.
AIRPORT REMARKS: Attended continuously. 100LL self serve fuel. Extsv hel
  tfc west of rwy.
AIRPORT MANAGER: 817-459-5571
WEATHER DATA SOURCES: ASOS 127.375 (817) 557-0251.
COMMUNICATIONS: CTAF 128.625
Ⓡ **REGIONAL APP/DEP CON** 118.1 124.3 125.2 125.8 135.975 (North)
  125.8 135.975 (South) 118.1 125.8
TOWER 128.625 (1300–0300Z‡) **GND CON/CLNC DEL** 121.875
CLNC DEL 118.85 (RGNL APP CON when twr clsd)
AIRSPACE: CLASS D svc 1300–0300Z‡; other times CLASS G.
RADIO AIDS TO NAVIGATION: NOTAM FILE FTW.
  MAVERICK (VH) (H) VORW/DME 113.1   TTT   Chan 78   N32°52.15´
    W97°02.43´   186° 12.6 NM to fld. 536/6E.
    All acft arriving DFW are requested to turn DME off until departure
    due to traffic overload of Maverick DME
  DME unusable:
    180°–190° byd 10 NM
    240°–260° byd 20 NM blo 3,500´
  VOR unusable:
    105°–110° byd 40 NM
  ILS/DME 111.55 I-GKY Chan 52(Y) Rwy 34. Class IE. LOC unusable byd 15° right of course. Unmonitored when
    ATCT clsd.

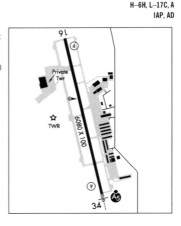

ARVILLA N33°03.98´ W96°03.68´ NOTAM FILE GVT.   DALLAS–FT WORTH
  (T) TACAN 109.6   MJF Chan 33 at Majors. 543/5E.   L–17D
    DME unusable:
      024°–034° byd 16 NM blo 3,000´
      080°–095° byd 5 NM
    TACAN AZIMUTH unusable:
      024°–034° byd 16 NM blo 3,000´
      080°–095° byd 5 NM
      212°–222° byd 12 NM blo 3,500´

TEXAS 247

ASPERMONT

STONEWALL CO (T6Ø) 1 NE UTC−6(−5DT) N33°10.22′ W100°11.84′ **DALLAS–FT WORTH**
1744 B NOTAM FILE FTW L−17B
RWY 17−35: H4000X60 (ASPH) S−12.5 MIRL 0.7% up S
  RWY 35: P−line.
AIRPORT REMARKS: Unattended. Agricultural activity May–Sep. Gate locked.
  Call AMGR for combination or access. 940−200−0894 AMGR cell.
AIRPORT MANAGER: 940−989−3393
COMMUNICATIONS: CTAF 122.9
CLEARANCE DELIVERY PHONE: For CD ctc Fort Worth ARTCC at 817−858−7584.
RADIO AIDS TO NAVIGATION: NOTAM FILE ABI.
  ABILENE (VH) (H) VORTACW 113.7 ABI Chan 84 N32°28.88′
    W99°51.81′ 328° 44.6 NM to fld. 1809/10E.
  VOR unusable:
    163°−236° byd 40 NM blo 18,000′
    237°−247° byd 40 NM blo 7,000′
    248°−250° byd 40 NM blo 18,000′
    251°−255° byd 40 NM blo 4,500′
    251°−255° byd 46 NM blo 18,000′

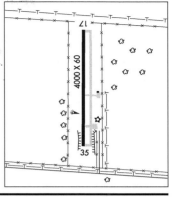

ATHENS MUNI (F44) 3 SE UTC−6(−5DT) N32°09.83′ W95°49.70′ **DALLAS–FT WORTH**
444 B NOTAM FILE FTW L−17D
RWY 18−36: H3988X60 (ASPH) S−25 MIRL IAP
  RWY 18: PAPI(P2L)—GA 3.0° TCH 37′. Fence.
  RWY 36: PAPI(P2L)—GA 4.0° TCH 47′. Trees. Rgt tfc.
SERVICE: S4 **FUEL** 100LL, JET A **OX** 3, 4
AIRPORT REMARKS: Attended 1400Z‡—dusk. Feral hcgs on and invof arpt.
AIRPORT MANAGER: 903−675−0066
WEATHER DATA SOURCES: AWOS−3PT 119.6 (903) 670−1247.
COMMUNICATIONS: CTAF/UNICOM 123.0
®**FORT WORTH CENTER APP/DEP CON** 135.25
CLEARANCE DELIVERY PHONE: For CD ctc Fort Worth ARTCC at
  817−858−7584.
RADIO AIDS TO NAVIGATION: NOTAM FILE FTW.
  FRANKSTON (L) (L) VORW/DME 111.4 FZT Chan 51 N32°04.48′
    W95°31.85′ 283° 16.1 NM to fld. 305/6E.
  VOR portion unusable:
    270°−293° byd 5 NM blo 8,000′
    293°−295° byd 25 NM blo 3,500′
    295°−340° byd 20 NM

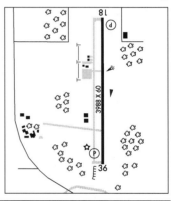

SC, 25 JAN 2024 to 21 MAR 2024

TEXAS

ATLANTA

HALL–MILLER MUNI (ATA)(KATA) 2 SW UTC–6(–5DT) N33°06.15′ W94°11.70′
280 B NOTAM FILE FTW
RWY 05–23: H3800X60 (ASPH) S–12.5 MIRL 0.3% up SW
  RWY 05: REIL. PAPI(P2L)—GA 4.0° TCH 29′. Trees.
  RWY 23: REIL. PAPI(P2L)—GA 4.0° TCH 30′. Trees.
RWY 15–33: 2264X75 (TURF)   0.5% up NW
  RWY 15: Trees.
  RWY 33: Trees.
SERVICE: **FUEL** 100LL **LGT** Actvt REIL rwy 05 and rwy 23; MIRL rwy 05/23—CTAF.
AIRPORT REMARKS: Attended irregularly. Fuel avbl 24 hrs self-serve. Feral hogs and deer on arpt. Rwy 05 trrn slopes +20′ 670′ fm thr. Rwy 15 marked with 1′ yellow plastic pipes. Rwy 23, 24′ mkd powerline 500′ dstc. Rwy 33, 42′ mkd powerline, 285′ dstc.
AIRPORT MANAGER: 903-796-2192
WEATHER DATA SOURCES: AWOS–3 118.250 (903) 799–4066.
COMMUNICATIONS: CTAF 122.9
®**FORT WORTH CENTER APP/DEP CON** 123.925
CLEARANCE DELIVERY PHONE: For CD ctc Fort Worth ARTCC at 817-858-7584.
RADIO AIDS TO NAVIGATION: NOTAM FILE TXK.
  TEXARKANA (VH) (H) **VORTACW** 116.3   TXK   Chan 110   N33°30.83′ W94°04.39′   187° 25.4 NM to fld. 273/7E.
  ATLANTA NDB (MHW) 347   ATA   N33°06.25′ W94°11.40′   at fld. 263/4E. NOTAM FILE FTW.

MEMPHIS
L–17E
IAP

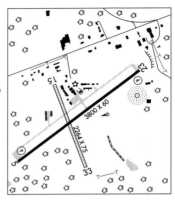

AUSTIN

AUSTIN EXEC (EDC)(KEDC) 12 NE UTC–6(–5DT) N30°23.85′ W97°33.98′
620 B NOTAM FILE EDC
RWY 13–31: H6025X100 (ASPH) D–101 MIRL 0.4% up NW
  RWY 13: REIL. PAPI(P4L)—GA 3.0° TCH 40′. Thld dsplcd 600′. Tree.
  RWY 31: REIL. PAPI(P4L)—GA 3.0° TCH 40′.
RWY 16–34: H1550X25 (ASPH) S–8 1.0% up N
SERVICE: S4 **FUEL** 100LL, JET A **LGT** ACTVT REIL Rwys 13 and 31; MIRL Rwy 13–31—CTAF. PAPI Rwys 13 and 31 opr consly.
AIRPORT REMARKS: Attended continuously. Rwys 16–34 CLOSED indefly. Rwy 16–34 extsv cracking, vegetation growing through. NW end of Rwy 13–31 and Twy A has a 16′ drop off at end of pavement. Rwy 13–31 twy edges are mkd by reflector posts.
AIRPORT MANAGER: 512-247-7678
WEATHER DATA SOURCES: AWOS–3 118.825 (512) 616–2967.
COMMUNICATIONS: CTAF 120.3 UNICOM 122.975
®**AUSTIN APP/DEP CON** 127.225
EXECUTIVE TOWER 120.3 (1200–0400Z‡)
GND CON 119.45 **CLNC DEL** 126.025 (Aus App/Dep when EDC twr clsd)
CLEARANCE DELIVERY PHONE: For CD ctc Austin Apch at 512-369-7865.
AIRSPACE: CLASS D svc 1200–0400Z‡; other times CLASS E.
RADIO AIDS TO NAVIGATION: NOTAM FILE AUS.
  CENTEX (VH) (H) **VORTACW** 112.8   CWK   Chan 75   N30°22.71′ W97°31.79′   295° 2.2 NM to fld. 593/6E.
  VOR unusable:
    180°–190° byd 40 NM
    200°–210° byd 40 NM
COMM/NAV/WEATHER REMARKS: VFR deps requesting ATC svc remain clear of the final apch crs of Rwys 17L and 17R. If the acft is initially eastbound, ctc AUS Apch Ctl on 127.22. If the acft is initially westbound ctc AUS Apch Ctl on 125.32. AUS Clearance Delivery 126.025.

SAN ANTONIO
H–7C, L–19C, 21A
IAP, AD

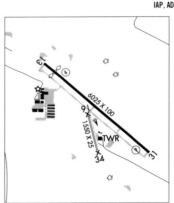

SC, 25 JAN 2024 to 21 MAR 2024

TEXAS

AUSTIN–BERGSTROM INTL (AUS)(KAUS) P (ARNG)   5 SE   UTC–6(–5DT)   N30°11.67′   **SAN ANTONIO**
W97°40.19′   H–7C, L–19C, 21A
542   B   LRA   Class I, ARFF Index D   NOTAM FILE AUS   IAP, AD

RWY 18R–36L: H12250X150 (CONC–GRVD)   S–75, D–210, 2D–618, 2D/2D2–913 PCN 98 R/B/W/T   HIRL
  RWY 18R: MALS. PAPI(P4L)—GA 3.0° TCH 60′. RVR–TR Rgt tfc.
  RWY 36L: MALS. PAPI(P4L)—GA 3.0° TCH 60′. RVR–TR
RWY 18L–36R: H9000X150 (CONC–GRVD)   S–75, D–210, 2D–618, 2D/2D2–913 PCN 92 R/B/W/T   HIRL   CL
  RWY 18L: ALSF2. TDZL. PAPI(P4L)—GA 3.0° TCH 74′. RVR–TMR Tower.
  RWY 36R: MALSR. TDZL. PAPI(P4L)—GA 3.0° TCH 59′. RVR–TMR Rgt tfc.

RUNWAY DECLARED DISTANCE INFORMATION
  RWY 18L: TORA–9000   TODA–9000   ASDA–9000   LDA–9000
  RWY 18R: TORA–12250 TODA–12250   ASDA–12250   LDA–12250
  RWY 36L: TORA–12250 TODA–12250   ASDA–12250   LDA–12250
  RWY 36R: TORA–9000   TODA–9000   ASDA–9000   LDA–9000

SERVICE: S2   **FUEL** 100LL, JET A   **OX** 3, 4   **MILITARY**— **FUEL** A+ (C512–530–5451) (NC–100LL, A) **FLUID** HPOX

NOISE: Noise abatemnent: All dep follow ATC instructions; climb ASAP to 4000′ or above. During the hrs 0600–1200Z‡ arrg acft will be assgnd Rwy 36L or Rwy 36R and departing acft will be assgnd Rwy 18L or Rwy 18R to avoid noise sensitive areas.

AIRPORT REMARKS: Attended continuously. Bird activity on and invof arpt. PPR engine maintenance run–ops call ops 512–530–7550. Declared low visibility conds require ATCT communication prior to push back. PPR GA acft on the passenger terminal apron, call ops 512–530–7550. Twy A clsd to acft with wingspan more than 171′. PPR for non State of Texas aircarft entering the State Ramp abeam Twy E. Call State Ops 512–936–8900 or freq. 131.375. TxIn R4 clsd to acft with wingspan more than 135 ft. TxIn C2 clsd to acft with wingspan more than 171 ft. TxIn R1, R3, R5 clsd to acft with wingspan more than 118 ft. TxIn C2 btwn Twy C and G1, and TxIn R1 clsd 0200–1400Z‡.

AIRPORT MANAGER: 512-530-2242
WEATHER DATA SOURCES: ASOS (512) 369–7881 WSP.
COMMUNICATIONS: UNICOM 122.95   **D–ATIS** 124.4 (512) 369–7867.
  AUSTIN RCO 122.2 (SAN ANGELO RADIO)
 ® **AUSTIN APP/DEP CON** 127.225 (East) 120.875 (South) 119.0 (West)
  AUSTIN TOWER 121.0 **GND CON** 121.9 **CLNC DEL** 125.5
  CPDLC (LOGON KUSA)
  PDC
AIRSPACE: CLASS C svc ctc APP CON.
RADIO AIDS TO NAVIGATION: NOTAM FILE AUS.
  CENTEX (VH) (H) VORTACW 112.8   CWK   Chan 75   N30°22.71′ W97°31.79′   207° 13.2 NM to fld. 593/6E.
  VOR unusable:
    180°–190° byd 40 NM
    200°–210° byd 40 NM
  ILS/DME 110.5   I–VNK   Chan 42   Rwy 18L.   Class IIIE.   DME also serves Rwy 36R.
  ILS/DME 110.95   I–GFQ   Chan 46(Y)   Rwy 18R.   Class IE.   DME also serves Rwy 36L.
  ILS/DME 110.95   I–BSM   Chan 46(Y)   Rwy 36L.   Class IE.   DME also serves Rwy 18R.
  ILS/DME 110.5   I–HCE   Chan 42   Rwy 36R.   Class IIE.   DME also serves Rwy 18L.

HELIPAD H1: H60X60 (CONC)
HELIPAD H2: H60X60 (CONC)
HELIPAD H3: H50X50 (CONC)

SAN MARCOS RGNL (HYI)(KHYI) 31 S UTC–6(–5DT) N29°53.57´ W97°51.78´ SAN ANTONIO
595 B NOTAM FILE HYI H–7C, L–19C, 21A
RWY 08–26: H6330X100 (ASPH) S–80 MIRL IAP, AD
  RWY 08: Fence.
  RWY 26: Crops.
RWY 13–31: H5601X100 (ASPH) S–60 MIRL 0.4% up NW
  RWY 13: MALS. PAPI(P2L)—GA 3.0° TCH 57´.
  RWY 31: PAPI(P2L)—GA 3.0° TCH 60´. Trees.
RWY 17–35: H5214X100 (ASPH) S–20 MIRL 0.4% up N
  RWY 17: PAPI(P2L)—GA 3.0° TCH 55´.
SERVICE: S5 **FUEL** 100LL, JET A **OX** 2, 4 **LGT** Actvt MALS 13; MIRL
  Rwys 08–26, 13–31 and 17–35 preset low intst; to incr intst—CTAF.
  PAPI Rwy 13, 31, 17 oper consly.
AIRPORT REMARKS: Attended 1200–0300Z‡. For aftr hrs serv
  800–229–2379. 100LL self service. 100LL and Jet A avbl full serve.
  Apn all ireg sfc.
AIRPORT MANAGER: 512-216-6039
WEATHER DATA SOURCES: AWOS–3PT (512) 353–8005
COMMUNICATIONS: CTAF 126.825 **ATIS** 120.825 (512–353–8005)
  (1300–0300Z‡)
Ⓡ **AUSTIN APP/DEP CON** 119.0
  TOWER 126.825 (1300–0300Z‡)
  GND CON/CLNC DEL 120.125 **CLNC DEL** 121.35 (When twr clsd)
  CLEARANCE DELIVERY PHONE: For CD ctc Austin Apch at 512-369-7865.
AIRSPACE: CLASS D svc 1300–0300Z‡ eff 01 Apr 2021; other times CLASS E.
RADIO AIDS TO NAVIGATION: NOTAM FILE AUS.
  CENTEX (VH) (H) VORTACW 112.8 CWK Chan 75 N30°22.71´ W97°31.79´ 205° 33.9 NM to fld. 593/6E.
  VOR unusable:
    180°–190° byd 40 NM
    200°–210° byd 40 NM
  GARYS NDB (LOMW) 272 RU N29°57.52´ W97°56.94´ 124° 6.0 NM to fld. 819/7E. NOTAM FILE HYI.
  ILS 108.7 I–RUM Rwy 13. Class IT. LOM GARYS NDB. ILS and LOM unmonitored. LOC unusable byd 30° left of
    course.

AVENGER FLD (See SWEETWATER on page 432)

BAILES (See ANGLETON on page 245)

TEXAS

BALLINGER

BRUCE FLD (E30) 5 SW UTC–6(–5DT) N31°40.47′ W99°58.62′ SAN ANTONIO
1739 B NOTAM FILE SJT L–19B
RWY 17–35: H3909X60 (ASPH) S–20 MIRL IAP
  RWY 17: PAPI(P2L)—GA 3.0° TCH 40′. Road.
SERVICE: FUEL 100LL LGT Dusk–Dawn. Actvt PAPI Rwy 17—CTAF.
  Airfield ltg not mntnd. Nmrs lgts ots.
AIRPORT REMARKS: Unattended. Deer on and invof arpt. For fuel call
  325–365–3511, cash or check only. Rwy 17–35 vegetation growing
  thru pavement.
AIRPORT MANAGER: (325) 365-3591
COMMUNICATIONS: CTAF 122.9
®SAN ANGELO APP/DEP CON 125.35 (1200–0300Z‡)
®FORT WORTH CENTER APP/DEP CON 126.15 (0300–1200Z‡)
CLEARANCE DELIVERY PHONE: For CD ctc san angelo Apch at 432-563-2123.
  when Apch clsd ctc Fort Worth ARTCC at 817-858-7584.
RADIO AIDS TO NAVIGATION: NOTAM FILE SJT.
  SAN ANGELO (VH) (H) VORTACW 115.1 SJT Chan 98 N31°22.50′
  W100°27.29′ 044° 30.4 NM to fld. 1886/10E.
  VOR unusable:
    111°–190° byd 40 NM
    191°–201° byd 40 NM blo 6,000′
    191°–201° byd 49 NM
    202°–255° byd 40 NM blo 7,000′
    202°–255° byd 71 NM
    256°–289° byd 40 NM blo 4,400′
    256°–289° byd 53 NM
    290°–314° byd 40 NM blo 5,000′
    290°–314° byd 46 NM
    315°–352° byd 40 NM

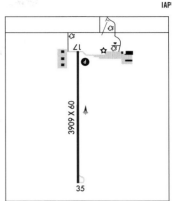

BAR V K (See BOLIVAR on page 258)

BAY CITY RGNL (BYY)(KBYY) 5 E UTC–6(–5DT) N28°58.39′ W95°51.81′ HOUSTON
45 B NOTAM FILE BYY H–7C, L–19D, 21A, GOMW
RWY 13–31: H5107X75 (ASPH) S–30, D–51, 2D–82 MIRL IAP
  RWY 13: REIL. PAPI(P2L)—GA 3.0° TCH 40′. Tree.
  RWY 31: REIL. Pole.
SERVICE: FUEL 100LL, JET A LGT MIRL Rwy 13–31 preset low intst SS–SR; to incr intst and ACTVT REIL Rwy 13—CTAF.
  PAPI Rwy 13 oprs consly. Rwy 31 REIL oprs on photocell.
AIRPORT REMARKS: Attended Mon–Fri 1400–2300Z‡. Arpt unattended holidays. After hrs attendant call arpt manager, fee
  $55/hr, two hour min. 100LL 24 hr self-service fuel. Twy reflectors on all twys.
AIRPORT MANAGER: 979-244-5037
WEATHER DATA SOURCES: AWOS–3 118.075 (979) 323–1801.
COMMUNICATIONS: CTAF/UNICOM 122.8
®HOUSTON CENTER APP/DEP CON 128.6
CLEARANCE DELIVERY PHONE: For CD ctc Houston ARTCC at 281-230-5622.
RADIO AIDS TO NAVIGATION: NOTAM FILE PSX.
  PALACIOS (VH) (H) VORTACW 117.3 PSX Chan 120 N28°45.87′ W96°18.37′ 054° 26.5 NM to fld. 16/8E.

BAY ELECTRIC SUPPLY HELIPORT (See LEAGUE CITY on page 363)

BAYTOWN

BAYTOWN (HPY)(KHPY) 3 N UTC–6(–5DT) N29°47.17′ W94°57.16′ **HOUSTON**
34 B NOTAM FILE CXO **COPTER**
RWY 14–32: H4334X60 (ASPH) S–24 MIRL L–19E, 21A
  RWY 14: REIL. PAPI(P2L)—GA 3.0° TCH 20′. Thld dsplcd 786′. Road. IAP
  RWY 32: REIL. PAPI(P2L)—GA 3.0° TCH 20′. Thld dsplcd 721′.
  P–line.
RUNWAY DECLARED DISTANCE INFORMATION
  RWY 14: TORA–4088 TODA–4088 ASDA–4088 LDA–3320
  RWY 32: TORA–4003 TODA–4003 ASDA–4003 LDA–3283
SERVICE: S4 FUEL 100LL, JET A+ LGT ACTVT REIL Rwy 14 and Rwy
  32; PAPI Rwy 14 and Rwy 32; MIRL Rwy 14–32—CTAF.
AIRPORT REMARKS: Attended 1400–2300Z‡.
AIRPORT MANAGER: 713-303-8638
COMMUNICATIONS: CTAF/UNICOM 122.8
®HOUSTON APP/DEP CON 134.45
CLEARANCE DELIVERY PHONE: For CD ctc Houston Apch at 281-443-5844 to
  cnl IFR call 281-443-5888.
RADIO AIDS TO NAVIGATION: NOTAM FILE CXO.
  TRINITY (VL) (DL) VORW/DME 114.75 MHF Chan 94(Y)
    N29°32.78′ W94°44.85′ 316° 17.9 NM to fld. 38/7E.
  VOR unusable:
    060°–079° byd 40 NM
    080°–090° byd 40 NM blo 6,000′
    080°–090° byd 50 NM blo 8,000′
    091°–109° byd 40 NM
    110°–190° blo 2,000′

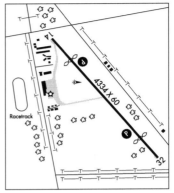

TEXAS

RWJ AIRPARK (54T)   7 E   UTC−6(−5DT)   N29°45.71´ W94°50.88´   HOUSTON
33   B   NOTAM FILE CXO   COPTER
RWY 08−26: H5035X40 (ASPH)   S−6   LIRL   H−7C, L−19E, 21A, GOMW
  RWY 08: Bldg.   IAP
  RWY 26: Thld dsplcd 939´. Road.
RWY 14−32: 3532X100 (TURF)   S−4
  RWY 14: Thld dsplcd 340´. Road.
  RWY 32: Thld dsplcd 600´. Road.
SERVICE: FUEL 100LL, JET A   LGT Rwy 08−26 LIRL lctd 15 ft fm rwy
  edge west, 4000 ft lgtd.
AIRPORT REMARKS: Attended Mon−Fri 1400−0000Z‡. For fuel services call
  281−383−2320. Twy too narrow for some acft. Rwy 08 rwy mkgs
  nstd, nrs 35 ft tall, thr bar 15 ins wide. Rwy 26 dsplcd thr mkgs nstd,
  nrs 35 ft tall, thr bar 15 ins wide. Rwy 08−26 east 1100 ft 60 ft wide.
  Rwy 08 28 ft pline (mkd and lgtd), 468 ft fm rwy end.
AIRPORT MANAGER: 512-825-9771
COMMUNICATIONS: CTAF/UNICOM 122.7
Ⓡ HOUSTON APP/DEP CON 134.45
CLEARANCE DELIVERY PHONE: For CD ctc Houston Apch at 281-443-5844 to
  cnl IFR call 281-443-5888.
RADIO AIDS TO NAVIGATION: NOTAM FILE CXO.
  TRINITY (VL) (DL) VORW/DME 114.75   MHF   Chan 94(Y)
    N29°32.78´ W94°44.85´   331° 13.9 NM to fld. 38/7E.
  VOR unusable:
    060°−079° byd 40 NM
    080°−090° byd 40 NM blo 6,000´
    080°−090° byd 50 NM blo 8,000´
    091°−109° byd 40 NM
    110°−190° blo 2,000´

BEAUMONT MUNI (BMT)(KBMT)   6 W   UTC−6(−5DT)   N30°04.21´ W94°12.91´   HOUSTON
32   B   NOTAM FILE CXO   L−19E, 21A, GOMW
RWY 13−31: H4001X75 (ASPH)   S−17   MIRL   IAP
  RWY 13: REIL. PAPI(P4L)—GA 3.0° TCH 40´. Thld dsplcd 332´. P−line. Rgt tfc.
  RWY 31: PAPI(P4L)—GA 4.0° TCH 40´. Thld dsplcd 67´. Road.
SERVICE: S4   FUEL 100LL, JET A   LGT Dusk−Dawn. MIRL Rwy 13−31 preset low intst; to incr intst actvt—CTAF.
AIRPORT REMARKS: Attended 1300−0100Z‡. Deer on and invof arpt. 100LL avbl 24 hrs self svc.
AIRPORT MANAGER: 409-866-0084
WEATHER DATA SOURCES: AWOS−3PT 118.425 (409) 8E6−2832.
COMMUNICATIONS: CTAF/UNICOM 123.0
  RCO 122.2 (MONTGOMERY COUNTY RADIO)
Ⓡ HOUSTON APP/DEP CON 121.3
  CLNC DEL 121.75
CLEARANCE DELIVERY PHONE: For CD ctc Houston Apch at 281-443-5844. To cnl IFR ctc Houston Apch at 281-443-5888.
RADIO AIDS TO NAVIGATION: NOTAM FILE BPT.
  (L) (L) VORW/DME 114.5   BPT   Chan 92   N29°56.76´ W94°00.97´   299° 12.7 NM to fld. 6/7E.
  GOODHUE NDB (MHW) 368   GDE   N30°04.23´ W94°12.66´   at fld. 30/7E. NOTAM FILE CXO. VFR only.
    NDB OTS indef

BEAUMONT/PORT ARTHUR

JACK BROOKS RGNL (BPT)(KBPT) 9 SE UTC–6(–5DT) N29°57.05´ W94°01.24´ HOUSTON
 15 B LRA Class I, ARFF Index A NOTAM FILE BPT H–7D, L–19E, 21A, GOMW
 RWY 12–30: H6751X150 (CONC–GRVD) S–90, D–170, 2S–175, IAP, AD
  2D–230 PCN 37 R/D/X/U HIRL
  RWY 12: MALSR. RVR–T Tree.
  RWY 30: REIL. VASI(V4L)—GA 3.0° TCH 54´. RVR–R Tree.
 RWY 16–34: H5071X150 (ASPH–CONC–GRVD) S–70, D–90, 2S–114,
  2D–145 PCN 26 R/D/X/U HIRL
  RWY 16: REIL. PAPI(P4R)—GA 3.0° TCH 53´.
  RWY 34: REIL. VASI(V4L)—GA 3.0° TCH 53´.
 RUNWAY DECLARED DISTANCE INFORMATION
  RWY 12: TORA–6751 TODA–6751 ASDA–6508 LDA–6508
  RWY 16: TORA–5070 TODA–5070 ASDA–5070 LDA–5070
  RWY 30: TORA–6751 TODA–6751 ASDA–6751 LDA–6751
  RWY 34: TORA–5070 TODA–5070 ASDA–5070 LDA–5070
 SERVICE: S2 **FUEL** 100LL, JET A **OX** 2 **LGT** When ATCT clsd REIL rwy
  16, 30 and 34; HIRL rwy 12–30 and 16–34 preset med intst. Actvt
  MALSR rwy 12—CTAF.
 AIRPORT REMARKS: Attended continuously. Bird activity on and invof arpt.
  First 4271 ft of Rwy 34 grvd. First 1000 ft Rwy 16 much darker than
  remainder of rwy. First 1000 ft of Rwy 16 PCN reported as
  28/F/D/X/U. Flight Notification Service (ADCUS) available.
 AIRPORT MANAGER: 409-719-4900
 WEATHER DATA SOURCES: ASOS 126.3 (409) 722-9396.
 COMMUNICATIONS: CTAF 119.5 **ATIS** 126.3 **UNICOM** 122.95
  BEAUMONT RCO 122.2 (MONTGOMERY COUNTY RADIO)
 ®**HOUSTON APP/DEP CON** 121.3
  BEAUMONT TOWER 119.5 (1200–0400Z‡) **GND CON** 124.85 **CLNC DEL** 118.3
 CLEARANCE DELIVERY PHONE: For CD when ATCT is clsd ctc Houston Apch at 281-443-5844 to cnl IFR at 281-443-5888.
 AIRSPACE: CLASS D svc 1200–0400Z‡; other times CLASS E.
  TRSA svc ctc APP CON 25 NM out
 RADIO AIDS TO NAVIGATION: NOTAM FILE BPT.
  BEAUMONT (L) (L) VORW/DME 114.5 BPT Chan 92 N29°56.76´ W94°00.97´ at fld. 6/7E.
  SABINE PASS (VL) (L) VORW/DME 115.4 SBI Chan 101 N29°41.20´ W94°02.28´ 356° 15.8 NM to fld.
  10/7E. NOTAM FILE CXO.
  ILS/DME 110.15 I–BPT Chan 38(Y) Rwy 12. Class IE. Unmonitored when ATCT clsd.

BEEVILLE

BEEVILLE MUNI (BEA)(KBEA) 3 SW UTC–6(–5DT) N28°21.85´ W97°47.52´ SAN ANTONIO
 273 B NOTAM FILE BEA L–20H, 21A, GOMW
 RWY 12–30: H4553X75 (ASPH) S–25 MIRL 0.5% up NW IAP
  RWY 12: PAPI(P2L)—GA 3.0° TCH 20´. Road.
  RWY 30: PAPI(P2L)—GA 3.0° TCH 43´. Trees.
 RWY 18–36: 2251X60 (TURF) 0.3% up N
  RWY 18: P–line.
  RWY 36: P–line.
 SERVICE: S2 **FUEL** 100LL, JET A **LGT** SS–SR MIRL Rwy 12–30 preset
  low intst, to incr intst actvt—CTAF.
 AIRPORT REMARKS: Unattended. 100LL 24hr self serv. On site attendant
  361–319–3448 also 361–542–6544. Rwy 18–36 thlds marked with
  3´ yellow cones.
 AIRPORT MANAGER: 361-358-4341
 WEATHER DATA SOURCES: AWOS–3 118.675 (361) 362–7627.
 COMMUNICATIONS: CTAF/UNICOM 122.8
 ®**HOUSTON CENTER APP/DEP CON** 134.6
 CLEARANCE DELIVERY PHONE: For CD ctc Houston ARTCC at 281-230-5622.
 RADIO AIDS TO NAVIGATION: NOTAM FILE SJT.
  THREE RIVERS (L) (L) VORTAC 111.4 THX Chan 51 N28°30.30´
   W98°09.03´ 106° 20.8 NM to fld. 266/8E.

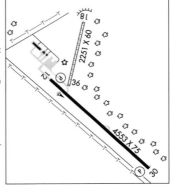

TEXAS

CHASE FLD INDUSTRIAL (TX2) 5 SE UTC–6(–5DT) N28°21.75′ W97°39.72′ SAN ANTONIO
184 B NOTAM FILE SJT H–7C, L–20H, 21A
RWY 13–31: H8000X200 (ASPH) MIRL IAP
SERVICE: FUEL JET A LGT MIRL Rwy 13–31 preset to low intst
SS–SR; to incr intst and actvt—122.8.
AIRPORT REMARKS: Unattended. The prev parl Rwy 13R–34L CLOSED.
Rwy 13–31 sfc rough and uneven, spcly btn Txys C2 and C5. Loose
stones thrut. Rwy 13–31 clsd to TGLS. Arpt fenced, gates locked, for
aces call AMGR.
AIRPORT MANAGER: 361-358-2023
COMMUNICATIONS: CTAF/UNICOM 122.8
HOUSTON CENTER APP/DEP CON 134.6
CLEARANCE DELIVERY PHONE: For CD ctc Houston ARTCC at 281-230-5622.
RADIO AIDS TO NAVIGATION: NOTAM FILE SJT.
THREE RIVERS (L) (L) VORTAC 111.4 THX Chan 51 N28°30.30′
W98°09.03′ 100° 27.2 NM to fld. 266°/8E.

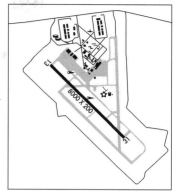

BENGER AIR PARK (See FRIONA on page 315)

BIG BEND RANCH STATE PARK (See PRESIDIO on page 404)

BIG LAKE

REAGAN CO (E41) 1 W UTC–6(–5DT) N31°11.92′ W101°28.51′ SAN ANTONIO
2706 B NOTAM FILE SJT L–19A
RWY 16–34: H5035X50 (ASPH) S–14 MIRL IAP
RWY 16: PAPI(P2L)—GA 3.0° TCH 30′. Thld dsplcd 1005′. Rgt tfc.
RWY 34: PAPI(P2L)—GA 3.5° TCH 40′. Pole.
RWY 09–27: H4001X60 (ASPH) 0.4% up E
RWY 27: Pole. Rgt tfc.
SERVICE: FUEL 100LL LGT ACTVT PAPI Rwy 16 and Rwy 34; MIRL
Rwy 16–34—CTAF.
AIRPORT REMARKS: Unattended. For fuel call 325-277-1551.
AIRPORT MANAGER: 325-650-1314
WEATHER DATA SOURCES: AWOS–3PT 118.4 (325) 884–2770.
COMMUNICATIONS: CTAF 122.9
®FORT WORTH CENTER APP/DEP CON 126.15
CLEARANCE DELIVERY PHONE: For CD ctc Fort Worth ARTCC at
817-858-7584.
RADIO AIDS TO NAVIGATION: NOTAM FILE SJT.
SAN ANGELO (VH) (H) VORTACW 115.1 SJT Chan 98 N31°22.50′
W100°27.29′ 249° 53.5 NM to fld. 1886′/10E.
VOR unusable:
111°–190° byd 40 NM
191°–201° byd 40 NM blo 6,000′
191°–201° byd 49 NM
202°–255° byd 40 NM blo 7,000′
202°–255° byd 71 NM
256°–289° byd 40 NM blo 4,400′
256°–289° byd 53 NM
290°–314° byd 40 NM blo 5,000′
290°–314° byd 46 NM
315°–352° byd 40 NM

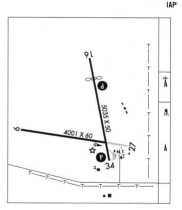

TEXAS

BIG SPRING MC MAHON–WRINKLE (BPG)(KBPG) 2 SW UTC–6(–5DT) N32°12.76′
W101°31.30′
2573 B NOTAM FILE BPG
RWY 17–35: H8802X100 (CONC) S–60, D–150, 2D–200 MIRL
 RWY 17: SSALS. PAPI(P4L)—GA 3.0° TCH 45′. Rgt tfc.
 RWY 35: PAPI(P4L)—GA 3.0° TCH 36′.
RWY 06–24: H4601X75 (ASPH)   MIRL 0.6% up NE
 RWY 06: PAPI(P2L)—GA 3.0° TCH 40′. Rgt tfc.
 RWY 24: PAPI(P2L)—GA 3.0° TCH 40′. Fence.
SERVICE: S4 **FUEL** 100LL, JET A **LGT** MIRL Rwys 06–24 and 17–35 preset low intst; to incr intst and actvt SSALS Rwy 17—CTAF.
AIRPORT REMARKS: Attended Mon–Fri 1400–2300Z‡. Prairie dogs on rwys and twys. Sandhill Cranes xng in the spring and fall. Fuel full and self serve. FBO 432–264–7124. Aft hrs 432–935–1238.
AIRPORT MANAGER: 432-264-2362
WEATHER DATA SOURCES: AWOS–3PT 118.025 (432) 264–7475.
COMMUNICATIONS: CTAF/UNICOM 122.8
 RCO 122.4 (SAN ANGELO RADIO)
 ® **FORT WORTH CENTER APP/DEP CON** 133.7
CLEARANCE DELIVERY PHONE: For CD ctc Fort Worth ARTCC at 817-858-7584.
RADIO AIDS TO NAVIGATION: NOTAM FILE BPG.
 (VL) (H) VORTACW 117.2 BGS Chan 119 N32°23.14′ W101°29.02′ 180° 10.5 NM to fld. 2670/11E.

DALLAS–FT WORTH
H–6G, L–6H
IAP

BIGGS AAF (FORT BLISS) (BIF)(KBIF) A 5 NE UTC–7(–6DT) N31°50.97′ W106°22.80′
3947 B LRA NOTAM FILE ABQ Not insp.
RWY 04–22: H13554X150 (CONC–GRVD) PCN 84 R/C/W/T HIRL
 RWY 04: REIL. PAPI(P4L)—GA 3.0° TCH 75′.
 RWY 22: SSALR. PAPI(P4L)—GA 3.0° TCH 75′. Rgt tfc.
ARRESTING GEAR/SYSTEM
 RWY 04 BAK–14 BAK–12B(B) (1500′).   BAK–14 BAK–12B(B) (2100′). **RWY 22**
SERVICE: **FUEL** JET A++ **LGT** ACTVT PAPI Rwy 04 and 22; 3–step HIRL Rwy 04–22—127.9. No twy edge lts at hot refuel area. SSALR OTS. **MILITARY**— **JASU** 4(A/M32A–86) 2(A/M32–95) **FUEL** A+ (1400–0600Z‡, C915–779–2831, 2 hr PN, after hr call out fee $150.) **FLUID** SP **TRAN ALERT** Opr 1300–0700Z‡ Mon–Fri, 1500–0700Z‡ Sat–Sun, exc hol.
NOISE: Noise abatement: VFR west arr/dep via mtn pass 15 NM NW of Biggs AAF. Avoid VFR ovft of city. Fly 1500′ AGL, 1500′ horizontal dist fm mtn dwellings.
MILITARY REMARKS: Attended Mon–Sun 1500–0700Z‡, except holidays. See FLIP AP/1 Supplementary Arpt Remark. No de–ice avbl, no off afld trnsp avbl for aircrew, 24 hr notice for lav and water svcs, 915–525–7087. **RSTD** PPR all acft 24 hr prior notice ctc Airfield Ops DSN 621–8811/8330, C915–744–8811/8330. Twr and svcs avbl for all acft with PPR. PPR time valid +/– 1 hr. All acft ctc Afld Ops via PTD 30 min prior to arr. Flt Ops and Tran Alert svc unavbl bfr 1 hr prior to PPR sked arr. **CAUTION** El Paso Intl Rwy 22 2 NM SE can be mistaken for Biggs AAF Rwy 22. Coyote haz. **TFC PAT** Fixed Wing 5000(1052′ AGL), Turbo Prop 5500(1552′ AGL), Rotary Wing 4500(552′ AGL), Jet 6000(2052′ AGL).
MISC Approval required for access to ramp. Intl garbage cap ltd. Expect delays unless placed in garbage bags prior to arrival. Hangar space extremely limited for transient acft. KBIF auto obsn and BAAF USAF wx avbl 24/7, DSN 621–1215/1214, C915–744–1215/1214, OT 25th OWS, Davis–Monthan AFB, DSN 228–6598/6599. Class D airspace eff 1500–0700Z‡ Mon–Sun, exc hol. OT Class E intl garbage cap ltd. Must be bagged prior to arr. Twy L south of Twy F dsgnd for rotary wing acft only. Clsd circuit TV opns, tsnt acft civ–mil inbd ctc afld opns via ptd at 60nm prior to ldg. Closed circuit TV opns, tsnt acft Civ–Mil inbd ctc afld opns via PTD at 60 NM prior to ldg. Acft svc/trans alert will not support lcl, round robin or out and back for trans acft.
AIRPORT MANAGER: 915-744-8088
COMMUNICATIONS: PTD 126.2
 ® **EL PASO APP CON** 119.15 353.5 (South–V16) 124.25 298.85 (North–V16)
 TOWER 127.9 342.25 (Mon–Sun 1500–0700Z‡)
 BLISS RDO 134.1 237.2 1500–0700Z‡ exc hol. **GND CON** 121.6 251.125
 ® **EL PASO DEP CON** 121.3 263.0
 EL PASO CLNC DEL 125.0 379.1 **PMSV** 373.7

EL PASO
H–4L, L–6F
DIAP, AD

CONTINUED ON NEXT PAGE

TEXAS

CONTINUED FROM PRECEDING PAGE

AIRSPACE: CLASS D svc 1500–0700Z‡ Mon–Sun; other times CLASS E..
RADIO AIDS TO NAVIGATION: NOTAM FILE ABQ.
  NEWMAN (VL) (H) VORTACW 112.4   EWM   Chan 71   N31°57.11´ W106°16.35´   210° 8.2 NM to fld. 4041/12E.
  TACAN AZIMUTH unusable:
    220°–255° byd 25 NM blo 12,000´
  DME unusable:
    220°–255° byd 25 NM blo 12,000´
  VOR unusable:
    001°–005° byd 40 NM
    030°–034° byd 40 NM
    042°–065° byd 40 NM
    066°–084° byd 40 NM blo 18,000´
    085°–130° byd 40 NM
    243°–260° byd 40 NM
    261°–279° byd 40 NM blo 18,000´
    280°–290° byd 40 NM
    304°–332° byd 40 NM
  ILS/DME 110.9 I–BIF Chan 46 Rwy 22. Class IE.
COMM/NAV/WEATHER REMARKS: Radar—See Terminal F_IP for Radar Minima.

BIRD DOG AIRFIELD (See KRUM on page 356)

BISHOP (See DECATUR on page 291)

BISHOP'S LANDING (See CELINA on page 269)

BISHOP–WINDHAM (Ø7R)   3 NE   UTC–6(–5DT)   N27°36.61´ W97°45.15´   **BROWNSVILLE**
55 B NOTAM FILE SJT   **L–20H, 21A**
RWY 15–33: H3200X50 (ASPH) S–12.5 MIRL
  RWY 15: Road.
  RWY 33: Road.
SERVICE: **LGT** Rwy 15–33 MIRLs OTS indefly.
AIRPORT REMARKS: Unattended. Intensive mil jet tfc 1300 ft AGL and abv from Kingsville NAS (NQI) 7 NM SW. Ctc Kingsville apch 119.9 for instrns.
AIRPORT MANAGER: 361-584-2567
COMMUNICATIONS: CTAF 122.9
CLEARANCE DELIVERY PHONE: For CD ctc Houston ARTCC at 281-230-5622.
RADIO AIDS TO NAVIGATION: NOTAM FILE CRP.
  CORPUS CHRISTI (VH) (H) VORTACW 115.5   CRP   Chan 102
    N27°54.23´ W97°26.69´   214° 24.0 NM to fld. 60/9E.
  TACAN AZIMUTH & DME unusable:
    024°–036° byd 35 NM blo 1,700´
    037°–023° byd 35 NM blo 2,000´
    265°–275°
  VOR unusable:
    340°–005° byd 40 NM blo 7,000´
    340°–005° byd 84 NM
    Byd 30 NM blo 1,500´
  TACAN AZIMUTH unusable:
    080°–085° byd 30 NM

BOERNE STAGE AIRFIELD (See SAN ANTONIO on page 415)

BOLIVAR

BAR V K (T38) P   1 N   UTC–6(–5DT)   N33°22.58´ W97°14.61´   DALLAS–FT WORTH
765   NOTAM FILE FTW   Not insp.
RWY 18–36: 2900X100 (TURF)   LIRL
   RWY 18: Thld dsplcd 200´. Road.
   RWY 36: Thld dsplcd 200´. Berm.
SERVICE: **LGT** ACTVT LIRL Rwy 18–36—122.825.
AIRPORT REMARKS: Unattended. Arpt clsd at ngt to non residents. Call for safety briefling and PPR for ngt opns. Wildlife on and invof rwy. Glider actvt on and invof arpt. PAEW on rwy. No fuel or otr svcs avbl. Use ctn for non–radio acft in pat. CAUTION: do not mistake north end 1400 ft long turf twy as rwy. Rwy soft when wet, call for current conds bfr use. Cell twr midfield inside downwind for Rwy 36. Grass mower will clear rwy aft low apch. Lgtd windsocks N twy W side and midfield on hngr E of rwy. Both rwy ends have 200 ft dsplcd thrs mkd by white mats, orange cone and green lgts. Ditch on both sides of rwy mid field outside of rwy lgts. Rwy 18–36 slopes; rolling trrn all quads.
AIRPORT MANAGER: 940-453-5256
COMMUNICATIONS: CTAF 122.85
CLEARANCE DELIVERY PHONE: For CD ctc Regional Apch at 972-615-2799.
COMM/NAV/WEATHER REMARKS: Lcl acft use MULTICOM 122.85 for tfc pat opns.

BONHAM

JONES FLD   (F00)   2 N   UTC–6(–5DT)   N33°36.79´ W96°10.76´   DALLAS–FT WORTH
618   B   NOTAM FILE FTW   L–17D, A
RWY 17–35: H4000X75 (ASPH)   S–12.5   MIRL   IAP
   RWY 17: PAPI(P2L)—GA 3.0° TCH 37´. Trees.
   RWY 35: PAPI(P2L)—GA 3.0° TCH 37´. P–line.
SERVICE: S4   **FUEL** 100LL, JET A+   **LGT** MIRL Rwy 17 and 35 SS–SR preset low. To ACTVT or incr intsty—CTAF. PAPI Rwy 17 and PAPI Rwy 35 opr consly.
AIRPORT REMARKS: Unattended. For arpt attendant call 903–583–7555 Mon–Fri 1400–2300Z‡, after hrs call Bonham Police Dept. 903–583–2141. 100LL self–serv. Jet A full serv. Call 903–227–5199. Extensive aerial AG ops Apr–Aug. Othr times ireg. For airframe repairs call 903–640–0233 or 903–583–5119.
AIRPORT MANAGER: 903-583-8623
WEATHER DATA SOURCES: AWOS–3PT 118.05 (903) 583–2082.
COMMUNICATIONS: CTAF/UNICOM 122.8
®**FORT WORTH CENTER APP/DEP CON** 127.6
CLEARANCE DELIVERY PHONE: For CD ctc Fort Worth ARTCC at 817-858-7584.
RADIO AIDS TO NAVIGATION: NOTAM FILE FTW.
   BONHAM (VH) (H) VORTACW 114.6   BYP   Chan 93   N33°32.25´ W96°14.05´   025° 5.3 NM to fld. 700/6E.
COMM/NAV/WEATHER REMARKS: UNICOM unmonitored.

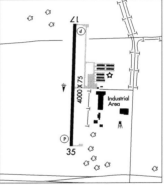

TEXAS

BORGER

HUTCHINSON CO (BGD)(KBGD)   2 N   UTC–6(–5DT)   N35°42.05´ W101°23.62´
3055   B   NOTAM FILE BGD
RWY 17–35: H6299X100 (ASPH)   S–60, D–100   MIRL   0.9% up S
  RWY 17: PAPI(P4L)—GA 3.0° TCH 58´.
  RWY 35: PAPI(P4R)—GA 3.0° TCH 41´. Trees.
RWY 03–21: H3897X100 (ASPH)   S–60, D–100   MIRL   0.5% up SW
  RWY 03: Trees.
SERVICE: **FUEL** 100LL, JET A, A+   **LGT** ACTVT PAPI Rwys 17 and 35;
   MIRL Rwys 03–21 and 17–35—CTAF.
AIRPORT REMARKS: Attended 1400–0000Z‡. Rwy 21, 100´ drop-off, 95´
   dstc. Rwy 3, 40´ drop-off, 150´ dstc.
AIRPORT MANAGER: 806-273-0137
WEATHER DATA SOURCES: ASOS 118.325 (806) 274–7318.
COMMUNICATIONS: CTAF/UNICOM 123.0
®**AMARILLO APP/DEP CON** 119.5 (1200–0600Z‡)
®**ALBUQUERQUE CENTER APP/DEP CON** 127.85 (0600–1200Z‡)
CLEARANCE DELIVERY PHONE: For CD ctc Albuquerque ARTCC at
   505-856-4861.
RADIO AIDS TO NAVIGATION: NOTAM FILE BGD.
   BORGER (L) TACAN   Chan 23   BGD (108.6)   N35°48.42´
   W101°22.93´   174° 6.4 NM to fld. 3130/11E.
   TACAN AZIMUTH unusable:
   220°–320° byd 10 NM blo 12,000´

DALLAS–FT WORTH
H–6G, L–15B
IAP

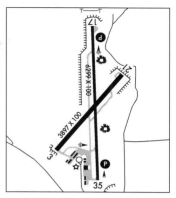

BORGER   N35°48.42´ W101°22.93´   NOTAM FILE BGD.
(L) TACAN 108.6   BGD   Chan 23   174° 6.4 NM to Hutchinson Co. 3130/11E.
TACAN AZIMUTH unusable:
220°–320° byd 10 NM blo 12,000´

DALLAS–FT WORTH
H–6G, L–15B

BOURLAND FLD (See FORT WORTH on page 308)

BOWIE MUNI (0F2)   4 NE   UTC–6(–5DT)   N33°36.10´ W97°46.53´
1101   B   NOTAM FILE FTW
RWY 17–35: H3603X60 (ASPH)   S–12.5   MIRL   0.5% up N
  RWY 17: PAPI(P2L)—GA 3.0° TCH 35´. Trees.
  RWY 35: PAPI(P2L)—GA 3.0° TCH 40´. Trees.
SERVICE: **FUEL** 100LL, JET A   **LGT** Dusk–dawn. Actvt PAPI Rwy 17 and
   35; MIRL 17–35—CTAF.
AIRPORT REMARKS: Attended Mon–Fri 1330–2230Z‡. For arpt attendant
   after hrs call 940–841–4156. Deer on and invof arpt. Ultralight
   activity on and invof arpt. Crop dusting Jan–Apr. 100LL and Jet A 24
   hr self–serve. Rwy 35 has 30 ft drop–off 190 ft dstc, both sides. Rwy
   17–35 pvmt lip 1.5 inches abv grade.
AIRPORT MANAGER: 940-841-4156
WEATHER DATA SOURCES: AWOS–3PT 118.75 (940) 872–2366.
COMMUNICATIONS: CTAF/UNICOM 122.8
®**FORT WORTH CENTER APP/DEP CON** 127.95
CLEARANCE DELIVERY PHONE: For CD ctc Fort Worth ARTCC at
   817-858-7584.
RADIO AIDS TO NAVIGATION: NOTAM FILE FTW.
   (H) (H) VORTACW 117.15   UKW   Chan 118(Y)   N33°32.15´
   W97°49.28´   024° 4.6 NM to fld. 1102/6E.

DALLAS–FT WORTH
L–17C, A
IAP

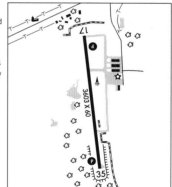

TEXAS

BRADY

CURTIS FLD (BBD)(KBBD) 3 NE UTC–6(–5DT) N31°10.76′ W99°19.44′   SAN ANTONIO
1827 B NOTAM FILE SJT   L–19B
RWY 17–35: H4605X75 (ASPH) S–21 MIRL 0.7% up N   IAP
  RWY 17: PAPI(P2L)—GA 3.0° TCH 40′.
  RWY 35: PAPI(P2L)—GA 3.0° TCH 48′. Tree.
RWY 08–26: 3520X110 (TURF) 0.3% up E
  RWY 08: Fence.
  RWY 26: Fence.
SERVICE: S4 FUEL 100LL, JET A LGT Dusk–Dawn. Actvt MIRL Rwy 17–35 —CTAF.
AIRPORT REMARKS: Attended Mon–Fri 1400–2300Z‡, Sat & Sun 1500–1900Z‡. Deer on and invof arpt. Extv mil hel opns on and invof arpt. Rwy 08–26 CLOSED except for tailwheel acft and helicopter. For fuel or attendant after hours call 325–456–1595. Call out avlbl, call for hol hrs. Rwy 08–26 sfc west end very rough, rwy paved at mid–field. Ovr ngt tie down fee.
AIRPORT MANAGER: 325-597-1461
WEATHER DATA SOURCES: AWOS–3 118.375 (325) 597–9139.
COMMUNICATIONS: CTAF/UNICOM 122.8
®HOUSTON CENTER APP/DEP CON 132.35
CLEARANCE DELIVERY PHONE: For CD ctc Houston ARTCC at 281-230-5622.
RADIO AIDS TO NAVIGATION: NOTAM FILE AQO.
  LLANO (L) (L) VORTACW 108.2 LLO Chan 19 N30°47.78′ W98°47.24′ 302° 35.9 NM to fld. 1207/8E.

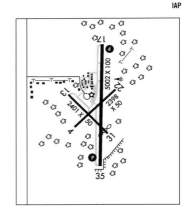

BRAZOS 538 BQX N28°18.84′ W95°37.20′
AWOS–3P 118.375   L–20I, 21A, GOMW

BRECKENRIDGE

STEPHENS CO (BKD)(KBKD) 2 S UTC–6(–5DT) N32°43.13′ W98°53.50′   DALLAS–FT WORTH
1284 B NOTAM FILE FTW   H–6H, L–17B
RWY 17–35: H5002X100 (ASPH) S–19 MIRL 0.6% up S   IAP
  RWY 17: PAPI(P2L)—GA 3.0° TCH 40′. Trees.
  RWY 35: PAPI(P2L)—GA 3.0° TCH 40′. Trees.
RWY 13–31: H2401X50 (ASPH) S–4 1.1% up SE
  RWY 13: Trees.
  RWY 31: Thld dsplcd 120′. Trees.
RWY 04–22: H2398X50 (ASPH) S–4 0.4% up SW
  RWY 04: Tree.
  RWY 22: Trees.
SERVICE: S4 FUEL 100LL, JET A LGT MIRL Rwy 17–35 preset low intst; to incr intst and actvt PAPI Rwys 17 and 35—CTAF.
AIRPORT REMARKS: Attended 1400–2300Z‡. After hrs on call.
AIRPORT MANAGER: 254-559-2190
WEATHER DATA SOURCES: AWOS–3 120.175 (254) 559–5525.
COMMUNICATIONS: CTAF/UNICOM 122.8

CONTINUED ON NEXT PAGE

TEXAS

CONTINUED FROM PRECEDING PAGE

BRECKENRIDGE RCO 122.5 (FORT WORTH RADIO)
Ⓡ FORT WORTH CENTER APP/DEP CON 127.0
RADIO AIDS TO NAVIGATION: NOTAM FILE FTW.
    MILLSAP (VH) (H) VORTACW 117.7   MQP   Chan 124   N32°43.57′ W97°59.85′   261° 45.3 NM to fld. 900/9E.
    VOR unusable:
      004°–009° byd 40 NM
      010°–054° byd 40 NM blo 3,800′
      010°–054° byd 46 NM blo 5,000′
      010°–054° byd 56 NM
      055°–066° byd 40 NM blo 3,800′
      055°–066° byd 50 NM
      230°–247° byd 40 NM
      248°–258° byd 40 NM blo 3,700′
      248°–258° byd 53 NM
      259°–270° byd 40 NM blo 6,000′
      259°–270° byd 63 NM
      271°–285° byd 40 NM
      312°–316° byd 40 NM
      325°–340° byd 40 NM blo 3,000′
      325°–340° byd 46 NM blo 5,000′
      325°–340° byd 66 NM
      353°–003° byd 40 NM blo 18,000′

BRENHAM MUNI (11R)   3 NE   UTC–6(–5DT)   N30°13.18′ W96°22.46′   **HOUSTON**
318   B   NOTAM FILE 11R   H–7C, L–19D, 21A, GOMW
  RWY 16–34: H6003X75 (ASPH)   S–30   MIRL   1.1% up N   **IAP**
  RWY 16: REIL. PAPI(P2L)—GA 3.0° TCH 36′. Tree.
  RWY 34: REIL. PAPI(P4L)—GA 3.5° TCH 48′. Trees.
  SERVICE: S4 **FUEL** 100LL, JET A **OX** 4 **LGT** Actvt MIRL Rwy
  16–34—CTAF.
  AIRPORT REMARKS: Attended Mon–Fri 1400–2300Z‡. 100LL 24 hr self-svc.
    Full svc avbl durg atndd hrs. For aft hrs svc 979–830–1361. 94′ lgtd
    radar ant, 1060′ west of Rwy 16 end. NOTE: See Special
    Notices—Aerobatic Practice Area.
  AIRPORT MANAGER: 979-337-7232
  WEATHER DATA SOURCES: AWOS–3 121.125 (979) 836–2303.
  COMMUNICATIONS: CTAF/UNICOM 123.075
Ⓡ **HOUSTON APP/DEP CON** 134.3
  CLEARANCE DELIVERY PHONE: For CD ctc Houston Apch at 281–443–5844 to
    cnl IFR call 281–443–5888.
  RADIO AIDS TO NAVIGATION: NOTAM FILE CLL.
    COLLEGE STATION (L) (L) VORTACW 113.3   CLL   Chan 80   N30°36.30′
      W96°25.24′   166° 23.2 NM to fld. 264/8E.
    TACAN unusable:
      101°–130° byd 25 NM blo 2,500′
      131°–148° byd 30 NM blo 2,500′
      149°–160° byd 30 NM blo 2,000′
      325°–349° byd 30 NM blo 2,500′
      350°–100° byd 25 NM blo 3,500′
    VOR unusable:
      024°–034° blo 4,000′
      024°–034° byd 20 NM
      131°–142° blo 7,000′
      142°–152° byd 30 NM
      152°–189° blo 7,000′

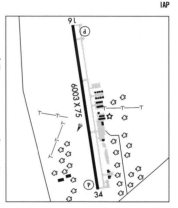

BRIDGEPORT MUNI (XBP)(KXBP)   4 SW   UTC–6(–5DT)   N33°10.44´ W97°49.71´   DALLAS–FT WORTH
864   B   NOTAM FILE XBP   L–17C, A
RWY 18–36: H5005X75 (ASPH)   S–30   MIRL   1.1% up S   IAP
  RWY 18: PAPI(P2L)—GA 3.0° TCH 51´. Tree.
  RWY 36: PAPI(P2L)—GA 3.5° TCH 46´.
SERVICE: S4   **FUEL** 100LL, JET A+
AIRPORT REMARKS: Attended Mon–Fri 1300–2200Z‡. 100LL fuel avbl 24 hrs self svc. Deer on and invof arpt.
AIRPORT MANAGER: 940-683-3435
WEATHER DATA SOURCES: AWOS–3PT 119.225 (940) 683–8027.
COMMUNICATIONS: CTAF/UNICOM 123.0
Ⓡ **FORT WORTH CENTER APP/DEP CON** 127.0
CLEARANCE DELIVERY PHONE: For CD ctc Fort Worth ARTCC at 817-858-7584.
RADIO AIDS TO NAVIGATION: NOTAM FILE FTW.
  BOWIE (H) (H) VORTACW 117.15   UKW   Chan 118(Y)   N33°32.15´
  W97°49.28´   175° 21.7 NM to fld. 1102/6E.

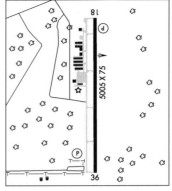

BROOKS CO (See FALFURRIAS on page 305)

BROWNFIELD
TERRY CO (BFE)(KBFE)   4 E   UTC–6(–5DT)   N33°10.39´ W102°11.58´   ALBUQUERQUE
3265   B   NOTAM FILE FTW   H–6G, L–6H
RWY 02–20: H5218X75 (ASPH)   S–50, D–65   MIRL   IAP
  RWY 02: PAPI(P2L)—GA 3.0° TCH 43´.
  RWY 20: PAPI(P2L)—GA 3.0° TCH 41´. Trees.
RWY 13–31: H2765X75 (ASPH)   S–12   0.4% up NW
  RWY 13: Trees.
  RWY 31: Road.
SERVICE: **FUEL** 100LL, JET A   **LGT** MIRL Rwy 02–20 preset low intensity, to increase intensity ACTIVATE—CTAF.
AIRPORT REMARKS: Unattended. Birds and wildlife on and invof arpt. 100LL fuel self svc 24 hrs.
AIRPORT MANAGER: (806) 543-9840
COMMUNICATIONS: CTAF/UNICOM 122.8
Ⓡ **LUBBOCK APP/DEP CON** 119.2   119.9
CLEARANCE DELIVERY PHONE: For CD ctc Fort Worth ARTCC at 817-858-7584.
RADIO AIDS TO NAVIGATION: NOTAM FILE LBB.
  LUBBOCK (L) (L) VORTACW 109.2   LBB   Chan 29   N33°42.30´
  W101°54.84´   193° 34.8 NM to fld. 3310/11E.
  VOR unusable:
    040°–050° byd 38 NM blo 5,300´
    210°–260° byd 25 NM blo 6,000´

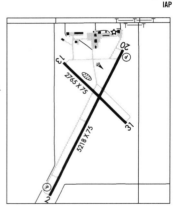

TEXAS

BROWNSVILLE/SOUTH PADRE ISLAND INTL (BRO)(KBRO)　4 E　UTC−6(−5DT)　N25°54.37′　　**BROWNSVILLE**
W97°25.56′　　　　　　　　　　　　　　　　　　　　　　　　　　　　　　　　　　　　　　H−7C, L−20H, 21A
　22　B　AOE　ARFF Index—See Remarks　NOTAM FILE BRO　　　　　　　　　　　　　　　IAP, AD
　RWY 13−31: H7399X150 (ASPH−GRVD)　S−75, D−170, 2S−175,
　　2D−240 PCN 67 R/D/X/T　HIRL
　　RWY 13: MALSR. RVR−T Tree.
　　RWY 31: PAPI(P4L)—GA 3.0° TCH 68′. RVR−R Tree.
　RWY 18−36: H6000X150 (ASPH−GRVD)　S−75, D−144, 2S−175,
　　2D−150 PCN 7 F/C/X/T　MIRL
　　RWY 18: PAPI(P4L)—GA 3.0° TCH 50′. Thld dsplcd 190′. Tree.
　　RWY 36: VASI(V4L)—GA 3.0° TCH 51′. Tree.
　RUNWAY DECLARED DISTANCE INFORMATION
　　RWY 13: TORA−7399　TODA−7399　ASDA−7399　LDA−7399
　　RWY 18: TORA−6000　TODA−6000　ASDA−6000　LDA−5810
　　RWY 31: TORA−7399　TODA−7399　ASDA−7399　LDA−7399
　　RWY 36: TORA−5532　TODA−5532　ASDA−5532　LDA−5532
　SERVICE: S4　**FUEL** 100LL, JET A　**OX** 1, 3　**LGT** When ATCT clsd
　　ACTVT MALSR Rwy 13—CTAF.
　AIRPORT REMARKS: Attended continuously. Birds on and invof arpt. For acft
　　svc call 956−542−5852 or 956−542−9111. Lgtd oil derricks lctn
　　aprxly 5 NM NE max 500 ft AGL. Class I, ARFF Index B. When ATCT
　　clsd req ARFF assistance thru Houston ARTCC or flt svc. PPR 24 hrs
　　for unsked acr opns with more than 30 psgr seats call AMGR. Txy J north of Txy H open to tfc under 12500 lbs. Landing
　　fee. Flight Notification Service (ADCUS) available.
　AIRPORT MANAGER: 956−542−4373
　WEATHER DATA SOURCES: ASOS 128.55 (956) 546−4540.
　COMMUNICATIONS: CTAF 118.9　ATIS 128.55　UNICOM 122.95
　　RCO 122.3 (SAN ANGELO RADIO)
　®VALLEY APP/DEP CON 119.5
　　TOWER 118.9 (1200−0600Z‡)　GND CON 121.9
　CLEARANCE DELIVERY PHONE: For CD when ATCT is clsd ctc crp Apch at 361−299−4230.
　AIRSPACE: CLASS D svc 1200−0600Z‡; other times CLASS E.
　RADIO AIDS TO NAVIGATION: NOTAM FILE BRO.
　　(H) (H) VORTACW 116.3　BRO　Chan 110　N25°55.44′ W97°22.52′　240° 2.9 NM to fld. 10/9E.
　　TACAN AZIMUTH unusable:
　　　360°−290° byd 24 NM
　　DME unusable:
　　　360°−290° byd 24 NM
　　VOR unusable:
　　　271°−290° byd 20 NM
　　　320°−335°
　　　360°−270° byd 24 NM
　　DEPOO NDB (LOMW) 393　BR　N25°59.02′ W97°30.55′　133° 6.5 NM to fld. 29/3E.
　　ILS/DME 110.3　I−BRO　Chan 40　Rwy 13.　Class IE.　LOM DEPOO NDB. Unmonitored when ATCT closed.

TEXAS

BROWNWOOD RGNL (BWD)(KBWD)   5 N   UTC−6(−5DT)   N31°47.62´ W98°57.39´   SAN ANTONIO
1387   B   NOTAM FILE BWD   MON Airport   H−6H, L−19C
RWY 17−35: H5599X100 (ASPH)   S−30   MIRL   0.3% up N   IAP
　RWY 17: MALS. PAPI(P4L)—GA 3.0° TCH 55´. Trees.
　RWY 35: PAPI(P4L)—GA 3.0° TCH 48´. Trees.
RWY 13−31: H4608X101 (ASPH)   S−25   MIRL
　RWY 31: Trees.
SERVICE: S4   **FUEL** 100LL, JET A   **LGT** ACTVT MALS Rwy 17; MIRL
　Rwy 13−31 and Rwy 17−35—CTAF.
AIRPORT REMARKS: Attended Mon−Fri 1300−2300Z‡, Sat−Sun
　1300−2100Z‡. Fuel avbl 24 hrs self svc. For fuel svc when arpt
　unatndd call 325−642−1026 or 325−643−1482. Airframe repairs on
　call 325−647−1876.
AIRPORT MANAGER: 325-643-1482
WEATHER DATA SOURCES: AWOS−3 118.325 (888) 297−9399.
COMMUNICATIONS: CTAF/UNICOM 122.8
　RCO 122.5 (FORT WORTH RADIO)
®**FORT WORTH CENTER APP/DEP CON** 127.45
CLEARANCE DELIVERY PHONE: For CD if una to ctc on FSS freq, ctc Fort Worth
　ARTCC at 817-858-7584.
RADIO AIDS TO NAVIGATION: NOTAM FILE BWD.
　(VL) (L) VORW/DME 113.55   BWD   Chan 82(Y)   N31°53.55´
　　W98°57.45´   172° 5.9 NM to fld. 1574/8E.
　VOR unusable:
　　010°−084° byd 40 NM
　　050°−080° byd 35 NM blo 5,500´
　　085°−099° byd 40 NM blo 5,000´
　　085°−099° byd 49 NM
　DME unusable:
　　050°−080° byd 35 NM blo 5,500´
　LOC 109.1   I−BWD   Rwy 17.   LOC unmonitored.

BRUCE FLD (See BALLINGER on page 251)

BRYAN

COULTER FLD   (CFD)(KCFD)   3 NE   UTC−6(−5DT)   N30°42.94´ W96°19.88´   HOUSTON
367   B   NOTAM FILE CFD   L−19D, 21A
RWY 15−33: H4000X75 (ASPH)   MIRL   IAP
　RWY 15: REIL. PAPI(P2L)—GA 3.5° TCH 40´. Trees.
　RWY 33: REIL. PAPI(P2L)—GA 3.5° TCH 40´. Brush.
SERVICE: S4   **FUEL** 100LL, JET A, A+   **LGT** MIRL Rwy 15−33 preset low
　intst; to incr intst—CTAF.
AIRPORT REMARKS: Attended Mon−Fri 1300−0000Z‡, Sat−Sun
　1500−2300Z‡. Deer on and invof arpt. Unlgtd hngrs 450 ft SW AER
　15. Unlgtd supplemental windsock 460´ sw AER 15.
AIRPORT MANAGER: 979-209-5233
WEATHER DATA SOURCES: AWOS−3PT 125.975 (979) 778−2544.
COMMUNICATIONS: CTAF/UNICOM 123.0
®**HOUSTON APP/DEP CON** 134.3
CLEARANCE DELIVERY PHONE: For CD ctc Houston Apch at 281-443-5844 to
　cnl IFR call 281-443-5888.
RADIO AIDS TO NAVIGATION: NOTAM FILE CLL.
　COLLEGE STATION (L) (L) VORTACW 113.3   CLL   Chan 80   N30°36.30´
　　W96°25.24´   027° 8.1 NM to fld. 264/8E.
　TACAN unusable:
　　101°−130° byd 25 NM blo 2,500´
　　131°−148° byd 30 NM blo 2,500´
　　149°−160° byd 30 NM blo 2,000´
　　325°−349° byd 30 NM blo 2,000´
　　350°−100° byd 25 NM blo 3,500´
　VOR unusable:
　　024°−034° blo 4,000´
　　024°−034° byd 20 NM
　　131°−142° blo 7,000´
　　142°−152° byd 30 NM
　　152°−189° blo 7,000´

TEXAS 265

BUFFALO (See AMARILLO on page 242)

BURNET MUNI/KATE CRADDOCK FLD (BMQ)(KBMQ) 1 SW UTC−6(−5DT) N30°44.34′ W98°14.32′   SAN ANTONIO
1283   B   NOTAM FILE BMQ   H−7B, L−19C
   RWY 01−19: H5001X75 (ASPH) S−30 MIRL 0.5% up N   IAP
     RWY 01: REIL. PAPI(P4L)—GA 3.0° TCH 43′. P−line. Rgt tfc.
     RWY 19: REIL. PAPI(P4L)—GA 3.03° TCH 45′. Trees.
   SERVICE: S4 FUEL 100LL, JET A LGT REIL RWY 01 and 19; PAPI RWY
     01 and 19; MIRL Rwy 01−19 preset low INTST; to INCR INTST and
     ACTVT—CTAF.
   AIRPORT REMARKS: Attended 1400−0000Z‡. For arpt attendant call
     512−756−6655. Deer invof arpt. Rwy 19 preferred calm wind rwy.
   AIRPORT MANAGER: 512-756-6655
   WEATHER DATA SOURCES: ASOS 119.925 (512) 756−7277.
   COMMUNICATIONS: CTAF/UNICOM 122.8
   ®HOUSTON CENTER APP/DEP CON 132.35
   CLEARANCE DELIVERY PHONE: For CD ctc Houston ARTCC at 281-230-5622.
   RADIO AIDS TO NAVIGATION: NOTAM FILE SJT.
     GOOCH SPRINGS (H) (H) VORTACW 112.5   AGJ   Chan 72   N31°11.13′
       W98°08.51′   186° 27.2 NM to fld. 1191/5E.

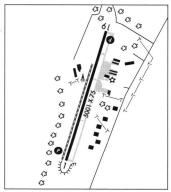

C DAVID CAMPBELL FLD−CORSICANA MUNI (See CORSICANA on page 280)

CABANISS FLD NOLF (NGW)(KNGW)   3 SW   N27°42.15′ W97°26.33′   BROWNSVILLE
   AIRSPACE: CLASS D svc 1400−0500Z‡ Mon−Thu, 1400−0100Z‡ Fri (DT 1300−0400Z Mon−Thu, 1300−0000Z   L−20H, 21A
     Fri); other times CLASS G.

CADDO MILLS MUNI (7F3)   2 SW   UTC−6(−5DT)   N33°02.17′ W96°14.59′   DALLAS−FT WORTH
542   B   NOTAM FILE FTW   L−17D, A
   RWY 13−31: H4000X150 (CONC) S−26   IAP
     RWY 13: Tree.
     RWY 31: Tree.
   RWY 18−36: H4000X75 (CONC) S−26 MIRL
     RWY 18: Tree.
     RWY 36: Tree.
   SERVICE: LGT ACTVT MIRL Rwy 18−36—CTAF.
   AIRPORT REMARKS: Attended Mon−Sat 1500−0000Z‡. Fcr arpt attendant
     other times, call 214−585−9953. Parachute Jumping. Rocket launch
     area adj to txy east of Rwy 13−31, midway. Rwy 13, Rwy 18, Rwy 31
     and Rwy 36 markings faded. Ramp on east−side of Rwy 13−31 in poor
     condition.
   AIRPORT MANAGER: 214-585-9953
   COMMUNICATIONS: CTAF/UNICOM 122.8
   ®FORT WORTH CENTER APP/DEP CON 132.025
   CLEARANCE DELIVERY PHONE: For CD ctc Fort Worth ARTCC at
     817-858-7784.
   RADIO AIDS TO NAVIGATION: NOTAM FILE FTW.
     BONHAM (VH) (H) VORTACW 114.6   BYP   Chan 93   N33°32.25′
       W96°14.05′   175° 30.0 NM to fld. 700/6E.
   COMM/NAV/WEATHER REMARKS: UNICOM not mnt.

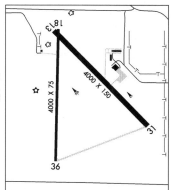

CAIN (See SLIDELL on page 426)

CALDWELL MUNI (RWV)(KRWV)   1 SW   UTC−6(−5DT)   N30°30.93´ W96°42.25´ **HOUSTON**
391   B   NOTAM FILE RWV   L−19D, 21A
RWY 15−33: H3252X50 (ASPH)   S−4   MIRL   0.9% up NW   IAP
 RWY 15: PAPI(P2L)—GA 3.0° TCH 42´. Trees.
 RWY 33: Thld dsplcd 242´. Trees.
SERVICE: FUEL 100LL   LGT Dusk−dawn, MIRL Rwy 15−33 preset low intst; to incr intst and actvt PAPI Rwy 15—CTAF. Rwy 15−33 Intens rwy lgts: photocell sensor.
AIRPORT REMARKS: Unattended. Rwy 15, 17 ft bldg. Penetrates trsn sfc, 104 ft fm rwy end, 260 ft R.
AIRPORT MANAGER: 979-599-4639
WEATHER DATA SOURCES: AWOS−3PT 118.35 (979) 567−6784.
COMMUNICATIONS: CTAF 122.9
®HOUSTON APP/DEP CON 134.3
CLEARANCE DELIVERY PHONE: For CD ctc Houston Apch at 281-443-5844 to cnl IFR call 281-443-5888.
RADIO AIDS TO NAVIGATION: NOTAM FILE CLL.
 COLLEGE STATION (L)(L) VORTACW 113.3   CLL   Chan 80
   N30°36.30´ W96°25.24´   242° 15.6 NM to fld. 264/8E.
  TACAN unusable:
   101°−130° byd 25 NM blo 2,500´
   131°−148° byd 30 NM blo 2,500´
   149°−160° byd 30 NM blo 2,000´
   325°−349° byd 30 NM blo 2,500´
   350°−100° byd 25 NM blo 3,500´
  VOR unusable:
   024°−034° blo 4,000´
   024°−034° byd 20 NM
   131°−142° blo 7,000´
   142°−152° byd 30 NM
   152°−189° blo 7,000´

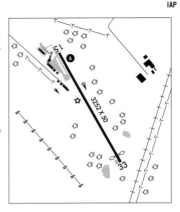

CALHOUN CO (See PORT LAVACA on page 403)

CAMERON MUNI AIRPARK (T35)   2 N   UTC−6(−5DT)   N30°52.74´ W96°58.33´   **HOUSTON**
402   B   NOTAM FILE FTW   L−19D, 21A
RWY 16−34: H3200X50 (ASPH)   S−19   MIRL
 RWY 16: PAPI(P2L)—GA 3.0° TCH 25´.
 RWY 34: PAPI(P2L)—GA 3.0° TCH 35´. Road.
SERVICE: FUEL 100LL, JET A   LGT MIRL Rwy 16−34 preset low intst; to incr intst actvt−CTAF.
AIRPORT REMARKS: Unattended. Rwy 16, 15 ft drop 155 ft byd thr. Rwy 34, 8 ft drop 150 ft byd thr. 106 ft ant 535 ft west of rwy cntrln.
AIRPORT MANAGER: 254-697-6646
WEATHER DATA SOURCES: AWOS−3P 124.1 (254) 605−0856.
COMMUNICATIONS: CTAF 122.9
CLEARANCE DELIVERY PHONE: For CD ctc Houston Apch at 281-443-5844 to cnl IFR call 281-443-5888.
RADIO AIDS TO NAVIGATION: NOTAM FILE CLL.
 COLLEGE STATION (L)(L) VORTACW 113.3   CLL   Chan 80   N30°36.30´ W96°25.24´   292° 32.9 NM to fld. 264/8E.
  TACAN unusable:
   101°−130° byd 25 NM blo 2,500´
   131°−148° byd 30 NM blo 2,500´
   149°−160° byd 30 NM blo 2,000´
   325°−349° byd 30 NM blo 2,500´
   350°−100° byd 25 NM blo 3,500´
  VOR unusable:
   024°−034° blo 4,000´
   024°−034° byd 20 NM
   131°−142° blo 7,000´
   142°−152° byd 30 NM
   152°−189° blo 7,000´

TEXAS

CANADIAN

HEMPHILL CO (HHF)(KHHF) 2 SW UTC–6(–5DT) N35°53.71´ W100°24.23´   DALLAS–FT WORTH
2396 B NOTAM FILE HHF   L–15C
RWY 04–22: H5004X75 (ASPH) S–30 MIRL   IAP
   RWY 04: REIL. PAPI(P2L)—GA 3.0° TCH 38´. Fence.
   RWY 22: REIL. PAPI(P2L)—GA 3.0° TCH 35´. Trees. Rgt tfc.
RWY 18–36: H3001X60 (ASPH) S–12.5 MIRL 1.0% up S
   RWY 18: Thld dsplcd 100´. Road. Rgt tfc.
   RWY 36: Fence.
SERVICE: FUEL 100LL, JET A, A++10   LGT Dusk–dawn. MIRL Rwy 04–22 and Rwy 18–36 preset low ints, to increase ints ACTIVATE—CTAF.
AIRPORT REMARKS: Attended Mon–Fri 1400–2300Z‡. 15´ ditch north of Rwy 04 thld extending 1000´ along left side of rwy.
AIRPORT MANAGER: (806) 679-4774
WEATHER DATA SOURCES: AWOS–3 119.025 (806) 323–8497.
COMMUNICATIONS: CTAF 122.9
®ALBUQUERQUE CENTER APP/DEP CON 127.85
CLEARANCE DELIVERY PHONE: For CD ctc Albuquerque ARTCC at 505-856-4861.
RADIO AIDS TO NAVIGATION: NOTAM FILE GAG.
   MITBEE (VH) (H) VORTACW 115.6 MMB Chan 103 N36°20.62´ W99°52.81´ 214° 37.0 NM to fld. 2426/10E.

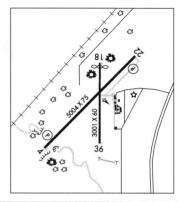

CANNON FLD (See SOMERSET on page 427)

CANTON–HACKNEY (7F5) 2 N UTC–6(–5DT) N32°35.17´ W95°51.76´   DALLAS–FT WORTH
500 NOTAM FILE FTW   L–17D
RWY 18–36: H3750X50 (ASPH) S–5.5 LIRL(NSTD)
   RWY 18: Thld dsplcd 103´.
   RWY 36: Thld dsplcd 70´. P–line.
SERVICE: LGT Rwy 18–36 NSTD LIRL, only middle 1,200´ of rwy lgtd on west side only.
AIRPORT REMARKS: Unattended. Arpt unsuitable for aircraft. Arpt CLOSED to acft over 10,000 lbs. Rwy 18–36 extsv loose stones and aggregate rwy and twy. Rwy 18–36 has 3´ posts and cable 75´ west of rwy cntrln. Rwy 18–36 no line of sight between thlds. Rwy 36 has 90 ft unmkd, unlgtd ant, 850 ft dstc, 190 ft L. Rwy 18 and Rwy 36 NSTD small rwy numbers only 35´ high, no dsplcd thld markings. Rwy 18 markings faded. Rwy 36 markings faded, NSTD color– white and yellow.
AIRPORT MANAGER: (903) 288-0392
COMMUNICATIONS: CTAF 122.9
CLEARANCE DELIVERY PHONE: For CD ctc Fort Worth ARTCC at 817-858-7584.
RADIO AIDS TO NAVIGATION: NOTAM FILE FTW.
   CEDAR CREEK (L) (L) VORTACW 114.8 CQY Chan 95 N32°11.14´ W96°13.09´ 031° 30.0 NM to fld. 400/6E.

TEXAS

CARRIZO SPRINGS
DIMMIT CO (CZT)(KCZT) 2 E UTC−6(−5DT) N28°31.34´ W99°49.42´   **SAN ANTONIO**
598   B   NOTAM FILE CZT   **H−7B, L−20G**
RWY 13−31: H5003X75 (ASPH)   S−30   MIRL   0.3% up NW   **IAP**
  RWY 13: PAPI(P4L)—GA 3.0° TCH 40´. Trees.
  RWY 31: PAPI(P4L)—GA 3.0° TCH 40´. Pole.
SERVICE: **FUEL** 100LL, JET A
AIRPORT REMARKS: Attended 1400−2300Z‡. Deer on or invof arpt. 100LL avbl avbl on request 830−876−2967. Rwy 31 unmkd, unlgtd elect transmission lines underlie apch. Landing fee.
AIRPORT MANAGER: 830-876-2967
WEATHER DATA SOURCES: AWOS−3 119.625 (830) 876−9243.
COMMUNICATIONS: CTAF/UNICOM 122.8
®**HOUSTON CENTER APP/DEP CON** 127.8
CLEARANCE DELIVERY PHONE: For CD ctc Houston ARTCC at 281-230-5622.
RADIO AIDS TO NAVIGATION: NOTAM FILE COT.
  COTULLA (VL) (H) VORTACW 115.8   COT   Chan 105   N28°27.72´
  W99°07.11´   267° 37.5 NM to fld. 522/9E.
  VOR unusable:
    008°−032° byd 40 NM

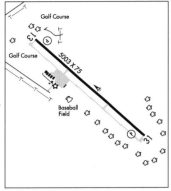

CARRIZO SPRINGS   FTN   N28°12.67´ W100°01.42´/758   **SAN ANTONIO**
AWOS−3 118.425 (956) 419−2913 AWOS associated with Faith Ranch airport (XA89).   **L−20G**

CARSWELL FLD (See FORT WORTH NAS JRB (CARSWELL FLD) on page 312)

CARTHAGE
PANOLA CO−SHARPE FLD (4F2) 2 E UTC−6(−5DT) N32°10.57´ W94°17.93´   **MEMPHIS**
248   B   NOTAM FILE FTW   **L−17E**
RWY 17−35: H4000X75 (ASPH)   MIRL   **IAP**
  RWY 17: PAPI(P4L)—GA 3.0°. Trees.
  RWY 35: PAPI(P4L)—GA 4.0°. Trees.
SERVICE: **FUEL** 100LL   **LGT** MIRL Rwy 17−35 preset low intst; to incr intst actvt—CTAF. PAPI opr consly.
AIRPORT REMARKS: Attended Mon−Fri 1400−2300Z‡. Deer on & invof rwy. 100LL avbl 24 hrs self-serve.
AIRPORT MANAGER: 903-693-7856
WEATHER DATA SOURCES: AWOS−3PT 121.125 (903) 690−0511.
COMMUNICATIONS: CTAF/UNICOM 122.8
®**SHREVEPORT APP/DEP CON** 119.3
CLEARANCE DELIVERY PHONE: For CD ctc Fort Worth ARTCC at 817-858-7584.
RADIO AIDS TO NAVIGATION: NOTAM FILE GGG.
  GREGG COUNTY (VL) (H) VORTACW 112.9   GGG   Chan 76
    N32°25.07´ W94°45.19´   115° 27.3 NM to fld. 329/7E.
  TACAN AZIMUTH unusable:
    045°−070° byd 25 NM blo 2,500´
    180°−225° byd 33 NM blo 3,500´
    258°−268° byd 26 NM blo 4,500´
    325°−340° byd 37 NM blo 2,500´
    248°−258° byd 34 NM blo 8,100´
  DME unusable:
    045°−070° byd 25 NM blo 2,500´
    180°−225° byd 33 NM blo 3,500´
    258°−268° byd 26 NM blo 4,500´
    325°−340° byd 37 NM blo 2,500´
  VOR unusable:
    138°−152° byd 40 NM
    188°−192° byd 40 NM
    210°−230° byd 40 NM

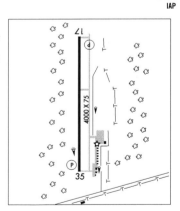

TEXAS

CASTROVILLE MUNI (CVB)(KCVB) 2 SE UTC–6(–5DT) N29°20.54′ W98°51.07′ SAN ANTONIO
774 B NOTAM FILE CVB L–19C
RWY 16–34: H5001X75 (ASPH) S–26, D–40 PCN 11 F/C/X/T MIRL IAP
  RWY 16: PAPI(P2L)—GA 3.0° TCH 40′. Road.
  RWY 34: PAPI(P2L)—GA 3.0° TCH 40′. Rgt tfc.
SERVICE: FUEL 100LL, JET A LGT MIRL Rwy 16–34 preset low intst;
  to incr intst actvt—CTAF.
AIRPORT REMARKS: Attended Mon–Fri 1400–2200Z‡. For aft hrs atndt call
  durg bus hrs. Deer on invof arpt. 100LL fuel avbl 24 hrs self svc. Jet A
  full serv durg atnd hrs. Bright lgts at ball park from Apr–July.
AIRPORT MANAGER: 830-538-2782
WEATHER DATA SOURCES: AWOS–3 119.25 (830) 931-0232.
COMMUNICATIONS: CTAF/UNICOM 122.8
®SAN ANTONIO APP/DEP CON 118.05
CLEARANCE DELIVERY PHONE: For CD ctc San Antonio Apch at
  210-805-5516.
RADIO AIDS TO NAVIGATION: NOTAM FILE SAT.
  SAN ANTONIO (VH) (H) VORTACW 116.8 SAT Chan 115 N29°38.64′
    W98°27.68′   221° 27.3 NM to fld. 1159/8E.
  VOR unusable:
    018°–022° byd 40 NM
    028°–032° byd 40 NM
    342°–347° byd 40 NM
    355°–002° byd 40 NM blo 18,000′

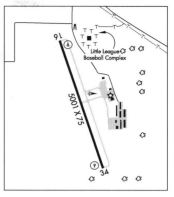

CEDAR CREEK N32°11.14′ W96°13.09′ NOTAM FILE FTW. DALLAS–FT. WORTH
(L) (L) VORTACW 114.8 CQY Chan 95 219° 13.3 NM to C David Campbell Fld–Corsicana Muni. H–6H, L–13C, 17D, A
  400/6E.

CEDAR MILLS (See GORDONVILLE on page 321)

CELINA
BISHOP'S LANDING (T80) 5 NE UTC–6(–5DT) N33°22.59′ W96°43.74′ DALLAS–FT WORTH
750 NOTAM FILE FTW
RWY 17–35: 1580X80 (TURF)
  RWY 17: Pole.
  RWY 35: Trees. Rgt tfc.
AIRPORT REMARKS: Unattended. Rwy 17–35 soft aft rain. Call amgr for fld conds. Rwy 17 p–line buried acrs apch. 35 ft poles
  0 ft dstc, 87 ft R, 96 ft L.
AIRPORT MANAGER: (214) 280-4408
COMMUNICATIONS: CTAF 122.9
CLEARANCE DELIVERY PHONE: For CD ctc Regional Apch at 972-615-2799.

- -

FOUR WINDS (9S1) 3 NE UTC–6(–5DT) N33°22.10′ W96°45.28′ DALLAS–FT WORTH
790 NOTAM FILE FTW
RWY 18–36: 2662X100 (TURF)
  RWY 18: Trees. Rgt tfc.
  RWY 36: Fence.
AIRPORT REMARKS: Attended dawn–dusk. All tfc remain west of the arpt. Rwy 17–20′ drop north of thr.
AIRPORT MANAGER: 214-803-7533
COMMUNICATIONS: CTAF 122.9
CLEARANCE DELIVERY PHONE: For CD ctc Regional Apch at 972-615-2799.

TEXAS

CENTER MUNI (F17) 3 NE UTC–6(–5DT) N31°49.90′ W94°09.39′ HOUSTON
319 B NOTAM FILE F17 H–6I, L–19E
RWY 17–35: H5501X75 (ASPH) S–30 MIRL 0.5% up N IAP
  RWY 17: PAPI(P2L)—GA 3.0° TCH 50′. Trees.
  RWY 35: PAPI(P2L)—GA 3.0° TCH 49′. Trees.
SERVICE: S6 **FUEL** 100LL, JET A+ **LGT** MIRL Rwy 17–35 preset low
  intst, to incr intst actvt—CTAF.
AIRPORT REMARKS: Attended Mon–Fri 1400–2100Z‡. Deer on and invof rwy.
  100LL self-svc fuel. Rwy 17–35 markings faded.
AIRPORT MANAGER: 936-598-8119
WEATHER DATA SOURCES: AWOS–3PT 128.775 (936) 598–3355.
COMMUNICATIONS: CTAF/UNICOM 122.8
  RCO 122.6 (MONTGOMERY COUNTY RADIO)
®**FORT WORTH CENTER APP/DEP CON** 126.325
CLEARANCE DELIVERY PHONE: For CD if una to ctc on FSS freq, ctc Fort Worth
  ARTCC at 817-858-7584.
RADIO AIDS TO NAVIGATION: NOTAM FILE DRI.
  ELM GROVE (L) (L) **VORTACW** 111.2 EMG Chan 49 N32°24.02′
    W93°35.71′ 213° 44.5 NM to fld. 160/7E.
    controlled by SHV RAPCON
  TACAN unusable:
    Byd 30 NM blo 2,000′
  VOR unusable:
    Byd 30.0NM blo 2,000′
  AMASON NDB (MHW) 341 CZJ N31°49.97′ W94°09.23′ at fld. 329/4E. NOTAM FILE CXO.

CENTER POINT N29°55.34′ W99°12.87′ NOTAM FILE ERV. SAN ANTONIO
  (VH) (H) VORTAC 117.5 CSI Chan 122 056° 7.5 NM to Kerrville Muni/Louis Schreiner Fld. 2079/8E. H–7B, L–19B
  RCO 122.1R 117.5T (SAN ANGELO RADIO)

CENTEX N30°22.71′ W97°31.79′ NOTAM FILE AUS. SAN ANTONIO
  (VH) (H) VORTACW 112.8 CWK Chan 75 015° 12.5 NM to Taylor Muni. 593/6E. H–7C, L–19C, 21A
  VOR unusable:
    180°–190° byd 40 NM
    200°–210° byd 40 NM

CHAMBERS CO (See ANAHUAC on page 244)

CHAMBERS CO/WINNIE STOWELL (See WINNIE/STOWELL on page 448)

CHAPARROSA RANCH N28°52.71′ W99°59.66′ NOTAM FILE SJT. SAN ANTONIO
  NDB (MHW) 385 CPZ 134° 14.3 NM to Crystal City Muni. 676/5E. NDB unmonitored 2300–1430Z‡ L–19B
  Mon–Fri.

CHARLES R JOHNSON (See PORT MANSFIELD on page 403)

CHASE FLD INDUSTRIAL (See BEEVILLE on page 255)

CHEROKEE CO (See JACKSONVILLE on page 348)

SC, 25 JAN 2024 to 21 MAR 2024

TEXAS

CHILDRESS MUNI (CDS)(KCDS) 4 W UTC–6(–5DT) N34°26.03′ W100°17.28′ DALLAS–FT WORTH
1954 B NOTAM FILE CDS H–6G, L–17B
RWY 18–36: H5949X75 (ASPH) S–21 MIRL(NSTD) IAP
 RWY 18: PAPI(P2L)—GA 3.0° TCH 40′. Pole.
 RWY 36: PAPI(P2L)—GA 3.0° TCH 40′.
RWY 04–22: H4425X60 (ASPH) S–21
SERVICE: FUEL 100LL, JET A1+ LGT MIRL Rwy 18–36 preset low intst;
 to incr intst ACTVT—CTAF. Rwy 18–36 NSTD MIRL Rwy 36 thld lgts
 60 ft south of rwy end. Rwy 18–36, nmrs lgts misg, out, incor color or
 orientation.
AIRPORT REMARKS: Attended 1400–2200Z‡. Rwy 04–22 CLOSED indefly.
 24 hr self svc 100LL and Jet A+. Full svc Jet A+ avbl durg oprg hrs;
 aft hrs call 940–937–8309. Rwy not mntnd; loose gravel and
 vegetation growing through the pavement. Some twys rough due to
 grass and weed encroachment. Agriculture opns near all paved sfcs.
AIRPORT MANAGER: 940-937-8309
WEATHER DATA SOURCES: ASOS 135.125 (940) 937–6337.
COMMUNICATIONS: CTAF/UNICOM 122.8
 RCO 122.4 (FORT WORTH RADIO)
® FORT WORTH CENTER APP/DEP CON 133.5
CLEARANCE DELIVERY PHONE: For CD ctc Fort Worth ARTCC at
 817-858-7584.
AIRSPACE: CLASS E svc continuous.
RADIO AIDS TO NAVIGATION: NOTAM FILE CDS.
 (VL) (H) VORTACW 117.0 CDS Chan 117 N34°22.14′ W100°17.34′ 351° 3.9 NM to fld. 1920/10E.

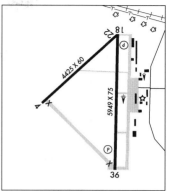

CHINA SPRING

WILDCAT CANYON (3T8) 4 NW UTC–6(–5DT) N31°40.71′ W97°21.75′ SAN ANTONIO
660 NOTAM FILE FTW
RWY 15–33: 2450X60 (TURF) 0.4% up NW
 RWY 15: Fence.
 RWY 33: Road.
AIRPORT REMARKS: Unattended. Deer and wild hogs on and invof rwy. 100′+ high tension power line (marked) 2500′ NW of
 Rwy 15 end.
AIRPORT MANAGER: 817-909-8044
COMMUNICATIONS: CTAF 122.9
CLEARANCE DELIVERY PHONE: For CD ctc Fort Worth ARTCC at 817-858-7584.

CISCO

CISCO MUNI (3F2) 3 N UTC–6(–5DT) N32°24.90′ W98°59.81′ DALLAS–FT WORTH
1621 B NOTAM FILE FTW L–17B
RWY 17–35: H3700X60 (ASPH) S–12 MIRL 0.7% up S
 RWY 17: Trees.
 RWY 35: Rgt tfc.
SERVICE: S2 LGT Nmrs rwy lgts out. Lgts obsc by vegetation.
AIRPORT REMARKS: Unattended. Deer and hogs on and invof arpt. Rwy
 17–35 thin asph is with seal coat. Extsv loose stones on pavement.
AIRPORT MANAGER: 254-442-2111
COMMUNICATIONS: CTAF 122.9
CLEARANCE DELIVERY PHONE: For CD ctc Fort Worth ARTCC at
 817-858-7584.
RADIO AIDS TO NAVIGATION: NOTAM FILE ABI.
 ABILENE (VH) (H) VORTACW 113.7 ABI Chan 84 N32°28.88′
 W99°51.81′ 085° 44.2 NM to fld. 1809/10E.
 VOR unusable:
  163°–236° byd 40 NM blo 18,000′
  237°–247° byd 40 NM blo 7,000′
  248°–250° byd 40 NM blo 18,000′
  251°–255° byd 40 NM blo 4,500′
  251°–255° byd 46 NM blo 18,000′

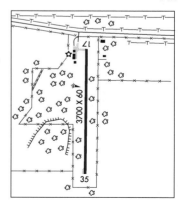

SC, 25 JAN 2024 to 21 MAR 2024

GREGORY M SIMMONS MEML (GZN)(KGZN) 3 WSW UTC−6(−5DT) N32°21.95′ W99°01.42′ DALLAS−FT WORTH
1711   NOTAM FILE FTW   L−17B
RWY 18−36: H6536X100 (CONC) S−150 MIRL   IAP
  RWY 18: PAPI(P4L)—GA 3.0° TCH 45′. Thld dsplcd 472′. Road. Rgt
    tfc.
  RWY 36: PAPI(P4L)—GA 3.2° TCH 48′. Pole.
RUNWAY DECLARED DISTANCE INFORMATION
  RWY 18: TORA−6536   TODA−6536   ASDA−6064   LDA−6064
  RWY 36: TORA−6536   TODA−6536   ASDA−6536   LDA−6536
SERVICE: S2 FUEL 100LL, JET A LGT ACTVT PAPI Rwy 18 and 36;
  MIRL Rwy 18−36 —CTAF.
AIRPORT REMARKS: Attended Mon−Fri 1400−2300Z‡. After hrs call
  254−433−1874. 100LL fuel 24 hr self serve. 260 ft AGL lgtd/mkd
  twr 0.74 SM E of rwy. 330 ft AGL lgtd/mkd twr 0.42 NM SE of rwy.
AIRPORT MANAGER: 254-433-1874
WEATHER DATA SOURCES: AWOS−4 118.0 (254) 442−1185.
COMMUNICATIONS: CTAF 122.9
®ABILENE APP/DEP CON 125.0
CLEARANCE DELIVERY PHONE: For CD ctc Fort Worth ARTCC at
  817-858-7584.
RADIO AIDS TO NAVIGATION: NOTAM FILE ABI.
  ABILENE (VH) (H) VORTACW 113.7 ABI Chan 84 N32°28.88′
    W99°51.81′   089° 43.2 NM to fld. 1809/10E.
  VOR unusable:
    163°−236° byd 40 NM blo 18,000′
    237°−247° byd 40 NM blo 7,000′
    248°−250° byd 40 NM blo 18,000′
    251°−255° byd 40 NM blo 4,500′
    251°−255° byd 46 NM blo 18,000′

CITY OF SLATON/LARRY T NEAL MEML (See SLATON on page 426)

CITY OF TULIA/SWISHER CO MUNI (See TULIA on page 436)

CLARENDON

SMILEY JOHNSON MUNI/BASS FLD (E34) 2 SE UTC−6(−5DT) N34°54.69′ W100°52.16′ DALLAS−FT WORTH
2833   B   NOTAM FILE FTW   L−17A
RWY 01−19: H4496X60 (ASPH) S−17 MIRL
  RWY 01: Berm.
SERVICE: LGT MIRL Rwy 01−19 preset low intst; to incr intst actvt—122.8. Actvt rotg bcn—122.8.
AIRPORT REMARKS: Unattended. No line of sight between rwy ends.
AIRPORT MANAGER: 806-874-3438
COMMUNICATIONS: CTAF 122.9
CLEARANCE DELIVERY PHONE: For CD ctc Albuquerque ARTCC at 505-856-4861.
RADIO AIDS TO NAVIGATION: NOTAM FILE CDS.
  CHILDRESS (VL) (H) VORTACW 117.0 CDS Chan 117 N34°22.14′ W100°17.34′ 309° 43.4 NM to fld. 1920/10E.

CLARK (See JUSTIN on page 350)

CLARKSVILLE/RED RIVER CTY−J D TRISSELL FLD (LBR)(KLBR) 3 SW UTC−6(−5DT) DALLAS−FT WORTH
  N33°35.56′ W95°03.85′   L−17D
440   B   NOTAM FILE LBR
RWY 18−36: H3000X50 (ASPH) S−10 MIRL 0.4% up N
  RWY 18: Trees.
  RWY 36: Trees.
AIRPORT REMARKS: Attended irregularly.
AIRPORT MANAGER: (903) 631-9531
COMMUNICATIONS: CTAF 122.9
CLEARANCE DELIVERY PHONE: For CD ctc Fort Worth ARTCC at 817-858-7584.
RADIO AIDS TO NAVIGATION: NOTAM FILE SLR.
  SULPHUR SPRINGS (L) DME 109.0   SLR   Chan 27   N33°11.92′ W95°32.57′   045° 33.7 NM to fld. 508.

SC, 25 JAN 2024 to 21 MAR 2024

TEXAS

CLEBURNE RGNL (CPT)(KCPT) 2 NW UTC−6(−5DT) N32°21.23′ W97°26.03′ **DALLAS−FT WORTH**
854   B   NOTAM FILE CPT H−6H, L−17C, A
RWY 15−33: H5697X100 (ASPH) S−30 MIRL IAP
  RWY 15: PAPI(P4L)—GA 3.0° TCH 39′. Thld dsplcd 185′. Trees. Rgt tfc.
  RWY 33: Pole.
SERVICE: S4 **FUEL** 100LL, JET A **LGT** ACTVT PAPI Rwy 15; MIRL Rwy 15−33—CTAF.
AIRPORT REMARKS: Attended Mon−Fri 1400−2300Z‡, Sat−Sun 1400−2200Z‡. 100LL 24 hr self−serve. For attendant aft hrs call 719−220−4584. Airframe repairs, no fabric or composite work.
AIRPORT MANAGER: 817-641-5456
WEATHER DATA SOURCES: AWOS−3 119.525 (817) 641−4135.
COMMUNICATIONS: CTAF/UNICOM 122.8
Ⓡ **REGIONAL APP/DEP CON** 135.975
CLEARANCE DELIVERY PHONE: For CD ctc Regional Apch at 972-615-2799.
RADIO AIDS TO NAVIGATION: NOTAM FILE FTW.
  GLEN ROSE (L) TACAN Chan 97 JEN (115.0) N32°09.58′
   W97°52.66′ 057° 25.4 NM to fld. 1300/6E.
  LOC/DME 111.25 I−CPT Chan 48(Y) Rwy 15. LOC unmonitored.

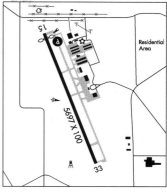

CLEVELAND MUNI (6R3) 4 NE UTC−6(−5DT) N30°21.39′ W95°00.48′ **HOUSTON**
150   B   NOTAM FILE CXO H−7C, L−19E, 21A, GOMW
RWY 16−34: H5001X75 (ASPH) S−30 MIRL IAP
  RWY 16: PAPI(P4L)—GA 3.0° TCH 52′. Trees.
  RWY 34: PAPI(P4L)—GA 3.0° TCH 45′. Trees.
SERVICE: S4 **FUEL** 100LL **LGT** Actvt PAPI Rwy 16 & Rwy 34; MIRL Rwy 16−34 —CTAF.
AIRPORT REMARKS: Attended Mon−Fri 1400−2200Z‡, Sat 1400−1800Z‡. For svc aft hrs call 281−761−5012. Rwy 16 calm wind rwy. To access arpt security gate use UNICOM freq. +25 ft trees 260 ft west of cntrln at thr.
AIRPORT MANAGER: 281-592-1282
WEATHER DATA SOURCES: AWOS−3 119.325 (281) 593−1754.
COMMUNICATIONS: CTAF/UNICOM 123.0
Ⓡ **HOUSTON APP/DEP CON** 119.7
CLEARANCE DELIVERY PHONE: For CD ctc Houston Apch at 281-443-5844 to cnl IFR call 281-443-5888.
RADIO AIDS TO NAVIGATION: NOTAM FILE CXO.
  DAISETTA (H) (H) VORTACW 116.9 DAS Chan 116 N30°11.38′
   W94°38.70′ 293° 21.3 NM to fld. 76/5E.
   VOR unusable:
    Byd 35 NM blo 1,600′
   TACAN AZIMUTH unusable:
    Byd 35 NM blo 1,600′
   DME unusable:
    Byd 35 NM blo 1,600′

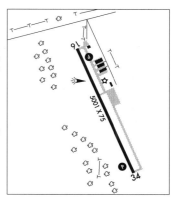

TEXAS

CLIFTON MUNI/ISENHOWER FLD (7F7)　2 N　UTC−6(−5DT)　N31°49.03′ W97°34.17′　　**SAN ANTONIO**
760　B　NOTAM FILE FTW　　**L−19B, A**
RWY 14−32: H3000X50 (ASPH)　S−13　MIRL　0.3% up NW
　RWY 14: PAPI(P2L)—GA 3.0° TCH 30′.
　RWY 32: PAPI(P2R)—GA 3.0° TCH 30′. Thld dsplcd 150′. Trees.
SERVICE: S4　**FUEL** 100LL　**OX** 4　**LGT** SS−SR MIRL Rwy 14−32 preset low intst; to incr intst—CTAF.
AIRPORT REMARKS: Attended Mon−Fri 1400−2230Z‡. Security gate locked after hrs., for access contact 254−675−6620. For arpt attendant on Sat and Sun−call 254−978−0020 or 254−253−0859, after hrs fee. Steep drop−off north of Rwy 14.
AIRPORT MANAGER: 254-675-3771
COMMUNICATIONS: CTAF/UNICOM 122.8
CLEARANCE DELIVERY PHONE: For CD ctc Fort Worth ARTCC at 817-858-7584.
RADIO AIDS TO NAVIGATION: NOTAM FILE ACT.
　WACO (VH) (H) VORTACW 115.3　　ACT　　Chan 100　　N31°39.73′ W97°16.14′　　292° 18.0 NM to fld. 507/9E.
　VOR unusable:
　　125°−149° byd 40 NM
　　149°−159° byd 47 NM
　　159°−187° byd 40 NM
　　188°−198° byd 40 NM blo 12,000′
　　199°−234° byd 40 NM
　　235°−245° byd 50 NM
　　246°−256° byd 40 NM blo 18,000′
　　246°−256° byd 52 NM
　　257°−267° byd 58 NM
　　268°−282° byd 40 NM
　　270°−335° byd 35 NM blo 4,000′
　　283°−293° byd 40 NM blo 6,000′
　　283°−293° byd 58 NM
　　294°−330° byd 40 NM

COCHRAN CO (See MORTON on page 385)

COLEMAN MUNI　(COM)(KCOM)　2 NE　UTC−6(−5DT)　N31°50.47′ W99°24.22′　　**SAN ANTONIO**
1697　B　NOTAM FILE FTW　　**L−19B**
RWY 15−33: H4506X75 (ASPH)　S−12.5　MIRL　0.4% up NW　　**IAP**
　RWY 15: Road.
　RWY 33: Trees.
SERVICE: S4　**FUEL** 100LL, JET A　**LGT** Rwy 15−33 MIRL preset to low, to incr ints and ACTIVATE—CTAF.
AIRPORT REMARKS: Attended Mon−Fri 1400−2300Z‡. Employee lives on premises. Rwy 15−33 nmrs cracks and pavement spalling.
AIRPORT MANAGER: 325-625-5495
WEATHER DATA SOURCES: AWOS−3PT 119.1 (325) 625−3563.
COMMUNICATIONS: CTAF/UNICOM 122.8
®**FORT WORTH CENTER APP/DEP CON** 127.45
CLEARANCE DELIVERY PHONE: For CD ctc Fort Worth ARTCC at 817-858-7584.
RADIO AIDS TO NAVIGATION: NOTAM FILE ABI.
　ABILENE (VH) (H) VORTACW 113.7　　ABI　　Chan 84　　N32°28.88′ W99°51.81′　　138° 44.9 NM to fld. 1809/10E.
　VOR unusable:
　　163°−236° byd 40 NM blo 18,000′
　　237°−247° byd 40 NM blo 7,000′
　　248°−250° byd 40 NM blo 18,000′
　　251°−255° byd 40 NM blo 4,500′
　　251°−255° byd 46 NM blo 18,000′

SC, 25 JAN 2024 to 21 MAR 2024

TEXAS

COLLEGE STATION

EASTERWOOD FLD (CLL)(KCLL)   3 SW   UTC–6(–5DT)   N30°35.28´ W96°21.75´   **HOUSTON**
321   B   Class I, ARFF Index B   NOTAM FILE CLL   **H–7C, L–19D, 21A**
RWY 17–35: H7000X146 (ASPH–CONC–GRVD)   S–78, D–94, 2D–156   **IAP, AD**
  PCN 29 R/D/X/T   HIRL
  RWY 17: VASI(V4R)—GA 3.0° TCH 51´. Tree.
  RWY 35: MALSR.
RWY 11–29: H5158X150 (ASPH–GRVD)   S–37, D–49 PCN 14 F/D/X/T
  MIRL
  RWY 11: VASI(V4L)—GA 3.0° TCH 50´. Tree.
  RWY 29: REIL. VASI(V4L)—GA 3.0° TCH 54´. Tree.
RUNWAY DECLARED DISTANCE INFORMATION
  RWY 11: TORA–5158   TODA–5158   ASDA–5158   LDA–5158
  RWY 17: TORA–7000   TODA–7000   ASDA–7000   LDA–7000
  RWY 29: TORA–5158   TODA–5158   ASDA–5158   LDA–5158
  RWY 35: TORA–7000   TODA–7000   ASDA–6932   LDA–6932
SERVICE: S4   **FUEL** 100LL, JET A, A+   **LGT** When twr clsd ACTIVATE
  MALSR Rwy 35; MIRL Rwy 11–29; HIRL Rwy 17–35—CTAF. REIL
  Rwy 29 preset low ints only.
AIRPORT REMARKS: Attended 1200–0400Z‡. 100LL svc 1200–0400Z‡.
  For fuel aft hrs PPR call 979–775–5255. Late night fee. CLOSED to
  unscheduled air carrier ops with more than 30 passenger seats except
  24 hours PPR call arpt manager 979–775–9920. Turn fee skedd FAR
  135 and all FAR 121 opns. Rwy 17–35 first 1850´ Rwy 35 conc. PAEW adjacent all rwys and twys 1200–2200Z‡.
  Surface conditions not reported from 2300–1100Z‡ (1700–0500 local) Mon–Fri & Sat–Sun. All rapid rfl mil Hel adz ATC
  for rapid rfl ops & procd to south ramp. Ctc UNICOM 122.95 for svc prior to lndg. Rapid rfl is avbl 1200–0400Z‡ dly.
  Spl rqs csdrd on case by case basis.
AIRPORT MANAGER: 979-775-9901
WEATHER DATA SOURCES: ASOS (979) 846–1708
COMMUNICATIONS: CTAF 118.5 **ATIS** 126.85 **UNICOM** 122.95
  COLLEGE STATION RCO 122.2 (MONTGOMERY COUNTY RADIO).
® **HOUSTON APP/DEP CON** 134.3
  TOWER 118.5 (1400–0300Z‡) **GND CON/CLNC DEL** 128.7 **CLNC DEL** 120.4 (when twr clsd)
CLEARANCE DELIVERY PHONE: For CD if una to ctc on FSS freq, ctc Houston ARTCC at 281-230-5622.
AIRSPACE: CLASS D svc 1400–0300Z‡; other times CLASS E.
RADIO AIDS TO NAVIGATION: NOTAM FILE CLL.
  COLLEGE STATION (L) (L) VORTACW 113.2   CLL   Chan 80   N30°36.30´ W96°25.24´   101° 3.2 NM to fld. 264/8E.
  TACAN unusable:
    101°–130° byd 25 NM blo 2,500´
    131°–148° byd 30 NM blo 2,500´
    149°–160° byd 30 NM blo 2,000´
    325°–349° byd 30 NM blo 2,500´
    350°–100° byd 25 NM blo 3,500´
  VOR unusable:
    024°–034° blo 4,000´
    024°–034° byd 20 NM
    131°–142° blo 7,000´
    142°–152° byd 30 NM
    152°–189° blo 7,000´
  ROWDY NDB (LOM) 260   CL   N30°29.62´ W96°20.26´ 344° 5.8 NM to fld. LOM unmonitored.
  ILS/DME 110.55   I–CLL   Chan 42(Y)   Rwy 35.   Class IE.   LOM ROWDY NDB. Unmonitored when ATCT clsd. DME
    unmonitored. Glideslope unusable for coupled apchs blo 1,050´ MSL. LOM unmonitored.
COMM/NAV/WEATHER REMARKS: All acft prkg on SE ramp must ctc for svc or trnsp, UNICOM 122.95 or 979–775–5255.

COLLINSVILLE

SUDDEN STOP (T32)   1 NE   UTC–6(–5DT)   N33°34.29´ W96°54.43´   **DALLAS–FT WORTH**
720   NOTAM FILE FTW
RWY 17–35: 1550X60 (TURF)
  RWY 17: Trees.
  RWY 35: Road.
AIRPORT REMARKS: Attended continuously. Student training prohibited. Rwy soft when wet. Call to confirm cond. Rwy 17–35
  thlds unmarked.
AIRPORT MANAGER: 903-429-6343
COMMUNICATIONS: CTAF 122.9
CLEARANCE DELIVERY PHONE: For CD ctc Fort Worth ARTCC at 817-858-7584.

TEXAS

COLORADO CITY (T88) 6 NW UTC−6(−5DT) N32°28.11´ W100°55.27´
2214 B NOTAM FILE FTW
RWY 17−35: H5479X60 (ASPH) S−50 LIRL
AIRPORT REMARKS: Attended irregularly. Rwy 17−35 pavement from Rwy 35 thld lgts southward used as a twy and not maintained. Rwy 17−35 markings faded and peeling, no centerline.
AIRPORT MANAGER: 325-728-3464
COMMUNICATIONS: CTAF 122.9
CLEARANCE DELIVERY PHONE: For CD ctc Fort Worth ARTCC at 817-858-7584.
RADIO AIDS TO NAVIGATION: NOTAM FILE BPG.
  BIG SPRING (VL) (H) VORTACW 117.2 BGS Chan 119 N32°23.14´ W101°29.02´ 069° 29.0 NM to fld. 2670/11E.

DALLAS−FT WORTH
H−6G, L−17A

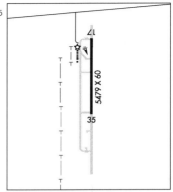

COLUMBUS

ROBERT R WELLS JR (66R) 3 S UTC−6(−5DT) N29°38.49´ W96°30.96´
242 B NOTAM FILE CXO
RWY 15−33: H3800X60 (ASPH) S−12.5 MIRL 0.3% up NW
  RWY 15: REIL. PAPI(P2L). Thld dsplcd 305´. Road.
  RWY 33: REIL. PAPI(P2L). Thld dsplcd 177´. Trees.
SERVICE: FUEL 100LL, JET A **LGT** ACTIVATE MIRL Rwy 15−33—CTAF.
AIRPORT REMARKS: Unattended. Deer and birds on and invof arpt. Ultra−light activity on and invof arpt. 100LL self svc fuel.
AIRPORT MANAGER: (979) 732-2604
WEATHER DATA SOURCES: AWOS−3 123.875 (979) 732−2514.
COMMUNICATIONS: CTAF 122.9
CLEARANCE DELIVERY PHONE: For CD ctc Houston Apch at 281-443-5844 to cnl IFR call 281-443-5888.
RADIO AIDS TO NAVIGATION: NOTAM FILE CXO.
  INDUSTRY (L) (L) VORTACW 110.2 IDU Chan 39 N29°57.36´ W96°33.73´ 165° 19.0 NM to fld. 419/8E.

HOUSTON
L−19D, 21A

COMANCHE CO−CITY (MKN)(KMKN) 2 NE UTC−6(−5DT) N31°55.22´ W98°35.95´
1387 B NOTAM FILE MKN
RWY 17−35: H4497X75 (ASPH) S−12.5 MIRL 0.3% up N
  RWY 17: PAPI(P2L)—GA 4.0° TCH 40´.
  RWY 35: PAPI(P2L)—GA 4.0° TCH 39´. Tree. Rgt tfc.
SERVICE: FUEL 100LL, JET A **LGT** Dusk−Dawn. MIRL Rwy 17−35 preset low intst; to incr intst actvt—CTAF.
AIRPORT REMARKS: Unattended. 100LL self svc fuel. Deer and wildlife on and invof arpt.
AIRPORT MANAGER: 325-330-0289
WEATHER DATA SOURCES: AWOS−3 118.575 (325) 356−7032.
COMMUNICATIONS: CTAF/UNICOM 123.075
  Ⓡ **FORT WORTH CENTER APP/DEP CON** 127.15
CLEARANCE DELIVERY PHONE: For CD ctc Fort Worth ARTCC at 817-858-7584.
RADIO AIDS TO NAVIGATION: NOTAM FILE SJT.
  GOOCH SPRINGS (H) (H) VORTACW 112.5 AGJ Chan 72 N31°11.13´ W98°08.51´ 327° 49.9 NM to fld. 1191/5E.

SAN ANTONIO
L−19C
IAP

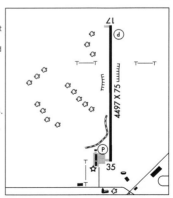

SC, 25 JAN 2024 to 21 MAR 2024

TEXAS

COMMERCE MUNI (2F7) 3 N   UTC–6(–5DT)   N33°17.57´ W95°53.79´ DALLAS–FT WORTH
516   B   NOTAM FILE FTW L–17D
RWY 18–36: H3907X60 (ASPH) S–13   MIRL IAP
 RWY 18: PAPI(P2L)—GA 3.0° TCH 40´. Trees.
 RWY 36: PAPI(P2L)—GA 3.0° TCH 40´. Tree.
SERVICE: S4 FUEL 100LL LGT MIRL Rwy 18–36 preset to low intst; to incr intst and actvt—CTAF.
AIRPORT REMARKS: Unattended. For attendant Mon–Fri 1400–2300Z‡ call 903–886–1101, after hrs call 903–886–1139 (Commerce Police Dept). 100LL avbl self serve. Rwy 18 mkgs faded. Rwy 36 mkgs faded.
AIRPORT MANAGER: 903-886-1101
COMMUNICATIONS: CTAF 122.9
®FORT WORTH CENTER APP/DEP CON 127.6
CLEARANCE DELIVERY PHONE: For CD ctc Fort Worth ARTCC at 817-858-7584.
RADIO AIDS TO NAVIGATION: NOTAM FILE SLR.
 SULPHUR SPRINGS (L) DME 109.0   SLR   Chan 27   N33°11.92´ W95°32.57´   288° 18.7 NM to fld. 508.

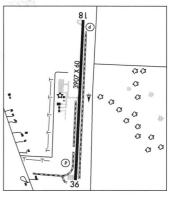

CONROE/NORTH HOUSTON RGNL (See HOUSTON on page 334)

CONWAY

EAGLES AERODROME (55T)   2 W   UTC–6(–5DT)   N35°12.87´ W101°24.66´ DALLAS–FT WORTH
3475   NOTAM FILE FTW
RWY 17–35: 5000X80 (TURF)   LIRL(NSTD)
 RWY 17: Fence.
 RWY 35: Fence. Rgt tfc.
SERVICE: LGT Arpt lgts opr dusk–0700Z‡. Rwy 17–35 NSTD LIRL, only center 3500´ lgtd, lights OTS indef.
AIRPORT REMARKS: Attended continuously. Rwy 17–35 surface rough. Wind turbines invof arpt. Deep tire ruts acrs rwy, aprxly 660´ fm north end.
AIRPORT MANAGER: 806-674-8993
COMMUNICATIONS: CTAF/UNICOM 122.8
CLEARANCE DELIVERY PHONE: For CD ctc Albuquerque ARTCC at 505-856-4861.

TEXAS

CORPUS CHRISTI INTL (CRP)(KCRP) P (CG) 5 W UTC−6(−5DT) N27°46.33′ W97°30.15′ **BROWNSVILLE**
46 B LRA Class I, ARFF Index B NOTAM FILE CRP MON Airport H−7C, L−20H, 21A, GOMW
RWY 13−31: H7510X150 (ASPH−GRVD) S−150, D−170, 2S−175, IAP, AD
2D−245 HIRL
  RWY 13: MALSR. PAPI(P4L)—GA 3.0° TCH 50′. RVR−T Pole. Rgt tfc.
  RWY 31: MALSR. PAPI(P4L)—GA 3.0° TCH 50′.
RWY 18−36: H6080X150 (ASPH−GRVD) S−150, D−170, 2S−175,
2D−245 HIRL
  RWY 18: MALSR. PAPI(P4L)—GA 3.0° TCH 50′. Pole.
  RWY 36: MALSR. RVR−T Rgt tfc.
RUNWAY DECLARED DISTANCE INFORMATION
  RWY 13: TORA−7510 TODA−7510 ASDA−7510 LDA−7510
  RWY 18: TORA−6080 TODA−6080 ASDA−6080 LDA−6080
  RWY 31: TORA−7510 TODA−7510 ASDA−7510 LDA−7510
  RWY 36: TORA−6080 TODA−6080 ASDA−6080 LDA−6080
SERVICE: S4 **FUEL** 100LL, JET A **OX** 1, 3 **MILITARY— FUEL** CG will use
FBO
AIRPORT REMARKS: Attended continuously. Birds on and invof arpt year round. Unmanned acft may be oprg 3 mi west of arpt drg dalgt hrs at or blw 400′ AGL. For svc after hrs call 361−438−1190. Cabaniss Fld located 5 miles southeast of arpt may be mistaken for Corpus Christi Intl arpt. VFR tfc may be operating in the Cabaniss Fld tfc pattern.
Cuddihy Fld (clsd arpt) is located 4 miles south of arpt may be mistaken for Corpus Christi Intl arpt. Acft at trml gates adz gnd ctl prior to push. Twr will provide progressive assistance.
MILITARY REMARKS: CG OFFL BUS, min 24 hr PPR. Ctc CORPUS CHRISTI AIR 345.0 15 min prior to entering CG ramp. No tran qrts or govt transportation avbl. If destn CG, incl CGAS CORPUS CHRISTI in rmk sec of flt plan. Sector Command Center: C361−939−0450.
AIRPORT MANAGER: 361−289−0171
WEATHER DATA SOURCES: ASOS (361) 289−0191
COMMUNICATIONS: ATIS 126.8 **UNICOM** 122.95
  RCO 122.2 (SAN ANGELO RADIO)
® **CORPUS APP/DEP CON** 120.9 Rwys 13 & 18 (340°−045°) 120.9 Rwys 31 & 36 (270°−045°) 124.8 Rwys 13 & 18 (150°−339°) 124.8 Rwys 31 & 36 (150°−269°) 125.4 (046°−149°)
  TOWER 119.4 **GND CON** 121.9 **CLNC DEL** 118.55
  CG CORPUS CHRISTI AIR 345.0 157.175(M83A)X
AIRSPACE: CLASS C svc ctc **APP CON**.
RADIO AIDS TO NAVIGATION: NOTAM FILE CRP.
  (VH) (H) VORTACW 115.5 CRP Chan 102 N27°54.23′ W97°26.69′ 192° 8.4 NM to fld. 60/9E.
    TACAN AZIMUTH & DME unusable:
      024°−036° byd 35 NM blo 1,700′
      037°−023° byd 35 NM blo 2,000′
      265°−275°
    VOR unusable:
      340°−005° byd 40 NM blo 7,000′
      340°−005° byd 84 NM
      Byd 30 NM blo 1,500′
    TACAN AZIMUTH unusable:
      080°−085° byd 30 NM
  ILS/DME 110.3 I−CRP Chan 40 Rwy 13. Class IE. DME also serves Rwy 31. Autopilot cpd apch NA blw 260′.
  LOC/DME 110.3 I−EKI Chan 40 Rwy 31. DME also serves Rwy 13.
  ILS/DME 109.5 I−OYC Chan 32 Rwy 36. Class IB. LOC unusable inside 1.6 DME.

TEXAS

CORPUS CHRISTI NAS (TRUAX FLD) (NGP)(KNGP) NAS, A   6 SE   UTC–6(–5DT)   BROWNSVILLE
N27°41.56´ W97°17.42´   H–7C, L–20H, 21A, GOMW
18   B   TPA—See Remarks   NOTAM FILE NGP   Not insp.   DIAP, AD
RWY 13R–31L: H8001X200 (PEM)   PCN 55 R/C/W/T   HIRL
  RWY 13R: SALSF. PAPI(P4L)—GA 3.0° TCH 47´. Rgt tfc.
  RWY 31L: REIL. PAPI(P4L)—GA 3.0° TCH 45´.
RWY 13L–31R: H5002X220 (ASPH)   PCN 47 F/B/W/T   HIRL
  RWY 13L: PAPI(P4L)—GA 3.0° TCH 46´.
  RWY 31R: PAPI(P4L)—GA 3.0° TCH 45´. Rgt tfc.
RWY 18–36: H5002X196 (ASPH)   PCN 41 F/B/W/T   HIRL
  RWY 18: REIL. PAPI(P4L)—GA 3.0° TCH 45´. Rgt tfc.
  RWY 36: REIL. PAPI(P4L)—GA 3.0° TCH 50´.
RWY 04–22: H5001X200 (ASPH)   PCN 33 F/B/W/T   HIRL
  RWY 04: REIL. PAPI(P4R)—GA 3.0° TCH 50´.
  RWY 22: REIL. PAPI(P4R)—GA 3.0° TCH 52´. Rgt tfc.
SERVICE: **OX** 1, 2, 3, 4   **LGT** Dusk–Dawn. When twr clsd actvt SALSF Rwy 13R; PAPI Rwys 04, 22, 13L, 31R, 31L, 18 and 36; HIRL Rwys 04–22, 13L–31R, 13R–31L, 18–36—CTAF. **MILITARY**— **JASU** 3(MSU–200, A/UA47A–5), MEPP–2(NC–8), 3(NC–10), 2(AM32A–108) **FUEL** F–24 **FLUID** SP PRESAIR LOX LHOXRB. LOX avbl only with 7 days prior notification of requirement. **OIL** MIL–PRF–23699 (NATO: 0–156) AND MIL–PRF–7808 L GRADE 3 (NATO: 148)
TRAN ALERT Tran acft exp delays fm 1500–2000Z‡ due ltd reful/svc. Maint extremely ltd before 1500Z‡, after 2000Z‡ and during non–work hrs.
MILITARY REMARKS: Opr Mon–Thu 1300–0500Z‡, Fri 1300–0100Z‡, CLOSED Sat, Sun and hol, other times check NOTAM. Base ops hrs 1230–0500Z‡ Mon–Thu; 1230–0100Z‡ Fri; clsd Sat, Sun and hol. Sierra twy clsd fm N of hngr 55 to the seawall, call AMGR at 361–961–2506 for aces. No lavatory svcs avbl here. **RSTD** Refueling/tran alert arrangements strongly recommended for all acft to avoid extv svcg/turnaround delays or parking in high FOD risk areas. PPR 48 hr all tran acft, DSN 861–2506/2507, C361–961–2506/2507. Flt planning DSN 861–2505/2513, C316–961–2505/2513. For civ air ldg pmt info ctc AFM C6361–961–2506/3395. Acft arr/dep prohibited one hr prior to afld opening due to afld preparations exc for Cust/Border Protection. Mission critical or other event rqr ctc base ops DSN 861–2506/2507/3395, C361–961–2506/2507/3395. USCG helopad located on seawall at 27 42 13N/ 97 16 42.5W clsd. Twy S, south of Ocean Drive, ltd to acft with a wingspan of 60´ or less. Bird bath lctd btwn Twy Y and Twy E, clsd. Sevice–Fluid–Lo avbl only with 7 days pn of rqmnt. Twy C, fm Twy B to Rwy 22 is ltd to TW4 acft only. **CAUTION** High mid–air potential, extreme vigilance rqr. Exercise extreme caution vcnty Waldron Fld NALF lctd 3 NM south. Bird act/BASH–See AP–1. See AP–1. Extv R/W test flgts conducted Mon–Sat fm town of Port O´Connor to Mustang Beach Arpt (KRAS), alg the coast fm 300–5000´. Nmrs birds vcnty afld, use ectreme ctn durg hvy rain events. If equipped, all acft shall utilize UHF ATC freq when assigned VHF. **TFC PAT** TPA—All tfc use ldg or taxi lgt while in arpt tfc area. Tran acft exp apch to full stop ldg only when single rwy ops are being conducted, practice apch not authorized. **CSTMS/AG/IMG** CSTMS, IMG avbl for acft arriving from overseas, plane arr from btn 1400–2100Z‡, C361–961–2506/2507. Pilots rqr to provide Identa Plate number to Inspector for billing. **MISC** Clsd twr ops: departing IFR acft shall obtain an IFR clnc and release from San Angelo FSS prior to tkof when the field is IFR via ground link or Corpus Christi apch by calling 361–299–4230. If the field is VFR, a VFR departure is authorized. Rwy 13L–31R clsd Sun 1400–1800Z‡. Rwy 13R–31L clsd Sun 1400–1800Z‡. Twy Y open fm intxn of Rwy 04–22 to apch end Rwy 13R. Acft operating to the sea wall use caution. Inbd heli ctc Corpus Christi Army Depot (CCAD) flt ops X–ray Charlie at 49.70, 139.0, 339.7, or DSN 861–0520/1020, C361–961–0520/1020. Tran and parts pickup acft park/fuel at Navy tran ramp (Separate PPR), DSN 861–2506/2507, C361–961–2506/2507. **A** Avoid flt over populated areas blo 1000´ AGL prior to Gulf shore line. Rotary wing acft destined for Corpus Christi Army Depot turn in will remain at least 1/4 NM off shore and 500´ prior to ctc Navy Corpus Twr. PPR all CCAD tran acft. Turn in will only be accepted dur nml duty hr, Mon–Fri 1300–2300Z‡. All R/W and F/W acft ldg/taxiing to seawall PPR DSN 861–2506/2507, C361–961–2506/2507. R/W acft make apch to helipad adj Hgr 44, ctc Ops/X–ray Charlie and gnd taxi to/fron parking. POC Avn Div, Hngr 44. Avoid overflt of bldg south of ramp area and ammo dump east of containment area. All acft with weapons arr CCAD after nml duty hr notify CCAD Security DSN 861–3313/3314, C361–961–3313/3314. Major maint avbl. Loading/unloading of air cargo mil/civ designated for CCAD will be scheduled for daylgt hr only. Dur times of natl emerg exceptions apvd by Director, Supply Corpus Christi Army Depot DSN 861–2557, C361–961–2557.
AIRPORT MANAGER: 361-961-3395
COMMUNICATIONS: CTAF 134.85   340.2 **ATIS** 127.9 290.9
Ⓡ **APP CON** 120.9 127.5 128.675 259.3 343.75 348.725 (120.9 343.75 all rwys exc as noted, 120.9 348.725 Hi–TACAN Rwy 13R, 127.5 259.3 Hi–TACAN 31L)
NAVY CORPUS TOWER 134.85 340.2 (North) 125.525 360.2 (South) (1300–0500Z‡ Mon–Thu, 1300–0100Z‡ Fri; clsd Sat, Sun and hol) No NOTAM MP: PAR Thurs 1300–1800Z‡. **NAVY CORPUS GND CON** 118.7 257.85
NAVY CORPUS CLNC DEL 314.3
BASE OPS 346.65 7965 **AIR** 345.0 5699 SSB. **PMSV METRO** 343.5 (Mon–Thu 1000–0500Z‡, Fri 1000–0100Z‡, clsd Sat, Sun and hol) (Radar wx advsy svc) **ARMY OPS** X–RAY CHARLIE 139.0 339.7 49.7
Ⓡ **DEP CON** 128.675 343.75

CONTINUED ON NEXT PAGE

SC, 25 JAN 2024 to 21 MAR 2024

TEXAS

CONTINUED FROM PRECEDING PAGE

AIRSPACE: CLASS D svc 1300–0500Z‡ Mon–Thu, 1300–0100Z‡ Fri, clsd Sat, Sun, and hol; other times by NOTAM; other times CLASS E.
RADIO AIDS TO NAVIGATION: NOTAM FILE NGP.
  TRUAX (L) TACAN   Chan 87   NGP (114.0)   N27°41.18´ W97°17.68´   at fld. 17/3E.
   No NOTAM MP: 1500–1800Z‡ 2nd Wed ea Month
   DME unusable:
     190°–305° byd 20 NM blo 2,000´
     333°–343° byd 10 NM blo 8,000´
   (VH) (H) VORTACW 115.5   CRP   Chan 102   N27°54.23´ W97°26.69´   138° 15.1 NM to fld. 60/9E.   NOTAM FILE CRP.
   TACAN AZIMUTH & DME unusable:
     024°–036° byd 35 NM blo 1,700´
     037°–023° byd 35 NM blo 2,000´
     265°–275°
   VOR unusable:
     340°–005° byd 40 NM blo 7,000´
     340°–005° byd 84 NM
     Byd 30 NM blo 1,500´
   TACAN AZIMUTH unusable:
     080°–085° byd 30 NM
  ILS/DME 111.3   I–NGP   Chan 50   Rwy 13R.   Class IT.   No NOTAM MP: 1800–0000Z‡ 2nd Thu ea Month. Glideslope unusable byd 6° left of course.
  ASR/PAR (PAR unsvc every Mon 0700L–1100L)
  COMM/NAV/WEATHER REMARKS: Radar see Terminal FLIP for Radar Minima.

CORSICANA

C DAVID CAMPBELL FLD–CORSICANA MUNI (CRS)(KCRS)   5 SE   UTC–6(–5DT)   N32°01.68´   DALLAS–FT WORTH
W96°24.04´   H–6H, L–19D, A
449   B   NOTAM FILE CRS   IAP
RWY 14–32: H5004X75 (ASPH)   S–26   MIRL   0.3% up NW
  RWY 14: REIL. VASI(V4R)—GA 3.0° TCH 26´. Road.
  RWY 32: REIL. PAPI(P2L)—GA 3.0° TCH 40´. Trees.
RWY 02–20: 3200X75 (TURF)   0.3% up NE
  RWY 02: P–line.
  RWY 20: Tree.
SERVICE: **FUEL** 100LL, JET A, MOGAS   **LGT** MIRL Rwy 14–32 preset med intst to incr intst and ACTVT PAPI Rwy 32—CTAF. VASI Rwy 14 opr consly.
AIRPORT REMARKS: Attended Mon–Fri 1430–2200Z‡, Sat 1430–2130Z‡. Deer on and invof arpt. 100LL avbl self-serve only. Rwy 02, 45 ft marked p-line at 935 ft acrs extdd cntrln.
AIRPORT MANAGER: 903-654-4857
WEATHER DATA SOURCES: ASOS 120.675 (903) 872-9321.
COMMUNICATIONS: CTAF/UNICOM 122.8
®**FORT WORTH CENTER APP/DEP CON** 135.25
CLEARANCE DELIVERY PHONE: For CD ctc Fort Worth ARTCC at 817-858-7584.
RADIO AIDS TO NAVIGATION: NOTAM FILE FTW.
  CEDAR CREEK (L) (L) VORTACW 114.8   CQY   Chan 95   N32°11.14´ W96°13.09´   219° 13.3 NM to fld. 400/6E.

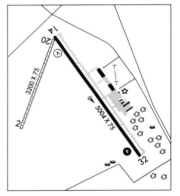

TEXAS

COTULLA–LA SALLE CO (COT)(KCOT) 1 NE UTC–6(–5DT) N28°27.34′ W99°13.03′ **SAN ANTONIO**
474 B NOTAM FILE COT H–7B, L–20G
RWY 13–31: H6005X75 (ASPH) S–25 MIRL 0.4% up NW IAF
  RWY 13: PAPI(P4L)—GA 3.0° TCH 45′.
  RWY 31: PAPI(P4L)—GA 3.0° TCH 45′. Ground. Rgt tfc.
SERVICE: S2 **FUEL** 100LL, JET A+ **OX** 3 **LGT** MIRL Rwy 13–31 preset
  low intst; to incr intst ACTVT—CTAF.
AIRPORT REMARKS: Attended 1400–0000Z‡. Arpt unattended Christmas.
  AMGR lives on airport. Fuel and svc avbl on call after hours
  830–879–3858. Ramp fee waived with minimum fuel purchase. Ocnl
  mil acft opns on and invof arpt. New arpt trml is opr; old trml is clsd.
AIRPORT MANAGER: 830-879-3858
WEATHER DATA SOURCES: ASOS 118.325 (830) 879–2861.
COMMUNICATIONS: CTAF/UNICOM 122.7
  RCO 122.2 (SAN ANGELO RADIO)
®**HOUSTON CENTER APP/DEP CON** 134.6
CLEARANCE DELIVERY PHONE: For CD if una to ctc on FSS freq, ctc Houston
  ARTCC at 281-230-5622.
RADIO AIDS TO NAVIGATION: NOTAM FILE COT.
  (VL) (H) VORTACW 115.8   COT   Chan 105   N28°27.72′
    W99°07.11′   257° 5.2 NM to fld. 522/9E.
    VOR unusable:
      008°–032° byd 40 NM

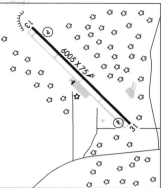

COULTER FLD (See BRYAN on page 264)

COVEY TRAILS (See FULSHEAR on page 315)

COWBOY N32°53.42′ W96°54.24′ NOTAM FILE FTW. **DALLAS–FT WORTH**
  (VH) (DH) VORW/DME 116.2   CVE   Chan 109   129° 3.8 NM to Dallas Love Fld. 443/6E. **COPTER**
    VOR unusable: H–6H, L–17C, A
      030°–035° byd 40 NM
      055°–060° byd 40 NM
      130°–140° byd 40 NM

COX FLD (See PARIS on page 397)

CRANE CO (E13)   1 NW   UTC–6(–5DT)   N31°24.69′ W102°21.63′ **SAN ANTONIO**
2555   B   NOTAM FILE SJT L–19A
RWY 12–30: H4258X70 (ASPH)   MIRL 0.4% up SE
  RWY 12: PAPI(P2L)—GA 3.5° TCH 52′.
  RWY 30: PAPI(P2L)—GA 3.0° TCH 40′. Thld dsplcd 488′. Pole.
RWY 15–33: H3395X50 (ASPH)
  RWY 15: Trees.
  RWY 33: Thld dsplcd 176′. P–line.
SERVICE: **FUEL** 100LL   **LGT** PAPI Rwy 12 and 30; MIRL Rwy 12–30 off SS–SR. CTAF to actvt 3 times low, 5 times med,
  7 times high.
AIRPORT REMARKS: Unattended. For fuel call 432–558–3571 (Sheriff dept). Rwy 12–30 pri sfc obstd by pumpjack 116′ fm
  cntrln 80′ NW of dsplcd thr on Rwy 30. +16′ pump jack 250′ west of Rwy 15 cntrln near thr. Rwy 15, 75′ pwrline
  crosses apch path 1800′ dstc.
AIRPORT MANAGER: 432-558-1100
COMMUNICATIONS: CTAF 122.9
CLEARANCE DELIVERY PHONE: For CD ctc Fort Worth ARTCC at 817-858-7584.
RADIO AIDS TO NAVIGATION: NOTAM FILE MAF.
  MIDLAND (L) (L) VORTACW 114.8   MAF   Chan 95   N32°00.56′ W102°11.42′   183° 36.8 NM to fld. 2860/11E.
    VOR unusable:
      010°–020° byd 8 NM blo 8,000′

CROCKETT

HOUSTON CO (DKR)(KDKR) 3 SE UTC−6(−5DT) N31°18.42′ W95°24.23′   **HOUSTON**
 348 B NOTAM FILE DKR   L−19D, 21A
 RWY 02−20: H4000X75 (ASPH) S−12 MIRL 0.5% up NE   **IAP**
  RWY 02: PAPI(P2L)—GA 3.0° TCH 35′. Tree.
  RWY 20: PAPI(P2L)—GA 3.0° TCH 35′. Pole.
 SERVICE: S4 **FUEL** 100LL **LGT** MIRL Rwy 02−20 preset low ints; to increase ints ACTIVATE—CTAF. MIRLs operate with photocell operating only at night with selectable ints on CTAF. Rwy 02 PAPI OTS indef. Rwy 20 PAPI OTS indef.
 AIRPORT REMARKS: Unattended. 100LL self−serve fuel.
 AIRPORT MANAGER: 936-544-3255
 WEATHER DATA SOURCES: AWOS−3PT 118.775 (936) 545−8510. Ceilings unavbl.
 COMMUNICATIONS: CTAF 122.9
 ®**HOUSTON CENTER APP/DEP CON** 134.8
 CLEARANCE DELIVERY PHONE: For CD ctc Houston ARTCC at 281-230-5622.
 RADIO AIDS TO NAVIGATION: NOTAM FILE CXO.
  LEONA (L) (L) VORTACW 110.8 LOA Chan 45 N31°07.44′ W95°58.08′ 061° 31.0 NM to fld. 346/8E.

CROSBYTON MUNI (8F3) 2 S UTC−6(−5DT) N33°37.43′ W101°14.45′   **DALLAS−FT WORTH**
 3018 B NOTAM FILE FTW   L−17A
 RWY 17−35: H3600X60 (ASPH) S−12 MIRL   **IAP**
  RWY 17: VASI(V2L)—GA 4.0°. P−line.
  RWY 35: VASI(V2L)—GA 4.0° TCH 23′. Trees.
 SERVICE: **LGT** Actvt MIRL Rwy 17−35—CTAF; opr on step 1 only. Rwy 17 and 35 VASI OTS indefly. Windsock lgt OTS indefly.
 AIRPORT REMARKS: Unattended. Seasonal aerial ag actvty. Rwy 17 and 35 markings faded.
 AIRPORT MANAGER: (806) 790-8533
 COMMUNICATIONS: CTAF/UNICOM 122.8
 ® **LUBBOCK APP/DEP CON** 119.2 119.9
 CLEARANCE DELIVERY PHONE: For CD ctc Fort Worth ARTCC at 817-858-7584.
 RADIO AIDS TO NAVIGATION: NOTAM FILE LBB.
  LUBBOCK (L) (L) VORTACW 109.2 LBB Chan 29 N33°42.30′ W101°54.84′ 087° 34.1 NM to fld. 3310/11E.
  VOR unusable:
   040°−050° byd 38 NM blo 5,300′
   210°−260° byd 25 NM blo 6,000′

CRYSTAL CITY MUNI (2Ø R) 1 NE UTC−6(−5DT) N28°41.85′ W99°49.06′   **SAN ANTONIO**
 608 NOTAM FILE SJT   L−20G
 RWY 13−31: H3550X100 (ASPH) S−21 MIRL 0.3% up SE
  RWY 13: Trees.
  RWY 31: Trees.
 SERVICE: **LGT** Lgts OTS indef. Lgt and windsock OTS indefly.
 AIRPORT REMARKS: Unattended. Arpt CLOSED indef. Apron and twy cracked with grass and loose grvl. Rwy 13 and 31 markings faded. Rwy 13−31 all paved surfaces have pot holes, loose gravel, and grass. Rwy 13 and 31 mkgs faded.
 AIRPORT MANAGER: 830-854-1458
 COMMUNICATIONS: CTAF 122.9
 CLEARANCE DELIVERY PHONE: For CD ctc Houston ARTCC at 281-230-5622.
 RADIO AIDS TO NAVIGATION: NOTAM FILE COT.
  COTULLA (VL) (H) VORTACW 115.8 COT Chan 105 N28°27.72′ W99°07.11′ 282° 39.5 NM to fld. 522/9E.
  VOR unusable:
   008°−032° byd 40 NM

TEXAS

CUERO MUNI (T71) 1 E UTC–6(–5DT) N29°05.02′ W97°16.02′ SAN ANTONIO
214 B NOTAM FILE CXO L–19C, 21A
RWY 14–32: H2800X60 (ASPH) S–11 LIRL
  RWY 14: Thld dsplcd 243′. Pole.
  RWY 32: Thld dsplcd 192′. Trees.
AIRPORT REMARKS: Unattended. Deer and wild hogs on and invof arpt. Una to detemine opr status of rwy lgts. Svrl lgts misg or broken. Rwy 14–32 pvmnt cracking, loose stones. Rwy 32 thr dsplcd 202 ft at ngt. No rwy mkgs. No bldgs, no facilities.
AIRPORT MANAGER: 360-243-2041
COMMUNICATIONS: CTAF 122.9
CLEARANCE DELIVERY PHONE: For CD ctc Houston ARTCC at 281-230-5622.
RADIO AIDS TO NAVIGATION: NOTAM FILE PSX.
  PALACIOS (VH) (H) VORTACW 117.3 PSX Chan 120 N28°45.87′ W96°18.37′ 283° 54.1 NM to fld. 16/8E.

CULBERSON CO (See VAN HORN on page 438)

CURTIS FLD (See BRADY on page 260)

CYPRESS RIVER (See JEFFERSON on page 349)

DAINGERFIELD
GREATER MORRIS CO (8F5) 7 N UTC–6(–5DT) N33°08.88′ W94°42.01′ MEMPHIS
402 NOTAM FILE FTW L–17D
RWY 17–35: H3000X50 (ASPH)
  RWY 17: Tree.
  RWY 35: Trees.
AIRPORT REMARKS: Unattended. Rwy 17–35 extsv cracking, loose grvl and grass on rwy and twy. Rwy conds not mnt. No line of sight btn rwy ends. No bldgs, no facs. Rwy 17 markings faded. Rwy 35 no markings. No airframe or powerplant rprs avbl.
AIRPORT MANAGER: 903-445-1788
COMMUNICATIONS: CTAF 122.9
CLEARANCE DELIVERY PHONE: For CD ctc Fort Worth ARTCC at 817-858-7584.
RADIO AIDS TO NAVIGATION: NOTAM FILE FTW.
  QUITMAN (L) DME 114.0 UIM Chan 87 N32°52.83′ W95°22.01′ 064° 37.3 NM to fld. 517.

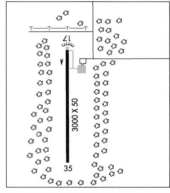

DAISETTA N30°11.38′ W94°38.70′ NOTAM FILE CXO. HOUSTON
(H) (H) VORTACW 116.9 DAS Chan 116 198° 7.3 NM to Liberty Muni. 76/5E. H–7C, L–19E, 21A, GOMW
VOR unusable:
  Byd 35 NM blo 1,600′
TACAN AZIMUTH unusable:
  Byd 35 NM blo 1,600′
DME unusable:
  Byd 35 NM blo 1,600′

DALHART MUNI (DHT)(KDHT) 3 SW UTC–6(–5DT) N36°01.35´ W102°32.84´ **WICHITA**
3991 B NOTAM FILE DHT MON Airport H–6G, L–15B
RWY 17–35: H6400X75 (ASPH) S–20, D–30 MIRL IAP
  RWY 17: REIL. PAPI(P4L)—GA 3.0° TCH 25´.
  RWY 35: REIL. PAPI(P4L)—GA 3.0° TCH 39´.
RWY 03–21: H5440X75 (ASPH) S–30 MIRL
  RWY 03: Tree.
  RWY 21: Antenna.
SERVICE: S4 **FUEL** 100LL, JET A1 **LGT** MIRL Rwys 03–21 and 17–35
  preset low intst; to incr intst and actvt PAPI Rwys 17 and 35—CTAF.
  Rwy 17 PAPI ots.
AIRPORT REMARKS: Attended 1400–0100Z‡. Large flocks of waterfowl invof
  Lake Rita Blanca 2 miles east during fall. For 100LL fuel aft hrs call
  806–244–5521 durg bus hrs. Ramp and twys pavement poor cond.
  Loose asph, stones, aggregate on sfc, pot holes and extsv cracking.
AIRPORT MANAGER: 806–244–5511
WEATHER DATA SOURCES: ASOS 134.075 (806) 249–5671.
COMMUNICATIONS: CTAF/UNICOM 122.95
  RCO 122.2 (FORT WORTH RADIO)
®**ALBUQUERQUE CENTER APP/DEP CON** 127.85
CLEARANCE DELIVERY PHONE: For CD if una to ctc on FSS freq, ctc Albuquerque
  ARTCC at 505–856–4561.
AIRSPACE: CLASS E.
RADIO AIDS TO NAVIGATION: NOTAM FILE DHT.
  (L) (L) VORTACW 112.0 DHT Chan 57 N36°05.49´ W102°02.68´ 170° 4.1 NM to fld. 4020/12E.
  TAC AZM unusable:
    240°–255° byd 15 NM
    320°–350° byd 15 NM

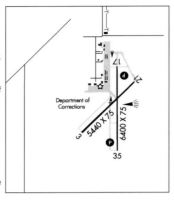

DALLAS

ADDISON (ADS)(KADS) 9 N UTC–6(–5DT) N32°58.11´ W96°50.19´ **DALLAS–FT WORTH**
645 B TPA—See Remarks NOTAM FILE ADS **COPTER**
RWY 16–34: H7203X100 (ASPH–GRVD) S–60, D–120 HIRL H–6H, L–17C, A
  RWY 16: MALSR. PAPI(P4R)—GA 3.0° TCH 60´. Thld dsplcd 979´. IAP, AD
    Road.
  RWY 34: REIL. PAPI(P4L)—GA 3.0° TCH 60´. Thld dsplcd 772´. Road.
RUNWAY DECLARED DISTANCE INFORMATION
  RWY 16: TORA–7203 TODA–7203 ASDA–7203 LDA–6224
  RWY 34: TORA–7203 TODA–7203 ASDA–7203 LDA–6431
ARRESTING GEAR/SYSTEM
  RWY 16: EMAS
SERVICE: S4 **FUEL** 100LL, JET A **OX** 2, 3 **LGT** Actvt MALSR Rwy 16;
  HIRL Rwy 16–34—CTAF.
NOISE: Noise sensitive areas surround arpt. Pilots req to use NBAA std
  noise procedures.
AIRPORT REMARKS: Attended 1200–0400Z‡. Birds on and invof arpt. No
  touch and go ldgs without arpt mgr apvl. Numerous 200´ bldgs within
  1 mile east, and south of arpt, transmission twrs and water tanks west
  of arpt. TPA—1601 (956) for light acft, 2001 (1356) for large acft.
  Be alert, rwy hldg ptn mrkgs lctd at the west edge of Twy A. User Fee
  arpt. CPB ofc hrs M–F 1600–0300Z‡. 214–208–3636. Flight
  Notification Service (ADCUS) available.
AIRPORT MANAGER: 972–392–4850
WEATHER DATA SOURCES: AWOS–3PT (972) 386–4855 LAWRS.
COMMUNICATIONS: CTAF 126.0 **ATIS** 133.4 972–628–2439 **UNICOM** 122.95
®**REGIONAL APP/DEP CON** 124.3
  TOWER 126.0 (1200–0400Z‡) **GND CON** 121.6 **CLNC DEL** 119.55
AIRSPACE: CLASS D svc 1200–0400Z‡; other times CLASS G.

CONTINUED ON NEXT PAGE

TEXAS

CONTINUED FROM PRECEDING PAGE

RADIO AIDS TO NAVIGATION: NOTAM FILE FTW.
   MAVERICK (VH) (H) VORW/DME 113.1   TTT   Chan 78   N32°52.15´ W97°02.43´   054° 11.9 NM to fld. 536/6E.
      All acft arriving DFW are requested to turn DME off until departure due to traffic overload of Maverick DME
      DME unusable:
         180°–190° byd 10 NM
         240°–260° byd 20 NM blo 3,500´
      VOR unusable:
         105°–110° byd 40 NM
   ILS/DME 110.1 I–ADS   Chan 38   Rwy 16.   Class IT.   Unmonitored when ATCT closed. DME also serves Rwy 34.
   ILS/DME 110.1 I–TBQ   Chan 38   Rwy 34.   Class IB.   Localizer unmonitored when ATCT closed. DME also serves
      Rwy 16.
COMM/NAV/WEATHER REMARKS: AWOS–3 info only avbl when ATCT clsd. ATIS avbl during twr hrs.

AIR PARK–DALLAS (F69)   16 NE   UTC–6(–5DT)   N33°01.41´ W96°50.22´   **DALLAS–FT WORTH**
   695   NOTAM FILE FTW   **COPTER**
   RWY 16–34: H3080X30 (ASPH)   **L–17C, A**
     RWY 16: Thld dsplcd 300´. Tree.
     RWY 34: Tree. Rgt tfc.
   SERVICE: S4
   AIRPORT REMARKS: Unattended. Rwy 16 apch, obstn lights lower than obstructions. Rwy 34 apch, obstruction light on bldg is
     lower than obstructions closer to rwy end. Rwy 34 mkd with 300 ft dsplcd thr.
   AIRPORT MANAGER: (214) 693-0513
   COMMUNICATIONS: CTAF 122.9
   CLEARANCE DELIVERY PHONE: For CD ctc Regional Apch at 972-615-2799.
   RADIO AIDS TO NAVIGATION: NOTAM FILE FTW.
     MAVERICK (VH) (H) VORW/DME 113.1   TTT   Chan 78   N32°52.15´ W97°02.43´   042° 13.8 NM to fld. 536/6E.
        All acft arriving DFW are requested to turn DME off until departure due to traffic overload of Maverick DME
        DME unusable:
           180°–190° byd 10 NM
           240°–260° byd 20 NM blo 3,500´
        VOR unusable:
           105°–110° byd 40 NM
   COMM/NAV/WEATHER REMARKS: Unicom freq: Arpt inside Addison Class D airspace. Ctc Addison twr 126.0 (1200–0400Z‡).

AIRPARK EAST (1F7)   23 E   UTC–6(–5DT)   N32°48.78´ W96°21.12´   **DALLAS–FT WORTH**
   510   B   NOTAM FILE FTW   **COPTER**
   RWY 13–31: H2630X30 (ASPH)   LIRL
     RWY 13: Tree. Rgt tfc.
     RWY 31: Trees.
   SERVICE: S4 **FUEL** 100LL
   AIRPORT REMARKS: Unattended. Pilots use caution, wind shear and turbulence when approaching Rwy 13. 4´ fence parallel
     to rwy, full len, 78´ west of rwy cntrln. Rwy 13–31, 15´ drop off each end. Rwy and twy shoulders broken, loose aggregate
     and stones, extensive cracking and spalling. Twy pavement rough and uneven. Rwy 13 and 31 ends nonstd RCLM mkgs
     8 in wide.
   AIRPORT MANAGER: 214-679-8277
   COMMUNICATIONS: CTAF/UNICOM 122.7
   CLEARANCE DELIVERY PHONE: For CD ctc Regional Apch at 972-615-2799.

DALLAS CBD HELIPORT (49T)   0 N   UTC–6(–5DT)   N32°46.30´ W96°48.12´   **DALLAS–FT WORTH**
   480   B   NOTAM FILE FTW   **COPTER**
   HELIPAD H1: H60X60 (CONC)   S–43   PERIMETER LGTS
   HELIPAD H2: H60X60 (CONC)   S–43   PERIMETER LGTS
   SERVICE: **LGT** Perimeter lgts OTS indefly.
   HELIPORT REMARKS: Unattended. Helipad H1 and H2 900´ bldgs NW, 500´ bldgs NE 1.2 mile dist. Helipad security
     214–939–2940. Helipad H1 perimeter lgts. Helipad H1 rooftop. Ingress/egress SW. Helipad H2 rooftop. Ingress/egress
     SE.
   AIRPORT MANAGER: 214-671-1296
   WEATHER DATA SOURCES: AWOS–3 135.425 (214) 670–1243. AWOS temp unreliable. AWOS freq OTS indef.
   COMMUNICATIONS: CTAF/UNICOM 123.05
   CLEARANCE DELIVERY PHONE: For CD ctc Regional Apch at 972-615-2799.

DALLAS EXEC (RBD)(KRBD) 6 SW UTC−6(−5DT) N32°40.88′ W96°52.13′   DALLAS–FT WORTH
661 B NOTAM FILE RBD   COPTER
RWY 13−31: H7136X100 (CONC−GRVD) S−40, D−90, 2D−130 MIRL   H−6H, L−17C, A
  RWY 13: REIL. PAPI(P4L)—GA 3.0° TCH 40′. Thld dsplcd 1085′.   IAP, AD
  Trees.
  RWY 31: REIL. PAPI(P4R)—GA 3.0° TCH 45′. Thld dsplcd 500′.
  Road.
RWY 17−35: H3800X150 (CONC) S−35, D−60, 2D−110 MIRL
  RWY 17: REIL. PAPI(P4R)—GA 3.0° TCH 43′.
  RWY 35: REIL.
RUNWAY DECLARED DISTANCE INFORMATION
  RWY 13: TORA−6766 TODA−7136 ASDA−6622 LDA−5537
  RWY 31: TORA−6051 TODA−7136 ASDA−7101 LDA−6601
SERVICE: S4 **FUEL** 100LL, JET A **OX** 1, 2 **LGT** When ATCT clsd MIRL
  Rwy 13−31 and 17−35 preset low intst; to incr intst ACTVT—CTAF.
AIRPORT REMARKS: Attended 1200−0200Z‡. On call aft hrs. 100LL fuel
  avbl 24 hr. Birds on and invof arpt.
AIRPORT MANAGER: 214-671-1296
WEATHER DATA SOURCES: ASOS (214) 330−5317 LAWRS.
COMMUNICATIONS: CTAF 127.25 **ATIS** 126.35 **UNICOM** 122.95
®**REGIONAL APP/DEP CON** 125.2
  EXECUTIVE TOWER 127.25 (1300−0300Z‡) **GND CON** 119.475
CLNC DEL 118.625
AIRSPACE: CLASS D svc 1300−0300Z‡; other times CLASS G.
RADIO AIDS TO NAVIGATION: NOTAM FILE FTW.
  MAVERICK (VH) (H) VORW/DME 113.1   TTT   Chan 78   N32°52.15′ W97°02.43′   136° 14.2 NM to fld. 536/6E.
    All acft arriving DFW are requested to turn DME off until departure due to traffic overload of Maverick DME
  DME unusable:
    180°−190° byd 10 NM
    240°−260° byd 20 NM blo 3,500′
  VOR unusable:
    105°−110° byd 40 NM
  ILS/DME 110.75 I−RBD Chan 44(Y) Rwy 31. Class IE. Unmonitored when ATCT closed.

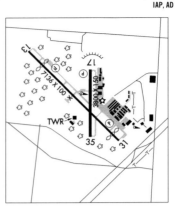

TEXAS

DALLAS LOVE FLD (DAL)(KDAL) 5 NW UTC−6(−5DT) N32°50.76′ W96°51.05′ DALLAS−FT WORTH
487 B Class I, ARFF Index C NOTAM FILE DAL COPTER
  RWY 13R−31L: H8800X150 (CONC−GRVD) S−120, D−250, 2S−175, 2D−388, 2D/2D2−875 H−6H, L−17C, A
    PCR 865 R/D/W/T HIRL CL IAP, AD
    RWY 13R: PAPI(P4R)—GA 3.0° TCH 52′. RVR−TM Thld dsplcd 489′. Rgt tfc.
    RWY 31L: MALSR. TDZL. PAPI(P4L)—GA 3.08° TCH 55′. RVR−TM Bldg.
  RWY 13L−31R: H7752X150 (CONC−GRVD) S−100, D−200, 2S−175, 2D−350 PCN 46 R/C/W/T HIRL CL
    RWY 13L: MALSR. TDZL. PAPI(P4R)—GA 3.0° TCH 57′. RVR−TR Thld dsplcd 399′.
    RWY 31R: MALSR. PAPI(P4L)—GA 3.0° TCH 55′. RVR−TR Pole. Rgt tfc.
  RUNWAY DECLARED DISTANCE INFORMATION
    RWY 13L: TORA−7752 TODA−7752 ASDA−7752 LDA−7352
    RWY 13R: TORA−8800 TODA−8800 ASDA−8800 LDA−8310
    RWY 31L: TORA−8800 TODA−8800 ASDA−8000 LDA−8000
    RWY 31R: TORA−7752 TODA−7752 ASDA−6952 LDA−6952
  SERVICE: S4 **FUEL** 100LL, JET A **OX** 1, 2, 3, 4
  NOISE: Noise sensitive areas all quadrants; noise abatement procedures in effect jet and acft over 12,500 lbs use Rwy 13R−31L between 0300−1200Z‡. For information call 214−670−5683.
  AIRPORT REMARKS: Attended continuously. Birds on and invof arpt. Bird activity Trinity River bottom 3 miles SW side. PAEW on arpt. Pvt pilot certificate or better rqrd to tkf or land. No student solo flts permitted. Twy K clsd thru tfc. K runup pad clsd 0600−1200Z‡. Acft using K runup pad btn 1200−0600Z‡ must obtain apvl fm arpt opns cntr 214−670−5683 prior to entering. Twy all clsd to acft wingspan 118 ft and gtr exc 1 hr PPR. 214−288−3069. Flight Notification Service (ADCUS) available. User fee arpt. Ldg fee arpt
  AIRPORT MANAGER: 214-670-5683
  WEATHER DATA SOURCES: ASOS (214) 353−1551 TDWR.
  COMMUNICATIONS: D−ATIS 120.15 (214) 358−5355
    DALLAS RCO 122.3 (FORT WORTH RADIO)
  ® **RGNL APP CON** 124.3 (North) 125.2 (South)
    LOVE TOWER 123.7 **GND CON** 121.75 **CLNC DEL** 127.5
  ® **RGNL DEP CON** 118.55 (East) 125.125 (West) 118.55 125.125 (Turbojets) 125.2 (South Props) 124.3 (North Props)
    CPDLC (LOGON KUSA)
    PDC
  AIRSPACE: CLASS B See VFR Terminal Area Chart.
  VOR TEST FACILITY (VOT) 113.3
  RADIO AIDS TO NAVIGATION: NOTAM FILE FTW.
    COWBOY (VH) (DH) VORW/DME 116.2 CVE Chan 109 N32°53.42′ W96°54.24′ 129° 3.8 NM to fld. 443/6E.
    VOR unusable:
      030°−035° byd 40 NM
      055°−060° byd 40 NM
      130°−140° byd 40 NM
    ILS/DME 111.5 I−DAL Chan 52 Rwy 13L. Class IIE. DME also serves Rwy 31R. DME unusable wi 1.3 NM fm thr; byd 30° left of course.
    ILS/DME 111.1 I−DPX Chan 48 Rwy 13R. Class IE. DME also serves Rwy 31L.
    ILS/DME 111.1 I−LVF Chan 48 Rwy 31L. Class IA. DME also serves Rwy 13R. LOC unusable byd 21° right of course.
    ILS/DME 111.5 I−OVW Chan 52 Rwy 31R. Class IIE. DME also serves Rwy 13L.

MCKINNEY NTL (TKI)(KTKI) 32 N UTC–6(–5DT) N33°10.62´ W96°35.33´   DALLAS–FT WORTH
589 B NOTAM FILE TKI   COPTER
RWY 18–36: H7002X150 (CONC) S–75, D–150, 2D–450 HIRL   H–6H, L–17C, A
  RWY 18: MALSR. PAPI(P4L)—GA 3.0° TCH 50´.   IAP, AD
  RWY 36: MALS. PAPI(P4L)—GA 3.0° TCH 50´. Rgt tfc.
SERVICE: S4 **FUEL** 100LL, JET A1+ **OX** 3 **LGT** When ATCT clsd actvt
  MALSR Rwy 18; MALS Rwy 36; PAPI Rwy 18 and 36; HIRL Rwy
  18–36—CTAF.
AIRPORT REMARKS: Attended 1200–0400Z‡. Bird activity invof arpt. Arpt
  admin 972-562-4053. NOTE: See Special Notices—Arrival Alert.
AIRPORT MANAGER: 972-562-3401
WEATHER DATA SOURCES: ASOS (972) 548–8525 ASOS broadcast over ATIS
  119.925 mhz.
COMMUNICATIONS: CTAF 118.825 **UNICOM** 122.95 **ATIS** 122.95
Ⓡ **REGIONAL APP/DEP CON** 124.3
  TOWER 118.825 (1200–0400Z‡) **GND CON** 121.875 **CLNC DEL** 121.35
  (when twr clsd)
AIRSPACE: CLASS D svc 1200–0400Z‡; other times CLASS G.
RADIO AIDS TO NAVIGATION: NOTAM FILE FTW.
  COWBOY (VH) (DH) VORW/DME 116.2 CVE Chan 109 N32°53.42´
  W96°54.24´ 037° 23.4 NM to fld. 443/6E.
  VOR unusable:
    030°–035° byd 40 NM
    055°–060° byd 40 NM
    130°–140° byd 40 NM
  ILS/DME 109.35 I–EFE Chan 30(Y) Rwy 18. Unmonitored when ATCT clsd.
COMM/NAV/WEATHER REMARKS: ASOS broadcast over ATIS 119.925 mhz.

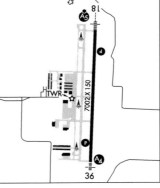

DALLAS SOUTH PORT (See PALMER on page 395)

TEXAS

DALLAS–FORT WORTH INTL (DFW)(KDFW)　12 NW　UTC–6(–5DT)　N32°53.83´ W97°02.26´　**DALLAS–FT WORTH COPTER**
606　B　LRA　Class I, ARFF Index E　NOTAM FILE DFW
RWY 18L–36R: H13401X200 (CONC–GRVD)　S–120, D–250, 2D–550, 2D/2D2–1066 PCN 83 R/B/W/T　H–6H, L–17C, A
HIRL　CL　IAP, AD
　RWY 18L: MALSR. TDZL. PAPI(P4L)—GA 3.0° TCH 70´. RVR–TMR
　RWY 36R: MALSR. TDZL. PAPI(P4L)—GA 3.0° TCH 66´. RVR–TMR
RWY 17C–35C: H13400X150 (ASPH–GRVD)　S–120, D–250, 2D–550, 2D/2D2–1120 PCN 93 R/B/W/T　HIRL　CL
　RWY 17C: ALSF2. TDZL. PAPI(P4L)—GA 3.0° TCH 74´. RVR–TMR
　RWY 35C: ALSF2. TDZL. PAPI(P4L)—GA 3.0° TCH 76´. RVR–TMR
RWY 17R–35L: H13400X200 (CONC–GRVD)　S–120, D–250, 2D–550, 2D/2D2–1049 PCN 81 R/B/W/T　HIRL　CL
　RWY 17R: MALSR. TDZL. PAPI(P4L)—GA 3.0° TCH 68´. RVR–TMR
　RWY 35L: MALSR. TDZL. PAPI(P4L)—GA 3.0° TCH 63´. RVR–TMR
RWY 18R–36L: H13400X150 (ASPH–GRVD)　S–120, D–250, 2D–490, 2D/2D2–985 PCN 90 R/C/W/T　HIRL　CL
　RWY 18R: ALSF2. TDZL. PAPI(P4L)—GA 3.0° TCH 74´. RVR–TMR
　RWY 36L: MALSR. TDZL. PAPI(P4L)—GA 3.0° TCH 72´. RVR–TMR
RWY 13R–31L: H9300X150 (CONC–GRVD)　S–120, D–250, 2D–485, 2D/2D2–1005 PCN 76 R/B/W/T　HIRL　CL
　RWY 13R: MALSR. TDZL. PAPI(P4L)—GA 3.0° TCH 71´. RVR–TR
　RWY 31L: REIL. PAPI(P4L)—GA 3.13° TCH 72´. RVR–TR
RWY 13L–31R: H9000X200 (CONC–GRVD)　S–120, D–250, 2D–550, 2D/2D2–1120 PCN 95 R/B/W/T　HIRL　CL
　RWY 13L: REIL. PAPI(P4L)—GA 3.0° TCH 82´. RVR–TMR Thld dsplcd 627´. 0.5% down.
　RWY 31R: MALSR. TDZL. PAPI(P4L)—GA 3.0° TCH 69´. RVR–TMR 0.5% up.
RWY 17L–35R: H8500X150 (CONC–GRVD)　S–120, D–250, 2D–550, 2D/2D2–1120 PCN 91 R/B/W/T　HIRL　CL
　RWY 17L: ALSF2. TDZL. PAPI(P4L)—GA 3.0° TCH 77´. RVR–TMR Antenna. 0.6% up.
　RWY 35R: ALSF2. TDZL. PAPI(P4R)—GA 3.0° TCH 73´. RVR–TMR 0.6% down.
LAND AND HOLD–SHORT OPERATIONS

LDG RWY	HOLD–SHORT POINT	AVBL LDG DIST
RWY 17C	TWY B	10460
RWY 18R	TWY B	10100
RWY 35C	TWY EJ	9050
RWY 36L	TWY Z	10650

RUNWAY DECLARED DISTANCE INFORMATION
　RWY 13L: TORA–9000　TODA–9000　ASDA–9000　LDA–8373
　RWY 13R: TORA–9300　TODA–9300　ASDA–9300　LDA–9300
　RWY 17C: TORA–13400 TODA–13400　ASDA–13400　LDA–13400
　RWY 17L: TORA–8500　TODA–8500　ASDA–8500　LDA–8500
　RWY 17R: TORA–13400 TODA–13400　ASDA–13400　LDA–13400
　RWY 18L: TORA–13401 TODA–13401　ASDA–13401　LDA–13401
　RWY 18R: TORA–13400 TODA–13400　ASDA–13400　LDA–13400
　RWY 31L: TORA–9300　TODA–9300　ASDA–9300　LDA–9300
　RWY 31R: TORA–8373　TODA–8373　ASDA–8373　LDA–8373
　RWY 35C: TORA–13400 TODA–13400　ASDA–13400　LDA–13400
　RWY 35L: TORA–13400 TODA–13400　ASDA–13400　LDA–13400
　RWY 35R: TORA–8500　TODA–8500　ASDA–8500　LDA–8500
　RWY 36L: TORA–13400 TODA–13400　ASDA–13400　LDA–13400
　RWY 36R: TORA–13401 TODA–13401　ASDA–13401　LDA–13401

CONTINUED ON NEXT PAGE

TEXAS
CONTINUED FROM PRECEDING PAGE

SERVICE: FUEL 100LL, JET A **OX** 1, 3
NOISE: See Special Notices–Noise Abatement Procedures.
AIRPORT REMARKS: Attended continuously. Birds on and invof arpt. Rwy 17L–35R CLOSED 0400–1200Z‡ exc PPR. Rwy 13R–31L CLOSED 0400–1200Z‡ except PPR. Rwy 13L–31R CLOSED 0400–1200Z‡ exc PPR. Visual screen 20´ AGL 1180´ south AER 35C. Visual screen 22´ AGL 1179´ south AER 35L. ASDE-X in use. Opr transponders with altitude reporting mode and ADS–B (if equipped) enabled on all airport surfaces. Runway Status Lights in operation. PPR for acft with wingspan 215´ or greater (GROUP VI), call arpt ops 972–973–3112 for flw–me svcs while taxiing to and from ramp and rwys. Arpt under const, PAEW in movement areas. A380 ops only auzd on Rwys 18R–36L and Rwy 18L–36R. B747–8 opns only auzd on Rwys 18R–36L, 18L–36R and 17R–35L. Ctc arpt opns for addnl info. Tkf distance for Rwy 17L from Twy Q2 is 8196´. Tkf distance for Rwy 35R from Twy Q9 is 8196´. Tkf distance for Rwy 17R from Twy EG is 13082´ and from Twy EH is 12816´. Tkf distance for Rwy 35L from Twy EQ is 13084´ and from Twy EP is 12811´. Tkf distance for Rwy 36R from Twy WP is 12815´, from Twy WQ is 13082´. Tkf distance for Rwy 18L from Twy WG is 13082´, from Twy WH is 12815´. Tkf distance for Rwy 17C from Twy EG is 13,082´. Tkf distance for Rwy 18R from Twy WG is 13,082´. Land And Hold Short signs on Rwy 17C at Twy B 10,460´ south of Rwy 17C thld, Rwy 18R at Twy B 10,100´ south of Rwy 18R thld, Rwy 35C at Twy EJ 9050´ north of Rwy 35C thld, Rwy 36L at Twy Z 10,650´ north of Rwy 36L thld, lgtd and marked with in–pavement pulsating white lgts. Acft using Terminal D gates or apron entrance/exit points 122 thru 150 must obtain approval from DFW ramp tower 129.825 prior to entering ramp and prior to pushback. Use extreme care at other times. Acft using terminal E gates E2–E17 must obtain approval from ramp 131.0 prior to entering ramp and prior to pushback. Acft using terminal E gates E–18–E38 must obtain approval from ramp 128.825 prior to entering ramp and prior to pushback. Acft using Terminal B Gates B1–B17, all Terminal D gates, and apron entry points 117–150 must obtain approval from Ramp 129.825 prior to entering ramp and prior to pushback. Acft using Terminal B Gates B18–B49 must obtain approval from Ramp 130.10 prior to entering ramp and prior to pushback. Acft using Terminal A Gates A8–A39 and Terminal C Gates C2–C12 must obtain approval from ramp 131.275 prior to entering ramp and prior to pushback. Acft using Terminal C Gates C14–C39 must obtain approval from Ramp 131.80 prior to entering ramp and prior to pushback. Acft using Twy HA north of Twy B must obtain approval from ramp 129.825 prior to entering ramp. Apron entrance/exit points 1 and 2 clsd to acft with wingspan greater than 89´ except PPR. Apron entrance/exit point 3 clsd to acft with wingspan greater than 214 ft except PPR. Apron entrance/exit points 5, 7, 42, 44, 48, 49, 51, 52, 117, 118 and 122 clsd to acft with wingspan greater than 118´. Apron entrance/exit points 31 and 39 clsd to acft with wingspan greater than 167´. Apron entrance/exit points 9, 32, 33, 34, 35, 36, 37, 38, and 53 clsd to acft with wingspan greater than 135´. Apron entrance/exit point 48 clsd to acft with wingspan greater than 195´. Apron entrance/exit point 124 clsd to acft with wingspan greater than 213´. Unless otherwise specified, all apron entrance/exit points clsd to acft with wingspan greater than 214´ except PPR. Terminal B apron taxilane btn apron entrance/exit point taxilanes 107 and 117 clsd to acft with wingspan 94´ and greater. Apron entrance/exit points 110, 111, 112, 113, 114, 115 and 116 clsd to acft with wingspan greater than 94´. Twy A6 clsd to acft with wingspan 171 ft and greater. Twys may rqr judgemental oversteering for large acft. PPR general aviation opns 0600–1100Z‡, call arpt ops 972–973–3112. PPR from arpt ops for general aviation acft to proceed to airline terminal gate exc to general aviation fac. PPR from the primary tenant airlines to opr within the central terminal area. Proper minimum object free area distances may not be maintained for ramp/apron taxi lanes. Twy edge reflectors along all twys. Apron entrance/exit points 22, 24, 105, and 107 clsd to acft with wingspan greater than 125 ft. Ldg fee. Flight Notification Service (ADCUS) available. NOTE: See Special Notices–Noise Abatement Procedures.
AIRPORT MANAGER: 972–973–3112
WEATHER DATA SOURCES: ASOS (972) 615–2608 LLWAS. TDWR.
COMMUNICATIONS: D–ATIS ARR 123.775 (972) 615–2701 **D–ATIS DEP** 135.925 (972) 615–2701 **UNICOM** 122.95
®**RGNL APP CON** 118.1 (Rwy 13R) 118.425 (Rwy 18L, Rwy 18R, Rwy 31R, Rwy 36L, Rwy 36R) 119.4 (Rwy 17L, Rwy 31R, Rwy 35R)
119.875 (West) 124.3 (North) 125.025 (East) 125.2 (South, Rwy 31R) 127.075 (Rwy 17C, Rwy 17R, Rwy 31L, Rwy 35L, Rwy 35C) 133.15 (Rwy 13R)
135.5 (Rwy 31R) 135.975 (South) 133.625 (West) 135.525 (East)
DFW TOWER 126.55 127.5 (E) 124.15 134.9 (W) **GND CON** 121.65 121.8 (E) 121.85 (W)
CLNC DEL 128.25
®**RGNL DEP CON** 118.1 135.975 124.825(North) 125.125 135.975(South) 126.475(West) 118.55(East)
CPDLC (LOGON KUSA)
PDC
AIRSPACE: CLASS B See VFR Terminal Area Chart.
RADIO AIDS TO NAVIGATION: NOTAM FILE FTW.
  MAVERICK (VH) (H) VORW/DME 113.1   TTT   Chan 78   N32°52.15´   W97°02.43´   359° 1.7 NM to fld. 536/6E.
    All acft arriving DFW are requested to turn DME off until departure due to traffic overload of Maverick DME
    DME unusable:
      180°–190° byd 10 NM
      240°–260° byd 20 NM blo 3,500´
    VOR unusable:
      105°–110° byd 40 NM
  ILS/DME 109.5 I–LWN   Chan 32   Rwy 13R.   Class IIE.   DME unusable wi 2.5 NM (4.2 DME).
  ILS/DME 110.3 I–FLQ   Chan 40   Rwy 17C.   Class IIIE.   DME also serves Rwy 35R.
  ILS/DME 111.75 I–PPZ   Chan 54(Y)   Rwy 17L.   Class IIIE.   DME also serves Rwy 35R.

CONTINUED ON NEXT PAGE
SC, 25 JAN 2024 to 21 MAR 2024

TEXAS

CONTINUED FROM PRECEDING PAGE

ILS/DME 111.35   I–JHZ   Chan 50(Y)   Rwy 17R.   Class IIE.   DME also serves Rwy 35L.
ILS/DME 110.55   I–CIX   Chan 42(Y)   Rwy 18L.   Class IT.   DME also serves Rwy 36R.
ILS/DME 111.9   I–VYN   Chan 56   Rwy 18R.   Class IIIE. DME also serves Rwy 36L.
ILS/DME 110.9   I–RRA   Chan 46   Rwy 31R.   Class IE.
ILS/DME 110.3   I–PKQ   Chan 40   Rwy 35C.   Class IIIE. DME also serves Rwy 17C. LOC unusable byd 16NM blw 3,700ft; byd 3° right of course byd 16nm.
ILS/DME 111.35   I–UWX   Chan 50(Y)   Rwy 35L.   Class IE.   LOC unusable byd 14 NM blo 3,400´. DME also serves Rwy 17R.
ILS/DME 111.75   I–AJQ   Chan 54(Y)   Rwy 35R.   Class IIIE. DME also serves Rwy 17L. LOC unusable byd 16 NM 5° right of course.
ILS/DME 111.9   I–BXN   Chan 56   Rwy 36L.   Class ID.   DME also serves Rwy 18R. LOC unusable byd 15 NM 5° right of course.
ILS/DME 110.55   I–FJN   Chan 42(Y)   Rwy 36R.   Class IE.   DME also serves Rwy 18L.

DAN E RICHARDS MUNI (See PADUCAH on page 394)

DAN JONES INTL (See HOUSTON on page 335)

DAVID WAYNE HOOKS MEML (See HOUSTON on page 336)

DECATUR

BISHOP   (76T)   6 E   UTC–6(–5DT)   N33°16.15´ W97°27.11´   DALLAS–FT WORTH
888   NOTAM FILE FTW   COPTER
  RWY 17–35: 3730X170 (TURF)   0.4% up N
    RWY 17: Trees.
    RWY 35: Road.
  SERVICE: S4
  AIRPORT REMARKS: Unattended. For rwy conds call 940–389–6100, or 940–389–6200. Rwy may be rough due to drought conds. Rwy soft aft hvy rain. 5 15 ft white poles alg W rwy edge.
  AIRPORT MANAGER: 940-389-6100
  COMMUNICATIONS: CTAF 122.9
  CLEARANCE DELIVERY PHONE: For CD ctc Regional Apch at 972-615-2799.

DECATUR MUNI   (LUD)(KLUD)   2 N   UTC–6(–5DT)   N33°15.26´ W97°34.83´   DALLAS–FT WORTH
1047   B   NOTAM FILE LUD   COPTER
  RWY 17–35: H4200X60 (ASPH)   S–12.5, D–17   MIRL   L–17C, A
    RWY 17: REIL. PAPI(P2L)—GA 3.5° TCH 23´. Tree.   IAP
    RWY 35: PAPI(P2L)—GA 3.5° TCH 40´. Trees. Rgt tfc.
  SERVICE: S4   **FUEL** 100LL, JET A   **LGT** Dusk–Dawn. MIRL Rwy 17–35 preset low intst; to incr intst actvt—CTAF.
  AIRPORT REMARKS: Attended 1400–2300Z‡. Deer and wildlife on and invof arpt. Gnd drops sharply 160´ north of Rwy 17 thr. Rwy 17–35 extensive pavement cracking. Due to rwy elev chg, acft not vsb at opposite end.
  AIRPORT MANAGER: 940-627-2855
  WEATHER DATA SOURCES: AWOS–3 118.225 (940) 627–2365.
  COMMUNICATIONS: CTAF/UNICOM 122.8
  ®**REGIONAL APP/DEP CON** 118.1
  CLEARANCE DELIVERY PHONE: For CD ctc Regional Apch at 972-615-2799.
  RADIO AIDS TO NAVIGATION: NOTAM FILE FTW.
    BOWIE (H) (H) VORTACW 117.15   UKW   Chan 118(Y)   N33°32.15´ W97°49.28´   138° 20.8 NM to fld. 1102/6E.

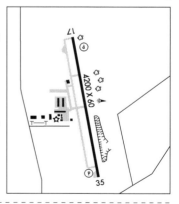

SC, 25 JAN 2024 to 21 MAR 2024

HERITAGE CREEK AIRSTRIP (58T) 9 SE UTC−6(−5DT) N33°09.96´ W97°28.79´   **DALLAS−FT WORTH**
883   NOTAM FILE FTW   **COPTER**
RWY 13−31: 3000X60 (TURF)   LIRL   0.8% up NW
  RWY 13: Tree.
  RWY 31: Tree. Rgt tfc.
SERVICE: S4   **LGT** ACTVT LIRL Rwy 13−31 —CTAF. Rwy defined by white "L" markers on each corner—nights: two lights each side of cntrln mark rwy ends.
AIRPORT REMARKS: Unattended. Deer and birds on and invof arpt. Parachute activity invof arpt. Remote controlled acft ops on arpt. All acft monitor CTAF due to the close proximity of Rhome Meadows arpt. Rwy 31 right tfc for fixed wing acft only; remain east of the rwy.
AIRPORT MANAGER: (817) 988-9745
COMMUNICATIONS: CTAF 122.9
CLEARANCE DELIVERY PHONE: For CD ctc Regional Apch at 972-615-2799.

LAZY G BAR RANCH (Ø9T) 5 NE UTC−6(−5DT) N33°16.88´ W97°29.80´   **DALLAS−FT WORTH**
931   NOTAM FILE FTW
RWY 17−35: 1600X40 (TURF−DIRT)
  RWY 17: Brush. Rgt tfc.
AIRPORT REMARKS: Unattended. Livestock on and invof arpt. For fld condition call arpt manager. Call ahead to confirm rwy is clear of livestock. Rough, rolling gradient. Full rwy not visible from ends. Center 20´ mowed.
AIRPORT MANAGER: (719) 221-7993
COMMUNICATIONS: CTAF 122.9
CLEARANCE DELIVERY PHONE: For CD ctc Regional Apch at 972-615-2799.

TRIPLE−ACE FLD (35X) 2 NE UTC−6(−5DT) N33°15.11´ W97°33.21´   **DALLAS−FT WORTH**
1010   NOTAM FILE 35X
RWY 02−20: 1271X40 (TURF)
  RWY 02: Road. Rgt tfc.
  RWY 20: Fence.
AIRPORT REMARKS: Unattended. Wildlife on and invof arpt. Acft oprg into or out of arpt will use Decatur Arpt freq 122.8 to communicate with Decatur Arpt tfc. Rwy soft aft rain. Call for ficons.
AIRPORT MANAGER: 940-627-6800
COMMUNICATIONS: CTAF 122.8

TEXAS

DEL RIO INTL (DRT)(KDRT) 2 NW UTC−6(−5DT) N29°22.45′ W100°55.63′   SAN ANTONIO
1002 B AOE Class I, ARFF Index A NOTAM FILE DRT   H−7B, L−19B
RWY 13−31: H6300X100 (ASPH) S−35, D−65, 2D−110 HIRL   IAP
  RWY 13: MALS. PAPI(P4L)—GA 3.0° TCH 47′. Thld dsplcd 300′. Tree.
    Rgt tfc.
  RWY 31: REIL. PAPI(P4L)—GA 3.0° TCH 62′. Tree.
RUNWAY DECLARED DISTANCE INFORMATION
  RWY 13: TORA−6300 TODA−6300 ASDA−6300 LDA−6000
  RWY 31: TORA−6000 TODA−6300 ASDA−5980 LDA−5980
SERVICE: S4 **FUEL** 100LL, JET A **LGT** ACTVT MALS Rwy 13; REIL Rwy
  31; HIRL Rwy 13−31; twy—CTAF.
AIRPORT REMARKS: Attended 1300−0100Z‡. After hrs call 830−768−0898.
  The National Weather Service releases weather ballons from the Del Rio
  Airport twice daily (1200 and 0000 ZULU).
AIRPORT MANAGER: (830) 734-4857
WEATHER DATA SOURCES: ASOS 118.525 (830) 703−8560.
COMMUNICATIONS: CTAF/UNICOM 122.8
  RCO 122.3 (SAN ANGELO RADIO)
®**APP/DEP CON** 119.6 (Mon−Fri 1300−0100Z‡, clsd Sat, Sun
  2100−2359Z‡ except holidays). Other hours ctc
®**HOUSTON CENTER APP/DEP CON** 125.75 (Mon−Fri 0100−1300Z‡, Sat 24,
  Sun 2359−2100Z‡ except holidays.)
CLNC DEL 120.5
CLEARANCE DELIVERY PHONE: For CD ctc Laughlin Apch at 830-298-5192, when Apch clsd ctc Houston ARTCC at
  281-230-5788.
RADIO AIDS TO NAVIGATION: NOTAM FILE DLF.
  LAUGHLIN (H) (H) VORTAC 114.4 DLF Chan 91 N29°21.65′ W100°46.30′ 269° 8.2 NM to fld. 1071/7E.
    VORTAC unmonitored when Del Rio apch ctl clsd.
    TACAN AZIMUTH unusable:
      161°−285° byd 15 NM
      No NOTAM MP: 0800−1200Z‡ Tue−Thu
    VOR unusable:
      045°−050° blo 3,000′
      161°−285° byd 15 NM
      286°−330° byd 25 NM blo 4,500′
      331°−359° byd 25 NM
      360°−160° byd 25 NM blo 4,500′
    DME unusable:
      161°−285° byd 15 NM
  KOTTI NDB (LOMW) 335 DR N29°26.56′ W100°59.54′ 132° 5.7 NM to fld. 1148/8E. NOTAM FILE DRT.
  ILS/DME 111.9 I-DRT Chan 56 Rwy 13. Class IE. LOM KOTTI NDB. ILS/DME unmonitored. KOTTI LOM
    unmonitored.

• • • • • • • • • • •

HELIPAD H1: H46X46 (CONC)
HELIPAD H2: H46X46 (CONC)
HELIPORT REMARKS: Helipad H1 and H2 lctd south end of main prkg ramp.

DELL CITY MUNI (2E5) 2 N UTC−7(−6DT) N31°56.86′ W105°11.51′   EL PASO
3703 B NOTAM FILE ABQ   L−6F
RWY 08−26: H4685X55 (ASPH) S−12.5 MIRL
  RWY 08: Road.
  RWY 26: Thld dsplcd 400′. Road.
AIRPORT REMARKS: Unattended. Dsplcd thld bar not painted.
AIRPORT MANAGER: 432-940-6658
COMMUNICATIONS: CTAF 122.9
CLEARANCE DELIVERY PHONE: For CD ctc Albuquerque ARTCC at 505-856-4861.
RADIO AIDS TO NAVIGATION: NOTAM FILE ABQ.
  SALT FLAT (L) (L) VORTACW 113.0 SFL Chan 77 N31°44.89′ W105°05.21′ 324° 13.1 NM to fld. 3730/12E.
    VORTAC unusable:
      010°−065° byd 29 NM blo 15,000′
      180°−190° byd 30 NM blo 9,500′
    TACAN AZIMUTH & DME unusable:
      065°−075° byd 10 NM
      265°−270° byd 26 NM

DENISON N33°49.59′ W96°40.13′ NOTAM FILE GYI.   DALLAS−FT. WORTH
  NDB (MHW) 341 DNI 176° 6.7 NM to North Texas Rgnl/Perrin Fld. 642/6E.   L−17C

DENTON ENTERPRISE (DTO)(KDTO)   3 W   UTC−6(−5DT)   N33°12.12′ W97°11.95′   DALLAS−FT WORTH COPTER
643   B   TPA—1443(800)   NOTAM FILE DTO   H−6H, L−17C, A
RWY 18L−36R: H7002X150 (ASPH)   S−70, D−100   MIRL   IAP, AD
 RWY 18L: MALSR. PAPI(P4L)—GA 3.0° TCH 50′.
 RWY 36R: PAPI(P4L)—GA 3.0° TCH 50′. Thld dsplcd 100′. Trees.
RWY 18R−36L: H5003X75 (ASPH)   S−30   MIRL   0.3% up N
 RWY 18R: PAPI(P4L)—GA 3.0° TCH 42′.
 RWY 36L: PAPI(P4L)—GA 3.0° TCH 42′.
RUNWAY DECLARED DISTANCE INFORMATION
 RWY 18L: TORA−7002   TODA−7002   ASDA−6502   LDA−6502
 RWY 36R: TORA−7002   TODA−7002   ASDA−6602   LDA−6502
SERVICE: S4   **FUEL** 100LL, JET A   **LGT** Dusk−dawn when ATCT clsd,
 MIRL Rwy 18L−36R and 18R−38L preset to low intst; to incr intst
 and ACTVT MALSR Rwy 18—CTAF.
AIRPORT REMARKS: Attended 1200−0400Z‡. Arpt closed to ultralights and
 gliders. Mowing opns on arpt May−Sept. Rwy 18L designated as a
 calm wind rwy.
AIRPORT MANAGER: 940−349−7736
WEATHER DATA SOURCES: ASOS 119.325 (940) 383−8457.
COMMUNICATIONS: CTAF 119.95 **ATIS** 119.325 **UNICOM** 122.95
® **REGIONAL APP/DEP CON** 118.1
 TOWER 119.95 (1200−0400Z‡)   **GND CON** 123.95 **CLNC DEL** 123.95
CLEARANCE DELIVERY PHONE: For CD when ATCT is clsd ctc Regional Apch
 at 972−615−2799.
AIRSPACE: CLASS D svc 1200−0400Z‡; other times CLASS G.
RADIO AIDS TO NAVIGATION: NOTAM FILE FTW.
 RANGER (VH) (H) VORTACW 115.7   FUZ   Chan 104   N32°53.37′ W97°10.77′   351° 18.7 NM to fld. 639/6E.
  VOR unusable:
   275°−290° byd 40 NM
   317°−327° byd 40 NM
 PINCK NDB (LOMW) 257   DT   N33°16.99′ W97°11.78′   178° 4.9 NM to fld. 739/4E.   NOTAM FILE DTO.
 ILS 109.1   I−DTO   Rwy 18L.   Class IT.   LOM PINCK NDB.   LOC unusable byd 10° left of course.

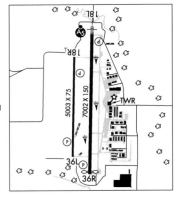

DENVER CITY (E57)   1 NW   UTC−6(−5DT)   N32°58.48′ W102°50.71′   ALBUQUERQUE
3575   B   NOTAM FILE FTW   H−6G, L−6H
RWY 04−22: H5780X50 (ASPH)   S−13   MIRL
 RWY 04: PAPI(P2L)—GA 4.5° TCH 64′. Thld dsplcd 350′. Road.
 RWY 22: PAPI(P2L)—GA 4.0° TCH 43′. Thld dsplcd 155′. P−line. Rgt
  tfc.
RWY 08−26: H3960X45 (ASPH)   S−13
 RWY 08: Thld dsplcd 179′. P−line.
 RWY 26: Thld dsplcd 526′. P−line. Rgt tfc.
SERVICE: **FUEL** 100LL, JET A
AIRPORT REMARKS: Attended irregularly. Fuel 100LL self−serve. Lgtd drilling
 rigs on and invof arpt. Rwy 26, entrance road and 20′ hangars inside
 prim sfc.
AIRPORT MANAGER: 806−592−5426
WEATHER DATA SOURCES: AWOS−3PT 118.275 (806) 592−3681.
COMMUNICATIONS: CTAF/UNICOM 122.8
CLEARANCE DELIVERY PHONE: For CD ctc Fort Worth ARTCC at
 817−858−7584.
RADIO AIDS TO NAVIGATION: NOTAM FILE HOB.
 HOBBS (L) (L) VORTACW 111.0   HOB   Chan 47   N32°38.29′
  W103°16.16′   036° 29.4 NM to fld. 3664/11E.

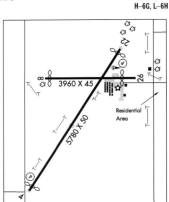

DEPOO   N25°59.02′ W97°30.55′   NOTAM FILE BRO.   BROWNSVILLE
 NDB (LOMW) 393   BR   133° 6.5 NM to Brownsville/South Padre Island Intl. 29/3E.

TEXAS

DESOTO HELIPORT (73T) 3 N UTC–6(–5DT) N32°37.90´ W96°51.31´ DALLAS–FT WORTH
649 B NOTAM FILE FTW COPTER
HELIPAD H1: H54X54 (CONC) PERIMETER LGTS
SERVICE: S4 **FUEL** 100LL, JET A **LGT** Perimeter lgts with recessed lgts srndg lndg pads.
HELIPORT REMARKS: Attended Mon–Fri 1500–0000Z‡. Self–serve fuel. Helipad H1 ingress/egress north and south. 49´ power
   pole 1,529´ north; 15´ rd, 500´ north; 42´ bldg., 270´ northeast; 35´ tree 783´ south; 33´ trees 85´ west; 36´
   building 276´ east. 1024´ MSL (310´ AGL) twr, 310 deg .73 mile from helipad. Inside KRBD Class D sfc area, ctc Dallas
   Exec twr 127.25.
AIRPORT MANAGER: 214-379-6790
COMMUNICATIONS: CTAF 122.9
CLEARANCE DELIVERY PHONE: For CD ctc Regional Apch at 972-615-2799.

DEVINE MUNI (23R) 2 W UTC–6(–5DT) N29°08.30´ W98°56.51´ SAN ANTONIO
702 B NOTAM FILE SJT L–19C
RWY 17–35: H3399X60 (ASPH) S–12.5 MIRL 0.8% up S IAP
   RWY 17: PAPI(P2L)—GA 3.0° TCH 33´. Road.
   RWY 35: PAPI(P2L)—GA 3.0° TCH 33´. Trees.
SERVICE: S4 **LGT** MIRL Rwy 17–35 preset low intst; to incr intst
   ACTVT—CTAF.
AIRPORT REMARKS: Attended Mon–Fri dawn–dusk. Deer on and invof arpt.
AIRPORT MANAGER: 830-538-4123
COMMUNICATIONS: CTAF 122.9
Ⓡ **HOUSTON CENTER APP/DEP CON** 134.95
CLEARANCE DELIVERY PHONE: For CD ctc Houston ARTCC at 281-230-5622.
RADIO AIDS TO NAVIGATION: NOTAM FILE SAT.
   SAN ANTONIO (VH) (H) VORTACW 116.8 SAT Chan 115 N29°38.64´
      W98°27.68´ 212° 39.4 NM to fld. 1159/8E.
   VOR unusable:
      018°–022° byd 40 NM
      028°–032° byd 40 NM
      342°–347° byd 40 NM
      355°–002° byd 40 NM blo 18,000´
   NDB (MHW) 359 HHH N29°08.30´ W98°56.36´ at fld.
      703/7E. NOTAM FILE SJT.

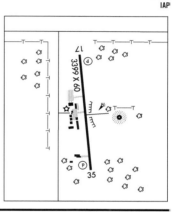

DICKINSON

TALON AIR HELIPORT (T34) 2 NE UTC–6(–5DT) N29°29.01´ W95°00.49´ HOUSTON
28 NOTAM FILE CXO
HELIPAD H1: 40X40 (TURF)
SERVICE: S2 **OX** 1, 2, 3, 4
HELIPORT REMARKS: Attended Mon–Fri 1400–2300Z‡. Ldg area not mkd. No windsock. Rcmdd apch fm the W, dept to the
   W. Trees in E apch close to ldg pad. Helipad H1 + 25´ trees east; + 25´ trees, 200´ west; 21´ bldg. north, + 25´ trees
   south. Airframe rprs: Overwater flight safety/survival gear, supplies, rental, re–certification, service.
AIRPORT MANAGER: 281-339-6000
COMMUNICATIONS: CTAF 122.9
CLEARANCE DELIVERY PHONE: For CD ctc Houston Apch at 281-443-5844 to cnl IFR call 581-443-5888.

TEXAS

DILLEY AIRPARK (24R) 2 NW UTC−6(−5DT) N28°41.13′ W99°11.35′   SAN ANTONIO
542   B   NOTAM FILE SJT   L−20G
RWY 12−30: H3400X60 (ASPH) S−12.5 LIRL 0.4% up SE
  RWY 12: Trees.
  RWY 30: Sign.
SERVICE: **LGT** Arpt lgts opr dusk−0500Z‡. Rotating bcn OTS indefly. Rwy
   12−30 LIRL OTS indefly.
AIRPORT REMARKS: Unattended.
AIRPORT MANAGER: 830-965-1624
COMMUNICATIONS: CTAF 122.9
CLEARANCE DELIVERY PHONE: For CD ctc Houston ARTCC at 281-230-5622.
RADIO AIDS TO NAVIGATION: NOTAM FILE COT.
  COTULLA (VL) (H) VORTACW 115.8   COT   Chan 105   N28°27.72′
   W99°07.11′   335° 13.9 NM to fld. 522/9E.
  VOR unusable:
    008°−032° byd 40 NM

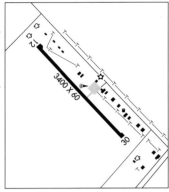

DIMMIT CO (See CARRIZO SPRINGS on page 268)

DIMMITT MUNI (T55) 2 N UTC−6(−5DT) N34°34.00′ W102°19.36′   ALBUQUERQUE
3883   B   NOTAM FILE FTW   H−6G, L−6H
RWY 01−19: H5500X60 (ASPH) S−15 MIRL
  RWY 01: Tree.
  RWY 19: Road. Rgt tfc.
SERVICE: **FUEL** 100LL   **LGT** Actvt MIRL Rwy 01−19—CTAF.
AIRPORT REMARKS: Unattended. For fuel call 806−647−2550 during
  business hrs. Rwy 01−19 Pavement spallling, cracks with vegetation
  growing through, loose stones and paint on sfc. Rwy 01 and 19
  Markings peeling off pavement.
AIRPORT MANAGER: 806-647-2155
COMMUNICATIONS: CTAF 122.9
CLEARANCE DELIVERY PHONE: For CD ctc Albuquerque ARTCC at
  505-856-4861.
RADIO AIDS TO NAVIGATION: NOTAM FILE FTW.
  TEXICO (VH) (H) VORTACW 112.2   TXO   Chan 59   N34°29.71′
   W102°50.38′   069° 26.0 NM to fld. 4060/11E.
  VOR unusable:
    095°−100° byd 40 NM
    120°−130° byd 40 NM
    210°−223° byd 40 NM blo 15,000′
    224°−251° byd 40 NM
    252°−262° byd 40 NM blo 18,000′
    263°−272° byd 40 NM blo 18,000′
    273°−283° byd 40 NM blo 6,000′
    273°−283° byd 46 NM blo 7,000′
    273°−283° byd 59 NM
    284°−319° byd 40 NM
    320°−035° byd 40 NM
  TACAN AZIMUTH unusable:
    222°−232°

DORCHESTER

TXAEROSPORT AERODROME (X65) 1 NE UTC−6(−5DT) N33°32.18′ W96°40.83′   DALLAS–FT WORTH
855   NOTAM FILE FTW
RWY 17−35: 3200X100 (TURF)
  RWY 17: Tree.
  RWY 35: Road.
SERVICE: S4
AIRPORT REMARKS: Attended Mon−Fri 1400−2300Z‡. Wildlife on and invof arpt. Rwy 17−35 mkd with orange tfc cones.
AIRPORT MANAGER: 469-502-9966
COMMUNICATIONS: CTAF 122.9
CLEARANCE DELIVERY PHONE: For CD ctc Fort Worth ARTCC at 817-858-7584.

SC, 25 JAN 2024 to 21 MAR 2024

TEXAS   297

DRAUGHON–MILLER CENTRAL TEXAS RGNL (See TEMPLE on page 434)

DRYDEN
TERRELL CO (6R6) 5 W UTC–6(–5DT) N30°02.79′ W102°12.79′   SAN ANTONIO
  2323 B NOTAM FILE SJT   L–19A
  RWY 13–31: H4526X75 (ASPH) S–30 MIRL 0.7% up NW
    RWY 13: Fence.
  RWY 04–22: H4525X75 (ASPH) S–30 0.3% up SW
    RWY 22: Brush.
  SERVICE: **LGT** Actvt MIRL Rwy 13–31—CTAF. Heli pad lgts 5 clicks 123.05.
  AIRPORT REMARKS: Attended Mon–Fri intmnt. Rwy 04–22 and Rwy 13–31 extensive cracking, loose stones on sfc. Rwy 13–31
    and Rwy 04–22 marking poor due to pavement deterioration.
  AIRPORT MANAGER: 432-345-6731
  COMMUNICATIONS: CTAF 122.9
  CLEARANCE DELIVERY PHONE: For CD ctc Houston ARTCC at 281-230-5622.
  RADIO AIDS TO NAVIGATION: NOTAM FILE FST.
    FORT STOCKTON (VH) (H) VORTACW 116.9   FST   Chan 116   N30°57.13′ W102°58.54′   133° 67.1 NM to fld.
      2893/11E.
    VOR unusable:
      020°–055° byd 20 NM blo 6,900′
      070°–086° byd 35 NM blo 6,400′
      106°–132° byd 30 NM blo 5,900′
      125°–202° byd 40 NM
      203°–213° byd 40 NM blo 18,000′
      214°–230° byd 40 NM
      245°–255° byd 40 NM
      315°–330° byd 30 NM blo 5,400′

DUBLIN MUNI (9F0) 2 SE UTC–6(–5DT) N32°04.09′ W98°19.52′   DALLAS–FT WORTH
  1495 B NOTAM FILE FTW   L–17B
  RWY 15–33: H3200X60 (ASPH) S–12.5 MIRL
    RWY 15: P–line.
  SERVICE: **FUEL** , UL94   **LGT** ACTIVATE MIRL Rwy 15–33 —123.5.
  AIRPORT REMARKS: Attended Wed–Fri 1500–0300Z‡, Sat 1500–2000Z‡.
    Deer and wildlife on and invof arpt.
  AIRPORT MANAGER: (254) 434-1082
  COMMUNICATIONS: CTAF 122.9
  CLEARANCE DELIVERY PHONE: For CD ctc Fort Worth ARTCC at 817-858-7584.
  RADIO AIDS TO NAVIGATION: NOTAM FILE FTW.
    GLEN ROSE (L) TACAN Chan 97   JEN (115.0)   N32°09.58′
      W97°52.66′   251° 23.5 NM to fld. 1300/6E.

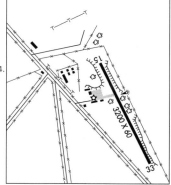

SC, 25 JAN 2024 to 21 MAR 2024

TEXAS

DUMAS

MOORE CO (DUX)(KDUX)   2 W   UTC−6(−5DT)   N35°51.45′ W102°00.80′   ALBUQUERQUE
3706   B   NOTAM FILE DUX   H−6G, L−15B
RWY 01−19: H6001X100 (ASPH)   S−30, D−45   MIRL   IAP
  RWY 01: PAPI(P4L)—GA 3.0° TCH 50′.
  RWY 19: PAPI(P4L)—GA 3.0° TCH 50′. Road.
RWY 14−32: H3100X60 (ASPH)   S−21, D−32   MIRL
  RWY 14: P−line.
SERVICE: S4   **FUEL** 100LL, JET A   **LGT** MIRL Rwy 01−19 preset low intst;
  to incr intst actvt—CTAF. PAPI Rwy 01 and 19 opr consly.
AIRPORT REMARKS: Attended 1400−2300Z‡. Parachute Jumping. Extensive
  cropdusting in summer. For services after hours, call 806−935−6995
  or 806−676−6412. 100LL self−serve fuel avbl 24 hrs with major credit
  card.
AIRPORT MANAGER: 806−935−6995
WEATHER DATA SOURCES: AWOS−3 118.075 (806) 934−3390.
COMMUNICATIONS: CTAF/UNICOM 122.8
®**ALBUQUERQUE CENTER APP/DEP CON** 127.85
CLEARANCE DELIVERY PHONE: For CD ctc Albuquerque ARTCC at
  505−856−4861.
RADIO AIDS TO NAVIGATION: NOTAM FILE DHT.
  DALHART (L) (L) VORTACW 112.0   DHT   Chan 57   N36°05.49′
    W102°32.68′   106° 29.4 NM to fld. 4020/12E.
  TAC AZM unusable:
    240°−255° byd 15 NM
    320°−350° byd 15 NM

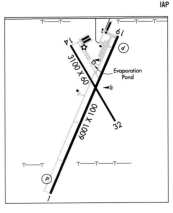

DUVAL—FREER (See FREER on page 314)

DYESS AFB (DYS)(KDYS) AF   5 SW   UTC−6(−5DT)   N32°25.11′ W99°51.39′   DALLAS—FT WORTH
1790   B   TPA—See Remarks   NOTAM FILE FTW   Not insp.   H−6H, L−17B
RWY 16−34: H13500X300 (PEM)   PCN 57 R/C/W/T   HIRL   DIAP, AD
  RWY 16: ALSF1. PAPI(P4L)—GA 2.6° TCH 48′. RVR−T
  RWY 34: ALSF1. PAPI(P4L)—GA 2.5° TCH 53′. RVR−T
RWY 163−343: 3500X60 (GRE)
RWY 164−344: H3498X60 (ASPH)   PCN 40 F/B/W/T
SERVICE: S4   **FUEL** JET A+   **OX** 2   **MILITARY**—   **JASU** 1(MD−3) 1(MA−1A) 1(AM32A−60A) 1(A/M32A−86) **FUEL** A++ **FLUID**
  LPOX De−ice **OIL** O−133−148−156 **TRAN ALERT** Svc avbl 1400−0400Z‡ Mon−Fri; clsd wkend and hol. No mil fleet svc avbl,
  ltd tran svc avbl.
NOISE: Quiet hr policy 0400−1000Z‡.

CONTINUED ON NEXT PAGE

TEXAS

CONTINUED FROM PRECEDING PAGE

MILITARY REMARKS: Opr hrs 1300–0559Z‡ Mon–Fri for all acft, 1500–2300Z‡ Sat-Sun for 7 BW and 317 AW only; clsd hol, hol wkend and AFGSC Fam Days. In case of aft hr emerg ntfy 7 BW Comd Post at 325–696–1921. **RSTD** PPR ctc afld mgmt at 7OSS.OSAA.AMOPS@us.af.mil for PPR req form DSN 461–2515/2258. Min 24 hr notice required and req no more than 7 days prior. PPR valid +/– 30 minutes of sked ldg. All diverts must ctc Afld Mgmt to confirm ramp space/tran svc avbl. Rwy 163–343 used as an assault strip. PPR valid +/– 30 minutes. PPR will not be issued for tran acft req Rwy 163–343 and Rwy 164–344. LZ164–444 has a non-std ltg sys. Tran acft must obtain briefing fm 317 OSK prior to ngt opns. without formal notification from 317 OSK, tran acft using Rwy 163–343 or 164–344 at ngt without lgt (overt or covert) and with respective MAJCOM/A3 apvl must notify Afld Mgmt and req separate NOTAM for unlgtd LZ opns. Inbd acft with DV code 6 or abv ctc afld ops 20 min prior arr Mon–Fri, ctc Comd Post on UHF or DSN 461–1921. 45 min prior wkend and hol. No arrival/departure when lightning within 5 NM without OG/CC approval. Twy G rstd to daylight ops only, exc navigation ops and maintenance tow. Park spots A1 and B1 avbl for taxi only. Parking spots A12, A13 and A20 are designated acft ground equipment (AGE) spots. ops only. Tye ramp clsd. B-52 acft ldg Dyess AFB must prvd at least 2–4 hrs notice bfr arr for afld prep. **CAUTION** Intensive training and formation flight of heavy acft in the immediate vicinity. Extensive VFR assault strip tfc west of Rwy 16–34. Afld signs require B52 acft exit Rwy 16–34 at Twy F. Acft lrgr than C130 only allowed 180 deg turns on conc sfc at N and S ends of Rwy 16–34. During bird watch condition moderate and severe, aircrews should comply with owning MAJCOM/Unit guidance, aircrews can obtain current bird watch condition fr ATIS/PTD. BASH Phase II in effect Apr–Jun and Sep–Nov. COMSEC stored at Command Post. Nmrs unmkd spalls thru out Rwy 16–34. Ctc afld mgmt ops DSN 461–2515 for further info. **TFC PAT** TPA—Rectangular 3000(1210), overhead 3500(1710). During VMC dep acft must remain at or blo 3000′ until fld boundary to ensure separation from VFR overhead. RSRS applies to all local acft, B–1 8000′, C–130, 5000′ separation, B–1 acft rqr minimum ceiling/visibility 1500′/3 statute miles and rwy surface dry. **CSTMS/AG/IMG** CSTMS avbl, ctc Security Forces DSN 461–2131/2132 24 hr in advance. **MISC** All AMC acft ctc AMCC prior to arrival DSN 461–1984, C 325–696–1984. Wx fcst svc avbl dur afld opr hrs; DSN 461–2524, C325–696–2524. All 175–1 wx req rqr 2 hr notice. Afld wx mnt by AN/FMQ–19 ASOS, augmented by human obsn when rqr. ATC will relay twr prev vis, RCR/RSC and VIRGA rmk to acft. Augmented sfc vis rstd 090°–160° by bldg. For customs refer to FCG or AP–1. Fire bottles lctd at N and S hammerheads.
WEATHER DATA SOURCES: ASOS 269.175.
COMMUNICATIONS: SFA   **ATIS** 269.175   **PTD** 139.3 372.2
Ⓡ **ABILEEN APP/DEP CON** 125.0 338.3 (E) 127.2 282.3 (W)
  TOWER 133.0 257.675 (UHF equipped acft shall use 257.675 to max extent possible.)   **GND CON** 118.35 275.8
  COMMAND POST (CALL– RAYMOND 37) 311.0 **PMSV METRO** 383.25 Altn PMSV, Sheppard AFB 339.65.
AIRSPACE: CLASS C svc ctc **APP CON**.
RADIO AIDS TO NAVIGATION: NOTAM FILE FTW.
  (L) TACAN   Chan 63   DYS (133.6)   N32°25.11′ W99°51.42′   at fld. 1784/5E.
    mp: 1100–1500Z‡ Mon
    No NOTAM MP: 1100–1500Z‡ Wed
    TACAN AZIMUTH unusable:
      096°–106° byd 25 NM blo 5,500′
      166°–178° byd 30 NM blo 5,500′
      179°–239° byd 20 NM blo 5,500′
      240°–260° byd 14 NM
      261°–272° byd 30 NM blo 5,500′
    DME unusable:
      131°–142° byd 39 NM blo 5,500′
      166°–178° byd 30 NM blo 5,500′
      179°–239° byd 20 NM blo 5,500′
      240°–260° byd 14 NM
      261°–272° byd 30 NM blo 5,500′
  ABILENE (VH) (H) VORTACW 113.7   ABI   Chan 84   N32°28.88′ W99°51.81′   165° 3.8 NM to fld.
    1809/10E.   NOTAM FILE ABI.
    VOR unusable:
      163°–236° byd 40 NM blo 18,000′
      237°–247° byd 40 NM blo 7,000′
      248°–250° byd 40 NM blo 18,000′
      251°–255° byd 40 NM blo 4,500′
      251°–255° byd 46 NM blo 18,000′
  TUSCOLA (L) (L) VORW/DME 111.6   TQA   Chan 53   N32°14.14′ W99°49.01′   340° 11.1 NM to fld. 2058/10E.
  ILS 109.9   I-TYY   Rwy 16.   Class ID.   Mp:1100–1500Z‡ Tue. No NOTAM MP: 1100–1500Z‡ Fri.
  ILS 109.9   I–DYS   Rwy 34.   Class IE.   Mp: 1100–1500Z‡ Tue. No NOTAM MP: 1100–1500Z‡ Fri.
  ASR
COMM/NAV/WEATHER REMARKS: Radar see Terminal FLIP for Radar Minima.

EAGLE LAKE (ELA)(KELA) 1 NE UTC−6(−5DT) N29°36.00′ W96°19.32′
HOUSTON
L−19D, 21A, GOMW
IAP

184 B NOTAM FILE ELA
RWY 17−35: H4280X60 (ASPH) S−12.5 MIRL
  RWY 17: PAPI(P2L)—GA 3.0° TCH 48′.
  RWY 35: PAPI(P2L)—GA 3.0° TCH 40′. Road. Rgt tfc.
SERVICE: FUEL 100LL, JET A **LGT** MIRL RWY 17−35 preset low, to INCR INTST ACTVT—CTAF.
AIRPORT REMARKS: Attended irregularly. For svc after hrs call 713−502−4064.
AIRPORT MANAGER: 979−234−2640
WEATHER DATA SOURCES: AWOS−3PT 128.475 (979) 234−2665.
COMMUNICATIONS: CTAF 122.9
®**HOUSTON APP/DEP CON** 124.225
CLEARANCE DELIVERY PHONE: For CD ctc Houston Apch at 281−443−5844 to cnl IFR call 281−443−5888.
RADIO AIDS TO NAVIGATION: NOTAM FILE ELA.
  (DH) DME 116.4 ELA Chan 111 N29°39.75′ W96°19.03′ 184° 3.7 NM to fld. 192.

EAGLE LAKE N29°39.75′ W96°19.03′ NOTAM FILE ELA.
HOUSTON
H−7C, L−19D, 21A, GOMW

(DH) DME 116.4 ELA Chan 111 184° 3.7 NM to Eagle Lake. 192.

EAGLE PASS
MAVERICK CO MEML INTL (5T9) 8 N UTC−6(−5DT) N28°51.43′ W100°30.81′
SAN ANTONIO
H−7B, L−19B
IAP

887 B AOE NOTAM FILE SJT
RWY 13−31: H5506X100 (ASPH) MIRL
  RWY 13: Brush.
  RWY 31: Brush.
SERVICE: FUEL 100LL, JET A **LGT** Dusk−Dawn. MIRL Rwy 13−31 preset low intst; to incr intst actvt—CTAF.
AIRPORT REMARKS: Attended Mon−Fri 1430−2000Z‡, Sat−Sun 1600−2200Z‡. Rwy 13−31 surface extsv cracking, vegetation. Rwy 13 and 31 markings faded. Aiming point in old rwy apprs bfr thr. Rwy 31 pavement marking indcs rwy 30. Old rwy mkgs show in paved area aprxly 300′ bfr each ewy end. Twys−extsv cracking, loose stones, vegation, no mrkgs, no lgts. Flight Notification Service (ADCUS) available.
AIRPORT MANAGER: 830−773−9636
WEATHER DATA SOURCES: AWOS−3 119.175 (830) 757−6795.
COMMUNICATIONS: CTAF/UNICOM 122.8
  EAGLE PASS RCO 122.3 (SAN ANGELO RADIO)
®**DEL RIO APP/DEP CON** 127.75 (Mon−Fri 1300−0100Z‡, clsd Sat, Sun 2100−2359Z‡ except holidays). Other times ctc
®**HOUSTON CENTER APP/DEP CON** 125.75 (Mon−Fri 0100−1300Z‡, Sat 24, Sun 2359−2100Z‡ except holidays.)
CLEARANCE DELIVERY PHONE: For CD ctc Laughlin Apch at 830−298−5192, when Apch clsd ctc Houston ARTCC at 281−230−5622.
RADIO AIDS TO NAVIGATION: NOTAM FILE DLF.
  LAUGHLIN (H) (H) VORTAC 114.4 DLF Chan 91 N29°21.65′ W100°46.30′ 149° 33.1 NM to fld. 1071/7E.
  VORTAC unmonitored when Del Rio apch ctl clsd.
  TACAN AZIMUTH unusable:
    161°−285° byd 15 NM
    No NOTAM MP: 0800−1200Z‡ Tue−Thu
  VOR unusable:
    045°−050° blo 3,000′
    161°−285° byd 15 NM
    286°−330° byd 25 NM blo 4,500′
    331°−359° byd 25 NM
    360°−160° byd 25 NM blo 4,500′
  DME unusable:
    161°−285° byd 15 NM

EAGLE'S NEST ESTATES (See MIDLOTHIAN on page 382)

EAGLES AERODROME (See CONWAY on page 277)

EAST BREAKS 165 EMK N27°49.12′ W94°19.37′
L−20J, 21A, GOMW

AWOS−3 119.475 Winds unreliable 090− 270 deg.

TEXAS

EAST BREAKS 643 VAF N27°21.22´ W94°37.52´
AWOS–3 119.525 Winds unreliable 225°–360° .

L–20J, 21A, H–7C, GOMW

EAST TEXAS RGNL (See LONGVIEW on page 367)

EASTERWOOD FLD (See COLLEGE STATION on page 275)

EASTLAND MUNI (ETN)(KETN)   1 N UTC–6(–5DT)   N32°24.89´ W98°48.58´   DALLAS–FT WORTH
  1468   B   NOTAM FILE FTW   H–6H, L–17B
  RWY 17–35: H5000X60 (ASPH) S–20   MIRL   0.4% up N   IAP
    RWY 17: PAPI(P2L)—GA 3.5° TCH 48´. Thld dsplcd 980´. Pole.
    RWY 35: PAPI(P2L)—GA 3.0° TCH 45´. Thld dsplcd 420´. Trees.
  SERVICE: S3   **FUEL** 100LL, JET A   **LGT** Actvt PAPI Rwy 17 and 35, MIRL Rwy 17–35—CTAF.
  AIRPORT REMARKS: Attended Mon–Fri 1400–0000Z‡. Aft fuel hrs call 254–488–1055. Trml avbl 24/7 for flt crews. 183 AGL,
    1617 MSL unltd/unmkd ant, 1000 fm Rwy 35 end, 1500 R.
  AIRPORT MANAGER: 254-629-1588
  WEATHER DATA SOURCES: AWOS–3PT 118.45 (254) 631–0493.
  COMMUNICATIONS: CTAF/UNICOM 122.8
  ®**FORT WORTH CENTER APP/DEP CON** 127.15
  CLEARANCE DELIVERY PHONE: For CD ctc Fort Worth ARTCC at 817-858-7584.
  RADIO AIDS TO NAVIGATION: NOTAM FILE FTW.
    MILLSAP (VH) (H) VORTACW 117.7   MQP   Chan 124   N32°43.57´ W97°59.85´   237° 45.2 NM to fld. 900/9E.
    VOR unusable:
      004°–009° byd 40 NM
      010°–054° byd 40 NM blo 3,800´
      010°–054° byd 46 NM blo 5,000´
      010°–054° byd 56 NM
      055°–066° byd 40 NM blo 3,800´
      055°–066° byd 50 NM
      230°–247° byd 40 NM
      248°–258° byd 40 NM blo 3,700´
      248°–258° byd 53 NM
      259°–270° byd 40 NM blo 6,000´
      259°–270° byd 63 NM
      271°–285° byd 40 NM
      312°–316° byd 40 NM
      325°–340° byd 40 NM blo 3,000´
      325°–340° byd 46 NM blo 5,000´
      325°–340° byd 66 NM
      353°–003° byd 40 NM blo 18,000´

EDINBURG

SOUTH TEXAS INTL AT EDINBURG   (EBG)(KEBG)   9 N   UTC–6(–5DT)   N26°26.50´ W98°07.33´   BROWNSVILLE
  75   B   NOTAM FILE EBG   H–7B, L–20H
  RWY 14–32: H5000X75 (ASPH) S–30   MIRL   IAP
    RWY 14: REIL. PAPI(P2L)—GA 3.0° TCH 42´.
    RWY 32: PAPI(P2L)—GA 3.0° TCH 45´.
  SERVICE: **FUEL** 100LL, JET A   **LGT** MIRL Rwy 14–32 preset low intst; to incr intst and ACTVT REIL Rwy 14—CTAF. PAPI
    Rwy 14 and Rwy 32 opr consly.
  AIRPORT REMARKS: Attended 1400–2300Z‡. 24 hrs self service 100LL & Jet A. Jet A also full serve. Wildlife actvty dly SS–SR.
    100 ft pole 595 ft NE of helipad. Twy has reflectors on pavement. Cust avbl. User fee arpt. M–F 1400–2200Z‡.
  AIRPORT MANAGER: 956-292-2047
  WEATHER DATA SOURCES: AWOS–3PT 118.025 (956) 587–0743.
  COMMUNICATIONS: CTAF/UNICOM 122.8
  ®**VALLEY APP/DEP CON** 126.55
  CLEARANCE DELIVERY PHONE: For CD ctc Corpus Christi Apch at 361-299-4230.
  RADIO AIDS TO NAVIGATION: NOTAM FILE HRL.
    HARLINGEN (L) (L) VORW/DME 113.65   HRL   Chan 83(Y)   N26°13.75´ W97°39.14´   292° 28.3 NM to fld. 32/5E.

EDNA

JACKSON CO (26R) 3 NE UTC−6(−5DT) N29°00.06′ W96°34.92′   **HOUSTON**
62   B   NOTAM FILE CXO   **L−19D, 21A**
RWY 15−33: H3393X70 (ASPH)   S−12.5   MIRL   **IAP**
   RWY 15: P−line.
SERVICE: S4   **FUEL** 100LL   **LGT** MIRL Rwy 15−33 preset to low. To incr
   intst and ACTVT—CTAF.
AIRPORT REMARKS: Unattended. 100LL avbl 24 hrs, self−serve. Twy has
   reflectors on pavement. To mnt aerobatic box—123.3. Heavy itinerant
   traffic on weekends. NOTE: See Special Notices—Aerobatic Practice
   Area.
AIRPORT MANAGER: 361−652−4163
COMMUNICATIONS: CTAF/UNICOM 122.8
®**HOUSTON CENTER APP/DEP CON** 135.05
CLEARANCE DELIVERY PHONE: For CD ctc Houston ARTCC at 281−230−5622.
RADIO AIDS TO NAVIGATION: NOTAM FILE PSX.
   PALACIOS (VH) (H) VORTACW 117.3   PSX   Chan 120   N28°45.87′
   W96°18.37′   306° 20.3 NM to fld. 16/8E.

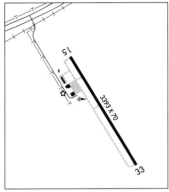

EDWARDS CO (See ROCKSPRINGS on page 411)

EL PASO INTL (ELP)(KELP) 4 NE UTC−7(−6DT) N31°48.44′ W106°22.58′   **EL PASO**
3962   B   TPA—See Remarks   AOE   Class I, ARFF Index C   NOTAM FILE ELP   **H−4L, L−6F**
RWY 04−22: H12020X150 (ASPH−CONC−GRVD)   S−100, D−180,   **IAP, AD**
   2D−350 PCN 70 R/B/X/T   HIRL
   RWY 04: REIL. PAPI(P4L)—GA 3.0° TCH 55′. RVR−TR
   RWY 22: MALSR. PAPI(P4R)—GA 3.0° TCH 70′. RVR−TR Rgt tfc.
   0.3% down.
RWY 08R−26L: H9025X150 (ASPH−CONC−GRVD)   S−100, D−180,
   2S−175, 2D−350 PCN 75 F/B/W/T   HIRL
   RWY 08R: REIL. PAPI(P4L)—GA 3.0° TCH 75′. Rgt tfc. 0.5% up.
   RWY 26L: MALSR. PAPI(P4R)—GA 3.0° TCH 75′. 0.3% down.
RWY 08L−26R: H5499X75 (CONC−GRVD)   S−60, D−180, 2S−175
   PCN 10 R/C/W/T   MIRL
   RWY 26R: Rgt tfc.
RUNWAY DECLARED DISTANCE INFORMATION
   RWY 04: TORA−12020 TODA−12020 ASDA−12020 LDA−12020
   RWY 08L: TORA−5499   TODA−5499   ASDA−5499   LDA−5499
   RWY 08R: TORA−9025   TODA−9025   ASDA−9025   LDA−9025
   RWY 22: TORA−12020 TODA−12020 ASDA−12020 LDA−12020
   RWY 26L: TORA−9025   TODA−9025   ASDA−9025   LDA−9025
   RWY 26R: TORA−5499   TODA−5499   ASDA−5499   LDA−5499
SERVICE: S4   **FUEL** 100LL, JET A1+   **OX** 2, 4
NOISE: Military users should review noise abatement procedures listed for Biggs AAF. Noise abatement procedures in effect,
   ctc tower for details.
AIRPORT REMARKS: Attended continuously. TPA small acft 5000 (1038); turbojet 5504 (1542); overhead apch 6004 (2042).
   Rwy 08L−26R not avbl for air carrier ops with more than 9 passenger seats. 24 hour PPR class A explosives ctc
   915−212−0333. Biggs AAF 2 NM northwest Rwy 22 can be mistaken for ELP Rwy 22. Engine power is rstd to idle power
   on one engine at a time for maximum 5 min on any terminal or parking aprons. Holding position markings for Rwy 08R
   apch and Rwy 04−22 are in close proximity to the terminal apron, review arpt diagram prior to pushback from the gate.
   Rwy 04−22, 206′ conc, 10,814′ asph, 1,000′ conc. Rwy 08R−26L, 7,780′ asph, 1,247′ conc. Twy A south of apch
   end of Rwy 4; Twy J NE of Twy K1; Twy K NE of Twy K1 btn Twy J and north cargo ramp; Twys U and Twy V south of
   Twy L; and Twy K2 not visible from ATCT. North bound tfc prohibited on Twy F south of AER 08R. Compass rose clsd
   permly. Cross−bleed starts or other pre−dep activity on movement areas only. Maintenance or other requirements needing
   longer or higher power ctc tower for directions to designated runup areas. NOTE: See Special Notices—Arrival Alert.

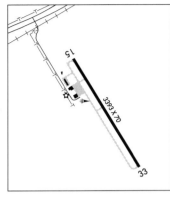

CONTINUED ON NEXT PAGE

TEXAS

CONTINUED FROM PRECEDING PAGE

AIRPORT MANAGER: 915-212-0333
WEATHER DATA SOURCES: ASOS (915) 774–9497 LLWAS. WSP.
COMMUNICATIONS: D–ATIS 120.0 (915) 774–9415 **UNICOM** 122.95
 RCO 122.6 (ALBUQUERQUE RADIO)
Ⓡ **APP CON** 124.25 (North–V16) 119.15 (South–V16)
 TOWER 118.3 **GND CON** 121.9 **CLNC DEL** 125.0
Ⓡ **DEP CON** 119.15
 PDC
AIRSPACE: CLASS C svc ctc **APP CON.**
VOR TEST FACILITY (VOT) 111.0
RADIO AIDS TO NAVIGATION: NOTAM FILE ELP.
 (VH) (H) VORTACW 115.2   ELP   Chan 99   N31°48.95′ W106°16.91′   252° 4.9 NM to fld. 4023/12E.
 DME unusable:
  260°–270° byd 30 NM blo 11,000′
  270°–310° byd 30 NM blo 10,000′
 VOR unusable:
  031°–075° byd 40 NM
  076°–099° byd 40 NM blo 18,000′
  100°–103° byd 40 NM
  258°–268° byd 40 NM blo 18,000′
  269°–294° byd 40 NM
  295°–305° byd 40 NM blo 18,000′
  295°–305° byd 48 NM blo 20,000′
  306°–309° byd 40 NM
  310°–070° byd 25 NM blo 12,000′
  314°–329° byd 40 NM
 LOC/DME 111.5   I–ETF   Chan 52   Rwy 04.   DME also serves Rwy 22. LOC unusable byd 24° left of course. LOC unusable byd 30° right of course.
 ILS/DME 111.5   I–ELP   Chan 52   Rwy 22.   Class IE.   DME also serves Rwy 4. DME unusable byd 16 NM restricted area R–5103A. LOC unusable byd 16 NM restricted area R–5103A.
 ASR

ELDORADO   (27R)   1 W   UTC–6(–5DT)   N30°51.73′ W100°36.65′   **SAN ANTONIO**
2448   B   NOTAM FILE SJT   **L–19B**
RWY 17–35: H4300X60 (ASPH)   S–12.5   MIRL
 RWY 17: PAPI(P2L)—GA 3.0° TCH 40′. Pole. Rgt tfc.
 RWY 35: PAPI(P2L)—GA 3.0° TCH 40′. Road.
SERVICE: FUEL 100LL   **LGT** MIRL Rwy 17–35 preset to low intst, to increase intst and ACTIVATE PAPI Rwy 17–35—CTAF.
AIRPORT REMARKS: Unattended. For fuel call 325–853–2036/2737 or 325–650–2256.
AIRPORT MANAGER: (325) 853-2593
COMMUNICATIONS: CTAF/UNICOM 123.0
CLEARANCE DELIVERY PHONE: For CD ctc san angelo Apch at 432-563-2123. when Apch clsd ctc Fort Worth ARTCC at 817-858-7584.
RADIO AIDS TO NAVIGATION: NOTAM FILE SJT.
 SAN ANGELO (VH) (H) VORTACW 115.1   SJT   Chan 98   N31°22.50′ W100°27.29′   185° 31.7 NM to fld. 1886/10E.
 VOR unusable:
  111°–190° byd 40 NM
  191°–201° byd 40 NM blo 6,000′
  191°–201° byd 49 NM
  202°–255° byd 40 NM blo 7,000′
  202°–255° byd 71 NM
  256°–289° byd 40 NM blo 4,400′
  256°–289° byd 53 NM
  290°–314° byd 40 NM blo 5,000′
  290°–314° byd 46 NM
  315°–352° byd 40 NM

ELLINGTON   (See HOUSTON on page 337)

TEXAS

ENNIS MUNI (F41) 2 W UTC−6(−5DT) N32°19.78´ W96°39.83´ DALLAS−FT WORTH
500 B NOTAM FILE FTW L−17C, A
RWY 16−34: H3999X50 (ASPH) S−18 MIRL IAP
 RWY 16: REIL. PAPI(P2L)—GA 3.0° TCH 35´. Ground. Rgt tfc.
 RWY 34: REIL. PAPI(P2L)—GA 3.0° TCH 35´. Thld dsplcd 255´. P−line.
SERVICE: S4 **FUEL** 100LL, JET A **LGT** ACTVT REIL RWY 16 and 34;
 PAPI RWY 16 and 34; MIRL Rwy 16−34, preset low INTST—CTAF.
AIRPORT REMARKS: Attended Mon−Fri 1400−2300Z‡. Parachute Jumping.
 Birds on and invof arpt. 100LL fuel self serve.
AIRPORT MANAGER: (972) 875-4279
COMMUNICATIONS: CTAF 122.9
®**REGIONAL APP/DEP CON** 125.3
CLEARANCE DELIVERY PHONE: For CD ctc Regional Apch at 972-615-2799.
RADIO AIDS TO NAVIGATION: NOTAM FILE FTW.
 CEDAR CREEK (L) (L) VORTACW 114.8 CQY Chan 95 N32°11.14´
  W96°13.09´ 285° 24.3 NM to fld. 400/6E.

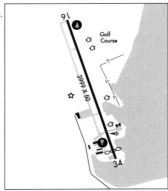

FABENS (E35) 1 NE UTC−7(−6DT) N31°31.03´ W106°08.82´ EL PASO
3680 B NOTAM FILE ABQ L−6F
RWY 08−26: H4197X60 (ASPH) S−12.5 MIRL 1.2% up E
 RWY 08: PAPI(P2L)—GA 3.0° TCH 42´. Thld dsplcd 173´. Fence.
 RWY 26: PAPI(P2L)—GA 4.0° TCH 73´. Antenna.
SERVICE: S4 **FUEL** 100LL **LGT** ACTVT rotg bcn and MIRL Rwy 08−26—CTAF. Rwy 08 and Rwy 26 PAPI OTS.
AIRPORT REMARKS: Attended 1400−2300Z‡. Rising terrain E of Rwy 08−26.
AIRPORT MANAGER: 915-764-3549
COMMUNICATIONS: CTAF/UNICOM 122.8
CLEARANCE DELIVERY PHONE: For CD ctc Albuquerque ARTCC at 505-856-4861.
RADIO AIDS TO NAVIGATION: NOTAM FILE ELP.
 EL PASO (VH) (H) VORTACW 115.2 ELP Chan 99 N31°48.95´ W106°16.91´ 147° 19.2 NM to fld. 4023/12E.
 DME unusable:
  260°−270° byd 30 NM blo 11,000´
  270°−310° byd 30 NM blo 10,000´
 VOR unusable:
  031°−075° byd 40 NM
  076°−099° byd 40 NM blo 18,000´
  100°−103° byd 40 NM
  258°−268° byd 40 NM blo 18,000´
  269°−294° byd 40 NM
  295°−305° byd 40 NM blo 18,000´
  295°−305° byd 48 NM blo 20,000´
  306°−309° byd 40 NM
  310°−070° byd 25 NM blo 12,000´
  314°−329° byd 40 NM

FAIRVIEW (See RHOME on page 408)

TEXAS

FALFURRIAS

BROOKS CO (BKS)(KBKS) 2 SE UTC−6(−5DT) N27°12.36′ W98°07.26′ **BROWNSVILLE**
112 B NOTAM FILE BKS **H−7B, L−20H**
RWY 17−35: H6006X75 (ASPH) S−52, D−80 MIRL **IAP**
 RWY 17: REIL. PAPI(P4L)—GA 3.0° TCH 45′. Tree.
 RWY 35: PAPI(P4L)—GA 3.0° TCH 45′.
RWY 14−32: H3018X60 (ASPH) S−4
 RWY 14: Trees.
SERVICE: FUEL 100LL, JET A LGT MIRL Rwy 17−35 preset low intst.
 To incr intst and ACTVT REIL Rwy 17; PAPI Rwys 17 and Rwy
 35—CTAF.
AIRPORT REMARKS: Attended Mar−Oct, Mon−Fri 1500−2200Z‡; Nov−Feb
 1500−2300Z‡. For attendant after hrs call 361−325−2909. 9 ft fence
 lctd aprx 900 ft north of Rwy 17. Rwy 14−32 single wheel 18000 lbs.
AIRPORT MANAGER: 361-325-2909
WEATHER DATA SOURCES: AWOS−3PT 118.125 (361) 325−4055.
COMMUNICATIONS: CTAF/UNICOM 122.8
®KINGSVILLE APP/DEP CON 119.9 (1345−0600Z‡) Mon−Thu;
 1345−2345Z‡ Fri; clsd Sat, Sun and hol exc by NOTAM, hrs subj to
 chg)
®HOUSTON CENTER APP/DEP CON 128.15 (0500−1300Z‡) Mon−Thu;
 2200−1300Z‡ Fri; 24 Sat, Sun and hol by NOTAM)
CLEARANCE DELIVERY PHONE: For CD ctc Houston ARTCC at 281-230-5622.
RADIO AIDS TO NAVIGATION: NOTAM FILE CRP.
 CORPUS CHRISTI (VH) (H) VORTACW 115.5 CRP Chan 102 N27°54.23′ W97°26.69′ 212° 55.2 NM to fld. 60/9E.
  TACAN AZIMUTH & DME unusable:
   024°−036° byd 35 NM blo 1,700′
   037°−023° byd 35 NM blo 2,000′
   265°−275°
  VOR unusable:
   340°−005° byd 40 NM blo 7,000′
   340°−005° byd 84 NM
   Byd 30 NM blo 1,500′
  TACAN AZIMUTH unusable:
   080°−085° byd 30 NM

FARLY N31°59.29′ W102°19.51′ NOTAM FILE MAF. **SAN ANTONIO**
 NDB (HW/LOM) 326 MA 104° 6.9 NM to Midland Intl Air And Space Port. 2957/9E. NDB unmonitored when **L−6H**
  ATCT clsd.

FAYETTE RGNL AIR CENTER (See LA GRANGE on page 357)

FERRIS RED OAK MUNI HELIPORT (See FERRIS/RED OAK on page 305)

FERRIS/RED OAK

FERRIS RED OAK MUNI HELIPORT (12T) 4 N UTC−6(−5DT) N32°31.79′ W96°43.87′ **DALLAS−FT WORTH**
510 NOTAM FILE FTW **COPTER**
HELIPAD H1: H40X40 (CONC)
HELIPORT REMARKS: Unattended. 5′ chain link perimeter fence, 80′−100′ from center of pad.
AIRPORT MANAGER: 972-544-2110
COMMUNICATIONS: CTAF 122.9
CLEARANCE DELIVERY PHONE: For CD ctc Regional Apch at 972-615-2799.

FISHER CO (See ROTAN/ROBY on page 413)

FLOYDADA MUNI (41F) 1 N UTC−6(−5DT) N34°00.09′ W101°19.82′ DALLAS−FT WORTH
3187 B NOTAM FILE FTW L−6H
RWY 17−35: H4600X60 (ASPH) S−15 MIRL IAP
  RWY 17: PAPI(P2L)—GA 3.0° TCH 40′.
  RWY 35: PAPI(P2L)—GA 3.0° TCH 39′. Bldg. Rgt tfc.
SERVICE: FUEL 100LL, JET A LGT Dusk−Dawn. MIRL Rwy 17−35 preset
  to low intst; to incr intst or actvt—CTAF.
AIRPORT REMARKS: Attended Mon−Sat 1400−0000Z‡. Extsv aerial ag ops.
AIRPORT MANAGER: 806-983-2314
COMMUNICATIONS: CTAF/UNICOM 122.8
®LUBBOCK APP/DEP CON 119.2 119.9
CLEARANCE DELIVERY PHONE: For CD ctc Fort Worth ARTCC at 817-858-7584.
RADIO AIDS TO NAVIGATION: NOTAM FILE PVW.
  PLAINVIEW (VL) (L) VORW/DME 112.9 PVW Chan 76 N34°05.17′
  W101°47.41′ 091° 23.5 NM to fld. 3400/11E.

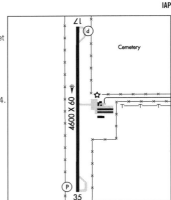

FLUFY N31°13.13′ W94°49.51′ NOTAM FILE LFK. HOUSTON
  NDB (LOMW) 350 LF 075° 4.0 NM to Angelina Co. 205/2E. NDB unmonitored.

FLYIN TIGER (See ANGLETON on page 245)

FLYING C (See SANGER on page 421)

FLYING H RANCH (See WHITESBORO on page 445)

FLYING V RANCH (See LOUISE on page 368)

FOLLETT/LIPSCOMB CO (T93) 1 E UTC−6(−5DT) N36°26.45′ W100°07.43′ WICHITA
2601 NOTAM FILE FTW L−15C
RWY 17−35: H4073X60 (ASPH) S−18 1.7% up S IAP
  RWY 17: P−line.
  RWY 35: Hill.
AIRPORT REMARKS: Unattended. No line of sight btn rwy ends. Rwy 17−35
  13′ wide strip of pavement alng west edge of rwy is spongy and will
  not support listed wheel weight. Rwy 17−35 extensive pavement
  cracking with vegetation growing through. loose stones on rwy. Rwy
  17−35 no pavement markings.
AIRPORT MANAGER: 806-653-2601
COMMUNICATIONS: CTAF 122.9
®KANSAS CITY CENTER APP/DEP CON 126.95
CLEARANCE DELIVERY PHONE: For CD ctc Kansas City ARTCC at
  913-254-8508.
RADIO AIDS TO NAVIGATION: NOTAM FILE GAG.
  MITBEE (VH) (H) VORTACW 115.6 MMB Chan 103 N36°20.62′
  W99°52.81′ 286° 13.2 NM to fld. 2426/10E.

TEXAS 307

FORT STOCKTON–PECOS CO (FST)(KFST) 2 NW UTC–6(–5DT) N30°54.92´ W102°54.77´   **SAN ANTONIO**
3011 B NOTAM FILE FST   H–6G, L–19A
  RWY 12–30: H7508X100 (ASPH) S–24 MIRL 0.3% up SE   IAF
    RWY 12: PAPI(P4L)—GA 3.0° TCH 45´. Tree.
    RWY 30: PAPI(P4L)—GA 3.0° TCH 45´. Road.
  RWY 07–25: 4961X150 (TURF) 0.6% up SW
    RWY 25: Trees.
  RWY 03–21: H4400X60 (ASPH)   MIRL 1.1% up SW
    RWY 03: P–line.
  RWY 16–34: 3981X100 (TURF) 1.0% up SE
    RWY 16: Brush.
    RWY 34: Tree.
  RWY 11–29: 3348X100 (TURF) 0.3% up SE
    RWY 29: Road.

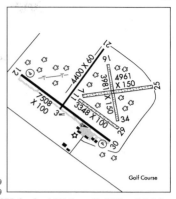

  SERVICE: **FUEL** 100LL, JET A+ **LGT** MIRL Rwy 03–21 and 12–30
    preset low intst; to incr intst actvt—CTAF. PAPI Rwy 12 and 30 opr
    consly. Rwy 12 and 30 VGSI unusbl byd 8 deg right of RCL.
  AIRPORT REMARKS: Attended 1400–2300Z‡. For fuel and services after
    hours call 432–336–9900 or UNICOM. 24 hr self service avbl with
    major credit card. Rwy 07–25, Rwy 11–29, and Rwy 16–34 not
    mntnd; has tall weeds, grass and thorns. Rwy 11 thr not mkd. Rwy 29
    thr not mkd. 3210´ tower 2 miles northeast. Turf Rwy 07–25, 11–29
    16–34 rough. Rwy ends 16 and 25 not inspected due to fld conds. NOTE: See Special Notices—Model Aircraft Activity.
  AIRPORT MANAGER: 432-336-6261
  WEATHER DATA SOURCES: ASOS 118.525 (432) 336–7591.
  COMMUNICATIONS: CTAF/UNICOM 122.8
    RCO 122.2 (SAN ANGELO RADIO)
  ®**ALBUQUERQUE CENTER APP/DEP CON** 135.875
  CLEARANCE DELIVERY PHONE: For CD if una to ctc on FSS freq, ctc Albuquerque ARTCC at 505-856-4561.
  RADIO AIDS TO NAVIGATION: NOTAM FILE FST.
    (VH) (H) VORTACW 116.9   FST   Chan 116   N30°57.13´ W102°58.54´   113° 3.9 NM to fld. 2893/11E.
    VOR unusable:
      020°–055° byd 20 NM blo 6,900´
      070°–086° byd 35 NM blo 6,400´
      106°–132° byd 30 NM blo 5,900´
      125°–202° byd 40 NM
      203°–213° byd 40 NM blo 18,000´
      214°–230° byd 40 NM
      245°–255° byd 40 NM
      315°–330° byd 30 NM blo 5,400´

SC, 25 JAN 2024 to 21 MAR 2024

FORT WORTH

BOURLAND FLD (5ØF)　17 SW　UTC–6(–5DT)　N32°34.91´ W97°35.45´　　　DALLAS–FT WORTH COPTER
873　B　NOTAM FILE FTW　　　　　　　　　　　　　　　　　　　　　　　　　L–17C, A
RWY 17–35: H4049X60 (ASPH)　　MIRL　0.9% up N　　　　　　　　　　　　IAP
　RWY 17: VASI(V2L)—GA 3.0° TCH 23´. Thld dsplcd 392´. Road.
　RWY 35: VASI(V2L)—GA 3.5° TCH 28´. Thld dsplcd 215´. Trees.
SERVICE: FUEL 100LL, JET A　**LGT** ACTVT MIRL Rwy 17–35—CTAF.
　VASI Rwys 17 and 35 opr consly.
AIRPORT REMARKS: Attended Mon–Sat dalgt hours. For svcs aft hrs call
　817-752-4701. Deer on and invof rwy. 100LL self serve. Arpt clsd
　to tsnt student tfc. Arpt clsd to acft ovr 12,500 lb max GWT. Rwy hold
　short lines NSTD 25 ft fm rwy edge.
AIRPORT MANAGER: 817-752-4701
COMMUNICATIONS: CTAF/UNICOM 123.0
ⓇREGIONAL APP/DEP CON 135.975
CLEARANCE DELIVERY PHONE: For CD ctc Regional Apch at 972-615-2799.
RADIO AIDS TO NAVIGATION: NOTAM FILE FTW.
　MILLSAP (VH) (H) VORTACW 117.7　　MQP　Chan 124　N32°43.57´
　　W97°59.85´　　104° 22.3 NM to fld. 900/9E.
　VOR unusable:
　　004°–009° byd 40 NM
　　010°–054° byd 40 NM blo 3,800´
　　010°–054° byd 46 NM blo 5,000´
　　010°–054° byd 56 NM
　　055°–066° byd 40 NM blo 3,800´
　　055°–066° byd 50 NM
　　230°–247° byd 40 NM
　　248°–258° byd 40 NM blo 3,700´
　　248°–258° byd 53 NM
　　259°–270° byd 40 NM blo 6,000´
　　259°–270° byd 63 NM
　　271°–285° byd 40 NM
　　312°–316° byd 40 NM
　　325°–340° byd 40 NM blo 3,000´
　　325°–340° byd 46 NM blo 5,000´
　　325°–340° byd 66 NM
　　353°–003° byd 40 NM blo 18,000´

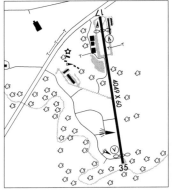

TEXAS 309

FORT WORTH MEACHAM INTL (FTW)(KFTW) 5 N UTC−6(−5DT) N32°49.19´ W97°21.75´ **DALLAS−FT WORTH**
710 B TPA—See Remarks ARFF Index—See Remarks NOTAM FILE FTW **COPTER**
RWY 16−34: H7502X150 (CONC−GRVD) S−80, D−100, 2S−127, **H−6H, L−17C, A**
2D−190, 2D/2D2−350 PCN 30 R/C/W/U HIRL 0.5% up N **IAP, AD**
RWY 16: MALSR. PAPI(P4R)—GA 3.0° TCH 59´. RVR−T Pole.
RWY 34: MALS. RVR−R Rgt tfc.
RWY 17−35: H4005X75 (ASPH) S−12.5, D−50 PCN 11 F/C/X/U MIRL
RWY 17: PAPI(P2L)—GA 3.75° TCH 56´. Berm. Rgt tfc.
RWY 35: PAPI(P2L)—GA 3.25° TCH 43´.
RUNWAY DECLARED DISTANCE INFORMATION
RWY 16: TORA−7502 TODA−7502 ASDA−7502 LDA−7502
RWY 34: TORA−7502 TODA−7502 ASDA−7455 LDA−7455
SERVICE: S4 **FUEL** 100LL, JET A, A1+ **OX** 1, 3 **LGT** Rwy 17−35 LED
lgt can appr brgtr than Rwy 16−34; ensure cor rwy alnmt.
AIRPORT REMARKS: Attended continuously. Birds on and invof arpt. Rwy
09−27 CLOSED indef. Class IV, ARFF Index A. ARFF Index A or higher
available all users with PPR. Helo skidding opns prohibited on Rwy
17−35. If skidding is rqrd, coord with ATCT to use Twy B. Rwy 17−35
Twys B, B1, C and D west of Rwy 16−34, Twy M east of Twy A, H, J,
Txl G SE of Txl N clsd to acft with more than 30 psgr seats. Rwy
17−35 designed for acft with wingspan of 49 ft or less. Twys B and
B1 designed for acft with wingspan less than 79 ft. Rwy 16−34 and
Twys A, A1, and M designed for acft with wingspan less than 171 ft.
All other Twys designed for acft with wingspan of less than 118 ft. Mkd US CUST pkrg southeast of Txl G and Txl N intxn.
PPR for acr opns with more than 30 psgr seats−24 hr notice rqrd−call Arpt Ops 817−994−0653. TPA—Rwy 17−35 R/W
1300(590) AGL, F/W 1500(790) AGL, Rwy 16−34 1500(790) AGL, Jets 2000(1290) AGL. Arpt fees for use of cust
svcs will be could imt upon ldg by city of Fort Worth Arpt opns psnl. User fee arpt. NOTE: See Special Notices—Arrival
Alert.
AIRPORT MANAGER: 817 392−5400
WEATHER DATA SOURCES: ASOS (817) 740−3346
COMMUNICATIONS: ATIS 120.7
  RCO 122.6 (FORT WORTH RADIO)
®**RGNL APP/DEP CON** 118.1 124.3 125.2 125.8 125.9 135.975 (North) 118.1 125.8 135.975 (South) 124.3 125.2
125.8
  MEACHAM TOWER 118.3 **GND CON** 121.9 **CLNC DEL** 124.65
AIRSPACE: CLASS D.
VOR TEST FACILITY (VOT) 108.2
RADIO AIDS TO NAVIGATION: NOTAM FILE FTW.
  RANGER (VH) (H) VORTACW 115.7 FUZ Chan 104 N32°53.37´ W97°10.77´ 240° 10.1 NM to fld. 639/6E.
  VOR unusable:
   275°−290° byd 40 NM
   317°−327° byd 40 NM
  MUFIN NDB (LOMW) 365 FT N32°53.59´ W97°22.40´ 165° 4.4 NM to fld. 744/8E.
  ILS/DME 109.9 I−FTW Chan 36 Rwy 16. Class IT. LOM MUFIN NDB. DME also serves Rwy 34.
  ILS/DME 109.9 I−UXT Chan 36 Rwy 34. Class IB. DME also serves Rwy 16.
• • • • • • • • • • • • • • • • •
HELIPAD H1: H35X35 (CONC)
HELIPAD H2: H35X35 (CONC)
HELIPORT REMARKS: H1 and H2 helipads are VMC dalgt use only; non−movement area. Hels repositioning byd imt prkg apron
  and under their own pwr must ctc ATC.

SC, 25 JAN 2024 to 21 MAR 2024

TEXAS

FORT WORTH SPINKS (FWS)(KFWS) 14 S UTC–6(–5DT) N32°33.91´ W97°18.51´ DALLAS–FT WORTH COPTER
700 B NOTAM FILE FWS H–6H, L–17C, A
 RWY 18R–36L: H6002X100 (ASPH) S–60, D–70, 2D–100 MIRL IAP, AD
  RWY 18R: PAPI(P4L)—GA 3.0° TCH 40´. P–line. Rgt tfc.
  RWY 36L: MALSR. PAPI(P4L)—GA 3.0° TCH 50´.
 RWY 18L–36R: 3660X60 (TURF)
  RWY 36R: Ground. Rgt tfc.
 SERVICE: S4 FUEL 100LL, JET A LGT ACTVT MALSR Rwy 36L—CTAF.
  When ATCT clsd MIRL Rwy 18R–36L preset on med intst.
 NOISE: Noise abatement procedure: Avoid noise sensitive areas all
  quadrants of arpt; maintain altitudes at or above 1000 ft AGL over
  these areas.
 AIRPORT REMARKS: Attended 1300–0400Z‡. Birds invof arpt. 100LL
  self–serve. Rwy 18L–36R avbl only during dalgt/VFR and dry weather
  sfc conds. Rotorcraft opns prohibited in self svc fuel areas. Rotorcraft
  opns prohibited on Twy A btn Twy H and Twy A2. Hel skidding opns
  prohibited.
 AIRPORT MANAGER: 817-392-5430
 WEATHER DATA SOURCES: AWOS–3PT 120.025 (817) 426–4172.
 COMMUNICATIONS: CTAF 124.625 ATIS 120.025 UNICOM 122.5
 ®REGIONAL APP/DEP CON 135.975
  TOWER 124.625 (1300–0200Z‡) GND CON 119.475
 CLEARANCE DELIVERY PHONE: For CD when ATCT is clsd ctc Regional Apch at
  972-615-2799.
 AIRSPACE: CLASS D svc 1300–0200Z‡; other times CLASS G.
 RADIO AIDS TO NAVIGATION: NOTAM FILE FTW.
  RANGER (VH) (H) VORTACW 115.7 FUZ Chan 104 N32°53.37´ W97°10.77´ 193° 20.5 NM to fld. 639/6E.
   VOR unusable:
    275°–290° byd 40 NM
    317°–327° byd 40 NM
  ILS 110.95 I–JZW Rwy 36L. Class IB. Unmonitored.

HICKS AIRFIELD (T67) 14 NW UTC–6(–5DT) N32°55.87´ W97°24.70´ DALLAS–FT WORTH COPTER
855 B TPA—See Remarks NOTAM FILE FTW L–17C, A
 RWY 14–32: H3740X60 (ASPH) MIRL
  RWY 14: PAPI(P2L)—GA 3.0° TCH 20´. Thld dsplcd 340´. Railroad.
  RWY 32: PAPI(P2L)—GA 3.0° TCH 20´. Thld dsplcd 191´. Railroad.
 SERVICE: S4 FUEL 100LL
 AIRPORT REMARKS: Unattended. 100LL fuel avbl 24 hr self–serve. Ultralight ops invof arpt. Uncontrolled vehicle tfc invof
  hangars and on twys. Calm wind Rwy 14. Rwy 14–32 railroad parallel and adj to rwy on SW side within primary sfc.
  TPA—1500.
 AIRPORT MANAGER: (817) 779-4664
 COMMUNICATIONS: CTAF/UNICOM 123.05
  CLNC DEL 125.9
 CLEARANCE DELIVERY PHONE: For CD ctc Regional Apch at 972-615-2799.
 RADIO AIDS TO NAVIGATION: NOTAM FILE FTW.
  RANGER (VH) (H) VORTACW 115.7 FUZ Chan 104 N32°53.37´ W97°10.77´ 276° 12.0 NM to fld. 639/6E.
   VOR unusable:
    275°–290° byd 40 NM
    317°–327° byd 40 NM

TEXAS

KENNETH COPELAND (4T2)   18 NW   UTC−6(−5DT)   N32°58.66′ W97°29.54′   DALLAS−FT WORTH
693   B   NOTAM FILE FTW   COPTER
RWY 17−35: H5943X127 (ASPH−CONC)   LIRL   0.5% up N   H−6H, L−17C, A
  RWY 17: Antenna.   IAP
  RWY 35: Trees.
SERVICE: LGT ACTVT LIRL Rwy 17−35; twy—CTAF.
AIRPORT REMARKS: Unattended. Tnst acft 3 hrs PPR. Rwy 17−35 outer 50′ of each side of rwy is asph, center 40′ is conc on Rwy 17 end, asph on Rwy 35 end. Asph cracking with loose aggregate. Twy A poor cond, outer 18 ft of each side is asph, cntr 39 ft is conc. Extsv hel act in area. 260′ AGL twr 0.7 NM NW Rwy 17 end.
AIRPORT MANAGER: 817-252-3510
COMMUNICATIONS: CTAF/UNICOM 123.075
®**REGIONAL APP/DEP CON** 125.8
CLEARANCE DELIVERY PHONE: For CD ctc Regional Apch at 972-615-2799.
RADIO AIDS TO NAVIGATION: NOTAM FILE FTW.
  RANGER (VH) (H) VORTACW 115.7   FUZ   Chan 104   N32°53.37′ W97°10.77′   283° 16.7 NM to fld. 639/6E.
  VOR unusable:
    275°−290° byd 40 NM
    317°−327° byd 40 NM

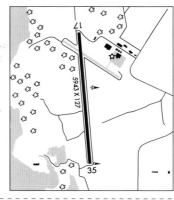

PEROT FLD/FORT WORTH ALLIANCE (AFW)(KAFW)   14 N   UTC−6(−5DT)   N32°59.42′   DALLAS−FT WORTH
W97°19.17′   COPTER
723   B   ARFF Index—See Remarks   NOTAM FILE AFW   H−6H, L−17C, A
RWY 16R−34L: H11125X150 (CONC−GRVD)   D−200, 2S−175,   IAP, AD
  2D−400, 2D/2D2−870 PCN 82 R/B/W/T   HIRL
  RWY 16R: REIL. PAPI(P4R)—GA 3.0° TCH 82′. Railroad. Rgt tfc. 0.4% down.
  RWY 34L: REIL. PAPI(P4L)—GA 3.0° TCH 74′. Thld dsplcd 716′. Fence. 0.7% up.
RWY 16L−34R: H11000X150 (CONC−GRVD)   D−200, 2S−175,
  2D−400, 2D/2D2−870 PCN 82 R/B/W/T   HIRL   CL
  RWY 16L: ALSF2. TDZL. RVR−TMR Rgt tfc. 0.4% down.
  RWY 34R: MALSR. TDZL. RVR−TMR P−line. 0.7% up.
RUNWAY DECLARED DISTANCE INFORMATION
  RWY 16L: TORA−10600 TODA−10600   ASDA−10600   LDA−10600
  RWY 16R: TORA−11010 TODA−11010   ASDA−10410   LDA−10410
  RWY 34L: TORA−11010 TODA−11010   ASDA−11010   LDA−10409
  RWY 34R: TORA−11000 TODA−11000   ASDA−11000   LDA−11000
SERVICE: S4   **FUEL** 100LL, JET A1+   **OX** 4
AIRPORT REMARKS: Attended continuously. Class IV, ARFF Index A. ARFF Index E available. PPR for air carrier ops with more than 30 passenger seats, call 817−890−1000 or 800−318−9268. Portions of Twy H movement area east of Twy A is not visible from ATCT. Prior arrangements required for airframe or power plant repairs for design group III and above. User fee arpt. Flight Notification Service (ADCUS) available.
AIRPORT MANAGER: 817-890-1000
WEATHER DATA SOURCES: ASOS (817) 491−6188
COMMUNICATIONS: ATIS 126.925
  RGNL APP/DEP CON 118.1 124.3 125.2 125.8 125.9 135.975
  ALLIANCE TOWER 135.15   120.825 (Helicopters)   **CLNC DEL** 128.725   **GND CON** 132.65
AIRSPACE: CLASS D svc continuous.
RADIO AIDS TO NAVIGATION: NOTAM FILE FTW.
  RANGER (VH) (H) VORTACW 115.7   FUZ   Chan 104   N32°53.37′ W97°10.77′   305° 9.3 NM to fld. 639/6E.
  VOR unusable:
    275°−290° byd 40 NM
    317°−327° byd 40 NM
  ILS/DME 110.25   I−UPE   Chan 38(Y)   Rwy 16L.   Class IIIE.   DME also serves Rwy 34R.
  ILS/DME 110.25   I−JVX   Chan 38(Y)   Rwy 34R.   Class ID.   DME also serves Rwy 16L.
COMM/NAV/WEATHER REMARKS: Emerg frequency not available. ARINC frequency 129.75 avbl.

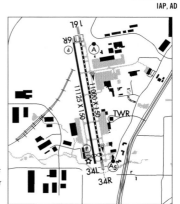

SYCAMORE STRIP (9F9) 8 S UTC−6(−5DT) N32°37.62′ W97°21.24′ DALLAS−FT WORTH
762 TPA—1562(800) NOTAM FILE FTW COPTER
RWY 17−35: H3375X30 (CONC) LIRL(NSTD) L−17C, A
 RWY 17: Pole. Rgt tfc.
 RWY 35: Thld dsplcd 175′. Railroad.
 SERVICE: S2 **FUEL** 100LL **LGT** LIRL Rwy 17−35 call ahead
  817−293−0510 M−F 1500−2300Z‡. Rwy 17−35 NSTD LIRL—single
  white thr lgt each side, NSTD 15′ fm rwy edge. 2766′ usbl at ngt. Rwy
  35 thr 609′ at ngt.
 AIRPORT REMARKS: Attended 1500−2300Z‡. Ultralight activity on and in
  vicinity of arpt. Rwy 35 thld relocated 609′ at ngt. Rwy 17−35 7′ wall
  76′ east of centerline parallel and adjacent rwy on 1730′ north end of
  rwy. Arpt clsd to transient acft except 2 hrs PPR call 817−293−0510.
  Lndg fee for all tnst acft. Windsock may be unreliable due to proximity
  of trees.
 AIRPORT MANAGER: 817−293−0510
 COMMUNICATIONS: CTAF/UNICOM 122.8
 CLEARANCE DELIVERY PHONE: For CD ctc Regional Apch at 972−615−2799.
 RADIO AIDS TO NAVIGATION: NOTAM FILE FTW.
  RANGER (VH) (H) VORTACW 115.7 FUZ Chan 104 N32°53.37′
  W97°10.77′ 203° 18.0 NM to fld. 639/6E.
  VOR unusable:
   275°−290° byd 40 NM
   317°−327° byd 40 NM

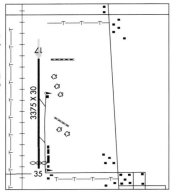

FORT WORTH NAS JRB (CARSWELL FLD) (NFW)(KNFW) N (AFRC) 5 W UTC−6(−5DT) DALLAS−FT WORTH
N32°46.15′ W97°26.49′ COPTER
650 B TPA—See Remarks NOTAM FILE NFW Not insp. H−6H, L−17C, A
RWY 18−36: H11999X200 (CONC) PCN 107R/B/W/T HIRL DIAP, AD
 RWY 18: REIL. PAPI(P4L)—GA 3.0° TCH 62′. Rgt tfc.
 RWY 36: ALSF1. PAPI(P4L)—GA 3.0° TCH 58′.
RWY 17S−35S: H3998X60 (CONC)
ARRESTING GEAR/SYSTEM
 RWY 18 HOOK E28(B) (1251′).   HOOK E28(B) (1375′). **RWY 36**
SERVICE: S4 **MILITARY—** **JASU** 1(NCPP−105) 1(NC−8) 4(AM32A−86D) 7(AM32A−60A) **FUEL** Opr 1200−0430Z‡. JA **FLUID**
 SP PRESAIR Ltd LOX. LOX svc not avbl with/non−removable LOX converters UFN. **OIL** O−133−148 Ltd JOAP. **TRAN ALERT**
 No priority basis. Ltd tran svc/maint avbl, emerg only. Hgr space/fleet svc/de−ice unavbl. Tran acft ctc twr on GND freq
 prior eng start/ taxiing. 48 hr PN for PPR acft rqr dly tran/ATC svc. Rules of ATC svc brief rqr for acft opr out of NAS Ft.
 Worth.
 MILITARY REMARKS: Opr Mon−Fri 1300−0500Z‡, Sat and Sun 1500−2300Z‡, other times by NOTAM. See FLIP AP/1
  Supplementary Arpt Remark. **RSTD** PPR all acft ctc air ODO C817−825−6411, DSN 739−5175. PPR all acft parking ANG
  ramp, DSN 874−3256, C817−852−3256, normal opr Tue−Fri 1130−2215Z‡, clsd Sat, Sun, Mon, and hol. All tran acft
  ctc ANG OPS 226.9 15 min prior to ldg. **CAUTION** Taxi on centerline, increase interval. Four−engine acft, secure outboard
  engine. Moderate and strong winds reduced at touchdown point Rwy 18 by Lockheed Complex.
  TFC PAT TPA—Rectangular 1700 (1050), overhead 2200 (1550), Helicopter 1200 (550). **CSTMS/AG/IMG** US military
  customs schedule Mon−Fri 1400−2200Z‡ 48 hr prior notice through NAS Security DSN 739−5200, C817−782−5200.
  MISC Rwy 18 first 1000 ft concrete, 6700 ft hi−friction asphalt, 2800 ft grooved concrete, remaining 1500 ft concrete,
  Twy B east of Twy F 50 ft. Twy A will be clsd between Twy F and the ramp from 1630−1730 local, Tue thru Fri, and at
  other times as disseminated by NOTAM. Flight Plan Dispatch DSN 739−7531, C817−782−7531. On site Wx forecasting
  available, ctc 1−888−PILOT−WX (1−888−745−6899) for forecasting svc. Duty driver not avbl. Lockheed/Martin—Official
  Business Only. For access, ctc Lockheed Martin flt ops DSN 838−5677, C817−763−3624. See FLIP AP/1 Supplementary
  Arpt Remark for additional information. **AFRC** DSN 739−6888. NOTE: See Special Notices—Aerobatic Practice Area.
 COMMUNICATIONS: SFA ATIS 351.675 (1300−0500Z‡)
 Ⓡ **RGNL APP/DEP CON** 118.1 124.3 125.2 125.8 125.9 135.975 257.95 282.275 306.95 343.65 (North) 125.8 135.975
  (South) 118.1 125.8
  NAVY FORT WORTH TOWER 120.95 269.325 284.725 (Mon−Fri 1300−0500Z‡, Sat−Sun 1500−2300Z‡ other times by
  NOTAM.)
  NAVY FORT WORTH GND CON 121.675 279.575 **NAVY FORT WORTH ARR** 128.775 371.875 (Mon−Fri 1300−0500Z‡, clsd Sat,
  Sun and hol.) **GND CON** 121.675 **CLNC DEL** 126.4 254.325
  PMSV METRO 342.55 **BASE OPS** 291.775 **LOCKHEED** 284.1 292.5 (Mon−Fri 1300−0000Z‡)
  ROPER OPS 226.9

CONTINUED ON NEXT PAGE

TEXAS

CONTINUED FROM PRECEDING PAGE

AIRSPACE: CLASS D.
RADIO AIDS TO NAVIGATION: NOTAM FILE NFW.
   NAS JRB FORT WORTH (L) TACAN Chan 24   NFW (108.7)   N32°46.28´ W97°26.36´   at fld. 631/4E.
    TACAN unavbl 0500–1300Z‡
    No NOTAM MP: 1330–1530Z‡ Wed
    TACAN AZIMUTH unusable:
      180°–320° byd 20 NM blo 4,000´
    DME unusable:
      180°–320° byd 20 NM blo 4,000´
   ILS/DME 108.7 I–NFW Chan 24 Rwy 18. Class IB. No NOTAM MP: 1300–1600Z‡ Mon and Wed . ILS not avbl
    when twr clsd.
   ILS 109.3 I–FWH Rwy 36. Class IB. LOC unavbl when ATCT clsd.
   ASR/PAR 1300–0500Z‡ Mon–Fri, exc hol
COMM/NAV/WEATHER REMARKS: Radar see Terminal FLIP for Radar Minima.

FOUR WINDS (See CELINA on page 269)

FOX STEPHENS FLD / GILMER MUNI (See GILMER on page 319)

FRANKLIN CO (See MOUNT VERNON on page 386)

FRANKSTON
AERO ESTATES (T25)   3 NE   UTC–6(–5DT)   N32°04.91´ W95°27.15´   **DALLAS–FT WORTH**
  445   NOTAM FILE FTW
RWY 09–27: 3100X60 (TURF)   LIRL
  RWY 09: VASI(V2L). Pole. Rgt tfc.
  RWY 27: Trees.
SERVICE: **LGT** ACTIVATE LIRL Rwy 09–27, VASI Rwy 09, lighted wind cone—CTAF, 3 clicks slow.
AIRPORT REMARKS: Attended irregularly. Deer on and invof rwy. All acft monitor CTAF due to proximity to Paradise Point pvt.
  arpt north of arpt. Rwy 09 rgt tfc pat: All acft remain south of the rwy. Rwy 09–27 marked with 18´ numerals on 40´ by
  50´ asph pad. Student Pilot training is not authorized except by residents of Aero Estates.
AIRPORT MANAGER: 903-617-7860
COMMUNICATIONS: CTAF 122.9
CLEARANCE DELIVERY PHONE: For CD ctc Fort Worth ARTCC at 817-858-7584.

 • • • • • • • • • • • • • • • • •

HELIPAD H1: 50X50 (TURF)
HELIPORT REMARKS: 14´ bldg 200´ north and 20´ bldg 200´ west of landing pad. 43´ trees 152´ north, 30´ pole 70´ east,
  38´ trees 280´ south, 25´ pole 205´ west.

AERO ESTATES SPB (TX1)   3 NE   UTC–6(–5DT)   N32°04.75´ W95°25.95´   **DALLAS–FT WORTH**
  345   NOTAM FILE FTW
WATERWAY 17W–35W: 5268X300 (WATER)
AIRPORT REMARKS: Unattended.
AIRPORT MANAGER: 903-617-7860
COMMUNICATIONS: CTAF 122.9
CLEARANCE DELIVERY PHONE: For CD ctc Fort Worth ARTCC at 817-858-7584.

FRANKSTON   N32°04.48´ W95°31.85´   NOTAM FILE FTW.   **HOUSTON**
  (L) (L) **VORW/DME** 111.4 FZT Chan 51 283° 16.1 NM to Athens Muni. 305/6E.   **H–6I, L–17D**
    VOR portion unusable:
      270°–293° byd 5 NM blo 8,000´
      293°–295° byd 25 NM blo 3,500´
      295°–340° byd 20 NM

TEXAS

FREDERICKSBURG

GILLESPIE CO (T82)   3 SW   UTC–6(–5DT)   N30°14.60′ W98°54.55′   SAN ANTONIO
1695   B   NOTAM FILE T82   H–7B, L–19C
RWY 14–32: H5001X75 (ASPH)   S–30 PCN 21 F/C/X/T   MIRL   IAP
0.3% up NW
  RWY 14: PAPI(P2L)—GA 3.0° TCH 43′. Fence. Rgt tfc.
  RWY 32: PAPI(P2L)—GA 3.0° TCH 37′. Road.
SERVICE: S4   **FUEL** 100LL, JET A   **LGT** MIRL Rwy 14–32
  ACTVT—CTAF (5 clicks – low intst, 7 clicks – med intst).
AIRPORT REMARKS: Attended 1400–0000Z‡. 100LL 24 hr self serve.
  Seasonal ffr air opns in and out of arpt. 75 ft tank 300 ft SE of rotg
  bcn. FBO: 830–997–3313.
AIRPORT MANAGER: 830-990-5764
WEATHER DATA SOURCES: AWOS–3 120.0 (830) 990–2716.
COMMUNICATIONS: CTAF/UNICOM 122.7
HOUSTON CENTER APP/DEP CON 134.2
  GCO 121.725 (HOUSTON ARTCC – 6 CLICKS; FSS – 4 CLICKS)
CLEARANCE DELIVERY PHONE: For CD if una via GCO ctc Houston ARTCC at
  281-230-5622.
RADIO AIDS TO NAVIGATION: NOTAM FILE T82.
  STONEWALL (VH) (H) VORTAC 113.8   STV   Chan 85   N30°12.41′
    W98°42.35′   274° 10.8 NM to fld. 1530/8E.
  TACAN AZIMUTH unusable:
    056°–066° byd 30 NM blo 3,000′
    067°–055° byd 30 NM blo 3,300′
  DME unusable:
    056°–066° byd 30 NM blo 3,000′
    067°–055° byd 30 NM blo 3,300′
  VOR unusable:
    056°–066° byd 30 NM blo 3,000′
    067°–055° byd 30 NM blo 3,300′
    110°–122° byd 40 NM blo 5,500′
    110°–122° byd 46 NM
    123°–210° byd 40 NM
    230°–240° byd 40 NM

FREEDOM FLD (See LINDSAY on page 364)

FREER

DUVAL–FREER (T19)   1 NE   UTC–6(–5DT)   N27°53.32′ W98°36.00′   BROWNSVILLE
564   B   NOTAM FILE SJT   L–20H
RWY 14–32: H3200X60 (ASPH)   S–24   RWY LGTS(NSTD)
  RWY 14: Trees.
  RWY 32: Trees.
SERVICE: **LGT** Rwy 14–32 NSTD fixtures. Svrl rwy and thr lgts inop or misg. Lgts mounted on non-frangible steel rods.
AIRPORT REMARKS: Unattended. Apron and twy, no marking. Rwy 14–32 broken asphalt, loose stones on rwy, vegetation
  encroaching along edges. No trml fac. To have gate unlocked, call 361–394–6002 (police dept).
AIRPORT MANAGER: 361-453-1325
COMMUNICATIONS: CTAF 122.9
CLEARANCE DELIVERY PHONE: For CD ctc Houston ARTCC at 281-230-5622.
RADIO AIDS TO NAVIGATION: NOTAM FILE SJT.
  THREE RIVERS (L) (L) VORTAC 111.4   THX   Chan 51   N28°30.30′ W98°09.03′   205° 43.9 NM to fld. 266/8E.

TEXAS

FRIONA

BENGER AIR PARK (X54) 2 NE UTC–6(–5DT) N34°39.25′ W102°41.51′   ALBUQUERQUE
4003   NOTAM FILE FTW   L–6H
RWY 04–22: H3013X60 (ASPH)   S–13
  RWY 04: Bldg.
RWY 17–35: 2700X150 (TURF)
  RWY 17: Trees.
SERVICE: FUEL 100LL, JET A
AIRPORT REMARKS: Attended dalgt hours. Attended Mon–Fri winter months. Rwy 04–22 sfc pot holes and grvl. Rwy 04–22 agri acft opns on NW side of rwy. Rwy 17–35 +3′ vegetation, rwy not mntned. Rwy not inspected.
COMMUNICATIONS: CTAF 122.9
CLEARANCE DELIVERY PHONE: For CD ctc Albuquerque ARTCC at 505-856-4861.
RADIO AIDS TO NAVIGATION: NOTAM FILE FTW.
  TEXICO (VH) (H) VORTACW 112.2   TXO   Chan 59   N34°29.71′ W102°50.38′   026° 12.0 NM to fld. 4060/11E.
  VOR unusable:
    095°–100° byd 40 NM
    120°–130° byd 40 NM
    210°–223° byd 40 NM blo 15,000′
    224°–251° byd 40 NM
    252°–262° byd 40 NM blo 18,000′
    263°–272° byd 40 NM blo 18,000′
    273°–283° byd 40 NM blo 6,000′
    273°–283° byd 46 NM blo 7,000′
    273°–283° byd 59 NM
    284°–319° byd 40 NM
    320°–035° byd 40 NM
  TACAN AZIMUTH unusable:
    222°–232°

FULSHEAR

COVEY TRAILS (X09) 3 E UTC–6(–5DT) N29°41.41′ W95°50.43′   HOUSTON
130   B   NOTAM FILE CXO
RWY 17–35: 3352X100 (TURF)   LIRL(NSTD)
  RWY 17: VASI(V2L). Thld dsplcd 315′. Tree.
  RWY 35: Thld dsplcd 250′. Tree.
SERVICE: LGT Dusk–0400Z‡. ACTVT LIRL Rwy 17–35 aft 0400Z‡—CTAF. VASI Rwy 17 opr consly. Rtg bcn dusk–0400Z‡. Rwy 17–35 NSTD LIRL; 2800 ft of rwy lgtd at night btn dsplcd thrs.
AIRPORT REMARKS: Unattended. Rwy 17–35 soft areas, unretracted sprinkler heads on rwy. Base legs and turns to final apch must be within .75 NM of the rwy ends. Cell twr, 1.5 miles south of Rwy 17 end. Ldg fee.
AIRPORT MANAGER: 281-685-7540
COMMUNICATIONS: CTAF/UNICOM 122.725
CLEARANCE DELIVERY PHONE: For CD ctc Houston Apch at 281-443-5844 to cnl IFR call 281-443-5888.

GAINES CO (See SEMINOLE on page 422)

TEXAS

GAINESVILLE MUNI (GLE)(KGLE) 3 W UTC−6(−5DT) N33°39.13′ W97°11.84′ DALLAS−FT WORTH
846 B NOTAM FILE GLE H−6H, L−17C, A
RWY 18−36: H6000X100 (ASPH) S−30, D−50 MIRL 0.9% up N IAP, AD
  RWY 18: REIL. PAPI(P2R)—GA 3.0° TCH 45′. P−line.
  RWY 36: REIL. PAPI(P2L)—GA 3.0° TCH 45′.
RWY 13−31: H4307X75 (ASPH) S−15 0.8% up NW
  RWY 13: Trees.
SERVICE: S4 **FUEL** 100LL, JET A+ **LGT** Dusk−Dawn. MIRL Rwy
  18−36 preset low intst; to incr intst ACTVT—CTAF. PAPI Rwys 18 and
  36 opr consly.
AIRPORT REMARKS: Attended 1400−2300Z‡. 100LL self−serve and full
  serve. Rwy 13 has aim points. Rwy 31 has aim points. Rwy 13−31
  markings faded. Hel skid ldg prohibited on all paved sfcs.
AIRPORT MANAGER: 940−668−4565
WEATHER DATA SOURCES: AWOS−3 118.375 (940) 612−3549.
COMMUNICATIONS: CTAF/UNICOM 123.0
Ⓡ **FORT WORTH CENTER APP/DEP CON** 124.75
  CLEARANCE DELIVERY PHONE: For CD ctc Fort Worth ARTCC at
    817−858−7584.
RADIO AIDS TO NAVIGATION: NOTAM FILE FTW.
  BOWIE (H) (H) VORTACW 117.15 UKW Chan 118(Y) N33°32.15′
    W97°49.28′   071° 32.0 NM to fld. 1102/6E.

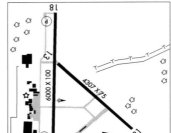

GALVESTON

SCHOLES INTL AT GALVESTON (GLS)(KGLS) 3 SW UTC−6(−5DT) N29°15.92′ HOUSTON
  W94°51.63′ COPTER
  6 B LRA NOTAM FILE GLS MON Airport H−7C, L−19E, 21A, GOMW
RWY 18−36: H6001X150 (CONC) S−74, D−92, 2D−162 MIRL IAP, AD
  RWY 18: REIL. PAPI(P4L)—GA 3.0° TCH 44′.
  RWY 36: REIL. PAPI(P4L)—GA 3.0° TCH 45′. Bldg.
RWY 14−32: H6000X150 (ASPH−CONC) S−90, D−115, 2D−192 HIRL
  RWY 14: MALSR. PAPI(P4L)—GA 3.0° TCH 52′.
  RWY 32: REIL. PAPI(P4L)—GA 3.0° TCH 46′. Bldg.
RUNWAY DECLARED DISTANCE INFORMATION
  RWY 14: TORA−6000 TODA−6000 ASDA−6000 LDA−6000
  RWY 18: TORA−6001 TODA−6001 ASDA−6001 LDA−6001
  RWY 32: TORA−6000 TODA−6000 ASDA−6000 LDA−6000
  RWY 36: TORA−6001 TODA−6001 ASDA−6001 LDA−6001
SERVICE: S4 **FUEL** 100LL, JET A **LGT** HIRL Rwy 14−32, MIRL Rwy
  18−36 preset med intst. When ATCT clsd ACTVT MALSR Rwy
  14—CTAF.
AIRPORT REMARKS: Attended 1200−0200Z‡. Flocks of birds invof arpt blw
  200 ft AGL. Hels oprg on and invof arpt. 100LL aft hrs svc
  409−750−0195. 178 ft lgtd bldg 2000 ft NE of Rwy 18 thr. PAEW adj
  rwys and twys. Rwy 14−32 first 1,300′ NW end is conc. Flight
  Notification Service (ADCUS) available.
AIRPORT MANAGER: 409−797−3590
WEATHER DATA SOURCES: ASOS 123.950 (409) 740−5483.
COMMUNICATIONS: CTAF 120.575 **UNICOM** 123.05
  GALVESTON RCO 122.2 (MONTGOMERY COUNTY RADIO)
Ⓡ **HOUSTON APP/DEP CON** 134.45
  TOWER 120.575 (1200−0000Z‡) **GND CON** 118.625 **CLNC DEL** 135.35
  CLEARANCE DELIVERY PHONE: For CD when ATCT is clsd ctc Houston Apch at 281−443−5844 to cnl IFR at 281−443−5888.
AIRSPACE: CLASS D svc 1200−0000Z‡; other times CLASS E.
RADIO AIDS TO NAVIGATION: NOTAM FILE GLS.
  (VH) (DH) VORW/DME 113.0 VUH Chan 77 N29°16.16′ W94°52.06′ at fld. 4/6E.
    VOR unusable:
      285°−295° byd 35 NM blo 2,500′
  ILS 111.7 I−GLS Rwy 14.

GALVESTON 209B GVW N29°07.82′ W94°32.79′/121 HOUSTON, HOUSTON TAC
  AWOS−3 118.25 (832) 917−1465 L−19E, L−21A, GOMW

GARDEN BANKS 668 GUL N27°18.23′ W93°32.30′
  AWOS−3 119.025 Winds unreliable. L−21B, GOMW

TEXAS 317

GARLAND/DFW HELOPLEX HELIPORT (T57) 2 SW UTC−6(−5DT) N32°53.22′ W96°41.10′   DALLAS−FT WORTH
601 B NOTAM FILE FTW   COPTER
HELIPAD H1: H105X105 (CONC)   PERIMETER LGTS
HELIPAD H2: H54X54 (CONC)
SERVICE: S4 **FUEL** 100LL, JET A **LGT** Peri lgts low intst SS−SR, to incr intst—CTAF.
HELIPORT REMARKS: Attended Mon−Sat 1400−0000Z‡, Sun 1500−2300Z‡. Helipad H1 egress/ingress north and south.
   Helipad H1 648′ twr 1 mile north, 34′ bldg 170′ north, 48′ antenna 352′ east, 30′ bldg 442′ south, 35′ bldg 379′
   west. Helipad H2 egress/ingress N. Rwy H2 under construction.
AIRPORT MANAGER: 214-349-7000
COMMUNICATIONS: CTAF/UNICOM 123.05
CLEARANCE DELIVERY PHONE: For CD ctc Regional Apch at 972-615-2799.

GARNER FLD (See UVALDE on page 437)

GARYS   N29°57.52′ W97°56.94′   NOTAM FILE HYI.   SAN ANTONIO
NDB (LOMW) 272 RU 124° 6.0 NM to San Marcos Rgnl. 819/7E.

GATESVILLE MUNI (GOP)(KGOP)   3 W UTC−6(−5DT)   N31°25.26′ W97°47.79′   SAN ANTONIO
905 B NOTAM FILE GOP   L−19C, 21A
RWY 17−35: H3400X60 (ASPH) S−12 MIRL 0.3% up S
   RWY 17: PAPI(P2L)—GA 3.0° TCH 30′. Trees.
   RWY 35: PAPI(P2L)—GA 3.0° TCH 30′. Trees.
SERVICE: S4 **FUEL** 100LL **OX** 1, 2, 3, 4 **LGT** Dusk−Dawn. MIRL Rwy 17−35 preset low intst, to incr intst actvt—CTAF.
AIRPORT REMARKS: Attended Mon−Fri 1400−2300Z‡. 100LL avbl 24 hrs self serve. Low flying military jet acft and helicopter
   in vicinity.
AIRPORT MANAGER: 254-865-8951
WEATHER DATA SOURCES: AWOS−3PT 119.725 (254) 865−6742. AWOS precipitation unreliable.
COMMUNICATIONS: CTAF 122.9
CLEARANCE DELIVERY PHONE: For CD ctc Fort Worth ARTCC at 817-858-7584.
RADIO AIDS TO NAVIGATION: NOTAM FILE SJT.
   GOOCH SPRINGS (H) (H) VORTACW 112.5   AGJ   Chan 72   N31°11.13′ W98°08.51′   046° 22.7 NM to fld. 1191/5E.

GAV AIR (See WHARTON on page 444)

GEORGE BUSH INTCNTL/HOUSTON (See HOUSTON on page 339)

GEORGE WEST
LIVE OAK CO (8T6)   2 N   UTC−6(−5DT)   N28°21.77′ W98°06.99′   SAN ANTONIO
129 B NOTAM FILE SJT   L−20H
   IAP
RWY 13−31: H3799X60 (ASPH)   MIRL
   RWY 13: PAPI(P2L)—GA 3.0° TCH 53′. P-line.
   RWY 31: PAPI(P2L)—GA 3.0° TCH 45′.
SERVICE: **FUEL** 100LL, JET A **LGT** Dusk−Dawn. MIRL Rwy 13−31
   preset low intst, to incr intst actvt—122.7.
AIRPORT REMARKS: Unattended. Birds on and invof arpt. 100LL self-serve.
   75′ elec transmission line, 600′ W of and parl to rwy cntrln, full len.
   For assistance or hngr call 361−449−2559 or 361−449−6315 (cell).
AIRPORT MANAGER: 361-449-6176
WEATHER DATA SOURCES: AWOS−3PT 119.05 (361) 449−1119.
COMMUNICATIONS: CTAF 122.9
Ⓡ **HOUSTON CENTER APP/DEP CON** 134.6
CLEARANCE DELIVERY PHONE: For CD ctc Houston ARTCC at 281-230-5622.
RADIO AIDS TO NAVIGATION: NOTAM FILE SJT.
   THREE RIVERS (L) (L) VORTAC 111.4   THX   Chan 51   N28°30.30′
      W98°09.03′   160° 8.7 NM to fld. 266/8E.

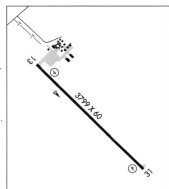

TEXAS

GEORGETOWN EXEC (GTU)(KGTU)   3 N   UTC–6(–5DT)   N30°40.73´ W97°40.76´   SAN ANTONIO
790   B   NOTAM FILE GTU   H–7C, L–19C, 21A
RWY 18–36: H5004X100 (ASPH–GRVD)   S–30, D–60   MIRL   IAP, AD
0.8% up N
  RWY 18: REIL. PAPI(P4L)—GA 3.0° TCH 35´. Trees.
  RWY 36: REIL. PAPI(P4L)—GA 3.0° TCH 50´. Trees. Rgt tfc.
RWY 11–29: H4099X75 (ASPH)   S–12.5   MIRL   0.7% up NW
  RWY 11: Tree.
  RWY 29: Tree. Rgt tfc.
SERVICE: S4   **FUEL** 100LL, JET A1+   **OX** 1, 2, 3, 4   **LGT** Aftr twr hrs,
MIRL Rwy 18–36 preset low intst; to incr intst and actvt REILS Rwy
18–36 and MIRL Rwy 11–29—CTAF. PAPI Rwy 18 and 36 ops
consly.
AIRPORT REMARKS: Attended 1300Z‡–0100Z‡. Deer on and in vicinity of
arpt. Mil hel opns prohibited btn 0300–1300Z‡. Rwy 18–36 clsd to
hel skid ldg to prevent dmg to groovrd sfc. Portions of Twy F not visible
from tower. NOTE: See Special Notices—Aerobatic Practice Area.
AIRPORT MANAGER: 512-930-8464
WEATHER DATA SOURCES: AWOS–3PT (512) 869–3430 LAWRS.
COMMUNICATIONS: CTAF 120.225   ATIS 118.6   UNICOM 123.0
®**AUSTIN APP/DEP CON** 119.0
TOWER 120.225   (1300–0400Z‡)   **GND CON** 119.125
CLNC DEL 119.125 **CLNC DEL** 121.1 (when twr clsd)
CLEARANCE DELIVERY PHONE: For CD ctc Austin Apch at 512-369-7865.
AIRSPACE: CLASS D svc 1300–0400Z‡; other times CLASS E.
RADIO AIDS TO NAVIGATION: NOTAM FILE AUS.
  CENTEX (VH) (H) VORTACW 112.8   CWK   Chan 75   N30°22.71´ W97°31.79´   331° 19.6 NM to fld. 593/6E.
    VOR unusable:
    180°–190° byd 40 NM
    200°–210° byd 40 NM

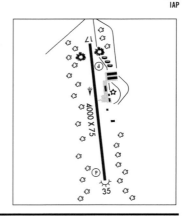

GIDDINGS–LEE CO (GYB)(KGYB)   3 W   UTC–6(–5DT)   N30°10.16´ W96°58.80´   HOUSTON
484   B   NOTAM FILE GYB   L–19D, 21A
RWY 17–35: H4000X75 (ASPH)   S–12.5   MIRL   1.1% up N   IAP
  RWY 17: PAPI(P2L)—GA 3.75° TCH 34´. Trees.
  RWY 35: PAPI(P2L)—GA 3.4° TCH 45´. Trees.
SERVICE: S4   **FUEL** 100LL, JET A
AIRPORT REMARKS: Attended Mon–Fri 1500–0000Z‡. Deer and invof
arpt. 100LL and Jet A 24 hr self serve.
AIRPORT MANAGER: 979-542-6081
WEATHER DATA SOURCES: AWOS–3 119.225 (979) 542–0382.
COMMUNICATIONS: CTAF/UNICOM 123.05
®**AUSTIN APP/DEP CON** 127.225
CLEARANCE DELIVERY PHONE: For CD ctc Austin Apch at 512-369-7865.
RADIO AIDS TO NAVIGATION: NOTAM FILE CXO.
  INDUSTRY (L) (L) VORTACW 110.2   IDU   Chan 39   N29°57.36´
  W96°33.73´   293° 25.2 NM to fld. 419/8E.

GILLESPIE CO (See FREDERICKSBURG on page 314)

TEXAS

GILMER

FOX STEPHENS FLD / GILMER MUNI (JXI)(KJXI)   2 S   UTC–6(–5DT)   N32°41.88′ W94°56.93′   **MEMPHIS**
415   B   NOTAM FILE JXI   L–17D
RWY 18–36: H3998X60 (ASPH)   S–12   MIRL   IAP
  RWY 18: PAPI(P2L)—GA 3.75° TCH 32′. P–line.
  RWY 36: Trees.
SERVICE: S4   **FUEL** 100LL, JET A
AIRPORT REMARKS: Attended Mon–Fri 1430–2300Z‡. PAEW invof rwys.
  Fuel A full svc avbl 1430–2300Z‡, Mon–Fri.
AIRPORT MANAGER: 903-843-2552
WEATHER DATA SOURCES: AWOS–3PT 120.250 (903) 734–7313.
COMMUNICATIONS: CTAF 122.9
®**LONGVIEW APP/DEP CON** 124.275 (1200–0400Z‡)
®**FORT WORTH CENTER APP/DEP CON** 132.025 (0400–1200Z‡)
CLEARANCE DELIVERY PHONE: For CD ctc Fort Worth ARTCC at
  817-858-7584.
RADIO AIDS TO NAVIGATION: NOTAM FILE FTW.
  QUITMAN (L) DME 114.0   UIM   Chan 87   N32°52.83′
  W95°22.01′   117° 23.8 NM to fld. 517.

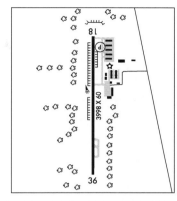

GLADEWATER MUNI (Ø7F)   2 SW   UTC–6(–5DT)   N32°31.73′ W94°58.31′   **MEMPHIS**
297   B   NOTAM FILE FTW   L–17D
RWY 14–32: H3299X75 (ASPH)   S–12.5   MIRL   0.3% up SE   IAP
  RWY 14: PAPI(P2L)—GA 3.0° TCH 44′. Trees.
  RWY 32: Trees.
RWY 17–35: H2300X50 (ASPH)   S–7
  RWY 17: Trees.
  RWY 35: Trees.
SERVICE: **FUEL** 100LL
AIRPORT REMARKS: Attended 1400–2300Z‡. Parachute Jumping. For
  service after hours call 903–295–8860. Rwy 17–35 nmrs cracks,
  loose stones.
AIRPORT MANAGER: 903-845-2586
COMMUNICATIONS: CTAF 122.9
®**LONGVIEW APP/DEP CON** 124.275 (1200–0400Z‡)
®**FORT WORTH CENTER APP/DEP CON** 126.325 (0400–1200Z‡)
CLEARANCE DELIVERY PHONE: For CD ctc Fort Worth ARTCC at
  817-858-7584.
RADIO AIDS TO NAVIGATION: NOTAM FILE GGG.
  GREGG COUNTY (VL) (H) VORTACW 112.9   GGG   Chan 76
    N32°25.07′ W94°45.19′   294° 12.9 NM to fld. 329/7E.
  TACAN AZIMUTH unusable:
    045°–070° byd 25 NM blo 2,500′
    180°–225° byd 33 NM blo 3,500′
    258°–268° byd 26 NM blo 4,500′
    325°–340° byd 37 NM blo 2,500′
    248°–258° byd 34 NM blo 8,100′
  DME unusable:
    045°–070° byd 25 NM blo 2,500′
    180°–225° byd 33 NM blo 3,500′
    258°–268° byd 26 NM blo 4,500′
    325°–340° byd 37 NM blo 2,500′
  VOR unusable:
    138°–152° byd 40 NM
    188°–192° byd 40 NM
    210°–230° byd 40 NM

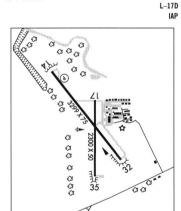

GLEN ROSE   N32°09.58′ W97°52.66′   NOTAM FILE FTW.   **DALLAS–FT WORTH**
  (L) TACAN 115.0   JEN   Chan 97   276° 15.6 NM to Stephenville Clark Rgnl. 1300/6E.   **H–6H, L–17C**

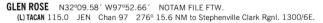

GODLEY

ARESTI AERODROME (2Ø T) 2 NW UTC−6(−5DT) N32°28.24′ W97°33.62′ DALLAS−FT WORTH
985 NOTAM FILE
RWY 14−32: 2500X60 (TURF)
  RWY 14: P−line. Rgt tfc.
  RWY 32: P−line. Rgt tfc.
NOISE: Noise sensitive area 1 mi west of AER 14.
AIRPORT REMARKS: Attended continuously. PPR 30 min prior at 817−304−4658. Pilots rqd to ctc aprt opns at 817−304−4658 for safety brief and ldg auth. Arpt sfc cond not rprtd. PPR 30 min prior at 817−304−4658. Aerobatic box 1 mi north of Rwy 14 thr, 300 ft AGL to 3500 ft AGL. Student trng PPR. Do not taxi on non−mowed areas. The flwg opns prohibited: ultralights, pwrd prchts, sailplanes, auto−gyros, paja, ag opns, airships. Unctld vehicle tfc invof hngrs and rwy. Fqt mowing opns. 30 ft unmkd p−line, parallel to and 60 ft SW of rwy edge, full length, partially obscured by trees. Three 60 ft antennas, 145 ft NE of rwy edge, mid−field. Ldg fee.
AIRPORT MANAGER: 817-304-4658
COMMUNICATIONS: CTAF 122.9
CLEARANCE DELIVERY PHONE: For CD ctc Regional Apch at 972-615-2799.

GOLDTHWAITE MUNI (T37) 2 SW UTC−6(−5DT) N31°25.74′ W98°36.50′ SAN ANTONIO
1458 B NOTAM FILE FTW L−19C
RWY 01−19: H3200X60 (ASPH) S−12.5 MIRL 0.4% up N
  RWY 01: PAPI(P2L)—GA 3.0° TCH 40′. Trees.
  RWY 19: PAPI(P2L)—GA 3.0° TCH 40′. Tree.
SERVICE: **LGT** MIRLS Rwy 01−19 pre−set low intst; to incr intst and ACTVT−CTAF. PAPI Rwy 01 and 19 opr consly.
AIRPORT REMARKS: Attended 1400−2300Z‡. Deer on and invof arpt.
AIRPORT MANAGER: 325-648-3186
COMMUNICATIONS: CTAF 122.9
CLEARANCE DELIVERY PHONE: For CD ctc Fort Worth ARTCC at 817-858-7584.
RADIO AIDS TO NAVIGATION: NOTAM FILE SJT.
  GOOCH SPRINGS (H) (H) VORTACW 112.5 AGJ Chan 72 N31°11.13′ W98°08.51′ 296° 28.1 NM to fld. 1191/5E.

GOLIAD NOLF (NGT)(KNGT) N 5 N UTC−6(−5DT) N28°36.70′ W97°36.75′ SAN ANTONIO
322 NOTAM FILE SJT H−7C, L−20H, 21A
RWY 17−35: H8001X150 (PEM) PCN 9 R/B/W/T HIRL
  RWY 17: TDZL. PAPI(P4L)—GA 3.0° TCH 54′.
  RWY 35: TDZL. PAPI(P4L)—GA 3.0° TCH 53′.
RWY 11−29: H8000X150 (PEM) PCN 8 R/B/W/T HIRL
  RWY 11: TDZL. PAPI(P4L)—GA 3.0° TCH 54′. Brush.
  RWY 29: TDZL. PAPI(P4L)—GA 3.0° TCH 53′. Brush.
SERVICE: **LGT** Rwy 17 PAPI unusable byd 8° right of centerline.
MILITARY REMARKS: Opr 1400Z‡ —sunset Mon−Fri. Opr outside publ hr proh. Others rqr PPR 72 hr for afld use ctc Corpus Christi NAS Base OPS C361−961−2505/2506/2507, DSN 861−2505/2507. PPR strictly enforced. TRAWING 4 exclusive use. **CAUTION** Student training activity, high mid−air potential, extreme vigilance req. All acft check−in with RDO prior to arrival on CTAF. **SERVICE** Avbl only during hrs of opr. No svc avbl.
AIRPORT MANAGER: 361-961-2247
WEATHER DATA SOURCES: ASOS 353.675.
COMMUNICATIONS: CTAF 132.875
®**HOUSTON CENTER APP/DEP CON** 135.05 353.6
CLEARANCE DELIVERY PHONE: For CD ctc Houston ARTCC at 281-230-5622.
RADIO AIDS TO NAVIGATION: NOTAM FILE SJT.
  THREE RIVERS (L) (L) VORTAC 111.4 THX Chan 51 N28°30.30′ W98°09.03′ 069° 29.1 NM to fld. 266/8E.

TEXAS

GONZALES

ROGER M DREYER MEML (T2Ø) 2 NW UTC–6(–5DT) N29°31.75′ W97°27.86′   SAN ANTONIO
354 B NOTAM FILE T20   L–19C, 21A
RWY 15–33: H3200X50 (ASPH) S–21 MIRL
  RWY 15: Trees.
  RWY 33: Tower. Rgt tfc.
SERVICE: **FUEL** 100LL   **LGT** MIRL Rwy 15–33 preset on low intst; to incr intst ACTVT—123.0.
AIRPORT REMARKS: Unattended. 100LL self–serve. Rwy 33 5 ft hill, 80 ft right and left of cntrln from thr north 500 ft. Rwy 33, 100′ elec tranmission line acrs S apch, 2400′ dstc, mkd and lgtd.
AIRPORT MANAGER: 830-672-2815
WEATHER DATA SOURCES: AWOS–3 125.875 (830) 519–4254.
COMMUNICATIONS: CTAF 122.9
CLEARANCE DELIVERY PHONE: For CD ctc Austin Apch at 512-369-7865.
RADIO AIDS TO NAVIGATION: NOTAM FILE AUS.
  CENTEX (VH) (H) VORTACW 112.8   CWK   Chan 75   N30°22.71′ W97°31.79′   170° 51.0 NM to fld. 593/6E.
  VOR unusable:
    180°–190° byd 40 NM
    200°–210° byd 40 NM

GOOCH SPRINGS   N31°11.13′ W98°08.51′   NOTAM FILE SJT.   SAN ANTONIO
(H) (H) VORTACW 112.5   AGJ   Chan 72   205° 5.5 NM to Lampasas. 1191/5E.   H–6H, L–19C

GOODHUE   N30°04.23′ W94°12.66′   NOTAM FILE CXO.   HOUSTON
NDB (MHW) 368   GDE   at Beaumont Muni. 30/7E. (VFR only).
  NDB OTS indef

GORDONVILLE

CEDAR MILLS (3TØ)   3 N   UTC–6(–5DT)   N33°50.36′ W96°48.60′   DALLAS–FT WORTH
640   NOTAM FILE FTW
RWY 07–25: 3000X60 (TURF)
  RWY 07: Trees.
  RWY 25: Tree.
AIRPORT REMARKS: Unattended. Wildlife on and invof of arpt. Rwy 25 end 70′ fm lake, 10′ drop off. Rwy 25 end, 80′ tree, 34′ fm W edge of rwy. 40′ trees 75′ N and 80′ trees 90′ S of Rwy 25 cntrln. Rwy 07–25 slopes down 24′ fm W to E twd lake.
AIRPORT MANAGER: 903-523-4222
COMMUNICATIONS: CTAF 122.9
CLEARANCE DELIVERY PHONE: For CD ctc Fort Worth ARTCC at 817-858-7584.

GRAFORD

POSSUM KINGDOM (F35)   12 SW   UTC−6(−5DT)   N32°55.40´ W98°26.21´   DALLAS–FT WORTH
1008   B   NOTAM FILE FTW   L−17B
   IAP
RWY 02−20: H3500X60 (ASPH)   S−24   MIRL
  RWY 02: PAPI(P2L)—GA 3.5° TCH 33´. Trees.
  RWY 20: PAPI(P2L)—GA 3.5° TCH 30´. Trees.
SERVICE: LGT ACTVT MIRL Rwy 02−20—CTAF.
AIRPORT REMARKS: Unattended. Wildlife invof arpt. NOTE: See Special Notices—Aerobatic Practice Area.
AIRPORT MANAGER: 940-779-2321
COMMUNICATIONS: CTAF 122.9
Ⓡ **FORT WORTH CENTER APP/DEP CON** 127.0
CLEARANCE DELIVERY PHONE: For CD ctc Fort Worth ARTCC at 817-858-7584.
RADIO AIDS TO NAVIGATION: NOTAM FILE FTW.
  MILLSAP (VH) (H) VORTACW 117.7   MQP   Chan 124   N32°43.57´ W97°59.85´   289° 25.2 NM to fld. 900/9E.
  VOR unusable:
    004°−009° byd 40 NM
    010°−054° byd 40 NM blo 3,800´
    010°−054° byd 46 NM blo 5,000´
    010°−054° byd 56 NM
    055°−066° byd 40 NM blo 3,800´
    055°−066° byd 50 NM
    230°−247° byd 40 NM
    248°−258° byd 40 NM blo 3,700´
    248°−258° byd 53 NM
    259°−270° byd 40 NM blo 6,000´
    259°−270° byd 63 NM
    271°−285° byd 40 NM
    312°−316° byd 40 NM
    325°−340° byd 40 NM blo 3,000´
    325°−340° byd 46 NM blo 5,000´
    325°−340° byd 66 NM
    353°−003° byd 40 NM blo 18,000´

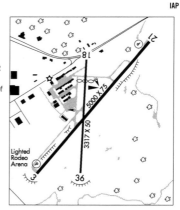

GRAHAM MUNI (RPH)(KRPH)   2 E   UTC−6(−5DT)   N33°06.64´ W98°33.29´   DALLAS–FT WORTH
1123   B   NOTAM FILE RPH   H−6H, L−17B
   IAP
RWY 03−21: H5000X75 (ASPH)   S−12   MIRL
  RWY 03: PAPI(P2L)—GA 3.0° TCH 40´. Trees.
  RWY 21: PAPI(P2R)—GA 3.0° TCH 40´. Trees.
RWY 18−36: H3317X50 (ASPH)   S−8   0.4% up S
  RWY 18: Thld dsplcd 639´. Road.
  RWY 36: Road.
SERVICE: S4   **FUEL** 100LL, JET A, A+   **LGT** MIRL Rwy 03−21 SS−SR preset to low, to incr intst ACTVT—CTAF.
AIRPORT REMARKS: Attended Mon−Fri 1400−2300Z‡. Wldlife on and invof arpt. Call prior to arrival for hangar availability at 940-549-6150.
AIRPORT MANAGER: 940-549-6150
WEATHER DATA SOURCES: AWOS−3P 118.025 (940) 521-0685.
COMMUNICATIONS: CTAF/UNICOM 122.975
Ⓡ **FORT WORTH CENTER APP/DEP CON** 127.0

CONTINUED ON NEXT PAGE

TEXAS

CONTINUED FROM PRECEDING PAGE

CLEARANCE DELIVERY PHONE: For CD ctc Fort Worth ARTCC at 817-858-7584.
RADIO AIDS TO NAVIGATION: NOTAM FILE FTW.
   MILLSAP (VH) (H) VORTACW 117.7   MQP   Chan 124   N32°43.57′ W97°59.85′   300° 36.4 NM to fld. 900/9E.
   VOR unusable:
     004°–009° byd 40 NM
     010°–054° byd 40 NM blo 3,800′
     010°–054° byd 46 NM blo 5,000′
     010°–054° byd 56 NM
     055°–066° byd 40 NM blo 3,800′
     055°–066° byd 50 NM
     230°–247° byd 40 NM
     248°–258° byd 40 NM blo 3,700′
     248°–258° byd 53 NM
     259°–270° byd 40 NM blo 6,000′
     259°–270° byd 63 NM
     271°–285° byd 40 NM
     312°–316° byd 40 NM
     325°–340° byd 40 NM blo 3,000′
     325°–340° byd 46 NM blo 5,000′
     325°–340° byd 66 NM
     353°–003° byd 40 NM blo 18,000′

GRANBURY RGNL (GDJ)(KGDJ)   2 W   UTC–6(–5DT)   N32°26.58′ W97°49.28′   **DALLAS–FT WORTH**
   835   B   NOTAM FILE GDJ   **L–17C, A**
   RWY 01–19: H5201X75 (CONC)   MIRL   1.0% up S   **IAP**
     RWY 01: PAPI(P2L)—GA 3.0° TCH 40′.
     RWY 19: PAPI(P2L)—GA 3.0° TCH 40′. Rgt tfc.
   SERVICE: S4   **FUEL** 100LL, JET A   **LGT** MIRL Rwy 01–19 preset low
     intst; to incr intst ACTVT—CTAF.
   AIRPORT REMARKS: Attended 1300–0100Z‡. 100LL 24 hr self serve. For
     Jet A aft hrs call 817–579–8533 durg ofc hrs. Overnight tie–down fee
     waived with fuel purchase.
   AIRPORT MANAGER: 817-579-8533
   WEATHER DATA SOURCES: AWOS–3PT 118.925 (817) 573–7514.
   COMMUNICATIONS: CTAF/UNICOM 123.0
   Ⓡ**FORT WORTH CENTER APP/DEP CON** 127.15
   CLEARANCE DELIVERY PHONE: For CD ctc Fort Worth ARTCC at
     817-858-7584.
   RADIO AIDS TO NAVIGATION: NOTAM FILE FTW.
     GLEN ROSE (L) TACAN   Chan 97   JEN (115.0)   N32°09.58′
       W97°52.66′   004° 17.2 NM to fld. 1300/6E.

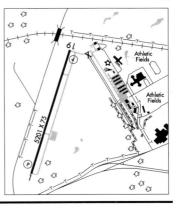

TEXAS

GRAND PRAIRIE MUNI (GPM)(KGPM) 4 SW UTC−6(−5DT) N32°41.93′ W97°02.82′ DALLAS−FT WORTH
590 B TPA—See Remarks NOTAM FILE GPM COPTER
RWY 18−36: H4001X75 (CONC) S−30 MIRL L−17C, A
  RWY 18: VASI(V4L)—GA 3.0° TCH 26′. Trees. IAP, AD
  RWY 36: REIL. VASI(V4L)—GA 4.0° TCH 37′. Road. Rgt tfc.
SERVICE: S4 **FUEL** 100LL, JET A **OX** 1, 2 **LGT** MIRL Rwy 18−36
  preset low intst; to incr intst and ACTVT REIL Rwy 36 aft ATCT
  clsd—CTAF.
AIRPORT REMARKS: Attended Mar−Oct Mon−Sat 1300−0200Z‡, Nov−Feb
  Mon−Sat 1400−0000Z‡, Sun 1400−0000Z‡. Extsv hel tfc west side
  of arpt. TPA—1400 (812) fixed wing, 1200 (612) rotary wing. West
  grass for rotary wing use only.
AIRPORT MANAGER: (972) 237−7591
WEATHER DATA SOURCES: AWOS−3P 118.475 (972) 606−1433.
COMMUNICATIONS: CTAF 128.55 UNICOM 123.075
Ⓡ **REGIONAL APP/DEP CON** 135.975
  TOWER 128.55 (1200−0200Z dalgt time; 1400−0000Z standard
  time) **GND CON** 121.15
CLEARANCE DELIVERY PHONE: For CD when ATCT is clsd ctc Regional Apch
  at 972-615-2799.
AIRSPACE: CLASS D svc 1200−0200Z dalgt time, 1400−0000Z standard
  time; other times CLASS G.
RADIO AIDS TO NAVIGATION: NOTAM FILE FTW.
  MAVERICK (VH) (H) VORW/DME 113.1   TTT   Chan 78   N32°52.15′ W97°02.43′   176° 10.2 NM to fld. 536/6E.
    All acft arriving DFW are requested to turn DME off until departure due to traffic overload of Maverick DME
    DME unusable:
      180°−190° byd 10 NM
      240°−260° byd 20 NM blo 3,500′
    VOR unusable:
      105°−110° byd 40 NM

• • • • • • • • • • • • • • • •
HELIPAD H1: H50X50 (CONC)   PERIMETER LGTS

GRANITE SHOALS/ BOB SYLVESTER AIRPARK (2G5) 1 E UTC−6(−5DT) N30°35.36′ W98°22.22′ SAN ANTONIO
860 NOTAM FILE 2G5
RWY 02−20: 2000X50 (TURF−DIRT)
  RWY 02: Trees.
  RWY 20: Road.
AIRPORT REMARKS: Unattended. Arpt is dalgt use only. Nmrs deer often on rwy.
AIRPORT MANAGER: 830-598-2424
COMMUNICATIONS: CTAF 122.9
CLEARANCE DELIVERY PHONE: For CD ctc Houston ARTCC at 281-230-5622.

GRAY N31°01.97′ W97°48.83′ NOTAM FILE GRK. SAN ANTONIO
  (T) (T) VORW/DME 111.8 GRK Chan 55 332° 2.2 NM to Robert Gray AAF. 963/7E. L−19C, 21A

GREATER MORRIS CO (See DAINGERFIELD on page 283)

TEXAS

325

GREENVILLE

MAJORS (GVT)(KGVT) P (AF)   4 SE   UTC−6(−5DT)   N33°04.07′ W96°03.92′   DALLAS−FT WORTH
535   B   NOTAM FILE GVT   H−6H, L−17D
RWY 17−35: H8030X150 (ASPH)   S−26   MIRL   IAP, DIAP, AD
  RWY 17: MALS. PAPI(P4L)—GA 3.0° TCH 74′. Trees. 0.4% up.
  RWY 35: REIL. PAPI(P4L)—GA 3.0° TCH 66′. Trees. 0.3% up.
SERVICE: S2   **FUEL** 100LL, JET A   **LGT** ACTVT MALS Rwy 17; REIL Rwy 35; MIRL Rwy 17−35—CTAF.
MLITARY—JASU 1(B−10) 1(B−10A) 1(MD−3) 1(MA−1) 1(MA−3) **FUEL** (NC−100LL, A)
AIRPORT REMARKS: Attended Sun−Thu 1330−2300Z‡, Fri−Sat 1330−0000Z‡. When ATCT clsd and there is an emerg or incident on arpt, ctc 903−457−5333. 100LL self svc avbl 24 hours. Parachute Jumping. PPR for PAJA onto Majors Field. Twy A clsd. 89 ft high intst radio freq ant 3700 ft east of Rwy 35 at end of abndd pavement. Twy E lgts located 47 ft from pavement edge. Acft not vsb fm opposite end of rwy. Nmrs mil acft on fld for modification.
AIRPORT MANAGER: 903-457-3168
WEATHER DATA SOURCES: AWOS−3 133.425 (903) 455−7703.
COMMUNICATIONS: CTAF 118.65 UNICOM 122.95
Ⓡ **FORT WORTH CENTER APP/DEP CON** 132.025   360.75
  TOWER 118.65   385.425 (1330−2200Z‡) Mon−Fri, irregular other hrs)
  GND CON 121.7   335.8 **AFMCLO FLT** 349.6
CLEARANCE DELIVERY PHONE: When ATCT clsd, for CD ctc Fort Worth ARTCC at 817-858-7584.
AIRSPACE: CLASS D svc 1330−2200Z‡ Mon−Fri; other times CLASS G.
RADIO AIDS TO NAVIGATION: NOTAM FILE FTW.
  BONHAM (VH) (H) VORTACW 114.6   BYP Chan 93   N33°32.25′ W96°14.05′   157° 29.4 NM to fld. 700/6E.
  ARVILLA (T) TACAN Chan 33   MJF (109.6)   N33°03.98′ W96°03.68′   at fld. 543/5E. NOTAM FILE GVT.
    DME unusable:
    024°−034° byd 16 NM blo 3,000′
    080°−095° byd 5 NM
    TACAN AZIMUTH unusable:
    024°−034° byd 16 NM blo 3,000′
    080°−095° byd 5 NM
    212°−222° byd 12 NM blo 3,500′
  SULPHUR SPRINGS (L) DME 109.0   SLR   Chan 27   N33°11.92′ W95°32.57′   254° 27.5 NM to fld. 508.   NOTAM FILE SLR.
  ILS/DME 110.5   I−GVT   Chan 42   Rwy 17.   Class IT.   Glideslope unusable for cpd apch blw 900 MSL.

GREGORY M SIMMONS MEML (See CISCO on page 272)

GROESBECK   N31°34.89′ W96°32.95′   NOTAM FILE FTW.   HOUSTON
(L) DME 108.8   GNL   Chan 25   026° 4.0 NM to Mexia−Limestone Co. 514.   L−19D, A
  DME unusable:
  150°−205° byd 30 NM blo 2,500′
  230°−310° byd 30 NM blo 2,400′
  345°−035° byd 35 NM blo 2,500′

GROVETON–TRINITY CO (33R)   3 NW   UTC–6(–5DT)   N31°05.06´ W95°09.85´   HOUSTON
340   B   NOTAM FILE CXO   L–19E, 21A
RWY 16–34: H3500X60 (ASPH)   S–8   LIRL
  RWY 16: Trees.
  RWY 34: Trees.
SERVICE: LGT ACTIVATE LIRL Rwy 16–34—CTAF.
AIRPORT REMARKS: Unattended. Deer and feral hogs on and invof arpt.
AIRPORT MANAGER: 936-642-1746
COMMUNICATIONS: CTAF 122.9
CLEARANCE DELIVERY PHONE: For CD ctc Houston ARTCC at 281-230-5622.
RADIO AIDS TO NAVIGATION: NOTAM FILE LFK.
  LUFKIN (VH) (H) VORTACW 112.1   LFK   Chan 58   N31°09.75´ W94°43.01´   254° 23.5 NM to fld. 207/5E.
  TACAN AZIMUTH unusable:
    260°–275° byd 30 NM
    275°–260° byd 30 NM blo 2,500´
  DME unusable:
    260°–275° byd 30 NM
    275°–260° byd 30 NM blo 2,500´
  VOR unusable:
    305°–312° byd 40 NM
    313°–323° byd 40 NM blo 2,300´
    313°–323° byd 66 NM
    324°–330° byd 40 NM

GRUVER MUNI (E19)   2 SW   UTC–6(–5DT)   N36°14.02´ W101°25.93´   WICHITA
3205   B   NOTAM FILE FTW   L–15B
RWY 02–20: H4698X60 (ASPH)   S–12.5   MIRL   0.4% up SW   IAP
  RWY 02: Fence.
  RWY 20: Fence.
SERVICE: LGT Actvt MIRL Rwy 02–20—CTAF.
AIRPORT REMARKS: Unattended. Extsv pavement cracking, potholes at Rwy 20 thr.
AIRPORT MANAGER: 806-733-2424
COMMUNICATIONS: CTAF 122.9
®ALBUQUERQUE CENTER APP/DEP CON 127.85
CLEARANCE DELIVERY PHONE: For CD ctc Albuquerque ARTCC at 505-856-4861.
RADIO AIDS TO NAVIGATION: NOTAM FILE BGD.
  BORGER (L) TACAN   Chan 23   BGD (108.6)   N35°48.42´ W101°22.93´   344° 25.7 NM to fld. 3130/11E.
  TACAN AZIMUTH unusable:
    220°–320° byd 10 NM blo 12,000´

GUADALUPE PASS   N31°49.97´ W104°48.55´   EL PASO
RCO 122.5 (ALBUQUERQUE RADIO)   L–6G

GUTHRIE   VUF   N33°38.23´ W100°20.86´/1787   DALLAS–FT WORTH
AWOS–3PT 120.20 (806) 596–4616 VUF AWOS–3PT is associated with 6666 Ranch airport 6TE6.   L–17B

GUTHRIE   N33°46.70´ W100°20.17´   NOTAM FILE FTW.   DALLAS–FT. WORTH
(L) DME 114.5   GTH   Chan 92   010° 15.2 NM to Dan E Richards Muni. 1941.   H–6G, L–17B

H H COFFIELD RGNL (See ROCKDALE on page 410)

HALE CO (See PLAINVIEW on page 400)

HALL–MILLER MUNI (See ATLANTA on page 248)

TEXAS

HALLETTSVILLE MUNI (34R)   3 S   UTC–6(–5DT)   N29°23.40´ W96°57.36´   HOUSTON
278   B   NOTAM FILE CXO   L–19D, 21A
RWY 17–35: H3210X60 (ASPH)   S–7   MIRL
   RWY 17: Trees.
   RWY 35: Trees.
SERVICE: **FUEL** 100LL   **LGT** MIRL Rwy 17–35 preset low intst; to incr intst ACTVT—CTAF.
AIRPORT REMARKS: Unattended. 100LL 24 hr self serve. Rwy 17 and Rwy 35 rwy mkgs discolored.
AIRPORT MANAGER: 361-798-2201
COMMUNICATIONS: CTAF 122.9
CLEARANCE DELIVERY PHONE: For CD ctc Houston ARTCC at 281-230-5622.
RADIO AIDS TO NAVIGATION: NOTAM FILE VCT.
   VICTORIA (L) (L) VORW/DME 109.0   VCT   Chan 27   N28°54.02´ W96°58.74´   356° 29.3 NM to fld. 125/6E.
   VOR unusable:
     345°–355° byd 30.0 NM

HAMILTON MUNI (MNZ)(KMNZ)   2 S   UTC–6(–5DT)   N31°39.96´ W98°08.92´   SAN ANTONIO
1305   B   NOTAM FILE FTW   H–6H, L–19C
RWY 18–36: H5012X75 (ASPH)   S–30   MIRL   IAP
   RWY 18: PAPI(P2L)—GA 3.0° TCH 38´.
   RWY 36: PAPI(P2L)—GA 3.0° TCH 40´.
SERVICE: **FUEL** 100LL, JET A   **LGT** MIRL Rwy 18–36 SS–SR preset
low intst; to incr intst actvt—CTAF.
AIRPORT REMARKS: Attended Intmt. Fuel avbl 24 hrs self serve. For
attendant aft hrs call 979–571–9821. Glider opns invof arpt.
Glider tow avbl. 254-386-3939
AIRPORT MANAGER: 254-386-3939
WEATHER DATA SOURCES: AWOS–3PT 118.525 (254) 386–8211.
COMMUNICATIONS: CTAF/UNICOM 122.7
®**GRAY APP/DEP CON** 120.075
CLEARANCE DELIVERY PHONE: For CD ctc Fort Worth ARTCC at
817-858-7584.
RADIO AIDS TO NAVIGATION: NOTAM FILE SJT.
   GOOCH SPRINGS (H) (H) VORTACW 112.5   AGJ   Chan 72
    N31°11.13´ W98°08.51´   354° 28.8 NM to fld.
    1191/5E.

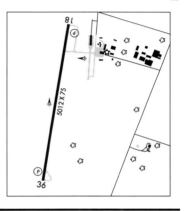

SC, 25 JAN 2024 to 21 MAR 2024

HARLINGEN

VALLEY INTL (HRL)(KHRL) 3 NE UTC–6(–5DT) N26°13.63′ W97°39.31′ BROWNSVILLE
  36 B Class I, ARFF Index B NOTAM FILE HRL H–7C, L–20H, 21A
  RWY 17R–35L: H8301X150 (ASPH–GRVD) S–160, D–200, 2S–175, IAP, AD
    2T–561, 2D–350, 2D/D1–593, 2D/2D2–700, C5–840 HIRL
    RWY 17R: MALSR. Rgt tfc.
    RWY 35L: PAPI(P4R)—GA 3.0° TCH 59′.
  RWY 13–31: H7257X150 (ASPH–GRVD) S–160, D–200, 2S–175,
    2D–350, 2D/2D2–700 HIRL
    RWY 13: REIL. PAPI(P4L)—GA 3.0° TCH 59′.
    RWY 31: MALSR. PAPI(P4L)—GA 3.0° TCH 55′.
  RWY 17L–35R: H5949X150 (ASPH) S–160, D–200, 2D–350 MIRL
    RWY 17L: REIL.
    RWY 35R: Thld dsplcd 190′. Rgt tfc.
  RUNWAY DECLARED DISTANCE INFORMATION
    RWY 13: TORA–7257 TODA–7257 ASDA–7257 LDA–7257
    RWY 17L: TORA–5949 TODA–5949 ASDA–5949 LDA–5949
    RWY 17R: TORA–8301 TODA–8301 ASDA–8301 LDA–8301
    RWY 31: TORA–7257 TODA–7257 ASDA–7257 LDA–7257
    RWY 35L: TORA–8301 TODA–8301 ASDA–8301 LDA–8301
    RWY 35R: TORA–5949 TODA–5949 ASDA–5949 LDA–5759
  SERVICE: S4 **FUEL** 100LL, JET A **OX** 3 **LGT** When ATCT CLSD ACTVT
    MALSR Rwy 17R and Rwy 31—CTAF.
  AIRPORT REMARKS: Attended 1200–0600Z‡. Migratory birds on and in vicinity of arpt. When ATCT clsd req ARFF thru Corpus
    Approach or flt svc. User fee arpt.
  AIRPORT MANAGER: 956-430-8605
  WEATHER DATA SOURCES: ASOS 124.85 (956) 428–7297. LAWRS.
  COMMUNICATIONS: CTAF 119.3 **ATIS** 124.85 **UNICOM** 122.95
    HARLINGEN RCO 122.2 (SAN ANGELO RADIO)
  ®**VALLEY APP/DEP CON** 120.7
    HARLINGEN TOWER 119.3 (1200–0600Z‡) **GND CON** 121.7
  CLEARANCE DELIVERY PHONE: For CD when ATCT is clsd ctc crp Apch at 361-299-4230.
  AIRSPACE: CLASS C svc ctc **APP CON** svc 1200–0600Z‡ other times CLASS E.
  RADIO AIDS TO NAVIGATION: NOTAM FILE HRL.
    HARLINGEN (L) (L) VORW/DME 113.65 HRL Chan 83(Y) N26°13.75′ W97°39.14′ at fld. 32/5E.
    SEBAS NDB (LOMW) 338 HR N26°18.31′ W97°39.45′ 173° 4.7 NM to fld. 28/5E.
    ILS/DME 111.5 I–HRL Chan 52 Rwy 17R. Class IB. LOM SEBAS NDB. Unmonitored when ATCT closed. Localizer
      backcourse unusable 1 NM inbound. Localizer backcourse unusable byd 15° left and right of course.
  COMM/NAV/WEATHER REMARKS: Emergency frequency 121.5 not available at tower.

HARRISON CO (See MARSHALL on page 374)

HARRISON FLD OF KNOX CITY (See KNOX CITY on page 355)

TEXAS

HASKELL MUNI (15F)   2 N   UTC–6(–5DT)   N33°11.49´ W99°43.07´   DALLAS–FT WORTH
   1625   B   NOTAM FILE FTW   L–17B
RWY 18–36: H3420X50 (ASPH)   S–13   MIRL   1.0% up S   IAP
   RWY 18: Thld dsplcd 206´. P–line.
   RWY 36: Road.
SERVICE: **FUEL** 100LL   **LGT** ACTVT MIRL Rwy 18–36—122.8. Nmrs
   lts out, obscured by vegetation.
AIRPORT REMARKS: Unattended. For 100LL fuel wkdays 1400–2300Z‡
   call 940–207–1855; nights and weekends call 940–864–2345. No
   line of sight between rwy ends. Rwy 18–36 nmrs cracks, spalling,
   loose stones, vegetation growing. Rwy 18 and Rwy 36 mkg poor.
AIRPORT MANAGER: (940) 864-2333
COMMUNICATIONS: CTAF 122.8
Ⓡ **FORT WORTH CENTER APP/DEP CON** 133.5
CLEARANCE DELIVERY PHONE: For CD ctc Fort Worth ARTCC at
   817-858-7584.
RADIO AIDS TO NAVIGATION: NOTAM FILE ABI.
   ABILENE (VH) (H) VORTACW 113.7   ABI   Chan 84   N32°28.88´
     W99°51.81´   360° 43.2 NM to fld. 1809/10E.
   VOR unusable:
     163°–236° byd 40 NM blo 18,000´
     237°–247° byd 40 NM blo 7,000´
     248°–250° byd 40 NM blo 18,000´
     251°–255° byd 40 NM blo 4,500´
     251°–255° byd 46 NM blo 18,000´

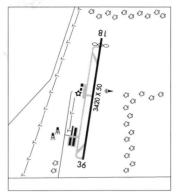

HAWTHORNE FLD   (See KOUNTZE/SILSBEE on page 356)

HEARNE MUNI   (LHB)(KLHB)   1 SW   UTC–6(–5DT)   N30°52.33´ W96°37.33´   HOUSTON
   285   B   NOTAM FILE LHB   L–19D, 21A
RWY 18–36: H4001X75 (ASPH)   S–17   MIRL   IAP
SERVICE: **FUEL** 100LL   **LGT** MIRL Rwy 18–36 opr via phototcell dusk
   to dawn, preset low intst; to incr intst actvt—123.3.
AIRPORT REMARKS: Unattended. Parachute Jumping. NOTE: See Special
   Notices–Hearne, TX–Model Aircraft Activity.
AIRPORT MANAGER: 979-279-3461
WEATHER DATA SOURCES: AWOS–3 118.675 (979) 280–5596.
COMMUNICATIONS: CTAF 122.9
Ⓡ **HOUSTON APP/DEP CON** 134.3
CLEARANCE DELIVERY PHONE: For CD ctc Houston Apch at 281-443-5844 to
   cnl IFR call 281-443-5888.
RADIO AIDS TO NAVIGATION: NOTAM FILE CLL.
   COLLEGE STATION (L) (L) VORTACW 113.3   CLL   Chan 80
     N30°36.30´ W96°25.24´   319° 19.1 NM to fld. 264/8E.
   TACAN unusable:
     101°–130° byd 25 NM blo 2,500´
     131°–148° byd 30 NM blo 2,500´
     149°–160° byd 30 NM blo 2,000´
     325°–349° byd 30 NM blo 2,500´
     350°–100° byd 25 NM blo 3,500´
   VOR unusable:
     024°–034° blo 4,000´
     024°–034° byd 20 NM
     131°–142° blo 7,000´
     142°–152° byd 30 NM
     152°–189° blo 7,000´

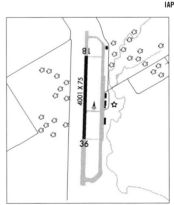

330 TEXAS

HEBBRONVILLE

JIM HOGG CO (HBV)(KHBV) 3 NW UTC−6(−5DT) N27°20.97´ W98°44.22´ BROWNSVILLE
663 B NOTAM FILE HBV H−7B, L−20H
RWY 13−31: H5003X75 (ASPH) S−30, D−72, 2S−91 MIRL IAP
  RWY 13: PAPI(P2L)—GA 3.0° TCH 39´. Trees.
  RWY 31: PAPI(P2L)—GA 3.0° TCH 43´. Tree.
SERVICE: FUEL JET A LGT MIRL Rwy 13−31 preset low intst; to incr intst ACTVT—CTAF. PAPI Rwy 13 oprs consly.
AIRPORT REMARKS: Unattended. Attendant on call. For jet A, call 361−850−3430. Rwy 13−31 gross weight pavement strength provided by arpt manager. Large acft exiting Rwy 31 should back taxi on rwy due to obstn on twy.
AIRPORT MANAGER: 956-693-7751
WEATHER DATA SOURCES: AWOS−3 118.075 (361) 527−2109. Ceiling not avbl.
COMMUNICATIONS: CTAF/UNICOM 122.8
®HOUSTON CENTER APP/DEP CON 127.8
CLEARANCE DELIVERY PHONE: For CD ctc Houston ARTCC at 281-230-5622.
RADIO AIDS TO NAVIGATION: NOTAM FILE LRD.
  LAREDO (VH) (H) VORTACW 117.4 LRD Chan 121 N27°28.72´ W99°25.06´ 093° 37.2 NM to fld. 583/9E.
  VOR unusable:
    080°−126° byd 40 NM
    127°−137° byd 40 NM blo 4,500´
    127°−137° byd 56 NM
    138°−160° byd 40 NM
    190°−260° byd 40 NM

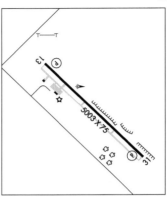

HEMPHILL CO (See CANADIAN on page 267)

HENDERSON

RUSK CO (RFI)(KRFI) 3 W UTC−6(−5DT) N32°08.50´ W94°51.10´ MEMPHIS
442 B NOTAM FILE FTW L−17D
RWY 17−35: H4006X75 (ASPH) S−22 MIRL IAP
  RWY 17: PAPI(P2L)—GA 3.0° TCH 40´. Tree.
  RWY 35: PAPI(P2L)—GA 3.0° TCH 40´. Trees.
RWY 12−30: H3002X75 (ASPH) S−22
  RWY 12: Trees.
  RWY 30: Trees.
SERVICE: FUEL 100LL
AIRPORT REMARKS: Attended 1400−2300Z‡. 100LL 24 hrs self serve. Rwy 12−30 extensive cracking, markings faded.
AIRPORT MANAGER: 903-657-7081
WEATHER DATA SOURCES: AWOS−3 119.375 (903) 657−0384.
COMMUNICATIONS: CTAF/UNICOM 122.8
®LONGVIEW APP/DEP CON 124.275 (1200−0400Z‡)
®FORT WORTH CENTER APP/DEP CON 135.25 (0400−1200Z‡)
CLEARANCE DELIVERY PHONE: For CD ctc Fort Worth ARTCC at 817-858-7584.
RADIO AIDS TO NAVIGATION: NOTAM FILE GGG.
  GREGG COUNTY (VL) (H) VORTACW 112.9 GGG Chan 76 N32°25.07´ W94°45.19´ 190° 17.3 NM to fld. 329/7E.
  TACAN AZIMUTH unusable:
    045°−070° byd 25 NM blo 2,500´
    180°−225° byd 33 NM blo 3,500´
    258°−268° byd 26 NM blo 4,500´
    325°−340° byd 37 NM blo 2,500´
    248°−258° byd 34 NM blo 8,100´
  DME unusable:
    045°−070° byd 25 NM blo 2,500´
    180°−225° byd 33 NM blo 3,500´
    258°−268° byd 26 NM blo 4,500´
    325°−340° byd 37 NM blo 2,500´
  VOR unusable:
    138°−152° byd 40 NM
    188°−192° byd 40 NM
    210°−230° byd 40 NM

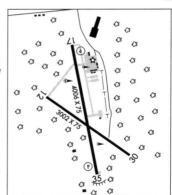

SC, 25 JAN 2024 to 21 MAR 2024

TEXAS   331

HEREFORD MUNI (HRX)(KHRX) 4 NE   UTC–6(–5DT)   N34°51.64´ W102°19.55´   ALBUQUERQUE
3788   B   NOTAM FILE FTW   H–6G, L–6H
RWY 02–20: H6100X100 (CONC–GRVD)   MIRL   IAP
  RWY 02: PAPI(P4L)—GA 3.0° TCH 52´. P–line.
  RWY 20: PAPI(P4L)—GA 3.0° TCH 48´.
RWY 14–32: 3807X135 (TURF)
  RWY 14: P–line.
  RWY 32: P–line.
SERVICE: S4   FUEL 100LL, JET A   LGT MIRL Rwy 02–20 preset low intst
  SS–SR. To actvt MIRL Rwy 02–20 or incr intst–CTAF. PAPI Rwy 02
  and 20 opr consly.
AIRPORT REMARKS: Attended 1400–2300Z‡. 100LL 24 hrs self–serve. Rwy
  14–32 thlds marked with concrete markers. Rwy 14–32 rough sfc.
AIRPORT MANAGER: 806-344-7710
WEATHER DATA SOURCES: AWOS–3 118.05 (806) 258-7283.
COMMUNICATIONS: CTAF/UNICOM 122.8
®AMARILLO APP/DEP CON 119.5 121.15 (1200–0600Z‡)
®ALBUQUERQUE CENTER APP/DEP CON 127.85 (0600–1200Z‡)
CLEARANCE DELIVERY PHONE: For CD ctc Albuquerque ARTCC at
  505-856-4861.
RADIO AIDS TO NAVIGATION: NOTAM FILE FTW.
  TEXICO (VH) (H) VORTACW 112.2   TXO Chan 59   N34°29.71´
    W102°50.38´   038° 33.6 NM to fld. 4060/11E.
  VOR unusable:
    095°–100° byd 40 NM
    120°–130° byd 40 NM
    210°–223° byd 40 NM blo 15,000´
    224°–251° byd 40 NM
    252°–262° byd 40 NM blo 18,000´
    263°–272° byd 40 NM blo 18,000´
    273°–283° byd 40 NM blo 6,000´
    273°–283° byd 46 NM blo 7,000´
    273°–283° byd 59 NM
    284°–319° byd 40 NM
    320°–035° byd 40 NM
  TACAN AZIMUTH unusable:
    222°–232°

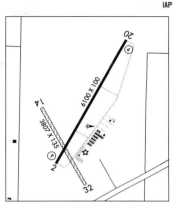

HERITAGE CREEK AIRSTRIP (See DECATUR on page 292)

HICKS (See PONDER on page 401)

HICKS AIRFIELD (See FORT WORTH on page 310)

HIGGINS/LIPSCOMB CO (1X1) 1 S UTC–6(–5DT) N36°06.35´ W100°01.54´   WICHITA
2566   NOTAM FILE FTW   L–15C
RWY 18–36: H3969X60 (ASPH) S–12.5 0.7% up N   IAP
  RWY 18: Thld dsplcd 196´. Fence.
AIRPORT REMARKS: Unattended. No line of sight btn rwy ends. 120´ AGL
  water twr, 2000´ NW of Rwy 18 end, unlgtd.
AIRPORT MANAGER: 806-862-4131
COMMUNICATIONS: CTAF 122.9
®KANSAS CITY CENTER APP/DEP CON 126.95
CLEARANCE DELIVERY PHONE: For CD ctc Kansas City ARTCC at
  913-254-8508.
RADIO AIDS TO NAVIGATION: NOTAM FILE GAG.
  MITBEE (VH) (H) VORTACW 115.6   MMB Chan 103   N36°20.62´
    W99°52.81´   196° 15.9 NM to fld. 2426/10E.

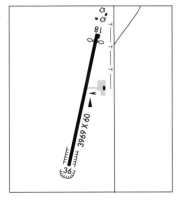

SC, 25 JAN 2024 to 21 MAR 2024

TEXAS

HILLSBORO MUNI (INJ)(KINJ)   5 N   UTC−6(−5DT)   N32°05.02′ W97°05.84′   DALLAS−FT WORTH
686   B   NOTAM FILE INJ   L−17C, A
RWY 16−34: H3998X60 (ASPH)   S−12.5   MIRL   0.3% up N   IAP
  RWY 16: PAPI(P2L)—GA 3.0° TCH 40′.
  RWY 34: PAPI(P2L)—GA 3.0° TCH 40′.
SERVICE: S4   **FUEL** 100LL, JET A   **LGT** MIRL Rwy 16−34 SS−SRpreset low intst; to incr intst—CTAF. PAPI Rwy 16 and 34 opr consly. VGSI unusbl byd 9 degs right of rwy cntrln.
NOISE: Noise sensitive area: Extend pattern on tkof and lndg Rwy 16 to avoid flying over houses to the southeast and east side of arpt.
AIRPORT REMARKS: Attended Mon−Fri 1400−2300Z‡. Skydiving actvty invof arpt. For fuel after hrs call 254−582−8604, self serve avbl with credit card.
AIRPORT MANAGER: 254-582-3731
WEATHER DATA SOURCES: AWOS−3PT 118.725 (254) 582−0063.
COMMUNICATIONS: CTAF 122.9
®**WACO APP/DEP CON** 127.65 (1200−0600Z‡)
®**FORT WORTH CENTER APP/DEP CON** 133.3 (0600−1200Z‡)
CLEARANCE DELIVERY PHONE: For CD ctc Fort Worth ARTCC at 817-858-7584.
RADIO AIDS TO NAVIGATION: NOTAM FILE ACT.
WACO (VH) (H) VORTACW 115.3   ACT   Chan 100   N31°39.73′ W97°16.14′   010° 26.7 NM to fld. 507/9E.
VOR unusable:
  125°−149° byd 40 NM
  149°−159° byd 47 NM
  159°−187° byd 40 NM
  188°−198° byd 40 NM blo 12,000′
  199°−234° byd 40 NM
  235°−245° byd 50 NM
  246°−256° byd 40 NM blo 18,000′
  246°−256° byd 52 NM
  257°−267° byd 58 NM
  268°−282° byd 40 NM
  270°−335° byd 35 NM blo 4,000′
  283°−293° byd 40 NM blo 6,000′
  283°−293° byd 58 NM
  294°−330° byd 40 NM

HONDO
SOUTH TEXAS RGNL AT HONDO (HDO)(KHDO)   2 NW   UTC−6(−5DT)   N29°21.55′ W99°10.65′   SAN ANTONIO
930   B   TPA—1730(800)   NOTAM FILE HDO   H−7B, L−19B
RWY 17L−35R: H6002X100 (CONC)   S−30, D−45, 2D−90   IAP, DIAP
  PCN 103R/C/W/T   MIRL   0.3% up N
  RWY 17L: PAPI(P4L)—GA 3.0° TCH 45′.
  RWY 35R: PAPI(P4L)—GA 3.0° TCH 45′. Rgt tfc.
RWY 13−31: H5545X150 (CONC)   S−30, D−45, 2D−90   0.3% up NW
  RWY 13: Thld dsplcd 98′. Rgt tfc.
RWY 08−26: H3451X75 (CONC)   S−30, D−45, 2D−90
RWY 17R−35L: H3224X140 (ASPH)   S−30, D−45, 2D−90   0.3% up N
  RWY 17R: Rgt tfc.
SERVICE: S2   **FUEL** 100LL, JET A
AIRPORT REMARKS: Attended Mon−Fri 1330−2300Z‡. Deer on and invof arpt. 100LL 24 hr self serve. Full serve Jet A and AVGAS on request, 830−426−3810. 2 hr prior notice, aft hrs. Rwy 08−26 width is 75′ unmarked, overall pavement width is 150′. Bring own ropes for tie down. NOTE: See Special Notices—Unmanned Aircraft System Activity.
AIRPORT MANAGER: 830-426-3810
WEATHER DATA SOURCES: ASOS 119.675 (830) 426−3060.
COMMUNICATIONS: CTAF/UNICOM 122.725
®**HOUSTON CENTER APP/DEP CON** 134.95
CLEARANCE DELIVERY PHONE: For CD ctc Houston ARTCC at 281-230-5622.
RADIO AIDS TO NAVIGATION: NOTAM FILE SAT.
SAN ANTONIO (VH) (H) VORTACW 116.8   SAT   Chan 115   N29°38.64′ W98°27.68′   238° 41.2 NM to fld. 1159/8E.
VOR unusable:
  018°−022° byd 40 NM
  028°−032° byd 40 NM
  342°−347° byd 40 NM
  355°−002° byd 40 NM blo 18,000′

TEXAS

HORIZON (See SAN ANTONIO on page 415)

HORSESHOE BAY RESORT (DZB)(KDZB)　0 N　UTC–6(–5DT)　N30°31.62´ W98°21.53´　SAN ANTONIO
1093　B　NOTAM FILE SJT　　　　　　　　　　　　　　　　　　　　　　　　　　　H–7B, L–19C
RWY 17–35: H5977X100 (ASPH)　D–100　HIRL
　RWY 17: Thld dsplcd 300´.
　RWY 35: Tree. Rgt tfc.
SERVICE:　FUEL 100LL, JET A+　**OX** 1, 2, 3, 4　**LGT** HIRL Rwy 17–35 preset low intst; to incr intst ACTVT—CTAF. Rotg bcn oprs 24/7.
AIRPORT REMARKS: Attended 1300—0100Z‡. Deer invof of rwy. Rwy 35 rgt tfc not mkd on gnd. Rwy 17 ft drop off. TGL and trng flights prohibited. Rwy 17 preferred for dep. Rwy 17 35 ft pline, 375 ft R of cntrln, parl to Rwy 17 end north 3600 ft.
AIRPORT MANAGER: 830-598-6386
WEATHER DATA SOURCES: AWOS–3 119.775 (830) 598–2059.
COMMUNICATIONS: CTAF/UNICOM 122.8
CLEARANCE DELIVERY PHONE: For CD ctc Houston ARTCC at 281-230-5622.
RADIO AIDS TO NAVIGATION: NOTAM FILE T82.
　STONEWALL (VH) (H) VORTAC 113.8　STV　Chan 85　N30°12.41´ W98°42.35´　035° 26.3 NM to fld. 1530/8E.
　　TACAN AZIMUTH unusable:
　　　056°–066° byd 30 NM blo 3,000´
　　　067°–055° byd 30 NM blo 3,300´
　　DME unusable:
　　　056°–066° byd 30 NM blo 3,000´
　　　067°–055° byd 30 NM blo 3,300´
　　VOR unusable:
　　　056°–066° byd 30 NM blo 3,000´
　　　067°–055° byd 30 NM blo 3,300´
　　　110°–122° byd 40 NM blo 5,500´
　　　110°–122° byd 46 NM
　　　123°–210° byd 40 NM
　　　230°–240° byd 40 NM

HORSESHOE BEND (See WEATHERFORD on page 443)

HOUSTON

CONROE/NORTH HOUSTON RGNL (CXO)(KCXO) P (AR)   37 N   UTC–6(–5DT)   N30°21.20´   **HOUSTON**
W95°24.90´   H–7C, L–19D, 21A, GOMW
245   B   NOTAM FILE CXO   IAP, AD
RWY 14–32: H7501X150 (CONC)   S–60, D–100 PCN 36 R/B/W/T   HIRL
  RWY 14: MALSR. PAPI(P4L)—GA 3.0° TCH 47´. Trees.
  RWY 32: REIL. PAPI(P2L)—GA 3.0° TCH 50´.
RWY 01–19: H5000X100 (CONC)   S–30, D–75, 2S–95   MIRL
  RWY 01: PAPI(P2L)—GA 3.15° TCH 49´. Trees.
  RWY 19: PAPI(P2L)—GA 3.0° TCH 49´. Trees.
RUNWAY DECLARED DISTANCE INFORMATION
  RWY 01: TORA–5000   TODA–5000   ASDA–5000   LDA–5000
  RWY 19: TORA–5000   TODA–5000   ASDA–5000   LDA–5000
SERVICE: S4   **FUEL** 100LL, JET A   **OX** 3, 4   **LGT** HIRL Rwy 14–32 preset low intst; to incr intst and actvt REIL Rwy 32—CTAF.
MILITARY— FUEL A+ (1200–0300Z‡, C936–494–4252)
NOISE: Avoid noise sensitive area 10 miles SW quad of arpt.
AIRPORT REMARKS: Attended Mon–Fri 1400–2300Z‡, Sat–Sun 1400–2200Z‡. Extv mil hel actvy on arpt. Hels use right–hand tfc. Extv student pilot (sunrise to sunset). User fee arpt: Intl arpt U.S. Cust user fee arpt. Call U.S. Cust 936–441–7750.
AIRPORT MANAGER: 936-788-8311
WEATHER DATA SOURCES: ASOS (936) 760–4237
COMMUNICATIONS: CTAF 124.125 **ATIS** 118.325
  MONTGOMERY COUNTY RCO 122.2 (MONTGOMERY COUNTY RADIO)
®**HOUSTON APP/DEP CON** 119.7
  TOWER 124.125 (1200–0300Z‡) **GND CON** 120.45
  CLNC DEL 120.45   119.55 (when twr clsd)
  CLEARANCE DELIVERY PHONE: For CD when ATCT clsd ctc Houston Apch at 281-443-5844, to cnl IFR at 281-443-5888.
AIRSPACE: CLASS D svc 1200–0300Z‡; other times CLASS E.
RADIO AIDS TO NAVIGATION: NOTAM FILE IAH.
  HUMBLE (H) (H) VORTACW 116.6   IAH   Chan 113   N29°57.42´ W95°20.74´   346° 24.0 NM to fld. 81/5E.
    VORTAC monitored by ATCT
    VOR portion unusable:
      060°–070° byd 35 NM
      175°–185° byd 20 NM blo 3,000´
      Byd 30 NM blo 2,000´
    DME unusable:
      015°–090° byd 30 NM blo 2,000´
      130°–320° byd 30 NM blo 2,000´
      175°–185° byd 20 NM blo 3,000´
      230°–250°
    TACAN AZIMUTH unusable:
      040°–055° blo 5,000´
      150°–320° blo 4,500´
      150°–320° byd 10 NM
  ALIBI NDB (LOMW) 281   CX   N30°25.92´ W95°28.58´   141° 5.7 NM to fld. 371/5E.   NOTAM FILE CXO.
  ILS/DME 108.7   I-CXO   Chan 24   Rwy 14.   Class IA.   LOM ALIBI NDB.

TEXAS

DAN JONES INTL (T51)   22 NW   UTC–6(–5DT)   N30°02.57´ W95°40.03´   **HOUSTON**
166   B   NOTAM FILE CXO   **COPTER**
RWY 17–35: H3440X50 (ASPH–TURF)   LIRL(NSTD)   L–19D, 21A, GOMW
  RWY 17: Thld dsplcd 255´. Tree.
  RWY 35: Thld dsplcd 380´. P–line.
SERVICE: S4   **FUEL** 100LL   **LGT** SS–SR, ACTIVATE LIRL Rwy 17–35—CTAF. For rotating bcn call 936–521–9887. Rwy 17–35 NSTD LIRL, NSTD colors, single thr lgt each rwy end. 2240 ft of rwy usbl for ngt opns. Rwy 17 thr relctd 300 ft for ngt opns; Rwy 35 thr relctd 900´ ft for ngt opns.
AIRPORT REMARKS: Attended dawn to 0600Z‡. Arpt CLOSED midnight to dawn. Deer on rwys. Cattle invof rwy. PPR for rotor wing acft. Rwy 17 thr bar 2 ft wide. Rwy 17–35 north end 2365 ft X 30 ft asph. Rwy 17 thr dsplcd 255 ft days only. Rwy 35 thr dsplcd 400 ft days only. Rwy 17–35 4 ft fence 53 ft east of cntrln. Left hand tfc 500´ and 1000´ MSL. North–south transitional acft west of fld. Ldg fee.
AIRPORT MANAGER: 936-521-9887
COMMUNICATIONS: CTAF/UNICOM 122.8
CLEARANCE DELIVERY PHONE: For CD ctc Houston Apch at 281-443-5844 to cnl IFR call 281-443-5888.
RADIO AIDS TO NAVIGATION: NOTAM FILE CXO.
  NAVASOTA (VH) (H) VORW/DME 115.9   TNV   Chan 106   N30°17.31´ W96°03.49´   118° 25.1 NM to fld. 247/8E.
    DME unusable:
    005°–072° byd 18 NM blo 3,000´
    073°–077° byd 18 NM blo 2,000´
    078°–106° byd 18 NM blo 3,000´
    VOR unusable:
    000°–039° byd 18 NM blo 3,000´
    025°–085° byd 40 NM
    040°–090°
    086°–145° byd 18 NM blo 6,000´
    091°–145° byd 35 NM
    146°–359° byd 18 NM blo 2,000´
    215°–230° byd 40 NM
    240°–255° byd 40 NM blo 2,100´
    240°–255° byd 52 NM
    256°–260° byd 40 NM
    261°–271° byd 39 NM blo 5,000´
    261°–271° byd 59 NM blo 7,000´
    261°–271° byd 82 NM
    272°–328° byd 40 NM
    329°–339° byd 40 NM blo 5,000´
    329°–339° byd 61 NM blo 6,000´
    329°–339° byd 83 NM
    340°–005° byd 40 NM

TEXAS

DAVID WAYNE HOOKS MEML (DWH)(KDWH)   17 NW   UTC–6(–5DT)   N30°03.71´   **HOUSTON**
W95°33.17´   **COPTER**
152   B   NOTAM FILE DWH   **H–7C, L–19D, 21A, GOMW**
RWY 17R–35L: H7009X100 (ASPH)   S–30, D–85   HIRL   **IAP, AD**
  RWY 17R: REIL. PAPI(P4R)—GA 3.0° TCH 52´. Thld dsplcd 1007´.
    Road.
  RWY 35L: REIL. PAPI(P4L)—GA 3.0° TCH 41´. Trees.
RWY 17L–35R: H3500X35 (ASPH)   S–12.5
  RWY 35R: Thld dsplcd 208´. Antenna. Rgt tfc.
RUNWAY DECLARED DISTANCE INFORMATION
  RWY 17R: TORA–7009   TODA–7009   ASDA–7009   LDA–6002
  RWY 35L: TORA–6700   TODA–6700   ASDA–6700   LDA–6700
SERVICE: S4   **FUEL** 100LL, JET A, A1+   **OX** 2   **LGT** When ATCT clsd
  actvt REIL Rwys 17R and 35L; HIRL Rwy 17R–35L—CTAF. 17R
  REIL lctd at dsplcd thld.
NOISE: Noise sensitive area SW of arpt. All mil acft departing Rwy 17R
  climb rwy hdg 650 ft MSL prior to turns or rejoin.
AIRPORT REMARKS: Attended continuously. Birds and deer on and invof
  arpt. Hel practice area west of ATCT at or blo 600 ft. Twys A and B
  clsd east of Rwy 17R indef. Acft 25000 lbs and ovr are rstrd to Twys
  C, P, E (btn Twys P and G), Twy G (north of Twy E), ramps A and C
  and the tomball jet cntr ramp. All other twys rstrd to acft below 25000
  lbs. Twys D and K rstrd to acft 12500 lbs and blw. Twy K rstrd to
  piston acft only. Twys unlgtd. After SS large acft use Twy P btn Twys E and C. Intersection where Twys Papa, Echo, Juliette
  and Kilo meet is referred to as the triangle. Four hel prkg spots lctd east of Twy K.
AIRPORT MANAGER: 281-376-5436
WEATHER DATA SOURCES: ASOS (281) 251–7853
COMMUNICATIONS: CTAF 118.4 **ATIS** 128.375 **UNICOM** 122.95
  ® **HOUSTON APP/DEP CON** 119.3
  HOOKS TOWER 118.4 (West) 127.4 (East) (1300–0400Z‡)   **GND CON** 121.8 **CLNC DEL** 119.45
CLEARANCE DELIVERY PHONE: For CD when ATCT clsd, ctc Houston Apch on CD freq or call 281-443-5844. for IFR cancellation
  when ATCT clsd, call 281-443-5888.
AIRSPACE: CLASS D svc 1300–0400Z‡; other times CLASS G.
RADIO AIDS TO NAVIGATION: NOTAM FILE IAH.
  HUMBLE (H) (H) VORTACW 116.6   IAH   Chan 113   N29°57.42´ W95°20.74´   295° 12.5 NM to fld. 81/5E.
    VORTAC monitored by ATCT
    VOR portion unusable:
      060°–070° byd 35 NM
      175°–185° byd 20 NM blo 3,000´
      Byd 30 NM blo 2,000´
    DME unusable:
      015°–090° byd 30 NM blo 2,000´
      130°–320° byd 30 NM blo 2,000´
      175°–185° byd 20 NM blo 3,000´
      230°–250°
    TACAN AZIMUTH unusable:
      040°–055° blo 5,000´
      150°–320° blo 4,500´
      150°–320° byd 10 NM
  LOC/DME 110.5   I–HEW   Chan 42   Rwy 17R.   DME unmonitored.

• • • • • • • • • • • • • • • •

WATERWAY 17W–35W: 2530X100 (WATER)
  WATERWAY 17W: Berm.
  WATERWAY 35W: Berm. Rgt tfc.
SEAPLANE REMARKS: Rwy 17W marked by buoy. Rwy 35W marked by buoy.

TEXAS

ELLINGTON (EFD)(KEFD) P (ANG CG NASA ARNG)   15 SE   UTC−6(−5DT)   N29°36.44′   **HOUSTON**
W95°09.53′   **COPTER**
33   B   TPA—See Remarks   LRA   Class IV, ARFF Index A   NOTAM FILE EFD   **H−7C, L−19E, 21A, GOMW**
RWY 17R−35L: H9001X150 (CONC−GRVD)   S−100, D−190, 2S−175,   **IAP, AD**
2D−590, 2D/2D2−800 PCN 120R/B/W/T   HIRL   CL
  RWY 17R: MALSF. TDZL. PAPI(P4L)—GA 3.0° TCH 48′. RVR−TR
  RWY 35L: MALSF. TDZL. PAPI(P4L)—GA 3.0° TCH 32′. RVR−TR Rgt
  tfc.
RWY 04−22: H8001X150 (CONC−GRVD)   S−100, D−164, 2S−175,
2D−300, 2D/2D2−668 PCN 110R/B/W/T   HIRL   CL
  RWY 04: PAPI(P4L)—GA 3.0° TCH 50′. RVR−TR Rgt tfc.
  RWY 22: MALSR. TDZL. PAPI(P4L)—GA 3.0° TCH 50′. RVR−TR
RWY 17L−35R: H4609X75 (CONC)   S−24, D−63, 2S−80, 2D−145,
2D/2D2−300 PCN 12 R/C/W/T
  RWY 35R: Rgt tfc.
RUNWAY DECLARED DISTANCE INFORMATION

	TORA	TODA	ASDA	LDA
RWY 04:	8001	8001	8001	8001
RWY 17L:	4609	4609	4609	4609
RWY 17R:	9001	9001	9001	9001
RWY 22:	8001	8001	8001	8001
RWY 35L:	9001	9001	9001	9001
RWY 35R:	4609	4609	4609	4609

ARRESTING GEAR/SYSTEM
  RWY 17R BAK−14 BAK−12B(B) (1500′).   BAK−14 BAK−12B(B) (1850′). **RWY 35L**
  RWY 04 BAK−14 BAK−12B(B) (1563′).   BAK−14 BAK−12B(B) (1496′). **RWY 22**
SERVICE: S4   **FUEL** 100LL, JET A   **OX** 2, 4   **MILITARY**— **A−GEAR** Potential for tail hook skip on Rwy 17R−35L and Rwy
04−22 due to centerline lgt within 200′ of Rwy A−G. A−Gear lgtd mrk placement exceeds 75′ from rwy edge. **JASU** 1(−95)
1(−86) 1(JETEX5) **FUEL** A++(Mil), A, A+, J8 (C281−484−6551.) (NC−100LL) **FLUID** LHOX HPOX
NOISE: NS ABTMT: Noise sensitive areas S and E of fld. Jet acft rstd to str−in full stop ldg only btn 0400−1300Z‡ dly,
0400−1900Z‡ Sun. On dep jet acft min use of after burners and climb rwy hdg to 1000′ prior to turns or rejoin.
AIRPORT REMARKS: Attended continuously. Caution:nmrs small acft with extv trng in area of arpt. Nmrs birds on and invof arpt
all quadrants. Be alert for mil acft at 1600′ MSL making overhead apchs. Arpt clsd to acft with wingspan 171′ or greater
exc 24 hrs PPR 281−433−1612. 70′ AGL tanks lctd 1400′ northeast of Rwy 17R apch. Street lgts lctd 700′ east of
Rwy 17R apch may be mistaken for apch lgts. TPA—VFR rectangular 1100(1067), overhead 1600(1567), lgt acft
600(567). Twy B unlgtd east of Rwy 17R−35L, dalgt use only. Rwy 17L−35R btn Twy C and Twy G dual purpose rwy/twy
with twy lgts. Parking ramp capacity TDT−710. Rwy 17R arresting barriers 1500′ lctd in safety area 14" lip each side of
rwy. Rwy 35L arresting barriers 1849′ lctd in safety area 14" lip each side of rwy. Rwy 04 arresting barriers 1563′ lctd
in safety area 14" lip each side of rwy. Rwy 22 arresting barriers 1496′ lctd in safety area 14" lip each side of rwy. PPR
for unscheduled air carrier ops, ctc 281−433−1612. Rwy 17L−35R and Twy B east of Rwy 17R−35L not avble for air
carrier acft. NSTD afld mrk on ANG acft prk apn. Space Launch Activity Area—See Special Notices.
MILITARY REMARKS: See FLIP AP/1 Supplementary Arpt Remarks. UAS ops within Ellington Class D airspace, opr hrs vary.
  ANG ANG ramp clsd to all acft exc Official Business only. 24 hrs PPR, ctc Base OPS 1200−2130Z‡ Tue−Fri, clsd wkend &
  hol. DSN 454−2142, C281−929−2142. Comd Post avbl 24 hr DSN 454−2716, C281−929−2716. All other tran acft
  ctc FBO 281−484−6551. BASH PHASE II cond Jun−Sep for migratory birds. BASH PHASE I Oct−May. **CG** Minimum 24
  hr PPR exc CG msn, C713−578−3000.
AIRPORT MANAGER: 713-847-4200
WEATHER DATA SOURCES: AWOS−3 135.575 (713) 847−4430.
COMMUNICATIONS: ATIS 135.575 269.9 (713) 847−4430   UNICOM 122.95
Ⓡ **HOUSTON APP/DEP CON** 134.45 284.0
  TOWER 126.05 253.5   **GND CON** 121.6 275.8
  ARNG OPS 41.00 (1230−2200Z‡ Mon−Fri, prior req only) 142.2 Call Texan ops.
  LONE STAR COMD POST 142.2   **ANG OPS COMD POST** 288.5
AIRSPACE: CLASS D.

CONTINUED ON NEXT PAGE

TEXAS
CONTINUED FROM PRECEDING PAGE

RADIO AIDS TO NAVIGATION: NOTAM FILE CXO.
  TRINITY (VL) (DL) VORW/DME 114.75   MHF   Chan 94(Y)   N29°32.78´ W94°44.85´   273° 21.8 NM to fld. 38/7E.
    VOR unusable:
      060°–079° byd 40 NM
      080°–090° byd 40 NM blo 6,000´
      080°–090° byd 50 NM blo 8,000´
      091°–109° byd 40 NM
      110°–190° blo 2,000´
  (L) TACAN   Chan 31   EFD (109.4)   N29°36.36´ W95°09.58´   at fld. 29/5E.   NOTAM FILE EFD.
    DME unusable:
      065°–090° byd 30 NM
    TACAN AZIMUTH unusable:
      065°–090° byd 30 NM
  ILS 110.3   I–LPV   Rwy 17R.   Class IE.
  ILS 110.1   I–FNF   Rwy 22.   Class IE.
  ILS 111.1   I–EFD   Rwy 35L.   Class IT.

TEXAS   339

GEORGE BUSH INTCNTL/HOUSTON (IAH)(KIAH)   15 N   UTC–6(–5DT)   N29°59.07´   **HOUSTON**
W95°20.49´   **COPTER**
96   B   LRA   Class I, ARFF Index E   NOTAM FILE IAH   H–7C, L–19E, 21A, GOMW
RWY 15L–33R: H12001X150 (CONC–GRVD) S–100, D–200, 2S–175,   IAP, AD
  2D–400, 2D/2D2–800 PCN 72 R/A/W/T   HIRL CL
  RWY 15L: PAPI(P4R)—GA 3.0° TCH 58´. RVR–TMR
  RWY 33R: MALSR. RVR–TMR
RWY 09–27: H10000X150 (CONC–GRVD)   D–210, 2S–175, 2D–560
  PCN 67 R/A/W/T HIRL CL
  RWY 09: MALSR. PAPI(P4R)—GA 3.0° TCH 71´. RVR–TMR
  RWY 27: ALSF2. TDZL. PAPI(P4L)—GA 3.0° TCH 70´. RVR–TMR
RWY 15R–33L: H10000X150 (CONC–GRVD) S–75, D–200, 2S–175,
  2D–400, 2D/2D2–873 PCN 94 R/B/W/T HIRL CL
  RWY 15R: MALSR. TDZL. PAPI(P4L)—GA 3.0° TCH 71´. RVR–TMR
  RWY 33L: TDZL. PAPI(P4L)—GA 3.0° TCH 59´. RVR–TMR
RWY 08R–26L: H9402X150 (CONC–GRVD) S–75, D–210, 2S–175,
  2D–498, 2D/2D2–873 PCN 72 R/A/W/T HIRL CL
  RWY 08R: MALSR. TDZL. PAPI(P4L)—GA 3.0° TCH 72´. RVR–TMR
  RWY 26L: ALSF2. TDZL. PAPI(P4R)—GA 3.0° TCH 71´. RVR–TMR
RWY 08L–26R: H9000X150 (CONC–GRVD) S–75, D–210, 2S–175,
  2D–409, 2D/2D2–873 PCN 72 R/A/W/T HIRL CL
  RWY 08L: ALSF2. TDZL. RVR–TMR
  RWY 26R: ALSF2. TDZL. RVR–TMR

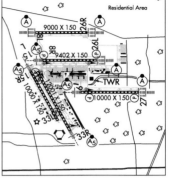

LAND AND HOLD–SHORT OPERATIONS

LDG RWY	HOLD–SHORT POINT	AVBL LDG DIST
RWY 08R	TWY NP	9019
RWY 26L	TWY NE	9010

RUNWAY DECLARED DISTANCE INFORMATION
  RWY 08L: TORA–9000 TODA–9000   ASDA–9000   LDA–9000
  RWY 08R: TORA–9402 TODA–9402   ASDA–9402   LDA–9402
  RWY 09: TORA–10000 TODA–10000 ASDA–10000 LDA–10000
  RWY 15L: TORA–12001 TODA–12001 ASDA–12001 LDA–12001
  RWY 15R: TORA–10000 TODA–10000 ASDA–10000 LDA–10000
  RWY 26L: TORA–9402 TODA–9402   ASDA–9402   LDA–9402
  RWY 26R: TORA–9000 TODA–9000   ASDA–9000   LDA–9000
  RWY 27: TORA–10000 TODA–10000 ASDA–10000 LDA–10000
  RWY 33L: TORA–10000 TODA–10000 ASDA–10000 LDA–10000
  RWY 33R: TORA–12001 TODA–12001 ASDA–12001 LDA–12001
SERVICE: S4   **FUEL** 100LL, JET A   **OX** 2
NOISE: Noise sensitive area north, east and west of arpt.
AIRPORT REMARKS: Attended continuously. Birds on and invof arpt. Wildlife haz bats invof IAH. Rwy 09–27 clsed to acft with
  wingspan 215´ and above. ASDE–X in use. Opr transponders with altitude reporting mode and ADS–B (if equipped)
  enabled on all airport surfaces. Acft equipped with dual antennas should use top antenna. GBAS apch svc vol 20 NM fr
  thld, all GLS apchs. Rwy status lgts are in opn. Rwy 15L–33R magnetic anomalies may affect compass hdg for tkof. North
  ramp north and south taxilanes clsd to acft with wing spans greater than 125´. Taxilane RC clsd to acft with wingspan
  greater than 135´. Twy NR clsd to acft with wing spans greater than 125´ between Twy WD and Twy WB. Twy NR btn
  Twy NC and Twy WW clsd to acft wingspan more than 214´. Twy SF btn Rwy 09–27 up to and including the east bridge
  clsd to acft with wingspan 215´ and over. Twy WW run–up pad for Rwy 15L clsd acft with wingspan 135´ and over. Twy
  WW btn Twy NR and Twy WB clsd to acft wingspan more than 214´. Pilots and crews should be aware of dep turns on
  crs in excess of 180°. Pilot readback of direction of turns is highly encouraged. The flwg mov areas are not vsb fm the
  ATCT: portions of Twys WA and WB fm Twy WH to the AER 33R; Twys WA and WB fm Twy WD north for 400´; Twy WD
  fm Twy WA to Twy NR; Twy NR; Twy WL fm Rwy 15L to Twy WB and Twy WM. Taxilane RA, RB, RC, R2, and Twy SC
  north of Twy SB are designated non–movement areas operated by UAL ramp ctl. Twy SF btn Twy NB and Txl RA is dsgnd
  non–mov area. Dual twy ops Twy NK btn Twy NB and North Ramp, west cntrln rstd to acft max wing spans 125´ and
  east cntrln max wing spans 214´. Twy NR btn Twy WW and WB is designated non–movement area. Twy NK btn Twy NB
  and terminal D ramp simultaneous acft ops prohibited when middle taxilane in use. Twy WC west of Rwy 15R–33L rstrd
  to acft with 118´ wingspan and blw. Twy WA and Twy WB magnetic anomalies may affect compass hdg. Twy NA lgt all
  between Twy WP and Twy NP not standard. 9´ AGL unmarked security fence adjacent to FBO and corporate base operator
  ramps and non–movement area taxilanes. Ldg fee. Flight Notification Service (ADCUS) available. Apron terminal alpha
  north ramp north–south txl clsd to acft wingspan more 125 ft. Apron terminal alpha north ramp spot 5 clsd to acft
  wingspan more than 118 ft. Apron terminal alpha north ramp east–west txl clsd to acft wingspan more than 118 ft. Apron
  terminal alpha north ramp spot 6 clsd to acft wingspan more than 125 ft. Twy WD btn Twy NR and Twy WB clsd to acft
  wingspan more than 171´. Twy NJ btn Twy NB and Terminal C Ramp simultaneous acft ops prohibited when middle
  taxilane in use, middle taxilane clsd to acft wingspn more than 214´. Dual twy opns Twy NJ btn Twy NB and Terminal C
  ramp; west cntrln rstrd to acft max wing spans 118´ and east cntrln max wing spans 118´.

CONTINUED ON NEXT PAGE
SC, 25 JAN 2024 to 21 MAR 2024

TEXAS

CONTINUED FROM PRECEDING PAGE

AIRPORT MANAGER: 281-233-1131
WEATHER DATA SOURCES: ASOS (281) 443-6397 TDWR.
COMMUNICATIONS: D-ATIS 124.05 (281-209-8665) **UNICOM** 122.95
   HOUSTON RCO 122.4 (MONTGOMERY COUNTY RADIO)
® **HOUSTON APP CON** 124.35 (West) 120.05 (East)
® **HOUSTON DEP CON** 123.8 (West) 119.7 (North) 127.125
   TOWER 135.15 (Rwy 09 and Rwy 27) 127.3 (Rwy 15R-33L and Rwy 15L-33R) 125.35 (Rwy 08R and Rwy 26L)
   120.725 (Rwy 08L and Rwy 26R) **GND CON** 121.7 (Rwy 15L-33R, and Rwy 15R-33L) 118.575 (Rwy 08L-26R, Rwy
   08R-26L and Rwy 09-27)
   GND METERING 119.95 **CLNC DEL** 128.1
   CPDLC (LOGON KUSA)
   PDC
AIRSPACE: CLASS B See VFR Terminal Area Chart.
RADIO AIDS TO NAVIGATION: NOTAM FILE IAH.
   HUMBLE (H) (H) VORTACW 116.6   IAH   Chan 113   N29°57.42′ W95°20.74′   003° 1.7 NM to fld. 81/5E.
     VORTAC monitored by ATCT
     VOR portion unusable:
       060°-070° byd 35 NM
       175°-185° byd 20 NM blo 3,000′
       Byd 30 NM blo 2,000′
     DME unusable:
       015°-090° byd 30 NM blo 2,000′
       130°-320° byd 30 NM blo 2,000′
       175°-185° byd 20 NM blo 3,000′
       230°-250°
     TACAN AZIMUTH unusable:
       040°-055° blo 5,000′
       150°-320° blo 4,500′
       150°-320° byd 10 NM
   ILS/DME 111.55 I-BZU Chan 52(Y) Rwy 08L. Class IIIE.
   ILS/DME 109.7 I-IAH Chan 34 Rwy 08R. Class IE. DME also serves Rwy 26.
   ILS/DME 110.9 I-UYO Chan 46 Rwy 09. DME also serves Rwy 27.
   ILS 111.15 I-LKM Rwy 15R. Class IE. LOC unusable byd 30° right of course. DME unusable byd 25° left of course.
   ILS/DME 109.7 I-JYV Chan 34 Rwy 26L. Class IIIE. DME also serves Rwy 08.
   ILS/DME 111.55 I-OND Chan 52(Y) Rwy 26R. Class IIIE.
   ILS/DME 110.9 I-GHI Chan 46 Rwy 27. Class IIIE. DME also serves Rwy 09.
   ILS 111.9 I-CDG Rwy 33R. Class IE.

HOUSTON EXEC (TME)(KTME)   28 W   UTC-6(-5DT)   N29°48.30′ W95°53.87′   **HOUSTON**
   166   B   NOTAM FILE CXO   **H-7C, L-19D, 21A, GOMW**
   RWY 18-36: H6610X100 (ASPH) D-101 MIRL   **IAP, AD**
     RWY 18: REIL. PAPI(P4L)—GA 3.0° TCH 40′. P-line.
     RWY 36: REIL. PAPI(P4L)—GA 3.0° TCH 40′. Rgt tfc.
   SERVICE: S4 **FUEL** 100LL, JET A **OX** 3, 4 **LGT** Actvt MIRL Rwy
     18-36, REIL Rwy 18 and 36—CTAF.
   NOISE: Noise sensitive area east of arpt in effect, avoid housing area.
   AIRPORT REMARKS: Attended continuously. Birds on and invof arpt.
   AIRPORT MANAGER: 281-945-5000
   WEATHER DATA SOURCES: AWOS-3 119.525 (281) 945-5451. or
     713-932-8437.
   COMMUNICATIONS: CTAF 126.975 **UNICOM** 122.975 **ATIS** 119.525 (24 hr
     281-945-5451)
® **HOUSTON APP/DEP CON** 123.8
     TOWER 126.975 (1200-0400Z‡)
     GND CON 132.075 **CLNC DEL** 132.075
   CLEARANCE DELIVERY PHONE: For CD when ATCT is clsd ctc Houston Apch at
     281-443-5844 to cnl IFR at 281-443-5888.
   AIRSPACE: CLASS D svc 1200-0400Z‡; other times CLASS E.
   RADIO AIDS TO NAVIGATION: NOTAM FILE ELA.
     EAGLE LAKE (DH) DME 116.4   ELA   Chan 111   N29°39.75′
       W96°19.03′   069° 23.5 NM to fld. 192.

TEXAS

HOUSTON FORT BEND (2H5)   33 SW   UTC–6(–5DT)   N29°29.95´ W95°53.90´   HOUSTON
105   NOTAM FILE CXO
RWY 17–35: 4400X100 (TURF)
   RWY 17: Fence.
   RWY 35: P–line.
AIRPORT REMARKS: Unattended. Arpt has perimeter fence, gates locked, ctc arpt manager for access. Rwy deliniated by mowing.
AIRPORT MANAGER: 713-725-3267
COMMUNICATIONS: CTAF 122.9
CLEARANCE DELIVERY PHONE: For CD ctc Houston Apch at 281-443-5844 to cnl IFR call 281-443-5888.

HOUSTON/SOUTHWEST (AXH)(KAXH)   15 SW   UTC–6(–5DT)   N29°30.37´ W95°28.62´   HOUSTON COPTER
69   B   NOTAM FILE CXO   H–7C, L–19D, 21A, GOMW
RWY 09–27: H5002X100 (ASPH)   S–60, D–75, 2D–100   MIRL   IAP
   RWY 09: REIL. PAPI(P2L)—GA 3.5° TCH 50´. Road.
   RWY 27: REIL. PAPI(P2L)—GA 3.0° TCH 43´. Road.
SERVICE: S4   **FUEL** 100LL, JET A+   **OX** 3   **LGT** MIRL Rwy 09–27
preset low intst dusk–dawn, to incr intst & ACTVT REIL Rwy 09 and Rwy 27—CTAF.
AIRPORT REMARKS: Attended continuously. Hel tfc invof arpt. Rwy 09 calm wind rwy.
AIRPORT MANAGER: 281-431-2581
WEATHER DATA SOURCES: AWOS–3 123.625 (281) 431–6572.
COMMUNICATIONS: CTAF/UNICOM 123.0
®**APP/DEP CON** 123.8
   CLNC DEL 120.8
CLEARANCE DELIVERY PHONE: For CD ctc Houston Apch at 281-443-5844.
to cnl IFR ctc Houston Apch at 281-443-5888.
RADIO AIDS TO NAVIGATION: NOTAM FILE CXO.
   TRINITY (VL) (DL) VORW/DME 114.75   MHF   Chan 94(Y)
   N29°32.78´ W94°44.85´   260° 38.3 NM to fld. 38/7E.
   VOR unusable:
      060°–079° byd 40 NM
      080°–090° byd 40 NM blo 6,000´
      080°–090° byd 50 NM blo 8,000´
      091°–109° byd 40 NM
      110°–190° blo 2,000´
   LOC/DME 108.9   I–AXH   Chan 26   Rwy 09.

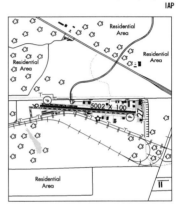

PEARLAND RGNL (LVJ)(KLVJ)   17 S   UTC–6(–5DT)   N29°31.28´ W95°14.53´   HOUSTON COPTER
44   B   NOTAM FILE LVJ   L–19E, 21A, GOMW
RWY 14–32: H4313X75 (CONC)   S–30   MIRL   IAP, AD
   RWY 14: Trees.
   RWY 32: Road.
SERVICE: S4   **FUEL** 100LL, JET A   **LGT** MIRL Rwy 14–32 SS–SR preset low intst; incr intst and actvt—CTAF.
AIRPORT REMARKS: Attended 1400–01000Z‡. Banner towing SR–SS. Hel traffic invof arpt. Rwy 14 and Rwy 32 hels use right–hand traffic. Rwy 14 calm wind rwy. Lgtd oil derrick 116´ AGL, 0.65 NM southeast of arpt. Rwy 14 25 ft lgtd poles in trees 520 ft fm thr. Rwy 14–32 safety area ireg sfc irrigation ditches E and W side adj 40´, 10´ drop.
AIRPORT MANAGER: 281-482-7551
WEATHER DATA SOURCES: ASOS 118.525 (281) 992–1853.
COMMUNICATIONS: CTAF/UNICOM 122.725
®**HOUSTON APP/DEP CON** 134.45
   CLNC DEL 124.0
CLEARANCE DELIVERY PHONE: For CD ctc Houston Apch at 281-443-5844.
to cnl IFR ctc Houston Apch at 281-443-5888.
RADIO AIDS TO NAVIGATION: NOTAM FILE GLS.
   SCHOLES (VH) (DH) VORW/DME 113.0   VUH   Chan 77   N29°16.16´
   W94°52.06´   302° 24.7 NM to fld. 4/6E.
   VOR unusable:
      285°–295° byd 35 NM blo 2,500´

SC, 25 JAN 2024 to 21 MAR 2024

SUGAR LAND RGNL (SGR)(KSGR) P 17 SW UTC−6(−5DT) N29°37.33′ W95°39.39′ **HOUSTON**
81 B NOTAM FILE SGR **COPTER**
RWY 17−35: H8000X100 (CONC) S−80, D−120, 2S−152, 2D−200, H−7C, L−19D, 21A, GOMW
  2D/2D2−600 HIRL IAP, AD
  RWY 17: REIL. PAPI(P2R)—GA 3.5° TCH 52′. Thld dsplcd 380′. Trees.
  RWY 35: REIL. PAPI(P4L)—GA 3.0° TCH 56′. Thld dsplcd 1984′.
    P−line.
SERVICE: S4 **FUEL** 100LL, JET A+ **OX** 1, 2 **LGT** When ATCT clsd actvt
  REIL Rwy 17 and 35; HIRL Rwy 17−35−CTAF.
NOISE: Noise abatement proc: Noise sensitive areas—info avbl at trml.
AIRPORT REMARKS: Attended 1100−0500Z‡. Birds on and invof arpt.
  100LL avbl 24 hrs self serve. For Jet A+ aft hrs call 281−275−2400
  durg atndd hrs. Sfc conds not rprtd Fri 10:00 pm to Sun 10:00 pm.
  Rwy 17−35 surface not grvd. Nitrogen avbl dur business hrs. No tgls
  aft twr closes. No int deps for multi−engine acft. Ramp fee for civ acft
  waived with fuel purchase. Mil and corporate gnd transportation
  prvdd. LRA M−F 1400−1800Z‡ & 1900−2300Z‡. Otr times by appt.
AIRPORT MANAGER: 281−275−2100
WEATHER DATA SOURCES: ASOS 118.125 (281) 242−7605.
COMMUNICATIONS: CTAF 118.65 **ATIS** 118.125 (1200−0400Z‡) **UNICOM**
  122.95
Ⓡ **HOUSTON APP/DEP CON** 123.8
  SUGAR LAND TOWER 118.65 (1200−0400Z‡)
  GND CON 121.4 **CLNC DEL** 121.4 **CLNC DEL** 119.25 (When twr clsd)
CLEARANCE DELIVERY PHONE: For CD when ATCT is clsd ctc Houston Apch at 281−443−5844 to cnl IFR at 281−443−5888.
AIRSPACE: CLASS D svc 1200−0400Z‡; other times CLASS E.
RADIO AIDS TO NAVIGATION: NOTAM FILE ELA.
  EAGLE LAKE (DH) DME 116.4 ELA Chan 111 N29°39.75′ W96°19.03′ 094° 34.6 NM to fld. 192.
  ILS/DME 110.7 I−TXH Chan 44 Rwy 35. Class IT.

TEXAS

WEST HOUSTON (IWS)(KIWS)   13 W   UTC–6(–5DT)   N29°49.09´ W95°40.36´   HOUSTON
111   B   NOTAM FILE CXO   COPTER
RWY 15–33: H3953X75 (ASPH)   S–18, D–44   HIRL   L–19D, 21A, GOMW
  RWY 15: REIL. PAPI(P2R)—GA 3.7° TCH 43´. Trees.   IAP
  RWY 33: REIL. PAPI(P2L)—GA 3.7° TCH 44´. Road.
SERVICE: S4   **FUEL** 100LL, JET A+   **OX** 1, 2, 3, 4   **LGT** HIRL Rwy
  15–33 preset low intst; to incr intst and ACTVT REIL Rwy 15 and Rwy
  33—CTAF.
AIRPORT REMARKS: Attended continuously. 20 ft deep, 25 ft wide ditch,
  0–166 ft dstc acrs apch. No TGLs btn 0400–1200Z‡. No ngt hel trng.
  No mult trng flts by hels. Rwy 15 nstd NPI markings due to rwy len.
  No aiming point. Rwy 33 nstd MPI markings due to rwy len. No aiming
  point. Facility fee charged to non–patrons, waived with minimum
  purchase.
AIRPORT MANAGER: 281-492-2130
COMMUNICATIONS: CTAF/UNICOM 123.05
 ® **APP/DEP CON** 123.8
  CLNC DEL 121.15
CLEARANCE DELIVERY PHONE: For CD ctc Houston Apch at 281-443-5844.
  to cnl IFR ctc Houston Apch at 281-443-5888.
RADIO AIDS TO NAVIGATION: NOTAM FILE IAH.
  HUMBLE (H) (H) VORTACW 116.6   IAH   Chan 113   N29°57.42´
  W95°20.74´   239° 19.0 NM to fld. 81/5E.
  VORTAC monitored by ATCT
  VOR portion unusable:
    060°–070° byd 35 NM
    175°–185° byd 20 NM blo 3,000´
    Byd 30 NM blo 2,000´
  DME unusable:
    015°–090° byd 30 NM blo 2,000´
    130°–320° byd 30 NM blo 2,000´
    175°–185° byd 20 NM blo 3,000´
    230°–250°
  TACAN AZIMUTH unusable:
    040°–055° blo 5,000´
    150°–320° blo 4,500´
    150°–320° byd 10 NM
COMM/NAV/WEATHER REMARKS: WX info avbl on 125.575, 281–579–9820. ASRI 129.875.

344 TEXAS

WILLIAM P HOBBY (HOU)(KHOU) 8 SE UTC−6(−5DT) N29°38.75´ W95°16.63´   HOUSTON
46   B LRA Class I, ARFF Index C NOTAM FILE HOU   COPTER
  RWY 04−22: H7602X150 (CONC−GRVD) S−75, D−200, 2S−168,   H−7C, L−19E, 21A, GOMW
    2T−461, 2D−400, 2D/D1−444, C5−717 HIRL CL   IAP, AD
    RWY 04: ALSF2. TDZL. PAPI(P4R)—GA 3.0° TCH 58´. RVR−TMR
    RWY 22: MALS. PAPI(P4L)—GA 3.0° TCH 49´. RVR−TMR Pole.
  RWY 13R−31L: H7602X150 (ASPH−GRVD) S−75, D−195, 2S−168,
    2T−461, 2D−220, 2D/D1−444, C5−717 HIRL CL
    RWY 13R: MALSR. TDZL. PAPI(P4R)—GA 3.0° TCH 52´. RVR−T Thld
      dsplcd 1034´. Pole.
    RWY 31L: TDZL. REIL. PAPI(P4L)—GA 3.0° TCH 76´. RVR−T Road.
  RWY 13L−31R: H5148X100 (CONC−GRVD) S−30, D−45, 2D−80 MIRL
    RWY 13L: PAPI(P4L)—GA 3.0° TCH 60´.
  RUNWAY DECLARED DISTANCE INFORMATION
    RWY 04: TORA−7602 TODA−7602 ASDA−7602 LDA−7602
    RWY 13L: TORA−5148 TODA−5148 ASDA−5148 LDA−5148
    RWY 13R: TORA−7602 TODA−7602 ASDA−7602 LDA−6568
    RWY 22: TORA−7602 TODA−7602 ASDA−7602 LDA−7602
    RWY 31L: TORA−7602 TODA−7602 ASDA−7602 LDA−7602
    RWY 31R: TORA−5148 TODA−5148 ASDA−5148 LDA−5148
  SERVICE: S2 **FUEL** 100LL, JET A, A1 **OX** 1, 2, 3, 4

Rwy 13L−31R: 5148 X 100

  AIRPORT REMARKS: Attended continuously. Numerous birds on and invof
    arpt. Arpt clsd to acft with wing span over 125 ft excp 24 hrs PPR call
    opns 713−417−5710. ASDE−X in use. Opr transponders with alt rprtg mode and ADS−B (if equipped) enabled on all arpt
    sfcs. Pilots/crew should be aware of dep turns in excess of 180 degs. Read back of drctn of turns is highly encouraged.
    Cust ramp has mult obstns; large acft will be asgnd an altn area by ATCT. Acft in tkof ptn on Rwy 22 be alert for poss
    radio intfc or null on freq 118.7. Use upper ant if so equipped. Twy G cntrln to parked acft on west side only 68´. Twy G
    cntrln to edge of adjacent svc veh road on west side only 48´. Due to complex rwy confign; when tax to thrs 13L and 13R
    check compass hdg bfr departing. Acft southbound on Twy C to Rwy 31L thr use extreme care; Twy C makes a 45 deg
    dogleg to the left xng Twy K.
  AIRPORT MANAGER: 713−845−6555
  WEATHER DATA SOURCES: ASOS (713) 847−1462 **TDWR.**
  COMMUNICATIONS: D−ATIS 124.6 (713) 847−1491 **UNICOM** 122.95
    HOBBY RCO 122.2 (MONTGOMERY COUNTY RADIO)
  ® **HOUSTON APP CON** 119.175 119.625 134.45 (South) 124.35 (West) 120.05 (East)
  ® **HOUSTON DEP CON** 134.45 (South) 123.8 (West) 119.7 (North)
    HOBBY TOWER 118.7
    HOUSTON GND CON 121.9 **CLNC DEL** 125.45 **PRE−TAXI CLNC** 125.45
    CPDLC (LOGON KUSA)
    PDC
  AIRSPACE: CLASS B See VFR Terminal Area Chart.

CONTINUED ON NEXT PAGE

SC, 25 JAN 2024 to 21 MAR 2024

TEXAS
CONTINUED FROM PRECEDING PAGE

VOR TEST FACILITY (VOT) 108.4
RADIO AIDS TO NAVIGATION: NOTAM FILE IAH.
  HUMBLE (H) (H) VORTACW 116.6   IAH   Chan 113   N29°57.42′ W95°20.74′   164° 19.0 NM to fld. 81/5E.
    VORTAC monitored by ATCT
    VOR portion unusable:
      060°–070° byd 35 NM
      175°–185° byd 20 NM blo 3,000′
      Byd 30 NM blo 2,000′
    DME unusable:
      015°–090° byd 30 NM blo 2,000′
      130°–320° byd 30 NM blo 2,000′
      175°–185° byd 20 NM blo 3,000′
      230°–250°
    TACAN AZIMUTH unusable:
      040°–055° blo 5,000′
      150°–320° blo 4,500′
      150°–320° byd 10 NM
  ILS/DME 109.9   I–HUB   Chan 36   Rwy 04.   Class IIIE.   DME also serves Rwy 22.
  ILS/DME 111.3   I–PRQ   Chan 50   Rwy 13R.   Class IE.   DME also serves Rwy 31L.
  LOC/DME 109.9   I–OIB   Chan 36   Rwy 22.   DME also serves Rwy 04. DME unusable byd 34° left of course.
  ILS/DME 111.3   I–UPU   Chan 50   Rwy 31L.   Class IE.   DME also serves Rwy 13R.

HOUSTON   MCJ   N29°42.83′ W95°23.80′/45   **HOUSTON**
AWOS–3PT 119.575   **H–7C, L–19E, 21A, GOMW**

HOUSTON CO (See CROCKETT on page 282)

HUBER AIRPARK CIVIC CLUB LLC (See SEGUIN on page 421)

HUDSPETH   N31°34.12′ W105°22.58′   NOTAM FILE ABQ.   **EL PASO**
  (VL) (H) VORTACW 115.0   HUP   Chan 97   123° 43.2 NM to Culberson Co. 4390/12E.   **H–4L, 6F, L–6F**
    VOR unusable:
      025°–050° byd 40 NM
      065°–075° byd 40 NM
      076°–086° byd 40 NM blo 9,000′
      076°–086° byd 51 NM blo 14,500′
      085°–091° byd 40 NM
      092°–102° byd 40 NM blo 11,000′
      103°–118° byd 40 NM
      119°–129° byd 40 NM blo 9,400′
      119°–129° byd 58 NM
      130°–140° byd 40 NM
      270°–305° byd 40 NM
      315°–345° byd 40 NM

HUMBLE   N29°57.42′ W95°20.74′   NOTAM FILE IAH.   **HOUSTON**
  (H) (H) VORTACW 116.6   IAH   Chan 113   003° 1.7 NM to George Bush Intcntl/Houston. 81/5E.   **COPTER**
    VORTAC monitored by ATCT   **H–7C, L–19E, 21A, GOMW**
    VOR portion unusable:
      060°–070° byd 35 NM
      175°–185° byd 20 NM blo 3,000′
      Byd 30 NM blo 2,000′
    DME unusable:
      015°–090° byd 30 NM blo 2,000′
      130°–320° byd 30 NM blo 2,000′
      175°–185° byd 20 NM blo 3,000′
      230°–250°
    TACAN AZIMUTH unusable:
      040°–055° blo 5,000′
      150°–320° blo 4,500′
      150°–320° byd 10 NM

HUNT (See PORTLAND on page 403)

TEXAS

HUNTSVILLE MUNI (UTS)(KUTS)   2 NW   UTC–6(–5DT)   N30°44.81´ W95°35.23´   **HOUSTON**
363   B   NOTAM FILE UTS   H–7C, L–19D, 21A
RWY 18–36: H5005X100 (ASPH)   S–27   MIRL   1.3% up S   IAP
  RWY 18: REIL. PAPI(P4L)—GA 3.0° TCH 26´. Trees.
  RWY 36: REIL. PAPI(P4L)—GA 3.0° TCH 40´. Pole.
SERVICE: S4   **FUEL** 100LL, JET A, A+   **OX** 1   **LGT** MIRL Rwy 18–36 preset low intst; to incr intst and ACTVT REIL Rwy 18 and Rwy 36—CTAF.
AIRPORT REMARKS: Attended dawn-dusk. Rwy 18–36 pvmt extsv cracking, sfc spalling, vegetation growing through.
AIRPORT MANAGER: 936-295-8136
WEATHER DATA SOURCES: ASOS 119.425 (936) 291–7997.
COMMUNICATIONS: CTAF/UNICOM 122.8
  RCO 122.3 (MONTGOMERY COUNTY RADIO)
®**HOUSTON CENTER APP/DEP CON** 134.8
CLEARANCE DELIVERY PHONE: For CD if una to ctc on FSS freq, ctc Houston ARTCC at 281-230-5222.
RADIO AIDS TO NAVIGATION: NOTAM FILE CXO.
  LEONA (L) (L) VORTACW 110.8   LOA   Chan 45   N31°07.44´ W95°58.08´   131° 29.9 NM to fld. 346/8E.
  NDB (MHW) 308   UTS   N30°44.44´ W95°35.45´   at fld. 943/6E.   NOTAM FILE UTS.

HUTCHINSON CO   (See BORGER on page 259)

INDUSTRY   N29°57.36´ W96°33.73´   NOTAM FILE CXO.   **HOUSTON**
(L) (L) **VORTACW** 110.2   IDU   Chan 39   165° 19.0 NM to Robert R Wells Jr. 419/8E.   H–7C, L–19D, 21A, GOMW
RCO 122.4 (MONTGOMERY COUNTY RADIO)

INGLESIDE

MCCAMPBELL–PORTER (TFP)(KTFP)   2 N   UTC –6(–5DT)   N27°54.78´ W97°12.69´   **BROWNSVILLE**
18   B   NOTAM FILE SJT   H–7C, L–20I, 21A, GOMW
RWY 13–31: H4999X75 (ASPH)   MIRL   IAP
  RWY 13: REIL. PAPI(P2L)—GA 3.0° TCH 39´.
  RWY 31: REIL. PAPI(P2L)—GA 3.0° TCH 33´.
SERVICE: S4   **FUEL** 100LL, JET A+   **LGT** MIRL Rwy 13–31 preset low ints; to incr intst actvt—CTAF.
AIRPORT REMARKS: Attended 1400–2230Z‡. Fuel full serv & self serve.
AIRPORT MANAGER: 361-226-0112
WEATHER DATA SOURCES: AWOS–3 118.775 (361) 758–8961.
COMMUNICATIONS: CTAF/UNICOM 122.7
®**CORPUS APP/DEP CON** 120.9
CLEARANCE DELIVERY PHONE: For CD ctc Corpus Christi Apch at 361-299-4230.
RADIO AIDS TO NAVIGATION: NOTAM FILE CRP.
  CORPUS CHRISTI (VH) (H) VORTACW 115.5   CRP   Chan 102   N27°54.23´ W97°26.69´   078° 12.4 NM to fld. 60/9E.
    TACAN AZIMUTH & DME unusable:
      024°–036° byd 35 NM blo 1,700´
      037°–023° byd 35 NM blo 2,000´
      265°–275°
    VOR unusable:
      340°–005° byd 40 NM blo 7,000´
      340°–005° byd 84 NM
      Byd 30 NM blo 1,500´
    TACAN AZIMUTH unusable:
      080°–085° byd 30 NM

TEXAS

IRAAN MUNI (2FØ) 1 SE UTC−6(−5DT) N30°54.37´ W101°53.39´ SAN ANTONIO
2200 B NOTAM FILE SJT L−19A
  RWY 14−32: H4085X60 (ASPH) S−12.5 RWY LGTS(NSTD)
    RWY 14: Thld dsplcd 500´. P−line.
    RWY 32: Thld dsplcd 490´.
  RWY 07−25: H2755X50 (ASPH) S−12.5 0.9% up E
    RWY 07: Pole.
    RWY 25: Brush.
  SERVICE: FUEL 100LL LGT Rwy 14−32 LIRL out of svc. Rwy 14−32 NSTD dspld thld lgts.
  AIRPORT REMARKS: Unattended. Wildlife on and invof arpt. Rising trrn southwest and west of arpt. 110LL 24 hr self−serve. Nstd dsplcd thr lgts Rwys 14 and 32. Rwy 32, 15´ drop off at rwy end. Rwy 07−25 markings are faded. Rwy 07−25 sfc has loose, extsv cracking, pot holes on cl. Rwy 07−25 markings faded. Rwy 14−32 Intens rwy lgts: nstd fixtures, not frangible, nstd layout, nstd colors. Rwy 14 tresh dsplcd: and 32 thrs dsplcd not lghtd. Day opns only.
  AIRPORT MANAGER: 432−639−2841
  COMMUNICATIONS: CTAF 122.9
  CLEARANCE DELIVERY PHONE: For CD ctc Houston ARTCC at 281−230−5622.
  RADIO AIDS TO NAVIGATION: NOTAM FILE FST.
    FORT STOCKTON (VH) (H) VORTACW 116.9 FST Chan 116 N30°57.13´ W102°58.54´ 082° 56.1 NM to fld.
    2893/11E.
    VOR unusable:
      020°−055° byd 20 NM blo 6,900´
      070°−086° byd 35 NM blo 6,400´
      106°−132° byd 30 NM blo 5,900´
      125°−202° byd 40 NM
      203°−213° byd 40 NM blo 18,000´
      214°−230° byd 40 NM
      245°−255° byd 40 NM
      315°−330° byd 30 NM blo 5,400´

IRESH N31°01.45´ W97°42.49´ NOTAM FILE ILE. SAN ANTONIO
  NDB (LOWM) 278 IL 012° 3.9 NM to Skylark Fld. 853/5E. L−19C, 21A
  NDB unusable:
    066°−294° byd 15 NM
    295°−065° byd 5 NM due to military restricted area

IRONHEAD (See SANGER on page 421)

JACK BROOKS RGNL (See BEAUMONT/PORT ARTHUR on page 254)

JACKSBORO MUNI (21F) 1 NE UTC−6(−5DT) N33°13.67´ W98°08.79´ DALLAS−FT WORTH
1062 B NOTAM FILE FTW L−17C
  RWY 18−36: H3220X75 (ASPH) S−4 MIRL 1.2% up S
    RWY 18: Pole.
    RWY 36: Trees.
  SERVICE: FUEL 100LL
  AIRPORT REMARKS: Unattended. Birds on and invof arpt. Arpt gate locked−combination 1581. Pilot lounge/restroom code 1114 unlck.
  AIRPORT MANAGER: 940−507−3147
  COMMUNICATIONS: CTAF 122.9
    RCO 122.4 (FORT WORTH RADIO)
  RADIO AIDS TO NAVIGATION: NOTAM FILE FTW.
    BOWIE (H) (H) VORTACW 117.15 UKW Chan 118(Y) N33°32.15´ W97°49.28´ 216° 24.6 NM to fld. 1102/6E.

JACKSON CO (See EDNA on page 302)

TEXAS

JACKSONVILLE

CHEROKEE CO (JSO)(KJSO) 6 SE UTC–6(–5DT) N31°52.16´ W95°13.04´ **HOUSTON**
678 B NOTAM FILE JSO H–6I, L–19E
RWY 14–32: H5006X75 (ASPH) S–30 MIRL 0.4% up NW IAP
  RWY 14: REIL. PAPI(P4L)—GA 3.0° TCH 30´.
  RWY 32: PAPI(P4L)—GA 3.0° TCH 28´. Tree.
SERVICE: S4 **FUEL** 100LL, JET A **LGT** Dusk–dawn, MIRL Rwy 14–32
  preset low intst; to incr intst and to ACTVT REIL Rwy 14—CTAF.
AIRPORT REMARKS: Attended Mon–Sat 1400–2300Z‡. 100LL 24 hrs
  self–serve.
AIRPORT MANAGER: 903–586–8219
WEATHER DATA SOURCES: AWOS–3 119.075 (903) 586–0124.
COMMUNICATIONS: CTAF/UNICOM 122.7
®**LONGVIEW APP/DEP CON** 128.75 (1200–0400Z‡)
®**FORT WORTH CENTER APP/DEP CON** 135.25 (0400–1200Z‡)
CLEARANCE DELIVERY PHONE: For CD ctc Fort Worth ARTCC at
  817-858-7584.
RADIO AIDS TO NAVIGATION: NOTAM FILE FTW.
  FRANKSTON (L) (L) VORW/DME 111.4 FZT Chan 51 N32°04.48´
  W95°31.85´ 121° 20.2 NM to fld. 305/6E.
  VOR portion unusable:
    270°–293° byd 5 NM blo 8,000´
    293°–295° byd 25 NM blo 3,500´
    295°–340° byd 20 NM

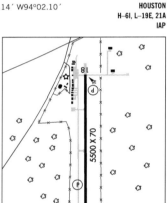

JASPER CO/BELL FLD (JAS)(KJAS) 4 SW UTC–6(–5DT) N30°53.14´ W94°02.10´ **HOUSTON**
213 B NOTAM FILE JAS H–6I, L–19E, 21A
RWY 18–36: H5500X70 (ASPH) S–21 MIRL 0.6% up N IAP
  RWY 18: PAPI(P2L)—GA 3.5° TCH 41´. Trees.
  RWY 36: PAPI(P2L)—GA 3.5° TCH 45´. Trees.
SERVICE: S4 **FUEL** 100LL, JET A **LGT** MIRL Rwy 18–36 preset low intst;
  to incr intst actvt—CTAF. PAPI Rwy 18 and 36 oprs consly.
AIRPORT REMARKS: Attended 1400–2300Z‡. Arpt attendant after hrs
  409–381–8151.
AIRPORT MANAGER: 409-384-2612
WEATHER DATA SOURCES: AWOS–3 118.375 (409) 489–1603.
COMMUNICATIONS: CTAF/UNICOM 122.8
  RCO 122.5 (MONTGOMERY COUNTY RADIO)
®**HOUSTON CENTER APP/DEP CON** 126.95
CLEARANCE DELIVERY PHONE: For CD if una to ctc on FSS freq, ctc Houston
  ARTCC at 281-230-5622.
RADIO AIDS TO NAVIGATION: NOTAM FILE LFK.
  LUFKIN (VH) (H) VORTACW 112.1 LFK Chan 58 N31°09.75´
  W94°43.01´ 110° 38.9 NM to fld. 207/5E.
  TACAN AZIMUTH unusable:
    260°–275° byd 30 NM
    275°–260° byd 30 NM blo 2,500´
  DME unusable:
    260°–275° byd 30 NM
    275°–260° byd 30 NM blo 2,500´
  VOR unusable:
    305°–312° byd 40 NM
    313°–323° byd 40 NM blo 2,300´
    313°–323° byd 66 NM
    324°–330° byd 40 NM

SC, 25 JAN 2024 to 21 MAR 2024

TEXAS

JAYTON

KENT CO (22F) 1 S UTC–6(–5DT) N33°13.75′ W100°34.15′ DALLAS–FT WORTH
2008 B NOTAM FILE FTW L–17A
RWY 17–35: H3300X50 (ASPH) S–12.5 LIRL 0.6% up N
   RWY 17: Road.
   RWY 35: Trees.
AIRPORT REMARKS: Unattended. Agricultural activity on arpt May–Sep.
AIRPORT MANAGER: 806-237-3373
COMMUNICATIONS: CTAF 122.9
CLEARANCE DELIVERY PHONE: For CD ctc Fort Worth ARTCC at 817-858-7584.
RADIO AIDS TO NAVIGATION: NOTAM FILE FTW.
   GUTHRIE (L) DME 114.5 GTH Chan 92 N33°46.70′ W100°20.17′ 200° 34.9 NM to fld. 1941.

JEFFERSON

CYPRESS RIVER (24F) 3 E UTC–6(–5DT) N32°44.66′ W94°18.28′ MEMPHIS
221 B NOTAM FILE FTW L–17E
RWY 05–23: H3200X60 (ASPH) S–12.5 LIRL
   RWY 05: PAPI(P2L)—GA 3.5° TCH 45′. Trees.
   RWY 23: PAPI(P2L)—GA 3.5° TCH 45′. Trees.
SERVICE: **FUEL** 100LL **LGT** Rwy 05 unusbl byd 9 deg left of RCL. Rwy 23 unusbl byd 7 deg left of RCL.
AIRPORT REMARKS: Attended irregularly. Deer on and invof arpt. 100LL 24 hour self svc.
AIRPORT MANAGER: 903-240-7707
COMMUNICATIONS: CTAF 122.9
CLEARANCE DELIVERY PHONE: For CD ctc Fort Worth ARTCC at 817-858-7584.
RADIO AIDS TO NAVIGATION: NOTAM FILE SHV.
   BELCHER (H) (H) VORTACW 117.4 EIC Chan 121 N32°46.28′ W93°48.60′ 259° 25.1 NM to fld. 190/7E.

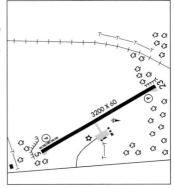

MANNING FLD (6F7) 4 N UTC–6(–5DT) N32°49.62′ W94°21.27′ MEMPHIS
320 NOTAM FILE FTW
RWY 07–25: 3600X100 (TURF) 2.1% up W
   RWY 07: Road.
   RWY 25: Fence.
AIRPORT REMARKS: Attended continuously. Ultralight activity on and in vicinity of arpt. Rwy 07–25 rolling trrn. 84′ rise in rwy elev fm Rwy 25 to Rwy 07 end. No line of sight between rwy ends. Rwy 07–25 mowed 30′ wide. Rwy 25 10–60′ trees along edge of rwy, both sides. Rwy 07 has 28′ power pole 88′ dstc, 162′ L.
AIRPORT MANAGER: 903-578-1504
COMMUNICATIONS: CTAF 122.9
CLEARANCE DELIVERY PHONE: For CD ctc Fort Worth ARTCC at 817-858-7584.

JIM HOGG CO (See HEBBRONVILLE on page 330)

JOE VAUGHN SPRAYING (See KRESS on page 356)

JONES FLD (See BONHAM on page 258)

JUNCTION

KIMBLE CO (JCT)(KJCT) 1 NE UTC−6(−5DT) N30°30.67′ W99°45.77′ SAN ANTONIO
1754 B NOTAM FILE JCT H−7B, L−19B
RWY 17−35: H5004X75 (ASPH) S−30 MIRL 1.0% up N IAP
  RWY 17: PAPI(P4L)—GA 3.5° TCH 50′. Hill.
  RWY 35: PAPI(P4L)—GA 3.0° TCH 45′. Trees.
RWY 08−26: 2255X130 (TURF) 1.0% up W
  RWY 26: Trees.
SERVICE: S4 **FUEL** 100LL, JET A+ **LGT** MIRL Rwy 17−35 preset low intst, to incr intst ACTVT—CTAF. PAPI Rwy 17 OTS. PAPI Rwy 35 OTS.
AIRPORT REMARKS: Attended continuously. Rwy 08−26 thlds mkd with white tires. Fqt mil trng flts conducting low apchs to arpt.
AIRPORT MANAGER: 325-446-2820
WEATHER DATA SOURCES: ASOS 119.275 (325) 446−2552.
COMMUNICATIONS: CTAF/UNICOM 122.8
  JUNCTION RCO 122.3 (SAN ANGELO RADIO)
® **HOUSTON CENTER APP/DEP CON** 125.75
CLEARANCE DELIVERY PHONE: For CD ctc Houston ARTCC at 281-230-5622.
RADIO AIDS TO NAVIGATION: NOTAM FILE JCT.
  JUNCTION (H) (H) VORTACW 116.0 JCT Chan 107 N30°35.88′ W99°49.05′ 143° 5.9 NM to fld. 2282/8E.
  VOR unusable:
    070°−101° byd 15 NM blo 4,900′
    070°−101° byd 30 NM blo 6,900′

JUSTIN

CLARK (3T6) 3 N UTC−6(−5DT) N33°08.02′ W97°17.82′ DALLAS−FT WORTH
705 NOTAM FILE FTW COPTER
RWY 17−35: H1800X22 (ASPH) 0.3% up N
  RWY 17: Bldg.
AIRPORT REMARKS: Unattended. 5 ft fence 50−75 ft east of and parallel to rwy. Rwy 17−35 loose stones on rwy. Rwy 17−35 no cntrln stripe.
AIRPORT MANAGER: (972) 741-4520
COMMUNICATIONS: CTAF 122.9
CLEARANCE DELIVERY PHONE: For CD ctc Regional Apch at 972-615-2799.

PROPWASH (16X) 3 W UTC−6(−5DT) N33°04.84′ W97°21.51′ DALLAS−FT WORTH
804 B NOTAM FILE FTW COPTER
RWY 17−35: H3000X60 (ASPH) LIRL L−17C, A
  RWY 17: Tree. Rgt tfc.
  RWY 35: Tree.
SERVICE: **LGT** ACTIVATE rotating bcn—CTAF. ACTIVATE LIRL Rwy 17−35—CTAF.
AIRPORT REMARKS: Unattended.
AIRPORT MANAGER: 713-542-9570
COMMUNICATIONS: CTAF 122.9
CLEARANCE DELIVERY PHONE: For CD ctc Regional Apch at 972-615-2799.
RADIO AIDS TO NAVIGATION: NOTAM FILE FTW.
  RANGER (VH) (H) VORTACW 115.7 FUZ Chan 104 N32°53.37′ W97°10.77′ 316° 14.6 NM to fld. 639/6E.
  VOR unusable:
    275°−290° byd 40 NM
    317°−327° byd 40 NM

PROSE FLD (XA0) 4 SSW UTC−6(−5DT) N33°08.89′ W97°16.80′ DALLAS−FT WORTH
685 NOTAM FILE FTW
RWY 18−36: 1660X60 (TURF)
  RWY 18: Thld dsplcd 320′. Road.
  RWY 36: Thld dsplcd 180′. Pole. Rgt tfc.
AIRPORT REMARKS: Unattended.
AIRPORT MANAGER: 940-479-2763
COMMUNICATIONS: CTAF 122.9
CLEARANCE DELIVERY PHONE: For CD ctc Regional Apch at 972-615-2799.

KELLY FLD (See SAN ANTONIO on page 416)

TEXAS

KELLY N29°23.50′ W98°34.86′ NOTAM FILE SKF.
   (L) TACAN 112.0 KSY Chan 57 at Kelly Fld. 687/4E. TACAN unmonitored when ATCT clsd.
      No NOTAM MP: 0600–1430Z‡ Wed
   TACAN AZIMUTH unusable:
      163°–188° byd 14 NM blo 2,700′
      298°–318° byd 20 NM blo 4,600′
      346°–356° byd 16 NM blo 3,400′
   DME unusable:
      163°–188° byd 14 NM blo 2,700′
      298°–318° byd 20 NM blo 4,600′
      346°–356° byd 16 NM blo 3,400′

SAN ANTONIO
L–19C

KENEDY RGNL (2R9) 1 NW UTC–6(–5DT) N28°49.50′ W97°51.93′
289 B NOTAM FILE SJT
RWY 16–34: H3218X60 (ASPH) S–11 MIRL 0.5% up N
  RWY 16: REIL. PAPI(P2L)—GA 3.0° TCH 44′. Sign. Rgt tfc.
  RWY 34: PAPI(P2L)—GA 3.6° TCH 48′. Trees.
SERVICE: S4 **FUEL** 100LL, JET A **LGT** MIRL Rwy 16–34 and twy lgts preset low intst; to incr intst ACTVT—CTAF. Rwy 34 VGSI rstrd 7 degs left due to obsts.
AIRPORT REMARKS: Attended Mon–Fri dalgt hours. Deer on and invof arpt. Acft airframe and power plant repairs on call 830–299–2295.
AIRPORT MANAGER: (830) 583–5930
WEATHER DATA SOURCES: AWOS–3PT 118.45 (830) 583–8080.
COMMUNICATIONS: CTAF/UNICOM 123.0
Ⓡ **HOUSTON CENTER APP/DEP CON** 134.6
CLEARANCE DELIVERY PHONE: For CD ctc Houston ARTCC at 281-230-5622.
RADIO AIDS TO NAVIGATION: NOTAM FILE SJT.
  THREE RIVERS (L) (L) VORTAC 111.4 THX Chan 51 N28°30.30′ W98°09.03′ 030° 24.3 NM to fld. 266/8E.

SAN ANTONIO
L–20H, 21A
IAP

KENNETH COPELAND (See FORT WORTH on page 311)

KENT CO (See JAYTON on page 349)

KENT N31°00.83′ W104°12.41′ NOTAM FILE SJT.
  NDB (MHW) 225 XAA 268° 29.9 NM to Culberson Co. 4357/7E.

EL PASO
L–6J

KERRVILLE MUNI/LOUIS SCHREINER FLD (ERV)(KERV) 5 SE UTC–6(–5DT) N29°58.60′
W99°05.13′
1617 B NOTAM FILE ERV
RWY 12–30: H6004X100 (ASPH) S–22.4, D–73.7 PCN 23 F/C/W/T
  MIRL 0.3% up SE
  RWY 12: REIL. PAPI(P4L)—GA 3.0° TCH 40′. Thld dsplcd 687′.
  RWY 30: REIL. PAPI(P4L)—GA 3.0° TCH 40′.
RWY 03–21: H3597X58 (ASPH) S–15 MIRL 1.2% up NE
  RWY 03: PAPI(P2L)—GA 3.5° TCH 25′. Tree.
  RWY 21: PAPI(P2L)—GA 3.5° TCH 25′. Trees.
RUNWAY DECLARED DISTANCE INFORMATION
  RWY 12: TORA–6000 TODA–6000 ASDA–6000 LDA–5313
  RWY 30: TORA–6000 TODA–6000 ASDA–5300 LDA–5300
SERVICE: S4 **FUEL** 100LL, JET A **OX** 3 **LGT** Dusk–Dawn. MIRL Rwys 12–30 and 03–21 preset low intst; to incr intst and actvt REIL Rwy 12 and 30—CTAF.
AIRPORT REMARKS: Attended 1200–0400Z‡. Deer on and invof arpt. Rwy 12 calm wind rwy. FBO phone 830–257–8840, aft hrs atndt 830–496–0332.
AIRPORT MANAGER: 830–896–9399
WEATHER DATA SOURCES: AWOS–3 118.125 (830) 895–2204.
COMMUNICATIONS: CTAF/UNICOM 122.7
Ⓡ **HOUSTON CENTER APP/DEP CON** 134.95
CLEARANCE DELIVERY PHONE: For CD ctc Houston ARTCC at 281-230-5622.
RADIO AIDS TO NAVIGATION: NOTAM FILE ERV.
  CENTER POINT (VH) (H) VORTAC 117.5 CSI Chan 122 N29°55.34′ W99°12.87′ 056° 7.5 NM to fld. 2079/8E.
  LOC 109.1 I–ERV Rwy 30.

SAN ANTONIO
H–7B, L–19C
IAP

KESTREL AIRPARK (See SAN ANTONIO on page 417)

KICKAPOO DOWNTOWN (See WICHITA FALLS on page 446)

KILLEEN

SKYLARK FLD (ILE)(KILE) 3 E UTC–6(–5DT) N31°05.15´ W97°41.19´
SAN ANTONIO
848 B NOTAM FILE ILE
H–6H, L–19C, 21A
RWY 01–19: H5495X100 (ASPH–AFSC) S–17, D–50 MIRL
IAP
RWY 01: REIL. PAPI(P4L)—GA 3.0° TCH 72´. Thld dsplcd 854´. Road. Rgt tfc.
RWY 19: REIL. PAPI(P4L)—GA 3.0° TCH 45´. P–line.
RUNWAY DECLARED DISTANCE INFORMATION
RWY 01: TORA–5495 TODA–5495 ASDA–5495 LDA–4651
RWY 19: TORA–5495 TODA–5495 ASDA–5295 LDA–5295
SERVICE: S2 **FUEL** 100LL, JET A **LGT** SS–SR. MIRL Rwy 01–19 preset low intst; to incr intst and ACTVT twy lights—CTAF.
AIRPORT REMARKS: Attended 1400–0000Z‡. NOTE: See Special Notices Section—Model Aircraft Activity.
AIRPORT MANAGER: 254-501-8728
WEATHER DATA SOURCES: AWOS–3PT 128.575 (254) 690–3131.
COMMUNICATIONS: CTAF/UNICOM 122.7
®**GRAY APP/DEP CON** 120.075
 CLNC DEL 121.7
CLEARANCE DELIVERY PHONE: For CD ctc Fort Worth ARTCC at 817-858-7584.
AIRSPACE: CLASS E.
RADIO AIDS TO NAVIGATION: NOTAM FILE GRK.
 GRAY (T) (T) VORW/DME 111.8   GRK Chan 55   N31°01.97´
 W97°48.83´   057° 7.3 NM to fld. 963/7E.
 IRESH NDB (LOMW) 278 IL N31°01.45´ W97°42.49´   012° 3.9 NM to fld. 853/5E. NOTAM FILE ILE.
 NDB unusable:
  066°–294° byd 15 NM
  295°–065° byd 5 NM due to military restricted area
 LOC/DME 108.3 I–ILE Chan 20 Rwy 01. LOM IRESH NDB.

KIMBLE CO (See JUNCTION on page 350)

KINGSVILLE

KLEBERG CO (IKG)(KIKG)   9 W   UTC−6(−5DT)   N27°33.05´ W98°01.86´   BROWNSVILLE
130   B   NOTAM FILE SJT   H−7B, L−20H
RWY 13−31: H6000X75 (ASPH)   S−35, D−47, 2D−70   MIRL   IAF
  RWY 13: REIL. PAPI(P4L)—GA 3.0° TCH 39´. Trees.
  RWY 31: REIL. PAPI(P4L)—GA 3.0° TCH 41´. Tree.
SERVICE: S4   **FUEL** 100LL, JET A   **OX** 3   **LGT** MIRL Rwy 13−31 preset low
  intst; to incr intst & ACTIVATE REIL Rwys 13 and 31— CTAF.
AIRPORT REMARKS: Attended Mon−Sat 1400−2300Z‡, Sat−Sun
  1400−2100Z‡. Parachute Jumping. Birds on & invof arpt. Rwy 13 and
  Rwy 31 mkgs faded/discolored. Ldg fee for turbine & jet acft. Fee waived
  with mnm fuel purchase.
AIRPORT MANAGER: 361-592-1225
WEATHER DATA SOURCES: AWOS−3P 119.075 (361) 592−9152.
COMMUNICATIONS: CTAF/UNICOM 122.7
®**KINGSVILLE APP/DEP CON** 119.9 (1345−0600Z‡ Mon−Thu; 1345−2345Z‡
  Fri; clsd Sat, Sun and hol exc by NOTAM, hrs subj to chg)
®**HOUSTON CENTER APP/DEP CON** 128.15 (0500−1300Z‡ Mon−Thu;
  2200−1300Z‡ Fri; 24 Sat, Sun and hol by NOTAM)
CLEARANCE DELIVERY PHONE: For CD ctc Houston ARTCC at 281-230-5622.
RADIO AIDS TO NAVIGATION: NOTAM FILE CRP.
  CORPUS CHRISTI (VH) (H) VORTACW 115.5   CRP   Chan 102
    N27°54.23´ W97°26.69´   227° 37.7 NM to fld. 60/9E.
  TACAN AZIMUTH & DME unusable:
    024°−036° byd 35 NM blo 1,700´
    037°−023° byd 35 NM blo 2,000´
    265°−275°
  VOR unusable:
    340°−005° byd 40 NM blo 7,000´
    340°−005° byd 84 NM
    Byd 30 NM blo 1,500´
  TACAN AZIMUTH unusable:
    080°−085° byd 30 NM

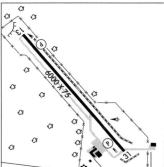

KINGSVILLE NAS (NQI)(KNQI) NAS 3 E UTC–6(–5DT) N27°30.27´ W97°48.50´ **BROWNSVILLE**
50 B NOTAM FILE SJT Not insp. H–7C, L–20H, 21A, GOMW
RWY 17L–35R: H8001X197 (PEM) PCN 60 R/C/W/T HIRL CL DIAP, AD
  RWY 17L: OLS. WAVE-OFF. REIL.
  RWY 35R: ALSF1. OLS. WAVE-OFF. REIL. PAPI(P4L)—GA 3.0° TCH 51´.
RWY 13L–31R: H8000X198 (PEM) PCN 49 R/C/W/T HIRL
  RWY 13L: OLS. WAVE-OFF. REIL.
  RWY 31R: OLS. WAVE-OFF. REIL. PAPI(P4L)—GA 3.0° TCH 51´.
RWY 13R–31L: H8000X198 (PEM) PCN 48 R/C/W/T HIRL
  RWY 13R: OLS. WAVE-OFF. REIL. PAPI(P4L)—GA 3.0° TCH 34´.
  RWY 31L: OLS. WAVE-OFF. REIL.
RWY 17R–35L: H8000X198 (PEM) PCN 56 R/C/W/T HIRL
  RWY 17R: OLS. WAVE-OFF. REIL. PAPI(P4L)—GA 3.0° TCH 51´.
  RWY 35L: OLS. WAVE-OFF. REIL.
ARRESTING GEAR/SYSTEM
RWY 17L HOOK E28(B) (1675').	HOOK E28(B) (1516'). **RWY 35R**
RWY 13L HOOK E28(B) (1050').	HOOK E28(B) (1500'). **RWY 31R**
RWY 13R HOOK E28(B) (1550').	HOOK E28(B) (1503'). **RWY 31L**
RWY 17R HOOK E28(B) (1250').	HOOK E28(B) (1600'). **RWY 35L**

SERVICE: **OX** 2 **LGT** Avbl only durg hrs of opn. OLS GS 3.25°. **MILITARY**— **JASU** 1(NC–10) 1(GTC–85) **FUEL** JAA **FLUID** SP PRESAIR LOX **OIL** O–148–156 **TRAN ALERT** Exp svcg delays wkend. Svc not avbl Sun til 2300Z‡. Tran must supervise svcg. Drag chute repack unavbl.
MILITARY REMARKS: Opr Mon–Thu 1345–0600Z‡, Fri 1345–2345Z‡. Clsd Sat, Sun and fed hol exc by NOTAM. Hrs subject to chg. Fld subj early/no notice closure. **RSTD** PPR for non–Chief of Naval Air Trng acft ctc Base OPS dur fld opr hr DSN 876–6108, C361–516–6108. For CALP processing ctc afld mgr via base ops. **CAUTION** Heavy jet inst trng dur fld opr hr. Bird and large wildlife haz. Avoid over flt of chemical plant 5 NM North. **TFC PAT** Arr tsnt acft exp enr descent. Use ldg/taxi lgt for final portion of inst apch dur VFR. **MISC** Durg FCLP periods or single rwy opns practice apchs for trans acft may be denied. Practice apchs for trans acft may be permitted at all other times but dlys or wave–offs should be anticipated.
TRAN ALERT Expc svcg dlas wkend. Svc not avbl Sun til 2300Z‡. Tran crew is responsible for fueling acft. Drag chute repack unavbl. Tran acft ctc app con 25 nm out.
AIRPORT MANAGER: 361-516-4331
COMMUNICATIONS: **SFA ATIS** 276.2 (Avbl 20 mins prior to opr hrs til completion of opr hrs or closure)
Ⓡ **APP CON** 119.9 290.45 (1345–0600Z‡ Mon–Thu; 1345–2345Z‡ Fri; clsd Sat, Sun and hol exc by NOTAM, hrs subj to chg)
Ⓡ **HOUSTON CENTER APP CON** 128.15 350.3 (0500–1300Z‡ Mon–Thu; 2200–1300Z‡ Fri; 24 Sat, Sun and hol by NOTAM)
  TOWER 124.1 377.05 (1345–0600Z‡ Mon–Thu; 1345–2345Z‡ Fri; clsd Sat; Sun and hol exc by NOTAM, hrs subj to chg)
  GND CON 239.05 **CLNC DEL** 328.4
Ⓡ **DEP CON** 121.05 266.8 (1345–0600Z‡ Mon–Thu; 1345–2345Z‡ Fri; clsd Sat, Sun and hol exc by NOTAM, hrs subj to chg)
Ⓡ **HOUSTON CENTER DEP CON** 128.15 350.3 (0500–1300Z‡ Mon–Thu; 2200–1300Z‡ Fri; 24 Sat, Sun and hol by NOTAM)
  PMSV METRO 225.6 (Mon–Thu 1345–0600Z‡; Fri 1345–2345Z‡; clsd Sat, Sun and hol exc by NOTAM. Also avbl 1 hr prior to and dur NOTAM afld hrs) **BASE OPS** 274.8
AIRSPACE: CLASS D airspace svc Mon–Thu 1345–0600Z‡, Fri 1345–2345Z‡, clsd Sat, Sun and hol exc by NOTAM, hrs subj to chg; ot CLASS G..
RADIO AIDS TO NAVIGATION: NOTAM FILE SJT.
  (H) TACAN Chan 125 NQI (117.8) N27°29.95´ W97°48.34´ at fld. 45/4E.
  ILS/DME 110.9 I–NQI Chan 46 Rwy 13R. Auto coupled apchs not authorized blw 439´ MSL. ILS performance CLASS IE.
  ASR/PAR
COMM/NAV/WEATHER REMARKS: Tran acft ctc App Con 25 NM out. Radar see Terminal FLIP for Radar Minima.

TEXAS

KIRBYVILLE (T12)　2 SW　UTC–6(–5DT)　N30°38.79′ W93°54.89′　　**HOUSTON**
　121　NOTAM FILE CXO　　　　　　　　　　　　　　　　　　　　　　　　　　　L–19E, 21A
RWY 13–31: H3746X50 (ASPH)　S–8
　RWY 13: Thld dsplcd 326′. Fence.
　RWY 31: Thld dsplcd 226′. Trees.
RWY 04–22: H1983X45 (ASPH)　S–8
　RWY 04: Trees.
　RWY 22: Trees.
AIRPORT REMARKS: Unattended. Rwy 04–22 CLOSED indefly. Deer on and invof arpt. PAEW during daylight. Rwy not suitable for acft, rough and uneven, loose stones on rwy, vegetation growing. Dirt piles adjacent. Rwy 13–31 potholes and loose aggregate.
AIRPORT MANAGER: 409-384-2612
COMMUNICATIONS: CTAF 122.9
CLEARANCE DELIVERY PHONE: For CD ctc Houston ARTCC at 281-230-5622.
RADIO AIDS TO NAVIGATION: NOTAM FILE BPT.
　BEAUMONT (L) (L) VORW/DME 114.5　　BPT　Chan 92　　N29°56.76′ W94°00.97′　　000° 42.3 NM to fld. 6/7E.

KLEBERG CO　(See KINGSVILLE on page 353)

KNOX CITY

HARRISON FLD OF KNOX CITY (F75)　1 N　UTC–6(–5DT)　N33°26.29′ W99°48.77′　　**DALLAS–FT WORTH**
　1500　B　NOTAM FILE FTW　　　　　　　　　　　　　　　　　　　　　　　　　　L–17B
RWY 01–19: H3200X50 (ASPH)　S–10　MIRL
　RWY 01: Tree.
　RWY 19: PAPI(P2L)—GA 3.75° TCH 27′. Trees.
SERVICE:　**LGT** MIRL Rwy 01–19 preset low intst dusk–0500Z‡ to incr intst or aft 0500Z‡ ACTVT—CTAF.
AIRPORT REMARKS: Unattended. Rwy 19, 20 ft pumpjack 125 ft right of cntrln 40 ft south Rwy 19 thr. Rwy 19 +20 ft trees 105 ft right, 0–200 ft south of rwy thr.
AIRPORT MANAGER: 940-658-3313
COMMUNICATIONS: CTAF 122.9
CLEARANCE DELIVERY PHONE: For CD ctc Fort Worth ARTCC at 817-858-7584.
RADIO AIDS TO NAVIGATION: NOTAM FILE FTW.
　GUTHRIE (L) DME 114.5　　GTH　Chan 92　　N33°46.70′
　　W100°20.17′　　128° 33.2 NM to fld. 1941.

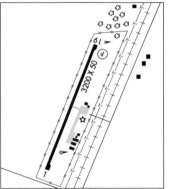

KOTTI　N29°26.56′ W100°59.54′　NOTAM FILE DRT.　　　　　　　　　　　　　　**SAN ANTONIO**
　NDB (LOMW) 335　DR　132° 5.3 NM to Del Rio Intl. 1148/8E.　　　　　　　　L–19B

KOUNTZE/SILSBEE

HAWTHORNE FLD (45R) 3 SE UTC–6(–5DT) N30°20.18′ W94°15.45′ **HOUSTON**
71 B NOTAM FILE CXO L–19E, 21A, GOMW
RWY 13–31: H4303X76 (ASPH) S–12.5 MIRL IAP
  RWY 13: PAPI(P2L)—GA 3.0° TCH 29′. Tree.
  RWY 31: PAPI(P2L)—GA 4.0° TCH 31′. Tree.
SERVICE: FUEL 100LL, JET A LGT MIRL RWY 13–31 preset low ints dusk–dawn; to incr ints ACTIVATE—CTAF. Rwy 31 PAPI OTS.
AIRPORT REMARKS: Attended 1400–2330Z‡. 24 hr self serve fuel. Rwy and twy markings including hold lines faded.
AIRPORT MANAGER: (409) 782-7620
COMMUNICATIONS: CTAF/UNICOM 122.8
®HOUSTON APP/DEP CON 121.3
CLEARANCE DELIVERY PHONE: For CD ctc Houston Apch at 281-443-5844 to cnl IFR call 281-443-5888.
RADIO AIDS TO NAVIGATION: NOTAM FILE CXO.
  DAISETTA (H) (H) VORTACW 116.9 DAS Chan 116 N30°11.58′ W94°38.70′ 061° 22.0 NM to fld. 76/5E.
  VOR unusable:
    Byd 35 NM blo 1,600′
  TACAN AZIMUTH unusable:
    Byd 35 NM blo 1,600′
  DME unusable:
    Byd 35 NM blo 1,600′

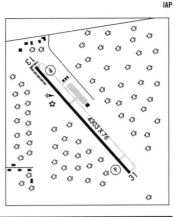

KRESS

JOE VAUGHN SPRAYING (29F) 1 N UTC–6(–5DT) N34°23.57′ W101°45.60′ **DALLAS–FT WORTH**
3500 NOTAM FILE FTW
RWY 17–35: 3900X60 (DIRT)
  RWY 17: Road.
  RWY 35: Fence.
SERVICE: S4 FUEL 100LL, JET A
AIRPORT REMARKS: Attended Mon–Fri 1400–0000Z‡, Sat–Sun irregular. JET A for ag acft only. 5′ fence 40′ west of rwy cntrln full length of rwy. Rwy 17 +30′ pline 46′ fm thr 77′ right cntrln. 25′ bldgs 45′ right of cntrln at Rwy 35 end. Rwy 17–35 sfc rough.
AIRPORT MANAGER: 806-684-2732
COMMUNICATIONS: CTAF/UNICOM 122.7
CLEARANCE DELIVERY PHONE: For CD ctc Fort Worth ARTCC at 817-858-7584.

KRUM

BIRD DOG AIRFIELD (E58) 8 E UTC–6(–5DT) N33°18.39′ W97°20.83′ **DALLAS–FT WORTH**
895 NOTAM FILE FTW
RWY 18–36: 2830X250 (TURF)
  RWY 18: Thld dsplcd 340′. Bldg.
  RWY 36: Thld dsplcd 400′. Tree.
AIRPORT REMARKS: Unattended. Rwy measured 200′ wide. Rwy 18–36 dspcld thlds marked with one white tire each side of rwy. $100 ldg fee all acft.
AIRPORT MANAGER: 940-367-1992
COMMUNICATIONS: CTAF 122.9
CLEARANCE DELIVERY PHONE: For CD ctc Regional Apch at 972-615-2799.

LA GRANGE

FAYETTE RGNL AIR CENTER (3T5)   2 W   UTC–6(–5DT)   N29°54.48´ W96°57.00´   HOUSTON
 324   B   NOTAM FILE 3T5   H–7C, L–19D, 21A
 RWY 16–34: H5000X75 (ASPH) S–30   MIRL   0.3% up SE   IAP, AD
  RWY 16: REIL. PAPI(P2L)—GA 3.0° TCH 42´. Tree.
  RWY 34: REIL. PAPI(P2L)—GA 3.0° TCH 31´. Tree.
 SERVICE: FUEL 100LL, JET A   LGT Dusk–dawn. MIRL Rwy 16–34 preset
  low intst; to incr intst ACTVT—CTAF.
 AIRPORT REMARKS: Attended 1500–2300Z‡. Fuel 24 hrs self serve. After hrs
  atndt, Call 979–242–3316 during atnd hrs. For arpt attendant after hrs
  call 979–966–9139. NOTE: See Special Notices—Aerobatic Practice
  Area.
 AIRPORT MANAGER: 979-242-4056
 WEATHER DATA SOURCES: AWOS–3 124.175 (979) 242–5777.
 COMMUNICATIONS: CTAF/UNICOM 122.7
 ®AUSTIN APP/DEP CON 120.875
  GCO 121.725 (AUSTIN APCH CTL and FLIGHT SERVICES)
 CLEARANCE DELIVERY PHONE: For CD ctc Austin Apch at 512-369-7865.
 RADIO AIDS TO NAVIGATION: NOTAM FILE CXO.
  INDUSTRY (L) (L) VORTACW 110.2   IDU   Chan 39   N29°57.36´
   W96°33.73´   254° 20.4 NM to fld. 419/8E.

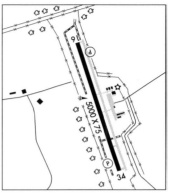

LA PORTE MUNI (T41)   3 NW   UTC–6(–5DT)   N29°40.16´ W95°03.85´   HOUSTON
 25   B   NOTAM FILE CXO   COPTER
 RWY 12–30: H4165X75 (ASPH)   S–23   MIRL   L–19E, 21A, GOMW
  RWY 12: REIL. PAPI(P4L)—GA 3.0° TCH 47´. Thld dsplcd 190´. Trees.   IAP
  RWY 30: Thld dsplcd 402´. Fence.
 RWY 05–23: H2998X75 (ASPH)   S–25   MIRL
  RWY 05: Pole.
  RWY 23: Trees.
 SERVICE: S4 FUEL 100LL, JET A   LGT ACTVT REIL Rwy 12; PAPI Rwy
  12; MIRL Rwys 05–23 and 12–30—CTAF. Rwy 12 PAPI unusbl byd 8
  deg left of rwy cntrln.
 AIRPORT REMARKS: Attended dalgt hours. Fuel avbl self serve 24 hrs.
 AIRPORT MANAGER: 281-471-9650
 WEATHER DATA SOURCES: AWOS–3PT 120.275 (281) 471–2206.
 COMMUNICATIONS: CTAF/UNICOM 122.7
 ®HOUSTON APP/DEP CON 134.45
  CLNC DEL 125.6
 CLEARANCE DELIVERY PHONE: For CD ctc Houston Apch at 281-443-5844. to
  cnl IFR ctc Houston Apch at 281-443-5888.
 RADIO AIDS TO NAVIGATION: NOTAM FILE CXO.
  TRINITY (VL) (DL) VORW/DME 114.75   MHF   Chan 94(Y)   N29°32.78´
   W94°44.85´   287° 18.1 NM to fld. 38/7E.
  VOR unusable:
   060°–079° byd 40 NM
   080°–090° byd 40 NM blo 6,000´
   080°–090° byd 50 NM blo 8,000´
   091°–109° byd 40 NM
   110°–190° blo 2,000´

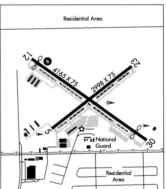

LA WARD

SHANK N BANK (TXØ)   7 SW   UTC–6(–5DT)   N28°44.40´ W96°28.09´   HOUSTON
 29   NOTAM FILE TX0   H–7C, L–20I, 21–A
 RWY 09–27: H5002X75 (ASPH)   MIRL
  RWY 09: REIL. PAPI(P2L)—GA 3.0° TCH 45´. Tree.
  RWY 27: REIL. PAPI(P2L)—GA 3.0° TCH 45´. Tree. Rgt tfc.
 SERVICE: LGT ACTVT REIL Rwy 09 and 27; PAPI Rwy 09 and 27; MIRL Rwy 09–27—CTAF.
 AIRPORT REMARKS: Unattended. Arpt fenced. Gates locked. For access ctc amgr.
 AIRPORT MANAGER: 361-408-0793
 COMMUNICATIONS: CTAF/UNICOM 122.8
 CLEARANCE DELIVERY PHONE: For CD ctc Houston ARTCC at 281-230-5622.

TEXAS

LAGO VISTA TX/RUSTY ALLEN (RYW)(KRYW) 2 NE UTC–6(–5DT) N30°29.92´ W97°58.17´
SAN ANTONIO
L–19C, 21A
IAP

1230 B NOTAM FILE RYW
RWY 15–33: H3808X50 (ASPH) S–12.5 MIRL 0.6% up NW
  RWY 15: PAPI(P2L)—GA 4.0° TCH 56´. Trees.
  RWY 33: PAPI(P2L)—GA 3.5° TCH 43´. P–line.
RUNWAY DECLARED DISTANCE INFORMATION
  RWY 15: TORA–3808 TODA–3808 ASDA–3808 LDA–3808
  RWY 33: TORA–3808 TODA–3808 ASDA–3808 LDA–3808
SERVICE: **FUEL** 100LL **LGT** MIRL Rwy 15–33 preset low intst; to incr intst ACTVT—CTAF. PAPI Rwys 15 and 33 opr consly.
AIRPORT REMARKS: Attended Mon–Fri 1400–0000Z‡. Deer on and invof arpt. Rwy 15 calm wind rwy. Rwy 15–33 GWT per AMGR.
AIRPORT MANAGER: 737-202-4378
WEATHER DATA SOURCES: AWOS–3PT 119.375 (512) 267–1365.
COMMUNICATIONS: CTAF/UNICOM 122.725
®**AUSTIN APP/DEP CON** 119.0
CLEARANCE DELIVERY PHONE: For CD ctc Austin Apch at 512-369-7865.
RADIO AIDS TO NAVIGATION: NOTAM FILE AUS.
  CENTEX (VH) (H) VORTACW 112.8 CWK Chan 75 N30°22.71´ W97°31.79´ 282° 23.9 NM to fld. 593/6E.
  VOR unusable:
    180°–190° byd 40 NM
    200°–210° byd 40 NM
COMM/NAV/WEATHER REMARKS: UNICOM not mnt.

LAJITAS INTL (T89) 4 E UTC–6(–5DT) N29°16.63´ W103°41.15´
EL PASO
H–7A, L–6J

2630 NOTAM FILE T89 Not insp.
RWY 07–25: H6501X100 (CONC) MIRL 0.3% up E
  RWY 25: Rgt tfc.
SERVICE: **FUEL** 100LL, JET A
AIRPORT REMARKS: Attended 1400–2300Z‡. For service call 432–424–5000. Notice rqrd for all incoming tfc. No TGLS. Ldg fee.
AIRPORT MANAGER: 432-424-3544
WEATHER DATA SOURCES: AWOS–3 119.275 (432) 424–3095.
COMMUNICATIONS: CTAF/UNICOM 122.7
CLEARANCE DELIVERY PHONE: For CD ctc Albuquerque ARTCC at 505-856-4861.
RADIO AIDS TO NAVIGATION: NOTAM FILE MRF.
  MARFA (VL) (DH) VORW/DME 115.9 MRF Chan 106 N30°17.90´ W103°57.29´ 156° 62.7 NM to fld. 4834/11E.
  DME unusable:
    025°–035° byd 30 NM
  VOR unusable:
    220°–225° byd 40 NM
    290°–309° byd 40 NM
    310°–320° byd 40 NM blo 11,000´
    310°–320° byd 58 NM
    321°–333° byd 40 NM
    334°–344°
    345°–130° byd 40 NM

LAKE DALLAS

LAKEVIEW (3ØF) 1 NE UTC–6(–5DT) N33°07.88´ W97°00.85´
DALLAS–FT WORTH
COPTER

535 NOTAM FILE FTW
RWY 18L–36R: H2815X30 (ASPH) S–4
  RWY 18L: Trees.
  RWY 36R: Pole.
RWY 18R–36L: 2600X75 (TURF)
  RWY 18R: Trees.
  RWY 36L: P–line.
AIRPORT REMARKS: Unattended. Arpt CLOSED to tnst students. Birds on and invof arpt. Rwy 18L–36R lake 350´ fm north end of rwy, 170´ fm south end. Portions of rwy may be under water during heavy rains. Rwy 36 30´ trees, 30´–65´ right, parallel to rwy. Gate locked 24 hrs. No touch and go landing permitted. Powered parachutes and balloons prohibited. Rwy 18L–36R pavement uneven with loose stones, vegetation and pot holes. Rwy 18R–36L boats and trailers parked along west edge of rwy. Rwy 18R–36L defined by mowing. Una to dtrm lctn of rwy, not inspd.
AIRPORT MANAGER: 214-850-8180
COMMUNICATIONS: CTAF 122.9
CLEARANCE DELIVERY PHONE: For CD ctc Regional Apch at 972-615-2799.

SC, 25 JAN 2024 to 21 MAR 2024

TEXAS 359

LAKEVIEW (See LAKE DALLAS on page 358)

LAKEWAY AIRPARK (3R9) 2 SW UTC−6(−5DT) N30°21.45′ W97°59.67′   **SAN ANTONIO**
909 TPA—See Remarks NOTAM FILE SJT   **L−19C, 21A**
RWY 16−34: H3930X70 (ASPH) S−9 0.6% up S   **IAP**
  RWY 16: Thld dsplcd 782′. Tree.
  RWY 34: Thld dsplcd 624′. Trees.
SERVICE: **FUEL** 100LL
NOISE: Mntn rwy hdg til 1 mi and 400 ft AGL (1300 ft MSL) for noise abatement.
AIRPORT REMARKS: Unatndd. Aprt CLOSED SS−SR. No ngt opns per city ordinance. Deer on and in vicinity of arpt. 100LL fuel self-svc. Numerous objects in prim sfc. Rwy rises fm S to N to 32 ft. Acft not visible at opposite end. No TGLs. No low passes. Arpt opns ltd to acft with max gwt 12,500 lbs or less by city ordinance. Ultralight and glider opns prohibited. Bldgs, trees and parked acft near rwy. 3 ft non-frangible signs 10 ft fm edge at dsplcd thr, both sides. No coml opns per city ordinance. Rwy 34, 30 ft mkd pwr lines acrs apch 155′ dstc. Rwy 34, 30 ft mkd elec tmtn lines crs thru apch 200 ft dstc. All acft, inclg rotary wing, left tfc. TPA 1900 MSL. Lndg fee for turbines and jets. Ovngt tiedown fee.
AIRPORT MANAGER: 512-261-4385
COMMUNICATIONS: CTAF/UNICOM 123.0
®**AUSTIN APP/DEP CON** 119.0
CLEARANCE DELIVERY PHONE: For CD ctc Austin Apch at 512-369-7865.
RADIO AIDS TO NAVIGATION: NOTAM FILE AUS.
  CENTEX (VH) (H) VORTACW 112.8   CWK   Chan 75   N30°22.71′   W97°31.79′   261° 24.1 NM to fld. 593/6E.
  VOR unusable:
    180°−190° byd 40 NM
    200°−210° byd 40 NM
COMM/NAV/WEATHER REMARKS: 2−way radio coms rqrd on CTAF. Aprt wx SR−SS click mike 5X on CTAF.

Rwy 16-34: 3930 X 70

LAMESA MUNI (LUV)(KLUV) 2 NE UTC−6(−5DT) N32°45.38′ W101°55.21′   **DALLAS−FT WORTH**
2999 B NOTAM FILE FTW   **H−6G, L−6H**
RWY 16−34: H5002X75 (ASPH) S−20 MIRL   **IAP**
  RWY 16: PAPI(P2L)—GA 3.0° TCH 31′. Road.
  RWY 34: PAPI(P2L)—GA 3.0° TCH 32′.
RWY 07−25: H4006X60 (ASPH) S−12 MIRL
  RWY 07: Tree.
  RWY 25: Road.
SERVICE: S4 **FUEL** 100LL, JET A1+ **LGT** SS−SR. **SVC** Pwr plant rprs: Acft maint 806−759−7250.
AIRPORT REMARKS: Unattended. For A1+ fuel svc call 806−759−9270, 806−759−7747 or 806−759−7250. Rwy 07−25, due to grade, acft on rwy end not vsb fm opposite end.
AIRPORT MANAGER: (806) 759-7747
WEATHER DATA SOURCES: AWOS−3PT 124.175 (806) 872−0659.
COMMUNICATIONS: CTAF/UNICOM 122.8
®**FORT WORTH CENTER APP/DEP CON** 132.6
CLEARANCE DELIVERY PHONE: For CD ctc Fort Worth ARTCC at 817-858-7584.
RADIO AIDS TO NAVIGATION: NOTAM FILE BPG.
  BIG SPRING (VL) (H) VORTACW 117.2   BGS   Chan 119   N32°23.14′ W101°29.02′   304° 31.3 NM to fld. 2670/11E.

SC, 25 JAN 2024 to 21 MAR 2024

TEXAS

LAMPASAS (LZZ)(KLZZ)   3 N   UTC–6(–5DT)   N31°06.37′ W98°11.76′   SAN ANTONIO
1214   B   NOTAM FILE SJT   L–19C
RWY 16–34: H4202X75 (ASPH)   S–12.5   MIRL   1.4% up NW   IAP
 RWY 16: PAPI(P2L)—GA 3.0° TCH 40′. Trees.
 RWY 34: PAPI(P2L)—GA 3.0° TCH 40′.
SERVICE: FUEL 100LL   **LGT** ACTVT MIRL Rwy 16–34—CTAF.
AIRPORT REMARKS: Unattended. Deer on and invof arpt. For atndnt aft hrs call 512–556–6235. (Police Dept). 100LL 24 hr self svc.
AIRPORT MANAGER: (512) 734-0228
WEATHER DATA SOURCES: AWOS–3 119.075 (512) 556–6392.
COMMUNICATIONS: CTAF/UNICOM 122.8
 RCO 122.4 (SAN ANGELO RADIO)
®**GRAY APP/DEP CON** 120.075
RADIO AIDS TO NAVIGATION: NOTAM FILE SJT.
 GOOCH SPRINGS (H) (H) VORTACW 112.5   AGJ   Chan 72   N31°11.13′ W98°08.51′   205° 5.5 NM to fld. 1191/5E.

LANCASTER RGNL (LNC)(KLNC)   2 S   UTC–6(–5DT)   N32°34.66′ W96°43.05′   DALLAS–FT WORTH
501   B   NOTAM FILE LNC   COPTER
RWY 13–31: H6500X100 (ASPH)   S–20, D–60   MIRL   0.4% up NW   H–6H, L–17C, A
 RWY 13: PAPI(P4L)—GA 3.0° TCH 45′.   IAP
 RWY 31: PAPI(P4L)—GA 3.0° TCH 50′. Trees. Rgt tfc.
SERVICE: S4   FUEL 100LL, JET A+   **LGT** ACTVT MIRL Rwy 13–31—CTAF.
AIRPORT REMARKS: Attended Mon–Thu 1300–0000Z‡, Fri–Sun 1300–0100Z‡. Arpt unatndd Thanksgiving, Christmas Eve 1800Z‡ thru Christmas. Wildlife on and invof arpt. Full on auto–rotations, sliding skid ldgs or tkfs by skid type helicopters on any paved sfc not authorized. N ramp hel prkg circles rotary wing use only, apch and dep NA.
AIRPORT MANAGER: 972-227-5721
WEATHER DATA SOURCES: AWOS–3PT 118.975 (972) 227–0471.
COMMUNICATIONS: CTAF/UNICOM 122.7
®**REGIONAL APP/DEP CON** 118.1 125.025 125.2 125.27 125.9 135.975
 GCO Avbl on freq 121.725 (DALLAS/FORT WORTH TRACON)
CLEARANCE DELIVERY PHONE: For CD ctc Regional Apch at 972-615-2799.
RADIO AIDS TO NAVIGATION: NOTAM FILE FTW.
 COWBOY (VH) (DH) VORW/DME 116.2   CVE   Chan 109   N32°53.42′ W96°54.24′   147° 21.0 NM to fld. 443/6E.
 VOR unusable:
  030°–035° byd 40 NM
  055°–060° byd 40 NM
  130°–140° byd 40 NM

LANE AIRPARK (See ROSENBERG on page 412)

LAREDO INTL (LRD)(KLRD) 3 NE UTC–6(–5DT) N27°32.65′ W99°27.70′ BROWNSVILLE
508 B AOE Class I, ARFF Index B NOTAM FILE LRD H–7B, L–20C
RWY 18R–36L: H8743X150 (CONC–GRVD) S–90, D–190, 2S–140, IAP, AD
2D–415, 2D/2D2–820 HIRL
  RWY 18R: MALSR. PAPI(P4L)—GA 3.0° TCH 50′.
  RWY 36L: PAPI(P4L)—GA 3.0° TCH 50′. Thld dsplcd 120′. Rgt tfc.
  0.4% up.
RWY 18L–36R: H8236X150 (CONC–GRVD) S–90, D–190, 2S–175,
2D–360 HIRL
  RWY 18L: PAPI(P4L)—GA 3.0° TCH 51′.
  RWY 36R: Rgt tfc. 0.4% up.
RWY 14–32: H5927X150 (CONC) S–50, D–60, 2D–125 MIRL
0.6% up NW
  RWY 14: VASI(V4L)—GA 3.0° TCH 55′.
  RWY 32: VASI(V4L)—GA 3.0° TCH 71′. Road. Rgt tfc.

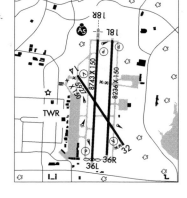

RUNWAY DECLARED DISTANCE INFORMATION

RWY 14: TORA–5927	TODA–5927	ASDA–5927	LDA–5927
RWY 18L: TORA–8236	TODA–8236	ASDA–8236	LDA–8236
RWY 18R: TORA–8743	TODA–8743	ASDA–8743	LDA–8743
RWY 32: TORA–5927	TODA–5927	ASDA–5927	LDA–5927
RWY 36L: TORA–8743	TODA–8743	ASDA–8743	LDA–8623
RWY 36R: TORA–8236	TODA–8236	ASDA–8236	LDA–8236

ARRESTING GEAR/SYSTEM
  RWY 18R: EMAS
SERVICE: S7 **FUEL** 100LL, JET A **OX** 2, 4 **LGT** When ATCT clsd ACTVT MALSR Rwy 18R—CTAF. MIRL Rwy 14–32; HIRL
Rwys 18L–36R and Rwy 18R–36L preset med intst.
AIRPORT REMARKS: Attended continuously. Birds on and invof arpt. JP4 fuel avbl. Rwy 14–32 rstrd to acft less than 60000 lbs
DTW. Rwy 14–32 not avbl for Part 121 acft opns. Twy C clsd btn Rwy 18L–36R and Rwy 18R indefly. Federal Inspection
Station fee. Federal Inspection Station is lctd on the West General Aviation/Cargo apron. Lndg fee assessed for any "for
hire" acft.
AIRPORT MANAGER: 956-795-2000
WEATHER DATA SOURCES: AWOS–3PT (956) 712–8640 LAWRS SAWRS(WHEN ATCT CLSD).
COMMUNICATIONS: CTAF 120.1 **ATIS** 125.775 **UNICOM** 122.95
  RCO 122.3 (SAN ANGELO RADIO)
® **HOUSTON CENTER APP/DEP CON** 127.8
  TOWER 120.1 (1200–0600Z‡) **GND CON** 121.8
CLEARANCE DELIVERY PHONE: For CD if una to ctc on FSS freq, ctc Houston ARTCC at 281-230-5622.
AIRSPACE: CLASS D svc 1200–0600Z‡, other times CLASS E.
RADIO AIDS TO NAVIGATION: NOTAM FILE LRD.
  (VH) (H) VORTACW 117.4 LRD Chan 121 N27°28.72′ W99°25.06′ 320° 4.6 NM to fld. 583/9E.
  VOR unusable:
    080°–126° byd 40 NM
    127°–137° byd 40 NM blo 4,500′
    127°–137° byd 56 NM
    138°–160° byd 40 NM
    190°–260° byd 40 NM
  ILS/DME 111.9 I–LRD Chan 56 Rwy 18R. Class IE. Unmonitored when ATCT closed. Localizer backcourse
  unusable byd 20° left of course. DME unusable byd 20° left of localizer backcourse. Localizer backcourse unusable byd
  25° right of course.
COMM/NAV/WEATHER REMARKS: Emerg frequency 121.5 not avbl at twr.

TEXAS

LAUGHLIN AFB (DLF)(KDLF) AF 5 E UTC–6(–5DT) N29°21.56´ W100°46.68´ SAN ANTONIO
1082   B   NOTAM FILE DLF   Not insp. H–7B, L–19B
 DIAP, AD
RWY 13C–31C: H8852X150 (PEM)   PCN 35 F/A/W/T   HIRL
  RWY 13C: ALSF1. PAPI(P4L)—GA 3.0° TCH 38´.
  RWY 31C: PAPI(P4L)—GA 3.0° TCH 55´.
RWY 13L–31R: H8316X150 (PEM)   PCN 51 R/B/W/T   HIRL
  RWY 13L: PAPI(P4L)—GA 3.0° TCH 40´.
  RWY 31R: PAPI(P4L)—GA 3.0° TCH 42´.
RWY 13R–31L: H6571X150 (ASPH)   PCN 31 F/B/W/T   MIRL
  RWY 31L: Thld dsplcd 330´.
ARRESTING GEAR/SYSTEM
  RWY 13C BAK–15 CHAG (151' OVRN). BAK–15 CHAG (155' OVRN). **RWY 31C**
  RWY 13L BAK–15 CHAG (115' OVRN). BAK–15 CHAG (155' OVRN). **RWY 31R**
SERVICE: S4 **LGT** Rwy 13C–31C PAPI opr dur opr hr, GS 3.0°. Rwy 13C–31C PAPI/ILS RPI´s not coincidental. Rwy 31C apch lgt not avbl UFN. Three sets of missing twy end lgt – int of Twy G and D, Twy G and E, Twy G and F. 4 missing rwy edge lgt on Rwy 13C–31C opposite int with Twy J and Twy D. 3 groups twy lgts instl greater than 10´ from twy edges: Twy B and Twy G both sides of int, Twy C and Twy G both sides of int. East side Twy G adj apn. Doubleblue twy entrance/exit lgt missing; Twy A and Rwy 13L/31R north side, Twy A and Rwy 13R/31L south side, Twy H and Rwy 13C/31C southwest side, Twy E and Rwy 13R–31L southwest side. **MILITARY— A–GEAR** BAK–15 on dep end Rwy 13C–31C and Rwy 13L–31R. Opposite end apch over raised barrier is proh. **JASU** 1(MD–3M) 1(MA–1A) 1(MC–1A) 1(MC–11) 1(A/M32A–86) **FUEL** A++, A++100 **FLUID** SP PRESAIR LHOX LOX **OIL** O–148 SOAP **TRAN ALERT** Opr dur afld hr.
NOISE: Noise Abatement: AETC quiet hr policy in effect daily 0400–1200Z‡dly, no tkof, low apch or touch and go ldg.
MILITARY REMARKS: Opr weekdays Mon–Fri 1300–0100Z‡, Sun 2000–2300Z‡, Clsd to all acft exc emerg OT, Sat and hol; OT by NOTAM. **RSTD** All acft cross departure end of all rwys at or blo 1600´ MSL for VMC departure. Rwy 13R–31L for lcl use only. T–1 and smaller acft only on Twys B, C, D, E and H. Rwy 31L thld dsplcd 330´, do not land prior to rwy thld, dsplcd thld may be used for tkf on Rwy 31L and ldg rollout on Rwy 13R–do not use opposite end dsplcd thld for tkf computations or tkf roll. Twy G1 for use by T6 acft only. Overhead apch not auth for tran acft dur stu trng opr. Exp radar vectors for ILS, LOC or straight–in apch and full stop ldg dur stu trng. PPR, ctc Base OPS DSN 732–5308, C830–298–5308. All acft with wingspan larger than C–130 rstd. **CAUTION** Twenty–seven security lgt poles along edge of prk apron have no obst lgts. All departuring acft cross 2 DME at or blo 3000´ to ensure separation from civ corridor. Rwy Supervisor Units lctd 230´ west of Rwy 13C abeam the 7000´ remaining marker, 236´ west of Rwy 31C abeam the 7000´ remaining marker and 221´ east of Rwy 31R abeam 5500´ remaining marker. Twy J VFR daytime only, no edge lgts installed. Lgtd wind cone 249´ west of Rwy 13C cntrln, south of Twy A. Lgtd wind cone 211´ west of Rwy 13C cntrln, north of Twy E. Potential transit/divert UAS ops within lcl terminal area. **TFC PAT** Due to close proximity of rwys, once established on final apch, tran acft will remain aligned with Rwy 13C–31C to avoid T–6 tfc ldg Rwy 13R–31L at 2100´ and tfc ldg Rwy 13L–31R at 2100´–2600´. **MISC** All acft dep VFR shall ctc CLNC DEL 335.8 for Class C Airspace climb out inst prior to taxi. Acft opr within the Rwy Supervisory Unit practice area are not Class C participants. Rwy Supervisory Unit practice area defined in AP/1. Airfield opns does not have ability to store comsec. Command post has ltd avbl storage. Ctc command post DSN 732–5167, c830–298–5167. Airfield opns does not have ability to store comsec. Command post has ltd avbl storage. Ctc command post DSN 732–5167, C830–298–5167. Fire fighting capabilities max 2300 gal. Wide–body acft (C17/C5) exp 30 min or longer svc time due to the use of 1.5 hose. **RWY** First 300´ Rwy 13C–31C is grvd conc, middle 8252´ is grvd asph. First 1000´ Rwy 13L–31R grvd conc, middle 6315´ grvd asph. Rwy Cond Reading (RCR) unavbl. Rwy Cond Code (RwyCC) not rptd. No rwy sfc cond avbl when twr clsd.
AIRPORT MANAGER: 830-298-5308
COMMUNICATIONS: SFA (Tfc permitting.) **ATIS** 114.4 269.9 (Mon–Fri 1300–0100Z‡, Sun 2000–2300Z‡ exc hol) **PTD** 372.2
®**DEL RIO APP CON** 119.6 259.1 (Mon–Fri 1300–0100Z‡, clsd Sat, Sun 2100–2359Z‡ exc hol), other times ctc
®**HOUSTON CENTER APP CON** 125.75 346.4 (Mon–Fri 0100–1300Z‡, Sat 24, Sun 2359–2100Z‡ exc hol)
 TOWER 125.2 307.375 (Mon–Fri 1300–0100Z‡, Sun 2100–2359Z‡ exc hol)
 GND CON 275.8 **CLNC DEL** 120.5 335.8
®**DEL RIO DEP CON** 119.6 296.7 (Mon–Fri 1300–0100Z‡, clsd Sat, Sun 2100–2359Z‡ exc hol), other times ctc
®**HOUSTON CENTER DEP CON** 125.75 346.4
 COMD POST 372.2 (Call BIG RANCH) **PMSV METRO** 354.6 Wx HS. Afld wx maintained by AN/FMQ–19 and augmented by observer as req. Backup wx obsn view ltd, rstd from 120°–320° by flt line fac.
AIRSPACE: CLASS C svc ctc **APP CON** svc 1300–0100Z‡ Mon–Fri, 2100–2359Z‡ Sun exc hol; other times CLASS G.

CONTINUED ON NEXT PAGE

TEXAS

CONTINUED FROM PRECEDING PAGE

RADIO AIDS TO NAVIGATION: NOTAM FILE DLF.
  (H) (H) VORTAC 114.4   DLF   Chan 91   N29°21.65´ W100°46.30´   at fld. 1071/7E. VORTAC unmonitored when Del Rio apch ctl clsd.
  TACAN AZIMUTH unusable:
    161°–285° byd 15 NM
    No NOTAM MP: 0800–1200Z‡ Tue–Thu
  VOR unusable:
    045°–050° blo 3,000´
    161°–285° byd 15 NM
    286°–330° byd 25 NM blo 4,500´
    331°–359° byd 25 NM
    360°–160° byd 25 NM blo 4,500´
  DME unusable:
    161°–285° byd 15 NM
  ILS 110.3 I–DLF Rwy 13C. Unavbl when app clsd. No NOTAM MP: 0800–1200Z‡ Mon–Fri. Wheel crossing height (WCH) GROUP 1: 29´; GROUP 2: 24´; GROUP 3: 19´; GROUP 4: 14´.
  ILS 108.9 I–ILH Rwy 31C. No NOTAM MP: 1000–1200Z‡ Tue–Thu. Unmonitored when app clsd.

LAZY G BAR RANCH (See DECATUR on page 292)

LEAGUE CITY
BAY ELECTRIC SUPPLY HELIPORT (T95) 3 SW UTC–6(–5DT) N29°29.30´ W95°06.45´   **HOUSTON**
  26   NOTAM FILE CXO   **COPTER**
  HELIPAD H1: H90X90 (CONC)   PERIMETER LGTS
  HELIPORT REMARKS: Unattended. 197 ft electric transmission lines and electric power lines north of landing pad, clockwise from 270 deg to 085 deg, not marked or lighted.
  AIRPORT MANAGER: 281-332-3466
  COMMUNICATIONS: CTAF 122.9
  CLEARANCE DELIVERY PHONE: For CD ctc Houston Apch at 281-443-5844 to cnl IFR call 281-443-5888.

LEAKEY
REAL CO (49R) 1 N UTC–6(–5DT) N29°44.73´ W99°45.65´   **SAN ANTONIO**
  1640   NOTAM FILE SJT   **L–19B**
  RWY 15–33: H3975X50 (ASPH) S–11 LIRL(NSTD)
    RWY 15: Thld dsplcd 240´. Trees.
    RWY 33: Thld dsplcd 270´. Trees.
  SERVICE: LGT Rwy 15–33 NSTD LIRL due to color. Rwy 15–33 LIRL OTS indef.
  AIRPORT REMARKS: Unattended. Ultralight act adj to rwy. Do not use turf taxiway from apron to Rwy 33 end. Rwy 15 and Rwy 33 dsplcd thr unlgtd.
  AIRPORT MANAGER: 830-232-5304
  COMMUNICATIONS: CTAF 122.9
  CLEARANCE DELIVERY PHONE: For CD ctc Laughlin Apch at 830-298-5192, when Apch clsd ctc Houston ARTCC at 281-230-5622.
  RADIO AIDS TO NAVIGATION: NOTAM FILE ERV.
    CENTER POINT (VH) (H) VORTAC 117.5   CSI   Chan 122   N29°55.34´ W99°12.87´   242° 30.4 NM to fld. 2079/8E.

LEONA N31°07.44´ W95°58.08´ NOTAM FILE CXO.   **HOUSTON**
  (L) (L) VORTACW 110.8   LOA   Chan 45   168° 12.7 NM to Madisonville Muni. 346/8E.   **H–6I, L–19D, 21A**

LEVELLAND MUNI (LLN)(KLLN) 2 S UTC–6(–5DT) N33°33.15´ W102°22.35´ ALBUQUERQUE
3514 B NOTAM FILE FTW H–6G, L–6H
RWY 17–35: H6110X75 (ASPH) S–30 MIRL(NSTD) IAP
  RWY 17: PAPI(P4L)—GA 3.0° TCH 47´. Tree.
  RWY 35: REIL. PAPI(P4L)—GA 3.0° TCH 39´. Rgt tfc.
RWY 08–26: H2072X55 (ASPH)
  RWY 08: Road. Rgt tfc.
  RWY 26: Brush.
SERVICE: S4 **FUEL** 100LL, JET A **LGT** MIRL Rwy 17–35 preset low ints, to increase ints ACTIVATE—CTAF. Rwy 17–35 NSTD MIRL, NSTD lenses. Rwy 35 PAPI OTS.
AIRPORT REMARKS: Attended Mon–Fri 1400–2200Z‡. Fuel self-svc at pump.
AIRPORT MANAGER: 806-897-4774
WEATHER DATA SOURCES: AWOS–3PT 121.125 (806) 897–4770.
COMMUNICATIONS: CTAF/UNICOM 122.8
®**LUBBOCK APP/DEP CON** 119.2 119.9
CLEARANCE DELIVERY PHONE: For CD ctc Fort Worth ARTCC at 817-858-7584.
RADIO AIDS TO NAVIGATION: NOTAM FILE LBB.
  LUBBOCK (L) (L) VORTACW 109.2 LBB Chan 29 N33°42.30´ W101°54.84´ 237° 24.7 NM to fld. 3310/11E.
  VOR unusable:
    040°–050° byd 38 NM blo 5,300´
    210°–260° byd 25 NM blo 6,000´

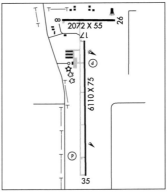

LIBERTY MUNI (T78) 6 NE UTC–6(–5DT) N30°04.67´ W94°41.91´ HOUSTON
70 B NOTAM FILE CXO L–19E, 21A, GOMW
RWY 16–34: H3801X75 (ASPH) S–10 MIRL IAP
  RWY 16: PAPI(P2L)—GA 3.0° TCH 23´. Trees.
  RWY 34: Trees.
SERVICE: S4 **FUEL** 100LL, JET A **LGT** ACTIVATE MIRL Rwy 16–34—CTAF.
AIRPORT REMARKS: Attended 1400–0000Z‡. 100LL 24 hr self-svc fuel.
AIRPORT MANAGER: (281) 660-2337
WEATHER DATA SOURCES: AWOS–3PT 120.775 (936) 587–4150.
COMMUNICATIONS: CTAF 122.9
®**HOUSTON APP/DEP CON** 119.3
CLEARANCE DELIVERY PHONE: For CD ctc Houston Apch at 281-443-5844 to cnl IFR call 281-443-5888.
RADIO AIDS TO NAVIGATION: NOTAM FILE CXO.
  DAISETTA (H) (H) VORTACW 116.9 DAS Chan 116 N30°11.38´ W94°38.70´ 198° 7.3 NM to fld. 76/5E.
  VOR unusable:
    Byd 35 NM blo 1,600´
  TACAN AZIMUTH unusable:
    Byd 35 NM blo 1,600´
  DME unusable:
    Byd 35 NM blo 1,600´

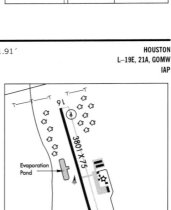

LINDSAY
FREEDOM FLD (7T0) 3 S UTC–6(–5DT) N33°35.62´ W97°13.13´ DALLAS–FT WORTH
885 NOTAM FILE FTW
RWY 17–35: 2400X60 (TURF)
  RWY 17: Road. Rgt tfc.
  RWY 35: Road.
AIRPORT REMARKS: Unattended. Ocnl livestock on rwy. No student tfc, no hels. 34 ft p–line, 69 ft dstc, 82 ft L of rwy CL. Lines buried under apch. +40´ pole 80´ left 60´ from Rwy 17. Rwy soft after rain. Call to confirm cond.
AIRPORT MANAGER: 940-736-6464
COMMUNICATIONS: CTAF 122.9
CLEARANCE DELIVERY PHONE: For CD ctc Fort Worth ARTCC at 817-858-7584.

TEXAS

LITTLEFIELD TAYLOR BROWN MUNI (LIU)(KLIU) 3 W UTC–6(–5DT) N33°55.44′ W102°23.20′ **ALBUQUERQUE**
3616 B NOTAM FILE FTW L–6H
RWY 01–19: H4021X60 (ASPH) S–12 MIRL IAP
  RWY 01: PAPI(P2L)—GA 3.0° TCH 40′. Tree.
  RWY 19: PAPI(P2L)—GA 3.0° TCH 40′. Tree.
RWY 13–31: H2513X40 (ASPH) S–5 0.4% up NW
  RWY 13: Road.
  RWY 31: P–line.
SERVICE: S2 **FUEL** 100LL **LGT** SS–SR
AIRPORT REMARKS: Attended 1400–2300Z‡. For fuel after hrs call 806–777–5030, 806–778–1418 or 806–241–0761. Glider operations sunrise to sunset weekends. Hangars obstruct transitional surface Rwy 13–31.
AIRPORT MANAGER: 806-777-5030
COMMUNICATIONS: CTAF/UNICOM 122.8
®**LUBBOCK APP/DEP CON** 119.2 119.9
CLEARANCE DELIVERY PHONE: For CD ctc Fort Worth ARTCC at 817-858-7584.
RADIO AIDS TO NAVIGATION: NOTAM FILE LBB.
  LUBBOCK (L) (L) VORTACW 109.2 LBB Chan 29 N33°42.30′
  W101°54.84′ 288° 27.0 NM to fld. 3310/11E.
  VOR unusable:
    040°–050° byd 38 NM blo 5,300′
    210°–260° byd 25 NM blo 6,000′

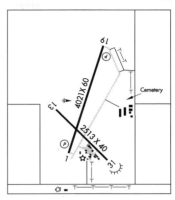

LIVE OAK CO (See GEORGE WEST on page 317)

LIVINGSTON MUNI (00R) 5 SW UTC–6(–5DT) N30°41.15′ W95°01.08′ **HOUSTON**
151 B NOTAM FILE CXO L–19E, 21A
RWY 12–30: H3704X60 (ASPH) S–11 MIRL IAP
  RWY 12: Trees.
  RWY 30: Trees.
SERVICE: S4 **FUEL** 100LL
AIRPORT REMARKS: Attended Mon–Fri 1400–2300Z‡, Sat–Sun 1800–2300Z‡.
AIRPORT MANAGER: 936-327-4311
COMMUNICATIONS: CTAF/UNICOM 122.7
®**HOUSTON CENTER APP/DEP CON** 125.175
CLEARANCE DELIVERY PHONE: For CD ctc Houston ARTCC at 281-230-5622.
RADIO AIDS TO NAVIGATION: NOTAM FILE LFK.
  LUFKIN (VH) (H) VORTACW 112.1 LFK Chan 58 N31°09.75′ W94°43.01′ 204° 32.5 NM to fld. 207/5E.
  TACAN AZIMUTH unusable:
    260°–275° byd 30 NM
    275°–260° byd 30 NM blo 2,500′
  DME unusable:
    260°–275° byd 30 NM
    275°–260° byd 30 NM blo 2,500′
  VOR unusable:
    305°–312° byd 40 NM
    313°–323° byd 40 NM blo 2,300′
    313°–323° byd 66 NM
    324°–330° byd 40 NM

TEXAS

LLANO MUNI (AQO)(KAQO)   2 NE   UTC−6(−5DT)   N30°47.05′ W98°39.59′   SAN ANTONIO
1102   B   NOTAM FILE AQO   L−19C
  RWY 17−35: H4202X75 (ASPH) S−20   MIRL   IAP
    RWY 17: PAPI(P2L)—GA 2.75° TCH 40′. Trees. Rgt tfc.
    RWY 35: PAPI(P2L)—GA 2.75° TCH 40′. Brush.
  RWY 13−31: 3209X150 (TURF)   0.6% up NW
    RWY 31: Trees. Rgt tfc.
  SERVICE: S4 FUEL 100LL, JET A   LGT MIRL Rwy 17−35 preset low
    intst; to incr intst ACTVT—CTAF.
  AIRPORT REMARKS: Attended Tue−Thu 1400−2300Z‡, Fri−Mon
    1300−2300Z‡. Deer on and invof arpt. 100LL self svc. Rwy 13−31
    thr mkd with white tires.
  AIRPORT MANAGER: 325-247-5635
  WEATHER DATA SOURCES: AWOS−3 119.425 (325) 247−2189.
  COMMUNICATIONS: CTAF/UNICOM 123.05
  ®HOUSTON CENTER APP/DEP CON 132.35
  CLEARANCE DELIVERY PHONE: For CD ctc Houston ARTCC at 281-230-5622.
  RADIO AIDS TO NAVIGATION: NOTAM FILE AQO.
    (L) (L) VORTACW 108.2   LLO   Chan 19   N30°47.78′
    W98°47.24′   088° 6.6 NM to fld. 1207/8E.

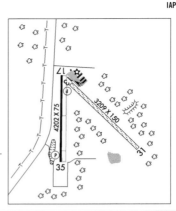

LLANO   N30°47.78′ W98°47.24′   NOTAM FILE AQO.   SAN ANTONIO
  (L) (L) VORTACW 108.2   LLO   Chan 19   088° 6.6 NM to Llano Muni. 1207/8E.   H−7B, 6G, L−19C

LOCKHART MUNI (50R)   2 S   UTC−6(−5DT)   N29°51.02′ W97°40.35′   SAN ANTONIO
532   B   NOTAM FILE SJT   L−19C, 21A
  RWY 18−36: H4001X75 (ASPH) S−12.5   MIRL   IAP
    RWY 18: PAPI(P2L)—GA 3.5° TCH 24′. Tree.
    RWY 36: PAPI(P2L)—GA 3.0° TCH 25′. Tree.
  SERVICE: S4 FUEL 100LL   LGT MIRL Rwy 18−36 preset low intst; to incr
    intst actvt—CTAF.
  AIRPORT REMARKS: Attended 1400−2300Z‡. Excp major hol. Wildlife invof
    arpt. Parallel twy has green centerline reflectors. + 280′ lgtd water twr
    2.1 mi S of Rwy 36. Rwy 18 and 36 mkgs discolored, peeling.
  AIRPORT MANAGER: 512-398-6452
  COMMUNICATIONS: CTAF/UNICOM 122.8
  ®AUSTIN APP/DEP CON 120.875
  CLEARANCE DELIVERY PHONE: For CD ctc Austin Apch at 512-369-7865.
  RADIO AIDS TO NAVIGATION: NOTAM FILE AUS.
    CENTEX (VH) (H) VORTACW 112.8   CWK   Chan 75   N30°22.71′
    W97°31.79′   187° 32.5 NM to fld. 593/6E.
    VOR unusable:
      180°−190° byd 40 NM
      200°−210° byd 40 NM

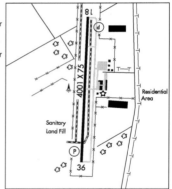

SC, 25 JAN 2024 to 21 MAR 2024

TEXAS

LONGVIEW

EAST TEXAS RGNL (GGG)(KGGG) 8 S UTC–6(–5DT) N32°23.04´ W94°42.69´ **MEMPHIS**
366 B ARFF Index—See Remarks NOTAM FILE GGG H–6I, L–17D
RWY 13–31: H10000X150 (ASPH–GRVD) S–95, D–155, 2S–175, IAP, AD
2D–288 PCN 51 F/C/X/T HIRL
  RWY 13: MALSR. RVR–T Thld dsplcd 800´.
  RWY 31: PAPI(P4L)—GA 3.0° TCH 50´. RVR–R
RWY 18–36: H6110X150 (ASPH–GRVD) S–95, D–155, 2S–175,
2D–280 PCN 29 F/C/X/T MIRL
  RWY 18: PAPI(P4L)—GA 3.0° TCH 59´. Tree.
  RWY 36: PAPI(P4R)—GA 3.0° TCH 50´. Tree.
LAND AND HOLD–SHORT OPERATIONS

LDG RWY	HOLD–SHORT POINT	AVBL LDG DIST
RWY 31	18–36	8100
RWY 36	13–31	4080

RUNWAY DECLARED DISTANCE INFORMATION
  RWY 13: TORA–10000 TODA–10000 ASDA–10000 LDA–9200
  RWY 18: TORA–6109 TODA–6109 ASDA–6109 LDA–6109
  RWY 31: TORA–10000 TODA–10000 ASDA–9200 LDA–9200
  RWY 36: TORA–6109 TODA–6109 ASDA–6109 LDA–6109
SERVICE: S4 **FUEL** 100LL, JET A **OX** 3, 4 **LGT** HIRL Rwy 13–31 preset
med intst; to incr intst actvt—CTAF. When ATCT clsd actvt MALSR Rwy
13—CTAF. MIRL Rwy 18–36 not avbl when ATCT clsd. Rwy 36 PAPI
unsbl byd 8° right of rwy centerline.

AIRPORT REMARKS: Attended 1200–0300Z‡. Birds on and invof arpt (seasonal). For fuel after hrs call 903–643–8748. Class
I, ARFF Index A. PPR for unscheduled air carrier ops with more than 30 passenger seats. Index B avbl on request. See
Special Notices — Extensive Flight Training Advisory
AIRPORT MANAGER: 903-234-3194
WEATHER DATA SOURCES: ASOS (903) 643–4029 LAWRS.
COMMUNICATIONS: CTAF 119.2 **ATIS** 119.65 **UNICOM** 122.95
  GREGG RCO 122.2 (FORT WORTH RADIO)
®**LONGVIEW APP/DEP CON** 128.75 (West, 7000 and blw) 124.675 (West, 5000 and blw) 124.275 (East 4000 ft and blw)
  127.325 (At or blw 4000 ft) (East 4500–12000 ft) (1200–0400Z‡)
®**FORT WORTH CENTER APP/DEP CON** 126.325 (0400–1200Z‡)
  EASTEX TOWER 119.2 (1200–0400Z‡) **GND CON** 121.6
AIRSPACE: CLASS D svc 1200–0400Z‡; other times CLASS G.
  TRSA ctc APP CON within 30 NM
RADIO AIDS TO NAVIGATION: NOTAM FILE GGG.
  GREGG COUNTY (VL) (H) VORTACW 112.9 GGG Chan 76 N32°25.07´ W94°45.19´ 127° 2.9 NM to fld. 329/7E.
  TACAN AZIMUTH unusable:
    045°–070° byd 25 NM blo 2,500´
    180°–225° byd 33 NM blo 3,500´
    258°–268° byd 26 NM blo 4,500´
    325°–340° byd 37 NM blo 2,500´
    248°–258° byd 34 NM blo 8,100´
  DME unusable:
    045°–070° byd 25 NM blo 2,500´
    180°–225° byd 33 NM blo 3,500´
    258°–268° byd 26 NM blo 4,500´
    325°–340° byd 37 NM blo 2,500´
  VOR unusable:
    138°–152° byd 40 NM
    188°–192° byd 40 NM
    210°–230° byd 40 NM
  VEELS NDB (LOMW) 410 GG N32°27.33´ W94°47.85´ 131° 6.1 NM to fld. 263/3E.
  ILS 109.5 I–GGG Rwy 13. Class IA. LOM VEELS NDB. Unmonitored when ATCT closed.

TEXAS

LOUISE

FLYING V RANCH (T26) 1 SE UTC–6(–5DT) N29°06.50′ W96°23.93′ HOUSTON
60 NOTAM FILE CXO
RWY 14–32: 2990X80 (TURF)
 RWY 14: Tree.
 RWY 32: Tree. Rgt tfc.
SERVICE: S4
AIRPORT REMARKS: Attended continuously. Rwy edge mkd with white tires. Rwy 14 creek/ravine 10–15 ft drop-off at thr east side of cntrln. Rwy 32 has 4 ft berm, 60 ft dstc acrs apch.
AIRPORT MANAGER: 979-541-3321
COMMUNICATIONS: CTAF/UNICOM 122.8
CLEARANCE DELIVERY PHONE: For CD ctc Houston ARTCC at 281-230-5622.

LUBBI N33°39.76′ W101°43.39′ NOTAM FILE LBB. DALLAS–FT. WORTH
 NDB (LOMW) 272 LD 265° 4.9 NM to Lubbock Preston Smith Intl. 3198/6E.

LUBBOCK

LUBBOCK EXEC AIRPARK (F82) 5 S UTC–6(–5DT) N33°29.14′ W101°48.76′ DALLAS–FT WORTH
3200 B NOTAM FILE FTW L–6H
RWY 17–35: H3500X70 (ASPH) S–13 LIRL
RWY 07–25: 1500X110 (TURF)
 RWY 07: P–line.
SERVICE: S4 **FUEL** 100LL, JET A
AIRPORT REMARKS: Attended 1300–0300Z‡ After hrs 806–789–6437, 806–589–8143. Fuel avbl 24 hrs with major credit card. Farm equip oprs AER 17, 25, 35. Rwy 07–25 35′ trees alg N rwy edge. Rwy 07–25 rwy rough with bare spots. Rwy defined by mowing.
AIRPORT MANAGER: 806-745-4967
COMMUNICATIONS: CTAF/UNICOM 122.8
CLEARANCE DELIVERY PHONE: For CD ctc Fort Worth ARTCC at 817-858-7584.
RADIO AIDS TO NAVIGATION: NOTAM FILE LBB.
 (L) (L) VORTACW 109.2 LBB Chan 29 N33°42.30′ W101°54.84′ 148° 14.1 NM to fld. 3310/11E.
 VOR unusable:
  040°–050° byd 38 NM blo 5,300′
  210°–260° byd 25 NM blo 6,000′

TEXAS

LUBBOCK PRESTON SMITH INTL (LBB)(KLBB) 4 N UTC–6(–5DT) N33°39.82´ W101°49.23´ **DALLAS–FT WORTH**
3282 B LRA Class I, ARFF Index C NOTAM FILE LBB MON Airport **H–6G, L–6H**
RWY 17R–35L: H11500X150 (CONC–GRVD) S–100, D–170, 2S–175, **IAP, AD**
2D–350 PCN 65 R/B/W/T HIRL
  RWY 17R: MALSR. PAPI(P4R)—GA 3.0° TCH 69´. RVR–T Rgt tfc.
  0.4% down.
  RWY 35L: VASI(V4L)—GA 3.0° TCH 54´. RVR–R 0.3% up.
RWY 08–26: H8003X150 (CONC–GRVD) S–100, D–170, 2S–175,
2D–350 PCN 71 R/B/W/T HIRL
  RWY 08: REIL. PAPI(P4L)—GA 3.0° TCH 50´. RVR–R Rgt tfc.
  RWY 26: MALSR. PAPI(P4L)—GA 3.0° TCH 50´. RVR–T
RWY 17L–35R: H2891X74 (ASPH) S–12.5
  RWY 35R: Road. Rgt tfc.
RUNWAY DECLARED DISTANCE INFORMATION
  RWY 08: TORA–8003 TODA–8003 ASDA–8003 LDA–8003
  RWY 17L: TORA–2891 TODA–2891 ASDA–2891 LDA–2891
  RWY 17R: TORA–11500 TODA–11500 ASDA–11500 LDA–11500
  RWY 26: TORA–8003 TODA–8003 ASDA–8003 LDA–8003
  RWY 35L: TORA–11500 TODA–11500 ASDA–11500 LDA–11500
  RWY 35R: TORA–2891 TODA–2891 ASDA–2891 LDA–2891
SERVICE: S4 **FUEL** 100LL, JET A, A1+ **OX** 1, 2, 3, 4

AIRPORT REMARKS: Attended continuously. Nmrs birds on & invof arpt.
PAEW adj Rwy 08–26 and Rwy 17R–35L. Psgr trml ramp aces rstd to acr & otr with prior pmsn, call 806–775–2044.
Rwy 17L–35R rstd to gen avn acft 12,500 lbs or less. Rwy 17L–35R; Twy B and Twy D; Txl E and Txl E1 not avbl for
acr acft with over 9 psgr seats. Twy B and Twy D; Txl E and Txl E1 rstd to acft weighing less than 50,000 lbs. Twy L
between Twy F and Twy J clsd to more than 120,001 lbs. East ramp delineated txl & apron area rstd to 120,000 lbs dual
tand acft; 89,000 lbs dual sngl wheel acft, 60,000 lbs sngl wheel acft. All otr east ramp pavements rstd to acft less than
12,500 lbs sngl wheel acft. Flight Notification Service (ADCUS) available.
AIRPORT MANAGER: 806-775-3126
WEATHER DATA SOURCES: ASOS (806) 766–6432 WSP.
COMMUNICATIONS: ATIS 125.3 (806) 766–6404 **UNICOM** 122.95
  RCO 122.2 (FORT WORTH RADIO)
® **APP/DEP CON** 119.2 119.9
  TOWER 120.5 **GND CON** 121.9 **CLNC DEL** 125.8
AIRSPACE: CLASS C svc ctc **APP CON.**
RADIO AIDS TO NAVIGATION: NOTAM FILE LBB.
  (L) (L) **VORTACW** 109.2 LBB Chan 29 N33°42.30´ W101°54.84´ 107° 5.3 NM to fld. 3310/11E.
    VOR unusable:
    040°–050° byd 38 NM blo 5,300´
    210°–260° byd 25 NM blo 6,000´
  LUBBI NDB (LOMW) 272 LD N33°39.76´ W101°43.39´ 265° 4.9 NM to fld. 3198/6E.
  ILS/DME 111.7 I–LBB Chan 54 Rwy 17R. Class IA.
  ILS 111.9 I–LDT Rwy 26. Class IA. LOM LUBBI NDB. GP unusable for cpd apch blw 3,370´ MSL.

TEXAS

LUFKIN

ANGELINA CO (LFK)(KLFK) 7 SW UTC–6(–5DT) N31°14.04´ W94°45.00´ HOUSTON
296 B NOTAM FILE LFK MON Airport H–6I, L–19E, 21A
RWY 07–25: H5400X100 (ASPH) S–60, D–90 MIRL IAP
  RWY 07: MALSR. Tree.
  RWY 25: PAPI(P4L)—GA 3.0° TCH 45´. Trees.
RWY 16–34: H4311X100 (ASPH) S–30 MIRL 0.4% up NW
  RWY 16: VASI(V4L)—GA 3.0° TCH 48´. Tree.
  RWY 34: VASI(V4L)—GA 3.0° TCH 55´. Thld dsplcd 107´. Trees.
SERVICE: S2 **FUEL** 100LL, JET A+ **LGT** Dusk–dawn. MIRL Rwy 07–25 & Rwy 16–34 preset med intst; to incr intst and ACTVT MALSR Rwy 07—CTAF. PAPI Rwy 25; VASI Rwy 16 & Rwy 34 opr consly.
AIRPORT REMARKS: Attended Mon–Fri 1300–0100Z‡, Sat–Sun 1500–0100Z‡. 100LL svc fee chrgd for fuel aft 0100Z‡; call 936–635–1542. Rwy 16–34 296 ft paved stopway NW end. Rwy 34: 100 ft x 199 ft paved safety area. NOTE: See Special Notice–Houston ARTCC.
AIRPORT MANAGER: 936-634-7511
WEATHER DATA SOURCES: ASOS 120.625 (936) 637–9420.
COMMUNICATIONS: CTAF/UNICOM 123.0
  LUFKIN RCO 122.2 (MONTGOMERY COUNTY RADIO)
®**HOUSTON CENTER APP/DEP CON** 125.175
CLEARANCE DELIVERY PHONE: For CD if una to ctc on FSS freq, ctc Houston ARTCC at 281-230-5622.
AIRSPACE: CLASS E.
RADIO AIDS TO NAVIGATION: NOTAM FILE LFK.
  LUFKIN (VH) (H) VORTACW 112.1 LFK Chan 58 N31°09.75´ W94°43.01´ 333° 4.6 NM to fld. 207/5E.
    TACAN AZIMUTH unusable:
      260°–275° byd 30 NM
      275°–260° byd 30 NM blo 2,500´
    DME unusable:
      260°–275° byd 30 NM
      275°–260° byd 30 NM blo 2,500´
    VOR unusable:
      305°–312° byd 40 NM
      313°–323° byd 40 NM blo 2,300´
      313°–323° byd 66 NM
      324°–330° byd 40 NM
  FLUFY NDB (LOMW) 350 LF N31°13.13´ W94°49.51´ 075° 4.0 NM to fld. 205/2E. NDB unmonitored.
  ILS 111.3 I–LFK Rwy 07. Class IB. LOM FLUFY NDB. Unmonitored.
COMM/NAV/WEATHER REMARKS: UNICOM mnt fm 1200–0100Z‡.

LUFKIN N31°09.75´ W94°43.01´ NOTAM FILE LFK. HOUSTON
(VH) (H) VORTACW 112.1 LFK Chan 58 333° 4.6 NM to Angelina Co. 207/5E. H–6I, L–19E, 21A
  TACAN AZIMUTH unusable:
    260°–275° byd 30 NM
    275°–260° byd 30 NM blo 2,500´
  DME unusable:
    260°–275° byd 30 NM
    275°–260° byd 30 NM blo 2,500´
  VOR unusable:
    305°–312° byd 40 NM
    313°–323° byd 40 NM blo 2,300´
    313°–323° byd 66 NM
    324°–330° byd 40 NM
RCO 122.2 (MONTGOMERY COUNTY RADIO)

TEXAS

MADISONVILLE MUNI (51R)   3 SW   UTC–6(–5DT)   N30°54.77´ W95°57.12´   HOUSTON
287   B   NOTAM FILE CXO   L–19D, 21A
RWY 18–36: H3202X50 (ASPH)   S–4   MIRL   0.8% up N   IAP
  RWY 18: Trees.
  RWY 36: Trees.
  SERVICE: FUEL   100LL, JET A
  AIRPORT REMARKS: Unattended. Parachute Jumping. Self svc avbl 24–7. Arpt gate locked from 0400–1200Z‡ call 936–348–2748.
  AIRPORT MANAGER: 936-755-0371
  COMMUNICATIONS: CTAF 122.9
  Ⓡ HOUSTON APP/DEP CON 134.8
    CLNC DEL Ctc Houston APP CON at 281–230–5553
  CLEARANCE DELIVERY PHONE: For CD ctc Houston ARTCC at 281-230-5622.
  RADIO AIDS TO NAVIGATION: NOTAM FILE CXO.
    LEONA (L) (L) VORTACW 110.8   LOA   Chan 45   N31°07.44´ W95°58.08´   168° 12.7 NM to fld. 346/8E.

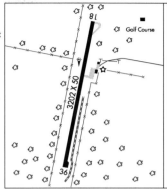

MAJOR SAMUEL B CORNELIUS FLD (See SPEARMAN on page 428)

MAJORS (See GREENVILLE on page 325)

MANNING FLD (See JEFFERSON on page 349)

MANVEL
WOLFE AIR PARK (3T2)   2 NE   UTC–6(–5DT)   N29°28.75´ W95°19.59´   HOUSTON
55   NOTAM FILE CXO   COPTER
RWY 02–20: 2910X80 (TURF)   RWY LGTS(NSTD)
  RWY 02: Trees.
  RWY 20: Road.
  SERVICE: LGT Solar lights.
  AIRPORT REMARKS: Attended dalgt hours. First 400 ft of each end of rwy unusbl when wet. Ditch xng Rwy 20 thr. No tsnt tgls.
  AIRPORT MANAGER: 915-449-9100
  COMMUNICATIONS: CTAF 122.9
  CLEARANCE DELIVERY PHONE: For CD ctc Houston Apch at 281-443-5844 to cnl IFR call 281-443-5888.

TEXAS

MARFA MUNI (MRF)(KMRF) 3 N UTC–6(–5DT) N30°22.27´ W104°01.05´ EL PASO
4849 B NOTAM FILE MRF MON Airport H–7A, L–6J
RWY 13–31: H6203X75 (ASPH) S–18 MIRL IAP
   RWY 13: PAPI(P2L)—GA 3.0° TCH 40´.
   RWY 31: PAPI(P2L)—GA 3.0° TCH 40´. Tree.
RWY 04–22: H5309X75 (ASPH) S–18 0.4% up NE
RWY 09–27: 2825X60 (DIRT)
   RWY 09: Fence.
SERVICE: **FUEL** 100LL, JET A **LGT** MIRL Rwy 13–31 preset low intst;
   to incr intst actvt—CTAF.
AIRPORT REMARKS: Attended 1400–2200Z‡. Wildlife on and invof arpt.
   Glider opns on and invof arpt. 100LL, Jet–A, self serve avbl 24 hrs.
   Parallel twy adjacent Rwy 04–22 clsd exc btn Twy A and Rwy 13–31.
   105 ft AGL lgtd water twr 1168 ft SW of AER 31. Twy A northwest of
   Rwy 04–22 clsd to acft more than 18000 lb. Ldg fee waived with min
   fuel purchase.
AIRPORT MANAGER: 432-295-3906
WEATHER DATA SOURCES: AWOS–3PT 134.025 (432) 729–3364.
COMMUNICATIONS: CTAF/UNICOM 122.8
   RCO 122.5 (SAN ANGELO RADIO)
®**ALBUQUERQUE CENTER APP/DEP CON** 135.875
CLEARANCE DELIVERY PHONE: For CD if una to ctc on FSS freq, ctc
   Albuquerque ARTCC at 505-856-4561.
RADIO AIDS TO NAVIGATION: NOTAM FILE MRF.
   (VL) (DH) VORW/DME 115.9 MRF Chan 106 N30°17.90´ W103°57.29´ 312° 5.4 NM to fld. 4834/11E.
     DME unusable:
       025°–035° byd 30 NM
     VOR unusable:
       220°–225° byd 40 NM
       290°–309° byd 40 NM
       310°–320° byd 40 NM blo 11,000´
       310°–320° byd 58 NM
       321°–333° byd 40 NM
       334°–344°
       345°–130° byd 40 NM

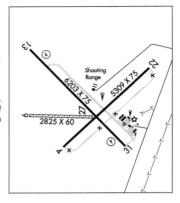

MARIAN AIRPARK (See WELLINGTON on page 444)

MARLIN (T15) 3 NE UTC–6(–5DT) N31°20.44′ W96°51.12′ HOUSTON
411   B   NOTAM FILE FTW L–19D, 21A
RWY 17–35: H3021X50 (ASPH) S–4 RWY LGTS(NSTD) IAP
  RWY 17: Trees.
  RWY 35: Thld dsplcd 90′. Fence.
  SERVICE: **LGT** Rwy 17–35 north 2900′ lgtd. Rwy thr markings not coincident with thr lgts. Vegetation obscs lgts.
AIRPORT REMARKS: Unattended. Windsock may be unrel due to trees in proximity and mast not ver.
AIRPORT MANAGER: 254-275-0051
COMMUNICATIONS: CTAF 122.9
Ⓡ **WACO APP/DEP CON** 127.65 (1200–0600Z‡)
Ⓡ **FORT WORTH CENTER APP/DEP CON** 133.3 (0600–1200Z‡)
CLEARANCE DELIVERY PHONE: For CD ctc Fort Worth ARTCC at 817-858-7584.
RADIO AIDS TO NAVIGATION: NOTAM FILE ACT.
  WACO (VH) (H) VORTACW 115.3 ACT Chan 100 N31°39.73′
    W97°16.14′   123° 28.8 NM to fld. 507/9E.
    VOR unusable:
      125°–149° byd 40 NM
      149°–159° byd 47 NM
      159°–187° byd 40 NM
      188°–198° byd 40 NM blo 12,000′
      199°–234° byd 40 NM
      235°–245° byd 50 NM
      246°–256° byd 40 NM blo 18,000′
      246°–256° byd 52 NM
      257°–267° byd 58 NM
      268°–282° byd 40 NM
      270°–335° byd 35 NM blo 4,000′
      283°–293° byd 40 NM blo 6,000′
      283°–293° byd 58 NM
      294°–330° byd 40 NM

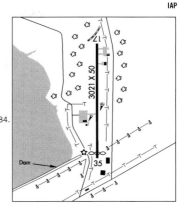

MARSHALL

HARRISON CO (ASL)(KASL)   3 SE   UTC−6(−5DT)   N32°31.23′ W94°18.47′   MEMPHIS
357   B   NOTAM FILE FTW   H−6I, L−17E
RWY 15−33: H5002X100 (ASPH)   S−20   MIRL   0.7% up NW   IAP
  RWY 15: REIL. Trees.
  RWY 33: REIL. Trees.
RWY 02−20: H3299X60 (ASPH)   S−20
  RWY 02: Trees.
  RWY 20: Trees.
SERVICE: S4   **FUEL** 100LL, JET A   **OX** 1, 2, 3, 4   **LGT** MIRL rwy 15−33
  preset low intst; to incr intst and actvt REIL rwy 15 and rwy 33—CTAF.
AIRPORT REMARKS: Attended Mon−Sat 1400−2300Z‡, Sun irregular. For
  emergency service after hours call 903−938−1394. For arpt attendant
  on Sun call 903−938−1394.
AIRPORT MANAGER: 903-938-1394
WEATHER DATA SOURCES: AWOS−3PT 118.675 (903) 938−2060.
COMMUNICATIONS: CTAF/UNICOM 122.8
Ⓡ **SHREVEPORT APP/DEP CON** 119.9
CLEARANCE DELIVERY PHONE: For CD ctc Fort Worth ARTCC at
  817-858-7584.
RADIO AIDS TO NAVIGATION: NOTAM FILE GGG.
  GREGG COUNTY (VL) (H) VORTACW 112.9   GGG   Chan 76   N32°25.07′
  W94°45.19′   068° 23.4 NM to fld. 329/7E.
  TACAN AZIMUTH unusable:
    045°−070° byd 25 NM blo 2,500′
    180°−225° byd 33 NM blo 3,500′
    258°−268° byd 26 NM blo 4,500′
    325°−340° byd 37 NM blo 2,500′
    248°−258° byd 34 NM blo 8,100′
  DME unusable:
    045°−070° byd 25 NM blo 2,500′
    180°−225° byd 33 NM blo 3,500′
    258°−268° byd 26 NM blo 4,500′
    325°−340° byd 37 NM blo 2,500′
  VOR unusable:
    138°−152° byd 40 NM
    188°−192° byd 40 NM
    210°−230° byd 40 NM

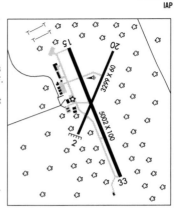

TEXAS

MASON CO (T92) 3 SE UTC−6(−5DT) N30°43.93´ W99°11.04´
1514 B NOTAM FILE SJT
RWY 18–36: H3716X50 (ASPH) LIRL
  RWY 18: Trees.
SERVICE: **FUEL** 100LL
AIRPORT REMARKS: Unattended. Deer on and invof rwy. 100LL 24 hrs self serve. For assistance call 325−347−5252 (County Sheriff). Hvy tsnt tfc Nov−Jan.
AIRPORT MANAGER: 325−347−5556
COMMUNICATIONS: CTAF 122.9
Ⓡ **HOUSTON CENTER APP/DEP CON** 132.35
CLEARANCE DELIVERY PHONE: For CD ctc Houston ARTCC at 281−230−5622.
RADIO AIDS TO NAVIGATION: NOTAM FILE AQO.
  LLANO (L) (L) VORTACW 108.2 LLO Chan 19 N30°47.78´ W98°47.24´ 251° 20.9 NM to fld. 1207/8E.

SAN ANTONIO
L−19C
IAP

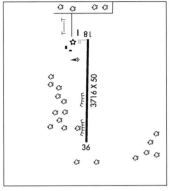

MAVERICK CO MEML INTL (See EAGLE PASS on page 300)

MAVERICK N32°52.15´ W97°02.43´ NOTAM FILE FTW.
(VH) (H) **VORW/DME** 113.1 TTT Chan 78 359° 1.7 NM to Dallas−Fort Worth Intl. 536/6E.
  All acft arriving DFW are requested to turn DME off until departure due to traffic overload of Maverick DME
  DME unusable:
    180°−190° byd 10 NM
    240°−260° byd 20 NM blo 3,500´
  VOR unusable:
    105°−110° byd 40 NM

DALLAS−FT. WORTH
COPTER
H−6H, L−17C, A

MC ALLEN INTL (MFE)(KMFE) 2 S UTC-6(-5DT) N26°10.55´ W98°14.32´
BROWNSVILLE
H-7B, L-20H
IAP, AD

107   B   AOE   Class I, ARFF Index C   NOTAM FILE MFE
RWY 14-32: H7120X150 (ASPH-GRVD) S-90, D-190, 2D-280
   PCN 285F/A/X/T   HIRL
RWY 14: MALSR. Thld dsplcd 137´. Road.
RWY 32: REIL. VASI(V2L)—GA 3.0° TCH 53´.
RWY 18-36: H2639X60 (ASPH) S-12.5 PCN 103F/A/X/T MIRL
   0.3% up N
RWY 18: PAPI(P2L)—GA 4.0° TCH 35´. Pole.
RUNWAY DECLARED DISTANCE INFORMATION
   RWY 14: TORA-7120 TODA-7120 ASDA-7120 LDA-6983
   RWY 18: TORA-2638 TODA-2638 ASDA-2638 LDA-2638
   RWY 32: TORA-7120 TODA-7120 ASDA-7120 LDA-7120
   RWY 36: TORA-2638 TODA-2638 ASDA-2638 LDA-2638
SERVICE: S4 **FUEL** 100LL, JET A **OX** 3 **LGT** When ATCT clsd actvt
   MALSR Rwy 14; HIRL Rwy 14-32; MIRL Rwy 18-36—CTAF. PAPI
   Rwy 18 OTS indefly.
NOISE: Jet or large propeller acft training prohibited (including practice
   apchs; touch and go landings and practice instrument apch
   procedures) due to noise abatement procedures effective
   0500-1200Z‡. When departing arpt fly rwy heading until reaching
   1000´ AGL before making procedure turn.
AIRPORT REMARKS: Attended 1200-0601Z‡. For svcs after hrs call
   956-686-1774. Birds on and invof airport (seasonal). For ARFF when ATCT clsd ctc Mc Allen arpt ops 956-681-1500.
   No 180° locked wheel turns on Rwy 14-32. Rwy 18-36 not avbl for acr opns. Twy C btn Twy C2 and the apch end of
   Rwy 18 not vsb fm ATCT. No acft eng run-ups on trml apn.
AIRPORT MANAGER: 956-681-1500
WEATHER DATA SOURCES: ASOS (956) 664-8212
COMMUNICATIONS: CTAF 118.5 **ATIS** 128.5 **UNICOM** 122.95
   RCO 122.2 (SAN ANGELO RADIO)
®**VALLEY APP/DEP CON** 126.55
   TOWER 118.5 (1200-0600Z‡) **GND CON** 121.8
CLEARANCE DELIVERY PHONE: For CD when ATCT is clsd ctc crp Apch at 361-299-4230.
AIRSPACE: CLASS D svc 1200-0600Z‡; other times CLASS E.
RADIO AIDS TO NAVIGATION: NOTAM FILE MFE.
   (H) (DH) VORW/DME 117.2 MFE Chan 119 N26°10.43´ W98°14.45´ at fld. 95/9E.
   MISSI NDB (LOMW) 330 MF N26°15.23´ W98°18.63´ 136° 6.1 NM to fld. 160/4E.
   ILS/DME 111.7 I-MFE Chan 54 Rwy 14. Class IE. LOM MISSI NDB. Unmonitored. DME also shared with Rwy 32.
   ILS/DME 111.7 I-LLM Chan 54 Rwy 32. Class IE. DME also shared with Rwy 14.

MC CAMEY
UPTON CO (E48) 1 SW UTC-6(-5DT) N31°07.51´ W102°13.52´
SAN ANTONIO
L-19A

2433   B   NOTAM FILE SJT
RWY 10-28: H4100X75 (ASPH) S-30 MIRL
RWY 10: PAPI(P2L). P-line. Rgt tfc.
RWY 28: PAPI(P2L). Trees.
SERVICE: **LGT** MIRL Rwy 10-28 preset to low, to incr intst—CTAF.
AIRPORT REMARKS: Unattended.
AIRPORT MANAGER: 432-413-8589
COMMUNICATIONS: CTAF 122.9
CLEARANCE DELIVERY PHONE: For CD ctc Albuquerque ARTCC at 505-856-4861.
RADIO AIDS TO NAVIGATION: NOTAM FILE FST.
   FORT STOCKTON (VH) (H) VORTACW 116.9 FST Chan 116 N30°57.13´ W102°58.54´ 064° 40.0 NM to fld.
      2893/11E.
   VOR unusable:
      020°-055° byd 20 NM blo 6,900´
      070°-086° byd 35 NM blo 6,400´
      106°-132° byd 30 NM blo 5,900´
      125°-202° byd 40 NM
      203°-213° byd 40 NM blo 18,000´
      214°-230° byd 40 NM
      245°-255° byd 40 NM
      315°-330° byd 30 NM blo 5,400´

MC GREGOR EXEC (See WACO on page 440)

TEXAS

MC KINLEY FLD (See PEARSALL on page 398)

MC KINNEY

AERO COUNTRY (T31)   4 W   UTC−6(−5DT)   N33°12.51´ W96°44.52´   DALLAS−FT WORTH
765   B   TPA—1800(1035)   NOTAM FILE FTW   COPTER
RWY 17−35: H4352X60 (ASPH−TURF)   S−6.5   MIRL(NSTD)
  RWY 17: Thld dsplcd 300´. Tree.
  RWY 35: Thld dsplcd 245´. Hill.
SERVICE: S4   **FUEL** 100LL   **LGT** MIRL Rwy 17−35 preset low intst SS−SR; to incr intst actvt—CTAF. Rwy 17−35 Nstd MIRL; only south 3002´ is lgtd.
NOISE: Noise sensitive areas around arpt. Tkf and landing only on designated runway recommended.
AIRPORT REMARKS: Unattended. Ultralight activity on and invof arpt. Watch for autos, pedestrians, signs and trash cans on twy. Arpt CLOSED to tnst flt trng, no tnst TGL. 100LL 24 hrs self−serve. Alpha twy 20´ wide, twy to fuel system 18´ wide. Steep downslope 50´ east of cntrln, south end. Rwy hold short lines 75´ from rwy centerline. 50´ trees 125´ east of rwy cntrln fm north end of rwy to 3050´ south. For drone operation requests and permission, see arpt web site www.aerocountry.org. Residential airpark, vehicles on twys. Tkof and lndg only on rwy. Other areas not maintained for acft opns. Rwy 17−35 3002 ft asph on S end, 1350 ft turf on N end. Rwy 17−35 restricted to acft less than 6500 lbs. Rwy 17 dsplcd thr only mkd on west side of rwy. The calm wind rwy is Rwy 17. No tnst prkg area. Due to rwy slope, acft not vsb fm opposite end.
AIRPORT MANAGER: 972-346-8109
COMMUNICATIONS: CTAF 122.9
CLEARANCE DELIVERY PHONE: For CD ctc Regional Apch at 972-615-2799.

MC LEAN/GRAY CO (2E7)   3 E   UTC−6(−5DT)   N35°14.81´ W100°32.81´   DALLAS−FT WORTH
2835   B   NOTAM FILE FTW   L−15C
RWY 17−35: H3225X50 (ASPH)   S−12.5   RWY LGTS(NSTD)
  RWY 17: Tree.
  RWY 35: Road.
SERVICE: **LGT** Rotating bcn OTS indefly. Rwy 17−35 Nonstd fruit jar lgts on non−frangible metal conduit. Nonstd colors.
AIRPORT REMARKS: Unattended. Wildlife on and invof arpt. No line of sight between rwy ends.
AIRPORT MANAGER: 806-662-7331
COMMUNICATIONS: CTAF 122.9
CLEARANCE DELIVERY PHONE: For CD ctc Albuquerque ARTCC at 505-856-4861.

MCCAMPBELL−PORTER (See INGLESIDE on page 346)

MCKINNEY NTL (See DALLAS on page 288)

MEMPHIS MUNI (F21)   1 NE   UTC−6(−5DT)   N34°44.38´ W100°31.78´   DALLAS−FT WORTH
2102   B   NOTAM FILE FTW   L−17A
RWY 17−35: H4670X75 (ASPH)   S−10   MIRL
  RWY 35: Trees.
RWY 08−26: 2750X70 (TURF)
  RWY 08: Road.
  RWY 26: Trees.
SERVICE: **LGT** ACTIVATE MIRL Rwy 17−35—CTAF.
AIRPORT REMARKS: Unattended. Rwy 08 and Rwy 26 thrs mrkd with red and white metal markers. Acft ldg Rwy 08, plan touchdown byd paved rwy. Rwy 08−26 trsn acrs paved Rwy 17−35 rough.
AIRPORT MANAGER: 806-259-3001
COMMUNICATIONS: CTAF 122.9
CLEARANCE DELIVERY PHONE: For CD ctc Albuquerque ARTCC at 505-856-4861.
RADIO AIDS TO NAVIGATION: NOTAM FILE CDS.
  CHILDRESS (VL) (H) VORTACW   117.0   CDS   Chan 117   N34°22.14´ W100°17.34´   322° 25.2 NM to fld. 1920/10E.

TEXAS

MENARD CO (T5Ø)   3 NW   UTC–6(–5DT)   N30°55.95′ W99°48.55′   SAN ANTONIO
1933   B   NOTAM FILE SJT   L–19B
RWY 15–33: H4100X60 (ASPH)   S–12.5   MIRL
  RWY 15: PAPI(P2L)—GA 3.0° TCH 33′. Thld dsplcd 480′. Trees.
  RWY 33: PAPI(P2L)—GA 3.0° TCH 33′. Road.
SERVICE: LGT MIRL Rwy 15–33 preset low intst, to incr intst actvt CTAF. PAPI Rwys 15 and 33 oprs consly. Rwy 15 and
  33 PAPI OTS.
AIRPORT REMARKS: Unattended. Birds on and invof arpt. Rwy 15 and Rwy 33 markings faded–barely visible.
AIRPORT MANAGER: 325-396-4789
COMMUNICATIONS: CTAF 122.9
CLEARANCE DELIVERY PHONE: For CD ctc Houston ARTCC at 281-230-5622.
RADIO AIDS TO NAVIGATION: NOTAM FILE JCT.
  JUNCTION (H) (H) VORTACW 116.0   JCT   Chan 107   N30°35.88′ W99°49.05′   353° 20.0 NM to fld. 2282/8E.
  VOR unusable:
    070°–101° byd 15 NM blo 4,900′
    070°–101° byd 30 NM blo 6,900′

MESQUITE METRO (HQZ)(KHQZ)   3 E   UTC–6(–5DT)   N32°44.82′ W96°31.83′   DALLAS–FT WORTH
447   B   NOTAM FILE HQZ   COPTER
RWY 18–36: H6000X100 (CONC)   S–70, D–100, 2D–100   MIRL   H–6H, L–17C, A
  RWY 18: RLLS. REIL. PAPI(P4L)—GA 3.0° TCH 55′. Tree.   IAP, AD
  RWY 36: RLLS. REIL. PAPI(P4L)—GA 3.0° TCH 42′. Fence.
SERVICE: S4   FUEL 100LL, JET A   OX 1   LGT ACTIVATE RLLS Rwy 18
  and Rwy 36; REIL Rwy 18 and Rwy 36; PAPI Rwy 18 and Rwy 36;
  MIRL Rwy 18–36–preset low ints, to increase ints—CTAF.
AIRPORT REMARKS: Attended 1400–0200Z‡. Birds, coyotes, and wild hogs
  on and invof arpt. 100LL self-serve avbl 24 hrs. For attendant after hrs
  call 214-244-1959.
AIRPORT MANAGER: 972-216-4130
WEATHER DATA SOURCES: AWOS–3 118.175 (972) 222-7631.
COMMUNICATIONS: CTAF 120.3   UNICOM 123.05
Ⓡ REGIONAL APP/DEP CON 125.2
  TOWER 120.3 (1300–0300Z‡)   GND CON 118.85
CLEARANCE DELIVERY PHONE: For CD when ATCT is clsd ctc Regional Apch at
  972-615-2799.
AIRSPACE: CLASS D svc 1300–0300Z‡; other times CLASS G.
RADIO AIDS TO NAVIGATION: NOTAM FILE FTW.
  COWBOY (VH) (DH) VORW/DME 116.2   CVE   Chan 109   N32°53.42′
    W96°54.24′   108° 20.7 NM to fld. 443/6E.
  VOR unusable:
    030°–035° byd 40 NM
    055°–060° byd 40 NM
    130°–140° byd 40 NM

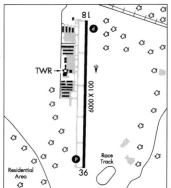

SC, 25 JAN 2024 to 21 MAR 2024

TEXAS

MEXIA–LIMESTONE CO (LXY)(KLXY)   3 SW   UTC–6(–5DT)   N31°38.47′ W96°30.87′   **HOUSTON**
545   B   NOTAM FILE LXY   H–6H, L–19D, A
RWY 18–36: H5000X75 (ASPH)   S–30   MIRL   IAP
  RWY 18: PAPI(P2L)—GA 3.0° TCH 25′.
  RWY 36: PAPI(P2L)—GA 3.0° TCH 24′.
SERVICE: S4   **FUEL** 100LL, JET A1+   **OX** 1, 2   **LGT** ACTVT: MIRL Rwy 18–36 SS–SR—CTAF. Rwy 18 PAPI OTS. Rwy 36 PAPI OTS.
AIRPORT REMARKS: Attended Mon–Fri 1400–0000Z‡. Exc hols 1500–2100Z‡. Otr times on call. For aftr hrs atndt, call AMGR during atnd hrs. 100LL self-serve fuel avbl 24 hrs.
AIRPORT MANAGER: 254-562-2857
WEATHER DATA SOURCES: AWOS–3 127.275 (254) 472–9370.
COMMUNICATIONS: CTAF/UNICOM 122.8
®**WACO APP/DEP CON** 127.65
®**FORT WORTH CENTER APP/DEP CON** 133.3
CLEARANCE DELIVERY PHONE: For CD ctc Fort Worth ARTCC at 817-858-7584.
RADIO AIDS TO NAVIGATION: NOTAM FILE FTW.
  GROESBECK (L) DME 108.8   GNL   Chan 25   N31°34.89′ W96°32.95′   026° 4.0 NM to fld. 514.
  DME unusable:
    150°–205° byd 30 NM blo 2,500′
    230°–310° byd 30 NM blo 2,400′
    345°–035° byd 35 NM blo 2,500′

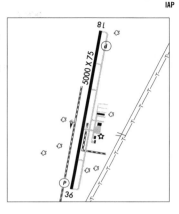

MIAMI–ROBERTS CO (3E0)   3 NE   UTC–6(–5DT)   N35°42.84′ W100°36.19′   **DALLAS–FT WORTH**
2720   NOTAM FILE FTW   L–15C
RWY 02–20: H4060X50 (ASPH)   S–12.5   LIRL
  RWY 02: Trees.
  RWY 20: Thld dsplcd 390′. Hill. Rgt tfc.
SERVICE: **LGT** Actvt LIRL Rwy 02–20—CTAF.
AIRPORT REMARKS: Unattended.
AIRPORT MANAGER: 806-868-3721
COMMUNICATIONS: CTAF 122.9
CLEARANCE DELIVERY PHONE: For CD ctc Albuquerque ARTCC at 505-856-4861.
RADIO AIDS TO NAVIGATION: NOTAM FILE BGD.
  BORGER (L) TACAN   Chan 23   BGD (108.6)   N35°48.42′ W101°22.93′   087° 38.4 NM to fld. 3130/11E.
  TACAN AZIMUTH unusable:
    220°–320° byd 10 NM blo 12,000′

MID VALLEY (See WESLACO on page 444)

MID–WAY RGNL (See MIDLOTHIAN/WAXAHACHIE on page 382)

MIDLAND

MIDLAND AIRPARK (MDD)(KMDD) 3 N UTC–6(–5DT) N32°02.19′ W102°06.09′ ALBUQUERQUE
2805 B NOTAM FILE MDD H–6G, L–6H
RWY 07–25: H5571X75 (ASPH–RFSC) S–18.5 MIRL IAP
  RWY 07: PAPI(P2L)—GA 3.0° TCH 40′. Thld dsplcd 550′. Pole.
  RWY 25: VASI(V4L)—GA 3.0° TCH 53′. Pole. Rgt tfc.
RWY 16–34: H3977X75 (ASPH) S–18.5 MIRL
  RWY 16: PAPI(P2L)—GA 3.0° TCH 40′. Road.
  RWY 34: PAPI(P2L)—GA 3.0° TCH 40′. Trees. Rgt tfc.
RUNWAY DECLARED DISTANCE INFORMATION
  RWY 07: TORA–5571 TODA–5571 ASDA–5571 LDA–5022
SERVICE: S4 **FUEL** 100LL, JET A **OX** 1, 3 **LGT** MIRL Rwy 07–25 and 16–34 preset low intst; to incr intst and actvt VASI Rwy 25; PAPI Rwy 07, 16 and 34—CTAF.
AIRPORT REMARKS: Attended Mon–Sun 1200–0200Z‡. Birds invof arpt (seasonal). For 100LL aft hrs call 432–685–7000 durg bus hrs to sched appointment. Oprs on non–paved surfaces are prohibited without 24 hr PPR.
AIRPORT MANAGER: 432-560-2200
WEATHER DATA SOURCES: AWOS–3 118.125 (432) 687–4605.
COMMUNICATIONS: CTAF/UNICOM 122.7
Ⓡ **MIDLAND APP/DEP CON** 124.6 (1200–0600Z‡)
Ⓡ **FORT WORTH CENTER APP/DEP CON** 133.1 (0600–1200Z‡)
  CLNC DEL 121.8
CLEARANCE DELIVERY PHONE: For CD when 121.8 is OTS ctc Midland Apch at 432–563–2123. When Apch clsd ctc Fort Worth ARTCC at 817–858–7584.
RADIO AIDS TO NAVIGATION: NOTAM FILE MAF.
  (L) (L) **VORTACW** 114.8 MAF Chan 95 N32°00.56′ W102°11.42′ 059° 4.8 NM to fld. 2860/11E.
  VOR unusable:
    010°–020° byd 8 NM blo 8,000′

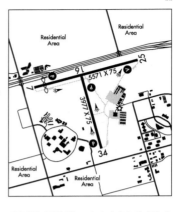

TEXAS

MIDLAND INTL AIR AND SPACE PORT (MAF)(KMAF) 8 SW UTC–6(–5DT) N31°56.55´ W102°12.12´ **SAN ANTONIO**
2872 B ARFF Index—See Remarks NOTAM FILE MAF MON Airport **H–6G, L–6H**
RWY 16R–34L: H9501X150 (ASPH–GRVD) S–160, D–200, 2S–175, **IAP, AD**
 2D–350, 2D/2D2–700 PCN 53 F/B/X/T HIRL
  RWY 16R: PAPI(P4L)—GA 3.0° TCH 50´.
  RWY 34L: REIL. PAPI(P4L)—GA 3.0° TCH 50´. Pole.
RWY 10–28: H8302X150 (ASPH–GRVD) S–160, D–200, 2S–175,
 2D–350, 2D/2D2–700 PCN 53 F/B/X/T HIRL
  RWY 10: MALSR. PAPI(P4L)—GA 3.0° TCH 54´. RVR–T
  RWY 28: MALS. PAPI(P4R)—GA 3.0° TCH 53´. RVR–R Thld dsplcd 691´.
RWY 04–22: H4605X75 (ASPH) S–30, D–60 PCN 19 F/B/X/T MIRL
  RWY 04: Pole.
  RWY 22: Road.
RWY 16L–34R: H4247X100 (ASPH) S–30, D–60 PCN 19 F/B/X/T
 MIRL 0.4% up N
  RWY 16L: Fence.
  RWY 34R: Road.

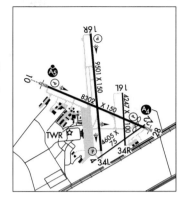

RUNWAY DECLARED DISTANCE INFORMATION
  RWY 04: TORA–4605 TODA–4605 ASDA–4605 LDA–4605
  RWY 10: TORA–8302 TODA–8302 ASDA–8177 LDA–8177
  RWY 16L: TORA–4247 TODA–4247 ASDA–4247 LDA–4247
  RWY 16R: TORA–9501 TODA–9501 ASDA–9501 LDA–9501
  RWY 22: TORA–4605 TODA–4605 ASDA–4605 LDA–4605
  RWY 28: TORA–8302 TODA–8302 ASDA–8302 LDA–7610
  RWY 34L: TORA–9501 TODA–9501 ASDA–9501 LDA–9501
  RWY 34R: TORA–4247 TODA–4247 ASDA–4247 LDA–4247
SERVICE: S4 **FUEL** 100LL, JET A, A1 **OX** 2, 4 **LGT** ATC ctl. When ATCT clsd HIRL Rwys 10–28 and 16R–34L preset on low intst. When ATCT clsd ACTVT MALSR Rwy 10; MALS Rwy 28; MIRL Rwys 04–22 and 16L–34R—CTAF.
AIRPORT REMARKS: Attended continuously. Bird activity on and invof arpt. Rwys 04–22 and 16L–34R clsd to acft over 60,000 lbs. Rwy 10–28 E 692´ CLOSED to acft over 60,000 lbs. Rwy 16R–34L 180° turn prohibited to acft 60,000 lbs and abv. Rwy 10–28 180° turn prohibited to acft 60,000 lbs or abv. Taxiways B and F north Rwy 10–28 clsd to acft over 60,000 lbs. Nmrs oil rigs invof arpt at or blw 200´ AGL. Class I, ARFF Index C. For ARFF svc btn 0600–1200Z‡ dly ctc FSS at 800–992–7433. All runup pads are ltd usage to ACFT 60000 lbs or blw. Acr ops are prohibited on Rwy 16L–34R and Rwy 04–22. Rwys 04–22 and 16L–35R are CLOSED to acft over 60,000 lbs. Oprs on non paved sfc are prohibited wo 24 hr PPR. Ldg fee. User Fee arpt.
AIRPORT MANAGER: 432-560-2200
WEATHER DATA SOURCES: ASOS (432) 561–5935 LLWAS.
COMMUNICATIONS: CTAF 118.7 **ATIS** 126.8 **UNICOM** 122.95
  RCO 122.6 (SAN ANGELO RADIO)
Ⓡ **APP/DEP CON** 124.6 (241°–136°) 121.1 (137°–240°) (1200–0600Z‡)
Ⓡ **FORT WORTH CENTER APP/DEP CON** 133.1 (0600–1200Z‡)
  TOWER 118.7 (1200–0600Z‡) **GND CON** 121.9 **CLNC DEL** 118.05
CLEARANCE DELIVERY PHONE: For CD if una to ctc on FSS freq, ctc Fort Worth ARTCC at 817-858-7584.
AIRSPACE: CLASS C svc ctc **APP CON** svc (per TWR/NOTAM 1200–0600Z‡); other times CLASS E.
VOR TEST FACILITY (VOT) 108.2
RADIO AIDS TO NAVIGATION: NOTAM FILE MAF.
  (L) (L) VORTACW 114.8 MAF Chan 95 N32°00.56´ W102°11.42´ 177° 4.0 NM to fld. 2860/11E.
   VOR unusable:
    010°–020° byd 8 NM blo 8,000´
  FARLY NDB (HW/LOM) 326 MA N31°59.29´ W102°19.51´ 104° 6.9 NM to fld. 2957/9E. NDB unmonitored when ATCT clsd.
  ILS/DME 110.3 I–MAF Chan 40 Rwy 10. Class IE. LOM FARLY NDB. ILS/DME unmonitored when ATCT clsd.
  ASR (1200–0600Z‡)

TEXAS

SKYWEST INC (7T7)   9 S   UTC–6(–5DT)   N31°51.31′ W102°04.44′   SAN ANTONIO
2805   NOTAM FILE SJT   H–6G, L–6H
RWY 16–34: H5000X42 (ASPH)   S–12.5   RWY LGTS(NSTD)   0.5% up S
  RWY 16: Brush.
  RWY 34: Brush.
RWY 06–24: H2800X45 (ASPH)
  RWY 06: Brush.
  RWY 24: Brush.
SERVICE: S6   FUEL 100LL, MOGAS   LGT Rwy 16–34 NSTD solar rwy lgts, 4 clear lgts each end.
AIRPORT REMARKS: Attended dawn–dusk. Fuel is self serve. Deer on and invof arpt. Rwy 06–24 markings NSTD due to incorrect size. Rwy 16–34 markings NSTD due to incorrect size, edge reflectors entire length.
AIRPORT MANAGER: (432) 682-5055
COMMUNICATIONS: CTAF 122.9
CLEARANCE DELIVERY PHONE: For CD ctc Midland Apch at 432-563-2123. When Apch clsd ctc Fort Worth ARTCC at 817-858-7584.
RADIO AIDS TO NAVIGATION: NOTAM FILE MAF.
  MIDLAND (L) (L) VORTACW 114.8   MAF   Chan 95   N32°00.56′ W102°11.42′   136° 11.0 NM to fld. 2860/11E.
  VOR unusable:
    010°–020° byd 8 NM blo 8,000′

MIDLOTHIAN

EAGLE'S NEST ESTATES (T56)   4 NE   UTC–6(–5DT)   N32°30.77′ W96°55.61′   DALLAS–FT WORTH
780   B   NOTAM FILE FTW   COPTER
RWY 17–35: H3216X36 (CONC)   MIRL   1.0% up N   L–17C, A
  RWY 17: REIL. TRCV(TRIL)—GA 5.0°. Thld dsplcd 332′. Trees.
  RWY 35: REIL. TRCV(TRIL)—GA 5.0°. Thld dsplcd 272′. Trees. Rgt tfc.
SERVICE: LGT ACTVT MIRL Rwy 17–35, REILs Rwy 17 and 35, TRIL Rwy 17 and 35—122.975. Rqr for a day and night lkofs/lndgs due to no line of site from opposite ends of rwy. ACTIVATE rotating beacon—CTAF.
AIRPORT REMARKS: Unattended. Rwy 17–35 strobes mark thrs. Rwy 17 has 37′ poles 401′ fm dsplcd thr, 125′ L and R of cntrln. Acft cannot be seen from opposite end of rwy. Rwy end 35: 43′ tree 200′ from dsplcd thld, 84′ right of centerline. Rwy 17 NSTD mkgs on rwy. Rwy 35 rises 12′ from pavement end to dsplcd thld.
AIRPORT MANAGER: 972-775-6403
COMMUNICATIONS: CTAF 122.975
CLEARANCE DELIVERY PHONE: For CD ctc Fort Worth ARTCC at 817-858-7584.

MIDLOTHIAN/WAXAHACHIE

MID–WAY RGNL (JWY)(KJWY)   5 SE   UTC–6(–5DT)   N32°27.50′ W96°54.75′   DALLAS–FT WORTH
727   B   NOTAM FILE JWY   COPTER
RWY 18–36: H6500X100 (ASPH)   S–30, D–90   MIRL   0.6% up N   H–6H L–17C, A
  RWY 18: REIL. PAPI(P4R)—GA 3.0° TCH 40′.   IAP
  RWY 36: PAPI(P4L)—GA 3.0° TCH 40′.
SERVICE: S4   FUEL 100LL, JET A   LGT Actvt REIL Rwy 18; MIRL Rwy 18–36—CTAF. PAPI Rwy 18 and Rwy 36 opr consly.
AIRPORT REMARKS: Attended Mar–Oct Mon–Sat 1400–0100Z‡, Sun 1500–0100Z‡. Attended Nov–Feb Mon–Sat 1400–0000Z‡, Sun 1500–0000Z‡. For fuel and services after hrs call 214–762–8286 or 972–979–5723. Glider ops on arpt.
AIRPORT MANAGER: 972-923-0080
WEATHER DATA SOURCES: AWOS–3 119.575 (972) 937–4747.
COMMUNICATIONS: CTAF/UNICOM 122.975
ⓇREGIONAL APP/DEP CON 125.2
CLEARANCE DELIVERY PHONE: For CD ctc Regional Apch at 972-615-2799.
RADIO AIDS TO NAVIGATION: NOTAM FILE FTW.
  MAVERICK (VH) (H) VORW/DME 113.1   TTT   Chan 78   N32°52.15′ W97°02.43′   159° 25.4 NM to fld. 536/6E.
  All acft arriving DFW are requested to turn DME off until departure due to traffic overload of Maverick DME
  DME unusable:
    180°–190° byd 10 NM
    240°–260° byd 20 NM blo 3,500′
  VOR unusable:
    105°–110° byd 40 NM

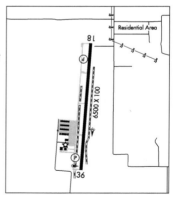

TEXAS 383

MILLSAP N32°43.57' W97°59.85' NOTAM FILE FTW. **DALLAS–FT WORTH**
(VH) (H) VORTACW 117.7 MQP Chan 124 307° 4.6 NM to Mineral Wells Rgnl. 900/9E. **H–6H, L–17C, A**
VOR unusable:
004°–009° byd 40 NM
010°–054° byd 40 NM blo 3,800'
010°–054° byd 46 NM blo 5,000'
010°–054° byd 56 NM
055°–066° byd 40 NM blo 3,800'
055°–066° byd 50 NM
230°–247° byd 40 NM
248°–258° byd 40 NM blo 3,700'
248°–258° byd 53 NM
259°–270° byd 40 NM blo 6,000'
259°–270° byd 63 NM
271°–285° byd 40 NM
312°–316° byd 40 NM
325°–340° byd 40 NM blo 3,000'
325°–340° byd 46 NM blo 5,000'
325°–340° byd 66 NM
353°–003° byd 40 NM blo 18,000'

MINEOLA WISENER FLD (3F9) 1 W UTC–6(–5DT) N32°40.60' W95°30.66' **DALLAS–FT WORTH**
430 B NOTAM FILE FTW **L–17D**
RWY 18R–36L: 3234X60 (TURF) **IAP**
RWY 18R: Trees.
RWY 36L: Trees.
RWY 18L–36R: H3203X40 (ASPH) S–10 LIRL 0.8% up N
RWY 18L: Trees.
RWY 36R: Trees.
SERVICE: S4 FUEL 100LL LGT Actvt LIRL rwy 18L/36R—CTAF. Rwy 18L–36R thr at both rwy ends mkd by two red lgts.
AIRPORT REMARKS: Attended continuously. 100LL fuel self-svc. Rwys 18L mkd thr dsplcd 140 ft. Rwy 36R mkd thr dsplcd 140 ft. Rwy 18L–36R sfc has some loose aggregate and several rough patches at thrs.
AIRPORT MANAGER: (903) 569-1929
COMMUNICATIONS: CTAF/UNICOM 122.8
®LONGVIEW APP/DEP CON 128.75 (1200–0400Z‡)
®FORT WORTH CENTER APP/DEP CON 132.85 (0400–1200Z‡)
CLEARANCE DELIVERY PHONE: For CD ctc Fort Worth ARTCC at 817-858-7584.
RADIO AIDS TO NAVIGATION: NOTAM FILE FTW.
QUITMAN (L) DME 114.0 UIM Chan 87 N32°52.83' W95°22.01' 211° 14.2 NM to fld. 517.

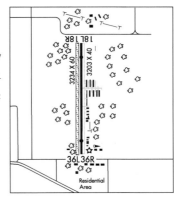

MINEOLA/QUITMAN
WOOD CO/COLLINS FLD (JDD)(KJDD) 5 N UTC–6(–5DT) N32°44.53' W95°29.79' **DALLAS–FT WORTH**
433 B NOTAM FILE JDD **L–17D**
RWY 18–36: H4002X60 (ASPH) S–12.5 MIRL 0.8% up S **IAP**
RWY 18: PAPI(P2L)—GA 3.0° TCH 30'. Trees.
RWY 36: PAPI(P2L)—GA 3.0° TCH 42'. Trees.
SERVICE: S4 FUEL 100LL, JET A LGT-Rwy 36 PAPI unusbl 6 degs left of cntrln. MIRL Rwy 18–36 preset low intst dusk–dawn; to incr intst ACTVT—CTAF. PAPI Rwy 18 and Rwy 36 opr consly.
AIRPORT REMARKS: Attended Mon–Fri 1500–2300Z‡. Wildlife invof arpt. 100LL self serve fuel.
AIRPORT MANAGER: 903-768-2100
WEATHER DATA SOURCES: AWOS–3 118.9 (903) 768–3065.
COMMUNICATIONS: CTAF/UNICOM 122.8
®LONGVIEW APP/DEP CON 128.75 (1200–0400Z‡)
®FORT WORTH CENTER APP/DEP CON 132.85 (0400–1200Z‡)
CLEARANCE DELIVERY PHONE: For CD ctc Fort Worth ARTCC at 817-858-7584.
RADIO AIDS TO NAVIGATION: NOTAM FILE FTW.
QUITMAN (L) DME 114.0 UIM Chan 87 N32°52.83' W95°22.01' 218° 10.6 NM to fld. 517.

TEXAS

MINERAL WELLS RGNL (MWL)(KMWL) 3 SE UTC–6(–5DT) N32°46.90´ W98°03.61´   DALLAS–FT WORTH
974 B NOTAM FILE MWL MON Airport   H–6H, L–17C, A
RWY 13–31: H5996X100 (ASPH) S–50, D–145, 2S–175 MIRL   IAP
  0.9% up SE
  RWY 13: PAPI(P4L)—GA 3.0° TCH 40´. Thld dsplcd 300´. Fence.
  RWY 31: PAPI(P4L)—GA 3.0° TCH 53´. Thld dsplcd 400´. Trees.
RWY 17–35: H4188X100 (ASPH) S–50, D–145, 2S–175 MIRL
  1.0% up S
  RWY 17: PAPI(P2R)—GA 3.0° TCH 43´. Trees.
  RWY 35: PAPI(P2L)—GA 4.0° TCH 46´. Thld dsplcd 286´. Trees.
SERVICE: **FUEL** 100LL, JET A **LGT** MIRL Rwy 13–31 and Rwy 17–35
  preset low intst; to incr intst ACTVT—CTAF. Rwy 35 PAPI unusable
  byd 3° left of centerline.
AIRPORT REMARKS: Attended 1200–0200Z‡. For fuel after hrs call
  940–328–7770. Rwy 13–31 rwy ends not visible from opposite end.
AIRPORT MANAGER: 940-328-7809
WEATHER DATA SOURCES: ASOS 135.075 (940) 325–2457.
COMMUNICATIONS: CTAF/UNICOM 122.725
  RCO 122.2 (FORT WORTH RADIO)
 ® **FORT WORTH CENTER APP/DEP CON** 127.0
CLEARANCE DELIVERY PHONE: For CD if una to ctc on FSS freq, ctc Fort Worth
  ARTCC at 817-858-7584.
AIRSPACE: CLASS E svc continuous.
RADIO AIDS TO NAVIGATION: NOTAM FILE FTW.
  MILLSAP (VH) (H) VORTACW 117.7   MQP   Chan 124   N32°43.57´ W97°59.85´   307° 4.6 NM to fld. 900/9E.
  VOR unusable:
    004°–009° byd 40 NM
    010°–054° byd 40 NM blo 3,800´
    010°–054° byd 46 NM blo 5,000´
    010°–054° byd 56 NM
    055°–066° byd 40 NM blo 3,800´
    055°–066° byd 50 NM
    230°–247° byd 40 NM
    248°–258° byd 40 NM blo 3,700´
    248°–258° byd 53 NM
    259°–270° byd 40 NM blo 6,000´
    259°–270° byd 63 NM
    271°–285° byd 40 NM
    312°–316° byd 40 NM
    325°–340° byd 40 NM blo 3,000´
    325°–340° byd 46 NM blo 5,000´
    325°–340° byd 66 NM
    353°–003° byd 40 NM blo 18,000´
  ILS/DME 109.55 I–VMH Chan 32(Y) Rwy 31. Class IE. Unmonitored.

MISSI N26°15.23´ W98°18.63´ NOTAM FILE MFE.   BROWNSVILLE
  NDB (LOMW) 330 MF 136° 6.1 NM to Mc Allen Intl. 160/4E.

SC, 25 JAN 2024 to 21 MAR 2024

TEXAS

MONAHANS

ROY HURD MEML (E01) 1 SW UTC−6(−5DT) N31°34.95´ W102°54.54´   SAN ANTONIO
2615   B   NOTAM FILE SJT   L−19A
RWY 12−30: H4268X75 (ASPH)   S−15   MIRL   IAP
  RWY 12: PAPI(P2L)—GA 3.0° TCH 24´. P-line.
  RWY 30: Tree.
RWY 01−19: H2922X75 (ASPH)   S−15   MIRL
  RWY 01: Tank.
  RWY 19: Tree.
SERVICE: S2   **FUEL** 100LL, JET A   **LGT** Actvt PAPI Rwy 12; MIRL Rwy 01−19 & 12−30—CTAF.
AIRPORT REMARKS: Attended 1300−2300Z‡. Wildlife and birds on and invof arpt. Down slope off end of Rwy 30. Rwy 19 apch−325 AGL. 2953 MSL antenna, 1.45 NM NE of arpt.
AIRPORT MANAGER: 432-940-2633
COMMUNICATIONS: CTAF/UNICOM 122.8
®**FORT WORTH CENTER APP/DEP CON** 133.1
CLEARANCE DELIVERY PHONE: For CD ctc Fort Worth ARTCC at 817-858-7584.
RADIO AIDS TO NAVIGATION: NOTAM FILE INK.
  WINK (VH) (H) VORTACW 112.1   INK   Chan 58   N31°52.49´ W103°14.63´   125° 24.5 NM to fld. 2860/11E.
  VOR unusable:
    256°−267° byd 40 NM blo 10,000´
    256°−267° byd 58 NM blo 18,000´
    268°−280° byd 40 NM
    281°−291° byd 40 NM blo 24,000´
    292°−305° byd 40 NM
    306°−320° byd 111 NM
    306°−320° byd 40 NM blo 15,000´

MONTGOMERY CO   N30°21.11´ W95°24.87´   HOUSTON
RCO 122.2 (MONTGOMERY COUNTY RADIO)   L−19D

MOORE CO (See DUMAS on page 298)

MORTON

COCHRAN CO (F85) 2 E UTC−6(−5DT) N33°43.88´ W102°44.10´   ALBUQUERQUE
3747   B   NOTAM FILE FTW
RWY 04−22: H2710X60 (ASPH)   S−12   MIRL
  RWY 04: Thld dsplcd 160´. Road.
  RWY 22: VASI(V2L)—GA 3.0° TCH 11´. Road.
RWY 17−35: H1775X39 (ASPH)   S−12
  RWY 35: Road.
AIRPORT REMARKS: Unattended. Rwy 17−35 clsd night. 4171´ MSL, 399´ AGL twr, 1.5 nm SW.
AIRPORT MANAGER: 806-266-5508
COMMUNICATIONS: CTAF 122.9
CLEARANCE DELIVERY PHONE: For CD ctc Fort Worth ARTCC at 817-858-7584.

MOUNT PLEASANT RGNL (OSA)(KOSA)   3 S   UTC–6(–5DT)   N33°05.81′ W94°57.71′   MEMPHIS
364   B   NOTAM FILE OSA   H–6I, L–17D
RWY 17–35: H6004X100 (ASPH)   S–30   MIRL   0.4% up N   IAP
  RWY 17: REIL. PAPI(P4L)—GA 3.0° TCH 40′.
  RWY 35: REIL. PAPI(P4L)—GA 3.0° TCH 45′. Trees.
SERVICE: S4   FUEL 100LL, JET A   LGT REIL Rwy 17 and 35, MIRL Rwy
  17–35 pre-set on low SS–SR. To actvt daytime and incr intst—CTAF.
  PAPI Rwy 17 and 35 opr consly.
AIRPORT REMARKS: Attended 1300–0000Z‡. Deer and wildlife on and invof
  arpt. For Jet A aft hrs call 903–575–4004. 100LL avbl 24 hrs self serv.
  No line of sight between rwy ends.
AIRPORT MANAGER: 903–575–4020
WEATHER DATA SOURCES: AWOS–3 119.775 (903) 575–4027.
COMMUNICATIONS: CTAF/UNICOM 122.7
®FORT WORTH CENTER APP/DEP CON 132.025
CLEARANCE DELIVERY PHONE: For CD ctc Fort Worth ARTCC at
  817–858–7584.
RADIO AIDS TO NAVIGATION: NOTAM FILE FTW.
  QUITMAN (L) DME 114.0   UIM   Chan 87   N32°52.83′
  W95°22.01′   058° 24.2 NM to fld. 517.
• • • • • • • • • •
HELIPAD H1: H44X44 (CONC)

MOUNT SELMAN
TARRANT FLD (6X0)   2 N   UTC–6(–5DT)   N32°05.85′ W95°17.69′   DALLAS–FT WORTH
590   NOTAM FILE FTW
RWY 12–30: 2700X30 (TURF)   1.8% up SE
  RWY 12: Trees.
  RWY 30: Trees.
AIRPORT REMARKS: Unattended. RC model acft ops on rwy near windsock and twy. 2059′ MSL lgtd antenna 2.75 miles SW
  of arpt. Rwy 30 has 25′ mkd p–line acrs apch at thr. Rwy 12–30 NE end of rwy rough.
AIRPORT MANAGER: 903–574–1760
COMMUNICATIONS: CTAF 122.9
CLEARANCE DELIVERY PHONE: For CD ctc Fort Worth ARTCC at 817–858–7584.

MOUNT VERNON
FRANKLIN CO (F53)   2 NW   UTC–6(–5DT)   N33°12.92′ W95°14.23′   DALLAS–FT WORTH
412   B   NOTAM FILE FTW   L–17D
RWY 13–31: H3900X60 (ASPH)   S–12.5   MIRL   0.4% up SE   IAP
  RWY 13: PAPI(P2L)—GA 3.0° TCH 37′. Trees.
  RWY 31: PAPI(P2L)—GA 3.0° TCH 38′. Trees.
AIRPORT REMARKS: Unattended.
AIRPORT MANAGER: (903) 588–2643
COMMUNICATIONS: CTAF/UNICOM 123.0
®FORT WORTH CENTER APP/DEP CON 132.025
CLEARANCE DELIVERY PHONE: For CD ctc Fort Worth ARTCC at 817–858–7584.
RADIO AIDS TO NAVIGATION: NOTAM FILE FTW.
  QUITMAN (L) DME 114.0   UIM   Chan 87   N32°52.83′ W95°22.01′   018° 21.1 NM to fld. 517.

MUFIN   N32°53.59′ W97°22.40′   NOTAM FILE FTW.   DALLAS–FT WORTH
NDB (LOMW) 365   FT   165° 4.4 NM to Fort Worth Meacham Intl. 744/8E.   COPTER

TEXAS

MULESHOE MUNI (2T1)   4 SE   UTC–6(–5DT)   N34°11.11′ W102°38.47′   ALBUQUERQUE
3779   B   NOTAM FILE FTW   H–6G, L–6H
  RWY 07–25: H5100X60 (ASPH)   S–12.5   MIRL   IAP
    RWY 07: PAPI(P2L)—GA 3.0° TCH 40′. Pole.
    RWY 25: PAPI(P2L)—GA 3.0° TCH 40′.
  SERVICE: **FUEL** 100LL   **LGT** Actvt PAPI Rwy 07 and 25; MIRL Rwy 07–25—122.8.
  AIRPORT REMARKS: Unattended. Deer on invof arpt. Fuel: 100LL: For emergency fuel call 806–272–4569, Central Dispatch.
  AIRPORT MANAGER: 806-272-4528
  COMMUNICATIONS: CTAF 122.9
  ®**FORT WORTH CENTER APP/DEP CON** 126.45
  CLEARANCE DELIVERY PHONE: For CD ctc Fort Worth ARTCC at 817-858-7584.
  RADIO AIDS TO NAVIGATION: NOTAM FILE FTW.
    TEXICO (VH) (H) VORTACW 112.2   TXO   Chan 59   N34°29.71′ W102°50.38′   141° 21.0 NM to fld. 4060/11E.
    VOR unusable:
      095°–100° byd 40 NM
      120°–130° byd 40 NM
      210°–223° byd 40 NM blo 15,000′
      224°–251° byd 40 NM
      252°–262° byd 40 NM blo 18,000′
      263°–272° byd 40 NM blo 18,000′
      273°–283° byd 40 NM blo 6,000′
      273°–283° byd 46 NM blo 7,000′
      273°–283° byd 59 NM
      284°–319° byd 40 NM
      320°–035° byd 40 NM
    TACAN AZIMUTH unusable:
      222°–232°

MUNDAY MUNI (37F)   3 E   UTC–6(–5DT)   N33°28.12′ W99°35.17′   DALLAS–FT WORTH
1474   B   NOTAM FILE FTW   L–17B
  RWY 17–35: H3200X50 (ASPH)   S–4   LIRL
    RWY 35: P–line.
  SERVICE: **LGT** ACTVT LIRL 17–35—CTAF.
  AIRPORT REMARKS: Attended Mon–Fri 1400–2200Z‡.
  AIRPORT MANAGER: 940-422-4331
  COMMUNICATIONS: CTAF 122.9
  CLEARANCE DELIVERY PHONE: For CD ctc Fort Worth ARTCC at 817-858-7584.
  RADIO AIDS TO NAVIGATION: NOTAM FILE FTW.
    GUTHRIE (L) DME 114.5   GTH   Chan 92   N33°46.70′ W100°20.17′   116° 41.9 NM to fld. 1941.

MUSTANG BEACH   (See PORT ARANSAS on page 401)

TEXAS

NACOGDOCHES A L MANGHAM JR RGNL (OCH)(KOCH) 3 SW UTC−6(−5DT) N31°34.67′ HOUSTON
W94°42.61′ H−6I, L−19E
343 B NOTAM FILE OCH IAP
RWY 18−36: H5000X75 (ASPH) S−23.6 MIRL
  RWY 18: REIL. PAPI(P2L)—GA 3.0° TCH 37′. Trees.
  RWY 36: MALSR. PAPI(P2L)—GA 3.0° TCH 53′. Trees.
SERVICE: S4 **FUEL** 100LL, JET A+ **LGT** Dusk−dawn, MIRL Rwy 18−36
  preset low intst. To incr intst & ACTVT MALSR Rwy 36; REIL Rwy
  18—CTAF. **FUEL** 24 hr self serve 100LL and Jet A+ with major cc; fuel
  serve 100LL & Jet A+ avbl fm truck drg bus hrs or with arranged aft
  hrs call out. Arpt tel nr is 936−560−9567; otr nrs posted at arpt.
AIRPORT REMARKS: Attended 1400−2300Z‡. Birds on and invof arpt. 35 ft
  AGL ant 400 ft west of cntrln Rwy 18−36. Rwy 18−36 no line of sight
  btn rwy ends. NOTE: See Special Notices—Model Aircraft Activity.
AIRPORT MANAGER: 936-560-9567
WEATHER DATA SOURCES: AWOS−3PT 135.625 (936) 564−5074.
COMMUNICATIONS: CTAF/UNICOM 123.0
®**HOUSTON CENTER APP/DEP CON** 125.375
CLEARANCE DELIVERY PHONE: For CD ctc Houston ARTCC at 281-230-5622.
RADIO AIDS TO NAVIGATION: NOTAM FILE LFK.
  LUFKIN (VH) (H) VORTACW 112.1 LFK Chan 58 N31°09.75′
  W94°43.01′ 356° 24.9 NM to fld. 207/5E.
  TACAN AZIMUTH unusable:
    260°−275° byd 30 NM
    275°−260° byd 30 NM blo 2,500′
  DME unusable:
    260°−275° byd 30 NM
    275°−260° byd 30 NM blo 2,500′
  VOR unusable:
    305°−312° byd 40 NM
    313°−323° byd 40 NM blo 2,300′
    313°−323° byd 66 NM
    324°−330° byd 40 NM
  NADOS NDB (MHW/LOM) 253 OC N31°29.13′ W94°43.21′ 360° 5.5 NM to fld. 360/5E. NOTAM FILE OCH.
  ILS/DME 111.5 I−OCH Chan 52 Rwy 36. Class IA. LOM NADOS NDB. DME unmonitored. Glideslope unusable
    byd 5° left of course. LOC unusable inside 0.3 NM fm thld. Autopilot coupled approach NA below 740 MSL.
COMM/NAV/WEATHER REMARKS: High intsty student pilot trng in and arnd arpt. Mnt 122.75 for student areas of actvty.

NADOS N31°29.13′ W94°43.21′ NOTAM FILE OCH. HOUSTON
  NDB (MHW/LOM) 253 OC 360° 5.5 NM to Nacogdoches A L Mangham Jr Rgnl. 360/5E. L−19E, 21A

NAS JRB FORT WORTH N32°46.28′ W97°26.36′ NOTAM FILE NFW. DALLAS−FT WORTH
  (L) TACAN 108.7 NFW Chan 24 at Fort Worth NAS JRB (Carswell Fld). 631/4E. H−6H, L−17C, A
    TACAN unavbl 0500−1300Z‡
    No NOTAM MP: 1330−1530Z‡ Wed
    TACAN AZIMUTH unusable:
      180°−320° byd 20 NM blo 4,000′
    DME unusable:
      180°−320° byd 20 NM blo 4,000′

TEXAS

NAVASOTA MUNI (60R)   2 SW   UTC–6(–5DT)   N30°22.03´ W96°06.78´   HOUSTON
229   B   NOTAM FILE CXO   H–7C, L–19D, 21A
RWY 17–35: H5003X75 (ASPH)   S–30   MIRL   0.7% up N   IAP
 RWY 17: REIL. PAPI(P2L)—GA 3.0° TCH 45´. Tree.
 RWY 35: REIL. PAPI(P2L)—GA 3.0° TCH 46´. Trees.
SERVICE: S4   **FUEL** 100LL, JET A   **LGT** ACTVT PAPI Rwy 17 and Rwy 35;
  MIRL Rwy 17–35—123.3.
AIRPORT REMARKS: Unattended. 16 ft mkd pwr line Rwy 17, 1300 ft dstc;
  50 ft pwr line, 2500 ft dstc.
AIRPORT MANAGER: 936-825-6450
WEATHER DATA SOURCES: AWOS–3PT 120.925 (936) 825–0798.
COMMUNICATIONS: CTAF 122.9
®**HOUSTON APP/DEP CON** 134.3
CLEARANCE DELIVERY PHONE: For CD ctc Houston Apch at 281-443-5844 to
  cnl IFR call 281-443-5888.
RADIO AIDS TO NAVIGATION: NOTAM FILE CXO.
  (VH) (H) VORW/DME 115.9   TNV   Chan 106   N30°17.31´
    W96°03.49´   321° 5.5 NM to fld. 247/8E.
   DME unusable:
    005°–072° byd 18 NM blo 3,000´
    073°–077° byd 18 NM blo 2,000´
    078°–106° byd 18 NM blo 3,000´
   VOR unusable:
    000°–039° byd 18 NM blo 3,000´
    025°–085° byd 40 NM
    040°–090°
    086°–145° byd 18 NM blo 6,000´
    091°–145° byd 35 NM
    146°–359° byd 18 NM blo 2,000´
    215°–230° byd 40 NM
    240°–255° byd 40 NM blo 2,100´
    240°–255° byd 52 NM
    256°–260° byd 40 NM
    261°–271° byd 39 NM blo 5,000´
    261°–271° byd 59 NM blo 7,000´
    261°–271° byd 82 NM
    272°–328° byd 40 NM
    329°–339° byd 40 NM blo 5,000´
    329°–339° byd 61 NM blo 6,000´
    329°–339° byd 83 NM
    340°–005° byd 40 NM

NAVASOTA   N30°17.31´ W96°03.49´   NOTAM FILE CXO.   HOUSTON
 (VH) (H) VORW/DME 115.9   TNV   Chan 106   321° 5.5 NM to Navasota Muni. 247/8E.   H–7C, L–19D, 21A, GOMW
   DME unusable:
    005°–072° byd 18 NM blo 3,000´
    073°–077° byd 18 NM blo 2,000´
    078°–106° byd 18 NM blo 3,000´
   VOR unusable:
    000°–039° byd 18 NM blo 3,000´
    025°–085° byd 40 NM
    040°–090°
    086°–145° byd 18 NM blo 6,000´
    091°–145° byd 35 NM
    146°–359° byd 18 NM blo 2,000´
    215°–230° byd 40 NM
    240°–255° byd 40 NM blo 2,100´
    240°–255° byd 52 NM
    256°–260° byd 40 NM
    261°–271° byd 39 NM blo 5,000´
    261°–271° byd 59 NM blo 7,000´
    261°–271° byd 82 NM
    272°–328° byd 40 NM
    329°–339° byd 40 NM blo 5,000´
    329°–339° byd 61 NM blo 6,000´
    329°–339° byd 83 NM
    340°–005° byd 40 NM

TEXAS

NEW BRAUNFELS NTL (BAZ)(KBAZ) 4 E UTC–6(–5DT) N29°42.35′ W98°02.59′ SAN ANTONIO
658 B NOTAM FILE BAZ H–7B, L–19C
RWY 13–31: H6503X100 (ASPH) S–30, D–60 MIRL IAP, AD
  RWY 13: MALS. REIL. PAPI(P4L)—GA 3.0° TCH 50′.
  RWY 31: PAPI(P4L)—GA 3.0° TCH 50′.
RWY 17–35: H5364X100 (ASPH) S–25 MIRL
  RWY 17: Thld dsplcd 522′.
  RWY 35: P–line.
SERVICE: S4 **FUEL** 100LL, JET A, A+ **LGT** Actvt MIRL Rwy 13–31,
  Rwy 17–35—CTAF.
AIRPORT REMARKS: Attended 1300–0100Z‡. Birds invof arpt. 100LL 24 hr
  self svc. For full serve fuel call 830–221–4290; aft hrs call
  830–221–4100. High per mil acft oprg at Randolph AFB AUX
  (Seguin).
AIRPORT MANAGER: 830-221-4290
WEATHER DATA SOURCES: ASOS 119.325 (830) 629–7979.
COMMUNICATIONS: CTAF 127.05 **ATIS** 119.325 **UNICOM** 122.7
Ⓡ **SAN ANTONIO APP CON** 124.35
Ⓡ **SAN ANTONIO DEP CON** 128.05
TOWER 127.05 (1300–0100Z‡) **GND CON** 120.175
CLNC DEL 134.75 When BAZ twr clsd.
CLEARANCE DELIVERY PHONE: For CD when ATCT is clsd ctc sat Apch at
  210-805-5516.
AIRSPACE: CLASS D svc 1300–0100Z‡; other times CLASS G.
RADIO AIDS TO NAVIGATION: NOTAM FILE SAT.
SAN ANTONIO (VH) (H) VORTACW 116.8 SAT Chan 115 N29°38.64′ W98°27.68′ 072° 22.2 NM to fld. 1159/8E.
  VOR unusable:
    018°–022° byd 40 NM
    028°–032° byd 40 NM
    342°–347° byd 40 NM
    355°–002° byd 40 NM blo 18,000′

NEWMAN N31°57.11′ W106°16.35′ NOTAM FILE ABQ. EL PASO
  (VL) (H) VORTACW 112.4 EWM Chan 71 210° 8.2 NM to Biggs AAF (Fort Bliss). 4041/12E. H–4L, L–6F
  TACAN AZIMUTH unusable:
    220°–255° byd 25 NM blo 12,000′
  DME unusable:
    220°–255° byd 25 NM blo 12,000′
  VOR unusable:
    001°–005° byd 40 NM
    030°–034° byd 40 NM
    042°–065° byd 40 NM
    066°–084° byd 40 NM blo 18,000′
    085°–130° byd 40 NM
    243°–260° byd 40 NM
    261°–279° byd 40 NM blo 18,000′
    280°–290° byd 40 NM
    304°–332° byd 40 NM

SC, 25 JAN 2024 to 21 MAR 2024

TEXAS

NEWTON MUNI (61R)   3 NE   UTC–6(–5DT)   N30°53.04´ W93°44.55´   **HOUSTON**
322   B   NOTAM FILE CXO   L–19E, 21B
RWY 14–32: H4000X60 (ASPH)   S–12.5   LIRL   0.9% up NW
  RWY 14: Trees.
  RWY 32: Trees.
AIRPORT REMARKS: Unattended.
AIRPORT MANAGER: 409-379-5691
COMMUNICATIONS: CTAF/UNICOM 122.8
  RCO 122.2 (MONTGOMERY COUNTY RADIO)
CLEARANCE DELIVERY PHONE: For CD ctc Polk Apch at 337-531-2352.
RADIO AIDS TO NAVIGATION: NOTAM FILE LFK.
  LUFKIN (VH) (H) VORTACW 112.1   LFK   Chan 58   N31°09.75´
  W94°43.01´   103° 52.9 NM to fld. 207/5E.
  TACAN AZIMUTH unusable:
    260°–275° byd 30 NM
    275°–260° byd 30 NM blo 2,500´
  DME unusable:
    260°–275° byd 30 NM
    275°–260° byd 30 NM blo 2,500´
  VOR unusable:
    305°–312° byd 40 NM
    313°–323° byd 40 NM blo 2,300´
    313°–323° byd 66 NM
    324°–330° byd 40 NM

NORTH TEXAS RGNL/PERRIN FLD (See SHERMAN/DENISON on page 425)

NUECES CO (See ROBSTOWN on page 410)

ODESSA–SCHLEMEYER FLD (ODO)(KODO)   5 NE   UTC–6(–5DT)   N31°55.28´ W102°23.23´   **SAN ANTONIO**
3004   B   NOTAM FILE ODO   H–6G, L–6H
RWY 11–29: H6200X100 (ASPH)   S–30   MIRL   IAP
  RWY 11: MALS. PAPI(P4L)—GA 3.0° TCH 40´. Trees.
  RWY 29: MALS. PAPI(P4L)—GA 3.0° TCH 40´. P–line.
RWY 02–20: H5703X75 (ASPH)   S–14   MIRL   0.9% up NE
  RWY 02: PVASI(PSIL)—GA 3.0° TCH 38´. Road.
  RWY 20: PVASI(PSIL)—GA 3.0° TCH 38´. P–line.
RWY 16–34: H5003X75 (ASPH)   S–14   MIRL   0.6% up N
  RWY 16: PAPI(P2L)—GA 4.0° TCH 49´. Antenna.
  RWY 34: PAPI(P2L)—GA 4.0° TCH 39´. P–line.
SERVICE: S4   FUEL 100LL, JET A   OX 4   LGT MIRL Rwy 02–20,
  11–29, 16–34 preset low intst; to incr intst actvt—CTAF.
AIRPORT REMARKS: Attended 1200–0200Z‡. Wildlife actvy incrd. For fuel
  after hours call 432-367-5881 or self serve. 340´ AGL obstruction
  twr 2.2 NM SW of arpt lgts OTS.
AIRPORT MANAGER: 432-367-5881
WEATHER DATA SOURCES: ASOS 119.275 (432) 363-9719.
COMMUNICATIONS: CTAF/UNICOM 123.0
®MIDLAND APP/DEP CON 124.6 (1200–0600Z‡) CLNC DEL 121.7
®FORT WORTH CENTER APP/DEP CON 133.1 (0600–1200Z‡)
CLEARANCE DELIVERY PHONE: For CD when 121.7 is OTS ctc Midland Apch
  at 432-563-2123. When Apch clsd ctc Fort Worth ARTCC at 817-858-7584.
RADIO AIDS TO NAVIGATION: NOTAM FILE MAF.
  MIDLAND (L) (L) VORTACW 114.8   MAF   Chan 95   N32°00.56´ W102°11.42´   231° 11.3 NM to fld. 2860/11E.
  VOR unusable:
    010°–020° byd 8 NM blo 8,000´

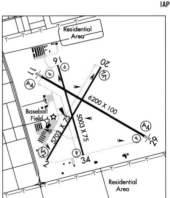

OLD HOPPE PLACE (See AGUA DULCE on page 239)

OLDHAM CO (See VEGA on page 438)

TEXAS

OLNEY MUNI (ONY)(KONY) 3 SW UTC−6(−5DT) N33°21.05′ W98°49.15′   **DALLAS−FT WORTH**
1275   B   NOTAM FILE FTW   **H−6H, L−17B**
    RWY 17−35: H5101X75 (ASPH−RFSC)   S−43, D−50, 2D−84   MIRL   **IAP**
    0.3% up N
      RWY 17: VASI(V2L)—GA 3.0° TCH 29′. Trees.
      RWY 35: VASI(V2R)—GA 3.0° TCH 37′. Road.
    RWY 04−22: H5100X75 (ASPH−RFSC)   S−43, D−50, 2D−84
      RWY 04: Trees.
      RWY 22: P−line.
    RWY 13−31: H5099X75 (ASPH)   S−43, D−50, 2D−84   0.6% up NW
      RWY 13: Road.
      RWY 31: Road.
    SERVICE: **FUEL** 100LL   **LGT** MIRL Rwy 17−35 preset to low intst, to incr
    intst ACTVT—CTAF.
    AIRPORT REMARKS: Attended Mon−Fri 1400−2300Z‡. Ocnl aerial ag opns.
    Self svc fuel avbl. Rwy 13−31 cntr 1600 ft by 75 ft overlaid with no
    grass encroachment. Rwy 13−31 first third and last third of rwy extsv
    cracks w/vegetation growing through. Loose stones.
    AIRPORT MANAGER: 940-564-5616
    COMMUNICATIONS: CTAF/UNICOM 122.8
    ®**FORT WORTH CENTER APP/DEP CON** 133.5
    CLEARANCE DELIVERY PHONE: For CD ctc Fort Worth ARTCC at 817-858-7584.
    RADIO AIDS TO NAVIGATION: NOTAM FILE SPS.
      WICHITA FALLS (H) (H) VORTACW 112.7   SPS   Chan 74   N33°59.24′ W98°35.61′   187° 39.8 NM to fld. 1133/10E.

ORANGE CO (ORG)(KORG) 3 SW UTC−6(−5DT) N30°04.11′ W93°48.24′   **HOUSTON**
13   B   NOTAM FILE ORG   **H−7D, L−19E, 21B, GOMW**
    RWY 04−22: H5500X75 (ASPH)   S−27   MIRL   **IAP**
      RWY 04: REIL. PAPI(P2L)—GA 3.0° TCH 22′. Trees.
      RWY 22: REIL. PAPI(P2L)—GA 3.0° TCH 21′. Trees.
    RWY 13−31: 3000X50 (TURF)
      RWY 13: Tree.
      RWY 31: Trees.
    SERVICE: S4 **FUEL** 100LL, JET A   **LGT** MIRL Rwy 04−22 preset low
    intst; to incr intst and ACTVT REIL Rwy 04 and 22—CTAF.
    AIRPORT REMARKS: Attended 1300−2300Z‡. Rwy 13−31 CLOSED indefly.
    Rwy 13−31 rwy not mntnd, rwy sfc rough, deep ruts, not suitable for
    acft. Trees obstruct primary sfc Rwy 13−31. 3 ft open drainage culvert
    at thr, 31 ft both sides.
    AIRPORT MANAGER: (409) 882-7861
    WEATHER DATA SOURCES: AWOS−3 118.975 (409) 670−9591.
    COMMUNICATIONS: CTAF/UNICOM 122.8
    ®**HOUSTON APP/DEP CON** 121.3
    CLEARANCE DELIVERY PHONE: For CD ctc Houston Apch at 281-443-5844 to
    cnl IFR call 281-443-5888.
    RADIO AIDS TO NAVIGATION: NOTAM FILE BPT.
      BEAUMONT (L) (L) VORW/DME 114.5   BPT   Chan 92   N29°56.76′
      W94°00.97′   049° 13.3 NM to fld. 6/7E.

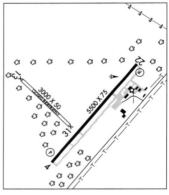

TEXAS

ORANGE GROVE NALF (NOG)(KNOG) NAF 8 N UTC–6(–5DT) N27°53.81´ W98°02.61´ BROWNSVILLE
257 B TPA—See Remarks NOTAM FILE SJT Not insp. H–7B, L–20H
RWY 13–31: H8001X198 (PEM) PCN 19 R/C/W/T MIRL DIAP, AD
RWY 01–19: H8000X198 (PEM) PCN 25 R/C/W/T MIRL
ARRESTING GEAR/SYSTEM
  RWY 13 HOOK E28(B) (1500').   HOOK E28(B) (1501'). **RWY 31**
  RWY 01 HOOK E28(B) (1500').   HOOK E28(B) (1500'). **RWY 19**
SERVICE: **LGT** OLS GS 3.25°. **MILITARY**— **FUEL** J8, JAA **FLUID** SP PRESAIR **OIL** O–156 **TRAN ALERT** No tran maint or svc avbl. Refuel CNATRA acft only.
MILITARY REMARKS: Attended continuously. Opr hrs by NOTAM in support of TRAWING–2 flt opr. **RSTD** CNATRA use only except in emerg, NALF admin. DSN 876–6140. NAS Kingsville Base OPS DSN 876–6108. **CAUTION** Student jet training in vicinity during opr hr. Bird and large wildlife hazard. **TFC PAT** TPA—Jet break altitude 1300(1043). Use ldg/taxi lgt on final apch during VFR condition.
COMMUNICATIONS: ATIS 254.35 (Mon–Thu 1330–2130Z‡. Fri 1330–1930Z‡)
®**KINGSVILLE APP/DEP CON** 119.9 300.4 (1345–0600Z‡ Mon–Thu; 1345–2345Z‡ Fri; clsd Sat, Sun and hol exc by NOTAM, hrs subj to chg)
®**HOUSTON CENTER APP/DEP CON** 128.15 350.3 (0500–1300Z‡ Mon–Thu; 2200–1300Z‡ Fri; 24 Sat, Sun and hol by NOTAM)
  TOWER 128.4 318.85 281.425 (318.85 Ldg Signal Officer) (Mon–Fri 1330–2130Z‡, clsd Sat, Sun and hol by NOTAM; hrs subject to change in support of TRAWING–2 flt opr.) **GND CON** 229.4 **CLNC DEL** 229.4
  PMSV METRO 225.6 (At Kingsville NAS)
AIRSPACE: CLASS D svc 1330–2130Z‡ Mon–Fri, clsd Sat, Sun and hol by NOTAM; other times CLASS G.
RADIO AIDS TO NAVIGATION: NOTAM FILE SJT.
  (T) TACAN Chan 63 NOG (133.6) N27°53.72´ W98°02.56´ at fld. 236/5E.
    TACAN opers 1300–2130Z‡ Mon–Fri
  KINGSVILLE (H) TACAN Chan 125 NQI (117.8) N27°29.95´ W97°48.34´ 328° 27.0 NM to fld. 45/4E.
  ILS/DME 110.5 I–NOG Chan 42 Rwy 13. Class IE. ILS scheduled for maintenance 3rd Tue each Month.
COMM/NAV/WEATHER REMARKS: Radar see Terminal FLIP for Radar Minima.

OX RANCH (See UVALDE on page 437)

OZONA MUNI (OZA)(KOZA) 1 N UTC–6(–5DT) N30°44.11´ W101°12.13´ SAN ANTONIO
2377 B NOTAM FILE SJT H–6G, L–19A
RWY 16–34: H6003X75 (ASPH) S–30 MIRL 0.4% up N IAP
  RWY 16: PAPI(P4L)—GA 3.0° TCH 39´. Trees.
  RWY 34: PAPI(P4L)—GA 3.0° TCH 35´. Pole.
SERVICE: S4 **FUEL** 100LL, JET A **LGT** MIRL Rwy 16–34 preset low intst; to incr intst actvt—CTAF.
AIRPORT REMARKS: Attended Mon–Fri 1400–2300Z‡. 100LL aft hrs call 325–226–2628.
AIRPORT MANAGER: 325-392-2030
WEATHER DATA SOURCES: AWOS–3PT 118.425 (325) 392–2051.
COMMUNICATIONS: CTAF/UNICOM 122.8
®**HOUSTON CENTER APP/DEP CON** 125.75
CLEARANCE DELIVERY PHONE: For CD ctc Houston ARTCC at 281-230-5622.
RADIO AIDS TO NAVIGATION: NOTAM FILE SJT.
  SAN ANGELO (VH) (H) VORTACW 115.1 SJT Chan 98 N31°22.50´ W100°27.29´ 215° 54.3 NM to fld. 1886/10E.
  VOR unusable:
    111°–190° byd 40 NM
    191°–201° byd 40 NM blo 6,000´
    191°–201° byd 49 NM
    202°–255° byd 40 NM blo 7,000´
    202°–255° byd 71 NM
    256°–289° byd 40 NM blo 4,400´
    256°–289° byd 53 NM
    290°–314° byd 40 NM blo 5,000´
    290°–314° byd 46 NM
    315°–352° byd 40 NM

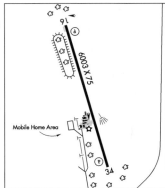

TEXAS

PADUCAH

DAN E RICHARDS MUNI (3F6)   1 E   UTC–6(–5DT)   N34°01.66′ W100°16.92′   DALLAS–FT WORTH
1860   B   NOTAM FILE FTW   L–17B
RWY 18–36: H3186X50 (ASPH)   S–8.5   MIRL   0.3% up N   IAP
  RWY 36: Berm.
SERVICE: LGT MIRL Rwy 18–36 preset low ints; to increase ints ACTVT—CTAF.
AIRPORT REMARKS: Unattended. Rwy 18, 10 ft drop off 60 ft dstc. Rwy 18–36 marked as 17–35.
AIRPORT MANAGER: (806) 492-3613
COMMUNICATIONS: CTAF 122.9
®FORT WORTH CENTER APP/DEP CON 133.5
CLEARANCE DELIVERY PHONE: For CD ctc Fort Worth ARTCC at 817-858-7584.
RADIO AIDS TO NAVIGATION: NOTAM FILE FTW.
  GUTHRIE (L) DME 114.5   GTH   Chan 92   N33°46.70′ W100°20.17′   010° 15.2 NM to fld. 1941.

• • • • • • • • • • • •

HELIPAD H1: H25X25 (ASPH)
HELIPORT REMARKS: H1 not maintained. Loose gravel and grass encroachment on surface.

PALACIOS MUNI   (PSX)(KPSX)   3 NW   UTC–6(–5DT)   N28°43.65′ W96°15.06′   HOUSTON
14   B   NOTAM FILE PSX   H–7C, L–20I, 21A, GOMW
RWY 08–26: H5001X150 (CONC)   S–46, D–58, 2D–105   IAP
  RWY 08: Trees.
  RWY 26: Trees.
RWY 13–31: H5001X150 (CONC)   S–46, D–58, 2D–105   MIRL
  RWY 13: REIL.
  RWY 31: REIL. Tree.
RWY 18–36: H5001X75 (CONC)   S–46, D–58, 2D–105
  RWY 18: Tree.
  RWY 36: Tree.
SERVICE: LGT MIRL Rwy 13–31 preset on low intst, to incr intst ACTVT—CTAF.
AIRPORT REMARKS: Unattended. Rwy 08–26 and Rwy 18–36 tall vegetation on rwy. Rwy 13–31 mkgs faded. Vegetation on twy. Courtesy car avbl.
AIRPORT MANAGER: 361-230-5394
WEATHER DATA SOURCES: ASOS 118.025 (361) 972–0101.
COMMUNICATIONS: CTAF/UNICOM 122.8
  RCO 122.2 (MONTGOMERY COUNTY RADIO)
®HOUSTON CENTER APP/DEP CON 135.05
CLEARANCE DELIVERY PHONE: For CD if una to ctc on FSS freq, ctc Houston ARTCC at 281-230-5622.
AIRSPACE: CLASS E.
RADIO AIDS TO NAVIGATION: NOTAM FILE PSX.
  (VH) (H) VORTACW 117.3   PSX   Chan 120   N28°45.87′ W96°18.37′   119° 3.7 NM to fld. 16/8E.

TEXAS

PALESTINE MUNI (PSN)(KPSN)   4 NW   UTC–6(–5DT)   N31°46.78´ W95°42.38´   **HOUSTON**
423   B   NOTAM FILE PSN   H–6I, L–19D
RWY 18–36: H5005X100 (ASPH)   S–45, D–70, 2D–135   MIRL   IAP
  RWY 18: PAPI(P4L)—GA 3.0° TCH 45´. Tree.
  RWY 36: REIL. PAPI(P4L)—GA 3.0° TCH 35´. Trees.
RWY 09–27: H4002X75 (ASPH)   S–45, D–70, 2D–135   MIRL
  0.9% up W
  RWY 09: Trees.
  RWY 27: Trees.
SERVICE: FUEL 100LL, JET A   **LGT** MIRL Rwy 18–36 preset low intst
  dusk–dawn; to incr intst ACTVT—CTAF. Rwy 36 REIL OTS indefly.
AIRPORT REMARKS: Attended Mon–Sat 1400–2300Z‡. For svc aft hrs call
  903–724–2225. Rwy 09–27 clsd daily SS–SR, perm.
AIRPORT MANAGER: 903–723–0111
WEATHER DATA SOURCES: AWOS–3PT 118.025 (903) 729–3641.
COMMUNICATIONS: CTAF/UNICOM 122.7
Ⓡ **FORT WORTH CENTER APP/DEP CON** 135.25
CLEARANCE DELIVERY PHONE: For CD ctc Fort Worth ARTCC at
  817-858-7584.
RADIO AIDS TO NAVIGATION: NOTAM FILE FTW.
  FRANKSTON (L) (L) VORW/DME 111.4   FZT   Chan 51   N32°04.48´
  W95°31.85´   201° 19.8 NM to fld. 305/6E.
  VOR portion unusable:
    270°–293° byd 5 NM blo 8,000´
    293°–295° byd 25 NM blo 3,500´
    295°–340° byd 20 NM

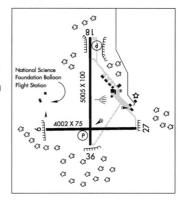

PALMER
DALLAS SOUTH PORT (T13)   3 N   UTC–6(–5DT)   N32°28.64´ W96°41.13´   **DALLAS–FT WORTH**
474   NOTAM FILE FTW
RWY 17–35: 3800X100 (TURF)
  RWY 17: Fence.
  RWY 35: Trees.
SERVICE: FUEL 100LL
AIRPORT REMARKS: Unattended. 100LL self–serve fuel. Rwy 35 starts 300´ frm road. Mkd w/ white tires. Windsock at rwy
  end, 100´ R. Second windsock midfield.
AIRPORT MANAGER: (214) 926-3457
COMMUNICATIONS: CTAF 122.9
CLEARANCE DELIVERY PHONE: For CD ctc Regional Apch at 972-615-2799.

PALO DURO   (See AMARILLO on page 242)

TEXAS

PAMPA

PERRY LEFORS FLD (PPA)(KPPA)   5 NW   UTC–6(–5DT)   N35°36.78′ W100°59.78′   DALLAS–FT WORTH
3245   B   NOTAM FILE PPA   H–6G, L–15B
RWY 17–35: H5862X100 (ASPH)   S–16   MIRL   IAP
  RWY 17: PAPI(P2L)—GA 3.0° TCH 45′.   Road.
  RWY 35: PAPI(P2L)—GA 3.0° TCH 45′.
RWY 05–23: H4500X75 (ASPH)   S–17   MIRL
  RWY 23: P–line.
SERVICE: S4   **FUEL** 100LL, JET A1+   **LGT** Dusk–Dawn. MIRL Rwy
  05–23 and 17–35 preset low intst; to incr intst actvt—CTAF.
AIRPORT REMARKS: Attended 1300–0100Z‡ hours. Antelope on and invof
  rwys. For fuel after hours call 806–395–1117, 806–662–8209. No
  line of sight btn both rwy ends.
AIRPORT MANAGER: (806) 669-8007
WEATHER DATA SOURCES: AWOS–3 118.725 (806) 669–1333.
COMMUNICATIONS: CTAF/UNICOM 122.7
®**ALBUQUERQUE CENTER APP/DEP CON** 127.85
CLEARANCE DELIVERY PHONE: For CD ctc Albuquerque ARTCC at
  505-856-4861.
RADIO AIDS TO NAVIGATION: NOTAM FILE BGD.
  BORGER (L) TACAN   Chan 23   BGD (108.6)   N35°48.42′
  W101°22.93′   111° 22.2 NM to fld. 3130/11E.
  TACAN AZIMUTH unusable:
    220°–320° byd 10 NM blo 12,000′

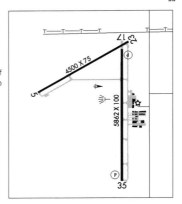

PAMPA   BPC   N35°53.36′ W101°01.81′/2772   DALLAS–FT WORTH
AWOS–3PT 118.1 (806) 665–5504 AWOS–3PT associated with Mesa Vista Ranch airport TX13.   L–15B

PANDE   N35°08.79′ W101°48.33′   NOTAM FILE AMA.   DALLAS–FT. WORTH
  NDB (LOMW) 251   AM   040° 6.6 NM to Rick Husband Amarillo Intl. 3609/8E. NDB unmonitored when   L–15B
  ATCT clsd.

PANHANDLE–CARSON CO (T45)   1 NE   UTC–6(–5DT)   N35°21.70′ W101°21.91′   DALLAS–FT WORTH
3454   B   NOTAM FILE FTW   L–15B
RWY 17–35: H4404X60 (ASPH)   S–12.5   MIRL   IAP
  RWY 17: Road.
  RWY 35: Road. Rgt tfc.
SERVICE: **FUEL** 100LL   **LGT** MIRL Rwy 17–35 preset low ints, to increase
  ints ACTIVATE–123.5.
AIRPORT REMARKS: Unattended.
AIRPORT MANAGER: 806-537-3517
COMMUNICATIONS: CTAF/UNICOM 122.7
®**AMARILLO APP/DEP CON** 119.5 (1200–0600Z‡)
®**ALBUQUERQUE CENTER APP/DEP CON** 127.85 (0600–1200Z‡)
CLEARANCE DELIVERY PHONE: For CD ctc Albuquerque ARTCC at
  505-856-4861.
RADIO AIDS TO NAVIGATION: NOTAM FILE FTW.
  (H) (H) VORTACW 116.6   PNH   Chan 113   N35°14.10′
  W101°41.94′   057° 18.1 NM to fld. 3595/8E.

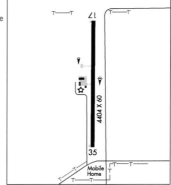

PANHANDLE   N35°14.10′ W101°41.94′   NOTAM FILE FTW.   DALLAS–FT WORTH
  (H) (H) VORTACW 116.6   PNH   Chan 113   at Rick Husband Amarillo Intl. 3595/8E.   H–6G, L–15B

PANOLA CO–SHARPE FLD (See CARTHAGE on page 268)

SC, 25 JAN 2024 to 21 MAR 2024

PARIS

COX FLD (PRX)(KPRX)   6 E   UTC-6(-5DT)   N33°38.20′ W95°27.05′   DALLAS–FT WORTH
548   B   NOTAM FILE PRX   H-6I, L-17D
RWY 17–35: H6002X100 (ASPH)   S-30   MIRL   IAP
  RWY 17: PAPI(P4L)—GA 3.0° TCH 40′.
  RWY 35: PAPI(P4L)—GA 3.0° TCH 40′. Trees.
RWY 03–21: H4624X150 (CONC)   S-26   0.3% up NE
  RWY 03: Trees.
  RWY 21: Trees.
RWY 14–32: H4624X150 (CONC)   S-26
  RWY 14: Trees.
RUNWAY DECLARED DISTANCE INFORMATION
  RWY 03: TORA–4624   TODA–4624   ASDA–4624   LDA–4624
  RWY 14: TORA–4624   TODA–4624   ASDA–4624   LDA–4624
  RWY 17: TORA–6002   TODA–6002   ASDA–6002   LDA–6002
  RWY 21: TORA–4624   TODA–4624   ASDA–4624   LDA–4624
  RWY 32: TORA–4624   TODA–4624   ASDA–4624   LDA–4624
  RWY 35: TORA–6002   TODA–6002   ASDA–6002   LDA–6002
SERVICE: S2   **FUEL** 100LL, JET A   **LGT** MIRL Rwy 17–35 preset low intst dusk–dawn; to incr intst actvt—CTAF. PAPI Rwy 17 and 35 oprs consly.
AIRPORT REMARKS: Attended Mon–Sat 1400–2300Z‡. For arpt attendant durg bus hrs call 903–784–4648. Arpt attndd 1400–0100Z durg dalgt savings time. 100LL fuel avbl 24 hr self serve. Jet A fuel avbl at nights call 903–784–1071. Rwy 03–21 and Rwy 14–32 not avbl for acr opns with more than 30 psgr seats. Rwy 14–32 no line of sight btn rwy ends. Twy lgts from trml apron to Rwy 17–35 on midfield twy only. Rwy 03–21 rwy cond not mntnd. Vegetation growing through cracks. Rwy 03 pavement mkgs faded. Rwy 21 pavement mkgs faded.
AIRPORT MANAGER: 903–784–4648
WEATHER DATA SOURCES: AWOS–3PT 119.675 (903) 737–8784.
COMMUNICATIONS: CTAF/UNICOM 122.975
  PARIS RCO 122.2 (FORT WORTH RADIO)
  ®**FORT WORTH CENTER APP/DEP CON** 124.875
  CLEARANCE DELIVERY PHONE: For CD if una to ctc on FSS freq, ctc Fort Worth ARTCC at 817-858-7584.
RADIO AIDS TO NAVIGATION: NOTAM FILE PRX.
  PARIS (L) (L) VORW/DME 113.6   PRX   Chan 83   N33°32.54′ W95°26.90′   352° 5.6 NM to fld. 510/7E.
• • • • • • • • • • • • • • • • • • •
HELIPAD H1: H40X40 (CONC)

PARKER CO (See WEATHERFORD on page 443)

PEARLAND

SKYWAY MANOR (T79)   3 W   UTC-6(-5DT)   N29°33.34′ W95°19.63′   HOUSTON
55   NOTAM FILE CXO   COPTER
RWY 17–35: 2525X70 (TURF)
  RWY 17: P–line.
  RWY 35: Trees.
AIRPORT REMARKS: Attended irregularly. Nmrs objects in prim sfc entr rwy len—bldgs, fences, trees and brush. No tgls. Rwy 17–35 soft when wet.
AIRPORT MANAGER: 281–723–8403
COMMUNICATIONS: CTAF 122.9
  CLEARANCE DELIVERY PHONE: For CD ctc Houston Apch at 281-443-5844 to cnl IFR call 281-443-5888.

PEARLAND RGNL (See HOUSTON on page 341)

TEXAS

PEARSALL

MC KINLEY FLD (T3Ø) 4 S UTC–6(–5DT) N28°49.34´ W99°06.54´   **SAN ANTONIO**
586 NOTAM FILE SJT   H–7B, L–20H
RWY 13–31: H5027X60 (ASPH) S–15 LIRL(NSTD) 0.6% up NW   IAP
  RWY 13: Thld dsplcd 168´. Road.
  RWY 31: Thld dsplcd 154´. P–line.
SERVICE: FUEL JET A   LGT Rwy 13–31 NSTD LIRL; spacing 20 ft fm edge and 300 ft btn lgts.
AIRPORT REMARKS: Attended continuously. Rwy 13–31 markings faded. Dsplcd thrs not lgtd, 4705 ft avbl ngt. Lndg fee.
AIRPORT MANAGER: 830-334-7306
COMMUNICATIONS: CTAF/UNICOM 122.8
®HOUSTON CENTER APP/DEP CON 134.6
CLEARANCE DELIVERY PHONE: For CD ctc Houston ARTCC at 281-230-5622.
RADIO AIDS TO NAVIGATION: NOTAM FILE COT.
  COTULLA (VL) (H) VORTACW 115.8   COT   Chan 105   N28°27.72´
    W99°07.11´   352° 21.6 NM to fld. 522/9E.
  VOR unusable:
    008°–032° byd 40 NM

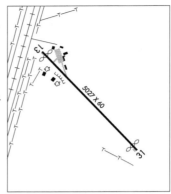

PECOS MUNI (PEQ)(KPEQ) 2 SW UTC–6(–5DT) N31°22.94´ W103°30.64´   **EL PASO**
2613 B NOTAM FILE PEQ   H–6G, L–6J
RWY 14–32: H6236X80 (ASPH) S–25, D–37 MIRL   IAP
  RWY 14: PAPI(P2L)—GA 3.0° TCH 40´. Brush.
  RWY 32: PAPI(P2L)—GA 3.0° TCH 40´.
RWY 09–27: H5953X80 (ASPH) S–25, D–37 MIRL 0.3% up W
  RWY 27: P–line.
SERVICE: S4 FUEL 100LL, JET A1+   LGT MIRL Rwy 14–32 preset low ints, to incr ints and ACTIVATE MIRL Rwy 09–27—CTAF. PAPI Rwy 14 and Rwy 32 opr continuously. Rwy 14 PAPI OTS.
AIRPORT REMARKS: Attended continuously. For fuel after hours contact UNICOM 122.8 or call 432-447-2488.
AIRPORT MANAGER: (512) 422-5396
WEATHER DATA SOURCES: AWOS–3 118.175 (432) 445–3867.
COMMUNICATIONS: CTAF/UNICOM 122.8
  RCO 122.1R 116.5T (SAN ANGELO RADIO)
®ALBUQUERQUE CENTER APP/DEP CON 135.875
CLEARANCE DELIVERY PHONE: For CD if una to ctc on FSS freq, ctc Albuquerque ARTCC at 505-856-4561.
RADIO AIDS TO NAVIGATION: NOTAM FILE PEQ.
  (VL) (L) VOR/DME 116.5   PEQ   Chan 112   N31°28.16´
    W103°34.49´   137° 6.2 NM to fld. 2650/11E.
  VOR unusable:
    254°–260° byd 40 NM

PEROT FLD/FORT WORTH ALLIANCE (See FORT WORTH on page 311)

PERRY LEFORS FLD (See PAMPA on page 396)

TEXAS

PERRYTON OCHILTREE CO (PYX)(KPYX)   3 E   UTC–6(–5DT)   N36°24.78′ W100°45.09′   **WICHITA**
2918   B   NOTAM FILE PYX   H–6G, L–15C
   RWY 17–35: H5701X75 (ASPH)   S–12.5   MIRL   **IAP**
     RWY 17: PAPI(P4L)—GA 3.0° TCH 40′. Pole.
     RWY 35: VASI(V2L)—GA 3.5° TCH 23′. Road.
   RWY 04–22: 3280X144 (TURF)
     RWY 22: P–line.
   SERVICE: S4   **FUEL** 100LL, JET A1+   **LGT** Dusk–dawn. MIRL Rwy 17–35 preset low intst; to incr intst and actvt PAPI 17 —CTAF.
   AIRPORT REMARKS: Attended Mon–Sat 1400–2300Z‡, Sun 1900–2300Z‡. For 100LL fuel aft hrs call 806–435–4226 or 806–228–5573. Rwy 04–22 thrs mkd with buried plates. Sfc rough with lrg animal holes. Rwy 04–22 south 1000′ clsd indefly. 2280′ avbl.
   AIRPORT MANAGER: 806-435-4226
   WEATHER DATA SOURCES: AWOS–3 118.175 (806) 435–9963.
   COMMUNICATIONS: CTAF/UNICOM 122.8
  ® **KANSAS CITY CENTER APP/DEP CON** 126.95
   CLEARANCE DELIVERY PHONE: For CD ctc Kansas City ARTCC at 913-254-8508.
   RADIO AIDS TO NAVIGATION: NOTAM FILE PYX.
     NDB (MHW) 266   PYX   N36°24.74′ W100°44.86′   at fld. 2917/7E.

PINCK   N33°16.99′ W97°11.78′   NOTAM FILE DTO.   **DALLAS–FT WORTH**
   NDB (LOMW) 257   DT   178° 4.9 NM to Denton Enterprise. 739/4E.

PINELAND MUNI (T24)   1 SW   UTC–6(–5DT)   N31°14.01′ W93°58.91′   **HOUSTON**
260   B   NOTAM FILE CXO   L–19E, 21A
   RWY 17–35: H3700X75 (ASPH)   S–14   MIRL
     RWY 17: Trees.
     RWY 35: Trees.
   SERVICE: **LGT** ACTIVATE MIRL Rwy 17–35—CTAF.
   AIRPORT REMARKS: Unattended. Extensive pavement cracking with vegetation growing thru. Loose aggregate on rwy. Rwy 17–35 no markings.
   AIRPORT MANAGER: 409-584-2390
   COMMUNICATIONS: CTAF/UNICOM 122.8
   CLEARANCE DELIVERY PHONE: For CD ctc Houston ARTCC at 281-230-5622.
   RADIO AIDS TO NAVIGATION: NOTAM FILE LFK.
     LUFKIN (VH) (H) VORTACW 112.1   LFK   Chan 58   N31°09.75′ W94°43.01′   078° 38.1 NM to fld. 207/5E.
       TACAN AZIMUTH unusable:
         260°–275° byd 30 NM
         275°–260° byd 30 NM blo 2,500′
       DME unusable:
         260°–275° byd 30 NM
         275°–260° byd 30 NM blo 2,500′
       VOR unusable:
         305°–312° byd 40 NM
         313°–323° byd 40 NM blo 2,300′
         313°–323° byd 66 NM
         324°–330° byd 40 NM

PLAINS

YOAKUM CO (F98) 1 NW UTC–6(–5DT) N33°13.03´ W102°49.81´   **ALBUQUERQUE**
3705   B   NOTAM FILE FTW   **H–6G, L–6H**
  RWY 03–21: H5001X75 (ASPH)   MIRL   0.6% up NE   **IAP**
    RWY 21: Pole.
  RWY 17–35: H3924X60 (ASPH)   S–12.5   MIRL
    RWY 17: P–line.
    RWY 35: Pole.
  SERVICE: **FUEL** 100LL   **LGT** Dusk–Dawn. MIRL Rwy 03–21 and 17–35 preset low intst; to incr intst actvt—CTAF.
  AIRPORT REMARKS: Attended irregularly. 100LL fuel self serve.
  AIRPORT MANAGER: 806-592-1267
  COMMUNICATIONS: CTAF 122.9
  ®**FORT WORTH CENTER APP/DEP CON** 132.6
  CLEARANCE DELIVERY PHONE: For CD ctc Fort Worth ARTCC at 817-858-7584.
  RADIO AIDS TO NAVIGATION: NOTAM FILE HOB.
    HOBBS (L) (L) **VORTACW** 111.0   HOB   Chan 47   N32°38.29´ W103°16.16´   021° 41.2 NM to fld. 3664/11E.

PLAINVIEW

HALE CO (PVW)(KPVW) 1 S UTC–6(–5DT) N34°10.09´ W101°43.04´   **DALLAS–FT WORTH**
3374   B   NOTAM FILE PVW   **H–6G, L–6H**
  RWY 04–22: H5997X100 (ASPH)   S–27   MIRL   **IAP**
    RWY 04: REIL. VASI(V4L)—GA 3.5° TCH 51´. Pole.
    RWY 22: REIL. VASI(V4L)—GA 3.5° TCH 54´. Bldg.
  RWY 13–31: H4000X100 (ASPH)   S–27   MIRL
    RWY 13: P–line.
    RWY 31: Road.
  SERVICE: **FUEL** 100LL, JET A1+   **LGT** REIL Rwy 04–22; MIRL Rwy 04–22 and Rwy 13–31 SS–SR preset to low intst. To incr intst actvt–CTAF. VASI Rwy 22—CTAF. VASI Rwy 04 opr consly. Unusbl byd 7 deg left of rwy cntrln.
  AIRPORT REMARKS: Attended 1400–0000Z‡. Unatnd Thanksgiving and Christmas. No line of sight to Rwy 13–31 fm Rwy end 22.
  AIRPORT MANAGER: 806-293-4121
  WEATHER DATA SOURCES: AWOS–3 119.675 (806) 291–8679.
  COMMUNICATIONS: CTAF/UNICOM 123.0
    RCO 122.2 (FORT WORTH RADIO)
  ®**LUBBOCK APP/DEP CON** 119.2
    CLNC DEL 118.2
  CLEARANCE DELIVERY PHONE: For CD if una to ctc on FSS freq, ctc Fort Worth ARTCC at 817-858-7584.
  RADIO AIDS TO NAVIGATION: NOTAM FILE PVW.
    PLAINVIEW (VL) (L) **VORW/DME** 112.9   PVW   Chan 76   N34°05.17´ W101°47.41´   025° 6.1 NM to fld. 3400/11E.
  COMM/NAV/WEATHER REMARKS: IFR departures ctc Lubbock Clnc Del on the ramp at Hale Co via freq 121.7.

PLEASANTON MUNI (PEZ)(KPEZ) 3 W UTC–6(–5DT) N28°57.25´ W98°31.20´   **SAN ANTONIO**
430   B   NOTAM FILE SJT   **L–19C**
  RWY 16–34: H4000X75 (ASPH)   S–4   MIRL   0.8% up NW   **IAP**
    RWY 16: PAPI(P2L)—GA 4.0° TCH 25´. Thld dsplcd 405´. Road.
    RWY 34: PAPI(P2L)—GA 3.0° TCH 35´. Fence.
  SERVICE: **FUEL** 100LL, JET A   **LGT** MIRL Rwy 16–34 preset low intst, to incr intst ACTVT—CTAF.
  AIRPORT REMARKS: Unattended. For services call 830–569–3155. 100LL self serve.
  AIRPORT MANAGER: (830) 569-3155
  WEATHER DATA SOURCES: AWOS–3 118.575 (830) 569–5749.
  COMMUNICATIONS: CTAF/UNICOM 122.7
  ®**SAN ANTONIO APP CON** 118.05
  ®**SAN ANTONIO DEP CON** 125.7 **CLNC DEL** 121.375
  CLEARANCE DELIVERY PHONE: For CD if una to ctc via freq, ctc San Antonio Apch at 210-805-5516.
  RADIO AIDS TO NAVIGATION: NOTAM FILE SJT.
    THREE RIVERS (L) (L) **VORTAC** 111.4   THX   Chan 51   N28°30.30´ W98°09.03´   316° 33.2 NM to fld. 266/8E.

POETRY FLYING RANCH (See ROCKWALL on page 412)

TEXAS

PONDER

HICKS (74T) 2 E UTC–6(–5DT) N33°10.98′ W97°15.28′   DALLAS–FT WORTH
725   NOTAM FILE FTW   H–6H, L–17C
RWY 17–35: 2364X90 (TURF)
  RWY 17: Bldg. Rgt tfc.
  RWY 35: Fence.
AIRPORT REMARKS: Unattended. Tfc in the pat shall remain at or below 1,300 ft MSL. Rwy defined by mowing. 30 ft trees, 40 ft R and L of rwy cntrln. 6 ft washout along W side of rwy. Rwy rough and uneven. Arpt fenced. Gates locked. No public ingress or egress.
AIRPORT MANAGER: 940-479-2114
COMMUNICATIONS: CTAF 122.9
CLEARANCE DELIVERY PHONE: For CD ctc Regional Apch at 972-615-2799.

PORT ARANSAS

MUSTANG BEACH (RAS)(KRAS) 2 SW UTC–6(–5DT) N27°48.71′ W97°05.33′   BROWNSVILLE
5   B   NOTAM FILE RAS   L–20I, 21A, GOMW
RWY 12–30: H3482X70 (ASPH)   MIRL   IAP
  RWY 12: PAPI(P2L)—GA 3.0° TCH 20′.
  RWY 30: PAPI(P2L)—GA 3.2° TCH 22′. Tree.
SERVICE: **FUEL** 100LL
AIRPORT REMARKS: Attended irregularly. Parachute Jumping. 100LL 24 hr self serv. Rwy 12–30: rwy sfc seal–peastones. Considerable amt of loose stones on rwy & twy. Rwy 12 has a –3 ft drop off near end of rwy, Rwy 30 has a 3 ft ditch 180 ft from end of rwy. Rwy 30 29 ft power line 1133 ft from thld left and right of centerline. 48 ft power line 1791 ft from thld left and right of centerline. Overnight tiedown fee.
AIRPORT MANAGER: 361-749-4008
WEATHER DATA SOURCES: AWOS–3 118.425 (361) 749-0537.
COMMUNICATIONS: CTAF 122.9
 Ⓡ**CORPUS APP/DEP CON** 125.4
CLEARANCE DELIVERY PHONE: For CD ctc Corpus Christi Apch at 361-299-4230.
RADIO AIDS TO NAVIGATION: NOTAM FILE CRP.
  CORPUS CHRISTI (VH) (H) VORTACW 115.5   CRP   Chan 102   N27°54.23′ W97°26.69′   097° 19.7 NM to fld. 60/9E.
  TACAN AZIMUTH & DME unusable:
    024°–036° byd 35 NM blo 1,700′
    037°–023° byd 35 NM blo 2,000′
    265°–275°
  VOR unusable:
    340°–005° byd 40 NM blo 7,000′
    340°–005° byd 84 NM
    Byd 30 NM blo 1,500′
  TACAN AZIMUTH unusable:
    080°–085° byd 30 NM

PORT ISABEL–CAMERON CO (PIL)(KPIL) 10 NW UTC–6(–5DT) N26°09.97´ W97°20.75´ **BROWNSVILLE**
19 B NOTAM FILE PIL   H–7C, L–20H, 21A
RWY 13–31: H8001X200 (ASPH–CONC) S–105, D–135, 2D–230 MIRL   IAP
  RWY 13: REIL. PAPI(P2L)—GA 2.0° TCH 27´.
  RWY 31: REIL. PAPI(P2L)—GA 3.0° TCH 41´.
RWY 08–26: H5317X150 (CONC) S–50, D–60, 2D–110
  RWY 08: Fence.
  RWY 26: Trees.
RWY 03–21: H5000X150 (ASPH–CONC) S–30, D–45, 2D–90
  RWY 03: Brush.
  RWY 21: Tree.
RWY 17–35: H4200X75 (ASPH–CONC) S–30, D–45, 2D–90
  RWY 35: Tower.
SERVICE: S2 **FUEL** 100LL, JET A **OX** 2 **LGT** Rwy 13 REIL OTS. Rwy 31 REIL OTS.
AIRPORT REMARKS: Attended 1400–2300Z‡. Parachute Jumping. 100LL & Jet A avbl self serve & full serv. Rwy 03–21 pavement has heavy grass encroachment. Rwy 08–26 rough pavement. Rwy has heavy grass encroachment. No position holding markings on numerous twys apchng rwy intersections. Loose gravel/pavement at intersection of Rwy 13 and northeast twy connecting Rwy 13 and Rwy 21. Rwy 03–21 and Rwy 08–26 markings faded.
AIRPORT MANAGER: (956) 761-3700
WEATHER DATA SOURCES: ASOS 118.525 (956) 233–1954.
COMMUNICATIONS: CTAF/UNICOM 122.8
Ⓡ **VALLEY APP/DEP CON** 119.5
  CLNC DEL 119.2
CLEARANCE DELIVERY PHONE: For CD ctc Corpus Christi Apch at 361-299-4230.
RADIO AIDS TO NAVIGATION: NOTAM FILE BRO.
  BROWNSVILLE (H) (H) VORTACW 116.3 BRO Chan 110 N25°55.44´ W97°22.52´ 357° 14.6 NM to fld. 10/9E.
  TACAN AZIMUTH unusable:
    360°–290° byd 24 NM
  DME unusable:
    360°–290° byd 24 NM
  VOR unusable:
    271°–290° byd 20 NM
    320°–335°
    360°–270° byd 24 NM

TEXAS

PORT LAVACA

CALHOUN CO (PKV)(KPKV) 3 NW UTC−6(−5DT) N28°39.20´ W96°40.96´   **HOUSTON**
32   B   NOTAM FILE PKV   H−7C, L−20I, 21A, GOMW
   RWY 14−32: H5004X75 (ASPH)   S−26   MIRL   **IAP**
      RWY 14: PAPI(P2L)—GA 3.0° TCH 45´. Road.
      RWY 32: PAPI(P2L)—GA 3.0° TCH 45´. Road. Rgt tfc.
   RWY 05−23: 2432X60 (TURF)
      RWY 05: Tree.
      RWY 23: Thld dsplcd 428´.
   SERVICE: S4   **FUEL** 100LL, JET A   **LGT** ACTVT MIRL Rwy 14−32—CTAF.
   AIRPORT REMARKS: Attended 1400−2300Z‡. 100LL and Jet A avbl 24 hrs
      self serve. Jet A also avbl by truck. RC model acft opr at Rwy 05 end.
   AIRPORT MANAGER: 361-552-1228
   WEATHER DATA SOURCES: AWOS−3 118.275 (361) 552−3060.
   COMMUNICATIONS: CTAF/UNICOM 122.8
   ®**HOUSTON CENTER APP/DEP CON** 135.05
   CLEARANCE DELIVERY PHONE: For CD ctc Houston ARTCC at 281-230-5622.
   RADIO AIDS TO NAVIGATION: NOTAM FILE PSX.
      PALACIOS (VH) (H) VORTACW 117.3   PSX   Chan 120   N28°45.87´
      W96°18.37´   244° 20.9 NM to fld. 16/8E.

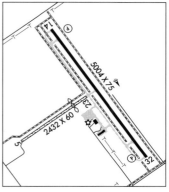

PORT MANSFIELD

CHARLES R JOHNSON (T05) 1 NW UTC−6(−5DT) N26°33.61´ W97°26.36´   **BROWNSVILLE**
10   B   NOTAM FILE SJT   L−20H, 21A
   RWY 12−30: H3200X50 (ASPH)   S−21   MIRL
      RWY 12: P−line.
      RWY 30: P−line.
   SERVICE: **LGT** MIRL Rwy 12−30 preset low intst; to increase intst ACTVT—CTAF.
   AIRPORT REMARKS: Unattended. Harbor superintendent´s ofc attended 1400−2250Z‡. Deer & birds on & invof arpt. Rwy 12
      and Rwy 30 rwy mkgs discolored. Fee for ovngt tie down.
   AIRPORT MANAGER: 956-944-2325
   COMMUNICATIONS: CTAF 122.9
   CLEARANCE DELIVERY PHONE: For CD ctc Corpus Christi Apch at 361-299-4230.
   RADIO AIDS TO NAVIGATION: NOTAM FILE HRL.
      HARLINGEN (L) (L) VORW/DME 113.65   HRL   Chan 83(Y)   N26°13.75´ W97°39.14´   025° 22.9 NM to fld. 32/5E.

PORTLAND

HUNT (9R5) 2 NW UTC−6(−5DT) N27°53.20´ W97°20.98´   **BROWNSVILLE**
40   NOTAM FILE SJT
   RWY 14L−32R: H2650X20 (ASPH)   S−9   0.6% up NW
      RWY 14L: P−line. Rgt tfc.
      RWY 32R: Brush.
   RWY 14R−32L: 1400X60 (TURF−GRVL)
      RWY 14R: Rgt tfc.
   NOISE: Noise abatement procedures in effect. Call arpt manager at 361-643-3950.
   AIRPORT REMARKS: Unattended. Rwy 14R−32L CLOSED indef. Wind turbines N of arpt. Rwy 14L−32R has severe grass
      encroachment, pot holes, and loose gravel on rwy. Rwy 14R−32L heavy rutting along entire rwy length. Rwy 14L−32R
      limited line of sight between thlds; southern 600´ of rwy drops off approximately 8´. Rwy 32R ground drops off
      approximately 10´ at thld.
   AIRPORT MANAGER: 361-643-3950
   COMMUNICATIONS: CTAF 122.9
   CLEARANCE DELIVERY PHONE: For CD ctc Corpus Christi Apch at 361-299-4230.

POSSUM KINGDOM (See GRAFORD on page 322)

404   **TEXAS**

POST–GARZA CO MUNI (5F1)   2 E   UTC–6(–5DT)   N33°12.20´ W101°20.29´   **DALLAS–FT WORTH**
    2545   B   NOTAM FILE FTW   **L–6H**
    RWY 17–35: H4200X60 (ASPH)   S–16   MIRL
        RWY 17: PAPI(P2L)—GA 3.0° TCH 20´.
        RWY 35: Road.
    RWY 06–24: H2210X60 (ASPH)   S–16   MIRL   1.0% up SW
        RWY 06: Trees.
        RWY 24: Fence.
    AIRPORT REMARKS: Attended intmnt. Deer and feral hogs on and invof arpt.
    AIRPORT MANAGER: (806) 759-7561
    COMMUNICATIONS: CTAF 122.9
    CLEARANCE DELIVERY PHONE: For CD ctc Fort Worth ARTCC at 817-858-7584.
    RADIO AIDS TO NAVIGATION: NOTAM FILE LBB.
        LUBBOCK (L) (L) VORTACW 109.2   LBB   Chan 29   N33°42.30´ W101°54.84´   125° 41.7 NM to fld. 3310/11E.
          VOR unusable:
            040°–050° byd 38 NM blo 5,300´
            210°–260° byd 25 NM blo 6,000´

PRESIDIO

BIG BEND RANCH STATE PARK (3T9)   23 E   UTC–6(–5DT)   N29°28.27´ W103°56.19´   **EL PASO**
    4250   NOTAM FILE SJT   **H–7A, L–6J**
    RWY 08–26: H5500X80 (ASPH)
        RWY 08: Brush.
        RWY 26: Brush.
    AIRPORT REMARKS: Unattended. Phone extension 224. Arpt located 26 miles from ranch gate, road very rough. Hills
        surrounding arpt.
    AIRPORT MANAGER: 432-358-4444
    COMMUNICATIONS: CTAF 122.9
    CLEARANCE DELIVERY PHONE: For CD ctc Albuquerque ARTCC at 505-856-4861.

PRESIDIO LELY INTL (PRS)(KPRS)   5 N   UTC–6(–5DT)   N29°38.05´ W104°21.69´   **EL PASO**
    2938   B   LRA   NOTAM FILE PRS   **H–7A, L–6J**
    RWY 17–35: H5200X75 (ASPH)   S–30   MIRL   0.9% up N   **IAP**
        RWY 17: PVASI(PSIL)—GA 3.0° TCH 19´. Brush.
        RWY 35: PVASI(PSIL)—GA 3.0° TCH 37´. Tree.
    SERVICE: S2   **FUEL** 100LL, JET A   **LGT** MIRL Rwy 17–35 preset low intst;
        to incr intst actvt—CTAF. Rwy 17 and Rwy 35 PVASI unusable byd 7°
        left and right of final course.
    AIRPORT REMARKS: Attended Mon–Fri 1400–2200Z‡. 100LL, Jet A, self
        serve abvl 24 hrs. Acft lndg fm Mexico notify Cust and Img Presidio TX
        ETA at arpt 30 min prior to arr.
    AIRPORT MANAGER: 361-480-6933
    WEATHER DATA SOURCES: AWOS–3PT 118.0 (432) 229–4805.
    COMMUNICATIONS: CTAF/UNICOM 122.8
    ®**ALBUQUERQUE CENTER APP/DEP CON** 135.875
    CLEARANCE DELIVERY PHONE: For CD ctc Albuquerque ARTCC at
        505-856-4861.
    RADIO AIDS TO NAVIGATION: NOTAM FILE MRF.
        MARFA (VL) (DH) VORW/DME 115.9   MRF   Chan 106   N30°17.90´
          W103°57.29´   197° 45.1 NM to fld. 4834/11E.
          DME unusable:
            025°–035° byd 30 NM
          VOR unusable:
            220°–225° byd 40 NM
            290°–309° byd 40 NM
            310°–320° byd 40 NM blo 11,000´
            310°–320° byd 58 NM
            321°–333° byd 40 NM
            334°–344°
            345°–130° byd 40 NM

PROPWASH   (See JUSTIN on page 350)

PROSE FLD   (See JUSTIN on page 350)

TEXAS

QUANAH MUNI (FØ1)   2 SW   UTC–6(–5DT)   N34°16.63´ W99°45.58´   DALLAS–FT WORTH
1603   B   NOTAM FILE FTW   L–17B
RWY 18–36: H4452X60 (ASPH)   S–12.5   MIRL
   RWY 18: Road.
   RWY 36: PAPI(P2L)—GA 3.0° TCH 44´.
RWY 11–29: 2270X70 (TURF)
   RWY 29: Thld dsplcd 360´. Road.
RWY 06–24: 2268X70 (TURF)   0.4% up SW
   RWY 24: Thld dsplcd 500´. Pole.
SERVICE: S4   **FUEL** 100LL   **LGT** MIRL Rwy 18–36 preset low intst; to incr intst ACTVT—CTAF.
AIRPORT REMARKS: Unatndd. For fuel or maint call 940–839–7588. Rwy 24 dsplcd thr unmarked. Rwy 29 dsplcd thr unmarked. Width of turf rwys based on the area mowed.
AIRPORT MANAGER: 940-839-7588
COMMUNICATIONS: CTAF/UNICOM 122.7
CLEARANCE DELIVERY PHONE: For CD ctc Fort Worth ARTCC at 817-858-7584.
RADIO AIDS TO NAVIGATION: NOTAM FILE CDS.
   CHILDRESS (VL) (H) VORTACW 117.0   CDS   Chan 117   N34°22.14´ W100°17.34´   092° 26.9 NM to fld. 1920/10E.

QUINLAN

ROCKIN M (T14)   3 NE   UTC–6(–5DT)   N32°57.15´ W96°05.75´   DALLAS–FT WORTH
473   B   NOTAM FILE FTW
RWY 18–36: 3120X60 (TURF)   LIRL
   RWY 18: Trees.
   RWY 36: Trees.
AIRPORT REMARKS: Attended intermittently. Arpt fenced. Gate locked. Call for aces. Rwy 18 and Rwy 36 marked with yellow cones. Rwy 18–36 solar powered LIRL. Rwy soft when wet call to confirm cond. Rwy soft 10´ alg both edges, full len. 12´ brush, 90´ each side of rwy cntrln.
AIRPORT MANAGER: 214-335-4768
COMMUNICATIONS: CTAF 122.9
CLEARANCE DELIVERY PHONE: For CD ctc Fort Worth ARTCC at 817-858-7584.

QUITMAN   N32°52.83´ W95°22.01´   NOTAM FILE FTW.   DALLAS–FT WORTH
   (L) DME 114.0   UIM   Chan 87   052° 5.7 NM to Winnsboro Muni. 517.   H–6I, L–17D

RALPH M HALL/ROCKWALL MUNI (See ROCKWALL on page 412)

SC, 25 JAN 2024 to 21 MAR 2024

TEXAS

RANDOLPH AFB (RND)(KRND) AF 13 NE UTC–6(–5DT) N29°31.73′ W98°16.68′ **SAN ANTONIO**
761 B TPA—See Remarks NOTAM FILE RND Not insp. **H–7B, L–19C**
RWY 15R–33L: H8352X200 (PEM) PCN 22 R/C/W/T HIRL **DIAP, AD**
 RWY 15R: PAPI(P4L)—GA 3.0° TCH 46′.
 RWY 33L: PAPI(P4L)—GA 3.0° TCH 50′.
RWY 15L–33R: H8351X200 (CONC) PCN 54 R/A/W/T HIRL
 RWY 15L: ALSF1. PAPI(P4L)—GA 3.0° TCH 46′. RVR–T
 RWY 33R: ALSF1. PAPI(P4L)—GA 3.0° TCH 43′. RVR–T
ARRESTING GEAR/SYSTEM
 RWY 15R BAK–15 CHAG (250′ OVRN). BAK–15 CHAG (250′ OVRN). **RWY 33L**
 RWY 15L BAK–15 CHAG (250′ OVRN). BAK–15 CHAG (250′ OVRN). **RWY 33R**
SERVICE: S1 **OX** 1, 2 **LGT** ALS Rwy 15L nstd len 2100′. Rwy 15L and 33R ILS and PAPI GS are not coincidental.
 MILITARY— **JASU** 3(MC–2A) (GTC–85) 9(ESSEX B809) 6(SGNC) **FUEL** A++ **FLUID** SP PRESAIR LHOX LOX **OIL**
 O–133–148–156 SOAP–Not avbl wknd. **TRAN ALERT** De–icing unavailable, tran aircraft must use follow–me to park.
 NOISE: Noise abatement: Departing and arr acft will use min pwr settings consistent with acft flt manuals and comply with
 all ATC instr.
 MILITARY REMARKS: Attended Mon–Fri 1300–0100Z‡, clsd wknd and Federal hol. BASH Phase II in effect 1 Mar–30 Nov, exp
 heavy migration. Yr round bird activity highest in early to mid morning and after 2230Z‡ dly. **RSTD** PPR 48 hr PN rqr, ctc
 Base OPS DSN 487–2943, C210–652–2943, Afld Mgr DSN 487–8160/8166, C210–652–8160/8166, PAX Terminal,
 DSN 487–5287, C210–652–5287. Acft must adhere to PPR arr block +/– 30 min of scheduled ldg. Exp radar vector
 for ILS for VFR straight in apch and full stop ldg dur stu trng. Recommend all wide body acft taxi with inboard eng only
 on Twys A, D and G. ARFF, USAF Core Set 1, NFPA Cat 1–4. **CAUTION** Dur VMC dep acft must remain blw 1300′ Rwy
 15R–33L, 2100′ Rwy 15L–33R until past departure end to ensure separation from VFR overhead tfc pat unless otherwise
 cleared by ATC. **TFC PAT** TPA—Overhead Rwy 15L–33R 2600 (1839), Rwy 15R–33L 1800 (1039). **MISC** Fleet svc
 unavbl. No glycol avbl. Acft with Code 7 and abv ctc PTD with block time 60 miles prior ldg. First 1000 ft Rwy 15R and
 first 2500 ft Rwy 33L conc, middle 4852 ft asph. Rwy Cond Code (RwyCC) not rptd.
 COMMUNICATIONS: ATIS 290.525 **HANGOVER ATIS** 327.8 (Mon–Fri 1300–0000Z‡, clsd weekend and Federal holiday **PTD** 372.2
 ® **SAN ANTONIO APP CON** 124.45 335.625
 ® **SAN ANTONIO DEP CON** 127.1 290.225
  TOWER 128.25 294.7 (Mon–Fri 1300–0100Z‡, clsd wknd and Federal hol) **GND CON** 119.65 275.8 **CLNC DEL** 338.35
  (Rwy 15L–33R)
  PMSV METRO 239.8 (Full svc avbl 0500–0200Z‡ Mon–Fri, 1700–2200Z Sun, as rqr, clsd Sat and federal hol at DSN
  487–2992, C210–652–2992. AN/FMQ–19 ASOS in use, augmented by human observer as nec dur afld op hr. Backup
  wx obsn view ltd, rstd fr S–NW by flightline fac and trees. Ctc 26 OWS DSN 331–2616/2690/2603,
  C318–529–2616/2690/2603 dur wx flt closure or evac. When possible, provide 2 hr PN for all rqr briefs.)
  HANGOVER TWR 120.5 291.1 **HANGOVER GND** 124.75 353.75
 AIRSPACE: CLASS D svc 1300–0100Z‡ Mon–Fri, clsd Sat–Sun and fed hol; other times CLASS E.
 RADIO AIDS TO NAVIGATION: NOTAM FILE RND.
  (T) (T) VORTACW 112.3 RND Chan 70 N29°31.15′ W98°17.11′ at fld. 735/5E.
   No NOTAM MP: 0430–1230Z‡ Tue and Thu (1500/5+1)
   VOR unusable:
   190°–270° blo 4,000′
   190°–270° byd 6 NM blo 9,000′
   270°–360°
   360°–100° blo 4,000′
   360°–100° byd 14 NM
  (L) TACAN Chan 36 DHK (109.9) N29°32.22′ W98°16.07′ at fld. 728/5E.
   No NOTAM MP: 0430–1230Z‡ Tue and Thu (1500/5+1)
   DME unusable:
   225°–260° byd 35 NM blo 2,900′
  ILS 109.9 I–TRT Rwy 15L. No NOTAM MP: 0430–1230Z‡ Mon and Wed (1,500/5+1). Glideslope critical areas
   unprotected.
  ILS 111.3 I–UNY Rwy 15R. No NOTAM MP: 0430–1230Z‡ Mon and Wed (1,500/5+1).
  ILS 111.1 I–VQE Rwy 33L. Class IT. Coupled apch unusable blo 953′. No NOTAM MP: 0430–1230Z‡ Mon and
   Wed (1,500/5+1).
  ILS 109.3 I–RND Rwy 33R. No NOTAM MP: 0430–1230Z‡ Mon and Wed (1,500/5+1).
 COMM/NAV/WEATHER REMARKS: Freqs 128.25/294.7 and 120.5/291.1 for tfc ctl Rwy 15R–33L when student trng in progress.

TEXAS

RANGER MUNI (F23) 2 S UTC–6(–5DT) N32°27.09′ W98°40.89′ DALLAS–FT WORTH
1470 NOTAM FILE FTW
RWY 01–19: 3415X75 (TURF) 0.4% up N
  RWY 01: Trees.
  RWY 19: Trees.
RWY 18–36: 1850X80 (TURF)
  RWY 18: Bldg.
  RWY 36: Tree.
AIRPORT REMARKS: Attended dalgt hours. Deer on and invof arpt. Pedestrian tfc on fld at times. Rwy 01 and Rwy 19 thr mkd by white tires.
AIRPORT MANAGER: 254-433-1267
COMMUNICATIONS: CTAF 122.9
CLEARANCE DELIVERY PHONE: For CD ctc Fort Worth ARTCC at 817-858-7584.

RANGER N32°53.37′ W97°10.77′ NOTAM FILE FTW. DALLAS–FT WORTH
(VH) (H) VORTACW 115.7 FUZ Chan 104 305° 9.3 NM to Perot Fld/Fort Worth Alliance. 639/6E. COPTER
  VOR unusable: H–6H, L–17C, A
    275°–290° byd 40 NM
    317°–327° byd 40 NM

RANKIN (49F) 1 W UTC–6(–5DT) N31°13.62′ W101°57.18′ SAN ANTONIO
2543 NOTAM FILE SJT
RWY 17–35: 3000X35 (GRVL–DIRT) 1.1% up N
  RWY 17: Hill.
  RWY 35: Trees.
AIRPORT REMARKS: Unattended. Arpt gate locked. For aces call Sheriff's ofc 432–693–2411. Rwy not mkd, dfclt to dtrm lctn of rwy in fld. Ditch acrs north end of rwy hidden by vegetation. Rwy 17–35 rwy surface rough and uneven.
AIRPORT MANAGER: 432-413-8589
COMMUNICATIONS: CTAF 122.9
CLEARANCE DELIVERY PHONE: For CD ctc Houston ARTCC at 281-230-5622.

REAGAN CO (See BIG LAKE on page 255)

REAL CO (See LEAKEY on page 363)

REFUGIO

ROOKE FLD (RFG)(KRFG) 3 W UTC–6(–5DT) N28°17.75′ W97°19.56′ SAN ANTONIO
54 B TPA—854(800) NOTAM FILE SJT L–20H, 21A
RWY 14–32: H4361X60 (ASPH) S–9 MIRL
  RWY 14: PAPI(P2L)—GA 3.0° TCH 35′.
  RWY 32: Thld dsplcd 166′. Rgt tfc.
SERVICE: **FUEL** 100LL **LGT** MIRL Rwy 14–32 SS–SR preset low. To incr intst—CTAF. Rwy 14 PAPI opr consly.
AIRPORT REMARKS: Attended intmnt. Wildlife on and invof arpt. Glider actvty on and invof arpt. Fuel avbl 24 hrs self svc with credit card. Rwy 14–32 rwy line of sight ltd btn rwy ends. Rwy 14 and Rwy 32 rwy markings faded.
AIRPORT MANAGER: 361-438-1775
COMMUNICATIONS: CTAF/UNICOM 122.8
CLEARANCE DELIVERY PHONE: For CD ctc Houston ARTCC at 281-230-5622.
RADIO AIDS TO NAVIGATION: NOTAM FILE CRP.
  CORPUS CHRISTI (VH) (H) VORTACW 115.5 CRP Chan 102 N27°54.23′ W97°26.69′ 006° 24.3 NM to fld. 60/9E.
    TACAN AZIMUTH & DME unusable:
      024°–036° byd 35 NM blo 1,700′
      037°–023° byd 35 NM blo 2,000′
      265°–275°
    VOR unusable:
      340°–005° byd 40 NM blo 7,000′
      340°–005° byd 84 NM
      Byd 30 NM blo 1,500′
    TACAN AZIMUTH unusable:
      080°–085° byd 30 NM

RHOME

FAIRVIEW (7ØT)   3 NE   N33°05.67´ W97°25.63´   DALLAS–FT WORTH
  915   NOTAM FILE FTW
  RWY 17–35: 2861X60 (TURF)   LIRL(NSTD)
    RWY 17: Thld dsplcd 300´. Road. Rgt tfc.
    RWY 35: Thld dsplcd 300´. Road.
  SERVICE: **LGT** ACTVT LIRL five clicks 122.7. Rwy 17–35 LIRL 19 ft from edge of rwy. NSTD colors.
  AIRPORT REMARKS: Unattended. Wildlife on and invof arpt. VFR day only use for tsnt acft. Rwy 17 and Rwy 35 dsplcd thr mkd with white L shape markers. Tsnt acft tgls prohibited. Ditches both sides of rwy; possible flooding after rain. For ficons call 757-777-8728.
  AIRPORT MANAGER: 757-574-5277
  COMMUNICATIONS: CTAF 122.9

RHOME MEADOWS (T76)   6 N   UTC–6(–5DT)   N33°08.96´ W97°29.77´   DALLAS–FT WORTH
  900   NOTAM FILE FTW   COPTER
  RWY 13–31: 3700X60 (TURF)
    RWY 13: Thld dsplcd 260´. Fence. Rgt tfc.
    RWY 31: Fence. Rgt tfc.
  AIRPORT REMARKS: Unattended. All acft monitor CTAF due to the close proximity to Heritage Creek airstrip. 120´ cell tower 2000´ west of rwy. Rwy 13 right tfc for fixed wing acft only, remain west of the rwy. Rwy 31 rgt tfc for ultralights only, remain east of the rwy. Rwy 13 dsplcd thld not marked. Rwy 31 end soft when wet. Rwy defined by mowing. Rwy dimensions indef. Dsplcd thr and rwy ends not mkd. Rwy 13–31 sfc rough and uneven. Grass not mowed full length.
  AIRPORT MANAGER: 817-320-2024
  COMMUNICATIONS: CTAF 122.9
  CLEARANCE DELIVERY PHONE: For CD ctc Regional Apch at 972-615-2799.

RICK HUSBAND AMARILLO INTL   (See AMARILLO on page 242)

RIO GRANDE CITY MUNI (67R)   3 NW   UTC–6(–5DT)   N26°25.46´ W98°50.76´   BROWNSVILLE
  290   B   NOTAM FILE SJT   L–20H
  RWY 16–34: H4000X75 (ASPH)   S–12.5   MIRL
  SERVICE: **LGT** MIRL Rwy 16–34 preset low intst; to incr intst ACTVT—CTAF.
  AIRPORT REMARKS: Unattended. Arpt gate clsd and locked call 956-487-5312 for access. No public phone within arpt property. Terminal bldg locked.
  AIRPORT MANAGER: 956-487-5312
  COMMUNICATIONS: CTAF 122.9
  CLEARANCE DELIVERY PHONE: For CD ctc Houston ARTCC at 281-230-5622.
  RADIO AIDS TO NAVIGATION: NOTAM FILE LRD.
    LAREDO (VH) (H) **VORTACW** 117.4   LRD   Chan 121   N27°28.72´ W99°25.06´   145° 70.1 NM to fld. 583/9E.
    VOR unusable:
      080°–126° byd 40 NM
      127°–137° byd 40 NM blo 4,500´
      127°–137° byd 56 NM
      138°–160° byd 40 NM
      190°–260° byd 40 NM

RIVER FALLS   (See AMARILLO on page 243)

TEXAS 409

ROANOKE

AERO VALLEY (52F) 3 NW UTC–6(–5DT) N33°02.99′ W97°13.93′   DALLAS–FT WORTH
643   B   NOTAM FILE FTW   COPTER
RWY 17–35: H3500X40 (ASPH)   S–8   LIRL   L–17C, A
  RWY 17: Thld dsplcd 400′. Road.
  RWY 35: Thld dsplcd 320′. Trees.
SERVICE: S4   FUEL 100LL   LGT Rwy mkgs, lighting do not coincide with published values.
AIRPORT REMARKS: Attended Mon–Sat 1500–2300Z‡. Turf area btn rwy and twys unsafe for acft. Full rwy avbl for tkof. Rwy 17, 18′ rd crosses through apch, 40′ from rwy end. Vehicles crossing. The following operations are prohibited: ultralights, powered parachutes, sailplanes, gliders, auto–gyros, skydiving, AG–operations, and airships. Uncontrolled vehicle traffic invof hangars and twys. Non–based flt schools rqr prior written pmsn.
AIRPORT MANAGER: 682-237-9039
COMMUNICATIONS: CTAF 122.9
CLEARANCE DELIVERY PHONE: For CD ctc Regional Apch at 972-615-2799.
RADIO AIDS TO NAVIGATION: NOTAM FILE FTW.
  RANGER (VH) (H) VORTACW 115.7   FUZ   Chan 104   N32°53.37′ W97°10.77′   339° 10.0 NM to fld. 639/6E.
  VOR unusable:
    275°–290° byd 40 NM
    317°–327° byd 40 NM

ROBERT GRAY AAF (GRK)(KGRK) MIL/CIV A   6 SW   UTC–6(–5DT)   N31°04.04′ W97°49.74′   SAN ANTONIO
1015   B   TPA—See Remarks   Class I, ARFF Index E   NOTAM FILE GRK   H–6H, L–19C, 21A
RWY 15–33: H9997X200 (ASPH–CONC)   PCN 59 R/B/W/T   HIRL   IAP, DIAP, AD
  RWY 15: MALSR. PAPI(P4L)—GA 3.0° TCH 53′. RVR–T
  RWY 33: MALSR. PAPI(P4L)—GA 3.0° TCH 50′. Thld dsplcd 194′. 0.4% up.
SERVICE: FUEL JET A   MILITARY— JASU 1(AM32–95) LASS 1(TUG TMD–250) 1(ESSEX B809) FUEL A++ PPR only. (A, 1000–0230Z‡, OT C254–501–8750).
AIRPORT REMARKS: Attended continuously. PPR all civil acft, ctc arpt manager.
MILITARY REMARKS: See FLIP AP/1 Supplementary Arpt Remarks. PPR all civil acft ctc arpt manager at 254–501–8704 or OPS 254–501–8750. RSTD PPR mil ramp DSN 738–9200/9209, C254–288–9200/9209 civ ramp (KFHRA) C254–501–8750. Twy D and Twy B from Twy C to AER 33 not authorized for DoD acft that rqr Class B rwy. Twy B from Twy C to Twy E rstd to acft with wingspan 200′ or less. Twy B from Twy C to AER 15 RSTD to acft with an ACN of 24 of less. CAUTION Extv copter opr vcnty Fort Cavazos, some wo conspicuous mrk and blend with terrain. Extensive helicopter SOD ops. Extensive UAS acft within Class D airspace and btn Class D airspace and R6302. TFC PAT Tfc pat altitude left and rgt. TPA—Rotary Wing 1500 (485), UAS 2000 (985) west tfc only, Fixed Wing 2500 (1485), pure jet/overhead 3000 (1985). CSTMS/AG/IMG CSTMS avbl. 72hr prior notice rqr. During normal duty hr ctc Provost Marshal's office CSTMS DSN 737–3535/3508, C254–287–3535/3508, other times ctc base ops DSN 738–9200, C254–288–9200. USDA AG inspection not avbl. MISC 50′ fuel svc safety zone enforced during all refuel ops. Ltd parking. Base OPS approval for ramp access. Clsd circuit TV opr. No de–ice capability. All inbound PPR acft ctc PTD 20 min prior ldg. Base OPS fax DSN 738–1930, C254–288–1930. Rwy 33 first 1000′ PEM remaining 8997′ GRVD. Wx visibility obstruction rstd S through NW. Precision approach radar not avbl (Exc emergency) from 0500–1300Z‡. 24 hr notice rqr for lavatory and water svc. Space A passenger ops prohibited, inbound and outbound. No off afld tran aircrew transportation avbl. Wide body acft 180° turns allowed only on conc areas at each EOR Rwy 15–33. Wide body acft movement on the south ramp auth only under control of follow–me and ground marshal personnel. Water twr 1182′ east side of afld.
AIRPORT MANAGER: 254-501-8701
COMMUNICATIONS: CTAF 120.75   ATIS 124.9   UNICOM (CIV) 122.825   PTD 125.05 305.15
® GRAY APP/DEP CON 120.075 323.15
  TOWER 120.75   285.5   GRAY GND CON 121.8 279.5   CLNC DEL 126.2 251.1
  PMSV GRAY METRO 41.2 306.5 (3 CWS, Robert Gray AAF, DSN 738–9400/9620 C254–288–9400/9620. Full svc avbl H24 or remote briefing svc avbl 26 OWS Barksdale AFB, DSN 331–2651, C318–529–2651) RANGE CTL 30.45 38.3
  FT HOOD FLT FLW 141.175 357.5
AIRSPACE: CLASS D svc continuous.
RADIO AIDS TO NAVIGATION: NOTAM FILE GRK.
  GRAY (T) (T) VORW/DME 111.8   GRK   Chan 55   N31°01.97′ W97°48.83′   332° 2.2 NM to fld. 963/7E.
  GOOCH SPRINGS (H) (H) VORTACW 112.5   AGJ   Chan 72   N31°11.13′ W98°08.51′   109° 17.6 NM to fld. 1191/5E. NOTAM FILE SJT.
  ILS 111.1   I–GRK   Rwy 15.   Class IT.
  ILS/DME 109.25   I–BTJ   Chan 30(Y)   Rwy 33.   Class IE.
  ASR/PAR
COMM/NAV/WEATHER REMARKS: Radar see Terminal FLIP for Radar Minima.

ROBERT R WELLS JR (See COLUMBUS on page 276)

ROBINSON   N31°30.23′ W97°04.18′   NOTAM FILE FTW.   SAN ANTONIO
NDB (MHW) 400   ROB   355° 8.0 NM to TSTC Waco. 392/3E.   L–19D, 21A, A

SC, 25 JAN 2024 to 21 MAR 2024

ROBSTOWN

NUECES CO (RBO)(KRBO) 2 SW UTC−6(−5DT) N27°46.69′ W97°41.41′ **BROWNSVILLE**
80 B NOTAM FILE RBO L−20H, 21A, GOMW
RWY 13−31: H3700X75 (ASPH) S−11 MIRL IAP
  RWY 13: Road.
  RWY 31: Trees.
SERVICE: S2 **FUEL** 100LL **LGT** MIRL Rwy 13−31 preset low intst; to incr intst actvt—122.8.
AIRPORT REMARKS: Attended Mon–Fri 1400–1800Z‡, Mon–Fri 1900–2300Z‡. 100LL avbl 24 hrs. 1049 ft MSL towers 3 NM east of arpt.
AIRPORT MANAGER: 361-387-1700
WEATHER DATA SOURCES: AWOS−3 118.175 (361) 767−1982.
COMMUNICATIONS: CTAF 122.9
ⓇKINGSVILLE APP CON 119.9 (1345−0600Z‡ Mon–Thu; 1345−2345Z‡ Fri; clsd Sat, Sun and hol exc by NOTAM, hrs subj to chg)
ⓇHOUSTON CENTER APP CON 128.15 (0500−1300Z‡ Mon–Thu; 2200−1300Z‡ Fri; 24 Sat, Sun and hol by NOTAM)
ⓇCORPUS DEP CON 120.9
CLEARANCE DELIVERY PHONE: For CD ctc Houston ARTCC at 281-230-5622.
RADIO AIDS TO NAVIGATION: NOTAM FILE CRP.
  CORPUS CHRISTI (VH) (H) VORTACW 115.5   CRP   Chan 102   N27°54.23′ W97°26.69′   231° 15.1 NM to fld. 60/9E.
   TACAN AZIMUTH & DME unusable:
     024°−036° byd 35 NM blo 1,700′
     037°−023° byd 35 NM blo 2,000′
     265°−275°
   VOR unusable:
     340°−005° byd 40 NM blo 7,000′
     340°−005° byd 84 NM
     Byd 30 NM blo 1,500′
   TACAN AZIMUTH unusable:
     080°−085° byd 30 NM

ROCKDALE

H H COFFIELD RGNL (RCK)(KRCK) 2 SE UTC−6(−5DT) N30°37.88′ W96°59.37′ **HOUSTON**
474 B NOTAM FILE CXO
RWY 17−35: H2962X50 (ASPH)   LIRL(NSTD) 0.7% up S
  RWY 17: Road.
  RWY 35: Trees.
SERVICE: **FUEL** 100LL **LGT** Rwy 17−35 NSTD LIRL – household type fixtures, oprg status of lgt unkn. NSTD spacing. Rotating bcn OTS indef.
AIRPORT REMARKS: Unattended. For fuel call 512−446−2511 after 2300Z‡ and weekends call 512−446−3436. +40 ft ant on hgr E side of rwy.
AIRPORT MANAGER: (512) 760-6991
COMMUNICATIONS: CTAF 122.9
CLEARANCE DELIVERY PHONE: For CD ctc Houston Apch at 281-443-5844 to cnl IFR call 281-443-5888.

ROCKIN M (See QUINLAN on page 405)

ROCKING L (See SONORA on page 428)

TEXAS

ROCKPORT
ARANSAS CO (RKP)(KRKP) 4 N UTC−6(−5DT) N28°05.17′ W97°02.62′ SAN ANTONIO
24 B NOTAM FILE RKP H−7C, L−20I, 21A, GOMW
IAP
RWY 14−32: H5608X100 (ASPH) S−45, D−80, 2S−101, 2D−140 MIRL
  RWY 14: REIL. PAPI(P4L)—GA 3.0° TCH 35′. Brush.
  RWY 32: PAPI(P4L)—GA 3.0° TCH 25′. Thld dsplcd 565′. P−line. Rgt tfc.
RWY 18−36: H4498X100 (ASPH) S−45, D−80, 2S−101, 2D−140 MIRL
  RWY 18: PAPI(P2L)—GA 3.0° TCH 39′. Trees. Rgt tfc.
  RWY 36: PAPI(P2L)—GA 3.0° TCH 42′. P−line.
SERVICE: S4 **FUEL** 100LL, JET A+ **LGT** MIRL Rwy 14−32 and Rwy 18−36 preset low intst. To incr intst and actvt REIL Rwy 14—CTAF.
AIRPORT REMARKS: Attended 1330−2330Z‡.
AIRPORT MANAGER: 361-790-0141
WEATHER DATA SOURCES: ASOS 119.275 (361) 729−2372.
COMMUNICATIONS: CTAF/UNICOM 123.05
  ROCKPORT RCO 122.3 (SAN ANGELO RADIO)
Ⓡ **CORPUS APP/DEP CON** 120.9
  CLNC DEL 121.7
AIRSPACE: CLASS E.
RADIO AIDS TO NAVIGATION: NOTAM FILE CRP.
  CORPUS CHRISTI (VH) (H) VORTACW 115.5   CRP   Chan 102
    N27°54.23′ W97°26.69′   054° 23.9 NM to fld. 60/9E.
  TACAN AZIMUTH & DME unusable:
    024°−036° byd 35 NM blo 1,700′
    037°−023° byd 35 NM blo 2,000′
    265°−275°
  VOR unusable:
    340°−005° byd 40 NM blo 7,000′
    340°−005° byd 84 NM
    Byd 30 NM blo 1,500′
  TACAN AZIMUTH unusable:
    080°−085° byd 30 NM

ROCKSPRINGS
EDWARDS CO (ECU)(KECU) 4 SE UTC−6(−5DT) N29°56.82′ W100°10.43′ SAN ANTONIO
2372 B NOTAM FILE ECU MON Airport L−19B
IAP
RWY 14−32: H4050X50 (ASPH) S−13 MIRL
  RWY 14: Thld dsplcd 278′. Trees.
  RWY 32: Trees.
AIRPORT REMARKS: Unattended. Nighttime opn dsplcd thr lgts are set 288′ fm Rwy 14 end. Access through security gate use field elev.
AIRPORT MANAGER: 830-683-6122
WEATHER DATA SOURCES: AWOS−3 118.175 (830) 683−2425.
COMMUNICATIONS: CTAF 122.9
Ⓡ **DEL RIO APP/DEP CON** 119.6 (Mon−Fri 1300−0100Z‡, clsd Sat, Sun 2100−2359Z‡, except holidays). Other hrs ctc
Ⓡ **HOUSTON CENTER APP/DEP CON** 125.75 (Mon−Fri 0100−1300Z‡, Sat 24, Sun 2359−2100Z‡ except holidays.)
CLEARANCE DELIVERY PHONE: For CD ctc Laughlin Apch at 830-298-5192, when Apch clsd ctc Houston ARTCC at 281-230-5622.
RADIO AIDS TO NAVIGATION: NOTAM FILE ECU.
  ROCKSPRINGS (VL) (H) VORTAC 114.55   RSG   Chan 92(Y)
    N30°00.88′ W100°17.99′   112° 7.7 NM to fld. 2310/10E.
  VOR unusable:
    000°−010° byd 40 NM
    015°−035° byd 40 NM
    065°−095° byd 40 NM
    250°−280° byd 40 NM
    315°−322° byd 40 NM blo 6,000′
    315°−322° byd 56 NM
    323°−359° byd 40 NM

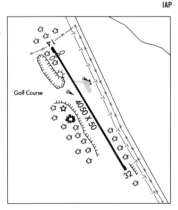

ROCKSPRINGS N30°00.88′ W100°17.99′ NOTAM FILE ECU. SAN ANTONIO
  (VL) (H) VORTAC 114.55 RSG Chan 92(Y) 112° 7.7 NM to Edwards Co. 2310/10E. H–7B, L–19B
  VOR unusable:
    000°–010° byd 40 NM
    015°–035° byd 40 NM
    065°–095° byd 40 NM
    250°–280° byd 40 NM
    315°–322° byd 40 NM blo 6,000′
    315°–322° byd 56 NM
    323°–359° byd 40 NM
  RCO 122.4 (SAN ANGELO RADIO)
  RCO 122.1R 114.55T (SAN ANGELO RADIO)

ROCKWALL
  POETRY FLYING RANCH (T48) 15 SE UTC–6(–5DT) N32°52.09′ W96°13.15′ DALLAS–FT WORTH
    500 NOTAM FILE FTW
    RWY 13–31: 3344X50 (TURF)
      RWY 13: Thld dsplcd 335′. Trees.
      RWY 31: Thld dsplcd 336′. Fence.
    AIRPORT REMARKS: Unattended. Wildlife on and invof rwy.
    AIRPORT MANAGER: 214-704-1593
    COMMUNICATIONS: CTAF/UNICOM 123.0
    CLEARANCE DELIVERY PHONE: For CD ctc Fort Worth ARTCC at 817-858-7584.

  RALPH M HALL/ROCKWALL MUNI (F46) 2 E UTC–6(–5DT) N32°55.84′ W96°26.73′ DALLAS–FT WORTH
    574 B NOTAM FILE F46 COPTER
    RWY 17–35: H3373X45 (ASPH) S–12 LIRL L–17C, A
      RWY 17: Thld dsplcd 470′. P-line. IAP
      RWY 35: Thld dsplcd 289′. Trees. Rgt tfc.
    SERVICE: S4 **FUEL** 100LL, JET A+ **LGT** Actvt LIRL Rwy 17–35—CTAF.
    AIRPORT REMARKS: Attended 1400–dusk. 100LL self-svc fuel. No line of sight between rwy ends. Several areas rwy and txy pavement lip greater than 3 inches at edge. Rwy 17 50′ drop off at apch end of pavement; steep down slope all sides of dsplcmt.
    AIRPORT MANAGER: 972-771-0151
    WEATHER DATA SOURCES: AWOS–3PT 121.25 (972) 772–6699.
    COMMUNICATIONS: CTAF/UNICOM 122.8
    Ⓡ **REGIONAL APP/DEP CON** 124.3
    CLEARANCE DELIVERY PHONE: For CD ctc Regional Apch at 972-615-2799.
    RADIO AIDS TO NAVIGATION: NOTAM FILE FTW.
      COWBOY (VH) (DH) VORW/DME 116.2 CVE Chan 109 N32°53.42′ W96°54.24′ 078° 23.8 NM to fld. 443/6E.
      VOR unusable:
        030°–035° byd 40 NM
        055°–060° byd 40 NM
        130°–140° byd 40 NM

  ROGER M DREYER MEML (See GONZALES on page 321)

  ROOKE FLD (See REFUGIO on page 407)

ROSENBERG
  LANE AIRPARK (T54) 3 SE UTC–6(–5DT) N29°31.39′ W95°46.78′ HOUSTON
    94 NOTAM FILE CXO L–19D, 21A
    RWY 13–31: H2890X35 (ASPH)
      RWY 13: Trees.
      RWY 31: Tree.
    SERVICE: S2 **FUEL** 100LL, JET A, A+
    AIRPORT REMARKS: Attended Mon–Fri dalgt hrs. Aces gates locked ngts and wkends. Fuel avbl Mon–Fri 1400–2300Z‡. Agricultural aerial application opn.
    AIRPORT MANAGER: 281-342-5451
    COMMUNICATIONS: CTAF 122.9
    CLEARANCE DELIVERY PHONE: For CD ctc Houston Apch at 281-443-5844 to cnl IFR call 281-443-5888.
    RADIO AIDS TO NAVIGATION: NOTAM FILE ELA.
      EAGLE LAKE (DH) DME 116.4 ELA Chan 111 N29°39.75′ W96°19.03′ 106° 29.3 NM to fld. 192.

SC, 25 JAN 2024 to 21 MAR 2024

TEXAS

ROTAN/ROBY
FISHER CO (56F) 3 SE UTC−6(−5DT) N32°49.46′ W100°24.77′ — DALLAS–FT WORTH
1941 B NOTAM FILE FTW — L−17A
RWY 16−34: H3300X60 (ASPH) S−12.5 MIRL
  RWY 16: Trees.
  RWY 34: Road.
RWY 07−25: 2800X50 (TURF)
  RWY 07: Thld dsplcd 200′. Fence.
  RWY 25: Trees.
AIRPORT REMARKS: Unattended. Intensive seasonal low level agricultural acft act invof arpt. Rwy 16−34 no pavement markings. Rwy 16−34 pea stone seal coat. Extsv loose stones. Rwy 07 dsplcd thld marked with 20 white tires on each side.
AIRPORT MANAGER: 325-776-2151
COMMUNICATIONS: CTAF 122.9
CLEARANCE DELIVERY PHONE: For CD ctc Fort Worth ARTCC at 817-858-7584.
RADIO AIDS TO NAVIGATION: NOTAM FILE ABI.
  ABILENE (VH) (H) VORTACW 113.7 ABI Chan 84 N32°28.88′ W99°51.81′ 297° 34.6 NM to fld. 1809/10E.
    VOR unusable:
      163°−236° byd 40 NM blo 18,000′
      237°−247° byd 40 NM blo 7,000′
      248°−250° byd 40 NM blo 18,000′
      251°−255° byd 40 NM blo 4,500′
      251°−255° byd 46 NM blo 18,000′

ROWDY N30°29.63′ W96°20.27′ NOTAM FILE CLL. — HOUSTON
NDB (LOMW) 260 CL 344° 5.8 NM to Easterwood Fld. 230/3E. — L−19D, 21A

ROY HURD MEML (See MONAHANS on page 385)

RUSK CO (See HENDERSON on page 330)

RWJ AIRPARK (See BAYTOWN on page 253)

SABINE PASS N29°41.20′ W94°02.28′ NOTAM FILE CXO. — HOUSTON
(VL) (L) VORW/DME 115.4 SBI Chan 101 356° 15.8 NM to Jack Brooks Rgnl. 10/7E. — H−7D, L−19E, 21A, GOMW

SALADO (2TX) 2 S UTC−6(−5DT) N30°55.23′ W97°32.40′ — SAN ANTONIO
689 NOTAM FILE SJT
RWY 02−20: H3494X40 (ASPH)
  RWY 02: P−line.
  RWY 20: Trees.
RWY 01−19: 3190X100 (TURF−DIRT) 0.3% up S
  RWY 19: Rgt tfc.
AIRPORT REMARKS: Unattended. Rwy 01−19 defined by mowing. Two antennas 1/2 to 3/4 miles north of arpt.
AIRPORT MANAGER: 512-222-8893
COMMUNICATIONS: CTAF 122.9
CLEARANCE DELIVERY PHONE: For CD ctc Fort Worth ARTCC at 817-858-7584.

SALT FLAT N31°44.89′ W105°05.21′ NOTAM FILE ABQ. — EL PASO
(L) (L) VORTACW 113.0 SFL Chan 77 324° 13.1 NM to Dell City Muni. 3730/12E. — L−6F
  VORTAC unusable:
    010°−065° byd 29 NM blo 15,000′
    180°−190° byd 30 NM blo 9,500′
  TACAN AZIMUTH & DME unusable:
    065°−075° byd 10 NM
    265°−270° byd 26 NM

SAN ANGELO RGNL/MATHIS FLD (SJT)(KSJT)   7 SW   UTC–6(–5DT)   N31°21.46′ W100°29.78′

SAN ANTONIO
H–6G, L–19B
IAP, AD

1919   B   Class I, ARFF Index B   NOTAM FILE SJT
RWY 18–36: H8054X150 (ASPH–GRVD)   S–70, D–100, 2S–127
  PCN 67 F/A/W/T   MIRL
  RWY 18: REIL. PAPI(P4L)—GA 3.0° TCH 45′. Thld dsplcd 902′. Road.
  RWY 36: PAPI(P4L)—GA 3.0° TCH 48′.
RWY 03–21: H5940X150 (ASPH–GRVD)   S–70, D–100, 2S–127
  PCN 115F/A/W/T   HIRL   0.4% up SW
  RWY 03: MALSR. RVR–T
  RWY 21: VASI(V4L)—GA 3.0° TCH 52′. RVR–R
RWY 09–27: H4406X75 (ASPH)   S–70, D–100, 2S–127
  PCN 39 F/A/W/T   MIRL
  RWY 09: Road.
  RWY 27: Road.
RUNWAY DECLARED DISTANCE INFORMATION
  RWY 03: TORA–5940   TODA–5940   ASDA–5940   LDA–5940
  RWY 09: TORA–4406   TODA–4406   ASDA–4406   LDA–4406
  RWY 18: TORA–8054   TODA–8054   ASDA–8054   LDA–7152
  RWY 21: TORA–5940   TODA–5940   ASDA–5940   LDA–5940
  RWY 27: TORA–4406   TODA–4406   ASDA–4406   LDA–4406
  RWY 36: TORA–7152   TODA–7152   ASDA–7152   LDA–7152
SERVICE: S4   **FUEL** 100LL, JET A   **OX** 1, 2, 4   **LGT** Dusk–dawn. When
ATCT clsd MIRL Rwy 18–36 preset low intst. To incr intst and actvt MALSR Rwy 03; REIL Rwy 18; PAPI Rwys 18 and 36; HIRL Rwy 03–21; MIRL Rwy 09–27—CTAF.
AIRPORT REMARKS: Attended 1200–0400Z‡. Fee for fuel after hrs call 325–656–1836/1837. PPR 12 hrs for unsked acr opns with over 30 psgr seats call AMGR 325–659–6409.
AIRPORT MANAGER: 325-659-6409
WEATHER DATA SOURCES: ASOS 128.45 (325) 949–6686.
COMMUNICATIONS: CTAF 118.3 **ATIS** 128.45 **UNICOM** 122.95
  RCO 122.2 (SAN ANGELO RADIO)
®️ **APP/DEP CON** 125.35 (1200–0300Z‡)
®️ **FORT WORTH CENTER APP/DEP CON** 126.15 (0300–1200Z‡)
  TOWER 118.3 (1300–0300Z‡)   **GND CON** 121.9
CLEARANCE DELIVERY PHONE: For CD if una to ctc on FSS freq, ctc Fort Worth ARTCC at 817-858-7584.
AIRSPACE: CLASS D svc 1300–0300Z‡; other times CLASS E.
RADIO AIDS TO NAVIGATION: NOTAM FILE SJT.
  (VH) (H) VORTACW 115.1   SJT   Chan 98   N31°22.50′ W100°27.29′   234° 2.4 NM to fld. 1886/10E.
  VOR unusable:
    111°–190° byd 40 NM
    191°–201° byd 40 NM blo 6,000′
    191°–201° byd 49 NM
    202°–255° byd 40 NM blo 7,000′
    202°–255° byd 71 NM
    256°–289° byd 40 NM blo 4,400′
    256°–289° byd 53 NM
    290°–314° byd 40 NM blo 5,000′
    290°–314° byd 46 NM
    315°–352° byd 40 NM
  WOOLE NDB (LOMW) 356   SJ   N31°16.78′ W100°34.57′   036° 6.2 NM to fld. 2127/5E.
  ILS/DME 109.7   I-SJT   Chan 34   Rwy 03.   Class IE.   LOM WOOLE NDB. ILS/DME unmonitored when ATCT clsd.
    Glideslope unusable for coupled apch blw 2,685′ MSL.
  ASR (1200–0600Z‡)

TEXAS

SAN ANTONIO

BOERNE STAGE AIRFIELD (5C1) 20 NW UTC–6(–5DT) N29°43.39´ W98°41.67´   SAN ANTONIO
1384 B NOTAM FILE SJT   L–19C
  RWY 17–35: H5006X60 (ASPH) LIRL   IAP, AD
    RWY 17: Thld dsplcd 629´. Fence. Rgt tfc.
    RWY 35: Thld dsplcd 1086´. Trees.
  SERVICE: S4 FUEL 100LL, JET A
  NOISE: Noise abatement procedures in effect ctc AMGR. All ldg turbine acft must be stage 3 or better. No tgls, stop and go or low apchs.
  AIRPORT REMARKS: Attended continuously. Glider act on and invof arpt. . Rwy 35 +35 ft lgtd pwr poles at 125 ft and 300 ft fm thr, 125 ft L of cntrln.
  AIRPORT MANAGER: 830-981-2345
  WEATHER DATA SOURCES: AWOS–3 118.725 (830) 755–9099.
  COMMUNICATIONS: CTAF/UNICOM 123.0
  ®SAN ANTONIO APP/DEP CON 125.1
  CLEARANCE DELIVERY PHONE: For CD ctc San Antonio Apch at 210-805-5516.
  RADIO AIDS TO NAVIGATION: NOTAM FILE SAT.
    SAN ANTONIO (VH) (H) VORTACW 116.8 SAT Chan 115 N29°38.64´ W98°27.68´ 283° 13.1 NM to fld. 1159/8E.
    VOR unusable:
      018°–022° byd 40 NM
      028°–032° byd 40 NM
      342°–347° byd 40 NM
      355°–002° byd 40 NM blo 18,000´
  COMM/NAV/WEATHER REMARKS: UNICOM unmnt.

HORIZON (74R) 9 S UTC–6(–5DT) N29°17.08´ W98°29.90´   SAN ANTONIO
551 NOTAM FILE SJT
  RWY 11–29: 2360X80 (TURF) 0.5% up W
    RWY 11: Trees.
    RWY 29: Trees.
  RWY 16–34: 2250X100 (TURF) 1.0% up N
    RWY 16: Trees.
    RWY 34: Trees.
  AIRPORT REMARKS: Unattended. Wild hogs on or invof arpt. No line of sight btn Rwys 34 and 29. Rwy 11–29 rough and uneven, not rglrly mntnd. Not suitable for acft.
  AIRPORT MANAGER: 210-748-8672
  COMMUNICATIONS: CTAF 122.9
  CLEARANCE DELIVERY PHONE: For CD ctc San Antonio Apch at 210-805-5516.

TEXAS

KELLY FLD (SKF)(KSKF) CIV/MIL AF (ANG AFRC)   4 SW   UTC−6(−5DT)   N29°23.05′ W98°34.87′   **SAN ANTONIO**
691   B   NOTAM FILE SKF   H−7B, L−19C
RWY 16−34: H11550X150 (CONC)   PCN 58 R/B/W/T   HIRL   IAP, DIAP, AD
  RWY 16: ALSF1. PAPI(P4L)—GA 3.0° TCH 89′. RVR−TR
  RWY 34: ALSF1. PAPI(P4R)—GA 3.0° TCH 93′. RVR−TR
ARRESTING GEAR/SYSTEM
  RWY 16 BAK−14 BAK−12A(B) (1853′).   BAK−14 BAK−12A(B) (1677′) HOOK MB100 (60′ OVRN). **RWY 34**
SERVICE: S4   **FUEL** 100LL, JET A+   **OX** 1, 2   **LGT** Rwy 34 PAPI (NSTD), located on right (east) side of Rwy 34. Twy F: No twy end lgts. **MILITARY**— **A−GEAR** BAK−12A(B) cables raised by BAK−14 device O/R to ctl twr. Potential for hook skip at BAK−12 cable sys due to irreg edges and uneven depths within 200′ of arresting sys. **JASU** (A/M32A−86D, A/M32A−95 LASS) **FUEL** A++, A+, J8, (J8 1200−0600Z‡, call out fee $50, 2 hr prior notice for defueling and reservice) Mil fuel unavbl Sat 0400−1200Z‡. (Mil) **FLUID** SP PRESAIR LHOX LOX LHNIT **OIL** O−133−148−156 SOAP − Avbl 2000−0600Z‡ Mon, 1230−0600Z‡ Tue−Thu, 1230−2230Z‡ Fri **TRAN ALERT** Opr 1130−0430Z‡ Mon−Fri, 1330−0230Z‡ Sat−Sun, clsd Federal hol; OT 2 hr PN rqr ctc AMOPS. 1 hr PN for all acft svc; ctc AMOPS DSN 945−6802, C210−925−6802 or PTD to avoid delays. Una to support tran acft lcl sorties.
NOISE: Quiet hrs 0500−1200Z‡ dly departure and full−stop ldg only. Acft arr btn 0500−1200Z‡ exp full stop ldg. No after burner tkof during these times without prior coord and apvl.
AIRPORT REMARKS: Probability of hydroplaning at all speeds entire rwy. Acft with wingspan larger than 93′ not authorized in Arm/DeArm Pads. Civ ramp lctd northeast of rwy. Twy G west of Twy H is for 149FW use. Ctc FBO 210−921−6100 for svc, JET A+, 100LL full service ARINC 129.725, 1200−0600Z‡, 2 hrs pn rqrd outside nml hrs. Acft using Avgas self−serve: do not deviate fm tax lns to/fm avgas self−serve to ensure safe dstc fm otr opns. 100LL fuel is full service at FBO. Apn PSA Ramp clsd in both drctns at Twy B at apn entrance to Twy C to all acft unless under tow. User fee arpt. Customs/AG/IMG rqr 72 hrs PN ctc FBO 1200−0600Z‡. 2 hr PN for defueling and reservice. For civilian operations, contact Port Operations 210−362−7875, PTD Airband 122.95. User fees applicable to civ acft.
MILITARY REMARKS: Attended continuously. **RSTD** Tran acft exp delays and may be ltd to one apch to a full stop for home stn formal trng unit ops and tactical arr and dep trng 1500−0400Z‡, Mon−Fri. Warning: Large successive flocks of cattle egrets, 5 to 50 in nr have been observed flying blw 300′ AGL across N end of rwy every morning at SR for up to 2 hrs, returning within 2 hrs of SS. BASH Phase II in eff 1 Mar−30 Nov. Req for PPR will be taken no earlier than 7 days prior to planned mission. At least 24 hr pn rqr for PPR, exc medevac, dv and other acft on a case by case basis apvd by DO. Ctc base ops DSN 945−6803, C210−924−6803. PPR good for +1/−1 hr PPR block time. Coord of PPR outside of block time by fone is rqrd. **CAUTION** North end underrun/ovrn 147′ paved, 853′ unpaved. Rwy and majority of twy pavement shoulders exceed standard dimensions and are not marked with yellow chevron, deceptive surface markings to indicate unusable. Heavy rubber deposits obscuring rwy markings at TDZS. **TFC PAT** Rectangular 1700 ft MSL, convl 2200 ft MSL, ftr type/overhead 2700 ft MSL. AETC arcft exp reduced rwy separation day/VFR. Tran ftr acft must notify twr on initial ctc of reduced separation is not desired. **CSTMS/AG/IMG** rqr 72 hrs PN ctc FBO. User fee arpt: Cstms; plant quarantine and IMG svc avbl ctc Base Opns 2 hrs PN. All psnl must clear IMG inbd. **MISC** USAF Acft will use tran alert svc and park on mil ramp; for qns ctc afld mgt opns C210−925−6803. Acft with Code 6 and abv ctc AMOPS phone patch/PTD with block time at least 1 hr before ldg. User fees applicable to civ acft. Official point of obsn does not allow a clear unobstructed view of rwy. WX technician view from North to SE is partially obstructed by trees, bldgs, and hangars. Technician relies on cooperative wx Watch with twr. High ints security lgts hinder ability to determine sky cond at ngt. AFRC PPR for use of AFRC ramp, DSN 945−4330, C210−925−4330. Rwy cond code (RWYCC) not rprtd. Ltd classified mtrls storage: excess and ts mtrls must go to 433 AW/CP. TACAN ck point /altm sign on Twy F and B sited opposite drctn of TACAN. **ANG** Opr Tue−Sat 1345−2230Z‡. PPR for use of ANG ramp, DSN 945−5934, C210−925−5934.
AIRPORT MANAGER: 210−925−5880
COMMUNICATIONS: ATIS 120.45 273.5 (24 hrs)   **PTD** 126.2 372.2   **PTD AIRBAND** 122.95
 ®**SAN ANTONIO APP CON** 118.05 125.1 127.1 289.2 307.0 353.5
   KELLY TOWER 124.3 322.35
   GND CON 121.8 289.4
 ®**SAN ANTONIO DEP CON** 125.7 290.225
   AFRC COMD POST 138.6 252.1 (502 ABW DSN 471−9363 C210−221−9363) **PMSV METRO** 239.8 (Full svc 24 hr, unless afld clsd by AMOPS via NOTAM. Wx DSN 945−5709 C210−925−5709. Afld wx is monitored by AN/FMQ−19 ASOS. Remote briefing svc avbl 26 OWS, Barksdale AFB DSN 331−2651, C318−529−2651.
AIRSPACE: CLASS D.

CONTINUED ON NEXT PAGE

TEXAS

CONTINUED FROM PRECEDING PAGE

RADIO AIDS TO NAVIGATION: NOTAM FILE SKF.
   (L) TACAN Chan 57 KSY (112.0) N29°23.50′ W98°34.86′ at fld. 687/4E. TACAN unmonitored when ATCT clsd.
   No NOTAM MP: 0600–1430Z‡ Wed
   TACAN AZIMUTH unusable:
     163°–188° byd 14 NM blo 2,700′
     298°–318° byd 20 NM blo 4,600′
     346°–356° byd 16 NM blo 3,400′
   DME unusable:
     163°–188° byd 14 NM blo 2,700′
     298°–318° byd 20 NM blo 4,600′
     346°–356° byd 16 NM blo 3,400′
   ILS 110.1 I–SKF Rwy 16. Class IT. No NOTAM MP: 0600–1430Z‡ Mon and Tue.
   ILS 110.7 I–OSQ Rwy 34. Class IT. No NOTAM MP: 0600–1430Z‡ Mon and Tue.
   ASR/PAR

KESTREL AIRPARK (1T7) 23 N UTC—6(—5DT) N29°48.71′ W98°25.56′   **SAN ANTONIO**
1261 NOTAM FILE SJT   **L–19C**
RWY 12–30: H3000X40 (ASPH)   RWY LGTS(NSTD) 1.4% up NW
  RWY 12: Trees.
  RWY 30: Road. Rgt tfc.
SERVICE: S4 **FUEL** 100LL **OX** 1 **LGT** Rwy 12–30 rwy lgts not at thrs–2780 ft avbl ngts.
AIRPORT REMARKS: Attended continuously. Self serv fuel. For assistance call 830–522–1885. Deer on and invof rwy. Rwy 30 rises rapidly at north end. 12 end 49 ft higher than 30 end. Tgl and low apchs prohibited for tran and coml acft. Tkofs rstrd btn 0400–1200Z‡. Hel trng ops prohibited. Use extreme ctn for high per MIL acft from Randolph AFB at or ABV 3000 FT MSL Mon–Fri 1600–0600Z‡ and when twr hrs extd by NOTAM, ocnl Sat and Sun. Rwy 12 120 ft rising trrn 0.4 mi NW of rwy end. Nonstd aiming point markings at 500 ft, 2490 ft remaining.
AIRPORT MANAGER: 210-504-8992
COMMUNICATIONS: CTAF/UNICOM 122.975
CLEARANCE DELIVERY PHONE: For CD ctc San Antonio Apch at 210-805-5516.
RADIO AIDS TO NAVIGATION: NOTAM FILE SAT.
  SAN ANTONIO (VH) (H) VORTACW 116.8 SAT Chan 115 N29°38.64′ W98°27.68′ 002° 10.2 NM to fld. 1159/8E.
  VOR unusable:
    018°–022° byd 40 NM
    028°–032° byd 40 NM
    342°–347° byd 40 NM
    355°–002° byd 40 NM blo 18,000′

TEXAS

SAN ANTONIO INTL (SAT)(KSAT) 7 N UTC−6(−5DT) N29°32.04´ W98°28.14´
809 B LRA Class I, ARFF Index C NOTAM FILE SAT MON Airport
SAN ANTONIO
H−7B, L−19C
IAP, AD

RWY 04−22: H8505X150 (CONC−GRVD) S−95, D−190, 2S−175, 2D−270 PCN 91 R/B/W/T HIRL CL
 RWY 04: MALS. PAPI(P4R)—GA 3.0° TCH 79´. RVR−T Pole. 0.3% down.
 RWY 22: REIL. PAPI(P4L)—GA 3.0° TCH 85´. RVR−R 0.5% up.
RWY 13R−31L: H8502X150 (CONC−GRVD) S−95, D−190, 2D−270 PCN 86 R/B/W/T HIRL CL
 RWY 13R: ALSF2. TDZL. PAPI(P4L)—GA 3.0° TCH 75´. RVR−TMR
 RWY 31L: MALSR. PAPI(P4L)—GA 3.0° TCH 82´. RVR−TMR Bldg.
RWY 13L−31R: H5519X100 (ASPH) S−59, D−120 PCN 61 F/C/W/T MIRL
 RWY 13L: REIL. PAPI(P4L)—GA 3.0° TCH 40´.
 RWY 31R: REIL. PAPI(P4L)—GA 3.0° TCH 60´.

RUNWAY DECLARED DISTANCE INFORMATION

RWY	TORA	TODA	ASDA	LDA
RWY 04:	8505	8505	8505	8505
RWY 13L:	5519	5519	5519	5519
RWY 13R:	8502	8502	8502	8502
RWY 22:	8505	8505	8505	8505
RWY 31L:	8502	8502	8502	8502
RWY 31R:	5519	5519	5519	5519

SERVICE: S4 **FUEL** 100LL, JET A **OX** 1, 2, 3, 4
NOISE: Noise sensitive areas exist on all sides of arpt, at pilots discretion climb as quickly and quietly as safely possible on departure and use consideration when flying over populated areas by minimizing flt and high pwr settings. Military aircraft: Departing and arriving aircraft will use minimum power settings consistent with aircraft flight manuals, afterburner takeoff is prohibited unless required for safety of flight. Engine run−ups are permitted btn 1200−0500Z‡.
AIRPORT REMARKS: Attended continuously. Numerous flocks of birds invof arpt. Glider/soaring ops aprx 17 miles northwest of arpt dur VFR. Rwy 13L−31R CLSD for const. Rwy 13L−31R not avbl part 121 for air carrier ops. Foreign mil acft with wingspans less than 100´ must report to general aviation ramp federal inspection station for cstms processing, ctc arpt mgmt at 210−207−3433. Arpt restricted to acft with wingspan greater than 171´, PPR with 24hr OPS 210−207−3433. Required for authorization. PPR with arpt ops for acft powering back from terminal gates. Acft taxiing on Rwy 04 northeast bound look for hold short to Rwy 31L. Acft taxiing on Twy N southwest bound look for hold short to Rwy 31R. Apron East Cargo Ramp intersection of Rwy 04−22 and Twy D aircraft are requested to apply the minimum thrust when crossing the rwy to avoid damage due to jet blast. The following twys are not avbl for acft 59000 lbs or over: Twy A, Twy M, Twy H northwest of Twy Z and Twy E east of Rwy 04−22. Inner ramp taxilane north of Terminal A and B is clsd to acft with wingspan greater than 135´. Acft at Terminal A and B advise gnd ctl prior to push. Twy L clsd northbound. Twys L and B clsd to acft with wingspans greater than 118´ exiting Rwy 31L. Twy S btn apch end Rwy 13L and Rwy 13R−31L clsd to acft wingspan more than 100´. Twy R between apch end Rwy 13L and Twy D clsd to acft wingspan more than 100´. Twy Z clsd to acft with wingspan greater than 118´. Gnd run−up enclosure avbl 24 hrs. Terminal Gates A1, A2, A6, A7 and A8, A15 & A17 use only with PPR call opns 210−207−3433. C130 and C17 type acft must park on west ramp to clear cstms. All intl general aviation clear U.S. Cstms at North Fixed Base Operator Ramp east side, call U.S. CSTMS 210−821−6965 upon arr. Flight Notification Service (ADCUS) available.
AIRPORT MANAGER: 210−207−3444
WEATHER DATA SOURCES: ASOS (210) 805−5583 WSP.
COMMUNICATIONS: D−ATIS 118.9 (210−805−5515) **UNICOM** 122.95
 RCO 122.3 (SAN ANGELO RADIO)
® **APP/DEP CON** 128.05 (091°−140° SAT) 125.1 (271°−359° SAT) 124.45 (360°−090° SAT) 118.05 (141°−270° SAT)
 TOWER 119.8 **GND CON** 121.9 **CLNC DEL** 121.375 126.7
 CPDLC (LOGON KUSA)
 PDC
AIRSPACE: CLASS C svc ctc **APP CON.**
VOR TEST FACILITY (VOT) 110.4
RADIO AIDS TO NAVIGATION: NOTAM FILE SAT.
 (VH) (H) VORTACW 116.8   SAT   Chan 115   N29°38.64´ W98°27.68´   176° 6.6 NM to fld. 1159/8E.
  VOR unusable:
   018°−022° byd 40 NM
   028°−032° byd 40 NM
   342°−347° byd 40 NM
   355°−002° byd 40 NM blo 18,000´
 ILS/DME 109.7 I−SAT   Chan 34   Rwy 04.   Class IE. Unmonitored.
 ILS/DME 110.9 I−ANT   Chan 46   Rwy 13R. Class IIE. DME also serves Rwy 31L.
 ILS/DME 110.9 I−IZR   Chan 46   Rwy 31L. Class IE.   DME also serves Rwy 13R.

TEXAS

SAN GERONIMO AIRPARK (8T8) 10 W UTC−6(−5DT) N29°30.61′ W98°47.91′   SAN ANTONIO
1040 NOTAM FILE SJT   L−19C
  RWY 17−35: H3000X40 (ASPH) 1.1% up N
    RWY 17: Trees.
    RWY 35: Trees.
  AIRPORT REMARKS: Unattended. Rwy 17−35 shoulders soft and muddy when wet. Wildlife on and invof arpt. Limit 3 TGLs durg daytime. Powered parachutes prohibited. +15 ft hgrs 112 ft west along Rwy 17−35.
  AIRPORT MANAGER: 210-688-9072
  COMMUNICATIONS: CTAF 122.9
  CLEARANCE DELIVERY PHONE: For CD ctc San Antonio Apch at 210-805-5516.
  RADIO AIDS TO NAVIGATION: NOTAM FILE SAT.
    SAN ANTONIO (VH) (H) VORTACW 116.8 SAT Chan 115 N29°38.64′ W98°27.68′ 238° 19.4 NM to fld. 1159/8E.
    VOR unusable:
      018°−022° byd 40 NM
      028°−032° byd 40 NM
      342°−347° byd 40 NM
      355°−002° byd 40 NM blo 18,000′

STINSON MUNI (SSF)(KSSF) 6 S UTC−6(−5DT) N29°20.22′ W98°28.26′   SAN ANTONIO
578 B NOTAM FILE SSF   H−7B, L−19C
     IAP, AD
  RWY 09−27: H5000X100 (ASPH) S−30, D−75 MIRL
    RWY 09: REIL. PAPI(P4L)—GA 3.0° TCH 40′. Thld dsplcd 450′. Trees.
    RWY 27: REIL. PAPI(P4L)—GA 3.0° TCH 40′. Pole.
  RWY 14−32: H4128X100 (ASPH) S−12, D−20 MIRL 0.5% up NW
    RWY 14: REIL. PAPI(P2R)—GA 3.0° TCH 35′. Thld dsplcd 583′. Trees.
    RWY 32: REIL. PAPI(P4L)—GA 3.0° TCH 40′. Thld dsplcd 372′. Trees.
  SERVICE: S4 **FUEL** 100LL, JET A **LGT** MIRL Rwy 09−27 and Rwy 14−32 preset med ints when twr clsd.
  AIRPORT REMARKS: Attended 1300−0200Z‡. Numerous acft opr at or abv 2,500′ MSL in the Stinson Arpt traffic area under the ctl of San Antonio Apch. PAEW adjacent all twys and ramp areas Mon−Fri 1300−2359Z‡.
  AIRPORT MANAGER: 210-207-1800
  WEATHER DATA SOURCES: ASOS (210) 927−9391 LAWRS.
  COMMUNICATIONS: CTAF 118.2 **ATIS** 128.8 **UNICOM** 122.95
  Ⓡ **SAN ANTONIO APP/DEP CON** 125.7
    TOWER 118.2 (1300−0400Z‡) **GND CON** 121.7 **CLNC DEL** 121.7
  CLEARANCE DELIVERY PHONE: For CD when ATCT is clsd ctc sat Apch at 210-805-5516.
  AIRSPACE: CLASS D svc 1300−0400Z‡; other times CLASS G.
  RADIO AIDS TO NAVIGATION: NOTAM FILE SAT.
    SAN ANTONIO (VH) (H) VORTACW 116.8 SAT Chan 115 N29°38.64′ W98°27.68′ 174° 18.4 NM to fld. 1159/8E.
    VOR unusable:
      018°−022° byd 40 NM
      028°−032° byd 40 NM
      342°−347° byd 40 NM
      355°−002° byd 40 NM blo 18,000′
    (L) VORW 108.4 SSF N29°15.50′ W98°26.61′ 334° 4.9 NM to fld. 541/9E. NOTAM FILE SSF.
    occasional fm broadcast interference occurs on freq 108.4
    VOR unusable:
      020°−075° byd 15 NM
      090°−105° byd 20 NM
      135°−185° byd 10 NM
      195°−219° byd 9 NM
      220°−250°
      325°−350° byd 25 NM

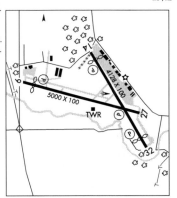

420 **TEXAS**

TWIN–OAKS (T94) 3 N UTC–6(–5DT) N29°34.21´ W98°28.10´ **SAN ANTONIO**
873 NOTAM FILE SJT
RWY 12–30: H2225X30 (ASPH) S–4
  RWY 12: Trees.
  RWY 30: Tree.
AIRPORT REMARKS: Unattended. Arpt clsd at ngt to tsnt acft. Houses, hngrs & trees in prim sfc. 6 ft fence lctd aprxly 70 ft E of rwy entr len. Rwy slopes up east to west. Rwy 12 end 41 ft higher than Rwy 30 end. No trml. Arpt fenced, gate locked. Public restrooms avbl 3rd bldg fm NW end, W side. Rwy 12 and Rwy 30 rwy markings NSTD due to size.
AIRPORT MANAGER: 210-494-3928
COMMUNICATIONS: CTAF 122.9
CLEARANCE DELIVERY PHONE: For CD ctc San Antonio Apch at 210-805-5516.
COMM/NAV/WEATHER REMARKS: Aprt inside San Antonio Class C sfc area. Ctc San Antonio ATCT, 119.8.

SAN AUGUSTINE CO (78R) 3 W UTC–6(–5DT) N31°32.43´ W94°10.20´ **HOUSTON**
443 B NOTAM FILE CXO **L–19E, 21A**
RWY 17–35: H3800X50 (ASPH) S–12 MIRL 1.3% up N
  RWY 17: Thld dsplcd 124´. Trees.
  RWY 35: Trees.
SERVICE: **LGT** MIRL Rwy 17–35 preset low ints, to incr ints ACTIVATE—CTAF. ACTIVATE rotating bcn—CTAF.
AIRPORT REMARKS: Unattended. Rwy 17–35 cracking and few potholes.
AIRPORT MANAGER: 936-275-2762
COMMUNICATIONS: CTAF 122.9
CLEARANCE DELIVERY PHONE: For CD ctc Houston ARTCC at 281-230-5622.
RADIO AIDS TO NAVIGATION: NOTAM FILE LFK.
  LUFKIN (VH) (H) VORTACW 112.3 LFK Chan 58 N31°09.75´ W94°43.01´ 046° 36.1 NM to fld. 207/5E.
  TACAN AZIMUTH unusable:
    260°–275° byd 30 NM
    275°–260° byd 30 NM blo 2,500´
  DME unusable:
    260°–275° byd 30 NM
    275°–260° byd 30 NM blo 2,500´
  VOR unusable:
    305°–312° byd 40 NM
    313°–323° byd 40 NM blo 2,300´
    313°–323° byd 66 NM
    324°–330° byd 40 NM

SAN GERONIMO AIRPARK (See SAN ANTONIO on page 419)

SAN MARCOS RGNL (See AUSTIN on page 250)

SAN SABA CO MUNI (81R) 3 N UTC–6(–5DT) N31°14.14´ W98°43.06´ **SAN ANTONIO**
1255 B NOTAM FILE SJT **L–19C**
RWY 13–31: H4206X60 (ASPH) S–12.5 MIRL 0.3% up NW **IAP**
  RWY 13: PAPI(P2L)—GA 3.0° TCH 40´.
  RWY 31: PAPI(P2L)—GA 3.0° TCH 40´. Road.
SERVICE: **FUEL** 100LL **LGT** ACTVT MIRL Rwy 13–31—CTAF.
AIRPORT REMARKS: Unattended. Deer on and invof arpt. Rwy 13, 10 ft ditch 30–180 ft dstc.
AIRPORT MANAGER: 325-372-3380
WEATHER DATA SOURCES: AWOS–3P 120.525 (325) 372–6027.
COMMUNICATIONS: CTAF/UNICOM 122.8
  HOUSTON CENTER APP/DEP CON 132.35
CLEARANCE DELIVERY PHONE: For CD ctc Houston ARTCC at 281-230-5622.
RADIO AIDS TO NAVIGATION: NOTAM FILE AQO.
  LLANO (L) (L) VORTACW 108.2 LLO Chan 19 N30°47.78´ W98°47.24´ 360° 26.5 NM to fld. 1207/8E.

TEXAS

SANGER

FLYING C (T87) 5 SW UTC–6(–5DT) N33°20.53´ W97°16.20´ DALLAS–FT WORTH
  775 NOTAM FILE FTW
  RWY 09–27: 1650X90 (TURF)
    RWY 09: Fence.
    RWY 27: Trees.
  RWY 17–35: 1400X140 (TURF)
    RWY 17: Trees.
    RWY 35: Trees.
  AIRPORT REMARKS: Unattended. For fld condition call arpt manager. Occasional livestock on fld.
  AIRPORT MANAGER: (972) 978-7127
  COMMUNICATIONS: CTAF 122.9
  CLEARANCE DELIVERY PHONE: For CD ctc Regional Apch at 972-615-2799.

IRONHEAD (T58) 3 SW UTC–6(–5DT) N33°19.91´ W97°13.82´ DALLAS–FT WORTH
  715 NOTAM FILE FTW
  RWY 18–36: 2500X200 (TURF)
    RWY 18: Fence.
    RWY 36: Tree.
  AIRPORT REMARKS: Unattended. Wildlife on and invof of arpt. Rwy 18–36 soft when wet, call for fld cond. Rwy 18–36 thld and edges marked with white tires. Arpt CLOSED to helicopter training. North 700´ Rwy 18–36 slopes down 25´, rwy ends not visible from opposite end.
  AIRPORT MANAGER: 940-458-7348
  COMMUNICATIONS: CTAF 122.9
  CLEARANCE DELIVERY PHONE: For CD ctc Regional Apch at 972-615-2799.

VULTURES ROW (6X8) 7 E UTC–6(–5DT) N33°20.40´ W97°06.18´ DALLAS–FT WORTH
  710 NOTAM FILE FTW
  RWY 18–36: 2700X50 (TURF)
    RWY 18: Tree.
    RWY 36: Trees.
  AIRPORT REMARKS: Unattended. Rwy 18–36 soft when wet, call for FICONS. Rwy 18–36 width mowed to 15´ wide drg hay season. Rwy 18 37´ powerlines mkd 110´ fm thr xng cntrln. HOP prohibited. No student pilots. Do not overfly house drctly N of rwy.
  AIRPORT MANAGER: 940-453-8126
  COMMUNICATIONS: CTAF 122.9
  CLEARANCE DELIVERY PHONE: For CD ctc Regional Apch at 972-615-2799.

SANTA ELENA U38 N26°49.26´ W98°29.10´/313 BROWNSVILLE
  AWOS–3T 135.975 U38 AWOS is associated with airport 38XS. L–20H

SCHOLES INTL AT GALVESTON (See GALVESTON on page 316)

SEBAS N26°18.31´ W97°39.45´ NOTAM FILE HRL. BROWNSVILLE
  NDB (LOMW) 338 HR 173° 4.7 NM to Valley Intl. 28/5E. L–20H, 21A

SEGUIN

HUBER AIRPARK CIVIC CLUB LLC (E70) 2 NW UTC–6(–5DT) N29°36.14´ W97°59.43´ SAN ANTONIO
  556 B NOTAM FILE SJT L–19C
  RWY 18–36: H3415X50 (ASPH) LIRL
    RWY 18: Tree.
  SERVICE: FUEL 100LL **LGT** Actvt LIRL Rwy 18–36—CTAF. Rwy 18–36 only cntr 3285 lgtd.
  AIRPORT REMARKS: Mon–Fri 1400–2300Z‡. 100LL self-serve. Rwy 18–36 mag brg 174–354.
  AIRPORT MANAGER: 830-379-9800
  COMMUNICATIONS: CTAF 122.9
  CLEARANCE DELIVERY PHONE: For CD ctc San Antonio Apch at 210-805-5516.
  RADIO AIDS TO NAVIGATION: NOTAM FILE SAT.
    SAN ANTONIO (VH) (H) VORTACW 116.8 SAT Chan 115 N29°38.64´ W98°27.68´ 088° 24.7 NM to fld. 1159/8E.
      VOR unusable:
        018°–022° byd 40 NM
        028°–032° byd 40 NM
        342°–347° byd 40 NM
        355°–002° byd 40 NM blo 18,000´

SEMINOLE

GAINES CO (GNC)(KGNC) 3 S UTC–6(–5DT) N32°40.52´ W102°39.16´ ALBUQUERQUE
3315 B NOTAM FILE GNC H–6G, L–6H
RWY 08–26: H5381X75 (ASPH) S–12.5 MIRL 0.6% up W IAP
  RWY 08: PAPI(P2L)—GA 3.0° TCH 24´.
  RWY 26: PAPI(P2L)—GA 3.0° TCH 20´. P–line.
RWY 17–35: H5002X75 (ASPH) S–12.5 MIRL 0.4% up N
  RWY 17: PAPI(P2L)—GA 3.0° TCH 23´. P–line.
  RWY 35: PAPI(P2L)—GA 3.0° TCH 37´. Trees.
SERVICE: S4 FUEL 100LL, JET A OX 1, 3 LGT MIRL Rwys 08–26 and
Rwy 17–35 preset low intst; to incr intst actvt—CTAF.
AIRPORT REMARKS: Attended Mon–Fri 1400–0000Z‡, Sat 1400–1800Z‡.
Parachute Jumping. Aft hrs svc: email Jonathan or call
432–955–7672. Rwy 08 and 26 markings faded.
AIRPORT MANAGER: 432-788-7357
WEATHER DATA SOURCES: AWOS–3 118.075 (432) 758–3102.
COMMUNICATIONS: CTAF/UNICOM 122.8
®FORT WORTH CENTER APP/DEP CON 132.6
CLEARANCE DELIVERY PHONE: For CD ctc Fort Worth ARTCC at
817-858-7584.
RADIO AIDS TO NAVIGATION: NOTAM FILE HOB.
  HOBBS (L) (L) VORTACW 111.0 HOB Chan 47 N32°38.29´
  W103°16.16´ 075° 31.3 NM to fld. 3664/11E.

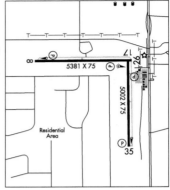

SEYMOUR MUNI (60F) 3 N UTC–6(–5DT) N33°38.91´ W99°15.68´ DALLAS–FT WORTH
1344 B NOTAM FILE FTW L–17B
RWY 17–35: H4300X60 (ASPH) S–4 MIRL IAP
  RWY 17: Fence.
  RWY 35: Hangar.
AIRPORT REMARKS: Unattended.
AIRPORT MANAGER: 940-889-0025
COMMUNICATIONS: CTAF 122.9
®FORT WORTH CENTER APP/DEP CON 133.5
CLEARANCE DELIVERY PHONE: For CD ctc Fort Worth ARTCC at 817-858-7584.
RADIO AIDS TO NAVIGATION: NOTAM FILE SPS.
  WICHITA FALLS (H) (H) VORTACW 112.7 SPS Chan 74 N33°59.24´ W98°35.61´ 229° 39.1 NM to fld. 1133/10E.

SHAMROCK MUNI (2F1) 3 NE UTC–6(–5DT) N35°14.08´ W100°11.12´ DALLAS–FT WORTH
2369 B NOTAM FILE FTW L–15C
RWY 17–35: H3600X60 (ASPH) S–15 MIRL
  RWY 17: Berm.
  RWY 35: Trees.
SERVICE: FUEL 100LL LGT MIRL Rwy 17–35 dusk–0600Z‡. Aft 0600Z‡ ACTVT—CTAF. Nmrs rwy lts out.
AIRPORT REMARKS: Unattended. Fuel self svc. Rwy 17–35, loose aggregate on rwy. Rwy 17 and Rwy 35 rwy mrkgs faded,
barely vsbl. Rwy 17–35, severe cracking. No twy mrkgs or hold lines.
AIRPORT MANAGER: 806-256-3281
COMMUNICATIONS: CTAF/UNICOM 122.8
CLEARANCE DELIVERY PHONE: For CD ctc Albuquerque ARTCC at 505-856-4861.

SHANK N BANK (See LA WARD on page 357)

TEXAS 423

SHEPPARD AFB/WICHITA FALLS MUNI (SPS)(KSPS) MIL/CIV AF   5 N   UTC–6(–5DT)   N33°59.33´   **DALLAS–FT WORTH**
W98°29.51´   **H–6H, L–17B**
1019   B   TPA—See Remarks   Class I, ARFF Index B   NOTAM FILE SPS   **IAP, DIAP, AD**
RWY 15R–33L: H13101X300 (CONC)   PCN 75 R/C/W/T   HIRL
  RWY 15R: MALSR. PAPI(P4L)—GA 3.0° TCH 55´. Rgt tfc.
  RWY 33L: MALSR. PAPI(P4L)—GA 3.0° TCH 56´.
RWY 15C–33C: H10003X150 (ASPH–CONC)   PCN 27 F/B/W/T   HIRL
  RWY 15C: ALSF1. PAPI(P4L)—GA 3.0° TCH 46´.
  RWY 33C: ALSF1. PAPI(P4L)—GA 3.0° TCH 48´.
RWY 18–36: H7021X150 (ASPH)   PCN 33 F/A/W/T   HIRL
  RWY 18: Rgt tfc.
  RWY 36: REIL.
RWY 15L–33R: H6000X150 (ASPH–CONC)   PCN 27 R/C/W/T   HIRL   0.3% up NW
  RWY 15L: REIL. PAPI(P4L)—GA 3.0° TCH 40´.
  RWY 33R: REIL. PAPI(P4L)—GA 3.0° TCH 40´.
ARRESTING GEAR/SYSTEM
  RWY 15R MA–1A CHAG (145 FT OVRN).   MA–1A CHAG (145 FT OVRN). **RWY 33L**
  RWY 15C BAK 15 (175 FT OVRN).   BAK 15 (175 FT OVRN). **RWY 33C**
SERVICE: S2   **FUEL** 100LL, JET A   **LGT** When ATCT clsd ACTVT MALSR Rwy 33L—CTAF. Rwy 15R–33L PAPI Rwy Reference Point and ILS Rwy Point of Intercept not coincidental. Rwy 15C–33C PAPI GS and ILS GS not coincidental. Rwy 15C SFL OTS UFN. **MILITARY**— **A–GEAR** MA–1A Rwy 15R–33L not raised, unless 80th FTW is flying, rqr 30 min PN when twr opr. Rwy 15C BAK–15 (175´ into ovrn). Rwy 33C BAK–15 (175´ into ovrn). Rwy 15R MA–1A CHAG (145´ ovrn). Rwy 33L MA–1A CHAG (145´ ovrn). **JASU** 3(AM32–95) 1(MC–1) 3(AM/32A–86D) **FUEL** A++ **FLUID** SP PRESAIR LOX **OIL** O–148. JOAP Results avbl 1345–2100Z‡ wkd exc hol. **TRAN ALERT** Opr 1200–0200Z‡ wkd, 1800–2300Z‡ Sun, clsd Sat and hol. Qualified weapons/munitions pers not avbl to safe ftr type acft.
AIRPORT REMARKS: Attended continuously. Migratory bird activity on and invof arpt from Oct–Apr. Mil arpt conducts high performance jet trng in a high density environment Mon–Fri 1300–0300Z‡ and when twr hrs extdd by NOTAM, ocnl Sat and Sun. Rwy 15C first 2000 ft and last 1000 ft conc; middle zone asph. Rwy 15L–33R first and last 1000´ conc, middle zone asph. Due to close proximity of Rwys 33L and 33C use vigilance with monitor gnd track for the Hi–TACAN Rwy 33C apch. Solo students not authorized. Wx obsn ltd to west due to hangar rstd view. TPA—lgt acft 1819(800), conventional and jet acft 2319(1300). Overhead Rwy 15R–33L 2819(1800).
MILITARY REMARKS: RSTD PPR, 24 hr PN rqr, ctc afld OPS DSN 736–2180/6474, C940–676–2180/6474. All tran acft must be chocked 30 minutes prior to tran alert closing, PPR expires 30 minutes prior to afld closing. All trans acft required to arrive with crew orders for security forces. Tran acft ltd to one apch to a full stop ldg and must taxi to prkg durg stu trng. Twy L and K clsd exc for mil base assigned acft and C–130 and smlr acft exiting Rwy 33C via Twy L and K. Pavement north of Twy Echo btn Rwy 18–36 and Airfield Ops Cntr apn unusbl. Remain on Twy Echo cntrln. **CAUTION** Do not confuse parallel twy with Rwy 15R–33L. Dur periods when ctl twr is clsd, exer caution when taxiing, the civ arpt is lctd to the S and the mil ramp is lctd to the W of the rwys. Fld Cond NOTAM (FICON) (RSC/RCR) not rprtd when twr clsd. ATC personnel in accordance with the cooperative wx Watch (CWW) will alert WX personnel on any unreported wx cond that could affect flt safety. Mil arpt conducts hi per jet trng in a hi density environment 1400–0400Z‡ Mon–Fri and when twr hr extn by NOTAM, ocnly Sat. Trans mil acft not auzd to arr/dep outside of publ hr. **MISC** Base OPS 1200–0200Z‡ wkd; 1800–2300Z‡ Sun; clsd Sat and hol. AETC fgtr acft exp reduced rwy separation. Day/VFR, similar type acft 3000´, dissimilar type acft 6000´, ngt 6000´ all AETC acft. For arr/dep req outside of published hrs ctc the Afld Ops Flt/Command Post at C940–676–2616, DSN 736–2616. Tran Mil acft will not receive support from Sheppard AFB outside of published hr. Expect no AF svc while prk at the rgn arpt. Tran AETC acft notify twr on initial ctc if reduced rwy separation is not desired. Ctc Base Taxi DSN 736–1843 C940–676–1843, or U–Drive DSN 736–6813 C940–676–6813 prior to arr. Mil wx advsy/warning avbl on req METRO. Wx obsv ltd to west due to rstd view. NOTE: See Special Notices—Aerobatic Practice Area.
AIRPORT MANAGER: 940-676-7119
WEATHER DATA SOURCES: ASOS (940) 855–9045 Obsn augmented dur afld opr hr.
COMMUNICATIONS: CTAF 119.75 279.525   ATIS 132.05 269.9 (Opr 1200–0200Z‡)   **UNICOM** 122.95 PTD Mnt 1200–0200Z‡ Mon–Fri, 1800–2300Z‡ Sun, exc hol.
  WICHITA FALLS RCO 122.65 (FORT WORTH RADIO)
Ⓡ **SHEPPARD APP CON** 118.2 269.025 (Mon–Fri 1200–0200Z‡, Sun 1800–0200Z‡; clsd Sat and hol, OT ctc FORT WORTH CENTER 133.5 350.35)
Ⓡ **SHEPPARD DEP CON** 118.2 120.4 269.025 316.075(Mon–Fri 1200–0200Z‡, Sun 1800–2300Z‡, exc hol, OT ctc FORT WORTH CENTER 133.5 350.35)
Ⓡ **FORT WORTH CENTER APP/DEP CON** 133.5 350.35 (Mon–Fri 0200–1200Z‡, Sun 2300–1800Z‡, Sat and hol 24 hrs)
  SHEPPARD TOWER 119.75 279.525 (Mon–Fri 1200–0200Z‡, Sun 1800–2300Z‡, clsd Sat and hol, OT use CTAF 119.75 279.525).   **GND CON** 125.5 289.4   **CLNC DEL** 121.2 282.525
  PMSV METRO 339.65 Wx opr hr 0500Z‡ Mon thru 0100Z‡ Sat, 1300–2200Z‡ Sun, clsd Sat and hol; opr hr may vary by lcl flying sked. Ctc C940–676–2730. KSPS ASOS remains opnl. Winds issued by twr are offl afld winds fm the cntr rwy.
CLEARANCE DELIVERY PHONE: For CD if una to ctc on FSS freq, ctc Fort Worth ARTCC at 817-858-7584.
AIRSPACE: CLASS D svc 1200–0200Z‡ Mon–Fri, 1800–2300Z‡ Sun, clsd Sat & hol; other times use CTAF 119.75 279.525; other times CLASS E.

CONTINUED ON NEXT PAGE
SC, 25 JAN 2024 to 21 MAR 2024

TEXAS

CONTINUED FROM PRECEDING PAGE

RADIO AIDS TO NAVIGATION: NOTAM FILE SPS.
   WICHITA FALLS (H) (H) VORTACW 112.7   SPS   Chan 74   N33°59.24´ W98°35.61´   079° 5.1 NM to fld. 1133/10E.
    (L) TACAN   Chan 45   SHP (110.8)   N33°58.96´ W98°29.26´   at fld. 992/5E.
     No NOTAM MP 0500–1200Z‡ Wed
    DME unusable:
     240°–260° byd 35 NM blo 3,500´
     261°–280° byd 30 NM blo 5,000´
    AZIMUTH unusable:
     261°–280° byd 30 NM blo 5,000´
   ILS 110.5 I–SHP Rwy 15C. Class IT. ILS unmntrd 0200–1100Z‡. ILS apch not radar mnt wkend and hol. Mp 0500–1200Z‡ dly.
   ILS/DME 109.7 I–SPS Chan 34 Rwy 33L. Class IE. ILS unmntrd 0200–1100Z‡. ILS apch not radar mnt wkend and hol. Mp 0600–1100Z‡ Mon, Tue.
   ASR (1200–0200Z‡)
COMM/NAV/WEATHER REMARKS: ASOS obsn augmented dur afld opr hr. ASOS is fixed sensor lctd near south end Rwy 15R–33L, measures clouds up to max hgt 12,000´. Radar see Terminal FLIP for Radar Minima

---

SHERMAN MUNI (SWI)(KSWI)   1 SE   UTC–6(–5DT)   N33°37.45´ W96°35.17´   **DALLAS–FT WORTH**
746 B   NOTAM FILE FTW   **L–17C, A**
RWY 16–34: H4000X75 (ASPH) S–19   MIRL   0.9% up NW   **IAP**
  RWY 16: Trees.
  RWY 34: P–line.
SERVICE: S4 **FUEL** 100LL **LGT** MIRL Rwy 16–34 preset low intst; to increase intst and ACTIVATE—CTAF.
AIRPORT REMARKS: Attended 1400–2300Z‡. Fuel avbl with major credit card. City ordinance mandates all tkfs on Rwy 34 commence at thld markings. High speed, low level passes are prohibited. Windsock not visible from Rwy 16 end. Twy mkgs and hold short lines poor. Hold line signs NSTD white.
AIRPORT MANAGER: 903-868-4412
COMMUNICATIONS: CTAF/UNICOM 122.8
®**FORT WORTH CENTER APP/DEP CON** 124.75
CLEARANCE DELIVERY PHONE: For CD ctc Fort Worth ARTCC at 817-858-7584.
RADIO AIDS TO NAVIGATION: NOTAM FILE FTW.
   BONHAM (VH) (H) VORTACW 114.6   BYP   Chan 93   N33°32.25´ W96°14.05´   280° 18.4 NM to fld. 700/6E.

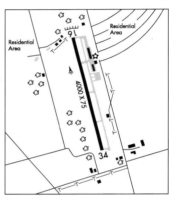

TEXAS

SHERMAN/DENISON

NORTH TEXAS RGNL/PERRIN FLD (GYI)(KGYI) 4 W UTC−6(−5DT) N33°42.85′ W96°40.46′ **DALLAS−FT WORTH**
749 B NOTAM FILE GYI **H−6H, L−17C, A**
RWY 17L−35R: H9000X150 (ASPH−CONC) S−75, D−100, 2S−127, **IAP, AD**
  2D−160 MIRL
  RWY 17L: MALSR. VASI(V4L)—GA 3.0° TCH 48′.
  RWY 35R: MALS. VASI(V4L)—GA 3.0° TCH 51′.
RWY 17R−35L: H4008X100 (ASPH−CONC)
RWY 13−31: H2277X60 (ASPH)
SERVICE: S4 **FUEL** 100LL, JET A **OX** 3 **LGT** Dusk−Dawn. MIRL Rwy
  17L−35R preset low intst, to incr intst and ACTVT MALSR Rwy 17L
  and MALS Rwy 35R—CTAF.
AIRPORT REMARKS: Attended 1300−0100Z‡. 100LL self serve. For fuel
  after hours call 903−786−2666; call−in fee. Rwy 17L dsgnd calm
  wind rwy. Txy mkgs and hold lines faded. Rwy 13−31 CLOSED
  permly. Extsv cracking and loose grvl. NOTE: See Special
  Notices—Aerobatic Practice Area.
AIRPORT MANAGER: 903−786−2904
WEATHER DATA SOURCES: AWOS−3 118.775 (903) 786−7790.
COMMUNICATIONS: CTAF 120.575 **ATIS** 118.775
  SHERMAN/DENISON RCO 122.3 (FORT WORTH RADIO)
®**FORT WORTH CENTER APP/DEP CON** 124.75
  TOWER 120.575 (1300−0100Z‡) **GND CON** 124.125
CLEARANCE DELIVERY PHONE: For CD if una to ctc on FSS freq, ctc Fort Worth ARTCC at 817−858−7584.
AIRSPACE: CLASS D svc 1300−0100Z‡; other times CLASS G.
RADIO AIDS TO NAVIGATION: NOTAM FILE FTW.
  BONHAM (VH) (H) VORTACW 114.6 BYP Chan 93 N33°32.25′ W96°14.05′ 290° 24.5 NM to fld. 700/6E.
  DENISON NDB (MHW) 341 DNI N33°49.59′ W96°40.13′ 176° 6.7 NM to fld. 642/6E. NOTAM FILE GYI.
  ILS 111.7 I−GYI Rwy 17L. Class IT. LOC unusable byd 25° right of course. Glideslope autocoupled approaches na
    blw 1,900′ MSL.

SINTON

ALFRED C 'BUBBA' THOMAS (T69) 2 W UTC−6(−5DT) N28°02.31′ W97°32.55′ **SAN ANTONIO**
48 B NOTAM FILE SJT **L−20H, 21A, GOMW**
RWY 14−32: H4323X55 (ASPH) S−8 MIRL **IAP**
  RWY 14: REIL. PAPI(P2L)—GA 3.0° TCH 19′. Thld dsplcd 250′. Road.
  RWY 32: REIL. PAPI(P2L)—GA 3.0° TCH 21′. Thld dsplcd 400′. Road.
RWY 03−21: 3100X50 (TURF)
  RWY 03: Road.
  RWY 21: P−line.
SERVICE: S4 **FUEL** 100LL, JET A+ **LGT** ACTVT REIL Rwy 14 and Rwy
  32; MIRL Rwy 14−32—CTAF.
AIRPORT REMARKS: Attended 1330−2300Z‡. Rwy 03−21 CLOSED indefly.
  Rwy 03−21 surface: rwy not mntnd, not inspd. Una to dtrm exact lctn
  of rwy. For fuel or svc call 361−364−3200. Aft hrs call
  361−548−1483 or 361−364−2251.
AIRPORT MANAGER: 361−226−0112
WEATHER DATA SOURCES: AWOS−3 118.25 (361) 364−1844.
COMMUNICATIONS: CTAF/UNICOM 122.8
  CORPUS CHRISTI RCO 122.2 (SAN ANGELO RADIO)
®**CORPUS APP/DEP CON** 120.9
CLEARANCE DELIVERY PHONE: For CD ctc Corpus Christi Apch at
  361−299−4230.
RADIO AIDS TO NAVIGATION: NOTAM FILE CRP.
  CORPUS CHRISTI (VH) (H) VORTACW 115.5 CRP Chan 102 N27°54.23′ W97°26.69′ 318° 9.6 NM to fld. 60/9E.
    TACAN AZIMUTH & DME unusable:
      024°−036° byd 35 NM blo 1,700′
      037°−023° byd 35 NM blo 2,000′
      265°−275°
    VOR unusable:
      340°−005° byd 40 NM blo 7,000′
      340°−005° byd 84 NM
      Byd 30 NM blo 1,500′
    TACAN AZIMUTH unusable:
      080°−085° byd 30 NM

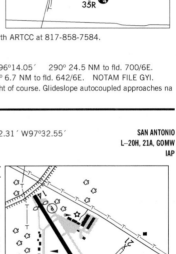

SC, 25 JAN 2024 to 21 MAR 2024

SKYLARK FLD (See KILLEEN on page 352)

SKYWAY MANOR (See PEARLAND on page 397)

SKYWEST INC (See MIDLAND on page 382)

SLATON
CITY OF SLATON/LARRY T NEAL MEML (F49) 2 N UTC–6(–5DT) N33°29.11´ W101°39.70´ DALLAS–FT WORTH
3127 B NOTAM FILE FTW L–6H
RWY 18–36: H4244X75 (ASPH) S–20 MIRL IAP
  RWY 18: PAPI(P2L)—GA 3.0° TCH 40´. Pole.
  RWY 36: PAPI(P2L)—GA 3.0° TCH 40´.
RWY 08–26: 1720X65 (TURF)
  RWY 08: Brush.
SERVICE: S2 **FUEL** 100LL, JET A **LGT** MIRL Rwy 18–36 nonstd PCL: 3–X on, 5–X off—CTAF. PAPI Rwy 18 OTS indefly. PAPI Rwy 36 OTS indefly.
AIRPORT REMARKS: BCAttended Mon–Fri 1400–2300Z‡. Aerobatic activity SR–SS, mod use on wkends. 5´ line-of-sight not avbl btn Rwy 18–36 ends. Rwy 08–26 sfc rough, CLOSED permly. 3457´ MSL, 348´ AGL twr, 1.75 nm SW of arpt.
AIRPORT MANAGER: 806-828-5892
COMMUNICATIONS: CTAF/UNICOM 123.0
Ⓡ**LUBBOCK APP/DEP CON** 119.2
CLEARANCE DELIVERY PHONE: For CD ctc Fort Worth ARTCC at 817-858-7584.
RADIO AIDS TO NAVIGATION: NOTAM FILE LBB.
  LUBBOCK (L) (L) VORTACW 109.2 LBB Chan 29 N33°42.30´ W101°54.84´ 125° 18.3 NM to fld. 3310/11E.
  VOR unusable:
    040°–050° byd 38 NM blo 5,300´
    210°–260° byd 25 NM blo 6,000´

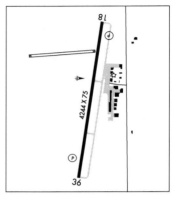

SLIDELL
AKROVILLE (3TX) 3 NE UTC–6(–5DT) N33°23.57´ W97°21.23´ DALLAS–FT WORTH
895 NOTAM FILE 3TX
RWY 18–36: 3001X60 (TURF)
  RWY 18: Fence.
  RWY 36: Road.
RWY 05–23: 1600X60 (TURF)
  RWY 05: Fence.
  RWY 23: Fence.
AIRPORT REMARKS: Attended irregularly. Birds, cows and wildlife invof rwys. APA acrobatic practice area co-lctd with arpt. Intsv aerobatic trng. Arpt fenced and gate locked. For ingress and egress, call 817–658–7479. PPR. Ctc amgr 24 hrs prior to arr, 817–658–7479. PPR ctc amgr 24 hrs prior to arr, 817–658–7479 for fld condsLoose rocks on rwy. Radio ctc recommended prior to ldg for adzy. Rwy 05–23 corners mkd with white barrels. Rwy 18–36 corners mkd with white barrels. Arpt rolling trrn. Acft not vsb at opposite rwy ends.
AIRPORT MANAGER: 817-658-4569
COMMUNICATIONS: CTAF 122.9
CLEARANCE DELIVERY PHONE: For CD ctc Regional Apch at 972-615-2799.

- -

CAIN (T28) 4 W UTC–6(–5DT) N33°21.27´ W97°26.34´ DALLAS–FT WORTH
890 NOTAM FILE FTW
RWY 18–36: 1200X50 (TURF)
  RWY 18: Fence.
  RWY 36: Brush. Rgt tfc.
AIRPORT REMARKS: Attended continuously. Deer on and invof arpt. Recommend STOL acft ops only. Rwy 18–36 rough, some portions gravel; call prior to use for rwy cond. Rwy 18–36 8–10´ rising terrain east of rwy. Rolling terrain, rwy ends not visible from each end.
AIRPORT MANAGER: 214-914-4809
COMMUNICATIONS: CTAF 122.9
CLEARANCE DELIVERY PHONE: For CD ctc Regional Apch at 972-615-2799.

SMILEY JOHNSON MUNI/BASS FLD (See CLARENDON on page 272)

TEXAS

SMITHVILLE CRAWFORD MUNI (84R) 2 N UTC–6(–5DT) N30°01.69´ W97°10.02´ SAN ANTONIO
323 B NOTAM FILE SJT L–19D, 21A
RWY 17–35: H4000X75 (ASPH) S–12.5 MIRL IAP
 RWY 17: PAPI(P2L)—GA 4.0° TCH 40´. Trees.
 RWY 35: PAPI(P2L)—GA 3.0° TCH 40´. Trees.
SERVICE: S4 FUEL 100LL LGT SS–SR Actvt MIRL Rwy 17–35 123.3;
 PAPI opr consly.
AIRPORT REMARKS: Attended Mon–Sat 1500–2300Z‡. Wildlife and
 livestock invof arpt. 35´ mkd/lgtd pline 1300´ dstc, acrs apch.
AIRPORT MANAGER: 512-237-3282
COMMUNICATIONS: CTAF 122.8
®AUSTIN APP/DEP CON 120.875 270.25
CLEARANCE DELIVERY PHONE: For CD ctc Austin Apch at 512-369-7865.
RADIO AIDS TO NAVIGATION: NOTAM FILE AUS.
 CENTEX (VH) (H) VORTACW 112.8 CWK Chan 75 N30°22.71´
  W97°31.79´ 132° 28.2 NM to fld. 593/6E.
 VOR unusable:
  180°–190° byd 40 NM
  200°–210° byd 40 NM

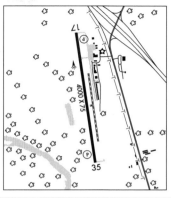

SNYDER

WINSTON FLD (SNK)(KSNK) 2 SW UTC–6(–5DT) N32°41.60´ W100°57.03´ DALLAS–FT WORTH
2430 B NOTAM FILE SNK H–6G, L–17A
RWY 17–35: H5599X100 (ASPH) S–24 MIRL IAP
 RWY 17: REIL. PAPI(P4R)—GA 3.0° TCH 33´. Rgt tfc.
 RWY 35: REIL. PAPI(P4L)—GA 3.0° TCH 30´.
RWY 08–26: H4200X75 (ASPH) S–24 1.3% up E
 RWY 08: Trees. Rgt tfc.
SERVICE: FUEL 100LL, JET A1 LGT Dusk–Dawn. MIRL Rwy 17–35
 preset low intst; to incr intst and actvt PAPI Rwys 17 and 35—CTAF.
 Rwy 35 PAPI unusbl byd 9 degs left and right of rwy cntrln.
AIRPORT REMARKS: Attended 1400–0000Z‡. Arpt unattended Thanksgiving,
 Christmas, and Easter.
AIRPORT MANAGER: 325-573-1122
WEATHER DATA SOURCES: AWOS–3 119.925 (325) 573–5724.
COMMUNICATIONS: CTAF/UNICOM 122.8
 SNYDER RCO 122.45 (FORT WORTH RADIO)
®FORT WORTH CENTER APP/DEP CON 127.45
CLEARANCE DELIVERY PHONE: For CD if una to ctc on FSS freq, ctc Fort Worth
 ARTCC at 817-858-7584.
RADIO AIDS TO NAVIGATION: NOTAM FILE BPG.
 BIG SPRING (VL) (H) VORTACW 117.2 BGS Chan 119 N32°23.14´
  W101°29.02´ 045° 32.7 NM to fld. 2670/11E.
 SNYDER NDB (MHW) 359 SDR N32°42.08´ W100°56.77´ at fld. 2434/8E. NOTAM FILE FTW.

SOMERSET

CANNON FLD (53T) 6 E UTC–6(–5DT) N29°12.93´ W98°32.98´ SAN ANTONIO
610 NOTAM FILE SJT
RWY 17–35: 2790X100 (TURF)
 RWY 17: Thld dsplcd 50´. Fence.
 RWY 35: Thld dsplcd 20´. Tree.
AIRPORT REMARKS: Attended continuously. Wildlife on and invof arpt. Rwy soft when wet, call for ficons. Rwy 17–35 south half
 rough edges. 30 ft mkd pline 500 ft N of Rwy 17 end. Rwys 17 and 35 dsplcd thrs mkd with white painted barrels. Rwy
 17–35 rolling terrain full length of rwy.
AIRPORT MANAGER: 210-842-0429
COMMUNICATIONS: CTAF/UNICOM 123.0
CLEARANCE DELIVERY PHONE: For CD ctc San Antonio Apch at 210-805-5516.

SONORA

ROCKING L (Ø1T)   26 ESE   UTC–6(–5DT)   N30°22.40′ W100°11.41′   SAN ANTONIO
  2339   NOTAM FILE   Not insp.
  RWY 18–36: 2432X50 (GRVL)
    RWY 18: Rgt tfc.
  AIRPORT MANAGER: 325-226-3445
  COMMUNICATIONS: CTAF 122.9

SONORA MUNI (SOA)(KSOA)   1 N   UTC–6(–5DT)   N30°35.14′ W100°38.91′   SAN ANTONIO
  2140   B   NOTAM FILE SOA   L–19B
  RWY 18–36: H4037X60 (ASPH)   S–12.5   MIRL   IAP
    RWY 18: REIL. PVASI(PSIL)—GA 3.0° TCH 25′. Thld dsplcd 93′. Trees.
    RWY 36: REIL. PVASI(PSIL)—GA 3.0° TCH 26′. Thld dsplcd 601′.
    P–line.
  SERVICE: **LGT** MIRL Rwy 18–36 preset med intst only. Actvt PVASI Rwys
    18 and 36—CTAF. Nstd lgt–incorrect colors, several lgts ots.
  AIRPORT REMARKS: Unattended. Rwy 18–36 markings faded.
  AIRPORT MANAGER: 325-387-2558
  WEATHER DATA SOURCES: AWOS–3 118.075 (325) 387–3801.
  COMMUNICATIONS: CTAF/UNICOM 122.8
  ®**HOUSTON CENTER APP/DEP CON** 125.75
  CLEARANCE DELIVERY PHONE: For CD ctc Houston ARTCC at 281-230-5622.
  RADIO AIDS TO NAVIGATION: NOTAM FILE ECU.
    ROCKSPRINGS (VL) (H) VORTAC 114.55   RSG   Chan 92(Y)
      N30°00.88′ W100°17.99′   322° 38.7 NM to fld. 2310/10E.
      VOR unusable:
        000°–010° byd 40 NM
        015°–035° byd 40 NM
        065°–095° byd 40 NM
        250°–280° byd 40 NM
        315°–322° byd 40 NM blo 6,000′
        315°–322° byd 56 NM
        323°–359° byd 40 NM
    NDB (MHW) 371   SOA   N30°34.91′ W100°38.82′   at fld. 2139/8E.   NOTAM FILE SOA. NDB unmonitored.

SOUTH TEXAS INTL AT EDINBURG (See EDINBURG on page 301)

SOUTH TEXAS RGNL AT HONDO (See HONDO on page 332)

SOUTHWEST LUBBOCK (See WOLFFORTH on page 449)

SPEARMAN

MAJOR SAMUEL B CORNELIUS FLD (E42)   1 N   UTC–6(–5DT)   N36°13.26′ W101°11.67′   WICHITA
  3090   B   NOTAM FILE FTW   H–6G, L–15B
  RWY 02–20: H5022X75 (ASPH)   S–12.5   MIRL   IAP
    RWY 02: PAPI(P2L)—GA 3.0° TCH 39′. Road.
    RWY 20: PAPI(P2L)—GA 3.0° TCH 40′.
  SERVICE: **FUEL** 100LL   **LGT** MIRL Rwy 02–20 preset low intst; to incr
    intst and ACTVT PAPI Rwys 02 and 20—CTAF. Rwy 02 PAPI OTS.
  AIRPORT REMARKS: Unattended. For fuel call 806–659–2422 and hangar
    space 806–659–2524 Mon–Sat 1330–0100Z‡. No line of sight
    between rwy ends.
  AIRPORT MANAGER: 806-659-2524
  WEATHER DATA SOURCES: AWOS–3P 118.925 (806) 644–6824.
  COMMUNICATIONS: CTAF 122.9
  ®**ALBUQUERQUE CENTER APP/DEP CON** 127.85
  CLEARANCE DELIVERY PHONE: For CD ctc Albuquerque ARTCC at
    505-856-4861.
  RADIO AIDS TO NAVIGATION: NOTAM FILE BGD.
    BORGER (L) TACAN   Chan 23   BGD (108.6)   N35°48.42′
      W101°22.93′   009° 26.4 NM to fld. 3130/11E.
      TACAN AZIMUTH unusable:
        220°–320° byd 10 NM blo 12,000′

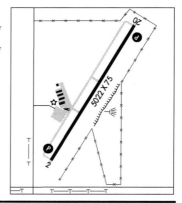

TEXAS
429

SPICEWOOD (88R) 2 E UTC–6(–5DT) N30°28.43′ W98°07.29′
SAN ANTONIO
830 NOTAM FILE SJT
L–19C
RWY 17–35: H4185X38 (ASPH) S–12.5
  RWY 17: Thld dsplcd 464′. Tree.
  RWY 35: Trees.
SERVICE: **FUEL** 100LL, JET A
AIRPORT REMARKS: Unatndd. Deer on and invof arpt. Arpt clsd at night exc for hel, medevac and mil flts. Arpt clsd to jet and turbo jet acft, exc for very light jets. Arpt clsd to TGL, ultralights and hang gldrs. No line of sight btn rwy ends. Rwy 17 calm wind rwy. Rotorcraft remain abv 500 AGL N of Rwy 17 to avoid residential area. Rotorcraft practice or autorotation prohibited. Rotorcraft arr and dep fly dctly to and fm prkg to avoid unec low–level txg.
AIRPORT MANAGER: 830-201-3111
COMMUNICATIONS: CTAF/UNICOM 122.8
CLEARANCE DELIVERY PHONE: For CD ctc Austin Apch at 512-369-7865.
RADIO AIDS TO NAVIGATION: NOTAM FILE AUS.
  CENTEX (VH) (H) VORTACW 112.8 CWK Chan 75 N30°22.71′ W97°31.79′ 275° 31.2 NM to fld. 593/6E.
  VOR unusable:
    180°–190° byd 40 NM
    200°–210° byd 40 NM

STAMFORD
ARLEDGE FLD (F56) 4 SE UTC–6(–5DT) N32°54.63′ W99°44.05′
DALLAS–FT WORTH
1561 B NOTAM FILE FTW
L–17B
RWY 17–35: H3707X60 (ASPH) S–4 MIRL
IAP
  RWY 17: Road.
RWY 08–26: 2211X50 (TURF)
RWY 13–31: 1702X50 (TURF–GRVL) 0.3% up NW
  RWY 13: Road.
  RWY 31: Road.
SERVICE: **S4** **FUEL** 100LL **LGT** Actvt MIRL Rwy 17–35—CTAF.
AIRPORT REMARKS: Unattended. Farm equipment invof arpt. Rwys 08–26 and 13–31 have rough sfc.
AIRPORT MANAGER: 325-773-2591
COMMUNICATIONS: CTAF/UNICOM 122.8
®ABILENE APP/DEP CON 127.2
CLEARANCE DELIVERY PHONE: For CD ctc Fort Worth ARTCC at 817-858-7584.
RADIO AIDS TO NAVIGATION: NOTAM FILE ABI.
  ABILENE (VH) (H) VORTACW 113.7 ABI Chan 84 N32°28.88′ W99°51.81′ 004° 26.5 NM to fld. 1809/10E.
  VOR unusable:
    163°–236° byd 40 NM blo 18,000′
    237°–247° byd 40 NM blo 7,000′
    248°–250° byd 40 NM blo 18,000′
    251°–255° byd 40 NM blo 4,500′
    251°–255° byd 46 NM blo 18,000′

STANTON MUNI (63F) 3 NW UTC–6(–5DT) N32°10.41′ W101°49.35′
DALLAS–FT WORTH
2731 NOTAM FILE SJT
L–6H
RWY 16–34: H4240X60 (ASPH) S–14
  RWY 16: Road. Rgt tfc.
  RWY 34: Road.
SERVICE: **LGT** Bcn OTS indefly.
AIRPORT REMARKS: Unattended. Nmrs 389′ wind turbines 1.25–3 mi NW, NE and E of arpt. Rwy 16–34 extensive cracking and loose stones.
AIRPORT MANAGER: 432-756-3301
COMMUNICATIONS: CTAF 122.9
CLEARANCE DELIVERY PHONE: For CD ctc midland Apch at 432-563-2123. when Apch clsd ctc Fort Worth ARTCC at 817-858-7584.
RADIO AIDS TO NAVIGATION: NOTAM FILE MAF.
  MIDLAND (L) (L) VORTACW 114.8 MAF Chan 95 N32°00.56′ W102°11.42′ 051° 21.2 NM to fld. 2860/11E.
  VOR unusable:
    010°–020° byd 8 NM blo 8,000′

STEPHENS CO (See BRECKENRIDGE on page 260)

TEXAS

STEPHENVILLE CLARK RGNL (SEP)(KSEP) 1 E UTC–6(–5DT) N32°12.92´ W98°10.66´ DALLAS–FT WORTH
1321 B NOTAM FILE SEP L–17C
RWY 14–32: H4209X75 (ASPH) MIRL 0.8% up NW IAP
  RWY 14: PAPI(P2L). Tree.
  RWY 32: PAPI(P2L). Trees.
SERVICE: S4 **FUEL** 100LL, JET A+ **LGT** Rwy 14 PAPI OTS indefly. Rwy 32 PAPI OTS indefly.
AIRPORT REMARKS: Attended Mon–Fri 1400–2300Z‡, Sat 1500–1930Z‡. Parachute Jumping. Skydiving and parachute actvty on and invof arpt. 100LL self–serve only.
AIRPORT MANAGER: 254-552-1224
WEATHER DATA SOURCES: AWOS–3PT 118.075 (254) 965–8672.
COMMUNICATIONS: CTAF/UNICOM 122.8
®**FORT WORTH CENTER APP/DEP CON** 127.35
CLEARANCE DELIVERY PHONE: For CD ctc Fort Worth ARTCC at 817-858-7584.
RADIO AIDS TO NAVIGATION: NOTAM FILE FTW.
  GLEN ROSE (L) TACAN Chan 97 JEN (115.0) N32°09.58´ W97°52.66´ 276° 15.6 NM to fld. 1300/6E.

STINSON MUNI (See SAN ANTONIO on page 419)

STONEWALL CO (See ASPERMONT on page 247)

STONEWALL N30°12.41´ W98°42.35´ NOTAM FILE T82. SAN ANTONIO
(VH) (H) VORTAC 113.8 STV Chan 85 274° 10.8 NM to Gillespie Co. 1530/8E. H–7B, L–19C
  TACAN AZIMUTH unusable:
    056°–066° byd 30 NM blo 3,000´
    067°–055° byd 30 NM blo 3,300´
  DME unusable:
    056°–066° byd 30 NM blo 3,000´
    067°–055° byd 30 NM blo 3,300´
  VOR unusable:
    056°–066° byd 30 NM blo 3,000´
    067°–055° byd 30 NM blo 3,300´
    110°–122° byd 40 NM blo 5,500´
    110°–122° byd 46 NM
    123°–210° byd 40 NM
    230°–240° byd 40 NM
  RCO 122.1R 113.8T (SAN ANGELO RADIO)

STRATFORD FLD (H70) 1 NE UTC–6(–5DT) N36°20.74´ W102°02.96´ WICHITA
3668 NOTAM FILE FTW L–15B
RWY 04–22: H3023X32 (ASPH) S–9 RWY LGTS(NSTD) 0.5% up SW
  RWY 04: Road.
  RWY 22: Road.
SERVICE: **LGT** Actvt LIRL Rwy 04–22 5 times—CTAF. Rwy 04–22 LIRL lctd 33´ fm edge of pavement. Nonstd solar thr lgts.
AIRPORT REMARKS: Unattended. Emergency fuel 100LL only. Sewage treatment plant located south of rwy. Rwy 04 and 22 not marked. Rwy 04 end, broken asph and loose stones.
AIRPORT MANAGER: (806) 753-7866
COMMUNICATIONS: CTAF 122.9
  DALHART RCO 122.2 (FORT WORTH RADIO)
CLEARANCE DELIVERY PHONE: For CD ctc Albuquerque ARTCC at 505-856-4861.
RADIO AIDS TO NAVIGATION: NOTAM FILE DHT.
  DALHART (L) (L) VORTACW 112.0 DHT Chan 57 N36°05.49´ W102°32.68´ 046° 28.5 NM to fld. 4020/12E.
    TAC AZM unusable:
      240°–255° byd 15 NM
      320°–350° byd 15 NM

SUDDEN STOP (See COLLINSVILLE on page 275)

TEXAS

SUGAR LAND RGNL (See HOUSTON on page 342)

SULPHUR SPRINGS MUNI (SLR)(KSLR) 2 NW UTC–6(–5DT) N33°09.59′ W95°37.27′ **DALLAS–FT WORTH**
489 B NOTAM FILE SLR H–6I, L–17D
RWY 01–19: H5001X75 (CONC) S–30, D–50 MIRL 0.4% up S IAP
  RWY 01: REIL. PAPI(P4L)—GA 3.0° TCH 56′. Fence.
  RWY 19: REIL. PAPI(P4L)—GA 3.0° TCH 40′.
SERVICE: S4 FUEL 100LL, JET A LGT ACTVT REIL Rwys 01 and
  19—CTAF. PAPI Rwys 01 and 19 opr consly. Rwy 19 PAPI byd 8 degs
  right of RCL unusbl.
AIRPORT REMARKS: Attended Mon–Sat 1400–0000Z‡, Sunday by request.
  For attendant after hrs call police dispatch 903–885–7602. For arpt
  attendant on Sun call 903–885–4911 during normal attendance hrs.
  100LL avbl 24 hrs self–serve. Birds on and invof arpt. Lgt sport acft oprg
  on west side of rwy. Rwy 01 has 45′ bldg 1,820′ dstc. Rwy 01, 44 ft
  unmkd p–line, 1530 ft dstc, 30:1; 62 ft tank, 1620 ft dstc, 10 ft L,
  27:1; 125 ft antenna, 1515 ft east of Rwy 01 end.
AIRPORT MANAGER: 903–885–4911
WEATHER DATA SOURCES: AWOS–3 118.35 (903) 885–9605.
COMMUNICATIONS: CTAF/UNICOM 123.075
®FORT WORTH CENTER APP/DEP CON 132.025
CLEARANCE DELIVERY PHONE: For CD ctc Fort Worth ARTCC at 817-858-7584.
RADIO AIDS TO NAVIGATION: NOTAM FILE SLR.
  (L) DME 109.0 SLR Chan 37 N33°11.92′
  W95°32.57′ 240° 4.6 NM to fld. 508.

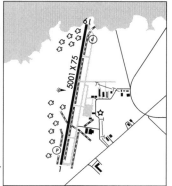

SUNRAY (X43) 1 NW UTC–6(–5DT) N36°01.75′ W101°49.73′ **WICHITA**
3507 NOTAM FILE FTW L–15B
RWY 02–20: 3760X50 (GRVL–DIRT)
  RWY 02: P–line.
  RWY 20: Road.
RWY 17–35: H3250X50 (ASPH) S–13 RWY LGTS(NSTD)
  RWY 17: Road.
  RWY 35: P–line.
SERVICE: LGT Rwy 17–35 low intens solar pwrd rwy lgts.
AIRPORT REMARKS: Attended irregularly. 10′ AGL gas well located 375′ east of south end Rwy 02–20. Aerial ag ops. Rwy
  35 LSO 40′ pwrline, 219′ dstc, 155′ L, 118′ R; 25′ RR, 265′ dstc, 0′ B. Rwy 17–35 hngrs, parked vehicles, pipe
  supplies, gravel piles, and acft obst prim sfc. Rwy 02–20 Sfc rough, crops and hay bales at rwy edge.
AIRPORT MANAGER: 806-948-4111
COMMUNICATIONS: CTAF 122.9
CLEARANCE DELIVERY PHONE: For CD ctc Albuquerque ARTCC at 505-856-4861.
RADIO AIDS TO NAVIGATION: NOTAM FILE BGD.
  BORGER (L) TACAN Chan 23 BGD (108.6) N35°48.42′ W101°22.93′ 291° 25.5 NM to fld. 3130/11E.
  TACAN AZIMUTH unusable:
  220°–320° byd 10 NM blo 12,000′

SUNRISE BEACH (2KL) 1 NE UTC–6(–5DT) N30°35.95′ W98°24.55′ **SAN ANTONIO**
854 NOTAM FILE SJT
RWY 12–30: 2649X110 (TURF) LIRL
  RWY 12: Tree.
  RWY 30: Tree. Rgt tfc.
SERVICE: S4 LGT Arpt lgts ops dusk–0430Z‡.
AIRPORT REMARKS: Unattended. Nmrs deer on and invof rwy. Ngt opns not rcmdd. No touch and go ldg ops. For acft svc call
  512–755–0399. Transient prkg west end of rwy by open hgr. Pkg lmtd to 72 hrs. Emerg helipad lctd east of wind sock
  and segmented crc. Rwy 12–30 irrigated aft 0430Z‡ ngtly. Trees in apch area and hngrs wi 60 ft of rwy. 20–30 ft trees
  alg both sides of rwy 75 ft each side of rwy cntrln. Rwy 12 thr mkd with white tires. Rwy 30 thr mkd with red lgts.
AIRPORT MANAGER: 408-564-9954
COMMUNICATIONS: CTAF 122.9
CLEARANCE DELIVERY PHONE: For CD ctc Houston ARTCC at 281-230-5622.

SWEETWATER

AVENGER FLD (SWW)(KSWW)   3 W   UTC–6(–5DT)   N32°28.04´ W100°27.99´   **DALLAS–FT WORTH**
2380   B   NOTAM FILE SWW   H–6G, L–17A
    RWY 17–35: H5840X100 (ASPH)   S–30   MIRL   0.5% up S   **IAP**
      RWY 17: REIL. PAPI(P4L)—GA 3.0° TCH 40´. Trees.
      RWY 35: REIL. PAPI(P4L)—GA 3.0° TCH 40´. Pole.
    RWY 04–22: H5658X75 (ASPH)   S–30   MIRL   0.8% up SW
      RWY 04: PAPI(P2L)—GA 3.0° TCH 40´. Trees.
      RWY 22: PAPI(P2L)—GA 3.0° TCH 40´. Pole.
    SERVICE: FUEL 100LL, JET A1+
    AIRPORT REMARKS: Attended 1400–0000Z‡. Holidays intmt. For fuel after
      hours call 325–235–8475.
    AIRPORT MANAGER: 325–235–8478
    WEATHER DATA SOURCES: AWOS–3 119.025 (325) 236–9652.
    COMMUNICATIONS: CTAF/UNICOM 122.8
    ®ABILENE APP/DEP CON 127.2
    CLEARANCE DELIVERY PHONE: For CD ctc Fort Worth ARTCC at
      817–858–7584.
    RADIO AIDS TO NAVIGATION: NOTAM FILE ABI.
      ABILENE (VH) (H) VORTACW 113.7   ABI   Chan 84   N32°28.88´
      W99°51.81´   259° 30.6 NM to fld. 1809/10E.
      VOR unusable:
        163°–236° byd 40 NM blo 18,000´
        237°–247° byd 40 NM blo 7,000´
        248°–250° byd 40 NM blo 18,000´
        251°–255° byd 40 NM blo 4,500´
        251°–255° byd 46 NM blo 18,000´

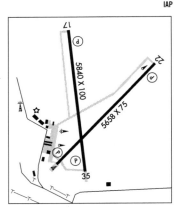

SYCAMORE STRIP (See FORT WORTH on page 312)

T–BAR (See TAHOKA on page 432)

TAHOKA

T–BAR   (2F4)   1 NW   UTC–6(–5DT)   N33°10.86´ W101°49.16´   **DALLAS–FT WORTH**
3126   B   NOTAM FILE FTW   **L–6H**
    RWY 17–35: H3278X50 (ASPH)   S–12.5   MIRL
      RWY 17: Rgt tfc.
      RWY 35: Road.
    RWY 08–26: 2543X33 (GRVL–DIRT)   S–10
      RWY 08: Road.
      RWY 26: Road. Rgt tfc.
    SERVICE: LGT MIRL Rwy 17–35 preset low intst; to incr intst actvt—CTAF.
    AIRPORT REMARKS: Attended irregularly. Extsv aerial ag opns May thru Oct. 20´ AGL irrigation equip 400´ north AER 35. Rwy
      08–26 thrs and rwy edges not defined.
    AIRPORT MANAGER: 806–561–4211
    COMMUNICATIONS: CTAF/UNICOM 122.8
    CLEARANCE DELIVERY PHONE: For CD ctc Fort Worth ARTCC at 817–858–7584.
    RADIO AIDS TO NAVIGATION: NOTAM FILE LBB.
      LUBBOCK (L) (L) VORTACW 109.2   LBB   Chan 29   N33°42.30´ W101°54.84´   160° 31.7 NM to fld. 3310/11E.
      VOR unusable:
        040°–050° byd 38 NM blo 5,300´
        210°–260° byd 25 NM blo 6,000´
    COMM/NAV/WEATHER REMARKS: UNICOM OTS indefly.

TALON AIR HELIPORT (See DICKINSON on page 295)

TARRANT FLD (See MOUNT SELMAN on page 386)

TEXAS

TAYLOR MUNI (T74) 2 W UTC–6(–5DT) N30°34.36′ W97°26.59′ SAN ANTONIO
600 B NOTAM FILE SJT L–19C, 21A
RWY 17–35: H4000X75 (ASPH) S–12.5 MIRL 1.3% up N IAP
  RWY 17: PAPI(P2L)—GA 3.0° TCH 40′. Rgt tfc.
  RWY 35: PAPI(P2L)—GA 3.0° TCH 57′. Thld dsplcd 249′. Trees.
SERVICE: S4 **FUEL** 100LL, JET A
AIRPORT REMARKS: Attended Mon–Sat 1400–2300Z‡. Helicopter svc also avbl. Numerous agricultural ops invof arpt during dalgt hrs. 200 ft AGL twr, 1000 ft east of rey centerline, apx mid point of rwy.
AIRPORT MANAGER: 512-352-5747
WEATHER DATA SOURCES: AWOS–3PT 119.75 (512) 352–4995.
COMMUNICATIONS: CTAF/UNICOM 122.8
ⓇAUSTIN APP/DEP CON 127.225
CLEARANCE DELIVERY PHONE: For CD ctc Austin Apch at 512-369-7865.
RADIO AIDS TO NAVIGATION: NOTAM FILE AUS.
  CENTEX (VH) (H) VORTACW 112.8 CWK Chan 75 N30°22.71′
    W97°31.79′ 015° 12.5 NM to fld. 593/6E.
  VOR unusable:
    180°–190° byd 40 NM
    200°–210° byd 40 NM

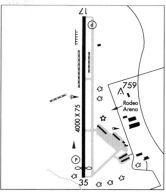

TEAGUE MUNI (68F) 3 NW UTC–6(–5DT) N31°39.71′ W96°18.63′ HOUSTON
525 B NOTAM FILE FTW L–19D, A
RWY 15–33: H3300X50 (ASPH) S–16 MIRL
  RWY 15: Trees.
  RWY 33: Tree.
SERVICE: **LGT** Beacon OTS. Rwy 15–33 nmrs rwy lgts OTS.
AIRPORT REMARKS: Unattended. For access gate call City Hall 254–739–2547, 1400–2300Z‡, after hrs call police 254–739–2553 or 903–389–3236. Mowing ops on arpt summer months. Radio control acft opr on ramp east of Rwy 15–33. Rwy 33 no rwy number.
AIRPORT MANAGER: (254) 739-5327
COMMUNICATIONS: CTAF 122.9
CLEARANCE DELIVERY PHONE: For CD ctc Fort Worth ARTCC at 817-858-7584.
RADIO AIDS TO NAVIGATION: NOTAM FILE FTW.
  CEDAR CREEK (L) (L) VORTACW 114.8 CQY Chan 95 N32°11.14′ W96°13.09′ 183° 31.7 NM to fld. 400/6E.

434 TEXAS

TEMPLE

DRAUGHON–MILLER CENTRAL TEXAS RGNL (TPL)(KTPL) 5 NW UTC–6(–5DT) N31°09.11´
W97°24.46´
682 B NOTAM FILE TPL
RWY 16–34: H7000X150 (ASPH–GRVD) S–55, D–70, 2D–110 MIRL
  RWY 16: MALSR.
  RWY 34: PAPI(P4L)—GA 3.0° TCH 34´.
RWY 03–21: H4740X100 (ASPH) S–31, D–37 MIRL
  RWY 21: PAPI(P4L)—GA 3.0° TCH 47´.
RUNWAY DECLARED DISTANCE INFORMATION
  RWY 03: TORA–4740 TODA–4740 ASDA–4740 LDA–4740
  RWY 16: TORA–7000 TODA–7000 ASDA–7000 LDA–7000
  RWY 21: TORA–4740 TODA–4740 ASDA–4740 LDA–4740
  RWY 34: TORA–7000 TODA–7000 ASDA–7000 LDA–7000
SERVICE: S4 **FUEL** 100LL, JET A, A1+ **LGT** Dusk–0400Z‡. ACTVT PAPI Rwy 21—CTAF. Aft 0400Z‡ MIRL Rwy 16–34 preset low intst; to incr intst and ACTVT MALSR Rwy 16—CTAF. MIRL Rwy 03–21 not avbl aft 0400Z‡.
AIRPORT REMARKS: Attended 1300–0200Z For aft hrs atndt 254–493–8530. Gldr opn 1.5 miles north of Rwy 16 thr. ARFF not avbl 0200–1300Z‡. ARFF protection meets Index B. 100LL and all fuels full and self svc. Military contract fuel avbl.
AIRPORT MANAGER: 254-298-5770
WEATHER DATA SOURCES: AWOS–3PT 134.975 (254) 774–8337.
COMMUNICATIONS: CTAF/UNICOM 123.0
  RCO 122.6 (SAN ANGELO RADIO)
® GRAY APP/DEP CON 120.075 CLNC DEL 125.9
AIRSPACE: CLASS E svc 1200–0500Z‡; other times CLASS G.
RADIO AIDS TO NAVIGATION: NOTAM FILE TPL.
  TEMPLE (L) DME 110.4 TPL Chan 41 N31°12.56´ W97°25.50´ 165° 3.6 NM to fld. 710.
  ILS/DME 111.5 I-TPL Chan 52 Rwy 16. Class IE. LOC unusable byd 20° right of course, Fort Hood MOA. Unmonitored.

SAN ANTONIO
H–6H, L–19C, 21A
IAP

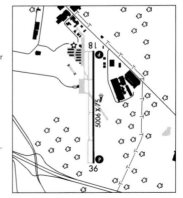

TERLINGUA RANCH (See ALPINE on page 241)

TERRELL CO (See DRYDEN on page 297)

TERRELL MUNI (TRL)(KTRL) 1 SE UTC–6(–5DT) N32°42.51´ W96°16.03´
474 B NOTAM FILE TRL
RWY 18–36: H5006X75 (ASPH) S–30 MIRL
  RWY 18: RLLS. REIL. PAPI(P4L)—GA 3.0° TCH 32´. Trees.
  RWY 36: REIL. PAPI(P4R)—GA 3.0° TCH 31´. Trees.
SERVICE: S4 **FUEL** 100LL, JET A **LGT** MIRL Rwy 18–36 preset low intst; to incr intst and actvt RLLS Rwy 18; PAPI Rwy 18 and 36—CTAF.
AIRPORT REMARKS: Attended 1400–0200Z‡. Birds on and invof arpt. For attendant after hours call 972–835–5395/5408.
AIRPORT MANAGER: (972) 551-6614
WEATHER DATA SOURCES: ASOS 119.275 (972) 551–1334.
COMMUNICATIONS: CTAF/UNICOM 123.075
® FORT WORTH CENTER APP/DEP CON 132.025
CLEARANCE DELIVERY PHONE: For CD ctc Fort Worth ARTCC at 817-858-7584.
RADIO AIDS TO NAVIGATION: NOTAM FILE FTW.
  CEDAR CREEK (L) (L) VORTACW 114.8 CQY Chan 95 N32°11.14´ W96°13.09´ 349° 31.4 NM to fld. 400/6E.

DALLAS–FT WORTH
H–6H, L–17D, A
IAP

TERRY CO (See BROWNFIELD on page 262)

TEXAS GULF COAST RGNL (See ANGLETON/LAKE JACKSON on page 245)

SC, 25 JAN 2024 to 21 MAR 2024

TEXAS 435

TEXICO N34°29.71′ W102°50.38′ NOTAM FILE FTW. ALBUQUERQUE
  (VH) (H) VORTACW 112.2 TXO Chan 59 026° 12.0 NM to Benger Air Park. 4060/11E. H–6G, L–6H
  VOR unusable:
    095°–100° byd 40 NM
    120°–130° byd 40 NM
    210°–223° byd 40 NM blo 15,000′
    224°–251° byd 40 NM
    252°–262° byd 40 NM blo 18,000′
    263°–272° byd 40 NM blo 18,000′
    273°–283° byd 40 NM blo 6,000′
    273°–283° byd 46 NM blo 7,000′
    273°–283° byd 59 NM
    284°–319° byd 40 NM
    320°–035° byd 40 NM
  TACAN AZIMUTH unusable:
    222°–232°

THREE RIVERS N28°30.30′ W98°09.03′ NOTAM FILE SJT. SAN ANTONIO
  (L) (L) VORTAC 111.4 THX Chan 51 160° 8.7 NM to Live Oak Co. 266/8E. H–7B, L–20H
  RCO 122.1R 111.4T (SAN ANGELO RADIO)

THROCKMORTON MUNI (72F) 1 NE UTC–6(–5DT) N33°10.80′ W99°08.99′ DALLAS–FT WORTH
  1273 B NOTAM FILE FTW L–17B
  RWY 17–35: H3723X60 (ASPH) S–12 LIRL
    RWY 17: Road.
    RWY 35: Trees.
  SERVICE: **LGT** Rwy 17 has nonstd dsplcd thr lgts. Rwy 35 does not have dsplcd thr lights. Rwy lts obscured by vegetation. Opr sts unkn.
  AIRPORT REMARKS: Unattended. Rwy 17–35 Nmrs conc & asph patches with cracks and loose grvl. Rwy uneven due to extsv patching. Rwy 17 and Rwy 35 rwy mkg poor.
  AIRPORT MANAGER: 940-849-4411
  COMMUNICATIONS: CTAF 122.9
  CLEARANCE DELIVERY PHONE: For CD ctc Fort Worth ARTCC at 817-858-7584.
  RADIO AIDS TO NAVIGATION: NOTAM FILE SPS.
    WICHITA FALLS (H) (H) VORTACW 112.7 SPS Chan 74 N33°59.24′ W98°35.61′ 200° 55.8 NM to fld. 1133/10E.

TOMHI N32°17.93′ W99°40.45′ NOTAM FILE ABI. DALLAS–FT. WORTH
  NDB (LOMW) 353 AB 352° 6.7 NM to Abilene Rgnl. 1895/5E.

TRADEWIND (See AMARILLO on page 243)

TRINITY N29°32.78′ W94°44.85′ NOTAM FILE CXO. HOUSTON
  (VL) (DL) VORW/DME 114.75 MHF Chan 94(Y) 011° 14.1 NM to Chambers Co. 38/7E. H–7C, L–19E, 21A, GOMW
  VOR unusable:
    060°–079° byd 40 NM
    080°–090° byd 40 NM blo 6,000′
    080°–090° byd 50 NM blo 8,000′
    091°–109° byd 40 NM
    110°–190° blo 2,000′

TRIPLE–ACE FLD (See DECATUR on page 292)

TRUAX N27°41.18′ W97°17.68′ NOTAM FILE NGP. BROWNSVILLE
  (L) TACAN 114.0 NGP Chan 87 at Corpus Christi Nas (Truax Fld). 17/3E. L–20H, 21A, GOMW
  No NOTAM MP: 1500–1800Z‡ 2nd Wed ea Month
  DME unusable:
    190°–305° byd 20 NM blo 2,000′
    333°–343° byd 10 NM blo 8,000′

TSTC WACO (See WACO on page 441)

TEXAS

TULIA

CITY OF TULIA/SWISHER CO MUNI (I06)   2 NW   UTC−6(−5DT)   N34°34.01´ W101°46.89´   DALLAS−FT WORTH
3503   B   NOTAM FILE FTW   L−6H
RWY 01−19: H4876X60 (ASPH)   S−12.5   MIRL   0.3% up S
  RWY 19: Road.
  SERVICE: FUEL 100LL LGT MIRL Rwy 01−19 preset low intst, to incr intst actvt—122.8.
  AIRPORT REMARKS: Unattended. Livestock invof arpt. Fuel avbl with credit card, for assistance call 806−995−3555. Rwy 18−36 mkd as Rwy 01−19.
  AIRPORT MANAGER: 806−995−3504
  COMMUNICATIONS: CTAF/UNICOM 122.7
  CLEARANCE DELIVERY PHONE: For CD ctc Fort Worth ARTCC at 817−858−7584.
  RADIO AIDS TO NAVIGATION: NOTAM FILE FTW.
    PANHANDLE (H) (H) VORTACW 116.6   PNH   Chan 113   N35°14.10´ W101°41.94´   178° 40.2 NM to fld. 3595/8E.

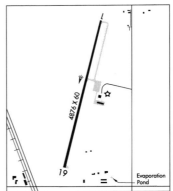

TUSCOLA   N32°14.14´ W99°49.01´   NOTAM FILE FTW.   DALLAS−FT. WORTH
  (L) (L) VORW/DME 111.6   TQA   Chan 53   340° 11.1 NM to Dyess AFB. 2058/10E.   H−6H, L−17B

TWIN−OAKS (See SAN ANTONIO on page 420)

TXAEROSPORT AERODROME (See DORCHESTER on page 296)

TYLER CO (See WOODVILLE on page 449)

TYLER POUNDS RGNL (TYR)(KTYR)   3 W   UTC−6(−5DT)   N32°21.21´ W95°24.18´   DALLAS−FT WORTH
544   B   Class I, ARFF Index B   NOTAM FILE TYR   H−6I, L−17D
RWY 04−22: H8334X150 (CONC−GRVD)   S−120, D−222, 2S−84,   IAP, AD
  2T−223, 2D−357, 2D/D1−212, C5−342 PCN 68 R/C/W/T   HIRL
  RWY 04: MALSR. PAPI(P4L)—GA 3.0° TCH 55´.
  RWY 22: REIL. PAPI(P4L)—GA 3.0° TCH 54´. Thld dsplcd 600´. Tree.
RWY 13−31: H5198X150 (ASPH−GRVD)   S−25, D−40 PCN 9 F/C/X/T   HIRL   0.5% up SE
  RWY 13: Pole.
  RWY 31: VASI(V4L)—GA 3.0° TCH 54´. Road.
RWY 18−36: H4832X150 (ASPH−GRVD)   S−109, D−172, 2D−289 PCN 43 F/B/X/T   MIRL   0.6% up S
  RWY 18: Tree.
  RWY 36: Tree.
RUNWAY DECLARED DISTANCE INFORMATION
  RWY 04: TORA−8334   TODA−8334   ASDA−7734   LDA−7734
  RWY 13: TORA−5198   TODA−5198   ASDA−5198   LDA−5198
  RWY 18: TORA−4832   TODA−4832   ASDA−4832   LDA−4832
  RWY 22: TORA−8334   TODA−8334   ASDA−8334   LDA−7734
  RWY 31: TORA−5198   TODA−5198   ASDA−5198   LDA−5198
  RWY 36: TORA−4832   TODA−4832   ASDA−4832   LDA−4832
SERVICE: S4   FUEL 100LL, JET A   OX 1, 3   LGT When ATCT clsd actvt MALSR Rwy 04; REIL Rwy 22; HIRL Rwy 04−22; MIRL Rwy 18−36; twy lgts—CTAF. HIRL Rwy 13−31 preset med intst, to incr intst actvt—CTAF. PAPI Rwy 04 and 22, VASI Rwy 31 opr consly. Rwy 22 VGSI unusbl byd 9 deg left and right of cntrln.
NOISE: Noise abatement procedures in effect Call 903−590−3048.
AIRPORT REMARKS: Attended 1100−0400Z‡. West side passenger terminal ramp access rstd to air carrier. Conditions not monitored btn the hrs of 9:30 PM and 6:30 AM local.

CONTINUED ON NEXT PAGE

TEXAS

CONTINUED FROM PRECEDING PAGE

　　AIRPORT MANAGER: 903-531-2343
　　WEATHER DATA SOURCES: ASOS (903) 535-9105 LAWRS.
　　COMMUNICATIONS: CTAF 120.1 ATIS 126.25 UNICOM 122.95
　　　　RCO 122.3 (FORT WORTH RADIO)
　　Ⓡ LONGVIEW APP/DEP CON 128.75 (1200-0400Z‡)
　　Ⓡ FORT WORTH CENTER APP/DEP CON 135.25 (0400-1200Z‡)
　　　　TOWER 120.1 (1230-0330Z‡) GND CON 121.9
　　CLEARANCE DELIVERY PHONE: For CD if una to ctc on FSS freq, ctc Fort Worth ARTCC at 817-858-7584.
　　AIRSPACE: CLASS D svc 1230-0330Z‡; other times CLASS G.
　　RADIO AIDS TO NAVIGATION: NOTAM FILE TYR.
　　　　(T) (T) VORW/DME 114.2　TYR　Chan 89　N32°21.35´ W95°24.21´　at fld. 537/6E.
　　　　DME unusable:
　　　　　　062°-092° byd 35 NM blo 2,200´
　　　　ILS/DME 111.95　I-TYR　Chan 56(Y)　Rwy 04.　Class IE.　Unmonitored when ATCT clsd. DME unusable byd 20° left of course.
　　COMM/NAV/WEATHER REMARKS: Helicopters operating inbound or outbound to/from the downtown hospitals state intention on 123.075.

UPTON CO (See MC CAMEY on page 376)

UTOPIA　U66　N29°33.04´ W99°31.03´/1278　　　　　　　　　　　　　　　　　　　　　　　SAN ANTONIO
　　AWOS-3T 121.125 (210) 384-5834 AWOS-3T ident associated with arpt Rancho Sabino Grande 6TX2.　　　L-19B

UVALDE

GARNER FLD　(UVA)(KUVA)　3 E　UTC-6(-5DT)　N29°12.68´ W99°44.62´　　　　SAN ANTONIO
　942　B　NOTAM FILE UVA　　　　　　　　　　　　　　　　　　　　　　　　　　　　　　　H-7B, L-19B
　　RWY 15-33: H5256X100 (ASPH)　S-30, D-40, 2D-40　MIRL　0.3% up NW　　　　　　　　　IAP
　　　　RWY 15: REIL. PAPI(P4L)—GA 3.0° TCH 36´. Trees.
　　　　RWY 33: REIL. PAPI(P4L)—GA 3.0° TCH 35´.
　　SERVICE: S4　FUEL 100LL, JET A　OX 1, 2, 3, 4　LGT Actvt REIL Rwy 15 and 33; MIRL Rwy 15-33—CTAF.
　　AIRPORT REMARKS: Attended 1300-0100Z‡. Self svc 100LL. Turf strip 3300 ft X 75 ft parl to and east of Rwy 15-33 used by crop dusters only.
　　AIRPORT MANAGER: 830-278-3315
　　WEATHER DATA SOURCES: AWOS-3 124.175 (830) 278-8862.
　　COMMUNICATIONS: CTAF/UNICOM 122.8
　　　　UVALDE RCO 122.5 (SAN ANGELO RADIO)
　　Ⓡ HOUSTON CENTER APP/DEP CON 134.95
　　CLEARANCE DELIVERY PHONE: For CD ctc Houston ARTCC at 281-230-5622.
　　RADIO AIDS TO NAVIGATION: NOTAM FILE ERV.
　　　　CENTER POINT (VH) (H) VORTAC 117.5　CSI　Chan 122　N29°55.34´ W99°12.87´　205° 50.8 NM to fld. 2079/8E.

- -

OX RANCH　(1ØX)　23 NW　UTC-6(-5DT)　N29°27.69´ W100°06.86´　　　　　　SAN ANTONIO
　1305　NOTAM FILE Not insp.　　　　　　　　　　　　　　　　　　　　　　　　　　　　　H-7B, L-19B
　　RWY 17-35: H5744X70 (CONC)　MIRL
　　　　RWY 17: REIL. PAPI(P2L)—GA 3.75° TCH 52´.
　　　　RWY 35: REIL. PAPI(P2L)—GA 3.3° TCH 60´. Rgt tfc.
　　SERVICE:　FUEL JET A1+　LGT Actvt PAPI Rwy 17 and 35; MIRL Rwy 17-35—CTAF.
　　AIRPORT REMARKS: Unattended. Wildlife on and invof arpt. Acft wingspan rstrd to 70 ft. Trng TGL prohibited. Hel trng prohibited. Ovngt prkg ltd due to ltd ramp space. Cdn prior to ldg, 830-275-4962, info@oxranch airport.com. Coml and student trng opns by pmt only. PPR for acft certd for 90500 TOG.
　　AIRPORT MANAGER: 830-275-4962
　　COMMUNICATIONS: CTAF 122.8
　　CLEARANCE DELIVERY PHONE: For CD ctc Del Rio Apch at 830-298-5192, when Apch clsd ctc Houston ARTCC at 281-230-5622.

VALLEY INTL (See HARLINGEN on page 328)

TEXAS

VAN HORN
CULBERSON CO (VHN)(KVHN) 3 NE UTC–6(–5DT) N31°03.47´ W104°47.03´ EL PASO
3957 B NOTAM FILE ABQ H–6F, L–6J
  IAP
RWY 03–21: H6005X76 (ASPH) S–15 MIRL(NSTD) 0.6% up SW
  RWY 03: PAPI(P2L)—GA 3.0° TCH 45´. Brush.
  RWY 21: PAPI(P2L)—GA 3.0° TCH 44´. Brush.
RWY 07–25: H5353X75 (ASPH) S–15 MIRL 0.9% up W
  RWY 07: Brush.
  RWY 25: Brush.
SERVICE: **FUEL** 100LL, JET A1+ **LGT** Actvt PAPI Rwy 03 and 21–CTAF. Rwy 21 has nstd lenses. North side has split clear/amber. South side has clear lenses.
AIRPORT REMARKS: Attended 1500–0000Z‡. For fuel call 432–283–2237 or 432–284–1418. Rwy 07–25 paint markings faded. Space Launch Activity Area – See Special Notices.
AIRPORT MANAGER: 432-283-2920
WEATHER DATA SOURCES: AWOS–3PT 119.925 (432) 283–2418.
COMMUNICATIONS: CTAF 122.9
  ALBUQUERQUE CENTER APP/DEP CON 135.875
CLEARANCE DELIVERY PHONE: For CD ctc Albuquerque ARTCC at 505-856-4861.
RADIO AIDS TO NAVIGATION: NOTAM FILE ABQ.
  HUDSPETH (VL) **(H) VORTACW** 115.0 HUP Chan 97 N31°34.12´ W105°22.58´ 123° 43.2 NM to fld. 4390/12E.
  VOR unusable:
   025°–050° byd 40 NM
   065°–075° byd 40 NM
   076°–086° byd 40 NM blo 9,000´
   076°–086° byd 51 NM blo 14,500´
   085°–091° byd 40 NM
   092°–102° byd 40 NM blo 11,000´
   103°–118° byd 40 NM
   119°–129° byd 40 NM blo 9,400´
   119°–129° byd 58 NM
   130°–140° byd 40 NM
   270°–305° byd 40 NM
   315°–345° byd 40 NM

VAN ZANDT CO RGNL (See WILLS POINT on page 447)

VEELS N32°27.33´ W94°47.85´ NOTAM FILE GGG. MEMPHIS
  NDB (LOMW) 410 GG 131° 6.1 NM to East Texas Rgnl. 263/3E.

VEGA
OLDHAM CO (E52) 2 SE UTC–6(–5DT) N35°13.84´ W102°23.93´ ALBUQUERQUE
3995 B NOTAM FILE FTW L–15B
RWY 17–35: H4200X60 (ASPH) S–20 MIRL
  RWY 17: PAPI(P2L). P–line.
  RWY 35: Fence.
SERVICE: **FUEL** 100LL, JET A **LGT** Actvt MIRL Rwy 17–35 and PAPI Rwy 17—CTAF.
AIRPORT REMARKS: Unattended. 100LL Fuel 24 hr self serve.
AIRPORT MANAGER: 806-639-2145
COMMUNICATIONS: CTAF 122.9
CLEARANCE DELIVERY PHONE: For CD ctc Albuquerque ARTCC at 505-856-4861.
RADIO AIDS TO NAVIGATION: NOTAM FILE FTW.
  PANHANDLE (H) (H) VORTACW 116.6 PNH Chan 113 N35°14.10´ W101°41.94´ 262° 34.4 NM to fld. 3595/8E.

TEXAS 439

VERNON

WILBARGER CO (F05)   4 N   UTC–6(–5DT)   N34°13.54´ W99°17.03´   DALLAS–FT WORTH
1265   B   NOTAM FILE F05   H–6H, L–17B
RWY 02–20: H5099X100 (ASPH)   S–30, D–40, 2D–60   MIRL   IAP
  RWY 02: Road.
  RWY 20: VASI(V4L)—GA 3.0° TCH 25´. Road.
RWY 16–34: H4304X80 (ASPH)   S–10   MIRL
  RWY 16: Road.
SERVICE: FUEL 100LL, JET A+
AIRPORT REMARKS: Attended Mon–Sat 1400–2300Z‡. Seasonal extsv
  aerial ag ops. 100LL self-serve. 100LL, Jet A+ full serve; aft hrs svc
  call 940–839–6365. Rwy 02–20 grass encroaching 13 ft each side.
AIRPORT MANAGER: 940-552-2182
WEATHER DATA SOURCES: AWOS–3 118.525 (940) 552–8600.
COMMUNICATIONS: CTAF/UNICOM 122.8
® ALTUS APP/DEP CON 125.1 (Mon–Fri 1500–0830Z‡ clsd weekends and
  holidays)
® FORT WORTH CENTER APP/DEP CON 128.4 133.5 (Mon–Fri
  0830–1500Z‡, 24 hrs weekends and holidays)
CLEARANCE DELIVERY PHONE: For CD ctc Fort Worth ARTCC at
  817-858-7584.
RADIO AIDS TO NAVIGATION: NOTAM FILE SPS.
  WICHITA FALLS (H) (H) VORTACW 112.7   SPS   Chan 74   N33°59.24´
    W98°35.61´   283° 37.2 NM to fld. 1133/10E.

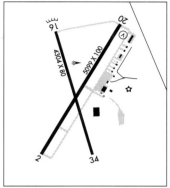

VICTORIA RGNL (VCT)(KVCT)   5 NE   UTC–6(–5DT)   N28°51.25´ W96°55.12´   HOUSTON
115   B   TPA—See Remarks   Class I, ARFF Index A   NOTAM FILE VCT   H–7C, L–20I, 21A
RWY 13–31: H9111X150 (ASPH–GRVD)   S–28, D–49, 2D–87   HIRL   IAP, AD
  RWY 13: MALSR.
  RWY 31: PAPI(P4L)—GA 3.0° TCH 55´. Rgt tfc.
RWY 18–36: H4908X75 (ASPH–GRVD)   S–28, D–49, 2D–87   MIRL
  RWY 18: REIL. PAPI(P2L)—GA 3.0° TCH 40´. Fence.
  RWY 36: REIL. PAPI(P2L)—GA 3.0° TCH 40´. Pole.
RUNWAY DECLARED DISTANCE INFORMATION
  RWY 13: TORA–9111   TODA–9111   ASDA–9111   LDA–9111
  RWY 18: TORA–4908   TODA–4908   ASDA–4908   LDA–4908
  RWY 31: TORA–9111   TODA–9111   ASDA–9111   LDA–9111
  RWY 36: TORA–4908   TODA–4908   ASDA–4908   LDA–4908
SERVICE: S2   FUEL 100LL, JET A   LGT HIRL Rwy 13–31 preset low intst,
  to incr intst and actvt MALSR Rwy 13—CTAF. MIRL Rwy 18–36 preset
  med intst only. PAPI Rwys 31, 18 and 36 opr consly.
AIRPORT REMARKS: Attended Mon–Fri 1200–0300Z‡. Ad ap bird act.
  Between 0400–1300Z‡ all unscheduled air carrier ops with more than
  9 passenger seats contact ARFF 361–582–5889. TPA for jets
  1715(1600); for turbo prop, light aircraft, rotorcraft 1215(1100).
AIRPORT MANAGER: 361-575-4558
WEATHER DATA SOURCES: ASOS 119.025 (361) 578–9916.
COMMUNICATIONS: CTAF 126.075   ATIS 119.025   UNICOM 122.7
  RCO 122.2 (MONTGOMERY COUNTY RADIO)
® HOUSTON CENTER APP/DEP CON 135.05
  TOWER 126.075 (1300–0400Z‡)   GND CON 120.525
CLEARANCE DELIVERY PHONE: For CD if una to ctc on FSS freq, ctc Houston ARTCC at 281-230-5622.
AIRSPACE: CLASS D svc 1300–0400Z‡; other times CLASS E.
RADIO AIDS TO NAVIGATION: NOTAM FILE VCT.
  (L) (L) VORW/DME 109.0   VCT   Chan 27   N28°54.02´ W96°58.74´   125° 4.2 NM to fld. 125/6E.
    VOR unusable:
    345°–355° byd 30.0 NM
  ILS/DME 111.5   I–VCT   Chan 52   Rwy 13.   Class IE.   Unmonitored when ATCT clsd.

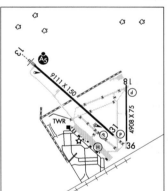

• • • • • • • • • • • • • • • • • • • •

HELIPAD H1: H60X60 (ASPH)

VULTURES ROW (See SANGER on page 421)

SC, 25 JAN 2024 to 21 MAR 2024

WACO

MC GREGOR EXEC (PWG)(KPWG)   4 W   UTC–6(–5DT)   N31°29.10′ W97°18.99′   SAN ANTONIO
592   B   NOTAM FILE PWG   H–6H, L–19D, 21A
RWY 17–35: H5501X75 (ASPH)   S–30, D–50   MIRL   0.4% up N   IAP
  RWY 17: REIL. PAPI(P4L)—GA 3.0° TCH 36′. Trees.
  RWY 35: PAPI(P4L)—GA 3.0° TCH 46′. Trees.
RWY 04–22: H3484X55 (ASPH)   S–12
  RWY 04: Trees.
SERVICE: S4   **FUEL** 100LL, JET A1+   **OX** 1, 2, 3, 4   **LGT** ACTIVATE REIL Rwy 17—CTAF.MIRL Rwy 17–35 preset low ints, to increase ints ACTIVATE—CTAF.
AIRPORT REMARKS: Attended 1300–2200Z‡. 100LL aft hrs fuel call 254–379–8204. Military fuel contract. Calm wind less than 5 knots use Rwy 17. 2550′ MSL twrs, 8 miles south Rwy 35 end. Space Launch Activity Area — See Special Notices.
AIRPORT MANAGER: 254-848-5477
WEATHER DATA SOURCES: AWOS–3PT 135.525 (254) 848–4581.
COMMUNICATIONS: CTAF/UNICOM 122.8
Ⓡ **WACO APP CON** 127.65 **DEP CON** 126.125 (1200–0600Z‡)
Ⓡ **FORT WORTH CENTER APP/DEP CON** 133.3 (0600–1200Z‡)
  GCO 121.725 (WACO CLNC and FLIGHT SERVICES)
CLEARANCE DELIVERY PHONE: For CD if una via GCO ctc Fort Worth ARTCC at 817-858-7584.
RADIO AIDS TO NAVIGATION: NOTAM FILE ACT.
  WACO (VH) (H) VORTACW 115.3   ACT   Chan 100   N31°39.73′ W97°16.14′   184° 10.9 NM to fld. 507/9E.
  VOR unusable:
    125°–149° byd 40 NM
    149°–159° byd 47 NM
    159°–187° byd 40 NM
    188°–198° byd 40 NM blo 12,000′
    199°–234° byd 40 NM
    235°–245° byd 50 NM
    246°–256° byd 40 NM blo 18,000′
    246°–256° byd 52 NM
    257°–267° byd 58 NM
    268°–282° byd 40 NM
    270°–335° byd 35 NM blo 4,000′
    283°–293° byd 40 NM blo 6,000′
    283°–293° byd 58 NM
    294°–330° byd 40 NM
  ASR (1200–0600Z‡)

TEXAS

TSTC WACO (CNW)(KCNW) 8 NE UTC–6(–5DT) N31°38.27′ W97°04.45′ **SAN ANTONIO**
470 B NOTAM FILE FTW MON Airport H–6H, L–19D, A
    RWY 17L–35R: H8600X150 (ASPH) S–50, D–200, 2S–175, 2D–450 IAP, AD
    MIRL
      RWY 17L: MALSR. PAPI(P4R)—GA 3.0° TCH 52′.
      RWY 35R: PAPI(P4L)—GA 3.0° TCH 41′. Trees. Rgt tfc.
    RWY 17R–35L: H6291X75 (CONC) S–25, D–76, 2S–96, 2D–140
      RWY 17R: Rgt tfc.
      RWY 35L: Trees.
    SERVICE: S2 **FUEL** 100LL, JET A **LGT** When ATCT clsd MIRL Rwy
      17L–35R preset low intst; to incr intst and ACTVT MALSR Rwy 17L;
      PAPI Rwy 17L and Rwy 35R—121.7.
    AIRPORT REMARKS: Attended Mon–Fri 1200–0000Z‡. Extv flt trng in arpt tfc
      area sfc to 3000 ft AGL. APU avbl for jet acft. Rwy 17R–35L no lights.
      Used primarily for, but not limited to, taxiing and helicopter ops during
      non–daylight hours. Rwy 17R–35L green cntrln reflectors alg full len of
      rwy.
    AIRPORT MANAGER: 254-867-4802
    WEATHER DATA SOURCES: AWOS–3PT 134.225 (254) 867–3880. LAWRS.
    COMMUNICATIONS: CTAF 124.0 UNICOM 122.95
      WACO RCO 122.15 (FORT WORTH RADIO)
    ® **WACO APP CON** 127.65 **DEP CON** 126.125 (1200–0600Z‡)
    ® **FORT WORTH CENTER APP/DEP CON** 133.3 (0600–1200Z‡)
      TOWER 124.0 (1300–0500Z‡) **GND CON** 121.7
    AIRSPACE: CLASS D svc 1300–0500Z‡; other times **CLASS E.**
    RADIO AIDS TO NAVIGATION: NOTAM FILE ACT.
      WACO (VH) (H) VORTACW 115.3 ACT Chan 100 N31°39.73′ W97°16.14′ 089° 10.1 NM to fld. 507/9E.
      VOR unusable:
        125°–149° byd 40 NM
        149°–159° byd 47 NM
        159°–187° byd 40 NM
        188°–198° byd 40 NM blo 12,000′
        199°–234° byd 40 NM
        235°–245° byd 50 NM
        246°–256° byd 40 NM blo 18,000′
        246°–256° byd 52 NM
        257°–267° byd 58 NM
        268°–282° byd 40 NM
        270°–335° byd 35 NM blo 4,000′
        283°–293° byd 40 NM blo 6,000′
        283°–293° byd 58 NM
        294°–330° byd 40 NM
      ROBINSON NDB (MHW) 400 ROB N31°30.23′ W97°04.18′ 355° 8.0 NM to fld. 392/3E. NOTAM FILE FTW.
      ILS 110.7 I–CNW Rwy 17L. Unmonitored.
      ASR (1200–0600Z‡)

TEXAS

WACO RGNL (ACT)(KACT) 5 NW UTC–6(–5DT) N31°36.73´ W97°13.82´ SAN ANTONIO
516 B ARFF Index—See Remarks NOTAM FILE ACT H–6H, L–19D, A
RWY 01–19: H7107X150 (ASPH–GRVD) S–50, D–82, 2S–121, 2T–276, IAP, AD
2D–166, C5–466 HIRL
  RWY 01: PAPI(P4R)—GA 3.0° TCH 55´. RVR–R Thld dsplcd 102´.
  Road.
  RWY 19: MALSR. RVR–T
RWY 14–32: H5103X150 (ASPH–GRVD) S–50, D–82, 2S–104 MIRL
  RWY 14: REIL. PAPI(P4L)—GA 3.0° TCH 58´.
  RWY 32: PAPI(P4L)—GA 3.0° TCH 58´. Road.
RUNWAY DECLARED DISTANCE INFORMATION
  RWY 01: TORA–7107 TODA–7107 ASDA–7107 LDA–7005
  RWY 14: TORA–5103 TODA–5103 ASDA–5103 LDA–5103
  RWY 19: TORA–7107 TODA–7107 ASDA–6605 LDA–6605
  RWY 32: TORA–5103 TODA–5103 ASDA–5103 LDA–5103
SERVICE: S4 **FUEL** 100LL, JET A, UL94 **OX** 1 **LGT** When ATCT clsd:
  MALSR Rwy 19; HIRL Rwy 01–19 preset low intst, to incr intst
  actvt—CTAF. REIL Rwy 14; MIRL Rwy 14–32; twy lgts preset low intst
  when wind favors, otrw not avbl.
AIRPORT REMARKS: Attended 1030–0600Z‡. Class I, ARFF Index B. PPR for
  unscheduled air carrier ops call arpt manager 254–750–8657. NOTE:
  See Special Notices—Model Aircraft Activity.
AIRPORT MANAGER: 254-750-8657
WEATHER DATA SOURCES: ASOS (254) 759–3065
COMMUNICATIONS: CTAF 119.3 **ATIS** 123.85 **UNICOM** 122.95
  RCO 122.6 (FORT WORTH RADIO)
Ⓡ **APP CON** 127.65 (0600–1200Z‡)
Ⓡ **DEP CON** 126.125 (0600–1200Z‡)
Ⓡ **FORT WORTH CENTER APP/DEP CON** 133.3 (0600–1200Z‡)
  TOWER 119.3 (1200–0600Z‡) **GND CON** 121.9
CLEARANCE DELIVERY PHONE: For CD ctc waco Apch at 121.9 or ctc Fort Worth ARTCC at 817-858-7584.
AIRSPACE: CLASS D svc 1200–0600Z‡; other times CLASS E.
RADIO AIDS TO NAVIGATION: NOTAM FILE ACT.
  (VH) (H) VORTACW 115.3 ACT Chan 100 N31°39.73´ W97°16.14´ 137° 3.6 NM to fld. 507/9E.
  VOR unusable:
    125°–149° byd 40 NM
    149°–159° byd 47 NM
    159°–187° byd 40 NM
    188°–198° byd 40 NM blo 12,000´
    199°–234° byd 40 NM
    235°–245° byd 50 NM
    246°–256° byd 40 NM blo 18,000´
    246°–256° byd 52 NM
    257°–267° byd 58 NM
    268°–282° byd 40 NM
    270°–335° byd 35 NM blo 4,000´
    283°–293° byd 40 NM blo 6,000´
    283°–293° byd 58 NM
    294°–330° byd 40 NM
  ILS/DME 109.7 I–ACT Chan 34 Rwy 19. Class IE. ILS/DME unmonitored when ATCT closed.
  ASR (1200–0600Z‡)

WINGS FOR CHRIST INTL FLIGHT ACADEMY (73F) 8 NE UTC–6(–5DT) N31°37.43´ W97°01.35´ SAN ANTONIO
455 NOTAM FILE FTW
RWY 16–34: 3000X80 (TURF) RWY LGTS(NSTD)
  RWY 16: Thld dsplcd 315´. Fence.
  RWY 34: Trees. Rgt tfc.
SERVICE: S2 **LGT** ACTIVATE LIRL Rwy 16–34—CTAF.
AIRPORT REMARKS: Attended continuously. +4´ fence along both sides of rwy 70´ from centerline south half of rwy. Rwy 34
  40´ trees 90´ fm thr.
AIRPORT MANAGER: 254-723-3277
COMMUNICATIONS: CTAF 122.9
CLEARANCE DELIVERY PHONE: For CD ctc Fort Worth ARTCC at 817-858-7584.
COMM/NAV/WEATHER REMARKS: Arpt inside Class D airspace. Ctc TSTC twr 124.0.

TEXAS   443

WALDRON FLD NOLF (NWL)(KNWL) N   6 SSE   UTC–6(–5DT)   N27°38.15′ W97°18.81′   BROWNSVILLE
AIRSPACE: CLASS D svc 1330Z‡–SS Mon–Fri exc hol; other times CLASS G.   L–21A

WEATHERFORD

HORSESHOE BEND (F78)   12 SW   UTC–6(–5DT)   N32°34.37′ W97°52.35′   DALLAS–FT WORTH
715   NOTAM FILE FTW
RWY 17–35: 3000X30 (TURF)
  RWY 17: Fence.
  RWY 35: Tree.
AIRPORT REMARKS: Unattended. Deer and motor vehicles on rwy. Rwy 17 has 27 ft pole, 158 ft dstc, 54 ft L.
AIRPORT MANAGER: 817-886-2256
COMMUNICATIONS: CTAF 122.9
CLEARANCE DELIVERY PHONE: For CD ctc Fort Worth ARTCC at 817-858-7584.

PARKER CO   (WEA)(KWEA)   5 E   UTC–6(–5DT)   N32°44.78′ W97°40.95′   DALLAS–FT WORTH
991   NOTAM FILE FTW   L–17C, A
RWY 17–35: H2892X40 (ASPH)   S–7.5   LIRL(NSTD)   IAP
  RWY 17: Thld dsplcd 220′. Tree.
  RWY 35: Trees.
SERVICE: FUEL 100LL   **LGT** Rwy 17–35 NSTD dsplcd thr lgts, single green lgt each side of rwy.
AIRPORT REMARKS: Attended 1400–0000Z‡. Wildlife on and invof arpt. 100LL fuel 24 hrs self serve. Arpt clsd to transient student tfc. Clsd to ultralight tfc. Twy on west side of rwy clsd to public indef. Rwy 17–35 restricted to acft 7500 lbs or less.
AIRPORT MANAGER: (817) 822-7205
COMMUNICATIONS: CTAF/UNICOM 122.7
®**REGIONAL APP/DEP CON** 135.975
CLEARANCE DELIVERY PHONE: For CD ctc Regional Apch at 972-615-2799.
RADIO AIDS TO NAVIGATION: NOTAM FILE FTW.
  MILLSAP (VH) (H) **VORTACW** 117.7   MQP   Chan 124   N32°43.57′ W97°59.85′   077° 16.0 NM to fld. 900/9E.
  VOR unusable:
    004°–009° byd 40 NM
    010°–054° byd 40 NM blo 3,800′
    010°–054° byd 46 NM blo 5,000′
    010°–054° byd 56 NM
    055°–066° byd 40 NM blo 3,800′
    055°–066° byd 50 NM
    230°–247° byd 40 NM
    248°–258° byd 40 NM blo 3,700′
    248°–258° byd 53 NM
    259°–270° byd 40 NM blo 6,000′
    259°–270° byd 63 NM
    271°–285° byd 40 NM
    312°–316° byd 40 NM
    325°–340° byd 40 NM blo 3,000′
    325°–340° byd 46 NM blo 5,000′
    325°–340° byd 66 NM
    353°–003° byd 40 NM blo 18,000′

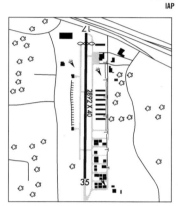

SC, 25 JAN 2024 to 21 MAR 2024

444 TEXAS

WELLINGTON
MARIAN AIRPARK (F06)　1 SE　UTC−6(−5DT)　N34°50.69′ W100°11.71′　　DALLAS–FT WORTH
2009　NOTAM FILE FTW　　　L−17B
RWY 12−30: H4035X60 (ASPH)　S−2.5　MIRL　0.3% up NW
　RWY 12: Thld dsplcd 525′. Road.
　RWY 30: Road.
RWY 17−35: H1819X60 (ASPH)　S−12.5　0.5% up N
　RWY 17: Thld dsplcd 219′. Road.
RWY 04−22: 1010X135 (TURF)　0.4% up NE
　RWY 22: Pole.
SERVICE: **FUEL** 100LL　**LGT** MIRL Rwy 12−30 preset to low to incr inst and ACTVT—CTAF.
AIRPORT REMARKS: Unattended. Extensive agricultural ops during spring and summer. Rwy 04−22 mkd with 3 ft barrel halves painted black and white. Rwy 12 and Rwy 30 markings faded, barely vsbl.
AIRPORT MANAGER: 806-447-2544
COMMUNICATIONS: CTAF 122.9
CLEARANCE DELIVERY PHONE: For CD ctc Fort Worth ARTCC at 817-858-7584.
RADIO AIDS TO NAVIGATION: NOTAM FILE CDS.
　CHILDRESS (VL) (H) VORTACW 117.0　CDS　Chan 117　N34°22.14′ W100°17.34′　359° 28.9 NM to fld. 1920/10E.

WESLACO
MID VALLEY (TXW)(KTXW)　1 NE　UTC−6(−5DT)　N26°10.72′ W97°58.44′　　BROWNSVILLE
70　B　LRA　NOTAM FILE TXW　　　L−20H
　　　　　　　　　　　　　　　　　　　　　　　　　　　　　　　　　　　　　　IAP
RWY 14−32: H6002X75 (ASPH)　S−12.5　MIRL
　RWY 14: PAPI(P4L)—GA 3.0° TCH 50′. Trees.
　RWY 32: REIL. PAPI(P4L)—GA 3.18° TCH 51′. Pole. Rgt tfc.
SERVICE: S4　**FUEL** 100LL, JET A　**LGT** MIRL Rwy 14−32 preset low intst; to incr intst and actvt REIL Rwy 32—CTAF.
AIRPORT REMARKS: Attended Mon−Sat 1300−0000Z‡. For atndnt aft hrs, call 956−469−0291 durg atndd hrs. Fuel avbl 24 hrs self−serve. 30′ pole 315′ northeast of helipad.
AIRPORT MANAGER: 956-969-0291
WEATHER DATA SOURCES: AWOS−3PT 118.575 (956) 447−0414.
COMMUNICATIONS: CTAF/UNICOM 122.8
Ⓡ **CORPUS APP/DEP CON** 122.65　**CLNC DEL** 125.95
RADIO AIDS TO NAVIGATION: NOTAM FILE HRL.
　HARLINGEN (L) (L) VORW/DME 113.65　HRL　Chan 83(Y)
　　N26°13.75′ W97°39.14′　255° 17.6 NM to fld. 32/5E.

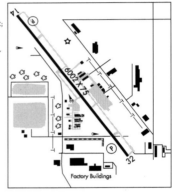

WEST HOUSTON (See HOUSTON on page 343)

WHARTON
GAV AIR (94R)　5 SE　UTC−6(−5DT)　N29°15.86′ W96°00.43′　　HOUSTON
90　NOTAM FILE CXO
RWY 15−33: H2167X20 (ASPH−DIRT)
　RWY 15: Tree. Rgt tfc.
　RWY 33: Tree.
AIRPORT REMARKS: Unattended. Arpt clsd 1 hr bfr SS til 1 hr aft SR daily.
AIRPORT MANAGER: 979-533-1388
COMMUNICATIONS: CTAF 122.9
CLEARANCE DELIVERY PHONE: For CD ctc Houston ARTCC at 281-230-5622.

TEXAS

WHARTON RGNL (ARM)(KARM) 5 SW UTC–6(–5DT) N29°15.26′ W96°09.26′
HOUSTON
100 B NOTAM FILE ARM
H–7C, L–19D, 21A, GOMW
IAP

RWY 14–32: H5004X75 (ASPH) S–22 MIRL
  RWY 14: PAPI(P4L)—GA 3.0° TCH 42′. Railroad. Rgt tfc.
  RWY 32: PAPI(P4L)—GA 3.0° TCH 42′.
SERVICE: S4 **FUEL** 100LL, JET A+ **LGT** MIRL Rwy 14–32 preset to low intst; to incr intst and actvt—CTAF. PAPI Rwy 14 and Rwy 32 opr consly.
AIRPORT REMARKS: Attended Mon–Sat 1400–2300Z‡. Otr times on req, call–in fee waived with min fuel purchase. Hang gldr actvt wi 5 NM of arpt up to 6000′ AGL. Hang gldr towing opns in grassy area left of DER 14. 100LL & Jet A self serve. Jet A also by truck. Svrl rwy/twy lgts out. Rwy 14–32 pavement cracking, svrl areas where pavement lip exceeds 3 inches.
AIRPORT MANAGER: 979-532-3210
WEATHER DATA SOURCES: AWOS–3 118.475 (979) 532–2791.
COMMUNICATIONS: CTAF/UNICOM 122.7
®**HOUSTON CENTER APP/DEP CON** 128.6
CLEARANCE DELIVERY PHONE: For CD ctc Houston ARTCC at 281-230-5622.
RADIO AIDS TO NAVIGATION: NOTAM FILE ELA.
  EAGLE LAKE (DH) DME 116.4 ELA Chan 111 N29°39.75′
  W96°19.03′ 161° 25.9 NM to fld. 192.

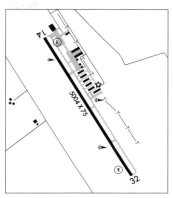

WHEELER MUNI (T59) 4 E UTC–6(–5DT) N35°27.07′ W100°12.00′
DALLAS–FT WORTH
2470 B NOTAM FILE FTW
L–15C
IAP

RWY 17–35: H3565X60 (ASPH) S–12 LIRL 1.1% up S
  RWY 35: Thld dsplcd 57′. Road.
SERVICE: **LGT** LIRL Rwy 17–35 nmrs lts OTS.
AIRPORT REMARKS: Unattended. 10 ft rising trrn 100 ft both sides of cntrln. Rwy pavement cracking with vegetation growing through.
AIRPORT MANAGER: 806-669-4182
COMMUNICATIONS: CTAF 122.9
®**ALBUQUERQUE CENTER APP/DEP CON** 127.85
CLEARANCE DELIVERY PHONE: For CD ctc Albuquerque ARTCC at 505-856-4861.
RADIO AIDS TO NAVIGATION: NOTAM FILE BGD.
  BORGER (L) TACAN Chan 23 BGD (108.6) N35°48.42′
  W101°22.93′ 099° 61.6 NM to fld. 3130/11E.
  TACAN AZIMUTH unusable:
  220°–320° byd 10 NM blo 12,000′

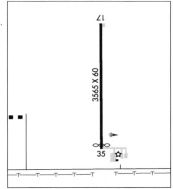

WHITESBORO
FLYING H RANCH (T29) 2 SW UTC–6(–5DT) N33°37.83′ W96°56.46′
DALLAS–FT WORTH
760 NOTAM FILE FTW

RWY 18–36: 2395X100 (TURF)
  RWY 18: Thld dsplcd 600′. Trees.
  RWY 36: Trees.
AIRPORT REMARKS: Unattended. Deer and hogs on and invof arpt. Rwy18–36 CLOSED exc 15 min PPR 214–802–8008. For fld cond call arpt manager. 75′ mkd pwr lines 900′ fm Rwy 18 acrs cntrln. Rwy 18–36 45′ tree aprx midpt of rwy, 100′ E of cntrln. No student trng. No touch and go opns. Rwy 18 dsplcd thr mkd with white conc tiles each side of rwy. Arpt phys ads 2227 West line. Whitesboro TX. Landing fee.
AIRPORT MANAGER: 214-802-8008
COMMUNICATIONS: CTAF 122.9
CLEARANCE DELIVERY PHONE: For CD ctc Fort Worth ARTCC at 817-858-7584.

WICHITA FALLS

KICKAPOO DOWNTOWN (CWC)(KCWC) 3 S UTC−6(−5DT) N33°51.64´ W98°29.42´   DALLAS−FT WORTH
1003 B NOTAM FILE FTW   L−17B
RWY 17−35: H4450X75 (CONC) S−30 MIRL 0.5% up S   IAP
   RWY 17: REIL. PAPI(P4L)—GA 3.0° TCH 37´. Thld dsplcd 150´. Fence.
   RWY 35: REIL. PAPI(P4L)—GA 3.0° TCH 41´. Thld dsplcd 250´. Road.
SERVICE: S4 **FUEL** 100LL, JET A **LGT** ACTVT REIL Rwy 17 and Rwy 35; MIRL Rwy 17−35—CTAF.
AIRPORT REMARKS: Attended 1200−0200Z‡. Do not mistake Kickapoo Downtown for Sheppard AFB/Wichita Falls Muni aprt 7 miles north. 100LL full and self serve 100LL and JET A. Intensive jet trainer tfc 2300−3000 ft MSL within Alert Area A−636. Remain blo 1800 ft MSL until in radar ctc with apch ctl for tfc advisories. Ants 2054 ft MSL 3.5 miles NW of arpt. NOTE: See Special Notices—Aerobatic Practice Area.
AIRPORT MANAGER: 940-766-1735
WEATHER DATA SOURCES: AWOS−3 119.625 (940) 766−2967.
COMMUNICATIONS: CTAF/UNICOM 122.7
® **SHEPPARD APP/DEP CON** 120.4 (Mon−Fri 1200−0200Z‡; Sun 1800−2300Z‡, clsd Sat and hol, OT ctc FORT WORTH CENTER 133.5 350.35)
® **FORT WORTH CENTER APP/DEP CON** 133.5 (Mon−Fri 0200−1200Z‡, Sun 2300−1800Z‡ Sat and holidays 24 hrs)
   CLNC DEL 121.2 940−676−8354
CLEARANCE DELIVERY PHONE: For CD ctc Fort Worth ARTCC at 817-858-7584.
RADIO AIDS TO NAVIGATION: NOTAM FILE SPS.
   WICHITA FALLS (H) (H) VORTACW 112.7   SPS   Chan 74   N33°59.24´ W98°35.61´   136° 9.2 NM to fld. 1133/10E.

WICHITA VALLEY (F14)   8 NW UTC−6(−5DT) N33°56.86´ W98°36.97´   DALLAS−FT WORTH
1005 NOTAM FILE FTW   L−17B
RWY 13−31: H3320X40 (ASPH) S−8, D−12.5 LIRL(NSTD)   IAP
0.7% up NW
   RWY 13: Road.
   RWY 31: Tree.
RWY 04−22: 3107X100 (TURF)
   RWY 04: P−line.
   RWY 22: Trees.
RWY 16−34: 2037X42 (TURF)   0.6% up S
   RWY 16: Fence.
   RWY 34: P−line.
SERVICE: FUEL 100LL **LGT** Rwy 13−31 NSTD LIRL. Rwy 13 thld lgts 2 green/red, Rwy 31 thld lgts 2 green/red.
AIRPORT REMARKS: Unattended. Self svc fuel. Intensive jet training tfc 2800−4500 ft MSL vicinity of arpt and Sheppard AFB 6 miles NE. Ctc apch control for tfc advisories. Unlighted tower 150´ AGL 2 miles S. Rwy 13 and Rwy 31, markings NSTD; nrs and cntrln small. NOTE: See Special Notices—Aerobatic Practice Area.
AIRPORT MANAGER: 940-781-7246
COMMUNICATIONS: CTAF/UNICOM 122.8
® **SHEPPARD APP/DEP CON** 118.2 (Mon−Fri 1200−0200Z‡, Sun 1800−2300Z‡, clsd Sat and hol, OT ctc FORT WORTH CENTER 133.5 350.35)
® **FORT WORTH CENTER APP/DEP CON** 133.5 (Mon−Fri 0200−1200Z‡, Sun 2300−1800Z‡, Sat and holidays 24 hrs)
CLEARANCE DELIVERY PHONE: For CD ctc Fort Worth ARTCC at 817-858-7584.
RADIO AIDS TO NAVIGATION: NOTAM FILE SPS.
   WICHITA FALLS (H) (H) VORTACW 112.7   SPS   Chan 74   N33°59.24´ W98°35.61´   195° 2.6 NM to fld. 1133/10E.

WICHITA FALLS N33°59.24´ W98°35.61´ NOTAM FILE SPS.   DALLAS−FT WORTH
(H) (H) **VORTACW** 112.7   SPS   Chan 74   195° 2.6 NM to Wichita Valley. 1133/10E.   H−6H, L−17B
RCO 122.65 (FORT WORTH RADIO)

WICHITA VALLEY (See WICHITA FALLS on page 446)

WILBARGER CO (See VERNON on page 439)

WILDCAT CANYON (See CHINA SPRING on page 271)

WILLIAM P HOBBY (See HOUSTON on page 344)

TEXAS

WILLS POINT
VAN ZANDT CO RGNL (76F) 3 SE UTC–6(–5DT) N32°40.89′ W95°59.05′   DALLAS–FT WORTH
522   B   NOTAM FILE FTW   L–17D
RWY 17–35: H3230X50 (ASPH) S–12   LIRL 0.6% up N
  RWY 17: Tree.
  RWY 35: Trees.
SERVICE: S2 **FUEL** 100LL
AIRPORT REMARKS: Attended Mon–Fri 1400–2300Z‡. 100LL fuel self serve 24 hrs. 68 ft antenna 810 ft east of rwy cntrln. 24 hr pilot aces to lounge. NOTE: See Special Notices—Model Aircraft Activity.
AIRPORT MANAGER: 903-873-3381
COMMUNICATIONS: CTAF/UNICOM 122.725
CLEARANCE DELIVERY PHONE: For CD ctc Fort Worth ARTCC at 817-858-7584.
RADIO AIDS TO NAVIGATION: NOTAM FILE FTW.
  CEDAR CREEK (L) (L) VORTACW 114.8   CQY   Chan 95   N32°11.14′ W96°13.09′   016° 32.0 NM to fld. 400/6E.

WINKLER CO (INK)(KINK)   3 NW   UTC–6(–5DT)   N31°46.79′ W103°12.10′   EL PASO
2822   B   NOTAM FILE INK   H–6G, L–6G
RWY 13–31: H5003X100 (ASPH) S–26, D–40   MIRL   IAP
  RWY 13: PAPI(P2L)—GA 3.0° TCH 22′. Brush.
  RWY 31: Brush.
RWY 04–22: H3514X100 (ASPH) S–26, D–40   MIRL
  RWY 04: Brush.
  RWY 22: P–line.
SERVICE: **FUEL** 100LL, JET A+ **LGT** MIRL Rwy 04–22 and 13–31 preset low intst; to incr intst and actvt PAPI Rwy 13—CTAF.
AIRPORT REMARKS: Attended Mon–Sat 1400–0000Z‡. Fuel avbl 24 hrs self serve or full service.
AIRPORT MANAGER: (432) 294-4247
WEATHER DATA SOURCES: ASOS 118.325 (432) 527-3320.
COMMUNICATIONS: CTAF/UNICOM 123.0
  RCO 122.3 (SAN ANGELO RADIO)
Ⓡ **FORT WORTH CENTER APP/DEP CON** 133.1
CLEARANCE DELIVERY PHONE: For CD if una to ctc on FSS freq, ctc Fort Worth ARTCC at 817-858-7584.
AIRSPACE: CLASS E.
RADIO AIDS TO NAVIGATION: NOTAM FILE INK.
  (VH) (H) VORTACW 112.1   INK   Chan 58   N31°52.49′ W103°14.63′   148° 6.1 NM to fld. 2860/11E.
  VOR unusable:
   256°–267° byd 40 NM blo 10,000′
   256°–267° byd 58 NM blo 18,000′
   268°–280° byd 40 NM
   281°–291° byd 40 NM blo 24,000′
   292°–305° byd 40 NM
   306°–320° byd 111 NM
   306°–320° byd 40 NM blo 15,000′

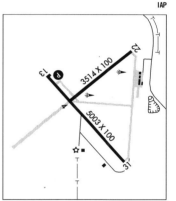

TEXAS

WINNIE/STOWELL

CHAMBERS CO/WINNIE STOWELL (T9Ø) 3 W UTC–6(–5DT) N29°49.13´ W94°25.86´ **HOUSTON**
24 B NOTAM FILE CXO L–19E, 21A
RWY 17–35: H3600X75 (ASPH) MIRL IAP
  RWY 17: PAPI(P2L)—GA 3.0° TCH 40´. Trees.
  RWY 35: PAPI(P2L)—GA 3.0° TCH 40´.
SERVICE: FUEL 100LL, JET A+ **LGT** MIRL Rwy 17–35 preset low intst dusk–0530Z‡, to incr intst or actvt aft 0530Z‡—CTAF.
AIRPORT REMARKS: Unattended. 110LL fuel self–svc.
AIRPORT MANAGER: 409-267-2719
COMMUNICATIONS: CTAF 122.95
Ⓡ **HOUSTON APP/DEP CON** 121.3
CLEARANCE DELIVERY PHONE: For CD ctc Houston Apch at 281-443-5844. to cnl IFR call 281-443-5888.
RADIO AIDS TO NAVIGATION: NOTAM FILE CXO.
  TRINITY (VL) (DL) **VORW/DME** 114.3 MHF Chan 94(Y) N29°32.78´ W94°44.85´ 038° 23.2 NM to fld. 38/7E.
  VOR unusable:
    060°–079° byd 40 NM
    080°–090° byd 40 NM blo 6,000´
    080°–090° byd 50 NM blo 8,000´
    091°–109° byd 40 NM
    110°–190° blo 2,000´

WINNSBORO MUNI (F51) 2 SE UTC–6(–5DT) N32°56.33´ W95°16.73´ **DALLAS–FT WORTH**
513 B NOTAM FILE FTW L–17D
RWY 01–19: H3215X50 (ASPH) S–12 MIRL 0.6% up N IAP
  RWY 01: Trees. Rgt tfc.
  RWY 19: Trees.
SERVICE: FUEL 100LL, MOGAS **LGT** ACTVT MIRL Rwy 01–19—CTAF.
AIRPORT REMARKS: Unattended. 100LL avbl 24 hr self serve.
AIRPORT MANAGER: 903-767-1060
COMMUNICATIONS: CTAF 122.9
Ⓡ **LONGVIEW APP/DEP CON** 128.75 (1200–0400Z‡)
Ⓡ **FORT WORTH CENTER APP/DEP CON** 132.85 (0400–1200Z‡)
CLEARANCE DELIVERY PHONE: For CD ctc Fort Worth ARTCC at 817-858-7584.
RADIO AIDS TO NAVIGATION: NOTAM FILE FTW.
  QUITMAN (L) **DME** 114.0 UIM Chan 87 N32°52.83´ W95°22.01´ 052° 5.7 NM to fld. 517.

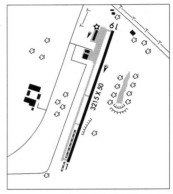

WINSTON FLD (See SNYDER on page 427)

TEXAS

WINTERS MUNI (77F) 2 SW UTC–6(–5DT) N31°56.83′ W99°59.15′   SAN ANTONIO
1871 B NOTAM FILE SJT   L–17B
  RWY 17–35: H3204X50 (ASPH) S–12 LIRL   IAP
    RWY 17: Fence.
    RWY 35: Fence.
  AIRPORT REMARKS: Unattended. Parl txy fm ramp south, gravel with potholes, unusbl. 4 ft fence 16–200 ft west of rwy.
  AIRPORT MANAGER: 325-665-4200
  COMMUNICATIONS: CTAF 122.9
  Ⓡ **ABILENE APP/DEP CON** 127.2
  CLEARANCE DELIVERY PHONE: For CD ctc Fort Worth ARTCC at 817-858-7584.
  RADIO AIDS TO NAVIGATION: NOTAM FILE ABI.
    ABILENE (VH) (H) VORTACW 113.7   ABI   Chan 84   N32°28.88′ W99°51.81′   181° 32.6 NM to fld. 1809/10E.
    VOR unusable:
      163°–236° byd 40 NM blo 18,000′
      237°–247° byd 40 NM blo 7,000′
      248°–250° byd 40 NM blo 18,000′
      251°–255° byd 40 NM blo 4,500′
      251°–255° byd 46 NM blo 18,000′

WOLFE AIR PARK (See MANVEL on page 371)

WOLFFORTH

SOUTHWEST LUBBOCK (T96) 7 S UTC–6(–5DT) N33°23.74′ W102°00.56′   ALBUQUERQUE
3265 NOTAM FILE   L–6H
  RWY 02–20: H2650X40 (ASPH)
    RWY 02: REIL. Rgt tfc.
    RWY 20: REIL.
  AIRPORT REMARKS: Unattended. Windsock lctd at each rwy end. Seasonal crops at each rwy end.
  AIRPORT MANAGER: 806-787-6681
  COMMUNICATIONS: CTAF 122.9
  CLEARANCE DELIVERY PHONE: For CD ctc Fort Worth ARTCC at 817-858-7584.
  RADIO AIDS TO NAVIGATION: NOTAM FILE LBB.
    LUBBOCK (L) (L) VORTACW 109.2   LBB   Chan 29   N33°42.30′ W101°54.84′   184° 19.1 NM to fld. 3310/11E.
    VOR unusable:
      040°–050° byd 38 NM blo 5,300′
      210°–260° byd 25 NM blo 6,000′

WOOD CO/COLLINS FLD (See MINEOLA/QUITMAN on page 383)

WOODVILLE

TYLER CO (Ø9R) 2 W UTC–6(–5DT) N30°46.51′ W94°27.51′   HOUSTON
388 B NOTAM FILE CXO   L–19E, 21A
  RWY 16–34: H4000X60 (ASPH) S–30 MIRL
    RWY 16: PAPI(P2L)—GA 3.0° TCH 38′. Thld dsplcd 178′. Trees.
    RWY 34: Trees.
  SERVICE: **LGT** Dusk–dawn. MIRL Rwy 16–34 preset low intst; to incr intst ACTVT—122.8.
  AIRPORT REMARKS: Unattended. Rwy 16 – 5 ft drop–off 25 ft fm west side, 400 ft south of thr; 20 ft drop–off 100 ft north of thr.
  AIRPORT MANAGER: 409-283-7623
  COMMUNICATIONS: CTAF 122.9
  CLEARANCE DELIVERY PHONE: For CD ctc Houston ARTCC at 281-230-5622.
  RADIO AIDS TO NAVIGATION: NOTAM FILE LFK.
    LUFKIN (VH) (H) VORTACW 112.1   LFK   Chan 58   N31°09.75′ W94°43.01′   145° 26.7 NM to fld. 207/5E.
    TACAN AZIMUTH unusable:
      260°–275° byd 30 NM
      275°–260° byd 30 NM blo 2,500′
    DME unusable:
      260°–275° byd 30 NM
      275°–260° byd 30 NM blo 2,500′
    VOR unusable:
      305°–312° byd 40 NM
      313°–323° byd 40 NM blo 2,300′
      313°–323° byd 66 NM
      324°–330° byd 40 NM

TEXAS

WOOLE N31°16.78´ W100°34.57´ NOTAM FILE SJT.   SAN ANTONIO
  NDB (LOMW) 356   SJ   036° 6.2 NM to San Angelo Rgnl/Mathis Fld. 2127/5E.   L–19B

YOAKUM CO (See PLAINS on page 400)

YOAKUM MUNI (T85)   1 N   UTC–6(–5DT)   N29°18.79´ W97°08.31´   SAN ANTONIO
  365   B   NOTAM FILE CXO   L–19D, 21A
  RWY 13–31: H3444X60 (ASPH)   S–12   MIRL   0.7% up NW   IAP
    RWY 13: Pole.
    RWY 31: Pole.
  AIRPORT REMARKS: Unattended. Rwy 13 and Rwy 31 mrkgs faded.
  AIRPORT MANAGER: (361) 293-6321
  COMMUNICATIONS: CTAF 122.9
  ®**HOUSTON CENTER APP/DEP CON** 132.8
    CLEARANCE DELIVERY PHONE: For CD ctc Houston ARTCC at 281-230-5622.
  RADIO AIDS TO NAVIGATION: NOTAM FILE ELA.
    EAGLE LAKE (DH) DME 116.4   ELA   Chan 111   N29°39.75´
      W96°19.03´   244° 47.8 NM to fld. 192.

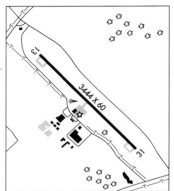

YOAKUM–DEFRENN AHP HELIPORT (HLR)(KHLR) A   1 NE   UTC–6(–5DT)   N31°08.26´ W97°42.85´   SAN ANTONIO
  910   B   TPA—See Remarks   NOTAM FILE SJT   Not insp.   L–19C, 21A
  HELIPAD 16–34: H2676X75 (ASPH)   PCN 9   F/C/W/T   MIRL   1.0% up N   DIAP, AD
  SERVICE: **LGT** MIRL AHP Rwy 16–34 opr 1400–0600Z‡ wkd exc fed hol OT PCL 119.65.   **MILITARY**— **FUEL**
    A++. Rapid refuel opr times by NOTAM **OIL** SOAP **TRAN ALERT** Ltd tran prk..
  MILITARY REMARKS: Attended Mon–Fri 1400–0600Z‡, except holidays. See FLIP AP/1 Supplementary Arpt Remarks. Rwy end
    16: mkg 16H. Rwy end 34: mkg 34H. H–1 and Twy J clsd 1200–1330Z‡ Mon–Fri exc hol. **RSTD** PPR all transient acft,
    C254–288–3811, DSN 738–3811 or C254–287–7585 DSN 737–7585 Rstd from Fixed Wing acft . No Base OPS svc
    avbl at Yoakum–Defrenn AHP, ctc Robert Gray Base OPS C254–288–9200, DSN 738–9200. Rapid refuel operational
    times by NOTAM. **CAUTION** Instrument final apch course cross 1 NM SW Skylark Fld. Ints copter opr vcnty Ft Cavazos. Some
    acft opr in area without conspicuous markings and blend with terrain. R6302 located 1.1 NM N of afld. Extensive UAS
    ACT within Class D airspace and btn Robert Gray AAF and R6302. **TFC PAT** TPA—Left and rgt tfc alt 1500´. **MISC** No trml
    fcst issued for Yoakum–Defrenn AHP. For remote briefing svc ctc Robert Gray AAF. C254–288–9620, DSN 738–9620 or
    26 OWS, Barksdale AFB, C318–529–2651, DSN 331–2651. Wx obsn fully automated via ASOS—C254–286–5692.
  AIRPORT MANAGER: 254-553-0501
  COMMUNICATIONS: ATIS 138.6 (Opr 1400–0600Z‡ Mon–Fri exc hol, OT ctc Robert Gray Twr 120.75 285.5)
    GRAY APP/DEP CON 120.075 323.15
    TOWER 119.65 269.45 (Mon–Fri 1400–0600Z‡, except holidays other times ctc Robert Gray Twr 120.75 285.5
    airborne; 133.85 225.4 on ground). **GND CON** 133.85 225.4 **CLNC DEL** 225.4
    PMSV GRAY METRO 306.5 WX obsn fully automated. Manual back–up provided for equipment/communication failure only
    during afld operating hrs. **RANGE CON** 30.45 38.30 **FORT HOOD FLT FOLLOWING** 141.175 357.5
  AIRSPACE: CLASS D.
  RADIO AIDS TO NAVIGATION: NOTAM FILE GRK.
    GRAY (T) (T) VORW/DME 111.8   GRK   Chan 55   N31°01.97´ W97°48.83´   032° 8.1 NM to fld. 963/7E.
    IRESH NDB (LOMW) 278   IL   N31°01.45´ W97°42.49´   352° 6.8 NM to fld. 853/5E. NOTAM FILE ILE.
    NDB unusable:
      066°–294° byd 15 NM
      295°–065° byd 5 NM due to military restricted area

TEXAS

ZAPATA CO (APY)(KAPY) 4 NE UTC–6(–5DT) N26°58.13´ W99°14.93´ **BROWNSVILLE**
422 B NOTAM FILE SJT H–7B, L–20G
RWY 12–30: H5000X60 (ASPH) S–12.5 MIRL
 RWY 12: Thld dsplcd 112´. Brush.
 RWY 30: Thld dsplcd 113´. Trees.
SERVICE: **FUEL** 100LL, JET A **LGT** Dusk–Dawn. MIRL Rwy 12–30 preset medium ints, to incr ints ACTIVATE—CTAF.
AIRPORT REMARKS: Attended irregularly.
AIRPORT MANAGER: 956-786-0000
WEATHER DATA SOURCES: AWOS–3 118.225 (956) 765–4069.
COMMUNICATIONS: CTAF/UNICOM 122.7
CLEARANCE DELIVERY PHONE: For CD ctc Houston ARTCC at 281-230-5622.
RADIO AIDS TO NAVIGATION: NOTAM FILE LRD.
 LAREDO (VH) (H) **VORTACW** 117.4 LRD Chan 121 N27°28.72´ W99°25.06´ 154° 31.8 NM to fld. 583/9E.
 VOR unusable:
  080°–126° byd 40 NM
  127°–137° byd 40 NM blo 4,500´
  127°–137° byd 56 NM
  138°–160° byd 40 NM
  190°–260° byd 40 NM

SPECIAL NOTICES

Bomb Disposal Area
McAlester, Oklahoma Vicinity

Bomb disposal area, one NM radius, MLC 240°/006, SFC to 2000 AGL. Times of use: Daily, 30 min after SR to 30 min before SS. Avoidance advised.

AEROBATIC PRACTICE AREA
Coushatta, LA, Red River Airport (0R7)

Aerobatic practice will be conducted at Red River Airport between the surface and 5,000 feet AGL within the boundaries of the airspace bounded on the west by the western edge of Rwy 17/35, extending northward and southward to the respective airport boundaries, extending eastward for 1.5 miles to an imaginary line connecting to the northeast and southeast corners, to create the practice area. The practice area is for waiver holders only. Pilots should use caution when operating within this area.

Crowley, LA, Le Gros Airport (3R2)

Aerobatic practice will be conducted at Le Gros Airport within the area defined as a semicircle extending southward from its diameter centered on the north end of the north/south taxiway at its intersection with the south edge of the east/west taxiway extending eastward 6,000 feet and westward 6,000 feet from the surface to 4,500 feet MSL. The practice area is for waiver holders only. Pilots should use caution when operating within this area.

Farmerville, LA, Union Parish Airport (F87)

Aerobatic practice will be conducted within a 2 NM radius of the Union Parish Airport, SFC to 4,000 feet MSL. The practice area is for waiver holders only. Pilots should use caution when operating within this area.

Jennings, LA, Jennings Airport (3R7)

Aerobatic practice will be conducted centered from 1 NM northwest of Jennings Airport, within an approx. 2.5 NM radius, 500 feet to 4,000 feet MSL. The practice area is for waiver holders only. Pilots should use caution when operating within this area.

Springhill Airport (SPH), Springhill, LA

Aerobatic practice conducted at the Springhill (SPH) Airport, from SFC to 5000 MSL, within the area defined as having its western boundary along the western edge of Rwy 18/36, extending northward 1000 feet beyond the north end of the runway; then eastward 150 feet to the eastern boundary; then southward parallel to the runway to a line which runs along the southern edge of Rwy 18/36, extending from its western edge 1500 feet to a point where it intersects the eastern boundary. The practice area is for waiver holders only. Pilots should use caution when operating within this area.

Sulphur, LA, Southland Field (UXL)

Aerobatic practice will be conducted at West Calcasieu Airport, Southland Field within a 2 NM radius of the Lake Charles VORTAC, LCH261014, SFC to 4,000 feet AGL. The practice area is for waiver holders only. Pilots should use caution when operating within this area.

Bristow, OK, Jones Memorial Airport (3F7)

Aerobatic practice will be conducted within 2 NM radius of Jones Memorial Airport (3F7), SFC to 6,000 feet AGL, SR–SS.

Cookson, OK, Tenkiller Lake Airpark (44M)

Aerobatic practice will be conducted at Tenkiller Airpark in a 3,000 foot box, beginning at the centerline of the approach end of RY23 and extending 400 feet beyond the departure end of RY23, thence extending 3,000 feet AGL. The practice area is for waiver holders only. Pilots should use caution when operating within this area.

Ketchum, OK, South Grand Lake Regional Airport (1K8)

Aerobatic practice will be conducted within 1 NM radius of the South Grand Lake Regional Airport (1K8), SFC to 4,500 feet AGL. The practice area is for waiver holders only. Pilots should use caution when operating within this area.

Nowata, OK, Nowata Airport (H66)

Aerobatic practice will be conducted centered from 3 NM northwest of the Nowata Airport (H66), SFC to 3,000 feet AGL. The practice area is for waiver holders only. Pilots should use caution when operating within this area.

Brenham, TX, Brenham Muni Airport (11R)

Aerobatic practice will be conducted within 2 NM radius of the Brenham Muni Airport (11R), 800 to 4,500 feet MSL. The practice area is for waiver holders only. Pilots should use caution when operating within this area.

Brenham, TX, Live Oak Ranch (TA17)

Aerobatic practice will be conducted within 2 NM radius of the center of Live Oak Ranch (TA17) from 900 feet MSL up to and including 4,500 feet MSL, SR–SS.

Celina, TX, Four Winds (9S1)

Aerobatic flight activity will be conducted at Four Winds Ranch, bound on the north by County Road 102, on the south by an imaginary line parallel to and 800 feet south of County Road 134, on the west by an imaginary line just east of the three lakes, and on the east by a tree line, SFC to 4,500 feet MSL, SR–SS.

SPECIAL NOTICES

Edna, TX, Jackson County Airport (26R)
Aerobatic practice will be conducted within 2 NM radius of the PSX307019.6 the area to the east of Jackson County Airport (26R), from SFC to 4,000 feet MSL, SR-SS. The practice area is for waiver holders only. Pilots should use caution when operating within this area.

Fort Worth, TX, Naval Air Station JRB (NFW)
Aerobatic practice will be conducted centered from 1 NM East and 3 NM West, North and South of NAS JRB Forth Worth (NFW) runway 17/35, from SFC to 6,000 feet MSL. The practice area is for waiver holders only. Pilots should use caution when operating within this area.

Georgetown, TX, Georgetown Muni (GTU)
Aerobatic practice activity will be conducted 4 NM East of GTU, surface to 5000 MSL, approximately 1 NM diameter at 19 DME on the 342 radial of the CWK VORTAC. Area is activated by coordination with GTU tower and Fort Worth NOTAM line.

Graford, TX, Possum Kingdom (F35)
Aerobatic practice will be conducted within 1 NM radius of MQP289929 3.5 NM west of Possum Kingdom Airport, SFC to 5,000 feet MSL. The practice area is for waiver holders only. Pilots should use caution when operating within this area.

LaGrange, TX, Fayette Regional Air Center (3T5)
Aerobatic flight activity will be conducted within a 2 NM radius of the Fayette Regional Airport (3T5), from 900 feet MSL up to and including 4,000 feet MSL. The practice area is for waiver holders only. Pilots should use caution when operating within this area.

Navasota, TX
Glider operations will be conducted within a 5 NM radius of the TNV VOR/DME 130/007, from SFC to 8000 feet MSL, SR-SS. Pilots should use caution when operating in this area.

Moonbow Field, Waxahachie, TX
Aerobatic flight practice will be conducted within 1 $^1/_2$ NM radius of TTT 148/024 from SFC to 3500 MSL. Pilots should use caution when operating within this area.

Sherman/Denison, TX, North Texas Rgnl/Perrin Field (GYI)
Aerobatic flight activity will be conducted within a 2 NM radius of the BYP290024.4, SFC to 5700´ MSL, SR-SS daily. The practice area is for waiver holders only. Pilots should use caution when operating in this area.

Slidell, TX, Akroville Airport (XA68)
Aerobatic practice will be conducted within 1.5 NM radius of the UKW108026, SFC to 4,000 feet MSL, SR-SS.

Wichita Falls, TX, Kickapoo Downtown Airport (CWC)
Aerobatic practice will be conducted within 1.5 NM radius of the SPS136009.2, SFC to 4,000 feet MSL, SR-SS.

SPECIAL NOTICES

MODEL AIRCRAFT ACTIVITY
Haskell, OK (2K9)
Model rocket activity will be conducted within a 1 NM radius of GNP092008, SFC to 9,000 feet MSL, SR–SS. For further information contact Flight Services at 1–800–WX–BRIEF (992–7433).

Oklahoma City, OK
Model rocket activity will be conducted within a 1 NM radius of IRW270023, SFC to 6,400 feet MSL, SR–SS. For further information, contact Flight Services at 1–800–992–7433.

Fort Stockton—Pecos Co (FST), TX
Model rocket activity will be conducted within a 2.6 NM radius of FST 146/014, SFC to 20,000 MSL, SR–SS. Model rocket activity will be conducted within a 2 NM radius of FST 212/9, SFC to 23,100 MSL, SR–SS.

Hearne, TX (LHB)
Model rocket activity will be conducted within a 1 NM radius of the Hearne Muni Airport (LHB) or the CLL 319/018 SFC to 12,500′ MSL, SR–SS. For further information, contact Flight Services at 1–800–992–7433.

Kileen (ILE), Texas, Vicinity
Model airplane activity conducted 1 NM radius ILE 138R/006NM, 10008 AGL and below. Intermittent launches daily.

Nacogdoches, TX (OCH)
Model Rocket activity will be conducted within a 1 NM radius of the Nacogdoches A L Mangham Jr. Rgnl Arpt (OCH) 045018, SFC to 3,000 feet MSL, SR–SS. For further information contact Flight Services at 1–800–WX–BRIEF (992–7433).

Wills Point, TX (76F)
Model rocket activity will be conducted within a 5 NM radius of TTT100051, SFC to 24,000 feet MSL, SR–SS. For further information, contact Flight Services at 1–800–992–7433.

Waco Rgnl, TX (ACT)
Model rocket activity will be conducted within a 5 NM radius of ACT 131014, SFC to 24,000 feet MSL, SR–SS. For further information, contact Flight Services at 1–800–992–7433.

DALLAS–FORT WORTH, TX, DALLAS–FORT WORTH INTL AIRPORT (DFW) NOISE ABATEMENT PROCEDURES
Successive or simultaneous departures from Runways 17R, 17C, 18R, 18L, 35L, 35C, 36L and 36R are authorized, with course divergence beginning within 5 miles from the departure end of parallel runways for non-RNAV aircraft, or 10 miles of the departure end of parallel runways for aircraft on an RNAV departure, due to noise abatement.

Office of Primary Responsibility (ORP): FAA/D10 (DFW) TRACON
Contact Information: 972-615-2532
Amended: November 2023

Robinsonville, Mississippi
Laser light activity will be conducted at the Grand Casino, Robinsonville, MS, N34°52′22″/W90°17′40″ MEM VOR 243R/18.3 NM, from 0000 to 0700 UTC daily. Laser light beams may be injurious to eyes within 300 feet vertically and 21,000 feet laterally. Flash blindness or cockpit illumination may occur beyond these distances.

Vicksburg, Mississippi
A permanent Laser Light Demonstration will be conducted at Harrah's Casino Hotel, Vicksburg, MS, (JAN VORTAC 255° Radial, 38 Nautical Miles, Latitude 32°21″N, Longitude 90°53″W), nightly from sunset until 12:00 A.M. Laser Light beam may be injurious to eyes if viewed within 1000 feet vertically and/or 3000 feet laterally of the light source. Cockpit illumination—flash blindness may occur beyond these distances.

SPECIAL NOTICES

SPECIAL NORTH ATLANTIC, CARIBBEAN AND PACIFIC AREA COMMUNICATIONS

VHF air–to–air frequencies enable aircraft engaged in flights over remote and oceanic areas out of range of VHF ground stations to exchange necessary operational information and to facilitate the resolution of operational problems.

Frequencies have been designated as follows: HOUSTON ARTCC

North Atlantic area:	123.45 MHz
Caribbean area:	123.45 MHz
Pacific area:	123.45 MHz

Secondary–Only Radar in the Vicinity of Lufkin, Texas

The Air Traffic Control Beacon Interrogator–6 (ATCBI—6) located at the Angelina County Airport (LFK), Lufkin, Texas, is the only source of radar data within an approximate 50 NM radius of LFK. This is a secondary radar system; therefore radar services are available on transponder equipped aircraft only.

CAUTION—HIGH DENSITY STUDENT FLYING
Little Rock AFB, AR

High density student flying training in the vicinity of Little Rock AFB and on low level Slow Routes (SR) within Arkansas; 0600–0200 Mon–Fri, occasional weekend. Extensive use of All American Drop Zone, Little Rock VORTAC 332° radial 15.0 NM, and Blackjack Drop Zone, Little Rock VORTAC 009° radial 33.0 NM; 0600–0200, Mon–Fri, occasional weekend. Drop Zones are used for personnel and cargo, including IMC (AWDS) drops. For further information, contact Little Rock AFB, Base Operations, on 1–501–988–6125.

East Texas Regional Airport, Longview, Texas

Extensive flight training activity within a 20 NM radius of the East Texas Regional Airport 9,000 MSL and below. These areas are in use from sunrise to sunset daily. Participating traffic reports on 123.5. It is advised to exercise caution when transiting this area and monitor 123.5.

CAUTION—VERTICAL LIGHTS ON BUILDING
Downtown Tulsa, Oklahoma

Approximately ten miles southwest of Tulsa International Airport in the area of downtown Tulsa, four 4,000–watt xenon lights are mounted on each corner of the roof of a 40–story building. Illumination is vertical and hours of use are daily, dusk to midnight.

BAYOU SAUVAGE NATIONAL WILDLIFE REFUGE, LA

Request aircraft remain at or above 2,000 ft in the vicinity of Bayou Sauvage National Wildlife Refuge bounded by Lake Pontchartrain to the Northwest and Northeast, Lake Borgue to the Southeast and New Orleans to the Southwest.

CAUTION–LARGE CONCENTRATION OF BATS
San Antonio, Texas, Vicinity

From April to October large concentration of bats are observed in the vicinity of Braken Cave located 5.5 miles east of SAT VORTAC. Most activity is observed around sunset and sunrise at altitudes up to 10,000 feet.

CAUTION–HIGH DENSITY AIR TRAFFIC AREA

Heavy helicopter and seaplane traffic exists over the Gulf of Mexico and adjacent onshore areas. Thousands of operations per month occur in this area in support of oil drilling and exploration.

Itinerant pilots traversing this area should familiarize themselves with offshore operating practices and frequencies through contact with the pertinent Flight Standards District Office (FSDO) or Flight Service Station.

SPECIAL NOTICES

MILITARY TRAINING ROUTES

The DOD Flight Information Publication AP/1B provides textual and graphic descriptions and operating instructions for all military training routes (IR, VR, SR) and refueling tracks/anchors. Complete and more comprehensive information relative to policy and procedures for IRs and VRs is published in FAA Handbook 7610.4 (Special Military Operations) which is agreed to by the DOD and therefore directive for all military flight operations. The AP/1B is the official source of route data for military users.

CIVIL USE OF MILITARY FIELDS:

U.S. Army, Air Force, Navy and Coast Guard Fields are open to civil fliers only in emergency or with prior permission.

Army Installations, prior permission is required from the Commanding Officer of the installation.

For Air Force installations, prior permission should be requested at least 30 days prior to first intended landing from either Headquarters USAF (PRPOC) or the Commander of the installation concerned (who has authority to approve landing rights for certain categories of civil aircraft. For use of more than one Air Force installation, requests should be forwarded direct to Hq USAF (PRPOC), Washington, D.C. 20330.

Use of USAF installations must be specifically justified.

For Navy and Marine Corps installations prior permission should be requested at least 30 days prior to first intended landing. An Aviation Facility License must be approved and executed by the Navy prior to any landing by civil aircraft.

Forms and further information may be obtained from the nearest U.S. Navy or Marine Corps aviation activity.

For Coast Guard fields prior permission should be requested from the Commandant, U.S. Coast Guard via the Commanding Officer of the field.

When instrument approaches are conducted by civil aircraft at military airports, they shall be conducted in accordance with the procedures and minimums approved by the military agency having jurisdiction over the airport.

AIRCRAFT LANDING RESTRICTIONS

Landing of aircraft at locations other than public use airports may be a violation of Federal or local law. All land and water areas are owned or controlled by private individuals or organizations, states, cities, local governments, or U.S. Government agencies. Except in emergency, prior permission should be obtained before landing at any location that is not a designated public use airport or seaplane base.

Landing of aircraft is prohibited on lands or waters administered by the National Park Service, U.S. Fish and Wildlife Service, U.S. Forest Service, and on many areas controlled by the U.S. Army Corps of Engineers, unless prior authorization is obtained from the respective agency.

FEDERAL AVIATION REGULATION 91.713

The provisions of FAR 91.713 will apply as follows:

Air traffic clearances to aircraft of Cuban registry not engaged in scheduled International Air Service in U.S. airspace will require that the flight plan be filed with appropriate authorities at least five days prior to the proposed departure time. Route changes while en route will normally not be authorized. The procedures set forth herein do not apply at this time to overflights by aircraft of Cuban registry engaged in scheduled International Air Service.

CONTROLLED FIRING

Camden, Harrell Fld, AR
6E Camden 2 NM radius surface–005 avoidance advised Mon–Fri daylight hours.
El Dorado, South Arkansas Rgnl
ELD 021/024 2 NM radius surface—500 AGL avoidance advised Mon–Fri daylight hours.
Texarkana Rgnl Webb Fld, AR.
.25 NM radius TXK 223010 2000/blo Mon–Thu. 1900–0500Z‡
.5 NM radius TXK 240014 1000/blo Mon–Sat SR–SS.

SPECIAL NOTICES

Camp Bullis Training Site
Controlled Firing Area (CFA)
Camp Bullis, TX

1. CFA Description:

    a. Boundaries: Beginning at

      Lat. 29°41′10.07″N., Long. 98°31′41.40″W. to
      Lat. 29°40′25.05″N., Long. 98°33′57.40″W. to
      Lat. 29°39′20.22″N., Long. 98°34′44.18″W. to
      Lat. 29°38′03.77″N., Long. 98°34′13.26″W. to
      Lat. 29°37′53.94″N., Long. 98°33′46.90″W. to
      Lat. 29°38′36.77″N., Long. 98°31′55.13″W. to
      Lat. 29°39′48.07″N., Long. 98°31′06.07″W. to
      Point of beginning.

    b. Altitudes: Surface to 3,000 feet AGL.

    c. Times of use: Approximately 70 times per year. Utilization will normally be 7 days per week, 0700–2300 local time. Give prior notice of all activities to Flight Service. Notify the Flight Service when activities are terminated each day.

2. Activities:

    a. M203 40mm Grenade Launcher, HE/Target Practice Training (TPT) rounds, average use 50 times per year.

    b. Heavy Demolitions Range, types of explosives will vary, but all are conventional (no nuclear, biological, or chemical), 20 times per year.

    c. Emergency destruction of illegal explosive devices will be unscheduled due to the nature of the event.

3. Using Agency: U.S. Army, Commander, Camp Bullis Training Site, Camp Bullis, TX

4. Effective date: The effective date is February 1, 2004. Biannual approval of the CFA is automatic upon receipt of a biannual status report from the Department of the Army Regional Representative containing a statement that the activities for which the area was established have not changed.

5. Conditions, Operating Limitations, and Safety Precautions:

    a. Camp Bullis Training Site will maintain observers with direct communications to the Range Towers located in positions that allow for sufficient visual surveillance of the entire area.

    b. Firing will cease upon observation of low-flying aircraft.

    c. The ceiling shall be at least 1,000 feet above the maximum ordinate of projectiles and/or debris.

    d. Visibility shall be sufficient to maintain visual surveillance of the entire CFA plus a distance of 5 statute miles beyond the CFA in all directions.

    e. All user responsibilities, precautionary measures, and surveillance requirements listed in FAA Order 7400.2 shall be complied with.

    f. All activities will be contained within the designated impact area at Camp Bullis.

6. With the exception of the emergency destruction of unsafe explosive devices, the following information shall be filed with the Flight Service in sufficient time to permit a NOTAM to be transmitted at least 2 hours prior to scheduled operations:

    a. Location of the CFA.

    b. Time of use.

    c. Activity to be conducted.

    d. Maximum altitudes.

    e. User.

7. Any violation of the conditions, as outlined above, shall be the basis for the FAA to withdraw authorization of the CFA.

CONTROLLED FIRING AREA
CAMP STANLEY, SAN ANTONIO, TEXAS

The Military has established a controlled firing area bordered by the following geographic coordinates: beginning at N29°40′37″/W98°37′53″; thence to N29°41′17″/W98°35′49″; to N29°43′51″/W98°35′50″; to N29°43′51″/W98°37′23″; to point of beginning. Operating SR–SS daily, SFC to 1,500 feet AGL (2,500 feet MSL).

SPECIAL NOTICES

FIREFIGHTING TRAFFIC AREAS

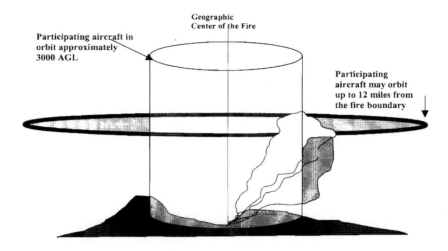

Pilots are advised to stay clear of Firefighting Traffic Areas. Remain 15 miles from the area of activity. If you must over-fly the area, do so at an altitude of 5000 feet AGL above. However, to remain safe and out of the way of working aircraft, it is best to circumnavigate the area.

The wild-land fire environment can be very complex and involve a large number and variety of aircraft types including fixed and rotary wing aircraft. Some of the aircraft are small single and multi-engine command and control platforms that can be especially difficult to see and may give the appearance that the fire is not staffed. The aircraft participating in firefighting can orbit as far out as 12 miles from the perimeter of the fire. Any intrusion by aircraft not directly involved in the firefighting operation could delay the delivery of much needed retardant or water to ground firefighters and will adversely affect the safety of participating aircraft. Please stay well away from wild-land fires even if you feel that aircraft are not working the fire; they may be en route or unseen.

If you see a fire developing along your route, report it immediately to air traffic control who will advise the US Forest Service. The firefighting community would welcome this information.

EL PASO INTERNATIONAL AIRPORT (ELP) ARRIVAL ALERT

Landing West
RWY 26R and RWY 26L and TWY Y

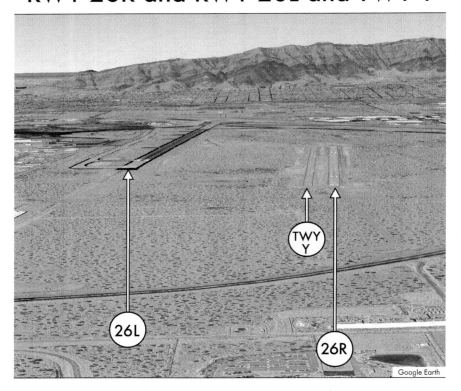

RWY 26L is over 3500 ft. longer and twice the width of RWY 26R. RWY 26R threshold is over 2000 ft. closer than RWY 26L. Pilots confuse TWY Y for RWY 26R.

**Not for Navigational Purposes
For Situational Awareness Only**

Office of Primary Responsibility (OPR): ATO, Runway Safety
Contact Information: (202) 856-1942
Original: January 2024

FORT WORTH MEACHAM INTERNATIONAL AIRPORT (FTW) ARRIVAL ALERT

Landing South
RWY 16 and RWY 17 and TWY A

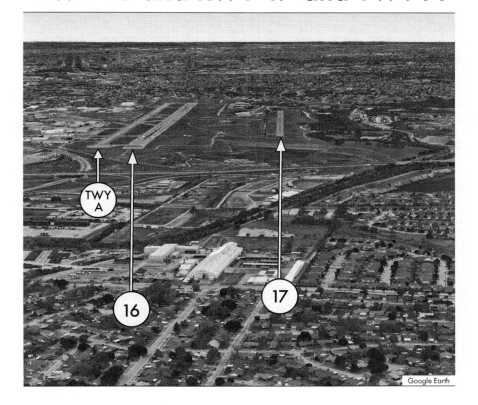

Pilots confuse RWY 17 for RWY 16. RWY 16 is over 3500 ft. longer, twice the width and over 1700 ft. closer than RWY 17. Pilots confuse TWY A for RWY 16.

**Not for Navigational Purposes
For Situational Awareness Only**

FORT WORTH MEACHAM INTERNATIONAL AIRPORT (FTW) ARRIVAL ALERT

Landing North RWY 34 and RWY 35 and TWY A

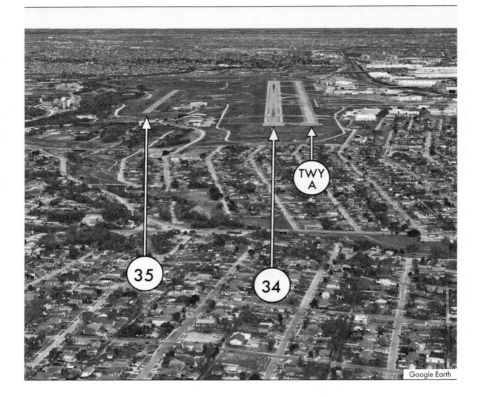

Pilots confuse RWY 35 for RWY 34. RWY 34 is over 3500 ft. longer, twice the width and over 1700 ft. closer than RWY 35. Pilots confuse TWY A for RWY 34.

Not for Navigational Purposes
For Situational Awareness Only

FORT WORTH MEACHAM INTERNATIONAL AIRPORT (FTW) ARRIVAL ALERT

Wrong Airport Landing
Landing North
FTW and JRB Carswell FLD (NFW)

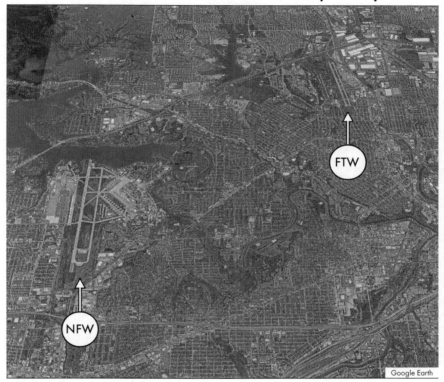

NFW is approximately 5.5 miles Southwest of FTW Airport and its RWY is 4500 ft. longer and 50 ft. wider than FTW RWY 16/34. Pilots confuse NFW RWY 18 with FTW RWY 16. Pilots confuse NFW RWY 36 with FTW RWY 34.

Not for Navigational Purposes
For Situational Awareness Only

Office of Primary Responsibility (OPR): ATO, Runway Safety
Contact Information: (202) 856-1942
Original: January 2024

MCKINNEY INTL (TKI) ARRIVAL ALERT

Landing South
RWY 18 and TWY B

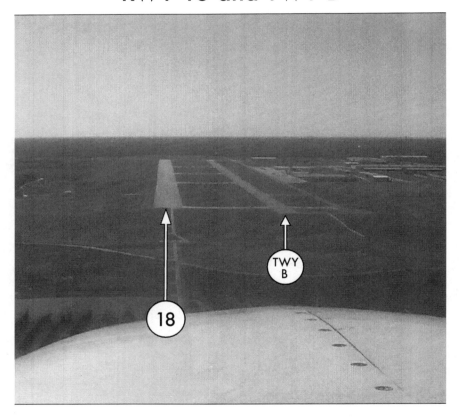

Pilots sometimes confuse TWY B for RWY 18.

Not for Navigational Purposes
For Situational Awareness Only

SPECIAL NOTICES

MCKINNEY INTL (TKI) ARRIVAL ALERT

Landing North RWY 36 and TWY B

Pilots sometimes confuse TWY B for RWY 36.

**Not for Navigational Purposes
For Situational Awareness Only**

Office of Primary Responsibility (OPR): ATO, Runway Safety
Contact Information: (202) 856-1942
Amended: January 2024

REGULATORY NOTICES

The following narratives summarize the FAR Part 93 Special Air Traffic Rules, and Airport Traffic Patterns in effect as prescribed in the rule. This information is advisory in nature and in no way relieves the pilot from compliance with the specific rules set forth in FAR Parts 91 and 93.

Special Airport Traffic Areas prescribed in Part 93 are depicted on Sectional Aeronautical Charts, Enroute Low Altitude Charts, and where applicable, on VFR Terminal Area Charts.

OPERATIONS RESERVATIONS FOR HIGH DENSITY TRAFFIC AIRPORTS KENNEDY, LAGUARDIA, AND WASHINGTON REAGAN NATIONAL

The Federal Aviation Administration (FAA) has designated New York's Kennedy and LaGuardia Airports and Washington Reagan National Airport as High Density Traffic Airports (HDTA), Title 14, Code of Federal Regulations, part 93, subpart K, and has prescribed air traffic rules and requirements for operating aircraft (excluding helicopters) to and from those airports during certain hours.

Reservations are required for operations from 6 a.m. through 11:59 p.m. local time at LaGuardia Airport and Washington Reagan National Airport. Reservations at Kennedy Airport are required from 3 p.m. through 7:59 p.m. local time.

Reservation procedures are detailed in Advisory Circular 93-1, Reservations for Unscheduled Operations at High Density Traffic Airports. A copy of the advisory circular is available on the FAA website at http://www.faa.gov. Reservations for unscheduled operations are allocated through the Enhanced Computer Voice Reservation System (e-CVRS) accessible via telephone or the Internet. This system may not be used to make reservations for scheduled air carrier or commuter flights.

The toll-free telephone number for accessing e-CVRS is 1-800-875-9694 and is available for calls originating within the United States, Canada, and the Caribbean. Users outside the toll-free areas may access e-CVRS by calling the toll number of 703-707-0568. The Internet web address for accessing the e-CVRS is http://www.fly.faa.gov/ecvrs. If you have any questions about reservation requirements or are experiencing problems with the system, you may telephone the Airport Reservation Office at the Air Traffic Control System Command Center at (703) 904-4452.

Requests for instrument flight rules (IFR) reservations will be accepted beginning 72 hours prior to the proposed time of operation at the high-density airport. For example, a request for an 11 a.m. reservation on a Thursday will be accepted beginning at 11 a.m. on the previous Monday.

IFR reservations must be obtained prior to IFR landing or takeoff at an HDTA during slot controlled hours. An air traffic control (ATC) clearance does not constitute a reservation. A reservation does not constitute permission to operate at an HDTA if additional operational limits or procedures are required by NOTAM and/or regulation.

Aircraft involved in medical emergencies will be handled by ATC without regard to a reservation after obtaining prior approval of the ATC System Command Center on (703) 904-4452. ATC will accommodate declared other emergency situations without regard to slot reservations.

NOTE: Visual flight rule (VFR) reservations via ATC for unscheduled operations at LaGuardia are not authorized from 7 a.m. through 8:59 a.m. local time and 4 p.m. through 6:59 p.m. local time, Monday through Friday and Sunday evenings, unless otherwise announced by NOTAM. Both IFR and VFR operations during those time periods must obtain an advance reservation through e-CVRS.

FAA TELEPHONE NUMBERS AND NWS

FSS TELEPHONE NUMBERS

Flight Service Station (FSS) facilities process flight plans and provide flight planning and weather briefing services to pilots. FSS services in the contiguous United States, Hawaii and Puerto Rico, are provided by a contract provider at two large facilities. In Alaska, FSS services are delivered through a network of three hub facilities and 14 satellite facilities, some of which operate part-time and some are seasonal. Because of the interconnectivity between the facilities, all FSS services including radio frequencies are available continuously using published data.

Further information can be found in the Aeronautical Information Manual (AIM).

NATIONAL FSS TELEPHONE NUMBER

Pilot Weather Briefings 1-800-WX-BRIEF (1-800-992-7433)

OTHER FSS TELEPHONE NUMBERS (except in Alaska)

Medevac Flights Only 1-877-LIF-GRD3 (1-877-543-4733)

FLIGHT RESTRICTED ZONE FLIGHTS

Pilots wishing to fly within the Flight Restricted Zone (FRZ) must call the Washington ARTCC Flight Data Unit at 703-771-3476.

FAA TELEPHONE NUMBERS AND NWS KEY AIR TRAFFIC FACILITIES

Air Traffic Control System Command Center
Main Number.........................540–422–4100

AIR ROUTE TRAFFIC CONTROL CENTERS (ARTCCs)

ARTCC NAME	*24 HR RGNL DUTY OFFICE TELEPHONE #	BUSINESS HOURS	BUSINESS TELEPHONE #	**CLEARANCE DELIVERY TELEPHONE #
Albuquerque	817–222–5006	7:30 a.m.–4:00 p.m.	505–856–4300	505–856–4561
Anchorage	907–271–5936	7:30 a.m.–4:00 p.m.	907–269–1137	
Atlanta	404–305–5180	7:30 a.m.–5:00 p.m.	770–210–7601	770–210–7692
Boston	404–305–5156	7:30 a.m.–4:00 p.m.	603–879–6633	603–879–6859
Chicago	817–222–5006	8:00 a.m.–4:00 p.m.	630–906–8221	630–906–8921
Cleveland	817–222–5006	8:00 a.m.–4:00 p.m.	440–774–0310	440–774–0490
Denver	206–231–2099	7:30 a.m.–4:00 p.m.	303–342–1600	303–651–4257
Ft. Worth	817–222–5006	7:30 a.m.–4:00 p.m.	817–858–7500	817–858–7584
Honolulu	310–725–3300	7:30 a.m.–4:00 p.m.	808–840–6100	808–840–6201
Houston	817–222–5006	7:30 a.m.–4:00 p.m.	281–230–5300	281–230–5622
Indianapolis	817–222–5006	8:00 a.m.–4:00 p.m.	317–247–2231	317–247–2411
Jacksonville	404–305–5180	8:00 a.m.–4:30 p.m.	904–549–1501	904–845–1592
Kansas City	817–222–5006	7:30 a.m.–4:00 p.m.	913–254–8500	913–254–8508
Los Angeles	661–265–8200	7:30 a.m.–4:00 p.m.	661–265–8200	661–575–2079
Memphis	404–305–5180	7:30 a.m.–4:00 p.m.	901–368–8103	901–368–8453
Miami	404–305–5180	7:00 a.m.–3:30 p.m.	305–716–1500	305–716–1731
Minneapolis	817–222–5006	8:00 a.m.–4:00 p.m.	651–463–5580	651–463–5588
New York	718–995–5426	8:00 a.m.–4:40 p.m.	631–468–1001	631–468–1425
Oakland	310–725–3300	6:30 a.m.–3:00 p.m.	510–745–3331	
Salt Lake City	206–231–2099	7:30 a.m.–4:00 p.m.	801–320–2500	801–320–2568
San Juan	404–305–5180	7:30 a.m.–5:00 p.m.	787–253–8663	787–253–8664
Seattle	206–231–2099	7:30 a.m.–4:00 p.m.	253–351–3500	253–351–3694
Washington	718–995–5426	8:00 a.m.–4:30 p.m.	703–771–3401	703–771–3587

*Facilities can be contacted through the Rgnl Duty Officer during non–business hours.
**For use when numbers or frequencies are not listed in the airport listing

MAJOR TERMINAL RADAR APPROACH CONTROLS (TRACONs)

TRACON NAME	*24 HR RGNL DUTY OFFICE TELEPHONE #	BUSINESS HOURS	BUSINESS TELEPHONE #
Atlanta	678–364–6131	7:00 a.m.–3:30 p.m.	678–364–6000
Chicago	817–222–5006	8:00 a.m.–4:00 p.m.	847–608–5509
Dallas–Ft. Worth	817–222–5006	7:30 a.m.–4:00 p.m.	972–615–2500
Denver	425–227–1389	7:30 a.m.–4:00 p.m.	303–342–1500
Houston	817–222–5006	7:30 a.m.–4:00 p.m.	281–230–8400
New York	718–995–5426	8:00 a.m.–4:30 p.m.	516–683–2901
Northern CA	310–725–3300	7:00 a.m.–3:30 p.m.	916–366–4001
Potomac	718–995–5426	8:00 a.m.–4:30 p.m.	540–349–7500
Southern CA	310–725–3300	7:30 a.m.–4:00 p.m.	858–537–5800

*Facilities can be contacted through the Rgnl Duty Officer during non–business hours.

SC, 25 JAN 2024 to 21 MAR 2024

FAA TELEPHONE NUMBERS AND NWS KEY AIR TRAFFIC FACILITIES

DAILY NAS REPORTABLE AIRPORTS

AIRPORT NAME	*24 HR RGNL DUTY OFFICE TELEPHONE #	BUSINESS HOURS	BUSINESS TELEPHONE #
Albuquerque Intl Sunport, NM	817–222–5006	8:00 a.m.–5:00 p.m.	505–842–4366
Andrews AFB, MD	718–995–5426	8:00 a.m.–4:30 p.m.	301–735–2380
Baltimore/Washington Intl Thurgood Marshall, MD	718–995–5426	8:00 a.m.–4:30 p.m.	410–962–3555
Boston Logan Intl, MA	404–305–5156	7:30 a.m.–4:00 p.m.	617–455–3100
Bradley Intl, CT	404–305–5156	7:30 a.m.–4:00 p.m.	203–627–3428
Burbank/Bob Hope, CA	310–725–3300	7:00 a.m.–5:30 p.m.	818–567–4806
Charlotte Douglas Intl, NC	404–305–5180	8:00 a.m.–4:30 p.m.	704–344–6487
Chicago Midway, IL	817–222–5006	8:00 a.m.–4:00 p.m.	773–884–3670
Chicago O'Hare Intl, IL	817–222–5006	8:00 a.m.–4:00 p.m.	773–601–7600
Cleveland Hopkins Intl, OH	817–222–5006	8:00 a.m.–4:00 p.m.	216–352–2000
Covington/Cincinnati, OH	817–222–5006	8:00 a.m.–4:30 p.m.	859–372–6440
Dallas–Ft. Worth Intl, TX	817–222–5006	8:30 a.m.–5:00 p.m.	972–615–2531
Dayton Cox Intl, OH	817–222–5006	7:30 a.m.–4:00 p.m.	937–415–6800
Denver Intl, CO	425–227–1389	7:30 a.m.–4:00 p.m.	303–342–1600
Detroit Metro, MI	817–222–5006	8:00 a.m.–4:00 p.m.	734–955–5000
Fairbanks Intl, AK	907–271–5936	7:30 a.m.–4:00 p.m.	907–474–0050
Fort Lauderdale Intl, FL	404–305–5180	7:00 a.m.–3:30 p.m.	305–356–7932
George Bush Intercontinental/Houston, TX	817–222–5006	7:30 a.m.–4:00 p.m.	713–230–8400
Hartsfield–Jackson Atlanta Intl, GA	678–364–6131	7:00 a.m.–3:30 p.m.	404–559–5800
Honolulu (Daniel K Inouye Intl), HI	310–725–3300	7:30 a.m.–4:00 p.m.	808–840–6100
Houston Hobby, TX	817–222–5006	8:00 a.m.–5:00 p.m.	713–847–1400
Indianapolis Intl, IN	817–222–5006	8:00 a.m.–4:00 p.m.	317–484–6600
Kahului/Maui, HI	310–725–3300	7:30 a.m.–4:00 p.m.	808–877–0725
Kansas City Intl, MO	817–222–5006	7:30 a.m.–4:00 p.m.	816–329–2700
Las Vegas McCarran, NV	310–725–3300	7:30 a.m.–4:00 p.m.	702–262–5978
Los Angeles Intl, CA	310–725–3300	7:00 a.m.–3:30 p.m.	310–342–4900
Louis Armstrong New Orleans Intl, LA	817–222–5006	7:00 a.m.–4:30 p.m.	504–471–4300
Memphis Intl, TN	404–305–5180	7:30 a.m.–4:00 p.m.	901–322–3350
Miami Intl, FL	404–305–5180	7:00 a.m.–4:00 p.m.	305–869–5400
Minneapolis/St. Paul, MN	817–222–5006	8:00 a.m.–4:00p.m.	612–713–4000
Nashville Intl, TN	404–305–5180	7:00 a.m.–3:30 p.m.	615–781–5460
New York Kennedy Intl, NY	718–995–5426	8:00 a.m.–4:30 p.m.	718–656–0335
New York La Guardia, NY	718–995–5426	8:00 a.m.–4:30 p.m.	718–335–5461
Newark Liberty Intl, NJ	718–995–5426	7:30 a.m.–4:00 p.m.	973–565–5000
Norman Y. Mineta San Jose Intl, CA	310–725–3300	7:30 a.m.–4:00 p.m.	408–982–0750
Ontario Intl, CA	310–725–3300	7:30 a.m.–4:00 p.m.	909–983–7518
Orlando Intl, FL	404–305–5180	7:30 a.m.–5:00 p.m.	407–850–7000
Philadelphia Intl, PA	718–995–5426	8:00 a.m.–4:30 p.m.	215–492–4100
Phoenix Sky Harbor Intl, AZ	310–725–3300	7:30 a.m.–4:00 p.m.	602–379–4226
Pittsburgh Intl, PA	718–995–5426	8:00 a.m.–4:30 p.m.	412–269–9237
Portland Intl, OR	425–227–1389	7:30 a.m.–4:00 p.m.	503–493–7500
Raleigh–Durham, NC	404–305–5180	8:00 a.m.–4:30 p.m.	919–380–3125
Ronald Reagan Washington National, DC	718–995–5426	8:00 a.m.–4:30 p.m.	703–413–0330
Salt Lake City, UT	425–227–1389	7:30 a.m.–4:00 p.m.	801–325–9600
San Antonio Intl, TX	817–222–5006	8:00 a.m.–4:30 p.m.	210–805–5507
San Diego Lindbergh Intl, CA	310–725–3300	8:00 a.m.–4:30 p.m.	619–299–0677
San Francisco Intl, CA	310–725–3300	7:00 a.m.–3:30 p.m.	650–876–2883
San Juan Intl, PR	404–305–5180	7:30 a.m.–5:00 p.m.	787–253–8663
Seattle–Tacoma Intl, WA	425–227–1389	7:30 a.m.–4:00 p.m.	206–768–2900
St. Louis Lambert, MO	817–222–5006	7:30 a.m.–4:00 p.m.	314–890–1000
Tampa Intl, FL	404–305–5180	7:30 a.m.–4:00 p.m.	813–371–7700
Ted Stevens Anchorage Intl, AK	907–271–5936	7:30 a.m.–4:00 p.m.	907–271–2700
Teterboro, NJ	718–995–5426	8:00 a.m.–4:30 p.m.	201–288–1889
Washington Dulles Intl, DC	718–995–5426	8:00 a.m.–4:30 p.m.	571–323–6375
West Palm Beach, FL	404–305–5180	8:00 a.m.–4:30 p.m.	561–683–1867
Westchester Co, NY	718–995–5426	8:00 a.m.–4:30 p.m.	914–948–6520

*Facilities can be contacted through the Rgnl Duty Officer during non–business hours.

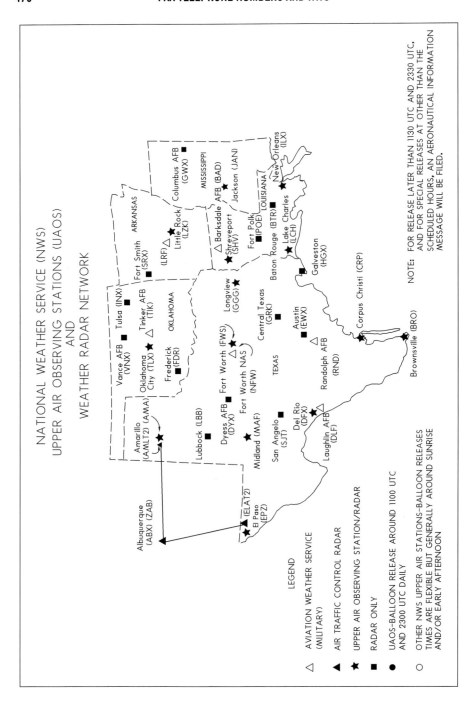

AIR ROUTE TRAFFIC CONTROL CENTERS

Air Route Traffic Control Center frequencies and their remoted transmitter sites are listed below for the coverage of this volume. Bold face type indicates high altitude frequencies, light face type indicates low altitude frequencies. To insure unrestricted IFR operations within the high altitude enroute sectors, the use of 720 channel communications equipment (25 kHz channel spacing) is required.

®ALBUQUERQUE CENTER   H–4–5–6–7, L–5–6N–6S–7–8–10–15–17–19   (KZAB)

Alamogordo – 132.65 **132.65** 257.6 **257.6**
Amarillo – **134.75 132.125** 127.85 121.5 **121.5 307.05** 285.475 243.0 **243.0 239.35**
Animas – 134.45 **133.0** 128.2 **126.225 341.7** 327.15 **285.5 281.5**
Bagdad – **134.325** 259.3
Buckeye – 126.45 288.3
Carlsbad – 135.875 121.5 **121.5** 292.15 243.0 **243.0**
Childress – **127.85 285.475**
Childs Peak – **135.15 132.45** 126.45 **371.9 350.2** 288.3
Clines Corner – 133.65 **133.65** 132.8 **125.075** 118.65 346.35 284.6 **284.6 269.475**
Douglas – 121.5 **121.5**
El Paso/A/ – 135.875 **120.975** 292.15 **278.3**
El Paso/B/ – 128.2 **125.525** 285.5 **269.45**
Fort Stockton – 135.875 **133.225 120.975** 292.15 **278.3 270.35** 243.0 **243.0**
Globe Nr 1 – **135.725** 132.9 **132.9 126.225 341.7** 339.8 239.0 **239.05**
Globe Nr 2 – **135.15** 125.4 **350.2** 269.3 243.0 **243.0**
Guadalupe Pass – **133.225** 121.5 **121.5 270.35** 243.0 **243.0**
Mesa Rica – **128.675 125.075 360.8 279.5**
Mount Dora – **133.05 128.225** 127.85 **291.6** 285.475 **269.35** 243.0 **243.0**
Phoenix – 125.25 307.0
Prescott – **135.375** 128.45 127.675 121.5 **121.5 370.9** 306.2 298.9 243.0 **243.0**
Raton – 132.8 346.35
Roswell – 132.65 **132.65** 121.5 **121.5** 257.6 **257.6**
Sandia Mountain – 132.8 346.35
Silver City – 134.45 327.15 243.0 **243.0**
Tesuque Peak – 132.8 **120.95** 346.35 **263.1**
Truth Or Consequences – 128.2 **126.225** 121.5 **121.5 341.7** 285.5 243.0 **243.0**
Tucson – 134.45 **133.0** 327.15 **281.5** 243.0 **243.0**
Tucumcari – **132.325** 126.85 121.5 **121.5** 285.6 267.9 **251.1** 243.0 **243.0**
West Mesa – **134.6** 133.65 **133.65 126.925** 124.325 121.5 **121.5 353.85** 288.25 284.6 **251.15** 243.0 **243.0**
Winslow – **133.925 128.125** 127.675 **317.75** 306.2 **282.35**
Zuni – **134.6** 132.9 **132.9 126.925** 124.325 121.5 **121.5 120.55 353.85** 288.25 **285.4 251.15** 243.0 **243.0 239.05**

AIR ROUTE TRAFFIC CONTROL CENTERS

Ⓡ **FORT WORTH CENTER** – 121.5 **121.5**   H–6, L–6N–6S–15–17–18–19–21–22, A–2
                                                                                                                       (KZFW)

Abilene – 127.45 317.7 290.3 282.2
Ardmore – **132.975** 128.4 124.75 121.5 **121.5 351.85** 323.0 269.375 243.0
Big Spring – 133.7 **120.275** 350.2 **319.25**
Brownwood – 127.45 346.3 290.3
Center – **126.275 270.325**
Childress – 121.5 **121.5** 243.0 **243.0**
Clinton-Sherman – **132.45** 128.4 126.3 **363.1** 339.8 269.375
Cumby – 132.85 132.025 **126.575** 360.75 **322.45** 317.75
Dalhart – 121.5 **121.5** 243.0 **243.0**
Dodd City/A – 124.875 370.95
Dodd City/B – 127.6 254.3
Dublin – **134.25 128.325** 351.9 **290.55**
Dublin/A – 135.375 354.05
Dublin/B – 127.15 314.0
El Dorado – 128.2 121.5 **121.5** 278.8 **278.8** 269.1 243.0 **243.0**
Fort Worth – 364.8
Frankston – 135.25 **134.025** 265.1 **227.4**
Gainesville – 126.775 124.75 328.4 323.0
Hobart – 121.5 **121.5** 243.0 **243.0**
Hobbs – 133.1 298.95
Jacksboro – 121.5 **121.5**
Lubbock – 132.6 **125.525 120.775** 348.0 **327.1** 295.9 292.1 **274.5** 269.05 243.0 **243.0**
Marshall – **120.475 323.3**
Mc Alester – **135.45** 132.2 121.5 **121.5** 338.35 288.3 **288.3 257.925** 243.0 **243.0**
Midland/A – 133.1 **132.075** 121.5 **121.5** 298.95 **278.8** 243.0 **243.0**
Midland/B – 364.8
Mineral Wells – 127.0 **120.35** 360.6 **307.35**
Mineral Wells/A – 127.15 314.0
Monroe – 126.325 121.5 **121.5** 346.25 243.0 **243.0**
Oklahoma City – **132.45 363.1** 298.9
Okmulgee – 132.2 338.35
Paducah – 133.5 126.45 **124.525 120.775** 350.35 **348.65 335.5 327.1** 316.1
Paris – **134.475** 123.925 121.5 **121.5 352.05** 306.925
Plainview – 126.45 316.1
San Angelo – 126.15 **120.275** 322.55 **319.25**
Seven Points – **135.75** 126.75 **379.25** 298.85
Shreveport – **135.55 132.275** 126.325 **364.8** 346.25 **307.25 285.65 269.275** 243.0 **243.0**
Snyder – 132.6 269.05 257.2
Texarkana – **134.475** 126.575 123.925 121.5 **121.5 352.05 322.45** 269.475 243.0 **243.0**
Tulsa – 364.8
Tyler – 135.25 **134.025** 279.65 **251.15**
Waco – 133.3 269.5
Wichita Falls Nr 1 – **132.925** 124.525 364.8 348.65 269.25 254.275 **254.275**
Wichita Falls Nr 2 – 133.5 127.95 350.35 322.325 281.525 **281.525**
Wink – 121.5 **121.5** 243.0 **243.0**

SC, 25 JAN 2024 to 21 MAR 2024

AIR ROUTE TRAFFIC CONTROL CENTERS

Ⓡ HOUSTON CENTER – 121.5 **121.5** 124.7 243.0 **243.0** 307.4 **321.3**   H–6–7–8–9, L–17–18–19–20–21–22
Alexandria – **132.7** 121.5 **121.5** 120.975 **348.75** 299.6 288.1 **288.1** 243.0 **243.0**   (KZHU)
Atlantis – 135.775 **135.775** 134.9 132.65 **132.65** 120.35
Austin – 132.15 127.725 **126.425 371.85** 279.6 273.55
Beaumont – 133.8 126.95 **123.825** 363.05 351.8 **279.625**
Boxer – 132.65 **132.65** 120.35
Cameron County – 133.4 132.65 **132.65**
College Station – 134.8 128.075 125.15 **123.725** 351.95 **319.15** 288.275 269.6
East Breaks – 127.85 306.3
East Cameron – 127.85 120.35
Eugene Island – 132.65 **132.65** 120.35 269.55 **269.55**
Fort Stockton – 125.75 346.4
Fredericksburg – 134.2 **129.65 363.25** 307.3
Galveston – 133.8 132.65 127.85 351.8 269.55 **269.55**
Grand Isle – 135.775 **135.775** 134.9 132.65 **132.65** 132.175 **132.175 370.9** 353.55 **353.55** 290.45 251.05 **251.05**
Hattiesburg – 126.8 **119.725** 327.8 **285.6**
High Island – 133.4 132.65 **132.65** 127.85 269.55 **269.55**
Intracoastal City – 127.85 120.35
Junction – 121.5 **121.5**
Keathley Canyon 875 – 132.65 **132.65** 127.85
Kerrville – 134.95 269.4
Kingsville – **133.75** 133.4 128.15 **354.0** 350.3
Lacombe – **126.875** 126.35 121.025 338.25 **327.05** 317.775
Lafayette – **134.925** 126.35 121.5 **121.5** 338.25 **263.1** 243.0 **243.0**
Lake Charles – **132.95** 124.7 121.5 **121.5 360.65** 317.4 243.0 **243.0**
Laredo – 135.425 **133.75** 127.8 121.5 **121.5 375.825 354.0** 319.1 317.625 307.2
Lometa – 132.35 372.0 317.5
Lufkin – 134.8 **132.775** 126.95 125.175 121.5 **121.5** 363.05 **335.65** 285.575 269.6 243.0 **243.0**
Many – 121.5 **121.5**
Mc Comb – 126.8 121.5 **121.5** 327.8
Mobile – 132.6 127.65 **125.775** 121.5 **121.5** 322.4 316.075 285.475 **277.4** (FOR T38 USE) 243.0 **243.0**
Natchez – 120.975 299.6
Newton – 134.8 **128.175 353.85** 269.6
Palacios – 128.6 360.8
Rock Springs – **132.4** 125.75 346.4 **324.3** (FOR T38 USE) **322.7** (FOR T38 USE) **299.2 267.9** (FOR T38 USE)
Rockport – 133.4
San Antonio – 132.8 **125.625 354.0** 343.7 **318.8** 306.9 251.075
San Antonio A – **301.4** (FOR T38 USE) **254.375 239.275**
Sealy – 132.15 128.6 **126.425 371.85** 360.8 279.6
South Timbalier – **135.775** 134.9 290.45
Three Rivers – 134.6 322.5 243.0
Uvalde – 134.95 127.8 319.1 307.2 269.4
Venice – 135.775 **135.775**
Victoria – 135.05 **124.725** 353.6 **291.75**
Virgo – 134.9

AIR ROUTE TRAFFIC CONTROL CENTERS

Ⓡ **KANSAS CITY CENTER** – 121.5 **121.5** 243.0 **243.0 CPDLC (LOGON KUSA)**   H–5–6, L–10–15–16–27, A–2
   (KZKC)
Anthony – **133.2** 121.5 **121.5** 118.35 **292.125** 285.625
Butler – 125.55 327.0
Chanute – 132.9 121.5 **121.5** 279.5
Chillicothe – 125.25 235.975
Clinton – 121.5 **121.5**
Columbia – 134.5 121.5 **121.5** 119.475 316.1 **279.6** 243.0 **243.0**
Decatur – 124.3 269.15
Edna – 128.6 282.325
Effingham – **135.05** 124.3 **290.4** 269.15
Emporia – **132.25** 127.725 120.2 323.2 **281.425** 270.25
Farmington – **132.65** 127.475 **120.825** 346.275 **319.0** 307.8
Gage – **132.825** 126.95 121.5 **121.5** 379.2 243.0 **243.0**
Garden City – **133.45** 125.2 285.425 **281.4** 243.0 **243.0**
Hutchinson – **134.3** 118.8 **353.9** 322.425 **273.6**
Independence – 121.65
Jacksonville – 127.275 307.1
Kansas City – **133.8 360.85**
Kirksville – **134.625** 132.6 370.9 **269.3**
Knob Noster – 135.575 323.15
Lawrence – 121.825
Liberal – **134.675** 134.0 121.5 **121.5** 257.625 **235.775**
Manhattan – 127.35 121.5 **121.5** 257.975
Maples – 128.35 284.675
Marion – 127.475 346.275
Mount Vernon – 127.7 351.825
Oklahoma City – 127.8 319.1
Olathe – 121.5 **121.5** 243.0 **243.0**
Ponca City – 127.8 121.5 **121.5** 319.1 243.0 **243.0**
Quincy – 126.225 121.5 **121.5** 317.775
Richland – 128.35 124.1 353.925 284.675
Russell – 124.4 121.5 **121.5** 322.4
Saint Charles – 125.9 327.1
Saint Joseph – 127.9 251.1
Saint Louis – **133.15** 128.35 121.5 **121.5** 355.6 284.675 243.0 **243.0**
Salina – 134.9 **125.175** 121.5 **121.5** 363.2 **269.625**
Springfield – **133.475** 127.5 **277.4** 269.4
Springfield, Il – 126.15
Topeka – 123.8 343.7
Tulsa – 128.8 **127.625** 354.1 **285.525**
Vichy – 121.5 **121.5**
CENTER REMARKS: CPDLC (LOGON KUSA)

AIR ROUTE TRAFFIC CONTROL CENTERS

®MEMPHIS CENTER – 121.5 **121.5** 243.0 **243.0**   H–5–6–9–10–12, L–15–16–17–18–22–25–26
Bowling Green – 121.5 **121.5** 243.0 **243.0**   (KZME)
Brinkley – 135.3 126.85 335.8 **317.45** 281.55
Cape Girardeau – 121.5 **121.5**
Centerville – 125.85 **124.275** 379.25 **296.7 288.35**
Columbus – **134.775** 127.1 320.4 **294.7** 275.4 269.4
Dyersburg – 121.5 **121.5** 243.0 **243.0**
Fayetteville – **132.55** 126.1 121.5 **121.5 353.8** 269.0 243.0 **243.0**
Flippin – 121.5 **121.5**
Greenville – 135.875 **133.075 124.925 322.35 282.25** 269.35
Greenwood – 132.5 121.5 **121.5** 259.1 243.0 **243.0**
Harrison – 126.85 121.5 **121.5** 281.55 243.0 **243.0**
Hot Springs – 128.475 377.15
Huntsville – 120.8 307.0
Jackson – 132.5 121.5 **121.5 296.7 285.2** 259.1 243.0 **243.0**
Jackson Tn – 121.5 **121.5** 243.0 **243.0**
Jonesboro – 121.5 **121.5** 243.0 **243.0**
Little Rock – **132.425 323.25**
Louisville – 132.75 **362.6 282.1** 263.0 **243.0**
Mckellar – 134.65 132.3 **126.45** 124.35 **354.0** 343.625 318.1 316.15
Memphis – **118.625 269.9**
Meridian – **128.275** 125.975 121.5 **121.5** 351.7 **307.275** 289.9 **285.4** 243.0 **243.0**
Muscle Shoals – 121.5 **121.5** 243.0 **243.0**
Nashville – 133.85 **124.125 118.875** 285.5 **269.425 257.75**
Nashville/Joelton – 132.9 290.3
Paducah – 133.65 121.5 **121.5** 292.15 243.0 **243.0**
Pine Bluff – 135.875 121.5 **121.5** 269.35 243.0 **243.0**
Rich Mountain – 126.1 121.5 **121.5** 307.375 269.0
Russellville – 128.475 377.15 307.325 243.0 **243.0**
Shelbyville – 128.15 323.125
Troy – 133.65 **122.275 354.15** 292.15
Tupelo – 135.9 **135.9** 134.4 128.5 **127.375 295.0 285.55** 279.55 273.55 **273.55**
Walnut Ridge – **132.375** 120.075 289.4 **257.6**

FLIGHT SERVICE STATION COMMUNICATION FREQUENCIES

VHF frequencies available at Flight Service Stations and at their remote communication outlets (RCO's) are listed below for the coverage of this volume. 'T' indicates transmit only and 'R' indicates receive only. RCO's available at NAVAID's are listed after the NAVAID name. RCO's not at NAVAID's are listed by name.

ALBUQUERQUE RADIO
ALAMOGORDO RCO 122.4
ALBUQUERQUE RCO 122.3
ANIMAS RCO 122.5
ANTON CHICO VORTAC 117.8T 122.1R
CARLSBAD RCO 122.4
CIMARRON VORTAC 116.4T 122.1R
CLINES CORNERS RCO 122.3
CLOVIS RCO 122.5
CONCHAS LAKE RCO 122.6
CORONA VORTAC 115.5T 122.1R
DEMING RCO 122.2
EL PASO RCO 122.6
FARMINGTON RCO 122.4
GALLUP RCO 122.6
GALLUP VORTAC 115.1T 122.1R
GUADALUPE PASS RCO 122.5
HOBBS RCO 122.2
LAS VEGAS RCO 122.6
ROSWELL RCO 122.5
RUIDOSO RCO 122.25
SANTA FE RCO 122.2
SILVER CITY RCO 122.3
SILVER CITY VOR/DME 115.75T 122.1R
SOCORRO VORTAC 116.8T 122.1R
TAOS RCO 122.2
TAOS VORTAC 115.8T 122.1R
TRUTH OR CONSEQUENCES RCO 122.2
TUCUMCARI VORTAC 122.35
WEST MESA RCO 122.5
ZUNI RCO 122.2

DE RIDDER RADIO
ALEXANDRIA RCO 122.2
FIGHTING TIGER VORTAC 122.2
GRAND ISLE RCO 122.4
LAFAYETTE RCO 122.35
LAKE CHARLES RCO 122.3
LEEVILLE VORTAC 113.5T 122.1R
MANY RCO 122.3
MONROE RCO 122.4
NEW ORLEANS RCO 122.6
PATTERSON RCO 122.5
RUSTON RCO 122.3
SHREVEPORT RCO 122.6
TIBBY VOR/DME 112.0T 122.1R

FLIGHT SERVICE STATION COMMUNICATION FREQUENCIES

FORT WORTH RADIO
ABILENE RCO 122.6
AMARILLO RCO 122.3
BRECKENRIDGE RCO 122.5
BROWNWOOD RCO 122.5
CHILDRESS RCO 122.4
DALHART RCO 122.2
DALLAS RCO 122.3
FORT WORTH RCO 122.6
GREGG COUNTY VORTAC 122.2
JACKSBORO RCO 122.4
LUBBOCK RCO 122.2
MINERAL WELLS RCO 122.2
PARIS RCO 122.2
PLAINVIEW VOR/DME 122.55
SHERMAN/DENISON RCO 122.3
SNYDER RCO 122.45
TYLER RCO 122.3
WACO RCO 122.6
WICHITA FALLS RCO 122.65

GREENWOOD RADIO
BIGBEE RCO 122.4
GREENVILLE VOR/DME 114.25T 122.1R
GREENWOOD RCO 122.2
GULFPORT VORTAC 109.0T 122.1R
HOLLY SPRINGS VORTAC 122.3
JACKSON RCO 122.2
LAUREL RCO 122.3
MC COMB RCO 122.2
MC COMB VORTAC 116.7T 122.1R
MERIDIAN VORTAC 117.0T 122.1R
NATCHEZ RCO 122.6
SIDON VORTAC 114.7T 122.1R
TUPELO VOR/DME 122.5

JONESBORO RADIO
BATESVILLE RCO 122.3
EL DORADO RCO 122.2
FAYETTEVILLE RCO 122.3
FAYETTEVILLE/SPRINGDALE/RO RCO 122.55
FLIPPIN RCO 122.35
FORT SMITH VORTAC 122.2
HARRISON RCO 122.45
HOT SPRINGS VOR/DME 110.0T 122.1R
JONESBORO RCO 122.2
LITTLE ROCK RCO 122.4
PINE BLUFF RCO 122.6
SOCIAL HILL RCO 122.2
TEXARKANA RCO 122.2
WALNUT RIDGE RCO 122.5
WALNUT RIDGE VORTAC 114.5T 122.1R

FLIGHT SERVICE STATION COMMUNICATION FREQUENCIES

MC ALESTER RADIO
ARDMORE RCO 122.6
BARTLESVILLE RCO 122.4
CLINTON – SHERMAN RCO 122.5
GAGE RCO 122.3
HOBART RCO 122.2
MC ALESTER RCO 122.3
MUSKOGEE RCO 122.5
NORMAN RCO 122.4
PONCA CITY RCO 122.2
RICH MOUNTAIN RCO 122.6
STILLWATER RCO 122.3
TULSA RCO 122.2
WILEY POST RCO 122.4
WOODRING RCO 122.6

MONTGOMERY COUNTY RADIO
BEAUMONT RCO 122.2
CENTER RCO 122.6
COLLEGE STATION RCO 122.2
GALVESTON RCO 122.2
HOBBY RCO 122.2
HOUSTON RCO 122.4
HUNTSVILLE RCO 122.3
INDUSTRY VORTAC 122.4
JASPER RCO 122.5
LUFKIN RCO 122.2
MONTGOMERY COUNTY RCO 122.2
NEWTON RCO 122.2
PALACIOS RCO 122.2
VICTORIA RCO 122.2

SAN ANGELO RADIO
ALICE RCO 122.6
AUSTIN RCO 122.2
BIG SPRING RCO 122.4
BROWNSVILLE RCO 122.3
CENTER POINT VORTAC 117.5T 122.1R
CORPUS CHRISTI RCO 122.2
COTULLA RCO 122.2
DEL RIO RCO 122.3
EAGLE PASS RCO 122.3
FORT STOCKTON RCO 122.2
HARLINGEN RCO 122.2
JUNCTION RCO 122.3
LAMPASAS RCO 122.4
LAREDO RCO 122.3
MARFA VOR/DME 122.5
MC ALLEN RCO 122.2
MIDLAND RCO 122.6
PECOS VOR/DME 116.5T 122.1R
ROCKPORT RCO 122.3
ROCKSPRINGS RCO 122.4
ROCKSPRINGS VORTAC 114.55T 122.1R
SAN ANGELO RCO 122.2
SAN ANTONIO RCO 122.3
STONEWALL VORTAC 113.8T 122.1R
TEMPLE RCO 122.6
THREE RIVERS VORTAC 111.4T 122.1R
UVALDE RCO 122.5
WINK RCO 122.3

VOR RECEIVER CHECKPOINTS and VOR TEST FACILITIES

The use of VOR airborne and ground checkpoints is explained in Aeronautical Information Manual, Basic Flight Information and ATC Procedures.

NOTE: Under columns headed "Type of Checkpoint" & "Type of VOT Facility" G stands for ground. A/ stands for airborne followed by figures (2300) or (1000–3000) indicating the altitudes above mean sea level at which the check should be conducted. Facilities are listed in alphabetical order, in the state where the checkpoints or VOTs are located.

ARKANSAS
VOR RECEIVER CHECKPOINTS

Facility Name (Arpt Name)	Freq/Ident	Type Check Pt. Gnd. AB/ALT	Azimuth from Fac. Mag	Dist. from Fac. N.M.	Checkpoint Description
Harrison (Boone County)	112.5/HRO	G	135	4.4	Intersection of Twy A and B.
Jonesboro (Jonesboro Muni)	115.85/JBR	G	229	3.9	On NE ramp in front of airline terminal.
Pine Bluff (Pine Bluff Rgnl Arpt Grider Fld)	116.0/PBF	G	184	3.9	North end of N/S twy AER 18.

LOUISIANA
VOR RECEIVER CHECKPOINTS

Facility Name (Arpt Name)	Freq/Ident	Type Check Pt. Gnd. AB/ALT	Azimuth from Fac. Mag	Dist. from Fac. N.M.	Checkpoint Description
Lafayette (Lafayette Rgnl/Paul Fournet Fld)	109.8/LFT	G	355	0.5	On Twy F run up area Rwy 04L.
	109.8/LFT	G	341	0.9	On Twy B run up area Rwy 11.
	109.8/LFT	G	039	0.8	On Twy B run up area Rwy 29.
	109.8/LFT	G	025	1.4	Twy J run up area 22L.

VOR TEST FACILITIES (VOT)

Facility Name (Airport Name)	Freq.	Type VOT Facility	Remarks
Shreveport Rgnl	108.6	G	

MISSISSIPPI
VOR RECEIVER CHECKPOINTS

Facility Name (Arpt Name)	Freq/Ident	Type Check Pt. Gnd. AB/ALT	Azimuth from Fac. Mag	Dist. from Fac. N.M.	Checkpoint Description
Caledonia (Columbus AFB)	115.2/CBM	G	302	1.3	North Hammerhead (VTAC).
	115.2/CBM	G	152	0.7	South Hammerhead, F Twy.
Greenville Mid–Delta	114.25/GLH	G	185	2.3	At intersection of Twy B and D.
Gulfport (Gulfport-Biloxi Intl)	109.0/GPT	G	089	0.8	DME, east ramp Twy A near.
Meridian (Key Field)	117.0/MEI	G	127	4.0	On ramp in front of terminal building.

VOR TEST FACILITIES (VOT)

Facility Name (Airport Name)	Freq.	Type VOT Facility	Remarks
Jackson–Evers Intl	111.0	G	

SC, 25 JAN 2024 to 21 MAR 2024

VOR RECEIVER CHECKPOINTS and VOR TEST FACILITIES

OKLAHOMA

VOR RECEIVER CHECKPOINTS

Facility Name (Arpt Name)	Freq/Ident	Type Check Pt. Gnd. AB/ALT	Azimuth from Fac. Mag	Dist. from Fac. N.M.	Checkpoint Description
Bartlesville (Bartlesville Muni)	117.9/BVO	G	166	4.5	On parallel twy opposite terminal. OTS indef.
Lawton (Lawton–Fort Sill Rgnl)	109.4/LAW	G	349	4.6	On taxiway between terminal and Rwy 17–35.
Ponca City (Ponca City Rgnl)	113.2/PER	G	089	2.9	At apch end Rwy 17 on Twy A.
	113.2/PER	G	107	3.2	South of ramp on Twy A.
Stillwater (Stillwater Rgnl)	108.4/SWO	G	176	4	On Twy A btn A3 and A4..
Wiley Post (Wiley Post)	113.4/PWA	G	150	0.5	On runup pad to Rwy 35R.
	113.4/PWA	G	007	0.7	On runup area to Rqy 17L.
Woodring (Enid Woodring Rgnl)	109.0/ODG	G	352	0.5	On ramp W of terminal.

VOR TEST FACILITIES (VOT)

Facility Name(Airport Name)	Freq.	Type VOT Facility	Remarks
Oklahoma City Rogers (Will Rogers World)	112.15	A/G	Within 10 NM radius between 3000´ and 5000´. VOT unusable east of Rwy 17L–35R.
Tulsa International	109.0	G	

VOR RECEIVER CHECKPOINTS and VOR TEST FACILITIES

TEXAS

VOR RECEIVER CHECKPOINTS

Facility Name (Arpt Name)	Freq/Ident	Type Check Pt. Gnd. AB/ALT	Azimuth from Fac. Mag	Dist. from Fac. N.M.	Checkpoint Description
Alice (Alice International)	114.5/ALI	G	272	0.5	On twy near FBO.
Borger (Hutchinson Co)	108.6/BGD	G	173	6.7	On twy intxn at N end of ramp.
Brownsville (Brownsville/South Padre Island Intl)	116.3/BRO	G	247	3.2	On hold line Rwy 13R.
Childress Muni	117.6/CDS	G	353	3.7	At the apron and the twy from Rwy 04-22.
Gregg Co (East Texas Rgnl)	112.3/GGG	G	128	2.4	At N end of ramp on twy to Rwy 13.
Humble (George Bush Intercontinental/Houston)	116.6/IAH	G	339	2.2	On runup pad Rwy 08.
Laredo (Laredo International)	117.4/LRD	G	318	4.8	On runup area of Twy A.
Laughlin (Laughlin AFB)	114.4/DLF	G	198	0.5	On ramp AER 31L.
	114.4/DLF	G	275	0.9	On ramp AER 13R.
McAllen (McAllen Miller Intl)	117.2/MFE	G	331	0.6	On cargo ramp.
Randolph (Randolph AFB)	112.3/RND	G	337	1.0	On AER 15R.
San Angelo (San Angelo Rgnl/Mathis Field)	115.1/SJT	G	237	2.6	On E edge of ramp in front of ATCT.
Scholes (Scholes Intl at Galveston)	113.0/VUH	G	088	0.5	On main terminal ramp.
Tyler (Tyler Pounds Rgnl)	114.2/TYR	G	082	0.5	At intersection Twys D and H.
Victoria (Victoria Rgnl)	109.0/VCT	G	128	3.2	At approach end of Rwy 13.
Wichita Falls (Sheppard AFB/Wichita Falls Muni)	112.7/SPS	G	093	5.5	On Twy C runup area Rwy 33L.
	112.7/SPS	G	075	5.3	On Twy G AER 33R.
	112.7/SPS	G	064	5.2	On Twy K AER 15L.
	112.7/SPS	G	068	4.7	On Twy H runup area Rwy 15R.

VOR TEST FACILITIES (VOT)

Facility Name (Airport Name)	Freq.	Type VOT Facility	Remarks
Dallas Love Field	113.3	G	
El Paso International	111.0	G	Used for ground only. Unusable on the west side of hangars south of the intersection of Twy A and the centerline of Rwy 04-22.
Fort Worth Meacham Intl	108.2	A/G	Used for ground and airborne test. For airborne use within 10 NM radius of Fort Worth Meacham Intl clockwise from 220°-270° between 2000´ and 5000´.
Houston (William P. Hobby)	108.4	G	
Midland Intl Air & Space Port	108.2	G	
San Antonio International	110.4	G	

SC, 25 JAN 2024 to 21 MAR 2024

PARACHUTE JUMPING AREAS

The following tabulation lists all reported parachute jumping areas in the area of coverage of this directory. Unless otherwise indicated, all activities are conducted during daylight hours and under VFR conditions. NOTAM D's may be issued to advise users of specific dates and times if outside the times /altitudes that are published. The busiest periods of activity are normally on weekends and holidays, but jumps can be expected at anytime during the week at the locations listed. Parachute jumping areas within restricted airspace are not listed.

All times are local and altitudes MSL unless otherwise specified.
Contact facility and frequency is listed at the end of the remarks, when available, in bold face type.
Refer to Federal Aviation Regulations Part 105 for required procedures relating to parachute jumping.
Organizations desiring listing of their jumping activities in this publication should contact Flight Service, tower, or ARTCC.
Qualified parachute jumping areas will be depicted on the appropriate visual chart(s).

Note: (c) in this publication indicates that the parachute jumping area is charted.

To qualify for charting, a jump area must meet the following criteria:
  (1) Been in operation for at least 1 year.
  (2) Log 1,000 or more jumps each year.

In addition, parachute jumping areas can be nominated by FAA Regions if special circumstances require charting.

LOCATION	DISTANCE AND RADIAL FROM NEAREST VOR/VORTAC OR GEOGRAPHIC COORDINATES	MAXIMUM ALTITUDE	REMARKS
ARKANSAS			
Black Jack Drop Zone	33 NM; 010° Little Rock	3,000 AGL	Mon-Fri 0600-2330 and occasional weekends.
Camp Chaffee, Arrowhead Drop Zone	6 NM; 160° Ft. Smith	3,000	Mon-Fri 0600-2300 and occasional weekends.
Camp Robinson—All American Drop Zone	15 NM; 332° Little Rock	3,000	Mon-Fri 0600-0200 and occasional weekends.
(c) Little Rock, Blackjack Drop Zone	33 NM; 009° Little Rock	3,000	Mon-Fri 0600-0200 and occasional weekends.
(c) Little Rock, Conway Drop Zone	24 NM; 334° Little Rock	12,500 AGL	0800-SS weekends and occasional weekdays.
(c) Siloam Springs, Smith Fld Arpt	18 NM; 256° Razorback	15,000	5 NM radius. Fri–Mon 0700–0000.
Texarkana	9 NM; 160° Texarkana	13,000 AGL	0800-SS weekends and occasional weekdays.
LOUISIANA			
(c) Baton Rouge	13NM; 060° Fighting Tiger	13,000	Daily SR–SS.
Bodcaw	16 NM; 083° Belcher	13,000	Daily SR–SS.
(c) Breaux Bridge, Bordelon Airpark	9 NM; 042° Lafayette	12,000	Daily SR–SS.
(c) Covington, St Tammy Rgnl Arpt	15.1 NM; 238° Picayune	10,500	3 NM radius. Sat-Sun SR–SS. **Louis Armstrong New Orleans Intl Tower 133.15.**
(c) Mansfield, CE 'Rusty' Williams Arpt	22 NM; 196° Elm Grove	13,000	3 NM radius. Daily SR–SS.
(c) Opelousas, St Landry Parish—Ahart Fld Arpt	25 NM; 340° Lafayette	11,500	3 NM radius. Weekends 0700–1800.
(c) Slidell, Slidell Arpt	13.8 NM; 195° Picayune	14,500 AGL	3 NM radius. Daily SR–SS. **Louis Armstrong New Orleans Intl Tower 133.15.**
MISSISSIPPI			
Artesia, Carson Drop Zone	11 NM; 188° Bigbee	2,000 AGL	Occasional use.
(c) Batesville, Panola Co Arpt	26 NM; 220° Holly Springs	10,500 AGL	5 NM radius. Sat–Sun 0900–SS.
Coldwater Drop Zone	20 NM; 170° Memphis	3,000	0600-2330 Mon–Fri and occasional weekends. Military use.
Greenwood, Camp McCain Drop Zone	31.9 NM; 067° Sidon	17,999	5 NM radius. Weekdays and weekends, occasional nights, seldom holidays.
Grenada, Grenada Muni Arpt	32.6 NM; 048° Sidon	17,999	5 NM radius. Weekends, occasional nights, seldom holidays. Military use.
Hattiesburg, Safee Drop Zone	25 NM; 135° Eaton	3,000 AGL	Occasional use.
Rolling Fork, Wade Arpt	32 NM; 180° Greenville	12,500	10 NM radius. Daily.
Strong	6.5 NM; 289° Caledonia	12,500	Weekends and holidays SR–SS.
West Point, King Drop Zone	7 NM; 305° Bigbee	2,000 AGL	Occasional use.

PARACHUTE JUMPING AREAS

LOCATION	DISTANCE AND RADIAL FROM NEAREST VOR/VORTAC OR GEOGRAPHIC COORDINATES	MAXIMUM ALTITUDE	REMARKS
OKLAHOMA			
(c) Chickasha, Redhills Arpt	23 NM; 212° Will Rogers	12,000	1 NM radius. Daily SR–SS.
(c) Cushing, Cushing Muni Arpt	50 NM; 245° Tulsa	14,000	5 NM radius. Daily SR until 1 hour after SS.
(c) Eldorado, Altus AFB, Sooner Drop Zone	22 NM; 247° Altus	12,500 AGL	1 NM radius. Mon–Fri 0700–0200 and occasional weekends.
Fort Sill, Frisco Ridge Drop Zone	15 NM; 360° Lawton	13,900 AGL	2 NM radius. Sat 0900–1500.
Fort Sill, Henry Post AAF	14.5 NM; 023° Lawton	1,100 AGL	Weekends SR–SS. Military use.
(c) Grandfield, Grandfield Muni Arpt	21 NM; 324° Wichita Falls	13,500	5 NM radius. SR–SS weekends and holidays; occasional weekdays.
(c) Haskell, Haskell Arpt	12.8 NM; 041° Okmulgee	12,000	4 NM radius. Weekends, holidays SR–SS. Occasional weekday and night jumps. Tulsa Intl Tower 124.0.
(c) Hugo	28.6 NM; 350° Paris	13,000	3 NM radius. Daily SR–SS.
Ketchum, South Grand Lake Rgnl Arpt		12,000	1 NM radius. Daily 0530–2000.
Miami, Miami Rgnl Arpt	54.6 NM; 077° Bartlesville	13,000	3 NM radius. Daily SR–SS.
Okmulgee, Okmulgee Rgnl Arpt	4.3 NM; 241° Okmulgee	15,000	3 NM radius. Sat-Sun and holidays SR–SS.
(c) Skiatook, Skiatook Muni Arpt	15 NM; 310° Tulsa	13,000	5 NM radius. Daily SR–SS, occasional ngts.
Tahlequah, Tahlequah Muni Arpt	41 NM; 105° Tulsa	13,500	5 NM radius. Daily SR–SS.
TEXAS			
Abilene, Dyess AFB	4 NM; 170° Abilene	3,300	5 NM radius. Daily SR–SS.
Amarillo, Buffalo Fld	13.5 NM; 213° Panhandle	15,000	Daily SR–SS.
(c) Bronte	27 NM; 023° San Angelo	6,500	1 NM radius. Mon–Fri 0900–2359. **40th Airlift Squadron 139.75 (COM), 314.2 (MIL). 40th Airlift Squadron, 325-696-3660.**
(c) Brownwood, Heartbreak Drop Zone	15 NM; 169° Brownwood	6,500	1 NM radius. Fridays 0900–1300. **Camp Bowie Training Facility 139.75 (COM), 314.2 (MIL) 40th Airlift Squadron, 325–696–3660.** Military Use.
(c) Caddo Mills, Caddo Mills Muni Arpt, Dallas Skydive Ctr	30 NM; 174° Bonham	17,500	1.5 NM radius. Daily 0700–SS. **Caddo Mills 122.8/Fort Worth Center 132.02.**
Camp Bullis, Hall Drop Zone	6.5 NM; 305° San Antonio	2,500 AGL	2 NM radius. Continuous.
(c) Camp Swift, Blackwell Drop Zone	15 NM; 119° Centex	1,500 AGL	Daily, occasional ngts.
Dumas, Moore Co Arpt	29 NM; 106° Dalhart	13,700	3 NM radius. SR–2359 weekends and holidays, 1700–2359 weekdays.
Ennis Muni Arpt	24 NM; 285° Cedar Creek	12,000	3 NM radius. Sat–Sun, Holidays.
(c) Fentress Airpark (Pvt)		15,000	5 NM radius. Daily SR–SS and occasional nights. **Austin–Bergstrom Intl Tower. 123.55.**
(c) Galveston	4.7 NM; 214° Scholes	14,500	1 NM radius. SR–SS. **Houston ARTCC 120.57.**
(c) Galveston	2.0 NM; 190° Scholes	14,500	1 NM radius. SR–SS. **Houston ARTCC 120.57.**
(c) Galveston	1.8 NM; 098° Scholes	14,500	1 NM radius. SR–SS. **Houston ARTCC 120.57.**
(c) Galveston	7.93 NM; 121° Trinity	10,500	1 NM radius. SR–SS. **Houston ARTCC 134.45.**

PARACHUTE JUMPING AREAS

LOCATION	DISTANCE AND RADIAL FROM NEAREST VOR/VORTAC OR GEOGRAPHIC COORDINATES	MAXIMUM ALTITUDE	REMARKS
(c) Gladewater Muni Arpt	14 NM; 295° Gregg Co	14,000	3 NM radius. 0700–2200 daily.
(c) Greenville, Majors Arpt	28.9 NM; 155° Bonham	17,999	1.5 NM radius centered at 33°04´50"N/096°02´53"W excluding the area west of County Rd 3303 on the south side and including 200 yards west of County Rd 3303 on the north half. SR–SS. **Fort Worth Center 132.02.**
(c) Hearne Muni, Brown Drop Zone	19 NM; 319° College Station	17999	5 NM radius. Mon-Fri 0600-2400 lcl. Some weekends if weather affects the weekday PJA and some nights after 2400 lcl. **Houston Tracon 134.3.**
(c) Hillsboro Muni	26.7 NM; 010° Waco	17,500	5 NM radius. 0700–2200, weekends and some holidays. **Waco Rgnl Twr 127.65.**
(c) Killeen, Ft. Hood, Antelope Drop Zone	14.5 NM; 087° Gooch Springs	13,000 AGL	Continuous.
(c) Killeen, Ft. Hood, Rapido Drop Zone	25 NM; 053° Gooch Springs	13,000 AGL	0.5 NM radius. Continuous.
(c) Kingsville, Kleberg Co Arpt	11.5 NM; 175° Alice	12,500	Weekdays, 1200–SS; Sat, Sun, holidays 0700–SS.
(c) Lexington Airfield (Pvt) Arpt	30 NM; 238° College Station	15,500	2 NM radius. Daily SR–Midnight.
(c) Madisonville Muni Arpt	12.7 NM; 168° Leona	17,999	5 NM radius. Daily SR–SS and occasional ngts. **Houston Center 134.8**
(c) Midlake Arpt	7 NM; 084° Stinson	15,000	1 NM radius. Daily SR–SS and occasional ngts.
(c) Mineral Wells, Fort Wolters Drop Zone	8.8 NM; 336° Millsap	3,000	.5 NM radius. Time of use: Any.
New Albany-Union County Airport		5000	1 NM radius.
(c) Nome, Farm Air Service (Pvt) Arpt	21 NM; 278° Beaumont	13,500	3 NM radius. Sat, Sun and holidays SR–SS. **Houston Center 124.7.**
(c) Port Aransas–Mustang Beach Arpt	23 NM; 100° Corpus Christi	13,500	2 NM radius. Daily SR–SS. Intersection of access road 1–A and dune road, 1 mile south of Mustang Beach Arpt. **Corpus Christi Intl ATCT–TRACON 125.4.**
(c) Rockdale, Cameron/Milano Drop Zone	27.5 NM; 278° College Station	17999	5 NM radius. Mon-Fri 0600-2400 lcl. Some weekends if weather affects the weekday PJA and some nights after 2400 lcl. **Houston Tracon 134.3.**
(c) Rosebud, Buster Drop Zone	35.7 NM; 313° College Station	17999	5 NM radius. Mon-Fri 0600-2400 lcl. Some weekends if weather affects the weekday PJA and some nights after 2400 lcl. **Houston Tracon 134.3.**
(c) Rosebud, Grace Drop Zone	38.4 NM; 311° College Station	17999	5 NM radius. Mon-Fri 0600-2400 lcl. Some weekends if weather affects the weekday PJA and some nights after 2400 lcl. **Houston Tracon 134.3.**
(c) Rosharon, B&B Airpark (Pvt) Arpt	31.5 NM; 274° Scholes	16,500	2 NM radius. All days; SR–SS. **Houston Tracon 134.34**
Seagoville Arpt	30.3 NM; 115° Maverick	13,000	SR–SS weekends and holidays and occasional days.
(c) Seminole, Gaines Co Arpt	31.2 NM; 075° Hobbs	14,000	10NM radius, Daily SR–SS. **Fort Worth Center 132.6.**
Stephenville Clark Rgnl	31.2 NM; 188° Millsap	13,000	5 NM radius. SR–SS weekends and holidays. **Ft. Worth Center 127.15.**

PARACHUTE JUMPING AREAS

LOCATION	DISTANCE AND RADIAL FROM NEAREST VOR/VORTAC OR GEOGRAPHIC COORDINATES	MAXIMUM ALTITUDE	REMARKS
Terrell Muni Arpt	32 NM; 349° Cedar Creek	13,500	2 NM radius. SR–SS weekends and holidays, occasional weekdays.
(c) Trenton, Tri–Co Aerodrome	8.6 NM; 230° Bonham	14,500	2 NM radius. Daily 0800–2200. Hi–density jump area, pilots are advised to monitor **Fort Worth ARTCC 124.875**.
(c) Waller, Skydive Houston (Pvt) Arpt	18.9 NM, 151° Navasota	24,000 AGL	3 NM radius. Continuous.

ered within this tabulation, and listed alphabetically by airport name, are all private-use airports charted on the U.S. IFR
486

SUPPLEMENTAL COMMUNICATION REFERENCE

Contained within this tabulation, and listed alphabetically by airport name, are all private-use airports charted on the U.S. IFR Enroute Low and High Altitude charts in the United States, having terminal approach and departure control facilities. Additionally, listed by country, are all Canadian and Mexican airports that appear on the U.S. IFR Enroute charts with approach and departure control services. All frequencies transmit and receive unless otherwise noted. Radials defining sectors are outbound from the facility.

UNITED STATES

FACILITY NAME	CHART & PANEL
Cabaniss Fld NOLF, TX (NGW)	L–20H, 21A
Corpus App/Dep Con 125.4 307.9	
Navy Cabaniss Tower 119.65 299.6 (Mon–Thu 1400–0500Z‡, Fri 1400–0100Z‡)	
Fentress NALF, VA (NFE)	H–10I, 12I, L–35D
Oceana App/Dep Con 123.9 266.8	
Fry, OH (Ø0H8)	L–27E
Columbus App/Dep Con 118.425	
Gila Bend AF AUX, AZ (GXF)	H–4J, L–5B
Luke App/Dep Con 125.45 263.125 (South) (Mon–Thu 1300–0530Z, Fri 1300–0130Z, clsd weekends and hol)	
Glasgow Industrial, MT (Ø7MT)	H–1E, 2G, L–13D
Salt Lake Center App/Dep Con 126.85 305.2	
Joe Williams NOLF, MS (NJW)	H–6J, L–18G
Meridian App/Dep Con 276.4	
Bravo Tower 118.475 279.2 355.8 (Mon–Fri 1400–2330Z‡)	
Oak Grove MCOLF, NC (13NC)	L–35B
Cherry Point App/Dep Con 119.35 377.175	
Shell AHP, AL (SXS)	L–22I
Cairns App/Dep Con 133.45 239.275 (24 hrs Tue–Sat, 1200–0500Z‡ Sun–Mon) other times ctc	
Jax Center App/Dep Con 134.3 322.55	
Shell Tower 139.125 244.5 (1230–0600Z‡ Mon–Fri, exc hol)	
USAF Academy Bullseye Aux Airfield, CO (CO9Ø)	L–10F
ASOS 125.0	
Webster NOLF, MD (NUI)	H–10I, 12I,
Patuxent App/Dep Con 121.0 250.3	L–34E, 36I
Navy Webster Tower 127.0 358.0 (Mon–Fri, exc hol, other times on request, 1400–2200Z‡ or SS, whichever occurs first)	
For Clnc Del when NHK Apch is clsd ctc Potomac Apch at 866–640–4124	
Whitehouse NOLF, FL (NEN)	H–8H, L–21D, 24G
Jax Center App Con 127.775 377.075	
Jax Center Dep Con 127.775 379.9	
Whitehouse Tower 125.15 307.325 340.2 (Manned during scheduled operations only)	
William P Gwinn, FL (Ø6FA)	H–8I, L–23C
Palm Beach App/Dep Con 317.4	
Gwinn Tower 120.4 279.25 (Mon–Fri 1300–2100Z‡)	
Gnd Con 121.65 279.25	

CANADA

FACILITY NAME	CHART & PANEL
Abbotsford, BC (CYXX)	H–1B, L–12F
ATIS 119.8 (1500–0700Z‡)	
Victoria Trml App/Dep Con 132.7 (Avbl on ground)	
Tower 119.4 (Inner) 121.0 (Outer) 295.0 (1500–0700Z‡) Gnd Con 121.8	
MF 119.4 295.0 (0700–1500Z‡) (Shape irregular to 4500′)	
Amos/Magny, QC (CYEY)	H–11B
Montreal Center App/Dep Con 125.9	
Atikokan Muni, ON (CYIB)	L–14I
MF 122.3 (5 NM to 4500′ No ground station)	
Barrie–Orillia (Lake Simcoe Rgnl), ON (CYLS)	H–11B, L–31D
Toronto Center App/Dep Con 124.025	
Bar River, ON (CPF2)	L–31C
Toronto Center App/Dep Con 132.65	
Bathurst, NB (CZBF)	L–32J
Moncton Center App/Dep Con 134.25 AWOS 127.925	
Boundary Bay, BC (CZBB)	H–1B, L–1E
ATIS 125.5 (1500–0700Z‡)	
Vancouver App/Dep Con 132.3 363.8	
Tower 118.1 (Inner) 127.6 (Outer) (1500–0700Z‡) Gnd Con 124.3	
MF 118.1 (0700–1500Z‡ to 2000′. Vancouver Trml 125.2 above 2000′. Shape irregular to 2500′.)	
Brampton, ON (CNC3)	L–31D
Toronto Trml App/Dep Con 119.3	
Brandon Muni, MB (CYBR)	H–2H
Winnipeg Center App/Dep Con 132.25	
MF 122.1 (5 NM to 4000′)	

SC, 25 JAN 2024 to 21 MAR 2024

SUPPLEMENTAL COMMUNICATION REFERENCE

CANADA

FACILITY NAME	CHART & PANEL
Brantford, ON (CYFD)	L–31D
Toronto Trml App/Dep Con 128.27	
Brockville Rgnl Tackaberry ON (CNL3)	L–32G
Montreal Center App/Dep Con 134.675	
Bromont, QC (CZBM)	L–32G
Montreal Center App/Dep Con 132.35 MF 122.15 (5 NM to 3400′)	
AUTO 122.975	
Burlington Executive, ON (CZBA)	L–31D
Toronto Center App/Dep Con 119.3 AUTO 122.55	
Castlegar/West Kootenay Rgnl, BC (CYCG)	H–1C
Vancouver Center App/Dep Con 134.2 227.3	
MF 122.1 (5 NM to 6500′)	
Centralia/James T. Fld Muni, ON (CYCE)	H–10G, 11B, L–31D
Toronto Center App/Dep Con 135.30	
Charlottetown, PE (CYYG)	H–11E, L–32J
Moncton Center App/Dep Con 135.65 384.8 MF 118.0 (5 NM to 3200′)	
Chatham–Kent, ON (CYCK)	H–10G, L–30G
Cleveland Center App/Dep Con 132.25	
Collingwood, ON (CNY3)	H–11B, L–31D
Toronto Center App/Dep Con 124.02	
Cornwall Rgnl, ON (CYCC)	L–32G
Boston Center App/Dep Con 135.25 377.1	
Cranbrook/Canadian Rockies Intl, BC (CYXC)	H–1C
Vancouver Center App/Dep Con 133.6 MF 122.3 (5 NM to 6100′)	
Debert, NS (CCQ3)	H–11E, L–32J
Halifax Trml App/Dep Con 119.2 AUTO 122.275	
Digby, NS (CYID)	L–32J
Moncton Center App/Dep Con 123.9	
Downsview, ON (CYZD)	H–11B, L–31E
Toronto Center App/Dep Con 133.4	
MF 126.2 (1300–2300Z‡, 3 NM to 1700′)	
Drummondville, QC (CSC3)	L–32H
Montreal Center App/Dep Con 132.35	
Earlton (Timiskaming Rgnl), ON (CYXR)	H–11B
MF 122.0 (5 NM to 3800′)	
Elliot Lake Muni, ON (CYEL)	L–31C
Toronto Center App/Dep Con 135.4	
Fort Frances Muni, ON (CYAG)	L–14H
Minneapolis Center App/Dep Con 120.9	
Fredericton Intl, NB (CYFC)	H–11E, L–32I
ATIS 127.55 (1045–0345Z‡, OT AWOS)	
Moncton Center App/Dep Con 124.3 135.5 270.8	
Tower 119.0 (1045–0345Z‡) Gnd Con 121.7 (1045–0345Z‡)	
MF 119.0 (0345–1045Z‡, 5 NM to 3500′)	
Goderich, ON (CYGD)	H–11B, L–31D
Toronto Center App/Dep 135.3 266.3	
Greenwood, NS (CYZX)	H–11E, L–32J
ATIS 128.85 244.3 (1100–0000Z‡)	
App/Dep Con 120.6 335.9 Tower 119.5 236.6 324.3	
Gnd Con 133.75 289.4 Clnc Del 128.025 283.9	
Grimsby Air Park, ON (CNZ8)	L–31E
Toronto Trml App/Dep Con 128.27 268.75 Tower 125.0 308.475	
Halifax/Shearwater, NS (CYAW)	H–11E, L–32J
ATIS 129.175 308.8 (Ltd hrs)	
App/Dep Con 119.2 MF Shearwater Advisory 119.0 126.2 340.2 360.2 (Ltd hrs)	
Gnd Con 121.7 250.1	
Halifax/Stanfield Intl, NS (CYHZ)	H–11E, L–32J
ATIS 121.0	
Moncton Center App/Dep Con 135.3	
Tower 118.4 236.6 Gnd Con 121.9 275.8 Clnc Del 123.95	
Hamilton, ON (CYHM)	H–10H, 11B, L–11B
ATIS 128.1	
Toronto Trml App/Dep Con 119.7 Tower 125.0	
Gnd Con 121.6	
Kingston, ON (CYGK)	H–11C, L–31E, 32F
ATIS 135.55 (1115–0400Z‡)	
Montreal Center App/Dep Con 135.05 (0400–1115Z‡)	
MF 122.5 (1115–0400Z‡ 5 NM to 3300′)	

SUPPLEMENTAL COMMUNICATION REFERENCE
CANADA

FACILITY NAME	CHART & PANEL

Kitchener/Waterloo, ON (CYKF)
  ATIS 125.1 (1200–0400Z‡)
  Toronto Trml App/Dep Con 128.275
  Waterloo Tower 126.0 118.55 (1200–0400Z‡)   Gnd Con 121.8
  MF 126.0 (0400–1200Z‡ 5 NM to 4000′)   AWOS 125.1 (0400–1200Z‡)
	H–11B, L–31D

Lachute, QC (CSE4)
  Montreal Center App Con 124.65 268.3
  Montreal Center Dep Con 132.85 268.3
	L–32G

La Tuque, QC (CYLQ) Montreal Center App/Dep Con 134.5 AUTO 122.975	H–11C

Langley, BC (CYNJ)
  ATIS 124.5 (1630–0230Z, DT 1530–0330Z)
  Victoria Trml App/Dep Con 132.7 290.8   Tower 119.0 (1630–0230Z,
  DT 1530–0330Z)
  Gnd Con 121.9   MF 119.0 (0230–1630Z, DT 0330–1530Z 3 NM to 1900′)
	L–1E

Leamington, ON (CLM2) Detroit Approach App/Dep Con 134.3	L–30F

Lethbridge, AB (CYQL)
  ATIS 124.4 (1245–0545Z‡)
  Edmonton Center App/Dep Con 132.75 265.2   MF 121.0 (5 NM to 6000′)
	H–1D

Lindsay, ON (CNF4) Toronto Center App/Dep 134.25	L–31E, L–32F
Liverpool/South Shore Rgnl, NS (CYAU) Moncton Center App/Dep Con 123.9	L–32J

London, ON (CYXU)
  ATIS 127.8 (1120–0345Z‡)
  Toronto Center App/Dep 135.3 135.625
  Tower 119.4 125.65 (1120–0345Z‡)   Gnd Con 121.9
  MF 119.4 (0345–1120Z‡ 5 NM to 3000′)
	H–10G, 11B, L–30G, 31D

Manitowaning/Manitoulin East Muni, ON (CYEM) Toronto Center App/Dep Con 135.4 260.9	L–31C
Maniwaki, QC (CYMW) Montreal Center App/Dep Con 126.57	L–32G

Mascouche, QC (CSK3)
  MF 122.35 (5 NM to 2500′. No gnd station. Excluding the portion S of the
  N shore of Riviere des Milles–Iles and 1 NM around Lac Agile Mascouche arpt.)
	L–32G

Medicine Hat, AB (CYXH)
  ATIS 124.875 (1245–0345Z)
  MF 122.2 (1245–0345Z 5 NM to 5400′)
	H–1D

Midland/Huronia, ON (CYEE) Toronto Center App/Dep Con 124.025	L–31D
Miramichi, NB (CYCH) Moncton Center App/Dep Con 123.7	H–11E, L–32J

Moncton/Greater Moncton Intl, NB (CYQM)
  ATIS 128.65
  App/Dep 124.4   Tower 120.8 236.6   Gnd Con 121.8 275.8
  Apron Advisory 122.075
	H–11E, L–32J

Mont–Laurier, QC (CSD4) Montreal Center App/Dep Con 126.57	L–32G

Montreal Intl (Mirabel), QC (CYMX)
  ATIS 125.7
  Montreal Center App/ Dep Con 124.65 268.3
  MF 119.1 (7 NM shape irregular to 2000′) (03–11Z (DT 02–10Z))
  (emerg only 450–476–3141)   VFR Advisory 134.15
  GND 121.8 (11–03Z (DT 10–02Z))   TWR 119.1 (11–03Z (DT 10–02Z))
  (emerg only 450–476–3141)
  GND Advisory 121.8 (03–11Z (DT 02–10Z)) (emerg only 450–476–3141)
  (PTC avbl)
	H–11C, 12K, L–32G

Montreal/Pierre Elliott Trudeau Intl, QC (CYUL)
  ATIS 133.7
  Montreal Trml App Con 118.9 126.9 132.85 268.3
  Tower 119.3 119.9 124.3 (old port) 267.1
  Gnd Con 121.0 (West) 121.9 (East) 275.8
  Clnc Del 125.6   Apron 122.275 (West) 122.075 (East)
  Montreal Trml Dep Con 120.42 (SE–S–SW) 124.65 (W–NW–NE) 268.3
  VFR Advisory 134.15
	H–11C, 12K, L–32G

SUPPLEMENTAL COMMUNICATION REFERENCE

CANADA

FACILITY NAME	CHART & PANEL

Montreal/St–Hubert, QC (CYHU)
  ATIS 124.9 (Apr–Oct Mon–Fri 1045–0500Z‡, Apr–Oct Sat–Sun 1045–0300Z‡,
  Nov–Mar Mon–Fri 1045–0400Z‡, Nov–Mar Sat–Sun 1045–0100Z‡)
  Montreal Center App/Dep Con 125.15 268.3
  St. Hubert Tower 118.4 (VFR Arr North) 121.3 (VFR Arr South and East) (Apr–Oct
  Mon–Fri 1045–0500Z‡, Apr–Oct Sat–Sun 1045–0300Z‡, Nov–Mar Mon–Fri
  1045–0400Z‡, Nov–Mar Sat–Sun 1045–0100Z‡)
  Gnd Con 126.4 (Apr–Oct Mon–Fri 1045–0500Z‡, Apr–Oct Sat–Sun 1045–0300Z‡,
  Nov–Mar Mon–Fri 1045–0400Z‡, Nov–Mar Sat–Sun 1045–0100Z‡)   MF 118.4
  (Apr–Oct Tues–Sat 0500–1045Z‡, Apr–Oct Sun–Mon 0300–1045Z‡, Nov–Mar
  Tues–Sat 0400–1045Z‡, Nov–Mar Sun–Mon 0100–1045Z‡)
  5 NM shape irregular to 2000´)   VFR Advisory 134.15
  MIL 135.9 322.1 (438 Sqn Ops)
	H–11C, L–32G

Muskoka, ON (CYQA)
  Timmins Radio App/Dep Con 122.3
  MF 122.3 (5 NM to 3900´)
	H–11B, L–31D

Nanaimo, BC (CYCD)
  ATIS 128.425 (1–877–517–2847)(1400–0500Z)
  Victoria Trml App/Dep 120.8 121.075 252.3   MF 122.1 291.8 1330–0530Z‡
  (5 NM to 2500´)
  GND ADV 122.6 (1330–0530Z (DT 1230–0430Z)) (emerg only 250–245–4032)
  (PTC avbl)
	H–1B, L–1E

North Bay, ON (CYYB)
  ATIS 124.9 (1130–0330Z‡)
  Toronto Center App/Dep 127.25
  MF 118.3 (1130–0330Z‡ 7 NM to 5000´)
	L–31E

Oshawa, ON (CYOO)
  ATIS 125.675 (1130–0330Z‡)
  Toronto Trml App/Dep Con 133.4
  Tower 120.1 (1130–0330Z‡)   Gnd Con 118.4
  MF 120.1 (0330–1130Z‡ 5 NM to 3000´)
	L–31E

Ottawa/Carp, ON (CYRP)
  ATIS 121.15
  Ottawa Trml App/Dep Con 127.7
	L–31E, 32F

Ottawa/Gatineau, QC (CYND)
  Ottawa Trml App/Dep Con 127.7 128.175
  MF 122.3 (5 NM shape irregular to 2500)
  VFR Advisory Ottawa Trml 127.7
  GND ADV 122.6 1130–0215Z (DT 1030–0115Z) (emerg only 819–643–2961)
	H–11C, L–32G

Ottawa/MacDonald–Cartier Intl, ON (CYOW)
  ATIS 121.15
  Ottawa App Con 135.15 Tower 118.8 (VFR South) 120.1 (VFR North) 118.8 341.3
  Gnd Con 121.9 Clnc Del 119.4
  Ottawa Dep Con 128.175
	L–11C

Owen Sound/Billy Bishop Rgnl, ON (CYOS) Toronto Center App/Dep 132.575 290.6	L–31D
Pelee Island, ON (CYPT) Cleveland Center App/Dep Con 126.35 360.0	L–30F

Pembroke, ON (CYTA)
  Montreal Center App/Dep Con 135.2
  Petawawa Advisory 126.4 250.1 (Mon–Fri 1300–2130Z‡, OT PPR)
	H–11C, L–31E, 32F

Penticton, BC (CYYF)
  Vancouver Center App/Dep Con 133.5 351.3 MF 118.5 (5 NM to 4100)
  GND ADV 121.9 (emerg only 250–492–3001)
	H–1B

Peterborough, ON (CYPQ) Toronto Center App/Dep 134.25 MF 123.0 (5 NM to 3600´)	H–11B, L–31E, 32F
Pincher Creek, AB (CZPC) Edmonton Center App/Dep Con 132.75 265.2	H–1D

Pitt Meadows, BC (CYPK)
  ATIS 125.0 (1500–0700Z‡)
  Vancouver Center App Con 128.6 (Outer) 352.7
  Pitt Tower 126.3 (1500–0700Z‡) Gnd Con 123.8
  Vancouver Center Dep Con 132.3 (South) 363.8
  MF 126.3 (0700–1500Z‡) (3NM to 2500)
	L–1E

Quebec/Jean Lesage Intl, QC (CYQB)
  ATIS 134.6
  Montreal Center App/Dep Con 124.0 127.85 135.025 270.9 322.8
  Tower 118.65 236.6
  Gnd Con 121.9 250.0
	H–11D, L–32H

Riviere Du Loup, QC (CYRI) Montreal Center App/Dep Con 125.1 299.6	H–11D
Rouyn Noranda, QC (CYUY) Montreal Center App/Dep Con 125.9 MF 122.2 (5 NM to 4000´)	H–11B

SUPPLEMENTAL COMMUNICATION REFERENCE
CANADA

FACILITY NAME	CHART & PANEL
Saint John, NB (CYSJ) Moncton Center App/Dep Con 124.3 135.5 270.8 MF 118.5 (5 NM to 3400′)	H–11E, L–32J
Sarnia (Chris Hadfield), ON (CYZR) Toronto Center App/Dep Con 134.375	H–10G, 11B, L–30F
Sault Ste Marie, ON (CYAM) ATIS 133.05 (1130–0330Z‡) Toronto Center App/Dep Con 132.65 344.5 Tower 118.8 (1130–0330Z‡) Gnd Con 121.7 (1130–0330Z‡) MF 118.8 (0330–1130Z‡ 5 NM irregular shape to 3000′)	H–2K, L–31B
Sherbrooke, QC (CYSC) Montreal Center App/Dep Con 132.55 MF 123.5 (Ltd hrs 5 NM to 3800′)	H–11D, L–32H
South Renfrew Muni, ON (CNP3) Montreal Center App/Dep Con 124.275	L–31E, 32F
Southport, MB (CYPG) ATIS 120.85 (Mon–Fri 1400–2300Z‡ except holidays) Tower 126.2 384.2 (Mon–Fri 1400–2300Z‡ except holidays) Gnd Con 121.7 275.8	H–2H
Springwater Barrie Airpark, ON (CNA3) Toronto Center App/Dep Con 124.025	L–31D
St. Catherines/Niagara District, ON (CYSN) ATIS 128.525 (1215–0200Z‡) Toronto Trml App/Dep Con 133.4 MF 123.25 (1215–0200Z‡ 5 NM to 3300′)	H–10H, 11B, L–31E
St. Frederic, QC (CSZ4) Montreal Center App/Dep Con 135.025 270.9	L–32H
St. Georges, QC (CYSG) Montreal Center App/Dep Con 132.35 MF 122.15 (5 NM 3900′ ASL)	H–32H, L–11D
St. Jean, QC (CYJN) Montreal Center App/Dep Con 125.15 268.3 Tower 118.2 (Apr–Oct 1230–0230Z‡ Nov–Mar 1300–0200Z‡) Gnd Con 121.7	L–32G
Sudbury, ON (CYSB) ATIS 127.4 Toronto Center App/Dep Con 135.5 MF 125.5 (7 NM to 4000′) Clnc Del 121.8 (PTC avbl)	H–31B, 10G, L–31D
Summerside, PE (CYSU) Moncton Center App/Dep Con 124.4 384.8	H–11E, L–32J
Thunder Bay, ON (CYQT) ATIS 128.8 Winnipeg Center App/Dep Con 132.125 Tower 118.1 (1100–0400Z‡) Gnd Con 121.9 (1100–0400Z‡) App/Dep 119.2 MF 118.1 (0400–1100Z‡ 5 NM to 4000′)	H–2J, L–14J
Timmins/Victor M. Power, ON (CYTS) ATIS 124.95 Toronto Center App/Dep Con 128.3 MF 122.3 (5 NM to 4000′)	H–11B
Toronto/Buttonville Muni, ON (CYKZ) Toronto Trml App/Dep Con 133.4 MF 124.8 (No gnd station. 5 NM shape irregular 2000 ASL)	L–31E
Toronto/Billy Bishop Toronto City Airport, ON (CYTZ) ATIS 133.6 (1130–0400Z‡) App/Dep Con 133.4 Tower 118.2 119.2 (1130–0400Z‡) Gnd Con 121.7 (1130–0400Z‡)	L–31E
Toronto/Lester B Pearson Intl, ON (CYYZ) ATIS 120.825 133.1 App Con 132.8 124.475 125.4 Dep Con 127.575 128.8 Tower 118.35 118.7 Gnd Con 121.9 121.65 119.1 Clnc Del 121.3 (1200–0400Z‡) A–CDM Coordinator 122.875 (122.825) Apron Tow Coordinator 136.525	H–11B, L–31D
Trenton, ON (CYTR) ATIS 135.45 257.7 App/Dep Con 128.4 324.3 Tower 128.7 236.6 Gnd Con 121.9 275.8 Clnc Del 124.35 286.4	H–11C, L–31E, 32F
Trenton/Mountain View, ON (CPZ3) Trenton Mil Advisory 268.0 or 122.35	H–11C, L–31E, 32F
Trois–Rivieres, QC (CYRQ) Montreal Center App/Dep Con 128.225 MF 122.35 (5 NM to 3200′)	H–11C, L–32H
Val–D'or, QC (CYVO) Montreal Center App/Dep Con 125.9 308.3 MF 118.5 (1030–0325Z‡ 5 NM to 4000′)	H–11B

SC, 25 JAN 2024 to 21 MAR 2024

SUPPLEMENTAL COMMUNICATION REFERENCE

CANADA

FACILITY NAME	CHART & PANEL
Vancouver Intl, BC (CYVR) ATIS 124.6 App Con 128.6 128.17 (Outer) 133.1 134.225 (Inner) 352.7 Dep Con 126.125 (north) 132.3 (south) 363.8 Tower 118.7 (south) 119.55 (north) VFR 124.0 125.65 226.5 236.6 Gnd Con 121.7 (south) 127.15 (north) 275.8 Clnc Del 121.4	H–1B, L–1E
Victoria Intl, BC (CYYJ) ATIS 118.8 (0800–1400Z‡) App Con 125.45 Dep Con 125.95 Tower 119.1 (Outer) 119.7 (Inner) 239.6 Gnd Con 121.9 361.4 (1400–0800Z‡ OT ctc Kamloops 119.7) Clnc Del 126.4 (1400–0800Z‡)	H–1B, L–1E
Victoriaville, QC (CSR3) Montreal Center App Con 132.35 AUTO 122.17 (bil)	L–32H
Waterville/Kings Co Muni, NS (CCW3) Greenwood Trml App/Dep Con 120.6 335.9 Greenwood Tower 119.5 324.3	L–32J
Wiarton, ON (CYVV) Toronto Center App/Dep Con 132.575 MF 122.2 (5 NM to 3700′)	H–11B, L–31D
Windsor, ON (CYQG) ATIS 134.5 (1200–0300Z‡) Detroit App/Dep Con 118.95 132.35 134.3 284.0 Tower 124.7 (1200–0300Z‡) Gnd Con 121.7 (1200–0300Z‡) MF 124.7 (0300–1200Z‡ 6 NM irregular shape to below 3000′) VFR Advisory Detroit App Con 134.3 AWOS 134.5 (0300–1200Z‡)	H–10G, L–8J
Yarmouth, NS (CYQI) Moncton Center App/Dep Con 123.9 368.5 MF 123.0 (5 NM to 3100′)	H–11E, L–32I

MEXICO

FACILITY NAME	CHART & PANEL
Chihuahua Intl/General R Fierro Villalobos Intl (MMCU) ATIS 127.9 Chihuahua App Con 121.0 Chihuahua Tower 118.4	L–6I
Ciudad Juarez Intl/Abraham Gonzalez Intl (MMCS/CJS) Juarez App Con 119.9 Juarez Tower 118.9	H–4L, L–6F
Del Norte Intl (MMAN) ATIS 127.55 (1300–0300Z‡) Monterrey App 119.75 120.4 Tower 118.6 Gnd 122.0	H–7B, L–20G
Durango Intl (MMDO/DGO) ATIS 132.1 Tower 118.1 Durango Info 122.3	H–7A
Matamoros Intl/General Servando Canales Intl (MMMA) Matamoros App Con 118.0 Matamoros Tower 118.0	H–7C, L–21A
Mexicali Intl/General Rodolfo Sanchez Taboada Intl (MMML) ATIS 127.6 (1400–0200Z‡) Mexicali App Con 118.2 Mexicali Tower 118.2 Mexicali Info 123.9 122.3	H–4I, L–4J, 5A
Monterrey Intl/General Mariano Escobedo Intl (MMMY) Monterrey ATIS 127.7 Monterrey App Con 119.75 120.4 Monterrey Dep Con 119.75 Monterrey Tower 118.1 Monterrey Gnd 121.9 Monterrey Clnc Del 123.75 (1200–0400Z‡) Monterrey Info 122.45	H–7B, L–20G
Nuevo Laredo/Quetzalcoatl (MMNL/NLD) Nuevo Laredo App Con 118.3 Nuevo Laredo Tower 118.3	H–7B, L–20G
Reynosa Intl/General Lucio Blanco Intl (MMRX) Reynosa App Con 127.2 Reynosa Tower 118.8	H–7B, L–20H
Saltillo Intl/Plan De Guadalupe Intl (MMIO/SLW) Saltillo App Con 127.4 Saltillo Tower 118.4	H–7B
Tijuana Intl/General Abelardo L Rodriguez Intl (MMTJ) ATIS 127.9 Tijuana App Con 119.5 120.3 Tijuana Tower 118.1 Tijuana Clnc Del 122.35 Tijuana Info 132.1	H–4I, L–4H
Torreon Intl (MMTC) App Con 119.6 Tower 118.5 Info 122.3	H–7A

PREFERRED IFR ROUTES

PREFERRED IFR ROUTES

A system of preferred routes has been established to guide pilots in planning their route of flight, to minimize route changes during the operational phase of flight, and to aid in the efficient orderly management of the air traffic using federal airways. The preferred IFR routes which follow are designed to serve the needs of airspace users and to provide for a systematic flow of air traffic in the major terminal and en route flight environments. Cooperation by all pilots in filing preferred routes will result in fewer traffic delays and will better provide for efficient departure, en route and arrival air traffic service.

The following lists contain preferred IFR routes for the low altitude stratum and the high altitude stratum. The high altitude list is in two sections; the first section showing terminal to terminal routes and the second section showing preferred direction route segments. Also, on some high altitude routes low altitude airways are included as transition routes.

The following will explain the terms/abbreviations used in the listing:

1. Preferred routes beginning/ending with an airway number indicate that the airway essentially overlies the airport and flight are normally cleared directly on the airway.
2. Preferred IFR routes beginning/ending with a fix indicate that aircraft may be routed to/from these fixes via a Standard Instrument Departure (SID) route, radar vectors (RV), or a Standard Terminal Arrival Route (STAR).
3. Preferred IFR routes for major terminals selected are listed alphabetically under the name of the departure airport. Where several airports are in proximity they are listed under the principal airport and categorized as a metropolitan area; e.g., New York Metro Area.
4. Preferred IFR routes used in one direction only for selected segments, irrespective of point of departure or destination, are listed numerically showing the segment fixes and the direction and times effective.
5. Where more than one route is listed the routes have equal priority for use.
6. Official location identifiers are used in the route description for VOR/VORTAC navaids.
7. Intersection names are spelled out.
8. Navaid and distance fixes (e.g., ARD201113) have been used in the route description in an expediency and intersection names will be assigned as soon as routine processing can be accomplished. Navaid radial (no distance stated) may be used to describe a route to intercept a specified airway (e.g., MIV MIV101 V39); another navaid radial (e.g., UIM UIM255 GSW081); or an intersection (e.g., GSW081 FITCH).
9. Where two navaids, an intersection and a navaid, a navaid and a navaid radial and distance point, or any navigable combination of these route descriptions follow in succession, the route is direct.
10. The effective times for the routes are in UTC. During periods of daylight saving time effective times will be one hour earlier than indicated. All states observe daylight saving time except Arizona, Puerto Rico and the Virgin Islands. Pilots planning flight between the terminals or route segments listed should file for the appropriate preferred IFR route.
11. (90–170 incl) altitude flight level assignment in hundred of feet.
12. The notations "pressurized" and "unpressurized" for certain low altitude preferred routes to Kennedy Airport indicate the preferred route based on aircraft performance.
13. All Preferred IFR Routes are in effect continuously unless otherwise noted.
14. Use current SIDs and STARSs for flight planning.
15. For high altitude routes, the portion of the routes contained in brackets [ ] is suggested but optional. The portion of the route outside the brackets will likely be required by the facilities involved.

LOW ALTITUDE

Terminals	Route	Effective Times (UTC)
HOUSTON(HOU)		
DALLAS(DAL)	(NON–TURBOJET (RNAV))STYCK (RNAV)–DP STYCK CQY YEAGR–STAR	
	or	
	(ALL OTHERS)LEONA–DP CQY YEAGR–STAR	
DALLAS–FORT WORTH(DFW)	(NON TURBOJET (RNAV))(DFW SOUTH FLOW)STYCK (RNAV)–DP STYCK CQY YEAGR–STAR	
	or	
	(NON TURBOJET (RNAV))(DFW NORTH FLOW)STYCK (RNAV)–DP STYCK CQY CEDAR CREEK–STAR	
	or	
	(ALL OTHERS)(DFW SOUTH FLOW)LEONA–DP CQY YEAGR–STAR	
	or	
	(ALL OTHERS)(DFW NORTH FLOW)LEONA–DP CQY CEDAR CREEK–STAR	
NEW ORLEANS(MSY)	(SFC–100; ALL OTHERS)SBI270016 SBI V198 TBD V552 OLEDD	
	or	
	(110–180; DME/DME/IRU OR GPS)ELOCO (RNAV)–DP LLA AWDAD AWDAD–STAR	
	or	
	(SFC–100; DME/DME/IRU OR GPS)ELOCO (RNAV)–DP SBI V198 TBD V552 OLEDD	
	or	
	(110–180; ALL OTHERS)SBI270016 SBI LLA AWDAD AWDAD–STAR	

PREFERRED IFR ROUTES

493

Terminals	Route	Effective Times (UTC)
HOUSTON(IAH)		
DALLAS(DAL)	(NON–TURBOJET (RNAV))STYCK (RNAV)–DP STYCK CQY YEAGR–STAR	
	or	
	(ALL OTHERS)LEONA–DP CQY YEAGR–STAR	
DALLAS–FORT WORTH(DFW)	(RNAV TURBOJET)(DFW NORTH FLOW)BLTWY (RNAV)–DP CRIED WHINY (RNAV)–STAR	
	or	
	(ALL OTHERS)(DFW SOUTH FLOW)LEONA–DP CQY YEAGR–STAR	
	or	
	(NON TURBOJET (RNAV))(DFW SOUTH FLOW)STYCK (RNAV)–DP STYCK CQY YEAGR–STAR	
	or	
	(NON TURBOJET (RNAV))(DFW NORTH FLOW)STYCK (RNAV)–DP STYCK CQY CEDAR CREEK–STAR	
	or	
	(RNAV TURBOJET)(DFW SOUTH FLOW)BLTWY (RNAV)–DP CRIED BEREE (RNAV)–STAR	
	or	
	(ALL OTHERS)(DFW NORTH FLOW)LEONA–DP CQY CEDAR CREEK–STAR	
NEW ORLEANS(MSY)	(SFC–100)LAKE CHARLES–DP LCH V20 AWDAD	
	or	
	(110–180; DME/DME/IRU OR GPS)(IAH WEST FLOW)MMUGS (RNAV)–DP GUSTI AWDAD AWDAD–STAR	
	or	
	(110–180; DME/DME/IRU OR GPS)(IAH EAST FLOW)GUMBY (RNAV)–DP GUSTI AWDAD AWDAD–STAR	
	or	
	(110–180; ALL OTHERS)LAKE CHARLES–DP LCH AWDAD–STAR	
TULSA(TUL)		
INDIANAPOLIS(IND)	EOS SGF FAM PXV TERGE SMUKE (RNAV)–STAR	
TERRE HAUTE(HUF)	EOS SGF FAM PXV V7 TTH	

HIGH ALTITUDE

Terminals	Route	Effective Times (UTC)
3R9,AUS,EDC,GTU,HYI,RYW,T74		
47N,CDW,LDJ,MMU,SMQ,TEB	ILEXY (RNAV)–DP ZENZI IAH GUSTI Q22 UMBRE SWNGR JAIKE (RNAV)–STAR	
MQS,PHL,PNE,TTN	ILEXY (RNAV)–DP ZENZI IAH GUSTI Q22 BEARI BBDOL PAATS (RNAV)–STAR	
NEW YORK(JFK)	ILEXY (RNAV)–DP ZENZI IAH GUSTI Q22 CATLN Q64 SAWED Q97 DLAAY RADDS SIE CAMRN–STAR	
NEWARK(EWR)	ILEXY (RNAV)–DP ZENZI IAH GUSTI Q22 UMBRE QUART PHLBO (RNAV)–STAR	
AMARILLO(AMA)		
AUSTIN(AUS)	SLIDE UCOKA DILLO LAIKS (RNAV)–STAR	
AUSTIN(AUS)		
BALTIMORE(BWI)	ILEXY (RNAV)–DP ZENZI IAH GUSTI Q22 CATLN Q56 KELLN Q58 PEETT THHMP RAVNN (RNAV)–STAR	
	or	
	(PART 121 & 129 ONLY)ILEXY (RNAV)–DP ZENZI LFK SUTTN J29 CARIN MEMFS Q34 NEALS BKW RAVNN (RNAV)–STAR	
BOSTON(BOS)	ILEXY (RNAV)–DP ZENZI LFK SUTTN J29 CARIN MEMFS Q34 RBV Q419 JFK ROBUC (RNAV)–STAR	
	or	
	ILEXY (RNAV)–DP ZENZI IAH GUSTI Q22 RBV Q419 JFK ROBUC (RNAV)–STAR	
HOUSTON(HOU)	(ALL OTHERS)ILEXY (RNAV)–DP ILEXY BLUBELL–STAR	
	or	
	(TURBOJETS)ILEXY (RNAV)–DP ILEXY KIDDZ (RNAV)–STAR	

SC, 25 JAN 2024 to 21 MAR 2024

PREFERRED IFR ROUTES

Terminals	Route	Effective Times (UTC)
HOUSTON(IAH)		
HOUSTON(IAH)	(TURBOJETS)(IAH EAST FLOW)ILEXY (RNAV)–DP ILEXY TTORO (RNAV)–STAR	
	or	
	(TURBOJETS)(IAH WEST FLOW)ILEXY (RNAV)–DP ILEXY MSCOT (RNAV)–STAR	
NEW YORK(JFK)	ILEXY (RNAV)–DP ZENZI LFK MEM J29 PXV ROD KLYNE Q29 JHW J70 LVZ LENDY–STAR	
NEW YORK(LGA)	ILEXY (RNAV)–DP ZENZI LFK SUTTN J29 CARIN MEMFS Q34 GVE KORRY–STAR......................	
	or	
	ILEXY (RNAV)–DP ZENZI IAH GUSTI Q22 BURGG Q60 HURTS HUBBS PXT KORRY–STAR......................	
NEWARK METRO(CDW,MMU,TEB)	ILEXY (RNAV)–DP ZENZI LFK SUTTN J29 CARIN MEMFS Q34 GVE JAIKE (RNAV)–STAR...........................	
NEWARK(EWR)	ILEXY (RNAV)–DP ZENZI LFK SUTTN J29 CARIN MEMFS Q34 GVE PHLBO (RNAV)–STAR...........................	
PHILADELPHIA(PHL)	ILEXY (RNAV)–DP ZENZI LFK SUTTN J29 CARIN MEMFS Q34 GVE PAATS (RNAV)–STAR...........................	
WASHINGTON(DCA)	ILEXY (RNAV)–DP ZENZI LFK SUTTN J29 CARIN MEMFS Q34 NEALS BKW TRUPS (RNAV)–STAR	
	or	
	ILEXY (RNAV)–DP ZENZI IAH GUSTI Q22 CATLN Q56 KIWII WAVES CAPSS (RNAV)–STAR	
WASHINGTON(IAD)	ILEXY (RNAV)–DP ZENZI LFK SUTTN J29 CARIN MEMFS Q34 HITMN HVQ GIBBZ (RNAV)–STAR	
	or	
	ILEXY (RNAV)–DP ZENZI IAH GUSTI Q22 BURGG Q60 JAXSN DORRN CAVLR (RNAV)–STAR	
BATON ROUGE(BTR)		
ATLANTA(ATL)	(TURBOJETS)(ATL EAST OPERATION)PAYTN SHYRE GNDLF (RNAV)–STAR	
	or	
	(TURBOJETS)(ATL WEST OPERATION)PAYTN SHYRE HOBTT (RNAV)–STAR	
HOUSTON(HOU)	(TURBOJETS– DME/DME/IRU OR GPS)(HOU WEST FLOW)SALVO LFT SLYCE PUCKS (RNAV)–STAR ...	
	or	
	(TURBOPROPS – DME/DME/IRU OR GPS)SALVO LFT BBURT TKNIQ (RNAV)–STAR......................	
	or	
	(TURBOJETS– DME/DME/IRU OR GPS)(HOU EAST FLOW)SALVO LFT SLYCE BAYYY (RNAV)–STAR....	
HOUSTON(IAH)	(TURBOJETS & TURBOPROPS – DME/DME/IRU OR GPS)(IAH WEST FLOW)SALVO LFT LINKK (RNAV)–STAR..	
	or	
	(TURBOJETS & TURBOPROPS – DME/DME/IRU OR GPS)(IAH EAST FLOW)SALVO LFT NNCEE (RNAV)–STAR..	
DALLAS(DAL)		
BALTIMORE(BWI)	LNDRE (RNAV)–DP LOOSE Q34 NEALS BKW RAVNN (RNAV)–STAR..	
BOSTON(BOS)	LNDRE (RNAV)–DP BSKAT J131 PXV KLYNE Q29 JHW Q82 PONCT JFUND (RNAV)–STAR.....................	
	or	
	LNDRE (RNAV)–DP FORCK ELD IZAAC Q30 VLKNN THRSR TWOUP Q22 RBV Q419 JFK ROBUC (RNAV)–STAR...	
DETROIT(DTW)	(DME/DME/IRU OR GPS REQUIRED)(DTW NORTH FLOW)LNDRE (RNAV)–DP BSKAT LIT J131 PXV WWODD LECTR (RNAV)–STAR	
	or	
	(DME/DME/IRU OR GPS REQUIRED)(DTW SOUTH FLOW)LNDRE (RNAV)–DP BSKAT LIT J131 PXV WWODD HANBL (RNAV)–STAR	
NEW YORK(LGA)	LNDRE (RNAV)–DP FORCK ELD IZAAC Q30 VLKNN THRSR TWOUP Q22 BURGG Q60 HURTS HUBBS PXT KORRY–STAR..	

SC, 25 JAN 2024 to 21 MAR 2024

PREFERRED IFR ROUTES 495

Terminals	Route	Effective Times (UTC)
NEWARK(EWR)................................	LNDRE (RNAV)–DP FORCK ELD IZAAC Q30 VLKNN THRSR TWOUP Q22 UMBRE QUART PHLBO (RNAV)–STAR................................	
PHILADELPHIA(PHL)	LNDRE (RNAV)–DP LOOSE Q34 GVE PAATS (RNAV)–STAR	
WASHINGTON(DCA)	LNDRE (RNAV)–DP LOOSE Q34 NEALS BKW TRUPS (RNAV)–STAR	
WASHINGTON(IAD)	LNDRE (RNAV)–DP LOOSE Q34 HITMN HVQ GIBBZ (RNAV)–STAR	
DALLAS–FORT WORTH(DFW)		
47N,CDW,LDJ,MMU,SMQ,TEB	FORCK (RNAV)–DP FORCK ELD IZAAC Q30 VLKNN THRSR TWOUP Q22 UMBRE SWNGR JAIKE (RNAV)–STAR	
BALTIMORE(BWI).............................	TRYTN (RNAV)–DP LOOSE Q34 NEALS BKW RAVNN (RNAV)–STAR	
BOCA RATON(BCT)............................	(WATER)MRSSH ZALEA HRV Q105 BLVNS Y290 GAWKS VUUDU (RNAV)–STAR................................	
	or	
	MRSSH (RNAV)–DP ZALEA MCB J50 CEW J2 DEFUN VUUDU (RNAV)–STAR................................	
BOSTON(BOS)....................................	FORCK (RNAV)–DP FORCK ELD IZAAC Q30 VLKNN THRSR TWOUP Q22 RBV Q419 JFK ROBUC (RNAV)–STAR	
	or	
	ZACHH (RNAV)–DP BSKAT J131 PXV KLYNE Q29 JHW Q82 PONCT JFUND (RNAV)–STAR	1100–0300
CHARLOTTE(CLT)..............................	FORCK (RNAV)–DP FORCK IZAAC Q30 VLKNN THRSR BESTT JONZE (RNAV)–STAR............................	
CHICAGO(ORD)	(RNAV TURBOJET)DALLAS–DP OKM J181 BAYLI BENKY (RNAV)–STAR	
CLEVELAND METRO(CLE,CGF,BKL,LNN,LPR)	(RNAV TURBOJET)ZACHH (RNAV)–DP BSKAT LIT J131 PXV DRUGA ROKNN (RNAV)–STAR................	
COVINGTON(CVG)	(RNAV TURBOJET)ZACHH (RNAV)–DP BSKAT LIT J131 PXV SARGO (RNAV)–STAR................................	
DENVER(DEN)	LOWGN (RNAV)–DP ROLLS LBL HALEN NIIXX (RNAV)–STAR	
DETROIT SATS(DET,ARB,PTK,YIP,CYQG)	ZACHH (RNAV)–DP BSKAT LIT J131 PXV VHP FWA LYNTN	
DETROIT(DTW)	(DME/DME/IRU OR GPS REQUIRED)(DTW NORTH FLOW)ZACHH (RNAV)–DP BSKAT LIT J131 PXV WWODD LECTR (RNAV)–STAR................................	
	or	
	(DME/DME/IRU OR GPS REQUIRED)(DTW SOUTH FLOW)ZACHH (RNAV)–DP BSKAT LIT J131 PXV WWODD HANBL (RNAV)–STAR................................	
FORT LAUDERDALE(FLL)	MRSSH (RNAV)–DP ZALEA MCB J50 CEW J2 DEFUN TEEKY (RNAV)–STAR	
	or	
	(WATER)MRSSH (RNAV)–DP ZALEA HRV Q105 BLVNS Y290 OCHHO VNECK TEEKY (RNAV)–STAR	
LOUISVILLE(SDF)	TRYTN (RNAV)–DP LOOSE Q34 HITMN MBELL MBELL (RNAV)–STAR	
MIAMI(MIA)	(WATER)MRSSH (RNAV)–DP ZALEA HRV Q105 BLVNS Y290 GAWKS FROGZ (RNAV)–STAR...................	
	or	
	MRSSH (RNAV)–DP ZALEA MCB J50 CEW J2 DEFUN FROGZ (RNAV)–STAR	
NEW YORK(JFK).................................	FORCK (RNAV)–DP FORCK ELD IZAAC Q30 VLKNN THRSR HRTWL Q64 SAWED Q97 DLAAY RADDS SIE CAMRN–STAR	
NEW YORK(LGA)	FORCK (RNAV)–DP FORCK ELD IZAAC Q30 VLKNN THRSR TWOUP Q22 BURGG Q60 JAXSN HPW HUBBS PXT KORRY–STAR	
NEWARK(EWR)	FORCK (RNAV)–DP FORCK ELD IZAAC Q30 VLKNN THRSR TWOUP Q22 UMBRE QUART PHLBO (RNAV)–STAR	
PHILADELPHIA(PHL)	TRYTN (RNAV)–DP LOOSE Q34 GVE PAATS (RNAV)–STAR	
PITTSBURGH(PIT)	ZACHH (RNAV)–DP BSKAT LIT J131 PXV HNN FEWGA (RNAV)–STAR	

SC, 25 JAN 2024 to 21 MAR 2024

PREFERRED IFR ROUTES

Terminals	Route	Effective Times (UTC)
SAN JOSE(SJC)	(TURBOJET)HRPER (RNAV)–DP HULZE TCC J76 FTI J58 ILC KNGRY RAZRR (RNAV)–STAR	
WASHINGTON(DCA)	TRYTN (RNAV)–DP LOOSE Q34 NEALS BKW TRUPS (RNAV)–STAR	
WASHINGTON(IAD)	TRYTN (RNAV)–DP LOOSE Q34 HITMN HVQ GIBBZ (RNAV)–STAR	
WEST PALM BEACH(PBI)	MRSSH (RNAV)–DP ZALEA MCB J50 CEW J2 DEFUN VUUDU (RNAV)–STAR	
	or	
	(WATER)MRSSH (RNAV)–DP ZALEA HRV Q105 BLVNS Y290 GAWKS VUUDU (RNAV)–STAR	
WINDSOR LOCKS(BDL)	TRYTN (RNAV)–DP LOOSE MEMFS Q29 JHW Q82 MEMMS WILET STELA–STAR	
	or	
	TRYTN (RNAV)–DP LOOSE Q34 RBV Q419 DPK DEER PARK–STAR	

DALLAS/FORT WORTH METRO

Terminals	Route	Effective Times (UTC)
CHICAGO(MDW)	FUZ J181 MAGOO ENDEE (RNAV)–STAR	
CHICAGO(ORD)	FUZ J181 BDF BRADFORD–STAR	1200–0400
HOUSTON(HOU)	(NON–TURBOJETS)JOE POOL–DP ELLVR BLUBELL–STAR	
	(RNAV TURBOJET)ARDIA (RNAV)–DP ELLVR NNEAL KIDDZ (RNAV)–STAR	
HOUSTON(IAH)	(RNAV TURBOJET)(IAH EAST FLOW)DARTZ (RNAV)–DP TORNN GUSHR (RNAV)–STAR	
	or	
	(NON–ADVANCED NAV ONLY)JOE POOL–DP BILEE RIICE–STAR	
	or	
	(RNAV TURBOJET)(IAH WEST FLOW)DARTZ (RNAV)–DP TORNN DRLLR (RNAV)–STAR	
SAN FRANCISCO(SFO)	(RNAV TURBOJET)HRPER (RNAV)–DP HULZE TCC J76 FTI J58 OAL MOD	

FAYETTEVILLE/SPRINGDALE/ROGERS(XNA)

Terminals	Route	Effective Times (UTC)
CHICAGO(ORD)	SGF BAYLI BRADFORD–STAR	
	or	
	EOS SGF WELTS TRTLL (RNAV)–STAR	
	or	
	EOS SGF WELTS SHAIN (RNAV)–STAR	
NEW YORK(LGA)	EOS SGF STL WWSHR TEESY J146 ETG MILTON–STAR	

FORT WORTH(FTW)

Terminals	Route	Effective Times (UTC)
LOUISVILLE(LOU)	TXK Q34 HITMN MBELL MBELL (RNAV)–STAR	

GULFPORT(GPT)

Terminals	Route	Effective Times (UTC)
HOUSTON(HOU)	(TURBOJETS– DME/DME/IRU OR GPS)(HOU EAST FLOW)HRV KCEEE BAYYY (RNAV)–STAR	
	or	
	(TURBOPROPS)HRV BBURT TKNIQ (RNAV)–STAR	
	or	
	(TURBOJETS– DME/DME/IRU OR GPS)(HOU WEST FLOW)HRV KCEEE PUCKS (RNAV)–STAR	
HOUSTON(IAH)	(TURBOJETS & TURBOPROPS–DME/DME/IRU OR GPS)(IAH EAST FLOW)HRV NNCEE (RNAV)–STAR	
	or	
	(TURBOJETS & TURBOPROPS – DME/DME/IRU OR GPS)(IAH WEST FLOW)HRV LINKK (RNAV)–STAR	

HOUSTON(HOU)

Terminals	Route	Effective Times (UTC)
ALBUQUERQUE(ABQ)	(DME/DME/IRU OR GPS)RETYR (RNAV)–DP JCT J15 CME	
ATLANTA(ATL)	(TURBOJETS)(ATL WEST OPERATION)ELOCO (RNAV)–DP LLA HRV PAYTN SHYRE HOBTT (RNAV)–STAR	
	or	
	(TURBOJETS)(ATL EAST OPERATION)ELOCO (RNAV)–DP LLA HRV PAYTN SHYRE GNDLF (RNAV)–STAR	
AUSTIN(AUS)	(DME/DME/IRU OR GPS)RETYR (RNAV)–DP MNURE WLEEE (RNAV)–STAR	
BIRMINGHAM(BHM)	STRYA (RNAV)–DP DPATY MEI LYMPH	

SC, 25 JAN 2024 to 21 MAR 2024

PREFERRED IFR ROUTES

497

Terminals	Route	Effective Times (UTC)
BOCA RATON(BCT)	ELOCO (RNAV)–DP LLA HRV SJI J2 DEFUN VUUDU (RNAV)–STAR	
	or	
	(WATER)ELOCO (RNAV)–DP LLA LEV Y290 GAWKS VUUDU (RNAV)–STAR	
BOSTON(BOS)	ELOCO (RNAV)–DP LLA HRV Q56 CATLN Q22 RBV Q419 JFK ROBUC (RNAV)–STAR	
BWI,DMW,MTN	(TURBOJETS)ELOCO (RNAV)–DP LLA HRV Q56 KELLN Q58 PEETT THHMP RAVNN (RNAV)–STAR	
CHARLESTON(CHS)	ELOCO (RNAV)–DP LLA HRV SJI J2 DEFUN CABLO ALLMA SAV BAGGY (RNAV)–STAR	
CHARLESTON(CRW)	LURIC (RNAV)–DP ORRTH CRAMM BNA SWAPP Q34 FOUNT HVQ	
CHARLOTTE(CLT)	(TURBOJETS)ELOCO (RNAV)–DP LLA HRV Q56 CATLN MGMRY BESTT JONZE (RNAV)–STAR	1400–0100
CHICAGO(MDW)	(DME/DME/IRU OR GPS)INDIE (RNAV)–DP TPAKK LIT J101 STL PIA MOTIF–STAR	
CHICAGO(ORD)	(DME/DME/IRU OR GPS)INDIE (RNAV)–DP TPAKK LIT J101 STL TRTLL (RNAV)–STAR	
	or	
	STYCK (RNAV)–DP WTSON BYP MLC RZC SGF WELTS TRTLL (RNAV)–STAR	
	or	
	(DME/DME/IRU OR GPS)INDIE (RNAV)–DP TPAKK LIT J180 FTZ TRTLL (RNAV)–STAR	
CLEVELAND METRO(CLE,CGF,BKL,LNN,LPR)	(RNAV TURBOJET)INDIE (RNAV)–DP TPAKK LIT J131 PXV DRUGA ROKNN (RNAV)–STAR	
COLORADO SPRINGS(COS)	(TURBOJETS – DME/DME/IRU OR GPS)STYCK (RNAV)–DP DOLEY ADM MMB LBL LAA OZZZY (RNAV)–STAR	
COLUMBIA(CAE)	ELOCO (RNAV)–DP LLA HRV Q56 CATLN MGMRY THRSR IRQ CAE	
COLUMBUS(CMH)	INDIE (RNAV)–DP TPAKK LIT J131 PXV GETTA JAKTZ (RNAV)–STAR	
COVINGTON(CVG)	(DME/DME/IRU OR GPS)INDIE (RNAV)–DP TPAKK LIT J131 SARGO (RNAV)–STAR	
CPK,FAF,LFI,NGU,ORF,PHF,PVG	ELOCO (RNAV)–DP LLA HRV Q56 CATLN Q64 HRTWL Q54 NUTZE DRONE DRONE–STAR	
DALLAS(DAL)	(TURBOJETS)(DAL NORTH FLOW)WYLSN (RNAV)–DP MAJKK MNNDO (RNAV)–STAR	
	or	
	(TURBOJETS)(DAL SOUTH FLOW)WYLSN (RNAV)–DP MAJKK REDDN (RNAV)–STAR	
	or	
	(ALL OTHERS)GIFFA YEAGR–STAR	
DALLAS–FORT WORTH(DFW)	(RNAV TURBOJET)(DFW SOUTH FLOW)BLTWY (RNAV)–DP CRIED BEREE (RNAV)–STAR	
	or	
	(RNAV TURBOJET)(DFW NORTH FLOW)BLTWY (RNAV)–DP CRIED WHINY (RNAV)–STAR	
	or	
	(ALL OTHERS)CRIED CEDAR CREEK–STAR	
DENVER(DEN)	STYCK (RNAV)–DP DOLEY ADM ROLLS LBL HALEN NIIXX (RNAV)–STAR	
DES MOINES(DSM)	(DME/DME/IRU OR GPS)STYCK (RNAV)–DP WTSON BYP TUL J25 DSM	
DETROIT(DTW)	(DME/DME/IRU OR GPS REQUIRED)(DTW SOUTH FLOW)INDIE (RNAV)–DP TPAKK LIT J131 PXV WWODD HANBL (RNAV)–STAR	
	or	
	(DME/DME/IRU OR GPS REQUIRED)(DTW NORTH FLOW)INDIE (RNAV)–DP TPAKK LIT J131 PXV WWODD LECTR (RNAV)–STAR	
FAYETTEVILLE/SPRINGDALE/ROGERS(XNA)	(DME/DME/IRU OR GPS)INDIE (RNAV)–DP INDIE PGO RZC	
FORT LAUDERDALE(FLL)	ELOCO (RNAV)–DP LLA HRV SJI J2 DEFUN TEEKY (RNAV)–STAR	
	or	
	(WATER)ELOCO (RNAV)–DP LLA LEV Y290 OCHHO VNECK TEEKY (RNAV)–STAR	

SC, 25 JAN 2024 to 21 MAR 2024

PREFERRED IFR ROUTES

Terminals	Route	Effective Times (UTC)
FORT MYERS(RSW)	ELOCO (RNAV)–DP LLA HRV SJI J2 DEFUN CABLO BULZI Q81 NICKI PLYER TYNEE (RNAV)–STAR.............. or ELOCO (RNAV)–DP LLA LEV Y290 BAGGS TYNEE (RNAV)–STAR..	
GMU,GSP,GYH,SPA	ELOCO (RNAV)–DP LLA HRV Q56 CATLN MGMRY BESTT WORXS (RNAV)–STAR	
GRAND RAPIDS(GRR)	(DME/DME/IRU OR GPS)INDIE (RNAV)–DP TPAKK LIT J101 STL J19 RBS OXI ELX VIO.........................	
INDIANAPOLIS(IND)	(TURBOJETS)INDIE (RNAV)–DP TPAKK LIT J131 PXV TERGE SMUKE (RNAV)–STAR............................	
JACKSONVILLE(JAX)	ELOCO (RNAV)–DP LLA HRV SJI J2 DEFUN CABLO CAPPS MARQO (RNAV)–STAR	
KANSAS CITY(MCI)	(RNAV TURBOJET/TURBOPROP)STYCK (RNAV)–DP WTSON BYP TUL STASN WUTNG (RNAV)–STAR..	
KNOXVILLE(TYS)	(DME/DME/IRU OR GPS)STRYA (RNAV)–DP DPATY MEI VUZ VXV	
LAS VEGAS(LAS)	RETYR (RNAV)–DP JCT J86 INW HAHAA RKSTR (RNAV)–STAR..	
LEXINGTON(LEX)	(DME/DME/IRU OR GPS)LURIC (RNAV)–DP ORRTH CRAMM BNA UNCKL	
LOS ANGELES(LAX)	(DME/DME/IRU OR GPS)RETYR (RNAV)–DP JCT J86 ELP J50 SSO J4 TNP SEAVU–STAR	
LOUISVILLE(SDF)	(TURBOJET)INDIE (RNAV)–DP TPAKK LIT J131 PXV ALENN DAMEN (RNAV)–STAR............................	
MEMPHIS(MEM)	(TURBOJETS – DME/DME/IRU OR GPS)LURIC (RNAV)–DP HAWES FAYEE HOBRK (RNAV)–STAR	
MIAMI(MIA)	(WATER)ELOCO (RNAV)–DP LLA LEV Y290 GAWKS FROGZ (RNAV)–STAR .... or ELOCO (RNAV)–DP LLA HRV SJI J2 DEFUN FROGZ (RNAV)–STAR..	
MILWAUKEE(MKE)	(DME/DME/IRU OR GPS)INDIE (RNAV)–DP LURIC LIT J101 JOT	
MINNEAPOLIS(MSP)	(TURBOJETS)STYCK (RNAV)–DP WTSON BYP TUL J25 MCI ROKKK NITZR (RNAV)–STAR	1000–0300
MQS,PHL,PNE,TTN	(TURBOJETS)ELOCO (RNAV)–DP LLA HRV Q56 CATLN Q22 BEARI BBDOL PAATS (RNAV)–STAR	
NASHVILLE(BNA)	(TURBOJETS – DME/DME/IRU OR GPS)LURIC (RNAV)–DP HAWES SUTTN J29 MEM CHSNE (RNAV)–STAR..	
NEW ORLEANS(MSY)	(DME/DME/IRU OR GPS)ELOCO (RNAV)–DP LLA AWDAD AWDAD–STAR... or (ALL OTHERS)SBI270016 SBI LLA AWDAD AWDAD–STAR..	
NEW YORK(JFK)	(TURBOJETS)ELOCO (RNAV)–DP LLA HRV Q56 CATLN Q64 SAWED Q97 DLAAY RADDS SIE CAMRN–STAR	
NEW YORK(LGA)	ELOCO (RNAV)–DP LLA HRV Q56 CATLN Q22 BURGG Q60 HURTS	
NEWARK(EWR)	(TURBOJETS)ELOCO (RNAV)–DP LLA HRV Q56 CATLN Q22 UMBRE QUART PHLBO (RNAV)–STAR	
OAKLAND(OAK)	(TURBOJET)RETYR (RNAV)–DP JCT J86 BLD J92 BTY RUSME OAKES (RNAV)–STAR	
OKLAHOMA CITY(OKC)	(DME/DME/IRU OR GPS)STYCK (RNAV)–DP DOLEY ADM DECKK IRW	
OMAHA(OMA)	(DME/DME/IRU OR GPS)STYCK (RNAV)–DP WTSON BYP HTHWY TIMMO (RNAV)–STAR............................	
ONTARIO(ONT)	(DME/DME/IRU OR GPS)RETYR (RNAV)–DP JCT J86 ELP SSO J4 BXK J212 PSP SETER–STAR	
ORLANDO(MCO)	ELOCO (RNAV)–DP LLA HRV SJI J2 DEFUN GRNCH (RNAV)–STAR.. or (WATER)ELOCO (RNAV)–DP LLA LEV Y280 CHRGE PRICY (RNAV)–STAR...	
PENSACOLA(PNS)	(DME/DME/IRU OR GPS)ELOCO (RNAV)–DP LLA HRV SJI V241 PENSI..	
PITTSBURGH(PIT)	(DME/DME/IRU OR GPS)LUFKIN–DP LIT J131 PXV ROD BSV JESEY (RNAV)–STAR..	

SC, 25 JAN 2024 to 21 MAR 2024

PREFERRED IFR ROUTES

499

Terminals	Route	Effective Times (UTC)
PORTLAND(PDX)	(DME/DME/IRU OR GPS)RETYR (RNAV)–DP JCT J15 IMB JOTBA HHOOD (RNAV)–STAR	
	or	
	(TURBOJETS)STYCK (RNAV)–DP DOLEY FUZ HNKER ALS JNC J15 IMB JOTBA HHOOD (RNAV)–STAR	
RALEIGH/DURHAM(RDU)	ELOCO (RNAV)–DP LLA HRV Q56 CATLN MGMRY THRSR IRQ PYRES DMSTR (RNAV)–STAR	
RICHMOND(RIC)	(TURBOJETS & TURBOPROPS)ELOCO (RNAV)–DP LLA HRV Q56 CATLN Q22 BURGG Q60 JAXSN KELCE DUCXS (RNAV)–STAR	
SALT LAKE CITY(SLC)	(TURBOJETS – DME/DME/IRU OR GPS)RETYR (RNAV)–DP JCT J15 JNC HELPR LEEHY (RNAV)–STAR	
SAN ANTONIO(SAT)	(NON–ADVANCED NAV ONLY)INDUSTRY–DP IDU MARCS–STAR	
	or	
	RETYR (RNAV)–DP WAILN BRAUN (RNAV)–STAR	
SAN DIEGO(SAN)	(DME/DME/IRU OR GPS)RETYR (RNAV)–DP JCT J2 HOGGZ LUCKI (RNAV)–STAR	
SAN FRANCISCO(SFO)	(DME/DME/IRU OR GPS)STYCK (RNAV)–DP DOLEY FUZ SPS J76 FTI J58 MLF J80 OAL	
	or	
	(DME/DME/IRU OR GPS)RETYR (RNAV)–DP JCT J86 BLD J92 OAL	
SAN JOSE(SJC)	(TURBOJET)RETYR (RNAV)–DP JCT J86 ELP Q4 BOILE MAKRS TROXX SILCN (RNAV)–STAR	
SANTA ANA(SNA)	(DME/DME/IRU OR GPS)RETYR (RNAV)–DP JCT J86 ELP J50 TFD J212 PSP KAYOH–STAR	
SAVANNAH(SAV)	(DME/DME/IRU OR GPS)ELOCO (RNAV)–DP LLA HRV SJI J2 CEW ALLMA JANIE	
SEATTLE(SEA)	(TURBOJETS)STYCK (RNAV)–DP DOLEY ADM ROLLS LBL LAA J52 FQF J20 PDT CHINS–STAR	
ST LOUIS(STL)	(TURBOJETS – DME/DME/IRU OR GPS)INDIE (RNAV)–DP TPAKK LIT ARG BOOSH (RNAV)–STAR	
TAMPA(TPA)	ELOCO (RNAV)–DP LLA LEV Y280 CHRGE RAYZZ (RNAV)–STAR	
	or	
	ELOCO (RNAV)–DP LLA HRV SJI J2 DEFUN MAATY (RNAV)–STAR	
TUCSON(TUS)	(DME/DME/IRU OR GPS)RETYR (RNAV)–DP JCT J86 ELP ZONNA (RNAV)–STAR	
TULSA(TUL)	(DME/DME/IRU OR GPS)STYCK (RNAV)–DP WTSON BYP TUL	
WASHINGTON(DCA)	(TURBOJETS)ELOCO (RNAV)–DP LLA HRV Q56 KIWII WAVES CAPSS (RNAV)–STAR	
WASHINGTON(IAD)	(TURBOJETS)ELOCO (RNAV)–DP LLA HRV SJI CATLN Q22 BURGG Q60 JAXSN DORRN CAVLR (RNAV)–STAR	
WEST PALM BEACH(PBI)	ELOCO (RNAV)–DP LLA HRV SJI J2 DEFUN VUUDU (RNAV)–STAR	
	or	
	(WATER)ELOCO (RNAV)–DP LLA LEV Y290 GAWKS VUUDU (RNAV)–STAR	
WICHITA(ICT)	(DME/DME/IRU OR GPS)STYCK (RNAV)–DP DOLEY ADM IRW HUSKA	
WINDSOR LOCKS(BDL)	ELOCO (RNAV)–DP LLA HRV Q56 CATLN Q22 RBV Q419 DPK DEER PARK–STAR	
HOUSTON(IAH)		
ALBUQUERQUE(ABQ)	(DME/DME/IRU OR GPS)(IAH WEST FLOW)BNDTO (RNAV)–DP CRGER LOWGO J15 CME	
	or	
	(DME/DME/IRU OR GPS)(IAH EAST FLOW)PITZZ (RNAV)–DP CRGER LOWGO J15 CME	

SC, 25 JAN 2024 to 21 MAR 2024

PREFERRED IFR ROUTES

Terminals	Route	Effective Times (UTC)
ATLANTA(ATL)	(TURBOJETS)(IAH WEST ATL WEST)MMUGS (RNAV)–DP LCH Q24 PAYTN SHYRE HOBTT (RNAV)–STAR....	
	or	
	(TURBOJETS)(IAH EAST ATL WEST)GUMBY (RNAV)–DP LCH Q24 PAYTN SHYRE HOBTT (RNAV)–STAR....	
	or	
	(TURBOJETS)(IAH WEST ATL EAST)MMUGS (RNAV)–DP LCH Q24 PAYTN SHYRE GNDLF (RNAV)–STAR....	
	or	
	(TURBOJETS)(IAH EAST ATL EAST)GUMBY (RNAV)–DP LCH Q24 PAYTN SHYRE GNDLF (RNAV)–STAR....	
AUSTIN(AUS)	(DME/DME/IRU OR GPS)(IAH EAST FLOW)PITZZ (RNAV)–DP MNURE WLEEE (RNAV)–STAR..........	
	or	
	(DME/DME/IRU OR GPS)(IAH WEST FLOW)BNDTO (RNAV)–DP MNURE WLEEE (RNAV)–STAR..........	
BALTIMORE(BWI)	(TURBOJETS)(IAH EAST FLOW)GUMBY (RNAV)–DP GUSTI Q22 CATLN Q56 KELLN Q58 PEETT THHMP RAVNN (RNAV)–STAR...	
	or	
	(TURBOJETS)(IAH WEST FLOW)MMUGS (RNAV)–DP GUSTI Q22 CATLN Q56 KELLN Q58 PEETT THHMP RAVNN (RNAV)–STAR...	
BIRMINGHAM(BHM)	STRYA (RNAV)–DP DPATY MEI LYMPH...................	
BOCA RATON(BCT)	(WATER/IAH LDG W)MMUGS (RNAV)–DP LLA LEV Y290 GAWKS VUUDU (RNAV)–STAR.............................	
	or	
	(WATER/IAH LDG E)GUMBY (RNAV)–DP LLA LEV Y290 GAWKS VUUDU (RNAV)–STAR.............................	
	or	
	(IAH WEST FLOW)MMUGS (RNAV)–DP GUSTI AWDAD SJI J2 DEFUN VUUDU (RNAV)–STAR...................	
	or	
	(IAH EAST FLOW)GUMBY (RNAV)–DP GUSTI AWDAD SJI J2 DEFUN VUUDU (RNAV)–STAR........................	
BOSTON(BOS)	(IAH EAST FLOW)GUMBY (RNAV)–DP GUSTI Q22 RBV Q419 JFK ROBUC (RNAV)–STAR	1100–0300
	or	
	(IAH WEST FLOW)MMUGS (RNAV)–DP GUSTI Q22 RBV Q419 JFK ROBUC (RNAV)–STAR	1100–0300
CHARLESTON(CHS)	(IAH EAST FLOW)GUMBY (RNAV)–DP GUSTI SJI J2 DEFUN CABLO ALLMA SAV BAGGY (RNAV)–STAR	
	or	
	(IAH WEST FLOW)MMUGS (RNAV)–DP GUSTI SJI J2 DEFUN CABLO ALLMA SAV BAGGY (RNAV)–STAR	
CHARLESTON(CRW)	LURIC (RNAV)–DP ORRTH CRAMM BNA SWAPP Q34 FOUNT HVQ..	
CHARLOTTE(CLT)	(TURBOJETS)(IAH EAST FLOW)GUMBY (RNAV)–DP GUSTI Q22 CATLN BESTT JONZE (RNAV)–STAR ..	1400–0100
	or	
	(TURBOJETS)(IAH WEST FLOW)MMUGS (RNAV)–DP GUSTI Q22 CATLN BESTT JONZE (RNAV)–STAR ..	1400–0100
CHICAGO(MDW)	(DME/DME/IRU OR GPS)INDIE (RNAV)–DP TPAKK LIT J101 SPI POOGY ENDEE (RNAV)–STAR...............	
CHICAGO(ORD)	STYCK (RNAV)–DP WATSN BYP MLC RZC SGF WELTS TRTLL (RNAV)–STAR	
	or	
	(DME/DME/IRU OR GPS)INDIE (RNAV)–DP TPAKK LIT J101 STL TRTLL (RNAV)–STAR	
	or	
	(DME/DME/IRU OR GPS)INDIE (RNAV)–DP TPAKK LIT J180 FTZ TRTLL (RNAV)–STAR	
CLEVELAND METRO(CLE,CGF,BKL,LNN,LPR)	(RNAV TURBOJET)INDIE (RNAV)–DP TPAKK LIT J131 PXV DRUGA ROKNN (RNAV)–STAR....................	
COLORADO SPRINGS(COS)	(TURBOJETS – DME/DME/IRU OR GPS)STYCK (RNAV)–DP DOLEY ADM MMB LBL LAA OZZZY (RNAV)–STAR..	

SC, 25 JAN 2024 to 21 MAR 2024

PREFERRED IFR ROUTES

501

Terminals	Route	Effective Times (UTC)
COLUMBIA(CAE)	(DME/DME/IRU OR GPS)(IAH WEST FLOW)MMUGS (RNAV)–DP GUSTI Q22 CATLN MGMRY THRSR IRQ CAE	
	or	
	(IAH EAST FLOW)GUMBY (RNAV)–DP GUSTI Q22 CATLN MGMRY THRSR IRQ CAE	
COLUMBUS(CMH)	INDIE (RNAV)–DP TPAKK LIT J131 PXV GETTA JAKTZ (RNAV)–STAR	
COVINGTON(CVG)	(DME/DME/IRU OR GPS)INDIE (RNAV)–DP TPAKK LIT J131 PXV SARGO (RNAV)–STAR	
DALLAS(DAL)	(RNAV TURBOJET)(DAL SOUTH FLOW)WYLSN (RNAV)–DP MAJKK REDDN (RNAV)–STAR	
	or	
	(RNAV TURBOJET)(DAL NORTH FLOW)WYLSN (RNAV)–DP MAJKK MNNDO (RNAV)–STAR	
	or	
	(ALL OTHERS)GIFFA YEAGR–STAR	
DALLAS–FORT WORTH(DFW)	(ALL OTHERS)CRIED CEDAR CREEK–STAR	
	or	
	(RNAV TURBOJET)(DFW SOUTH FLOW)BLTWY (RNAV)–DP CRIED BEREE (RNAV)–STAR	
	or	
	(RNAV TURBOJET)(DFW NORTH FLOW)BLTWY (RNAV)–DP CRIED WHINY (RNAV)–STAR	
	or	
	(NON–TURBOJET (RNAV))BLTWY (RNAV)–DP CRIED CEDAR CREEK–STAR	
DENVER(DEN)	STYCK (RNAV)–DP DOLEY ADM ROLLS LBL HALEN NIIXX (RNAV)–STAR	
DES MOINES(DSM)	(DME/DME/IRU OR GPS)STYCK (RNAV)–DP WTSON BYP TUL J25 DSM	
DETROIT(DTW)	(DME/DME/IRU OR GPS REQUIRED)(DTW SOUTH FLOW)INDIE (RNAV)–DP TPAKK LIT J131 PXV WWODD HANBL (RNAV)–STAR	
	or	
	(DME/DME/IRU OR GPS REQUIRED)(DTW NORTH FLOW)INDIE (RNAV)–DP TPAKK LIT J131 PXV WWODD LECTR (RNAV)–STAR	
FAYETTEVILLE/SPRINGDALE/ROGERS(XNA)	(DME/DME/IRU OR GPS)INDIE (RNAV)–DP INDIE PGO RZC	
FORT LAUDERDALE(FLL)	(IAH EAST FLOW)GUMBY (RNAV)–DP GUSTI AWDAD SJI J2 DEFUN TEEKY (RNAV)–STAR	
	or	
	(WATER/IAH LDG W)MMUGS (RNAV)–DP LLA LEV Y290 OCHHO VNECK TEEKY (RNAV)–STAR	
	or	
	(IAH WEST FLOW)MMUGS (RNAV)–DP GUSTI AWDAD SJI J2 DEFUN TEEKY (RNAV)–STAR	
	or	
	(WATER/IAH LDG E)GUMBY (RNAV)–DP LLA LEV Y290 OCHHO VNECK TEEKY (RNAV)–STAR	
FORT MYERS(RSW)	(TURBOJETS)(IAH EAST FLOW)GUMBY (RNAV)–DP LLA LEV Y290 BAGGS TYNEE (RNAV)–STAR	
	or	
	(IAH EAST FLOW)GUMBY (RNAV)–DP GUSTI AWDAD SJI J2 DEFUN CABLO BULZI Q81 NICKI PLYER TYNEE (RNAV)–STAR	
	or	
	(TURBOJETS)(IAH WEST FLOW)MMUGS (RNAV)–DP LLA LEV Y290 BAGGS TYNEE (RNAV)–STAR	
	or	
	(IAH WEST FLOW)MMUGS (RNAV)–DP GUSTI AWDAD SJI J2 DEFUN CABLO BULZI Q81 NICKI PLYER TYNEE (RNAV)–STAR	
GRAND RAPIDS(GRR)	(DME/DME/IRU OR GPS)INDIE (RNAV)–DP TPAKK LIT J101 STL J19 RBS OXI ELX VIO	

SC, 25 JAN 2024 to 21 MAR 2024

PREFERRED IFR ROUTES

Terminals	Route	Effective Times (UTC)
GREER(GSP)	(IAH WEST FLOW)MMUGS (RNAV)–DP GUSTI Q22 CATLN MGM BESTT WORXS (RNAV)–STAR .... or (IAH EAST FLOW)GUMBY (RNAV)–DP GUSTI Q22 CATLN MGM BESTT WORXS (RNAV)–STAR	
INDIANAPOLIS(IND)	(TURBOJETS)INDIE (RNAV)–DP TPAKK LIT J131 PXV TERGE SMUKE (RNAV)–STAR............................	
JACKSONVILLE(JAX)	(IAH EAST FLOW)GUMBY (RNAV)–DP GUSTI SJI J2 DEFUN CABLO CAPPS MARQO (RNAV)–STAR...... or (IAH WEST FLOW)MMUGS (RNAV)–DP GUSTI SJI J2 DEFUN CABLO CAPPS MARQO (RNAV)–STAR......	
KANSAS CITY(MCI)	(RNAV TURBOJET/TURBOPROP)STYCK (RNAV)–DP WTSON BYP TUL STASN WUTNG (RNAV)–STAR..	
KNOXVILLE(TYS)	(DME/DME/IRU OR GPS)(IAH WEST FLOW)MMUGS (RNAV)–DP LCH MEI VUZ VXV............................ or (DME/DME/IRU OR GPS)STRYA (RNAV)–DP DPATY MEI VUZ VXV .... or (DME/DME/IRU OR GPS)(IAH EAST FLOW)GUMBY (RNAV)–DP LCH MEI VUZ VXV............................	
LAS VEGAS(LAS)	(IAH WEST FLOW)BNDTO (RNAV)–DP CRGER ELP J86 INW HAHAA RKSTR (RNAV)–STAR .... or (IAH EAST FLOW)PITZZ (RNAV)–DP CRGER ELP J86 INW HAHAA RKSTR (RNAV)–STAR............................	
LEXINGTON(LEX)	(DME/DME/IRU OR GPS)LURIC (RNAV)–DP ORRTH CRAMM BNA UNCKL	
LOS ANGELES(LAX)	(DME/DME/IRU OR GPS)(IAH EAST FLOW)PITZZ (RNAV)–DP CRGER ELP J50 SSO J4 TNP SEAVU–STAR or (DME/DME/IRU OR GPS)(IAH WEST FLOW)BNDTO (RNAV)–DP CRGER ELP J50 SSO J4 TNP SEAVU–STAR	
LOUISVILLE(SDF)	(TURBOJET)INDIE (RNAV)–DP TPAKK LIT J131 PXV ALENN DAMEN (RNAV)–STAR............................	
MEMPHIS(MEM)	(TURBOJETS – DME/DME/IRU OR GPS)LURIC (RNAV)–DP LURIC ELD HOBRK (RNAV)–STAR	
MIAMI(MIA)	(IAH EAST FLOW)GUMBY (RNAV)–DP GUSTI AWDAD SJI J2 DEFUN FROGZ (RNAV)–STAR .... or (WATER/IAH LDG E)GUMBY (RNAV)–DP LLA LEV Y290 GAWKS FROGZ (RNAV)–STAR .... or (IAH WEST FLOW)MMUGS (RNAV)–DP GUSTI AWDAD SJI J2 DEFUN FROGZ (RNAV)–STAR .... or (WATER/IAH LDG W)MMUGS (RNAV)–DP LLA LEV Y290 GAWKS FROGZ (RNAV)–STAR	
MILWAUKEE(MKE)	(DME/DME/IRU OR GPS)INDIE (RNAV)–DP LURIC LIT J101 JOT	
MINNEAPOLIS(MSP)	(TURBOJETS)STYCK (RNAV)–DP WTSON BYP TUL J25 MCI ROKKK NITZR (RNAV)–STAR	1000–0300
MQS,PHL,PNE,TTN	(TURBOJETS)(IAH EAST FLOW)GUMBY (RNAV)–DP GUSTI Q22 BEARI BBDOL PAATS (RNAV)–STAR .. or (TURBOJETS)(IAH WEST FLOW)MMUGS (RNAV)–DP GUSTI Q22 BEARI BBDOL PAATS (RNAV)–STAR ..	
NASHVILLE(BNA)	(TURBOJETS – DME/DME/IRU OR GPS)LURIC (RNAV)–DP HAWES SUTTN J29 MEM CHSNE (RNAV)–STAR...	
NEW ORLEANS(MSY)	(DME/DME/IRU OR GPS)(IAH WEST FLOW)MMUGS (RNAV)–DP GUSTI AWDAD AWDAD–STAR .... or (DME/DME/IRU OR GPS)(IAH EAST FLOW)GUMBY (RNAV)–DP GUSTI AWDAD AWDAD–STAR	

PREFERRED IFR ROUTES

Terminals	Route	Effective Times (UTC)
NEW YORK(JFK)	(IAH WEST FLOW)MMUGS (RNAV)–DP GUSTI Q22 CATLN Q64 SAWED Q97 DLAAY RADDS SIE CAMRN–STAR	
	or	
	(IAH EAST FLOW)GUMBY (RNAV)–DP GUSTI Q22 CATLN Q64 SAWED Q97 DLAAY RADDS SIE CAMRN–STAR	
NEW YORK(LGA)	(IAH EAST FLOW)GUMBY (RNAV)–DP GUSTI Q22 BURGG Q60 HURTS HUBBS PXT KORRY–STAR…	
	or	
	(IAH WEST FLOW)MMUGS (RNAV)–DP GUSTI Q22 BURGG Q60 HURTS HUBBS PXT KORRY–STAR…	
NEWARK(EWR)	(TURBOJETS)(IAH EAST FLOW)GUMBY (RNAV)–DP GUSTI Q22 UMBRE QUART PHLBO (RNAV)–STAR	
	or	
	(TURBOJETS)(IAH WEST FLOW)MMUGS (RNAV)–DP GUSTI Q22 UMBRE QUART PHLBO (RNAV)–STAR	
NORFOLK(ORF)	(IAH WEST FLOW)MMUGS (RNAV)–DP GUSTI Q22 CATLN Q64 HRTWL Q54 NUTZE DRONE DRONE–STAR	
	or	
	(IAH EAST FLOW)GUMBY (RNAV)–DP GUSTI Q22 CATLN Q64 HRTWL Q54 NUTZE DRONE DRONE–STAR ..	
OAKLAND(OAK)	(TURBOJET)(WEST FLOW)BNDTO (RNAV)–DP CRGER ELP J86 BLD J92 BTY RUSME OAKES (RNAV)–STAR	
	or	
	(TURBOJET)(EAST FLOW)PITZZ (RNAV)–DP CRGER ELP J86 BLD J92 BTY RUSME OAKES (RNAV)–STAR ..	
OKLAHOMA CITY(OKC)	(DME/DME/IRU OR GPS)STYCK (RNAV)–DP DOLEY ADM DECKK IRW	
OMAHA(OMA)	(DME/DME/IRU OR GPS)STYCK (RNAV)–DP WTSON BYP HTHWY TIMMO (RNAV)–STAR	
ONTARIO(ONT)	(DME/DME/IRU OR GPS)(IAH WEST FLOW)BNDTO (RNAV)–DP CRGER ELP SSO J4 BXK J212 PSP SETER–STAR	
	or	
	(DME/DME/IRU OR GPS)(IAH EAST FLOW)PITZZ (RNAV)–DP CRGER ELP SSO J4 BXK J212 PSP SETER–STAR	
ORLANDO(MCO)	(IAH EAST FLOW)GUMBY (RNAV)–DP LLA LEV Y280 CHRGE PRICY (RNAV)–STAR	
	or	
	(IAH EAST FLOW)GUMBY (RNAV)–DP GUSTI AWDAD SJI J2 DEFUN GRNCH (RNAV)–STAR	
	or	
	(WATER/IAH WEST FLOW)MMUGS (RNAV)–DP LLA LEV Y280 CHRGE PRICY (RNAV)–STAR	
	or	
	(IAH WEST FLOW)MMUGS (RNAV)–DP GUSTI AWDAD SJI J2 DEFUN GRNCH (RNAV)–STAR	
PENSACOLA(PNS)	(DME/DME/IRU OR GPS)(IAH WEST FLOW)MMUGS (RNAV)–DP GUSTI SJI V241 PENSI	
	or	
	(DME/DME/IUR OR GPS)(IAH EAST FLOW)GUMBY (RNAV)–DP GUSTI SJI V241 PENSI	
PITTSBURGH(PIT)	(DME/DME/IRU OR GPS REQUIRED)INDIE (RNAV)–DP TPAKK LIT J131 PXV ROD BSV JESEY (RNAV)–STAR	
PORTLAND(PDX)	(DME/DME/IRU OR GPS)(IAH EAST FLOW)PITZZ (RNAV)–DP CRGER LOWGO J15 IMB JOTBA HHOOD (RNAV)–STAR	
	or	
	(TURBOJETS)STYCK (RNAV)–DP DOLEY FUZ HNKER ALS JNC J15 IMB JOTBA HHOOD (RNAV)–STAR	
	or	
	(DME/DME/IRU OR GPS)(IAH WEST FLOW)BNDTO (RNAV)–DP CRGER LOWGO J15 IMB JOTBA HHOOD (RNAV)–STAR	

SC, 25 JAN 2024 to 21 MAR 2024

PREFERRED IFR ROUTES

Terminals	Route	Effective Times (UTC)
RALEIGH/DURHAM(RDU)	(IAH WEST FLOW)MMUGS (RNAV)–DP GUSTI Q22 CATLN MGMRY THRSR IRQ PYRES DMSTR (RNAV)–STAR	
	or	
	(IAH EAST FLOW)GUMBY (RNAV)–DP GUSTI Q22 CATLN MGMRY THRSR IRQ PYRES DMSTR (RNAV)–STAR	
RICHMOND(RIC)	(TURBOJETS & TURBOPROPS)(IAH EAST FLOW)GUMBY (RNAV)–DP GUSTI Q22 BURGG Q60 JAXSN KELCE DUCXS (RNAV)–STAR	
	or	
	(TURBOJETS & TURBOPROPS)(IAH WEST FLOW)MMUGS (RNAV)–DP GUSTI Q22 BURGG Q60 JAXSN KELCE DUCXS (RNAV)–STAR	
SALT LAKE CITY(SLC)	(TURBOJETS – DME/DME/IRU OR GPS)(IAH WEST FLOW)BNDTO (RNAV)–DP CRGER JCT J15 JNC HELPR LEEHY (RNAV)–STAR	
	or	
	(TURBOJETS – DME/DME/IRU OR GPS)(IAH EAST FLOW)PITZZ (RNAV)–DP CRGER JCT J15 JNC HELPR LEEHY (RNAV)–STAR	
SAN ANTONIO(SAT)	(NON–ADVANCED NAV ONLY)INDUSTRY–DP IDU MARCS–STAR	
	or	
	(IAH WEST FLOW)BNDTO (RNAV)–DP WAILN BRAUN (RNAV)–STAR	
	or	
	(IAH EAST FLOW)PITZZ (RNAV)–DP WAILN BRAUN (RNAV)–STAR	
SAN DIEGO(SAN)	(DME/DME/IRU OR GPS)(IAH WEST FLOW)BNDTO (RNAV)–DP CRGER ELP J2 HOGGZ LUCKI (RNAV)–STAR	
	or	
	(DME/DME/IRU OR GPS)(IAH EAST FLOW)PITZZ (RNAV)–DP CRGER ELP J2 HOGGZ LUCKI (RNAV)–STAR	
SAN FRANCISCO(SFO)	(DME/DME/IRU OR GPS)(IAH WEST FLOW)BNDTO (RNAV)–DP CRGER ELP J86 BLD J92 OAL	
	or	
	(DME/DME/IRU OR GPS)(IAH EAST FLOW)PITZZ (RNAV)–DP CRGER ELP J86 BLD J92 OAL	
SAN JOSE(SJC)	(TURBOJET)(EAST FLOW)PITZZ (RNAV)–DP CRGER ELP Q4 BOILE MAKRS TROXX SILCN (RNAV)–STAR	
	or	
	(TURBOJET)(WEST FLOW)BNDTO (RNAV)–DP CRGER ELP Q4 BOILE MAKRS TROXX SILCN (RNAV)–STAR	
SANTA ANA(SNA)	(DME/DME/IRU OR GPS)(IAH EAST FLOW)PITZZ (RNAV)–DP CRGER ELP J50 TFD J212 PSP KAYOH–STAR	
	or	
	(DME/DME/IRU OR GPS)(IAH WEST FLOW)BNDTO (RNAV)–DP CRGER ELP J50 TFD J212 PSP KAYOH–STAR	
SAVANNAH(SAV)	(DME/DME/IRU OR GPS)(IAH EAST FLOW)GUMBY (RNAV)–DP GUSTI SJI J2 CEW ALLMA JANIE	
	or	
	(DME/DME/IRU OR GPS)(IAH WEST FLOW)MMUGS (RNAV)–DP GUSTI SJI J2 CEW ALLMA JANIE	
SEATTLE(SEA)	(TURBOJETS)STYCK (RNAV)–DP DOLEY ADM ROLLS LBL LAA J52 FQF J20 PDT CHINS–STAR	
ST LOUIS(STL)	(TURBOJETS – DME/DME/IRU OR GPS)INDIE (RNAV)–DP TPAKK LIT ARG BOOSH (RNAV)–STAR	

PREFERRED IFR ROUTES

Terminals	Route	Effective Times (UTC)
TAMPA(TPA)	(TURBOJETS)(IAH EAST FLOW)GUMBY (RNAV)–DP GUSTI AWDAD SJI J2 DEFUN MAATY (RNAV)–STAR	
	or	
	(TURBOJETS)(IAH WEST FLOW)MMUGS (RNAV)–DP GUSTI AWDAD SJI J2 DEFUN MAATY (RNAV)–STAR	
	or	
	(IAH EAST FLOW)GUMBY (RNAV)–DP LLA LEV Y280 CHRGE RAYZZ (RNAV)–STAR	
	or	
	(IAH WEST FLOW)MMUGS (RNAV)–DP LLA LEV Y280 CHRGE RAYZZ (RNAV)–STAR	
TUCSON(TUS)	(DME/DME/IRU OR GPS)(IAH EAST FLOW)PITZZ (RNAV)–DP CRGER ELP ZONNA (RNAV)–STAR	
	or	
	(DME/DME/IRU OR GPS)(IAH WEST FLOW)BNDTO (RNAV)–DP CRGER ELP ZONNA (RNAV)–STAR	
TULSA(TUL)	(DME/DME/IRU OR GPS)STYCK (RNAV)–DP WTSON BYP TUL	
WASHINGTON(DCA)	(TURBOJETS)(IAH EAST FLOW)GUMBY (RNAV)–DP GUSTI Q22 CATLN Q56 KIWII WAVES CAPSS (RNAV)–STAR	
	or	
	(TURBOJETS)(IAH WEST FLOW)MMUGS (RNAV)–DP GUSTI Q22 CATLN Q56 KIWII WAVES CAPSS (RNAV)–STAR	
WASHINGTON(IAD)	(TURBOJETS)(IAH WEST FLOW)MMUGS (RNAV)–DP GUSTI Q22 BURGG Q60 JAXSN DORRN CAVLR (RNAV)–STAR	
	or	
	(TURBOJETS)(IAH EAST FLOW)GUMBY (RNAV)–DP GUSTI Q22 BURGG Q60 JAXSN DORRN CAVLR (RNAV)–STAR	
WEST PALM BEACH(PBI)	(WATER/IAH LDG W)MMUGS (RNAV)–DP LLA LEV Y290 GAWKS VUUDU (RNAV)–STAR	
	or	
	(IAH EAST FLOW)GUMBY (RNAV)–DP GUSTI AWDAD SJI J2 DEFUN VUUDU (RNAV)–STAR	
	or	
	(WATER/IAH LDG E)GUMBY (RNAV)–DP LLA LEV Y290 GAWKS VUUDU (RNAV)–STAR	
	or	
	(IAH WEST FLOW)MMUGS (RNAV)–DP GUSTI AWDAD SJI J2 DEFUN VUUDU (RNAV)–STAR	
WICHITA(ICT)	(DME/DME/IRU OR GPS)STYCK (RNAV)–DP DOLEY ADM IRW HUSKA	
WINDSOR LOCKS(BDL)	(IAH WEST FLOW)MMUGS (RNAV)–DP GUSTI Q22 RBV Q419 DPK DEER PARK–STAR	
	or	
	(IAH EAST FLOW)GUMBY (RNAV)–DP GUSTI Q22 RBV Q419 DPK DEER PARK–STAR	
JACKSON(JAN)		
HOUSTON(HOU)	(TURBOJETS – DME/DME/IRU OR GPS)AEX WAPPL (RNAV)–STAR	
	or	
	(NON–TURBOJETS – DME/DME/IRU OR GPS)AEX CESAN CESAN (RNAV)–STAR	
HOUSTON(IAH)	(NON–TURBOJETS – DME/DME/IRU OR GPS)AEX GESNR (RNAV)–STAR	
	or	
	(TURBOJETS–DME/DME/IRU OR GPS)(IAH EAST FLOW)AEX SKNRD (RNAV)–STAR	
	or	
	(TURBOJETS–DME/DME/IRU OR GPS)(IAH WEST FLOW)AEX DOOBI (RNAV)–STAR	
LITTLE ROCK(LIT)		
HOUSTON(HOU)	(NON–TURBOJETS–DME/DME/IRU OR GPS)J180 SWB CESAN CESAN (RNAV)–STAR	
	or	
	(TURBOJETS–DME/DME/IRU OR GPS)J180 SWB WAPPL (RNAV)–STAR	

SC, 25 JAN 2024 to 21 MAR 2024

PREFERRED IFR ROUTES

506

Terminals	Route	Effective Times (UTC)
HOUSTON(IAH)	(TURBOJETS, TURBOPROPS)(IAH WEST FLOW)LIT J180 SWB ZEEKK (RNAV)–STAR	
	or	
	(TURBOJETS, TURBOPROPS)(IAH EAST FLOW)LIT J180 SWB GESNR (RNAV)–STAR	
NEW ORLEANS METRO(MSY,NEW)		
47N,CDW,LDJ,MMU,SMQ,TEB	CATLN Q22 UMBRE SWNGR JAIKE (RNAV)–STAR ..	
BOSTON(BOS)	CATLN Q22 RBV Q419 JFK ROBUC (RNAV)–STAR ..	
CHICAGO(ORD).................................	(TURBOJETS – RNAV 1)(ORD EAST FLOW)SQS FTZ SHAIN (RNAV)–STAR	
	or	
	(TURBOJETS (RNAV 1))(ORD WEST FLOW)SQS FTZ TRTLL (RNAV)–STAR	
COVINGTON(CVG)	(DME/DME/IRU OR GPS)J35 MEM J29 PXV SARGO (RNAV)–STAR...	
DALLAS–FORT WORTH(DFW)	(RNAV TURBOJET)(DFW NORTH FLOW)AEX PNUTS WHINY (RNAV)–STAR	
	or	
	(ALL OTHERS)AEX CEDAR CREEK–STAR................	
	or	
	(RNAV TURBOJET)(DFW SOUTH FLOW)AEX PNUTS BEREE (RNAV)–STAR	
DENVER(DEN)	J58 FUZ J21 ADM ROLLS LBL HALEN NIIXX (RNAV)–STAR...	
DETROIT(DTW)	(DME/DME/IRU OR GPS REQUIRED)(DTW NORTH FLOW)MCB J35 MEM J29 PXV WWODD LECTR (RNAV)–STAR...	
	or	
	(DME/DME/IRU OR GPS REQUIRED)(DTW SOUTH FLOW)MCB J35 MEM J29 PXV WWODD HANBL (RNAV)–STAR...	
HOUSTON(HOU)	(TURBOJETS – DME/DME/IRU OR GPS)(HOU EAST FLOW)KCEEE BAYYY (RNAV)–STAR	
	or	
	(TURBOJETS – DME/DME/IRU OR GPS)(HOU WEST FLOW)KCEEE PUCKS (RNAV)–STAR	
	or	
	(TURBOPROPS – DME/DME/IRU OR GPS)BBURT TKNIQ (RNAV)–STAR...	
HOUSTON(IAH).................................	(TURBOJETS & TURBOPROPS – NON–ADVANCED NAV ONLY)JEPEG GILCO–STAR	
	or	
	(TURBOJETS & TURBOPROPS – DME/DME/IRU OR GPS)(IAH EAST FLOW)JEPEG NNCEE (RNAV)–STAR	
MQS,PHL,PNE,TTN	(TURBOJETS – DME/DME/IRU OR GPS)CATLN Q22 BEARI BBDOL PAATS (RNAV)–STAR	
NEW YORK(JFK)	CATLN Q64 SAWED Q97 DLAAY RADDS SIE CAMRN–STAR...	
NEWARK(EWR)	(TURBOJETS – DME/DME/IRU OR GPS)CATLN Q22 UMBRE QUART PHLBO (RNAV)–STAR	
TAMPA(TPA).....................................	REDFN Y280 CHRGE RAYZZ (RNAV)–STAR	
WASHINGTON(DCA)...........................	CATLN Q56 KIWII WAVES CAPSS (RNAV)–STAR	
WASHINGTON(IAD)	CATLN Q22 BURGG Q60 JAXSN DORRN CAVLR (RNAV)–STAR...	
WINDSOR LOCKS(BDL)	CATLN Q22 RBV Q419 DPK DEER PARK–STAR	
NEW ORLEANS(MSY)		
ATLANTA(ATL)..................................	(TURBOJETS)(ATL EAST OPERATION)PAYTN SHYRE GNDLF (RNAV)–STAR	
	or	
	(TURBOJETS)(ATL WEST OPERATION)PAYTN SHYRE HOBTT (RNAV)–STAR	
AUSTIN(AUS)	(DME/DME/IRU OR GPS)LCH WEEED WLEEE (RNAV)–STAR...	
BALTIMORE(BWI)	(TURBOJETS)CATLN Q56 KELLN Q58 PEETT THHMP RAVNN RAVNN (RNAV)–STAR............................	
CHARLOTTE(CLT)	(TURBOJETS)CATLN BESTT JONZE (RNAV)–STAR ...	1400–0100
CLEVELAND(CLE)..............................	(RNAV TURBOJET)LBY MERDN HITMN Q139 IIU ROKNN (RNAV)–STAR...	

SC, 25 JAN 2024 to 21 MAR 2024

PREFERRED IFR ROUTES

507

Terminals	Route	Effective Times (UTC)
FORT LAUDERDALE(FLL)	CEW J2 DEFUN TEEKY (RNAV)–STAR .... or (WATER)BLVNS Y290 OCHHO VNECK TEEKY (RNAV)–STAR	
HOUSTON(IAH)	(TURBOJETS & TURBOPROPS – DME/DME/IRU OR GPS)(IAH WEST FLOW)JEPEG LINKK (RNAV)–STAR	
LOUISVILLE(SDF)	MCB J35 MEM BNA MBELL MBELL (RNAV)–STAR ..	
MIAMI(MIA)	CEW J2 DEFUN FROGZ (RNAV)–STAR .... or (WATER)BLVNS Y290 GAWKS FROGZ (RNAV)–STAR	
NEW YORK(LGA)	CATLN Q22 BURGG Q60 HURTS HUBBS PXT KORRY–STAR	
ORLANDO(MCO)	(WATER)REDFN Y280 CHRGE PRICY (RNAV)–STAR or CEW J2 DEFUN GRNCH (RNAV)–STAR	
SAN ANTONIO(SAT)	LCH IAH BRAUN (RNAV)–STAR .... or LCH IAH IDU MARCS–STAR	
TAMPA(TPA)	CEW J2 DEFUN MAATY (RNAV)–STAR	
OKLAHOMA CITY(OKC)		
CHICAGO(MDW)	TUL SGF MAGOO MOTIF–STAR .... or TRUPR (RNAV)–DP TRUPR WELTS MAGOO ENDEE (RNAV)–STAR	
CHICAGO(ORD)	(TURBOJET)TUL EOS WELTS BRADFORD–STAR...... or (TURBOJET)TRUPR (RNAV)–DP TRUPR TUL EOS WELTS SHAIN (RNAV)–STAR .... or (TURBOJET)TRUPR (RNAV)–DP TRUPR TUL EOS WELTS TRTLL (RNAV)–STAR	
HOUSTON(HOU)	(NON–TURBOJETS)CVE ELLVR BLUBELL–STAR ...... or (TURBOJETS – DME/DME/IRU OR GPS)CVE ELLVR NNEAL KIDDZ (RNAV)–STAR	
HOUSTON(IAH)	(TURBOJETS, TUBOPROPS)(IAH WEST FLOW)CVE DRLLR (RNAV)–STAR .... or (TURBOJETS, TUBOPROPS)(IAH EAST FLOW)CVE GUSHR (RNAV)–STAR	
SAN ANTONIO(SAT)		
47N,CDW,LDJ,MMU,SMQ,TEB.............	CHURN Q56 CATLN Q22 UMBRE SWNGR JAIKE (RNAV)–STAR	
ATLANTA(ATL)	(TURBOJETS)(ATL EAST OPERATION)CHURN Q24 PAYTN SHYRE GNDLF (RNAV)–STAR .... or (TURBOJETS)(ATL WEST OPERATION)CHURN Q24 PAYTN SHYRE HOBTT (RNAV)–STAR	
BALTIMORE(BWI)..............................	CHURN Q56 KELLN Q58 PEETT THHMP RAVNN (RNAV)–STAR .... or (PART 121 AND 129 ONLY)CHURN Q56 BLUMS IAH J101 LFK SUTTN J29 CARIN MEMFS Q34 NEALS BKW RAVNN (RNAV)–STAR	
BOSTON(BOS)..................................	CHURN Q56 BLUMS IAH J101 LFK SUTTN J29 CARIN MEMFS Q34 RBV Q419 JFK ROBUC (RNAV)–STAR or CHURN Q56 CATLN Q22 RBV Q419 JFK ROBUC (RNAV)–STAR	
DENVER(DEN)	ALAMO–DP HENLY ABI J17 PNH ZIGEE NIIXX (RNAV)–STAR	
DETROIT(DTW)	(DTW NORTH FLOW)CHURN Q56 BLUMS IAH J29 PXV WWODD LECTR (RNAV)–STAR............................ or (DTW SOUTH FLOW)CHURN Q56 BLUMS IAH J29 PXV WWODD HANBL (RNAV)–STAR............................	
HOUSTON(HOU)	(TURBOJETS)CHURN Q56 WEMAR BELLR BELLR (RNAV)–STAR	

SC, 25 JAN 2024 to 21 MAR 2024

PREFERRED IFR ROUTES

Effective Times (UTC)

Terminals	Route
HOUSTON(IAH)	(TURBOJETS)(IAH WEST FLOW)CHURN Q56 WEMAR GMANN TEJAS (RNAV)–STAR
	or
	(TURBOJETS)(IAH EAST FLOW)CHURN Q56 WEMAR GMANN HTOWN (RNAV)–STAR
MQS,PHL,PNE,TTN	CHURN Q56 CATLN Q22 BEARI BBDOL PAATS (RNAV)–STAR
NEW YORK(JFK)	CHURN Q56 CATLN Q64 SAWED Q97 DLAAY RADDS SIE CAMRN–STAR
	or
	CHURN WEMAR BLUMS IAH J101 LFK MEM J29 PXV ROD KLYNE Q29 JHW J70 LVZ LENDY–STAR
NEW YORK(LGA)	CHURN Q56 BLUMS IAH J101 LFK SUTTN J29 CARIN MEMFS Q34 GVE KORRY–STAR
	or
	CHURN Q56 CATLN Q22 BURGG Q60 HURTS HUBBS PXT KORRY–STAR
NEWARK METRO(CDW,MMU,TEB)	CHURN Q56 BLUMS IAH J101 LFK SUTTN J29 CARIN MEMFS Q34 GVE JAIKE (RNAV)–STAR
NEWARK(EWR)	CHURN Q56 BLUMS IAH J101 LFK SUTTN J29 CARIN MEMFS Q34 GVE PHLBO (RNAV)–STAR
	or
	Q56 CATLN Q22 UMBRE QUART PHLBO (RNAV)–STAR
PHILADELPHIA(PHL)	CHURN Q56 BLUMS IAH J101 LFK SUTTN J29 CARIN MEMFS Q34 GVE PAATS (RNAV)–STAR
WASHINGTON(DCA)	CHURN Q56 BLUMS IAH J101 LFK SUTTN J29 CARIN MEMFS Q34 NEALS BKW TRUPS (RNAV)–STAR
	or
	CHURN Q56 KIWII WAVES CAPSS (RNAV)–STAR
WASHINGTON(IAD)	CHURN Q56 CATLN Q22 BURGG Q60 JAXSN DORRN CAVLR (RNAV)–STAR
	or
	CHURN Q56 BLUMS IAH J101 LFK SUTTN J29 CARIN MEMFS Q34 HITMN HVQ GIBBZ (RNAV)–STAR
TULSA(TUL)	
CHICAGO(MDW)	SGF MAGOO MOTIF–STAR
	or
	SGF MAGOO ENDEE (RNAV)–STAR
CHICAGO(ORD)	SGF WELTS TRTLL (RNAV)–STAR
	or
	SGF BAYLI BRADFORD–STAR
	or
	SGF WELTS SHAIN (RNAV)–STAR
HOUSTON(HOU)	(TURBOJETS – DME/DME/IRU OR GPS)OKM CVE ELLVR NNEAL KIDDZ (RNAV)–STAR
HOUSTON(IAH)	(TURBOJETS & TURBOPROPS – DME/DME/IRU OR GPS)(IAH EAST FLOW)OKM CVE GUSHR (RNAV)–STAR
	or
	(TURBOJETS & TURBOPROPS – DME/DME/IRU OR GPS)(IAH WEST FLOW)OKM CVE DRLLR (RNAV)–STAR

PREFERRED IFR ROUTES
SPECIAL HIGH ALTITUDE PREFERRED DIRECTION ROUTES

Terminals	Route	Effective Times (UTC)
TRAFFIC ENTERING ZHU VIA GULF OF MEXICO LANDING ORLANDO METRO AREA (TURBOJETS)		
NORTHBOUND	IRDOV M580 MINOW M215 SNOMN CIGAR PRICY (RNAV)–STAR	
NORTHBOUND	MYDIA M219 CULLY CIGAR PRICY (RNAV)–STAR....	
NORTHBOUND	PISAD M215 SNOMN CIGAR PRICY (RNAV)–STAR...	

HIGH ALTITUDE—PREFERRED DIRECTION ROUTES

Airway	Segment Fixes	Direction Effective	Effective Times (UTC)
J180	LITTLE ROCK, AR to HOUSTON, TX	SW BND	1200–0400
Q34	TEXARKANA, AR to ROBBINSVILLE, NJ	NE BND	1100–0300

TOWER ENROUTE CONTROL (TEC)
SOUTH CENTRAL TEXAS and LOUISIANA

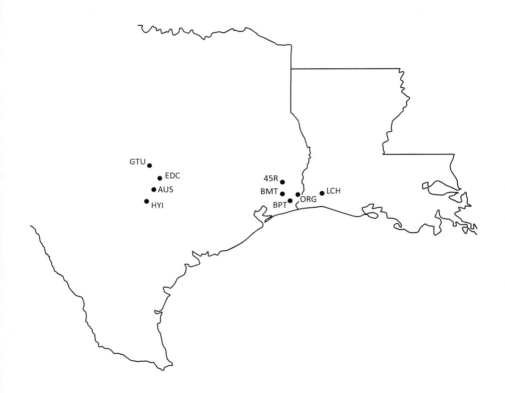

TOWER ENROUTE CONTROL (TEC)
FOR
SOUTH CENTRAL TEXAS AND LOUISIANA

Within the national airspace system it is possible for a pilot to fly IFR from one point to another without leaving approach control airspace. This is referred to as "Tower Enroute" which allows flight beneath the enroute structure. The tower enroute concept has been expanded (where practical) by reallocating airspace vertically/geographically to allow flight planning between city pairs while remaining within approach control airspace. Pilots are encouraged to use the TEC route descriptions provided in the South Central U.S. Chart Supplement when filing flight plans. Other airways which appear to be more direct between two points may take the aircraft out of approach control airspace thereby resulting in additional delays or other complications. All published TEC routes are designed to avoid enroute airspace and the majority are within radar coverage. The following items should be noted before using the graphics and route descriptions.

1. The graphic is not to be used for navigation nor detailed flight planning. Not all city pairs are depicted. It is intended to show geographic areas connected by tower enroute control. Pilots should refer to route descriptions for specific flight planning.

2. The route description contains three columns of information after geographic area listed in the heading, where the departure airport is located; i.e., the airport/airports of intended landing using FAA three letter/letter–two number identifiers, the specific route (airway, radial, etc.), the altitudes allowed for the routes.

3. The word "DIRECT" will appear as the route when radar vectors will be used or no airway exists. Also this indicates that a Standard Instrument Departure (SID) or Standard Terminal Arrival (STAR) may be applied by ATC.

4. Routes beginning and ending with an airway indicate that the airway essentially overflies the airport or radar vectors will be applied.

5. Although all airports are not listed under the destination column, IFR flight may be planned to satellite airports in the proximity of major airports via the same routing.

6. The altitudes shown are to be used for the route. This allows for separation of various arrival routes, departure routes, and overflights to, from, and over all airports in the Houston area.

TOWER ENROUTE CONTROL

FROM: AUS

TO:	ROUTE	ALTITUDE
45R	TNV V306 DAS	050 OR 070
BMT	TNV V306 DAS	050 OR 070
BPT	TNV V306 DAS	050 OR 070
LCH	TNV V306 DAS	050 OR 070
ORG	TNV V306 DAS	050 OR 070

FROM: EDC

TO:	ROUTE	ALTITUDE
45R	TNV V306 DAS	050 OR 070
BMT	TNV V306 DAS	050 OR 070
BPT	TNV V306 DAS	050 OR 070
LCH	TNV V306 DAS	050 OR 070
ORG	TNV V306 DAS	050 OR 070

FROM: GTU

TO:	ROUTE	ALTITUDE
45R	CLL T254 LCH	050 OR 070
BMT	CLL T254 LCH	050 OR 070
BPT	CLL T254 LCH	050 OR 070
LCH	CLL T254 LCH	050 OR 070
ORG	CLL T254 LCH	050 OR 070

FROM: HYI

TO:	ROUTE	ALTITUDE
45R	WEMAR T466 SBI	050 OR 070
BMT	WEMAR T466 SBI	050 OR 070
BPT	WEMAR T466 SBI	050 OR 070
LCH	WEMAR T466 SBI	050 OR 070
ORG	WEMAR T466 SBI	050 OR 070

MINIMUM OPERATIONAL NETWORK (MON) AIRPORT LISTING

STATE	CITY	AIRPORT NAME	LOCATION IDENTIFIER
AR	BENTON	SALINE COUNTY RGNL	SUZ
AR	JONESBORO	JONESBORO MUNI	JBR
AR	SPRINGDALE	SPRINGDALE MUNI	ASG
AR	TEXARKANA	TEXARKANA RGNL-WEBB FIELD	TXK
LA	BATON ROUGE	BATON ROUGE METROPOLITAN, RYAN FIELD	BTR
LA	LAKE CHARLES	LAKE CHARLES RGNL	LCH
LA	NEW ORLEANS	LOUIS ARMSTRONG NEW ORLEANS INTL	MSY
LA	SHREVEPORT	SHREVEPORT RGNL	SHV
MS	GREENWOOD	GREENWOOD-LEFLORE	GWO
MS	JACKSON	JACKSON-MEDGAR WILEY EVERS INTL	JAN
MS	MC COMB	MC COMB/PIKE COUNTY/JOHN E LEWIS FIELD	MCB
MS	TUNICA	TUNICA MUNI	UTA
OK	ARDMORE	ARDMORE MUNI	ADM
OK	HOBART	HOBART RGNL	HBR
OK	LAWTON	LAWTON-FORT SILL RGNL	LAW
OK	PONCA CITY	PONCA CITY RGNL	PNC
TX	BROWNWOOD	BROWNWOOD RGNL	BWD
TX	CORPUS CHRISTI	CORPUS CHRISTI INTL	CRP
TX	DALHART	DALHART MUNI	DHT
TX	GALVESTON	SCHOLES INTL	GLS
TX	LUBBOCK	LUBBOCK PRESTON SMITH INTL	LBB
TX	LUFKIN	ANGELINA COUNTY	LFK
TX	MARFA	MARFA MUNI	MRF
TX	MIDLAND	MIDLAND INTL AIR AND SPACE PORT	MAF
TX	MINERAL WELLS	MINERAL WELLS RGNL	MWL
TX	ROCKSPRINGS	EDWARDS COUNTY	ECU
TX	SAN ANTONIO	SAN ANTONIO INTL	SAT
TX	WACO	TSTC WACO	CNW

AIRPORT DIAGRAMS

In support of the Federal Aviation Administration's Runway Incursion Program, selected towered airport diagrams have been published in the Airport Diagram section of the Chart Supplement. Diagrams will be listed alphabetically by associated city and airport name. Airport diagrams, depicting runway and taxiway configurations, will assist both VFR and IFR pilots in ground taxi operations. The airport diagrams in this publication are the same as those published in the U.S. Terminal Procedures Publications. For additional airport diagram legend information see the U.S. Terminal Procedures Publication.

NOTE: Some text data published under the individual airport in the front portion of the Chart Supplement may be more current than the data published on the Airport Diagrams. The airport diagrams are updated only when significant changes occur.

PILOT CONTROLLED AIRPORT LIGHTING SYSTEMS

Available pilot controlled lighting (PCL) systems are indicated as follows:
1. Approach lighting systems that bear a system identification are symbolized using negative symbology, e.g., Ⓐ, Ⓥ, ✪.
2. Approach lighting systems that do not bear a system identification are indicated with a negative "Ⓛ" beside the name.
A star (★) indicates non-standard PCL, consult Chart Supplement, e.g., Ⓛ*
To activate lights, use frequency indicated in the communication section of the chart with a Ⓛ or the appropriate lighting system identification e.g., UNICOM 122.8 Ⓛ, Ⓐ, Ⓥ

KEY MIKE	FUNCTION
7 times within 5 seconds	Highest intensity available
5 times within 5 seconds	Medium or lower intensity (Lower REIL or REIL-off)
3 times within 5 seconds	Lowest intensity available (Lower REIL or REIL-off)

CHART CURRENCY INFORMATION

Date of Latest Revision   09365

The Date of Latest Revision identifies the Julian date the chart was added or last revised for any reason. The first two digits indicate the year, the last three digits indicate the day of the year (001 to 365/6) in which the latest revision of any kind has been made to the chart.

FAA Procedure ⎯⎯⎯⎯⎯⎯→ Orig 31DEC09 ←⎯⎯⎯⎯⎯⎯ Procedure Amendment
Amendment Number ⎯⎯⎯→ Amdt 2B 12MAR09 ←⎯⎯⎯ Effective Date

The FAA Procedure Amendment Number represents the most current amendment of a given procedure. The Procedure Amendment Effective Date represents the AIRAC cycle date on which the procedure amendment was incorporated into the chart. Updates to the amendment number & effective date represent procedural/criteria revisions to the charted procedure, e.g., course, fix, altitude, minima, etc.

NOTE: Inclusion of the "Procedure Amendment Effective Date" will be phased in as procedures are amended. As this occurs, the Julian date will be relocated to the upper right corner of the chart.

MISCELLANEOUS

★ Indicates a non-continuously operating facility, see Chart Supplement.
For Civil (FAA) instrument procedures, "RADAR REQUIRED" in the planview of the chart indicates that ATC radar must be available to assist the pilot when transitioning from the en route environment. "Radar required" in the pilot briefing portion of the chart indicates that ATC radar is required on portions of the procedure outside the final approach segment, including the missed approach. Some military procedures also have equipment requirements such as "Radar Required", but do not conform to the same charting application standards used by the FAA. Distances in nautical miles (except visibility in statute miles and Runway Visual Range in hundreds of feet). Runway Dimensions in feet. Elevations in feet. Mean Sea Level (MSL). Ceilings in feet above airport elevation. Radials/bearings/headings/courses are magnetic. Horizontal Datum: Unless otherwise noted on the chart, all coordinates are referenced to North American Datum 1983 (NAD 83), which for charting purposes is considered equivalent to World Geodetic System 1984 (WGS 84).

Terrain is scaled within the neat lines (planview boundaries) and does not accurately underlie not-to-scale distance depictions or symbols.

AIRPORT DIAGRAMS

515

24025
LEGEND
INSTRUMENT APPROACH PROCEDURES (CHARTS)

AIRPORT DIAGRAM/AIRPORT SKETCH

Runways

Hard Surface	Other Than Hard Surface	Stopways, Taxiways, Parking Areas	Metal Surface

Closed Runway	Closed Surface	Non-Movement	Under Construction	Water Runway

Helicopter Alighting Areas (H) ⊞ [H] ⚠ ⊞

Negative Symbols used to identify Copter Procedures landing point.................... ● ⊞ ▣ ▲ ⊞

NOTE:
Landmark features depicted on Copter Approach insets and sketches are provided for visual reference only.

Runway TDZ elevation.....................TDZE 123

ARRESTING GEAR: Specific arresting gear systems; e.g., BAK12, MA-1A etc., shown on airport diagrams, not applicable to Civil Pilots. Military Pilots refer to appropriate DOD publications.

Runway Slope........ ← 0.3% Down......0.8% UP →
(shown when rounded runway slope is ≥ 0.3%)

uni-directional   bi-directional   Jet Barrier

ARRESTING SYSTEM [   ] (EMAS)

NOTE:
Runway Slope measured to midpoint on runways 8000 feet or longer.

REFERENCE FEATURES

Displaced Threshold...........................
Hot Spot ....
Runway Holding Position Markings...........
Buildings..
Self-Serve Fuel ##............................
Tanks...
Obstructions.....................................
Airport Beacon #..............................
Runway Radar Reflectors......................
Bridges..
Control Tower #................................ TWR
                                  Unlit   Lit
Wind Cone.......................................
Landing Tee......................................
Tetrahedron.....................................

When Control Tower and Rotating Beacon are co-located, Beacon symbol will be used and further identified as TWR.

See appropriate Chart Supplement for information.

Runway Weight Bearing Capacity or Pavement Classification Number (PCN)/Pavement Classification Rating (PCR) is shown as a codified expression. Refer to the appropriate Supplement/Directory for applicable codes e.g., RWY 14-32 PCR 560 R/B/W/T; S-75, D-185, 2D-325, 2D/2D2-1120

U.S. Navy Optical Landing System (OLS) "OLS" location is shown because of its height of approximately 7 feet and proximity to edge of runway may create an obstruction for some types of aircraft.

Approach light symbols are shown in the Flight Information Handbook.

Airport diagram scales are variable.

True/magnetic North orientation may vary from diagram to diagram

Coordinate values are shown in 1 or ½ minute increments. They are further broken down into 6 second ticks, within each 1 minute increments.

Positional accuracy within ± 600 feet unless otherwise noted on the chart.

Runway length depicted is the physical length of the runway (end-to-end, including displaced thresholds if any) but excluding areas designated as stopways.

A [D] symbol is shown to indicate runway declared distance information available, see appropriate Chart Supplement for distance information.

NOTE:
All new and revised airport diagrams are shown referenced to the World Geodetic System (WGS) (noted on appropriate diagram), and may not be compatible with local coordinates published in DoD FLIP. (Foreign Only)

The airport sketch box includes the final approach course or final approach course extended.

HS 1   A5   FIELD ELEV 174   Displaced Threshold   Runway Identification   Visual Screen
        0.7% UP →
20   9000 X 200   ← 023.2°   1000 X 200   EMAS

Runway End Elevation   ELEV 164   Runway Dimensions (in feet)   Runway Heading (Magnetic)   Movement Area Dimensions (in feet)

SCOPE
Airport diagrams are specifically designed to assist in the movement of ground traffic at locations with complex runway/taxiway configurations. Airport diagrams are not intended to be used for approach and landing or departure operations. For revisions to Airport Diagrams: Consult FAA Order 7910.4.

LEGEND

SC, 25 JAN 2024 to 21 MAR 2024

AIRPORT DIAGRAMS
HOT SPOTS

An "Airport surface hot spot" is a location on an aerodrome movement area with a history or potential risk of collision or runway incursion, and where heightened attention by pilots/drivers is necessary.

A "hot spot" is a runway safety related problem area on an airport that presents increased risk during surface operations. Typically it is a complex or confusing taxiway/taxiway or taxiway/runway intersection. The area of increased risk has either a history of or potential for runway incursions or surface incidents, due to a variety of causes, such as but not limited to: airport layout, traffic flow, airport marking, signage and lighting, situational awareness, and training. Hot spots are depicted on airport diagrams as open circles or polygons designated as "HS 1", "HS 2", etc. and tabulated in the list below with a brief description of each hot spot. Hot spots will remain charted on airport diagrams until such time the increased risk has been reduced or eliminated.

CITY/AIRPORT	HOT SPOT	DESCRIPTION
ARKANSAS		
LITTLE ROCK		
BILL AND HILLARY CLINTON NTL/ADAMS FLD (LIT)	HS 1	Wrong Rwy Departure Risk – Rwy 36 and Rwy 04L thlds in close proximity and share single hold lines at both Twy A and Twy F. Ensure correct rwy alignment.
LOUISIANA		
BATON ROUGE		
BATON ROUGE METRO, RYAN FLD (BTR)	HS 1	Complex int Twy A, Twy B, Twy D and Twy K W of Rwy 13–31 and Rwy 04L–22R.
	HS 2	Rwy 04R–22L and Twy E in close proximity, pilots sometime confuse the runway as Twy E.
	HS 3	Acft taxiing fr Twy F, turning onto Twy E southbound, sometime crosses the Rwy 13–31 hold bar wo authorization.
	HS 4	Pilots exiting Rwy 13 onto Twy E sometimes exits onto Rwy 04R–22L wo authorization.
HOUMA		
HOUMA–TERREBONNE (HUM)	HS 1	Rwy Incursion Risk: Complex intersection Twy H, Twy E and Twy B east of Rwy 18–36 & Rwy 12–30.
	HS 2	Remain alert due to numerous copter ops
LAFAYETTE		
LAFAYETTE RGNL/PAUL FOURNET FLD (LFT)	HS 1	Twy D and Twy C may experience ramp congestion and a short taxi transition to Rwy 11. Be alert not to enter Rwy 11–29 without ATC approval. Acft on the Terminal Ramp, contact Ground Control prior to push back.
	HS 2	Twy F and Twy J extend across Rwy 11–29, and Twy B extends across Rwy 04L–22R, all in close proximity. Be alert for Rwy Holding Position Markings.
	HS 3	Twy F East of Rwy 04L has max weight restriction. Some acft exiting Rwy 22L at Twy H have entered Twy F instead of making the sharp right turn onto Twy J.
NEW ORLEANS		
LAKEFRONT (NEW)	HS 1	Rwy Incursion Risk at Twy F and Rwy 09–27 – Wide intersection.
	HS 2	Rwy Incursion Risk at Twy F and Rwy 27– Hold Line is at Apron exit on Twy F.
	HS 3	Rwy Incursion Risk at Twy B and Rwy 36L– Apron exit east of Rwy 36L is inside Hold Lines.
NEW ORLEANS		
LOUIS ARMSTRONG NEW ORLEANS INTL (MSY)	HS 1	Limited wingtip clearance on Twy G near Concourse Bravo due to acft pushbacks. Maint vigilance exiting Rwy 11/29 on Twy G8 and when taxing on Twy G. High Traffic area.
	HS 2	Green painted ovrn for Rwy 11–29 can be misinterpreted for Twy E when landing Rwy 02–20.
	HS 3	Rwy 11–29 and Twy G6, hi No of rwy crossings.
MISSISSIPPI		
COLUMBUS		
COLUMBUS AFB (CBM)	HS 1	Maint vigilance numerous twys in area of Rwy 13R.
	HS 2	Rwy incursion risk for Rwy 13R/31L, Twy M.
	HS 3	Rwy incursion risk for Rwy 13R/31L, Twy J, Twy E.

SC, 25 JAN 2024 to 21 MAR 2024

AIRPORT DIAGRAMS

CITY/AIRPORT	HOT SPOT	DESCRIPTION
OKLAHOMA		
ALTUS		
ALTUS AFB (LTS)	HS 1	Acft taxiing on Twy B between Spot 47 and Twy D.
NORMAN		
UNIVERSITY OF OKLAHOMA WESTHEIMER (OUN)	HS 1	Rwy 03-21 hold marking is in close proximity to the ramp.
	HS 2	Rwy 03-21 hold marking is in close proximity to the ramp.
	HS 3	Rwy 03-21 hold marking is a short taxi distance from Rwy 18-36.
	HS 4	Pilots taxiing westbound on Twy B risk incursion of Rwy 18-36 if they miss the turn to Twy C.
TEXAS		
AUSTIN		
AUSTIN–BERGSTROM INTL (AUS)	HS 1	Drivers northbound on E svc road may be unaware of acft from Rwy 36R exiting at Twy G and Twy H.
AUSTIN		
SAN MARCOS RGNL (HYI)	HS 1	Rwy incusion/wrong rwy departure risk. Ensure correct rwy alignment. Complex airfield geometry at rwy/rwy int.
	HS 2	Rwy incusion/wrong rwy depature risk. Ensure correct rwy alignment. Complex airfield geometry. Rwy thlds in close proximity.
BEAUMONT/PORT ARTHUR		
JACK BROOKS RGNL (BPT)	HS 1	South end of Twy B not visible from ctl twr.
COLLEGE STATION		
EASTERWOOD FLD (CLL)	HS 1	Rwy holding posn markings non typical lctn. Pilots sometime incorrectly cros the holding posn markings on Twy B when taxied to Rwy 11.
DALLAS		
ADDISON (ADS)	HS 1	Twy A and Rwy 16-34. Holding Position Markings have been moved back to the edge of Twy A.
	HS 2	Twy J and Rwy 16-34. Holding Position Markings have been moved back to the edge of Twy A.
	HS 3	Twy H and Rwy 16-34. Holding Position Markings have been moved back to the edge of Twy A.
	HS 4	Twy G and Rwy 16-34. Holding Position Markings have been moved back to the edge of Twy A.
	HS 5	Twy F and Rwy 16-34. Holding Position Markings have been moved back to the edge of Twy A.
	HS 6	Twy E and Rwy 16-34. Holding Position Markings have been moved back to the edge of Twy A.
	HS 7	Twy D and Rwy 16-34. Holding Position Markings have been moved back to the edge of Twy A.
	HS 8	Twy C and Rwy 16-34. Holding Position Markings have been moved back to the edge of Twy A.
	HS 9	Twy A and Rwy End 34. Holding Position Markings have been moved back to the edge of Twy A prior to turn off parallel twy.
DALLAS		
DALLAS LOVE FLD (DAL)	HS 1	Acft NW bound on Twy A sometimes cross relctd Rwy 13L hold short line.
EL PASO		
EL PASO INTL (ELP)	HS 1	Rwy 08R apch considered act, do not proceed on or cross wo ATC clnc especially when taxiing to Rwy 04 via the terminal ramp.
GEORGETOWN		
GEORGETOWN EXEC (GTU)	HS 1	Acft taxiing on Twy A should exp to giveway to acft exiting Rwy 18-36 at Twy J.
	HS 2	Acft taxiing on Twy A should exp to giveway to acft exiting Rwy 18-36 at Twy D.
HARLINGEN		
VALLEY INTL (HRL)	HS 1	Southeast corner of the airport and coincident thlds of Rwy 31 and Rwy 35R may cause confusion for departing acft.

AIRPORT DIAGRAMS

CITY/AIRPORT	HOT SPOT	DESCRIPTION
HOUSTON CONROE/NORTH HOUSTON RGNL (CXO)	HS 1	Twy F west of Twy D not visible from ctl twr.
HOUSTON DAVID WAYNE HOOKS MEML (DWH)	HS 1	Rwy Incursion Risk– Ramp accessible to inadequately trained drivers; inadequate signage leaving ramp.
	HS 2	Rwy Incursion Risk– Complex twy intersection near Rwy 17L.
	HS 3	Rwy Incursion Risk– Previous Incursions occuring Twy E at Rwy 17R–35L.
	HS 4	Rwy Incursion Risk – Int of Twy G and Rwy 17L–35R. Acft exiting Rwy 17R–35L at Twy G sometimes fail to turn onto Twy F and enter Rwy 17L–35R wo a clnc.
	HS 5	Rwy Incursion Risk – Int of Twy H and Rwy 17L–35R. Acft exiting Rwy 17R–35L at Twy H sometimes fail to turn onto Twy F and enter Rwy 17L–35R wo a clnc.
	HS 6	Rwy Incursion Risk – Incursions occuring on Twy K at Rwy 17L.
HOUSTON SUGAR LAND RGNL (SGR)	HS 1	Twy E int with Twy A and Twy A3 incr likelihood of conflicts btn acft due to short dist fr Rwy 17–35.
HOUSTON WILLIAM P HOBBY (HOU)	HS 1	Rwy Incursion Risk– Twy G at Rwy 13R: Numerous incursions, pilots inadvertently miss Hold Lines on Twy G at Rwy 13R.
	HS 2	Rwy Incursion Risk: Twy E crosses Rwy 13L in close proximity; Complex afld geometry along Twy E resulting in numerous incursions associated with pilots inadvertently crossing Hold–lines.
MC ALLEN MC ALLEN INTL (MFE)	HS 1	Rwy 14 hold short marking lctd on Twy A is perpendicular to Rwy 14.
MIDLAND MIDLAND INTL AIR AND SPACE PORT (MAF)	HS 1	Twy B and Twy P merge.
	HS 2	Area not visible from twr. Limited air tfc services provided.
NEW BRAUNFELS NEW BRAUNFELS NTL (BAZ)	HS 1	Wrong Rwy Departure Risk – Rwy 13 intersection Twy D and Rwy 17 threshold in close proximity. Ensure correct rwy alighnment. Rwy 13 and Rwy 17 share the same hold short line at Twy D.
SAN ANGELO SAN ANGELO RGNL/MATHIS FLD (SJT)	HS 1	Rwy 18–36 at the int of Rwy 09–27 is a hi energy areas where extra caution is nec dur rwy crossings.
	HS 2	Rwy 18–36 at the int of Twy D is a hi energy areas where extra caution is nec dur rwy crossings.
	HS 3	Rwy 03 Hold Short Line is a Hot Spot where acft are required to hold when req a Rwy 36 Departure and ops are being conducted on Rwy 03–21.

SC, 25 JAN 2024 to 21 MAR 2024

AIRPORT DIAGRAMS

CITY/AIRPORT	HOT SPOT	DESCRIPTION
SAN ANTONIO		
KELLY FLD (SKF)	HS 1	The unpaved portion of the north overrun.
	HS 2	Int of Rwy 16–34, Twy D, and Twy G.
SAN ANTONIO		
SAN ANTONIO INTL (SAT)	HS 1	Rwy 04 at Rwy 31L. Acft taxiing on Rwy 04 sometimes fail to hold short of Rwy 31L.
	HS 2	Twy G and Twy N in close proximity of Rwy 31L. Acft taxiing northbound on Twy N sometimes fail to make the turn onto Twy G and enter Rwy 31L without approval.
TYLER		
TYLER POUNDS RGNL (TYR)	HS 1	Rwy Incursion Risk: Complex int Twy K, Twy K2 leads to the approach end of 2 Rwy's, Rwy 18–36, and Rwy 13–31.
WICHITA FALLS		
SHEPPARD AFB/WICHITA FALLS MUNI (SPS)	HS 1	Rwy 18–36 and Twy E. High number of vehicle traffic and crossings.
	HS 2	Twy G and Rwy 15R–33L. High numbers of aircraft and vehicles crossing and entering runway.
	HS 3	Twy G and Rwy 15C–33C. High numbers of aircraft and vehicles crossing and entering runway.

SC, 25 JAN 2024 to 21 MAR 2024

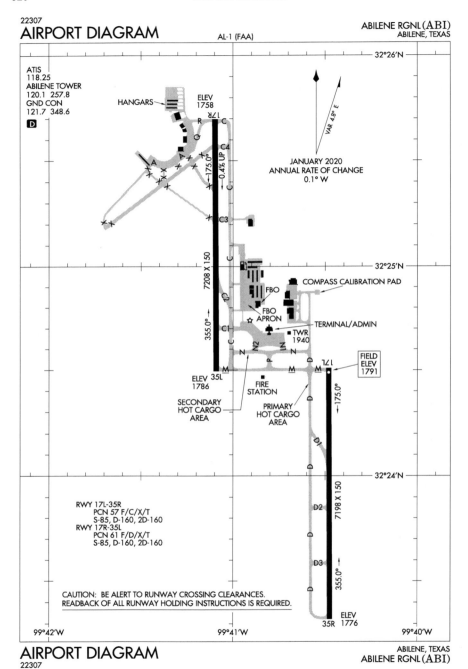

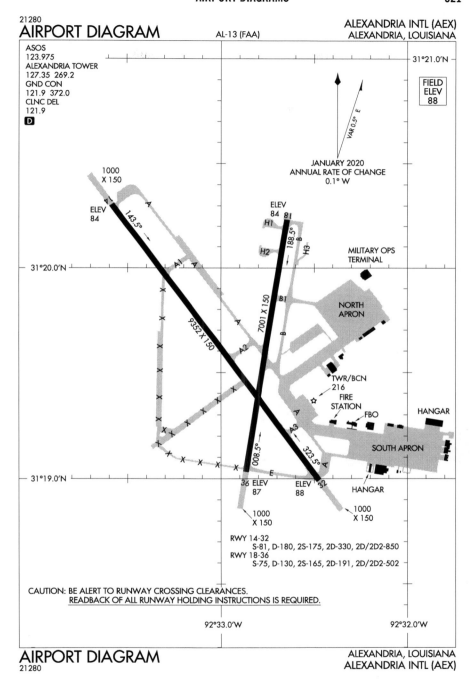

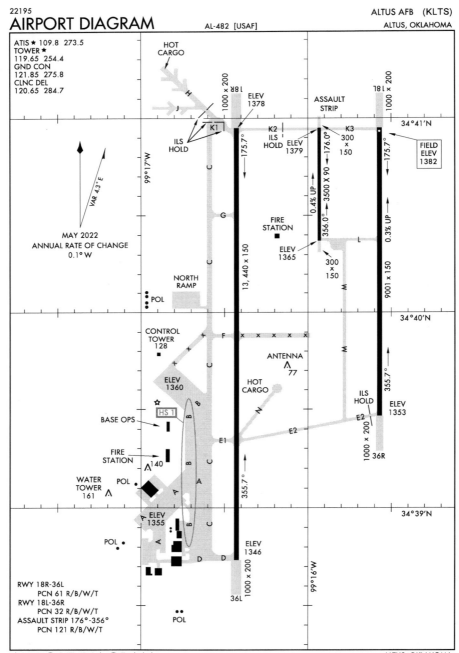

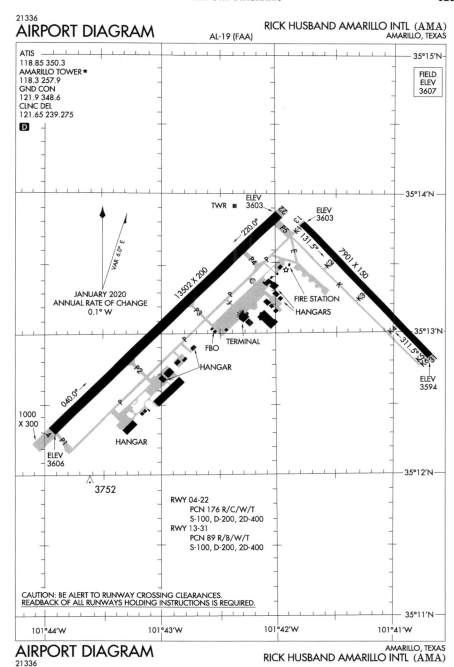

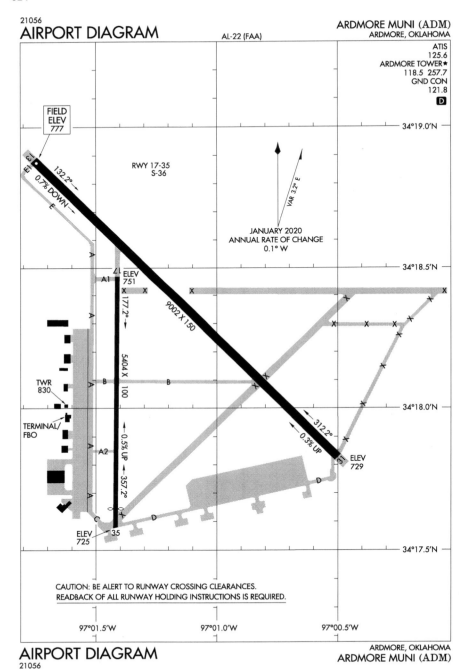

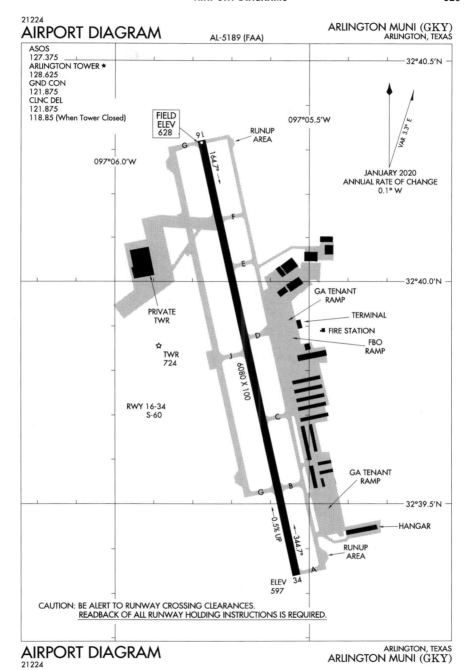

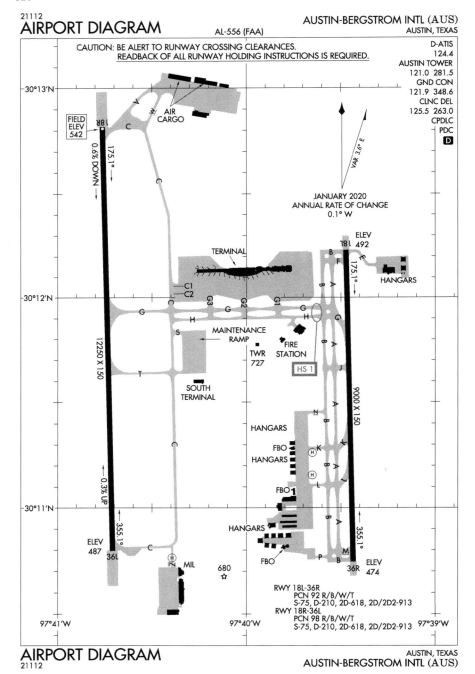

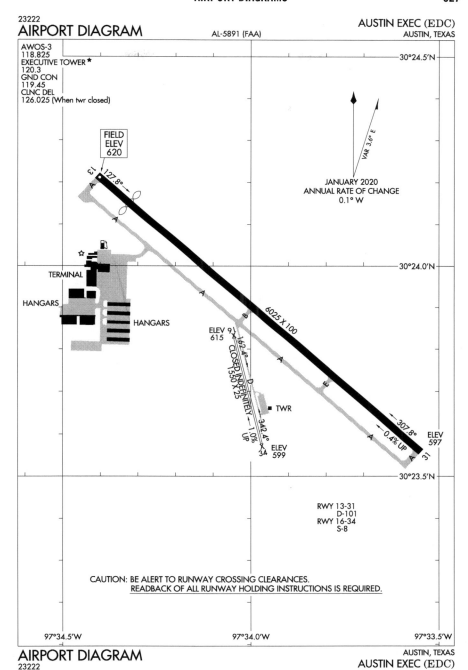

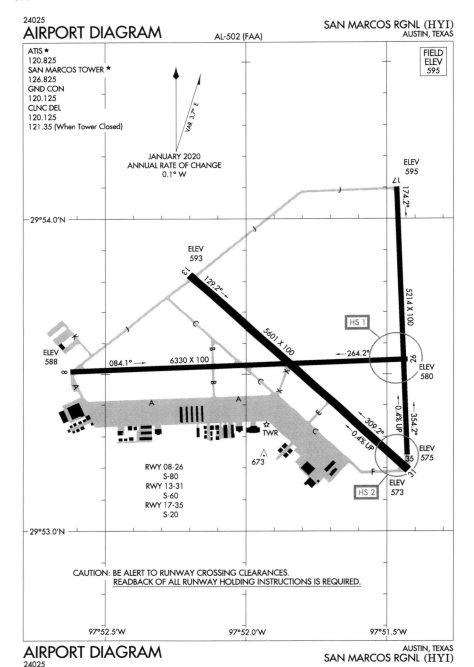

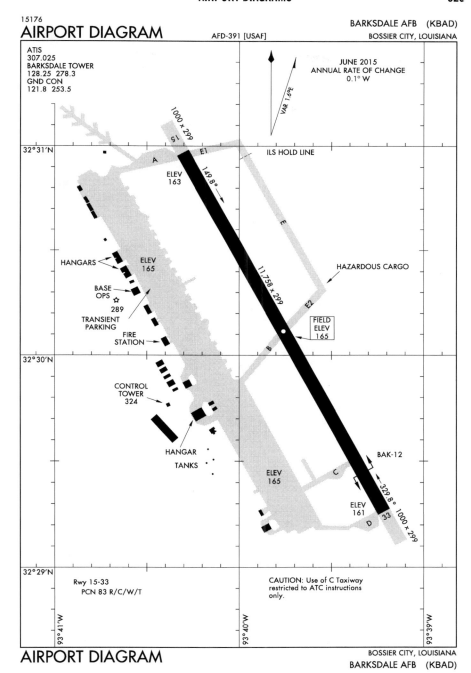

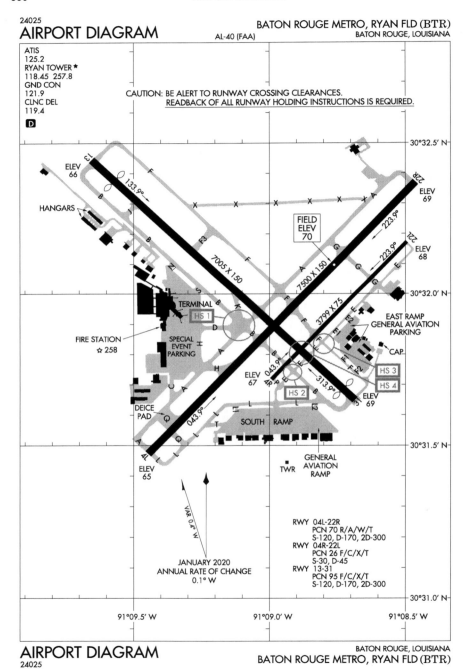

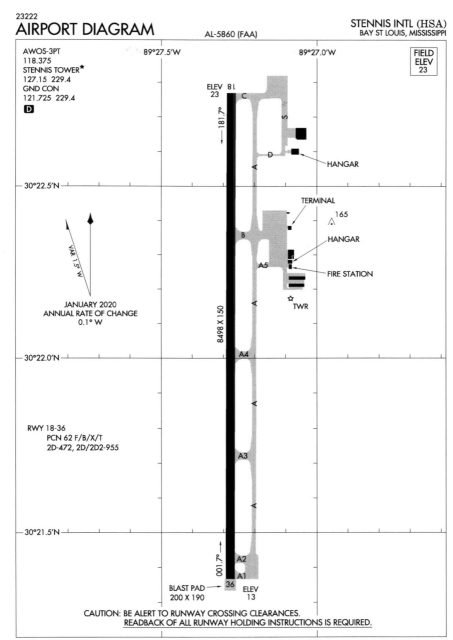

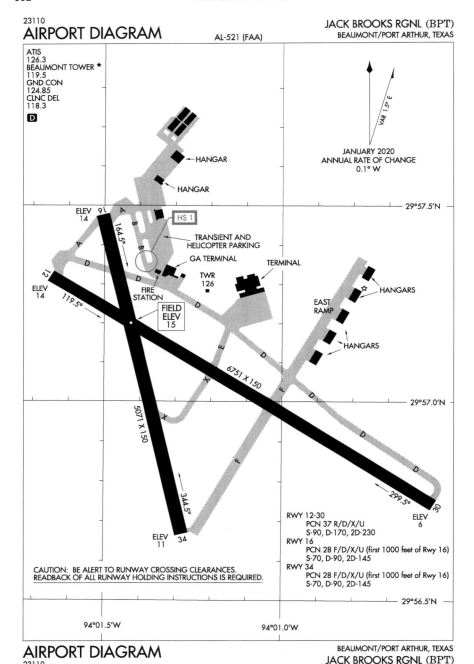

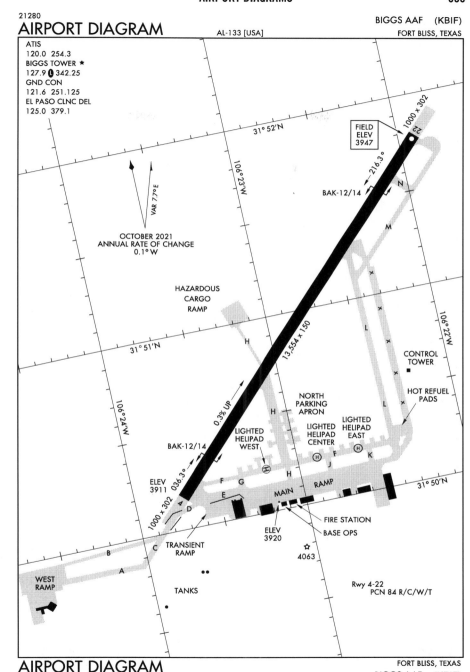

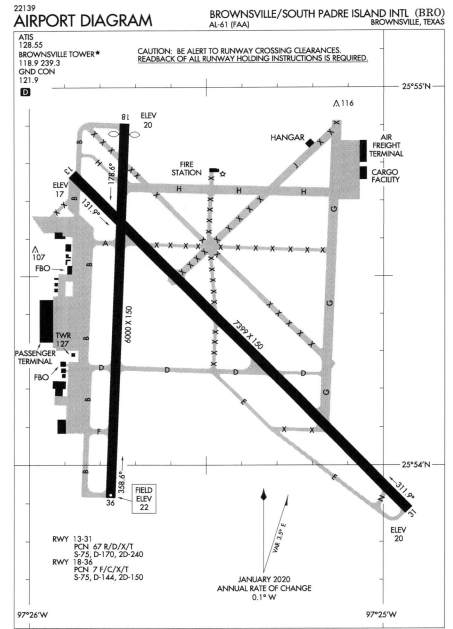

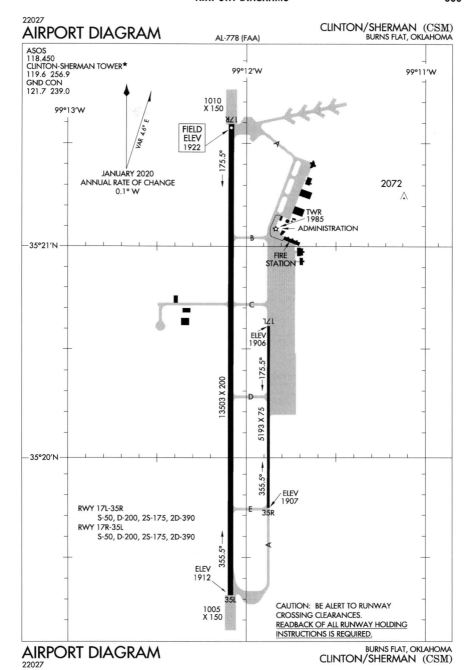

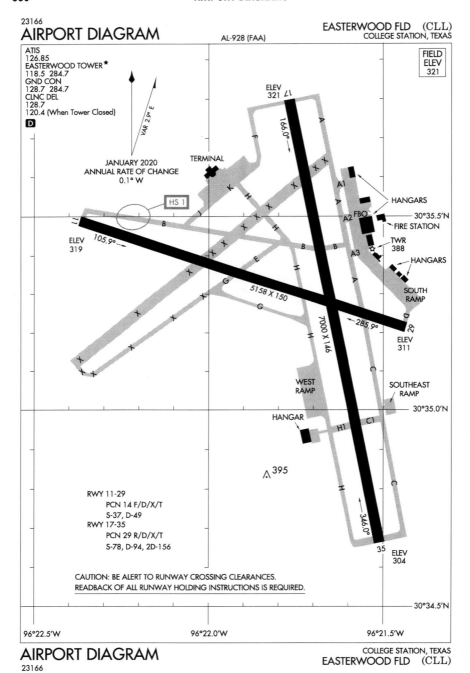

AIRPORT DIAGRAMS

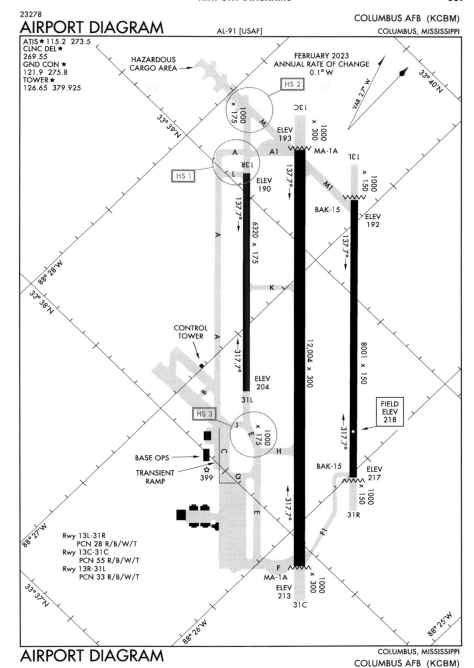

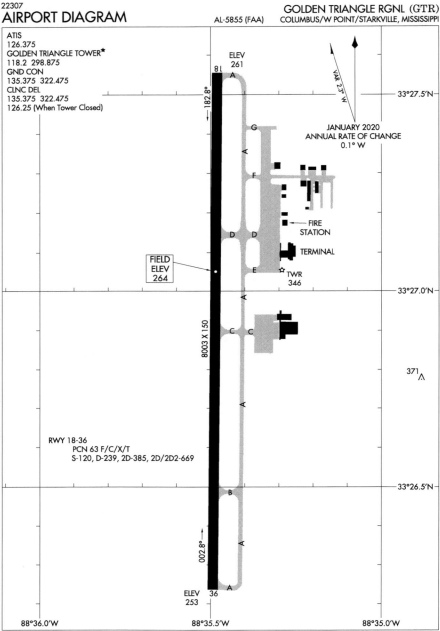

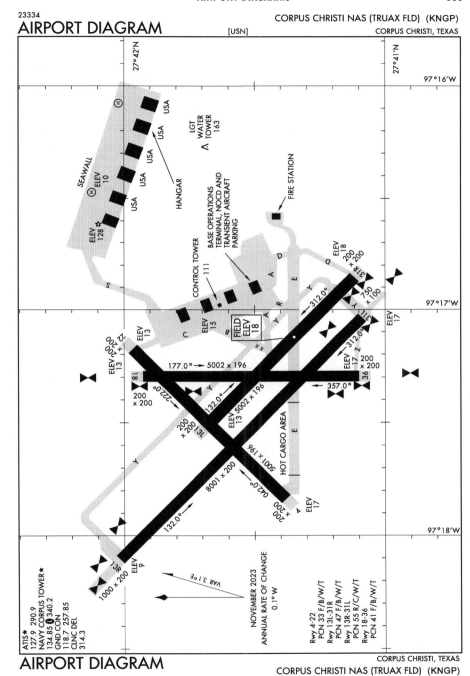

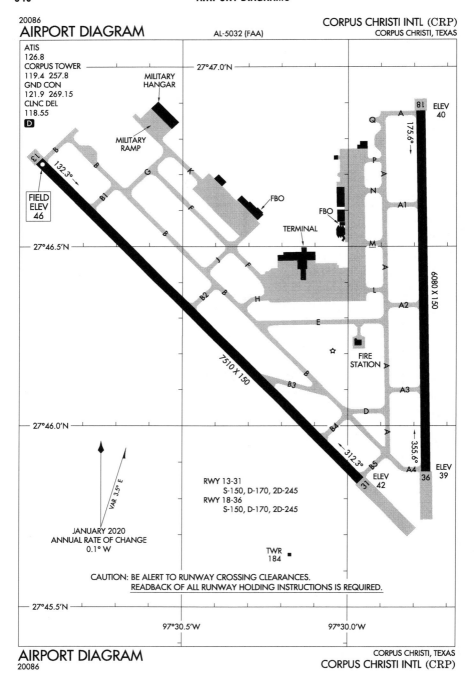

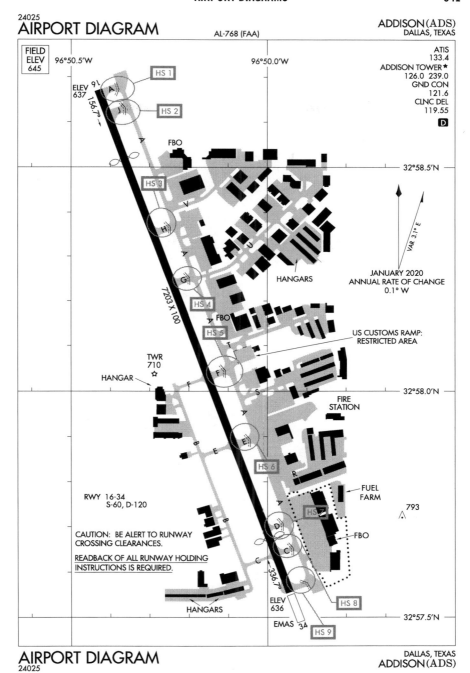

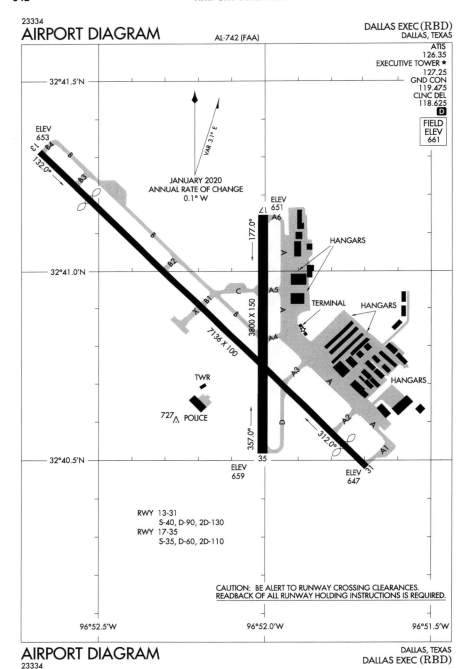

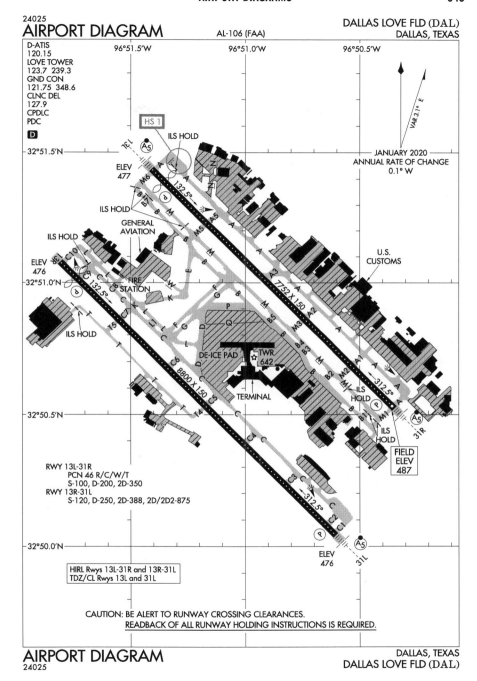

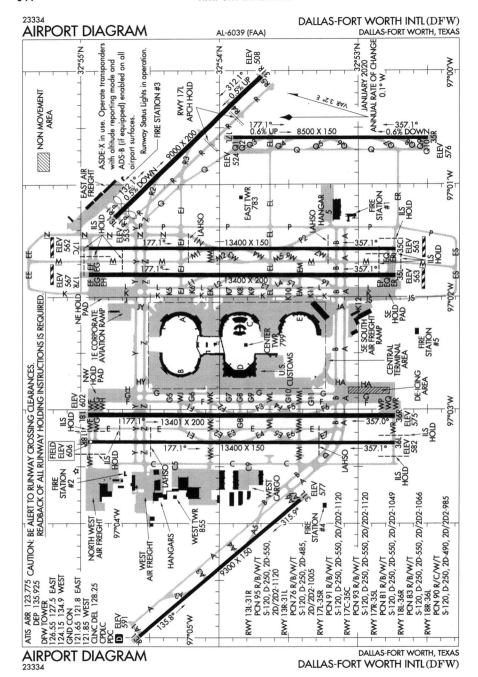

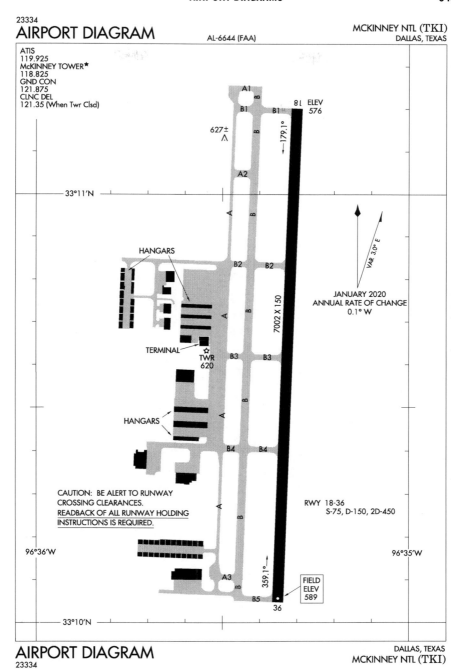

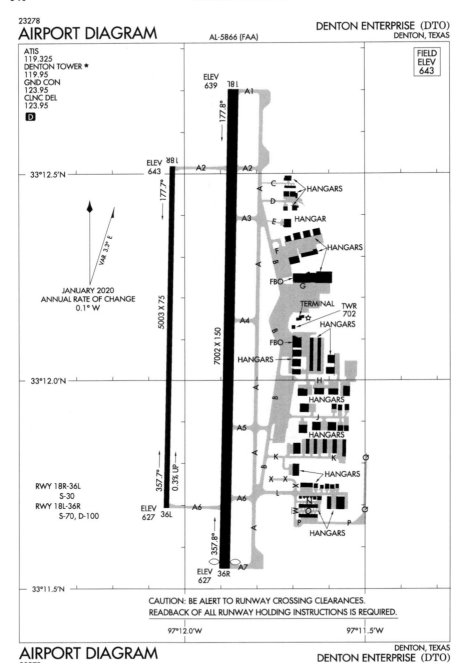

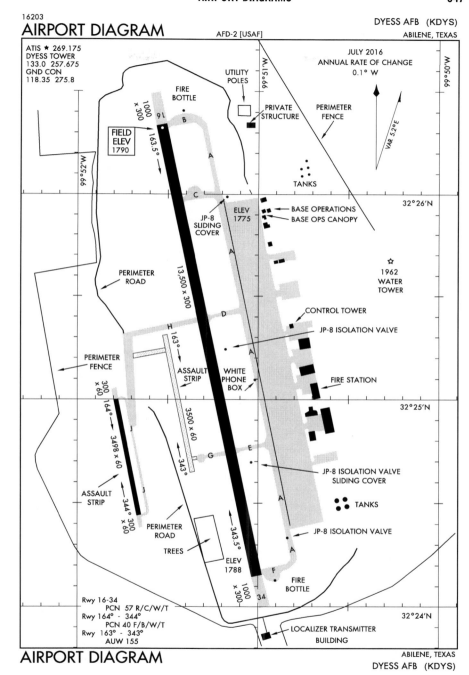

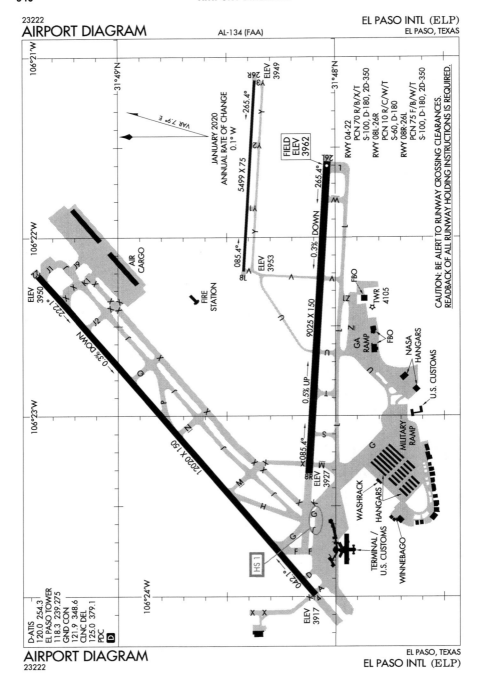

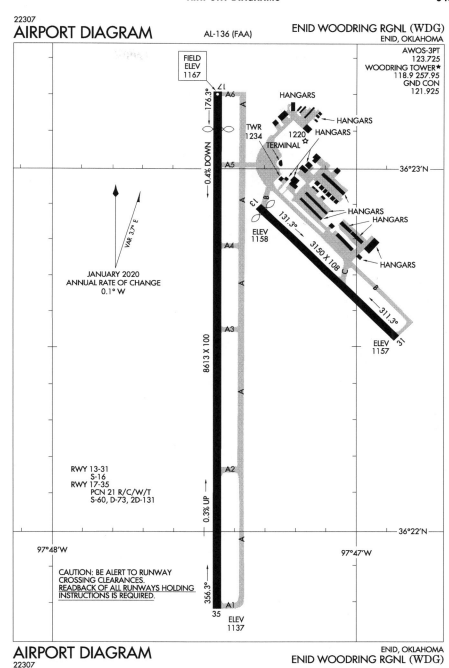

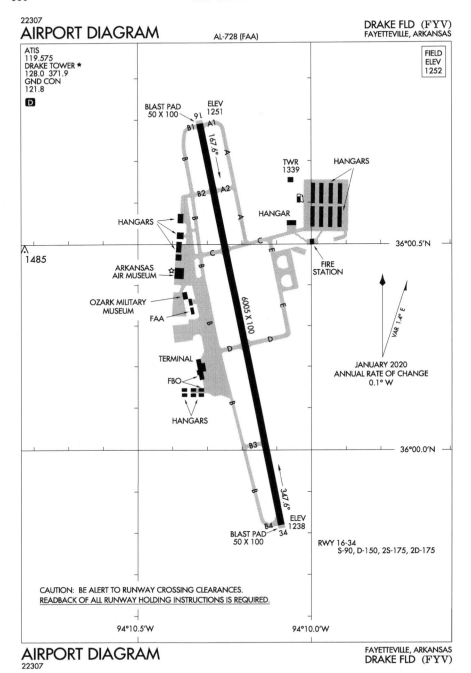

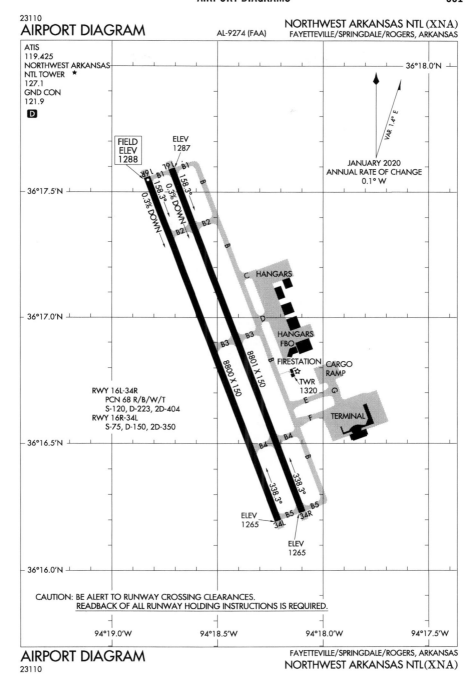

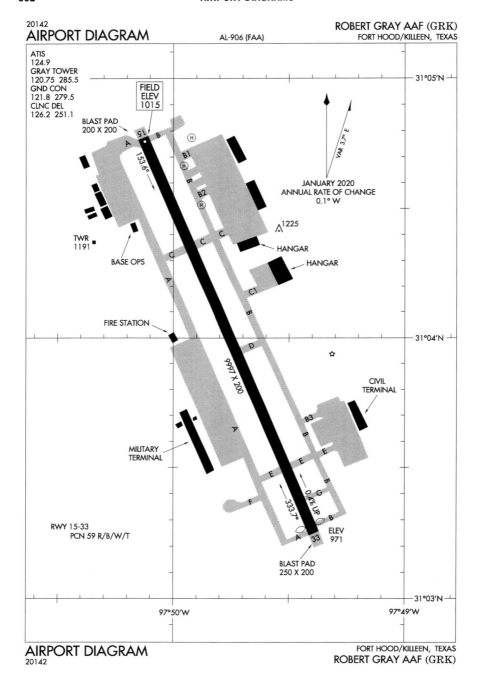

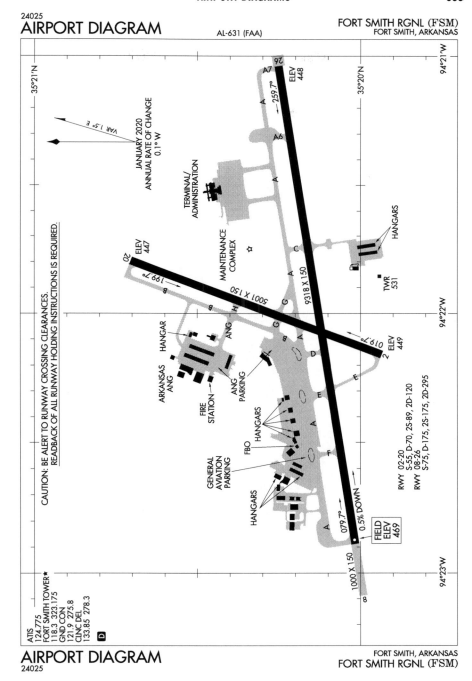

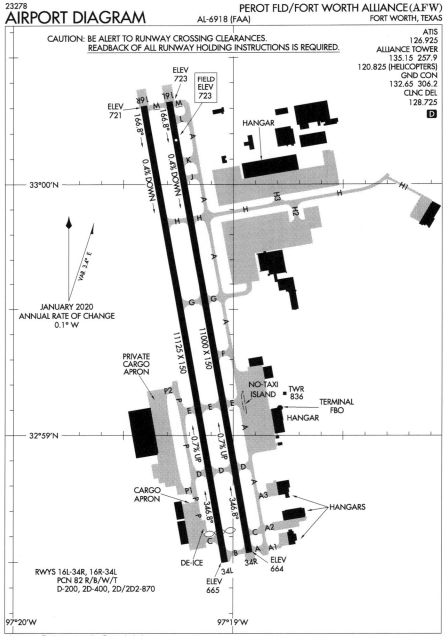

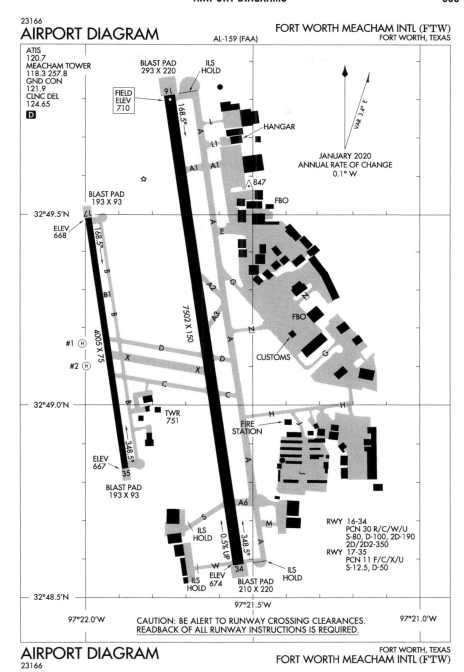

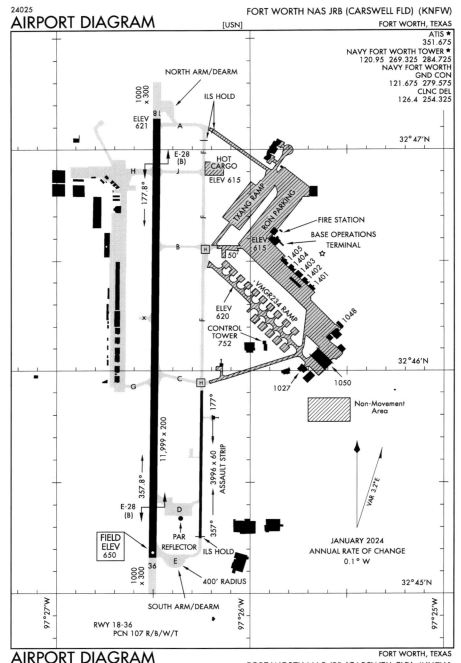

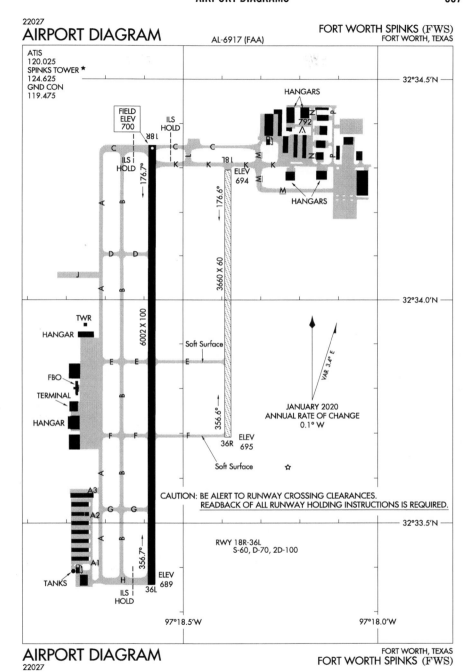

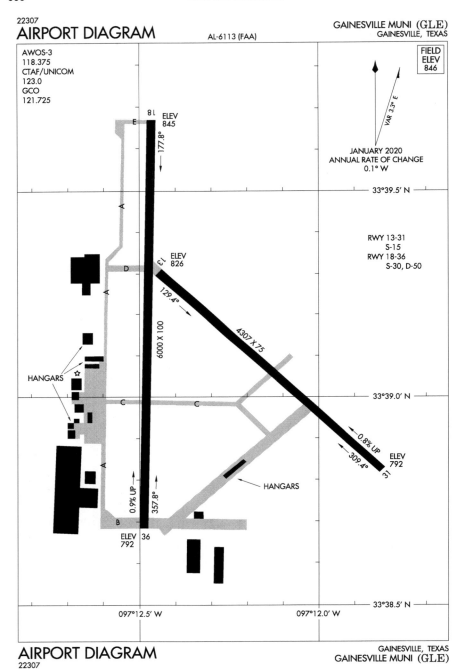

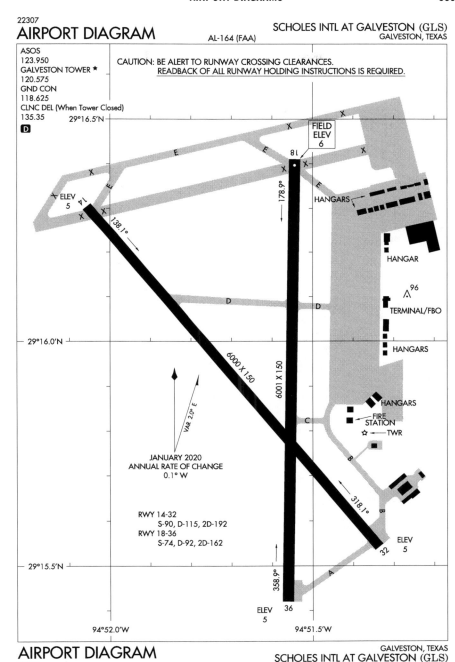

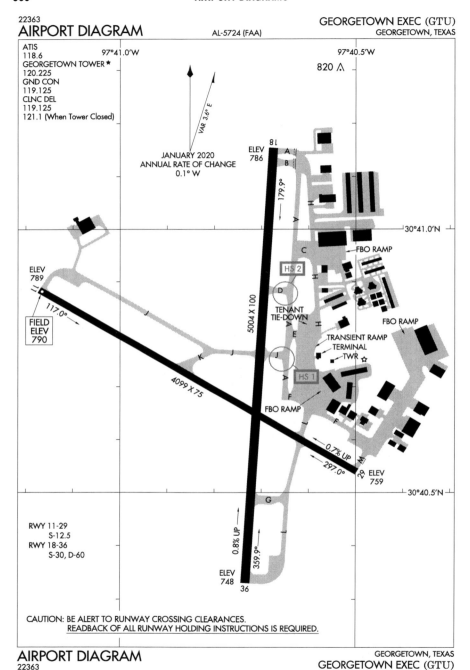

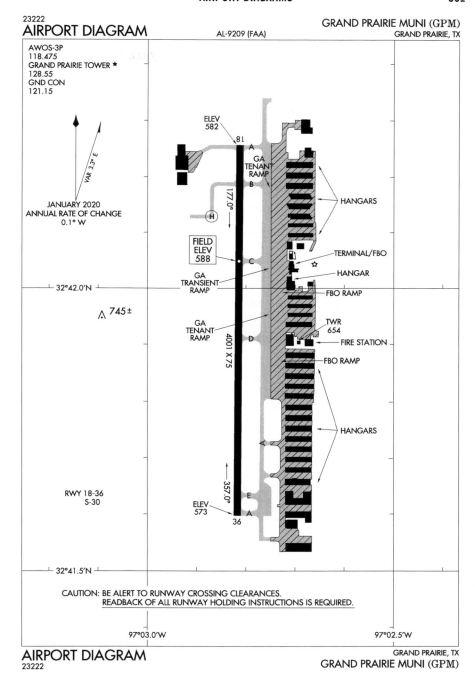

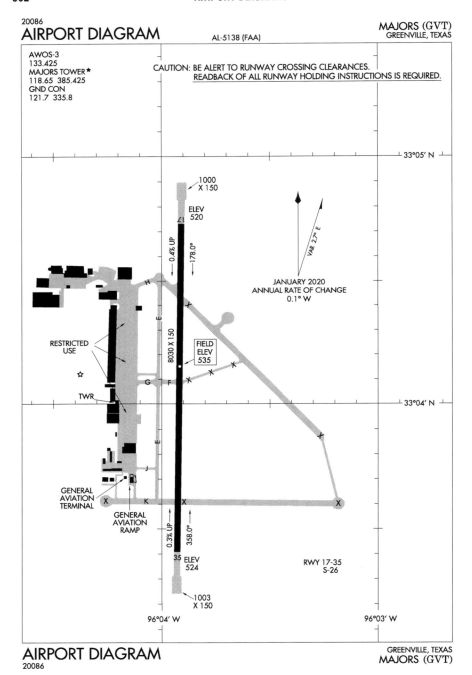

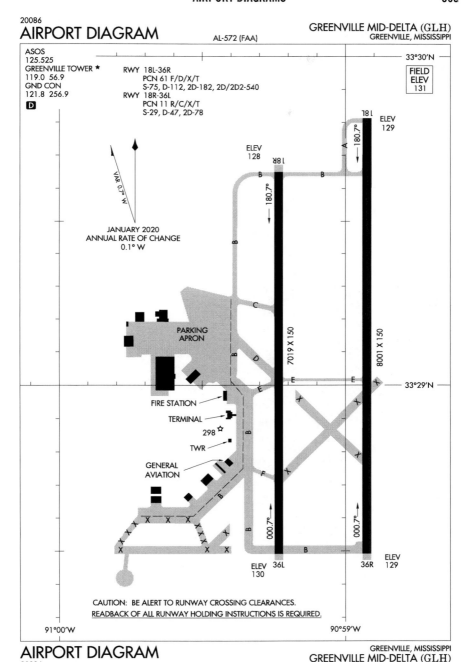

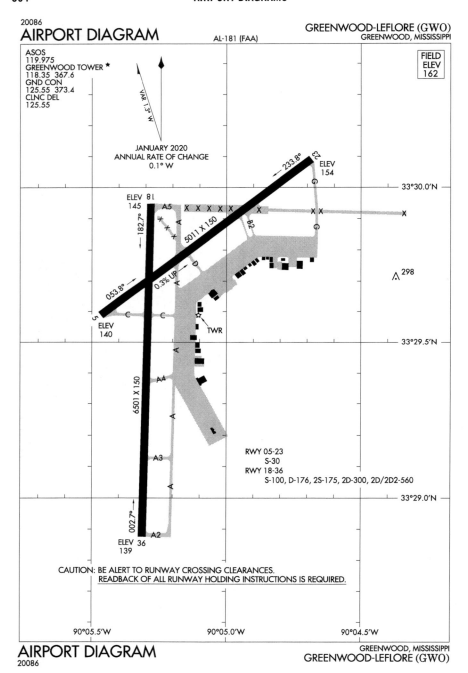

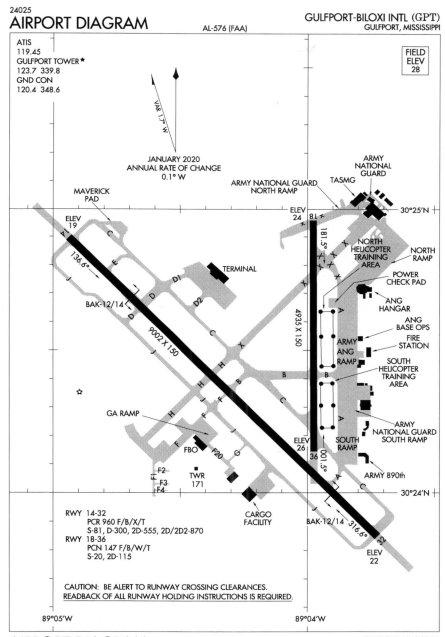

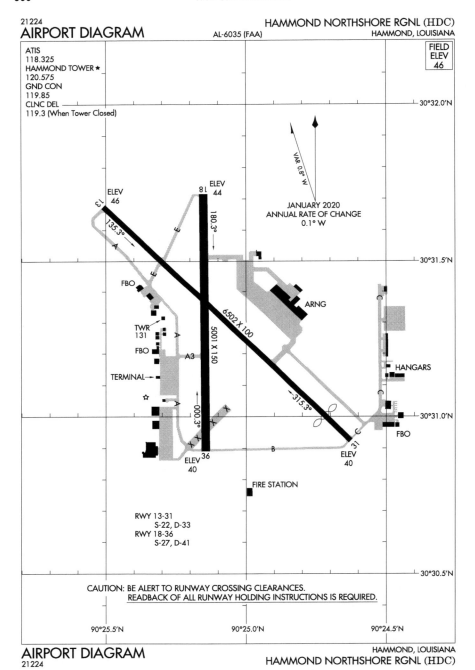

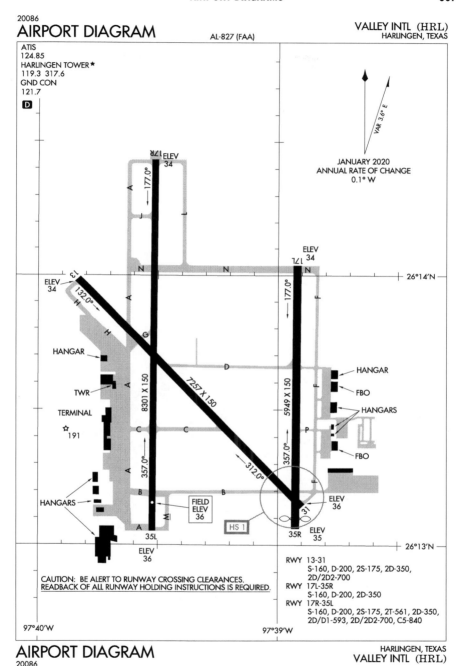

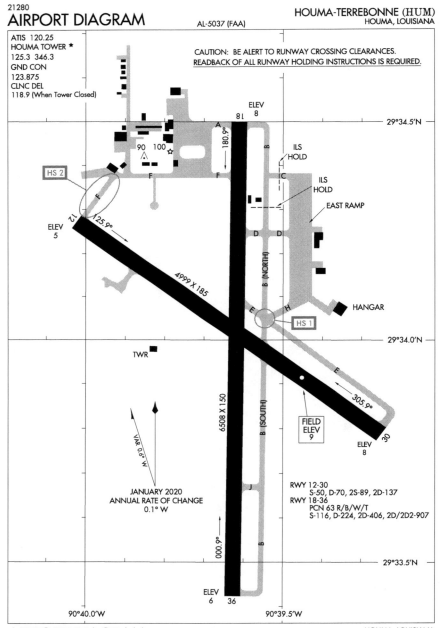

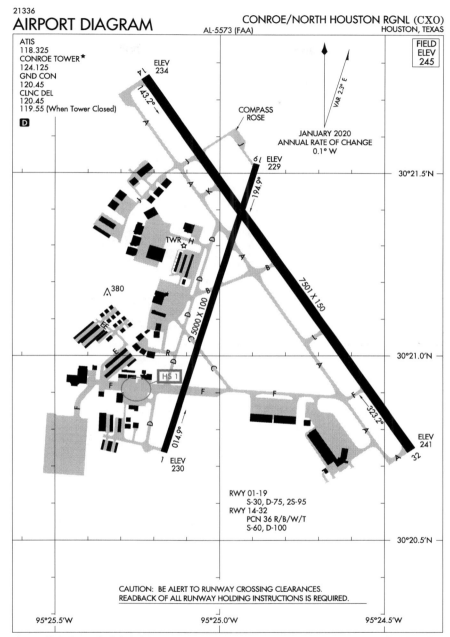

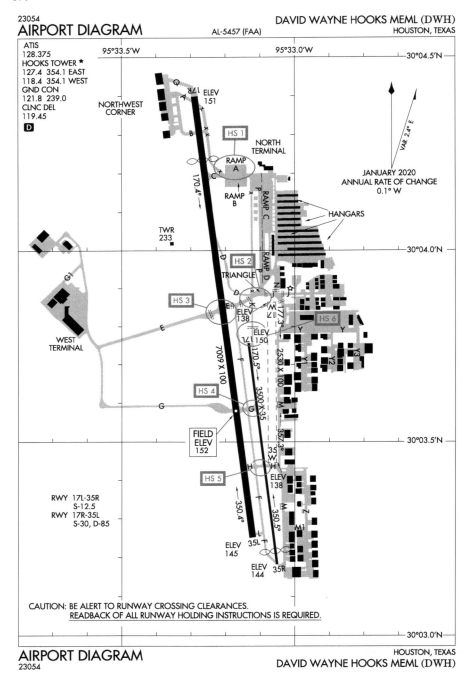

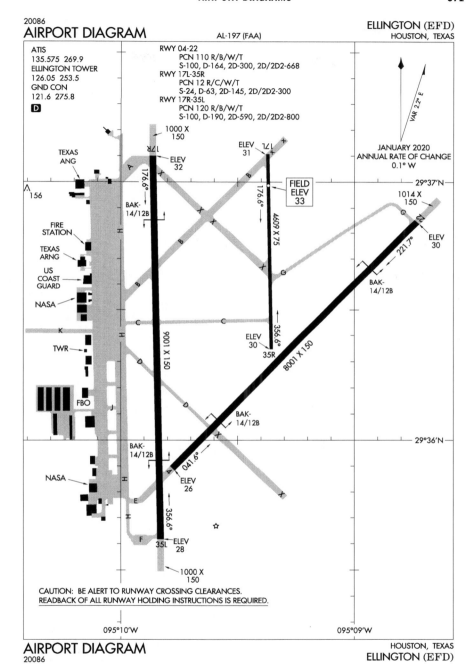

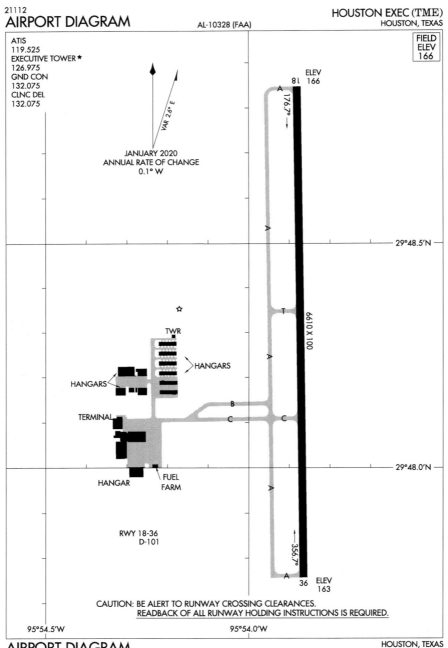

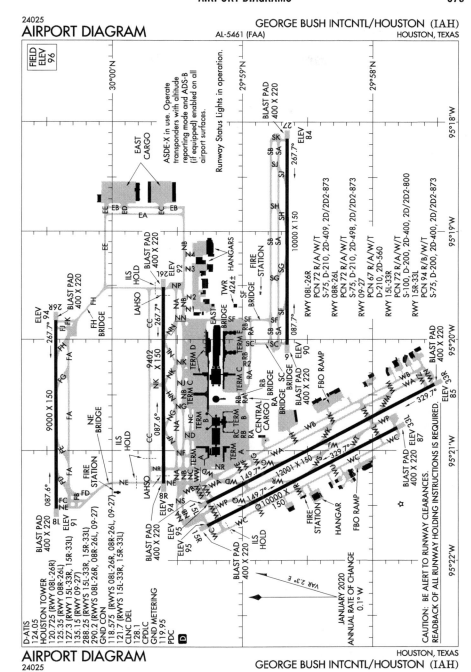

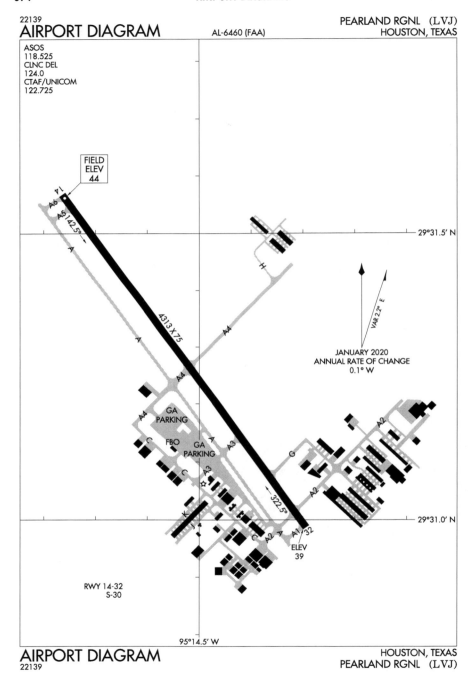

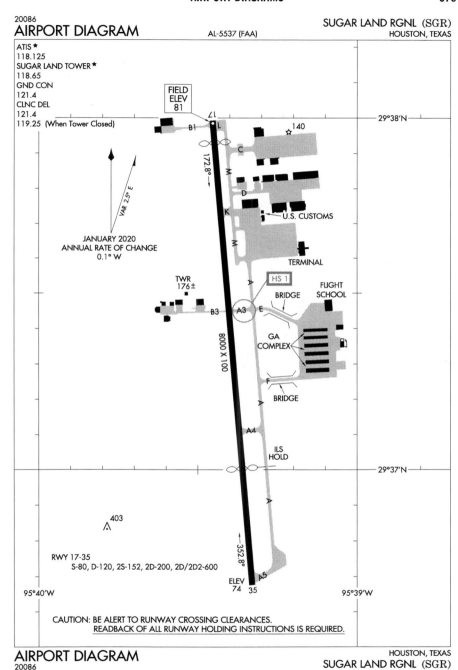

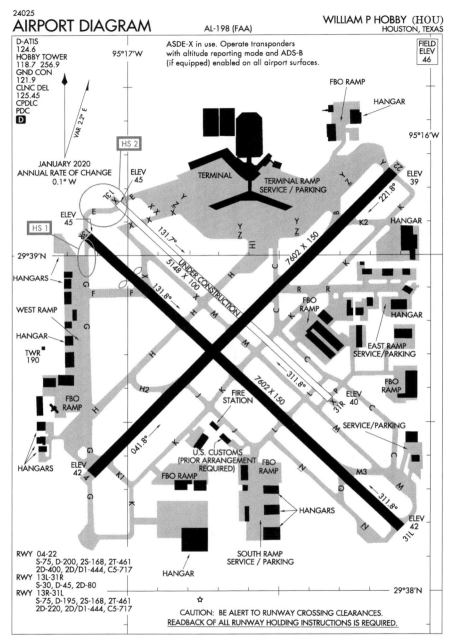

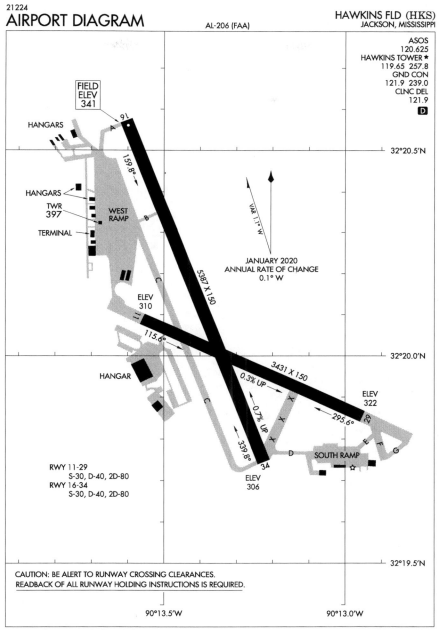

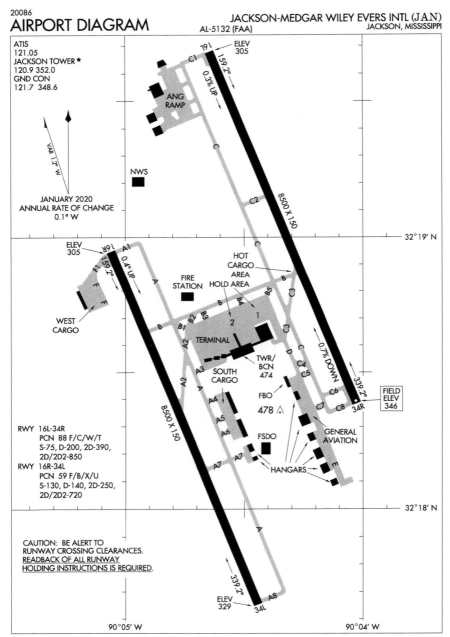

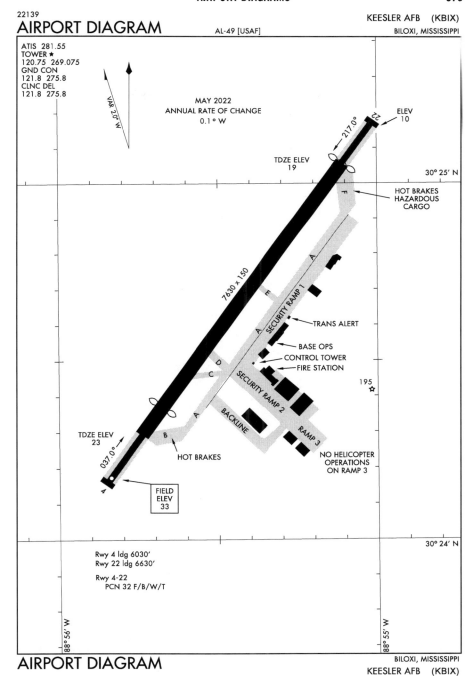

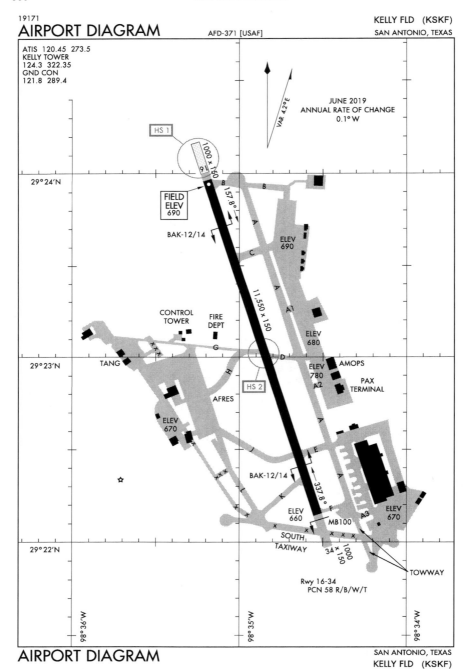

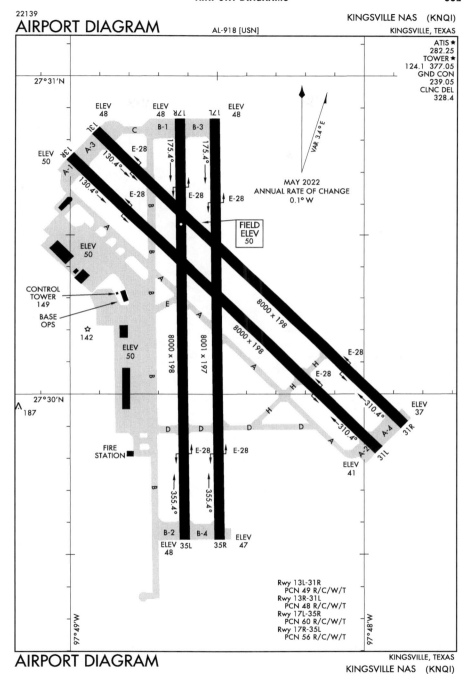

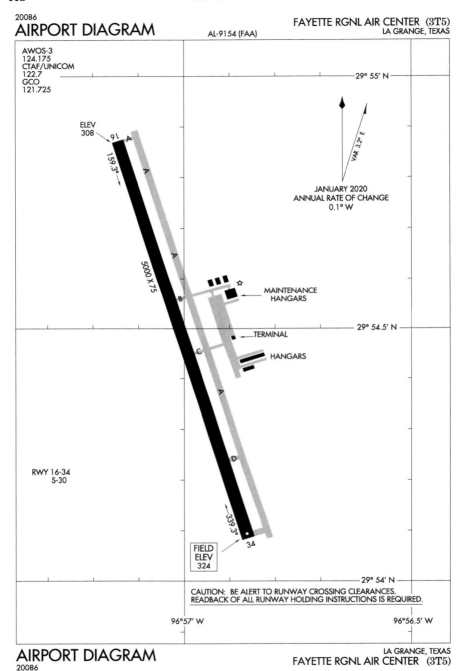

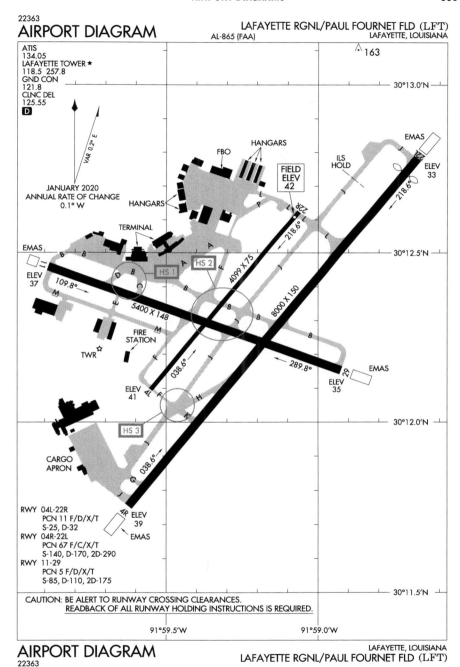

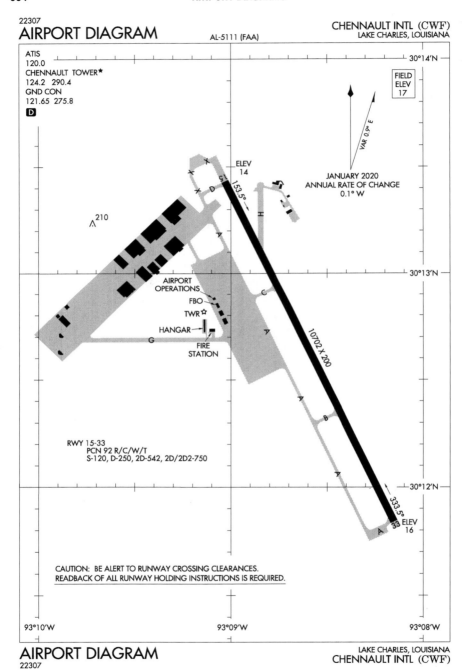

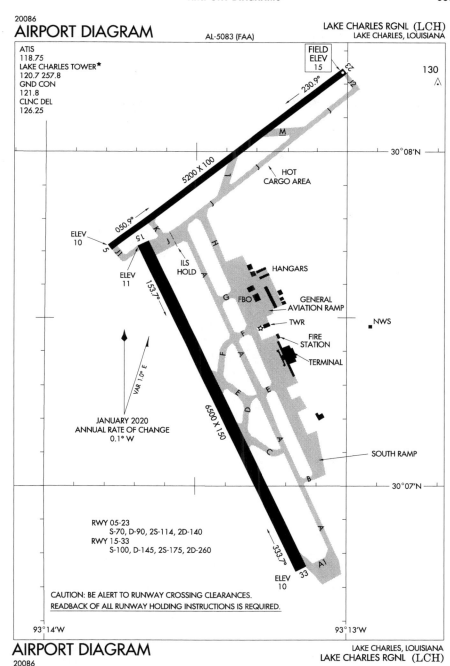

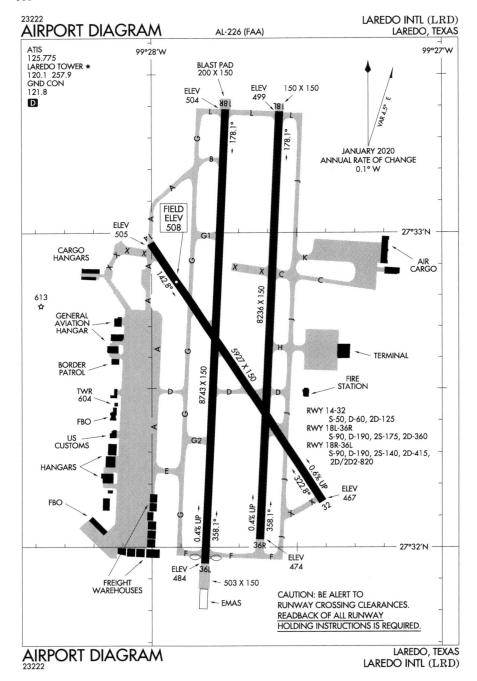

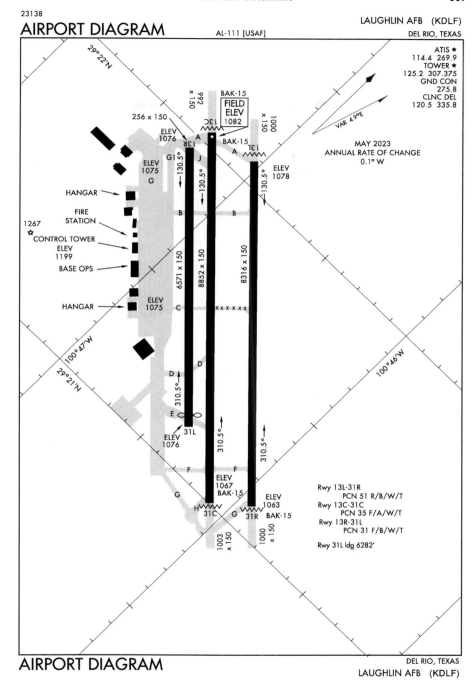

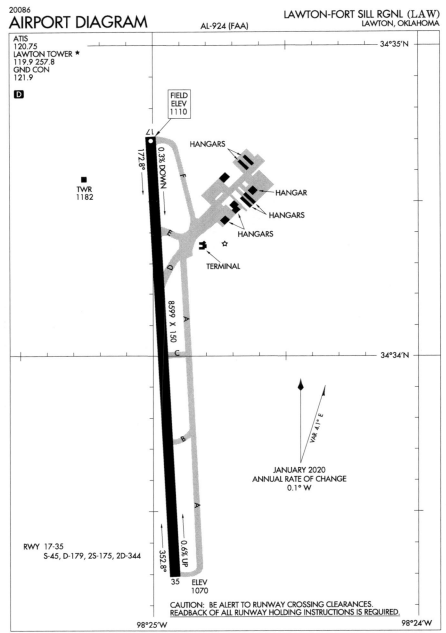

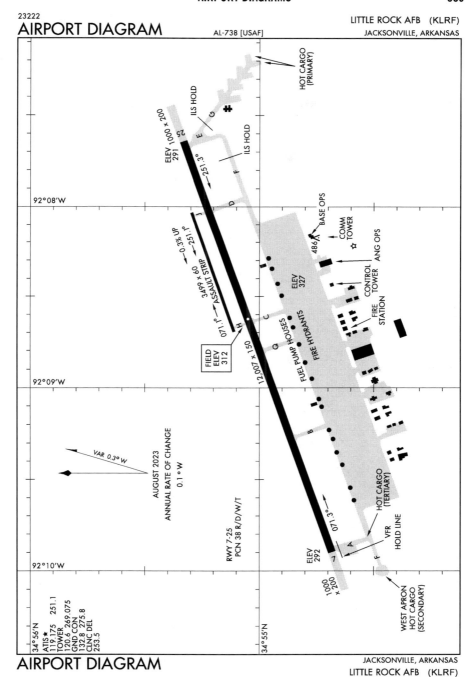

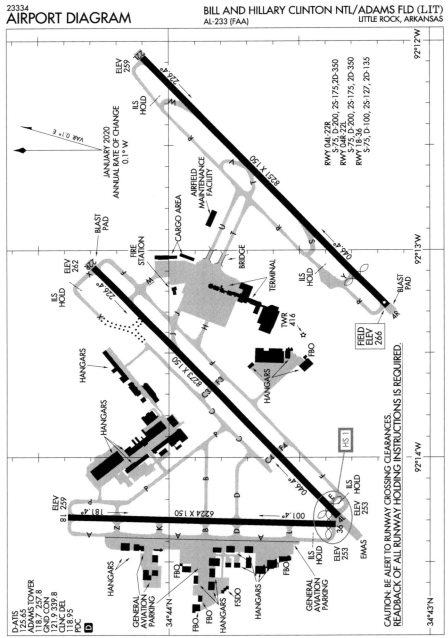

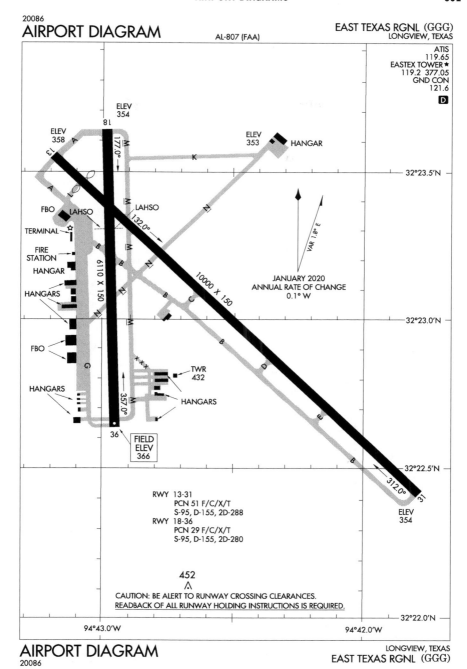

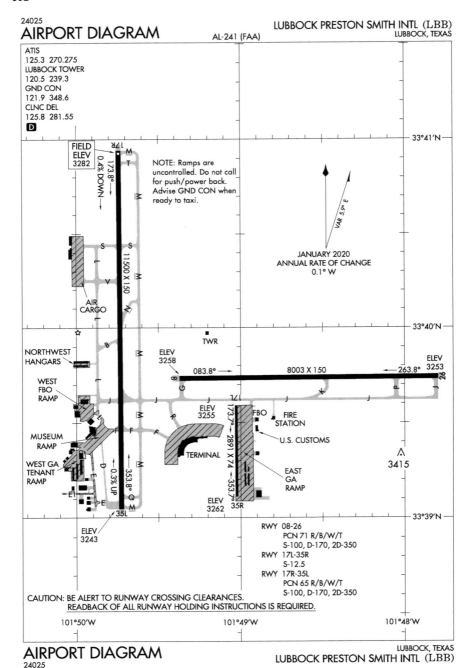

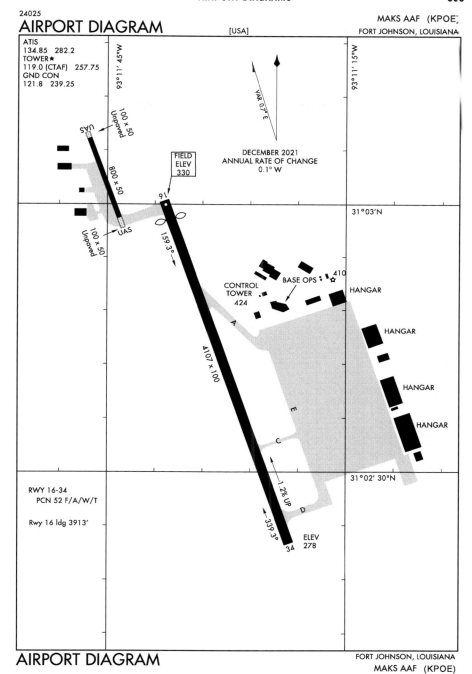

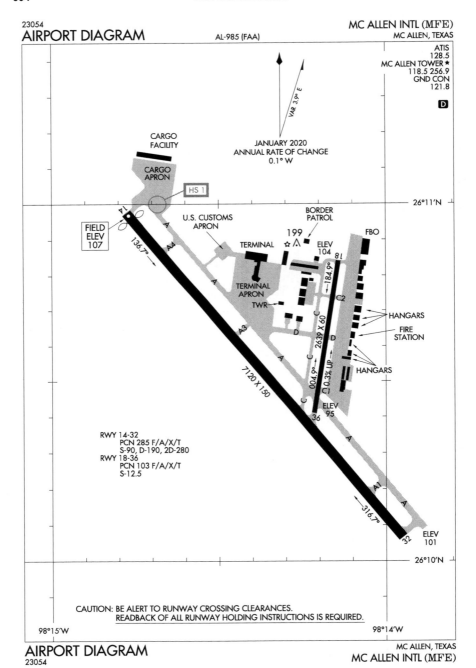

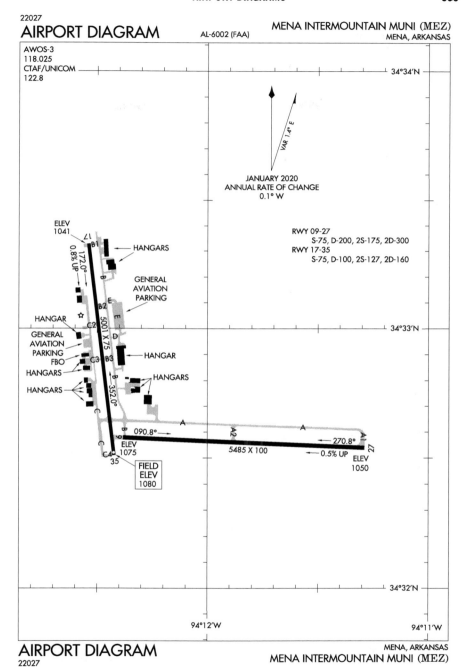

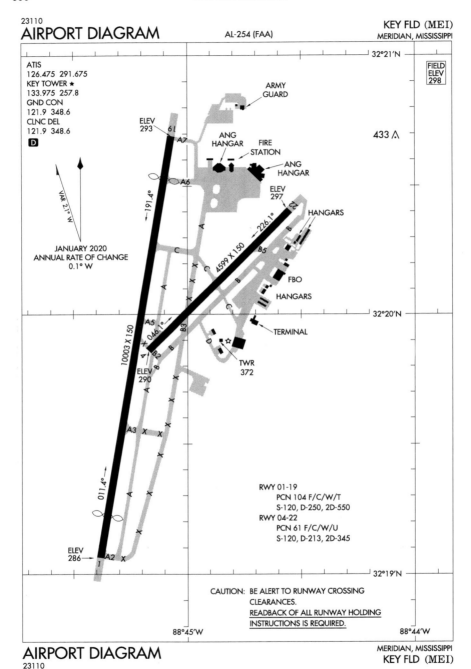

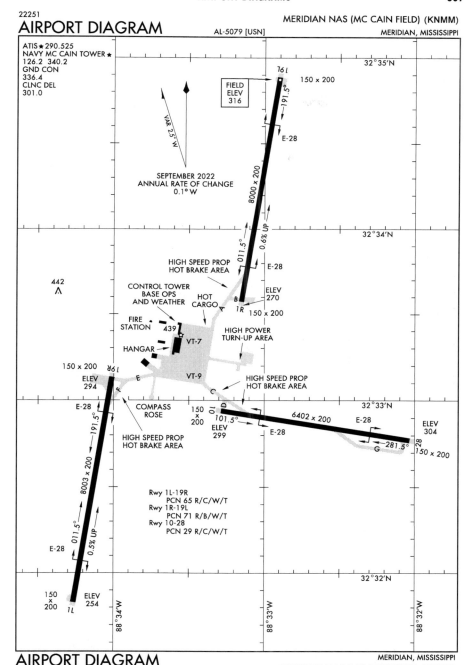

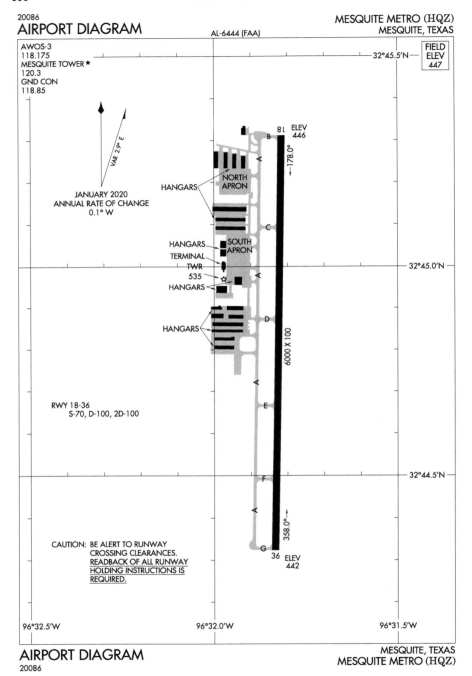

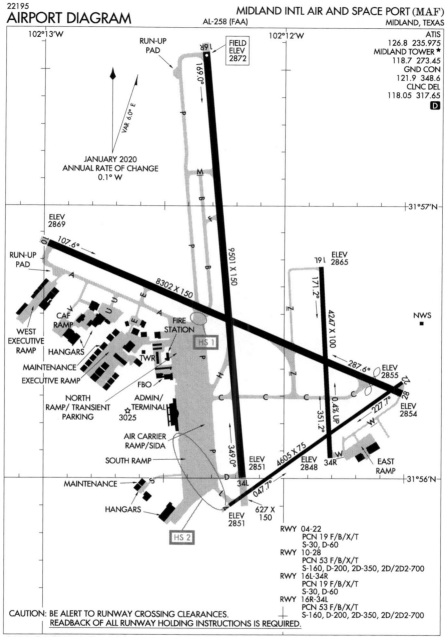

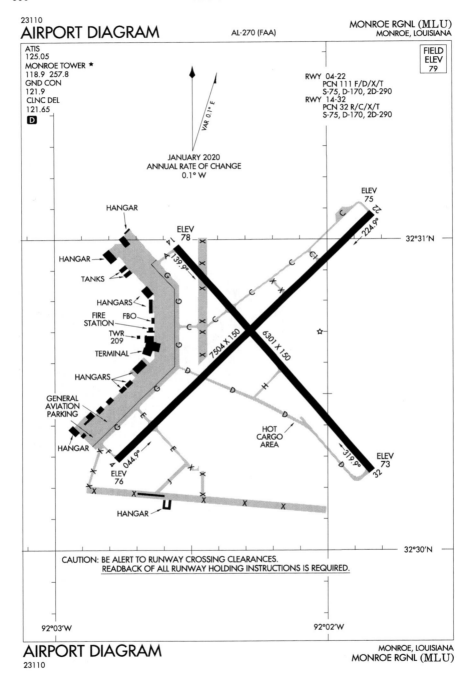

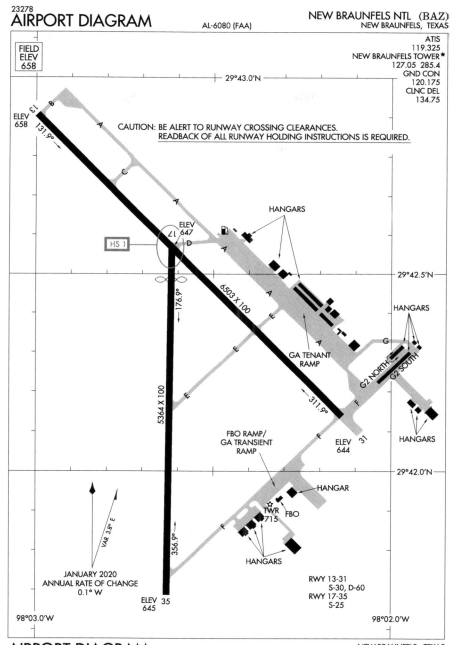

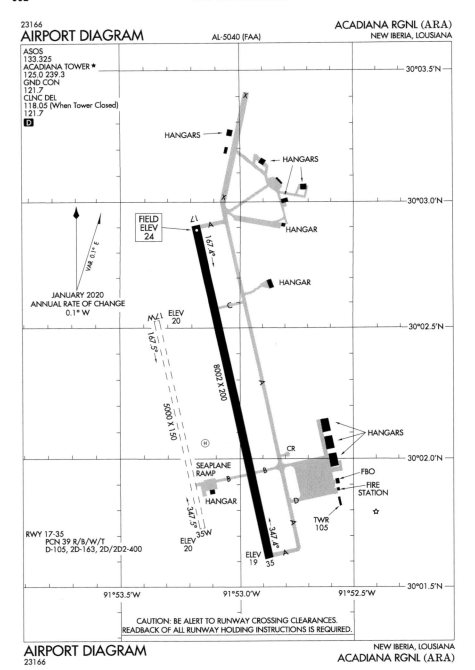

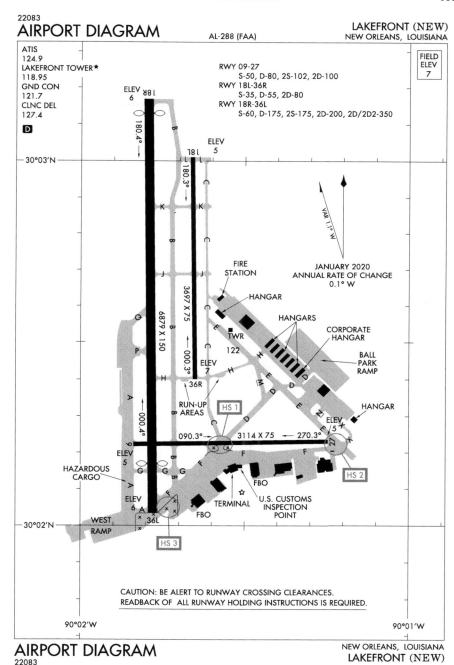

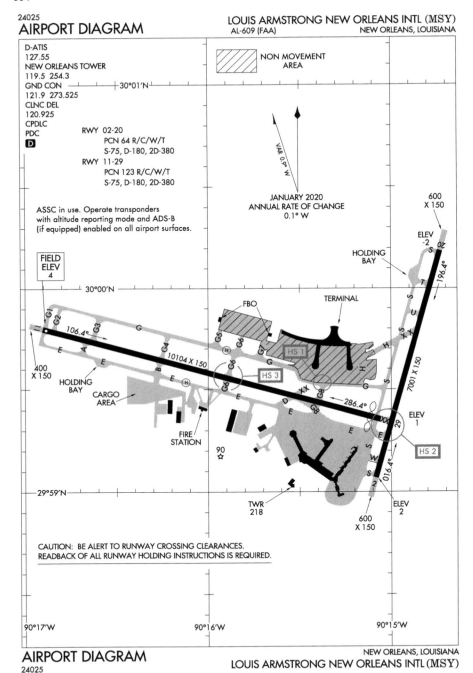

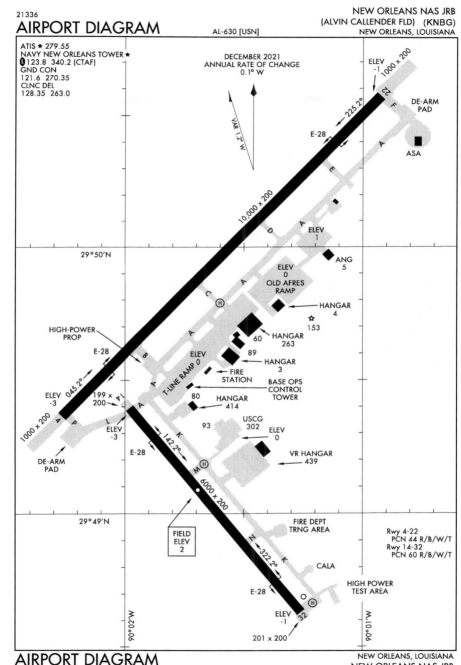

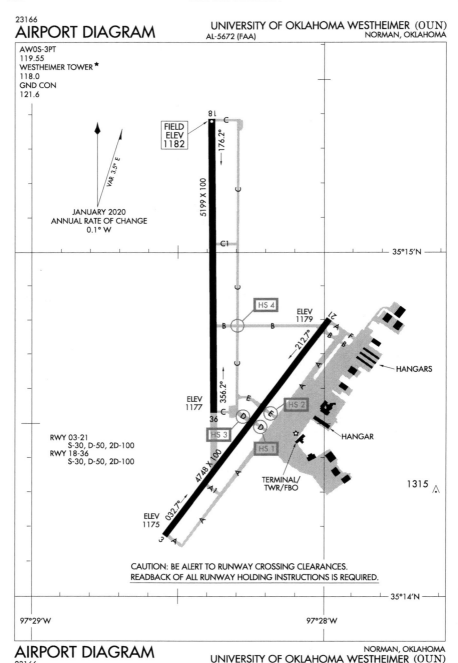

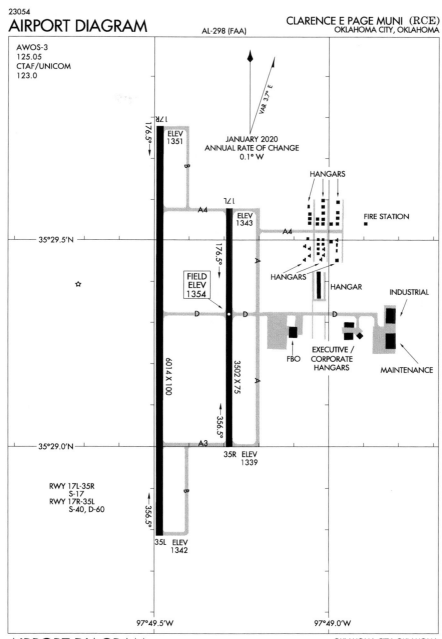

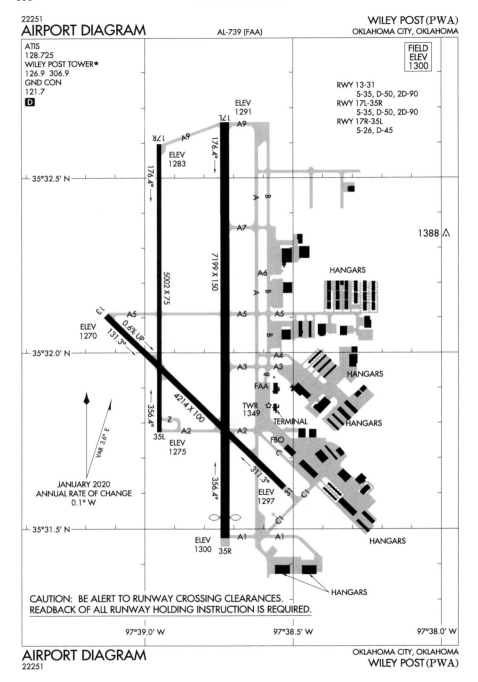

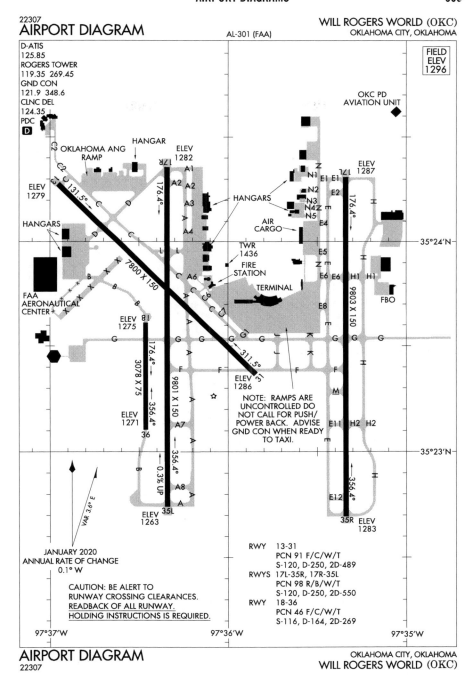

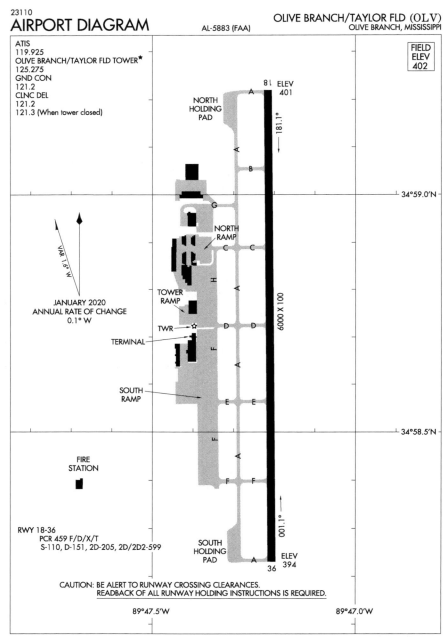

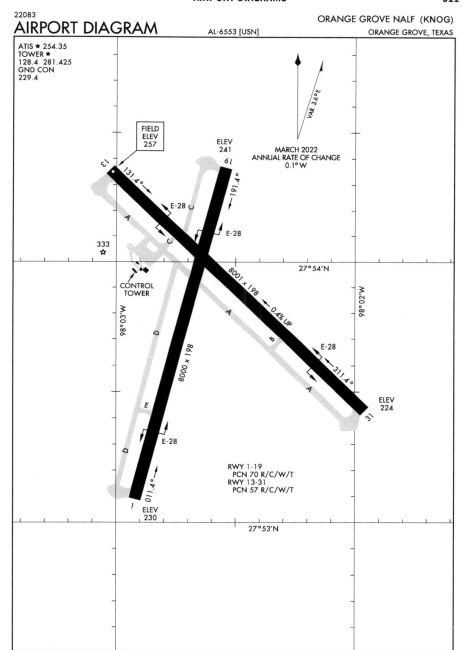

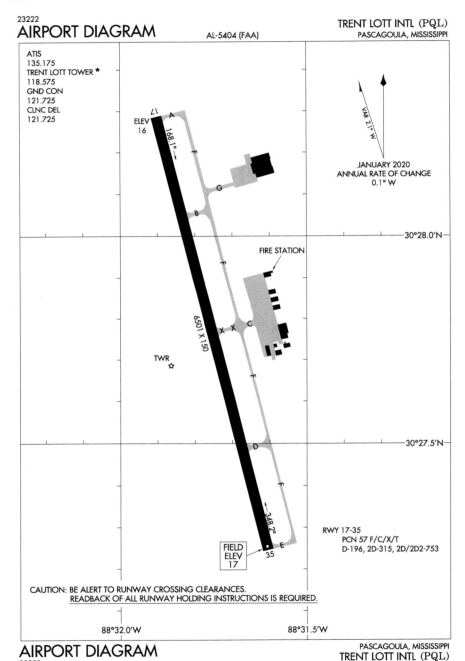

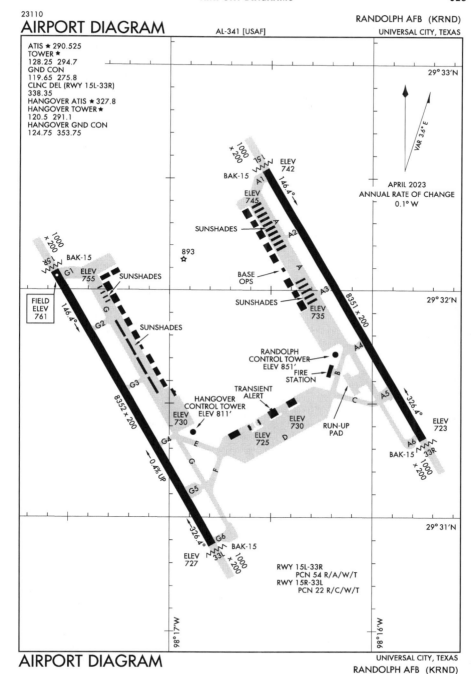

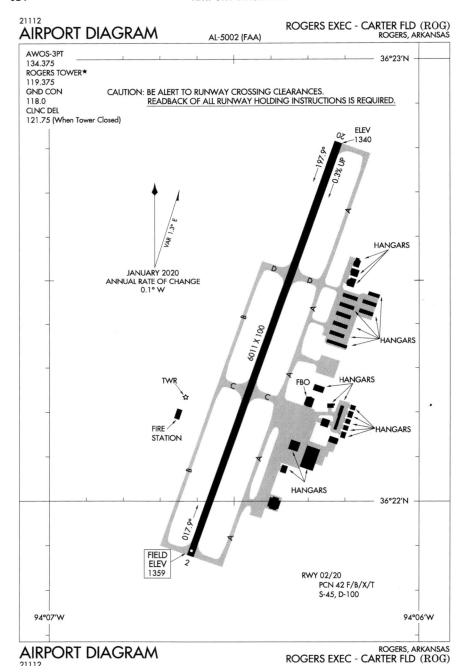

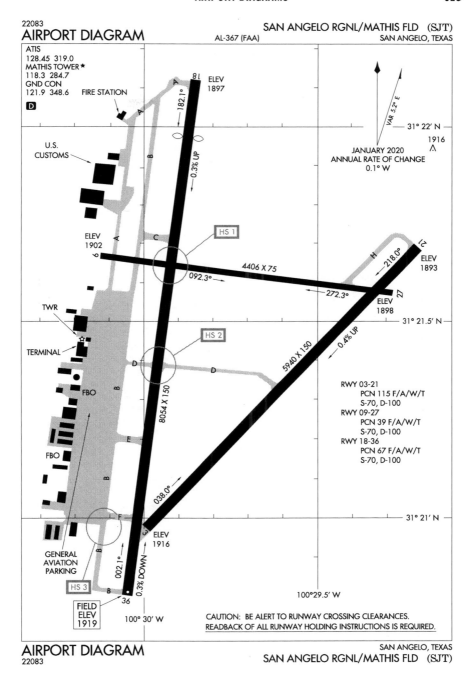

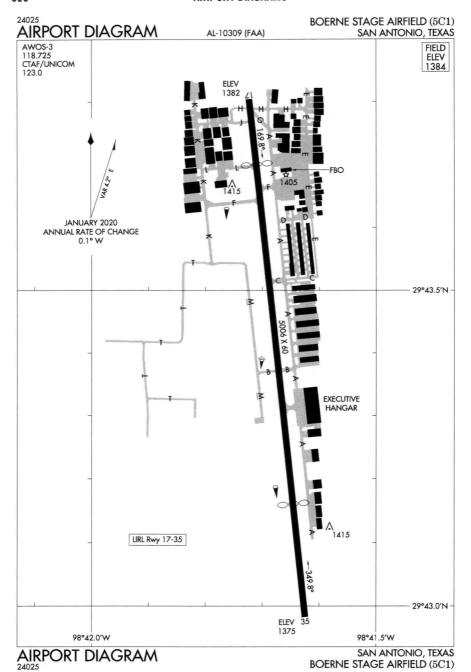

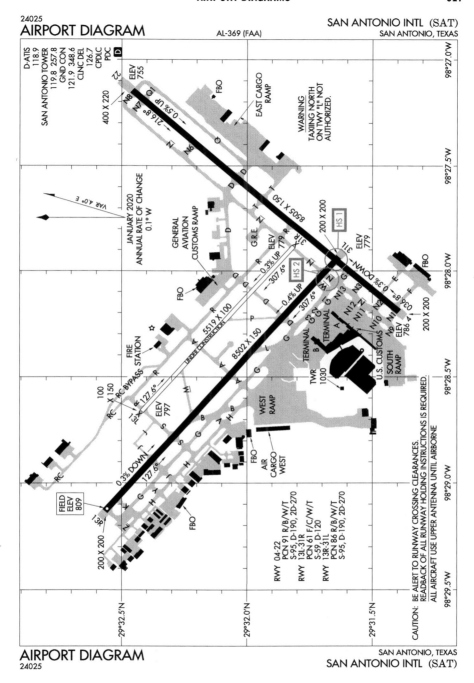

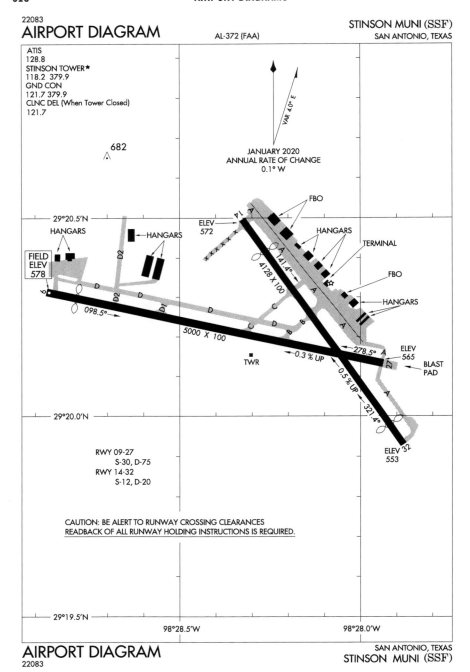

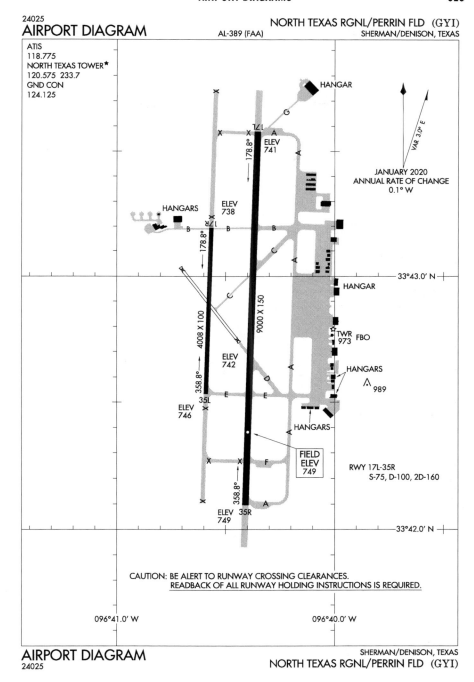

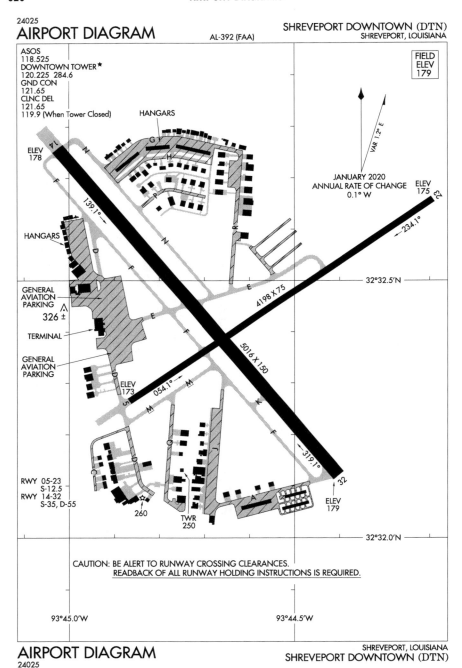

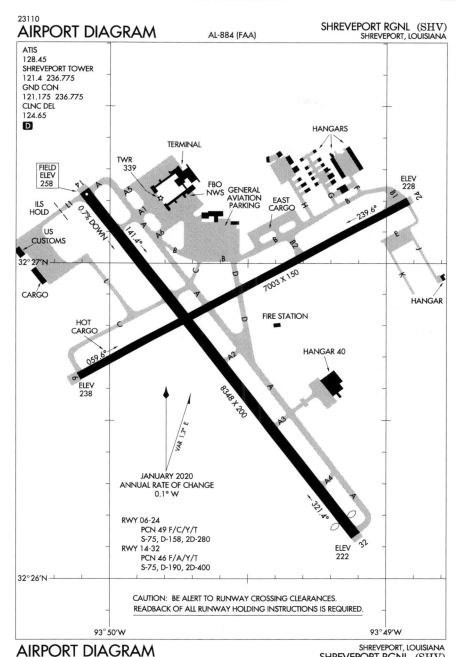

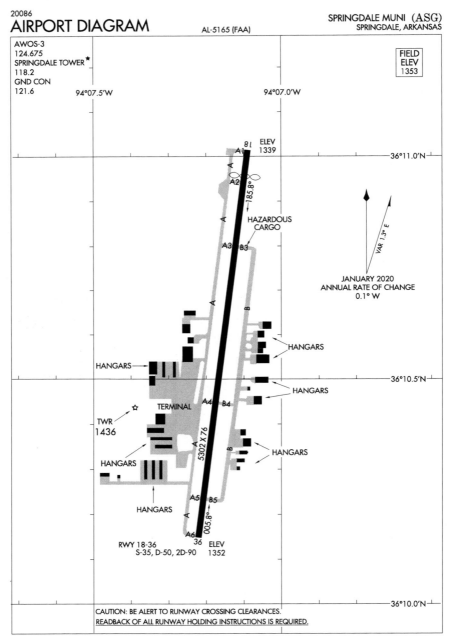

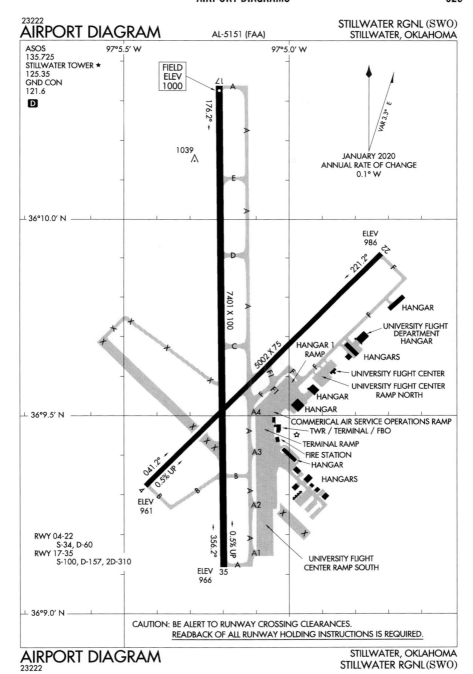

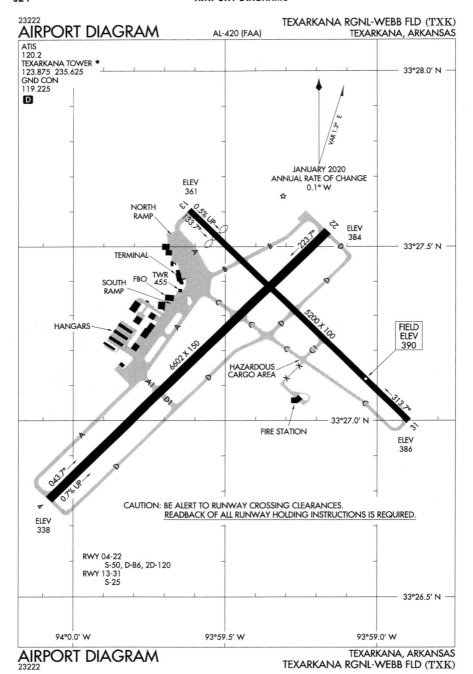

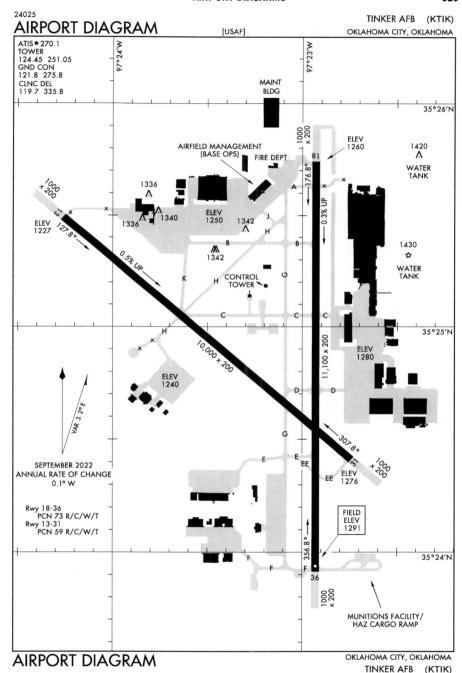

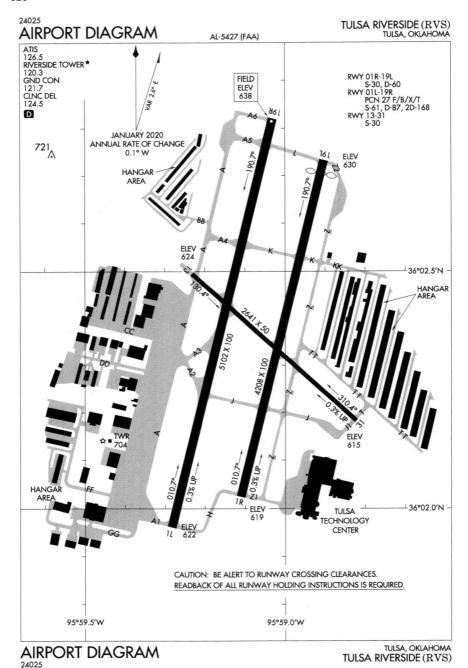

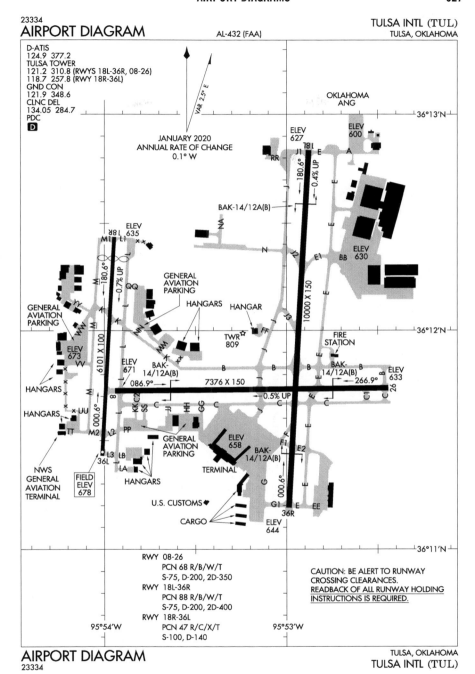

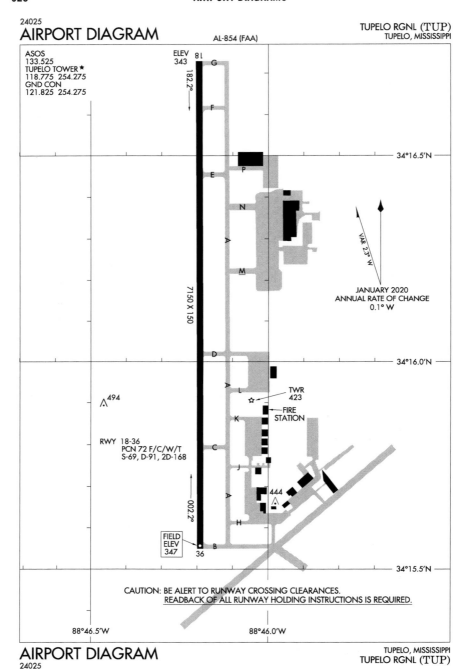

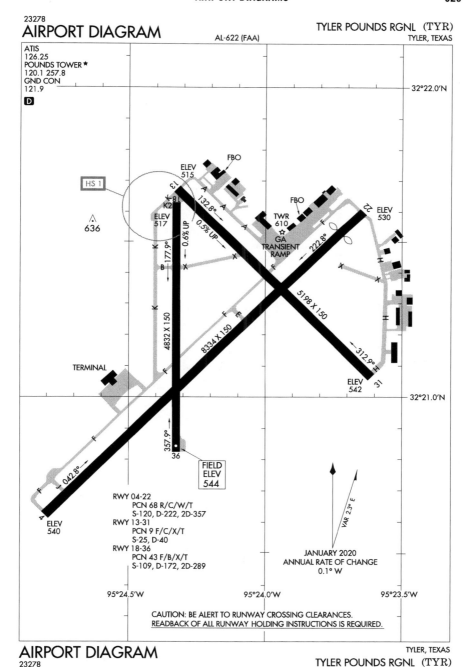

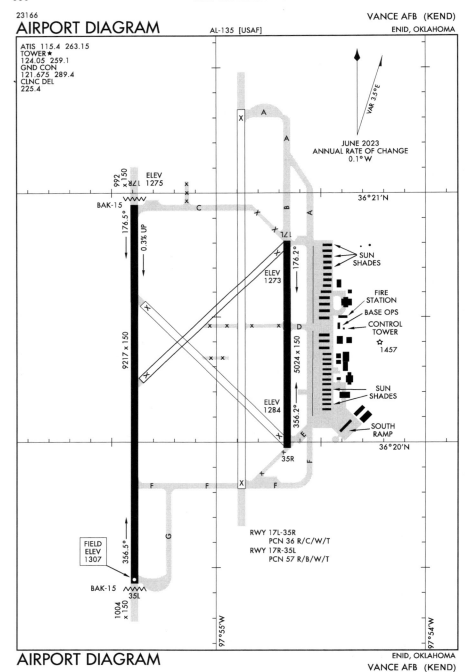

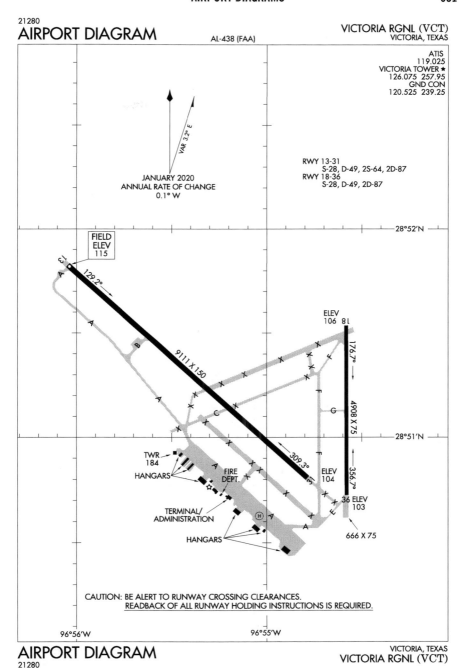

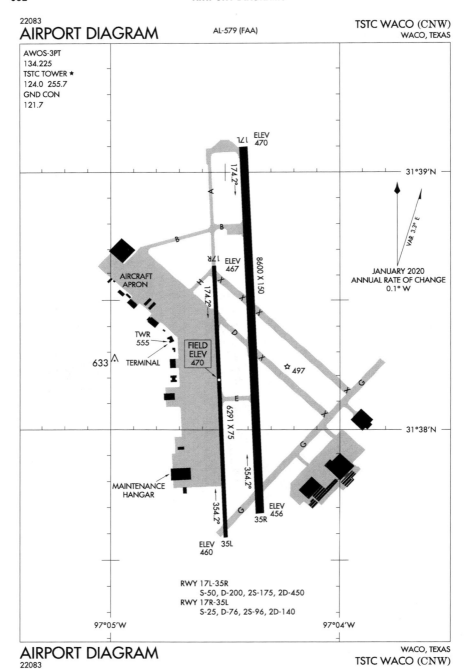

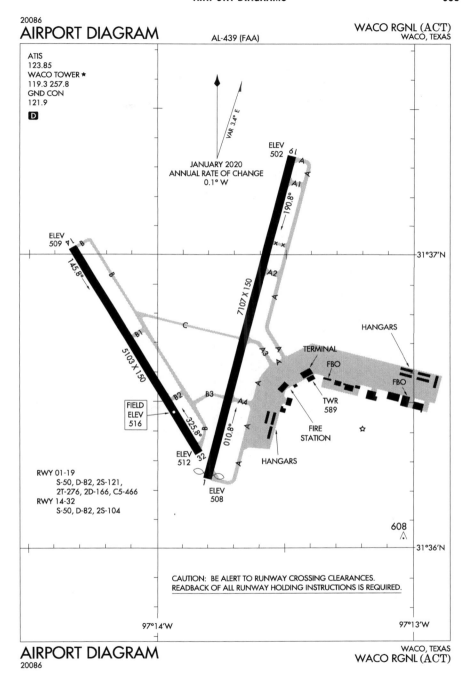

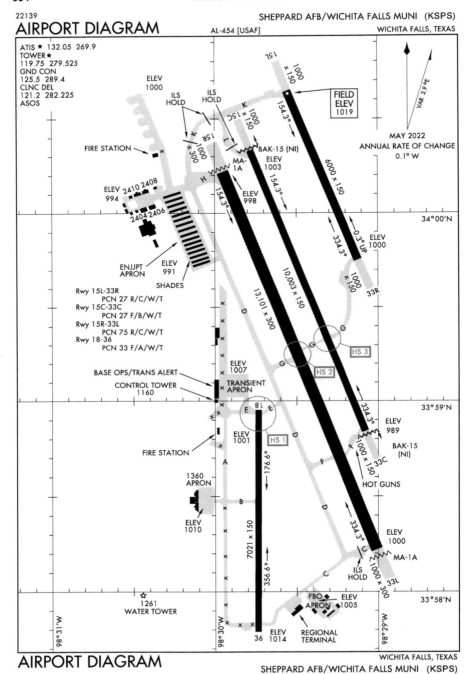

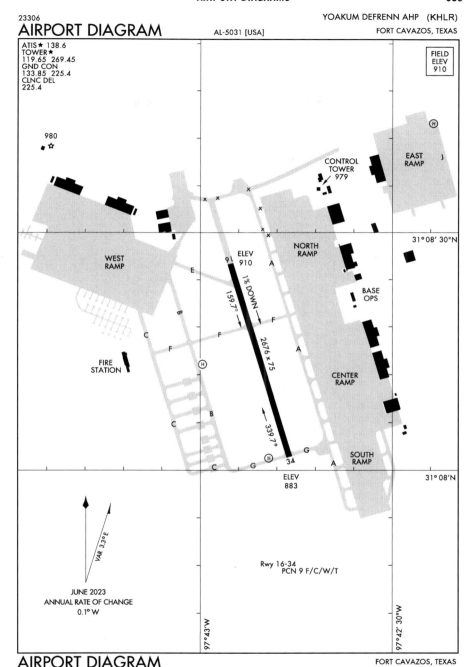

Submitting Pilot Weather Reports (PIREPs)

1. **UA - Routine PIREP / UUA - Urgent PIREP**

2. **/OV - Location:** Use Airport or NAVAID identifiers only.
   - Location can be reported as a single fix, radial DME, or a route segment (Fix- Fix)
   Examples: /OV LAX, /OV LAX-SLI120005, /OV PDZ-PSP.

3. **/TM – Time:** When conditions occurred or were encountered.
   - Use 4 digits in UTC.
   Examples: /TM 1645, /TM 0915

4. **/FL - Altitude/Flight Level**
   - Use 3 digits for hundreds of feet. If not known, use UNKN.
   Examples: /FL095, /FL310, /FLUNKN

5. **/TP - Type aircraft:** Required if reporting Turbulence or Icing
   - No more than 4 characters, use UNKN if the type is not known.
   Examples: /TP P28A, /TP RV8, /TP B738, /TP UNKN

6. **/SK – Sky Condition/Cloud layers:**
   - Report cloud coverage using contractions: FEW, SCT, BKN, OVC, SKC
   - Report bases in hundreds of feet: BKN005, SCT015, OVC200
   - If bases are unknown, use UNKN
   - Report cloud tops in hundreds of feet: TOP120
   Examples: /SK BKN035, /SK SCT UNKN-TOP125, /SK OVC095-TOP125/ SKC

7. **/WX - Weather:** Flight visibility is always reported first. Append FV reported with SM.
   - Report visibility using 2 digits: FV01SM, FV10SM
   - Unrestricted visibility use FV99SM.
   - Use standard weather contractions e.g.: RA, SH, TS, HZ, FG, -, +
   Examples: /WX FV01SM +SHRA, /WX FV10 SM -RA BR.

8. **/TA - Air temperature (Celsius):** Required when reporting icing
   - 2 digits, unless below zero, then prefix digits with M.
   Examples:/TA 15, /TA 04 /TA M06

9. **/WV - Wind:** Direction in 3 digits, speed in 3 or 4 digits, followed by KT.
   Examples: /WV 270045KT, /WV 080110KT

10. **/TB - Turbulence:**
    - Report intensity using LGT, MOD, SEV, or EXTRM
    - Report duration using INTMT, OCNL or CONS when reported by pilot.
    - Report type using CAT or CHOP when reported by pilot.
    - Include altitude only if different from /FL.
    - Use ABV or BLO when limits are not defined.
    - Use NEG if turbulence is not encountered.
    Examples: /TB OCNL MOD, /TB LGT CHOP, /LGT 060, /TB MOD BLO 090, / TB NEG

11. **/IC - Icing:**
    - Report intensity using TRACE, LGT, MOD or SEV
    - Report type using RIME,CLR, or MX
    - Include altitude only if different than /FL.
    - Use NEG if icing not encountered.
    Examples: /IC LGT-MOD RIME, /IC SEV CLR 028-045, /IC NEG

12. **/RM - Remarks:** Use to report phenomena that does not fit in any other field.
    - Report the most hazardous element first.
    - Name of geographic location from /OV field fix.
    Examples: /RM LLWS +/-15KT SFC-003 DURC RWY22 JFK
    /RM MTN WAVE, /RM DURC, /RM DURD, /RM MULLAN PASS
    /RM BA RWY 02L BA MEDIUM TO POOR 3IN DRY SN OVER COMPACTED SN

Examples of Completed PIREPS

UA /OV RFD /TM 1315 /FL160 /TP PA44 /SK OVC025-TOP095/OVC150 /TA M12 /TB INTMT LGT CHOP

UA /OV DHT360015-AMA /TM 2116 /FL050 /TP PA32 /SK BKN090 /WX FV05SM –RA /TA 04 /TB LGT /IC NEG

UUA /OV PDZ010018 /TM 1520 /FL125 /TP C172 /WV 270048KT TB SEV 055-085 /RM CAJON PASS

PIREP FORM

3 or 4 letter Identifier

___ ___ ___ ___   1. **UA** _____ **UUA** _____
                          Routine   Urgent

2. **/OV**	Location
3. **/TM**	Time
4. **/FL**	Altitude/Flight Level
5. **/TP**	Aircraft Type

Items 1 through 5 are mandatory for all PIREPs

6. **/SK**	Sky Condition
7. **/WX**	Flight Visibility & Weather
8. **/TA**	Temperature (Celsius)
9. **/WV**	Wind
10. **/TB**	Turbulence
11. **/IC**	Icing
12. **/RM**	Remarks

FAA Form 7110-2 (9/19) Supersedes Previous Edition

Made in the USA
Coppell, TX
28 January 2024

28303572R10350